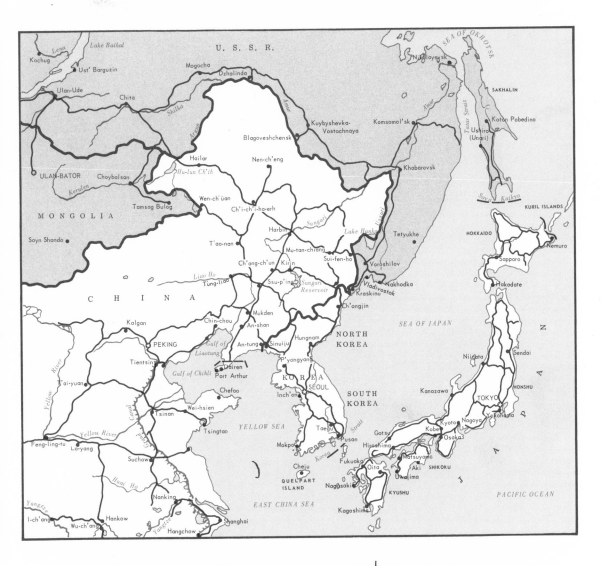

NORTHEAST CHINA,
KOREA AND JAPAN
AFTER WORLD WAR II

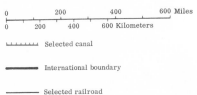

| | 0 | | 200 | | 400 | | 600 Miles |
| 0 | | 200 | | 400 | | 600 Kilometers | |

⊔⊔⊔⊔⊔⊔ Selected canal

━━━━ International boundary

──── Selected railroad

Paul H. Clyde
Sometime Professor of History, Duke University

Burton F. Beers
Professor of History, North Carolina State University

5th EDITION

The Far East

*A History of
the Western Impact
and
the Eastern Response
(1830-1970)*

Prentice-Hall, Inc., Englewood Cliffs, New Jersey

© Copyright 1971, 1966, 1958, 1952, 1948
by Prentice-Hall, Inc.
Englewood Cliffs, New Jersey.

Printed in the United States of America
Library of Congress Catalog Card Number: 72-144100

13-302976-X

Current Printing (last digit):
10 9 8 7 6 5 4 3 2

Prentice-Hall International, Inc. London
Prentice-Hall of Australia, Pty. Ltd., Sydney
Prentice-Hall of Canada, Ltd., Toronto
Prentice-Hall of India Private Limited, New Delhi
Prentice-Hall of Japan, Inc., Tokyo

Contents

Preface, xiv

The Romanization of Chinese and Japanese, xvi

The Antiquity of China and Japan (table), xx

List of Illustrations, xxiii

chapter 1

**On History
in General,
and This History
in Particular**

1

History defined.   The two histories.
The nature of the past.
Problems in the study of Asia.
The continent of Asia.   The Far East.
The theme of this history.
Problems in the study and teaching of history.

chapter 2

**Ways of Life
in Old China**

10

The antiquity of China.   Chinese history.
The ideas by which Old China lived.
The general character of Old China.
Philosophy and religion.
The character of Chinese painting.
Class structure.   Science.

v

chapter 3

Ideas on
Government
in Old China

27

Early schools of political thought. The philosophers, or Confucians.
Confucian political precepts.   Confucian political institutions: the
monarchy; ministers and departments; the censors; the law;
the provinces; local government; economic theory and taxation;
education and government; civil service examinations; tradition
vs. innovation.

chapter 4

Ways of Life
in Old Japan

39

Men of bronze and iron.   Religion in primitive Japan.
Political origins: Yamato.
Japan builds a Chinese city: The Nara period, 710–784.
The Heian period, 794–1185.   Kyoto and the New Japan.
Chinese institutions become Japanese.
Kamakura: Military dictatorship, 1185–1338.
The Hojo Regency, 1205–1333.   The Ashikaga Shogunate, 1336–1573.
Dictators reunite Japan.

chapter 5

The West Discovers
Eastern Asia

53

The Nestorian missions.   The renewal of European interest in China.
The Portuguese reach China.   The development of Catholic missions.
Early trade with China.   The West discovers Japan.
Japanese foreign policy.   A period of shifting interests.
The Canton trade.

chapter 6

China Submits:
The Treaty System

71

Lin acts: The British react.   The Nanking and Bogue treaties.
Early American interests in China.
The first enunciation of American policy.
The reception of the first treaties.   China and foreign affairs.

chapter 7

China, 1848–1860:
The New
Sino-Western Order
in East Asia

84

The T'ai-p'ing rebellion.   The rebellion and the foreign powers.
The foreign inspectorate of customs.
The obligations of extraterritoriality.   The growth of the opium trade.
Demands for treaty revision.   A so-called judicial murder.
The affair of the Lorcha Arrow.   The approach to Peking.
The treaties of Tientsin, 1858.   Legalization of the opium trade.
The renewal of hostilities.   The Peking convention.
Russia and China.

chapter 8

Japan, 1603–ca. 1840: The Making and Breaking of the Tokugawa Regime
100

Men who knew their own minds. The Tokugawa political system. The character of Tokugawa Japan: the philosophy; the economy; the arts; the roots of a new Japan. Summary.

chapter 9

Japan, 1840–1865: The Collapse of Isolation
112

Early attempts to open Japan. Treaties with foreign powers. Townsend Harris in Japan. Domestic politics and foreign affairs.

chapter 10

Japan, 1865–1889: from Feudal to Constitutional Government
122

The end of the Shogunate. The Restoration, 1868. The abolition of feudalism. The era of enlightened government (Meiji). The material transformation. Appearance of representative institutions. A constitution is shaped. Drafting the constitution. The essentials of the constitution.

chapter 11

Japan: Economic and Cultural Bases of the Meiji Government
137

Government in industry. The place of *Zaibatsu*. Political parties in Meiji Japan. The economic base of the Meiji parties. The political philosophy of Meiji. The union of traditional religion and modern politics. The disintegrating family structure. The place of Shintoism. Western intellectual imports. The temper of Meiji Japan.

chapter 12

China, 1860–1890: An Uneasy Interlude
151

The collapse of the T'ai-p'ing. China's military establishment. Implications of regional militarism. The co-operative policy, 1861–1867. Chinese missions abroad. The Burlingame mission. The problem of treaty revision. *(Continued)*

The development of Christian missions.
The treaty status of missionaries.
Treaty revision and the Margary affair.
Immigration: principle and practice.
The Chinese become a political question.

chapter 13

China,
1860–1890:
Reform Versus
Revolution

168

The role of questionable assumptions.   China's first response.
The policy of conciliation.
The "Restoration" of T'ung-chih, 1862–1874.
The appeal of Western technology, 1860–1870.
T'ung-wen Kuan, or Interpreters' College.   Chinese students abroad.
The audience question.   Efforts toward industrialization.
Government supervision: merchant operation.
The nature of Chinese leadership, 1860–1890.
The quality of leadership at Peking.   A nineteenth century contrast.

chapter 14

China and Her
Dependent States

180

Traditional Chinese "foreign relations."
The relationships of inequality.
The case of the Ryukyu (Liu-ch'iu) Islands.   The case of Korea.
The dependencies of Ili, Annam, Burma, Sikkim.   China and Korea.
The Tientsin Convention, 1885.
Immediate background of the Sino-Japanese War.
Korea: A European problem.   Immediate preliminaries to the war.
The war.   The treaty of Shimonoseki, April 17, 1895.

chapter 15

1895–1899:
China and
the Powers

192

The triple intervention.   European background of the intervention.
Financing the war and the peace.
The Russo-Chinese agreements of 1896.
The Chinese Eastern railway.   The Yamagata-Lobanov agreement.
Germany and the Far East.   Russia leases Port Arthur.
France leases Kwangchou Bay.
Great Britain: Kowloon, Wei-hai-wei.   The Philippines.

chapter 16

China, 1890–1901:
Artless Reform
and Blind Reaction

209

Reform and Christian missions.   The first Chinese reformers.
The hundred days of reform.   The reaction again in power.
The threatened partition of China.   The open door policy.
The Hay open door notes.   The Boxer catastrophe.
China's political integrity.   The international Boxer settlement.

chapter 17

China, 1901–1910:
The Empress Dowager
Tries Reform

222

Educational reform.   Military reform.
Constitutional reform.   Liang Ch'i-ch'ao.
Sun Yat-sen.   Economic reform.
Opium suppression.   A decade of reform in summary.

chapter 18

1902–1910:
Manchuria
and Korea

232

Foundations of the Anglo-Japanese alliance.   Japan and Russia.
The war and American policy. The stakes of the Russo-Japanese War.
Military campaigns in Manchuria.
The United States and the problem of peace.
The Treaty of Portsmouth.   Japan's new position in Korea.
Steel rails and politics in Manchuria.
The Sino-Japanese treaty of Peking.   Jurisdiction in
Manchuria after 1905.   Intensification of international rivalry.
Britain and France in Manchuria, 1907.
The United States and Manchuria, 1905–1910.
The shift to dollar diplomacy.   The Knox neutralization proposal.
The annexation of Korea.
Summation of American attitudes and policy.

chapter 19

China, 1911–1916:
The Gray Dawn
of a Republic

249

Flood, famine, and taxes.   Centralization versus provincial autonomy.
The revolution of 1911.   Effects of the revolution in Peking.
The policy of Yuan Shih-K'ai.   The peace negotiations.
Early phases of Yuan's government.
Dollar diplomacy and the revolution.
Separatist movements in border territories.
Analysis of the old first republic.

chapter 20

Japan, 1889–1918:
Economic Growth
and Evolution of
Oligarchical Government

258

The basis of oligarchical government.
Japan, 1889–1918:
The oligarchy versus the parties.
Oligarchic-party ententes, 1895–1900.
The oligarch as party leader, 1900–1918.
Economic and social bases of oligarchy.

chapter 21

Japan and China
in World War I,
1914–1918

267

War comes to East Asia.   The twenty-one demands.
The course of negotiations.   Chinese politics, 1915–1917.
China enters the war.   Peace.
Japan at Versailles.   China enters the conference.
The debate at Paris.   China's balance sheet of war.

chapter 22

The Legacies
of War
in East Asia,
1918–1924

282

The Siberian intervention.
The question of Allied intervention in Russia.
Theory and practice in Siberia.   The end of inter-Allied intervention.
The Four-Powered consortium.   The Washington disarmament
conference.   The way to disarm is to disarm.   The Four-Power pact.
Limiting naval armament.   The Far Eastern conference.
Japanese immigration.   In summary.

chapter 23

Japan,1918–1931:
Experiments with
Party Government

299

The basis of the new politics.   The Hara government, 1918–1921.
The Kato governments, 1924–1926.
The Tanaka government, 1927–1929.
The Minseito Cabinet, 1929–1931.   Party government: a summary.
Responsible government and world politics.
Japan and Russia, 1922–1929.   A period of Sino-Japanese amity.
Tanaka and the positive policy.   Japan and the League of Nations.
Naval rivalry in the Pacific.

chapter 24

China, 1916–1931:
Warlords,
The Kuomintang,
and Nationalism

310

An era of warlordism.   The growth of national feeling.
The new *Kuomintang*.   The passing of Sun Yat-sen.
China's revolution and the foreign powers.
Soviet policy and the Chinese revolution.
The Canton soviet and the powers.   Nanking's new treaty relations.

chapter 25

The Manchurian
Crises,
1929–1937

324

The Russo-Chinese crisis of 1929.   Sino-Japanese issues in Manchuria.
September 18, 1931 and after.
The report of the commissions of inquiry.
Manchuria: interpretations.   Consolidation of Manchukuo after 1932.
Further Japanese advances.

chapter 26

Politics
in Japan
and China,
1931–1941

336

Japan, 1931: the political atmosphere.   The new Japanism.
Extremists seek control.   Chinese politics, 1931 and after.
The national government and the *Kuomintang*.
The *Kuomintang* as ruling party.
Communist opposition to the *Kuomintang*.
Japan and the *Kuomintang*.

chapter 27

From the
Marco Polo Bridge
to Pearl Harbor,
1937–1941

352

Marco Polo Bridge: hostilities but not war.
The propagation of puppet regimes.
Resistance in independent China.
The Sino-Japanese conflict in world politics.
The new order in East Asia.   Japan starts south.
America moves toward war.   Pearl Harbor.

chapter 28

"Colonial"
Southeast Asia, I:
The Philippines
under
American Rule

367

The Republicans in the Philippines.
Construction of a colonial government.
The period of the Taft policy.   The changing Philippines.
Characteristics of early American policy.
The Democrats revive independence.
Independence and political expediency.   The Philippines accept.
The constitution of the Commonwealth.
Political parties in the Philippines.   Education in the Philippines.
The Philippine experiment in perspective.   The socioeconomic system.
Paradoxes in American policy.

chapter 29

"Colonial"
Southeast Asia, II:
The British,
French, and Dutch

380

Netherlands India.
Burma.
Malaya.
Siam or Thailand.
Indochina.
Southeast Asia on the eve of World War II.

chapter 30

East Asia in
World War II,
1941–1952

398

Military offensives and the diplomacy of war, 1941–1945.
Japan during the war: the economic pattern, the
search for effective government. China during the war.

chapter 31

The Occupation
of Japan,
1945–1952

415

Japan as a victim of war. The American concept of occupation.
The occupation at work. The new political structure.
Educational reforms. The new social and economic patterns.
Politics during the occupation. Economic rebuilding, 1948–1950.
The Japanese peace treaty.

chapter 32

From Kuomintang
to Communist China,
1945–1949

428

The Nationalist attempt to gain control.
Efforts at political settlement. A case of crumbling foundations.
The Communist military victory.
The Nationalist defeat in perspective.
Repercussions in the United States.
Communist China and the powers.

chapter 33

China under
Communism:
1949 and After

440

Political and administrative foundations.
The role of the Communist party. Reshaping the masses.
The balance sheet on social reform. Economic development.
Communist China and world affairs. Aspects of contemporary China.

chapter 34

Toward
a New Japan:
1952 and After

460

Economic recovery.   Economic development.
Rising living standards.
Social change.   Political change.
Government and politics.
Political parties.   New Japan.

chapter 35

Korea
and Taiwan
since 1945
474

Korea (postwar status; war in Korea; two Koreas).
Taiwan (*Kuomintang*-Nationalist occupation; government;
economic development; relations with the larger world).

chapter 36

The New
Southeast Asia:
1941 and After

491

The Japanese occupation.
The Philippines.   Burma.   Malaya.
Indochina.   Vietnam.   Laos.
Cambodia.   Thailand.
The balance sheet of the post-war years.

chapter 37

The New
Southeast Asia
in
World Affairs
512

Co-operation and rivalry in the early years of independence.
Southeast Asia in world politics.   The Laotian crisis.
The cold war in Vietnam.   The search for peace.
International perspectives on the new Southeast Asia.
Southeast Asia in American policy.

524   *Index*

Preface to the Fifth Edition

This **fifth** edition, like its predecessors, is addressed to college and university students and to the general reader seeking a systematic introduction to the history of Eastern Asia during the past one hundred and forty years. As in previous editions, the emphasis is on the impact of the West on Eastern Asia and the resulting response of Asia to the Western invasion. While the focus is therefore international rather than national, the basic theme is not diplomacy or international relations as such, but rather the clash of emerging national aims and cultural ambitions as East and West have met.

The pressures constantly felt in a new edition to expand on recent events at the expense of the more distant past have been resisted to the best of our ability. It has been our business to provide the student, so far as we can, with historical perspective. In this particular narrative there can be no valid historical evaluation or perspective for those who are unwilling to grapple with the foundations that were laid in the nineteenth and in the early twentieth centuries. It was this period in the Far East that prepared the way for Pearl Harbor, the Communist conquest of China, and for the Korean and the Vietnam wars.

The authors take pleasure in acknowledging their debt to a host of scholars, past and present, without whose patient research no synthesis such as this could have been written. The aim has been to present as far as possible in very limited space a chronological development of the narrative, to include enough specific data to illustrate the complexity of historical evidence, to suggest shadings that must always be present in historical interpretation, and to stimulate the reader, young or old, to further study of an intense and vital drama in which he is already a member of the cast.

In the preparation of a relatively brief survey of this kind covering a vast and exceedingly complex area where diverse cultures are meeting in an age of intense conflict, we have been forced of necessity to be highly selective in the choice of materials to be included. It is our belief, however, that the story presented is a valid introduction to an historical scene in which much of the more recent evidence is as yet untouched by research and analysis. We would hold that our interpretations are in accord with the evidence presently available but we make no claim to infallibility. The interpretation of historical events and movements is in some major degree a subjective process. It is our hope that the narrative presented here will stimulate students to pursue the subject further in wide reading and research, in analysis of all the evidence, and in the building of their own interpretations and conclusions.

A Note on Reading and Sources

Every student who aspires to study history and who is not content merely to scratch the surface will learn sooner or later that there is no substitute for planned, extensive, and intensive reading. This survey is intended to give him an effective start on the long and rough road to an historical understanding of the Far East. Its purpose is therefore limited. Further travel along this amazing road is the function of the individual instructor and student. To assist them in this adventure we have provided guides to further reading, but here too there are limitations. Within the past two decades, useful and scholarly literature on the history of the Far East has multiplied many times. Even a highly selective bibliography would now fill many volumes the size of this one. While therefore the reading lists and references cited in this study are selective in the extreme, we have attempted, so far as space would permit, to include those that are representative of recent scholarship and most likely, in our judgment, to meet the immediate needs of instructor and student. Certainly every user of this survey should be familiar with and use the annual bibliographies published by The Association for Asian Studies. In the main, sources cited in footnotes and in the reading lists are in the English language, but the reader is reminded that voluminous sources of great value also exist in other European languages as well as in Chinese and in Japanese. English titles in the reading lists that are available in paperback editions are marked with an asterisk.

The following colleagues made suggestions for the present edition: George Lensen, Florida State University; David Lu, Bucknell University; David Maynard, Foothill College; Paul S. Dull, University of Oregon; and Stephen Uhalley, Jr., Duke University. Raymond Esthus, Tulane University, made detailed comments based on a critical reading of Chapters 1–35. Mrs. Elizabeth B. Bond assisted with the preparation of the manuscript. We gratefully acknowledge their generous aid.

P.H.C.
B.F.B.

The Romanization
of Chinese and Japanese

Chinese personal and place names are written by the Chinese in Chinese characters that are intelligible only to students of the Chinese language. These names are reproduced in the phonetic languages of the West by attempting to write the sound, a process known as transliteration or romanization. This process is not as simple as it may seem because within China itself, Chinese characters are pronounced in various ways. The Mandarin or Peking dialect is, however, generally regarded as standard. This would seem to resolve the matter, but unfortunately the sounds of the Mandarin dialect do not always have exact equivalents in English. Thus the Mandarin sounds are indicated by some conventionalized system of English letters and accents in which the English letters do not necessarily have the normal English sound but instead represent certain Mandarin sounds.

The problem is one with which Western sinologists have long experimented with results somewhat less than adequate. The most commonly used system is the Wade-Giles spelling, which in simplified form is generally followed in this book. However as news from Eastern Asia has commanded more space in the Western press, there has come into common use a postal or journalistic spelling, which is often used in these pages to avoid confusing the student unfamiliar with the Wade-Giles spelling. For example, we spell the name of the old capital of the Manchu Empire in journalistic style as Peking; the Wade-Giles spelling would be Pei-ching. A closer approach in the conventional sounds of the English letters would be Bei-jing. The commonly used transcriptions for Chinese words are defective, chiefly in three respects: (1) they fail to use the letters *b, d, g*, and they use *j*, not with its hard sound, but for a sound closer to the English *r;* (2) they use English vowels to represent the Chinese semi-vowels in such syllables as *tzu* and *shih;* and (3) the un-English apostrophe in the Wade-Giles romanization is frequently forgotten and dropped, with the result that different Chinese pronunciations are represented by the same English letters. Since speakers of English inevitably tend to pronounce words as they are spelled, such words as "Peking" are pronounced in a way that would be unintelligible to a Chinese.

The following is a simplified guide to pronunciation in the Peking dialect according to the Wade system.

VOWELS (as in Italian)

a as in "father"

e as in "Edward"

i like the *e* in "me"

o like "aw" (but often like the *u* in "cut")

u as in "lunar"

ê like the *u* in "under"

ih like the *e* in "her" (no real equivalent in English)

ü like French *u* or German *ü*

u is practically unpronounced

CONSONANTS

The apostrophe following a consonant indicates aspiration; the lack of the apostrophe indicates the lack of aspiration, which sounds to our ears very much like voicing. Therefore:

(Unaspirated)

ch sounds like the *j* in "jam"

k like the *g* in "gun"

p like the *b* in "bat"

t like the *d* in "doll"

ts and *tz* sound like *dz*

j between French *j* and English *r*

(Aspirated)

ch' as in "chin"

k' as in "kin"

p' as in "pun"

t' as in "tap"

ts' and *tz'* like the *ts* of "Patsy"

Most of the other consonants are similar to those in English. In the following pages the diacritical ˆ ˘ ¨ marks other than the apostrophe are omitted.

Other systems of romanization are used in other Western languages. A more recent system of romanization which is not commonly used, is the Homer H. Dubs revision of C. S. Gardner's romanization. It is an attempt to modify the Wade-Giles spelling to avoid the difficulties noted above. It also represents the distinction between *ts* and *ch*, and *hs* and *s* before the vowels *i* and *ü*. This distinction is retained in most of China. Actually, only a specially devised alphabet can be entirely phonetic. The Dubs-Gardner romanized spelling has the advantage of suggesting approximate pronunciation in letters pronounced as they are more frequently in English.

Some examples of the three systems follow:

Postal or journalistic spelling	Wade-Giles spelling	Dubs spelling (and approximate pronunciation)
Chekiang	Che-chiang	Je-jiang
Kwangtung	Kuang-tung	Guang-dung
Paoting	Pao-ting	Bao-ding
Peking	Pei-ching	Bei-jing
Peiping	Pei-p'ing	Bei-ping
Tientsin	T'ien-chin	Tien-dzin
Hupeh	Hu-pe	Hu-be
Kuling	Ku-ling	Gu-ling
Kweilin	Kuei-lin	Guei-lin
Tali	Ta-li	Da-li
Lanchow	Lan-chou	Lan-jou
Kweiyang	Kuei-yang	Guei-yang
Chang Po-ling	Chang Po-ling	Jang Bo-ling
Hsinking	Hsin-ching	Sin-jing
Chihtang	Chih-t'ang	Jzh-tang
Szechuan	Ssu-ch'uan	Sz-chuan
Jehol	Je-ho	Re-ho
Tsingtao	Ch'ing-tao	Tsing-dao
Tsinan	Chi-nan	Dzi-nan
Sun Yat-sen	Sun I-hsien	Sun Yi-sien
Canton	Kuang-chou	Guang-jou
Wuchang	Wu-ch'ang	Wu-chang
Yenan	Yen-an	Yen-an
Kaifeng	K'ai-feng	Kai-feng
Kunming	K'un-ming	Kun-ming

In both Chinese and Japanese personal names, the surname comes first, followed by the given name. However, in the following pages it has seemed best to use the form with which American readers are most likely to be familiar. Thus, for example, Li Hung-chang, Feng Yu-hsiang, Chiang K'ai-shek, but T. V. Soong. The same procedure has been followed with Japanese names. However fewer Japanese given names are known to the American public, and in general the rule of surname followed by given name has been adopted. There are, however, some cases in which even this simple rule cannot be followed. There is a growing tendency among some authors and publishers to use the English word order for Japanese and Chinese personal names in title pages and book citations. In such cases there is no choice but to follow the same practice. For the romanization of Japanese words, the Hepburn system is used in which each syllable ends in a vowel, with the exception of the few syllables ending with the consonant *n*. There are as many syllables in a word as there are vowels. No syllable is accented, though there are long vowels which really constitute two syllables, as in Osaka. The long mark has been omitted in the following pages. Consonants in Japanese are sounded much as they are in English. Vowels are sounded as follows: *a* as in father; *i* as "ee" in feet; *u* as "oo" in food; *e* as in met; *o* as in home.

There is much variation in the spelling of Korean words in English and other western languages. During the long period of Japanese rule in Korea, 1910–1945, most maps used in the West employed the romanization of place names used by the Japanese. After 1945 there was a return to the romanized forms of the Korean terms. Perhaps the most satisfactory method of transliteration of Korean words and names is the McCune-Reischauer system (see *Transactions of the Royal Asiatic Society*, Korea Branch, XXIX, 1939) which resembles the Wade-Giles and Hepburn systems for Chinese and Japanese respectively. Consonants are sounded as in English, vowels as in Italian. The wider variation of vowel sounds in Korean than that represented in the English alphabet is usually indicated by certain diacritical notations. Some vowel sounds by way of example are: *o* pronounced as *a* in above, *o* as in moss, *u* as in full, *ae* as in bag, *oe* as the German *o*. Aspirated sounds are indicated by '. See George M. McCune, *Korea Today* (1950), xii-xiii.

The English meaning of a few common Chinese words in their romanized form will aid the beginning student.

chuan, stream
chung, middle or central (Chung Kuo, The Middle Kingdom)
fu, obsolete ending in name of a city
hai, sea
ho, river (in north China)
hsien, county
hu, lake
huang, yellow
hung, red
kiang, river (in central and south China)
ling, range, pass
nan, south
pai, white
peh, pei, north
shan, mountain
si, hsi, west
tai, large, great
t'ien, heaven
tung, east
wan, bay

The Antiquity of China and Japan

Christian Calendar	Dynasties of China	The World of Japan	Beyond East Asia	
B.C. 1300	Shang or Yin 1523–1027 B.C. (*Anyang*)		Tutankhamen, Egypt / Moses	1300
1200			Iron Age / Fall of Troy to the Greeks	1200
1100		PRE-HISTORY: Migrations from the Asiatic continent; tribal warfare.		1100
1000			Rigveda / David and Solomon, Judah	1000
900	Chou 1027–256 B.C.			900
800				800
700			Legendary Founding of Rome / Zoroaster	700
600	(Confucius)		Gautama, founder of Buddhism / Darius	600
500			Thermopylae / Parthenon completed	500
400			Alexander, Socrates / Chandragupta, Aristotle	400
300			Asoka	300
200	Ch'in, 221–207 B.C.		Hannibal	200

Timeline scale (top): 100 | 0 | 100 | 200 | 300 | 400 | 500 | 600 | 700 | 800 | 900

World events:
- Julius Caesar
- Jesus
- Kanishka
- Marcus Aurelius
- Mani
- Rome sacked by Alaric
- Attila
- Mohammed
- Harum Al Rashid
- Charlemagne

Japan:
- Founding of the Japanese State: Yamato
- (Shotoku Taishi)
- Nara, 710–784
- Heian 794–1185

China:
- Former Han 202 B.C.–A.D. 8 (*Sian*)
- Hsin, A.D. 8–23 (*Loyana*)
- Later Han 25–220
- 3 Kingdoms
- Western Chin
- Tsin
- Wei 386–534
- Sung / Ch'i / Liang / Ch'en
- Ch'i / Chou
- Sui, 590–618
- Tang 618–906
- 5 Dynasties
- 10 Kingdoms 907–979

Timeline scale (bottom): 100 | A.D. 0 | 100 | 200 | 300 | 400 | 500 | 600 | 700 | 800 | 900

Christian Calendar	Dynasties of China		The World of Japan	Beyond East Asia	
1000	Sung 960–1126	Liao 947–1127	Fujiwara (late Heian)	Lief Ericsson	1000
1100				William the Conqueror	1100
1200	Southern Sung 1127–1279	Chin 1127–1234	Kamakura 1185–1333	Magna Carta	1200
1300	Yuan (Mongols) 1260–1368			The Polos	1300
1400	Ming 1368–1644 (Nanking, Peking)		Ashikaga 1336–1573	John Wycliffe	1400
1500				Columbus Magellan; Henry VIII	1500
1600			Tokugawa 1603–1867	Shakespeare	1600
1700	Ch'ing (Manchus) 1644–1912 (Peking)			Glorious Revolution	1700
1800				U.S. Independence The French Revolution War of 1812 Crimean War	1800
1900			Meiji, 1868–1912		1900
1911	Republic (Nanking)		Taisho, 1912–1926	Two World Wars	1911
1941			Showa, 1926–		1941
1949	Communist China (Peking)			Korean War	1949
1970				Vietnam War	1970

Illustrations

China: Great Periods in History.   11
China with an Outline of the U.S.A.   12
The Mongol Empire, 1300 A.D.; and
     The Ming Empire, 15th century.   14
Japan.   40
Canton and Hong Kong.   62
Shanghai, 1930: International Settlement
     and French Concession.   80
Shanghai and the Yangtze.   86
Russo-Chinese Border Regions, 1860.   98
Japan in the 1850s.   114
Japan 1875–1890.   127
Principal Features of the Government of
     Japan under the Constitution of 1889
     (chart).   131
China in the Era of the Taiping
     Rebellion.   153
Japan 1891–1904.   189
Foreign Encroachment on China,
     1895–1911.   194
The Philippine Islands.   202
Japan 1905–1909.   237
The Kwantung (Liaotung) Peninsula.   241
The Shantung Peninsula.   268
Japan 1910–1919.   277

The Sino-Russian Frontier.   284
Japan 1920–1930.   290
The Kuomintang's Conquest of China,
     1926–1928.   317
Japan 1931–1933.   328
Japan's Projected Autonomous Region
     in North China.   334
The Shifting Base of Communist Power.   348
Five Years in China, 1937–1942.   354–55
The Advance of Colonialism in Southeast
     Asia.   369
Colonial Indonesia.   381
Indonesia with an Outline of the U.S.A.   383
Singapore Straits.   387
The Malayan Federation, July 1965.   388
Allied Counter-Attacks, 1943–1945.   399
The Kurile Islands and Sakhalin.   418
Government of Japan under the
     Constitution of 1947.   421
Agriculture in Communist China.   443
Industry in Communist China.   444
Divided Korea.   477
Nationalist China.   487
Principal Cities and Transportation Routes
     in the Indochina Area.   513

To Mary Kestler Clyde and Pauline Cone Beers

We are by nature observers, and thereby learners.

——Emerson

History's value . . . is, indeed, not scientific, but moral: by liberalizing the mind, by deepening the sympathies, by fortifying the will, it enables us to control, not society, but ourselves—a much more important thing; it prepares us to live more humanely in the present and to meet rather foretell the future.

——Becker

On History in General
and This History in Particular

chapter 1

History, of all intellectual disciplines, is the most used and the most abused. Perhaps this fact is not surprising because "Mr. Everyman," as Carl Becker once said, is an historian of sorts though he may be unaware of it. The performance of "Mr. Everyman's" simplest daily chores is possible only because his historical experience, such as it may be, tells him how to perform them, and to what purpose.

HISTORY DEFINED

History, in the broadest sense of the word, is the record of things thought, said, and done. Consciously or unconsciously all men and women cherish their history for many reasons. Among other things, it is a main avenue to understanding or misunderstanding the present. Its systematic pursuit in the quest of truth provides stern intellectual discipline. If it is good history it is even stranger than fiction. Its power to provide enjoyment is unsurpassed and, for those with a practical turn of mind, it is the principal means by which "Mr. Everyman," including "Mr. Student," may anticipate the future.

THE TWO HISTORIES

There are actually two histories. First, there is history in theory, in the absolute, the actual series of thoughts and events that once occurred. Second, there is history in all its raw distortions, the series each individual affirms and holds in memory. The latter has been called the history of the specious present. This history of the specious present is troublesome, because people everywhere believe in it as the epitome of their traditions and prejudices, wishful thinking, folklore, misinformation, and emotionalism. The power of this kind of history is very great, and is derived not from reality or truth but from what men wish to think and to believe. Naturally there is some correspondence between the two histories, and it is the business of the historian to make the correspondence as exact as possible. The degree of coincidence that may be achieved is determined by the ability of historians to write and of readers to recognize valid history and thereby minimize man's dependence on the history of the specious present.

Accordingly, the perceptive student will need to grapple at an early stage with baffling questions. What is an historical fact? What is the nature of its verification or proof? Another way of putting this problem is to ask whether the raw material of history, the so-called facts, general or particular, can be classified. Can they be described as objective or subjective? Is there a distinction between historical fact and historical interpretation? Does each have a function? How can the abuse of such functions be discovered, especially in the case of historical subjects on which men tend to disagree, sometimes violently? In dealing with such subjects, the historian is sometimes thought to be subversive, as the evidence he unearths and the conclusions which follow often run counter to man's deep-seated prejudices.[1]

THE NATURE OF THE PAST

History, the record of things thought, said, and done, is concerned with the past no matter whether the idea or the event in question occurred one minute ago or a thousand years ago. Moreover, history, to the uninitiated, may appear to be an easy subject until it is discovered that the past is not a simple but rather a very complex, elusive thing. To the question, "What has happened in the world in the twentieth century?" there is not one, but a variety of different answers. The physical scientist will not give the same answer as the biologist. The anthropologist, the political scientist, the sociologist, the humanist will each have his own answer and his own emphasis. There may well be areas where all answers coincide, indicating where educated men and women are in agreement; but, since each answer is drawn from a specialized background, its point of emphasis may reveal an aspect of reality or history overlooked or belittled by other intellectual disciplines.

History may thus have many points of emphasis depending on whether the historian is primarily interested in political, social, economic, artistic, scientific, or philosophical matters. All of these various approaches to history will have at least one

[1] See Carl Becker, "Everyman His Own Historian," *American Historical Review* 37 (1932): 221–36.

thing in common; they will all be concerned with change: for example, when, how, and why change takes place. In some eras of history changes in man's ideas and institutions occur with great speed and produce major alterations in the values of his society. The landing of two Americans on the moon and their safe return to earth is a dramatic example. Such periods are described as revolutionary, and it is one of these revolutionary eras in a particular part of the world which forms the principal subject of this book.

PROBLEMS IN THE STUDY OF ASIA

As the title has indicated, this study is concerned with extraordinary things that have been taking place in an area of the world known conventionally as the Far East but more properly as Eastern Asia. At the center of this geographical area is the world's oldest extant civilization—the Chinese—whose continuing stability until recently was unmatched by any society. Yet today this Chinese society is among the least stable or predictable forces in the world community. Indeed it may well be that the political and social history of the world in the century ahead will be determined as much by the temper of China as by the behavior of any other major state.

Few students in the 1970s will deny the importance of Asian studies. America's recent involvement in Asian wars—the Pacific War, 1941–45; the Korean War, 1950–52; and the Vietnam War of the 1960s—has highlighted the Orient's role in a world crisis. Yet it is not easy for Americans to acquire a thorough knowledge of China and other Asian countries. Until recent years American intellectual horizons seldom extended beyond the Western World. When in 1898 President William McKinley acknowledged that he was somewhat uncertain about just where the Philippine Islands might be, his confession was one to which most of his fellow countrymen could also subscribe. The political geography of Asia, when it was thought of at all, was considered a subject that might well be left to academicians with a fancy for strange and outlandish regions of the world. To be sure, there were Americans—traders, businessmen, sea captains, missionaries, and historians—who were not strangers to Asia's lands and peoples; but apart from these special groups, very few Americans had any systematic politico-geographical knowledge of China, Japan, India, or the lesser countries of the East. A popular school history, published in 1863 in New York, advised its readers that "China, a vast country of eastern Asia, may be almost said to have no history of any interest to the general reader, it has so few revolutions or political changes to record." [2]

There are of course many historical factors that explain the Americans' neglect of the larger world. As men built a new society in the United States they found satisfaction in certain negative rather than positive realities of geography, because realities such as the Atlantic Ocean enabled them to achieve that political separation from Europe which they so ardently desired. Geography was not a means by which cultural, political, or economic influence could be furthered. Later, when this new nation had acquired a coastline on the Pacific, men saw, to be sure, visions of a great commerce with Asia; they even pictured the Pacific as an American lake. Yet they were more than ever dominated by a philosophy of political isolation, and it was thus very satisfying that the Pacific Ocean was wide and the "teeming millions" of Asia were far away. If, as many American forefathers saw it, there was little reason to be concerned about the political affairs of Europe (since they were largely a matter of the sinister rivalries of kings), there was even less to recommend the civilizations of Asia, inhabited as the continent was by Oriental despots and a heathen, "uncivilized" society.

"The march of events," however, often has scant respect for man's deep-rooted habits and traditions. American participation in

Asia's recent military and political crises has given thousands of Americans an undreamed of familiarity with those same distant lands which their fathers and grandfathers had called strange and outlandish. Furthermore, this growing contact has been accompanied by a measure of educational reform. In some of America's larger universities, centers devoted to research on Asian societies have been established; graduate and undergraduate courses, few of which were available before 1941, have multiplied; and in a few American localities the study of Asia has even been incorporated into the public schools' curricula. Yet, in spite of these changes, American education at all levels remains predominantly European-centered. Asia studies "still remain on the fringe of things. . . ." [3] In consequence, the "liberally" educated student, even in the 1970s, may complete this schooling with little knowledge beyond the Western tradition. This is not to suggest, of course, that for Americans an emphasis on European institutions and their American derivatives is less than imperative. It does not follow, however, that Asian studies, as newcomers to American education, are "exotic," or that students should be encouraged to regard them as a special field of study. In reality the civilizations of the Occident and Orient are so interwoven that education built on the exclusion of one or the other can hardly be called education at all for it ignores half of human experience.[4]

THE CONTINENT OF ASIA

Eastern Asia, though an immense area in itself, is but a part of the world's largest continent, Eurasia. Asia is pre-eminent among all the continents in both size and altitude. Covering one-third of the land surface of the world, Asia comprises some

---

[2] Marcius Willson, *Outlines of History* (1863): 286–87. At the very moment when Willson was writing, China was in the grip of the T'ai-p'ing rebellion, the most devastating upheaval any society had known.

[3] Holden Furber, "Asia and the West as Partners Before 'Empire' and After," *Journal of Asian Studies*, 28 (1969): 720.

[4] See Ward Morehouse, "Asia and Africa in Today's World," *Teachers College Record*, 63 (1962): 551–56; and John K. Fairbank, "Assignment for the '70's," *American Historical Review*, 74 (1969): 861–79.

18,500,000 square miles. It is larger than the combined area of North and South America, and more than four times the size of Europe. If considered in terms of linear distance, Asia extends for some 6,000 miles from east to west and for more than 5,000 miles from its most northerly to its most southerly point. However, the most compelling characteristic of Asia's physical formation is neither its unique size nor its towering altitudes, but rather its "gigantic development of plateau." This plateau extends for some 9,000 miles in a great arc from the eastern Mediterranean to the Bering Strait, widening in some areas to nearly 2,000 miles in the heart of the Tibetan tableland. As geographers measure this plateau, it covers nearly two-fifths of Asia's land mass, but it supports only a limited and mostly pastoral population.

Asia's physical diversity is matched by an even greater social diversity including three major civilizations, the Chinese, the Hindu, and the Islamic. Asia is therefore only a geographical term, since Asia as a social unit has no existence at all.[5]

Of the estimated three and one half billion inhabitants of the world (1970), more than half live in Asia. Most of this multitude is in the southern and eastern fringes of the continent: in India, China, Japan, Korea, and the East Indies. Important, too, is the fact that the overwhelming proportion of this vast population are tillers of the soil. Just prior to World War II, Japan was the only Asiatic country with a highly developed industry, and even in Japan some 50 per cent of the population still lived by the soil.

The climates of Asia are varied, yet there are certain broad features that may be said to affect the continent as a whole. Of these the best known, and, to the early European navigators the most useful, was the monsoon. The monsoon is comprised of seasonal winds blowing south and westerly from the heart of the continent in the winter or dry season, and north and easterly from the Indian Ocean in the summer or wet season. From the sixteenth to the mid-nineteenth century, it was on the spring or summer monsoon that the European navigators sailed to Canton, and on the winter monsoon they turned their course homeward. But of greater importance to the population of Asia was the fact that the wet monsoon brought the seasonal rains that made it possible for so many to live on the land in southern Asia. Farther inland, where the moisture did not reach, were the arid and semi-arid regions of the Mongolian plateau.

Land configuration and climate in Asia are reflected not only in the distribution of Asia's population but also in its racial and cultural traits. In Asia, immense size, virtually impassable barriers of mountain and desert, and extreme variations of climate generally precluded communication over the continent as a whole. Furthermore, it should be observed that geography not only separated the great civilizations of Asia one from another, but it also isolated these people, until very recent times, from other centers of civilization such as Western Europe. Indeed it may be said that this isolation remained for practical purposes unbroken until as recently as the late nineteenth century. When the barriers of separation were finally broken by an expanding Western World, the Far East was overwhelmed. There had been no preparation in Asia to meet the modern West, which had been enriched and empowered by all that Europe had achieved since the Renaissance in government, trade, invention, science, industry, and literature.

THE FAR EAST

Eastern Asia comprises those lands of the Asiatic continent and adjacent islands that lie east of longitude 90° east of Greenwich. The mainland includes eastern Siberia, Korea or Chosen, China and its borderland territories—Manchuria, Mongolia, Sinkiang or Chinese Turkestan, and Tibet; to the south, Burma, Siam (Thailand), Indochina (Vietnam, Laos, Cambodia, and Cochin China), and Malaya; and the insular areas, Japan, the Philippines, and the East Indies

[5] John M. Steadman, "The Myth of Asia," *The American Scholar* 25 (1956): 163–75.

or Indonesia. To the eighteenth- and nineteenth-century Americans as well as to the Europeans, the term Far East was more descriptively suggestive than it is today, since, in those days, mariners sailing to China skirted Africa and sailed eastward. Thus in a very real sense China and the lands immediately surrounding it were the Far East. For Americans of the mid-twentieth century, the region is neither east nor far.

THE THEME OF THIS HISTORY

Throughout the past 150 years, as noted, Eastern Asia has been the stage for a revolution perhaps unequalled in all history in the breadth and depth of its penetration. It has involved two great movements. The first was the expansion of Western civilization in all its aspects and power into the old and traditional societies of Middle and Eastern Asia. This movement, which began in the early nineteenth century and is usually called the "Impact of the West," had all but conquered Asia in military and political power by the beginning of the twentieth century. By that time, however, the second aspect of this revolution was well under way. The response of Asia to the Western impact was at first faltering, uneven, and uncharted, but by the end of World War II it had gathered an irresistible momentum. The result in mid-twentieth century was a new Eastern Asia—chaotic, often irresponsible, jealous of its "rights" and its newfound political freedom, torn between the fiercely opposed Western ideologies of democracy and communism (both of which few Asians understood). While the Asians were overwhelmed by poverty in the resources and skills that could raise their world to new standards, they were also suspicious that bounty from the West would substitute an economic for the older political "enslavement."

There are, of course, many avenues of approach to a study of the modern Far East. The avenue that will be found here is that of history. Asia's revolution is a product of historical growth. The successes and the failures in the meeting of East and West can be understood only in the light of the disciplined background knowledge that history should provide. Within broad topics, therefore, this is a chronological survey, since time and history are inseparable. The study begins with a descriptive survey of some principal ideas and institutions of Old China and Old Japan. These, the major countries of the Far East, had developed rich and enduring civilizations very unlike the cultural background of the modern Western World. A study of the Western impact must therefore provide some foundations in historic Asiatic values.

For example, a concept that has one meaning in the United States may have quite another meaning in China. In the West, the concepts of individual freedom and of law as preservers of individual rights have been regarded as foundations of just government. In China, individualism (a foreign notion for which a term had to be coined) suggests unordered selfishness rather than a high ideal. Likewise, law in China, compared to its role in Western society, has little to do with the rights of individuals but is of great importance as an administrative tool to be used in the interest of the state. Thus the assumption, often entertained by Americans, that the Chinese would react like Americans to a given proposal, is, at best, rather far-fetched.[6]

The most conspicuous aspects of the meeting of West and East have been in the areas of war and diplomacy, often termed the field of international relations. Yet, formal international relations alone have not been the sole means of contact, nor have they been necessarily the most significant. Accordingly, emphasis will be given in this study to the West-East traffic in ideas and values and to the institutions through which man gives expression to them. Asia's contemporary revolutions were born in the migration of ideas from West to East that spanned the past century. Here, too, attention will be given to the way in which the Asians received Western thought. It is re-

[6] See John K. Fairbank, *China: the People's Middle Kingdom and the U.S.A.* (1967).

markable that the West has given surprisingly little attention to this key subject until so recently as World War II. The result has been a shocking failure to understand Asia's aspirations, the sources from which they arose, or the means she might use to achieve them.

Perhaps, too, it is well to be reminded again that the following narrative is in itself only an introduction to Eastern Asia's recent experience with the West. The vastness and the variety, the age and the wealth of Eastern Asia's civilizations as they have entered upon the modern age cannot be disposed of within the covers of a single book. The purpose here is to provide some foundations on which those who would know the China or the Japan of tomorrow may first learn how they came to be as they are today.

This story of the Western impact and of Eastern Asia's response has led the authors of this study to develop a stimulus-response theory of history which, they feel, has particular applicability in the narrative to be related in these pages. However, it should not be assumed that this theory alone is a complete avenue of approach to the history of Eastern Asia in the nineteenth and twentieth centuries.

PROBLEMS IN THE STUDY AND TEACHING OF HISTORY

The question of how a student may best study history, or how a teacher may best teach it has no one simple answer. There was a time when the student who, under a good deal of prodding, had memorized the names and dates of the kings of England and the presidents of the United States was regarded as one who was on the right track. In reality, what this victim had done was to develop his memory and thus prepare himself to grapple with the kings of France and, if he were so disposed, with the emperors of China. In the study of history, one should remember that mastering the names and dates of the kings of England may be a very useful first step, but it should not be confused with history.

More recently, over the past fifty or so years, the teaching of history, at least to beginning college students, has taken the form of broad-structured survey courses in which large classes of students listen to lectures, occasionally brilliant but more often quite pedestrian. Save in exceptional cases, this system has only limited justification since much that is dispensed in lectures can be found in far better form in reputable books. The lecture system is most useful where it amplifies and integrates evidence the student has already acquired.

In contemporary times, efforts have been and are being made to find more meaningful ways by which the beginning student may discover whether history is relevant to him. The rationale of these newer approaches is that history, which has been completely prestructured for the student, denies to him the stimulus of discovery. This theory postulates that students learn best what they discover for themselves, and this is doubtless quite true. Thus, in history, the most important thing for a student to learn first is how to learn, what to learn, and to what purpose. In this approach, the student is confronted with documents, the raw materials of history—original manuscripts, letters, eyewitness accounts, treaties, diplomatic and other official or unofficial correspondence. He is assigned the task of learning how to use these sources, how to draw conclusions from them, and how to test these conclusions. He thereby takes the first step toward creating his own structure of the subject. He is on the way to becoming an historian, which is another way of saying he will have some sense of what history is and what it can mean.

As a matter of fact, none of these approaches to the study of history is either new or exclusive. Each of them has its proper place. History is as broad and all-inclusive as man's comprehension. What men have sought and will seek to find in history is far more complex and varied than the processes by which a computer spews out its answers. No two students will enter the maze of history in precisely the same way or with identical objectives. What teachers and students need to bear in mind is that somewhere there is what Carl Becker called history in the absolute—the actual thoughts and deeds that once occurred. It is the search for this absolute, even if unattainable, which justifies the writing and the study of history.

In the contemporary world of America and elsewhere, an encouraging sign is the increasing desire of students for intellectual pursuits that are "relevant." This desire, in fact, is essential in the study of history. Relevance, which may be defined as that which bears upon or is connected with the matter at hand, may in some cases of the immediate present be self-evident; more frequently, relevance is a subtle and elusive thing. In the case of history, the student's ultimate discovery of relevance should be a primary goal and an unending search, but its attainment, even in some limited measure, requires first the labor and the patience necessary to master the fundamentals and the content of the subject. There can be no historical relevance for those who are unwilling to struggle with the learning process. The student of history is called upon constantly to distinguish between what is historically relevant and what is less so. Interpretation of the historical evidence must provide the answer, not the whim of an individual or a group. Contemporaneity alone is not the badge of relevance.

Asking the Right Questions

Again, the student of history, like the professional historian, needs to develop the capacity to seek historical meaning by asking the questions that can direct the quest for answers. Sometimes the appropriate questions and the answers to them are relatively simple. It may be important, for example, to determine the exact date of a given event in order to relate it to other events on which it is presumed to have had an effect. How does the historian go about this task? Some historical questions are far more profound and far more frustrating. It will be noted in succeeding pages of this book that governments, even entire societies, have made specific plans for the future and have adopted careful programs of action to implement this

future. Yet the programs of action, even when applied with vigor, have produced conditions and results which were the antithesis of what the government or the society was attempting to achieve. How is this kind of phenomenon to be explained?

Language and Meaning

There is an additional pitfall into which the scholar and student of history can easily fall. Precise thought and precise language to give it expression are not easily come by. For example, there will be frequent reference in the pages which follow to "modernization" and "Westernization" in the past century or so of Far Eastern history. The trouble is that these terms are not precise in meaning. They may easily convey very different concepts to different people. At best they are convenient labels which continue in use for want of something better.[7]

Furthermore, as the student or the general reader enters upon the narrative that is contained in this book, he should note that the writing and the study of history in the latter part of the twentieth century are beset with difficulties that are in some measure unique. By way of example, one may recall that in the first half of this century so-called scientific history written by conservative evolutionists seemed less satisfying than it once had been. The experimental and skeptical approach of science played havoc with inherited values, and many historians attempted to become social scientists with a problem orientation. The result was the charge that subjective values had been so much a part of written history as to reduce the product to an act of faith based on a framework of assumptions within an orthodox body of opinion.[8]

[7] On this perplexing subject of ideas and language, the student should consult: Knight Biggerstaff, "Modernization—And Early Modern China," *Journal of Asian Studies* 25 (1966): 607–20; Ardath Burks, "Modernization in Korea," *ibid.* 27 (1968): 609–12; and Marius B. Jansen, ed., *Changing Japanese Attitudes Toward Modernization* (1965),* especially ch. 1 by John Whitney Hall. [Note: The asterisk indicates a paperback edition.]

[8] See John Higham *et al., History* (1965).*

In a word, the nature and functions of history itself have been called in question in a time of world crisis. A major difference between this present crisis and earlier ones is related to the charge that in some major degree man has lost his capacity to believe. The idea is suggested by some contemporary slogans: "the end of ideology" and "God is dead." Man's growing critical faculties and his sense of relativity have reduced his capacity to replace old ideologies with new ones or to replace an old with a new religion.

As the reader enters upon the following historical introduction to an aspect of modern Far Eastern history—the Western impact and the Asian response during the past century—he will find it helpful to be conscious of the pitfalls and the limitations of history in general and of this phase of history in particular.

In this chapter, suggestions have been given as to the nature of history itself. It has been noted that while history, even at its best, is an imperfect product, it is, nevertheless, an indispensable factor in the human quest for understanding. It has also been suggested that creative study and research in history require of both teacher and student disciplined methodology of the highest order. When disciplined methodology is absent, the record of history will present what men wish to believe rather than what they ought to know.

Finally, these opening pages have remarked on some special problems that confront American and other Western students as they attempt to grapple with the modern Far East. Far Eastern languages by their nature and diversity are a major, though not an insurmountable, hurdle. Far more persistent as an obstacle is the long-standing American assumption that the Far East can be known and understood through the medium of traditional American mores and values. The task of overcoming these and other special problems is not easy, but it can be rewarding.

FOR FURTHER READING

BIBLIOGRAPHIES. American Historical Association, comp. and ed., *A Guide to Historical Literature* (1961). American Universities Field Staff, *A Select Bibliography: Asia, Africa, Eastern Europe, Latin America* (1960), with *Supplements* (1961 and 1963). S. F. Bemis and G. G. Griffin, *Guide to the Diplomatic History of the United States, 1775–1921* (1935). *Bibliography of Asian Studies,* pub. annually by The Association for Asian Studies, formerly The Far Eastern Association. Charles O. Hucker, *China, A Critical Bibliography;* and Bernard S. Silberman, *Japan and Korea, A Critical Bibliography* (1962). R. J. Kerner, *Northeastern Asia: A Selected Bibliography* (2 vols., 1939). Hyman Kublin, comp., *An Introductory Reading Guide to Asia* (3rd rev. ed., 1962). W. L. Langer and H. F. Armstrong, *Foreign Affairs Bibliography: a Selected and Annotated List of Books on International Relations, 1919–1932* (1933). Clifford H. MacFadden, *A Bibliography of Pacific Area Maps* (1941).

GEOGRAPHY AND PEOPLE. Inez Adams, "Rice Cultivation in Asia," *American Anthropologist* 50 (April-June, 1948), 256–82. Daniel R. Bergsmark, *Economic Geography of Asia* (1935) is still a useful introductory survey. L. H. D. Buxton, *The Peoples of Asia* (1925). George B. Cressey, *Asia's Lands and People* (3rd ed., 1963), perhaps the most useful and comprehensive survey of the physical environment and cultural features. E. H. G. Dobby, *Monsoon Asia* (1961), useful reference, of uneven quality. Norton S. Ginsburg, ed., *The Pattern of Asia* (1958), general geography of Asia. Pierre Gourou, Joseph E. Spencer, and Glenn T. Trewartha, *The Development of Upland Areas in the Far East* (1949). Albert Herrman, *Historical and Commercial Atlas of China* (1935 and 1963). Albert Herrmann, *An Historical Atlas of China.* New edition edited by Norton Ginsburg (1966). Lionel

W. Lyde, *The Continent of Asia* (London, 1933), a detailed, technical study. Rhoads Murphey, *An Introduction to Geography* (1961), an excellent geography with maps, charts, and illustrations. Louis Richard, *Comprehensive Geography of the Chinese Empire and Dependencies* (Shanghai, 1908), historically still very useful. L. Dudley Stamp, *Asia* (3rd ed., 1935). Guy Wint, ed., *Asia: A Handbook* (1966), handles the problems of Asia systematically and concisely.

GOVERNMENT AND POLITICS. Three important general studies are: George McTurnan Kahin, ed., *Major Governments of Asia* (1958; second ed., 1963), a symposium on political systems and processes in China, Japan, India, Pakistan, and Indonesia in modern times; Robert E. Ward and Roy C. Macridis, eds., *Modern Political Systems: Asia* (1963); and Paul M. A. Linebarger, Chu Djang, and Ardath Burks, *Far East Governments and Politics* (1954).

TREATY COLLECTIONS. Carnegie Endowment for International Peace, *Treaties and Agreements with and Concerning China, 1919–1929* (1929). China, the Maritime Customs, *Treaties, Conventions, etc., Between China and Foreign States* (2 vols., 2nd ed., Shanghai, 1917). Henry Chung, *Korean Treaties* (1919). Hertslet's, *China Treaties* (2 vols., 3rd ed., London, 1908). League of Nations, *Treaty Series* (London, 1920-). J. V. A. MacMurray, ed., *Treaties and Agreements with and Concerning China, 1894–1919* (2 vols., 1921). W. M. Malloy, ed., *Treaties, Conventions, International Acts, Protocols and Agreements Between the United States and Other Powers* (3 vols., 1909–1923). W. F. Mayers, *Treaties Between the Empire of China and Foreign Powers* (3rd ed., Shanghai, 1901). David Hunter Miller, ed., *Treaties and Other International Acts of the United States of America* (8 vols., 1931–1948) scholarly and meticulous. W. W. Rockhill, *Treaties and Conventions with or Concerning China and Korea, 1894–1904*

(1904). United States, *Treaties and Other International Agreements* (1950 and subsequent years).

UNITED STATES DOCUMENTS. *The Annals of Congress* (1789–1824), *Register of Debates* (1825–1837), *The Congressional Globe* (1833–1873), and *The Congressional Record* (1873 to date), illuminating material from the debates in Congress on foreign relations. *Papers Relating to the Foreign Relations of the United States* (1861 and subsequent years), annual volumes contain selections from American diplomatic correspondence with liberal sections devoted to the Far East.

LITERATURE IN TRANSLATION. Two excellent anthologies include: G. L. Anderson, ed., *Masterpieces of the Orient* (1961);* John D. Yohannan, ed., *A Treasury of Asian Literature* (1956).

PERIODICALS. Many of the more definitive studies on aspects of modern Far Eastern history are scattered throughout an extensive periodical literature, in the journals of learned and professional societies, and in popular and semi-popular periodicals. The following is a selected list of some of these journals: *The American Historical Review, American Journal of International Law, American Political Science Review, Annals of the American Academy of Political and Social Science, Asian Survey, The China Quarterly, Contemporary Japan,* The Foreign Policy Association, *Bulletins and Reports, The Harvard Journal of Asiatic Studies, The Journal of Asian Studies* (before 1957 *The Far Eastern Quarterly*), *Pacific Affairs, The Journal of Modern History, The Pacific Historical Review, Philippine Social Science Review, Political Science Quarterly, Transactions of the Asiatic Society of Japan, Transactions and Proceedings of the Japan Society of London,* United Nations Department of Economic Affairs, *Economic Survey of Asia and the Far East, United States Naval Institute Proceedings.*

Ways of Life
in Old China

chapter 2

The civilization of China is one of the oldest and one of the richest known to man. Yet, until recently, it has been given little attention in the United States. This neglect is curious because for more than a century the American people thought themselves the friends of China, and, during the same period, the United States government adhered to a policy of friendly relations with China. In principle at least, the United States was the defender of China's political integrity. Nevertheless, the richness of China's thought and culture has occupied an extraordinarily small corner in the scheme of American education and in the recesses of American thought. Europe, in contrast to America, has often been more conscious of the intellectual gifts China could offer, but even in Europe enthusiasm for things Chinese has been sporadic. The result is that although there is a long history of intercourse between China and the Western world, the two civilizations have actually never ceased to be strangers. Thus, before entering upon the story of the growth of contacts between China and the West, it will be helpful to review briefly some of the highlights of China's institutional history.

THE ANTIQUITY OF CHINA

Students are sometimes struck, and perhaps irritated, by the seemingly curious ways and the outmoded ideas of their elders. The few years that separate the younger generation from the older can make a vast difference in the point of view. Similar tensions are apt to be present when a young nation such as the United States is thrown into daily contact with a very old civilization such as China's. The American people, for example, have been an independent politico-social group for almost 200 years, and this appears quite a respectable age until it is recalled that the Chinese people have been a social group developing an integrated cultural heritage for more than 3,000 years. This important factor of time and age may be stated another way. The United States has been regarded as the leader of the contemporary "Free World" for some four decades, but China was regarded as the cultural center of the Far Eastern world both ancient and modern for something like two millenniums. It should not be surprising then if the American sense of values and the Chinese sense of values do not always add up to the same thing. Nor should it be surprising to learn that the Chinese called their land

CHINA: GREAT PERIODS IN HISTORY

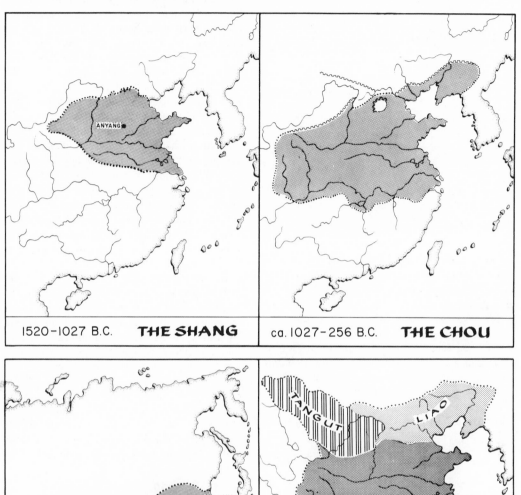

1520-1027 B.C.	**THE SHANG**	ca. 1027-256 B.C.	**THE CHOU**
100 A.D.	**THE HAN EMPIRE**	1100 A.D.	**SUNG, TANGUT**

Adapted with permission from L. Carrington Goodrich, A Short History of the Chinese People *(New York: Harper & Row) 1943.*

CHINA
WITH OUTLINE OF U S A
ON SAME SCALE

Chung-kuo, the central country, or, as the name often appeared in Western literature, The Middle Kingdom, a name which might lead one to suspect that the Chinese of today, even as the Chinese of yesterday, are culturally a very proud people. Indeed, an educated Chinese, whether he be a Confucian, or a Communist, is an heir to a rich and ancient cultural tradition revealing itself in an immense and varied society, unrivalled in age by any political or social community the world has ever known.

CHINESE HISTORY

The chronological chart of China, page xx suggests some perspective in this matter of time. At the beginning of the Christian era, China was already an old society. Sometime within the sixteenth to the eleventh centuries B.C., her learned men had even created a system of writing that employed most of the important principles involved in the intricate modern Chinese written characters. Time was already calculated by a calendar which was frequently adjusted to keep it in step with the seasons of the year. This matter of adjustability was quite important. In an agricultural country and among a credulous people, a ruler might easily lose his job and his head, too, if the

seasons went astray.[1] The greatest names in Chinese history—Confucius, and that vague figure, Lao-tzu, together with other great philosophers who have left their mark on every succeeding generation in China—belong to the ancient days of the Chou dynasty, 1027–256 B.C. Between 221 and 207 B.C., the succeeding Ch'in rulers had made their king into China's first emperor, Shih Huang Ti, and had completed the Great Wall along the northern frontier, thus emphasizing what was Chinese and what was foreign, and therefore inferior and barbarian.

Ch'in indeed witnessed the beginnings of one of the great revolutions in China's history, a revolution comparable only with that now taking place in twentieth-century China. This early revolution sought to destroy the ancient feudal system, thereby laying the foundations for a relatively centralized bureaucratic state. The extent of this ruthless social upheaval is suggested by the fact that the kings of the earlier feudal China were aristocrats who claimed divine ancestry and, together with the nobility, were the sole possessors of political power, whereas Liu Pang, founder of the Han dynasty, 202 B.C., was born a poor peasant. The contributions of the Ch'in revolution, however, were not always constructive. Shih Huang Ti is also remembered for his "burning of the books" by which he vainly hoped to narrow and discipline the course of Chinese intellectual development.[2]

The Han, 202 B.C.–A.D. 8 and 25–220 A.D.

It is hardly surprising that the Chinese have liked to call themselves the Sons of Han, for Han is one of the richest and most inspiring periods in China's long history. The forces which had struck at the political and social systems of the old feudal China also

[1] The basic study is H. G. Creel, *The Birth of China* 1954).° See also K. S. Latourette, *The Chinese: Their History and Culture* (3rd ed., 1946). A brief survey, convenient as an introduction, is L. Carrington Goodrich, *A Short History of the Chinese People* (1943; 3rd ed., 1959).°

[2] C. P. Fitzgerald, *China: A Short Cultural History* (London, 1935; rev. ed., 1950).°

prepared the way for an era of discovery, expansion, and conquest which made China a great power dominating the eastern half of Asia.

Han culture enriched China's life in seemingly numberless ways: in literature and the arts, in government, science, and industry. Here began the painstaking search and research to rediscover the proscribed classics. Here was laid the foundation for the Confucian conquest of the Chinese mind, of which more will be said later.

The creative qualities of Han culture were amazingly varied. A lunar calendar was developed with great mathematical accuracy. A seismograph detected earthquakes so slight that people did not notice them. Glaced pottery was being made at the close of the Han period. Elaborately embroidered silks were woven for both domestic and foreign trade. Han ladies improved on nature with face powder and rouge. Literature became richer in expression. Manuscripts were collected in an imperial library, and the first standard histories were written on paper which appears to have been made from rags.[3]

The T'ang Dynasty, 618–906

It was four centuries after the fall of Han before China again entered a period of greatness. T'ang China is usually called the most brilliant period of that country's history. Education was officially encouraged. Civil service examinations, an idea adapted from the previous Sui dynasty, were stressed. Though the state cult of Confucius was later favored, religious tolerance prevailed in general. Laws were codified, and commerce was encouraged by extension of the canal system. In the middle of the eighth century the T'ang Empire covered not only the greater part of what in the nineteenth century was known as China Proper, but also south and central Manchuria and the vast area of Turkestan far to the west. T'ang rulers, endowed with great political perception, challenged the growing

[3] Richard Wilhelm, *A Short History of Chinese Civilization* (1929); and John K. Shryock, *The Origin and Development of the State Cult of Confucius* (1932).

political power of Buddhism and other religions, subjecting them to the State or suppressing them. Architecture and sculpture reached new peaks of excellence. Ch'ang-an, the capital of T'ang China, with a population of nearly two million in 742, was architecturally one of the world's finest cities. Ch'ang-an formed the model for Japan's first permanent capital, Nara. T'ang was also the great age of Chinese poets: Li Po, Tu Fu, Wang Wei, Po Chu-i, and Wei Ying-wu. Two great encyclopedias were compiled. The short story, which formerly dealt only with the world of spirits, entered the more human and mundane field of life and love. Block printing was invented.

The Sung Empire, 960–1279

With the fall of the T'ang Empire, China was again overtaken by political confusion. Between 907 and 960, a succession of the so-called "Five Dynasties" maintained a precarious hold on what remained of the T'ang Empire. In general this was a period of rule by "licentious tyrants," of such sensual refinements as the binding of women's feet (which seems to have been imposed first upon dancing girls), and a period of general breakdown in the entire economic and political structure of society. Out of this chaos, however, rose the Sung empire, which, with the exception of the years 1127–1135, ruled China from 960 to 1279. Sung China at its height was a period of general advancement in the livelihood of the people. Even the common folk began to sit on chairs instead of the floor. Sung was also a period of renaissance in the arts and in education. Unlike T'ang, when the poets excelled, under Sung the writers of prose took the lead. Porcelain, landscape painting, block printing, and Neo-Confucianism were particularly famous in the Sung dynasty. There was also advance in the science of algebra, probably introduced through the Arab trade. All in all, the civilization of Sung China probably outstripped any of its contemporary rivals so that Shao Yung might well have said: "I am happy because I am a human and not an animal; a male, and not a female; a Chinese,

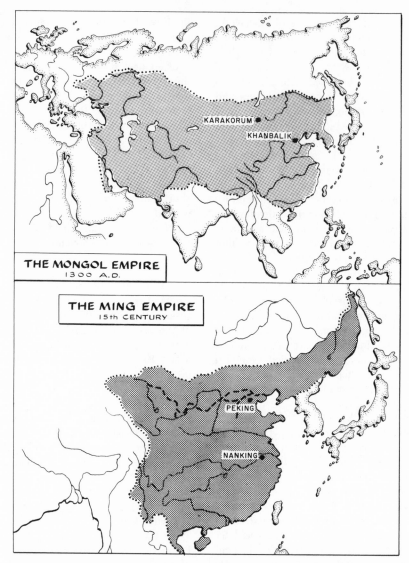

THE MONGOL EMPIRE
1300 A.D.

THE MING EMPIRE
15th CENTURY

Adapted with permission from L. Carrington Goodrich, A Short History of the Chinese People *(New York: Harper & Row) 1943.*

and not a barbarian; and because I live in Loyang, the most wonderful city in all the world." [4]

The Mongols, 1260–1368

After three centuries of Sung rule, China was conquered by the Mongols. Near

[4] Quoted by L. Carrington Goodrich, *A Short History of the Chinese People* (rev. ed., 1963),* 163.

the end of the thirteenth century, the greater Mongol Empire extended from the eastern seaboard of China and as far north as the Amur in a continuous broad belt across the heart of Asia to the borders of Arabia and far into European Russia. The Mongols, in their advance upon China, controlled Mongolia by 1206, overran Korea in 1231, and made Cambaluc (Peking) their eastern winter capital in 1264. Under Kublai Khan's leadership, Yunnan was conquered, Annam was reduced to vassalage, and two unsuccessful expeditions were dispatched against Japan. China had become a part of the world empire. It was the period when, as will be seen in later chapters, the world was shrinking; ideas as well as goods travelled the caravan routes from Peking to the Danube.

The Ming, 1368–1644;
The Ch'ing (Manchu), 1644–1912

With the fall of the Mongol power after a century of rule, China passed under the control of its last native Chinese dynasty, the Ming, which in mid-seventeenth century was overcome by another alien conqueror, the Manchus, who ruled until the establishment of the Republic in 1912.

THE IDEAS BY WHICH
OLD CHINA LIVED

China's long history from its beginning to the end of the Manchu dynasty in 1912 may be labeled conveniently as the Age of Old China to distinguish it from Republican China, 1912–1949, or Communist China after 1949. These latter periods, as indicated by the chart, p. xx , are barely perceptible when compared with the long course of Chinese history. To say, therefore, in any basic historical sense, that an idea or philosophy or institution is "Chinese" means that it was born and nurtured as a part of Old China.

While this Old China was, in the main, a remarkably stable and enduring society, it was not the unchanging society Western observers often thought it to be. In fact, Old China, at one time or another, produced an almost infinite variety of ideas and institutions, some of which survived into modern times. For example, Sung China was remarkable for its diversity of thought and for a relative absence of official orthodoxy.

For the purposes of this history, the Ch'ing or Manchu period (1644–1912) is of particular importance because it was in this period that China was faced with the impact

of European, and later American, expansion. In a sense, Manchu China lay between what was traditional and what is modern. The Manchu period, like all Chinese history, left notable legacies to the China of today. Many of these legacies are derived from ancient China, but the Ch'ing period placed its peculiar stamp upon them. The Manchu era made at least five significant contributions to the form of early modern China:

1. It was a period of empire building, geographically and historically speaking. During most of the age of Old China, the area of effective Chinese jurisdiction was some 1,500,000 square miles (about half the area of the United States), whereas in the late Ch'ing period, the empire covered some 4,275,000 square miles.
2. The Ch'ing period also gave to China a major population problem. In previous periods, China's peak population was probably 100,000,000. Yet by 1850, despite an unfavorable population-land ratio and worsening economic conditions, China's population had reached 430,000,-000. In 1968, China's estimated population was some 700,000,000.
3. The key to Manchu success in conquest lay in a policy of systematic sinicization. The supreme test of this policy came in 1851 when, in the T'ai-p'ing rebellion (of which the reader will hear more later), the bulk of the scholar-official class fought to sustain their "foreign" Manchu masters.
4. In the Manchu period, too, political, economic, and social institutions achieved greater maturity, and interregional integration became more pronounced.
5. Finally, the Ch'ing period, particularly in the eighteenth century, was one of enrichment and fulfillment. The variety of articles for mass and elite consumption was notable. Substantial segments of the population enjoyed a rising standard of living. The rich could afford to be extravagant. It became fashionable for the elite to cultivate artistic and scholarly avocations.[5]

However, even when due allowance is made for the distinctive features that set apart one period of Chinese history from an-

[5] For the development of this subject see Ping-ti Ho, "The Significance of the Ch'ing Period in Chinese History," *Journal of Asian Studies* 26 (1967): 189–95.

other, the fact remains that the Chinese way of life has exhibited an amazingly constant character. At its center were a number of ideas, ideals, and goals forming the common denominator of China's political, social, and philosophical thought.

The Meaning of Life

Educated Chinese have always been more concerned with the world of nature and of man than with the elusive world of the supernatural. The church and the priesthood played a lesser role in China than in most great civilizations. This is not to say that there were no religious motivations in China. They were present, but they expressed themselves principally through ancestor worship. The point to note is that ancestor worship belonged to the single family group. It could not become an institutionalized national or international church. The idea of divinity was, of course, not absent. Sacred mountains and other forms of nature were worshipped, as was the supreme Chinese divinity, *T'ien*, or Heaven; but these forces remained abstract and were rarely personified. An important consequence was that the Chinese were remarkably free from religious intolerance or bigotry. When persecution occurred it was occasioned not by religious ideas as such, but by religious movements that sought to control the State. Finally, the Chinese were not enticed by proffered rewards in heaven or tormented by threats of everlasting punishment in hell. Such notions did not appear in China until introduced by Buddhism and other alien faiths. In a comparative sense, then, the Chinese were not a religious people.[6]

The Social Philosophy

If the educated Chinese were not greatly concerned about other-worldliness, they were very much preoccupied with this world, namely, with nature and with man, which they considered to be one great unity. As a part of this unity, man was certainly important, but he was not the supreme tri-

[6] An adequate discussion of the subject is Derk Bodde, "Dominant Ideas," *China,* H. F. MacNair, ed. (1946), 18–28.

umph of creation which Christian religious thought has attempted to make of him. The idea was that if man was to be in harmony with the universal unity (God), he would adjust himself to the universe, that is, to nature. In contrast, the modern West has sought what it calls "happiness" in bending nature to the will of man. Traditional Chinese ideas could not have approved an A-bomb, much less an H-Bomb. Furthermore, within the universal unity of man and nature, man's problem was to find and practice the means of getting along with his fellow men. Long before the Christian era began, Chinese thinkers were well aware that so-called progress and growth in material power merely increase the tribulations of men unless they have first solved the riddle of human relations. This Chinese concern with the immediate troubles and pleasures of human existence is what is usually meant when the Chinese are described as a very "practical" people.

Harmony and Stability

Concerned with human problems here and now, the Chinese developed a temporal mindedness that laid great stress on man's experience. They thus became great compilers of history, from which it was believed man could learn how to behave. Since rulers often prefer the history of the specious present, these official historical writings perpetuated the ideas thought to be most valid. Moreover, the society that the Chinese recorded in such detail was very complex and rich in ideas. Here it will be sufficient to note merely a few of the concepts that exercised an extraordinary power over the Chinese mind.

A Society of Status. The society of Old China was one of status. Man was born into a particular social status and, in general, was supposed to remain there. It was possible, however, and in some cases considered desirable, for individuals to rise to higher stations.

Duties and Obligations. Great stress was laid on man's duties in his particular station rather than on his rights, since only if one's duties were performed diligently would the larger group of which he was a part benefit.

The Place of the Individual. Rugged individualism, as exalted in the modern West, was not counted a virtue in Old China. On the contrary, it was not the individual but the family or clan which formed the basis for social structure. The first obligations of an individual were not directed to himself, to his nation, or to his government, but to his family. He expressed these obligations by the worship of his ancestors, by caring for and obeying the family elders, and by breeding and rearing sons to perpetuate the family and its name. The family in turn was the individual's social security, protecting him from a world that was often hard and cold. It was this closely knit family or clan, perhaps more than any other institution, which preserved Chinese civilization in and through periods of great political chaos. The primacy of the family in Chinese thought meant also that ideas such as nationalism and patriotism, so inseparable from modern Western thought, exercised little influence in Old China save in a nonpolitical, cultural sense.

The Nature of Government. In Old China there were clear and pronounced ideas on government and on the position of the ruler. The state in Old China was, in theory, one large family. The Chinese word for nation, *kuo-chia,* means nation-family. The emperor was "the parent of the people." Government was therefore paternalistic. At the same time it was recognized that if the emperor were to exert the proper influence he must live himself by the highest moral standards and select ministers and officials of like character. Moreover, if inferiors were expected to obey, superiors were expected to rule with high moral regard for the rights of lesser men. Americans take great pride in their government *by law,* but Old China held that the best government was achieved through moral persuasion and example. Laws there were, but they were regarded

as a secondary instrument of government. In other words, in Old China it was believed that government should be *by men* who understood and applied right conduct rather than by inflexible rules of law (see Chapter 3.).

Moral Foundations. In the West, Christianity has emphasized man's depravity; one has to be born again. Old China, in contrast, proceeded from the more optimistic premise that man was by nature fundamentally good. In Chinese thought, sin never achieved the exalted status it has often enjoyed in some other civilizations. Old China held that the positive force was man's goodness, which could be cultivated by learning. As a result, stress was laid upon education. The good man, through learning, achieved wisdom and thus became a superior being.

THE GENERAL CHARACTER OF OLD CHINA

The foregoing sketch of some ideas that shaped the body and spirit of Old China makes it quite clear that this traditional society was very unlike modern Western Europe and America. These differences are hardly susceptible to easy generalization, but the following suggestions are to be noted. First, China, like most ancient empires, operated under a government that was centralized politically and decentralized economically. Second, in this empire most large-scale activity, whether political, economic, military, or religious, was controlled by a great and numerous official bureaucracy. Third, this bureaucratic state was dominantly agrarian, deriving its income from the agricultural production of an illiterate but intelligent peasantry which, in addition to growing the food, provided the conscript labor for public works such as the Great Wall or Grand Canal, and the conscript armies for defense or conquest. Fourth, the bureaucracy of government officials who presided over the construction of public works, who administered the revenue, or who decided on war or peace came from the small literate element of the population who could conduct public affairs in the beautiful but difficult system of ideographic writing of the Chinese language. Since it required many years of education to master the written language and the great literature of the classics, it followed that only the sons of men of wealth could afford a classical education. So it was that the landed gentry reared educated sons (scholars), scholars became officials, officials ran the empire and invested their wealth in land. As a result, the ideal man of leadership in Old China was not a merchant, a trader, a general, or a priest, but rather a landlord-scholar-official. Fifth, the family or clan controlled the individual. The individual was subservient to the family, and society governed its conduct by ethics rather than by legal codes. The supremacy of law and the freedom of the individual under law acquired at no time the position they have had in the West.

PHILOSOPHY AND RELIGION

In the seventeenth and eighteenth centuries, the European Enlightenment waxed eloquent on the subject of Confucianism as "a humanistic ethic independent of revealed religion." More recently, philosophic Taoism and then Buddhism have had their appeal to particular Western audiences. Yet traditional Chinese thought cannot be catalogued easily among the systems the West has labeled philosophy. The pre-eminent Chinese thinkers were mystics, moralists, and political theorists rather than the creators of metaphysical systems or developers of rational thought. For the most part, too, they were not religious prophets; they did not appeal to divine revelation, but neither did they appeal to reason. They were more inclined to appeal to tradition.[7]

[7] A. C. Graham, "The Place of Reason in the Chinese Philosophical Tradition," in Raymond Dawson, ed., *The Legacy of China* (Oxford, 1964), 28–56. Chinese seeming indifference to logical problems may be related to the uninflected words and structure of the Chinese language.

Religious Attitudes

The statement was made earlier that in a comparative sense the Chinese were not a religious people. While this statement is true, it can easily be misleading. To assume that because of this statement the Chinese lacked moral and ethical motivations of the highest order or that they lacked a sense of reverence would be a grave error. Because their religious motivations were different from those of many Western peoples does not mean that these motivations were inferior.

From earliest times the Chinese have had a great variety of popular religious cults followed by the common people and at times by the aristocracy. For the most part the Confucian intellectuals and bureaucrats paid little attention to these cults except when they assumed a dangerous political tone. Educated Chinese revered Heaven (*Hao-t'ien*), their ancestors, and sometimes notable names such as Confucius, Buddha, and Lao-tzu, while the common folk were free to put their trust in a great variety of heavens and to fear, if they were so inclined, a vast number of hells. They placed great reliance on charms and magic through which they hoped to appease the spirits who controlled their fortunes. From this it will be seen that while the educated looked upon Confucianism, Taoism, and even Buddhism as primarily systems of philosophy, the masses regarded them as religions founded by supernatural beings. Thus there was a marked tendency for the educated and the uneducated to go separate ways in matters of religion. Moreover, neither the intellectuals nor the common people followed exclusively Confucianism or Taoism or Buddhism. On the contrary, the Chinese accepted all three as different roads to the same destination.

The great names associated with early Chinese philosophy and religion are Lao-tzu,[8] Confucius, and Mo Ti. All three were revolutionary in their thinking. Applying the

[8] Contemporary scholarship, in particular the research of Homer H. Dubs, is inclined to consider Lao-tzu not as an older contemporary of Confucius, but as living in a much later period, that is, at the end of the fourth century B.C. See Homer H. Dubs, "Taoism," *China,* H. F. MacNair, ed. (1946), 266.

language of modern politics to ancient religion, Lao-tzu represented the extreme Left; Confucius, the Center, though leaning toward the Left; and Mo Ti, the Right. Lao-tzu was a thorough heretic in religion and a revolutionary in philosophy. Confucius was a humanist and an agnostic. Mo Ti, devoutly religious, sought to preserve the early indigenous faith by purifying it and infusing it with new life.

Taoist Philosophy and Religion

Taoism, one of the world's greatest pre-systematic bodies of thought, had its beginnings as a magnificent mystical philosophy which has continued to influence the Chinese mind. In the course of time, Taoism also assumed a secondary form as a popular religion garbed in the trappings of superstition. As a philosophy, Taoism has appealed strongly to China's intellectuals; as a religion, rapidly losing its appeal in the twentieth century, it has played an immense role in the lives of the credulous masses.

Of the traditional founder of these two great systems, the sage Lao-tzu (venerable master), nothing is known with any certainty. Indeed, his very existence is doubted by some scholars. But the teachings ascribed to him have affected China profoundly. His philosophy resented the idea that God is a personal being, and sought to replace it by the idea of *Tao* (the Way or Road or Process). To Lao-tzu the *Tao* was a natural process, something "being so of itself"; thus, there was no need to construct any divine plan or purpose: "the *Tao* always does nothing; and yet it achieves everything." This was a quietistic philosophy, which, if applied, would affect every phase of society. In politics, the best government was the least government. Literature, knowledge, and civilization were undesirable, for "when the world knows beauty to be beauty, there is ugliness; when it knows goodness to be good, there is evil."

Taoism by its very nature was the antithesis of and the great opponent of Confucianism. The attack of Taoism was directed against moral idealism and political realism. "Heaven and Earth [the great gods of Old China] are not humane," said Lao-tzu. The universe was neither kindly nor righteous, but went its way, ignoring human desires or human standards of conduct. Thus, efforts to reform morals or to right wrongs were a waste of time, since these efforts were an attempt to control the universe. Since the universe was not moral, there was no point to man's cultivation of virtue. The way to avoid evil was not to stress good, but to reach beyond both good and evil to the pure essence of the universe, the Way or *Tao*. The answer then was to be found in effortlessness, in nonaction. "The sage," said Lao-tzu, "relies on actionless activity and carries on wordless teaching."

Posterity has dealt with Lao-tzu much as it has dealt with other great teachers. Although he probably did not consider himself a religious leader, he was credited by later generations with founding a religion. Early chroniclers affirmed that he was born of a virgin. The wisdom ascribed to him was published, probably with much padding, in the second century B.C., in a delightful book called the *Tao-Te-Ching*.[9] Many of the virtues which Lao-tzu extolled, such as patience, humility, calmness, and deliberation, appealed to thoughtful men; but his quietistic doctrines, reminiscent of some forms of Hindu philosophy, were beyond the understanding of the masses. Hence, out of Lao-tzu's "natural way," succeeding generations of priests built the religion of Taoism, a thing miraculous and supernatural. In time Taoism became "the most elaborate and complicated system of magic, myths, spells, charms, in-

---

[9] See Dubs, "Taoism," *China*, 266–89. The *Tao Te Ching* is one of the most remarkable documents in the history of religion. Arthur Waley's effective translation (see "For Further Reading") renders the title as *The Way and Its Power*. The nature and the purpose of the *Tao Te Ching* are elusive. The book is really a collection of brief passages of verse and prose designed to provoke meditation and contemplation. For example: "The way that can be followed (or the road that can be charted) is not the true way. The word that can be spoken is not the true word. In modern times the *Tao Te Ching* has been interpreted as primitive scientific empiricism, as a restatement of the philosophy of the Upanishads, and as a statement of Zen doctrine. In any event it is a book no student should miss.

cantations, demonology, and all similar forms of superstitious practice that any society has developed." [10] Taoism's control of the world of spirits gave it a foremost place in the scheme of ancestor worship. Man's every act was affected by spirits, either friendly or hostile. Herein lay the power of the Taoist priest to determine the appropriate time for building a house, for celebrating a wedding, or for burying a corpse. Here, too, the practical, matter-of-fact Chinese mind found relief in a world of the unreal: the world of romance, and of spirits—a world of mysteries. Taoism was mysticism, some would say superstition, but it was also poetry.

Confucianism:
The Traditional Philosophy

The history of China without Confucius would be like the history of America without Washington and Jefferson. China, of course, has not always been dominated by the lives of those who professed to be Confucians. Yet Confucianism has affected China more profoundly and continuously than any other philosophy. It gave China a remarkable humanistic philosophy, a recognition that the true bases of society are social and mundane as well as divine.

Confucius (K'ung Fu-tzu, 551–479 B.C.) was not merely an academic theorist. He was also a practical statesman, who, however, spent most of his life moving about the country engaged in teaching. Most of his students were young men of the upper classes for whom politics was the only honorable profession. Confucius presented to them a code of high moral ideas of such force that it became the dominant philosophy of official China and, until 1911, remained as authoritative as the Bible was,

[10] Paul Monroe, *China: A Nation in Evolution* (1928), 102. Traditional Chinese geomancy (*feng shui*) held that the prosperity of descendants depended on a properly located grave. While Westerners in China scoffed at such ideas, Chinese sometimes noted that the foreigner took steps to accommodate his own dead in ways suggesting that he, too, was not immune to the influence of *feng shui*. See Andrew L. March, "An Appreciation of Chinese Geomancy," *Journal of Asian Studies* 27 (1968): 253–67.

until a century ago, in Western thought. In fact, Confucianism was so much a part of the Chinese character that it was in a sense taken for granted. The Chinese said little about it, just as Burke rarely quotes the Bible. Yet this Confucian tradition was in the background of every educated person's mind, since every candidate for official position concentrated on it for years; he memorized longer accounts of the Confucian classics than early Americans memorized from the Bible, and, what is more important, became expert in applying it.

The Bible of Confucianism consists of the Five Classics and the Four Books. The Five Classics, comprising the most ancient and venerated works, contain: (1) *the Book of Changes*, an elaborate guide to divination with a philosophical interpretation of the sixty-four hexagrams; (2) the *Book of History*, a fragmentary history covering the period 2400–619 B.C.; (3) the *Book of Poetry*, a collection of some three hundred poems of the Chou period; (4) the *Book of Rites*, dealing with ceremonial procedure; and (5) the *Spring and Autumn Annals*, a history of the state of Lu. While tradition holds that Confucius wrote or edited these works, the *Five Classics* actually derived from the work of many authors. Confucius as a teacher may have used the *Book of Poetry*, the *Book of History*, and the *Spring and Autumn Annals*.

Over a thousand years after the close of the Chou period, four texts, known as the Four Books, were selected from the mass of classical literature. These were: (1) the *Analects*, or dialogues of Confucius with his disciples; (2) the *Book of Mencius*, containing the sayings of the sages; (3) the *Great Learning*, an outline of Confucian ethics; and (4) the *Doctrine of the Mean*, a similar treatise. To these basic works must be added the voluminous commentaries, comprising thousands of volumes, produced through the tireless industry of Confucian scholars both ancient and modern.

The classics and the commentaries provided a minutely detailed plan for human conduct. It was not sufficient to describe how Confucius spoke or acted; details were provided as to his posture when in bed and even the length of his night shirt. All life, in a word, was measured by the Confucian code. Thus it was possible for a wise man to be master of himself at all times and in all circumstances.

Since Confucius was a humanist, his philosophy, broadly considered, was a code of conduct by which man might govern himself in his relations with his fellow men. Five relations considered of prime importance were: the relation of prince and minister, of parent and child, of husband and wife, of elder and younger brother, and of friend and friend. Five constant virtues were stressed: benevolence, righteousness, propriety, wisdom, and fidelity. The application of these virtues to human relations would, in the Confucian view of things, achieve the true end of life. Life would be simple, the family happy, and social relations harmonious. Confucianism expressed the practical, matter-of-fact, mundane tendencies in the Chinese character. It was not a supernatural religion. To the Confucianist, the idea that men live in order to die, as taught by Christianity, is incomprehensible. When his disciples asked concerning the gods, Confucius replied that he knew little about them. He appears to have been mildly skeptical of the supernatural, on the theory that if man could not understand life, it was unreasonable to suppose that he could understand death. Yet Confucianism included and inculcated the state religion and the sacrifices to the gods. Confucius attended these and taught them. But the common accompaniments of supernatural religion were left to the state and the people. There was a state priestcraft, but no Confucian priestcraft. The concept of a future life was vague, but not nonexistent. Matters such as apostolic succession, miracles, sacraments, and the future life were left for other cults to manage as they would. Without the promise of rewards or punishment from the unknown spiritual world, Confucianism directed man in his duty both to his family and to society as a whole.

From what has been said, it should not be assumed that Confucianism lacked a metaphysical tradition. In various ways and at various times neo-Confucianism was much concerned with problems of epistemology.

Buddhism

Perhaps it should be said at this point that there is no easy way for a person of one culture to gain a real understanding of a religion of another culture. A background based on the Judeo-Christian tradition is certainly likely to influence one's approach to a "foreign" faith such as Buddhism. The real problem then is to see the "foreign" religion as it is seen by those who accept it, and to gain some understanding how one generation attempts to transmit its religious beliefs to succeeding generations.[11]

Buddhism was introduced into China according to official tradition about the beginning of the Christian Era.[12] In reality, however, no one knows when or in what fashion the Chinese acquired their first knowledge of Buddhism. Gautama, the traditional founder, is said to have been born in northern India on the border of Nepal about 563 B.C. Despite his noble birth he became dissatisfied with the transient character of worldly things, renounced the world, and began his wanderings in search of truth. His problem was the perplexing one of achieving release from the burden of constant trouble that beset human life, and of achieving the spiritual training necessary to that end. Whether Gautama regarded himself as the founder of a religion or merely as a teacher of ethics need not be argued here. The fact of importance is that from his central theme —the moral life with its virtues of love, wisdom, and the suppression of desire—his followers did erect a religion whose influence has been of the greatest significance. Centuries after Gautama's death his followers divided, and it was the northern as distinct from the southern Buddhist movement that spread its influence to Nepal, Tibet, Mongolia, Cochin China, China, Korea, and Japan. The most influential sect in this northern school of Buddhism developed the

[11] Kenneth W. Morgan, *Asian Religions* (1964).*
[12] The term "Buddha" is not a proper name but a title meaning "The Enlightened One."

idea of the Western Paradise (Heaven), a concept that was lacking in Gautama's original teaching. Buddhism thus concerns itself deeply with man's after-life, whereas Confucianism is interested primarily in the earthly life.

China in many ways might have appeared an unpromising field for Buddhism. The emphasis on introspection and the inner life did not seem to harmonize with the practical philosophy of the Confucian mind. Buddhism in its exhortations to the celibate life could, it would seem, have little appeal in a land of ancestor worship.[13] Yet Buddhism was widely accepted in China and was one of the dominant elements in Chinese thought. This is explained by the fact that during the years of its introduction the leading intellectuals of China were already deeply immersed in the closely related speculations of Lao-tzu, while popular Taoism was widely practiced among the common people. Buddhism therefore appealed to both the learned and the illiterate. Its elaborate ritual made a natural appeal to the masses. As a religion it was more comprehensive than Taoism, while as a philosophy it was emphasizing the spiritual aspect so lacking in the Confucian ethical code of conduct. Both Buddhism and Taoism became popular because Confucianism had so little to offer to the unsophisticated minds of the common people. In times of chaos when life was in constant danger, there was the very human tendency to turn in desperation to some supernatural power. This was a refuge Confucianism did not offer.

Buddhism, however, brought more to China than the spiritual satisfactions of religion. Indian science and art came too. Chinese astronomy and the written language were enriched through the adoption of foreign methods and terms; Chinese sculpture and painting took on new and deeper forms; block printing was used in the making of Buddhist and other books. These were permanent contributions to China's culture. In time, Buddhism as a religion tended to give

place to the rising influence of Neo-Confucianism; yet much of the nobility of Buddhist thought and spirit remained.

THE CHARACTER OF CHINESE PAINTING

Closely linked with Chinese thought is Chinese art. It is hardly necessary here to attempt a description of Old China's marvelous creations in bronze, jade, textiles, lacquer, enamels, and ceramics, but a word should be said about Chinese painting and calligraphy which in many ways represent the summit of China's artistic expression. Since Chinese thought tended to center on keeping man in tune with the universe or nature, landscape painting sought generalized conceptions of nature and man's place in it. Thus, in general, the painter was not concerned with particular events or objects but rather with ultimate meanings to be found in nature. In calligraphy the Chinese gentleman-scholar sought to perfect his mastery of form, movement, and balance. Unlike the modern Western abstract expressionist who seeks form only, the Chinese artist calligrapher was in search of meaning beyond form.[14]

CLASS STRUCTURE

The foregoing dominant ideas, philosophies, and religions marking some principal lines of thought in Old China were not shared with equal consciousness by all Chinese. The society in which these ideas held sway was composed of two major groups: (1) the gentry, and (2) the people in general. There were major distinctions of great importance between these two groups.

The gentry was the dominant class of Old China. Members of this group were distinguished from their fellows by many factors. They derived their income from land

---

[13] Buddhism adjusted itself to ancestor veneration. Who could tell better than the Buddhist priest what became of the spirits of deceased ancestors?

[14] Chiang Yee, *Chinese Calligraphy* (London, 1954), and Michael Sullivan, "The Heritage of Chinese Art," in Dawson, ed., *Legacy of China*, 198–99.

which they themselves did not cultivate, from government office, or from academic, intellectual pursuits, and in more recent times from banking, industry, and commerce. Within the gentry class were the intellectuals since, in the main, only the sons of gentry could afford an education and thus pass the civil service examinations which provided the principal avenue to government office. Through their control of land the gentry controlled the economy, and through their monopoly of learning they shaped the patterns of intellectual, social, and political life.

Among the nongentry, the largest and most significant group, forming indeed the great mass of the people, was the peasantry. In an overwhelmingly agricultural society, they were the cultivators of the land, some as farmers who owned and cultivated their land, others as tenants, and still others as nonlandowning laborers. Even as late as the mid-twentieth century something like 75 or 80 per cent of China's population belonged to the peasantry. The remainder of the nongentry elements of the population included handicraftsmen, small merchants, servants, soldiers, priests, actors, and, in more recent times, factory workers.

It is rather important to note here that the traditional China that Western students of history come to know first, the China of the great philosophers such as Confucius, of the great dynasties and systems of government, the China of literature and art, was in a major degree the China of the gentry. Historical writing has often left the impression that the picture of China's gentry was also a picture of the Chinese as a whole, an implication open to some question. This seeming misrepresentation can be understood, however, when it is recognized that the institutionalized patterns of gentry thought and behavior were regarded by all Chinese society as the ideal patterns even if for the most part they were unattainable save by the favored few. Dynasties might rise or fall and conquerors come and go, yet from the third century B.C. until the nineteenth century, the gentry patterns remained the ideal patterns for all Chinese. In this sense the history of China's gentry, so inseparable from the political, economic, intellectual, literary, and artistic growth of culture, was the history of China.[15]

SCIENCE

Finally, it should be noted that one of the striking contrasts between modern Western civilization and the civilization of traditional China was that the former produced what is called modern science while the latter did not. Chinese discoveries in empirical science were of course very extensive. These included findings in astronomy, biology, geology, archaeology, mathematics, and geography to mention only a few of the major areas. More specifically, the Chinese knew how to compute celestial distances. They had classified more than one hundred plant species before 500 A.D. Cast iron was produced in Western Chou 1500 years in advance of the West. The Chinese knew of the magnetic north in Shang times and had a magnetized needle to indicate direction as early as Chou. A Chinese map of the third century A.D. was almost as accurate as Ptolemy's. The Chinese were probably the inventors of glass (Chou period). They invented gunpowder (T'ang), made the first bomb (1161), and probably the first cannon (about 1250). They were the first to produce paper (105 A.D.), porcelain, and printing (600 A.D.). They produced moveable type in the twelfth century.

China was also responsible for the first successful immunization technique. A seismograph was used in China as early as the

[15] Chinese literature is, of course, an indispensable key to the flavor of Old China's culture. In both prose and poetry the Chinese created a remarkable heritage. In general, Chinese writers were exponents of Confucian doctrine. They sought to influence people to be moral in the Confucian sense. They viewed literature as a pragmatic vehicle. As a matter-of-fact, practical people, their literature was thus utilitarian rather than aesthetic. Writers were not concerned with art for art's sake. The best introduction to the subject is Liu Wu-chi, *An Introduction to Chinese Literature* (1966).* Also C. T. Hsia, *The Classic Chinese Novel: A Critical Introduction* (1968).

second century. It also appears that medieval Chinese anatomy was far more advanced than has generally been thought. What needs to be noted is that, while Chinese achievements in these areas were in some measure technical rather than scientific, there was in ancient and medieval China a large body of naturalistic theory. There was systematic experimentation and a great deal of surprisingly accurate measurement. The theories, however, remained medieval, since the European Renaissance, with its mathematization of hypotheses, did not occur in China.[16] It must be clear, then, that there is no foundation for the belief commonly held in the West that there was never any science or technology in China. Part of this misunderstanding may result from a problem in definition. What may be called "modern science" originated only in Western Europe in the sixteenth and seventeenth centuries. But this is not the same thing as "science in its entirety" whose foundations were laid by ancient and medieval peoples in every major society including the Chinese.

FOR FURTHER READING

BIBLIOGRAPHIES. Henri Cordier, *Bibliotheca Sinica* (5 vols., 2nd ed., Paris 1904–24). Yuan Tung-li, *China in Western Literature* (1958), continues Henri Cordier. J. K. Fairbank, ed., *Bibliographical Guide to Modern China: Works in Western Languages* (mimeographed, 1948). L. C. Goodrich and H. C. Fenn, *A Syllabus of the History of Chinese Civilization and Culture* (6th rev. ed., 1958). Charles O. Hucker, *China, A Critical Bibliography* (1962). Charles O. Hucker, *Chinese History: A Bibliographic Review* (1958), issued by the Service Center for Teachers of History, American Historical Association. Charles S. Gardner, comp., *A Union List of Selected Western Books on China in Ameri-*

can *Libraries* (1938), a carefully selected list of 350 books and 21 periodicals of great importance. Kwang-ching Liu, *Americans and Chinese: A Historical Essay and a Bibliography* (1963).

GEOGRAPHY, THE PEOPLE, AND THE ECONOMY. George B. Cressey, *Land of the 500 Million: A Geography of China* (1955), indispensable. George B. Cressey, *China's Geographic Foundation: A Survey of the Land and Its People* (1934), also highly recommended. Rhoads Murphey, *Shanghai: Key to Modern China* (1953), an historio-geographic monograph of rare interest and value. Theodore Shabad, *China's Changing Map: A Political and Economic Geography of the Chinese People's Republic* (1956), a competent, if dull, reference work. On China's population, note Ho Ping-ti, *Studies on the Population of China, 1368–1953* (1959), a major study in socioeconomic history, and John S. Aird, *The Size, Composition, and Growth of the Population of Mainland China* (1961). On the Chinese economy, note E. Stuart Kirby, *Introduction to the Economic History of China* (London, 1954), and Solomon Adler, *The Chinese Economy* (1957), an attempt to provide an introductory economic history of China. Chi Ch'ao-t'ing, *Key Economic Areas in Chinese History* (London, 1936), describes water-control measures and the shifts in China's economic center. Shen Tsung-han, *Agricultural Resources of China* (1951), an excellent study. Yang Lien-sheng, *Money and Credit in China, A Short History* (1952). Gerald F. Winfield, *China: The Land and the People* (rev. ed., 1950), presents the interrelations among deeply rooted mores, economic conditions, and problems of political change. Lin Yutang, *My Country and My People* (1935), a fascinating portrayal, generally reliable, but idealized. Pearl S. Buck, *The Good Earth* (1931),* reissued repeatedly, is a novel on Chinese peasant life. F. H. King, *Farmers of Forty Centuries, or Permanent Agriculture in China, Korea and Japan* (1926; reissued 1948), a standard description of the agrarian foundations of Chinese life. Fei Hsiao-t'ung, *Peasant Life in China* (London, 1939) is based on a detailed study of a Chi-

---

[16] Joseph Needham, "Science and China's Influence on the World," *Legacy of China*, Dawson, ed., 234–308. Note also Sung Ying-hsing, *T'ien-kung k'ai-wu: Chinese Technology in the Seventeenth Century,* translated and annotated by E-tu Zen Sun and Shiou-chuan Sun (1966).

nese village. Morton H. Fried, *Fabric of Chinese Society: A Study of the Social Life of a Chinese County Seat* (1953). Feng Han-chi, *The Chinese Kinship System* (1948).° Olga Lang, *Chinese Family and Society* (1946).

HISTORY. Chang Kwang-chih, *The Archaeology of Ancient China* (1963), cultural growth of early China and its surrounding regions during a period extending from approximately 1500 B.C. to the founding of the Ch'in Dynasty in 221 B.C. Cheng Te-kun, *Archaeology in China* (Cambridge, England, 1959), one of the best studies. Li Chi, *The Beginnings of Chinese Civilization: Three Lectures Illustrated with Finds at Anyang* (1957), an authoritative brief survey of archaeological origins. Thomas F. Carter and L. C. Goodrich, *The Invention of Printing in China and its Spread Westward* (rev. ed., 1955), a monumental study in Chinese cultural history. W. T. deBary, ed., *Sources of Chinese Tradition* (1960), the most convenient and comprehensive collection of source readings on Chinese civilization from early times. Etienne Balazs, *Chinese Civilization and Bureaucracy: Variations on a Theme* (1964), a splendid sampling of the brilliant studies by the late Hungarian-French authority on Old China. Hu Chang-tu, *et al.*, *China: Its People, Its Society, Its Culture* (1960), a survey covering all major aspects of Chinese history, culture, and life. S. Wells Williams, *The Middle Kingdom* (2 vols., 1901), the work most widely read by Americans in the nineteenth and early twentieth centuries. Joseph Needham, *Science and Civilization in China* (Vols. 1–4, Cambridge, England, 1954–1965). Wolfram Eberhard, *History of China* (1950), translated by E. W. Dickes, a sociological interpretation emphasizing the continuity of gentry domination. Lin Yutang, *Imperial Peking: Seven Centuries of China* (1961), a picture of China's traditional humanism. Arthur W. Hummel, ed., *Eminent Chinese of the Ch'ing Period (1644–1912)* (2 vols., 1943–1944), an indispensable study. Ho Ping-ti, *The Ladder of Success in Imperial China* (1962), a statistical study of elite mobility in Ming and Ch'ing times. Franz Michael, *The Origin of Manchu Rule*

in China (1942), the basic work on the Manchu conquest. E-tu Zen Sun and John De Francis, eds., trans., *Chinese Social History* (1956), essays covering the period from the Chou to the Ch'ing dynasty. Richard L. Walker, *The Multi-State System of Ancient China* (1953) describes the relations between the various Chou states. Hsu Cho-yun, *Ancient China in Transition: An Analysis of Social Mobility, 722–222 B.C.* (1965). Marcel Granet, *Chinese Civilization*, trans. Kathleen E. Innes and Mabel R. Brailsford (1951), a sociological interpretation of early literary remains. Woodbridge Bingham, *The Founding of the T'ang Dynasty: The Fall of the Sui and the Rise of the T'ang* (1941). René Grousset, *The Rise and Splendour of the Chinese Empire*, trans. A. Watson-Gandy and T. Gordon (1953), episodic but successful in conveying the flavor of China's cultural glories. René Grousset, *Conqueror of the World. The Life of Chingis-Khan.* Marian McKellar and Denis Sinor, trans. (1966). B. Y. Vladimirtsov, *The Life of Chinghis Khan* (London, 1930).

PHILOSOPHY AND RELIGION. Chan Wing-tsit, *An Outline and an Annotated Bibliography of Chinese Philosophy* (1959). H. G. Creel, *Confucius and the Chinese Way* (1960), first published in 1949 as *Confucius the Man and the Myth*. Fung Yu-lan, *A Short History of Chinese Philosophy*, trans. and ed. by Derk Bodde (1948) provides the best coverage of the shorter works. Fung Yu-lan, *History of Chinese Philosophy*, trans. and ed. by Derk Bodde, (2 vols., 1952–53), a comprehensive and detailed work including political theory. Lewis Hodous, *Folkways in China* (London, 1929), a good introduction to popular religion. E. R. Hughes and K. Hughes, *Religion in China* (London, 1950) surveys early religious practices. Arthur Waley, *Three Ways of Thought in Ancient China* (1956), a study of the early philosophies. Arthur Waley, *The Analects of Confucius* (London, 1938), an able translation of the sayings of Confucius. Arthur Waley, trans., *The Way and Its Power: A Study of the Tao Te Ching and Its Place in Chinese Thought* (1958), an introduction to early Taoism. C. K. Yang, *Religion in Chinese Society* (1962). Holmes Welch, *The Parting of the Way: Lao Tzu and the Taoist Movement* (1957). Arthur F. Wright, ed., *Studies in Chinese Thought* (1953).* David S. Nivison and Arthur Wright, eds., *Confucianism in Action* (1959), essays on Confucianism in China and Japan. Arthur F. Wright, ed., *The Confucian Persuasion* (1960). Carsun Chang, *The Development of Neo-Confucian Thought* (2 vols., 1957, 1962).* Charles Eliot, *Hinduism and Buddhism, An Historical Sketch* (3 vols., 1954) traces the origins of Buddhism in India and its spread to China. Kenneth Ch'en, *Buddhism in China: A Historical Survey* (1964).

LITERATURE. Ch'en Shou-yi, *Chinese Literature: A Historical Introduction* (1961), a comprehensive survey of Chinese literature. James Legge, *The Chinese Classics* (5 vols., Hong Kong, 1960), a reprint with minor corrections and an added concordance. C. T. Hsia, *The Classic Chinese Novel: A Critical Introduction* (1968), an eloquent and critical appreciation. Lin Yutang, trans., *Famous Chinese Short Stories* (1952).* Cyril Birch, ed., *Anthology of Chinese Literature: From Early Times to the Fourteenth Century* (1965).* Robert Payne, *The White Pony* (1967),* an introduction to Chinese poetry. Arthur Waley, *Translations from the Chinese* (1941), an introduction to Chinese poetry.

Arhur Waley, *The Book of Songs* (London, 1937),* a fine translation of the classical anthology of poetry (*Shih Ching*). Arthur Waley, *The Poetry and Career of Li Po, 701–762* (London, 1950) gives a valuable approach to the T'ang and Sung dynasties. James J. Y Liu, *The Art of Chinese Poetry* (1962).* Burton Watson, *Early Chinese Literature* (1962) provides an account of Chinese writing from the time of the Chou dynasty to the middle of the Later Han dynasty. Some masterpieces of Chinese literature include: Wang Chi-chen, trans., *Dream of the Red Chamber* (rev. ed., 1958);* Clement Edgerton, trans., *The Golden Lotus* (4 vols., London, 1939); Wu Cheng-en, *Monkey*, trans. from the Chinese by Arthur Waley (1958);* Chow Chung-cheng, *The Lotus Pool*, trans. by Joyce Emerson (1961).

ART. Laurence Sickman and Alexander Soper, *The Art and Architecture of China* (1956). Dagny Carter, *Four Thousand Years of Chinese Art* (1948), one of the best of the shorter surveys. William Willets, *Chinese Art* (2 vols., 1958). Sherman E. Lee, *A History of Far Eastern Art* (1965). Ernest F. Fenollosa, *Epochs of Chinese and Japanese Art: An Outline History of East Asiatic Design* (2 vols., 1963),* reprint of a classic study.

Ideas
on Government
in Old China

chapter 3

Throughout their long history the Chinese have given a great deal of thought to the subject of government. They have had much to say about what government should be, what it should do, what ideas and ideals should guide it, and so forth. The Chinese were not always in agreement on these matters; nevertheless they developed a pattern of political principles and conduct which may be described in broad general terms. It is important that this be done at the outset, since it is difficult to understand the impact of the West upon China in the nineteenth and twentieth centuries without some basic knowledge of what kind of political society the West met in China.

The principal body of political thought that guided both the rulers and the ruled in China for some two thousand years prior to the beginning of the twentieth century was Confucianism. Two thousand years is a long time for any system to survive. What gave the Confucian political habit and tradition this power of survival? How shall its collapse in the twentieth century be explained?

As a point of departure, it is well to note that from the earliest times Chinese philosophy was concerned with ethics and politics. Confucius, the most famous of all Chinese political scientists, was a statesman as well as a teacher. In addition, politics in Old China was regarded as the most desirable profession for a young man of "good" family. Moreover, the ruling class—that is, the politicians—was the educated class. Education, in turn, meant mastery not only of the Confucian classics but also of the voluminous commentaries on them made by later scholars. Political problems were discussed, debated, and solved in terms of these classics and commentaries. An apt quotation from the classics could clinch a political argument. Scholarship was thus the key to passing the civil service examinations, which were the principal avenue to government office; and government office meant honor and perhaps wealth.

EARLY SCHOOLS OF POLITICAL THOUGHT

Although, as indicated, Confucianism as a body of political thought has had far greater influence in China than any other political philosophy or system, it has not been without rivals. It had its beginning far back in the pre-Christian era along with other schools of thought.[1] Fortunately for the Confucians, it was largely their philosophical works alone that survived the burning of the books by Ch'in Shih Huang Ti (259–210 B.C.). The relationship among the early schools of thought is not clear, save that no one of them was able to dominate the others. There were, for example, the *Yin-Yang* (Negative-Positive) School and the School of Names (the Logicians) whose followers have left little evidence of a well-considered theory of political action. Other schools have been more generous in apprising posterity of their political views. The *Tao* School, or Taoists, followers of Lao-tzu, have left one of the great living monuments of Chinese thought. Lao-tzu denied the necessity or the wisdom of a society built on elaborate laws and institutions. He would neither approve of nor be happy in society of the twentieth century, either in its democratic or its totalitarian forms. He would doubtless attribute the world's troubles to its departure from his *Tao* (way), which, in the philosophical sense, is the effortless union of man and nature.[2]

Chuang-tzu, a follower of Lao-tzu, went even further on the path of negativism. The best government was the least government and thus the essence of simplicity. Men should avoid distinctions between good and bad, high and low, the beautiful and the ugly, since these in turn lead to moralizing and therefore put an end to simplicity.[3]

A contrasting body of thought was advocated by the School of Law or the Legalists, represented by men of action such as Li Li (fifth century B.C.), Shang Yang (fourth century B.C.), and especially Han

Fei (third century B.C.). These men were codemakers, insistent upon a uniform body of laws and upon the theory of reward and punishment as the controller of human action.[4]

Again, there was in early China the Mo School, followers of Mo Ti (fifth century B.C.), who sought the interest of the people, opposed war as injurious to all, and wished the sovereign, aided by the ablest men, to reflect the will of the people and in turn to be obeyed by them. Mo Ti extolled a doctrine of mutual love, mutual benefit, and something of the democratic spirit, though not the democratic theory or the political machinery of the democratic state.[5]

THE PHILOSOPHERS, OR CONFUCIANS

Existing alongside these various schools that prescribed what government ought or ought not to be was the *Ju* School (the Confucians). So it may be said that Confucianism was not formed in a political vacuum but rather in close relationship with other competing ideas. It is not wholly surprising, then, to discover that Confucian teachings are exceedingly rich in that they have drawn upon practically all other teachings of early times. Confucius himself was a person who travelled widely and had almost unlimited contacts with men in all conditions. In consequence, what emerged on the death of Confucius was not one but some eight schools of Confucianism, among which could be found doctrines almost as unlike as those of the Taoists on the one hand and the Legalists on the other. Yet through all the divergent Confucian schools there was a common factor of humanism—"Man lives with and for other Men."

All the principles and values of Con-

---

[1] Ch'ien Tuan-sheng, *The Government and Politics of China* (1950). H. G. Creel, *Confucius and the Chinese Way* (1960)*; first published as *Confucius, the Man and the Myth* (1949).

[2] The recommended translation of Lao-tzu's *Tao-te ching* is by Arthur Waley, *The Way and Its Power* (London, 1934).*

[3] See Homer H. Dubs, "Taoism," *China,* H. F. MacNair, ed., 266–89. For translations from the work of Chuang-tzu see H. A. Giles, *Chuang Tzu, Mystic, Moralist, and Social Reformer* (2nd ed., London, 1926), and Fung Yu-lan, trans., *Chuang Tzu* (Shanghai, 1932).

[4] See J. J. L. Duyvendak, trans., *The Book of Lord Shang: A Classic of the Chinese School of Law* (London, 1928), a translation of Shang Yang's work, the *Shang-tzu.*

[5] See Mei Yi-pao, trans., *The Ethical and Political Works of Motse* (London, 1929); and Mei Yi-pao, *Motse, the Neglected Rival of Confucius* (London, 1934).

fucianism may be attributed to this theory of the position of man among men. Confucian ideas are concerned with what the Confucians called *Rites, Virtue, Names,* and the *Five Relationships.* Rites were the standards of sane, social living. To live by them was to practice *jen,* the greatest Virtue. Moreover, life was a matter of status (political, social, economic, or intellectual), which was indicated by a Name, since things must be known by what they are if there is not to be confusion. Only when persons are designated properly may responsibility be located, honors and punishments bestowed with confidence. From this marking of status come also the Five Relationships with their obligations and privileges already referred to in Chapter 2. Nevertheless, important as status and the Five Relationships were, it is to be noted that there was very little permanent stratification of social groups in Chinese society. A man could rise from humble birth to the Confucian "aristocracy of virtue" and find an illustrious place among scholars. On the other hand, he might lose virtue and fall.

Just as the foregoing humanistic concepts provided rules of conduct for private individuals, they also provided a Bible for statesmen on the assumption that "orderly political life must come from orderly private lives." The Confucian philosophy stressed the reciprocal nature of duties and obligations between the ruler and the ruled, and the primary duty of the ruler to give good government to the people. To do this, the ruler himself had to set a high moral standard and select with care the officials who served under him. The Confucian scholar became important because only he, by his knowledge of the rules of right conduct, could advise properly the "Son of Heaven" in his traditional duties of maintaining universal harmony between man and nature. In the *Analects,* Confucius said, "When a prince's personal conduct is correct, his government is effective without the issuing of orders. If his personal conduct is not correct, he may issue orders but they will not be followed." Right conduct gave the ruler his power.

On this basis the Confucian scholars established themselves as an essential part

of the government. Since the *Rites* tended to be "what was" rather than "what ought to be" (Confucius himself being a realist), the whole body of Confucian political thought tended to be conservative, stressed legitimacy, avoided the revolutionary, and found in monarchy a convenient instrument to promote a stable society.

The business of making over, so to speak, the early and fluid Confucian philosophy into an effective, applicable body of political dogma was largely the work of Former Han times (202 B.C. to A.D. 8) when the first great Chinese empire was consolidated. It was also at this time that a civil service examination system began to take shape whereby political office was virtually closed to all but Confucian scholars or at least to those who professed to be Confucian.[6]

During the first ten centuries of the Christian era, Confucianism, somewhat discredited by the fall of the eminently Confucian Han dynasty, encountered political rivals in Buddhism and Taoism. Nevertheless, by Sung times the challenge was met in the rise of Neo-Confucianism (the *Li* school of Sung and Ming times). Finally, under the Manchu dynasty, the leading Confucian school was known as the *Classicists.* These modern schools endowed Confucianism with a spirit of inertia and traditionalism in political thought, and thus the doctrine of absolute monarchy tempered by mildness persisted— the stereotyped ideal of the literati, the men who ruled China.[7]

CONFUCIAN POLITICAL PRECEPTS

Since the government of Old China was affected more by Confucianism than by any other philosophy, it is worthwhile to inquire

---

[6] See Ssu-yu Teng, "China's Examination System and the West," *China,* H. F. MacNair, ed., 441–51. See also H. G. Creel, "The Beginning of Bureaucracy in China: The Origin of the Hsien," *Journal of Asian Studies* 23 (February, 1964): 155–93.

[7] See Ch'ien Tuan-sheng, *The Government and Politics of China* (1950), 27–28.

into the nature of its more important political precepts. In the course of time, these precepts came to be so deeply rooted as to be taken for granted by the ruling bureaucracy. Among the first precepts was that of *unity*, both social and political. To students familiar with the chaotic and amorphous China of the early twentieth century, it may be surprising that Confucius taught: "As Heaven has not two suns, so the people should not have two kings." This was a doctrine frequently invoked when the state was threatened with political division.

Closely allied with this concept of political unity was the doctrine of *Heaven's Mandate*, which appears to have been taught by Confucius, but more particularly by his disciple Mencius. This doctrine taught that the supreme earthly ruler, the emperor, was elevated to his position through the favor of Heaven. The emperor was therefore the *Son of Heaven*, and by Heaven's Mandate maintained his rule. But Heaven did not lose control of its mandate. When an incapable or wicked ruler ascended the throne, Heaven withdrew the mandate and bestowed it on some righteous noble. It then became the duty of this noble to rebel, to overthrow the emperor, and to ascend the throne himself. In expounding this doctrine, Confucius was really idealizing the method by which dynasties in China were said to have been overthrown.

A number of important implications followed very naturally from this convenient doctrine of the Mandate of Heaven. It could be a justification for rebellion—a very significant point to the practical Chinese mind. It was also a justification for conquest, once the conquest had been achieved successfully. It could sanction submission on the part of a conquered people to the conqueror, since the latter undoubtedly held the Mandate of Heaven. However, the conqueror might also be resisted, for Mencius taught that Heaven sees as the people see and hears as the people hear. Therefore a conqueror who did not improve the lot of the people might be resisted. In modern times China has twice applied these political principles. She accepted the rule of the Mongols (1260–1368)

and of the Manchus (1644–1912) as long as these foreigners conferred substantial benefits upon her. She overthrew their rule once they had lost the Mandate of Heaven.

The principle of *political loyalty* was also affected by the doctrine of Heaven's Mandate. Although loyalty in the Confucian code was honored frequently to an extreme degree, it was not an absolute virtue. When the ruler had lost the Mandate of Heaven, it was the duty of the subject to be disloyal. The Western concept of the divine right of kings, demanding absolute loyalty to the throne, did not exist in the Confucian scheme of things. On the contrary, Confucianism called upon the people to pass judgment on their sovereign. As Mencius said: "The people are the water and the prince is the boat; the water can support the boat, but it can also sink it."

Again, the doctrine of Heaven's Mandate justified only a very limited use of force by a conqueror, for a conquest was not achieved by fighting but only by securing the favor of Heaven. Hence, force was only to subdue recalcitrants against the Will of Heaven. As a result, Chinese, generally speaking, have been pacifists. Mencius taught that there were no righteous wars, although some wars might be better than others. Lao-tzu and Mo Ti likewise condemned offensive war. Virtue was more likely to impress Heaven than brute force. Consequently, Confucianism justified military expeditions only when they could be interpreted as designed to restore order and preserve peace in a neighboring state. The record of Chinese history, to be sure, may appear as a contradiction of all this theorizing about peace, for actually the Chinese have warred as generously as other peoples; but their wars of conquest were conducted mostly by rulers who were not Confucians.[8] The Confucian theory alone does not of course explain why the Chinese

[8] However, the whole question of Chinese pacifism is a touchy one and cannot be disposed of easily. Most of China's dynasties were set up by brute force, as, for a recent example, the Communist conquest of 1949. This conquest was a simple matter of power, but the determination of the factors which create power is a very complex problem.

have in general avoided wars of conquest. Economic considerations have also played an important part. But it does appear that, had there been no Confucian pacifism, China would have warred upon its neighbors to a much greater extent than it has. In general, Old China preferred to let her neighbors alone, provided the neighbors did not meddle in Chinese affairs.

CONFUCIAN POLITICAL INSTITUTIONS

The Monarchy

The political institution of supreme importance in Old China was the monarchy, which operated on the theory of the emperor's unlimited power. In the case of most sovereigns the actual exercise of power could be and often was limited in various ways, but the theory of *absolutism* remained strong. As a result, in the course of time absolutism was taken for granted, sterility in political discussion was encouraged, and eventually the idea was developed that good government is government by men, since under unlimited power there could be no rule of law. But absolutism was made more palatable by the process of making it humane. In practice, of course, the imperial power was exercised not by the emperor himself but by various ambitious groups: kinsmen, eunuchs, generals, or powerful families, as the case might be.

Under the Manchu dynasty (1644–1912) the emperor was accountable for famine, flood, or pestilence because such things were believed to be a consequence of his misrule. As the father of the nation, he was clothed in theory with autocratic, absolute powers; yet these powers were not to be exercised in any arbitrary manner, but in conformity with customary practices established through the ages. The succession passed in the male line to whichever son an emperor might choose; the offspring of concubines were not excluded. When there was no direct heir, the succession passed to a lateral branch of the family of a younger generation. The new emperor was thus adopted as the son of his predecessor and performed the ancestral rites to the spirits of the departed sovereigns.

The authority of the Manchu emperor was not confined within definitive politico-geographic boundaries as was the case with European sovereigns, because the philosophical base of the Confucian monarchy was cultural rather than territorial or national. The territory over which he exercised direct rule included eighteen provinces, known as China Proper, and four great dependencies: Mongolia, Manchuria (which enjoyed a privileged status because it was the homeland of the dynasty), Tibet (after 1700), and Sinkiang (after 1872). Beyond these dependencies lay the tributary states, varying in number from time to time and recognizing, according to Confucian political ideas, the overlordship of the Middle Kingdom. Payment of tribute was one tangible evidence of inferior status (it was repaid by imperial gifts), and its bearers had come, in the course of Chinese history, from such distant lands as Arabia, Malabar, Ceylon, and eastern India, as well as from the adjacent kingdoms of Annam, Ryukyu, Sulu, and Korea. The theory and practice in these "foreign" relations will be treated in detail in Chapter 14.

As legislator and administrator, this autocratic Manchu emperor was bound by powerful controls: *custom*, the unwritten constitution of the Empire; and *precedent*, as defined in the edicts of his predecessors. He was influenced and not infrequently controlled by the opinions of his ministers and by those of his personal attendants within the palace. Under the guidance of the latter, he selected his empress from a group of daughters of Manchu nobles. Secondary consorts might be chosen from the same group. Finally, he might favor himself with an unlimited number of concubines from the families of Manchu nobles and freemen.[9]

The *nobility* consisted of the imperial clansmen who traced their descent directly

[9] For the methods and content of education by which in modern times a Manchu prince was prepared for the duties of an emperor see Harold L. Kahn, "The Education of a Prince: the Emperor Learns his Roles," *Approaches to Modern Chinese History*, Albert Feuerwerker, ed. (1967), 15-44.

to the founder of the dynasty; the hereditary nobility who were direct descendants of the eight princes who co-operated in the conquest of China; and finally, a number of Chinese families such as the household of the Duke of Yen, a descendant of Confucius.

Usually the function of the metropolitan administration at Peking was negative rather than positive: to check rather than to direct the actions of the provincial officials. In the middle of the nineteenth century, however, increasing contacts with Western states forced the central government, though reluctantly, to assume a more positive responsibility.

Ministers and Departments

In general, the imperial political structure at Peking consisted of six ministries or boards, namely: civil office (appointment of officials), revenue, ceremonies, war, punishments, and public works (canals, flood control). In addition to these six boards there were two other independent branches of government, the military establishment and the censorate. There were also a number of minor offices such as the imperial academy of literature, a court of review in criminal cases, and the office of history. Finally, in Ming times a grand secretariat of high officials assisted the emperor in administration, while the later Manchus created a grand council to advise on military and other important matters.

The ministers of state, the official servants of the emperor, varied in title, number, and power. Their ultimate function was to preserve the sovereign's power. Actually, they usurped for themselves whatever powers they could. The net product was the binding of public life to Confucianism. Scholarship led to the civil service examinations. Those who passed the examinations were Confucian scholars. These successful candidates might be appointed to political office. Thus, in normal times, Confucianism alone opened the door to political power.

The Censors

Among the more interesting political institutions of Old China was the *Court of Censors*. Originally there were two classifications of censors: (1) those whose function

it was to impeach erring officials, and (2) those who might protest against acts of the Court and propose remedies. In general, the censors provided a healthy and useful instrument of government. However, by Ming times (1368–1644), with the full development of monarchical rule, the censors tended to lose their function of remonstrating with the Court. How could a monarch who had become infallible submit to criticism and still maintain his prestige? [10]

The Law

In Old China, ideas on the nature and function of law were quite different from those that have developed in the West. Chinese legal theory found its origins in the Chinese view of an order of nature. It was necessary for man by his actions to keep in harmony with this order, and the ultimate function of the emperor was to see to it that this was done. In theory, at any rate, the emperor accomplished his mission by the moral example of his own virtuous conduct. Thus laws and regulations were thought to be unnecessary save in the case of uncivilized persons. Even here laws were regarded as only a secondary recourse in stimulating right conduct. From early times, however, the Chinese made certain compromises with

[10] Charles O. Hucker, "Confucianism and the Chinese Censorial System," *Confucianism in Action*, D. S. Nivison and A. F. Wright, eds., (1959), 182–208; also Hucker's "The Traditional Chinese Censorate and the New Peking Regime," *American Political Science Review*, 14 (1951): 1041–57; and Richard L. Walker, "The Control System of the Chinese Government," *Far Eastern Quarterly*, 7 (1947): 2–21. The Court of Censors was a time-honored and useful agency of government even if, at times, it was subject to great abuse. Its beginnings probably date back to the second century B.C.; it had become a major bureaucratic organ by Sung times, about 1100 A.D.; and it reached maturity and began its decline during the Ming dynasty. As with most governmental institutions, the effectiveness of the Censorate depended on the integrity and responsibility of the emperor and his high officials and on the character and backbone of the censors. Weak censors could be afraid of the court eunuchs, while a weak emperor could admonish his censors: "Don't harass me." See Hucker, *The Censorial System of Ming China* (1966).

this Confucian concept of law. In the third century B.C. the Legalists employed law as a bulwark of absolutism, while the eminently Confucian Han dynasty also took advantage of legal practices. Moreover, major codes were subsequently to appear in T'ang, Sung, Yuan, Ming, and Ch'ing times.

Thus Chinese (Confucian) law was derived from the moral character of the natural universe. It enjoyed no divine attributes. Confucius did not claim that his insights came from divine revelation. Therefore laws were not inflexible rules but were to be considered as suggestive examples of proper procedures. As a consequence morality stood above law. The sanction of law was to be found in reason and experience, which may suggest why a Chinese was apt to be a Confucian when in office and a Taoist out of office. Since harmony rather than abstract justice was the ideal, law was concerned with mutual self-respect, the principle of live and let live. In practice this meant that law was involved with the art of diplomacy and compromise which would take into account changing condition. The traditional skill of the Chinese in compromise and conciliation was an expression of their dislike of litigation and their distrust of the courts.

Moreover, Chinese law was made by the ruler, not by a legislature or by the decisions of the courts. Little was done to establish a body of legal doctrine. Most of the law was either penal or administrative. Since business, large or small, was an affair of the family, it was controlled by kinship and personal relations, so that private law was considered unnecessary. Thus there was no occasion to regard a big commercial firm as a legal individual. The rights of a contract were of less consequence than the preservation of the moral order. In Old China, the function of law was not to protect the political freedom or the private property of the individual. Yet it should be remembered that the Chinese were constantly concerned with achieving justice. The significant point is that they defined justice according to the values that seemed good to them.

It follows, therefore, that the study of Chinese law, especially as contrasted with Western law, presents problems which no student of Eastern Asia can afford to neglect. It is notable, for instance, that while the great dynasties from Tang to Ch'ing times compiled their legal codes, and while popular Chinese literature delighted in stories of court trials, the Chinese did not develop a science of jurisprudence or a legal profession as it is understood in the West. In seeking answers to the legal aspects of the Chinese mind, the student will find it helpful to pursue the following questions: What were the components of the traditional Chinese legal system? Who controlled and operated the system and to what purpose? Was it a single system or a plurality and, if the latter, how were the parts related? Was Chinese society, in theory or in practice, ruled by law?

For the introductory purposes of this survey, it is sufficient to note that from a Western point of view, the weakness of the Chinese system was that the application of the law rested with the administrative bureaucracy of the Empire. Thus the courts provided no check and were not intended to be a check on executive power. To a democratic society, dominated by the supremacy of law, the Chinese system was repugnant, but it was not so regarded in China. There was no popular concept of the law and the courts as the protectors of the individual. Indeed, the Chinese had a saying to the effect: "Avoid litigation; going to law is going to trouble." [11]

The Provinces

Under the impressive but rather passive metropolitan administration at Peking, the provinces of China Proper enjoyed a large measure of autonomy. Each province was divided for purposes of administration into *tao* or circuits, prefectures, and *hsien* which might be described as districts or counties. Over these various divisions presided a bu-

[11] A useful introduction is Sybille van der Sprenkel, *Legal Institutions in Manchu China* (London, 1962).* See also Derk Bodde and Clarence Morris, *Law in Imperial China* (1967), a distinctive study presenting the judicial process as it actually operated and not as it was supposed to operate.

reaucracy of officials whose status was determined by rank. In all there were nine ranks, each divided into upper and lower grades.

As long as the actions of these provincial officials did not run counter to Peking's general instructions, and as long as the appropriate revenues were forwarded promptly to the capital, a province was free to administer local affairs largely as it saw fit. This did not mean, however, that Peking had no control in the province. All provincial officials from the highest to the lowest were appointed, promoted, transferred, and dismissed by the central government. Appointment was made usually for a three-year term, and high officials were not assigned to office in the province of their birth. It followed that the personnel were constantly changing and that every official ruled among strangers. Moreover, officials sent to a given capital were likely to be chosen from various factions or cliques in order that each might act as a check on his fellows.

The principal official of the provincial administration was a governor. With him might be associated a Tatar general in command of the local Manchu garrison. There were also a treasurer who transmitted the revenues to Peking, a judge who passed on appeals from prefectural and district courts, a salt commissioner who controlled both the manufacture and sale of this article, a grain commissioner (in some provinces), and a literary chancellor who supervised the civil service examinations.

Local Government

As mentioned above, for purposes of administration, the province was divided into a number of units, the most important being the county or district. The county was composed of a walled city and the adjacent country with its towns and villages. In the case of larger cities, only half or a third of the city was included. The *magistrate*, supposedly a master of all the arts and problems of government, was the chief official. His functions were as many and varied as the problems of mankind. He collected all local revenues, with the exception of special taxes such as the salt tax and *likin*, the latter being an internal transit levy. He was judge in first instance in cases both civil and criminal. He was registrar of land, commissioner of famine and pestilence, and custodian of official buildings. In general, it was his business to preserve law and order and to have a care for both the physical and the moral welfare of the people. Thus the functions of the magistrate called for rare ability. Here it may be added that as local administrators the magistrates were free in general to pursue whatever course seemed good as long as they could raise the necessary finances without arousing public protest, and without offending higher officials or the Court.

Some local public functions could be and sometimes were performed by the local gentry. From this circumstance, however, it should not be concluded that Old China enjoyed local self-government. The gentry who performed these functions were not elected or formally appointed, nor did they constitute self-governing councils free from the interference of higher authorities. The gentry, nevertheless, formed an indispensable part of local government. It performed functions which the local government was unable or not qualified to perform. Put another way, the gentry was a local elite sharing with governing the control of local affairs. It was an informal power contrasting with the local government's formal power. Indeed, it was the only group empowered to represent the local community in discussions with officials or to take part in the governing process. The official class and the gentry class overlapped but did not coincide. In general, a man might be an official in his public capacity and a member of the gentry in his private capacity.

The term "gentry" (since there is no better designation) with its English connotations can be misleading when applied to the Chinese scene. Unlike the English gentry, whose status was hereditary, the composition of the Chinese gentry changed from time to time. Membership in the gentry depended on holding a degree or on receiving an official appointment regardless of whether the person owned landed property, the principal source of wealth. Many persons who owned land were not members of the gentry.

At the same time, the possession of wealth could ease one's course into gentry status. Wealth could mean leisure, the opportunity to get an education and to take the civil service examinations, and thus to get a degree. Of course when the govenment was hard pressed for money one could sometimes buy a degree.

There were two principal ways in which gentry influence played a part in local government. The first was the gentry relationship with the commoners. As the social elite of the community, its members might settle disputes. The commoners looked to the gentry for protection against injustice and for relief in times of distress. The second was the gentry relationship with the local officials. Only officials could make decisions, but the gentry could influence officials to initiate, modify, or withdraw an unwise decision. In a sense, therefore, the gentry were the eyes and the ears of local government and of public opinion.[12]

Within a county, the towns and villages were governed by their own officials, who were nominated by the village elders and confirmed in office by the magistrate. Within the village lay the real government of China, where the spirit of the family or the unity of the family expressed itself in a larger loyalty to the land that had supported the family or the clan. The government of the village was communal and largely invisible, for there were no mayor and councilors; it was a moral government of the elders based on "custom and usage, the unwritten law." This was the only government that most Chinese knew. As for Peking and the metropolitan administration, the villagers considered that "heaven was high and the emperor far away." [13]

[12] For extended treatment of local government and the role of the gentry see T'ung-tsu Ch'ü, *Local Government in China under the Ch'ing* (1962),* and Chang Chung-li, *The Chinese Gentry* (1966).*
[13] T'ung-tsu Ch'u, *Local Government in China under the Ch'ing* contains an excellent account of how officials who were "gentlemen" humanists without training in practical day-to-day problems of administration could function in charge of the courts, of security, of welfare, and, indeed, of things in general. In the early

Economic administration in Old China considered in its narrowest sense was concerned with the problem of extracting enough revenue to maintain the Court and the necessary public services. As in all agricultural societies, most revenue was derived directly from the land, which, though belonging in theory to the emperor, was in reality owned by individuals. At times the entire system of taxation rested on the land tax. Land and taxation, therefore, were major administration problems. Sometimes, as in the cases of salt and iron, the principle of government monopoly was applied. In general, some degree of economic regulation was regarded as a proper state function, and in times of great natural calamities this principle might be applied rather widely in public works and even in more direct measures of relief.

Education and Government

Although schools did exist in Old China and although some schools were subsidized, formal public education was not regarded as the function or duty of government. The wealthy employed private tutors for their children and in some cases established a free school as an act of benevolence, but the

years of the Manchu dynasty the imperial rulers were quite successful in maintaining a firm control over their vast realm, thus ensuring stability and the perpetuation of their power. They sought to protect various groups and sections of the vast rural population from undue encroachment so that most of the inhabitants of a rural area tended to accept alien Manchu rule as the best way to preserve local interests. In the long run, however, the Manchu system of local and rural control failed, partly because the system itself was imperfect, and also because the cumulative effects of physical want, economic and social inequities, and decaying administration drove the peasant to desperation. In a broader sense, developments of this kind are a reminder of a persistent conflict throughout Chinese history between bureaucracy and emperor. For an exhaustive treatment of this vital subject see Kung-chuan Hsiao, *Rural China: Imperial Control in the Nineteenth Century* (1960),* especially 501–18. Note also Lawrence D. Kessler, "Ethnic Composition of Provincial Leadership during the Ch'ing Dynasty," *Journal of Asian Studies* 28 (1969): 489–511.

average Chinese boy enjoyed no formal schooling. At the close of the nineteenth century, only a very small percentage of the people was literate, as Arthur W. Hummel has suggested in the usual sense of this word. However, the word "literate" is apt to be misleading when applied to a people so compact socially and so deeply rooted in their culture as were the Chinese. A Chinese, for instance, might not be able to read, and yet he could possess extraordinary traditional skills which would make him almost a cultured man.

The small literate group, however, provided the scholars, and scholarship in turn was of high importance, since only through learning could men rise to official position and honor. The basis of education was the Confucian classics and their commentaries, a knowledge of which required a much more extensive scholarship than, for example, a thorough knowledge of English literature. In addition, the extensive Chinese histories had to be known. Therefore there was much emphasis on memory. To be able by memory and in appropriate style to apply a classical phrase to the solution of a philosophical problem of politics was the goal of the scholar. Science, mathematics, and the development of independent and critical thought were regarded as of little consequence in fitting a man for the responsibilities of government.

Civil Service Examinations

Scholarship achieved its rewards when the candidate had passed one or all of the civil service examinations prescribed and conducted by the metropolitan government. This was the only proper avenue to public office and official distinction. There were four series of examinations, the first being held in the county and prefectural cities twice every three years. In the county only some 2 per cent of the candidates were permitted to pass. These were admitted a few weeks later to the prefectural examinatons, where somewhat more than 50 per cent were likely to be successful. These men were now eligible for minor posts and could qualify to enter the provincial examinations held every three

years in the provincial capitals. In great examination halls, as many as 14,000 candidates ate the food they brought along, wrote their essays, and slept in their "cells" for three separate sessions of three days each. During these sessions the candidates were permitted no recesses. Once a session had commenced and the walls between the rows of cells had been bricked up, the gates of the hall were locked, and none, not even the chief examiner, might enter or leave. Successful candidates in the provincial tests were eligible for the metropolitan examinations in Peking. In these about 6 per cent passed, and they, in turn, might enter the palace examinations held in the presence of the emperor.

The significance of the Chinese examination system can hardly be overestimated. It was the great carrier of tradition. It helped, under the Ming and Manchu dynasties, to freeze the old and rich Chinese culture into a fixed pattern. It encouraged exclusive reliance upon the wisdom of the past; it discouraged freedom and independence of thought and thus prepared the way for a cultural decline that was hastened by the concurrent impact of an expanding Europe on China. It was the principal agent by which Confucianism monopolized scholarship, and by which scholarship, in turn, monopolized politics. But it went even further. The examinations became a principal road to wealth as well as to official position. This wealth was usually invested in land. The landed gentry, the silk-gowned, frequently controlled public opinion. The official did well to defer to this class, for he was a member of it either in his person or in his interests, or in both.[14]

[14] Too frequently there was a wide gulf between theory and practice in the administration of the examination system. In addition to entry into the civil service through the examinations, many officials were admitted through the recommendation of their relatives who had attained high position. While this practice was looked down upon, a considerable fraction of the lesser officials entered office through this *yin* system. The question of the extent of social mobility in Old China and the relationship of mobility to the examination system can hardly be said to have been resolved. Note Ho Ping-ti, *The Ladder of Success in Imperial China* (1962).*

The foregoing sketch has suggested briefly the extraordinary influence Confucianism in its broadest aspects has exerted on the government of China. Now, in the later twentieth century, this unique background seems to have vanished. A new China, no longer merely rebellious but openly revolutionary, has challenged not only the future but also the hallowed Confucian past. Perhaps we might find this upheaval far more comprehensible if China's revolutionists had patterned their course on models provided by eighteenth- and nineteenth-century America. On the contrary, China's revolutionists, whether of *Kuomintang* or Communist persuasion, have striven toward their own peculiar goals. No student of history expects that China's dead past will determine the shape of things to come, but it would be equally naive to suppose that political principles by which China has lived for more than two thousand years and by which she was still living in the early years of the twentieth century can be discarded and destroyed quickly and completely. In what ways then will political tradition be likely to reassert itself even in the midst of revolutionary change?

Authoritarianism. It is clear that the Confucian tradition is one of authority exercised (sometimes humanely) by those who were above upon those who were below. Very little evidence has emerged from twentieth-century China to suggest that this tradition has been weakened seriously. Both the *Kuomintang* and the Communists have used it, the latter with seemingly more effect than the former.[15]

Ideological Control. Confucian China is one of the best examples history provides of a society that operated by ideological control rather than by organized governmental direction. In many respects Confucianism was to China what religion has sometimes been to the West, namely, an agency for control. An

[15] The authoritarian tradition is discussed ably by John K. Fairbank, *The United States and China* (rev. ed., 1962),* 97, 102–4.

ideology that captures the imagination, particularly in times of political corruption and popular distress, enjoys a marked advantage. Chinese Communists have attempted to capitalize on this ideological tradition.

Bureaucracy. Again, it is to be noted that in Confucian China government was by bureaucracy. For Americans steeped in the democratic tradition and only recently subjected to problems of bureaucracy, it might be difficult to sense the hold which this tradition has had upon China. It was not a tradition of responsible government as the West understands that term, but rather of the responsibility of one official to another. It followed that the people, given the foundation on which bureaucratic rule stood, were not concerned and did not regard it as their business to be concerned with affairs of state. The point is illustrated by an incident in 1851 at the time of the death of the Tao Kuang emperor. The intrepid traveller E. R. Huc, who with his fellow travellers was taking tea at an inn with some Chinese, attempted unsuccessfully to induce the latter into a political discussion. Finally, a worthy Chinese laid his hands paternally on Huc's shoulders and said, smiling ironically:

> *Listen to me, my friend! Why should you trouble your heart and fatigue your head by all these vain surmises? The Mandarins have to attend to affairs of state; they are paid for it. Let them earn their money then. But don't let us torment ourselves about what does not concern us. We should be great fools to want to do political business for nothing.*[16]

Moreover, bureaucracy in a society based on personal relationships lived on standardized forms of corruption practiced so generally and openly as to become accepted institutions. Yet whatever the shortcomings of the Chinese bureaucratic system may have been, the fact remains that as early as the beginning of the Christian era, the Chinese Empire in matters of political management had many bureaucratic features not unlike the super state of the twentieth

[16] E. R. Huc, *A Journey Through the Chinese Empire* (2 vols., 1859), I, 117.

century. Indeed, ancient Chinese bureaucracy when examined closely looks remarkably modern. For good or ill, it was one of China's great contributions to political theory and practice.[17]

Humanism. Although the Confucian tradition was authoritarian, it was also humanistic in that it concerned itself with human relationships and practical patterns of conduct. Although the sovereign was absolute, arbitrary, and without fear of any higher law, there was a constant regard for stability in human relationships. From this one may conclude that the Confucian tradition did not place the state completely above mankind. There was some regard for the individual. The worth of the individual, however, was measured in social, not in personal, terms. Success was not derived from personal initiative and individual accomplishment but from conformity with right conduct. Confucianism thus left a tradition and a principle not of individual but of social action.

Doubtless, China's past will not be the only force laboring to shape China's present and future; yet it is worth noting that the more the Chinese Communists try to create a new China, the more they seem to rely on Old Chinese ways of doing it.[18]

[17] See H. G. Creel, "The Beginnings of Bureaucracy in China: the Origin of the Hsien," *Journal of Asian Studies* 23 (1964): 155–83. The terms "feudalism" and "bureaucracy" have come to be used so loosely as to lose practically all meaning. It will thus be helpful to think of feudalism as a system of government in which a ruler personally delegates limited sovereignty over portions of his domain to vassals. Bureaucracy, in contrast, is a system of administration by means of professional functionaries whose functions are prescribed more or less definitely. A feudal vassal could do anything he was not expressly forbidden to do. A bureaucratic official could not properly do anything that was not part of his prescribed function.

[18] W. G. Beasley and E. G. Pulleybank, *Historians of China and Japan* (1961) should be consulted for the conceptions of history held by the traditional Chinese and Japanese historians. Both groups approached their task with purposes very unlike American historians of the twentieth century.

FOR FURTHER READING

Donald J. Munro, *The Concept of Man in Early China* (1969) traces the growth of the concept of man's innate moral equality. Ch'u T'ung-tsu, *Law and Society in Traditional China* (La Haye, 1961), a detailed analysis of the historical relationship between Chinese law and society, stressing the traditional Chinese concept that law is an instrument for maintaining social order. Ch'u T'ung-tsu, *Local Government in China under the Ch'ing* (1962) gives details on the administration of justice, taxation, public works, and social services. Hsiao Kung-chuan, *Rural China: Imperial Control in the Nineteenth Century* (1960),* a monumental work covering the whole range of government activities in town and village. Hsieh Pao-chao, *The Government of China 1644–1911* (1925), a useful introduction to the Manchu period. Charles O. Hucker, *The Traditional Chinese State in Ming Times, 1368–1644* (1961). E. A. Kracke, *Civil Service in Early Sung China, 960–1067* (1953)* deals with the techniques for maintaining administrative integrity among government personnel. Lin Mou-sheng, *Men and Ideas, An Informal History of Chinese Political Thought* (1942). Thomas T. Meadows, *The Chinese and Their Rebellions* (1954), a reissue of a standard work first published in 1856. Franz Michael, *The Origin of Manchu Rule in China* (1942), a study in the significance of the frontier. Karl A. Wittfogel, *Oriental Despotism: A Comparative Study of Total Power* (1957),* a detailed analysis of the author's theory of "hydraulic society" and bureaucratic despotism.

Two brief case studies of traditional government in action are Johanna M. Menzel, ed., *The Chinese Civil Service: Career Open to Talent?* (1963),* and John Meskill, ed., *Wang An-shih: Practical Reformer?* (1963).*

Ways of Life
in Old Japan

chapter 4

The Japanese and the Chinese are in many ways the product of the single civilization of China. From early times Japan drew heavily upon the profound learning of the Chinese: their arts, letters, and philosophy. It thus came about that there was much common ground in the cultural and intellectual life of these two great oriental states. Yet they did not become one people or one culture, and, indeed, their differences have often appeared quite as arresting as their similarities.

As already indicated, the impact of the Western world upon China in the past hundred years can be comprehended only by those who have some understanding of the Chinese institutional life upon which this Western impact exerted its influence. So too, in the case of Japan, the impact of the West cannot be separated from the ideas and the institutions by which the Japanese lived.

An historical sketch of this kind can perhaps best begin with the reminder that geography had its part in shaping the distinctive character of Japan no less than it did in the case of China. Japan's insular position, like that of the British Isles, gave a special character to Japan's life. It was possible for Japan at various times to avoid the main stream of continental life and thereby to protect its own individuality. On the other hand, Japan as often received invaders, immigrants, and a stream of continental cultural influence. Out of these importations, which they combined with their indigenous traditions, the Japanese fashioned a distinctive Japanese culture and a character which, though belonging to Asia, was unlike that of any other Asiatic people. Moreover, Japan's ancient cultural borrowings were voluntary; they were not forced by foreign military conquest. Japan was therefore free to reject this or to accept that, and to digest in comparative seclusion those things which she did take from China, permitting them to shape and color her own ideas but not to destroy them. Japan, as a result, has sometimes seemed to present the paradox of a people always ready to consider new teachings yet jealous to retain their own traditions. These circumstances have sometimes led to untenable opinions concerning the Japanese, as, for example, the belief that geography fostered a spirit of isolationism in Japan and a spirit of repugnance toward foreign intercourse.[1]

[1] G. B. Sansom, *The Western World and Japan* (1950), 167–69, a masterpiece of historical interpretation.

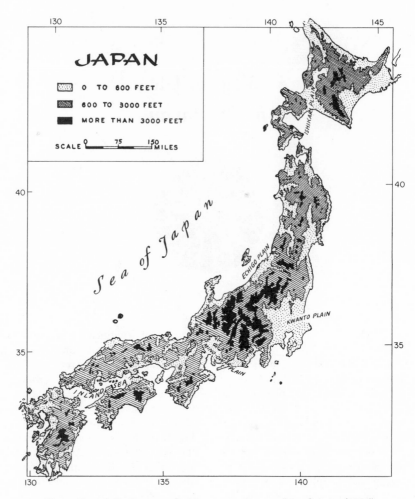

From Daniel R. Bergsmark, Economic Geography of Asia *(1935).*

The history of Japan, measured in terms of China's long past, is a comparatively brief story. When Confucius, around the year 500 B.C., was giving form and purpose to one of history's greatest codes of humanistic behavior (Confucianism), the history of Japan had hardly begun—though the islands may well have been at that time the battleground of rude and barbarous tribes.

The Japanese who peopled the country in its early history were a product of racial mixture but were predominantly Mongoloid and certainly akin to their neighbors in Korea and China. Most of them reached Japan through Korea. Some, of course, may have come from the southern coasts of China and Malaya by way of Formosa and the Ryukyu Islands. These Mongoloid folk were preceded in the islands by another people, by the ancestors of the present day Ainu, a people of proto-white stock but of a neolithic culture inferior to the new invaders from Korea. The Ainu, in time, were pushed to the east and north. In the mid-twentieth century only approximately 14,000 of this vanishing race still survived in Hokkaido.[2]

[2] J. Edward Kidder, *Japan, Before Buddhism* (1959), 86.

It was about the beginning of the Christian era that Japan was invaded by Mongoloid clans of horsemen who brought with them a superior civilization built of bronze and iron. These were the men who were shortly to establish in central Japan the original Japanese state known as Yamato. These invaders had already known something of the superior culture of China, for they brought into Japan not only the iron sword of northern Asia but also semi-precious stones often found in archaeological remains in Korea, and a round bronze mirror of Chinese origin. These three articles, the sword, the jewel, the mirror, became in time the historic symbols of authority for Japanese sovereigns. At first Yamato was merely one of many clan states, some of which were ruled by women. The idea of hereditary rights and of the soldier as aristocrat and ruler was probably strong among these people. These ideas were to show a marked capacity to survive in the Japanese mind.

RELIGION IN PRIMITIVE JAPAN

The religion of this young Japan was a simple nature worship involving, somewhat later under Chinese influence, some concepts of ancestor worship. This religion was Shinto, "the way of the gods," as it came to be known in the sixth century to distinguish it from Buddhism, which by that time had reached Japan from China. If the material culture of this early Japan was crude, its religious and social life were of a comparatively high order, for Shinto was based on "appreciation rather than fear." It thus followed that:

. . . *much that is kindly and gracious in the life of the Japanese today can be traced to those sentiments which caused their remote ancestors to ascribe divinity not only to the powerful and awe-inspiring, such as the sun and the moon and the tempest, or to the useful, such as the well and the cooking pot,* but also to the lovely and pleasant, such as the rocks and streams, the trees and flowers.[3]

In this "religion of love and gratitude rather than of fear," man's religious nature expressed itself through simple sentiments of awe in the presence of the wonders of nature. Anything in nature prompting this emotion of wonder was called *kami*. This word, usually translated into English as "god," actually means "above" and thus "superior." *Kami* stood for the simple Shinto idea of deity, and it is obviously important to remember this when attempting to understand the deification of living emperors in modern Japan and also of Japanese soldiers who died for their country.[4] In this Shinto reverence for nature the Sun Goddess occupied a central position. She was not only the central deity of early Shinto, but she also became the mythological ancestress of the Imperial Japanese House.

Purity, the chief virtue among the concepts of this early religion, was expressed in the first instance in physical cleanliness. To be ready for religious observance, one took a bath and put on clean garments. Here deeply rooted in time is the origin of a modern trait of the Japanese: their desire to be scrupulously clean.

During the past fifteen centuries there have been many attempts to transform Shinto into an organized and formalized religion, and in very recent times to employ it as a weapon to forge nationalism and fanaticism.

[3] G. B. Sansom, *Japan: A Short Cultural History* (rev. ed., 1962), 47; and E. O. Reischauer, *Japan: Past and Present* (3rd ed., 1964),* 12–13.

[4] Western historians and students of Japanese history, as well as Chinese history have the difficult problem of understanding Japan's past in its own terms, of avoiding the natural tendency to interpret it in the value system of the West. The problem is one of vocabulary as well as approach, as the word *kami* suggests. Western words do not always convey Japanese realities. The student should bear in mind that general terms such as feudalism, nationalism, family, and village have meant one thing in Europe and America but not necessarily the same thing in Japan. See John Whitney Hall, *Japanese History* (1961),* 18.

More will be said on these aspects of the subject in later pages.

POLITICAL ORIGINS: YAMATO

As the migrations from Korea continued through successive centuries, the later invaders pushed and fought their way through the Inland Sea to settle in the Yamato area of central Japan. There a clan emerged, stronger than its neighbors, absorbing some of its rivals until it could claim a shadowy overlordship throughout central and western Japan and in parts of southern Korea. The rise of this Yamato clan did not mean the destruction of all other clans, nor did it challenge their autonomous rights. It did mean that the priest-chief of Yamato assumed priority among all clan chiefs, and the cults of the Yamato clan tended to become the cults of the land as a whole. It was in this way that the Sun Goddess who, according to mythology, was the ancestress of the founder of the Yamato clan became the supreme deity of Japanese Shinto. Moreover, the chiefs of Yamato, by gaining some degree of supremacy over other clan chiefs, became the founders of the Japanese imperial family. In a word, the beginnings of the Japanese state go back to a time about the beginning of the Christian era, when the Yamato clan could at least claim some form of suzerainty over a group of lesser but associated clans.

This early clan age culture (approximately 250–600 A.D.) was in many respects a fairly sophisticated economic and political society, notably in the area of provincial administration. Yet it was soon to be revolutionized by an educational tidal wave that poured in upon it from China. The early Japanese had always had some indirect contacts with China, and new immigrant waves continued to carry the Chinese influence to Japan; but it was not until the sixth century that the Japanese, consciously recognizing how superior Chinese civilization was, sought actively to understand it and make much of it their own.

Somewhat earlier, perhaps before the beginning of the fifth century, Japan had some knowledge of the Chinese language and script. In 405 A.D. the arrival of a Sino-Korean scholar, Wani by name, as tutor to the heir apparent of Yamato, meant that the Chinese written language had been adopted officially by the Japanese court. These events paved the way for the general Chinese cultural impact that followed. Buddhism was introduced to the Yamato court in about the year 550 and won numerous converts. Many of these converts later journeyed to study in China and returned to Japan as the most effective missionaries of Chinese culture. These pro-Chinese, pro-Buddhist factions controlled the Japanese (Yamato) court and the way was thus cleared for the radical reforms that followed under the leadership of the crown prince, Shotoku Taishi, sometimes called the father of Japanese civilization.

Supported by the Chinese-Buddhist factions, Shotoku Taishi in 604 issued a code of moral injunctions superior to any political philosophy hitherto known in Japan. This code enunciated a Chinese theory that political power resided with the ruler. Shotoku Taishi and those who influenced him were seeking in Chinese political theory for a unifying force to break the heritage of clan and caste barriers. He was thus attempting to lay the foundations of a new political and economic life in Japan by a frontal assault on the old clan order. The movement was advanced further when, beginning in 607, Shotoku Taishi sent embassies to China accompanied by able young Japanese students who on their return became promoters of Chinese learning not only in government, but also in the whole range of artistic and cultural life.

By 645 the reformers were committed to remaking the Yamato state in the image of their magnificent neighbor, T'ang China. Some of their ideas toward this end were embodied in the *Taikwa* or Great Reform of 645–650 and the subsequent reforms which extended to 701. These edicts contemplated a new system of taxation, of local government, and of land tenure. In theory they all involved a greater centralization of power, but in practice they did not work out ideally. Powerful families who could not be deprived expediently of their lands were confirmed in their titles on the questionable assumption that they now held their lands from the throne. In addition they were given official posts or court rank. The central government also undertook to appoint governors for the provinces; but here too the practice was to confirm the existing authority of the most powerful local chief. Theoretically, all of this amounted to a political reorganization, but in reality the emphasis in the Great Reform was on the economic rather than on the political sphere. The reformers who controlled the court were not primarily concerned about extending their direct political control to remote regions. Their immediate concern was to find a more effective means of collecting wealth from the provinces.[5]

Even this early in their history the Japanese were showing an amazing zest for learning, a trait noted many centuries later by the first Europeans to reach Japanese shores. Moreover, these reforming Japanese were now thinking of their state as an empire and of their ruler as an all-powerful monarch in the Chinese tradition. However, the ruler, while attaining this new stature, retained his original and indigenous character as chief-priest. In this manner Japanese sovereigns came to play a dual role embodied in the single person of the emperor: he was the Shinto high priest of Japan's divine origins as well as an absolute secular ruler such as the Chinese had long had. In some very important cases the Japanese accepted the form of a Chinese idea or institution but rejected its spirit, as when the reformers amid all this Chinese flavor attempted to preserve the interests of a court aristocracy of birth at the expense of other groups. In China the aristocracy was one of learning rather than of birth.

[5] K. Asakawa, *The Early Institutional Life of Japan* (Tokyo, 1903; reissued 1963),* 295–96, 322ff.

JAPAN BUILDS A CHINESE CITY: THE NARA PERIOD, 710–784

The ancient city of Nara near the modern town of that name in the Yamato plain stood in eighth century Japan as the most striking tangible evidence of the Chinese influence. Prior to this time the Japanese had not been city builders, nor had they a permanent capital. Nara was their first great city and the first permanent capital. Ch'ang-an, capital of T'ang China and perhaps the greatest city in the world at that time, was the model—a rectangle with the imperial palace at the northern end and broad straight thoroughfares intersecting at right angles. Here was the actual design and structure of Chinese architecture transplanted into Japan. The city was not so large as the Chinese model. Nevertheless, some of its Buddhist temples such as Horyuji and Todaiji still stand in the twentieth century, the oldest wooden buildings in the world, and the only existing examples of the graceful Chinese architecture of T'ang.

It was at Nara that the imported Buddhism acquired tremendous influence as the new state religion. Buddhism in turn was one of the chief instruments through which the young bureaucratic government sought to strengthen its control by appointing the "right" men as chief abbots of the growing and powerful monasteries. Buddhist temples with their brilliant decorations dotted the near and the distant landscapes. Moreover, the cultured men of the Japanese court were steeped not only in Chinese religion, government, city-planning, and art, but also in the vehicle through which much of this learning came to Japan, namely, the classical written Chinese language.

When they discovered that the writing of history had always been an important concern of Chinese governments, these aristocrats of Nara felt that they too must have histories. Their first great chronicles, the *Kojiki* or *Records of Ancient Matters*, and the *Nihon Shoki* or *Chronicles of Japan* were completed in the early years of Nara, probably in 712 and 720 respectively.[6] Both of these chronicles, though official histories, are of immense importance in the study of early Japanese history. They have proven to be rather accurate accounts of the years after 400 A.D. For the earlier years, they present a wealth of mythology and tradition from which it has been possible to reconstruct much of that early and simpler Japan which existed before the coming of Chinese learning. However, historians are not always free to be *good* historians. Sometimes they are under pressure from politicians or from advocates of this or that theory to color what they have to say. So it would seem that the rulers of Nara were not content that history should record the simple myths and traditions handed down orally by professional chroniclers. On the contrary, it was thought that matters would be much improved if history should teach that the chiefs of Yamato were the unique and divine rulers of an old Japan no less glorious than its mighty neighbor China. Accordingly the historians created what had been called an impressive pseudo-history in which the Sun Goddess, a principal object of nature worship by the men of early Yamato, became the progenitress of the royal family and the grandmother of Japan's first emperor, who supposedly ascended the throne on February 11, 660 B.C. This date, which, of course, had not the slightest foundation in fact, may have been arrived at by projecting the founding of Japan a full Chinese time cycle of some 1,260 years into the past. In the twentieth century, as we shall see, these early Japanese chronicles were to be revived and used by supernationalists and superpatriots to serve the ends of a philosophy of 100 per cent Japanism.

In poetry as well as history, Nara was a great age. The great anthology of verse, the *Manyoshu* (Collection of One Thousand Leaves), has never since been surpassed in Japanese poetry.[7]

[6] *Kojiki* or *Records of Ancient Matters*, B. H. Chamberlain, trans. (2nd ed., Kobe, 1932) has been the standard translation. For the beginning student a new edition is recommended: *Kojiki*, Donald L. Philippi, trans. (Tokyo, 1968); W. G. Aston, *Nihongi: Chronicles of Japan* (2 vols., London, 1896).

[7] Nippon Gakujutsu Shinkokai, *The Manyo-*

Politically, Nara witnessed the beginnings of a movement in which the national government, such as it was, practically withered away due to the growth of tax-free estates, both secular and religious. Unlike the Chinese, the Japanese with their strong leanings toward clan loyalty and hereditary rights failed to develop a bureaucracy of education and learning to maintain the national domain and protect the central authority. As a consequence, the peasantry and their lands fell under the control of powerful local families with enough influence at the capital to escape the government tax collector. This meant the decline and impoverishment of the royal authority and the ultimate control of the weakened court by some powerful local family such as the Fujiwara clan, which came to the fore in the Nara period. All in all the close of the Nara era did not present a pretty picture. To be sure, artistic triumphs in temples and images were created, but they were the work of a government that lived far beyond its means, and which, through purchasing the favor of the powerful Buddhist priesthood by means of generous gifts from the public domain, had reduced the central authority to impotence and the peasants to the level of slaves.[8]

THE HEIAN PERIOD, 794–1185

The four centuries following the Nara period are in many respects the most fascinating and revealing period in Japanese history. Although the men who ruled at Nara were absorbed in the new learning from China, their successors in the age of Heian (meaning "peace and tranquility") had a deeper understanding of the processes of cultural borrowing, and therefore a more critical attitude toward Chinese learning in its new Japanese environment. By the ninth century the undiscriminating zeal for Chinese

shu. One Thousand Poems Selected and Translated from the Japanese (Tokyo, 1940, reissued ed., with the texts in Romaji and a new Foreword by Donald Keene, 1965). Also Earl Roy Miner, *An Introduction to Japanese Court Poetry* (1968).[°]

[8] R. K. Reischauer, *Early Japanese History* (2 vols., 1937).

learning had given place to critical analysis which sought to adapt the new ideas to the peculiar background and needs of Japan. In part this more critical point of view was due to the decay of T'ang China and the resulting end in 838 of Japanese embassies to the continent, but it should also be attributed to the growing intellectual maturity of the Japanese. It was in this period that the Japanese first showed their capacity not only to borrow and imitate but also to adapt and develop the ideas and institutions of other lands to their own purposes and in their own particular ways. It was in this period, for example, that Buddhism in Japan became a Japanese rather than an Indian or a Chinese Buddhism.

At the beginning of Heian, which was to witness the development of a mature native culture, the Buddhist church still retained the power to intimidate government. The capital was moved accordingly to Heiankyo (City of Peace), known today as Kyoto, where it was to remain until the Restoration of 1868. This astute maneuver to escape the political control of a powerful church was the work of the Emperor Kammu, who, when he had thus curbed the political power of the Buddhists, set about to fuse the church's religious power with the native cult of Shinto to create a national religion supporting the throne. The task of doing this was entrusted to two learned priest-patriots, Kobo-Daishi and Dengyo-Daishi, who became the founders respectively of the Shingon and the Tendai sects of Japanese Buddhism. Kobo-Daishi reconciled Buddhism with Shinto by a very neat doctrine which stated that the Buddhas had in part revealed themselves in Japan as Shinto deities. In this way a foreign Buddhism became a patriotic Japanese Buddhism and thus a bulwark of the central government.

KYOTO AND THE NEW JAPAN

The new capital, Kyoto, the most spacious city Japan had yet known, modelled after the T'ang capital of Ch'ang-an, became one of the world's most beautiful cities. Surrounded by and built into natural scenic beauty, it expressed the early maturing of

Japanese artistic expression. Here the Japanese Imperial Court, the court nobility (*Kuge*), the men of letters, and, to an even greater degree, the women of letters, created the masterpieces of classical Japanese literature. The second great anthology, the *Kokinshiu* (Poems Ancient and Modern), was completed in 922.[9] The age also brought forth Japan's ablest women of letters: Lady Murasaki no Shikibu, author of the *Genji Monogatari*[10] (ca. 1004), and Lady Sei Shonagon, author of the *Makura-no-soshi* (Pillow Sketches).[11] Kyoto was a cultured, refined, and effeminate city. Belles-lettres dominated its great literature. It was the great age of the novel and poetry, of diaries and essays in the sophisticated manner, and written in the native language. The duller pursuits of theology and the law were left to scholars who still wrote in rather bad Chinese.

The flowering of this early native literature in prose and poetry meant among other things that the Japanese had now acquired an adequate system for writing their native tongue. The creation of this system had taken place gradually through the ninth and tenth centuries. The method involved using simpler Chinese characters or parts of them as phonetic symbols usually representing a syllable such as *ka, mi, ku, se,* or *to*. This syllabary or *kana* was and still is written in

---

[9] T. Wakameda, trans., *Early Japanese Poets. Complete Translation of the Kokinshiu* (Tokyo, 1929). A complete translation but in inferior English.

[10] *Monogatari* means narrative. It is applied chiefly to fiction and sometimes to histories. Murasaki, like Fielding created the prose epic of real life.

[11] Arthur Waley, trans., *The Pillow Book of Lady Sei Shonagon* (1929 and 1953). The first complete English translation is Ivan Morris, *The Pillow Book of Sei Shōnagon* (2 vols., 1967). *The Pillow Book* is the earliest example of a rather unique form of Japanese writing. It is a collection of impressions, thoughts, descriptions, diary entries, lists of things liked or loathed, conversations, and poetry. It is one of the great works of Japanese literature. Also, Edward Seidensticker, trans., *The Gossamer Years: A Diary by a Noblewoman of Heian Japan* (1964),* and Ivan Morris, *The World of the Shining Prince: Court Life in Ancient Japan* (1964),* fascinating books of interest to the general reader and of instruction for the specialist.

two forms, the one cursive, the other angular, known respectively as *hiragana* and *katakana*. Although some poetry had been written in Japanese during earlier centuries by using unabbreviated Chinese characters, it was the new syllabary that made a real and rich Japanese literature possible. It was in the new phonetic medium that the court ladies, Sei and Murasaki and others, wrote their thirty-one syllable poems, their diaries, and their novels. This was a Japanese literature expressive of a distinct Japanese culture in which the Chinese influence was all but completely adapted to Japanese forms.

CHINESE INSTITUTIONS BECOME JAPANESE

It was also in the Heian period that the political and social institutions built in Japan during the previous centuries of Chinese influence were so altered as to leave in some cases little evidence of their original Chinese models. For example, in China the civilian-scholar-bureaucrat chosen through civil service examinations operated in a system in which the educated class, drawn in theory at least from all walks of life, was accepted as the proper ruling class. In Japan, too, as a result of the Chinese learning, the classics were studied and examinations held, but it was clan loyalties and hereditary rights that determined who was appointed to high office. In such a situation there was no group of public servants whose duty it was to preserve the national domain. The result was that the central government, instead of developing into the stature of its Chinese model, became an empty pretense.

The imperial family continued to enjoy great prestige because of its political background and its relation to Shinto, but in actual power it was reduced to a succession of puppet emperors in the control of a powerful family—the Fujiwara. This clan family, which had been a leader of the pro-Chinese factions in the seventh century, had acquired great wealth in lands, and finally gained complete control of the capital and the court by marrying its daughters to the young emperors.

Thus the Fujiwaras created a situation in which the clan monopolized the high if empty offices of state. Child emperors, the offspring of Fujiwara consorts, were placed on the throne, while heads of the Fujiwara house administered what was left of the state as regents *(sessho)* or as civil dictators *(kampaku)*.

Ambitious and capable men who were not members of the Fujiwara clan had no choice but to seek their fortunes in distant provinces. There, by various means and as a result of varying conditions, many of them acquired great manors and built the foundations of a frontier, military, vigorous society in striking contrast to effete Kyoto aristocracy. These new landed barons had very little concern for the stability of the central government. On the contrary, their ambition was to strengthen their own local independence.

During the last century of the Heian era, the feudal barons *(buke)* and their hardy soldiers *(bushi)* were beyond the control of Kyoto. The once powerful Fujiwara was forced to seek the aid of some of these new military upstarts to maintain order in the imperial capital. In the conflicts which ensued between the frontier warrior factions of Taira and Minamoto, the old civil government of Kyoto collapsed. Control of the next chapter in Japan's history was settled at the naval battle of Dan-no-ura, 1185, when the Taira were routed by their Minamoto rivals.

KAMAKURA: MILITARY DICTATORSHIP, 1185–1338

Minamoto Yoritomo, the victor, avoiding the mistake of his vanquished rival, Taira Kiyomori, set up his seat of government not at Kyoto but at the seaside village of Kamakura near the principal estates of his relatives and allies in eastern-central Japan, not far from the present-day Tokyo. At Kyoto he permitted the emperor, the Fujiwara, and the court nobility to carry on the forms of their make-believe civil government and to perpetuate the fiction that it was this emperor's government that actually ruled. The fiction was strengthened further when Yoritomo accepted from the emperor the title Shogun (generalissimo) which invested him with supreme command of all military forces. The implication was that Yoritomo commanded the emperor's army. Actually there was no emperor's army. What Yoritomo commanded was a powerful association of knights held together by family ties or by bonds of friendship arising from relations of mutual assistance. This military association under Yoritomo's leadership made up the real power and thus the real government. Moreover, with Yoritomo, the title of Shogun became hereditary and therefore of greatly increased significance.

The military administration that came into being at Kamakura was known significantly as the *Bakufu* (meaning literally "tent government"), a term used originally to designate the headquarters of an army in the field, and later the administrative headquarters of a military dictator. In addition, this Kamakura administration was not a national government in the modern sense of that term but a simple machinery to control and regulate the affairs of the knights making up the Minamoto faction. Since these knights were scattered throughout the land, many of them as estate managers, Kamakura was in a position to control all areas and classes. During the time of the Minamoto shoguns and their successors, the Hojo regents, the lands of the Minamoto and their vassals were scattered thickly throughout eastern Japan, and more thinly in other areas. Sometimes the lands of a vassal lay within the domain of some independent lord. The authority of the shogun was thus likely to vary from complete military control in some areas to a rather shadowy suzerainty in others. So long as the *Bakufu* retained able administrators its power was for all practical purposes supreme. The Shogun was a military dictator deriving his military power from the Minamoto faction. Within this sphere, the administration of Kamakura was direct and exclusive.

These bold statements, however, require some important shading. Yoritomo, although acting the part of a military dictator, recognized the sovereignty of the throne and considered himself as exercising authority delegated by the throne. The throne therefore did not disappear with the creation of the shogunate, even though the throne did lose all save *de jure* authority. Emperors continued to reign in Kyoto, where the throne retained at times "a certain social prestige and a certain negative authority." In this way the throne expressed rather vaguely a continuing concept of unity. It was significant that the throne should have carried this tradition, since Yoritomo probably did not think of himself as the ruler of all Japan or of Japan as a national unit. The twelfth century had already created a feudal society in which landed barons were virtually independent within their own estates. The barons did not recognize the military power of the throne, for the throne possessed no military power. The barons did recognize the military power of the Shogun, for he had the power, and it was expedient for them to do so. They were the more likely to bow to the Shogun's legal as well as military authority, since the former was derived from the throne and carried with it whatever prestige the throne possessed.

The Kamakura system was of importance for itself alone as a system by which Japanese society of that day was ordered and controlled; but it was perhaps even more important for the influence it was to exert on the Japanese character during the succeeding six centuries of feudalism (until 1871). Kamakura planted firmly in Japan the tradition of military rule, of dictatorship of the peculiar Japanese variety, and of the principle of dual government in which an emperor reigned but a shogun ruled. It preserved the theory of the political and religious role of the imperial family. In the nineteenth and the twentieth centuries this imperial tradition was to be reasserted as a vigorous force when Japan emerged as a modern nation state.[12]

[12] See Minoru Shinoda, *The Founding of the Kamakura Shogunate* (1960). Note the description of the Kamakura shogunate as a "private clan government based on vassalage but also empowered with certain public functions."

On Yoritomo's death, his wife's family, known by the name of Hojo, disposed of his heirs and proceeded to rule under the title of Regents, acting for puppet shoguns chosen from either the Fujiwara or the imperial families. Japan of the thirteenth century thus presented the amazing spectacle of a country headed by a sovereign who was emperor in name only, whose vestigial functions were assumed by an abdicated emperor, and whose real power was delegated to a hereditary military dictator (the shogun), but wielded by a hereditary regent acting for the dictator. It might be supposed that this absurd-appearing system, where the theoretical sources of power were so remote from the agencies exercising real power, would be meaningless and unworkable. Actually, the Hojo regents, men of great capacity, gave Japan a government more stable, honest, and efficient than it had previously known. The period, moreover, was one of spiritual vigor. Great teachers such as Honen (1133–1212), Shinran (1173–1262), and Nichiren (1222–1282), forsaking the classical Chinese for Japanese, touched and quickened the intellectual life of the people and made Buddhism a popular religion.[13]

In the midst of this moral and political awakening, the regency was called upon to repel the Mongol invasions of Kublai Khan, who in 1263 had become emperor of China. In 1274 and again in 1281, the Mongol armies were driven back by the Japanese, the fleets of the invaders being destroyed by providential typhoons. The Hojo regents, their vassals, and their feudal allies had been equal to the military task of defense, but they were unequal to the task of domestic reconstruction that followed the attempted invasions. The shogunate was bankrupt. Increased taxes brought on local rebellions. Vassals who had defended the nation and priests whose prayers had brought the typhoons wanted to be rewarded, as politicians usually do, but there were no new

[13] For Japan's great religious leaders, see Anesaki Masaharu, *History of Japanese Religion* (London, 1930).

lands for the Hojo to bestow. In 1333 the Hojo regency was destroyed by an ex-emperor who thought to restore the imperial rule. Instead there followed a new shogunate established by a rebellious general, Ashikaga Takauji, who had assisted in the destruction of the Hojo.

THE ASHIKAGA SHOGUNATE, 1336–1573

Politically, the Ashikaga Shogunate had little to recommend it. The Ashikaga shoguns who set up their capital at Kyoto never exercised effective control over the barons and the military caste. The result was incessant feudal strife, while for a time rival dynasties claimed the imperial throne. The disappearance of any real central authority meant that Japan was in the grip of factions seeking to gain control of feudal privileges in the form of lands or vassals. The cultural life of Japan during the period of Kamakura and Ashikaga thus was dominated by the rise of the military caste. Moreover, military men continued to rule Japan after Ashikaga on through the nineteenth and into the twentieth century. In a word, much of the Japanese national atmosphere of the twentieth century can be understood only in terms of what happened in Japan in the days of Yoritomo and his successors.

The Culture of Kamakura

The new culture of Kamakura, like its new political system, mirrored the warrior class of the provinces so unlike the literary dilettantes of the older Kyoto aristocracy. Symbolized by the hard, finely tempered steel of his sword, the ideal of the warrior was a life of self-discipline, like that of a Spartan or an ascetic. The supreme virtues were the personal loyalties of family ties and a stoical indifference to suffering. Where practiced, these virtues produced men of parochial horizon but of tough fiber. They read a new literature on the military exploits of the Taira and the Minamoto instead of the love diaries and novels of court ladies. With this newer austerity came a new interest in religion, particularly Buddhism, the evidences of which are still present in twentieth century Japan not only in monuments such as the Great Buddha at Kamakura but also in the religious thinking of the modern Japanese. This religious awakening took various forms. It created a popular Buddhism of the people which rested on faith in salvation in an afterlife rather than on philosophic enlightenment. It further developed the doctrine of Zen Buddhism, which cast aside formalized religion and faith in the saving power of a redeemer in favor of individual effort to discover the meaning of the universe. Zen made a special appeal to the fighting men of the *Bakufu*. Zen was self-reliant, did not depend on scriptures, and was unencumbered by any intricate philosophy. Its stern injunction to self-examination, its freedom from the emotional, its stress on individualism—each and all of these appealed to the rugged warriors of the *Bakufu*. Zen, the religion of the soldier, became in succeeding centuries a vital influence not only in the lives of military men but also on those whom they ruled.

The Culture of Ashikaga

Culturally, the Ashikaga period brought about a mingling of the provincial military-feudal society with the old civilian society of Kyoto. The Ashikaga shoguns, unlike their predecessors, set up their residence in Muromachi, a quarter of Kyoto. In Kyoto the military caste was influenced by the older civilian culture. Military men soon learned to covet the cultural trappings which wealth could buy in the capital. At this time, against a background of political chaos, Japan entered a period of cultural and economic growth.

Ashikaga was also a period of Zen culture. Leading artists were Zen priests who, because of their close contacts with China, brought to Japan new aspects of Chinese art and learning which soon blended with the native arts. For example, the *No* drama was developed as a major contribution to dramatic art. Japanese painting reached new heights of perfection in Chinese and native schools. Likewise, from Chinese inspiration the Japanese of Ashikaga developed as their own art

their unsurpassed landscape gardening, and their aesthetic masterpieces of flower arrangement (*ikebana*). The disciplinary diversion of the tea ceremony (*cha-no-yu*) was developed to foster the sophisticated virtues of urbanity and courtesy.[14]

The period of Ashikaga was also marked by the growth of Japanese trade and industry, and by the formation of merchants' guilds. In fostering foreign trade, some Ashikaga shoguns even accepted investiture as "Kings of Japan" from the Ming emperors of China. By the end of the Ashikaga period, Japan had developed economically far out of proportion to her political maturity. Thus the picture was not well balanced. Extravagance and dissipation were reflected in vast sums expended on the Kinkakuji (Golden Pavilion) and the Ginkakuji (Silver Pavilion). Wealthy barons rivalled each other in the construction of costly palaces and in indulgence in aesthetic amusements, while in contrast squalor infested the countryside and impoverished emperors sought a subsistence by selling their calligraphy in the market place.

DICTATORS REUNITE JAPAN

In summary then, the Ashikaga period, which had brought great economic growth and a brilliant development of the arts, had also fostered the collapse of the central authority, whether of emperor or shogun. In the domains of the great feudal lords, the daimyo, it had created the spirit and the reality of complete local independence. Each of these domains had become a political unit unto itself, a miniature state, in which the daimyo assisted by a bureaucracy of chosen military officers maintained his court and government at a central castle fortress from which he ruled his peasants, merchants, and soldiers as an independent sovereign. The tendency was for each daimyo to build up his military strength at the expense of his neighbors and rivals. By this process there emerged

[14] See Arthur L. Sadler, *The Japanese Tea Ceremony* (London, 1934); Harada Jiro, *Japanese Gardens* (1956).

finally a few daimyo of unrivalled strength who fought for control of the entire nation.

The first of these powerful figures moving toward the reunification of the land was Oda Nobunaga. By seizing Kyoto in 1568, and by destroying the military power of the central Buddhist monasteries, Nobunaga made himself master of central Japan. When he was assassinated in 1582, his ablest general, Hideyoshi Toyotomi, later known as the Japanese Napoleon, carried on the conquest. Wisely recognizing the force of tradition, he instilled new life into the hapless imperial court by having the throne bestow upon him the title of *kampaku,* regent or civil dictator; and he won military control of all Japan by defeating the powerful daimyo of Satsuma in Kyushu and his remaining rivals in the east and north. With these victories behind him he embarked on the conquest of China by way of Korea in 1592. His armies, however, numbering at times as many as 200,000 men, did not get beyond Korea. The resistance of the Koreans and the Chinese was too powerful, and on Hideyoshi's death in 1598 his armies were withdrawn.

Hideyoshi's successor as master of Japan was one of his own vassals and generals, Tokugawa Iyeyasu, whose home was at Yedo in east-central Japan. Iyeyasu first defeated Hideyoshi's rivals, then turned upon and destroyed Hideyoshi's family. Since neither Nobunaga nor Hideyoshi had been able to make his rule hereditary, Iyeyasu was consumed with a single ambition—to fashion a political structure that would preserve the newly acquired power in the Tokugawa family. In this ambition Iyeyasu and his successors met with astonishing success. The edifice they erected was the final and greatest of the shogunates, lasting from 1603 to 1868.[15]

[15] For the period in biography, see Walter Dening, *The Life of Toyotomi Hideyoshi, 1536–1598* (3rd ed., Kobe, 1930); and A. L. Sadler, *The Maker of Modern Japan: the Life of Tokugawa Iyeyasu* (London, 1937). John W. Hall and Richard K. Beardsley, *Twelve Doors to Japan* (1965) suggests briefly what different disciplines can reveal about Japan. The chapter "The Historical Dimension" makes observations on historiography and the periodization of Japanese history.

FOR FURTHER READING

REFERENCE WORKS. *Japan, The Official Guide* (Tokyo, 1964), accurate, informative with many fine maps. Basil Hall Chamberlain, *Things Japanese: Being Notes on Various Subjects Connected with Japan for the Use of Travellers and Others* (Kobe, 1939), an informative presentation which first appeared in 1890. It covers the field of Japanese culture from the "abacus" to "zoology."

BIBLIOGRAPHIES. Hyman Kublin, comp., *What Shall I Read on Japan: An Introductory Guide* (6th rev. ed., 1961), very selective but good. Bernard S. Silberman, *Japan and Korea. A Critical Bibliography* (1962), more recent and extensive. Paul H. Clyde, "Japan's March to Empire: Some Bibliographical Evaluations," *The Journal of Modern History 21* (1949): 333–43. Hugh Borton, *et al., A Selected List of Books and Articles on Japan in English, French and German* (rev. ed., 1954)* gives a broad coverage of many disciplines. A monumental series is Fr. von Wenckstern, *A Bibliography of the Japanese Empire* (Vol. I, Leiden, 1895; Vol. II, Tokyo, 1907), which is continued by Oskar Nachod, *Bibliography of the Japanese Empire 1906–1926* (2 vols., London, 1928), and the same author's *Bibliographie von Japan, 1927–1929* (Leipzig, 1931), and *Bibliographie von Japan 1930–1932* (Leipzig, 1935), continued by Hans Praesent and Wolf Hainisch, *Bibliographie von Japan, 1933–1935* (Leipzig, 1937).

HISTORIOGRAPHY. Hugh Borton, "A Survey of Japanese Historiography," *The American Historical Review 43* (April, 1938): 489–99. John W. Hall, "Historiography in Japan," in H. Stuart Hughes, *Teachers of History,* (1954), 284–304, very good on the approach and methodology of Japanese historians. John W. Hall's *Japanese History: A Guide to Japanese Reference and Research Materials* (1954) deals primarily with Japanese language materials. Note the essay by James W. Morley, "Historical Writing in Modern Japan," *The Development of Historiography,* ed. by M. A. Fitzsimons *et al.* (1954), 381–89. W. G. Beasley and E. G. Pulleybank, eds.,

Historians of China and Japan (1961) contains five chapters on Japanese historiography by various authorities.

GEOGRAPHY, PHYSICAL AND HUMAN, AND RESOURCES. Guy Harold Smith and Dorothy Good, with collaboration of Shannon McCune, *Japan: a Geographical View* (1943), a very able and readable factual view of Japan at the start of World War II. Glen T. Trewartha, *Japan: A Physical, Cultural and Regional Geography* (1945), a standard, technical study. Edward A. Ackerman, *Japan's Natural Resources and Their Relation to Japan's Economic Future* (1953), a comprehensive survey of Japan's resources for economic growth. Nasu Shiroshi, *Aspects of Japanese Agriculture* (1941). See also the wealth of material in E. B. Schumpeter, ed., *The Industrialization of Japan and Manchukuo, 1930–1940* (1940). Richard K. Beardsley, John W. Hall, and Robert E. Ward, *Village Japan* (1959) analyzes the people, customs, and values of a Japanese rural village. The earlier work by John F. Embree, *Suye Mura: A Japanese Village* (1939)* is a fascinating study of village life and manners. See also Carl W. Bishop, "The Historical Geography of Early Japan," *Geographical Review* 13 (January, 1923): 40–63.

POPULATION. Irene B. Taeuber, *The Population of Japan* (1958) deals with the question of population as related to economic development. E. F. Penrose, *Population Theories and Their Application with Special Reference to Japan* (1934), the ablest study prior to World War II.

THE AINU. Takakura Shinichiro, "The Ainu of Northern Japan, A Study in Conquest and Acculturation," *Transactions of the American Philosophical Society* (translated and annotated by John A. Harrison, New Series, Vol. 50, part 4, 1960). Neil Gordon Munro and Brenda Seligman, eds., *Ainu Creed and Cult* (1963).

HISTORY. Herschel Webb, *An Introduction to Japan* (2nd ed., 1960), a brief survey carefully prepared and well written. Hugh Borton, ed., *Japan* (1951), a collection of the

23 articles on various subjects prepared by specialists. G. B. Sansom, *A History of Japan to 1334* (1958); *A History of Japan, 1334–1615* (1961); and *A History of Japan, 1615–1867* (1963) completed the three-volume history from antiquity to the end of the Tokugawa period. These volumes are unrivalled in quality. Hugh Borton, *Japan's Modern Century* (2nd ed., 1970), a detailed history of Japan since 1850, rich in interpretation. Yanaga Chitoshi, *Japan Since Perry* (1949), factual and, for the period after 1853, takes on the proportions of a reference history. Richard Storry, *A History of Modern Japan* (1963), well written and organized. Arthur Tiedemann, *Modern Japan* (1962)* is a pocket edition containing several important documents. W. G. Beasley, *The Modern History of Japan* (1963),* an attempt to continue Sansom's three-volume study. James Murdock and Yamagata Isoh, *A History of Japan* (3 vols., 3rd impression, London, 1949), still useful though heavy in political matters and weak in interpreting the aesthetic side of Japan. Tsunoda Ryusaku, William T. deBary, Donald Keene, comps., *Sources of Japanese Tradition* (1960), a source of the very first importance covering all Japanese history, ancient and modern. Honjo Eijiro, *The Social and Economic History of Japan* (Kyoto, 1935). Takekoshi Yosaburo, *The Economic Aspects of the History of the Civilization of Japan* (3 vols., 1930) covering the pre-Restoration period is a translation of a well-known Japanese work, a mine of information.

SPECIAL STUDIES. Gerald J. Groot, *The Prehistory of Japan* (1951) depicts the Stone Age culture and relates it to comparable cultures. Anesaki Masaharu, *Prince Shotoku, the Sage Statesman* (Tokyo, 1948). K. Asakawa, *The Documents of Iriki, Illustrative of the Development of the Feudal Institutions of Japan* (1929). John H. Hall, *Government and Local Power in Japan: A Study of Bizen Province, 500–1700* (1966), an important re-examination of institutional history. Shinoda Minoru, *The Founding of the Kamakura Shogunate, 1180–1185* (1960) covers the formative stage in Japan's feudal system. Helen Craig McCullough, trans. (with introduction) *Yoshitsune: A Fifteenth-Century Japanese*

Chronicle (1966). Delmer M. Brown, *Money Economy in Medieval Japan: A Study in the Use of Coins* (1951) covers the period 1200 to 1600. Ruth Benedict, *The Chrysanthemum and the Sword: Patterns of Japanese Culture* (1946),* a brilliant study on the behavior of the Japanese people. Ishimoto Shidzue, *Facing Two Ways: The Story of My Life* (1935) depicts conflicts between traditional and modern Japan. Sugimoto Etsu, *A Daughter of the Samurai* (1925), a delicate and artistic account of old Japan presented through the medium of autobiography.

PHILOSOPHY AND RELIGION. Charles A. Moore, ed., *The Japanese Mind: Essentials of Japanese Philosophy and Culture* (1967). Joseph R. Kitagawa, *Religion in Japanese History* (1966), a thoughtful survey. E. Dale Saunders, *Buddhism in Japan* (1964) gives an over-all picture of Buddhism in Japan from the sixth century. Charles N. E. Eliot, *Japanese Buddhism* (London, 1935), a comprehensive study emphasizing early historical trends and developments. Anesaki Masaharu, *Nichiren, the Buddhist Prophet* (1949), a careful study of the life and teachings of the founder of a popular and militant Buddhist sect. William Barret, ed., *Zen Buddhism; Selected Writings of D. T. Suzuki* (1956)* contains selections from the prolific writings of the principal interpreter of Zen Buddhism to the West. Ono Motonori, *Shinto, the Kami Way* (1962), a good popular introduction to the indigenous religion of Japan.

LITERATURE. Donald Keene, *Japanese Literature: An Introduction for Western Readers* (1955),* is an excellent, brief treatment. The same author's *Anthology of Japanese Literature: from the Earliest Era to the Mid-Nineteenth Century* (1955)* contains superb translations from the prose, poetry, and drama of old Japan. Note also the same author's *Modern Japanese Literature: an Anthology* (1957).* Richard M. Dorson, *Folk Legends of Japan* (1962), an enjoyable collection of folk legends depicting traditional beliefs, fantasies and customs. Lord Redesdale (A. B. Mitford), *Tales of Old Japan* (London, 1905), a free translation of early Japanese stories. Arthur Waley, *Japanese Poetry: the "Uta"* (London, 1946),* a reprinting of an earlier collection of fine translations. Arthur Waley, *The No Plays of Japan* (1954),* a reprint of a standard collection. Murasaki Shikibu, *The Tale of Genji*, trans. by Arthur Waley (1960),* Japan's most famous novel written about the year 1000 by a lady-in-waiting at the Japanese court. Harold G. Henderson, *An Introduction to Haiku: an Anthology of Poems and Poets from Basho to Shiki* (1958),* a survey of Japan's most popular poetic medium.

ART AND MUSIC. Robert T. Paine and Alexander Soper, *The Art and Architecture of Japan* (1955). H. Minamoto, *An Illustrated History of Japanese Art*, trans. by Harold G. Henderson (Kyoto, 1935) contains reproductions with historical explanation. Charles S. Terry, *Masterworks of Japanese Art* (1956) provides excellent illustrated commentaries on the broader history of Japanese artistic achievement. Langdon Warner, *The Enduring Art of Japan* (1952),* a classic of perceptive evaluation. William P. Malm, *Japanese Music* (Tokyo, 1959), an extensive study of the traditional music.

The West
Discovers Eastern Asia

chapter 5

The discovery of Eastern Asia by the Western world is a subject that presents some very real problems. During the centuries since the first contacts were made, China, for example, has been described in various Western writings in conflicting terms: as being good and bad, weak and strong, rich and poor, wise and foolish. These Western views of China have changed from time to time. In the sixteenth century, the Jesuits thought they had found in China something akin to the ideal state. In the nineteenth century, Protestant missionaries found there a supreme example of depravity. How shall such contradictory conclusions be explained? Part of the answer is that the China of the sixteenth century was not the same as the China of the nineteenth century. But a much greater part of the answer is to be found in what the foreign observers wanted to see, and in what their own cultural backgrounds permitted them to see.

In any event, the history of Western contacts with the Far East is a long and fascinating story; it reaches back into the pre-Christian Era. In reality, the time at which Europe gained its first knowledge of China is not known with certainty. Perhaps it was as early as the sixth or even the seventh century B.C.[1] A remarkable overland traffic in silk from China to the Roman World had developed by the early years of the Christian Era. This traffic was primarily due to the Roman demand for silk, not to any Chinese demand for the products of Rome. This European demand for Chinese silk continued during the first six centuries of the Christian Era until the time when Europe was producing its own silk.

The sixth century in Central Asia witnessed the rise of the Turks and their westward advance until they had effected diplomatic contacts with the Roman World at Constantinople. This development did not lead to direct Roman contacts with China; however, it created in the Byzantine Greek literature, derived from Turkish sources, the most revealing picture of China to appear in European literature prior to the accounts of Marco Polo.

[1] For a detailed account of early relations between Europe and China, consult G. F. Hudson, *Europe and China* (London, 1931; reissued, 1961)* which covers the period to 1800. The student interested in how Asia has affected the West should consult Donald F. Lach, *Asia in the Making of Europe*, I, Books 1 and 2 (1965).

When Christianity, in one of its various forms, first reached China is not known. It is known that Nestorian missionaries of the Persian Church did reach China. The record of this Nestorian effort has been preserved on a monument erected at Sian in 781, though not discovered until the seventeenth century.[2] From this and other sources it now appears that the Nestorians reached T'ang China about 635, where they were honorably received by the emperor. Churches were built in several cities and, though the faith was persecuted at times, it appears to have been generally tolerated for two centuries. Then in 845, the emperor commanded the missionaries to renounce their priestly calling and to cease to pervert the institutions of the country.

During the Five Dynasties (907–960) and the Sung dynasty (960–1279) a very considerable foreign trade was conducted at Ch'uan-chou (Zayton) in Fukien, and at Canton in Kwangtung. Most of the foreign merchants in this trade were Moslem Arabs, who in general seem to have been well treated; they were permitted to settle in the country, to take Chinese wives, to adjust disputes among themselves according to their own laws, and, in some cases, to hold high office in the state. Among these southern foreigners there was also a colony of Jews. It was the Arab trade which eventually was to carry into Europe a knowledge of Chinese tea.

THE RENEWAL OF EUROPEAN INTEREST IN CHINA

Christian Europe was beset by unprecedented dangers in the thirteenth century. On the south and southeast lay the fanatical power of Islam. Directly to the east was the

rising threat of the Mongol Empire, whose armies in 1222 invaded Europe and defeated the Russians on the Dnieper. Simultaneously, other Mongol armies were advancing eastward upon North China. Before the close of the century, the empire built by Ghenghis Khan and his successors extended across the map of Eurasia from the western borders of Russia to the Pacific Ocean. Trade routes from Europe to China, closed for more than four centuries, were again opened. Europe was soon to expand upon the meager knowledge of China which it had gained in the days of the silk trade. Various motives inspired this new European interest in China and the empire of the Tatars. Christian Europe was not averse to the possibility of an alliance with the Mongols and the Chinese against the Moslems. The Crusades had created a new demand for the wares of the East. Finally, the Roman Catholic Church recognized in some measure the new opportunity to carry Christianity to the pagan world. Faith, fear, and the desire for material gain combined to inspire the embassies which Europe was soon to dispatch into Central Asia and the Far East.

Thus it was that during the thirteenth and fourteenth centuries, Europeans representing religious, political, or commercial interests did reach the capital of the Mongol Empire. John de Plano Carpini, a Franciscan, was received at the Great Khan's court in 1246. Two embassies from Louis IX of France followed in 1249 and 1252. In 1264 the two Venetian merchants, Nicolo and Maffeo Polo, were received in the court of Kublai Khan. Later, in 1275, the two brothers and Nicolo's son, Marco, entered the service of the Khan. From these beginnings came *The Book of Marco Polo* written at the close of the century when the Polos had returned to Europe. During the early years of the fourteenth century a small Christian community, the work of a Roman missionary, John of Monte Corvino, existed briefly at Cambaluc.[3]

Although as far back as 1300, Europe

---

[2] *Sian* is the generally used modern spelling for Hsian (Wade-Giles romanization). In the spelling *Hsianfu*, the *fu* ending is a Manchu dynasty form that was not used in Nationalist China. Again, the T'ang dynasty name was *Ch'ang-an* instead of *Hsian*.

[3] A fascinating account of the Polos and their adventures in East Asia is Henry H. Hart, *Marco Polo: Venetian Adventurer* (1967).

had played with the idea of a sea route to the East, it was not until two centuries later that this dream was brought to fulfillment when, in 1488, Portuguese navigators reached and passed the Cape of Good Hope. Ten years later (1498–1499), Vasco da Gama reached Calicut in India. Successors of da Gama reached Malacca in 1511. From these advanced trading posts, which now for the first time could be reached by an unbroken sea voyage, the Portuguese advanced to Java, Siam, Indochina, and the southern coasts of China Proper. Meanwhile, they had, by their naval warfare against the Arabs, become the commercial masters of the Arabian Sea.

The China which Portuguese traders were soon to visit was ruled by the last of the great Chinese dynasties, the Ming (1368–1644). The first century of Ming rule had been a period of commercial and maritime vigor dominated by a forceful naval diplomacy. Chinese fleets penetrated the South China Sea and the Indian Ocean, and tribute-bearing embassies from these areas visited China. However, after 1421, when the Ming capital was moved from Nanking to Peking, maritime interests were subject to increasing neglect.[4]

[4] In the story of early modern contacts between Europe and the Far East (about 1500 to 1800), it is well to note that it was the Asian states that fixed the terms in which these contacts took place. At the same time a handful of Western adventurers made Europe and Asia aware of each other in some limited degree. There was some recognition in Europe that major Asian civilizations were superior to the European and that Europe had much to learn from China's gifted craftsmen. The German philosopher Liebnitz suggested half seriously that the Emperor of China ought to send missionaries to Europe to teach human relations. Voltaire said the sovereigns of Europe ought to follow the example of the Ch'ien-lung emperor in supporting philosophy and the arts. See Lach, I, Book 1, xii-xiii, and Book 2, Chapter VIII, "Japan," and Chapter IX, "China."

Carlo M. Cipolla, *Guns, Sails, and Empires: Technological Innovations and the Early Phases of European Expansion, 1400–1700* (1966),* stresses the importance of technological innovation in sailing and warfare in enabling Europeans by the end of the fifteenth century to force their way to the Spice Islands, control sea

A Portuguese commerical expedition reached China from Malacca in 1514; and though the mariners were not permitted to land, they disposed of their goods at a considerable profit. This auspicious beginning led to an official Portuguese mission headed by Thomas Pires in 1517. This embassy was well received at Canton. However, in 1522 the Chinese attacked and destroyed the Portuguese trading post at Canton, though another was soon established nearby. Later, Portuguese traders were driven from Ningpo and Amoy. These misfortunes are not difficult to explain. Reports had already reached the Ming court that the Portuguese, far from being solely interested in peaceful commerce, were intent on conquest. Then in 1557 the Portuguese established themselves at Macao, a small peninsula joined by a narrow neck of land to Hsiang-shan, now called Chung-shan, which lies in the delta to the south of Canton. Here the Portuguese traders were under the jurisdiction of the Chinese authorities. They themselves, however, were usually allowed to handle cases involving only their own subjects. Beyond this, Chinese control—territorial, judicial, and fiscal—was absolute.[5] It remained so until 1849, at which time the Portuguese began to

routes, and establish empires. By replacing oarsmen in the galley with sails and placing men in the boarding party with guns, Europeans transcended the limitations of human energy and obtained decisive advantage over non-Europeans.

Raymond Dawson, *The Chinese Chameleon: an Analysis of European Conceptions of Chinese Civilization* (1967), finds that Europe has envisaged China in a series of stereotypes: "the mighty and wealthy kingdom" reported by Polo and other early travellers; the "model [state] even for Christians" visited by Jesuits; the static China of nineteenth century philosophers and historians; the isolated and insulated China of Kiplingesque imperialists; the "heathen Chinese" of evangelical Christians; and the "sinister" China of today. These stereotypes seem to owe as much in their making to the condition and need of the observer as to the actual state of the observed.

[5] H. B. Morse, *The Chronicles of the East India Company Trading to China* (5 vols., Oxford, 1926–29), I, 8–9.

persist in a claim to exclusive jurisdiction. Macao, nevertheless, was not recognized as Portuguese territory until the Protocol of Lisbon of 1887. Macao, from the time when the Portuguese first settled there until the cession of Hong Kong to Great Britain in 1842, remained the summer residence of Westerners engaged in the Canton trade.

The question naturally arises why China, after her expulsion of the Pires mission and her subsequent experience with the Portuguese lawlessness, tolerated these foreign merchants at all. In part it may be explained by the tendency of the Chinese imperial court to assert an authority which it was either unwilling or unable to enforce. Certainly the emperor could not bestow his imperial favor on surly Western barbarians who had respect neither for the dignity of the empire nor for its control over neighboring tributary states. Yet if there was profit to be derived from a limited commerce with the barbarian, he might be permitted to trade informally at a few ports. This was practical and therefore good Chinese doctrine. Actually the Chinese merchants at Canton desired the trade; there were provincial officials who for a consideration would permit the trade; and at Peking, metropolitan officials, likewise for a consideration, might pretend ignorance that there was any trade with the barbarian at all. The consequence was that trade prospered while the question of diplomatic recognition was ignored.[6]

[6] The system of foreign trade that prevailed under the Mings is the key to the politico-commercial difficulties that were to plague China's relations with the Western powers during the later eighteenth and nineteenth centuries. Under the Mings, foreign trade was considered primarily as an instrument for controlling the vassal states, not as a source of government revenue. Local officials, however, found in this trade a door to great wealth. The system worked very well in early Ming times, but with the arrival of the European barbarians (the Portuguese and those who followed them), who did not consider themselves as tributaries, it was subjected to new and powerful pressures. Chang Teh-ch'ang, "Maritime Trade at Canton during the Ming Dynasty," *Chinese Soc. and Pol. Science Rev.* 17, No. 2 (July, 1933): 264–82. Note also J. K. Fairbank, "Tributary Trade and China's Relations with the West," *Far Eastern Quarterly* 1 (1942): 129–49;

THE DEVELOPMENT OF CATHOLIC MISSIONS

The rediscovery of China by Portuguese traders renewed the missionary interest of the Roman Catholic Church. Francis Xavier, who in 1549 introduced Catholicism to Japan, was the first zealot in the new campaign to convert the Chinese. Xavier, however, died off the coast of Kwangtung (1552), thwarted in his ambition to carry Roman Catholicism to China. Xavier was followed by Matteo Ricci, an Italian Jesuit who reached Macao in 1582.[7] The religious propaganda of Ricci, his associates, and successors, based on their appeal to the scientific and scholarly interests of Chinese officialdom, met with notable success. Among the converts were many princes of the blood, mandarins, and other courtiers. Ricci prepared for the Chinese a map of the world, on which he tactfully placed China in the middle; his followers corrected the Chinese calendar; others were appointed by the emperor to the post of state astronomer. A century after Ricci's arrival at Canton, the K'ang-hsi emperor granted freedom of worship to the Roman churches throughout the empire.

These official favors, however, did not exempt the missionaries from persecution. In 1616 and again in 1664 some of the Jesuits were expelled from Peking and forced to return to Canton or Macao. In fact it is surprising that in the seventeenth century there was not more persecution. Neo-Confucianism under the Ming emperors was inclined to be fixed and intolerant; Buddhism and Taoism were permitted but were regulated closely. The imperial court under the late Mings and under the first Manchu rulers did not look

and J. K. Fairbank and Teng Ssu-yu, "On the Ch'ing Tributary System," *Harvard Journal of Asiatic Studies* 6 (1941): 135–246. The last article is also included in John K. Fairbank and Teng Ssu-yu, *The Ch'ing Administration, Three Studies* (1960),° 107–246.

[7] K. S. Latourette, *A History of Christian Missions in China* (1932), 91–98. Also, Jonathan Spence, *To Change China: Western Advisers in China 1620–1960* (1969), 3–33 on Adam Schall and Ferdinand Verbiest, later Jesuits at the Peking court.

with favor on an exclusive, authoritarian, and dogmatic religion such as Catholicism. Actually, seventeenth-century China, whatever its limitations may have been, was far more tolerant than Catholic Europe. At the very moment when the Papacy was seeking tolerance for its monks in China, Alva, as agent of the Counter Reformation, was seeking to crush heresy by the sword in the Netherlands.[8]

EARLY TRADE WITH CHINA

The Spaniards Reach the Philippines

Less than a decade after the first Portuguese navigators reached Canton, Spanish explorers were crossing the Pacific after rounding Cape Horn. In 1521, Ferdinand Magellan, a Portuguese by birth but sailing under the flag of Spain, discovered the Mariana or Ladrone (Robber) Islands, and later reached Samar in the Philippines. The Spaniards, however, were not seeking the Philippines or China, but the Spice Islands, which lay to the south. As it happened, these islands, by the line of demarcation of 1494, lay, as did also the Philippines, in the Portuguese half of the world. It was not, then, until some years later that Spain undertook conquest and exploration of the Philippines. Manila was founded in 1571, by which time the Chinese trade with the islands was considerable.

The Dutch in the Far East

Fresh from their successful struggle for national independence, the Dutch reached the Far East at the beginning of the seventeenth century. Organization of the United Dutch East India Company signalized the emerging commercial supremacy of the Netherlands and its determination, with England, to destroy the colonial and mercantile monopoly

[8] Christianity was finally proscribed by Peking in 1724. A full and excellent discussion of the origin and development of anti-missionary feeling and anti-foreignism in China during the seventeenth and eighteenth centuries is given in Earl H. Pritchard, *Anglo-Chinese Relations during the Seventeenth and Eighteenth Centuries* (1931), Chapter 6.

of Spain and Portugal. The Dutch attempted to open trade at Canton in 1604, and again in 1607, but on both occasions permission was denied, probably at the instigation of the Portuguese at Macao. Eventually the Dutch established themselves first on the Pescadores Islands and later (1624) on Taiwan (Formosa). During the seventeenth and eighteenth centuries the Dutch sent four embassies to Peking (1656, 1667, 1685–1686, and 1795) seeking formal contacts with the Manchu Court and commercial concessions. The ambassadors were required to perform the humiliating kowtow (nine prostrations), in return for which they received only meager commercial privileges. After 1729, however, the Dutch traded regularly at Canton.

The English Reach China

The first English vessel to reach Canton was dispatched in 1635 by the English East India Company. This was followed by a squadron of English vessels, commanded by Captain John Weddell, sent by the Courteen Association. Weddell arrived at Macao in 1637, proceeded to Canton, and at first met with opposition from the Chinese but was finally permitted to engage in trade. The English sent ships regularly to Canton after 1699, which is the probable date of the beginning of their permanent factory there.

Other European nations played an inconspicuous role in this early China trade. The first French ship to reach Canton arrived in 1698; the first Danish ship in 1731; the first Swedish ship in 1732; and the first Russian ship in 1753. The first American ship, *Empress of China*, sailed for China in 1784.

First Russian Contacts with China

While western Europeans in the sixteenth and seventeenth centuries were making their first contacts with China by the all-sea route, Russians were moving to the East by way of Siberia. These first adventurers were composed of a motley aggregation of explorers, fur traders, and fugitives from the law. Some of them reached the Pacific slope, while others established permanent settlements at Tobolsk, Tomsk, Yakutsk, Nertchinsk, and at other points across Siberia. In far eastern Sibera there was a natural tendency for the Russians to move south into the valley of the Amur River. Here they came into conflict with tribal peoples who, theoretically at least, recognized the overlordship of China. For some years there was intermittent conflict between the Russians and the Chinese at Albazin, a Muscovite outpost on the upper Amur. Not until 1689 was a boundary settlement effected by the Russo-Chinese Treaty of Nertchinsk, China's first treaty with a Western power. As a result of this settlement, in which the Chinese negotiators were assisted by Jesuit advisers, Peking retained and extended its sovereignty over the Amur Valley.[9] A number of Russian embassies were subsequently sent to Peking during the eighteenth century. A settlement of the Russo-Chinese northwestern boundary was reached in 1727, and permanent trading posts were established on the frontier. Permission was also given for establishment of a Russian church in Peking, and China sent to St. Petersburg her only embassy to a foreign court. Meanwhile in 1702, a Japanese castaway on Siberian shores had been carried to Moscow by the Russians.

THE WEST DISCOVERS JAPAN

It was more than two centuries after the travels of the Polos in China that Europeans set foot on the shores of Japan. The account generally accepted relates that in 1542 (Japanese sources say 1543) Portuguese sailors voyaging from Macao to Siam were blown from their course to the shores of Tanegashima, a small island off the southern coast of Kyushu, where they instructed the natives in the use of firearms. These visitors were followed closely by Fernando Mendez Pinto, to whom the discovery of Japan is usually credited. More Portuguese ships soon ap-

---

[9] Vincent Chen, *Sino-Russian Relations in the Seventeenth Century* (The Hague, 1966). At the time of their first contacts, the Russians knew so little of China that the chieftain of the new Russian settlement of Nertchinsk was demanding that the K'ang-hsi emperor recognize the overlordship of Russia.

peared, for the feudal lords of southern Japan readily accepted the idea of trade with the foreigners.

These commercial contacts with southern Japan aroused the interest of the Portuguese monks. Francis Xavier, a Jesuit who had been preaching in Goa, Travancore, and Malacca, landed at Kagoshima in 1549. For more than two years he pursued in this new field the most successful mission of his life. The Japanese, far from repelling the foreigner, welcomed both his commerce and his religion. Other Jesuits followed Xavier to Japan where their work soon testified to their aggressive spirit and to the tolerance of the Japanese. The missionaries were heard respectfully by all classes of the people, including Buddhist priests. This may be accounted for by certain similarities between the rites and ceremonials of Buddhism and Catholicism. Also, since Catholicism was introduced directly from India, many Japanese assumed that it was a reformed Buddhism. It may be questioned whether many of the Japanese converts possessed any profound understanding of the new Western religion, for it has been noted that Japanese is a difficult language and Christianity is hard to explain.

Other causes contributed to the early success of Christianity in Japan. The feudal barons desired the profits of the foreign trade, and those in southern Japan, where most of the trade was conducted, were eager to increase their own power at the expense of the shogun's government. These barons observed the deference paid by the Portuguese traders to the missionaries. They concluded that where the missionary was, there would be the trader.

The Spaniards in Japan

Until 1592 the Portuguese were the only Europeans to reach Japan. When Philip II of Spain ascended the throne of Portugal in 1581, he confirmed his Portuguese subjects in the exclusive right to the Japan trade. Four years later the Papacy conferred upon the Jesuits the sole right to enter Japan as missionaries. It was just at this time (1591) that Hideyoshi, planning the conquest of

China, sent an embassy to Manila demanding that the Spaniards there recognize Japan as their suzerain. The Spanish governor sent two missions to Japan, carrying among their number four Franciscan friars, who, in the guise of ambassadors, entered Japan in violation of the papal order. Other priests who soon followed were permitted to remain on the understanding that they should not preach Christianity. Having accepted this prohibition, the priests immediately proceeded to violate it by conducting services in Nagasaki, Kyoto, and Osaka. Hideyoshi had first been favorably disposed toward the foreign priests, but he had become suspicious of political implications in the Jesuit policy and conduct. In confirmation of his fears, he now observed the Spanish priests openly defying his authority, and promoting, as in China, sectarian feuds with their Jesuit colleagues. Finally, the idle boasting of a Spanish pilot to the effect that the missionary was preparing the way for political conquest led Hideyoshi to act. In 1597 a number of Franciscans, Japanese Jesuits, and Japanese laymen were crucified at Nagasaki. In explanation of this brutal act, it should be noted that ten years earlier, Hideyoshi, after subduing the daimyo of Satsuma, where most of the Christians lived, had issued an edict ordering the foreign missionaries to leave Japan within twenty days. This edict was directed against the priests, not against their religion, for the Japanese desired to continue the Portuguese trade. The edict was consequently modified to permit priests to accompany the Portuguese ships but not to remain in Japan. Nevertheless, for a number of reasons, the law was not enforced effectively.

JAPANESE FOREIGN POLICY

With the passing of Hideyoshi (1598), political control of Japan passed into the hands of Tokugawa Iyeyasu, the able founder of the last great shogunate. Iyeyasu's views on foreign policy and trade were probably more enlightened than any that prevailed at the time, even in Europe. During his rule, the Portuguese, the Spaniards, the Dutch

and the English were all welcomed in Japanese ports. The exclusion edict against foreign priests was not revoked; neither was it enforced. Spanish monks from Manila again entered Japan, and in 1608 the Papacy rescinded the restriction which had granted the field solely to the Jesuits.

In 1600 the first Dutch ship reached Japan. The pilot of the vessel was an English sailor, Will Adams, who, because of his natural wit and ability, was promptly employed by Iyeyasu as an adviser in matters of commerce and navigation. Other Dutch ships arrived in 1609, and a Dutch factory was built at Hirado near Nagasaki. News of these successes brought the first English ship to Hirado in 1613. Iyeyasu, influenced by Adams, offered the English a charter for free trade and urged them to construct a factory at his capital, Yedo, the modern Tokyo. The short-sighted English Captain Saris preferred to remain with his factory and trade at Hirado. There the business was handled incompetently and abandoned in 1623, at a time when the Dutch trade was prospering.

Iyeyasu was likewise interested in developing closer commercial relations with Spain. He communicated with the Spanish authorities in the Philippines, offered to open the ports of eastern Japan to Spanish ships, and allowed it to be understood that the edicts against the missionaries would not be enforced. But it soon appeared that Spain was more likely to send missionaries than traders. As a result, Iyeyasu became suspicious of Spanish motives. The Dutch and English asserted that priests were not essential to trade. Accordingly, in 1612 Iyeyasu proscribed the Christian faith. All the Franciscan churches and many of the Jesuit establishments were destroyed. Some Japanese converts were executed in Yedo (1613), and in the following year suppression of the faith was ordered throughout the land. However, most of the foreign missionaries were not harmed at this time, and many of the local barons refused to act against the native Christians in their domains. Hidetada, who succeeded Iyeyasu in 1616, executed some Spanish priests, yet the laws were still not fully enforced. The government sought rather to have the priests leave the country voluntarily, whereas native Christians were induced by peaceful means to abandon the faith. Actually this policy failed, for the priests were defiant, and most of the converts clung to their new-found religion.

The Policy of Exclusion and Seclusion

The Catholic priesthood and its converts were, it seemed to the shogun, creating a rival authority in Japan which the shogunate was no longer willing to tolerate. Accordingly, in 1624 the Spaniards were ordered to leave the country. Direct relations between Japan and the Philippines were severed. Then in 1636 Iyemitsu, son and successor of Hidetada, proscribed Japanese trade on the high seas. No Japanese vessel might proceed abroad; no Japanese subject could lawfully leave his country; those doing so and attempting to return would suffer death. The Dutch were still permitted to trade at Hirado, but at Nagasaki the Portuguese were forced to conduct their commerce virtually as prisoners on a small artificial island known as Deshima.

These forceful measures did not end the trouble. The Shimabara revolt of 1637, a movement occasioned by feudal oppression and Christian persecutions, involved a large number of Japanese converts and was believed to have been incited by the missionaries. The government acted promptly. Spanish and Portuguese subjects were forbidden to visit Japan. Furthermore, it was decreed that if any Portuguese ship came to Japan, the vessel and cargo would be burned and the crew put to death.[10]

In this manner Japan entered upon a long period of exclusion and seclusion. It had become *sakoku* or the closed country. The Dutch, to be sure, were permitted to carry on a limited trade confined to the island of Deshima in Nagasaki harbor, and the Chinese could send a few junks annually to the same port. Except for these contacts Japan was excluded from the outside world, and was to remain so for more than two centuries, the centuries (1638–1854) in which the Western powers built and consolidated their colonial empires.

Why did Japan adopt so drastic a policy as seclusion, a policy that was to prevail for more than two centuries? The persecution of Christians in Japan was not basically of religious origin. The Buddhist church and clergy were not prime instigators, and the antagonism of the ruling class to Christianity was, in the main, political since it was the faith of Japan's potential enemies. The seclusion policy should be regarded rather as the means by which Japan's rulers sought to avoid any foreign entanglements which might endanger their fundamental aim of maintaining peace and fostering prosperity.[11]

A PERIOD OF SHIFTING INTERESTS

In summary, then, it may be said that the sixteenth and seventeenth centuries were not wholly without promise in the new intercourse between Europe and the Far East. In China there was an intelligent and tolerant audience ready to listen while Jesuits lectured on Europe's science. In Japan, the commercial and economic ideas of Tokugawa Iyeyasu far surpassed in liberality the economic policies of contemporary leaders in Europe. Yet by 1638 Japan had closed her doors to all foreign intercourse save for the annual Dutch ship and a few Chinese junks at Nagasaki. China likewise adopted a policy of cultural if not commercial exclusion. Repelled by the exclusive philosophy of the Catholic Church and by the quarrelsome character and aggressive behavior of its rival religious orders, the Chinese government expelled the missionaries in 1724. Thus the trade between Europe and Japan was ended, while such trade as remained with China was confined to the single port of Canton where it faced an uncertain future.

[10] The nature of militant Christianity is treated ably by C. R. Boxer, *The Christian Century in Japan 1549–1650* (1951), Chapters VII and VIII.

[11] George Sansom, *A History of Japan 1615–1867* (1963), 44.

Yet in the eighteenth century it seemed that Europe might develop some appreciation of China as a source of things cultural and intellectual. Indeed, at the beginning of the century polite society in Europe spoke of Chinese art with ease and familiarity. The brilliant masquerades of the French court were dominated by the art of China. The work of many of Europe's rococo artists was enriched if not inspired by the elaborate arts of southern China. To Europeans, the word porcelain connoted China; in England it actually was called "china," and still is. Side by side with these Chinese influences upon the Paris *salon* were others playing upon the intellectual life of so-called "enlightened" Europe. European philosophers such as Leibnitz, La-Mettrie, and Quesnay found support in Confucian philosophy for the rational basis of their systems of "pure thought." The physiocrats derived in part their notions on the economic nature of the state from their conception of conditions in ancient China. Lastly, in the late eighteenth century Europe's "Back to Nature" movement and the development of a sentimental nature-worship found some of their inspiration in the form and symbolism of the Chinese garden. But as the eighteenth century drew to a close, China ceased to be a source of vital inspiration to either the art or the philosophy of Europe. This was due in part to the altered views and changed status of the Jesuits. To a great degree the intellectual bridge between China and Europe had been built by the Jesuits. They had found in China something akin to what they considered the ideal state, and they had so reported to Europe. But the expulsion of these missionaries by China and the later dissolution of the Jesuits in Europe destroyed the main carrier of Chinese thought and influence.[12]

With the passing of the Jesuit contact, Chinese cultural influence not only ceased to reach Europe, but such influence as persisted there was subjected to attack. Save for a few remnants here and there, the China of art, letters, and philosophy had by 1800 all but disappeared from the European mind. Yet quite another China was already making its appeal to Europe. This was a material China rather than an aesthetic one; an economic China rather than an intellectual one. Unlike the China that had appealed to the intellectuals of the European enlightenment, this was a China that appealed to the moneyed barons of the English East India Company. It was a China of statistics and markets, and, so the barons hoped, of larger and larger profits.

The emergence of this new attitude toward and interest in China was a product of a momentous transformation taking place in Europe itself during the late eighteenth and the early nineteenth centuries. It was in these years that the European nation-state reached a degree of maturity. It was a product of what might be called political technology. With it came equally marked changes in military technology. In a relatively brief span of time, leading European powers increased vastly their efficiency in the conduct of war and in the political management of their conquests.[13] Political centralization and hierarchy in political organization combined with the new military and industrial technology of the times to become the foundations of European power after 1750.

The birth of the nation-state also created a new international system based on the idea of the equality of states. Admission to this society of "equal" states required that a state (1) define clearly the nature and source of authority and thus the locus of responsibility, (2) subscribe to the concept of the sanctity of contract to guarantee systematic and predictable conduct in trade, and (3) accept the Western concept of the universality of law and its application to the individual. These were the components of a new and powerful European system which was to work its

[12] See Adolph Reichwein, *China and Europe* (1925) for a full discussion of intellectual and artistic contacts in the eighteenth century. Also W. W. Appleton, *A Cycle of Cathay: The Chinese Vogue in England during the Seventeenth and Eighteenth Centuries* (1951).

[13] See Theodore Ropp, *War in the Modern World* (rev. ed., 1962).*

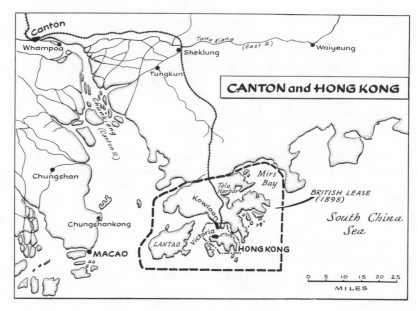

will in Eastern Asia as the nineteenth century advanced.

THE CANTON TRADE

Thus it was that in the later eighteenth century, Europe's cultural interest in China was replaced by a growing commercial interest—an interest that tended more and more to be monopolized by the British, which is to say, by the English East India Company. This did not mean that other nations were excluded from the trade of the China coast; but their share in it was circumscribed by political events. For instance, the Portuguese who had dominated the early trade (1517–ca. 1600), maintained themselves continuously at Macao during the seventeenth, eighteenth, and nineteenth centuries, enjoying the profits of a small but lucrative trade. The Dutch, who dominated the eastern trade in the seventeenth century, failed to maintain this lead against the British in China. France, defeated by Britain in the colonial struggle, was unable to bid seriously for the China trade. Thus the China trade increasingly became the property of the English East India Company. Britain's victories in the colonial wars, her established position in India, and her

primacy in the industrial revolution all served to stimulate her trade with the Far East. In fact, from 1750 until 1834 it may be said that China's relations with Europe were essentially her relations with the English East India Company.

For most of this period China's foreign trade, as noted, was confined to the single South China port of Canton. Thus, this commerce came to be known as the Canton trade. The peculiar circumstances surrounding this trade, the attitude of the Chinese toward the foreign barbarians, and the attitude of foreign barbarians in turn toward the "heathen" Chinese—all these had created by 1839 a crisis of dire proportions in the relations between Great Britain and China. It was this crisis and the wars which followed that were to determine the relations of China and the West for the succeeding century (1840–1940).

The primacy enjoyed by British trade was not, however, a reflection of British satisfaction with the commercial system that prevailed at Canton. On the contrary, the British, like all other foreign traders in China, regarded the system as exceedingly irksome. Accordingly, between 1787 and 1816 the British sent three embassies to Peking to establish a more reasonable system of trade. These successive embassies, headed by Charles Cathcart (1787), George Macartney (1792–94), and Lord Amherst (1816), all failed. These failures and the insults to which the British believed they had been subjected served to clarify the alternatives facing British policy at Canton. To British commercial interests and to the government it was becoming increasingly clear that there were three alternatives: (1) complete submission to a commercial system prescribed and controlled wholly by the Chinese; (2) complete abandonment of the trade (an unlikely course, since the trade was profitable even under the worst conditions); and (3) the application of force to compel the Chinese to do business on terms more pleasing to the West. Certainly a situation had arisen in which if Britishers and Chinese were to do business at Canton some accommodation would have to be found between their conflicting systems of foreign relations. The areas of disagreement were many and fundamental.[14]

[14] On the trade of various countries at Canton, see the tables compiled by Earl H. Pritchard, "The Struggle for Control of the China Trade," *The Pacific Historical Review* 3 (1934): 280–95. An essential study for the period is Michael Greenberg, *British Trade and the Opening of China 1800–42* (Cambridge, England, 1951). Also Pritchard, *Anglo-Chinese Relations during the Seventeenth and Eighteenth Centuries*, 189–90. Note also J. L. Cranmer-Byng, ed., *An Embassy to China: Being the Journal Kept by Lord Macartney during his Embassy to the Emperor Ch'ien-Lung, 1793-1794* (1963). Although the embassy did not achieve its purposes, Lord Macartney had the perception and the grace to write at the end of his journey: "Nothing could be more fallacious than to judge of China by any European standard." In attempting to get historical perspective on the conflicts which arose in and about the Canton trade, the reader will find it helpful to remember that the positions taken toward the Canton trade by the Manchu rulers of China seemed just as sensible to them as the views of Western traders appeared to Westerners. In attempting to understand the Manchu policy, the reader should recall that the Manchus were immersed in the very old social order of an agrarian-bureaucratic Chinese state mainly concerned in the power relations of an Inner Asian empire. There was no precedent and

The "Irregularities" of the Chinese Tariff

At the time the English East India Company was fast assuming leadership in the Canton trade, China had developed and was applying a tariff policy that was notable in that it was designed to encourage the import and to discourage the export trade. Such a policy was not likely to win British or other foreign approval. One feature of the Chinese tariffs appealed to the foreigners—the system was authorized by Peking. A system in which fiscal policy originated in the central government was quite understandable to western Europeans. But these same tariffs, though fixed by Peking, were interpreted and applied by local or provincial authorities who functioned only nominally under the Peking government. For the most part it would appear that the rates sanctioned by Peking were reasonable. But when these rates were interpreted and applied by the local customs authorities, the tariff became far from reasonable—such, at least, was the constant complaint of the foreign traders.

This complaint was not without some foundation. The chief Chinese customs officials and their staffs had every reason to seek rapid and ready fortunes. Each chief together with his staff enjoyed only a short term in office. He had paid heavily for the office; he continued to pay for the favor of the higher authorities; he was required to see that fixed contributions reached the imperial government; and he would indeed be short-sighted not to make provision for his own later days of retirement. All these ends he accomplished by a constant though irregular pressure on the foreign trade. These unpredictable exactions meant fortunes to the customs bureaucracy but were an abomination to the foreign traders. In general these merchants held that, although the imperial rates appeared to be moderate, they were so

no preparation for dealing creatively with the growth of the new maritime trade with Europe. Thus they attempted to apply at Canton the old administrative procedures of earlier dynasties. See John K. Fairbank, *Trade and Diplomacy on the China Coast* (1953),* I, 45–53.

little regarded in practice that it was scarcely possible to name any fixed charge, save on a few articles.[15] In fact, the policy of the local officials at Canton was to keep the foreigner in ignorance of the actual tariff schedule.

The Canton Monopoly: The Co-Hong

In the early nineteenth century, British traders, so it was said, found China as difficult to enter as Heaven and as difficult to get out of as Chancery. This was merely a way of saying that the Canton trade was a monopoly, and that the Chinese, at least a favored few of them, were the monopolists. There was nothing shocking to the English East India Company in the fact of monopoly. The Company itself was a monopoly. But when Chinese traders exacted monopoly profits at the expense of Western traders, monopoly as a principle lost some of its virtue.

The monopoly system that prevailed at Canton from 1757 to 1842 bore resemblance in some respects to commercial institutions and practices of Europe in the Middle Ages, namely, to the staple and the gild merchant or hanse. In Europe the gild merchant was a society whose primary purpose was to secure and hold a monopolistic privilege of carrying on trade. In China, the Co-hong, which corresponded to the gild merchant, was an instrumentality of imperial politics as well as of trade.

At the close of the eighteenth century, the Co-hong after a long and rather intricate history, had emerged as a group of twelve, later thirteen, so-called security merchants closely controlled by government, directly subject to the Hoppo (the Chinese commissioner of customs at Canton), enjoying a monopoly in the foreign trade. Every foreign vessel on arrival at Canton was "secured," that is, assigned to one of the Co-hong merchants who became responsible not only for the sale of the inbound cargo and provision for an outbound cargo but also for every operation of whatever kind connected with the arrival, stay, and departure of the ship. The Co-hong thus became the instrument for exacting a great revenue from the foreign trade for the benefit of the Hoppo and, indirectly, through him, of the Canton officials and the Court of Peking.[16] Finally, the Co-hong was to insure that foreigners observed the rules of the government and was to act as the sole medium of communication between the government and the foreign traders.[17]

The End of the Company's Monopoly, 1833

In 1833 there occurred an event of great significance. The English East India Company's monopolistic charter giving it exclusive control of English trade at Canton expired and Parliament did not renew it. So far as England was concerned, the trade was now open to any British merchant who had a mind to engage in it. This change foreshadowed grave complications in the commercial relations of Chinese and foreigners. Prior to 1833 the English traders at Canton had been under the control of a mere commercial agent, the chief factor of the Company there, but after 1833, with the abolition of the Company's monopoly, His Britannic Majesty was to be represented in the Canton trade by a "commissioned officer not only as a protector of his subjects and an overseer of their commercial activities, *but as a political and diplomatic representative*" of the British crown.[18] The Crown was not likely to bow without protest to those real or supposed indignities and to the "exactions" under which, at China's will, the *Fan-Kwei* (foreign devils)

---

[15] See Stanley F. Wright, *China's Struggle for Tariff Autonomy 1843–1938* (Shanghai, 1938), 1–5.

[16] Pritchard, *Anglo-Chinese Relations,* 141–42. The Hong merchants were among the world's greatest businessmen and traders of this period. Most popular with the American traders at Canton was the Hong merchant Houqua (Wu Ping-ch'ien). He is described by Thomas W. Ward of Salem as "very rich," "just in his dealings," "a man of honour and veracity," who "loves flattery and can be coaxed." Joseph Downs, "The American Trade with the Far East," in *The China Trade and Its Influences* (1941), 15.

[17] H. B. Morse, *The Gilds of China* (2nd ed., Shanghai, 1932), 78. See also John Barrow, *Travels in China* (1805), 414. Barrow was private secretary to the Earl of Macartney during the latter's mission to China.

[18] See W. C. Costin, *Great Britain and China 1833–1860* (Oxford, 1937).

had previously traded. This change in the status of British traders and of the agent who was to represent British interests at Canton set the stage for the ensuing Anglo-Chinese troubles that finally (1839–1842) resulted in the first Anglo-Chinese war, more frequently called the Opium War.

In 1833, Lord Napier, a Scottish peer of distinction, received a royal commission as First Superintendent of (British) Trade at Canton.[19] On his arrival at Macao (July, 1834) he proceeded to carry out his instructions, which, although they appeared proper enough from the Western point of view, were, if pressed, bound to result in conflict. Napier was required to announce his arrival "by letter to the Viceroy." He interpreted this to mean that he could not communicate through the Hong merchants. At the same time he was instructed not to arouse Chinese prejudice or to endanger the trade; he was not to call for armed assistance save in "extreme cases"; yet he was advised by Lord Palmerston that "the establishment of direct communications with the imperial court at Peking would be desirable." Neither Palmerston nor Napier appears to have realized that all these diplomatic eggs could not be carried in one basket with safety. A foreign naval officer and a representative of the British king simply could not be recognized by the Chinese unless he came as a bearer of tribute, as Napier did not.

Accordingly, at Canton, Napier announced his arrival by a letter to the Viceroy, which, of course, the latter refused to receive. This refusal was natural enough, for Napier had violated three important rules by which the Chinese controlled the foreigners. He had proceeded from Macao to the Canton factories, which were located on the bank of

[19] He was assisted by Sir John Francis Davis and Sir George Best Robinson as Second and Third Superintendents respectively, both of whom succeeded to the post of First Superintendent in the years following Napier's death. The fact that these officials were Superintendents of Trade precluded any possibility of their being treated as diplomatic equals by the Chinese officials. A merchant as such did not enjoy a station of honor in the official social scale of either Chinese or Japanese society.

the river outside the walled city, without asking and receiving China's official permission; he had attempted direct communication with the Viceroy, instead of using the medium of the Hong merchants; finally, he had termed his communication a *letter* instead of a *petition*, the form required by China of inferior tributary or vassal states. During this impasse Napier sickened and died, and for the ensuing five years (1834–1839) both the British and the Chinese governments followed a policy of indecision and drift.

The Legal Problem of Jurisdiction

The abolition of the English East India Company's monopoly at Canton precipitated in aggravated form another problem of long standing. This was the question of legal control over foreigners engaged in the trade at Canton. Most serious in Western eyes were those cases in which the Chinese demanded the surrender to Chinese justice of a foreigner accused of homicide in which a Chinese was the victim. There was already a long history of cases in which the Chinese and the foreigners had clashed on this point. One of the most notorious cases illustrative of the jurisdictional conflict was the Terranova affair. Terranova was an Italian seaman serving on the American ship *Emily* of Baltimore. In 1821, he was accused by the Chinese of having caused the death of a Chinese woman. Although convinced of his innocence and thoroughly aware that the Chinese would not give him a fair trial according to Western standards, the American merchant consul at Canton and the officers of the ship surrendered Terranova after the Chinese had stopped all American trade. Terranova was strangled, and the credit of the American merchants was saved.

In this conflict of jurisdictional interests all the faults were by no means on one side. It would appear that the Chinese authorities had no fixed desire to shield their own nationals from punishment; but they insisted that justice should take its course according to well-established Chinese ideas and methods. These the foreigners regarded as barbarous.

The Chinese attitude was equally understandable. Prior to the coming of the West-erners, China's foreign relations were con-fined substantially to bordering vassal states which acknowledged their inferiority. If Chi-nese law had been accepted by these vassals, there seemed to be no good reason why special legal concessions should be made to the Western barbarians. But the foreigners argued that no matter what China's legal theories might be, her courts were utterly corrupt. In cases involving foreigners, money, it was said, was more effective than evi-dence. A Chinese judge was disposed to give more credence to the testimony of a "civi-lized" Chinese than to that of an "uncivi-lized" barbarian. Furthermore, torture was usually applied to any victim who refused to confess. This method of extracting a con-fession, by no means unknown in the Western world at the time, appeared more sinister when applied by "yellow" men against "white."

Finally, it should be observed that the Chinese legal theory of responsibility was thoroughly obnoxious to the English and other foreigners at Canton.

The Yellow River bursts its banks; the governor of Honan begs the emperor to de-prive him of his titles, since he is responsible. A son commits an offence; the father is held responsible. A bankrupt absconds; his family are held responsible in body and estate. A shopman strikes a blow and goes into hiding; his employer is held responsible for his ap-pearance. A province is overrun by rebels; its governor is held responsible. . . . The result is that nothing which occurs goes unpun-ished; if the guilty person cannot be found, convicted, and punished, then the responsible person must accept the consequences—father, family, employer, village, magistrate, or viceroy.[20]

Social Restraints on the Foreigner at Canton

If the foreigner was aggrieved when China dictated the terms on which he might conduct his trade, he was exasperated when his personal life was treated in like man-ner. At Canton, the foreign factories were

situated on the river bank just outside the walled city. To this city the foreigner was denied access. His movements at Canton were confined to the narrow limits of the factory grounds. He was denied the use of sedan chairs—the most honorable conveyance for travel. He could not row on the river and only on rare occasions was he permitted to visit the flower gardens on the opposite bank. The markets of the walled city, with their variety of wares, were as far removed from his view as though they had been on the op-posite side of the globe. He could hire Chi-nese servants only by connivance, not by right. Neither wives nor other foreign women could accompany the traders to Canton. They were required to remain at Macao, where all the traders were forced to return at the close of the trading season.[21] Official China, which made these rules, looked upon the foreigner as a lower order of being and treated him accordingly. And yet, in contrast with these imposed social restraints, there were fre-quently the most friendly and intimate rela-tions among the traders, their Chinese agents, and the Hong merchants. At times the foreigner became restive, yet he was also timid. Despite all its impositions the Canton trade was profitable. On the whole, the for-eign trader was inclined to bear exasperating regulations rather than risk stoppage of the trade.

The Canton trade was, in brief, much more than a mere rivalry of merchants. It was a clash between essentially different commercial, legal, and political systems. To the foreigner, as Arthur Smith observed, it was "one long illustration of the Chinese talent for misunderstanding." Yet to the complaints of the foreigner the Chinese had a ready and plausible answer.

Why do you come here? We take in ex-change your articles of produce and manu-facture, which we really have no occasion for, and give you in return our precious tea, which nature has denied to your country; and yet you are not satisfied. Why do you so

---

[20] H. B. Morse, *The International Relations of the Chinese Empire* (3 vols., London, 1910–1918; Taiwan ed., 1963), I, 115.

[21] See Charles T. Downing, *The Fan-Qui or Foreigner in China* (2nd ed., London, 1840), III, 199–200.

often visit a country whose customs you dislike? [22]

The Chinese System of Foreign Relations

Moreover, the Canton trade, as it had developed by the 1830's, was both an example of and a challenge to China's theory and practice of foreign relations. The traditional Chinese system of foreign relations was one between China—the Middle Kingdom, the universal empire, and therefore the superior —on the one hand, and the lesser peoples— the outer barbarians and therefore the inferiors—on the other. In the Chinese view, the relationship was not one between equals. Historically, China had rarely been confronted by equals, but she had never been lacking in enemies on her borders, particularly in her great land frontier on the northeast. Foreign relations was therefore the problem of controlling the barbarians culturally even in those periods when the barbarian was able to invade and conquer China. The Chinese concept of their own superiority was one of cultural rather than of physical or material power; and this concept derived conviction from the Confucian emphasis on the power of example. Thus the idealized relationship between China and the outer barbarians required that the barbarian recognize the unique position of the Son of Heaven as the ruler of mankind and be submissive to him, while the emperor in turn was to be generous and benevolent to lesser peoples who showed him proper respect. This respect for and acceptance of Chinese suzerainty was given ritualistic expression and a measure of reality through the institution of *tribute* (usually native produce). The presentation of tribute at Peking by both the barbarians and also by the provinces of China itself signified membership in the Chinese Confucian society of peoples. In this ritual the tributary envoy might receive a patent of appointment, appointment to noble rank, and an imperial seal in addition to the hospitality of the Chinese court. In return the tributary performed the kowtow,

a symbol of submission. As elaborated at the Chinese court the kowtow consisted of three kneelings each involving three prostrations before the emperor. It was a ceremony that left no doubt as to who was above and who was below. To Westerners recently imbued with ideas of equality it was a repugnant performance, but to men of the Confucian order it was no more than good behavior. The emperor himself performed the kowtow at the altar of Heaven and to his parents.

The tribute system and its missions had survived because it served the interests of both the superior and the inferior, of China and the outer barbarian. It served the Chinese rulers as evidence that they did hold the Mandate of Heaven. This prestige was important to the dynasty not only in controlling the barbarians but also in maintaining its rule over its own people, the Chinese. It was also China's medium of diplomacy, the process by which she kept in touch with the outside world. On the other hand, the barbarians conformed to the tribute system and were prepared to accept inferior status partly because there was no alternative, but to an even greater degree because the tribute missions became an instrumentality for conducting commerce. China's system of foreign relations by the nineteenth century involved two inseparable factors—tribute and trade.

This background of the Chinese theory of foreign relations is an important key to understanding the explosive conditions created as Western traders congregated at Canton. What mattered to the rulers of China was the ethics of tribute; what mattered to the Western barbarians was the profits of trade and, after 1834, the concept of equality. Herein lay a fundamental conflict between Confucian and Western society. [23]

---

[22] Barrow, *Travels in China*, 413.

[23] Fairbank, *Trade and Diplomacy*, I, 23–53. The problem was intensified because China herself was ruled by the alien Ch'ing dynasty. For example, in the Canton conflict the imperial authorities in attempting to stir local Cantonese antiforeignism against the British discovered that this was a dangerous weapon which, if put to extensive use, might react against the local authority of the Manchu government itself.

The Economics of the Canton Trade

In spite of all the irritations that surrounded it, the Canton system of trade had been a profitable venture both for the English East India Company on the outside and for Chinese merchants and officials on the inside. Indeed so picturesque was this meeting of East and West in search of profits from teas and silks that the story of the old Canton trade before 1834 has often taken on the glamour of a fabulous and ideal age where merchants met as gentlemen. There is evidence to justify within some limits this glorification. At the same time the Canton system failed, and the economic reasons for this collapse should be noted.

A very conspicuous feature of the old Canton trading system was the pressing need for cargoes outbound to China to pay for exports of silk and tea. This need operated at the beginning of the nineteenth century in a complex of evolving and contradictory pressures. The Macartney (1792–1794) and the Amherst missions (1816) signified, under the influence of the industrial revolution, Britain's need for wider markets for increased manufactures. Yet in these same years the fortunes of the Company tended to be in decline. The way out of this contradiction came in part through what was known as the "country" trade.

As exports of silk and tea were growing rapidly between 1760 and 1800, there developed a distinctive British commerce, the "country" trade between India and China conducted by private individuals licensed by the Company in India and under its control at Canton. This country trade made up the third side of what was in reality a triangular commerce between Canton, London, and India. But it did far more than that. The country trade took over in large measure the old native Chinese junk trade of the Southeast Asia seas, carrying to Canton articles the Canton market would buy, such as cotton piece-goods and opium from India, and tin, camphor, and spices from the East Indies and Malaya. In this way imports to China were provided to pay for exports.

Equally important was the fact that the growth of this private trade and the ingenuity of the private traders in performing all manner of services (acting as the agents of private firms in London in banking and insurance, and as selling agents, etc.) meant that the Company's monopoly was becoming nominal rather than real. The private traders with their agency houses were therefore deeply involved in the Canton system while officially the monopoly of the Company still prevailed.

The Opium Traffic

To the foregoing picture of the Company's declining monopoly in the face of the resourceful pressures of the private traders was added the disrupting influence of opium, to the importation of which into China these traders turned much of their skill.

The first cause of this traffic lay in the unexplained development of a Chinese demand for opium. Since extensive cultivation of the poppy within China did not occur until after 1850, the demand could be met only by importation. Thus the demand within China plus the constant need at Canton for imports to balance the tea trade provided the economic bases for the growth of the traffic. As the Chinese demand grew, Indian opium came to surpass Indian raw cotton in balancing the trade. In time, too, opium production in India became an important source of government revenue there, thus tending to ensure opium's place in the China trade. As it happened, the phenomenal growth in the opium trade came just at the time the Company lost its monopoly at Canton. The two circumstances' coinciding brought on what may be called the Canton crisis of 1834–1840. The stimulus to this illegal traffic extended the opium business along the entire southeastern China coast to the mutual financial benefit of both foreign and Chinese merchants and of Chinese officials.

The rise of the opium trade presented the Peking government not only with a grave social problem but also with perplexing questions of regulations of the foreign trade, which was supposed to remain confined at Canton between the Co-hong and the foreign merchants. Nevertheless, the smuggling of opium was as prevalent at Canton as it became elsewhere. The dangers of opium, of course, had long been recognized by Peking. Importation and sale had been prohibited as early as 1729. But edicts were of no avail. The fact was that Chinese officials from the highest to the lowest "all connived at the continuous breach of the law provided only that they found therein their personal profit." [24]

Although Indian opium bulked largest in the trade and although the British occupied a conspicuous place as the carriers, all the foreign nationals represented at Canton were involved. Portuguese, French, American, and other ships carried Persian and Turkish rather than Indian opium. Indeed, prior to 1820 American cargoes of the Persian and Turkish drug were regarded as a threat to the East India Company's interest in the trade.[25] In a word, the Canton system, contrived to meet the limited contacts of the eighteenth century, could not control the expanding contacts of the nineteenth. The system was no longer a vehicle for legitimate Western commerce or a shield for China's theory and practice of foreign relations.[26]

[24] Morse, *The International Relations of the Chinese Empire*, I, 183.

[25] Charles C. Stelle, "American Trade in Opium to China Prior to 1820," *The Pacific Historical Review* 9 (1940): 425–44.

[26] See Fairbank, *Trade and Diplomacy* I, 56–73.

FOR FURTHER READING

EARLY CONTACTS. Donald F. Lach, *Asia in the Making of Europe*, I (Books 1 and 2): *The Century of Discovery* (1965), the first part of a unique study, massive and meticulous, of Asia and Europe in their historical interaction from 1500 to 1800. Donald F. Lach and Carol Flaumenhaft, eds., *Asia on the Eve of Europe's Expansion* (1965),* a

collection of contemporary accounts. Mark A. Stein, *On Ancient Central-Asian Tracks* (London, 1933). Leonardo Olschki, *Marco Polo's Asia: an Introduction to His "Description of the World Called Il Milione"*, John A. Scott, trans. (1960), a treasury of information on medieval Asia. Henry Yule, *The Book of Ser Marco Polo* (2 vols., London, 1921). Michael Prawdin, *The Mongol Empire: Its Rise and Legacy*, Eden and Cedar Paul, trans. (London, 1940).* A. C. Moule, *Christians in China Before the Year 1550* (London, 1930), of value as a source book. A. H. Rowbotham, *Missionary and Mandarin: The Jesuits at the Court of China* (1942), an evaluation of the impact of the Jesuits on China. George Harold Dunne, *Generation of Giants* (1962), the story of the Jesuits in China during the last decades of the Ming dynasty. Matthew Ricci, *China in the Sixteenth Century: The Journals of Matthew Ricci: 1583–1610*, Louis J. Gallagher, trans. (1953). Wang I-t'ung, *Official Relations Between China and Japan, 1368–1549* (1953) gives a description of the problems of Japanese piracy on the China coast during the Ming dynasty. Two studies by C. R. Boxer: *Fidalgos in the Far East, 1550–1770: Fact and Fancy in the History of Macao* (The Hague, 1948), a history of early Macao and Portuguese contacts with China; and, *Four Centuries of Portuguese Expansion, 1415–1825* (Johannesburg, 1961).* See also C. R. Boxer, ed., *South China in the Sixteenth Century* (London, 1953) contains accounts of Western travelers in China written between 1553 and 1576. Chang T'ien-tse, *Sino-Portuguese Trade from 1514 to 1644. A Synthesis of Portuguese and Chinese Sources* (Leyden, 1934). Lo-shu Fu, *A Documentary Chronicle of Sino-Western Relations, 1644–1820* (2 vols., 1967), a richly annotated selection of important official records from Chinese sources.

Early Russian penetration of East Asia is ably portrayed by Frank A. Golder, *Russian Expansion on the Pacific, 1641–1850* (1914). Note also Joseph Sebes, *The Jesuits and the Sino-Russian Treaty of Nerchinsk (1689). The Diary of Thomas Pereira, S. J.*

(Rome, 1961). V. S. Frank, "The Territorial Terms of the Sino-Russian Treaty of Nertchinsk, 1689," *The Pacific Historical Review* 16 (1947); 265–70.

SOUTHEAST ASIA. See Kristof Glamann, *Dutch-Asiatic Trade 1620–1740* (Copenhagen, 1958), a detailed examination of the Dutch East India Company in the early years.

BRITISH AND AMERICAN INTERESTS. Philip G. Rogers, *The First Englishman in Japan: The Story of Will Adams* (London, 1956). J. L. Cranmer-Byng, "Lord Macartney's Embassy to Peking in 1793," *Journal of Oriental Studies* 4 (1957–58). H. B. Morse, *The Trade and Administration of the Chinese Empire* (3rd rev. ed., London, 1920) treats Chinese institutions having a bearing on the foreign trade. Helen Augur, *Tall Ships to Cathay* (1951), an account of a New England firm's efforts to establish an Oriental trading company. R. Coupland, *Raffles, 1781–1826* (London, 1926), an excellent study of the founder of Singapore. A popular novel recreating the color of early Hong Kong, James Clavell, *Tai-pan* (1966).°

China Submits:
The Treaty System

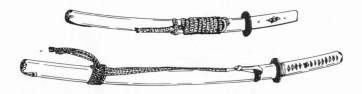

chapter 6

The clash of interests in the foreign trade at Canton and on the southeast China coast had become fundamental by 1835. The issues were not simple. Beyond the matter of profits in trade whether legitimate or contraband, these issues, to mention only the more striking, revolved about such things as: (1) the British desire for diplomatic representation and equality as against China's assumptions of superiority; (2) the free-trading aspirations of the foreigners against the controlled economy of the Co-hong; and (3) the rights of the individual in Western law as against Chinese concepts of collective responsibility. When to these basic conflicts were added the abolition of the East India Company's monopoly (1834) and the rapid expansion of the legal and the contraband trade, there was created a degree of confusion in Canton waters which neither the British nor the Manchu government could long ignore. The policy of drift following Napier's death (1834) could not be prolonged indefinitely.

China's immediate contribution to the coming crisis came from its anti-opium movement, which was first a moral protest against the drug evil as expressed in imperial edicts against the traffic, and second an economic protest resting on the mistaken belief that opium was the cause of the government's

fiscal troubles. The general Chinese belief was that as opium moved into China, silver, which was often used to pay for it, moved out. Although in some degree this was so, there were many other factors inducing the silver shortage. To the government, this shortage was a matter of grave concern. The Chinese people, who used copper coins in everyday transactions, were required to convert these to silver for purposes of tax payments. Thus, when silver became more valuable in relation to copper, the taxpayer suffered; the government, in turn, had to choose between facing popular resentment or accepting reduced tax revenue.[1] At any rate, the government resolved to end the opium trade, and for this purpose sent to Canton in 1839 a determined official, a rare character in the Chinese bureaucracy of the time, as Imperial Commissioner. This official was the famous Lin Tse-hsu (1785–1850), known to the foreigners as Commissioner Lin.

LIN ACTS: THE BRITISH REACT

Commissioner Lin was a man of thought as well as action, but his sources of information on the foreigners were at best very imperfect. A product of China's ignorance of

[1] J. K. Fairbank, *Trade and Diplomacy on the China Coast* (2 vols., 1953), I, 75–76.

barbarian power, he intended to reform the Canton system on China's own terms by attacking the problem unilaterally through the single target of opium. Accordingly, within a week of his arrival Lin had imprisoned the foreign traders in the factories and demanded delivery of the opium in their possession. The traders, through Captain Elliott, Superintendent of British trade, eventually surrendered some twenty thousand chests. To the astonishment of the foreign community this comfortable fortune, later valued at $6,000,-000, was mixed with salt and lime and sluiced into the river. War was now certain, for whereas Lin seems to have felt that his mission was accomplished, the British government could not do less than seek reparations.[2]

The first Anglo-Chinese war, which followed in 1840–1842, involved two campaigns. In the first (1840), the British took Canton only to withdraw in favor of an expedition up the China coast where they attacked Chinese garrisons and blockaded the mouth of the Yangtze. This advance brought the removal of Lin and the appointment of a Manchu, Ch'i-shan, to negotiate. He induced the British to return to the south where in January, 1841, an abortive convention was signed which included the transfer of Hong Kong to the British, the concession of diplomatic equality, an indemnity to the British,

[2] Lin's fascinating diary is found in Arthur Waley, *The Opium War Through Chinese Eyes* (1958).⁰ There is no definite answer to the question of whether the warfare of 1839–1842 should be called the Opium War or the First Anglo-Chinese War. It is a matter of the historian's individual judgment based on his reading of the evidence. Certainly the opium trade was the immediate occasion of the hostilities, but there were many other factors of long standing and of explosive potential. To Chinese, the conflict has always been "The Opium War"; yet the underlying conflict was not opium but rather the clash between China's tribute system and the Western theory of the equality of states. The problem here presents the student with a very nice case demonstrating the inadequacy of labels when applied to complex historical situations. See Hsin-pao Chang, *Commissioner Lin and the Opium War* (1964). This full and able treatment is more critical of British policy at Canton than some previous studies.

and provision for resumption of trade. For their trouble Ch'i-shan was promptly disgraced and Elliott recalled. In the view of their respective governments, Ch'i-shan had gone too far; Elliott, not far enough. Accordingly, the war was renewed in a second campaign (August, 1841–August, 1842). In March, 1842, the Manchu court began to consider negotiation.[3]

Meanwhile, Sir Henry Pottinger had arrived off the coast as Britain's chief representative. A British fleet moved northward, meeting no effective resistance. Early in August, 1842, Nanking, the southern capital, was at the mercy of British guns. The war was ended. The military defeat of China was decisive. A small British force, never more than 10,000 effectives, had broken what remained of Manchu military prestige. It was the beginning of a century of military defeats for China. Helpless, she sought peace on the deck of a British battleship, the *Cornwallis,* as it lay in the river off Nanking. In doing so China was choosing between danger and safety, not between what she considered right and wrong.

THE NANKING AND BOGUE TREATIES

The formal settlement of the first Anglo-Chinese war was embodied in two treaties: the Treaty of Nanking, August 29, 1842, and the supplementary Treaty of Hoomun Chai, signed at the Bogue, October 8, 1843.[4] The two treaties contained the basic principles that were to govern China's international status for a century. Later treaties between China and foreign states modified or amplified details, but the basic structure of principles contained in the first treaties remained

[3] P. C. Kuo, *A Critical Study of the First Anglo-Chinese War* (Shanghai, 1935), 194–99. See also D. E. Owen, *British Opium Policy in China and India* (1934), 167–75.

[4] For texts of all important nineteenth-century treaties with China, see China, the Maritime Customs, *Treaties, Conventions, etc., Between China and Foreign States* (2 vols., 2nd ed., Shanghai, 1917).

with little change until the end of the unequal treaty system in 1943.

Five ports, Canton, Amoy, Foochow,
Ningpo, and Shanghai, were opened to the
residence and trade of British merchants.
Britain was to appoint consular officers to
these ports. The island of Hong Kong was
ceded to Great Britain "in perpetuity." [5] The
Co-hong was abolished, and British merchants were "to carry on their mercantile
transactions with whatever persons they
please." China was to pay a total indemnity
of $21,000,000—$6,000,000 for the surrendered opium; $3,000,000 to cover debts
owed by Hong merchants to British subjects;
$12,000,000 for expenses occasioned by the
war. Correspondence between the chief British representative and high Chinese officials
was to be under the term "a communication,"
not "a petition."

China agreed to a uniform and moderate
tariff on exports and imports, which came
to be known as the 5 per cent ad valorem
treaty tariff. The duties fixed at this time
were not to be increased save by mutual
agreement. Thus, for the ensuing 88 years—
that is, until 1930—China was unable to fix
her tariffs of her own free will. In 1842,
however, China did not realize the importance of this act, nor was there anything in
the nature of a plot on the part of British
negotiators to violate China's sovereign rights
beyond meeting and correcting the circumstances in which the trade had been conducted. The British purpose was not to control China's fiscal policies but to provide a
modus operandi for the foreign trade. Since

this trade was still relatively small, and since
isolation was still China's prevailing philosophy, the principle of tariff autonomy had at
the time little of the significance it acquired
in later years.[6] Another motive behind the
tariff clause of the treaty was the aggressive
free trade philosophy that existed in Britain.
In general the free traders felt that they had
a divine mission to impose their creed on
the world.

The first treaty settlement likewise included provision for extraterritorial jurisdiction in criminal cases (Treaty of the Bogue,
Article IX)—a second major infringement on
China's exercise of sovereignty. It will be
recalled that for many years the foreign
traders and their governments had condemned
Chinese notions concerning the theory and
practice of justice. At Macao the Portuguese
had sought to retain exclusive jurisdiction
over their nationals, and in 1833 the British,
by order-in-council, provided their own court
at Canton with criminal and admiralty jurisdiction. Again, it was only in later years that
China realized the full implications of harbor-
ing in her seaports a foreign population over
which her courts had no power.

Although China regarded opium as the
primary cause of the war, the first treaty
settlement, aside from stipulating the payment of $6,000,000 for the opium seized, did
not mention the traffic at all. In the British
view, China was free to legalize and control
or prohibit imports, but enforcement of the
latter course would be China's responsibility.
The Chinese would not agree to legalization,
and thus the treaty was silent on this important question.

Finally, Britain secured the principle of
most-favored-nation treatment. Article VII
(Treaty of the Bogue) stated that should the
emperor hereafter grant additional privileges
or immunities to the subjects or citizens of

---

[5] G. B. Endacott, *A History of Hong Kong*
(London, 1958) is a competent treatment of this
British Crown colony from the beginning to the
end of World War II. Also the same author's
*Government and People in Hong Kong 1841–
1962* (Hong Kong, 1964) for the problems involved in providing a colonial government for a
predominantly Chinese populace. Even at the
end of the nineteenth century when Britain acquired by lease the New Territories on the
mainland, adjacent to Kowloon (acquired 1860),
a British colonial official was noting that the
Chinese villager "does not set great store by
cleanliness or better housing," did not understand British aims or ideas, or "our dismal condition of unrest" (p. 133).

[6] S. F. Wright, *China's Struggle for Tariff
Autonomy* (Shanghai, 1938), 45–48. Frederic
Wakeman, Jr., *Strangers at the Gate: Social Disorder in South China, 1839–1861* (1966), suggests that Cantonese hostility toward foreigners
in the wake of the war was not solely a matter
of anti-foreignism. It was also an expression of
regional antagonism toward the Peking government and its policies.

other foreign countries, the same privileges and immunities would be extended to British subjects.

The new status thus acquired by Great Britain and her traders in China prompted other powers to seek treaty relations. Between 1844 and 1847 three treaties were concluded by China: with the United States (July 3, 1844); with France (October 24, 1844); and with Norway and Sweden (March 20, 1847). Of these, by far the most important was the American. Its significance may best be seen by briefly reviewing the growth of American interests in China.

EARLY AMERICAN INTERESTS IN CHINA

Even before the days of independence some notable Americans had expressed themselves on China. Benjamin Franklin (1771) hoped America would increase in likeness to her. Thomas Jefferson (1785) held that China's policy of nonintercourse was ideally adapted to American use. John Quincy Adams (1822) praised the Chinese for recognizing the virtues of the decimal system. But to most Americans China was merely a vast and remote empire—as much a curiosity as if it had been on another planet.

John Ledyard, an American who accompanied Captain Cook to the Pacific (1776–1781), was among the first to tell his countrymen how furs from the northwest coast of American sold in Canton at enormous profit. The result was a voyage by the *Empress of China*, the first American ship to sail direct for Canton (1784).[7] The trade, thus begun, soon prospered. The Americans, like the European traders, sought Chinese silk and tea, and they encountered the same difficulties as the Europeans in finding an outbound cargo. Furs, ginseng, sandalwood,

opium, and silver constituted main items in the China-bound cargoes, and various routes were followed by the ships in the early American trade. Between 1784 and 1811 Americans were the most serious rivals of the British in the tea trade at Canton. Their ships were neither so large nor so numerous as those of the English East India Company, yet in the season 1805–1806 they carried from Canton 11 million pounds of tea in 37 ships, as against British exports of 22 million pounds in 49 ships.[8]

The position of the Americans at Canton contrasted in some respects with that of the British. The Americans traded with greater individual freedom, but they possessed neither the financial backing nor the prestige of the English company, nor did they enjoy any naval protection from their home government. The first official representative of the United States in China was Major Samuel Shaw, who, after a number of voyages to the Far East, was named consul, without salary, at Canton by the Continental Congress acting on the recommendation of John Jay. It would seem that the early American trader felt little need for official support so long as he was permitted to trade on equal terms with his British rivals. But as the tension grew between the British and the Chinese after 1834, the indifference of American merchants to official backing disappeared. In May, 1839, after Lin had forced the surrender of foreign-owned opium, a group of Americans at Canton memorialized Congress to send a commercial agent to negotiate a treaty, and a naval force to protect persons and property.[9] Although expressing no sympathy with the opium traffic, they found no excuses for the "robbery" of the British. They foresaw that England would use armed force, and they believed "that this is necessary." They recommended that the United States take *joint* action with England, France, and

---

[7] *The Empress of China*, 300 tons, carried as cargo "furs, foodstuffs, and ginseng—a wild root worth its weight in gold in the Orient as the 'dose of immortality.'" Robert Morris financed the voyage. Joseph Downs, "The American Trade with the Far East," in *The China Trade and Its Influences* (1941), 13.

[8] See K. S. Latourette, *History of Early Relations Between the United States and China (1784–1844)* (1917).

[9] For a selected group of representative documents on American policy, see Paul H. Clyde, *United States Policy Toward China: Diplomatic and Public Documents, 1839–1939* (1940; reissued 1964).

Holland to secure: (1) resident ministers at Peking; (2) a fixed tariff on exports and imports; (3) the liberty of trading at ports other than Canton; and (4) Chinese assent to the principle that, until their laws are made known and recognized, punishment for offenses committed by foreigners against Chinese or others shall not be greater than is applicable to a like offense by the laws of the United States or England.

When the opium crisis broke at Canton, the Americans turned over their opium to the British superintendent for surrender to the Chinese; but when the English withdrew to Macao, and later to Hong Kong, the Americans remained at Canton, and conducted a lucrative business carrying cargoes of British goods to Canton when British ships were no longer permitted to enter the river.

In the broad sense, America appeared ill-prepared to formulate a political policy toward China. A fair proportion of Americans who thought about China at all harbored all manner of distorted notions concerning her. The most prevalent opinion was that the Anglo-Chinese war was "another item in the sad catalogue of [British] outrages on humanity." When in 1841 John Quincy Adams suggested in an address that the principle of equality among states was the real cause of the war in China, the idea was so shocking to the editor of the *North American Review* that he refused to print Adams' manuscript. After the first American Protestant missionaries, Elijah C. Bridgman and David Abeel, were sent to Canton in 1829, the missionary press dwelt heavily on the vices of the "heathen Chinese." The Chinese were frequently pictured as masters of deceit, cruelty, gambling, rioting, indolence, and superstition. Worst of all was their preference for rice rather than for salvation. To many religious Americans there was a shocking satisfaction in the thought that China's "depravity" offered an unlimited field for American missions. Nor were these opinions merely the fulminations of fanatics. After seventeen years in China, S. Wells Williams, one of the ablest of missionaries, succumbed at times to the prevalent conclusion:

It is much easier [he wrote] loving the souls of the heathen in the abstract than in the concrete encompassed as they are in such dirty bodies, speaking forth their foul language and vile natures exhibiting every evidence of depravity.[10]

Any thoughtful American must have been at a loss to know what to believe about China when he read that the Chinese had "some very esteemable qualities" but were "false, dishonest, and distrustful."

THE FIRST ENUNCIATION OF AMERICAN POLICY

Out of the background of these inadequate ideas on China there emerged an official policy which, surprising as it may seem, so exactly expressed the reality of American interests that it survived for a century. President Tyler, on December 30, 1842, four months after the Treaty of Nanking had been signed, asked Congress to authorize appointment of a resident commissioner in China to protect the commerical and diplomatic affairs of the United States. This post was conferred upon Caleb Cushing of Massachusetts, brilliant lawyer, member of the Committee on Foreign Affairs, and intimate friend of the President. To Secretary of State Daniel Webster fell the task of preparing Cushing's instructions. The American envoy was to secure entry of American ships and cargoes into the open ports on terms as favorable as those enjoyed by the British. He was to employ the utmost tact; to impress the Chinese with the peaceful character of his mission; to visit Peking if possible; but in no case was he to perform the kowtow. The instructions concluded with these significant words—the essence of American policy:

Finally, you will signify, in decided terms and a positive manner, that the Government of the United States would find it impossible to remain on terms of friendship and regard with the Emperor, if greater privileges or commercial facilities should be allowed to the subjects of any other Government than should

[10] F. W. Williams, *The Life and Letters of Samuel Wells Williams* (1899), 174.

be granted to the citizens of the United States.

Cushing reached Macao in February 1844, welcomed neither by the Chinese, the British, nor the American communities. The treaties of Nanking and the Bogue were already in operation. Also, the Manchu negotiators had already applied, in 1842–1843, the old and well-established idea of equal treatment for all barbarians, so that the Americans enjoyed most-favored-nation treatment in fact without the asking. Thus the question arose as to what Cushing could do that had not already been done.[11]

In the face of Chinese procrastination on the subject of a treaty, Cushing intimated that he would proceed to Peking. This threat brought an imperial commissioner to Macao, and soon thereafter the first American treaty was signed (Treaty of Wang-hsia [Wang Hiya], July 3, 1844).[12] Although this treaty followed in general the principles contained in the British treaties, it was superior in point of clarity and in extending the principle of extraterritoriality to include civil as well as criminal cases. Thus the American treaty rather than the British became the basic document in China's foreign relations until the treaties of Tientsin were signed in 1858. Whereas the commercial policy set forth by Webster was in the main approved by American opinion, criticism of the Cushing mission was not lacking, although for the most part it was political in character—directed at the gold braid and plumes worn by the "pomp-

[11] Cushing's instructions are printed in Clyde, ed., *United States Policy Toward China,* 9–12. The Manchu emperor's formal approval of the equal extension of trading privileges had been given November 15, 1843, before the arrival of Cushing in China. Kenneth Ch'en, "The Cushing Mission: Was It Necessary?" *Chinese Soc. and Pol. Science Rev.* 23 (1939): 3–14.

[12] For a scholarly editing of this treaty, see Hunter Miller, ed., *Treaties and Other International Acts of the United States of America* IV. The prompt conclusion of the American treaty, once negotiations were begun, was due to Chinese "abhorrence of Cushing's intention to go to Peking," Ping Chia Kuo, "Caleb Cushing and the Treaty of Wanghia, 1844," *The Journal of Modern History* 5 (1933): 51. China was represented by Ch'i-ying.

ous" Cushing rather than at the purposes of the mission. Journals such as *Hunt's Merchants' Magazine,* which a few months previously had bitterly denounced England's motives in China, reversed themselves, found excuses for England's behavior, and supported her policy of treaty relations. And in Congress there was spirited support for Cushing, since no one knew "just how much of our tobacco might be chewed [in China] in place of opium."[13]

These more favorable reactions were not unanimous. There was a strong current of opinion that the China trade did not merit the publicity given it. Americans, it was said, might better direct their attention to the internal development of their own country. This was doubtless a very natural reaction in an America in the full tide of expansion on the frontier. Perhaps, too, the very positive character of this pioneer society reinforced the general American tendency to judge things Chinese solely in terms of American values, a tendency that contributed to tragic results in the twentieth century.

The Franco-Chinese treaty (October, 1844) followed the model of the British and American treaties. The French diplomats, however, appeared also in the role of "protectors" of Catholic missions. Their request for permission to build Roman Catholic missions at the five treaty ports, and for toleration to Chinese and foreign Christians, was granted by the emperor, though not as a part of the treaty. These concessions were extended later to Protestants.

THE RECEPTION OF THE FIRST TREATIES

The first treaty settlement viewed in retrospect reveals graphically its deep significance, but it must not be assumed that all this was clear to the contemporaries of Lin, Ch'i-ying, Pottinger, and Cushing. The fact that a handful of British troops and a small fleet had forced the Manchu court to terms did not signify necessarily that all was now

[13] *Congressional Globe,* 27th Cong., 3rd sess., 325.

well. The treaties themselves were an experiment. Would they in practice satisfy either the foreign traders and their governments or the reluctant Manchu court? Behind this question was a broad and vital problem. Did China's signature on the first treaties mean that she had broken positively with the past? Would her doors now be opened widely to Western influence, or, by evasion of the treaties, would she await the day when these doors might be closed again to a presumptuous, barbarian world?

The period from the First Anglo-Chinese War until the settlement of the second war (1861) illustrates nicely the persistence of the Chinese view that all Westerners were "irritating intruders." Confident of the greatness and self-sufficiency of her own rich culture, China, in 1844, was still confident that she could control the intruders and preserve her own integrity. The defeat in the "Opium" War and the imposition of the treaties were considered temporary reverses, unfortunate but not fatal. Within this overall official Chinese attitude were the more particular reactions of the ruling Manchu dynasty. This dynasty, already weakened in the nineteenth century by the declining capacity of its emperors, was confronted by recurring rebellion at home as well as by the intrusions of the Westerners at the ports. Faced by these trials, the Manchus attempted at times to use the lesser trading powers, France and the United States, in an effort to thwart the main antagonist, Great Britain. The mass of memorials that flowed to Peking from high officials at Canton and later from Shanghai insisted that the barbarian problem could best be handled by adroit "management." Accordingly, the emperor created a Barbarian Affairs Bureau to collect all records and information concerning foreign affairs, thus indicating that the government knew it was faced with a problem. In this picture, the United States by 1842 occupied a somewhat distinct position as the most important "neutral" state involved in the Anglo-Chinese struggle. Since the Americans had not joined Britain in the war, a number of Chinese officials played with the idea of "utilizing the American barbarians" in a general scheme of

"using barbarians to curb barbarians." Indeed, throughout the remainder of the nineteenth century, China relied heavily on the technique of playing one power against another in her effort to resist the Western impact and to preserve her political system.[14]

CHINA AND FOREIGN AFFAIRS

China's Method in Foreign Affairs

The Treaty of Nanking (1842) had ended the old Chinese system of dealing with the foreigners through the Co-hong and the factories at Canton. This development did not mean that China's foreign relations were patterned immediately on the Western model. In the strict sense of the term there really were no official Chinese foreign relations before 1841, nor were there to be any, even in a semi-orthodox sense of the term, until the establishment of the Tsungli Yamen in 1861 and the opening of Peking to residence of ministers of the treaty powers. Thus China's foreign affairs from 1841 to 1861 were in a formative stage.[15]

The embryonic organization China used to deal with the barbarians in these years was briefly as follows: The most important official dealing directly with the foreigners at the five recently opened treaty ports was the tao-t'ai, or Intendant of Circuit. He had jurisdiction over two or more prefectures and served as an intermediary in diplomatic intercourse with the foreigners while he also usually served as superintendent of customs, a post formerly held by the "hoppo," or superintendent of customs at Canton. A second official concerned with foreign affairs was the provincial governor (hsun-fu). Although the governor occasionally received the representative of a foreign state, he more frequently merely memorialized the

[14] Earl Swisher, *China's Management of the American Barbarians: A Study of Sino-American Relations, 1841–1861, with Documents* (1953), 1–54.

[15] The handling of foreign affairs was merely an aspect of the far larger problem of Chinese government administration as a whole. See John K. Fairbank and Teng Ssu-yu, *Ch'ing Administration* (1960),* especially 107–73.

throne on negotiations between the *tao-t'ai* and the foreigner, or shifted the problem down to the *tao-t'ai* or up to the governor-general. More important, therefore, in handling foreign affairs in the new treaty period was the governor-general (*tsung-tu*), whom Westerners usually called the "viceroy." His prominence in foreign affairs was due partly to the American treaty of 1844, which stated that communications to the court were to be transmitted through this official.

The highest official outside of Peking who dealt with foreign affairs was the imperial commissioner (*ch'in-ch'ai*). Ranking above the governor-general and with a direct commission from the emperor, he might be instructed to cope with any new or alarming crisis such as when Lin Tse-hsu was sent to Canton in 1839 to deal with the opium affair. When the Treaty of Nanking abolished the Co-hong as the agency for dealing with foreigners, the "diplomatic" function was taken over by the governor-general at Canton under the new title of "Imperial Commissioner charged with the superintendence of the concerns of foreign nations with China." All of the above officials were served by a host of underlings supposedly well versed in foreign affairs but whose knowledge, in this period at least, was anything but impressive or accurate.[16]

Central Machinery of Foreign Affairs

Throughout the nineteenth century Western diplomats in China felt, more often than not, that China's handling of foreign affairs was a colossus of purposeful evasion, capped with downright administrative incompetence. Evasion of foreign purposes there certainly was, but the charge of administrative incompetence has been greatly overdrawn. Actually Peking's handling of foreign affairs was centralized and orderly. All such matters were dealt with directly by the emperor and the highest organ of state, the Grand Council (*Chun Chi Ch'u*). Originally set up in 1729 to handle secret military affairs, the Council, as a kind of inner, intimate staff of the emperor, acquired the power

[16] Swisher, *China's Management of the American Barbarians*, 1–7.

to interfere with any political matter. It had become an agency of dynastic power negating traditional Chinese restrictions on imperial authority. This small group, some five officials personally responsible to the emperor, was obviously not a foreign office, for it dealt with matters of all kinds. Moreover, in the period 1841–1861 the Council was declining in character and initiative. In this picture it is clear that the emperor's authority was final; however, the degree of initiative he exercised and the degree of judgment exercised by the Councilors could vary greatly.

The working of this machinery for foreign affairs was regular and efficient according to the Chinese standards of that day. The foreign diplomat presented his credentials to the governor-general and imperial commissioner at Canton, or, if this had been done, he might, in specific cases of diplomatic business, deal with a governor-general, governor, or *tao-t'ai* at one of the treaty ports. The next step was a memorial from the high Chinese official to the emperor setting forth and reporting upon the business at hand. The important point is that the Western diplomat was dependent upon the case presented by the memorialist.

Chinese "Diplomatic" Officials

The Chinese official at the ports who dealt with representatives of the Western treaty power was separated from them culturally by barriers of language, tradition, philosophy, and custom. He was therefore apt to be in the opinion of the foreigner an inscrutable enigma or a thoroughly perverse and unreasonable being. There was, however, a Chinese side to this picture that was not always comprehended by Western envoy, merchant, or missionary. What manner of men were these Chinese officials, and what ideas concerning the foreigners did they entertain in the twenty years following the first treaty settlement?

Since these Chinese officials were numerous and held posts of varying importance, from the exalted station of the imperial high commissioner down the scale of rank to semi-official and even unofficial underlings, it is only possible to give here by a few selected examples some impression of their quality as men. Among the more prominent names known to the foreigners were those of Lin Tse-hsu who seized the opium, and Ch'i-ying or Kiying, who negotiated the first treaty settlement. The study of Lin's career is rewarding because in stature and influence he appears as among the greatest of Chinese statesmen of the nineteenth century. Tseng Kuo-fan and Li Hung-chang, who will be met with later in these pages, "excelled in the art of doing what was possible, [but] Lin surpassed them in the science of foreseeing what was inevitable." [17]

Lin, a native of Fukien, had first acquired fame as judicial commissioner in Kiangsu, where his judgments were regarded as so able he came to be known as "Lin, Clear as the Heavens." When, as his reputation grew, he memorialized the throne in 1838 on the opium question, he was called to Peking and, following nineteen audiences, was appointed imperial commissioner with full powers to examine and stamp out the evil of opium at Canton. The reader already knows what Lin did at Canton. However, when China was defeated in the war that followed and a British fleet lay off Tientsin, Lin was dismissed and ordered to Peking. Following a period of banishment to Chinese Turkestan, he was recalled in 1845 and thereafter served in a number of provincial posts. His fame rests not solely on his general administrative career or on his virtuosity in the opium drama at Canton. Beyond these accomplishments he was a pioneer in recognizing the power of the West. He advocated the study of Western geography and the introduction by China of Western methods and weapons of warfare as means of restoring Chinese power.

Ch'i-ying, known to contemporary Westerners as Kiying, was a Manchu imperial clansman. It was he who concluded the Treaty of Nanking with Great Britain in 1842, the Treaty of the Bogue in 1843, and the American Treaty of Wang-hsia in 1844. He also signed the later treaties with France and Sweden-Norway in 1844 and 1847 re-

[17] Chang, *Commissioner Lin and the Opium War*, 216–17.

spectively. His power in China's relations with the West was unrivalled until 1850, when, under a new emperor, he was denounced as having "oppressed the people to please the foreigners." Degraded in rank, he committed suicide in 1858. He was the victim of an uncompromising court party, and of the unpopularity of the first treaties.

Actually, the Manchu failure of 1842 was due in some measure to ignorance of the West. Even some of China's most distinguished dignitaries thought "it was because England had only a queen" that many of her subjects dared to be so unruly in China. Chinese scholars found the barbarian character "unfathomable," since it would do anything for profits. But there were reasons other than ignorance and misunderstanding for China's capitulation. The Manchu military structure had been designed to control the Chinese people, not to resist invasion from the sea.

The New Treaty Ports

The laboratory in which the new treaties were to be tried consisted of the five treaty ports: Canton, Amoy, Foochow, Ningpo, and Shanghai. In all these ports save Canton, the foreigner was a stranger, and to the vast population in the interior he was all but unknown. China and the Powers were entering upon a very unpredictable experiment. In the first years, 1843–1845, the way was paved for initial application of the Treaties by Ch'i-ying's policy of appeasement toward Pottinger. Thereafter, 1845–1853, there was to follow a progressive breakdown of the Treaty system. This was to lead in 1854 to the creation of the Foreign Inspectorate of Customs at Shanghai, one of the most significant developments in the evolving Sino-Western system of the nineteenth century.

Only two of the first treaty ports were destined to develop as great centers of the foreign trade—Shanghai and Canton. For a few years, commerce, particularly in black tea and in contract coolie labor to Cuba, flourished at Amoy. Trade at Foochow was negligible. Until the middle of 1844 not a foreign ship had entered its harbor. As a port Foochow suffered because its harbor

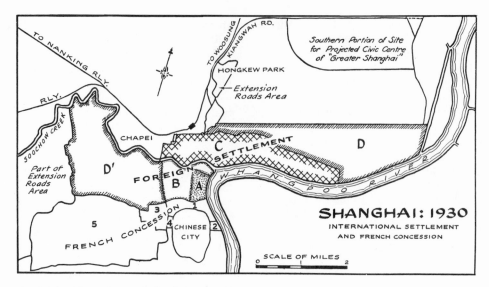

A. *Original boundaries of the foreign settlement.*
B. *Extension of the settlement boundaries, 1848.*
C. *The "American Settlement," 1863; incorporated with the foreign settlement the same year.*
D. *Further extension of the settlement, 1899.*
D' *Extension of 1899. (1) Original French concession, 1849; (2) Extended, 1861; (3) Extended, 1900; (4) Extended 1900; (5) Extended, 1914; The projected civic center of Shanghi was a project of the municipal government of the Chinese city.*

was poor, its population, under official encouragement, was anti-foreign, and its location was too close to Amoy. In the same way Ningpo was too close to Shanghai. Ningpo's later fame was due to missionary rather than commercial enterprise.

Shanghai was opened to foreign trade in November 1843. Situated on the Whangpoo River about twelve miles from where it joins the Yangtze at Woosung, and having a native population of some 270,000, it was already an important center of China's inland and coastal trade. Here traders were no longer hampered by such monopolistic agencies as the Co-hong. There was business and opportunity for all. In 1844, forty-four foreign ships of a total tonnage of more than 8,000 entered Shanghai. Eight years later the number of ships was 182, with a total tonnage of 78,000. Shanghai exports were valued in 1846 at $7,000,000; in 1853 at $23,000,000. By 1852 Shanghai accounted for more than half of China's export trade. Many factors contributed to this rapid growth. The city bordered

the great silk-producing areas; its situation at the mouth of the Yangtze was ideal for both the import and the export trade; and its inhabitants were free from the unhappy memories and the violent anti-foreignism so pronounced at Canton.

The Shanghai International Settlement

The treaty status under which foreign merchants lived at the new ports was a peculiar, not to say unique, system. At Canton and at many of the ports opened subsequently, the treaty powers obtained from China—that is, from the emperor—grants of land known as "concessions," where the traders could erect commercial structures and residences. The concession was leased by China to the foreign power concerned; the power subdivided the land into lots, granting these on long-term leases to its subjects and in some cases to other foreigners. Sometimes, as later at Tientsin, there were at one time in one open port as many as eight separate foreign "concessions." The foreign community of each concession provided, under authority of its home government, its own municipal government for the concession. Over this municipal government the consul of the given power presided. Thus at a treaty port there came to exist, in contiguous concession areas, a number of separate municipal governments, each exercising independent authority.

Shanghai met the problem in its own way. Since the local Chinese authorities there objected to the concession system, the first British consul accepted a plan whereby the Chinese authorities set apart an area of land on the river bank in which British subjects might acquire lots from Chinese owners. A British purchaser, having reached an agreement with a Chinese owner, reported it to the British consul, who in turn reported it to the Chinese local authority, the *tao-t'ai*. This latter functionary then issued to the British subject, through his consul, a title in the form of a perpetual lease, under which the foreign buyer paid a nominal annual rent to the Chinese government, the theory being that all land belonged to the emperor and could not be alienated by outright sale.[18]

The Shanghai "settlement," as this area and its peculiar system came to be known, was at first restricted to British control. Foreigners of non-British nationality secured land therein through the consent of the British consul. This proved particularly objectionable to Americans, and so in time the right of all foreigners to lease land within the settlement and to register such land at their own consulates was recognized. In this manner a system developed whereby each consul exercised jurisdiction over his own nationals in the common settlement area, and at the same time participated with his fellow consuls in supervision of settlement affairs.[19]

When the Shanghai settlement was first established, it was supposed that the area

[18] *Report of the Hon. Mr. Justice Feetham to the Shanghai Municipal Council* (4 vols., Shanghai, 1931–32), I, 27.

[19] For a brief period, separate American and French settlements existed at Shanghai, but in 1863 the American was merged with the British, forming the basis of what was to be known as the International Settlement. The French area continued to remain separate and came to be

would be inhabited exclusively by foreigners, and for some eight years this was so. In 1853 there were only 500 Chinese residents, most of whom were servants or shopkeepers supplying the needs of the 200-odd foreign residents. In this same year, however, Chinese authority in areas adjacent to the settlement having broken down completely as a result of rebellions and civil war, the foreign area was soon swarming with homeless and often destitute Chinese refugees. By 1854 the Chinese population of the settlement exceeded 20,000. In this manner the whole character of the settlement was changed, and it became imperative that this unorganized community, consisting of groups of foreigners belonging to different nations, each group living under its own national laws and subject to the jurisdiction of its own consul, should provide itself with effective municipal authority for both internal administration and protection against the rebellions on its borders. To accomplish this the foreign settlement community had to acquire some degree of unity under a municipal constitution having the approval of the consular authorities. Such a constitution was adopted by the foreign merchants (known as the "renters" of settlement land) in 1854. Under this instrument adequate governing powers over the Shanghai Settlement were placed in the hands of an elected and exclusively foreign municipal council. Here then was a situation unforeseen at the time the first treaty settlement was made (1842–1844).

Foreign Relations at Canton

While the new foreign trade at Shanghai grew rapidly under generally amicable conditions, its corresponding growth at Canton was marked by friction, mob violence, and open armed conflict. To understand this contrast, one should recall that at Canton the foreign traders and some Chinese had long been in contact and in many cases had made fortunes, but also at Canton had arisen the grievances, real and imaginary, and the hatreds that had finally produced war. At Canton the foreigner had been subjected to

known as the "French concession," though the term is not strictly accurate.

"insults" from the populace and high-handed Chinese officials. At Canton these same officials had bowed outwardly at least before the power of British guns. Now that the war had been won, the British proposed to assert their newly won privileges of equality. But the Chinese populace and many of the officials were by no means prepared to concede all this. The issue was soon drawn. No sooner had the city been officially opened in its new status as a treaty port (1843) than the intensity of its anti-foreignism became apparent. The mere presence of Caleb Cushing in South China and his threat to proceed to Peking called forth a popular manifesto from Canton: "Ye men of America may truly dread local extermination." Foreigners were not permitted access to the walled city, and Governor Davis of Hong Kong regarded this "degrading" exclusion as a factor "provoking the insolence of the people." The treaties, to be sure, did not explicitly provide for entrance into the city, but the British claimed that denial of the privilege violated the spirit of the treaties and indicated the resolve of both officials and populace to preserve the old exclusive superiority. Because of this intensity of feeling, it was agreed in 1846 to postpone the "opening" of the city. The temper of the populace, however, did not improve. Foreigners, including Englishmen and an American, were stoned in a nearby village in 1847; a British fleet attacked the Bogue Forts and blockaded the river; the viceroy thereupon agreed to open the city in April, 1849, but this settlement was not approved by the emperor. Peking in fact was torn between the demands of the foreigners and those of its own people. Until 1848, Ch'i-ying at Canton at least attempted to keep the people within the strict limits of the treaties, but his successors, Hsu Kwang-chin and Yeh Ming-ch'en, as will be seen, encouraged antiforeignism and thus contributed to a second war, which was already in the making.[20]

In summary it may be said that the First Treaty Settlement was merely the beginning, not the consummation, of a new order between China and the West. By 1852 it had become merely a matter of time until Britain (this time aided by France) would demand the enforcement of the treaties and the addition of new and greater commercial privileges. This result was the more certain because Chinese leadership had neither the power nor the will to concede fully what had already been granted. There were at this time three factors in the Chinese intellectual tradition shaping her resistance to the Western impact: (1) the beginnings of a nationalistic ideology created by Chinese scholars who had long resented the alien Manchu dynasty; (2) the existence of a well-established anti-Western political tradition, in part the product of Jesuit efforts in the seventeenth and eighteenth centuries to plant Western technology and religious philosophy in Chinese soil; and (3) the determination of the Manchu court to apply to the Western barbarians, as it always had applied to the barbarians of inner Asia, the Chinese theory of the Middle Kingdom as the universal empire to which all outsiders were to come as inferiors and bearers of tribute. Thus China's initial response to the modern West was one of complete intellectual resistance.[21]

These intellectual limitations which conditioned China's response to the West in the mid-nineteenth century revealed themselves in the opinions commonly held by the scholar-officials. In the Chinese documents of the time the conventional phrases applied to Britishers, Frenchmen, and Americans were vigorous and colorful. The barbarians were inherently cunning and malicious, impatient and with no understanding of values, insatiable and avaricious, self-seekers with the feelings of dogs and sheep, fickle and inconstant, and perverse in words. If there was any fine distinction to be drawn concerning the Americans, it was that they were weak and might therefore be used in turning one barbarian against another. As for America itself, the best that was known by the scholar-officials was that it was "maritime, uncultivated, and primitive."[22]

[20] T. F. Tsiang, "New Light on Chinese Diplomacy 1836–49," *The Journal of Modern History* 3 (1931): 590–91.

[21] Teng Ssu-yu and John K. Fairbank, *China's Response to the West* (1954),* 6–21.

[22] Swisher, *China's Management of the American Barbarians*, 44–48.

Li Chien-nung, *The Political History of China, 1840–1928*, ed. and trans. by Teng Ssu-yu and Jeremy Ingals (1956; New Delhi, 1963) ° contains valuable chapters on the mid-nineteenth century. Alfred K. L. Ho, "The Grand Council in The Ch'ing Dynasty," *Far Eastern Quarterly* 11 (February, 1952): 167–82. Foster Rhea Dulles, *China and America, the Story of Their Relations Since 1784* (1946), a useful general survey. Nathan A. Pelcovits, *Old China Hands and the Foreign Office* (1948) presents the thesis that the British government resisted efforts of its merchants to make the Middle Kingdom another India. Wu Wen-tsao, *The Chinese Opium Question in British Opinion and Action* (1928). George C. Allen and Audrey G. Donnithorne, *Western Enterprise in Far Eastern Economic Development: China and Japan* (1954) describes methods and policies pursued by Western firms. George Lanning and Samuel Couling, *The History of Shanghai* (2 vols., Shanghai, 1921–1923). Hallett Abend, *Treaty Ports* (1944), a popular treatment. Arthur H. Clark, *The Clipper Ship Era. An Epitome of Famous American and British Clipper Ships, Their Owners, Builders, Commanders, and Crews, 1843–1869* (1910). Gideon Ch'en, *Lin Tse-hsu, Pioneer Promoter of the Adoption of Western Means of Maritime Defense in China* (Peiping, 1934),° a valuable study of this Chinese official whose actions precipitated the First Anglo-Chinese War. Maurice Collis, *Foreign Mud* (1947), a popular account of the opium dispute at Canton and of the Anglo-Chinese war that followed. Teng Ssu-yu, *Chang Hsi and the Treaty of Nanking, 1842* (1944) presents an annotated translation of a Chinese diary kept during the First Anglo-Chinese War. E. J. Eitel, *Europe in China. The History of Hong Kong from the Beginning to the Year 1882* (London, 1895).

China, 1848–1860:
The New Sino-Western
Order in East Asia

chapter 7

The First Sino-Western treaties formed the beginnings of a new order for East Asia. These agreements called for treaty relations based on a theory of the equality of states to replace the Confucian theory of relations between people that were unequal. A victory of British arms had ordained a new order to regulate the meeting and the mingling of Western states with China's Confucian society. The creation of treaty ports, the arrival of consuls, the appearance of concessions and settlements, the application of the new treaty tariff and of extraterritoriality gave tangible evidence that an old order was passing and that a new one was appearing. These obvious changes from the procedures of pre-treaty days are easily stated, but the statement itself cannot present an adequate picture of the conflict in manners and values between Confucian China and an equality-minded West. Britain had won a war, but the settlement she had imposed was to operate in an alien environment where the Western barbarian, asserting his equality and thereby assuming the role of reformer, was not welcome. He was feared because of his military power, but he was not respected for his appreciation of values. Thus the opening

of the ports, the arrival of the first consuls and merchants, and the setting apart of concessions were merely the preliminary steps in the application of a new order the future of which was as yet unpredictable. Would this order, even if China observed the treaties, satisfy the commercial ambitions of the Westerners? How far and how rapidly could the Manchu government go toward enforcing a treaty system so repugnant to traditional Confucian concepts of foreign relations and trade? Answers to these and related questions form the basic history of the turbulent years in Sino-Western relations from 1848 to 1860. The outcome, as will be seen, was a compromise, acceptable but not satisfactory to either side.

The crisis confronting the Manchu Empire in the decade 1850 to 1860 was perhaps no less acute than that faced by Commissioner Lin at Canton in 1840. Great Britain had won the first war but there was some doubt as to who was winning the peace. By 1850 most of the foreigners in the five ports regarded the first treaty settlements as inadequate if not a complete failure. The major question was whether this settlement could be revised by diplomacy or would require resort to arms. This problem was ultimately resolved by conditions of political disintegration within China: conditions that, in a sense, deprived the Manchu government of both the will and the power either to enforce or repudiate the treaties and their broad implications. The days of the great K'ang-hsi emperor (1662–1722) and the Ch'ien-lung emperor (1736–1796) were long since past. China was devoid of great leadership.

Thus continuing conflict between China and the West was nurtured from three principal sources: (1) the decline of Manchu power, hastened by the T'ai-p'ing and other rebellions; (2) the incapacity of the official heirarchy to adjust itself to the new order of foreign intercourse with its broad social and economic implications; and (3) the growing co-operation and strength of the treaty powers in their quest for wider and more stable commercial relations with The Middle Kingdom.

THE T'AI-P'ING REBELLION

Rebellion is an old institution in China, sanctioned by Confucian philosophy and essential in the theory of the Mandate of Heaven. When a dynasty, for whatever reason, lost its ability to rule, it was obvious that Heaven had withdrawn the mandate. The duty of the subject to rebel was then clear. This ancient theory was to enjoy wide application in nineteenth-century China. In the two decades preceding the first British war, revolts had occurred with alarming frequency in Kwangsi, Shansi, Kweichow, Kiangsi, Hainan, Hupeh, and Formosa. By mid-century there were four rebellions of major proportions: Moslem rebellions in Yunnan (1855–73) and the Northwest (1862–73), the Nien rebellion (1853–68), and the T'ai-p'ing rebellion (1851–64). Of these upheavals the most serious by far was the T'ai-p'ing rebellion.

No single evil created all this disorder. China suffered from dynastic decline, official corruption, overtaxation, excessive land rents, and official discrimination against minority groups. Compounding these troubles was a population that had increased out of proportion to land under cultivation (in 1850 Chinese had reached 430 million, a 200 per

cent increase during Ch'ing rule, while arable land during the same period had expanded only 35 per cent). As a result of these circumstances and of economic dislocations created by growing foreign trade, the peasant was degraded to virtual serfdom. Thus a permanent, floating "population of paupers" provided the raw materials for rebellion.[1]

In these circumstances there appeared one Hung Hsiu-ch'üan, a native of Hua-hsien near Canton, the youngest and brightest son of a farm family. Young Hung passed the local examinations, but failed repeatedly in the provincial tests. To his background of disappointment and failure were added illness, visions, and some contacts with the Reverend Issachar Roberts, an American Baptist missionary at Canton. With the mental and spiritual equipment thus provided, Hung came to believe that he was commissioned to restore the worship of the true god. His original organization, the *Pai Shang-ti Hui* (Association of God Worshippers), soon recruited an enormous following from disaffected elements in Kwangsi. At first the movement appeared religious and iconoclastic, and, superficially at least, seemed to bear some resemblance to Protestantism. As the movement grew, its devastating armies moved north to the Yangtze and captured

[1] G. E. Taylor, "The Taiping Rebellion: Its Economic Background and Social Theory," *Chinese Soc. and Pol. Science Rev.* 16 (1933): 545–49. On the contemporary Nien Rebellion see Chiang Siang-tsch, *The Nien Rebellion* (1954) and Teng Ssu-yu, *The Nien Army and Their Guerrilla Warfare* (The Hague, 1961).° Note also Wen-Djang Chu, *The Moslem Rebellion in Northwest China 1862–1878* (The Hague, 1966). The Moslem rising spread from Shensi to Sinkiang covering almost one-fourth of China's territory. Like the T'ai-p'ing, the Moslem rebellion accounted for unknown millions of deaths. For conditions nurturing rebellion in south China on the eve of the T'ai-p'ing rebellion, Frederic Wakeman, Jr., *Strangers at the Gate* (1966). For still other indications of China's rebellious spirit see Nancy J. F. Evans, "Social Criticism in the Ch'ing: The Novel *Ching-hua yuan,*" and Maureen F. Dillon, "The Triads in Shanghai: The Small Sword Society Uprising, 1853–1855," *Papers on China.* Vol. 23. (Published and distributed by the East Asia Research Center, Harvard University, 1970), 52–66 and 67–86.

Nanking, where its capital was established in 1853. Meanwhile Hung had bestowed upon himself the title, *T'ien-wang* (Heavenly King), professed to rule over the *T'ai-p'ing T'ien-kuo* (The Heavenly Kingdom of Great Peace), and had set for his purpose the overthrow of the Manchu dynasty. In this new theocracy God was the Heavenly Father; Christ, the Divine Elder Brother; and the *T'ai-P'ing Wang* (Hung, himself) the Divine Younger Brother. The Christian factor in the movement was, in the main, the first five books of the Old Testament. Such was the notable achievement of this "soured and disappointed member of the learned proletariat."

SHANGHAI AND THE YANGTZE

THE REBELLION AND
THE FOREIGN POWERS

During the winter of 1853–1854, Hung and his rebels advanced to the north and reached the outskirts of Tientsin, but did not continue on to Peking. For another decade they dominated the Yangtze Valley in defiance of Manchu authority. A rebellion so widespread and promoting a government that threatened to rival, if not overthrow, the Manchus could not but attract the attention of the foreign powers. If the T'ai-p'ing were Christians, would they not be more amenable than the Manchus to foreign treaty relations, to the commercial, social, and political concepts of the Westerners? [2] The powers rea-

[2] Since in the later years of the T'ai-p'ing rebellion the foreign powers gave some support to the Manchu campaign of suppressing the rebels, it should be remarked that in the early stages of the revolt, the T'ai-p'ings do not appear to have been anti-foreign. British, French, and American contacts with the T'ai-p'ings in 1853–54 were, in the main, cordial. Because of their principles of human brotherhood, and their realistic appraisal of Western power, the rebels tended to invite Western support. Hung Jen-k'an, a cousin of the rebel leader and T'ai-p'ing foreign minister, was an advocate of the adoption of Western institutions. The Western powers, however, were half-hearted in such explorations. Note Teng Yuan Chung, "The Failure of Hung Jen-k'an's Foreign Policy," *Journal of Asian Studies* 28 (1968): 125–38; and Stephen Uhalley, Jr., "A New Look at the Diplomatic

lized the importance of defining their relation to the rebels in 1853, when the Chinese walled city of Shanghai, on the very border of the foreign settlements, was captured by a rebel band known as the "Small Swords." Civil war had thus reached the edge of the settlements, and retreating imperial authorities deserted the Shanghai customs house. This raised the question of whether Shanghai had become a free port, since the Chinese government was no longer capable of collecting the duties. British and American consular authorities notified their nationals that the consuls themselves would collect the duties during the absence of imperial authorities. The British consul required his merchants to deposit promissory notes, which in fact were never paid, while the Americans were at the disadvantage of having to pay in specie. Merchants who had no consular representative enjoyed favorable discrimination and paid nothing. British policy stipulated too that the Shanghai settlement was to remain neutral in the civil strife that surrounded it, but in reality foreign merchants constantly gave aid to the rebels in the sale of supplies. Many ships entered and cleared the port without the payment of duties. It was in these circumstances of confusion, discrimination, and uncertainty that the rate-payers of the settlement established their own Municipal Council.

Missions of 1853–54 to T'ai-p'ing-Held Nanking," *Chung Chi Journal* 6 (1967): 171–90. The ultimate collapse of the rebellion is discussed in Chapter 12 in its chronological context.

THE FOREIGN INSPECTORATE OF CUSTOMS

Also from this crisis, which in Shanghai had temporarily destroyed the power of the Peking government and threatened likewise the whole treaty structure built by the foreigners, there emerged a remarkable institution—the Foreign Inspectorate of Customs. By agreement between the *tao-t'ai* and the consuls of the three treaty powers, England, the United States, and France (June 29, 1854), provision was made for appointment of a board of foreign inspectors, for the creation of an adequate customs machinery, and for regulations that should define the relation of the Inspectorate to the *tao-t'ai*, the consuls, and the commercial public. At first the appointing power was given to the consuls, and it was the purpose of the British consul that the British should control the new Inspectorate, but within a year the British Foreign Office had ruled that the foreign inspectors were officials of China and not the nominees and delegates of foreign countries. Thus was formed the nucleus of a new Chinese customs administration, directed by foreign inspectors, which, in 1858, was extended to all the treaty ports, where it became a model of efficient government.[3]

Throughout these early years of the T'ai-p'ing revolt, the efforts of the major treaty powers to determine what policy they should follow relative to the T'ai-p'ings were hampered by the various attitudes toward the rebellion assumed by segments of public opinion in Europe and in America. In the United States, where "Manifest Destiny" had become the slogan of the decade, journalists

and other writers found evidence of a divine plan in the opening of China to Western trade, and the subsequent rebellion of the T'ai-p'ings was God's instrument, destined to overthrow the Manchu dynasty and to hasten the advent of a Chinese Christian republic. Once the T'ai-p'ings had prepared the way, it was said, China would progress to republicanism and Christianity aided by the educational forces of commercial intercourse and Christian missions. Few people evaluated or questioned the evidence on which these comforting predictions were based. It was enough that the predictions were in accord with what many Americans wanted to believe.

THE OBLIGATIONS OF EXTRATERRITORIALITY

It should also be noted that the growing crisis in the treaty system was not due solely to Chinese obstructionism and political decline. The Western governments were at times negligent in their obligations toward China. The application of extraterritoriality was a case in point. In acquiring extraterritorial jurisdiction over their nationals in China, the treaty powers had won a legal right of the greatest consequence. The practice of extraterritoriality carried with it grave responsibilities which, for many years, most of the powers treated with shameful disregard. At first only the British recognized and sought to meet their extraterritorial obligations.

Since under the extraterritorial grants China had surrendered the power of her own courts over foreigners, it became the duty of the treaty powers to provide competent consular courts in the treaty ports, and jails where criminals might be incarcerated. Prior to 1857, Great Britain alone took adequate steps to meet this need. A British criminal court, provided for in 1833, functioned at Canton after 1839. By act of Parliament (1843) British legal jurisdiction was authorized on foreign soil, as a result of which machinery was provided for the administration of extraterritoriality in China, including provision for jails. In contrast, American

[3] For detailed studies of the customs problem at Shanghai in this period, see J. K. Fairbank, "The Provisional System at Shanghai," *Chinese Soc. and Pol. Science Rev.* 18 (1934–35): 455–504, and 19 (1935–36): 65–124; "The Creation of the Foreign Inspectorate of Customs at Shanghai," *ibid.* 19 (1935–36): 469–514, and 20 (1936–37): 42–100; "The Definition of the Foreign Inspector's Status (1854–55): A Chapter in the Early History of the Inspectorate of Customs at Shanghai," *Nankai Social and Economic Quarterly* 9 (1936): 125–63; and *Trade and Diplomacy on the China Coast*, 371–461.

criminals in the China ports could be confined only on a national ship, or, as frequently happened, by courtesy in a British jail. In 1858 American criminals were released from the British jail in Shanghai because the American consul had no funds for jail expenses. Two years later the United States provided its first appropriation for consular jails in China.[4]

THE GROWTH OF THE OPIUM TRADE

Since 1842 the opium trade had continued to grow and to prosper. Although opium had provided the occasion for the first Sino-British war, the subsequent treaties had evaded the problem of control. Thus, although the importation of opium was still prohibited by the laws of China, foreigners and Chinese conspired to flood the market with this contraband and demoralizing drug.[5] It has been estimated that between 1840 and 1858 the annual imports increased almost 300 per cent. The effects upon the Chinese were devastating, but so long as the Chinese government would not or could not enforce its law, there was little hope that the foreigners would forego a trade so profitable.

DEMANDS FOR TREATY REVISION

By 1854, despite the growth of profitable trade at Shanghai and Canton, it was evident that the relations of China and the treaty powers were far from healthy. The abuses of extraterritoriality, a flagrant traffic in coolies to servitude in Cuba, the opium trade, and the gun-boat policy, (whereby one did the shooting first and the talking afterwards) at Canton, all served to reinforce the official

[4] For an extended treatment, see G. W. Keeton, *The Development of Extraterritoriality in China* (2 vols., London, 1928).

[5] *The Times* correspondent reported, 1857: "At present the [opium] trade is as open and as unrestrained in all the cities of China as the sale of hot-cross buns on Good Friday is in the streets of London." George Wingrove Cooke, *China: Being The Times Special Correspondence from China in the Years 1857–58* (1858), 179.

Chinese view that the foreign barbarians were an uncouth and troublesome lot with whom China should have as few dealings as possible. On his part, the foreigner, both merchant and consul, was convinced that China had no respect for treaties and no understanding of the benefits of free commerce and free access to markets. The foreigners now regarded the treaties of 1842–1844 as inadequate not only because China had frequently evaded them but also because these treaties confined foreign trade to the five ports. The foreign trader was still a stranger to China's vast interior; the foreign diplomat was still a stranger to Peking. Both the American and the French treaties of 1844 provided for revision after twelve years, and the British claimed this same privilege on the basis of most-favored-nation treatment. Under this claim the British held that the Treaty of Nanking would be subject to revision in 1854.

The scope of Britain's policy of treaty revision had been determined by February, 1854. The British government would insist on China's recognition of the *right* of immediate revision, but the actual revision might be delayed in view of China's domestic strife due to the T'ai-p'ing rebellion. Meanwhile, the British would seek co-operation with the Americans and the French, whose treaties would also soon be subject to revision. Britain would also seek "access generally to the whole interior of the Chinese Empire as well as to the cities on the coast: or failing this, . . . free navigation of the Yangtze Kiang and access to the cities on its banks up to Nanking . . ." Britain also wanted legalization of the opium trade, in order that it might be limited and controlled, and abolition of internal transit duties on goods imported or purchased for export. Finally, the British government desired "the permanent and honourable residence at the Court of Peking of a Representative of the British Crown" or provision for direct and unobstructed correspondence with that government These official British objectives also represented approximately those general principles beginning to appear in French and American policy.

The British desire to be represented diplomatically at Peking indicated, among other things, that they were no longer willing to tolerate the Chinese system whereby the Canton viceroy was entrusted by Peking with the actual conduct of foreign affairs. With this official alone the foreigners were expected to deal, and their experience had not recommended the system. In 1848 John W. Davis, the American commissioner, after great difficulty secured an interview with the viceroy for the purpose of presenting his credentials. He was treated "with extreme rudeness" by both viceroy and governor. In fact, after 1852 "the practice of ignoring the foreign representatives became a part of the settled policy of the Chinese government." [6] A French diplomat remained at Macao fifteen months vainly awaiting a personal interview with a qualified Chinese official. Of the various sucessors of Davis in the period to 1855, none succeeded in securing an interview. The high commissioner was always "too busy," and in any event would have to await the dawn of "an auspicious day." Two American commissioners, Humphrey Marshall and Robert McLane, went to Nanking hoping to make direct contact with responsible officials, only to be referred back to Canton. Thus in 1854 the foreign traders and most of their consular and diplomatic associates were of a mind not only to extend their commercial rights but also to convert China, forcibly if necessary, to Western concepts of international law and diplomacy.

England's plan for treaty revision did not imply an immediate resort to war. There was to be no precipitate action. Actually the British government hoped for a cooperative policy with France and the United States. Among American merchants in the treaty ports there was general support for Britain's policy of treaty revision. This was natural because the interests of British and American traders were in many respects identical. Some support for British policy was contained, too, in the dispatches of various American commissioners in China.

In view then of the general harmony between British and American expressions of policy, England's proposals to the United States (March, 1857) for a three-power alliance (the United States, France, and Great Britain) to effect revision of the treaties were not surprising. These proposals were declined, yet the dangers threatening American interests in China did prompt the appointment of William B. Reed as envoy extraordinary and minister plenipotentiary to the court of Peking.

By the early autumn of 1856, with the crisis of the Crimean War already past, Great Britain had determined on a diplomatic and naval move toward Peking to hasten revision of the treaties, to expand commercial intercourse, and to destroy the exclusiveness of Chinese policy at Canton.

A SO-CALLED JUDICIAL MURDER

In this forward policy Britain could count on the support of France, for in February, 1856, a French Catholic missionary, Auguste Chapdelaine, had been put to death by Chinese authorities at Sinlin in Kwangsi. Chapdelaine and some of his converts had been arrested on a charge that they were rebels—a natural enough charge, for Kwangsi had witnessed the beginnings of the T'ai-p'ing rebellion with its frosting of Christian flavor. The arrest, torture, and execution of the foreign priest and his followers are thus understandable according to Chinese ideas of the time. The Chinese magistrate could likewise rest his case on the fact that under the treaties no foreigners were allowed beyond the treaty ports. Furthermore, the testimony of Catholic missionaries themselves reveals that they indoctrinated their Chinese converts with the idea of looking to "France as their support and liberator" against persecution. [7] China's fault lay in the fact that the execution of the priest violated the extraterritorial rights of France.

News of this so-called "judicial murder"

[6] H. B. Morse, *The International Relations of the Chinese Empire* (3 vols., London, 1910–1918), I, 411.

[7] *Missions Etrangères* (Paris), Vol. DL. Quoted by W. C. Costin, *Great Britain and China* (Oxford, 1937), 202.

reached Canton in July, 1856. It was not unwelcome to Napoleon III. France was now in a position not only to assist Great Britain in forcing, if need be, a revision of the treaties, but also to aid the Catholic Church by political means in the spiritual conquest of China. By October, 1856, France and England were able to agree upon a common policy of force.

THE AFFAIR OF THE LORCHA ARROW

The incident that was to precipitate hostilities between Great Britain and China found its origin in a system by which Chinese coasting vessels acquired temporary register under foreign flags. During the years 1853–1854 southern Chinese rebels held positions so strong in the regions of Canton and Kowloon that communications between Whampoa (the Canton anchorage) and Hong Kong were frequently broken so far as the passage of Chinese vessels was concerned. Even Commissioner Yeh asked help from the despised foreigners. In 1855 English and American authorities, in order to maintain trade between Hong Kong and Canton, believed it was necessary to grant "English and United States flags with a passport to Chinese lighters for a single trip to and from Canton and Whampoa to be immediately returned and filed at the consulates by which they were issued." Out of this situation arose various ordinances of the colonial government of Hong Kong permitting residents of the colony, including Chinese, under prescribed conditions, to use the British flag on their vessels for this limited purpose. In time this right by ordinance was abused. Some vessels used the protection of the British flag to engage in the smuggling trade; others carried the flags of various foreign powers with no authority whatsoever for doing so; sometimes merchant consuls, without authority from their governments, issued foreign registry to native craft. As a result it was soon difficult for Chinese authorities to distinguish between the legitimate and the illegitimate use of foreign flags by native craft.

The lorcha *Arrow*, owned by a Chinese

The Approach to Peking

who had resided in Hong Kong for ten years, and commanded by a British subject, was boarded by Chinese police on October 8, 1856, while it was lying at anchor in the river at Canton. Twelve of her Chinese crew of fourteen were arrested on charges of piracy and removed to a Chinese war-junk. Harry Parkes, British consul at Canton, promptly demanded release of the captives on the ground that the *Arrow* was a British ship carrying colonial registry from Hong Kong, that she had been boarded without communication first having been made to the British consul, and that the British flag had been hauled down by the Chinese police. British authority at Hong Kong supported Parkes by demanding an apology and guarantees for the future.[8] The prisoners were eventually handed over by Yeh, but Consul Parkes refused to accept this release, since the captives were accompanied neither by a Chinese officer of rank nor by an apology.

British naval forces attacked the forts guarding the approach to Canton. On October 29, the walls of the city were breached, but though the British could attack the city, they had insufficient forces to occupy it. In the heat of these proceedings the American flag too was fired upon by Chinese forts—a

[8] The British registry on the *Arrow* had expired before the seizure. Chinese authorities disputed Parkes' allegation that the British flag had been lowered.

fire that was returned by American ships of war. Trade was now at an end, yet Commissioner Yeh refused all concessions.

In England, the British action was approved despite vigorous criticism from the opposition, and now that France was prepared for full co-operation in treaty revision, the British government appointed Lord Elgin to head a special embassy. Elgin's mission was not merely to solve local grievances at Canton or elsewhere. He was to extend the opportunities for foreign trade and to establish diplomatic representation at Peking. In other words, he was to revise the treaties thoroughly.

War was now certain. The "murder" of the French priest and the affair of the *Arrow* were the convenient pretexts for armed action, the real causes of which were far more fundamental than these incidents. China's obstructive policy was regarded by Britain as a menace both to her actual and to her potential commercial interests, while the conduct of Chinese officials—that of Yeh in particular—was looked upon as an insult to the Crown. Napoleon III was happy to be associated with the British policy. A victorious war in China would appeal to French business, and, by avenging the death of a priest and providing religious guarantees for the future, would not be unwelcome to French Catholics or to the Papacy.

After much delay due to diversion of British contingents to suppress the Indian Mutiny, British and French forces bombarded and captured Canton in December, 1857. British marines seized the venerable but proud and obstinate High Commissioner Yeh as this portly gentleman sought to escape over the back wall of his yamen. Fifteen months later he died, a prisoner of war, in India. Until 1860, Canton was ruled by Chinese officials acting at the command of a British and French commission.

Britain and France, on February 11, 1858, were joined by the representatives of the United States and Russia, William B. Reed and Count Putiatin, in simultaneous notes to Peking making clear the united demand of the powers for treaty revision and religious toleration, and suggesting negotia-

tions at Shanghai. To the Chinese demand that negotiations be conducted at Canton, the representatives of the powers replied by sailing north to the mouth of the Pei-ho, at the very gateway to Peking. Alarmed by this maneuver, the Chinese court appointed the viceroy of Chihli to negotiate, but his powers were regarded by Lord Elgin and Baron Gros (France) as inadequate. They believed that only an advance to Tientsin would bring the Chinese to terms. To this end they demanded the surrender of the Taku forts guarding the mouth of the river; and when this was refused, the forts were stormed and taken (May 20). Peking thereupon promptly appointed officials whose powers were regarded as adequate. Negotiations leading to new treaties were now conducted with all four powers, concurrently but separately. Before the end of June, 1858, the four treaties of Tientsin had been signed.[9]

THE TREATIES OF TIENTSIN, 1858

The treaties of Tientsin were a revision and an enlargement of principles and practices set forth in the first treaties of 1842–1844. Since England and France had employed force, it was their treaties that embodied the new and valuable concessions, which, however, by reason of the most-fav-

[9] An excellent study of contemporary British records is Douglas Hurd, *The Arrow War: An Anglo-Chinese Confusion* (1967). When seen in historical perspective, the affair of the lorcha *Arrow* was a weak excuse for a war. Sir John Bowring, the Governor of Hong Kong, was flexible in his treatment of the Chinese but inflexible toward their government. In the *Arrow* case "he provoked hostilities by magnifying a comparatively trivial incident. . . ." G. B. Endacott, *Government and People in Hong Kong 1841–1962* (Hong Kong, 1964), 56. An indispensable reference on China's relations with her neighbors and the Western powers (1858–1880) is Immanuel C. Y. Hsü, *China's Entrance into the Family of Nations* (1960). It has been stated with some justification that "it became ingloriously, yet very profitably, the role of the United States pacifically to follow England to China in the wake of war, and to profit greatly by the victories of British arms." Tyler Dennett, *Americans in Eastern Asia* (1922), 159.

ored-nation clause would be enjoyed likewise by Russia and the United States. In this sense the four treaties constituted a single settlement having a profound influence upon China's relations with the West.

The new and significant privileges won by the treaty powers in the Tientsin Treaties included:

1. The right to maintain a resident minister at Peking, or the right of the minister, at the discretion of the British government, to visit the capital. The British minister should "not be called upon to perform any ceremony derogatory to him as representing the sovereign of an independent nation on a footing of equality with that of China."
2. The right of travel in all parts of the interior under passports issued by the foreign consuls and countersigned by the local Chinese authorities.
3. The right of foreign ships to trade on the Yangtze River, and the opening of additional treaty ports.[10]
4. The right of missionaries to protection by the Chinese authorities, since "the Christian religion, as professed by Protestants or Roman Catholics, inculcates the practice of virtue, and teaches man to do as he would be done by." [11]

The Tientsin Treaties represented a common policy on the part of the four powers, for although England and France alone had used force, the United States and Russia insisted on most-favored-nation treatment. The most striking concession was the right of residence of foreign ministers at Peking, or at least the right of these ministers to visit the capital. The delay and evasion that China had constantly practiced in dealing with for-

eign governments would now be more difficult.

The grant of toleration to Christians, missionaries, and their Chinese converts has been a subject of much controversy. To toleration in principle there could be no objection, but in 1858 toleration was won as a result of war and was granted in the clause of a treaty exacted as a result of war. The missionaries were already well aware that many elements in Christian doctrine had proved disruptive of China's cultural heritage; yet, since the object of the missionaries was to make this heritage subservient to Christianity, they welcomed the new treaty status for themselves and for their religion. As a consequence after 1858 many Chinese felt quite justified in regarding Christianity as a political as well as a religious weapon of the West.

The right of foreigners to travel in the interior was another concession on which interpretation has differed widely. The traders of 1858 had complained bitterly of the restrictions that confined them to the treaty ports. They were businessmen intent on profits, and these same profits, they felt, would depend in turn on freedom of access to the entire country. Against this point of view the Chinese could argue that the people were not yet ready to receive foreigners beyond the port towns, and that because the foreigner enjoyed extraterritoriality and would when in the interior be far removed from his nearest consul, China could exercise over him only an ineffective control.

Since the powers were now bent on expanding their commerce with China, the opening of additional treaty ports (nine in China and one in Formosa) could not long be delayed. Nevertheless, the opening of the additional ports did occasion trouble, and in the case of Nanking the port was not opened until 1899. In addition, the admission of foreign vessels to the trade of the Yangtze could not be easily defended. It was the great artery to the richest areas of China. The fact that the foreigners could demand and be granted access to China's coasting and inland trade is the most eloquent testimony to the decay of the Manchu dynasty.

---

[10] To the five ports opened by the treaty of 1842 were added Chefoo in Shantung, Chinkiang in Kiangsu, Hankow in Hupeh, Kiukiang in Kiangsi, Kiungchow in Hainan, Newchwang in Manchuria, Swatow in Kwangtung, Wenchow in Chekiang, and Nanking in Kiangsu.

[11] All quotations are from the British treaty. The extraterritorial rights of foreigners were further defined in criminal cases. For a full account of the Tientsin negotiations see Immanuel C. Y. Hsu, *China's Entrance into the Family of Nations, the Diplomatic Phase, 1858–1880* (1960), 21–118.

Following the Tientsin settlement, negotiations were adjourned to Shanghai, where a revised schedule of rates in the conventional tariff was adopted, providing a general 5 per cent duty on exports and imports. But more significant than this revision was the legalization of the opium trade at a duty of 30 taels per 100 catties.[12] This new legal status of opium was a triumph for British policy, which, since 1842, had been consistent, and probably sound, despite the fact that it appeared to support a nefarious traffic. The British argument ran as follows: since the Nanking settlement, the importation of opium, a contraband trade, had increased rapidly. Although most of the opium was produced in India, other sources of supply were available, and therefore prohibition by the British authorities was not likely to prove effective in stopping the trade, though it would materially reduce Indian revenue. It was the business of China to enforce her laws against an illicit traffic. England would not give protection to subjects violating China's laws, but neither would she undertake to enforce the laws for China. Since China had failed to enforce the law against opium, the trade should be legalized at a fixed duty and strictly supervised.[13]

The attitude of the United States at this time to the opium question is also of interest. Minister Reed had been instructed that his government would not seek legalization of the opium traffic, and thus the treaty that

[12] One catty equals 1⅓ lbs.

[13] J. K. Fairbank, "The Legalization of the Opium Trade Before the Treaties of 1858," *Chinese Social and Political Science Review* 17 (1933): 215, points out that although the Imperial government in Peking took no steps to levy an official impost on opium trade before 1858, nevertheless "the unofficial or private taxation of the traffic by local [Chinese] authorities . . . appears to have been put gradually on a more regular basis." Thus the taxing of opium was applied by the Chinese authorities at some of the ports before the legalization clause was written into the treaties of 1858. Legalization served two purposes: it provided China with needed revenue, and it stabilized an important item of the foreign trade by placing it on a treaty basis.

Reed signed at Tientsin made no mention of opium. But later, in discussions with Lord Elgin, Reed came to the view that "any course is better than that which is now pursued." He therefore supported the principle of legalization, and his action in this respect was accepted by his government. American business in general approved of the Tientsin Treaties, since it was believed that, as trade with China continued to increase, cotton alone would probably more than repay the annual deficits on the imports of tea and silk.

THE RENEWAL OF HOSTILITIES

The treaties of Tientsin were approved by the Chinese government in 1858 before the British and French forces left Tientsin. They were not to become effective, however, until ratified copies had been exchanged *at Peking*. This was done without difficulty in the case of the Russian treaty. The new Russian minister, General Ignatiev, proceeded to Peking by the old overland route and was promptly received. The British, the French, and the American envoys, accompanied by ships of war, arrived at the mouth of the Pei-ho in June, 1859. Here it was discovered that the Chinese had strengthened the forts at Taku and had blocked the river's mouth. The envoys were informed, but only when it was too late, that they would be received at P'ei-t'ang ten miles farther north on the coast, but that China would repel any attempt to enter the river at Taku. The British and French therefore attempted to storm the forts and break the barrier—an attempt in which they failed utterly, and accordingly were forced to return to Shanghai.[14]

Hostilities had thus been precipitated and a second chapter in the *Arrow* War was now inevitable. Again, the question of responsibility is difficult to assess. The British envoy, Frederick Bruce, had been instructed

[14] During the engagement, the commander of the American naval forces, whose country was neutral, had nonetheless come to the assistance of his British cousins, explaining his action with the statement that "blood is thicker than water."

that it would be desirable for him to "reach Tientsin in a British ship of war," but that since definite rules of procedure could not be laid down in London the envoy was to use discretion when "to give way" and when "to stand firm." Thus Bruce, faced with dilatory Chinese correspondence and evasion followed by the blocking of the river at Taku, had come to the conclusion that this was the time "to stand firm." When he insisted on the approach through Taku and Tientsin he was not violating his instructions, but he *was* demanding something not granted by the British treaty. Actually neither British nor French policy in this instance could be justified in law. Both the policy and Bruce's decision were political. They rested on the conviction, for which there was considerable ground, that the Peking government had no intention to honor the extensive new concessions it had been forced to grant at Tientsin the previous year.

Meanwhile, John E. Ward, the American envoy, not restricted to any route or place for the exchange of his country's treaty, proceeded to P'ei-t'ang. At Tungchow the Chinese provided carts that carried him and his mission to Peking.[15] This was unfortunate for the dignity of the United States. Ward, a native of Georgia, was a Southern gentleman of some distinction, but being sadly ignorant of the finer points of Oriental procedure he permitted the Chinese to take full advantage of his inexperience. He should have demanded sedan chairs, the mode of conveyance used by high Chinese officials. The cart in which he did ride was the kind of vehicle used to carry Korean and other tribute-bearers to the Chinese capital. Over this cart floated banners describing Ward as a tribute-bearer from the United States. Upon his arrival in Peking, Ward was requested to perform the kowtow, which of course he refused to do, and with what must have been a splendid dignity informed the Chinese officials that "althought he was willing to 'bend the body and slightly crook the right knee,' he was accustomed to kneel only to

[15] The Ward correspondence is in U. S. Sen. Ex., doc. 36–1:(30), 569 ff.

God and woman." [16] Having delivered himself of this impressive statement, Ward returned to P'ei-t'ang, where copies of the ratified American treaty were exchanged.

Meanwhile, British and French reinforcements reached the Pei-ho. In August 1860, the Allies stormed the Taku forts and advanced on Tientsin and Peking. The Chinese retired in confusion, and when the foreigners entered the capital, the degenerate Manchu emperor had already fled with his court to Jehol, ostensibly on a hunting trip. During the Allied march on Peking, thirty-nine foreigners (twenty-six English and thirteen French, including the private secretary of Lord Elgin, who had replaced Bruce as Britain's plenipotentiary) were captured by the Chinese. At the time, the victims were presumably protected by a flag of truce, but the Chinese appear to have believed that by holding these hostages they would bring the Allies to adopt a more moderate policy. Twenty of the prisoners were already dead when the remaining survivors were released. As a result, Lord Elgin ordered the burning of the emperor's Summer Palace (Yuan Ming Yuan) situated outside the city, an achitectural monument which the French troops had already occupied and looted.[17]

THE PEKING CONVENTION, 1860

With the Chinese capital now at their mercy, the Allied envoys proceeded to the exchange of the ratified treaties of 1858, and to exact new concessions embodied in the Conventions of Peking, 1860. The Emperor of China expressed "his deep regret" that a "misunderstanding" had occurred at Taku the previous year; agreed that the British minister might "reside permanently" at Peking, consented to additional indemnities and

[16] Dennett, *Americans in Eastern Asia,* 342.

[17] The Summer Palace extended over an area more than six miles in length, situated at the foot of the first range of hills some five miles to the northwest of Peking. The grounds, which might be described as a great private park, included residences, temples, pagodas, gardens, and artificial hills, some of them 300 feet in height, surrounding a lake.

to the opening of Tientsin as a treaty port, legalized the coolie trade under regulation, and consented to the cession of Kowloon on the mainland opposite Hong Kong. The French convention secured the restoration to the Roman Catholic Church of all property confiscated since 1724, a provision that was to work great hardship on Chinese who had acquired the property. This fact does not appear to have troubled the French government or the Church. Both found a convenient justification for taking the property in an imperial edict of 1846, which had promised restoration of religious establishments to Roman Catholics. The Chinese text of the French convention (which was not authoritative) also contained a troublesome provision allowing French missionaries to rent and purchase land and to erect buildings in all provinces.[18]

The most curious phase of events in China during 1860 remains to be told. It was in this year that rebel bands associated with the T'ai-p'ing were threatening to advance upon the wealthy and populous city of Shanghai with its growing foreign settlement. In this extremity the Chinese authorities appealed to the English and French for protection, and these latter agreed to defend the Chinese city and the foreign settlement against any attack. On August 21, 1860, the British troops, assisted by some French, repelled the rebels from the walls of Shanghai. It was on this very day that British and French troops in the north were storming the Taku forts and beginning their march on Peking.

The new order in Sino-Western relations formalized by the Tientsin Treaties, 1858, and the Peking Treaties, 1860, has often been explained exclusively in terms of *imperialism*, a Western movement imposing itself upon an unco-operative China. This interpretation is sound, but it is not the entire explanation. Between 1840 and 1860 imperialism did work its way with China. There was also, however, a concurrent and complementary movement by means of which the Chinese state, long skilled in handling the barbarians of Inner Asia, adjusted itself to the new nineteenth-century Western intruders by drawing upon institutional devices fashioned from long experience. From the Chinese point of view there is evidence to suggest that the treaty system was added to the traditional tribute system with the idea of bringing the foreigner under the influence of the universal Confucian state. The new order was therefore not an exclusively Western creation. Seen in the perspective of Chinese historical experience with outer barbarians, the treaty ports were modern reflections of the stations assigned for ancient tributary trade. Consular jurisdiction could be compared to the method by which the chief of Arab traders was responsible for the actions of his countrymen in China (see page 54). The most-favored-nation principle could be interpreted as contemporary evidence of the benevolence of the Confucian sovereign toward all barbarians to the end of playing one against another. The treaty tariff, so antagonistic to potential Chinese industry, had its forerunner in the older and onerous Manchu policy of taxation on production and trade. Finally, even the employment of foreigners in Chinese government service had many precedents in China's history. Thus the period 1840 to 1860 witnessed the achievement of a compromise settlement in the form of a joint Chinese-Western administration in the treaty ports. Preeminent as an example of an institution of this dual administration was the Foreign Inspectorate of Customs at Shanghai. Imperialism alone therefore does not explain what was happening in Chinese-barbarian relations in the nineteenth century.[19]

RUSSIA AND CHINA

While the *Arrow* War had been running its course in China Proper, a new chapter was being enacted in Russo-Chinese re-

[18] For a full discussion of the social and political complications arising from this alleged right of Catholic missionaries, see Paul H. Clyde, *United States Policy Toward China* (1940; reissued 1964), 107–112.

[19] Fairbank, *Trade and Diplomacy*, I, 462–468.

lations in Northeast Asia. Although China had won a diplomatic victory at Nertchinsk (1689), she failed in the following years to consolidate her hold on the Amur country. While the Manchus themselves tended to migrate southward to China, Chinese migration to Manchuria was prohibited. Therefore the Amur Valley had persisted as an uncolonized, undeveloped, and unprotected frontier.

It was not until 1847 that Russia seriously undertook the task of advancing the frontier beyond the unsurveyed line of the Treaty of Nertchinsk. In 1847 the tsar appointed Count Nicholas Muraviev governor-general of eastern Siberia, with instructions to pursue special investigations of the Amur question. This renewed Russian interest in the Far East had been prompted by a number of developments. The British as a result of the Opium War had opened a new maritime door to the China trade, eclipsing the Russian caravans at Kiakhta. The activities of the British navy in the Pacific spurred the Russians with the desire to establish ports on their own Pacific coastline. Both eastern and western Siberia had grown in importance to Russia, particularly after 1825. The growth of settlements in Kamchatka, the expanding activities of the Russian-American Company in Alaska, and the development of the whaling industry in the Bering Sea—all these prophesied the growing importance of Russia's Pacific and China frontier. It is hardly surprising therefore that between 1847 and 1854 Russia reached a number of decisions that were to launch her on the new policy of the "Easterners" under the leadership of Muraviev.[20]

The Policy of Muraviev

The new governor-general applied his policy with promptness and decision. His first agents sailed down the Amur in 1848. This river, it will be recalled, was wholly within the territory of the Manchu empire according to the terms of the Treaty of Nertchinsk. The following year Russian officers explored the coasts of the sea of Okhotsk as far south as the mouth of the Amur. This was a preliminary survey in Russia's general plan to prevent occupation of the area by potential enemies: Great Britain and France. Nikolaievsk was founded at the mouth of the Amur (August, 1850). These were the first major violations of the Nertchinsk Treaty. They were to be followed by a vigorous pursuit of the new policy. Russian posts were founded at De Castries, Mariinsk, and Imperatorski Bay in 1852. Sakhalin Island was annexed in 1853.[21]

Up to this point China paid little attention to the Russian advance and seems to have ignored the deep significance of the new aggressive policy. Chinese border authorities were negligent, and most of the Manchurian troops had been withdrawn by 1853 to meet in China Proper the threatening northward march of the T'ai-p'ing rebels. Even had this not been the case, China's position in 1853 did not appear on the surface at least to be seriously threatened on the northern frontier. Officially the policy of the Russian government was still one of respect for the terms of the Nertchinsk Treaty. Nevertheless, by 1854 Muraviev had received the tsar's mandate to settle directly with Peking all questions concerning the eastern boundary. He was thus freed from all interference by the "Westerners" in the Russian ministry of foreign affairs. He was free to pursue his own grandiose scheme of making Russia a power on the Pacific, and, if need be, "the protector of China."[22]

The Crimean War had already broken out in Europe. In the Pacific the two great commercial pioneers, the Hudson's Bay Company and the Russian-American Company, had agreed to remain neutral, but this did not deter Great Britain and France from attacking Russia's Pacific base at Petropavlovsk. The real value of the Amur as a road for the transport of Russian supplies to the Pacific could no longer be denied even by the "Westerners." As a result, in April, 1854, Muraviev, on the pretext of military neces-

---

[20] T. C. Lin, "The Amur Frontier Question Between China and Russia, 1850–1860," *The Pacific Historical Review* 3 (1934): 1–27.

[21] *Ibid.*

[22] Anatole G. Mazour, "Dimitry Zavalishin: Dreamer of a Russian-American Empire," *The Pacific Historical Review* 5 (1936): 26–37.

sity, the defense of Kamchatka, sent his first major expedition down the entire length of the Amur. No attempt was made by the Chinese frontier forces to question or stop the Russians. More troops and munitions of war descended the river the following year, and the tsar informed Muraviev that the left bank of the Amur was now indispensable to Russia.

Now that Russia had occupied the river with her transports, contacts with the border Chinese authorities were inevitable. The first direct Russo-Chinese negotiations at Mariinsk in 1855 proved abortive. In 1856 Muraviev ordered his third major expedition down the river. The Chinese authorities protested, but the Russians replied with the stationing of garrisons at strategic points on the left bank of the river.

The Mission of Count Putiatin

Meanwhile Russia was preparing a double diplomatic assault on Peking. While Muraviev was yet on the Amur, Count Putiatin was sent to Peking to secure for Russia whatever commercial concessions should fall to England and France as a result of the *Arrow* War. He was also to seek a settlement of the Amur question. Putiatin was refused entry at Kiakhta but reached the mouth of the Pei-ho in August, 1857, by way of the Amur and the ocean route. To his overtures, the Chinese replied tersely that Russia should observe her treaty obligations. Blocked in his mission, Putiatin joined the British, French, and American envoys at Canton and proceeded north again with them to Tientsin, where in June, 1858, the four commercial treaties were signed. His influence on the Amur question was negligible. Not so with that of Muraviev.

During the progress of the *Arrow* War, Muraviev had not been idle in the north. Early in May, 1858, he succeeded in bringing the Chinese into conference at Aigun, where he demanded the river boundary which was to divide Manchuria from Siberia. China's protests received but scant consideration. On May 28, 1858, the Aigun Treaty was signed. In it Russia acquired all the territory on the left or northern bank of the Amur, while the land lying between the Ussuri River and the sea (the present Maritime Province) was to be held in joint control by both powers.[23] The Aigun agreement was thus signed two weeks before Putiatin signed the Russian Treaty of Tientsin, and without his knowledge.

Although China was in no position to successfully dispute Muraviev's advance, she refused to accept the Aigun Treaty in its entirety. China was prepared to cede those territories north of the Amur not already occupied by Chinese subjects, but she was not prepared to dispose of the Ussuri country. The local Kirin provincial authorities were accordingly commanded to prevent Russian encroachments. But this gesture was of no effect. When these officials failed, Peking might, and in fact did, order punishment of these helpless underlings. She might declare null and void the joint-control clause of the Aigun Treaty. Actually, China's impotence and Russia's strength remained unchanged.

Having thus pushed her boundary to the river, and having commenced penetration of the Trans-Ussuri region, Russia now directed her final attack through diplomacy in Peking. Early in the summer of 1859 General Ignatiev had reached the Chinese capital to exchange the ratified copies of the Russian Treaty of Tientsin. In addition it was his purpose to cultivate Russian interest in other ways. In his first diplomatic overtures he sought additional commercial privileges and the outright cession to Russia of the Trans-Ussuri lands. These requests were promptly refused, and the envoy was informed that China did not regard the Aigun settlement as binding. Here matters might have rested until such time as Muraviev was again prepared to use force. But, happily for Russia, other powers came unwittingly to her aid. By October, 1860, the British and French Allies, having broken Chinese resistance between Peking and Taku, had occupied the capital. The Manchu Dynasty appeared to

[23] The Chinese text of the treaty refers, in the case of territory to be held in common, only to the right bank of the Amur from the Ussuri to the sea, and not to the entire Maritime Province as is implied in the Russian text. T. C. Lin, "The Amur Frontier Question . . . ," 21.

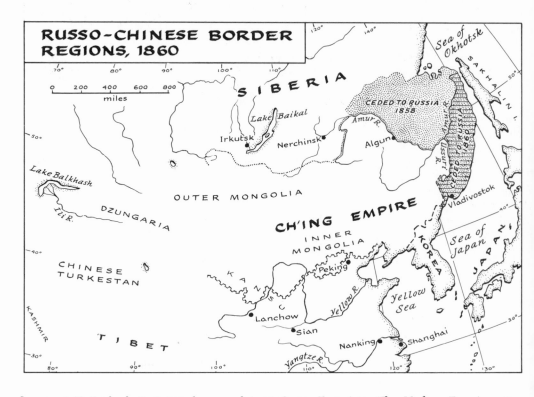

RUSSO-CHINESE BORDER REGIONS, 1860

Sources: J. K. Fairbank, E. G. Reischauer, and A. M. Craig, *East Asia, The Modern Transformation* (Boston: Houghton-Mifflin Co., 1965), 47; and Dun J. Lee, *The Ageless Chinese* (New York: Charles Scribners Sons, 1965), 416.

be on the verge of total collapse. The T'ai-p'ing rebels were laying waste the central coast; the capital lay at the mercy of British and French arms; the Summer Palace had already been looted and burned, while a cowardly emperor and his renegade court had fled to the mountains of Jehol. Baffled and perplexed by the misfortunes that pursued the dynasty, Prince Kung, brother of the emperor, remained in Peking to seek a settlement with the victorious "barbarians."

Here was Russia's opportunity. Ignatiev played on the fears of the frightened Prince. He would intervene, so he said, with the Allies and thus save Peking itself from the destruction that had already consumed the Summer Palace. For these services to China he would ask only an insignificant return: the rectification of a frontier, the cession of the Trans-Ussuri country. Prince Kung was not deceived, but assuredly he was defeated. On November 14, 1860, he signed with

Ignatiev the convention that, among other things, ceded the Manchurian coastline to Russia.

In large part Muraviev's dream had now been realized. By the close of 1860, Russian policy in China had enjoyed a success unparalleled by that of any other state. Like the United States, she had not participated as a belligerent in the *Arrow* War, yet she was to reap all the advantages, commercial and diplomatic, won by England and France in the Treaties of Tientsin. In the north, through a policy of force, but without declaration of war, she had opened the Mongolian frontier to her traders and had advanced her boundary along the course of the Amur and far south along the Pacific coast to the northern tip of Korea. By conquest and colonization, yet without war in the legal sense, she had deprived the Manchu empire of 350,000 square miles of territory. Manchuria was cut off from the sea on the east, whereas

Russia possessed a new and broad road to the ocean. Before Ignatiev signed the convention that transferred the Maritime Province, Russia proceeded to consolidate her new lands. At the southern extremity of the new coastal territory Muraviev selected the harbor and site of Russia's future fortress on the Pacific. The founding of Vladivostok, "dominion of the East," was a fitting culmination to the work, aggressive, unscrupulous, but successful, of one of Russia's great empire builders.[24]

FOR FURTHER READING

THE CHINESE SCENE AND PERSONALITIES. Huang Yen-yü, "Viceroy Yeh Ming-ch'en and the Canton Episode (1856–1861)," *Harvard Journal of Asiatic Studies* 6 (1941): 37–127, a documentary study of the person and the episode. Rhoads Murphey, *Shanghai, Key to Modern China* (1953) portrays the geographic and economic influences which made Shanghai a great port. Li Chien-nung, *The Political History of China 1840–1928*, trans. Teng Ssu-yu and Jeremy Ingals (1956).° A. W. Hummel, ed., *Eminent Chinese of the Ch'ing Period (1644–1912)* (2 vols. 1943–1944), a reference work of great value. Ch'en Ch'i-t'ien, *Tseng Kuo-fan*, trans. by Gideon Chen (Peiping, 1935; reissued, 1961).

THE T'AI-P'ING REBELLION. Teng Ssu-yu, *New Light on the History of the T'ai-p'ing Rebellion* (1950), and *Historiography of the Taiping Rebellion* (1962)° are important bibliographical surveys of historical studies with an excellent brief account of the rebellion itself. Franz Michael, "The Military Organization and Power Structure of China During the T'ai-p'ing Rebellion," *The Pacific Historical Review* 18 (1949): 469–83. Vincent Y. C. Shih, "The Ideology of the Taiping T'ien-kuo," *Sinologica*, 3 (1951), 1–15. W. J.

[24] R.K.I. Quested, *The Expansion of Russia in East Asia, 1857–1860* (Kuala Lumpur, 1968) is the most recent and best account of Sino-Russian negotiations. See also the same author's bibliographic review: "Further Light on the Expansion of Russia in East Asia, 1792–1860," *Journal of Asian Studies* 29 (1970): 327–45.

Hail, *Tseng Kuo-fan and the T'ai-p'ing Rebellion* (1927). E. P. Boardman, *Christian Influence Upon the Ideology of the T'ai-p'ing Rebellion* (1952), a study of the part played by Christianity in initiating and shaping the rebellion. John S. Gregory, *Great Britain and the Taipings* (1969). Laai Yi-faai, Franz Michael, and John C. Sherman, "The Use of Maps in Social Research: A Case Study in South China," *Geographical Review* 52 (1962): 92–111, a revealing study in content and method centering on the T'ai-p'ing period.

BRITISH INTERESTS. D. Bonner-Smith and E. W. R. Lumby, eds., *The Second China War, 1856–1860* (London, 1954) based on the archival materials reveals that the second China war was accelerated by Harry Parkes and that the lorcha *Arrow* was originally a pirate's boat. Grace Fox, *British Admirals and Chinese Pirates, 1832–1869* (London, 1940) suggests the influence of the Admiralty on British policy toward China from 1832–1869. Alexander Michie, *The Englishman in China* (2 vols. Edinburgh, 1900), the life in the Far East of Sir Rutherford Alcock. Laurence Oliphant, *Narrative of the Earl of Elgin's Mission to China and Japan in the Years 1857, '58, '59* (1860). Charles Collins, *Public Administration in Hong Kong* (London, 1952), a well-documented account of the development of administrative machinery in the British colony.

THE RUSSIAN ROLE. Robert J. Kerner, *The Urge to the Sea: the Course of Russian History* (1942). L. Pasvolsky, *Russia in the Far East* (1922), a brief, general introduction. D. J. Dallin, *The Rise of Russia in Asia* (1949) outlines the rise of Russia as an Asiatic power in the nineteenth and early twentieth centuries. A. Lobanov-Rotovsky, *Russia and Asia* (1933), a popular general survey. William Mandel, *The Soviet Far East and Central Asia* (1944) gives a more contemporary picture. Perry McDonough Collins, *Siberian Journey: Down the Amur to the Pacific, 1856–1857*, Charles Vevier, ed. (1962). Martin Norins, *Gateway to Asia: Sinkiang Frontier of the Chinese Far West* (1944).

Japan, 1603–ca. 1840:
The Making and Breaking of
the Tokugawa Regime

chapter 8

In returning to the subject of early modern Japan, the reader will recall (see p. 59) that at the beginning of the seventeenth century it appeared for a time that, under the enlightened leadership of Tokugawa Iyeyasu, Japan would pursue a policy of ever broader commercial contacts with the traders from the West, but that within a few years this policy had given place to one of exclusion and seclusion. Japan's rulers had become convinced that Catholic Christianity as taught by Portuguese and Spanish monks was a political threat to the state. Thus, in the seventeenth century when Europe had already set its course toward geographical discovery and expansion, toward far-flung trade and settlement, toward a liberal philosophy of man's rights and of respect for the individual, Japan was setting her course with determination against these infatuations of a modern age, was turning inward upon herself, was closing her doors to either entry or exit, while consolidating a political and social structure whose virtues would be stability and rigid conformity to orthodox values and habits of behavior.

Japan was entering upon one of the most significant periods in her history, the Tokugawa Shogunate, 1603–1867. The To-

kugawa period has often been interpreted as "an unhappy interlude" between Japan's first and second encounters with the West in the sixteenth and nineteenth centuries. There are some grounds for this interpretation. The period was an age of isolationism, of 100 per cent Japanism, of an effort to resist the modern world and to revive in some degree Japan's particular forms of feudalism. At the same time, Tokugawa Japan achieved much more than this interpretation would suggest. While the goal of the Tokugawa rulers was to crystallize society and in this sense to look backward, their regime actually produced basic changes that prepared Japan for modern nationhood. It is thus a period of great fascination and seeming contradictions.[1]

MEN WHO KNEW THEIR OWN MINDS

The *Bakufu*, it will be recalled, had achieved its mastery of Japan in battle and,

[1] For a detailed treatment of Tokugawa Japan, *see* Edwin O. Reischauer and John K. Fairbank, *East Asia: The Great Tradition* (1960), I, Chapter 13. A very useful broad reference is J. W. Hall, *Japanese History: New Dimensions of Approach and Understanding* (2nd ed., publication 34, A. H. A. Service Center for Teachers of History, 1966).

within a few decades, had sealed the country, in a major degree, from foreign influence. These steps were in a sense merely preliminaries to their major ambition, which was to create a political and social system that would preserve this newly won power for themselves and their descendants. The means they employed toward these ends were not a loose set of expedients designed to combat opposition where and when it might arise, but rather an integrated design of authoritarian rule for the entire nation. Under this plan the military power of the shogunate would remain so complete that no one would dare to challenge it. The result would be an age of unbroken peace and political stability buttressed by a social order resting on clearly defined and rigidly maintained class lines— that is, a society of status. In achieving this ambition of authoritarian stability the *Bakufu* could at first rely on a large measure of popular support. The efficient exercise of centralized power leading to peace and order was welcomed as a relief from the intolerable disorders of the late Ashikaga period. Stable absolutism was considered a refuge from the uncertainties of unstable feudalism that threatened to bring complete anarchy.

THE TOKUGAWA POLITICAL SYSTEM

The Tokugawa political system was notable because it survived with relatively little change for two and one-half centuries. Essentially conservative, the purpose of the system was negative—to prevent political change. In a long period of peace, it perpetuated forms of military administration devised earlier for periods when warfare was the rule. The first goal was political stability. This was achieved in considerable degree soon after the battle of Sekigahara (1600) which gave the Tokugawas an essential military supremacy over all Japan.

To ensure further this stability, Iyeyasu decided to rule indirectly through the old daimyo system. The central part of the country was assigned to the Tokugawa family and to other leaders who had been his vassals and allies prior to the victory at Sekiga-

hara. He was thus assured of a central power bloc and structure that could not easily be challenged. Beyond this, he treated his more distant and powerful enemies, such as Satsuma, with considerable generosity.

Moreover, Iyeyasu decided to return to the system of two capitals. The emperor's court was preserved at the old imperial city of Kyoto. There the emperor, surrounded by the civilian aristocracy, the *Kuge,* continued to preside over priestly affairs, etiquette, and the conferring of titles, the most important of the latter being "shogun" which was given to Iyeyasu. Iyeyasu, however, retained his headquarters at the fishing village of Yedo in eastern Japan where the lands of the Tokugawas and their allies were concentrated. The castle fortress he constructed there became the administrative center of the shogunate, and the new city that grew around the fortress was later to become the modern city of Tokyo. Some of the fortress' massive walls and moats may still be seen.

Also, it will be recalled that in these early years the Tokugawas moved Japan steadily toward a policy of isolation (see p. 60 ff.), involving the proscribing of Christianity, and ultimately a rigorous control and limitation of foreign trade. Iyeyasu had become convinced that Christianity could be a threat to his political order. In the case of foreign trade, the reasoning was that it was neither desirable nor indispensable, and that such trade as might be permitted should be a monopoly of government so as not to enrich those daimyo whose loyalty to the shogunate might be questioned. By these means, foreign influences and pressures were minimized and domestic stability was thereby increased.

In internal policy and administration, Iyeyasu and his successors preserved the old daimyo system. In reality it provided a sort of compromise between central control by Yedo and the local autonomy of the fiefs. The daimyo lands (*han*) numbered some 270. Each of these was a local autonomous government under strict Tokugawa supervision. The daimyo status of a lord depended on the rice production of his fief since the Tokugawas based their government primarily on agricultural income. In a political sense daimyo were classified in three groups: (1) *Shimpan* were descendants of Tokugawa shoguns who did not succeed to this high office. (2) *Fudai* were those daimyo who were descendants of men who had accepted Iyeyasu as their overlord prior to 1600. (3) *Tozama* daimyo were the descendants of lords who in 1600 had been equals, in theory at least, of Iyeyasu. The Tokugawa and the *fudai* lands occupied the central part of the country. The strongest *tozama*, potential enemies of the shogunate, were for the most part in the south and west. In time, smaller *fudai* holdings came to be located on the borders of these potential enemies. Although the daimyo governments did not pay taxes to the shogunate, they supported it by "presents" that were virtually compulsory. The shogunate was thus free from most of the obligations of local government and defense.

The Machinery of Control

It is quite apparent that the Tokugawa political system, which sanctioned local autonomy and independent military power among the daimyo, could be an invitation to revolt through alliances among discontented lords. The Tokugawas created barriers against any such development through a complex system of controls. One example will illustrate their political skill in this matter.

The Tokugawa shogunate refined and made mandatory the system of *sankin kotai* whereby the daimyo alternated in attendance on the shogun in Yedo. *Fudai* in central Japan alternated semi-annually, while other *fudai* and all *tozama* usually alternated annually. Their wives and children remained in Yedo as hostages when the daimyo returned to their fiefs. The great daimyo trains moving to and from Yedo along the Tokaido (road) between Yedo and Kyoto created the most picturesque scenes of Tokugawa Japan.[2]

[2] Oliver Statler, *Japanese Inn* (1961),* a delightful recapturing of Japanese life at an historic inn on the Tokaido which joined Kyoto and Yedo in Tokugawa days. See the delightful, ribald classic Ikku Jippensha, *Shank's Mare: Being a Translation of the Tokaido Volumes of Hizakurige*, Thomas Satchell, trans. (1960).* The transition from the pre-Tokugawa to the Toku-

This *sankin kotai* system was remarkably effective. It meant that half of the daimyo was always under the eye of the shogun at Yedo. The tendency was for them to become courtiers rather than effective rebels. Moreover, the expense of maintaining an elaborate establishment at the shogun's capital drained the resources of the daimyo and thus contributed to their subservience to the shogun.[3]

The Central Administration

Back in the days of Nara and Heian, Japan developed no adequate body of administrative officials loyal to or appreciative of a stable and healthy central government. By 1600, however, there was a body of educated men that Yedo could call into government service, and this the Tokugawas proceeded to do.

At the high level of policy making, the Tokugawas relied heavily on their Council of Elders (*Toshiyori*). A member of this Council acted as regent when the shogun was a minor. This Council was all important in fixing the relationships of the shogunate with the emperor's court and the feudal lords. The lesser vassals of the Tokugawa were regulated by a lower Council of Junior Elders (*Wakadoshiyori*). Under these high-ranking bodies was a large civil service, the bureaucracy proper, comprising executive, administrative, and judicial officials together with their still more numerous underlings handling all the various aspects of government. This personnel, as might be expected, was drawn, usually on an hereditary basis, from the Tokugawa and the *fudai* families. Among these officials there was in general a lack of any precise definition of responsibility, a circumstance which, although it can be explained in part on grounds of custom, was

gawa era is briefly but ably presented in E. O. Reischauer, *Japan: The Story of a Nation* (1970),* 78–98, and G. B. Sansom, *A History of Japan, 1615–1867* (1963). On the position of the emperor in Tokugawa Japan, H. D. Harootunian, "Between Principle and Personality," *Journal of Asian Studies*, 24 (1964): 115–21.

[3] For the detailed working of *sankin kotai* and its effects on the Tokugawa system see Toshio Tsukahira, *Feudal Control in Tokugawa Japan* (1966).*

also a matter of intentional policy whereby the individual was prevented from building his own little empire of power. In reality it added up to a system of government by council, not by individuals. This feature was common in government in all the various feudal domains and even in the local government of the peasant village as well as on the high plane of the shogunate. Indeed, government in the fiefs of the great lords varied little in organization from that of the shogunate. Each fief made its own laws and collected its own taxes very much on the pattern set by the Tokugawas. At the extreme local level, the village, government was directed and administered by village headmen and councilors under the watchful eye of district officers of the daimyo.[4]

THE CHARACTER OF TOKUGAWA JAPAN

The foregoing details will have suggested that the machinery of government in Tokugawa Japan was comparatively simple. It was possible and logical for this to be so because in Old Japan, as in Old China, the ordering and the controlling of society was sought through social rather than through political principles and agencies. This being so, it is essential to take careful note of the

[4] An able account of the Tokugawa central government or *Bakufu* is Conrad D. Totman, *Politics in the Tokugawa Bakufu, 1600–1843* (1967). A significant aspect of Tokugawa government was the ever-present group of officials at various levels of government held together by personal ties of loyalty and resulting common purposes. These cliques or factions were in a sense the political parties of that time. Note the later discussion of Japan's first modern political parties in Chapter 11. The political society created in Tokugawa Japan was, in fact, derived from three social systems: the "family" or *uji* (pre-Nara) system; the aristocratic (Nara and Heian) system; and finally, the samurai (Kamakura, Ashikaga, and Tokugawa) system. In some notable measure, Tokugawa Japan derived its traditional loyalties from the family system, and its bureaucratic and legal techniques from the aristocratic system. John Whitney Hall, *Government and Local Power in Japan, 500 to 1700* (1966).

social orders or classes as they existed in Tokugawa times. The influence of this social class structure often exerted itself after Japan had become a modern and partially Westernized state. The class system, moreover, was deeply rooted long before the Tokugawas came to power at the beginning of the seventeenth century. What the Tokugawas did was to distinguish the classes in elaborate detail and to encourage a rigid crystallization of them through more than two centuries of peace.

First in rank and in social prestige among the classes of society was the Imperial Family and the emperor's immediate vassals, the court nobles or *kuge*. The emperor, to whom land and income were granted by the shogunate, retained a real if somewhat uncertain traditional influence; but his political power had become a matter of theory only, and his court nobility subsisted on less income than that enjoyed by the poorest feudal lords. Theirs were the vaporous satisfactions of honor, not the tangible rewards of wealth.

Second in the social scale but first in power and privilege were the military men, the samurai. These made up the ruling class in Japan's military-feudal dictatorship. Within this class was a vast array of gradations from the shogun at the top to the foot soldier at the bottom. The principal ranks within this powerful caste in descending order of grade were: (1) the daimyo or great lords, some two hundred and seventy in number who were classified according to wealth, and all of whom enjoyed an annual rice income exceeding ten thousand *koku* (a *koku* is 4.96 bushels); (2) direct retainers of the shogun, known as *hatamoto* and *gokenin*, some of whom lived in Yedo performing civil or military duties; (3) *baishin*, who were retainers of daimyo or *hatamoto*, and who according to grade within their own class served as government advisers, administrative officials, or as foot soldiers, which last category was the most numerous within the samurai class; (4) *ronin*, or soldiers unattached to any lord; and (5) *goshi*, or samurai-peasants who acquired the status of active soldiers only in time of war. In the eighteenth century of the Tokugawa period

Japan's entire population was about thirty million, and of these the daimyo and their vassals numbered about two million, the *ronin* about four hundred thousand until about 1650.

The court nobility and the samurai belonged, in a society of status, to what may best be called the privileged classes. They were not permitted to engage in common manual labor. All others, and this included the vast majority, can hardly be said to have had no privileges, but it is certain that their privileges were few and quite unimpressive.

Heading, in the Confucian sense, this multitude of common men was the farmer or peasant who, like his betters in privileged society, was ranked and graded by various standards within his own class. The first rank among these plebians were the village headmen and councilors. In second rank came those farmers who owned their land. Finally there was the landless peasantry, the most numerous and poorest of all. It was from this group that the laboring force of the growing cities was recruited.

Differentiated from the farmer but of about the same social rank among common men were the artisans or craftsmen. They fashioned the simplest articles of daily use or created the marvellously tempered two-handed sword known as the soul of the samurai. Neither the farmer nor the craftsman was a person of power, but since they fed and armed the samurai they were accorded a measure of honor as useful members of society.

Ranking as the commonest of common men was the merchant or *chonin* class. In the feudal-military society of early Tokugawa days, the merchant class was looked upon by both shogunate and daimyo as a useful tool which, so long as it had no political influence, was not likely to endanger the feudal system. Long before the close of the Tokugawa era, however, this despised but tolerated merchant was to acquire an influence wholly out of proportion to his lowly social status.

Finally, if one scraped the bottom of the social barrel, one discovered the sub-stratum of mankind, the *eta* or the untouchables, who were professional players, tanners, and executioners. Below the *eta* was the lowest class of society, composed of beggars considered as less than human. One could be born into this class or be consigned to it as punishment for some crime. Districts were set apart where the untouchables were required to live unto themselves, since they could not even act as servants to commoners. In fine, they were classified as animals rather than humans, and were not even included in the census. The two names, *eta* and *hinin* were suppressed in 1871, and today descendents of these former classes are legally citizens.

The Philosophy

The goal of Tokugawa government was stability, but in seeking this end the shogunate did not confine itself to defining social classes, and to spying upon its enemies. It went beyond these matters to prescribe in minute detail the morals and the behavior of the entire populace. In the Western World morals had usually been left to the management of some church, but in Japan, as in China, ethics were the concern of government, and thus moral and political philosophy became one. As a consequence the fundamental laws of the shogunate were really codes of moral injunction, such as, for example, "Avoid what you like, and attend to unpleasant duties." Life was not considered to be the pursuit of happiness, but rather the performance of obligation. There was no place for freedom of thought because duty called for unqualified loyalty and obedience. The idea of progress was also excluded because this was a society of status in which each man occupied his proper place and was expected to stay in it. A more inflexible philosophy would be difficult to imagine.

The intellectual cornerstone upholding this Tokugawa scheme of government and society was Confucianism in its most conservative aspects, in which stress was laid on the "proper" relations between ruler and ruled. The Buddhist church had already been reduced to obedience to the state by Nobunaga and Hideyoshi, and the first Tokugawa shoguns had suppressed Christianity. Therefore, the way had already been cleared for the secular morality of the Confucians. The trend actually was not entirely new. Samurai had long prided themselves on their regard for courage, self-sacrifice, disregard of material wealth, and loyalty to one's lord. In theory, at least, all of these qualities had been the moral stock-in-trade of the soldier since long before the Tokugawas came to power. They were qualities that the shogunate wished to strengthen. But the problem was not as simple as this would suggest. The shogunate recognized that the samurai warlike spirit could, in times of peace, be inconvenient and even dangerous. Therefore the shogunate attempted to turn the minds of military men toward peaceful undertakings. What the consequences were to be we shall discover shortly.[5]

Such then was the pattern of permanence the Tokugawas tried to impose. At first their success seemed complete. For a long time the basic character of Tokugawa institutions remained substantially without change. Yet, almost from the beginning, processes of change were at work. Indeed, the advent of unbroken peace and the closing of the country to foreign intercourse created conditions that forced the Tokugawas to tolerate and

---

[5] The prescribed philosophy of Tokugawa times especially as it applied to the samurai or ruling caste is sometimes referred to as *Bushido*, the Way of the Warrior, a term of comparatively recent origin though the set of ideas for which it is the label are quite old. These ideas are not unlike those in the code of early European chivalry. Historically the code was the expression of early ideas on the duty of the soldier. Since Japan had been controlled by soldiers since the time of Yoritomo, there had been both the need and the opportunity to develop a set of principles on the duty of the soldier. These principles varied in degree from time to time and had not been highly conventionalized until well into the Tokugawa period, and then, in part at least, under the Confucian influence. In general, *Bushido* extolled "rectitude, courage, benevolence, politeness, sincerity, honor, disdain of money, and self-control" as ideals to be followed by the samurai. Since virtue is only as strong as those who profess it, this code was the measure of what a samurai was supposed to do, not of what he sometimes actually did.

even to encourage changes in a policy that was designed to resist change.

The Tokugawa government, class structure, and politico-moral philosophy suggest that Japan had fashioned for herself a way of life that must have been very bleak indeed. Nevertheless, could a Westerner have visited Yedo, Kyoto, or Osaka in, let us say, 1700, he would doubtless have been impressed not so much by the coldness of life as by its warmth, its vitality, its apparent prosperity, and its color. However gloomy the moral injunctions of shogun or daimyo might be, it was very evident that the city dwellers of this Japan were much concerned with the idea of progress and the pursuit of happiness. The processes of change so repugnant to Tokugawa philosophy were already in operation, and something of the nature of these changes must now be described.

The Economy

It was in the field of economics and commerce that the processes of change first became apparent. When military Japan settled down to a life of peace in the early 1600's, it was possible for trade to grow to proportions previously unknown. In peace, too, there was also less reason for local commercial restrictions, so that even though the country was still divided into the many domains of individual lords, the tendency was for the whole to become one economic unit. This tendency acquired strength from the nature of the shogun's government at Yedo, to which city under the system of *sankin kotai* came all the daimyo with their families and a host of retainers. This official and aristocratic populace of government officials, daimyo, and samurai created a demand for goods and services which only artisans and tradesmen could furnish. In these circumstances the relatively simple rice economy of the individual feudal domain gradually gave way to a money and credit economy managed by merchants, brokers, and bankers who controlled the rice markets and storehouses of such cities as Osaka and Yedo. The daimyo when in residence at Yedo converted rice revenue into cash, spending the proceeds on elaborate furnishings, dress, and lavish entertainment. Since his income in rice did not vary greatly, and since keeping up with the Joneses in Yedo was an expensive business, it was not difficult for a daimyo to find himself in debt to his social inferior the merchant—not a healthy or comfortable status for members of a ruling class.

Two points need to be emphasized in explaining how the mercantile class that had relatively limited legal rights and no military power could reach a point where it was able to exploit the military classes and the farmers. The first of these was the further development of Yedo as a large city which had to be supplied in part by imported food and which demanded a large supply of manufactured luxuries. These factors encouraged further the use of money and made the merchant indispensable. Yedo's growth, as indicated, resulted from the growth of government and the enforced residence there of the daimyo and their families. Had the daimyo remained in their castle towns, their consumptive habits and those of their retainers would have developed and changed much more slowly; likewise the use of money and the growth of a merchant class to cater to these expensive habits would have been retarded. In the second place, the military class by reason of its new consumptive habits became more and more dependent on the merchant. Once a taste for luxury had been acquired, the nobility was prepared to mortgage its future to the merchant rather than be eclipsed in the rivalry of social living. The merchant was not liquidated because without him the necessary food and luxuries would not have been forthcoming.[6]

Years of peace and the growth of the market also affected the farmers, who, in an overwhelmingly agricultural society, comprised about 80 per cent of the population. While in many ways Japanese farming changed very little over the centuries, production during the Tokugawa era shifted from a co-operative to an individual basis. Whereas in 1600, farming was conducted

[6] The complex situation which created and gave power to the merchants is portrayed in Charles D. Sheldon, *The Rise of the Merchant Class in Tokugawa Japan, 1600–1868* (1958).

by the co-operation of families organized into kinship groups sharing land, labor, tools, and sometimes food and housing, by the end of the Tokugawa period the individual family had become the main agent of agricultural production and the focus of economic interest. The implications of this shift extended well beyond the realm of economics. Economic change, previously an aspect of kinship and social relations, became a more independent force creating its own values. Thereby the exchange of goods was less a matter of social or ritual obligation and more a question of whether the price was right.[7]

Therefore by 1700, roughly a hundred years after the Tokugawas had first risen to power, Japan had not only modified her economy but had also acquired in her larger cities a prosperous middle class. Side by side then with the extravagance of the daimyo and their followers to maintain their social elegance, there appeared a new world of well-to-do merchants and their hirelings who had their own particular ideas on how to enjoy their money. These merchants and their associates, whom the samurai regarded as uncultivated persons of low and vulgar taste, soon created through their demands for entertainment a whole new world of popular arts in literature, the theater, painting, and in color prints.

The Arts

The new art was distinguished from older forms by its subject matter. It was an art that dealt with the doings and the aspirations of the newly rich commoners, their own colorful everyday life. Here were street scenes, theaters, tea-houses, or taverns of that time, the actors who had risen to stardom, and, as Sir George Sansom has said, "the easy-going ladies of the world of entertainment." The patrons of this new art were

[7] For the development of this fascinating and intricate subject, see Thomas C. Smith, *The Agrarian Origins of Modern Japan* (1965). Note in particular the changes that occurred in land holding, labor services, a subsistence to a marketing economy, the growth of rural industries, the use of agricultural technology, and especially in the development of new agricultural class relations.

the tradespeople. In time they developed their own standards and critics, so that eventually the old aristocratic monopoly over art was broken. The processes of change were in motion.[8]

In literature and in the theater, as in art, the city folk were not wholly satisfied with the classical romances and stage plays that were the traditional fare of the military class. The tastes of the city commoners, robust and sensuous, called forth a new group of authors whose stories and plays had a wide contemporary appeal. All of this brought books and plays and an appreciation of literature and acting to a growing populace of city dwellers. Yedo literature is important historically because it was another indication of change in the Tokugawa changeless pattern, and because the vacuous character of Yedo writing explains in some measure the easy inroads made by European literary influence and thought in the later Meiji period, when Japan had opened her doors to Western intercourse.

The Roots of a New Japan

These bright and attractive colors in Yedo's life of business and of the new arts need to be appraised against a background of contention—both social and economic. It has been suggested that the long period of peace the Bakufu was able to impose opened the way for a new society which in turn eventually destroyed the social and political order Iyeyasu had founded and laid the foundations for a new state and nation. This new society, far from being confined to the markets and pleasure haunts of Yedo, made itself felt in every aspect of the nation's life. Although the Tokugawas did not set out to build a modern national state, Japan during most of the Yedo period was taking the first steps in the direction of modern

[8] Hishigawa Motonobu was one of the great painters of this popular new art. The work of such men was the forerunner of the famous Japanese color print which testified to the widely developing artistic sense of the urban classes. The great print artists (Hiroshige, for example) became popular idols. They were the creators of Ukiyo, or Floating World. Ukiyo-e was a picture of the passing world of pleasure.

nationalism and industrialism. The Tokugawa period saw the beginnings of prolonged struggles between a rice agriculture and industry, between a local barter economy and a national money economy, between a feudal and military aristocracy and the power of commercial and then industrial capital, between the food supply and the population that had to be fed, between what was traditional and what was not. There was much dislocation and much suffering before the birth pains of this new society with its creeping capitalism had passed.

Since every society must provide a means of feeding and clothing itself, it follows that economic conditions are often a barometer of a society's contentment and therefore of its stability. Stability was a primary goal of the Yedo Bakufu, but the history of the period is a story of growing dissatisfaction with economic conditions. These dissatisfactions played their part in the gradual undermining of that "massive stability" which describes the early years of the Tokugawa system. The most obvious signs of unrest occurred in the countryside among the peasantry. Peasant uprisings were not peculiar to Tokugawa times, but they increased in number and violence under the Yedo Bakufu. Their causes were very complex and it is possible here to suggest only a few of the conditioning factors.

First of all was the important fact that the peasant was the only regular taxpayer. A large part of his rice crop he owed to his feudal lord for the support of the whole military aristocracy. Whatever new burdens the Bakufu might lay on the military or business classes were passed on by them to the peasant in the form of additional taxation or through currency or market manipulations. Since a peasant paid more to his lord in a good crop year than in a bad one, a bumper crop was a questionable blessing. Although the peasant did not "own" the land he cultivated, his tenure was secure through laws that prohibited transfer of land under cultivation. Nevertheless, with the appearance of a merchant class with funds for investment, ways were found to get around these laws and thus to create a new landlord class of city merchants who shared in the revenue derived from land on which the whole feudal state rested. However, the student should not jump to the simple conclusion that all the woes of the Tokugawa period can be laid at the door of a land tax on the peasantry. Actually in some areas the land tax remained static or declined slightly while the productivity of land was rising. Agrarian distress there certainly was, but it resulted not only from taxation but also from usury, flood, drought, extravagant spending, and adverse price movements. At the same time, by the end of the Tokugawa period there was a large class of relatively wealthy, ambitious, and educated peasant families.[9]

Closely allied to the burden of peasant taxation was the distressing problem of population. For the first half of the Tokugawa period population increased rapidly. Through the second half it remained practically stationary at about thirty million. The initial increase bore heavily on food supply. The growth of cities contributed to shortages of farm labor. The problem was aggravated by Japan's major dependence on a single food crop, rice, and her isolation from the outside world. In periods of crop failure there was no foreign trade, no imports and exports to relieve the crisis, and no effective means by which the price of rice could be controlled. In a fluctuating market it was the merchant who understood such matters who profited. Those who paid were the military caste and, most of all, the peasants.

The stability of the Bakufu was also undermined by its failure to pursue sound policies in public finance. It should be recognized that the Yedo government faced extraordinary difficulties. Its military triumph at the beginning of the seventeenth century imposed upon it responsibilities that were really national in scope, while the state was organized in a feudal pattern: the Bakufu derived regular revenue from its own domains only. The consequence was a state of chronic deficit relieved but little by drastic

economic policies effected from time to time. Because of the country's political organization there could be no recourse to national loans. Instead, the Bakufu resorted to emergency measures. Since the peasant was already taxed to the limit that agriculture could bear, and since forced "gifts" from the daimyo could not be demanded too frequently, most of the special emergency levies fell upon the merchant class in the large cities under Tokugawa control. Although these levies were called loans, frequently they were not repaid; and when these levies, as was often the case, failed to meet the government's financial plight, it could and did resort to debasement of the coinage. These expedients, which at best only postponed the day of judgment, aggravated economic conditions that were already bad by encouraging wild fluctuation of prices.

By the 1830s the once secure Tokugawa shogunate was infected by a deepening sense of crisis. The failure of officialdom to ease the peasant's lot was dramatized in 1837 by rebellion in Tokugawa's own ranks. Oshio Heihachiro, a minor official in the Bakufu's Osaka city administration, called upon an oppressed urban and rural populace to rise and kill "the heartless officials and the luxury living merchants who profited while the poor starved." This proved to be a minor flare-up, one quickly suppressed, but it was symptomatic of a popular inclination to attack authority. In territory least susceptible to Bakufu censorship, scholars were producing literature which questioned the shogun's position. Reinterpretation of Confucian classics and of Japan's political history produced a picture of the shogunate as a usurper of the Emperor's legitimate function, a government scarcely deserving loyal obedience. Finally, Tokugawa was challenged in its policy of seclusion by both the Russians and British who, becoming numerous in Japanese waters, pressed for the opening of trade.[10]

[9] Thomas C. Smith, "The Land Tax in the Tokugawa Period," *Journal of Asian Studies* 18 (1958): 3–19.

[10] John Whitney Hall, "Tokugawa Japan: 1800–1853," *Modern East Asia; Essays in Interpretation*, James B. Crowley, ed. (1970),* 62–94. The developing and increasingly divergent aims of education are treated in R. P. Dore, *Education in Tokugawa Japan* (1965). Even in an

SUMMARY

All these various conditions, trends, changes, and schools of thought gradually destroyed the Tokugawa pattern of permanence and created in its place a society whose formal structure of feudal dictatorship and rigid class lines was no longer an adequate vehicle by which this new nation could live, move, and have its being. Tokugawa feudalism had become a facade behind which grew the strivings and struggles of a disgruntled people. No class was exempt from the disturbing effects of these varied dislocations. In summary they added up to a complex anatomy of maladjustments:

1. At the top of the politico-social scale, many of the daimyo were plagued by the same financial ailments that beset the shogunate.
2. The samurai posed the perplexing problem of what to do with an idle standing army in a prolonged period of unbroken peace. As the finances of shogun and daimyo went from bad to worse, there was the irresistible tendency to cut the allowances of their samurai retainers. As a net result, the samurai had too little money and too much time on their hands.
3. The farmers, as the Tokugawa era moved into the nineteenth century, continued through peasant uprisings to protest against economic grievances magnified by periodic natural calamities of flood and famine.
4. The merchants, even with their wealth, were vulnerable and insecure. They were never free from the vexatious interference by government which often amounted to confiscation. Nevertheless, most of the merchants were not opposed to the regime even though many were angered by its restrictions. They resented the lowly social status from which their wealth had not freed them.

---

authoritarian society there was disagreement on the purposes of samurai education. The traditional view was that the primary purpose was to build moral character in a Confucian sense. Against this were those who said that the ruling warrior class would be better rulers if education gave them new and increased knowledge. By the beginning of the nineteenth century the educational system was remarkably diversified considering the time and place. Indeed, it had laid some firm foundations for the nation that was soon to emerge.

At the beginning of the seventeenth century, the Tokugawas had fashioned a society of seemingly "massive stability." For a time their plan was eminently successful. In the end, their regime of peace was their own undoing. By the end of the eighteenth century, stability was a memory. The political framework of the past still stood, but the society it was supposed to represent was no longer essentially feudal. The first steps toward modern nationhood had been taken.

In Tokugawa times, theory, such as it was, and practice did not always coincide. The original exclusion laws had appeared gradually. They were occasioned less by ideology than by the empirical demands of a particular situation. Even when exclusion did become a national policy its enforcement was uneven. For example, in 1720 the ban against Western books was modified to permit the study of geography, military science, and medicine. At best, exclusion, adopted without philosophical conviction, ran counter to Japan's natural economic needs. These problems were recognized early by some Japanese statesmen, Tanuma Okitsugu, for example, the most important minister in the shogunate in the late eighteenth century. The work of such statesmen indicates that Japan might have abandoned her seclusion policy voluntarily a half century before she was actually compelled to do so.[11]

The fact that the Tokugawa regime lasted for two and one-half centuries is testimony to its political and economic craftsmanship. Regulation, extended to every phase of life, would ensure stable, unchanging institutions. The policy of seclusion would be a barrier against contagion from without. Intellectually and spiritually the country would find contentment in neo-Confucianism and Buddhism. For a time, this planned society seemed to work quite well, but, in the longer view, institutions did change. In a period of

[11] The basic study is John W. Hall, *Tanuma Okitsugu, 1719–1788: Forerunner of Modern Japan* (1955).* The fascinating story of what the Japanese learned about the West in the crucial years, 1720–1830, is told by Donald Keene, *The Japanese Discovery of Europe, 1720–1830* (rev. ed., 1969).*

unbroken peace there was a lessening of samurai control. The rigid class structure weakened. The economic base shifted in some degree to the growing cities. An inflexible Confucianism failed to curb a new spirit of intellectual curiosity. Even in exclusion, Japan did acquire a view of Western natural science, military science, and philosophy. Thus was the way prepared for the downfall of the last great shogunate.[12]

[12] Grant Kohn Goodman, *The Dutch Impact on Japan, 1640–1853* (Leiden, 1967), especially 212–26.

FOR FURTHER READING

HISTORY. David M. Earl, *Emperor and Nation in Japan: Political Thinkers of the Tokugawa Period* (1964) deals with Confucian influence in Japan and with the samurai scholar, Yoshida Shoyin. Alexander Pernikoff, *"Bushido"* (1943), a wartime publication on this "unwritten" code for Japanese knighthood. Nitobe Inazo's *Bushido* (1905) though old, is more scholarly, balanced and penetrating. Daniel Spencer, "Japan's Pre-Perry Preparation for Economic Growth," *American Journal of Economics and Sociology* 17 (1958): 195–216, an analysis of Japanese economic conditions in the last century of the Tokugawa period; Robert Sakai, "Feudal Society and Modern Leadership in the Satsuma-Han," *Journal of Asian Studies* 16 (1957): 365–76, and his article, "The Satsuma-Ryukyu Trade and the Tokugawa Seclusion Policy," *Journal of Asian Studies* 23 (1964): 391–403, are important research papers from original sources. Equally important is Robert G. Flershem's "Some Aspects of Japan Sea Trade in the Tokugawa Period," *Journal of Asian Studies* 23 (1964), 405–16. Charles R. Boxer, *The Christian Century in Japan, 1549–1650* (1951), a scholarly, readable study of the impact of Christianity and the West upon Japan in early modern times. Dan F. Henderson, "Japanese Legal History of the Tokugawa Period, Scholars and Sources," *Five Studies in Japanese Politics*, Robert E. Ward, ed. (1957) includes analysis of the legal system itself. Hugh Borton, "Peasant Up-

risings in Japan of the Tokugawa Period," *Transactions*, Asiatic Society of Japan, Second Series, 16 (1938), 15, 219. Herschel Webb, *The Japanese Imperial Institution in the Tokugawa Period* (1968). John W. Hall and Marius B. Jansen, eds., *Studies in the Institutional History of Early Modern Japan* (1968). Peter Duus, *Feudalism in Japan* (1969)* G. B. Sansom, *A History of Japan: 1615–1867* (1963) is the most recent and the most definitive political and social history. H. D. Harootunian, *Toward Restoration: The Growth of Political Consciousness in Tokugawa Japan* (1970).

BIOGRAPHICAL STUDIES. Walter Dening, *The Life of Toyotomi Hideyoshi* (Tokyo, 1955), a fast moving but not always accurate sketch of the life of the sixteenth-century "Napoleon of Japan." Arthur Lindsay Sadler, *The Maker of Modern Japan: The Life of Tokugawa Iyeyasu, 1542–1616* (London, 1937) presents a portrait of the founder of the Tokugawa Shogunate. Philip G. Rogers, *The First Englishman in Japan: The Story of Will Adams* (London, 1956). J. W. Hall, *Tanuma Okitsuga, 1719–1788: Forerunner of Modern Japan* (1955).*

RELIGION. Robert N. Bellah, *Tokugawa Religion* (1957), a monumental study in motivation.

THE THEATER AND THE ARTS Arthur Lindsay Sadler, *Cha-no-yu: the Japanese Tea Ceremony* (London, 1934), and the same author's *The Art of Flower Arrangement in Japan. A Sketch of its History and Development* (1933). Faubion Bowers, *Japanese Theater* (1952),* and A. C. Scott, *The Kabuki Theatre of Japan* (London, 1955),* an extremely useful study of the traditional theatre.

LITERATURE. Howard Hibbett, *The Floating World in Japanese Fiction, Tales of the Ukiyo and Their Background* (1959). The *ukiyo-zoshi*, or "tales of the floating world," offer a glittering picture of the city life which flourished during the brilliant Genroku era (1680–1740). Ikku Jippensha, *Shank's Mare:*

Being a Translation of the Tokaido Volumes of Hizakurige, trans. by Thomas Satchell (Tokyo, 1960),* Japan's great comic novel of travel and ribaldry. Oliver Statler, *Japanese Inn* (1961),* a delightful recapturing of Japanese life at an historic inn on the Tokaido which joined Kyoto and Yedo in Tokugawa days. Ihara Saikaku, *Five Women Who Loved Love*, trans. by Wm. Theodore deBary (1956),* a collection of risqué tales of the eighteenth century by one of Japan's literary masters, is unsurpassed for its glimpses of contemporary urban life and manners.

Japan, 1840–1865:
The Collapse of Isolation

chapter 9

During the nineteenth century Japan experienced a revolution the consequences of which would be difficult to exaggerate. There were two major effects of this revolution which are of importance to this narrative. As a result of the first (the subject of this chapter), the 250-year-old policy of exclusion and seclusion was ended and replaced by a broad policy of intercourse with the West. As a result of the second (treated in Chapter 10), dual government, the shogunate, and the system of feudalism were replaced by a centralized administration, carried on in the name of the Mikado, and clothed in 1889 with a constitution deriving its form, if not its spirit, from Western political models.

The collapse in the middle of the nineteenth century of Japan's policy of isolation was a result not only of external pressures exerted by foreign states, but also of revolutionary social pressures within Japan itself. To put the matter another way, when in 1854 the Japanese signed a treaty with the United States, they were not reacting solely to American naval power; they were reacting also to the fundamental needs of their own society. For nearly 250 years the Tokugawa shoguns had sought to maintain a planned and fixed social economy. Their initial success and their ultimate failure have been discussed in the previous chapter. Thus, by mid-nineteenth century, Japan was living under a regime that was no longer adequate to meet new conditions. A new policy, both internal and external, was imperative and imminent.

While Japan was living within the exclusive walls of the Tokugawa dictatorship, Western states were developing a new society, new theories of government, new conceptions of national wealth, and new colonial empires. Between 1638 and 1854, the period of Japanese seclusion, Europe witnessed the Glorious Revolution in England, the perfecting of the absolute monarchy in France, the victory of England over France in the great colonial wars in America and India, the revolt of the thirteen English colonies, the French Revolution, the wars of Napoleon, and the beginnings of the Industrial Revolution with its emphasis on economic doctrines of laissez faire. In the first half of the nineteenth century, popular middle-class nationalism had triumphed over the crumbling edifice erected by Metternich. Both Europe and the United States (the latter had become a power on the Pacific with the acquisition of the Oregon Territory in 1846) were prepared for a new era of commercial and industrial expansion.

Western commerce was already invading every area of the globe. It certainly could not by-pass Japan for long. Already, in 1840–1842, England had fought successfuly her first commercial war in China.

Japan's knowledge of this changing and threatening Western world was imperfect and colored by lack of perspective. Yet the shogunate was by no means in complete ignorance of external affairs. Some considerable body of information had entered Japan through the medium of the Dutch at Nagasaki and through Chinese merchants.

EARLY ATTEMPTS TO OPEN JAPAN

Late in the eighteenth and early in the nineteenth centuries a number of Western powers attempted to open Japan to trade. Of these efforts, the most continuous were exerted by Russia. Contacts between Russians and Japanese dated back to 1697, the year of the first recorded encounter of a Japanese castaway and a Russian explorer. Down to 1875 when Russia obtained southern Sakhalin in exchange for her claims to the northern Kuriles, Russian objectives sought commercial and diplomatic relations with Japan and delineation of a Russo-Japanese frontier. During the eighteenth century when numerous Russian expeditions reached Japanese shores there was vigorous debate within Japan on what should be done.[1] The ultimate decision to continue exclusion was reached less by reference to tradition and to unalterable exclusion laws than to the fear that a Russian trade might be unprofitable and that the Russians entertained territorial ambitions.

By 1850 the United States was becoming as interested in Japan as it had previously, since 1842, been interested in China. Shipwrecked American seamen from the North Pacific whaling fleet cast upon Japanese shores were often treated as criminals. Some died from exposure; others were required to trample and spit on the Cross; all were ex-

[1] The definitive study is George A. Lensen, *The Russian Push Toward Japan: Russo-Japanese Relations, 1697–1875* (1959).

hibited in cages to the public gaze. Furthermore, America's expanding trans-Pacific trade from San Francisco to China passed through Japanese waters. Japanese ports were needed as coaling stations for the new trans-Pacific steamships. American business was already anticipating the opening of a lucrative trade with Japan. Influenced by these various motives, by petitions to Congress, and by what appeared to be an influential public interest, President Fillmore in 1852 selected Commodore Matthew C. Perry, a distinguished naval officer and a brother of the hero of Lake Erie fame, to command a naval expedition designed to open Japan to trade.

Public reaction to the mission was divided. While optimists hoped for its success, the pessimists referred to it as a "romantic notion" and "a matter of ridicule abroad and at home." A contributor to *Putnam's Magazine* thought Perry the instrument of a divine plan. Trade would follow Perry's mission and thus the merchants would open "a highway for the chariot of the Lord Jesus Christ. . . ." There were also voices that cautioned care lest the United States become involved in a war with Japan. The fact that the Japanese were "rude, intractable, selfish, and unsocial" was not sufficient reason for going to war with them. These reactions are not surprising, since both in the United States and Europe pseudo knowledge had produced strange and varied opinions of Japan and the Japanese. Estimates of Japan's area ranged from 9,000 to 266,000 square miles; of population density, from 184 to 4,000 per square mile; and of total population, from 15,000,000 to 50,-000,000. Yedo alone was said to have a population of at least 10,000,000. The Japanese of the "lowest orders" were said to have a yellow complexion, "like the color of cheese." As is usually true in such cases, fancy rather than fact determined what people had to say about Japan.

With a fleet of four ships, Perry entered Yedo (later Tokyo) Bay and anchored off Uraga, July 8, 1853. His arrival did not take the Japanese by surprise, for they had been warned of his coming by the Dutch; yet the appearance of the American squadron pre-

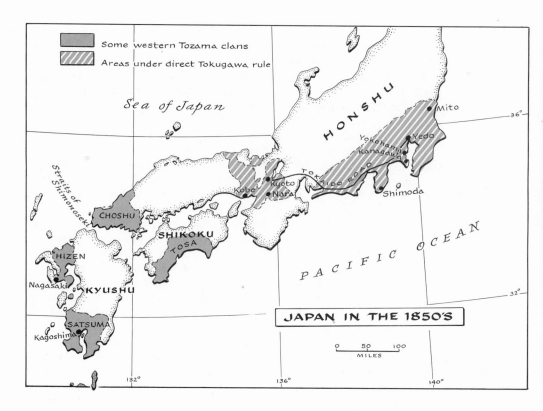

Source: E. O. Reischauer, *Japan, The Story of a Nation* (New York: Alfred A. Knopf, 1970), 84–85.

cipitated one of the great crises of Japanese history. While unaware of the real nature of this crisis, Perry proceeded to the task before him with firmness, dignity, and tact. He impressed the officials of the shogun's government with the power of his fleet—it contained the first steamers seen in Japanese waters—and with his own good will. He refused to retire to Nagasaki or to deal through the Dutch there. He demanded treatment suitable to the representative of a great power. In this behavior he was justified when, in opposition to Japanese law, President Fillmore's letter was received by two high officials of the shogun's court. Then Perry sailed away, but not without informing the Japanese that he would return the next year with a more powerful fleet to receive their answer.[2]

[2] Payson J. Treat, *Diplomatic Relations Between the United States and Japan* (2 vols., 1932; reprint, 1963), I, 11.

TREATIES WITH FOREIGN POWERS

Perry's visit confronted the shogun with the most serious decision ever faced by the Tokugawas. An Iyeyasu would have decided the matter on his own responsibility. Now, however, the shogunate had come on sorry days, and, faced with an issue of unparalleled importance, it took the unprecedented step of seeking the advice not only of the leading daimyo, but also of the emperor. The preponderant opinion favored repelling the foreigner, but some few recognized the futility of armed opposition.

Perry was already hastening his return, spurred by rumors that French and Russian squadrons planned to visit Japan. This time, with an augmented fleet of seven vessels, he entered Yedo Bay on February 13, 1854. Fortunately, the minority at the shogun's court had prevailed, and so at Kanagawa the negotiation of a treaty proceeded amid social activities of the utmost gaiety. Gifts presented to the Japanese by the United States included a miniature railway, telegraph, books, and a variety of liquors. All these delighted the Japanese.[3]

The treaty signed by Perry and the representatives of the shogun, March 31, 1854 (Treaty of Kanagawa), viewed superficially, was in many respects a disappointment. In reality it was little more than a convention covering shipwreck and supply. It provided for peace, for the opening of two ports for supplies (Shimoda immediately and Hakodate a year later), good treatment for shipwrecked American sailors, a limited trade under Japanese regulations, and for supplies for American ships—really a treaty of friendship. Yet viewed realistically, the treaty was a remarkable achievement against more than two centuries of Japanese exclusion. Perry's success was due to many factors: his own "firmness, sagacity, tact, dignity, patience, and determination"; the strength of his great naval squadron, the like of which the Japanese had never before seen; and his declaration that more ships would be sent if the just demands of the United States were not met. Reinforcing these attributes of Perry the diplomat were others over which he had no control, but without which he might well have failed: the recent frequent appearance of Russian vessels in Japanese waters, Japanese knowledge of China's defeat in 1842, and above all, those internal developments, described in Chapter 8, which had made Japan ripe for revolution. Any estimate of Perry as naval officer, diplomat, or statesman should consider not only his success in Japan but also the broader pattern of Pacific policy which he had in mind. To Perry the opening of Japan was not an end in itself but rather

one in a series of steps toward creating American maritime power in the Pacific. This pattern would include coaling stations and naval bases throughout the Pacific and especially in the Bonin Islands, the Liu-ch'iu (Ryukyu), and Formosa. Perry has sometimes been called the first American imperialist. He foresaw and supported a policy to which little heed was given at the time, but which was implemented in great detail in the next fifty years.

Perry's success was one of the most significant events in American history, though it was not so recognized then in the United States. Little attention was paid to it in the press, and it was almost ignored by President Pierce in his annual message to Congress, perhaps because it had been the work of a Whig government. Almost the only interest shown by Congress took the form of a protest that the cost of printing the report of the Perry mission was "outrageously extravagant." Moreover, the book was "full of pictures and most costly engravings of shells, and birds, and snakes, and bugs in Japan, with God knows how many maps that are appended to its surveys." Japan's exclusion policy had been ended. The decision that effected this momentous change was made by the shogun's government, but the United States had provided the occasion that forced the decision.

Representatives of other powers soon followed Perry to Japan and secured treaties similar though not identical with that of the United States. A British admiral, Sir James Stirling, negotiated a treaty at Nagasaki (October, 1854). The Russian Admiral, Count Putiatin, secured his treaty at Shimoda (February, 1855).[4] Finally the Dutch were released from their commercial confinement at Nagasaki and given a new treaty (January, 1856). The most-favored-nation clause made the provisions of each treaty the common

[3] See Francis L. Hawks, compiler, *Narrative of the Expedition of an American Squadron to the China Seas and Japan, Performed in the Years 1852, and 1854 under the Command of Commodore M. C. Perry, United States Navy* (published by order of Congress, 1856), 375. For the Americans as Japanese artists saw them, Oliver Statler, *The Black Ship Scroll: An Account of the Perry Expedition at Shimoda in 1854 and the Lively Beginnings of People-to-People Relations Between Japan and America* (1964).

[4] Several works by George A. Lensen, "Russians in Japan, 1858–1859," *The Journal of Modern History* 26 (1954): 162–73; "The Russo-Japanese Frontier," *History and Literature,* Florida State University Studies, No. 14, 1954, 23–40; *Russia's Japan Expedition of 1852 to 1855* (1964),* 111–26; and *Russia's Eastward Expansion* (1964).* See also W. G. Beasley, *Great Britain and the Opening of Japan* (London, 1951), 113–44.

property of the four powers, and expanded somewhat the rights Americans had won in the Perry treaty. These total and enlarged rights held by the four powers in 1856 included: (1) permission to secure supplies at Shimoda, Hakodate, and Nagasaki; (2) permission to trade through Japanese officials and under their regulations at these ports; (3) right of male residence at Nagasaki; (4) permission to appoint consuls at Shimoda and Hakodate; and (5) a limited extraterritorial jurisdiction.

Three of these treaties (the American, the British, and the Russian) were approved by the emperor in February, 1855. The importance of this was not realized at the time by the foreign powers. The treaties had been negotiated with the shogun's government and they were signed under the title of "tycoon" (great lord). By the foreigners it was assumed that the shogun was the proper authority to control diplomatic affairs. This of course was so, but what the foreigner did not know was the extent to which the authority of the shogun had already been weakened by internal dissension. This explains why the shogunate, when Perry arrived, was unwilling to accept full responsibility for signing a treaty. It had therefore referred the matter for approval to the emperor. Since the shogun's influence with the Imperial Court was still strong, the Imperial approval was given. With this approval the shogun could for a time silence the powerful opposition to the new policy.

The Imperial approval ensured general acceptance of the treaties, but the fact that the shogunate almost failed to secure the throne's favor revealed how the might of the *Bakufu* had declined. It had not been the habit of the Tokugawas or their predecessors to consider the will of the throne. They did so now because their old supremacy was little better than a political fiction, because they recognized the power of their feudal enemies, the *tozama* or outside lords of the Western clans (Satsuma, Choshu, Hizen and Tosa) who were enemies of the Tokugawa before 1600, and because there was bitter dissension within the Tokugawa clan itself. Indeed, even among those elements that favored signing the trea-

ties, the feeling was strong that no further concessions should be made to the foreigner— no general trade would be permitted and foreign contacts would be held to the bare treaty minimum.

TOWNSEND HARRIS IN JAPAN

Shortly after the Perry treaty was concluded, the American government sent its first consul general to reside at Shimoda. He was Townsend Harris of New York, a merchant familiar with the Far East and a man of excellent mind and character. Harris travelled by way of Siam, where he negotiated a treaty granting extraterritoriality and a conventional tariff. He reached Shimoda in August, 1856.

The village of Shimoda, some 60 miles from Yedo, on the southern extremity of the Izu Peninsula southwest of Yedo Bay, was possessed of an exceptionally poor harbor that had been all but ruined by a tidal wave the previous year. The town, shut off from the hinterland by ranges of hills, was remote from the high roads and markets, and, in a word, was peculiarly ill-adapted to the needs of Harris. The Japanese had hoped to isolate the consul, if one came, and the selection of Shimoda was admirable for this purpose. Here Harris was in virtual quarantine not only from the United States but also from Japan. Fourteen months elapsed before he was visited by an American naval vessel, and eighteen months before he received additional instructions from the Department of State. On one occasion he wrote in his journal that for ten months he had not received a letter from the United States, that his supply of Western food was exhausted, and that he had lost so much weight it appeared that a viceconsul had been cut out of him. His position was described as "one honest man against a host of liars."

The principal objective of the Harris mission was to secure a full commercial treaty. The prospects of success were small. From the moment Harris landed, the Japanese used every device of obstruction and deceit to discourage and defeat him. They asserted that he had no right to land, since

Japan had not approved his coming. With reluctance they assigned him an old temple as a residence. It was infested with mosquitoes, cockroaches, and large rats. The market sold him roosters that were too tough to eat. Police constantly guarded the temple on the pretext of protecting him. Wherever Harris or his Chinese servants went they were spied upon with the utmost suspicion. Japanese officials lied to him in the most flagrant manner. All this and much more Harris bore with patience, until after some months he was able to write in his journal: "The Japanese officials are daily becoming more and more friendly and more open in their communications with me. I hope this will grow and lead to good results by and by." This turn for the better in the relations between Harris and the shogun's officials must be attributed in large part to the patience, firmness, and unfailing honesty of this lonely bachelor American diplomat. He had set a high goal for himself. He proposed to serve the interests of his own country by leading Japan to a policy of full commercial intercourse, yet in so doing he was resolved not to take advantage of Japanese ignorance and lack of experience in international affairs. Harris, indeed, had become Japan's first instructor in world politics.

In June, 1857, Harris witnessed the first official fruits of his labors when the Japanese signed a convention that, among other things, granted formally to the United States all that was contained in the British, Russian, and Dutch treaties. This was merely a preliminary. The great work still remained. Harris had asked for an audience with the shogun in Yedo at which he would present a letter from the President. After much delay the request was granted. Harris himself described the astonishment of the officials as he stood in the presence of the shogun and looked "the awful 'Tycoon' in the face," spoke "plainly to him," and heard his reply —all this without any trepidation, or any "quivering of the muscles of the side." [5]

Without the support of gunboats or marines Harris had won a great diplomatic victory.

It now remained for Harris to approach his main task—negotiating a full commercial treaty. He sought to convince the shogunate that the limited intercourse established by the first treaties was no longer adequate or practical. By January, 1858, the shogunate had agreed to the principal terms of a treaty. As the details of the treaty were perfected, Harris continued to act as instructor to the Japanese in diplomacy and international law. He continued to be that rare type of patriot who believed that the honor of his own country depended on its consideration for the rights of others.

When the treaty was completed, Harris waited impatiently month after month for the Japanese to sign. In July an American warship reached Shimoda bringing news of the Tientsin Treaties with China. Harris saw in these reports both a danger and an opportunity. If the Europeans now turned their guns on Japan, his own policy would be in jeopardy. Could this potential threat from English and French warships be used to frighten the shogunate into signature of the new treaty with America? Harris believed it could, and in this he was right. Despite bitter division of opinion in the shogunate, the treaty was signed July 29, 1858. It was a great personal victory for Harris, and a great diplomatic victory for his country. The treaty provided for diplomatic representation at the capitals of both powers, for the opening of new treaty ports where consuls might be stationed, for extraterritoriality, civil and criminal, for prohibition of the opium trade, for the freedom of foreigners to practice their religion, for a conventional tariff, and for the principle of most-favored-nation treatment.

The Harris treaty became the fundamental document in Japan's foreign relations until 1894. European powers accepted it as a model for their new treaties concluded in the months immediately following: the Dutch,

[5] See M. E. Cosenza, ed., *The Complete Journal of Townsend Harris* (1930; rev. ed., 1959); and Carl Crow, *He Opened the Door of Japan* (1939). Also Henry Heusken, *Japan Journal, 1855–1861.* Jeannette C. van der Corput and Robert A. Wilson, trans. and eds. (1964), the fascinating journal of the young Dutchman who was secretary and translator to Townsend Harris.

August 18; the Russian, August 19; the British, August 26; and the French, October 7.[6] Ratifications of the Harris treaty were exchanged in Washington in 1860 by the first modern Japanese embassy to the Western World. Members of this embassy, the first Japanese to see the wonders of America, were influential promoters of Japan's subsequent modernization.

DOMESTIC POLITICS AND FOREIGN AFFAIRS

The shogunate had signed the Harris treaty. Could it enforce acceptance of the new policy by its enemies at home? These latter included not only the *tozama* lords but also powerful leaders within the Tokugawa family itself. During 1857 powerful opposition against the pro-foreign policy of the shogunate had again reasserted itself. Thus, when the shogunate sought the emperor's consent to signature of the Harris treaty, the request was denied. This explains why Harris was kept waiting. Furthermore, his treaty represented a new policy adopted by the *Bakufu without the consent of the Mikado.* The enemies of the Tokugawas were quick to see that by opposing this liberal foreign policy of the shogunate they could appear as loyal supporters of the "divine" emperor against a "usurping" shogun. It was clear too that the balance of power in Japan had so shifted as to enable the Imperial court to issue orders to the *Bakufu.* Therefore the court told the shogun that the new treaties could be accepted only until such time as the foreign barbarians could be expelled and the old policy of exclusion resumed. In this way the Imperial court at Kyoto became the center of an anti-foreign, anti-*Bakufu* party, deriving its support from the *tozama* lords, from

[6] For the Harris treaty and conventions, see Hunter Miller, ed., *Treaties, etc.* . . . (1931–), VII, 598–648, 947–1170. The Harris treaty was also a triumph for those Japanese who believed Japan must move into the modern world, not away from it. Pre-eminent among these was Ii Naosuke, richest of Japan's hereditary vassals (fudai daimyo). See Yoshida Tsunekichi, *Ii Naosuke* (Tokyo, 1963).

disgruntled allies of the Tokugawa clan, and from branch families of the Tokugawa house itself, such as the Mito group.

July, 1859, was a critical month both for the shogunate and for the new treaty powers. So great was the danger of murderous attacks upon foreigners that the shogunate, refusing to open Kanagawa, which lay on the *Tokaido* highway between Yedo and Kyoto, encouraged the foreigners to settle at Yokohama, farther down the bay and destined soon to become one of Japan's great seaports. The immediate danger was twofold. So-called ultra-patriots, samurai and *ronin,* who had detached themselves from their clans, were anxious to embarrass the shogunate by attacking foreigners. Many of the foreigners in turn had come directly from residence in China, where too frequently they had acquired the habit of regarding the Oriental as an inferior to be treated with little respect. This being so, it is surprising that in the years 1859 to 1865, when foreigners were denounced by every fanatical supporter of the throne, only twelve Westerners were killed. Two cases that had important repercussions on foreign relations may be mentioned. When in January, 1861, the interpreter at the American legation, Heusken by name, was murdered, the foreign representatives, with the exception of Harris, retired from Yedo to Yokohama in protest against the shogun's failure to give the legations adequate protection. Harris took the broader view that the administration was doing everything in its power to protect them. He therefore remained in Yedo, where for a time he was the only foreign diplomatic representative.

The second case had more serious consequences. In September, 1862, C. L. Richardson, a Britisher visiting from Hong Kong, was killed on the highway near Yokohama while riding with three compatriots, two men and a woman. The assassins were samurai in the feudal procession of the father of the Lord of Satsuma, a leader of the anti-shogun and anti-foreign party supporting the throne. This influential personage had just served upon the shogun a summons ordering him to appear in Kyoto to explain his conduct before the throne. There are various accounts as to what happened. There is no proof that Richardson intended to be offensive. Nevertheless, he and his companions failed to dismount while the feudal procession passed by. For this he sacrificed his life, and his companions were wounded. Although foreigners in Yokohama demanded immediate military action, saner counsel prevailed. Early in the following year (1863), the British government made the following demands: (1) payment of an indemnity of 100,000 pounds; (2) an indemnity of 25,000 pounds to be paid by the Satsuma clan; and (3) trial and execution of the assassins in the presence of a British naval officer.

These demands came at a most unhappy moment in the shogun's career. He had already been summoned to Kyoto to explain his conduct, which could mean only that those opposed to his government and his policy were now in control of the throne. This proved to be true, for the emperor ordered that all ports be closed to foreign commerce. Meanwhile, the negotiations on the British demands continued at Yokohama, where the British and the French now offered to use their naval forces on behalf of the shogun against the anti-foreign lords. This offer the shogun declined. In June the British indemnity was paid and the powers were notified of the emperor's exclusion decree. Their reply declared that the treaties must be enforced, which, of course, the shogun fully realized. For the moment his policy would be one of delay, while he entertained the hope that some change could be effected in the attitude of his domestic enemies.

According to the Imperial decree, the expelling of the foreigners and the discarding of the treaties were to be carried out by the shogun's government. However, the Lord of Choshu, a *tozama* daimyo whose lands controlled the western entrance to the inland sea, fired on an American ship lying off Shimonoseki. Later, French and Dutch vessels were also fired upon. Consequently, one American and several French war vessels hastened to attack the Choshu forts. It was evident that the shogun was unable to control the western barons. The British had already determined to take action against Satsuma to enforce compliance with the demands arising out of the Richardson affair. Accordingly, a British squadron appeared at Kagoshima in August, 1863. Here negotiations broke down, and the resulting bombardment, assisted by a typhoon and fire, destroyed more than half the town. Without securing acceptance of their demands, the British sailed away. Three months later envoys from Satsuma called upon the British *chargé*, agreeing to pay the indemnity and to continue the search for the guilty. They also requested assistance in securing in England a naval vessel for their clan. The significance of the incident is obvious. Anti-foreignism in Satsuma was in part a cloak hiding a determination to destroy the shogunate.

Events took an unusual turn at Kyoto where the anti-foreign and anti-shogunate forces were in control. Dissension appeared in these councils, where Choshu leaders were accused of attempting to seize the person of the emperor. Choshu troops were ordered to leave the capital, and when they attempted a *coup d'état*, the shogun was ordered by the emperor to deal with the rebellious clan. At this juncture, Sir Rutherford Alcock, the British minister, returned to Japan determined to unite the foreign powers in a joint expedition against Choshu. The purpose of this was to give needed support to the shogunate and to demonstrate to the hot-headed clans that it was no longer safe to tamper with the treaty rights of foreigners. Alcock's plan was supported by his diplomatic colleagues, and so, contrary to his instructions from London, he set about to organize a joint naval expedition, consisting of British, Dutch, and French ships, and one small American vessel, which sailed from Yokohama in August, 1864. No negotiations preceded the engagement off the Choshu coast. The fleet went straight to the task of silencing the batteries. On Choshu this lesson was as effective as the previous affair at Kagoshima. Clan leaders agreed to open the straits, not to repair the forts or to build new ones, and to pay an indemnity covering the cost of the expedition. This clan, too, now turned to the West for armaments and advice that would create an effective military machine. Since the shogun could not permit the foreign powers to negotiate with a single clan, a convention was soon concluded whereby the indemnities were assumed by the shogunate. Payment of large sums, however, proved most embarrassing to the government, and since the powers were more interested in new treaty ports and new concessions, the opportunity was favorable for a second naval demonstration.

Under the leadership of the new British minister, Sir Harry Parkes, it was planned to assemble the naval forces of the powers at Osaka, close to Kyoto, where pressure could be most effectively brought to bear upon the anti-foreign forces surrounding the throne. This time no American vessel participated, for none was available. The demands stated that two-thirds of the Shimonoseki indemnity would be remitted if Hyogo (Kobe) and Osaka were opened immediately, if the emperor gave his approval to the treaties, and if the tariff were reduced to a general 5 per cent. The reply was delivered on the final day permitted by the Allies' demands. The emperor—and this was most important of all—had agreed to ratify the treaties, the tariff would be reduced, and the full indemnity would be paid, for Japan was not prepared to open Hyogo and Osaka until 1868. Thus the most serious problem, the opposition of the imperialists to the treaties, was disposed of. The western daimyo were no longer aligned against the foreigners, but their determination to overthrow the shogunate and restore the emperor still remained.

The first phase of Japan's nineteenth-century revolution was now complete. The two-centuries-old policy of exclusion and seclusion had been abandoned not only by the weakened shogunate but also by the throne, which derived its power from the vital western clans. Japan had now accepted full treaty relations with the major Western powers. These treaties as in the case of those with China, imposed certain serious limitations upon Japan's sovereignty—extraterritoriality and the conventional tariff.

It should also be observed that Japan's anti-foreignism in these early years of contacts with the West should not be considered merely the emotional outburst of military patriots. Anti-foreignism did have deep cultural and political roots, but its appearance after Perry's arrival can be explained by the economic results of the opening of Japan to foreign commerce. The cost of living was increased by large exports of consumer goods. The price of tea soon doubled; that of raw silk tripled. Before 1867 the price of rice, Japan's main food, had increased twelvefold. This disastrous revolution in prices was induced in part by the outflowing of Japan's gold supply due to the high and fixed price of silver in Japan. Hardships resulting from this price revolution supported the case of those factions that, for whatever reasons, regarded anti-foreignism as a patriotic duty.

FOR FURTHER READING

HISTORY. Delmer M. Brown, *Nationalism in Japan: An Introductory Historical Analysis* (1955) surveys Japanese nationalism from earliest times. J. H. Gubbins, *The Making of Modern Japan* (London, 1922), still useful though superseded in many respects by more recent and thorough studies. Ienaga Saburo, *History of Japan* (4th ed., Tokyo, 1959),° an interpretative view of Japanese history by a foremost Japanese historian. George M. Beckmann, *The Modernization of China and Japan* (1962), a recent survey presenting excellent chapters on the Meiji transformation.

FOREIGN RELATIONS. Edwin O. Reischauer, *The United States and Japan* (1950),° an excellent survey of U.S.-Japanese relations. Payson Jackson Treat, *Japan and the United States, 1853–1921*, Revised and continued to 1928 (1928), a standard survey. Manfred C. Vernon, "The Dutch and the Opening of Japan by the United States," *The Pacific Historical Review* 28 (1959): 39–48.

SPECIAL STUDIES ON THE OPENING OF JAPAN. Arthur C. Walworth, *Black Ships off Japan; The Story of Commodore Perry's Expedition* (1946; reprint, 1966), a popular and readable account. Allan B. Cole, ed., *A Scientist with Perry in Japan, the Journal of Dr. James*

Morrow (1947); and *Yankee Surveyors in the Shogun's Seas: Records of the U.S. Surveying Expedition to the North Pacific Ocean, 1853–56* (1947). George Henry Preble, *The Opening of Japan: A Diary of Discovery in the Far East, 1853–1856*, Boleslaw Szczesniak, ed. (1962). Roger Pineau, ed., *The Japan Expedition, 1852–1854: The Personal Journal of Commodore Matthew C. Perry* (1968). Samuel Eliot Morison, *"Old Bruin": Commodore Matthew C. Perry, 1794–1858. The American Naval Officer Who Helped Found Liberia, Hunted Pirates in the West Indies, Practised Diplomacy with the Sultans of Turkey and the King of the Two Sicilies; Commanded the Gulf Squadron in the Mexican War, Promoted the Steam Navy and the Shell Gun, and Conducted the Naval Expedition which Opened Japan* (1967), a meticulous study.

SPECIAL STUDIES. F. C. Jones, *Extraterritoriality in Japan and the Diplomatic Relations Resulting in Its Abolition, 1853–1899* (1931). John A. Harrison, *Japan's Northern Frontier: A Preliminary Study in Colonization and Expansion with Special Reference to the Relations of Japan and Russia* (1953)* presents the story of Japanese fears of Russia and Britain to 1882. George A. Lensen, *Report from Hokkaido: The Remains of Russian Culture in Northern Japan* (Hakodate, 1954). Roger F. Hackett, "Nishi Amane—A Tokugawa-Meiji Bureaucrat," *Journal of Asian Studies* 18 (1959): 213–25, illustrates the interplay of change and continuity in nineteenth century Japan. Marius B. Jansen, "Takechi Zuizan and the Tosa Loyalist Party," *Journal of Asian Studies* 18 (1959): 199–212, a study of the Loyalist movement in Tosa.

Japan, 1865–1889:
from Feudal to
Constitutional Government

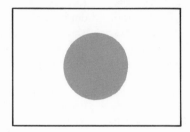

chapter 10

By 1865 the contending clan and other factions that controlled political power in Japan had accepted as a basic plank in the national policy the principle of diplomatic and commercial intercourse with the West. This was the first phase of the nineteenth-century revolution. But by whom should this new policy be controlled and carried on? The general economic distress, the weakness of the shogunate, its lack of national confidence, and more specifically its bankrupt prestige in the eyes of the western *tozama* clans—all these and other factors foreshadowed the need for sweeping changes in the whole structure of Japanese government if the nation was to acquire a strong position in its relations with the foreign powers. Neither dual government, nor the shogunate, nor military feudalism was designed to serve Japan adequately in her new relation with the outside world. The need was for a strong national government capable of controlling the clans and of creating a unified political structure that might deal with the foreigners on terms of equality.

The most vigorous and effective spokesmen of all elements disgruntled with the existing social and economic order, whether daimyo, *kuge*, samurai, *ronin*, merchants, or peasants, were certain able samurai of the western clans. These by capacity and experience had already become the real controllers of clan policy, the daimyo having been reduced to the role of puppets.

It was men of this stamp who planned and executed in its initial stages the political revolution which, between 1867 and 1889, destroyed the shogunate, stripped the Tokugawas of their lands and power, restored the emperor as the supreme ruler, abolished the feudal order, and bestowed upon the nation a centralized and constitutional but not a democratic government. This revolution, effected in scarcely more than twenty years, placed Japan before the turn of the twentieth century in that exclusive company known as "the Great Powers." It was a political, an economic, and in some degree a social revolution of transcending importance.[1]

[1] Here we are concerned with the political revolution. Its economic and social features will be discussed in Chapter 11. The student should bear in mind that the subject of the Restoration movement in Japan in the latter half of the nineteenth century cannot be disposed of in the brief survey presented in these pages. Marking Japan's entrance into the modern world, the Restoration has produced an impressive array of

The first step in these revolutionary changes occurred in 1867, when the daimyo of Tosa demanded the resignation of the Tokugawa shogun and the restoration of all power to the emperor. Since this demand was supported by the daimyos of Satsuma, Choshu, and Hizen, and by the strongest branch families of the Tokugawa clan—the daimyos of Owari and Echizen—the shogun was forced to comply, consoled by the thought that he would doubtless be chosen as chief adviser to the emperor under the new regime. This, however, was not the purpose of the revolutionists. These men were impelled by many and often mixed motives: (1) their newly found loyalty to the throne, (2) their hatred of the Tokugawa family, and (3) their own personal clan ambitions for power. Therefore, when the Tokugawas and their allies realized that the western clans were bent on their total destruction, they resorted to arms. In the brief civil war that followed, the Tokugawas were defeated. This was the end of Tokugawa power, and likewise the end of the shogunate and the ancient system of dual government. These stirring events opened the way for the restoration to full sovereign power, at least in theory, of a boy emperor, Mutsuhito, fourteen years of age, who was destined to go down in history as one of Japan's greatest rulers. He bore with dignity the reign-name of Meiji (enlightened government) from 1868 to 1912. By 1871, the formal structure of feudalism was also to disappear. These were revolutionary steps of enormous import.

theories respecting its causes and its historical meaning, and the last word on it has by no means been said as yet. Was it a spontaneous resurgence of loyalty to the throne? Was the emperor merely used by counterrevolutionary forces, as communist doctrine would hold? Was the Restoration caused by serious economic decline under the later Tokugawas? Was the Restoration a result of pressure from the West? See Marius B. Jansen, "The Meiji State, 1868–1912," *Modern East Asia:—Essays in Interpretation*, James B. Crowley, ed. (1970),° 95–121, a stimulating appraisal.

It might well have been expected that the disaffected samurai who engineered the Restoration of an emperor would have chosen rather to erect a new shogunate. Such an outcome was precluded by clan rivalries and by the fact that the anti-Tokugawa leadership could not recreate a *Bakufu* without destroying its own role which was innovative in attitude. They thus moved toward the only viable alternative, the Western model of the state. Their real problem was to choose between a liberal-democratic as against an absolute bureaucratic state. They chose the latter, because, among other reasons, speed was an imperative.

Meiji Government

During the past quarter of a century, Japan's Restoration has often been explained as simply the work of disgruntled lower-ranking or lower-class samurai who had the financial backing of merchant capitalists of Osaka and other cities.[2] While this interpretation undoubtedly has its place, it appears to have given undue emphasis to class and to economic motivation, important as these influences may have been.[3] Class and economic motivations do not explain very well the careers of the young political activists (*shishi*) who brought about the Restoration. Japanese politics from 1853 to 1868 often appeared to be one assassination following another; yet the end result was a purposeful movement toward national unity. Indeed these revolutionary characters gave to Japan a loyalty and a devotion to national interest that preserved the country from Western control.[4] In addition, it is beginning to appear that the Restoration and the radical reforms that were to follow it were achieved because the Restoration leaders were also strongly traditionalist and worked through traditional institutions. In a word, the Restoration and its immediate aftermath are best

[2] E. Herbert Norman, *Japan's Emergence as a Modern State* (1940), 102.
[3] See George B. Sansom, *The Western World and Japan* (1950).
[4] Marius B. Jansen, *Sakamoto Ryoma and the Meiji Restoration* (1961).

described as a perplexing interplay between traditionalism and reform sometimes influenced by class and economic motivation.[5]

The emperor was the logical one to wear the official mantle of authority under the new regime. Though often neglected by the shoguns and sometimes relegated to a position of abject poverty, the emperor, or rather "the magic power of the throne," was "such as to evoke the most passionate feelings of loyalty which were never completely dissipated." [6] This loyalty was soon developed by the Restoration leaders into a cult of emperor-worship deriving its immediate background from historical studies that stressed the "divinity" of the Imperial Family and the "illegitimate" character of Tokugawa rule. Fundamentally the new emperor-worship rested on what has been called a revival of "pure Shinto"—a Shintoism which, purged of Buddhist influence, was to stress as never before the emperor as the central and supreme deity of the nation.[7]

Since many of the daimyo and the samurai feared that power in the new regime would be monopolized by a few younger leaders, they caused the young Emperor Mutsuhito to issue in June, 1868, an Imperial Oath setting forth the principles on which the new imperial rule was to rest. This charter, a sort of Japanese Declaration of the Rights of Man, recognized, sometimes in ambiguous terms, the principles of public

discussion and debate by both the high and the low, and called for the abandonment of "absurd" practices of former times and for the pursuit of knowledge wherever it might be found.[8] Although the framers of this charter had in mind the samurai and not the people as a whole, it was to this same charter that the liberals of later nineteenth-century Japan appealed in their struggle for representative government. In 1868, however, these gropings of new political forces were extremely vague, and the framework of the new political order had not taken definite shape. For some fifteen years after the Restoration, one administration followed another. They were essentially caretaker governments as the nation sought a new political equilibrium.

THE ABOLITION OF FEUDALISM

It has already been pointed out that for many years economic and social adjustments had been taking place extra-legally in Japanese society, adjustments that revealed the incapacity of the feudal structure to meet new needs. The Restoration of 1868 in bestowing political power on the young samurai leaders of the western clans gave them the opportunity to destroy political feudalism to clear the ground for a truly national government.

The initiative in this development came again from the western clans of Satsuma, Choshu, Hizen, and Tosa, whose daimyo in 1869 returned their feudal domains to the emperor. These lords had been advised by their samurai leaders, who now controlled the emperor, that they were surrendering power only to receive greater power. Indeed the western lords were ordered to take up their residence in Tokyo, the former Yedo, to which the emperor had moved, and place their troops at the disposal of the sovereign's

[5] Albert M. Craig, *Chōshū in the Meiji Restoration* (1961). See also Bernard S. Silberman, *Ministers of Modernization: Elite Mobility in the Meiji Restoration, 1868–1873* (1964). Silberman suggests that: (1) the Restoration leaders were of the elite in their roles in clan government (there were few merchants among them) and their qualifications for leadership were enhanced not only by status but also by exposure to Western ideas; (2) the Meiji leadership enlarged its potential for success by pushing unqualified higher samurai and nobility upstairs rather then purging them; (3) growth of clan population and wealth contributed to the success of Meiji leadership making possible the pursuit by individuals of Dutch and other Western studies.

[6] Norman, *Japan's Emergence as a Modern State*, 27.

[7] D. C. Holtom, *Modern Japan and Shinto Nationalism* (1943; rev. ed., 1947; reprint, 1963), Chapters 1 and 2.

[8] For the text of the Imperial Oath, see W. W. McLaren, "Japanese Government Documents," *Transactions of the Asiatic Society of Japan* 42, Pt. 1 (Tokyo, 1914): 8. It is also quoted by Chitoshi Yanaga, *Japan Since Perry* (1949), 48; and Hugh Borton, *Japan's Modern Century* (1955), 72.

government. Thus strengthened in their position, the young samurai leaders were able through the emperor "to invite" the remaining daimyo to surrender their lands, and to follow this "invitation" with an imperial rescript (1871) abolishing fiefs and clans. Feudalism as a political structure was thus destroyed.

This sweeping change in the political edifice affected materially every class of society. Most of the daimyo viewed the change with apprehension, but they knew better than to oppose the great western clans. They were consoled with annual pensions of one-tenth of the nominal revenue from their former fiefs. Indeed, their financial position was greatly improved because (1) the nominal income was higher than the actual income; (2) they were no longer burdened with the support of their samurai; and (3) their debts in most instances were assumed by the new central government or were cancelled. However, none of the daimyo won political distinction in the new government.

Far different were the effects upon the samurai. This class numbered about 450,000 families in 1871. The samurai's income from his feudal lord, measured in rice, was already small. This income was cut in half; but he was permitted to lay aside the badge of his class, the two swords, and to enter the field of business or finance. All this, however, was highly bewildering to men whose sole profession had been that of bearing arms, who regarded the fief as owing them a living, and whose mental horizon was restricted to the military philosophy of *Bushido*. They now faced a society that deprived them of half their income, of their monopoly in bearing arms (the new conscript national army was made up largely of commoners), and, worst of all, directed them toward the despised walks of business. Some of the lesser samurai adjusted themselves with relative ease to the new order. Some were to emerge as the leaders of modern Japanese politics and business. But the majority could not make the adjustment. These malcontents, and their intellectual descendants were destined to play a significant role in Japan's later bid for world power.

Capitalistic groups—bankers, rice brokers, and wealthy merchants—welcomed the Restoration and the abolition of feudalism. Among these groups were families such as Mitsui and Sumitomo, who had helped to finance the Revolution of 1868–1871. For these services they were not to go unpaid. Many of the debts owed to these capitalists were assumed by the new government.

Most significant of all the effects stemming from the abolition of feudalism were those directly touching the farmers. In 1871 probably 80 per cent of Japan's population was composed of farmers, a majority of whom were independent cultivators. Yet within a few years "tenant land occupied 30 per cent of the area cultivated," a tendency that was accelerated in later years. In a word, the surreptitious acquisition of land by the new capitalistic landlord class, which had been going on before the Restoration, was now legalized; the peasant was freed from feudal obligations and became nominally a freeholder paying, not a tax in kind on the value of his crop, but a money tax on the value of his land. When in feudal days taxes were collected, the principle followed was "to see that the peasants had just enough to live on and no more." Thus under the "paternal" care of the feudal lord, the peasant "neither died nor lived." "In the new society [after 1871] they [the peasants] were free to choose their own fate; to live or die, to remain on the land or sell out and go to the city." [9] Thus the way was opened for the dispossession of the peasantry and the creation of "modern Japanese agriculture with its unique tenant-landlord relations."

THE ERA OF ENLIGHTENED GOVERNMENT (MEIJI)

The Restoration and the abolition of feudalism, together with the earlier adoption of the new policy of commercial inter-

[9] For population estimates and vocational distribution, see Ryoichi Ishii, *Population Pressure and Economic Life in Japan* (London, 1937), and A. E. Hindmarsh, *The Basis of Japanese Foreign Policy* (1936).

course with great Western maritime powers, were an essential prelude to the creation of a new Japan.

Prior to the Restoration, foreign travel had been forbidden. Japan's knowledge of the Western world was confined to what she had learned from the Dutch at Nagasaki, from the foreigners who had come in the wake of Perry, and from the limited company of Japanese who had gone abroad with or without government approval. It was a new and strange world that they saw. The scope of the impressions carried back to Japan by the first travellers in these years is illustrated by the report of the shogun's mission to the United States in 1860. Its observations covered every human activity from the constitutional position and behavior of the President to the plumbing and etiquette of the bathroom. As a result many of the earliest reforms were in education.

Here Japan's enthusiasm for the world of the West appeared to recognize no barriers. Following the mandate of the Imperial Oath (1868) that knowledge should be sought wherever it might be found, a department of education was set up (1871) under a law which proclaimed that "all people, high or low, and of both sexes, should receive education, so that there should not be found one family in the whole empire, nor one member of a family, ignorant and illiterate." This was a radical departure. Education in feudal Japan had been restricted to men of privileged society; now elementary education for all was to be compulsory. It was based on a modification of the American primary and secondary systems. Boys and girls, six years of age, were required to attend a four-year, later increased to a six-year, course. They were given instruction in elementary subjects plus special character training closely associated with reverence for and loyalty to the emperor. Secondary education prepared students for an immediate vocation or for entrance into a university. Normal schools turned out an ever-increasing supply of teachers, and in a few years the personnel needs of Japan's expanding trade and industry were met by commercial schools. Elementary training for girls was similar to that for the boys; secondary education, however, stressed woman's role as a wife and mother; and it was not until 1902 that the government made provision for higher education for women. Yet in this limited program for women, Japan was in advance of many Western states. In the organization of her universities for men Japan tended to follow the French model, and throughout the entire educational system the German insistence on vocational training was notable.

From whatever angle considered, this was a revolution in education, quite as striking as the political and economic revolutions of 1867–1871. The Japanese clamored for the new education with an unbounded but at times undiscriminating enthusiasm. Many mistakes were made, laws were frequently altered, and hurriedly trained teachers taught what they themselves did not understand. It was above all an educational system founded and shaped by the new Restoration government, a system that imparted to Japan's rising generations the strength and likewise the weakness of her revolutionary leaders. Two positive accomplishments are traceable to the new education: it created a literate people, and a nation that was technically abreast of the modern mechanical world of science. But as a purely intellectual force, the new education in the late nineteenth century did not create—in fact, was never intended to create— a democratic philosophy for free men. There was no Thomas Jefferson in Japan's historical heritage. Consequently, although Japan imported precipitately a host of forms and techniques of American education between 1870 and 1890, the spirit and ideals of this education did not thrive in the new environment. From the standpoint of the leaders of post-Restoration Japan, education could be useful only as it helped in the transition from a mediaeval to a modern autocratic state, only as it prevented "the predatory powers of America and Europe" from gaining "a stronghold in the economic life of the islands." Therefore education was limited to specific purposes: "national unification, unquestioning loyalty, the acquirement of modern scientific and economic technique, and the perfection of national defense."

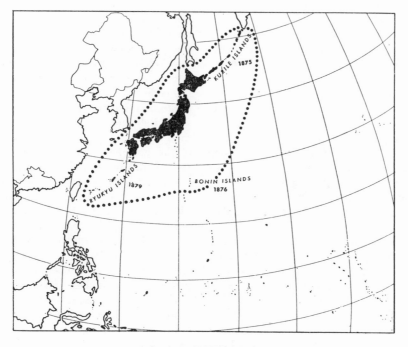

Japan 1875–1890
Reproduced from A War Atlas for Americans *(New York: Simon & Schuster) 1944, with permission from the publisher and from the U.S. Department of State, Department Division of Map Intelligence and Cartography.*

THE MATERIAL TRANSFORMATION

The technical, material transformation of Japan was rapid and dramatic. Every Western mechanical device of the time in trade, business, commerce, and transportation soon found its place in the Japanese scene. Foreign architecture and city planning appeared first in the seaports of Yokohama and Kobe. Japanese in foreign trade put on foreign dress, and, even in later days of the nineteenth century, those who were not too discriminating might be seen taking their summer evening stroll through the bazaars of Yokohama clad in a hard straw hat, white cotton gloves, a cane, native *geta* (wooden clogs), and, for the finishing touch, a suit of American model BVD's. A postal system and telegraph were established in 1871. In 1872 the first railroad, 18 miles long, began business. In 1897, 3,000 miles of railroad, mostly government owned, were in operation. In all these activities and many others the initiative of the government was evident

either through organization or subsidy. Shipping lines such as Nippon Yusen Kaisha (Japan Mail) (1885), and Osaka Shosen Kaisha were organized. Tonnage increased from 59,000 in 1885 to 1,115,000 in 1907. The textile industries were promoted by every modern means designed to improve and standardize the product and to assure its acceptance by the public. To meet the needs of currency reform and national credit, national banks, after the American model, made their appearance after 1872. The Central Bank of Japan was formed in 1882 as the financial bulwark of the government. This was followed among others by the Yokohama Specie Bank (1887) to finance foreign trade and to control exchange.

APPEARANCE OF REPRESENTATIVE INSTITUTIONS

The overwhelming enthusiasm of the Japanese for the newly discovered Western world was affected naturally enough by Western political philosophy and especially by the dominant liberalism of the nineteenth century. What philosophy and structure of government would Japan erect on the foundations of her Meiji Restoration? Her new educational program indicated already that the new government would be nationalistic and centralized in a peculiarly Japanese sense. Would it also be democratic, based on a popular constitution, a bill of rights, a broad franchise, political parties, and economic individualism as understood by powerful industrial and middle class groups in the Western democracies? [10]

The answer to these questions must be found in the sphere of domestic Japanese politics following the return (1873) of the Iwakura mission from Europe and America.[11] Impressed by the strength of the West, the members of this mission soon emerged as leaders of a so-called peace party in opposition to a war party composed of more belligerent samurai, who, for reasons to be explained later, desired a foreign war in Korea and Formosa. The war party soon withdrew from the government and thus formed a nucleus of potential political opposition. To strengthen its position, the government created a Ministry of Home Affairs, which had immediate control over prefectural and city governments. The opposition then attempted to assassinate Iwakura and demanded a national elective assembly. This the government refused, and a series of rebellions followed. As a concession, the government did call an Assembly of Local Governors (1875), which proved to be a rubber stamp for approval of government policies.

While the government continued to live under the protection of press censorship, it succeeded in defeating a desperate rising by opposition leaders from Satsuma. The Satsuma Rebellion (1877), led by Saigo Takamori, was a protest against the general policy of the government—against the conscription law (1873), against the importance of capitalistic interests in the new government, and against the refusal of the government to employ the ex-samurai in foreign war—a composite policy that threatened the very existence of samurai traditions. When, however, despite suppression of the rebellion, further assassinations of government leaders followed, prefectural assemblies (fuken-kai) were established. This was a faltering step toward representative government because the franchise in the assemblies was limited; prefectural governors initiated and could veto all bills, leaving to the assemblies nothing but the privilege of discussing budgets and finding ways to raise new taxes. Nevertheless, these assemblies encouraged the opposition to agitate for a national assembly. In response to the incessant demands of Itagaki, the government, while opposing anything in the form of a national parliament, did permit (1880) the calling of municipal assemblies.

A CONSTITUTION IS SHAPED

Political Parties

The immediate origins of the Imperial edict granting a national parliament involved, among other things, the financial corruption of the Satsuma and Choshu ex-samurai who controlled the government. When these practices were exposed publicly in 1881 by Okuma Shigenobu, there was mob violence in Tokyo. Government property was destroyed and the police were defied. A frightened government sought refuge behind the throne, while an imperial rescript announced that a national parliament would be created in 1890. For this turn of events

[10] On the political philosophy of the most interesting personality in modern Japanese politics see Jackson H. Bailey, "Prince Saionji and the Popular Rights Movement," *Journal of Asian Studies* 21 (1961): 49–63. Political thought in Meiji Japan may be described generally as a conflict between: a) liberal and democratic ideas derived from British, French, and American sources as against b) authoritarian and state centralist philosophy rooted in native Japanese doctrines of imperial sovereignty supported by German constitutional theories.

[11] Note Marlene J. Mayo, "A Catechism of Western Diplomacy: The Japanese and Hamilton Fish, 1872," *Journal of Asian Studies* 26 (1967): 389–410.

the Satsuma and Choshu leaders had only themselves to blame. They had excluded from office or had relegated to minor posts their colleagues from the less powerful clans such as Itagaki Taisuke and Goto Shojiro of Tosa. It was this disgruntled but able opposition that now used the pretext of graft in high places to force the issue of a national parliament and its natural concomitant, political parties.[12]

During 1881 and 1882 three so-called political parties made their appearance: the *Jiyuto* (Liberal Party) led by Itagaki, the *Kaishinto* (Progressive Party) headed by Okuma, and the *Rikken Teiseito* (Imperialist Party) supported by the government. For the moment these parties seemed to be concerned primarily with advocating one or another form of Western constitutional government. This interest in political theory and political forms was not entirely spurious, but it was secondary to economic and social considerations which will be discussed in the next chapter.

Constitutional Preparations

Meanwhile, as the political parties clamored for a popular and liberal constitution, the government set about the task of drafting a document that would preserve the

---

[12] It is not to be assumed that Itagaki and Goto were concerned primarily with the purification of Japanese politics. They, like many members of the government, began as poor if high ranking samurai and died immensely wealthy. Moreover, opposition came from within as well as from without. Okuma was in the government in 1881 when he did the exposing. Finally, these rivalries among the leadership were not solely of an ideological character. For example, Satsuma and Choshu were allies against the *Bakufu*, but once they were in power, interclan rivalries threatened their control. The Osaka conference called for quite another purpose, quieted interclan rivalries, and advanced the fortunes of Ito Hirobumi, the most effective spokesman for clan peace. See Andrew Fraser, "The Osaka Conference of 1875," *Journal of Asian Studies* 26 (1967): 589–610; Joyce C. Lebra, "Okuma Shigenobu and the 1881 Political Crisis," *ibid.* 18 (1959): 475–87; and Andrew Fraser, "The Expulsion of Okuma from the Government in 1881," *ibid.* 26 (1967): 213–36.

power of oligarchy. It created a commission on constitutional investigation headed by Ito Hirobumi. In 1884 a new nobility was created to draw together and unify the conservative and aristocratic elements that were to dominate the new government. It was also decided to create the executive branch prior to the adoption of the constitution. This would enable the executive to become a functioning organism familiar with its duties before it would be required to adjust itself to a parliament. Accordingly, a cabinet (*nai kaku*) was set up in 1885 modelled on the German cabinet of that day. Then in 1888 a new privy council was named with Ito, head of the constitutional commission, as president. As further preparation for the constitutional regime, a merit system was introduced into the civil service and new codes were prepared in both public and private law.

Japanese law of the earlier Restoration period had been derived from early Japanese law, which had been borrowed from China in the seventh and later centuries and codified extensively in the Tokugawa feudal society. As the Western powers entered into treaty relations with Japan, they objected to submitting their nationals to Japanese law and consequently demanded and secured extraterritorial jurisdiction, as they had also done in China. The Restoration government in its desire to preserve national independence was quick to recognize that the abolition of extraterritoriality would depend on the speed and effectiveness with which Japan adopted principles of jurisprudence acceptable to Europeans and Americans. Accordingly, a penal code and a code of criminal procedure, begun in 1873 and completed in 1880, were adopted in 1882. They were strongly influenced by French law. The larger task of constructing a civil code, begun in 1870, was completed and put into effect in 1899, in which year extraterritoriality was terminated. Civil law basically was also French. A code of civil procedure was operative as early as 1891, and adopted with the commercial code, German in origin, in 1899.

From the foregoing it will be noted that some of the more important instruments of a new government had been created and were in operation before the constitution itself was created. Although this procedure lent stability to political affairs in a period of transition, it also enabled the ruling faction, headed by Ito, to maintain its monopoly of power.

The foundations of a constitutional regime had been laid as early as 1868, when the Charter Oath was proclaimed. Two years later, in 1870, Ito visited the United States, where he studied the American constitutional system, delving deeply into the pages of the *Federalist*. More important in shaping Ito's ideas, however, was the advice of General Grant, given in 1879, that Japan in designing a constitution should give full regard to her own peculiar traditions. Then, in 1882, a year after the emperor had promised a constitution, Ito studied in Germany where the successes of Bismark had brought new prestige to the political philosophy and institutions of Prussia. Back in Japan and commissioned in 1884 to draft a constitution, Ito called on the services of three able assistants, all of whom had travelled abroad: Inouye Tsuyoshi, Ito Myoji, and Kaneko Kentaro. With Ito, these men constituted a bureau attached to the Imperial Household, thus precluding political pressure from the liberals. When the draft of the constitution was completed, it was ratified by the Privy Council, which was created by Ito for this specific purpose and was to be maintained under the constitution as the highest advisory body to the sovereign. Finally, when the work was complete, Emperor Mutsuhito on February 11, 1889, the anniversary of the traditional founding of the state of Yamato in 660 B.C., bestowed the constitution as a royal gift upon his people. Every precaution had already been taken to ensure an obedient and peaceful acceptance by the people at large. Tokyo under a special Peace Preservation Ordinance was subject to quasi-martial law. Most of the radical newspapers had already been suppressed, while the press in general was under strict instructions to refrain temporarily from all critical comment. As a consequence the public reception was peaceful.[13]

The constitution which emerged in 1889 has been described in various ways, none of which is very precise in meaning. For example, it has been seen as a document embodying Japanese political principles under the guise of representative institutions, a unique blend of authoritarianism and constitutionalism, a kind of hybrid—absolute constitutional monarchy. While there is nothing about the constitution that could be described as liberal, it would appear that its authors opposed extreme conservative views almost as vigorously as they rejected full parliamentary authority. The result was a distinctly Japanese product. Certainly, the Meiji leaders were reluctant to share political power. Yet in the constitutional struggle they did so, even if grudgingly. As Ito saw his task in drafting the constitution, it was to seek means of controlling and rendering as harmless as possible any encroachment by political parties in the area of political authority.[14]

[13] W. W. McLaren, *A Political History of Japan* (1916), 186; G. E. Uyehara, *The Political Development of Japan* (London, 1910), 109–23. The official interpretation of the constitution is by Ito Hirobumi, *Commentaries on the Constitution of the Empire of Japan,* Ito Myoji, trans. (2nd ed., Tokyo, 1906). Note particularly the concept of *kokumin,* the relation of nationalism and liberalism, the state and the individual as discussed by Barbara J. Teters, "Kuga's Commentaries on the Constitution of the Empire of Japan," *Journal of Asian Studies* 28 (1969): 321–37.

[14] George Akita, *Foundations of Constitutional Government in Japan, 1868–1900* (1967), and Joseph Pittau, S.J., *Political Thought in Early Meiji Japan, 1868–1889* (1967). Very dissimilar theories have developed with regard to the intent of the makers of the Meiji Constitution. Students of Japanese politics in the earlier part of this century stressed the authoritarian aspects of the constitution. More recent scholarship has tended to challenge this emphasis. A helpful presentation of major interpretations is Joseph Pittau, "The Meiji Political System: Different Interpretations," *Studies in Japanese Culture,* Joseph Roggendorf, ed. (Tokyo, 1963).

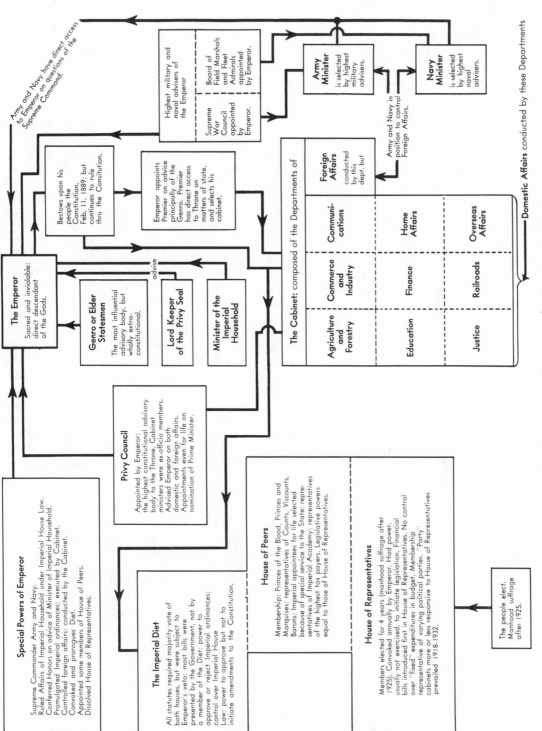

Army and Navy have direct access to Emperor on questions of the Supreme Command.

Highest military and naval advisers of the Emperor

Board of Field Marshals and Fleet Admirals appointed by Emperor.

Supreme War Council appointed by Emperor.

Army Minister is selected by highest military advisers.

Navy Minister is selected by highest naval advisers.

Army and Navy in position to control Foreign Affairs.

Foreign Affairs conducted by this dept. but

Bestows upon his people the Constitution, Feb. 11, 1889; but continues to rule thru the Constitution.

Emperor appoints Premier on advice principally of the Genro. Premier has direct access to Throne on matters of state, and selects his cabinet.

The Cabinet: composed of the Departments of

Agriculture and Forestry	Commerce and Industry	Communications
Education	Finance	Home Affairs
Justice	Railroads	Overseas Affairs

The Emperor

Sacred and inviolable: direct descendant of the Gods.

advise

Genro or Elder Statesmen

The most influential advisory body, but wholly extra-constitutional.

Lord Keeper of the Privy Seal

Minister of the Imperial Household

Privy Council

Appointed by Emperor: the highest constitutional advisory body to the Throne. Cabinet ministers were ex-officio members. Advised Emperor on both domestic and foreign affairs. Appointments even for life on nomination of Prime Minister.

Special Powers of Emperor

Supreme Commander Army and Navy. Ruled Affairs of Imperial Household under Imperial House Law. Conferred Honors on advice of Minister of Imperial Household. Promulgated Imperial ordinances; executed by Cabinet. Controlled foreign affairs; conducted by the Cabinet. Convoked and prorogues Diet. Appointed some members of House of Peers. Dissolved House of Representatives.

The Imperial Diet

All statutes required majority vote of both houses, but were subject to Emperor's veto: most bills were presented by the Government, not by a member of the Diet: power to approve or reject Imperial ordinances; control over Imperial House Law; power to approve but not to initiate amendments to the Constitution.

House of Peers

Membership: Princes of the Blood, Princes and Marquises; representatives of Counts, Viscounts, Barons; Imperial appointees for life selected because of special service to the State: representatives of the highest tax payers. Legislative powers equal to those of House of Representatives.

House of Representatives

Members elected for 4 years (manhood suffrage after 1925). Convoked annually by Emperor. Had power, usually not exercised, to initiate legislation. Financial bills introduced first in House of Representatives. No control over "fixed" expenditures in budget. Membership representative of varying political parties. "Party" cabinets more or less responsive to House of Representatives prevailed 1918-1932.

The people elect. Manhood suffrage after 1925.

─── Domestic Affairs conducted by these Departments

Principal Features of the Government of Japan under the Constitution of 1889

The Law and the Constitution of 1889

The fundamental law of the Empire consisted of the constitution, the Imperial House Law, Imperial ordinances, statutes, and international treaties.[15]

The nature of the constitution was best revealed by the position of the emperor. Since the constitution was a gift of the throne, only the emperor could initiate amendments. These required the consent of the House of Peers (*Kizoku-in*) and the House of Representatives (*Shugi-in*). Interpretation of the constitution rested with the courts, and, in a case of dispute, with the Privy Council.

The Imperial House Law occupied a unique position. It could not be affected by legislation, was beyond the control of the Diet, could be amended only by the emperor with advice of the Imperial Family Council and the Privy Council. The Imperial House Law, not the constitution, determined the succession.

Great powers were exercised by the emperor through imperial ordinances of three kinds: (1) prerogative—Imperial House Law; (2) administrative—executive acts in the interest of the general welfare; (3) emergency—to meet emergencies when the Diet was not in session. These last required at time of issue approval by the Privy Council (*Sumitsu-in*), and ultimately approval by the Diet, unless repealed before a new session. It is thus clear that in a very large field the ordinance powers of the emperor were beyond legislative control.

Statutes were enacted by majority vote of both houses of the Diet, whose powers over legislation were the same, save that money bills were to be presented first in the lower house. The emperor's veto power over all laws was made absolute. In practice, most legislation was initiated by the government. Treaties were to be ratified by the emperor with the consent of the Privy Coun-

[15] For a concise summary of the organization of Japan's government see R. K. Reischauer, *Japan: Government—Politics* (1939), Chapter 4.

cil. Treaties were to be regarded as superior to ordinary law: they were not subject to change by ordinance, but could not be in conflict with the constitution or the Imperial House Law.

The Power Elite and the Constitution

Japanese government was dominated after 1889 by a power elite composed of the Imperial Family, the *Genro* (Elder Statesmen), and the House of Peers. In this group were the former *kuge* (the civilian court nobility), the daimyo (the former great feudal lords), those samurai who engineered the Restoration, and finally, a select few from the professional classes.

The Emperor. The emperor's powers as defined by the constitution were extremely broad. He possessed the rights of sovereignty and exercised them within the constitution, convoked and prorogued the Diet, dissolved the House of Representatives, issued ordinances, determined the organization of the government, and acted on appointments and dismissals of all officials, save in those cases where other provision was made by the constitution. He exercised the administrative and command powers over the army and navy, declared war, made peace and concluded treaties, proclaimed martial law, conferred all high official ranks and honors, appointed and removed judges. All these constitutional powers and prerogatives of the emperor were to be exercised *only* on the advice of his advisers, whether ministers of state, ministers of the Imperial Household, or chiefs of the general staffs of the army and navy. The emperor, in a word, reigned but did not rule. The problem for the student of Japanese government in any period after 1889 is to discover which individuals and groups ruled through the sovereign.

The Genro (Elder Statesmen). From shortly after the promulgation of the constitution until 1931, the most powerful group in Japanese government and politics was the *Genro*. This group was extraconstitutional. It was composed of trusted and tried statesmen who had assumed leadership in the making of the new Japan, approximately in the years 1880–1900. These men exercised the real power in government under the constitution. No important decisions were made without their consent; in fact they made the decisions. Although the power of the *Genro* was contested as early as 1913, it was not until about 1922 that their supreme control in all important affairs of state, domestic and foreign, began to be questioned. The *Genro* illustrate clearly the fact that although constitutional government in Japan often appeared to be Western in structure and performance, actually it was not so. The *Genro* as personalities, not as constitutionalists, were the real makers of the new Japan in the later years of Meiji. They included Ito Hirobumi (Choshu), maker of the constitution, Yamagata Aritomo (Choshu), the builder of Japan's modern army, Inouye Kaoru (Choshu), influential in reforms in taxation, Oyama Iwao (Satsuma), a great soldier, and Matsukata Masayoshi (Satsuma), of great prominence in taxation and finance. These were the original members. Later, General Katsura Taro (Choshu) and Saionji Kimmochi (*kuge*) were added.[16]

Study of the appearance of the *Genro*, of why this decision-making structure emerged at a particular time and took a particular form, is a rewarding pursuit. The *Genro* was more than a manifestation of the general tendency in Japanese society to make decisions through group consensus. Since all the original members of the *Genro* held at one time or another prior to 1900 all major posts in the civil and military bureaucracy and the government, there was practically no distinction between bureaucracy and government. Moreover, in the late nineteenth century, Meiji leaders needed above all to find

a consensus on goals and to resolve the conflict between traditional Confucian moral education and so-called *jitsugaku* or education for practical affairs associated with Western learning as preparation for service in bureaucracy and government. In the case of Japan in this period there was no one person who could be entrusted with such decisions and such responsibility. Restraint was placed on the emergence of such a leader by the peculiar status of the emperor. Thus the small group character of the *Genro* was all but inevitable.[17]

The House of Peers. This body, the upper house of the legislature, included: (*1*) all Princes of the Blood who had reached majority; (*2*) princes and marquises twenty-nine years of age; (*3*) representatives of counts, viscounts, and barons, elected by their orders for terms of seven years; (*4*) Imperial appointees selected for life because of distinguished service to the state or in recognition of scholarship; (*5*) representatives of the Imperial Academy elected by their colleagues for seven-year terms; and (*6*) elected representatives of the highest taxpayers from each prefecture. This was a body distinguished for its conservatism of blood, wealth, and title. Its power was guaranteed by the constitution.

The Bureaucracy

The bureaucrats were the civil office holders. Their position was based on ability and on appointment. Their loyalties were to the aristocrats rather than to the common people. Of first importance among the bureaucratic elements was the Imperial Household Ministry. The Lord Keeper of the Privy Seal and the Minister of the Imperial Household headed this group. Both, because of their close personal relationship with the emperor,

---

[16] Ito was assassinated, 1909; Katsura died, 1913; Inouye, 1915; Oyama, 1916; Yamagata, 1922; Matsukata, 1924; Saionji, 1940. It is significant that no *Genro* was ever assassinated in Japan or by a Japanese. But as indicative of the weakening prestige of the group, attempts were made on the life of the aged Saionji.

[17] For further development of this subject see two articles by Bernard S. Silberman: "Bureaucratic Development and the Structure of Decision-Making in the Meiji Period: the Case of the *Genro*," and "Bureaucratic Development and the Structure of Decision-Making in Japan: 1868–1925," *Journal of Asian Studies* 27 (1967): 81–94; and 29 (1970): 347–62.

had great influence as advisers of the throne. It was through them that audience with the sovereign was secured. These ministers were appointed by the emperor on the advice of the prime minister.

The Privy Council. The second group in the bureaucracy was the Privy Council. Created in 1888, it was designed to review and accept the constitution and to be the highest constitutional advisory body to the emperor. Its membership numbered twenty-six, appointed for life by the emperor on the advice of the prime minister and with the approval of the President of the council. Ministers of state were ex-officio councilors. The council proved itself an effective curb against representative tendencies.

The Civil Service. The great body of civil servants—the rank and file of bureaucracy, numbering nearly half a million members—was selected by competitive examination. Usually the most rigid application of these examinations was in the Foreign Office (*Gaimusho*), whereas in the Home Ministry they were less effective in competition with the spoils system.[18]

The Military

In no modern state, save perhaps Prussia, has the professional soldier played so influential a role in politics as in Japan. The unbroken dominance of the military men, the samurai, began in the twelfth century. In Tokugawa times the soldier acquired a pre-eminent social status and a monopoly of political power. The Restoration of 1868 did not destroy the influence of the military class. It tended rather to transfer power from the upper to the middle and lower ranks among the former samurai. The military conscription law of 1873 destroyed, in theory at least, the distinction between samurai and commoner, but in reality the personnel of the army and navy, especially the professional officer class,

retained the old samurai tradition and attitude of moral and social superiority. The mentality continued to be that of a ruling class. Yet this superior attitude did not prevent the appearance of cliques among those who controlled the new army. As early as 1879, the three main military functions—operations and strategy, military administration, and training and inspection—were being carried out by three separate sections of the army. In 1885 when the cabinet was set up as a preliminary to constitutional government, only one of the three functions—military administration—was placed even under partial control of the civil government. Thus the principle of the separation of the command power (*tōsuiken*) from routine military administration (*gunsei*) was established even before the constitution. Under the constitution, the prime minister accepted the nominees of the services as the ministers of war and of the navy in his cabinet. The services thus had the power to destroy a government by forcing the resignation of a service minister and refusing to nominate a new one.[19]

The Politicians and the House of Representatives

The constitution provided for a bicameral legislature or Diet, which the Japanese

[18] Robert M. Spaulding, Jr., *Imperial Japan's Higher Civil Service Examinations* (1967). Modernization which destroyed the civil service examinations in China created a system of examinations in Japan.

[19] The background of the subject is discussed ably by Yale C. Maxon, *Control of Japanese Foreign Policy* (1957), especially Chapter 2. The army and the navy liked to think of themselves as unique guardians of the throne and of the so-called "national spirit." In practice, however, they were the most flagrant violators of the commands of the throne. An imperial rescript addressed to service men (1882) set forth that: "Service men should not involve themselves or interest themselves in politics." Under the Constitution they did not vote. Nevertheless, no group in Japanese society was more jealous of its political fortunes than the military. See K. W. Colegrove, *Militarism in Japan* (1936); also E. E. N. Causton, *Militarism and Foreign Policy in Japan* (1936); O. Tanin and E. Yohan, *Militarism and Fascism in Japan* (1934). Ernest L. Presseisen, *Before Aggression: Europeans Prepare the Japanese Army* (1965), demonstrates that in the modernization of the Japanese army after 1870 far more was involved than the selection of the German as the ideal military model.

called *gikai*. The purpose of the framers was to prevent the legislators from indulging in hasty legislation and to give decisive legislative power (in the House of Peers) to the aristocracy. The House of Representatives, according to the *Commentaries*, was to regard itself as "representatives of the people of the whole country," though prior to 1925 there were high property qualifications both for candidates and for the franchise. The constitution required annual sessions of the Diet, which were frequently supplemented by extraordinary sessions caused by frequent dissolutions. Originally the House of Representatives consisted of 300 members, but this number was increased to 381 in 1900, and to 466 in 1925, when manhood suffrage was adopted. All statutes required approval by the House of Representatives as well as by the House of Peers. The same applied to amendments to the constitution and to Imperial ordinances if these latter were to remain in effect after the Diet came into session. However, the Diet, and consequently the House of Representatives, held only limited control over the nation's finances. All items of so-called "fixed expenditures" were beyond its power: salaries, expenses of the Imperial Household, fixed budgets of administrative branches of the government, etc., such as the army and navy. Furthermore, the constitution provided, in Article LXXI, that: "When the Imperial Diet has not voted on the budget, or when the budget has not been brought into actual existence, the government shall carry out the budget of the preceding year." Thus the framers of the constitution were careful not to place control of the national purse in the hands of the representatives of the people.

The Ministry and the Cabinet

Under the constitution no formal provision was made for a cabinet. The constitution merely noted that: "The respective Ministers of State shall give their advice to the emperor, and be responsible for it." All laws, ordinances, rescripts, etc., required the counter-signature of a minister of state. But, as noted, a cabinet was created in 1885, and it continued to function as the ministry

under the constitution. The prime minister was selected by the emperor on the advice of the *Genro*. This is another way of saying that the cabinet's responsibility was primarily to the emperor, and only secondarily to the Diet.

Such, in brief, were some of the main structural features of Japan's national government as established by the constitution of 1889. Historians are still seeking a satisfactory explanation for the form that this Meiji political structure assumed. How and why did the Japanese bureaucracy acquire almost a complete monopoly of decision making and administration? Why did the institution of the emperor emerge as it did—that is, the emperor as the state? [20]

Some aspects of the economic, social, and cultural foundations undergirding this new political structure are described in the next chapter. The story of how the Meiji constitution was to work out in practice after 1889 will be found in Chapter 20.

FOR FURTHER READING

HISTORY AND POLITICS. G. B. Sansom, *The Western World and Japan; a Study in the Interaction of European and Asiatic Cultures* (1950), covering the period 1600–1900, this study attempts to place Japan within the context of world history. Fujii Jintaro, ed. and comp., *Outline of Japanese History in the Meiji Era*, Hattie K. Colton and Kenneth E. Colton trans. (Tokyo, 1958), concerned with political development. Ike Nobutaka, *Japanese Politics, an Introductory Survey* (1957), especially valuable for the treatment of social and cultural factors. Yanaga Chitoshi, *Japanese People and Politics* (1956),* an adequate treatment of the social and cultural dimensions of the political process in Japan. Robert A. Scalapino, *Democracy and the*

[20] For the application of structural-functional analysis in the area of political systems as an aid in finding answers, see Bernard S. Silberman, "E. H. Norman: Structure and Function in the Meiji State, a Reappraisal," *Pacific Affairs* 41 (1968–69): 553–59.

Party Movement in Prewar Japan, the Failure of the First Attempt (1953), a general history of politics in modern Japan with a sociological approach.

GOVERNMENT. Robert A. Wilson, *Genesis of the Meiji Government in Japan 1868–1871* (1957) presents the first stage of political reorganization after the Restoration. Harold Scott Quigley, *Japanese Government and Politics, an Introductory Study* (1932), valuable as a reference work. George M. Beckmann, *The Making of the Meiji Constitution, the Oligarchs and the Constitutional Development of Japan, 1868–1891* (1957), important for key constitutional documents. Sakata Yoshio, and John W. Hall, "The Motivation of Political Leadership in the Meiji Restoration," *Journal of Asian Studies* 16 (1956): 31–50. Junesay Iddittie, *The Life of Marquis Shigenobu Okuma* (Tokyo, 1956). Hamada Kengi, *Prince Ito* (Tokyo, 1936).

SPECIAL STUDIES. A. H. Mounsey, *The Satsuma Rebellion* (London, 1879), an account of the revolt of 1877. D. C. Holtom, *The National Faith of Japan; a Study in Modern Shinto* (1943), an extremely valuable study. Warren Smith, *Confucianism in Modern Japan: A Study of Conservatism in Japanese Intellectual History* (Tokyo, 1959). E. Herbert Norman, *Soldier and Peasant in Japan: The Origins of Conscription* (1943). John A. Harrison, "The Capron Mission and the Colonization of Hokkaido, 1868–1875," *Agricultural History*, 25 (1951): 135–42. Sir Ernest Satow, *A Diplomat in Japan* (London, 1921). Johannes Hirschmeier, *The Origins of Entrepreneurship in Meiji Japan* (1964).

Japan:
Economic and Cultural Bases
of the Meiji Government

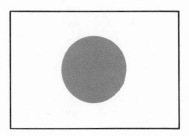

chapter II

The political history of Japan between the years 1853 and 1889 is the record of an extraordinary revolution under equally extraordinary leadership which was designed to bring Japan into the modern world, to transform overnight, as it were, an isolated, feudal society into a modern, centralized state and nation. This transformation from feudalism to centralization and from military dictatorship to constitutionalism would have been much more difficult without the foundations laid in the later years of the Tokugawa era when Japan's traditional society had already outlived its usefulness. Nevertheless, it may be said that in relation to the rapidity of change in the nature of the Japanese state, the Meiji revolution was unique. Although the concept of constitutionalism, as it appeared in late nineteenth-century Japan, was imported from the West, the political society created by this revolution cannot be described as Western. On the contrary, it was a peculiarly Japanese product colored by Western influence, shaped in some respects by Western forms, and occasionally partaking of the Western spirit; but its intellectual and philosophic foundations were, in the main, Japanese, derived principally from Japanese

historic ideals, political and social institutions, and from prevailing conditions within Japan. In a word, the political revolution of early Meiji acquires historical meaning only as it is related to the economic, social, and intellectual Japan that emerged in the four decades following Perry's expedition.

It will be convenient to deal first with some economic foundations that underlay this Meiji transformation. By 1871, with the framework of feudalism already destroyed, Japan was creating a new and unified political regime that would make invasion from abroad too dangerous and too uncertain an undertaking. This new Restoration government derived part of its economic power from the financial backing of the merchant-capitalists, and its leadership from the lesser but capable samurai of the Western Clans. These leaders steadfastly pursued until 1894 the goal of internal reconstruction—political, economic, and social. Only after the foundations of the new economic, social, and political Japan had been laid did they venture into the field of foreign expansion.[1]

[1] For detailed treatment of the decay of feudalism, of the rise of the merchant-capitalists, and of the appearance of lower samurai as political leaders of early Restoration Japan, see E. Herbert Norman, *Japan's Emergence as a*

The subject of industrialization and modernization is particularly significant in the case of Japan, since this country was the one major nation outside the European cultural sphere to industrialize successfully. How this was done is a matter of supreme importance to other states attempting to travel the same road. The answers are not simple because to be meaningful they must have something to say on what happens to other parts of a nation's social structure when, through industrialization, a society in new ways becomes more productive. For example, in the industrialized Japan of the late twentieth century as compared with the Japan of the late nineteenth century the locus of power, income, and prestige "depends to a much greater degree on demonstrated abilities and much less on ascribed characteristics." Changes in the ways in which people act may be symptomatic of far deeper changes in human relationships and status. For instance, as the student moves further into his examination of modern Japan, he may note that there has been a gradual withering away of some forms of deferential behavior between inferiors and superiors. Extreme forms of respectful speech are heard less frequently. Gift giving to superiors, which formerly was merely proper behavior, may come to be regarded as degrading forms of apple polishing. Subordinates bow less often and not so low. A taxi driver may take off his hat to an irate policeman, but he does not get down on his knees as the rickshawman did fifty or sixty years ago. In a word, the modern factory or the steel mill was to initiate extraordinary and sometimes unforeseen changes in the nature of Japanese society.[2]

Modern State (1940), 1–104; G. B. Sansom, Japan: A Short Cultural History (1962), Chapter 23; Honjo Eijiro, Social and Economic History of Japan (Kyoto, 1935). W. W. Lockwood, The Economic Development of Japan 1868–1938 (1954),* 3–37, gives a comprehensive summary of the foundations of industrialism in the Meiji period.

[2] For an introduction to this transformation of Japan see R. P. Dore, ed., Aspects of Social Change in Modern Japan (1967), especially 3–24.

GOVERNMENT IN INDUSTRY

The political and constitutional developments in Meiji Japan represent, therefore, only one aspect of the change that was taking place. This move toward constitutionalism of some sort acquires meaning only when seen in the context of an ultimate objective, namely, the building of a strong nation-state. It was clear, however, to the Meiji leadership that this objective could not be achieved by political forms alone. Controlled and expanding economic power would be indispensable, and this, in turn, meant rapid industrialization. Politics and economics were not separate entities. They moved hand in hand toward a common goal. For example, the Meiji leaders achieved at an early date a remarkable degree of political stability and created strong fiscal institutions. These were essential preludes to industrialization, but government went further than this. It pioneered in a number of industrial areas, particularly the strategic industries; it assisted in others, and thus paved the way for private enterprise, which was to provide the major part of Japan's remarkable and rapid industrial growth.

Strategic Industries

In undertaking to develop the strategic industries, the Meiji leadership had some foundations on which to build. The Tokugawa shogunate and some of the clans had initiated the work prior to 1868. Satsuma had created an iron industry. Western-style ships were constructed in the mid-fifties. Once the Meiji government was in power it took steps to strengthen existing plants it had inherited and to establish new ones. Hyogo (Kobe), Nagasaki, and Yokosuka became centers of shipbuilding; Osaka and Tokyo, centers of arms and ammunition. Government was equally vigorous in building communications, the telegraph and railroads. Many of the major cities were connected by telegraph as early as 1880. Because of the mountainous nature of the country, railroad building was difficult and costly yet indispensable. The first line linked Yokohama and Tokyo (19 miles); a second, Kobe, Osaka, and Kyoto.

Nonstrategic Industries

The Meiji government was also impelled into other industries such as textiles, machine tools, mining. These had to become machine industries to meet Western competition, to create a balance in foreign trade, to provide employment, and to meet from domestic sources the rising demand for foreign goods. Under Ito and his successors in the Ministry of Industry, established in 1870, the government set up its own plants or encouraged private ventures by providing subsidies and low interest rates. In the early years of Meiji, however, industrialization through private sources, even with government assistance, made little headway. Private capital was scarce, interest rates were high, the Japanese lacked experience with machinery, and, until communications could be expanded, transportation costs were excessive. The new woolen industry was developed entirely by government. Cotton yarn and piece goods were produced in the early years by means of heavy government subsidies. In the silk industry, government played only a minor part. Indeed, it was the silk industry which at this time, did more than any other to rectify Japan's unfavorable balance of trade.[3]

Under government direction Japan's early industrial pattern was different from that of the West. Japan's development emphasized heavy as well as light manufacturing. As Japan's economy expanded, and as private capital eventually assumed enlarged responsibilities, however, the capital value of light industry exceeded by far the value of other types of enterprise. Thus,

while Japan in the 1890's could boast of a substantial defense industry, her emergence as a heavy industry country did not occur until well into the present century.[4]

The policy of government-in-industry was followed closely until 1880, when the principle of "direct control" began to give place to "indirect protection." It was at this time that the government, which had carried on the initial development of industry, began to turn over specific enterprises to the financial oligarchy, the *Zaibatsu*, at amazingly low rates. By this means, industrial as well as financial capital came to be concentrated in the same hands. It should be added that the economic structure of nineteenth-century Meiji Japan was fashioned without a major resort to foreign loans.[5]

---

[3] Japan's success in building these industries so rapidly was due partly to the fact that essential foundations had been laid in the Tokugawa era. By the mid-1800's farm families often supplemented their income through one or another "by-employments," that is, part-time work in fishing, wood finishing, weaving, or shopkeeping. Thus, the new industrial system could draw upon a populace which could bring to the job usable crafts, clerical skills, and even managerial skills. Thomas C. Smith, "Farm Family By-employments in Preindustrial Japan," *Journal of Economic History*, 29 (1969): 687–715.

[4] Ranked by value of their capitalization, Japan's industries in 1912 assumed the following order: electricity, cotton spinning, gas, shipbuilding, paper, sugar refining, fertilizer, beer, wool cloth, cement, cotton cloth, sake, machinery, medicine, wool spinning, thread, electrical equipment, and milling. Among these top eighteen industries, shipbuilding was the only heavy industry.

[5] The philosophy of economic individualism, so important in England and America, played a much lesser role in Meiji Japan. In Japan, industrialization and related social changes took place, not under a completely transformed value system created by the Restoration, but under a legacy of traditional and pre-industrial values. As a consequence, the ideology of Japanese business in the late nineteenth century had qualities peculiarly its own. See Byron K. Marshall, *Capitalism and Nationalism in Prewar Japan: The Ideology of the Business Elite, 1868–1941* (1967). Differences also are to be noted in literature dealing with Western and Japanese business history. Western businessmen have become the subject of numerous biographies. Japanese entrepreneurs, however, as individuals, have been little studied. See Kozo Yamamura and Henry Rosovsky, "Entrepreneurial Studies in Japan," *Business History Review*, 44 (1970): 1–12, a bibliographical essay introducing a special issue devoted to Japanese business history. For the class origins of Japan's business pioneers and the role of government in Meiji industry, see Thomas C. Smith, *Political Change and Industrial Development in Japan: Government Enterprise, 1868–1880* (1955); and Johannes Hirschmeier, *The Origins of Entrepreneurship in Meiji Japan* (1964).

There was, therefore, a strong and peculiar focus of economic power which implemented Japan's modern industrialization. Although in modern Japanese industry the small technical unit was typical of a wide range of enterprise, these small units were often dependent on larger concerns which, in turn, were controlled, if not owned, by a very few financial-industrial groups having manifold interests. This state of affairs was encouraged because the Meiji and later governments were determined to hurry by industrialization the creation of national power and security in a country that lacked adequate material resources and technical experience. Scarcity of capital and entrepreneurial skill tended to concentrate industrialization in a few immense concerns known as the *Zaibatsu*.

The principal *Zaibatsu* were the families of Mitsui, Mitsubishi, Sumitomo, and Yasuda. Lesser but powerful groups often referred to as *Zaibatsu* included: Okura, Asano, Kuhara, Ogawa-Tanaka, Kawasaki, Shibusawa, Furukawa, and Mori. Mitsui were great financiers and traders far back in Tokugawa times; Mitsubishi, founded by the samurai family of Iwasaki, dated its greatness only as far back as the Formosan affair of 1875, when it had provided the ships for the government's expedition; Sumitomo mined copper and traded in rice in Tokugawa times; and Yasuda were money lenders. The modern rise to power of all four *Zaibatsu* is explained (1) by their capacity to aid the government industrially and financially, and (2) by the choice privileges which the government in return bestowed upon them. In short, they were principal instruments of national policy in the creation of national power.[6]

The economic control, direct and indirect, exercized by *Zaibatsu* was a product of their diversified interests. They owned and/or controlled banks, trust companies, insurance companies, and leading firms in every

line of industry. They also placed heavy investments in undertakings which they did not own or control. In some areas their position was monopolistic. The extent of this concentration of *Zaibatsu* power is suggested by the fact that, together, Mitsui, Mitsubishi, and Sumitomo, prior to World War II, controlled one-third of the copper production, one-half the coal, more than one-half of the merchant marine and a major proportion of the cargoes carried, large interests in oil importing, half the warehouse capacity, one-third of Japan's foreign trade, nearly all of the paper industry, more than 70 per cent of the flour milling, and about 40 per cent of raw and refined sugar.

From the point of view of modern Japanese politics as shaped by older historical patterns, it is important to observe that the *Zaibatsu* were family concerns. Control was a family partnership; the capital was owned exclusively by the family or sometimes by a group of families all having a common ancestor. By the holding of shares, and the appointment of managers and directors in the various concerns, the partnership or family council could direct all matters of policy. At times actual control was vested by the family in *Banto*, or managers, who were not regarded primarily as hired officials but rather as fellow members of the clan serving their overlord.

Government and Agriculture

This pattern of industrialization for early Meiji Japan was applied, however, in a society that was overwhelmingly agricultural. It is not surprising therefore that the leaders of Meiji applied themselves to the agricultural settlement with the same revolutionary vigor they were showing in politics and industry. The importance of their agricultural settlement can scarcely be overestimated, for it fashioned the unique features of much of Japan's twentieth-century social, as well as economic, structure. Since this agricultural settlement was an immensely complex affair only the barest outlines can be suggested here.[7]

---

[6] The four *Zaibatsu* proper were distinguished from the lesser groups by reason of their supremacy in finance as well as in industry and commerce.

[7] See Thomas C. Smith, *The Agrarian Origins of Modern Japan* (1959).*

In the later years of the Tokugawa *Bakufu*, the illegal alienation of land to a new landlord class had gone on at a considerable rate. Then, after 1867, the Restoration legalized the sale of land. Although this made the peasant a nominal free-holder, it also created the means through which he could be dispossessed through foreclosures on mortgaged land. This was a matter of significance, since in 1870 many of the peasants were small, independent cultivators. Meanwhile, the Restoration government was seeking a unified and workable system of taxation to provide the revenue with which it hoped to carry the burden of military expenditure, and the capital necessary for strategic industries. The answer was found in the land tax policy of 1873, which effected a radical revision in previous methods of taxation. It involved three principal changes: (1) the tax was to be fixed by the *value* of the land, not, as formerly, by the yield of the harvest; (2) the tax would be at a fixed rate (3 per cent), not adjustable, as it had been in feudal times, to good or bad seasons; and (3) the tax would be paid in money and not, as formerly, in kind (rice). In 1889, as government under the Meiji Constitution was inaugurated, 70 per cent of national revenues derived from this land tax, though in later years it provided a decreasing proportion of the total income.

The Land Tax and the Peasantry

How did the new policy of taxation affect the peasant? It meant in general a steady dispossession of the landowning peasantry and the accumulation of land in a new, wealthy, landowning class. Yet, unlike the eighteenth-century enclosures in England, this did not mean that the Japanese peasantry deserted the countryside and moved to the cities. Since Japanese landlords had always been able to collect excessively high rents, they preferred to retain the tenant on the land rather than to oust him and exploit the land themselves as capitalists. Thus the habit-bound peasant remained upon the land, paying exorbitant rents and sinking deeper and deeper into poverty. During Meiji Japan his economic

decline, caused principally by outrageous rents, was aided and abetted by other factors: (1) the decline of the older household industries, and (2) a marked increase in the rural population. The resulting conditions of extreme agricultural poverty were closely related to developments marking the expansion of the Japanese textile industries in the twentieth century. The younger generation in the tenant households, the girls in particular, moved to the cities seeking to increase the *family* income. The textile industry was thereby provided with low-cost labor.

Again, the depressed position of the peasant was conditioned by the size of the average unit of land cultivated by a single household. The growth of tenancy in Japan was not accompanied by any marked increase in the size of the lots cultivated. In 1874 the average holding cultivated by a peasant household was 2.35 acres. In 1909 it was 2.38 acres, and in 1914 (including the larger individual holdings in Hokkaido and Ryukyu) it was 2.61 acres. These figures covering both paddy and dry fields, were considerably larger than the averages for paddy field holdings alone. The perpetuation of small holdings was partly traceable to Japanese topography, but it was also a direct result of the agrarian settlement made in the early Meiji period. Furthermore, although the Japanese tenant-farmer assumed the risks involved in crop raising, the landlord, through high rent, took most of the profit. The composite results of this subsistence economy were far-reaching. The peasant could no longer resort to the common lands for fodder, wood, and implements. His household cotton industry was destroyed first by imported cotton and then by the rise of the urban industry in Japan; thus he was forced to turn chiefly to sericulture as the principle supplementary household industry.

The partial destruction of the old domestic industry created a home market for the products of Japan's new factory industries, but this expanding home market was subject to limitations such as lack of purchasing power. This limited purchasing power of the Japanese home market became in the late nineteenth and twentieth centuries one of the chief factors impelling Japanese industry to seek ever larger foreign markets for its goods—and the Japanese nation to use war to this end. Japan's case was not unique. Nevertheless, the direction of her national policy could not remain unaffected by the fact that the masses of labor—rural and un-skilled industrial—were unable to buy the products of their nation's industry.

In spite of the unhappy plight of the peasantry, the general growth of the Japanese economy was spectacular, especially in trade, in agriculture, and in handicraft industries that were not destroyed by Western imports. By the early twentieth century, agricultural output had doubled. The whole Japanese economy grew rapidly, not merely the technological machine industry that was run or subsidized in the earlier years by government.

POLITICAL PARTIES IN MEIJI JAPAN

The Meiji economic settlement also had a direct bearing on the character of Japan's early political parties. As mentioned in Chapter 10, three important political parties appeared in late nineteenth-century Japan: the *Jiyuto* (Liberal Party), the *Rikken Kaishinto* (Progressive Party), and the *Rikken Teiaeito* (Imperialist Party). All these parties boasted of their adherence to stated political principles and platforms. These principles and platforms, however, were usually exceedingly vague and broad; in any case, they were of secondary importance, since in Japanese political thought the emphasis was on the political leader rather than upon any body of principles. It followed then that political parties tended to be aggregations of individuals bound by personal loyalty to a particular man, as was the case in feudal times, rather than a group held together by loyalty to any set of political principles.[8] Although this was the generally prevailing tendency, it should not be assumed that Western political theory, constitutionalism, and liberalism, played no part in the thinking of

[8] R. K. Reischauer, *Japan: Government—Politics* (1939), 29–30, 95–97.

Japanese politicians and intellectuals, for indeed it did. Yet, at the same time, it would be wrong to assume that Japanese political parties were inspired primarily by Western concepts of constitutionalism, or that the early "liberal" in Japanese politics was a replica of the nineteenth-century English liberal.

From 1881, when the first party appeared, until about 1900, there seems to have been some genuine enthusiasm among the politicians for the principles of responsible government. But after 1900 until 1918 the power of the *Genro* and the special groups that supported them—aristocrats, bureaucrats, and militarists—was so entrenched that generally the party politicians gave up the struggle for liberal principles (for which there was no long background of tradition as there was in England); they then sought the spoils of office by selling their parliamentary support to the oligarchy. In turn, oligarchs such as Ito Hirobumi and militarists such as Katsura Taro accepted the presidency of major political parties. Considering such leaders, it becomes obvious why the parties could no longer stand effectively for liberal or responsible government.

THE ECONOMIC BASE OF THE MEIJI PARTIES

The *Jiyuto*, or Liberal Party, of 1881 presented the seemingly incongruous spectacle of liberalism promoted by a class of rural landowners. This was due to the peculiar character of Japan's rural economy in the Restoration era. Landed proprietors occupied a dual position. They collected the profits of agriculture in the form of land rent paid by tenants in rice. These profits, which the proprietors converted into money at the best possible rate, were usually invested either in land or in rural industries such as the manufacture of *sake* (rice wine) or *miso* (bean paste). Thus the landowner became a local rural industrialist, rice broker, or merchant. He thereby combined the functions of "semi-feudal landlord" with those of the commercial capitalist. It was in this latter capacity of commercial capitalist that the manufacturing-landlord entered politics in 1881, combining his efforts with other groups in the formation of the *Jiyuto*. He did so because he was opposed to the government's policy of financing its military and naval program by increasing taxation on the products he manufactured, and because he objected to paying the bulk of the nation's income in the form of the land tax while the government bestowed its favors and protection on the financial oligarchy of the cities. Other rural groups also had their special complaints. The tenant cultivator wanted reduction in his rent. Those who owned their land were already threatened with dispossession. Thus from these various groups, particularly from the landed, rural manufacturers, came the crusade for "Liberty and the People's Rights" with its subsequent development into the constitutional movement that culminated in the Constitution of 1889. In this sense Japanese liberalism sprang from the countryside and not from the cities. In contrast the ideological leadership of the movement came from quite a different group. This was a nucleus of samurai from Hizen and Tosa who had been pushed out of the new government bureaucracy by the samurai politicians of Satsuma and Choshu.

The second and rival political party, the *Kaishinto*, led by Okuma, included in its membership other disgruntled bureaucrats who were out of office, a scattering of liberal intellectuals who favored the British parliamentary system, and, significantly, from the economic point of view, some of the wealthier urban merchants and industrialists, including representatives of the Mitsubishi interests. In ideology, the *Kaishinto* was a mild reflection of the then current English liberalism and utilitarianism.

From 1880 until 1918 the oligarchy, led by the *Genro,* was able to channel within narrow limits all movements of political liberalism, and thus to uphold its authoritarian concepts on the economic and social structure of society. It accomplished this in a number of ways. It neutralized the parties by playing one against another. It won over to its own fold some of the party leaders by various means, not excluding that of bribing them with offices. Freedom of speech and of the press were seriously hampered long before the constitution was promulgated. The Press Law of 1875 and the Peace Preservation Ordinance of 1887 were the nineteenth-century manifestations of what came to be known in the twentieth century as the control of "dangerous thoughts." The first liberal political parties were for a time suppressed entirely, thus depriving the economically and socially depressed masses of any political leadership. What is more, when the resurrected Liberal Party (*Jiyuto*) took its place in the first Diet of 1890, it had been shorn of its liberalism. By 1900, when it became the *Seiyukai*, it was the party of the great landlords and rural capitalists.[9]

THE POLITICAL PHILOSOPHY OF MEIJI

The political and economic settlement which the Meiji leaders devised in the late nineteenth century was a product of deeply ingrained Japanese values and habits of thought. First in importance was the Confucian idea of unity. Whether it was the family, the clan, or the family-state, the individual was merely a part of these larger units, and only through them did his life acquire meaning and become an expression of what has sometimes been called loosely the Japanese spirit. In the West in modern times, science, philosophy, literature, even religion have struggled to free themselves from control by church or state. This quest for new and free roads to individualism has produced many types of individuals and all manner of standards of values with the resulting changes and conflicts between them: Christian versus Atheist, Protestant versus Catholic, Liberal versus Conservative. This self-seeking diversity did not make sense to the traditional Japanese mind in which phi-

[9] G. E. Uyehara, *The Political Development of Japan, 1867–1909* (London, 1910), 89–106; Yusuke Tsurumi, "The Liberal Movement in Japan," *The Reawakening of the Orient* (1925), 68 ff.; W. W. McLaren, *A Political History of Japan During the Meiji Era, 1867–1912* (1916), 153–77.

losophy, religion, economics, and politics were one and indivisible. Consequently, a Japanese was a Confucian, a Buddhist, and a Shintoist at one and the same time. Nothing, it was believed, should be permitted to interfere with this idea of oneness. There could be no place in the old Japanese society for the rugged individualism of the capitalist, the parochial school of an exclusive church, the class struggle of the communists, or even the conflicting platforms of political parties.

The application of this principle of unity to practical politics was best exemplified by the Japanese attitude toward the emperor system. In Shintoism the emperor was the descendant of the gods; in Buddhism, of the supreme Buddha; and in Confucianism, he was the fountain of the great virtues from which the good society would come. He symbolized the complete unity of the family-state in its philosophical, religious, political, and economic concerns.

An American school child learns at a tender age that "all men are created equal." Japanese children, however, learned to recognize inequality as a principle that is both self-evident and natural. As in the case of unity, the doctrine of inequality was sanctioned by the dominant systems of thought. Shintoism explained inequality in terms of blood, the emperor being what he was because of his direct descent from the Sun Goddess. The respective stations of all persons in society were determined by the stations of their divine ancestors. Buddhism gave equal stress to the inequality of men as they struggled toward salvation. Confucianism rated men as having superior or inferior virtue. One man was, therefore, not as good as another. Within the circle of Japanese culture he held a particular station that was determined by nobility of blood, Buddhist enlightenment, and Confucian virtue. This theory of society would not harmonize easily with the modern world into which Japan had begun to move even before the end of the Tokugawa period. How could a society that was moving toward new institutions be controlled during a period of unprecedented change? Since Japan was an agrarian society, much would depend on maintaining some stability in the rural life of the nation. Japan's

Meiji leadership met this problem in the following way.

During the Tokugawa era the actual control of rural Japan had been delegated downward so far that its recovery by a revitalized central administration could by no means be taken for granted. The Tokugawa system of delegation to local officials had worked well so long as the peasant remained loyal and disciplined, and so long as the traditional and feudal social and economic systems of rural Japan remained undisturbed. But in the last years of Tokugawa rule and the early years of the Restoration, disturbance within the traditional system was the order of the day. Cities grew in size, transportation improved, agriculture became more productive while industry invaded the countryside. These changes disrupted the stable structure of power in the villages. The result, among other things, was some peasant participation in the Restoration movement, the real nature of which the village dwellers neither knew nor understood. In rural Japan, nationalism and industrialization were meaningless terms, but the traditional language of loyalty and obligation (now directed to the throne) was understandable to samurai and peasant alike. Therefore it was this language of tradition that the leaders of Meiji used to support an orderly revolution. They used old values to justify a new society.

THE UNION OF TRADITIONAL RELIGION AND MODERN POLITICS

Although the separation of church and state dated back to the beginnings of American history, the principle is maintained only through constant vigilance by the community. In Japan, in contrast, church and state were regarded as one, or, to put the matter as the Japanese saw it, politics was a phase of ethics. The Japanese sovereign, descended directly from the gods, was both priest and emperor to his people. He was also a manifestation of the spirit of Buddhism. Confucianism, taken over by the Japanese from China, pictured him as the exponent of the Will of Heaven. The good society could not be independent of Heaven's Will, nor could it arise from any source other than Heaven's sovereign whose ideas obviously could not be subject to question, since God was on his side.

Freedom under constitutional law is a familiar concept to young American students, for it is the ideal of the American system of government. It stresses regulation arrived at in democratic fashion through the legislative process. It implies that law is the essential factor in safeguarding equal opportunity and the common good. A traditionally minded Japanese, however, did not see society in this light. Because of his indoctrination with unity, inequality, and ethics, he looked to man as the answer to good government. In other words, it was the will of the sovereign that was important to the welfare of society. Laws were simply an expression of what the sovereign believed to be best at a given time. Their purpose could not be the protection of individual freedom because this would violate the principle of unity. Furthermore, a society based on inequality meant that there were rulers and those who were ruled. Written law was considered a guide to the former rather than a protection of the latter.

The leadership of the Restoration movement was directed by able young samurai convinced that their own political power, as well as the safety of the state, could best be assured by the material products of modern industry and by the political ideals of an ancient and in part mythological past. Accordingly, while industrialization was fostered by all modern techniques, including government ownership and subsidization, "the system of beliefs and values . . . was pushed back, as it were, to an earlier age." A modern system of communication and education, employing thought control, propaganda, and censorship, was used to counter democratic ideals surging in from the West, and to revitalize traditional notions on unity, inequality, government by man, and the patriarchal state.[10]

This dual course, dictated by the Meiji leadership, toward what was materially modern but spiritually ancient has been present in varying degree in all modern societies. In Meiji Japan freedom of speech and of investigation asserted themselves stubbornly. Nevertheless, the material success of the Meiji leaders and their resulting and growing prestige enabled them to insist on orthodoxy in social and political matters. At no time was the atmosphere congenial to freedom of thought, to free public discussion, or to the formation of political parties that might challenge the views of the oligarchs. The appearance, therefore, of political associations in mid-nineteenth-century Japan must be examined through Japanese eyes, not as they might appear to an American hoping to see democracy arise in Japan.

Meiji political parties were associations rather than parties. Parties in the true sense of the word exist only where there is a keen *public* consciousness—a sense of the *public* and the *public welfare* or of *society* and its welfare. These concepts as Americans understand them did not exist in Japan, where, in place of "public servants," there was something quite different, namely, the emperor's officials, and where a man's obligations were to family and to state but not to society. When a man did step outside of the circle of family and state, he tended to be on an uncharted road with no signposts to guide him. In these circumstances he tended to fall back on a pattern which he did understand—the pattern of the family. He sought the protection and security of some prominent individual. There was thus established between the two a sort of son and father relationship. The existence of this kind of relationship bore heavily on the character of Japan's political parties. Therefore, despite the fact that feudalism was abolished formally in 1871, the essential character of the relationship between feudal lord and retainer lingered on in the new Japan and placed its stamp on the political process.

THE DISINTEGRATING FAMILY STRUCTURE

It is not proper, however, to dismiss the subject of Meiji political parties by saying that they were mere relics of familial

---

[10] For an effective treatment in detail, see Ike Nobutaka, *The Beginnings of Political Democracy in Japan* (1950), 195–201.

relations and feudalism. In the Meiji period and even after it, these influences were undoubtedly dominant, but they were not exclusive. The Meiji leaders to be sure, attempted to reimpose family structure and discipline of the samurai type on the entire population. In this, they enjoyed a large measure of success, but the success was not unqualified. One explanation is apparent. Industrialization and population growth created a shifting population, disrupting the compact family circle. During and after Meiji, rural Japan had a higher birth rate than urban Japan, yet rural population remained relatively stationary. With young men and women flocking to the city, family ties were weakened though by no means destroyed. Meiji literature was filled with the resulting conflict between family and individual.

THE PLACE OF SHINTOISM

The means by which traditional Japanism was made the inspiration of Meiji's modernization was best exemplified in the use made of the old and indigenous cult of Shinto. From the beginning of Meiji there was a conscious, deliberate, and organized effort not only to perpetuate old cultural values but also to give them new strength. These efforts created in the late nineteenth and early twentieth centuries out of Japan's mythological past a foundation for the modern Japanese state that was essentially religious in character. Marked by a high degree of organization and formalization, these religious foundations were clothed with a sancity that made them immune to free debate or criticism. Since they were concerned essentially with the origins of the state, their authority could be invoked at all times to stifle criticism and thereby negate the principles of democratic practices. This state religion, so intimately a part of modern Japanese nationalism, was commonly known as State or Pure Shinto to distinguish it from popular sectarian cults of Shinto that had no formal official standing.

For many centuries after its early, simple flowering, Shinto had been all but submerged by Buddhism, just as was Confucianism in China. But, with the rise of military feudalism, Shinto, taking on a new intellectual vigor, not only freed itself by degrees from Buddhist control but even asserted its superiority over Buddhism. This regeneration of Shinto, strongly nationalistic, sang the praises of early Japan as it was before the coming of Confucianism and Buddhism. In Tokugawa times, although the shoguns patronized Chinese learning and although Buddhism was the established religion, Shinto scholars nevertheless were able to revive interest in the *Kojiki*, to make it a Bible of nationalism and a proof of Japan's unique superiority. During the early nineteenth century, the popular appeal of the Shinto myths was revealed in the rise of numbers of Shinto sects which eventually attracted many adherents from among the common people, thus testifying to the inadequacy of modern Japanese Buddhism as a popular religious vehicle. One of the early decisions of the Meiji leaders involved the disestablishing of Buddhism and the reestablishing and revitalizing of Shinto. An Office of Shinto Affairs became one of the highest organs of the new state. By this means it was possible to reinvigorate Shinto and to use it consciously as the spiritual foundation of the new national state.

The nationalistic values in Shinto mythology were exploited to the full. From Japan's ancient myths re-emerged a pantheon of deities headed by the Sun Goddess, who was now ministered to by thousands of priests at tens of thousands of sacred places. The dogma of State Shinto cannot be treated here in detail, but its character may be suggested by three essential tenets of this politico-religious faith.

The first was the dogma, extolled in the first and third articles of the Meiji constitution, of unbroken, divine, imperial sovereignty. The emperor was divine because he was the living embodiment of the divine ancestors of the race. The second dogma of State Shinto, closely related to the first, was the belief in Japan as the land of the gods. Here the concept was that Japan, far from being merely the product of ordinary geographical and historical forces, was peculiarly endowed with grace by the divine ancestors. The third dogma was the belief in Japan's benevolent mission or destiny. Modern Japanese were taught that the land of the gods, uniquely formed, was possessed of a divine mission to extend its righteous sovereignty over less fortunate peoples. Thus the dogma of divine descent, the land of the gods, and benevolent destiny, all served to reinforce traditional Japanese thought, and, by so doing, to create a climate inhospitable to democratic ideas.[11]

WESTERN INTELLECTUAL IMPORTS

While Meiji Japan was peculiarly a Japanese creation, the occasion for its birth was the Western impact. For Japanese scholars and statesmen, it was a period of intense intellectual upheaval. In its simplest form, their intellectual problem may be stated as follows: How should Japan transform herself into a powerful nation-state on the models provided by the West while at the same time preserving her own cultural identity? In the case of Japan, the leading advocates of "Westernization" (the importation of Western ideas and institutions) were not aiming at upheaval or at the abandonment of Japanese values. Rather, the purpose was to discover and to adopt ideas and institutions that would ensure the orderly creation of a modern state. When, after 1865, the question of exclusion and seclusion was no longer a political issue, and when in 1868 the Charter Oath proclaimed that "wisdom and knowledge shall be sought in all parts of the world," Japanese scholars turned to things Western with a boundless and sometimes undiscriminating enthusiasm. At first the search was directed mainly to those fields of learning considered most essential in creating a modern state: Western theories of government, ideas and techniques in economics, finance, and commerce. Free trade versus protection was a

[11] The subject of Shinto nationalism is treated in great detail in D. C. Holtom, *Modern Japan and Shinto Nationalism* (1943; rev. ed., 1947; reprint, 1963).

lively subject of debate as early as the decade of the 1870s.

Philosophy and Law

The most progressive Japanese scholars derived their main foreign inspiration from such contemporaneous Western social philosophies as positivism and utilitarianism rather than from the European enlightenment of the eighteenth century.[12] Leaders in Japanese thought read John Stuart Mill (*System of Logic*), Jeremy Bentham (*Principles of Morals and Legislation*), and they read widely in the writings of Herbert Spencer (*Social Statistics*) whose advice, particularly on sociological matters, was often sought by the Meiji government. The influence of German idealistic philosophy was felt particularly after 1880 through the works of Nietzsche, Schopenhauer, and Hegel. In psychology Spencer's *Principles* were well known. In law, the Tokyo Imperial University, founded in 1886, offered instruction in English, French, and German jurisprudence. Japan's pioneer student in the field of constitutional and administrative law was Hozumi Yatsuka, and in international law, Ariga Nagas, later well known in the West. In the drafting of Japan's modern criminal code French influence was strong, since a French jurist, Gustave Boissanade, was legal adviser to the government. The later civil code, however, was framed under German direction, and a German scholar at Tokyo Imperial University, Herman Roessler, was adviser to

[12] On the thought of the Japanese intellectuals of the period see: Thomas R. H. Havens, "Comte, Mill, and the Thought of Nishi Amane in Meiji Japan," *Journal of Asian Studies* 27 (1968): 219–28; and George M. Wilson, "Kita Ikki's Theory of Revolution," *Journal of Asian Studies* 26 (1966): 89–99. The most influential proponent of the enlightenment as Japan moved into the new era was Fukuzawa Yukichi, the founder of Keio University. Critical of the old Confucian education and concerned with how man could best fulfill his obligations to society, he advocated a limited economic individualism. *The Autobiography of Fukuzawa Yukichi*, trans. Eiichi Kiyooka (Tokyo, 1950), and Carmen Blacker, *The Japanese Enlightenment: A Study of the Writings of Fukuzawa Yukichi* (Cambridge, England, 1964).

the drafting committee for the Constitution of 1889. Also, the legal framework for local government was patterned in some degree on the Prussian system as outlined for the Japanese by Albert Mosse.

In their search for the secrets of Western progress, the Japanese also turned to Western historical literature: Guizot's *History of Civilization in Europe*, and Buckle's *History of Civilization in England*. During the Tokugawa period, Japan had learned something of Western medicine through the Dutch at Deshima (Drs. Carl Thunberg and Philip Franz von Siebold). Japanese interest was further stimulated in 1860 by Dr. J. C. Hepburn, the first American medical missionary in Japan. After 1871, with the appointment of two German doctors to the faculty of Tokyo Imperial University, the influence of German medical science was pronounced.

Even before the Restoration government removed in 1873 the two-centuries-old ban against Christianity, British and American Protestant missionaries in some numbers had been well received. In 1875 the founding of Doshisha English School (later Doshisha University) in Kyoto marked the beginnings of Christian education by Japanese converts. Five additional Christian schools and colleges had been founded by 1890. At first the Christian movement was welcome, perhaps for itself but also because it contributed to Westernization. In time it met opposition from: (1) advocates of English empiricism who taught evolution and agnosticism, (2) zealots of Buddhism and Shintoism, and (3) extreme disciples of the new nationalism who held that Westernization was being carried too far. Although Christian theology made only a limited imprint in Meiji Japan, the influence of Christian principles of social responsibility and humanitarianism was, though indeterminate, by no means inconsiderable.

New Customs in a Bewildered Society

The social and intellectual temper of Japanese life from 1870 to 1900 was not only complex; it was also subject to constant and bewildering change. In the earlier years there was, as indicated, a mad mania for Westernization: a willingness to replace everything that was native with anything that was foreign. Confusion in thought was followed by confusion and contradiction in action. The dictum of the Charter Oath of 1868 that "absurd customs" would be discarded was at first taken very literally. Class distinctions were abolished. Buddhist priests were told to take wives, to raise families, and to eat beef. Since beef eating was common in the West, it was inferred that it must be a symbol of advanced civilization. Married women and former court nobles (*kuge*) were told to stop blackening their teeth and shaving their eyebrows. For men, the Western haircut, instead of long hair done in a top knot, came to symbolize that the wearer was modern and progressive.

Particularly in the early years of their new contacts with the West, the Japanese showed a deep sensitivity to Western opinion. Since they were determined to be well thought of by the "more advanced" Europeans and Americans, there was a general scramble to discard or to hide institutions and customs that might subject them to ridicule or moral scorn by the foreigners. Abortion and infanticide, both common practices in Tokugawa times, were now prohibited. Mixed bathing at public bath houses, the social clubs of feudal times, met a similar fate. By 1885, however, although the mania for things Western remained strong, it was countered by a conservative reaction—a demand for the preservation of Japanese values.

Literature and the Arts

Because the Meiji period was one of planned Westernization it was natural that in the early years its literature was centered on translations of European and American works. Many of the translators were not professional writers but students of politics, economics, and government, and the first translations were from the classics in these fields. In time literary as well as political and economic classics appeared in Japanese: *Earnest Maltravers, Hamlet, Aesop's Fables, The Lady* of the Lake, *The Arabian Nights, Julius Caesar,* and a host of others. By the mid-twentieth century in Japan one could obtain in translation almost any major work written in the West from Homer and Hesiod whose names in Japan are pronounced as Homelosu and Heshiodosu. In time these Western masterpieces together with the fast march of events in Japan itself produced a new creative Japanese literature.

THE TEMPER OF MEIJI JAPAN

It must be clear that Meiji Japan compresses itself into no easy historical nutshell. Indeed, it has much in common with Stephen Leacock's hero who rode off in all directions. This is not to imply that there was no purpose in the Meiji revolution. In fact, the purpose—to enable Japan to overtake the West and become overnight a powerful national state—was never in doubt. If there were confusions and contradictions, these were the natural garments of a people torn between the old and the new, between what was indigenous and what was foreign, between a native heritage they understood and alien cultures they could scarcely comprehend. Historically, the point to observe is that before the turn of the nineteenth century the pattern of the new Japan had been made and applied. In material things and purposes it was a modern and even a Western Japan, where politics was constitutional, where wages replaced kinship and loyalty, and where businessmen wore coats and trousers instead of the kimono. At the same time, the leaders directing this revolution were men of the samurai tradition, and they preserved and invigorated that tradition as the moral and spiritual foundation of the new nation.

An understanding of this late nineteenth century Japan involves the measurement of Western penetration and influence. This task is beset by many pitfalls. For example, it has often been assumed that Germany provided Ito with the model for the Meiji constitution. Certainly, Ito saw merits in the German structure, but it should not be forgotten, as Sir George Sansom notes, that Japan, it would seem, even without the German experience to draw upon, would have produced a political system almost precisely like the one adopted.[13] In Meiji Japan, Westernization and modernization were not always the same thing. It would seem that the Meiji leadership had taken deeply to heart the principle that "foreign ideas and institutions must be adopted *in degree* so that they appear to supplement and enrich the society rather than challenge and defy it. . . ."[14]

FOR FURTHER READING

HISTORY. G. C. Allen, *A Short Economic History of Modern Japan,* (rev. ed., 1962), main emphasis on industry, finance, and economic policy. G. C. Allen, *Modern Japan and Its Problems* (1928) contains excellent essays on many aspects of Japanese life. Takekoshi Yosaburo, *Economic Aspects of the History of the Civilization of Japan* (3 vols., London, 1930), rich in significant materials.

CAPITAL, TRADE, AND POPULATION. E. F. Penrose, *Population Theories and Their Application with Special Reference to Japan* (1934) is the best work on the subject. Henry Rosovsky, *Capital Formation in Japan 1868–1940* (1961), a major work on the Japanese economy. Ohara Keichi, ed., trans. and adapted by Okata Tamotsu, *Japanese Trade and Industry in the Meiji-Taisho Era* (Tokyo, 1957).

LANDLORD, PEASANT, AND VILLAGE. Robert K. Sakai, "Feudal Society and Modern Leadership in Satsuma-Han," *Journal of Asian Studies* 16 (1957): 365–76. John F. Embree, *Suye Mura; a Japanese Village* (1939),* a case study of a small village in Kyushu. R. P. Dore, "The Meiji Landlord: Good or Bad?"

[13] George B. Sansom, *The Western World and Japan* (1950), 358–63.
[14] Robert A. Scalapino, "Environmental and Foreign Contributions: Japan," *Political Modernization in Japan and Turkey,* R. E. Ward and D. A. Rustow, eds. (1964), 89.

Journal of Asian Studies 18 (1959): 343–56. Hani Setsuko, *The Japanese Family System* (Tokyo, 1948).

THE CULTURE OF MEIJI. Kaikoku Hyakunen Kinen Bunka Jigyo Kai, (Centenary Culture Council, ed.) *Japanese Culture in the Meiji Era* (10 vols., Tokyo, 1955–1958). Irwin Schiner, *Christian Converts and Social Protest in Meiji Japan* (1970), important reinterpretations of Meiji thought. Fukuzawa Yukichi, *The Autobiography of Fukuzawa Yukichi*, trans. Eiichi Kiyooka (Tokyo, 1950), the fascinating autobiography of the great pioneer in the introduction of things western into Japan. Lafcadio Hearn, *Japan; an Attempt at Interpretation* (Tokyo, 1955),° a romantic view of old Japan by a great nineteenth-century writer.

LITERATURE. Donald Keene, comp. and ed., *Modern Japanese Literature, an Anthology* (1956),° a selection from prose, poetry, and drama superbly rendered into English. Kokusai Bunka Shinkokai, *Introduction to Contemporary Japanese Literature* (Tokyo, 1939). Kunitomo Tadao, *Japanese Literature Since 1868* (Tokyo, 1938).

THE THEATRE. Zoe Kincaid, *Kabuki, the Popular Stage of Japan* (London, 1925), a detailed study based on secondary sources. Earle Ernst, *The Kabuki Theatre* (1956).° Faubion Bowers, *Japanese Theatre* (1952, 2nd printing, 1954),° a very good general introduction to the various forms of Japanese theatre with illustrations.

China, 1860–1890:
An Uneasy Interlude

chapter 12

In returning to the story of the Western impact on China, we should keep in mind that the years 1840 to 1860 had confronted the Ch'ing dynasty with unprecedented crises at home and in its relations with the Western powers. Within the compass of twenty years China had suffered humiliating defeat in the so-called Opium War and the *Arrow* War, had seen its capital invaded by British and French armies, and, far more significant, had pledged itself in treaties to conform to a theory of international relations founded on a concept of equal and sovereign states. In other words, Manchu-Chinese society in 1860 was faced with the business of revolutionizing its outlook upon and its approach to the "barbarian" society of the West. The record of how China sought to adjust to these new facts of life is a story of consuming interest and complexity.[1]

In 1861, as the first ministers of the treaty powers took up their residence in Peking, it seemed that the days of the Manchu dynasty might well be numbered. Nevertheless, the end of the dynasty was not yet

[1] See Liang Ch'i-ch'ao, *Intellectual Trends in the Ch'ing Period*, Immanuel C. Y. Hsu, trans. (1959), Part II.

to be. Indeed, during the T'ung-chih period (1862–1874), there was a short dynastic revival called the "Restoration." This "Restoration" must therefore be examined in the context of the continuing pressures of the Western treaty powers on the coast and of the T'ai-p'ing rebels in the interior.

Peking in 1860 was a "deserted" city— deserted by its emperor and his court. The Imperial entourage had fled to the mountains of Jehol when the British and French advanced on the capital. When the panic passed, the court had to return to set up an administration capable of enforcing the new treaties of 1858 and 1860. To this nervous capital came also, in the spring of 1861, Frederick Bruce and M. de Bourboulon, the British and French Ministers. Anson Burlingame, the new American Minister, arrived a few months later. These ministers were permitted to set up permanent residence in Peking, but when a representative of Prussia appeared, the Chinese, although granting him the commercial privileges won by the treaty powers, refused him residence at the capital. This refusal was significant because it revealed the power still exercised by the extreme anti-foreign party at court.

The newly arrived envoys of the Western powers were met in Peking by I-hsin, usually known as Prince Kung (1833–1898), a half-brother of the fugitive Hsien-feng emperor who had been left behind to deal as he could with the victorious British and French. Faced with the humiliation of signing the supplementary conventions of 1860, Prince Kung was convinced that China had no alternative but "to act according to the treaties and not allow the foreigners to go even slightly beyond them." His conclusion combined both wisdom and naïveté: wisdom in seeing that the treaties must be accepted and observed; naïveté in the assumption that the powers would remain satisfied with what the treaties contained.

To implement this new policy of treaty observance there was created, on the recommendation of Prince Kung and with imperial sanction, the Tsungli Yamen, a special body under the Grand Council which was to deal with all matters relating to the Western powers. The creation of this special board, which was often staffed with able and powerful officials, was a major step toward a ministry of foreign affairs (Wai-wu-pu), which was not established until 1901. Prince Kung had sensed the futility of China's blind resistance. Accordingly, as head of the Tsungli Yamen, he organized the beginnings of a Westernized Manchu army, revitalized the Peking administration, acted as regent for the child T'ung-chih emperor (1862–1874), and until his dismissal from the Tsungli Yamen in 1884 directed his influence toward maintaining peace with the Western powers on the theory that only through peace could China gain strength. A vital weakness in Prince Kung's policy was his inability, for reasons that will be apparent later, to reassert the influence of Peking in the provinces after the defeat of the T'ai-p'ings. Nor was he able to free himself wholly from the stifling influences of an ignorant, retrograde, and anti-foreign Manchu court.[2]

[2] On the role of the Tsungli Yamen, see Masataka Banno, *China and the West, 1858–1861: the Origins of the Tsungli Yamen* (1964), and the administrative history by S. M. Meng, *The Tsungli Yamen: Its Organization and Function* (1962).* Something of the atmosphere of this court is suggested by events of 1861. The Hsien-feng emperor, a mental and physical de-

THE COLLAPSE OF THE T'AI-P'ING

The T'ai-p'ing had continued to threaten the Manchu dynasty during the years 1851–63, a period in which the pressure of the foreign powers on the coast had been severe. The conditions, political, economic, and social, which had occasioned the uprisings, have already been suggested (see p. 85). The basic importance of the T'ai-p'ing movement lay not only in its weakening effect upon the Manchu dynasty already under threat from the foreign powers, but also in the fact that the T'ai-p'ing may be considered the opening phase of a profound reform and revolutionary process.

The real nature of the T'ai-p'ing movement is still a subject of research and debate among historians. Some conclusions that are emerging indicate (1) The political goal of the T'ai-p'ings was creation of a dynasty that was to be new in kind as well as name. Under the rule of the Heavenly King the T'ai-p'ings envisioned a state providing "a system of total control of all life . . . which had no parallel in Chinese history."[3] (2) T'ai-p'ing social and economic doctrine looked toward full-scale reorganization of Chinese life. Drawing upon ideas of the fatherhood of God and of the brotherhood and equality of

generate, had died at Jehol in August. Two court factions seeking control promptly appeared. The one was headed by Manchu princes; the other by an anti-foreign concubine who in 1856 had borne the sovereign his first and only son. Anti-foreignism, characteristic of the Court during the entire Hsien-feng period, left ample room for factionalism, and so it came about that under the influence of her enemies, the emperor had at his death named an administration from which she and Prince Kung were excluded. These circumstances drove the former concubine, now the junior Empress Dowager Tz'u-hsi, and Prince Kung to join forces. The princes were ruthlessly crushed. Since Prince Kung had saved the throne for her son, Tz'u-hsi repressed her violent and anti-foreign views, perhaps in gratitude, perhaps because it was expedient. Such was the uneasy court alliance on which Prince Kung was required to base his policy of peace with the powers.

[3] Franz Michael and Chang Chung-li, *The Taiping Rebellion: History and Documents* (2 vols., 1966), I, 84.

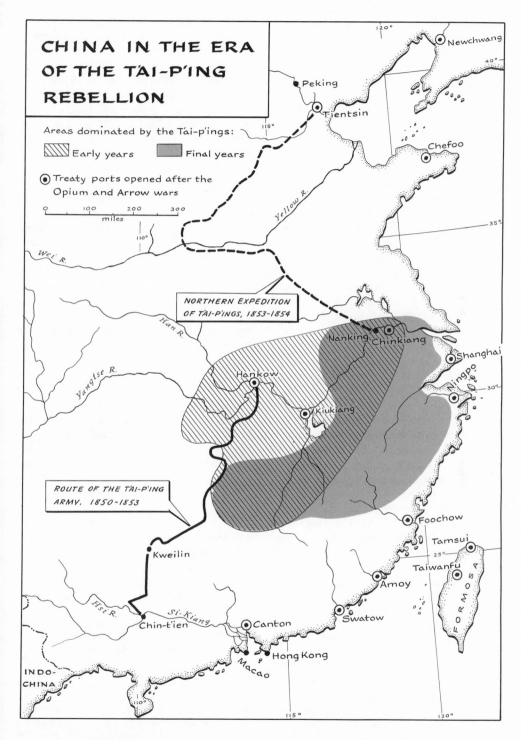

CHINA IN THE ERA OF THE TẠI-P'ING REBELLION

Areas dominated by the Tại-p'ings:

Early years

Final years

Treaty ports opened after the Opium and Arrow wars

0   100   200   300
miles

NORTHERN EXPEDITION OF TẠI-P'INGS, 1853-1854

ROUTE OF THE TẠI-P'ING ARMY, 1850-1853

Newchwang

Peking

Tientsin

Chefoo

Yellow R.

Wei R.

Han R.

Yangtse R.

Nanking   Chinkiang

Shanghai

Hankow   Ningpo

Kiukiang

Foochow

Tamsui

Kweilin

Taiwanfu

FORMOSA

Hsi R.   Si-Kiang

Chin-t'ien   Canton   Swatow

Amoy

Macao   Hong Kong

INDO-CHINA

Source: J. K. Fairbank, E. G. Reischauer, and Albert M. Craig, *East Asia, The Modern Transformation* (Boston: Houghton Mifflin Co., 1965), 160, 339.

153

all men, the rebels held that the state should provide security and protection for the aged, the handicapped, the widowed and the orphaned. Women were to be the equals of men, being permitted to enter military service, to take government examinations and to hold office. Such ancient customs as footbinding, prostitution, and polygamy were to be abolished, and movable goods were to be consigned to a public treasury for redistribution on the basis of need. In short, the T'ai-p'ing's creed embraced the vision of a revolutionized society, but among the rebels this vision was embraced mostly by the leadership. The great majority of T'ai-p'ings were peasants seeking redress of traditional grievances rather than the transformation of society. Thus, did the T'ai-p'ing upheaval mark the beginning of modern China's revolution, or was it in fact a more traditional peasant rebellion? To such questions history does not yet provide definitive answers.[4]

In any event, the fact remains that the destruction and devastation of life and property in the decade of the rebellion were almost beyond description. How many lives were destroyed, directly or indirectly, no one knows, but the estimates run as high as thirty million. In the beginning the movement was idealistic and disciplined. Its leadership included some men of ability and responsibility. Unfortunately, many of these men lost their lives in the early years and were replaced by men of lesser caliber. As a result, vast areas controlled by the T'ai-p'ing were subject to maladministration, while border areas were pillaged by both T'ai-p'ing and Imperial forces.

The ultimate collapse of the rebellion

cannot be ascribed to a single cause. Fundamental was its failure to win the support of the literati. These influential elements were alienated, to be sure, by Christian concepts in T'ai-p'ing ideology, but more especially by the T'ai-p'ing attack on the Confucian bureaucracy as intellectually hollow and socially corrupt.[5] The later T'ai-p'ing leadership found, among other things, the recesses of the harem more congenial than the edifice of reform. From what appeared as constructive beginnings, the movement headed toward destructive ends. Its leadership was eventually captured by the traditions and abuses against which it had taken up arms: provincialism, familism, and nepotism. This loss of the ardor for reform coincided with the revival of dynastic spirit at Peking under Prince Kung. Moreover, the T'ai-p'ings did not solve the problem of recruiting and training young leaders to perpetuate their new order. In the long view, T'ai-p'ing military leadership suffered the same decline as its political leadership. The military's failure to capture Peking was fatal.

If China was slow in meeting the threat of the T'ai-p'ing, she was not wholly without resolve. It was the T'ai-p'ing revolt that brought into prominence two of China's all too few great nineteenth-century leaders, Tseng Kuo-fan of Hunan and Li Hung-chang of Anhui. These men, unlike so many of their colleagues, had fought the rebellion from its beginnings; but it was not until after 1860 that they achieved, with foreign assistance, any major success.[6]

Among the foreigners who entered the Chinese military service to fight the T'ai-p'ing were Frederick Townsend Ward, an American soldier of fortune from Salem,

---

[4] The study by Michael and Chang cited above and Joseph Levenson's *The Problem of Monarchical Decay*, Vol. II of *Confucian China and Its Modern Fate* (3 vols., 1958–65) hold that the T'ai-p'ing upheaval was an attempted revolution. The argument is disputed in Vincent Y. C. Shih, *The Taiping Ideology: Its Sources, Interpretations and Inferences* (1967). For a brief discussion of the historiographic problems see Paul A. Cohen, "Ch'ing China: Confrontation with the West, 1850–1900," *Modern East Asia: Essays in Interpretation,* James B. Crowley, ed. (1970), 29–61.

[5] Joseph R. Levenson, *Confucian China and Its Modern Fate,* Vol. II (1964),* 112.

[6] Teng Ssu-yu, *New Light on the History of the Taiping Rebellion* (1950), especially 35–73. Also by the same author, "A Political Interpretation of Chinese Rebellions and Revolutions," *Tsing Hua Journal of Chinese Studies,* I (1958), 91–119. Eugene P. Boardman, *Christian Influence upon the Ideology of the Taiping Rebellion, 1851–1864* (1952), especially 41–105. Also Helmut G. Callis, *China, Confucian and Communist* (1959).

Massachusetts, organizer of a Chinese force known as the "Ever Victorious Army"; and Major Charles George Gordon of the British army, who took command of the "Ever Victorious Army" in 1863 after Ward's death. The military campaigns of Tseng, Li and their foreign colleagues, together with the aid of the British and the French governments, resulted in the slow but sure destruction of the rebel military power on the lower Yangtze. The city of Soochow, one of the strongest rebel bastions, fell in December, 1863. In the following year the T'ai-p'ing "Heavenly King," debauched, degenerate, committed suicide shortly before his capital Nanking fell before the armies of Tseng Kuo-fan. So ended the T'ai-p'ing Rebellion. During its course through the middle decades of the century, twelve of the richest provinces were devastated, millions of people were exterminated, and poverty and despair made an unprecedented conquest. In some respects the rebellion played a decisive part in the relations of China and the West. It helped to encourage European intervention in China. For instance, the conclusion of the treaties of 1858 and 1860 stamped the T'ai-p'ings as rebels. They could no longer be regarded as potential allies of the Western powers, nor as potential successors to the Manchus. Furthermore, the indemnities for the *Arrow* War depended on the fate of the Peking dynasty.[7]

CHINA'S MILITARY ESTABLISHMENT

The final suppression of the T'ai-p'ings is a reminder that the Confucian dynasty had narrowly escaped destruction from domestic foes. How, then, had it come to pass that Peking could show so little capacity to meet her enemies at home or from abroad?

When the crises of the mid-nineteenth century befell China, her military establishment, set up by the Manchus some two

[7] G. E. Taylor, "The Taiping Rebellion," *Chinese Social and Political Science Rev.* 16 (1933): 612–14; W. J. Hail, *Tseng Kuo-fan and the Taiping Rebellion* (1927), 290. For a graphic account of Ward and Gordon, see Jonathan Spence, *To Change China* (1969), 57–92.

centuries earlier, was all but useless as a fighting force. Prior to the conquest of China (1644), the Manchus had been organized in military-administrative groups, known as "banners," that served the civil and economic as well as the military activities of the Manchu rulers. After the conquest of China, the Manchus sought to rule their new subjects in a Chinese way while, at the same time, preserving their own identity as Manchus. The banner organization was thus maintained and banner garrisons were placed throughout the Empire. These garrisons were heaviest about Peking, along the northwestern frontier, and in the provincial capitals and larger cities. Although some Chinese, mainly from the northern frontier, had been admitted to the banners, these military units and their families remained a class apart from the conquered people.

With the consolidation of the Manchu conquest, the bannermen emerged as a hereditary privileged military group or caste, excluded from trade and labor though not always from the civil service. Like the samurai in Japan under the Tokugawa dictatorship, they were perpetuated through generations of comparative peace, losing their character and capacity as warriors and lapsing into the role of tragic and useless idlers.

The Manchus had also maintained in the provinces a second and Chinese military force known as the Army of the Green Standard. This force was descended from certain Chinese armies that had assisted the Manchus during the conquest. Some of these forces had been taken into the banners, but in the south, they remained distinct and formed the beginnings of a separate Chinese army under the Manchu rule.

Some of the Green Standard were used to assist the banner garrisons on the northwestern frontier or to help suppress rebellious factions in various parts of the empire, but the far greater portion appeared to be devoted to the detection and prevention of robbery and other crimes, of protecting government property, or of escorting criminals from one locale to another. The Green Standard could thus hardly be counted an army at all. Nevertheless, it was an integral part of the central bureaucratic administration through which the Manchus ruled China, and in the earlier and more vigorous years of the Dynasty the Green Standard had served understandable purposes.

As the leadership and competence of the Manchu dynasty declined in the late eighteenth and the nineteenth centuries, the military services, both the bannermen and the Green Standard, no longer served effectively the original purposes for which they were designed, and were next to useless against the guns and disciplined troops of the Western powers. Worst of all, corruption had depleted the services of whatever morale they once possessed. As the dynasty no longer led the nation, so the officers of the Green Standard no longer led their troops. It had become common practice for officers to use their men as servants, to ride in sedan chairs when an infrequent march was undertaken, to withhold soldiers' pay for their own use, to charge the government for companies at full strength when actually no more than a handful of men were really in service. In times of emergency or for purposes of some official inspection, units were hastily recruited to full strength by gathering in a rabble of bandits, idlers, and criminals who could be discharged just as promptly once the inspectors had moved on. Thus it was that Chinese diplomacy at Nanking in 1842 and at Tientsin and Peking in 1858 and 1860 operated in a vacuum: there was no effective military power behind it. This same lack of military power also had much to do with the early successes of the T'ai-p'ings and with their ability to remain in occupation of so much of central China long after their movement had lost direction and momentum.

As some few abler members of China's ruling class, the scholar gentry, witnessed this spectacle of crisis, it would seem that it was rebellion at home rather than the barbarian in the Treaty Ports that occasioned the more intense alarm. The immediate, and presumably the ultimate, purpose of the barbarians was trade, and this, it was assumed, could eventually be confined and controlled; whereas, the T'ai-p'ing rebels, entrenched in the heart of China, were pseudo-Christian, anti-Confucian, anti-Manchu, and thus a positive and immediate threat not only to the established governmental system but also to the personal vested interests of all who enjoyed the favor of those in power. Against this threatened calamity, some members of the official scholar gentry were moved to action in the interest of the dynasty, of the social-political system, and of their own stake therein.

In the beginning the resultant movement to create regional armies was nothing more than an effort by some of the gentry to organize local militia for the defense of their home communities against the T'ai-p'ings. Since the regular troops, the bannermen and the Green Standard, had failed to destroy the rebels, the central government was in the unhappy position where it must accept and even encourage this kind of local initiative. Accordingly, in 1853, the emperor ordered Tseng Kuo-fan, who had a reputation for scholarship and experience as an official at Peking, to organize forces in his native Hunan to fight the T'ai-p'ings. In a Confucian society Tseng's lack of military background was considered no drawback. He soon justified the Confucian theory that scholarship and virtue fit a man for any public service. His Hunan army, as it came to be known, was built on quality rather than numbers. His recruits were hardy loyal peasants, not the dregs of the slums and jails. Moreover, these soldiers were well paid and were led by officers selected for character and ability to lead. Early in its career this army gained its first battle training suppressing banditry in its home province, Hunan. This strategy gave Tseng control of the area from which his financial support had to come, demonstrated to the populace the value of the army, and guaranteed the necessary replacements in troops. Moreover, what was done by Tseng in Hunan was repeated by Li Hung-chang in Anhui and by a few men of initiative in other areas.[8]

[8] Among the important studies on the military power under the Manchus is Franz Michael, *The Origin of Manchu Rule in China* (1942). On the new military leaders of the nineteenth century, see Arthur W. Hummel, ed., *Eminent Chinese of the Ch'ing Period, 1644–1912,* 2 vols.

IMPLICATIONS OF REGIONAL MILITARISM

It was armies such as these which, bolstered with some foreign assistance, finally destroyed the incubus of the T'ai-p'ing. The military importance of these armies in preserving the life of the Manchu dynasty was thus immediate and apparent. It was not so apparent, that while these armies were saving the dynasty from the T'ai-p'ings they were not saving the dynasty from itself. This was so because, unlike the traditional armies, the banners and the Green Standard, which were closely integrated with the central political authority, the new nineteenth-century armies were not national: they were regional armies recruited from and financed by local areas. The financing of these armies by the local authorities who organized them meant that new sources of revenue had to be found by these same local authorities. One such source was a new tax called *likin* (literally one thousandth). *Likin* was a commercial tax on goods in transit imposed and collected by provincial or other local authorities.

The point to be noted in particular is

(1943). On politico-military aspects during the T'ai-p'ing rebellion, see Franz Michael, "Military Organization and Power Structure of China during the Taiping Rebellion," *The Pacific Historical Review* 18 (1949): 469–83; James T. K. Wu, "The Impact of the Taiping Rebellion on the Manchu Fiscal System," *The Pacific Historical Review* 19 (1950): 265–75; and Ralph L. Powell, *The Rise of Chinese Military Power, 1895–1912* (1955). Stanley Spector, *Li Hung-chang and the Huai Army: A Study in Nineteenth Century Chinese Regionalism* (1964). Note in particular the difficulties of evaluating the policies of Chinese leaders of this period. It seems fair to say, for example, that while Li Hung-chang took ample personal profit from his industrial enterprises (see Chapter 13), his primary concern was regional development and the strengthening of the state. In the years of the T'ai-p'ing rebellion, regional militarism, unlike its later tendencies, supported the central authority of Peking in important ways. See David Pong, "The Income and Military Expenditure of Kiangsi Province in the last years (1860–1864) of the Taiping Rebellion," *Journal of Asian Studies* 26 (1966): 49–65.

---

that Peking had little part in conceiving, directing, or controlling these matters. China was saved from the T'ai-p'ings, but it was not the dynasty that did the saving. All that was left for Peking was to acquiesce in what local leaders of initiative were doing by appointing them, as Prince Kung did, as governors or governors-general of provinces, and by placing its seal of approval on their selection of subordinates, on the local laws they passed, and on the taxes they collected. This meant that Peking was losing its power of control as the local and regional administration was being taken over by provincial leaders of the new militia armies. It meant, in addition, that after 1860 the nice balance which the dynasty had maintained between Manchu and Chinese officials began rapidly to favor the Chinese, many but not all of whom were of the scholar-official class. From 1861 to 1890 the number of Manchu governors-general appointed was ten, while the number of Chinese was thirty-four. Manchu governors appointed during the same period numbered thirteen, while the Chinese totaled 104.

The conclusion is inescapable that the structure of political power within China was altered radically during and following the T'ai-p'ing period. The centralized military organization effective in the early years of the dynasty had lost its practical power. Actual power, no longer centralized, was diffused at the military level in various provincial and therefore local areas. With this diffusion of military authority went also a comparable diffusion of fiscal authority and ultimately of Peking's administrative control. A governor or governor-general who owed his position to a local army, to local taxation, and to his control of local administration was not a mere servant of the dynasty. These beginnings in a conflict between centralism and regionalism were to continue, and in the twentieth century they were to have far-reaching results. These shiftings within China in the politico-military focus of power had a very direct bearing on China's relations with the foreign powers. The military impotence of Peking was a constant invitation to the Treaty Powers to take advantage of China's treaty violations to demand further treaty concessions.

THE CO-OPERATIVE POLICY, 1861–1867

Nevertheless, in a number of ways the years following the Peking settlement of 1860 gave promise of peaceful and constructive adjustment in China's relation with the powers. This was due very largely to the personalities of the four principal ministers who had established their legations in Peking: Anson Burlingame of the United States; Sir Frederick Bruce of Great Britain; M. Berthemy of France; and General L. de Balluseck of Russia, known popularly as the "Four B's." In this group Burlingame soon achieved a leadership that was the more remarkable because his own country was involved in civil war and because he himself was a novice in the diplomatic techniques of commercial imperialism.

Since Burlingame was under instructions to "consult and cooperate" with his diplomatic colleagues, he described for Secretary Seward in 1862 the principles through which the United States might apply in China a "co-operative" policy. These principles, approved by Seward, included:

1. No acquisition of Chinese territory by the United States.
2. No interference "in the political struggles of the Chinese further than to maintain our treaty rights."
3. Active assistance, in co-operation with other powers, to Chinese authorities in maintaining treaty rights against pirates, bandits, and rebels to the end that should the other powers "menace the integrity of the Chinese territory then the very fact that we had acted with them for law and order would give us greater weight against such a policy."

Burlingame believed that the danger of continuing foreign aggression was very real. To meet this danger he reiterated a principle already expressed by Humphrey Marshall nearly a decade earlier, to the effect that it would be sound policy for the Treaty Powers to guarantee the neutrality of China.

From 1862 until he retired as American Minister in 1867, Burlingame and his three colleagues applied the co-operative policy with some success. In essence the policy achieved two things. First, China, confronted by united diplomatic action from the powers, was held to a stricter observance of the treaties, and this lessened the danger of resort to the gunboat policy. Second, as a result of this increased diplomatic stability, there was less temptation to individual powers to take advantage of China's weakness. However, Chinese officialdom remained suspicious even of the co-operative policy.

CHINESE MISSIONS ABROAD

Since the Ch'ing court had excluded foreign envoys from Peking until forced to admit them in 1860, it is understandable that China was not represented in the West. Yet here, too, there were signs of what the West liked to call progress. At Peking after 1860 some members of the new Tsungli Yamen sought the advice of Burlingame and other foreigners on many matters of foreign affairs. But when in return the suggestion was made that China would be better informed by sending her own diplomats abroad, it was met by a chorus of objections and excuses. Finally, in 1866, as a kind of temporary substitute for regular diplomatic intercourse, the court approved a semi-official mission headed by an elderly Manchu official of low rank, Pin-ch'un. Since he was a person of little consequence, indignities he might suffer abroad could be ignored. Pin-ch'un visited widely throughout Europe. He paid little attention to political affairs but was greatly impressed by the spotless hotels, the brightly lighted streets that did not become muddy in the rain, and by Queen Victoria "unable to act without the sanction of a parliament." This was China's first modern diplomatic effort.[9]

[9] Knight Biggerstaff, "The First Chinese Mission of Investigation Sent to Europe," *The Pacific Historical Review* 6 (1937): 307–20.

Far more significant was China's invitation in 1867 to Burlingame, who was about to retire as American minister at Peking, to serve as one of China's first official envoys to the Treaty Powers. Prince Kung and his colleagues took this unprecedented action in the hope that misunderstandings might be removed, that there might be closer contact with foreign governments, and, most important, that in the approaching revision of the treaties the powers might be persuaded to show forbearance on the theory that China was already "progressing" as rapidly as could be, and that demands for further concessions would be inexpedient. Burlingame had so won the confidence of Peking that he was considered the ideal envoy to achieve these ends. Associated with him on a basis of equality in the mission were Chih Kang, a Manchu, and Sun Chia-ku, a Chinese.

The Burlingame mission was also due in some measure to the fact that after 1861 Prince Kung, Wen-hsiang (his chief assistant), Tseng Kuo-fan, and Li Hung-chang, "while no more favorably inclined toward revolutionary changes than their predecessors," were able to see that China must make adjustments to the West if she hoped to survive. It was against this background that the Tsungli Yamen in 1867 required the provincial governors to give Peking their views on what should be done when the foreign powers pressed for further treaty revision. The replies of these officials are of importance historically, since they reveal the attitude of high Chinese officials to the problem of foreign relations in general and to specific questions in particular; thus they provide an approach to the history of China's foreign relations during the next half century. In general the views expressed in this secret correspondence with Peking in 1867–1868 are a fair indication of the rough road China was to travel in foreign affairs. For the most part the opinions from the provinces may be summarized as follows: (1) foreigners and the countries from which they came were still held in low esteem; (2) no further treaty concessions should be granted to for-

eign merchants; and (3) no further expansion of foreign missionary activity should be permitted. Only three high officials who engaged in this correspondence (Li Hung-chang, Tseng Kuo-fan, and Shen Pao-chen) showed any understanding of the possible values to China of railways, telegraphs, steamships, and mining machinery. Perhaps not more than five of these officials sensed the gravity of the problems posed for China by an aggressive Western World.[10]

The Burlingame mission was received in America with an enthusiasm not unlike what small boys accord a circus. Burlingame, an idealist and above all an orator, gave free reign to his eloquence. He pictured China, the oldest nation, seeking Westernization and progress through America, the youngest of nations. He pictured a China that stood with arms extended to receive "the shining banners of Western civilization"—strange-sounding words to the ears of Prince Kung and his associates in Peking. Many an American editor assumed that Burlingame's words meant what they said. The *Farmer's Cabinet* of Amherst, New Hampshire, was moved to observe that China's exclusiveness was ended. This "must give an enormous development to our trade, and the interests of Christianity will be more effectively promoted by this action of the Chinese Emperor, than by any other political event of the last two centuries." Although Burlingame's intentions were of the best, he laid the foundations for a species of oratorical reporting on China that was to deceive the American public from that day to the present.

In Washington, Burlingame and his Chinese colleagues were received by President Johnson and the Congress. Burlingame and Secretary Seward then concluded (July 28) eight supplementary articles to the American Treaty of Tientsin. These articles provided that China might appoint consuls at United States ports, that Americans in China and Chinese in the United States should enjoy

[10] Knight Biggerstaff, "The Secret Correspondence of 1867–1868: Views of Leading Chinese Statesmen Regarding the Further Opening of China to Western Influence," *The Journal of Modern History* 22 (1950): 122–36.

complete freedom of religion, and that rights of residence and travel were to be available to the nationals of both countries. Moreover, the United States disavowed "any intention or right to intervene in the domestic administration of China in regard to the construction of railroads, telegraphs or other material internal improvements," China being conceded the right to determine the time for such improvements; and, finally, China and the United States recognized "the inherent and inalienable right of man to change his home and allegiance. . . ." [11]

On September 19 the mission reached London, where it received Lord Clarendon's assurance that the British government would show forbearance in seeking further commercial concessions and would deal only with the central government in seeking redress for wrongs to British subjects. From London the mission visited Paris, Belgium, Prussia, Denmark, Sweden, Holland, and Russia. In Russia, on February 23, 1870, Burlingame died of pneumonia. Meanwhile, although the foreign press in the treaty ports had heaped abuse on the mission, declaring that it did not represent the real purposes of Peking, the Chinese government did ratify the Seward-Burlingame articles, thus demonstrating its faith in an envoy who, though exceeding the stricter limits of his instructions, had presented China's case with enthusiasm, if not with complete candor. The general success of the Burlingame mission in weathering for the moment at least the problem of treaty revision inspired unwarranted confidence at the Manchu court, for now it seemed evident that the foreigners, for a price (the modest cost of the Burlingame mission), could be managed.

It required another ten years, however, before the Manchu court established its first diplomatic mission in Britain (1877). This mission provided a nice example of the pro-

[11] For the Burlingame mission, see Knight Biggerstaff, "The Official Chinese Attitude Toward the Burlingame Mission," *The American Historical Review*, 41 (1936): 682–702; and Knight Biggerstaff, "A Translation of Anson Burlingame's Instructions from the Chinese Foreign Office," *Far Eastern Quarterly*, 1 (1942): 277–79.

cesses by which China was learning, slowly, to comprehend the West. When Kuo Sung-t'ao, a loyal, learned, incorruptible official, and the first Chinese minister at London returned to Peking, he said, to the astonishment of his colleagues: "Confucius and Mencius have deceived us." By this he meant not that he was converted to Western ideas, but that he had learned there were ways other than the Chinese of governing civilized countries. For a distinguished Chinese official to acknowledge that there were barbarian governments untouched by Confucian culture that were both "civilized and rational" was unprecedented if not subversive. In the United States the first Chinese legation was opened in 1878 by Ch'en Lanpin and Yung Wing, who had been in charge of an educational mission. By 1880 China had legations in most of the leading Western states and Japan. But it was only through dire necessity, rather than a free positive choice, that China thus entered the world community.

THE PROBLEM OF TREATY REVISION

The British Treaty of Tientsin was subject to revision in 1868, but Lord Clarendon had assured Burlingame that the British government would exercise forbearance. This was significant. Chinese officialdom was convinced that the treaties offered too much; the British, and most of the foreign merchants in the ports, that they conceded too little. There was always the danger, too, that attacks upon foreigners by lawless or anti-foreign elements of the Chinese populace would lead to a resumption of the gunboat policy. Americans, like all foreigners, were subject to these armed attacks.

Skillful diplomacy was needed if the legal rights of the powers were to be observed, if the uncompromising demands of the merchants were to be curbed, and if Chinese officialdom was to be convinced that its best interests would be served by educating its people to a fuller observance of the treaties. A few Chinese officials did have some understanding of all this. Li Hung-chang, for example, advocated a more progressive policy. Discarding the view that foreigners were a plague on Chinese soil, he observed with brutal frankness that "The outrageous craft and malignity of the Chinese exceeds even that of the foreigners."

The foreign merchants in the treaty ports and Hong Kong also had their ideas on what should be done. They were appealing already to their home governments on the subject of treaty revision to redress their real or imagined grievances. However, Sir Rutherford Alcock, British Minister at Peking, believed that China could better be induced to adopt a progressive policy if coercion were not applied. He recognized that a moderate policy would never satisfy the merchants, and he added that they had no claim to consideration, since they refused to appreciate the difficulties of reform and progress in a land as old as China and since they themselves were guilty of "fraudulent practices and want of good faith." Accordingly, Lord Clarendon decided to delay pressing for treaty revision until 1872–1873, when the young T'ung-chih emperor would attain his majority. In this decision the other treaty powers concurred.

THE DEVELOPMENT OF CHRISTIAN MISSIONS

The question of treaty revision and, in fact, the larger problem of China's relations with the West were connected intimately with the so-called missionary problem. The reader is already familiar with some aspects of Roman Catholic missions in China during the sixteenth, seventeenth, and eighteenth centuries. In the nineteenth century, coincident with the opening of China and Japan, Protestant Christendom became active in the field of foreign missions. In 1805 the London Missionary Society sent Robert Morrison to China. He travelled on an American ship, because the English East India Company, fearful of offending the Chinese, refused him passage on a Company ship.[12] The American

---

[12] See K. S. Latourette, *A History of Christian Missions in China* (1929), 212.

Bible Society also entered the field. During the first year of its work in China (1822) the Society distributed 500 copies of the New Testament. Eighty years later it was giving away more than half a million copies, including an elegantly bound edition to the Empress Dowager on her sixtieth birthday. After 1830, American Protestantism was represented in China by an expanding group of churches and missionary societies.

THE TREATY STATUS OF MISSIONARIES

Christianity and those who preached it had acquired an international legal status in China as a result of the toleration clauses of the Tientsin Treaties of 1858; the Russian and the French treaties permitted the missionaries *to travel* with passports in the interior. The Chinese text of the Franco-Chinese Convention of 1860 conceded the right of missionaries *to reside* in the interior, to acquire land, build churches and schools, and to propagate Catholic doctrine without hindrance. The French text, which was the authoritative text, contained no such concessions, and was kept secret from the other legations at Peking for ten years. Whatever the explanation of this discrepancy in the texts its effects were explained clearly by Frederick F. Low, American Minister at Peking in 1870:

> The missionaries of this Roman Catholic Religious Faith have, in addition to the right of residence as Bishops and Priests, assumed to occupy a semi-official position which places them on an equality with the native officers where they reside. They also claimed the right to protect the native Christians from persecution, which practically constituted the missionaries the arbiters of their disputes and the judges of their wrongful acts, and removed this class from the control of their native rulers. The absolute right of the Roman Catholic Clergy to exercise, in the name and by the authority of the French Government, a protectorate over native Christians was claimed . . . and insisted upon by some of the earlier representatives of France in China.[13]

[13] To Secretary of State Hamilton Fish. Printed in Paul H. Clyde, *United States Policy Toward China* (1940, reissued 1964), 108, 112.

Chinese officialdom feared and resented these pretensions of the missionaries. Not only did the official see immediate political implications involving his own power, he was also suspicious of Christianity because it was an alien and exclusive faith that was frequently in conflict with fundamental concepts of Chinese social and religious life. It will not be difficult, then, to understand how easily the masses might be aroused to attacks upon missionaries and their property. All classes of the Chinese found ample evidence to support their distrust of the foreign missionary. His intolerant dogmas could scarcely be reconciled with Chinese philosophy, which was essentially tolerant, practical, and mundane. Christian love and Christian intolerance were difficult for many Chinese to reconcile. Christian theory did not seem to be practiced with much vigor by the foreign merchants in the ports. From these critical conclusions grew others less critical, born of ignorance and fanaticism. It was common belief that Christian hospitals and orphanages purchased from indigent mothers hapless infants, whose eyes were extracted to compound direful drugs which when taken converted the victim to Christianity.[14]

From a background of such suspicion, hatred, and fear came the so-called Tientsin Massacre of 1870. A Chinese mob destroyed a Roman Catholic orphanage and adjoining church, and killed the French consul, two priests, ten nuns, three Russians, and some thirty Chinese servants. Alarm soon spread to many of the treaty ports, and French, British, and American warships appeared off

[14] Paul A. Cohen, *China and Christianity: The Missionary Movement and the Growth of Chinese Antiforeignism, 1860–1870* (1963). Also James E. Kirby, Jr., "The Foochow Anti-Missionary Riot, August 30, 1878," *Journal of Asian Studies* 25 (1966): 665–79. In the view of Chinese officials, the missionary was unwelcome not only because of his religious ideology but also because he was a disturber of the peace. The missionary's appeal for protection (for which he was entitled under the treaties) imposed special burdens on Chinese officialdom. What the Western diplomat demanded, the Peking government might grant even if it was in no position to enforce the grant.

Tientsin. The demands of France led to the death penalty or banishment of some of the perpetrators. China paid an indemnity of 250,000 taels and sent a mission of apology to France. Peking proposed a number of rules to govern and safeguard the work of missionaries, but only the American Minister was willing even to discuss them.

Thus less than ten years after Burlingame had reached China, and two years after negotiation of the Burlingame-Seward Treaty, the policy of patience and forebearance was headed for rough weather. The responsibility for the Tientsin Massacre cannot be laid at the door of one country or one group of individuals. It was an ugly creation of Chinese officials and agitators, and of foreign missionaries, their church, and their governments.

During the remainder of the nineteenth and on into the twentieth century China's relations with the West continued to be complicated by the political and other implications of the Christian missionary movement. A balanced picture of the missionary at work must give full weight to the sincerity and humanity with which many missionaries labored. The educational and the medical work of the missions brought forth the highest praise. Nevertheless, George F. Seward, while American Minister at Peking (1876–1880), found that the majority of the grievances with which the legation was called upon to deal concerned missionaries. He regretted a situation that made the diplomatic agent of the American government the right arm of the propagandists of the Christian faith.

TREATY REVISION AND THE MARGARY AFFAIR

Foreign traders in the Far East had long speculated on the possibilities of reaching China's western provinces of Kweichow, Yunnan, and Szechuan by way of the Burma border. One expedition from British India had proceeded to Bhamo on the upper Irrawaddy in 1868; a second expedition, under the command of Colonel Horace A. Browne, was organized in 1874 to enter Yunnan. The British legation in Peking was asked to secure passports and an interpreter from the consular service. For this post Minister Wade selected Augustus Raymond Margary, who, travelling overland with six Chinese, reached Bhamo on January 17, 1875.

In February the Browne expedition left Bhamo. It was preceded by Margary and his Chinese, whose purpose was to discover whether the route might be travelled in safety. The answer to this question was given when Margary and five of his Chinese associates were killed by what seems to have been the premeditated act of armed Chinese. Responsibility for this outrage is not easily placed. The Burmese sovereign was opposed to the opening of trade routes, as were also the local Chinese authorities in Yunnan. The border tribes were irresponsible and frequently beyond Chinese control; yet the local Chinese authorities could scarcely be absolved of negligence if not connivance. What is really significant is that the murder of Margary was seized upon by British Minister Wade as an appropriate incident to be used in forcing a settlement with Peking of all outstanding Anglo-Chinese questions.

Wade formulated his demands promptly: (1) China to send a mission of investigation accompanied by British officers; (2) permission to be granted for a second expedition from India; (3) 150,000 taels to be placed at the British Minister's disposal; (4) the emperor to grant a fitting and satisfactory audience to Her Majesty's Minister; (5) British goods to be freed from all *likin* taxation; and (6) all British claims to be satisfied at once. On second thought Wade reduced his demands to the first three. In London the government approved one and two but reserved judgment on point three.

The Chinese government accepted the demands in principle but objected to the blunt manner of Wade's diplomacy. It was not until August, 1876, that Wade met with Li Hung-chang at Chefoo, where on September 13 an agreement known as the Chefoo Convention was signed. It was ratified by

China four days later, but not by Great Britain until July, 1885.[15]

The Chefoo Convention was an impressive document embodying three sections. The first, which dealt with the Yunnan-Margary case, provided for the issuance of proclamations in the provinces, the drawing up of regulations for the Burma-Yunnan frontier trade, a second mission from India, the stationing for five years of British officers at some city in Yunnan, an indemnity of 200,-000 taels for the families of those murdered, for expenses incident to the whole case, and for the claims of British merchants. Finally, China was to send a mission of apology to London.

Section two of the Convention dealt with "Official Intercourse." China was to invite the foreign powers to consider with her a code of procedure and official etiquette designed to insure proper treatment of the foreign ministers at Peking and of the consuls at the treaty ports. China was also to invite the powers to consider with her means of insuring more effective administration of justice at the treaty ports.

Section three, dealing with trade, provided for the opening of additional treaty ports (Ichang, Wuhu, Wenchow, and Pakhoi), for stationing a consul at Chungking, and for the opening of several ports of call on the Yangtze. Other clauses provided for defining more clearly the foreign settlement areas in the ports.

In general the Chefoo Convention was a substantial supplement to Britain's treaties of 1842, 1858, and 1860, in that it secured practically all the concessions the British Minister had been demanding over a period of nearly two years. However, the Convention was not well received by representatives of the other treaty powers. There were objections from the Russians, the Germans, and

[15] For text of the Chefoo Convention, see China, The Maritime Customs, *Treaties* (2 vols., 2nd ed., Shanghai, 1917), 491–505. Note S. T. Wang, *The Margary Affair and the Chefoo Agreement* (1940), and Immanuel Hsu, *China's Entrance into the Family of Nations* (1960), 176–79.

the French, a point of importance, since by the nature of its content most of the Convention required the ratification of these powers also. Some British merchants were also opposed to it, on the ground that it would be better to hold China to a strict observance of the 1858 settlement than to require new concessions of her. The Chefoo Convention illustrates not only how pressure was exerted on China to revise treaties but also how difficult it was to attain agreement among foreign powers themselves.

IMMIGRATION: PRINCIPLE AND PRACTICE

While these problems of treaty revision and interpretation were still being debated, China's relations with the United States were disturbed by the results of the emigration of Chinese laborers to California. During the nineteenth century Chinese emigration had been of two kinds: free emigration of coolie laborers, for the most part to California and Australia, and contract-labor emigration to Cuba and Peru, known as the coolie trade. After 1862 the coolie trade was prohibited in American ships, and was brought under rigid regulation in British vessels sailing from Hong Kong. Nevertheless, until 1874 this nefarious trade continued to flourish from the Portuguese settlement at Macao. S. Wells Williams wrote in 1866 from Peking that "the most flagitious acts have been committed by the Chinese natives upon each other, under the stimulus of rewards offered by foreigners to bring them coolies." Burlingame reported that in the season 1865–1866 there were sent to Cuba alone, mostly from Macao, 13,500 coolies at a cost of nearly $3,000,000.[16] Until this vicious traffic was brought to an end in 1874 there was no logic in Western moralizing on the shortcoming of China in international affairs.

In contrast with the pitiable condition of

[16] United States, Department of State, *China Despatches*, Vol. 23, No. 27, and Vol. 24, No. 130, in Clyde, ed., *United States Policy Toward China*, 76–79.

the Chinese coolie laborer in Cuba and Peru, the free laborer who went to California enjoyed a personal and an economic freedom he had not known in China. So relatively prosperous, indeed, was the lot of these immigrants that by 1880 there were 75,000 Chinese in California—9 per cent of the population. They had been attracted by news of the rich opportunities offered in the gold fields, by the demands for labor in the building of the first transcontinental railroad, and by the retail trade in San Francisco and other towns. At first the Chinese were welcomed. They provided cheap convenient labor, able to live on "the smell of a greasy rag." In the beginning, too, their qualities of industry and docility were thought of as virtues. This attitude prevailed until the great depression of the seventies, at which time the cry was raised that the "Chinaman" was robbing the white man's dinner pail and destroying his standard of living. The "Chinaman's" virtues now became vices. The New York *Nation* noted derisively in 1883 that on the Pacific Coast the Chinese were perpetuating "those disgusting habits of thrift, industry, and self-denial. . . ." It became clear, to those who wished so to think, that the Chinese had many other vices. They lived to themselves, frequently in hovels. They were impervious to the beneficent influence of Americanization. They gambled. They smoked smuggled opium, and, since they had no wives with them, they consorted with prostitutes. There was some truth in all these charges, but no evidence has yet been unearthed to indicate that in these respects the Chinese were any worse, or better, than virile immigrant "Americans" of Irish and other descent who at this time made up the vociferous element on the Pacific Coast.

Violence against the Chinese in word and deed reached a shameful intensity in 1877. San Francisco harbored the backwash of the depression of 1873: the scum of the labor market, rowdies, and political adventurers. In this group were many Irish, naturalized and unnaturalized, who readily accepted the leadership of one Denis Kearney, an Irish-born, recently naturalized agitator, famous for his charismatic power. It was Kearney who shouted as he held a noosed rope in his hand, "The Chinese must go!" "Christian" followers of Kearney held that the Chinese didn't have souls, and even if they did, they weren't worth saving. So the Chinese were attacked, their store windows broken, their freshly laundered clothing trampled in the gutter, their queues snipped with scissors, their bodies kicked and stoned. Finally, there were boycotts of Oriental labor, and cold-blooded murdering of some of the Chinese.[17]

THE CHINESE BECOME A POLITICAL QUESTION

What was basically an economic and sociological problem soon became political. Western politicians and members of Congress were determined to be rid of the Chinese. The attitude of the eastern states was one largely of indifference. As early as 1855 a governor of California was denouncing the Chinese to satisfy his constituents, anti-Chinese memorials were in circulation, and anti-Chinese bills were being offered in the legislature. Charges were made that the Chinese in California, like those in Cuba and Peru, were under servile contracts. The Civil War quieted the agitation for a time, and the transcontinental railroad construction that followed absorbed all available Chinese labor. The Central Pacific was finished in 1869, at which time the roads were employing nearly 10,000 men, of whom some 9,000 were Chinese who were noted to be "peaceable, industrious and economical, apt to learn and quite as efficient as white laborers." However, in defiance of all forecasts, the completion of the railways did not usher in prosperity. On the contrary, land values failed to rise, thousands of white and Chinese laborers were thrown out of employ-

[17] See M. R. Coolidge, *Chinese Immigration* (1909), Chapters 1–7, R. W. Paul, "The Origins of the Chinese Issue in California," *The Miss. Valley Hist. Rev.* 25 (1938): 181–96; and the study by H. F. MacNair, *The Chinese Abroad* (Shanghai, 1924).

ment, the California State Democratic platform of 1869 was rabidly anti-Negro, anti-railway, and anti-Chinese. The Republicans too found it expedient politically to be nominally anti-Chinese. In 1876 the California Senate sent to Congress, in the guise of an impartial investigation of the Chinese, a viciously partisan document designed to inflame race prejudice and win an election. Against this testimony were the words of a former American Minister at Peking, J. Ross Browne, usually regarded as severe in his judgments of the Chinese:

The Chinese do not seek to interfere in our political struggles; they are peaceful and law-abiding; they are always willing to bear their equal burden of taxes; and all they ask is to be treated with common humanity.[18]

The unhappy fate of the Chinese on the Pacific Coast made it abundantly clear that Seward and Burlingame had misjudged the nature of Sino-American relations when in 1868 they had written into their Sino-American treaty "the inherent and inalienable right of man to change his home and allegiance." It now appeared either that this principle itself was not valid or that many Americans were not so closely wedded to it as had been supposed. At any rate, the American government was faced with the embarrassing task of informing China that her people were not wanted here.

Prompt action by the federal government could not be delayed, for in 1879 Congress passed a law prohibiting any ship from bringing to the United States more than fifteen Chinese on any one trip. President Hayes vetoed the bill on the ground that it was virtual exclusion and therefore in violation of the Burlingame Treaty. In the West, Hayes was burned in effigy, while the East greeted his act as "wise and manly." Thereupon the President sent to China a commission composed of James B. Angell, William H. Trescot, and John F. Swift. One who is unfamiliar with the background traced here, and who reads only the instructions of Sec-

[18] United States, Department of State, *China Despatches,* Vol. 25, No. 1.

retary Evarts to the commission, June 1880, might well suppose that in that year it was the United States rather than China that suffered injury. The commissioners were to concern themselves with: (1) "making our commercial privileges more clear, more secure and more extensive"; (2) impressing upon the Chinese that if they could collect *likin* and other "discriminatory" taxes, they could also prevent their collection; (3) entertaining any ideas the Chinese might have for reconciling the systems of jurisprudence, American and Chinese, in applying extraterritoriality in China; and (4) explaining to the Chinese why "this Government finds great public interests to require in our relations to China and the movement of its population to our Pacific coast, what may appear to be a modification of our universal hospitality to foreign immigration." [19] In November 1880, the commission signed two treaties with China, the one commercial, the other giving the United States the right to "regulate, limit or suspend" but not to "absolutely prohibit" the immigration of Chinese laborers. When in response to this new treaty status Congress suspended Chinese immigration for twenty years, President Arthur vetoed the measure, April 1882, as "unreasonable," that is, not within the meaning of a "suspension." Again East and West were divided, but compromise was found in a second bill, in 1882, suspending Chinese immigration for ten years, a measure which the President accepted. The law of 1882 was amended and strengthened in 1884. In 1892 immigration was suspended for another ten years, and in 1894 China agreed by treaty to extend it to 1904. When exclusion by treaty ended in 1904, Congress renewed the exclusion without time limit.

Even this diplomatic settlement and the legislative program against the Chinese did not for a time put an end to anti-Chinese riots in the United States. Twenty-eight Chinese were murdered in Wyoming in 1885; the federal government was powerless to intervene in what was purely a state

[19] United States, Department of State, *China Instructions*, Vol. 3, No. 1.

matter. The best that Congress could do was to vote an indemnity.[20]

The facts of the Chinese immigration question in the late nineteenth century lead to conclusions that are not pleasant. On a number of points the evidence is perfectly clear. Most of the Chinese in the United States were here legally; as a group they were industrious and peaceable; their vices may have been different but it would be a wise man who could affirm that they were worse than those of other immigrants, or for that matter of native-born Americans. Indeed, the Chinese had been encouraged to come to the United States not only by economic opportunity but also by the diplomacy of two Americans, Seward and Burlingame. Burlingame was undoubtedly influenced by idealism, Seward by the more mundane considerations of cheap labor. Their combined motives resulted in the writing of a treaty in 1868 which embodied the ideal and the principle of free immigration. Within twelve years this ideal had become unworkable. Thereupon the problem was permitted to fall into the hands of demagogues, agitators, and political hoodlums, who thought of themselves as "100 per cent American." Their policy of total exclusion was even more barren in statesmanship than was the naive "free immigration" of Burlingame and Seward.

[20] Coolidge, *Chinese Immigration,* Chapters 9–17.

FOR FURTHER READING

THE CONFUCIAN TRADITION. David Nivison and Arthur F. Wright, eds., *Confucianism in Action* (1959). Arthur Wright, ed., *Confucian Persuasion* (1960); Arthur Wright and Denis Twitchett, eds., *Confucian Personalities* (1962); Joseph R. Levenson, *Confucian China and Its Modern Fate* (1958) and Vol. 2 (1964)*; and Joseph R. Levenson, *Modern China and Its Confucian Past* (1964) are authoritative and systematic studies on the most influential tradition. Mary Gertrude Mason, *Western Concepts of China and the Chinese, 1840–1876* (1939).

ECONOMICS AND COMMERCE. C. F. Remer, *The Foreign Trade of China* (Shanghai, 1926). Harold Hinton, *The Grain Tribute System of China, 1845–1911* (1956). Edwin G. Beal, *The Origin of Likin* (1958) treats economic developments in the late nineteenth century. Liu Kwang-ching, *Anglo-American Steamship Rivalry in China, 1862–1874* (1962), a good specialized study. Stanley F. Wright, *Hart and the Chinese Customs* (Belfast, 1950).

CHINA'S REBELLIONS. Thomas Taylor Meadows, *The Chinese and Their Rebellions* (1856, reprint 1953), a classic on the T'ai-p'ing upheaval. Teng Ssu-yu's *Historiography of the Taiping Rebellion* (1962),* a digest of sources on the T'ai-p'ing; and *The Nien Army and Their Guerilla Warfare, 1851–1868* (1961)* shows the relation of Nien rebels to the T'ai-p'ings and the Moslems, describes weapons and tactics, and shows the Nien influence in accelerating the fall of the Manchu dynasty. John S. Gregory, "British Intervention Against the T'ai-p'ing Rebellion," *Journal of Asian Studies* 19 (1959): 11–31. Teng Yuan-chung, "Reverend Issachar Jacox Roberts and the Taiping Rebellion," *Journal of Asian Studies* 23 (1963): 55–67.

W. L. Bales, *Tso Tsung-t'ang, Soldier and Statesman of Old China* (1937) treats the campaigns of the T'ai-p'ing rebellion.

ORIENTAL IMMIGRATION. R. D. McKenzie, *Oriental Exclusion* (1928), an extensive work covering the entire field. Alexander McLeod, *Pigtails and Gold Dust: A Panorama of Chinese Life in Early California* (1947). E. C. Sandmeyer, *The Anti-Chinese Movement in California* (1939) stresses the conflict between local and federal jurisdiction. Robert Seager, II, "Some Denominational Reactions to Chinese Immigration to California, 1856–1892," *The Pacific Historical Review* 28 (1959): 49–66. Thomas E. LaFargue, *China's First Hundred* (1942) narrates the career of Yung Wing and his education experiment. Paul A. Cohen, *China and Christianity: The Missionary Movement and the Growth of Chinese Antiforeignism, 1860–1870* (1963). Gunther P. Barth, *Bitter Strength: a History of the Chinese in the United States, 1850–1870* (1964), and Stuart Creighton Miller, *The Unwelcome Immigrant: The American Image of the Chinese, 1785–1882* (1969) deal with Chinese in America.

China, 1860–1890:
Reform Versus Revolution

chapter 13

China's record in the new world of Western diplomacy, 1860 to 1890, does not lend itself to easy analysis. The general failure to understand what was happening in China at the time was shared by both Chinese and foreigners. The contemporary official reaction on China in both America and Europe vacillated between hope and despair: hope that China would soon accept the virtues of Western modernization and despair that she would ever free herself from the dead hand of her past. Even so astute an observer as John Russell Young, American Minister at Peking, 1882 to 1885, saw only the surface manifestations of China's troubles. His dictum that China had largely herself to blame for her woes, that she had no government worthy of the name, and that her efforts in foreign affairs amounted to simple "trifling" was substantially true but it did not touch the core of China's real problem. The essence of that core was the intellectual reaction of the scholar-official class, the ruling bureaucracy, to the Western assault not simply upon China's seacoast but, more important, upon her institutions and the ideas and values from which they were created. Of this in-

tellectual reaction, the West knew almost nothing. The ways through which China's educated men sought to fathom the alien and powerful West and to protect their own culture from its contagion is therefore a subject of prime import.[1]

[1] The pioneer collection of documents on this subject is Teng Ssu-yu and John K. Fairbank, *China's Response to the West* (1954).*

It is vital for the Western student not to confuse modern Chinese conservatism of this period with Western conservatism. To be sure, they both wished to conserve but, beyond this, they had little in common. Western political conservatism was concerned to preserve "the Christian, antirationalist, aristocratic, and feudal strains of pre-Enlightenment European Society." Chinese conservatism of the later nineteenth century was bent on preserving Confucian, rationalist, gentry and non-feudal strains of earlier Chinese society. The Chinese conservative had no interest in Western political and philosophic ideas. He believed in a rational, cosmopolitan order and in a rational national order that might even subordinate private property to group interests. He believed in man's innate goodness, and in the ideal of the universal state. These beliefs bear no resemblance to the preoccupations of the modern Western conservative with a divine plan in history, a sense of sin, a distrust of reason, and a conviction that private property is sacred. See Mary C. Wright, *The Last Stand of Chinese Conservatism* (1957),* 1–3.

THE ROLE OF QUESTIONABLE ASSUMPTIONS

The historical puzzle posed by China's response in the nineteenth century to the Western impact was complicated by two decisive factors. The first was the Chinese attitude of superiority to, if not disdain of, the Western barbarian. The second was the capacity of Europeans and Americans to approach the Chinese question armed, for the most part, with very questionable assumptions on what China was and what it wanted to be. This capacity to see in China what one wanted to see rather than what was actually there was not new in the nineteenth century. It went back to far earlier European and later American contacts with China (see Chapter 5).

For example, Marco Polo, with an amazing flair for exaggeration, described China as a land of great material prosperity. Later, in the sixteenth and seventeenth centuries, the Jesuit missionaries depicted China (save for its religions) as an ideal society. Then came the assumption, widely cultivated by some notable historians (Leopold von Ranke), that China was timeless and unchanging. From this idea grew the notion that there was a peculiar Asiatic type of society. Thus "Asiatic" became far more than a geographical term. It began to connote an assortment of meanings, political, social, and philosophical, most of which were general, vague, and at best misleading. Lastly, whereas the Jesuits reported that China approached the ideal society, nineteenth century Protestantism found China to be anything but ideal. It was heathen and in a state of moral degradation which could hardly be described. In this view even the greatest minds of China were necessarily inferior.[2]

These misconceptions were expanded in the late nineteenth century. Burlingame had told his American audience of a China bent on mastering the fundamentals of Western civilization. These were sweet words to Americans in the era of Manifest Destiny.

They carried the implication that, given the chance, China would gladly foresake her own outmoded ways for the modern manners of America. This slender thesis was to intrude itself repeatedly into American thought on China from that day to the present. Certainly evidence from the later nineteenth century suggests that what many Americans chose to believe concerning China was fanciful, though well intentioned. In sharp contrast, the testimony of J. Ross Browne, who succeeded Burlingame as American Minister at Peking, 1868, was a direct and explicit denial of much that Burlingame had said. Browne's words, however, did not reach the American public. They were for the confidential ears of Secretary William H. Seward.

An impression [said Browne] seems to have obtained in the United States that the Government of China is peculiarly friendly to our country, and that great advantages to our commerce are about to accrue from this preference. . . .

I need scarcely say these anticipations are without foundation. The Government of China may have preferences; but it has no special regard for any foreign power.[3]

CHINA'S FIRST RESPONSE

The Canton crisis of 1834–1840 had revealed China's original intellectual response to the West. This response was preeminently Chinese. It did not assume that China might profit through learning from the West, and this was natural, since the Chinese tradition was self-sufficient and less disposed to borrow abroad than was, for instance, the Japanese tradition. At Canton, therefore, in 1839, Lin did what any able and traditional Chinese could be expected to do. He applied force against the British while at the same time, by letter, he delivered himself of a sermon to Queen Vic-

[2] Raymond Dawson, "Western Conceptions of Chinese Civilization," *The Legacy of China*, Raymond Dawson, ed. (Oxford, 1964), 1–27.

[3] United States, Department of State, *China Despatches* 25, No. 7, November 25, 1868, quoted by Paul H. Clyde, *United States Policy Toward China, 1839–1939* (1940; reissued 1964), 93–94. Note also Harold R. Isaacs, *Scratches on our Minds*, (1958),* 63 ff.

toria exhorting that lady to control her subjects within the bounds of Confucian virtue. This formula of force plus persuasion was the traditional method by which China had controlled the barbarians on her borders. Lin, however, although traditional, was also observant. The subsequent debacle at Canton convinced him that China should purchase and manufacture Western armaments, translate Western books, hire foreign technical advisers, and train Chinese technical personnel; but these ideas were so revolutionary that he confided them only to his most intimate friends. China was to wait another twenty years before embarking on these ventures. Meanwhile, the Chinese response, particularly at Canton, took the form of bitter and violent anti-foreignism, which meant anti-Westernism.[4]

THE POLICY OF CONCILIATION

Although Lin's policy failed and Chinese arms met defeat, China's traditional diplomatic arsenal was not thereby exhausted. If an enemy could not be forced and persuaded, it was good traditional policy to conciliate him through negotiation, and this was what the Ch'ing dynasty did when it accepted the first treaties of 1842–1844 and 1858–1860. Under this strategy the treaties were regarded officially as temporary devices for pacifying the barbarians and thereby bringing them under control. The great exponent of this policy was the imperial Manchu clansman, Ch'i-ying, who negotiated with Sir Henry Pottinger of Great Britain (1842), Caleb Cushing of the United States (1844), and Th. de Lagrene of France (1844). The policy of conciliation was not regarded as a concession to Western

ways or as a reform of Chinese ways. It was traditional procedure. At the same time, the agent of conciliation, even so distinguished an official as Ch'i-ying, was in constant danger of being denounced to the court as subversive on the theory of guilt by association. The barbarians being untouchable, there was a fine line of distinction between conciliation that was appeasement and conciliation that was not. Thus proper conciliation was a delaying tactic designed to hold and then to divide the enemy, to "manage" him adroitly by playing one barbarian against another.[5] On the positive side the period of conciliation, 1842–1860, produced, in time, a new type of Chinese official, a man familiar with the barbarians and presumed to know how to deal with them. Some of these new type officials were on friendly terms with foreigners, but it is important to note that their memorials to Peking continued to denounce the barbarian, his opium, his ignorance of Confucian virtue, and his religion.

THE "RESTORATION" OF T'UNG-CHIH, 1862–1874

The invasion of Peking by British and French troops in 1860 together with the pitiful flight of the dynasty to Jehol brought forth some tangible evidence that at least a few Chinese and Manchus saw the dire plight of the nation and were stirred to do something about it. The first efforts, as the reader knows, resulted in new Chinese institutions, such as the Tsungli Yamen, and the expansion of the customs service to cope more effectively with foreign affairs. Foreign advice and personnel were sought and accepted in the suppression of the T'ai-p'ings. There were even efforts at rehabilitation and relief from excessive taxation. These promising measures seemed to suggest that a new leadership, capable of adjusting to the aggressive West, was in command at Peking and in some of the provinces. Such was not the case. These hopeful signs were a "Restoration," not a revolution. The intel-

[4] Lin's letter to Queen Victoria and his comments on Western arms, etc., is in Teng and Fairbank, *China's Response*, 23–30. See this source for other documents referred to in this chapter. The perceptive student will wish to seek answers to the question: "Why have certain Western ideas been warmly received in China while others have been met with cold indifference?" See Benjamin Schwartz, "The Intellectual History of China," *Chinese Thought and Institutions*, John K. Fairbank, ed. (1957),* 15–30.

[5] Earl Swisher, *China's Management of the American Barbarians, 1841–1861* (1953), 1–54.

lectual temper was a revival of good but traditional Confucian ideas whereby through scholar-government and the practice of virtue China, it was said, would again become strong. It was a theory of self-strengthening propounded by scholar-officials who were not Western and who had no desire to become Western or to model their state on Western precedent and example. This T'ung-chih Restoration failed. It demonstrated that an effective modern state, even in favorable circumstances, could not be grafted on to a Confucian society. Yet more than half a century later so-called republican China under the *Kuomintang* had not learned this lesson. In the Restoration there was no desire to create a new society.

One of the notable creators of the Restoration mentality was Feng Kuei-fen, a Soochow scholar, versed in the classics, experienced in government, and possessed of a keen and cosmopolitan interest in modern scientific knowledge. As an associate of such men as Tseng Kuo-fan and Li Hung-chang he knew many foreigners, and was instrumental in opening a school of Western languages and science at Shanghai (1863). His essays, written about 1860 but not widely distributed until 1898, revealed him as perhaps the first to understand that Western pressures were a complex of ideas and power unlike any invasion China had previously known. He thereupon concluded that Western languages and sciences must be acquired and used to supplement Chinese knowledge. The superiority of Confucian ethics was not questioned. These would remain as the foundation and the principal structural form of Chinese society. Within technological limits Western learning could be useful. There was no thought of concessions to Western learning in general; indeed, Western books "which expound the doctrine of Jesus are generally vulgar, and not worth mentioning."

THE APPEAL OF WESTERN TECHNOLOGY, 1860–1870

The theory of Feng Kuei-fen that Western "know-how" should become the

servant of a Confucian society was shared and sometimes applied by the leaders of the "Restoration." Tseng Kuo-fan, Li Hung-chang, and Tso Tsung-t'ang (1812–1885), the great administrators of the period, were all advocates of Western weapons. Such ideas, however, were also stoutly opposed.

At the time of the downfall of the T'ai-p'ings, Tseng Kuo-fan (1811–1872) was probably the most influential man in China. He had employed foreigners and their weapons in his fight against the rebels. Long before the *Arrow* War (1857–1858) he had urged the building of a Chinese navy. He built arsenals in the provinces of Hunan and Kiangsi and, together with Li Hung-chang, the Kiangnan arsenal at Shanghai (1865). In these matters of armament Tseng was a Western convert. Yet he never deserted the Confucian ideal of the good statesman. His formula for dealing with the foreigners was to treat them with Confucian virtue. In treaty revision, for example, what could be conceded should be conceded; that which could not be conceded should be resisted with resolution. "We should never hem and haw [literally, half spit and half swallow]."

T'UNG-WEN KUAN, or INTERPRETERS' COLLEGE

Like Tseng, Li Hung-chang not only approved the use of Western arms but also took practical steps to secure them through the training of Chinese personnel in Western mathematics as applied to engineering. An Interpreters' College, T'ung-wen Kuan, had been approved at Peking and opened in 1862. Later its curriculum was expanded to include science and mathematics, since, as Prince Kung said, science was the secret of Western strength. Meanwhile, additional language schools had been founded at Shanghai (1863), at Canton (1864), and at Foochow (1866).[6]

[6] Knight Biggerstaff, *The Earliest Modern Government Schools in China* (1961) is indispensable for an understanding of the Chinese approach to Western learning. Problems confronted by W. A. P. Martin at this time in translating Wheaton's *Elements of International*

These innovations met opposition from high places at court led by the Grand Secretary Wo-jen, a Mongol scholar of great reputation, a tutor to the emperor, and head of the Hanlin Academy. His objections to Western learning expressed the traditionalism that was still dominant. Wo-jen declared that if mathematics was to be taught by Westerners the damage to China would be great. The way to establish and strengthen a nation, he said, was to lay emphasis on propriety and righteousness (Confucian virtues), not on power and plotting. No nation, he asserted, had ever raised itself from decline by the use of mathematics. As for other aspects of Westernism, he pointed out that Christianity had already deceived many ignorant Chinese.

Another great advocate of self-strengthening through Western methods and Chinese values was Tso Tsung-t'ang, the son of a Hunan peasant family. Tso became first a student and school teacher, but after failing three times to win his degree in the metropolitan examinations he turned from the classics to knowledge for "practical use." When his experimental steamboat built by native craftsmen and mechanics proved unsatisfactory, he sought the advice of French engineers. As one of the first advocates of a Chinese navy, he was author of the plan for a Foochow shipyard. In his later government career in the far northwest (Shensi, Kansu, and Sinkiang), he introduced a program of modernization in agriculture, transportation, and fiscal policy, and the suppression of graft. Tso's formula was to learn from the barbarians, but not to rely on them.

CHINESE STUDENTS ABROAD

Among the most revealing episodes in China's intellectual response was the effort

to educate young Chinese in the United States, Britain, and France. The training of Chinese in science and mathematics had already been undertaken at the T'ung-wen Kuan in Peking and elsewhere, but ultimately the need for young Chinese to study abroad gained some recognition. Two principal student missions followed. The first sent one hundred and twenty Chinese students to the United States between 1872 and 1881; the second sent thirty students to England and France for technical training. As in other matters it was Tseng Kuo-fan and Li Hung-chang who implemented these missions. Their memorial of 1871 to the Tsungli Yamen declared that there was no way to master Western ideas, techniques, and machines "unless we have actually seen them and practised with them for a long time." Or, as the Chinese proverb puts it, "To hear a hundred times is not as good as to see once."

In the United States the education of these Chinese students gave promise of significant results. The way for them had been paved by the enthusiasms of Yung Wing (1828–1912), the first Chinese to graduate from an American university (Yale '54). Then the venture ended as suddenly as it had begun. In 1881 the students were recalled for reasons that bear directly on China's intellectual response in this period. In part this premature death of China's efforts in foreign education was hastened by jealousies among those Chinese who administered the program in America, but more important, it would appear, was the discovery that the students were mastering American studies to the exclusion or at least the neglect of Chinese studies. This revelation was too much for the traditionalists in Peking, and even Li Hung-chang felt that China had gone too far, though there was a touch of understanding in his remark that it was hard for young Chinese abroad "to avoid indulging in foreign customs."

There were occasions, too, during this period when China made some grudging use of Western international law, not because Western law was good in itself or superior to Chinese law, but because China might use it

Law into Chinese are revealed by Hungdad Chiu, "The Development of Chinese International Law Terms and the Problem of their Translation into English," *The Journal of Asian Studies* 27 (1968): 485–501.

to confound the barbarians with their own rules.[7]

THE AUDIENCE QUESTION

The thirteen-year period from 1860 to 1873 had shown that the Ch'ing dynasty in its relations with the West as directed by Prince Kung was capable of some faltering steps toward adjustment to the new world of the West. At the same time this Manchu-Chinese capacity to take one step forward was countered more often than not by a genius for taking two steps backward. The granting by the emperor in 1873 of the first official audience at Peking to the ministers of the foreign powers resident there suggests how this genius worked. When a minister from a treaty power reached China, he would, if Western practice prevailed, be received in audience by the emperor to present his credentials. However, such an audience would imply that the Son of Heaven was a mere equal of Western sovereigns, an admission Peking could not bring itself to make. As late as 1867 the Court had been most careful in its instructions to the Burlingame mission to guard against committing the emperor on this point. Consequently, all requests for audience made by the envoys in Peking had been denied. From 1861 to 1873 the Tsungli Yamen was able to evade and delay a decision on the ground that the emperor was a minor. But this excuse could not be used indefinitely. The powers were in general agreement that eventually the audience must be insisted upon. It seemed that 1873, the year of the emperor's coming of age, would be the appropriate time.[8]

[7] Y. C. Wang, *Chinese Intellectuals and the West, 1872–1949* (1966). This exhaustive study of Chinese students abroad reaches the pessimistic conclusion that Chinese education abroad was a failure, a conclusion to which some exception has been taken.

[8] The Chinese attitude toward the audience question may be stated in this way: Apparently the Court was not unwilling to grant Imperial audiences during the 1860's. It merely demanded that foreign envoys conform to certain ceremonial

The date for the first audience was finally set for June 29, 1873. During the previous months the ministers of the Tsungli Yamen and the foreign envoys had engaged in an unprofitable wrangle, the former demanding that the foreigners kneel before the throne. Three bows were finally accepted as a substitute. Then came the appointed day when the T'ung-chih emperor entered the *Tzu Kuang Ko* (Throne Hall of Purple Effulgence) located in an Imperial park adjacent to but not in the Imperial Palace. The Japanese ambassador, Soyejima, outranking his European colleagues, was received first and alone. Then the representatives of the Western powers were led in together by Prince Kung: General Vlangaly of Russia, Frederick F. Low of the United States, Thomas F. Wade of Great Britain, M. de Geofroy of France, and M. Ferguson of the Netherlands. All bowed three times as they advanced to the center of the hall and placed their letters of credence on the Dragon Table. After the reading of a congratulatory address in French, the emperor acknowledged receipt of the letters by a slight inclination of the head and a few words in Manchu addressed to Prince Kung. The envoys now stepped backwards bowing repeatedly until they had reached the entrance to the Hall. The entire ceremony had taken less than half an hour.

So ended the first audience granted the foreign powers since the establishment of treaty relations. It was an event of primary importance to the powers, for, as Minister Low had said, friendly relations could not be cultivated unless the "arrogance and conceit" of high Chinese officials was curbed by a ceremonial recognition that China was not superior to the foreign barbarians. On the surface therefore the powers could pride themselves on a diplomatic, ceremonial victory. Their triumph, however, was not so complete as they supposed. The Manchu-Chinese Court had succeeded in snubbing

usages to which the foreign envoys objected. Hence came the desire of the Chinese to postpone grappling with the question. Note W. W. Rockhill, *Diplomatic Audiences at the Court of China* (London, 1905).

the foreigners at the very moment their equality was seemingly recognized. The *Tzu Kuang Ko* where the audience was held was a pavilion used for receiving tribute missions from the rulers of lesser kingdoms such as Korea, Burma, and the Ryukyu Islands. Furthermore, the envoys were not permitted to enter the grounds by the main gate but through a side entrance, just as lesser officials were required to enter at the side gate of a yamen. Finally, the Chinese account of the audience notes particularly that the foreign ministers were admitted "after an interval of some duration"; that is, after they had been kept waiting, a favorite method of making a caller feel his inferiority.

In reality, therefore, the audience had accomplished very little, for the Peking authorities were convinced that they had succeeded in maintaining their superior position. Moreover, a year and a half later (January 12, 1875) the T'ung-chih emperor died of smallpox. Under the influence of the Empress Dowager Tz'u-hsi, and against all precedent, the Court named as successor Tsai-tien, a child of the same generation as the deceased monarch. The new sovereign, the Kuang-hsu emperor (1875–1908), was a son of Tz'u-hsi's sister and of Prince Chun, her most ardent supporter in the Imperial Family. For the next fourteen years Tz'u-hsi, as regent, was again the ruler of China. This development did not smooth China's relations with the treaty powers.

EFFORTS TOWARD INDUSTRIALIZATION

The emphasis that Chinese leadership was placing in the late nineteenth century on the problem of defense against the West led inevitably to concern with industrialization. Here there was a natural train of thought, beginning with the idea that China must use Western arms and armament and ending with the conclusion that China herself must manufacture these arms. Mention has already been made of the building of arsenals and shipyards. In 1872, organization of the China Merchants Steam Navigation Company led to the opening of the Kaiping coal mines near

Tientsin. Transportation of the coal from mine to port called for railroad construction.

Here it may be helpful to recall that the idea of industrialization, already a century old in Europe, was still a very new idea in the China of Tseng and Li. It was therefore something to which the scholar-official mind of China had yet to be converted. When it was discovered that the first steamships built in China cost more than was anticipated and proved to be inferior to foreign ships, there were officials who advised abandoning the whole business. Li Hung-chang's protest against this proposed retreat from industrialization was expressed in a memorial of 1872: "Our scholars and officials have confined themselves to the study of stanzas and sentences and are ignorant of the greatest change of the last several thousand years." The seeming security of the "Restoration" had bred complacency.

As a result of the energy and foresight of Li and Tso a great variety of industrial enterprises were planned and some were actually established between 1863 and 1890. These included technical schools, arsenals, shipyards, machine factories, Western-style fortifications, coal and iron mines, a steamship company, a telegraph from Taku to Tientsin in 1879, plans for a navy and a naval school, the construction of railroads and a dockyard, and the establishment of textile mills. Yet for all its variety the movement toward industrialization was slow and ineffective.[9]

GOVERNMENT SUPERVISION: MERCHANT OPERATION

This failure of the early industrialization effort to meet China's goal of self-strengthening and defense was not due primarily to the advantages enjoyed by and the competition of the foreigners. In the same period Japan faced similar competition but succeeded in creating a strong industrial foundation based

[9] For the position occupied by Americans and the British in China's coastal shipping see Liu Kwang-ching, *Anglo-American Steamship Rivalry in China 1862–1874* (1962).

on initial government capital, operation, and control.

In China quite a different system of control and management was followed, one derived from traditional methods of economic administration. Under this system merchants provided a part of the capital, while the manager was apt to be of official status with influence enough to deal with local authorities in the matter of securing special privileges such as exemption from taxation. There might even be two managers, one to run the business, the other to manage the government. Thus, management was half business, half politics. Initially the purpose of the system was to enlist private capital from merchant sources. What happened more often than not was that officials, using the names of merchants, invested in these semi-government enterprises and placed their own relatives in charge as managers. The whole system went under the name of "official supervision and merchant operation."

The evils that resulted from this mingling of Confucian bureaucracy and Western business were described vividly in 1892 by a contemporary Chinese compradore-scholar, Cheng Kuan-ying, who knew many foreigners and much Western literature.

In recent days [he wrote], although the court has ordered the governors-general and governors to develop commerce and open all kinds of manufacturing bureaus, and has authorized the inviting of merchants to manage them, yet the officials and merchants have habitually been unable to get along together. . . . Businessmen who have undertaken many affairs, although they understand clearly that there are profits to be made, nevertheless hesitate to accept the invitation to manage government enterprises. . . . If a surplus or profit is made by the company, all the local officials request some contribution and overstep their proper duty to meddle in the company's affairs.[10]

Moreover, the modern-type enterprises started in China in this period failed to develop into a real industrial revolution. China continued to be preoccupied with

[10] From the writings of Cheng Kuan-ying, *ca.* 1892, printed in Teng and Fairbank, *China's Response,* 113–14.

dividing the static economic product among landlords, merchants, and officials. Thus there was no recognition for the need of increasing the product, and therefore no real undermining of traditional institutional barriers.[11]

THE NATURE OF CHINESE LEADERSHIP, 1860–1890

By the year 1890, China had passed through three decades of effort in "self-strengthening." What had the movement

[11] See Albert Feuerwerker, *China's Early Industrialization* (1958), 242–51. The tendency of Ch'ing to resist reform and to preserve institutions that should have been abolished is illustrated in the study by Harold C. Hinton, *The Grain Tribute System of China, 1845–1911* (1957).

For indispensable insights into political institutional developments in China from 1870 to the close of the century, the student should consult Albert Feuerwerker *et al.,* eds., *Approaches to Modern Chinese History* (1967), especially the essays by Kwang-ching Liu on Li Hung-chang, by John L. Rawlinson on the nineteenth century Chinese navy, by Paul A. Cohen on the ideas of Wang T'ao, and by Akira Iriye on Chinese public opinion. In these materials will be found at least a partial answer to the proposition that the Manchu dynasty survived as long as it did precisely because it was weak.

In the case of the mineral industries, the Ch'ing government in its early years had permitted small-scale local development as a supplementary factor in the general economy. Later the Ch'ing engaged in substantial participation itself through direct sponsorship, supervision, or financial subsidy and purchasing in the production and distribution of minerals and metals. In the late eighteenth century, government took the additional step of recruiting wealthy investors who were expected to carry the undertaking to a successful conclusion. This concept of *chao-shang* (recruiting investors) meant that private fortunes were called upon by government to meet the latter's needs. In such cases political motives were likely to be more influential than economic ones. The Hong merchants at Canton were a manifestation of *chao-shang.* E-tu Zen Sun, "Ch'ing Government and the Mineral Industries Before 1800," *Journal of Asian Studies* 27 (1968): 835–45.

On China's monetary system see Frank H. King, *Money and Monetary Policy in China, 1845–1895* (1965).

achieved? During the '60's there were signs that a new order was in the making, but during the 70's and 80's signs of self-strengthening were not easy to discern. The movement appeared to lose rather than to gain in strength. In explanation it may be noted that the entire period was in general one of peace in which the Western powers used the pressures of negotiation rather than of war; and it would appear that this softer policy was interpreted by the great majority of the scholar-bureaucrats to mean that the crisis was passed. If the crises of 1840 and 1860 were not forgotten, at least their forebodings seemed less ominous.

How shall this lack of sustained purpose be explained? Some of the factors involved are reasonably clear. Basic among these was the nature of the Confucian leadership which the mid- and later nineteenth century had produced. It was not that China had no men of political stature. Prince Kung, Tseng Kuo-fan, Li Hung-chang, Tso Tsung-t'ang and others were administrators of ability who perceived the danger of foreign control and sought a defense against it through Western scientific techniques. Beyond this point, however, they were unprepared to go. Their answer to the West was to use Western science to make China more Confucian. When it appeared, as in the case of Chinese students abroad, that Confucian values would thereby suffer, even China's most progressive leaders drew back. The students were recalled.

THE QUALITY OF LEADERSHIP AT PEKING

There were two areas in which Chinese leadership, or the lack of it, were of the greatest import: (1) at Peking in the Manchu court and the metropolitan administration, and (2) in the provinces, where vigorous administrators such as Tseng and Li held office.

At Peking the hopeful course set by Prince Kung in 1860 was soon abandoned. For five years as a member of the regency and as head of the Grand Council and of the Tsungli Yamen, he had shown an awareness

of China's plight and had wielded sufficient influence to direct policy accordingly. When, however, by 1865 the immediate threat of dynastic collapse had passed and the T'ai-p'ings had been suppressed, the incubus of court conservatism reasserted its power in the person of Tz'u-hsi, the Empress Dowager (1835–1908). This able and ambitious Manchu woman, a concubine of the Hsien-feng emperor (ruled 1851–1861) and mother of the T'ung-chih emperor (1856–1875), had become co-regent with the first wife when her son ascended the throne in 1862. Some reference has already been made to the uneasy alliance between Prince Kung and this remarkable woman. On the death of her childless son in 1875 she adopted and placed on the throne the son of Prince Kung's brother, Prince Chun, and her own sister, thereby maintaining her power as regent for the new child emperor, Kuang-hsu (ruled 1875–1908). From then on until her death in 1908, except for a brief period, 1889–1898, she was the power in the Peking government.

Two principal traits highlighted the character of this woman as a ruler. By the power of her inflexible will and her knowledge of human frailty she dominated the court and thereby the metropolitan administration. She won or controlled officials of court and government by an amazing assortment of methods. According to the need of the moment she exhorted, flattered, bribed, commanded, or pleaded to get what she wanted. By placing an increasing number of Chinese in high provincial office she strengthened the loyalty of the scholar-bureaucrats to the Manchu monarchy. At the same time the high price she placed on her official favors raised the fine art of bribery (gifts to the Empress Dowager) to new and fantastic levels.

Against her limited success in reviving the loyalty of Chinese officialdom was her incapacity to face repeated crises in foreign affairs. Though she usually followed the advice of her ministers, she hated the foreigners and their works. Moreover, there were few who could advise her with intelligence. As Li-Hung-chang wrote in 1881: "The stupidity and confusion of our scholar-officials, and the lack of men of ability in the court are really ridiculous."

From these circumstances came the confusion of the Empress Dowager's rule. Under her authority vast sums had been collected to give China a modern navy. The money was spent in rebuilding the Summer Palace. The warnings of Wen-hsiang, one of the able assistants of Prince Kung, were like a small voice calling in the wilderness: "When Your Majesty is concerned to work diligently, then your ministers . . . dare not follow their traditional dawdling habits. Otherwise . . . the disaster will be unspeakable." These were prophetic words, but the Empress Dowager did not understand them.

In the provinces the prospect for leadership had more substance. The efforts of Tseng,[12] Li, and others meant that there was some awakening among the scholar-bureaucrats. At the same time this awakening was so hedged about by mental obstructions and the carrion weight of traditionalism that not even Li saw the alternatives among which China might choose. The time had not yet come for Chinese-Manchu leadership to question the dead hand of the past. Moreover, and this is historically quite understandable, history had not bequeathed China a sense of political patriotism. The urge to adopt Western technology and science was often seen as a means whereby officials and merchants might make profits for themselves rather than as a method of saving the country from foreign aggression. Although the progressive governors were for the most part steadfast in their loyalty to Peking, their local successes in provincial finance and military affairs were at the expense of central authority and therefore at the expense of a unified and coherent effort to save the empire through self-strengthening.[13]

[12] Note Chen Shen Han-yin, "Tseng Kuo-fan in Peking, 1840–1852: His Ideas on Statecraft and Reform," *Journal of Asian Studies* 27 (1967): 61–80.

[13] Undoubtedly a significant factor in the general failure of the reform movement may best be described as bureaucratic inertia. Certainly Chinese leadership in this period was inept. At the same time individuals within the leadership were sometimes thwarted in efforts

The ways in which China and Japan responded in the nineteenth century to the Western impact form an arresting study in contrasts. How did it come about that the Japanese alone met the Western intrusion with vigor, seeking survival in strong, independent nationhood that readily employed modern science and technology to refashion traditional Japanese society on industrial foundations, while the Chinese in the same years failed to make a positive, constructive response? Satisfying answers are the more elusive because what actually happened was just the reverse of what informed contemporaries might well have predicted. They might have noted that Japan was at a grave physical disadvantage in the struggle for power and wealth. Her farmlands were crowded, her minerals scanty. She was not well located either as to materials or to markets. In mid-nineteenth century she was still bound by feudalism and by the self-conscious power of a warrior caste antagonistic to modernization. In contrast China might have seemed ready for the modern world. In location and wealth she was superior. She had traditions of freedom and social mobility, of private property, of pragmatism and materialism, of humane political ideals, and of knowledge as the key to office. All in all China appeared uniquely equipped to adopt

at reform by the very ideas and institutions that had given Chinese society its stability. In some measure these institutions were so hallowed by time and so infected by bureaucratic confusion and indecision and by widespread corruption and nepotism that, as one example, the maintenance of a respectable navy would have been impossible regardless of the number or quality of warships China might build or buy. Note John L. Rawlinson, *China's Struggle for Naval Development, 1839–1895* (1967). Another case in point was the use by Li Hung-chang of a traditional institution, the *mu-fu* (tent friends) system, a coterie of tried associates where the emphasis was on personal loyalty rather than on competence. Although the system had often worked in the past, it simply opened the door to abuse in the nineteenth century. Note Kenneth Folsom, *Friends, Guests, and Colleagues: the Mu-Fu System in the Late Ch'ing Period* (1968).

"the secular, rational, utilitarian democratic culture of the West." Yet it was Japan, not China, that embraced the modern world in the nineteenth century. No simple explanation can portray why and how this occurred but the following factors are suggestive of the processes at work.

1. Traditional philosophical attitudes, especially those attributable to Confucianism and Taoism, with their emphasis on indirection, may well have conditioned the Chinese response. In Japan the code of the samurai taught that an enemy was met by direct action, and most of Japan's Meiji leaders were samurai.
2. Most important in Japan's response was her capacity to combine the two essential conditions of successful adaptation and growth: (a) leadership in technological and social change, and (b) teamwork and discipline in organization giving order and momentum to the process of change. The fitness of the leaders to rule and the willingness of the majority to follow characterized Japanese organization.
3. Japan's response was aided by the fact that her society, above the family, was more pluralistic in structure than was China's. Initiative in Japan thus tended to be dispersed among a number of centers. Particular groups such as the business elite, barred from the hereditary aristocracy, had built their own money power undermining the ruling caste, or particular families such as the Western clans became the pioneers in Western technology and later the leaders of political revolution.
4. Japan's response was more vigorous because her internal crisis, unlike that of China, was potentially revolutionary. Within Japan the mid-century tensions were such that powerful elements of the ruling class were ready to adopt modernization even if it meant the downfall of feudalism and the liquidation of their own class.
5. Historically Japan was a frontier society, a cultural borrower, and, as it happened, the Western impact reached her shores at the precise moment when internal frictions had already prepared the way for great changes in her society.[14]

[14] W. W. Lockwood, "Japan's Response to the West: the Contrast with China," *World Politics* 9 (1956): 37–54. A more extended comparison is in Edward O. Reischauer and John K. Fairbank, *East Asia: the Great Tradition* (1960), I, Chapter 14.

FOR FURTHER READING

CONFUCIANISM AND REFORM. Banno Masataka, *China and the West 1858–1861, the Origin of the Tsungli Yamen* (1964), a detailed case study of the clash between Chinese and Western political traditions. Marion J. Levy, *The Family Revolution in Modern China* (1949).* Arthur F. Wright, ed., *Studies in Chinese Thought* (1953),* an important symposium in the field of intellectual history. Joseph R. Levenson, *Confucian China and Its Modern Fate: The Problem of Intellectual Continuity* (1958). William T. de-Bary, Chan Wing-tsit, Burton Watson, comps., *Sources of Chinese Tradition* (1960).* Chang Chung-li, *The Chinese Gentry: Studies on Their Role in Nineteenth Century Chinese Society* (1955)* emphasizes the scholarly bureaucratic foundation of the dominant social class. Fei Hsiao-t'ung, *China's Gentry*, rev. and ed. by Margaret Park Redfield (1953),* a study of political and social classes stressing the disruptive influences of Western commerce. Robert M. Marsh, *The Mandarins: the Circulation of the Elites in China, 1600–1900* (1961), a study of eminent Chinese to determine whether advancement in government service was due to bureaucratic factors or to family background. S. M. Meng, *The Tsungli Yamen: Its Organization and Functions* (1962).*

ECONOMICS AND INDUSTRY. Marion J. Levy, *The Rise of the Modern Chinese Business Class* (1949). Norman Jacobs, *The Origin of Modern Capitalism and Eastern Asia* (rev. ed., 1959) seeks an answer to the question: why did modern industrial capitalism arise in Japan and not in China? Ellsworth C. Carlson, *The Kaiping Mines (1877–1912)* (1957), a study of China's first modern coal-mining enterprise. Frank H. H. King, *Money and Monetary Policy in China, 1845–1895* (1965).

BIOGRAPHY. Two works by Chen Ch'i-t'ien: *Tseng Kuo-fan, Pioneer Promoter of the Steamship in China* (1961); and *Tso Tsung-*

t'ang (1961), brief biographies of China's first industrialists. C. John Stanley, *Late Ch'ing Finance: Hu Kuang-yung as an Innovator* (1961).

EDUCATION AND THE PRESS. Knight Biggerstaff, "Shanghai Polytechnic Institution and Reading Room: An Attempt to Introduce Western Science and Technology to the Chinese," *The Pacific Historical Review* 25, (1956): 127–49. Lin Yu-t'ang, *A History of the Press and Public Opinion in China* (1936).

China and
Her Dependent States

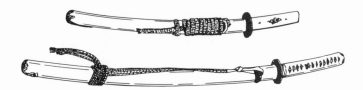

chapter 14

It has already been suggested that the increasing nineteenth-century contacts between the Westerners and the Chinese involved forces more complex than the balance sheet of a trader, the catechism of a missionary, or the etiquette of a diplomat. In their various callings, trader, missionary, and diplomat carried to China a Western civilization that was well on its way to Europeanizing the world. It was a vigorous and an aggressive civilization which assumed that man's material and, in some degree, even his spiritual, salvation rested on the national state and the colonial empire, on the Industrial Revolution and the development of commerce, on the conversion of the heathen to Christianity, and on the acceptance by "remote and backward peoples," such as the Chinese, of Western ideas of international law. But all these ideas were foreign to the traditional thought of nineteenth-century China. She could accept them only through changes which, in the light of her civilization, would be in the broadest sense revolutionary, but China was not yet prepared to undertake a revolution.[1]

[1] The traditional Chinese view of history had something to do with the slowness of Chinese modern adjustment. According to the tradi-

The Seward-Burlingame Treaty (1868) had conceded to China "the right to decide the time and manner and circumstances" of westernization; but treaties frequently fail to control the march of events. So it was that between 1870 and 1895 China's position in the Far East was challenged by the powers not only at Peking but also on the borders of the Empire in the "tributary" or dependent states. During this period the Middle Kingdom lost whatever control it had exercised previously in the Ryukyu Islands, Indochina, Burma, Korea, and in other areas.[2] Thereby a

tional view, "dynasty succeeded dynasty, each following the same cycle of rise in virtue and decay in vice—the same play presented over and over again, but each time with a new cast. It was this view of Chinese history which T. T. Meadows had in mind in mid-nineteenth century when he coined his famous description of the Chinese as the most rebellious but the least revolutionary of peoples. A change of dynasty meant new personnel, not new institutions." Meribeth Cameron, "The Periodization of Chinese History," *The Pacific Historical Review* 15 (1946): 173.

[2] In some cases (e.g., Burma, Sikkim, Annam) China had not exercised any control for a long time, so that despite theoretical dependence upon China, these states were really independent *de facto*. France and Britain, therefore, paid little attention to Chinese claims of overlordship.

fundamental principle of Chinese government —the relation between the superior and the inferior state—was destroyed. States that had recognized the overlordship of Peking were to become either independent or colonies of foreign powers. To understand how this came about and the consequences to China requires some discussion of the Chinese theory and practice of what in the West is called international relations.

TRADITIONAL CHINESE "FOREIGN RELATIONS"

It is perhaps best to begin by saying that Old China did not have a theory or practice of what the modern West has regarded as foreign relations. Nevertheless, Old China did have a very logical and impressive concept and practice of what may be called the Chinese world order. This concept, which matured over the centuries, was a product of historical circumstances which are readily understood.

It may be recalled that the societies of Eastern Asia had, as it were, a common cultural ancestor in ancient China. For example, Japan, Korea, Liu-ch'iu (Ryukyu), and Indochina came to be, in some major and varying degree, descendants of a Chinese cultural influence. The extent of China, her age, wealth, cultural richness, and power gave her an unrivalled pre-eminence over her neighbors. Thus there developed an Eastern World of which China was the center. She was in fact *Chung-kuo*, the Central Country or Middle Kingdom. Quite naturally, therefore, the Chinese came to regard their relations with neighboring peoples as a means by which the Chinese social order (Confucianism) would be bestowed upon less fortunate communities. As a result, *T'ien-tzu*, the Son of Heaven, would realize the desirable Confucian ideal of unity, of *T'ien-hsia*, "all under Heaven." In this concept of China as the center, there was a very pronounced assumption of Chinese superiority. China's neighbors were not considered her equals. Here was a reflection of the inequalities of status within Chinese society itself.

The formal relationship that came to prevail between China and her neighbors suggests the Confucian relationship of the elder and the younger brother. It was a relationship not always definite or uniform, but it was apt to include the following: (1) China, the superior, taught and admonished the lesser state; (2) the lesser state might be under close supervision or the contacts might be largely ceremonial; (3) the lesser sovereign received investiture from the Chinese emperor; (4) the lesser state could be required to furnish men and supplies when China engaged in missions of "correction"; (5) tribute-bearing missions from the lesser state were sent to China, thereby recognizing the primacy of China in the Confucian family of nations.[3]

In theory, and generally in practice, China did not seek through these means to control directly the internal affairs of the border states. In fact, the border states were largely autonomous so long as their rulers kept the peace, lived with their peoples on the Confucian model, and performed the ceremonial and other duties of their inferior status. In practice, however, many of the men who have controlled China have been politicians rather than pure Confucian theorists. It was possible for such men to use the theory of the superior and the inferior state to serve the ends of what today would be called power politics and thus to make the border states mere satellites of the Middle Kingdom.

With all influence flowing outward, with no competing cultures or authority against which the barriers of definite boundaries need be raised, China had no need for the legal concept of the state. Its control was through

[3] The nature of the Chinese world order is treated in John K. Fairbank, "China's World Order: The Tradition of Chinese Foreign Relations," *Encounter*, December, 1966, 1–7; Immanuel C. Y. Hsü, *China's Entrance into the Family of Nations* (1960), 3–18; M. Frederick Nelson, *Korea and the Old Orders in Eastern Asia* (1945), 3–20. Also, John K. Fairbank, ed., *The Chinese World Order* (1968) for an extended treatment.

ideas that could be confined within no physical boundaries. The marking off of a certain territory within which its word was the highest law and beyond which its precepts were unrecognized was not contemplated in Chinese theory. Furthermore the field of governmental influence embraced the entire social life of man, not certain fields that were deemed public such as foreign relations.

China's controls were applied "through propaganda, appeal to reason, and example, not through the enactment of law, enforced by the authority of the state." None of this, of course, was understood by the Western powers when in the nineteenth century they sought to open relations with China's border states. To the West it appeared that China was the "suzerain" over various "vassal" or "tributary" states. This was so; but these terms did not connote identical forms of control in the Western and in the Chinese system of things.

While China remained the center and the superior in a Confucian community of societies, and while China had no vital contacts with other civilizations, all was well; but when in the nineteenth century Western states sought relations not only with China but also with the border states, such as Korea, they precipitated a conflict between Confucian theory and Western concepts of international law and of the legal equality of states. In Korea, they found a people which to them was neither sovereign enough to conduct independent relations nor subject enough to throw responsibility for its actions on China.

THE CASE OF THE RYUKYU (LIU-CH'IU) ISLANDS

The island kingdom of Ryukyu, the chain of small islands reaching from Kyushu in southern Japan southward to Formosa, had sent tribute to China since late in the fourteenth century, a fact that placed it in the Confucian community of states over which China presided. However, feudal Japan also exercised certain political claims over Ryukyu. The royal family of Ryukyu was said to be related to the Minamoto clan; this may explain why it was that the Ryukyuans sent tribute to Japan in the fifteenth century. Early in the seventeenth century the Japanese Daimyo of Satsuma attacked the islands, brought the northern group under his immediate control, leaving the southern group semi-independent, a species of tributary status. Thus in the middle of the nineteenth century the unfortunate little state found itself tributary to both China and to Japan. In 1871 some Ryukyu islanders, wrecked on the shores of Formosa, were murdered by the aborigines. When China in response to Japanese overtures disclaimed responsibility for acts of the Formosans, Japan sent a military expedition to Formosa (1874). In addition, the Japanese continued to occupy a portion of the island, pending a settlement of the dispute with China. This was finally secured through British mediation; China agreed to indemnify the families of the murdered men and to pay for the roads Japan had built in Formosa. The significant implication of this settlement was that Japan was able to establish a legal claim as protector of the Ryukyu islanders. For a time China refused to accept this view, and Ryukyu continued to send tribute missions to Peking. Attempts at mediation by General U.S. Grant in 1879 also failed; but in that year the Ryukyuan king was removed to Tokyo, where he was granted a title of nobility, and the islands were incorporated into Japan as a prefecture under the name of Okinawa. In 1881 China finally accepted a situation which she was powerless to alter.[4] The Ryukyu incident is important because in this case Japan had succeeded in breaking the Confucian concept of international relations and in substituting for it the Western code of state responsibility.

THE CASE OF KOREA

The case of Korea was to be of far greater international consequence than that

[4] Payson J. Treat, *Diplomatic Relations between the United States and Japan 1853–1895* (2 vols., 1932), I, 473–75, 568–69; II, 71–78, 98–104, 126–27, 141–44; Hyman Kublin, "The Attitude of China During the Liu-ch'iu Controversy, 1871–1881," *The Pacific Historical Review* 18 (1949): 213–31.

of Ryukyu.[5] The earliest European contacts with Korea had occurred in 1593 when the Spanish Jesuit, Gregario de Cespedes, administered spiritual consolation to Japanese Christian soldiers during Hideyoshi's abortive invasion. A number of Dutch sailors were shipwrecked on Korean shores in the seventeenth century and later escaped to Japan. Some attempts were made to open trade toward the end of the eighteenth and the beginning of the nineteenth century. During these developments Catholic Christianity reached Korea by the way of the Jesuit mission in Peking, and, later, French priests entered the country surreptitiously. The conflict between Christianity and Confucianism, and the increase in the number of converts (there were some 9,000 in 1839) led in that year to the persecution and death of many converts and three priests. When in 1846 France sought explanations, she was informed that Korea was subordinate to China, to whom all questions of foreign relations must be referred. By this statement Korea was attempting to avoid relations with the West rather than to describe accurately her own status, for actually she had negotiated directly with foreign states such as Japan, though not with any other states that were outside the Confucian system.

After 1860 a number of powers attempted to trade with Korea: the British and the Russians in 1861, the French the following year. To a second Russian mission in 1866 the Koreans declared that they were a dependent state of China. This Korean policy was implemented from 1863 until 1898, by the regent, father of an infant king, who was vigorously anti-Western and anti-Christian, and who carried the title Taewongun.

France in Korea, 1866

In 1866 a great wave of anti-Christian persecution virtually wiped out the Christian community of some 18,000 converts; only three of a score of French priests escaped with their lives. A French force from China

prepared to attack Korea, and the Peking government was informed that, since China disclaimed any authority over Korea, France herself would seek satisfaction. The military-naval expedition that followed suffered a decisive defeat, and for a time France abandoned any further action. The fact that China did not assume any responsibility for the acts of Korea confirmed France in the belief that China had voluntarily surrendered any claim to suzerainty over this former tributary state.

The United States and Korea

The United States showed an official interest in Korea in 1866, when Secretary of State William H. Seward, thinking that Korea was about to be partitioned, proposed a joint Franco-American expedition. The French had brought back word from Korea that an American merchant ship, the *General Sherman*, had been wrecked on the Korean coast and that the natives had burned her and killed the crew. To Burlingame's inquiries at Peking, China replied that her connections with Korea were only "ceremonial." Seward's joint expedition was not undertaken, but American naval vessels did some charting on the Korean coast, and it was decided to seek a treaty with Korea for the protection of Americans shipwrecked there. When the American naval expedition reached Korea in May, 1871, it was fired upon. In retaliation, it destroyed a number of Korean forts, but got no treaty.[6] Indeed, the Koreans made it clear to China that they wished to continue the old Confucian relationship, and they hoped China would make this clear to the barbarians. This, China made little effort to do. Thus American diplomats in Peking, like their French colleagues, continued to hold the view that China had recently renounced control over Korea's foreign affairs in order to avoid responsibility for Korea's involvements with Western powers.

Japan and the Opening of Korea

Japan sent a mission to Korea in 1868 to

[5] For the background of traditional Korea, see Edwin O. Reischauer and John K. Fairbank, *East Asia: the Great Tradition* (1960), I, Chapter 10.

[6] C. O. Paullin, *Diplomatic Negotiations of American Naval Officers, 1788–1883* (1912), 282–328.

announce the restoration of the emperor and to seek the re-opening of relations. This mission and subsequent ones in 1869 and 1871 were treated with scant respect by the Taewongun's government, since Japan was regarded as a traitor to Confucian society because of her adoption of Western ways. Then, in 1875, a Japanese gunboat engaged in marine surveys on the Korean coast was fired upon. Here was an incident that could serve to bring Korea into treaty relations with Japan and at the same time detach Korea from its Confucian dependency on China. Recognizing, however, that her success in Korea might well depend on the attitude of China, Japan first dispatched to Peking a mission under Mori Arinori to seek a more definite Chinese avowal of Korea's independence. But China continued to maintain that the relationship was that of "dependence yet no control." Nevertheless, Li Hung-chang agreed to aid Japan in securing a friendly reception at Seoul.

The mission that Japan sent to Korea soon secured a treaty (February 26, 1876) which opened three Korean ports to trade and provided for diplomatic intercourse. In English translation, Article I reads: "Chosen, being an independent State (*tzu chu*), enjoys the same sovereign rights as does Japan." Some Chinese historians have, however, translated this article more favorably to China. For instance: "Chaohsien [Chosen or Korea] being an autonomous (*tzu chu*) state, shall enjoy the rights of equality with Japan." [7] Nevertheless, despite arguments over the precise meaning of Article I, certain points are quite clear. The Japanese intended by their treaty to make Korea "independent" as the West understood that term, whereas China on the other hand had no intention of altering the ancient relation in any way. As for the Korean government, it signed a "Western treaty" with Japan, making at the same time a mental reservation to continue the old Confucian relation with China.

[7] Hsu Shuhsi, *China and Her Political Entity* (1926), 109. *Tzu chu* is usually translated "self-governing" or "autonomous," rather than "sovereign" or "independent."

THE DEPENDENCIES OF ILI, ANNAM, BURMA, SIKKIM

Korea's status, hanging as it did at this time between the ancient Confucian ideology and a modern Western one, was soon to be clarified by events in China's other dependencies. In 1881 the inroads of Russia in the northwest resulted in the loss by China of the western part of Ili, which was ceded to Russia.[8] In 1885 the long story of French penetration into Indochina, dating back to the days of Louis XVI, was completed. In that year Annam, which had been a dependent state of China since Han times, fell completely under the control of France.[9] At the same time, Burma ceased to be a dependency of China. It had been a dependent state since its conquest by Kublai Khan in 1284. Lower Burma had passed to British control between 1824 and 1852. Now, in 1886, the British extended their jurisdiction over all Burma. China recognized British sovereignty in Burma, and Britain agreed that Burma might continue to send decennial tribute missions to Peking. Only one mission, that of 1895, was ever sent. Finally, in 1890, China recognized a British protectorate over Sikkim. All of these treaties concerning Ili, Annam, Burma, and Sikkim revealed that the old Chinese relationship to these states (dependence yet no control) was giving place to a new Western and legalistic relationship in

[8] Immanuel C. Y. Hsu, *The Ili Crisis: A Study of Sino-Russian Diplomacy, 1878–1881* (London, 1965).

[9] This outcome was not achieved without Sino-French hostilities, 1884–85, and ultimately a declaration of war by China. On Chinese naval strength which could be used against France see John L. Rawlinson, *China's Struggle for Naval Development, 1839–1895* (1967), 190–98.

The Sino-French controversy and hostilities resulting from expanding French control in Indochina show the methods by which the Peking government made its decisions in the face of the Western impact. It is clear that the power of the throne was limited by the power of high officials and also by the more numerous low-ranking conservative officialdom. See Lloyd E. Eastman, *Throne and Mandarins: China's Search for a Policy during the Sino-French Controversy 1880–1885* (1967).

which these states were recognized by China as the colonies or protectorates of Western powers. It was therefore apparent that Japan's attempt to establish the independence of Korea in 1876 was not an isolated occurrence but rather a part of a larger movement by which the dependencies of China were being detached from Peking.

CHINA AND KOREA

China recognized the danger of losing her ancient Confucian control over Korea. Following the loss of Ryukyu, Li Hung-chang noted that: "We can no longer refrain from devising ways and means for the security of Korea." Accordingly, China adopted a threefold course of action: she urged Korea to strengthen her military forces; she increased her diplomatic contacts with Korea in the hope of exercising greater influence at Seoul; and she urged Korea to conclude treaties with those powers which, unlike Japan and Russia, would be unlikely to have territorial ambitions. Of these powers the United States was the first to show a renewed interest in treaty relations with Korea. Commodore Robert W. Shufeldt was sent by the Navy Department to seek, with Japanese aid, a commercial treaty. The mission failed, but Shufeldt was encouraged by Li Hung-chang to seek a treaty through China's good offices. In 1882 the first American-Korean treaty was concluded. It provided among other things for the exchange of diplomatic and consular officers, for trade with Korea on the most favored-nation principle, and included the provision:

If other Powers deal unjustly or oppressively with either Government, the other will exert their good offices, on being informed of the case, to bring about an amicable arrangement, thus showing their friendly feelings.

Li had asked, and Shufeldt had refused, to include a clause acknowledging the dependence of Korea upon China. This matter was disposed of by a letter from the Korean king to the President acknowledging the subservient status. However, the United States took

the position, stated by Frederick T. Frelinghuysen, the Secretary of State,

. . . that we regarded Corea as de facto independent, and that our acceptance of the friendly aid found in China was in no sense a recognition of China's suzerain power.[10]

The principal European powers soon followed the example of the United States by securing treaties through China's good offices: Great Britain, 1883; Germany, 1883; Italy, 1884; Russia, 1884; and France, 1886. In each case Korea, while negotiating as a sovereign power in terms of the treaty, set forth in accompanying letters her dependent position upon China.

Korean Politics and Chinese Relations, 1882

Prior to the conclusion of these treaties, the international status of Korea had been affected by other developments. The first of these was China's intervention in a palace revolution at Seoul; the other, the conclusion of certain Sino-Korean trade regulations.

There were two major factions at the Korean court: the one, led by the family of the queen, favored relations with foreign powers; the other, led by the Taewongun was intensely anti-foreign. The rivalry of these two factions, together with bad economic conditions, led to a conspiracy (1882) to do away with the queen. The plot failed, but in the course of the fighting Korean mobs attacked the Japanese legation and drove its occupants to the coast, where they were rescued by a British ship. Both Japan and China now stepped into the picture by sending troops to restore order. China, claiming to act in her traditional Confucian capacity, seized the Taewongun and sent him to Tientsin for punishment. Japan on her part exacted from Korea an agreement providing for an apology, an indemnity, the right to station a legation guard at Seoul, and permission to travel in the interior. To the Western powers all this was thoroughly confusing. Here was China intervening in the internal affairs of

[10] United States, Department of State, *China Instructions*, Vol. 3, No. 30.

Korea, for which she professed to have no responsibility, using troops to restore order, issuing proclamations in the name of the king, and carrying off a member of the Royal House to answer for his deeds. On the other hand, here was Japan ignoring the Chinese and dealing directly with Korea.

The second development of 1882 was the conclusion by China and Korea of new regulations on trade. This agreement, asserting that there was no change in Korea's status "as a boundary state of China," gave to the Chinese advantages over other foreigners in matters of residence, travel, trade, and import duties. Again the question before the Western powers was how this sort of thing could be reconciled with their own Korean treaties negotiated on the assumption that Korea was now independent.

It was evident by 1882 that Chinese control over and intervention in Korea was becoming more pronounced. High Chinese military officers even proposed the annexation of Korea and war with Japan. Li Hung-chang, however, adopting measures short of this, sent P. G. von Mollendorff to Korea as Inspector-General of Korean Customs. He also sent a number of Chinese "commercial agents" who would "actually assist the King to decide political issues." Indeed, Korea had ceased to be merely a Confucian appendage of China, for Li Hung-chang was now asserting, "I am King of Korea whenever I think the interests of China require me to assert that prerogative." [11]

THE TIENTSIN CONVENTION, 1885

Japan too had become more active in Korea. She gave her support to the Progressive (Reform) party. By 1884 the Japanese minister at Seoul openly criticized the policies of China, adding that Japan would welcome complete Korean independence. In Decem-

[11] United States, Department of State, *China Despatches*, Vol. 65, No. 230, Young to Frelinghuysen, August 8, 1883. Also, Dong Jae Yim, "The Abduction of the Taewongun, 1882," *Papers on China*, Vol. 21. Published by the East Asian Research Center, Harvard University (1968): 99–130.

ber, 1884, the Korean Progressives seized the king and called upon the Japanese for military protection. Yuan Shih-k'ai, commanding Chinese troops, promptly drove the Japanese to the coast and restored the king to his conservative counsellors. For this affair, the Japanese exacted from Korea an indemnity; but they also sent a mission headed by Ito Hirobumi to Tientsin to discuss the Korean question with Li Hung-chang. The Convention of Tientsin (April 18, 1885) was a partial though not a complete victory for Japan. The two powers agreed to withdraw their troops from Korea, and, in the case of future disturbances, neither was to send troops *without notifying the other*. Thus, Japan gained a position of equality with China in the matter of military intervention.

However, between 1885 and 1894 Li Hung-chang so strengthened his control over Korea that the country became in fact a Chinese protectorate rather than a dependent state in the old Confucian sense. Li accomplished this end by various means. To the control which he already exercised through foreigners in the employ of the Korean government and through Chinese commercial agents, he added the appointment of Yuan Shih-k'ai as Chinese Resident in Korea, a post superior to that of a mere diplomatic representative. By the control which he exercised through these agents, Li attempted to destroy any idea in the minds of the powers that Korea was fully sovereign. Li also sought economic as well as political influence at Seoul. In 1885 China obtained a monopoly in the Korean telegraph, and attempted to get control over future loans sought by the Korean government. So successful was Li's policy that in 1892 even Japan approached Korea through China when seeking satisfaction for losses occasioned by certain Korean embargoes on the exportation of cargoes to Japan.

IMMEDIATE BACKGROUND OF THE SINO-JAPANESE WAR

The issue between China and Japan concerning the international status of Korea was clear by the early months of 1894. Summarized briefly, it may be stated as follows: (1) the impact of the West had already deprived China of her principal dependent states, Burma, Annam, Ili, and Sikkim—Korea alone remained; (2) Korea too appeared to be headed toward what the West called "sovereign independence" (this was indicated by the Japanese treaty of 1876, the American treaty of 1882, and the European treaties of 1883 and after); (3) Li Hung-chang, however, was determined to preserve China's influence in this strategic peninsula against the designs of either Japan or Russia, and to do so by Western as well as Confucian techniques if necessary; and, finally, (4) since no one of the Western powers was prepared to assert the fact as well as the principle of Korean independence, it remained for Japan to do so. When Japan did act it was relatively easy for her to give the impression that her motives were benevolent—to rescue Korea from China and Russia, and to bestow upon the Hermit Kingdom the independence, sovereignty, and progressive outlook which Japan herself enjoyed.[12]

KOREA: A EUROPEAN PROBLEM

However, even in 1894 Korea was not a question concerning Japan and China alone. It had already become "a sort of focal point for great European rivalries, as well as for Asiatic antagonisms." [13] The Russians wanted an ice-free port in Korea and the British were determined they should not have one. It was against such European rivalries that the Japanese policy of 1894 was launched.

By 1894, Japan's political position in Korea was woefully weak, but her economic position was showing steady growth. Ninety per cent of Korea's foreign trade was with

[12] The most detailed account of Japanese-Korean relations is Hilary Conroy, *The Japanese Seizure of Korea: 1868–1910* (1960).

[13] William L. Langer, *The Diplomacy of Imperialism, 1890–1902* (2 vols., 1935; 2nd. ed. in one vol., 1951), I, 168. Note Chapter 6 for a discussion of European aspects of the crisis.

Japan. Li had made strenuous efforts to counter Japan's economic advance. He was acquiring an army and navy, and was creating at Port Arthur a naval base. He was also planning a railway from Shanhaikwan to the Manchurian border near Vladivostok. News of this project created considerable excitement in Russia, where in 1891 the decision was made to build the Trans-Siberian Railway. This was looked upon in Europe as a decision of the utmost importance, and it was viewed with misgivings by both China and Japan. The Japanese believed that if Russia completed her system of communications, her advance into eastern Asia could not be stopped; yet they also believed that Korea must be independent or controlled by Japan if the Empire was to be secure. The Japanese also had domestic worries on their minds. The constitutional government inaugurated in 1890 was not going well. Cabinets that considered themselves responsible only to the emperor were faced with a succession of recalcitrant Diets that refused to accept naval estimates presented by the government until appealed to directly by the emperor.[14] With young and inexperienced parliamentarians in this mood, some of the bureaucrats and militarists in the government were ready to welcome a foreign war that would unite the home front.

IMMEDIATE PRELIMINARIES TO WAR

From 1871 until 1894 the peace party in Japan, headed in the later years by Ito Hirobumi, maintained its ascendancy over the militarists, and consequently there was no war over Korea. But after 1890 the "obstructive" tactics of the Diet gave the war party its opportunity. Only a pretext was needed, and this was soon forthcoming. The *Tong Hak* ("Eastern Learning Society"), originally a Korean religious sect, had acquired a political complexion, had drawn into its membership the politically oppressed, and had assumed a program that was antiforeign, anti-Christian, and anti-Japanese.

[14] Takeuchi Tatsuji, *War and Diplomacy in the Japanese Empire* (1935), 109–110.

When, as a result, rebellion finally occurred in the southern provinces, Korean government troops sent to quell the disturbance were themselves defeated. Acting on the advice of Yuan, Li Hung-chang promptly decided to send Chinese troops (June 6, 1894), and, in accord with the Tientsin Convention, notified Japan that he was doing so. Untactfully, China's notice referred to "our tributary state." Japan replied the same day that she too would send troops owing to the "grave nature" of affairs in the peninsula, and added that she had "never recognized Korea as a tributary state of China." By the time the Chinese and the Japanese troops arrived, the Koreans had already suppressed the revolt. A miracle perhaps could have prevented a clash, but miracles were not happening at Seoul. Japan proposed joint Sino-Japanese action to effect financial, administrative, and military reforms in Korea. China replied that she could not interfere in the internal administration of Korea and added that Japan had no right to do so. Japan then turned to the Korean government, demanding a declaration indicating whether Korea was tributary to China. When Korea's reply proved unsatisfactory to the Japanese, their troops seized the king, and a reorganized Korean government ordered Japan to expel Chinese troops. The Sino-Japanese War had begun. The declarations were issued on August 1, 1894.

THE WAR

The diplomatic front was by no means favorable to Japan when she embarked on a policy of war. Britain indicated that she would not agree to Japanese annexation of Korean territory. Russia too gave her diplomatic support to China, seemingly on the theory that it was better to have Korea controlled by a weak China than by a young and vigorous Japan. As a result, Japan gave assurances to the powers that she had no designs on Korean territory, was interested only in Korean reform, and, in the interests of European commerce, would refrain from attacking Shanghai. These assurances were accepted, probably because it was generally believed in the West that Japan would be defeated. But these early forecasts were shattered by the September victories of Japanese arms at Pingyang and the Yalu. It soon became evident that Chinese forces were no match for the small but relatively efficient Japanese military machine.

Indeed a diplomatic revolution was already under way. British opinion, reacting to the Japanese victories, invited France, Germany, Russia, and the United States to intervene jointly to seek a settlement that would include Korean independence, a European guarantee to Korea, and indemnity for Japan. The proposal was dropped when Germany and the United States refused to join. Li Hung-chang himself also sought the support of Europe and America to end the disastrous war before China was completely humbled.

During the winter months of January and February, 1895, the Japanese had taken Wei-hai-wei; their armies were crossing southern Manchuria; and in early March they had occupied Newchwang and Ying-kow, from which they might soon advance on a frightened and humiliated government in Peking. Here the Empress Dowager, instead of building a navy, had employed government funds to rebuild the Summer Palace. When the United States offered its good offices to both belligerents, Japan replied significantly that her objectives would not be reached "until China finds herself in a position to approach Japan directly on the subject of peace."

Indeed Li Hung-chang did send a succession of peace missions to Japan. Finally, when all these failed and when hope of European aid or of a victory for Chinese arms had vanished, Li himself accepted the humiliating task of asking for peace. As he left for Japan he still hoped for a diplomatic victory through European intervention, though he was warned by Charles Denby, American minister at Peking, that what China needed was a sincere, friendly *rapprochement* with Japan.

China's failure to prevent Korea's detachment from the tributary system has often

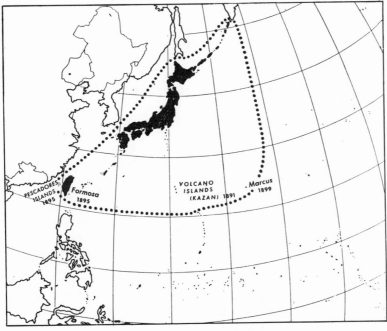

Japan   1891–1904

Reproduced from A War Atlas for Americans *(New York: Simon & Schuster, 1944) with permission from the publisher and from the U.S. Department of State, Division of Map Intelligence and Cartography.*

been explained simply by saying that her foreign policy was weak, inept, and uninformed. In a limited degree this interpretation is sound, but it should also take into account the fact that the Tsungli-yamen, though constantly blocked by the tradition-bound Board of Rites, did advance new ideas and did try new methods. In the Korean case the Tsungli-yamen showed remarkable flexibility. Its efforts were nullified not only by obstruction at home but also by the intransigence of the Koreans.[15]

THE TREATY OF SHIMONOSEKI
APRIL 17, 1895

Japan's military and naval victory marked the beginning of a new era in the Far East, the effects of which were to be

[15] Mary C. Wright, "The Adaptability of Ch'ing Diplomacy," *Journal of Asian Studies* 17 (1958): 363–81.

felt almost as much in Europe as in Asia. The immediate question was: "What would be Japan's demands?" The tables were now turned. At Tientsin in 1885 Ito had been forced to accept what China was willing to give. At Shimonoseki in 1895 China would be forced to give whatever Ito demanded. The specific nature of Japan's demands was not known until they were presented to the Chinese on April 1. They included (1) China to recognize the full and complete independence of Korea; (2) China to cede Japan Formosa,[16] the Pescadores, and the Liaotung Peninsula in South Manchuria; (3)

[16] Japan's interest in Formosa or Taiwan dated back to 1872. For a few brief weeks in the spring of 1895 the terms of the Shimonoseki settlement were challenged by the appearance of the Republic of Taiwan, "a republican state, autonomous but not sovereign, presided over by a ruler who sought to function as both a Taiwanese president and Chinese governor." See Harry J. Lamley, "The 1895 Taiwan Republic," *Journal of Asian Studies* 27 (1968): 739–62.

China to pay an indemnity of 300,000,000 taels; (4) China to conclude with Japan a new treaty of commerce, granting among other things most-favored-nation treatment to Japan and opening seven new treaty ports. Since neither Europe nor the United States was prepared to come actively at this time to China's aid, Li was forced to accept Japan's terms with some modifications. The Treaty of Shimonoseki (sometimes know as Bakan) was signed April 17, 1895.

The efficacy of war as a stabilizer of Japanese politics was immediately evident. By the declaration of war Ito and Japan's Elder Statesmen achieved notable results. The nation was unified; peace prevailed between the government and the Diet; huge war budgets (one of 150,000,000 yen) were passed without a dissenting vote; a resolution was adopted unanimously to appropriate any amount of funds needed for the prosecution of the war. Japan had indeed taken the first step in what was to be a vigorous policy of expansion on the Asiatic continent. With Port Arthur and the Liaotung Peninsula in her possession she could look forward to a controlling influence at Peking. In short, she had made it clear that both territorially and diplomatically she proposed to be a part of whatever pressures were exerted upon China.

For China the results of the war were no less momentous. The proud Middle Kingdom had been defeated by a people looked upon not only as inferior but also, by reason of their Westernization, as traitors to the Confucian ideal. In naval, military, and political affairs the Manchu government was revealed as decrepit and corrupt. To a few thoughtful Chinese it appeared that the dynasty had lost the Mandate of Heaven. Now with Japan's victory the old Confucian theory of international relations, which China had maintained for centuries, was destroyed. There was no longer in theory or in fact a far eastern Confucian world order. China was no longer the Middle Kingdom, for there were no longer any dependent states that recognized her superior status. Her efforts to protect herself from the inroads of the powers had been frustrated by the same institutional obstacles, by the same bureaucratic incubus that had blocked internal reform.

FOR FURTHER READING

GENERAL. Franz Michael, *The Origin of Manchu Rule in China, Frontier and Bureaucracy as Interacting Forces in the Chinese Empire* (1942) develops Chinese-nomad relations. Owen Lattimore, *Inner Asian Frontiers of China* (2nd ed., 1951),* a study of Chinese relations with frontier areas. L. A. Mills, *British Rule in Eastern Asia* (London, 1942), an excellent study of Hong Kong, the Straits settlements, and the Malay states. Tong Te-kong, *United States Diplomacy in China: 1844–1860* (1964) examines the crucial formative period in Sino-American relations prior to the "Open Door" policy.

LIU-CH'IU. Clarence Glacken, *The Great Loochoo: A Study in Okinawan Village Life* (1955). George H. Kerr, *Okinawa: the History of an Island People* (1958), a comprehensive history of the island group annexed by Japan in 1879 and occupied by the United States since 1945.

KOREA. Shannon McCune, *Korea's Heritage: A Regional and Social Geography* (1956). W. W. Rockhill, *China's Intercourse with Korea from the XVth Century to 1895* (London, 1905). *Korean-American Relations: Documents Pertaining to the Far Eastern Diplomacy of the United States*, Vol. 1, George M. McCune and John A. Harrison, eds. (1951), and Volume II, Spencer J. Palmer, ed. (1963). Fred H. Harrington, *God, Mammon, and the Japanese* (1962), a biography of Horace Allen, missionary, businessman, and first American Minister to Korea. Peter Hyun, trans. and introduction, *Voices of the Dawn; a Selection of Korean Poetry from the Sixth Century to the Present Day* (London, 1960)* contains masterpieces of Korean poetry and a helpful introduction to the history of Korean literature. Tyler Dennett, *Americans in Eastern Asia* (1922;

reprint, 1963) contains good chapters on Korea's nineteenth century foreign relations.

TIBET. Li Tieh-tseng, *Tibet: Today and Yesterday* (1960), a study of the history and foreign relations of Tibet. Shen Tsung-lien and Liu Shen-chi, *Tibet and the Tibetans* (1953), a short but very informative book. Charles Bell, *The People of Tibet* (Oxford, 1928). Charles Bell, *The Religion of Tibet* (Oxford, 1931), based on Tibetan as well as English sources. Helmut Hoffmann, *The Religions of Tibet* (1961). H. E. Richardson, *A Short History of Tibet* (1962) concentrates upon Tibet's international relations with China, Great Britain, Russia, and India in the twentieth century. Li Tieh-tseng, *The Historical Status of Tibet* (1956) covers the field from Tibet's dealings with T'ang China. Schuyler Cammann, *Trade Through the Himalayas: The Early British Attempts to Open Tibet* (1951) also covers early Ch'ing relations with Tibet. Robert Brainerd Ekvall, *Cultural Relations on the Kansu-Tibetan Border* (1939).

SOUTHEAST ASIA. R. O. Winstedt, *The Malays* (5th ed., London, 1958), a brief but fundamental survey of the land, people, and life of Malaya. Joseph Kennedy, *A History of Malaya, 1400–1959* (1962), a clear survey with excellent critical bibliography. Harold C. Hinton, *China's Relations with Burma and Vietnam* (1958). William A. Hanna, *The Formation of Malaysia* (1964), a chronicle of its beginnings and its problems. John L. Christian, *Modern Burma* (1942), a fine introductory study. D. G. E. Hall, *A History of South-east Asia* (London, 1955). C. A. Fisher, *South-east Asia, A Social, Economic and Political Geography* (1964), and George McTurnan Kahin, ed., *Governments and Politics of Southeast Asia* (1959; rev. ed, 1964). Brian Harrison, *South-East Asia, a Short History* (2nd rev. ed., 1963).

1895–1899:
China and the Powers

chapter 15

The Treaty of Shimonoseki not only placed Japan in the company of the so-called Great Powers, it precipitated a new and a dramatic era in the relations of China and the West. Until 1895, the major interest of the Western states in China was commercial. The traders had purchased China's silk and tea, and in return they had sold to China silver, opium, ginseng, sandalwood, furs, and, in the later years of the century, an expanding assortment of manufactured textiles, flour, and kerosene. There had been little penetration by the trader *into* China. Business was conducted in the treaty ports on the coast. Here the foreign merchants and their governments had surrounded themselves with certain protective agencies—the conventional tariff, extraterritoriality, concessions, and settlements —but apart from these guarantees to commerce, neither government nor merchants had been concerned primarily with China as a great frontier for capital investment or with the political controls that might be imposed upon China to that end. Between 1895 and 1899 much of this was changed, for in these years China did become a market for the investment, principally, of railroad capital. This development, considered so vital by

the industrialized states of the West, took the form of an international scramble by the powers for exclusive economic concessions and spheres of political interest. For a time it appeared that a complete political partitioning of China was imminent. The roots of this movement antedate the Sino-Japanese War, but it was Japan's victory in that war and her threat to dominate North China by the annexation of Port Arthur and Liaotung which precipitated the movement and endowed it with the full flavor of power politics.[1]

[1] The role of foreign investment in China's economic development was to become increasingly important and controversial in the twentieth century. Certainly during the past 100 years economic contact with the West has been a very important but not the only factor affecting the Chinese economy. The most common interpretation, especially by Chinese, has been that the foreign economic intrusion was detrimental to the Chinese economy—economic imperialism designed to subjugate China to the West. The most commonly used arguments in support of this view are that (1) foreign trade and investment ruined Chinese handicraft industries and disturbed agriculture, (2) foreign trade and investment drained wealth from China, and (3) foreign enterprises in China enjoyed special advantages which placed Chinese-owned modern enterprises at a hopeless disadvantage. These arguments against the foreign economic impact

THE TRIPLE INTERVENTION

193

China,
1890s:
Foreign
Pressures

Six days after the conclusion of the Treaty of Shimonoseki, on April 23, 1895, the representatives of Russia, Germany, and France in Tokyo presented to Count Hayashi, deputy foreign minister, notes which said that

. . . the possession of the Peninsula of Liaotung, claimed by Japan, would be a constant menace to the Capital of China, would at the same time render illusory the independence of Korea, and would henceforth be a perpetual obstacle to the peace of the Far East.

The three powers, protesting that in this manner they were giving new proof of their friendship, "advised" Japan to renounce possession of Liaotung. For a week the diplomatic scales hung in uneasy equilibrium. Japan offered to give up all of Liaotung save the southern tip with Port Aruthur. This offer the three powers rejected, and on May 5 Japan accepted their "advice" without qualification. She asked, however, that the Treaty of Shimonoseki be ratified in its original form prior to the retrocession, and that she be given additional indemnity. This the powers granted. Ratification took place at Chefoo where, significantly, a Russian squadron, wearing the gray paint of war and with its decks cleared for action, lay at anchor. The Liaotung Peninsula was returned to China by a convention signed November 8, 1895, in which China agreed to pay an additional indemnity of 30,000,000 Kuping taels.[2]

The Triple Intervention ended the temporary truce in Japan's domestic politics. During the Shimonoseki negotiations Prime Minister Ito and Foreign Minister Mutsu knew that an unfriendly European intervention was in the making. Accordingly, Mutsu, in an effort to forestall action by the powers, had insisted that Japan make no territorial demands on the mainland, but he was overruled by pressure of the military and naval staffs. The generals were determined to have a strategic foothold on the continent. Therefore, when the Japanese public, elated with the news of military and naval triumphs, learned that its government had bowed to a European intervention, indignation was widespread, and was not quieted until the emperor sanctioned an Imperial rescript stating that the retrocession in no way compromised the dignity or honor of the nation. Actually, the government was well aware that Japan had won the war but had lost the peace. For the brief duration of the war she had bid for and had held diplomatic leadership in the Far East. Then, with military victory achieved, Japan made certain her diplomatic defeat by permitting the militarists to have their way in demanding a territorial concession from which Japan could dominate Peking.

EUROPEAN BACKGROUND OF THE INTERVENTION

The reasons that led to this dramatic three-power intervention are clear, as are also the reasons why Britain did not participate. Up to the time of the war, British policy had been decidely pro-Chinese. However, it also favored independence for Korea while opposing any thought of Japanese annexations on the continent. Japan's demands were therefore disturbing to the British, for they upset whatever balance of power there was in the Far East; yet at the same time the British admired Japan's aggressive efficiency, and they were not in-

were believed strongly by the Manchu government in the last decades of the nineteenth century, as well as by more recent governments. Actually, the evidence now available tends to challenge the validity of all of these arguments in whole or in part. In following the economic aspects of the Western impact, especially from 1895 to 1937, the reader should consult Chiming Hou, *Foreign Investment and Economic Development in China, 1840–1937* (1965).

[2] The tael (Chinese, *liang*) was a unit of weight and when applied to silver was often used as a currency unit. There were in practice a number of taels of varying weight but generally of about 1⅓ ounces. In general, too, the currency tael was used as a standard money of account

and was seldom minted in coin. Transactions were carried on with silver ingots, checks or bank notes in taels, or Spanish-Mexican dollars.

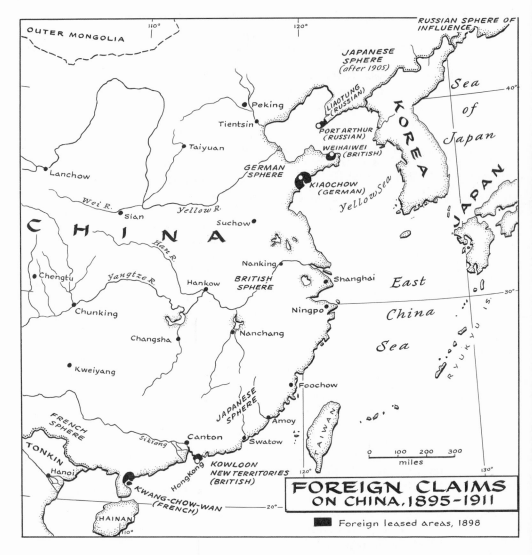

OUTER MONGOLIA

RUSSIAN SPHERE OF INFLUENCE

JAPANESE SPHERE (after 1905)

Peking

Tientsin

Taiyuan

Lanchow

LIAOTUNG (RUSSIAN)

PORT ARTHUR (RUSSIAN)

WEIHAIWEI (BRITISH)

KOREA

Sea of Japan

GERMAN SPHERE

KIAOCHOW (GERMAN)

Yellow Sea

JAPAN

Wei R.

Sian

Yellow R.

Suchow

C H I N A

Han R.

Nanking

Shanghai

East China Sea

BRITISH SPHERE

Chengtu

Yangtze R.

Hankow

Ningpo

Chunking

Changsha

Nanchang

RYUKYU IS.

Kweiyang

Foochow

JAPANESE SPHERE

FRENCH SPHERE

TAIWAN

Amoy

Sikiang

Canton

Swatow

0 100 200 300
miles

TONKIN

Hanoi

Hong Kong

KOWLOON NEW TERRITORIES (BRITISH)

FOREIGN CLAIMS ON CHINA, 1895-1911

KWANG-CHOW-WAN (FRENCH)

HAINAN

Foreign leased areas, 1898

Sources: J. K. Fairbank, E. O. Reischauer, and A. M. Craig, *East Asia: The Modern Transformation* (Boston: Houghton Mifflin Co., 1965), 399; and Dun J. Lee, *The Ageless Chinese* (New York: Charles Scribners Sons, 1965), 423.

sensible to the fact that the commercial clauses of the peace settlement could be very profitable to British business in China.

Until 1895, Russia had attempted to remain on friendly terms with Japan. She had ample opportunity to intervene in the war but at the time was more interested in preserving the status quo. All this, however, was changed by Japan's amazing victory. The Tsar changed his mind several times

and then, having the assurance of German and French support, decided to thwart Japan's Imperial ambitions.[3] In general, Russian policy in the long view was aiming at acquisition of an ice-free port on the Pacific. The Russians saw numerous advantages in

[3] George A. Lensen, "Japan and Tsarist Russia—the Changing Relationships, 1875–1917," *Jahrbucher fur Geschichte Osteuropas* (Wiesbaden, 1962), 337–48.

this course. It would exclude Japan from any share in the partition of China (a partition which the Japanese were already considering), and it would make Russia appear as the savior of China, which would thus dispose Peking favorably to subsequent Russian territorial demands.

Germany's participation in the intervention is explained largely by the fear that a partition of China was possible and that it would be well to be active in the events leading to that end. The Germans already had their eyes on several bases in the Far East, and the views of the German Foreign Office were influenced by von Brandt, who for a quarter of a century had been the leading German diplomat in the Orient. Furthermore, anything that encouraged the Russians to become involved in eastern Asia would presumably react to German advantage in Europe.

The participation of France is explained by considerations of general policy. France feared that the Japanese would resist, and that they would be joined by the British, which would thus precipitate a general conflict. Therefore, France favored letting the Japanese have their gains while the powers would seek their own territorial compensation elsewhere in China. When, however, Russia decided to act, France joined her in the interest of the Dual Alliance.

FINANCING THE WAR AND THE PEACE

While Japan paid for her diplomatic defeat with loss of her territorial gains in Manchuria, China paid for her unpreparedness with cold cash. Her efforts to float domestic loans during the war had failed. Chinese bankers had little interest in Li Hung-chang's Korean or Manchurian policies. Consequently, the Peking government financed the war with two loans totalling some £4,635,000 from the British Hong Kong and Shanghai Bank. After the war, China was confronted with the Japanese indemnity totalling 230,000,000 Kuping taels (about $172,000,000 gold). The Russians

were particularly anxious that this bill should be paid and thus effect the Japanese evacuation of Liaotung; but they were equally concerned that the indemnity be met in such fashion as to leave China in a kind of politico-financial dependence upon Russia, which thus would prevent the extension of British financial influence at Peking. The Germans and the French shared in this desire. The result was a Franco-Russian loan to China, July 6, 1895, of 400,000,000 francs. The political motive behind the loan was indicated by China's pledge not to grant to any foreign power any right of supervision or administration over any of its revenues, unless the same rights were extended to the Russian government. Witte, Russia's minister of finance, had won the first round in the financial battle for dominance at Peking. The Germans, who had not been admitted to the Franco-Russian loan, then joined the British bankers in a loan of £16,000,000, March 23, 1896. Two years later the Anglo-German banking group extended another loan in the sum of £16,000,000. The era of international European rivalry to finance and to control China had begun.

THE RUSSO-CHINESE AGREEMENTS OF 1896

The indemnity loans, virtually forced upon China by Russia and France in 1895, were not to be considered as adequate compensation for "the diplomatic aid" these powers had given Peking. The shape of future Russian policy was made clear during 1896. Since 1891 the Russians had been engaged in construction of the Trans-Siberian Railway. It was obvious that such a huge undertaking involving a line some 5,000 miles in length was not designed primarily to connect European Russia with Vladivostok or any other port which, like it, was icebound four or five months each year. Since as early as 1857 Russian statesmen had played with the idea of a Peking terminus for a Siberian railway. What Russia now wanted was a port in southern Korea or Manchuria; but in the months immediately following the peace this was out of the question unless she was prepared to fight Japan. However, by February, 1896, Russian fortunes in Korea took an unexpected turn for the better. The Koreans had not taken kindly to Japan's energetic suggestions on reform, and, when the Japanese Minister was implicated in the murder of the Korean queen, the king fled to the Russian legation in Seoul, from which he ruled the country for some time. Even this development did not result in immediate Russian seizures in Korea.

However, in December, 1895, Witte chartered the Russo-Chinese Bank, ostensibly a private corporation but officially approved and inspired. Baron Rosen called it a slightly disguised branch of the Russian treasury. The capital came from French banks. The new concern was to be the financial arm of the new Trans-Siberian Railway. Its powers were notable in that it could collect taxes, finance the business of local government, coin money, and secure commercial and industrial concessions. Its founders likewise assumed that the granting of special concessions to Russia would be promoted by a judicious bestowal of financial gifts upon suitable Chinese officials in Peking.

Another phase of the Russian far eastern plan concerned the route of the Trans-Siberian Railway from Lake Baikal to Vladivostok. To run the line wholly in Russian territory north of Manchuria and the Amur would entail 350 miles of additional construction through difficult terrain. If, however, it were run directly across Central Manchuria, it would be the first step to Russian control of all Manchurian commerce and of railroad development in North China. For a time, however, the Russians made little headway at Peking. The Chinese were well aware that Russian railway demands could not be pushed aside, but they hoped to strike a better bargain by sending Li Hung-chang to the coronation of the new tsar. Actually this arrangement was exactly what Witte wanted. Li was met at Port Said by Witte's agent, Prince Esper Ukhtomskii, whose colorful writings on the cultural and philosophical unity of the Russians and the Asiatics were well known. It was the role of

the Prince to prepare Li for Witte's more practical proposals on Russo-Chinese industrial unity in Manchuria. The argument as presented to Li was that Russia had plenty of territory and therefore no designs on that of China; that culturally the tie between the two nations was great; that by building the railroad across Manchuria, Russia would be in a position to aid China against attack; and finally that China herself was not in a position to finance or build the road. There seems little doubt that Li was bribed handsomely by Russian agents, but his decision was probably made basically on other grounds. He had given up hope of aid from England; he hated Japan intensely. Therefore, an alliance with and concessions to Russia seemed the natural answer.[4]

Moreover, Li was not alone in wishing to play Russia against Japan and other powers. Japan's victory in 1895 had awakened and alarmed the Chinese scholar-official mind as had no crisis in the previous half century. The Sino-Japanese War illumined the empty pretense of the program of self-strengthening and hustled the high command of the Confucian bureaucracy back again to the older weapon of playing one power against another, of using barbarian to fight barbarian. Even among Li's rivals there were supporters of his Russian policy, such as Chang Chih-tung (1837–1909). In 1895 Chang wrote that Russia was China's natural ally, "because England uses commerce to absorb the profits of China, France uses religion to entice the Chinese people, Germany has no territorial boundary with us, and the United States does not like to interfere in others' military affairs." As a result, China got the Russian alliance she wanted, but she did so by granting concessions which within two years precipitated the threatened break-up of the Empire.

The Russo-Chinese secret alliance, known as the Li-Lobanov Treaty, was signed on June 3, 1896. It was to remain in force for fifteen years. Among other things it provided: (1) for mutual assistance against any

[4] A. Yarmolinsky, ed., *The Memoirs of Count Witte* (1921), of great value but incomplete and unreliable in Witte's estimates of his own role.

Japanese aggression, (2) for the use of Chinese ports by Russia in the event of war, and (3) for China's consent to the construction of the Trans-Siberian Railway across Manchuria—construction and operation of the road to be accorded to the Russo-Chinese Bank. Although rumors of this agreement soon became public, it was not until many years later that the exact nature of the alliance was revealed.

THE CHINESE EASTERN RAILWAY

What the public did learn was that on September 8, 1896, the Russo-Chinese Bank and the Chinese government had agreed to the construction and operation by the Chinese Eastern Railway Company of a line of railway from Manchouli on the western border of Manchuria to Pogranichnaya (Suifenho) on the southeast border near Vladivostok. The statutes of the new Chinese Eastern Railway Company were to conform to Russian law; the president was to be named by China; but the Russian general manager would exercise the greater power. The political nature of the line was indicated by the fact that over the "lands actually necessary for the construction, operation, and protection of the line" the Company was to have "the absolute and exclusive right of administration." China was to grant reduced tariff rates to goods entering or leaving by the line; there was to be no interference with the movement of Russian troops or munitions; and the Company was to have "the complete and exclusive right to operate the line."

These terms were confirmed in December, 1896, when the Russian government sanctioned the statutes of the Chinese Eastern Railway Company. These statutes obligated the Company to construct telegraph lines and to carry Russian mails free. Although the Chinese government was to adopt measures for the protection of the line, the statutes provided that "the preservation of law and order on the lands assigned to the railway and its appurtenances shall be confided to police agents appointed by the Company." After eighty years the railroad was to become Chinese property without payment. Thirty-six years after its completion China could purchase it by paying to the Company the full outlay with interest. Construction of the Chinese Eastern Railway was completed in 1904. From this great trunk line, nearly 1,000 miles in length, Russia hoped to build a political and commercial empire, providing easy access to the Pacific and insuring Russian economic dominance in North China. This was the Russian policy called *peaceful penetration*.

THE YAMAGATA-LOBANOV AGREEMENT

Li Hung-chang was not the only distinguished Oriental guest at the Russian coronation in 1896. Japan was represented by Yamagata Aritomo, the most powerful of the Choshu clansmen, father of the modern Japanese army, and, in his day, the leading exponent of the military tradition. The Japanese wanted a compromise settlement of Russo-Japanese rivalry in Korea, a compromise that would maintain the balance until the army and navy expansion program could be effected. Accordingly, Yamagata proposed to the Rusians that the two powers divide Korea at the 38th parallel into a northern Russian sphere and a southern Japanese sphere, an arrangement that would give the Japanese control of Seoul, the capital. But the Russians turned down the offer. For the present they regarded it as good policy to play along with England and the United States, respecting the integrity of Korea. In the long run, they hoped to get control of the entire peninsula. As a result, two general and unsatisfactory compromise agreements were reached. At Seoul the Russian and Japanese representatives advised the Korean king to return as soon as possible to his palace from his refuge in the Russian legation. The Japanese were to withdraw most of their troops. This understanding reached at Seoul (May 26) was supplemented by the Yamagata-Lobanov Agreement made at Moscow (June 9). Both powers would support the Korean king's efforts to restore and maintain order; both would guarantee foreign loans so that adequate police could be maintained and foreign intervention avoided. Korea was thus recognized as a Russo-Japanese joint problem. A secret article provided that in case it became necessary to send troops to Korea, the two powers would consult with a view to fixing a neutral zone between their spheres of action. Korea had become a kind of joint protectorate.[5]

GERMANY AND THE FAR EAST

The German intervention against Japan in 1895 had been prompted not only by the desire to involve Russia in the Far East and thus weaken the Franco-Russian alliance in Europe, but also by the German ambition to secure a naval and commercial base in China. All during the last quarter of the nineteenth century, Germany had possessed very able scientific as well as diplomatic representation in the Far East. To the diplomatic and political knowledge concerning Asia from such men as von Brandt was added scientific, geographic, and social-economic data from such authorities as Ferdinand von Richthofen, perhaps the outstanding European authority of the time on China. It was he who dramatized for Europe the dire consequences that must follow when Asiatic labor was turned loose upon the world. It was he also who first pointed out the strategic and economic advantages of Kiaochou on the South Shantung coast; but for a time Germany appeared to be more interested in various islands on the Korean coasts, and in Wei-hai-wei, Chusan, Woosung, Amoy, Samsah Bay, and Mirs Bay.[6]

The German decision to take Kiaochou was made in the summer of 1897. This deci-

[5] William L. Langer, *The Diplomacy of Imperialism, 1890–1902* (1935; 2nd. ed. in one vol., 1951), I, 405–7.

[6] German commercial and colonial activity in the Pacific area dated back to the activities of Hamburg merchants in Samoa (1857); by 1885 Germany had possession of a large section of New Guinea, and of the Bismarck and the Marshall Islands.

sion rested on the enthusiasm of the Kaiser, on the reports of Admiral von Tirpitz, who was in command of the German far eastern fleet in 1896, and on the reports of German harbor-construction engineers. To avoid any collision with Russia, whose fleet had already wintered at Kiaochou, thus setting up a sort of priority in the place, the Kaiser appealed to the tsar and was seemingly given a green light. Accordingly, Germany notified China of her need for this harbor. Apparently the plan was for the German fleet, uninvited, to winter at Kiaochou—a friendly but unmistakable gesture calculated to bring the Chinese to terms. But the way was made easier when, in November 1897, two German Catholic missionaries were killed by Chinese robbers in southern Shantung. Admiral von Diederich landed German troops at Kiaochou Bay. For a time the Chinese government refused to come to terms. The mandarins were encouraged by the Russians to resist, but by January, 1898, the Russian opposition had subsided, and on March 6, Germany secured her agreement with China. This convention was prefaced with the remark that "The Imperial Chinese Government consider it advisable to give a special proof of their grateful appreciation of the friendship shown to them by Germany." How deep this "friendship" was, and how significant its results, may be judged from the terms of the convention. It provided, among other things: (1) a so-called "neutral" zone 50 kilometers wide surrounding Kiaochou Bay, in which zone China would permit the free movement of German troops, and in which China would take no measures without the consent of Germany; (2) a 99-year lease to Germany for both sides of the entrance to Kiaochou Bay, including the port of Tsingtao as a naval base; (3) the exercise by Germany during the term of the lease of sovereign powers over the leased area; (4) a Chinese pledge to "cede to Germany a more suitable place" in the event that the Germans returned the territory prior to the expiration of the lease; (5) a German pledge not to "sublet" the territory to another power; (6) permission for the construction of two railways by a Sino-German company in which the nationals of both powers might invest; (7) the right of Germans to mine coal within 30 *li* (10 miles) of the railways; and, finally, (8)

> . . . *the Chinese Government binds itself in all cases where foreign assistance, in persons, capital or material, may be needed for any purpose whatever within the Province of Shantung, to offer the said work or supplying of materials in the first instance to German manufacturers and merchants engaged in undertakings of the kind in question.*[7]

RUSSIA LEASES PORT ARTHUR

Germany's descent upon Kiaochou necessitated changes in Russia's plans. She had considered taking Kiaochou herself in the winter of 1895–1896. Although the Germans had taken the one good naval harbor in North China, there were still plenty of harbors in Korea. Back in Moscow in 1896 Li Hung-chang had even advised the Russians to take a Korean port. But when in late 1897 Russia turned to Korea and attempted to make a Russian the financial adviser of the king and to oust a Britisher, M'Leavy Brown, from control of the Korean customs, she was met with the appearance of a strong Anglo-Japanese squadron in the harbor of Chemulpo. Accordingly, in November, 1897, the Russian government began to consider occupation of the harbor of Talienwan on the Liaotung Peninsula in South Manchuria a few miles northeast of Port Arthur. In Peking, the Chinese government, though petitioned by some of the most powerful viceroys, such as Chang Chih-tung, to seek an alliance with Japan and England, had already determined on a policy of surrender. And so, in March 1898, less than three weeks after Germany had leased Kiaochou, China leased to Russia for twenty-five years the southern tip of the Liaotung Peninsula containing Port Arthur and Talienwan. This was the spot from which Russia, France, and

[7] John V. A. MacMurray, ed., *Treaties and Agreements with and concerning China, 1894–1919* (2 vols., 1921), 1, 112–16.

Germany had ousted Japan three years earlier. North of the leased area was to be a neutral zone stretching to the base of the peninsula. Finally, the convention granted to the Chinese Eastern Railway Company the right to connect Talienwan by rail with the main line in Central Manchuria. Thus, to quote the terms of the agreement, Russia's naval forces had acquired "an entirely secure base on the littoral of northern China."

FRANCE LEASES KWANGCHOU BAY

During the winter of 1897–1898, when Germany and Russia were maturing their plans at Kiaochou and Port Arthur, France did not appear disposed to play an active role in China. French political leaders were paying lip service to the principle of China's integrity. Yet it was obvious that France was not unaffected by the German and Russian moves. Since 1885 France has possessed a great empire of colonies and "protectorates" in Indochina. In that year China had renounced control over Annam, had agreed to respect Franco-Annamite agreements, and had promised to open two cities in Yunnan to French commerce. In 1895, French influence, now more strongly entrenched in northern Indochina (Annam and Tongking), was looking to industrial concessions across the frontier in China's southern provinces. Within a month of the famous Triple Intervention of that year, France reaped her first reward. In June 1895, it was agreed that

> . . . *for the exploitation of its mines in the provinces of Yunnan, Kwangsi, and Kwangtung, [China] may call upon, in the first instance, French manufacturers and engineers* . . .

The principle that the railways of Annam might be extended into China was also agreed upon. Following close on the heels of this agreement, France in June, 1896, secured from China a concession to construct a railroad in Kwangsi from the border of Tongking to Lungchow. In the same year a French expedition explored the interior of the island of Hainan, and in January China promised France never to alienate it to any other power. It is not surprising, then, that France was ready with new demands once Germany and Russia had taken action at Kiaochou and Port Arthur. The gains of France were extensive. In April 1898, China agreed not to alienate any of her territories on the border of Tongking (northern Annam). At the same time she agreed: (1) to grant France a concession for a railroad from Tongking to Yunnan-fu; (2) to lease to France for 99 years the bay of Kwang-chou as a naval station and coaling depot; and (3) to appoint Frenchmen as advisers to the newly proposed Chinese postal service. These measures were designed not only to give France a strategic foothold and industrial concessions in South China, but also to draw Chinese commerce away from British influence at Hongkong and Canton and to center it under French control in the Gulf of Tongking.

GREAT BRITAIN: KOWLOON, WEI-HAI-WEI

The British government during 1897–1898 had failed to place any effective restraints on the development of German, Russian, or French policy in China. British policy had been basically commercial rather than political, but it could hardly remain unaffected by the new position now occupied in China by the other great European powers. In other words, if leaseholds, preferential concessions, and special spheres were to be the order of the day, it behooved England, so ran the argument, to have her share. From February through July, 1898, Britain and China concluded a series of agreements of the utmost importance. China agreed: (1) never to alienate any territory in the Yangtze Valley; (2) that the Inspector-General of the Chinese Maritime Customs should be a British subject so long as British trade predominated; (3) to lease Wei-hai-wei to Britain as a naval harbor "for so long a period as Port Arthur shall remain in the occupation of Russia"; (4) to extend the

British territory of Kowloon in a 99-year lease over the entire peninsula lying between Deep Bay and the Mirs Bay. With this British advance should be noted also an Anglo-German loan to China in the amount of £ 16,000,000, and various preliminary agreements between the Hongkong and Shanghai Banking Corporation and Chinese authorities concerning the financing of the Shanghai-Nanking and the Peking-Newchwang Railways. By November, 1898, the British had secured nine railroad concessions totaling 2,800 miles; the Russians, three concessions, 1,500 miles; the Belgians, one concession, 650 miles; the French, three concessions, 300 miles.[8]

These developments, culminating in the spring and summer of 1898, made it quite evident that the integrity of China was worth very little. Germany, Russia, and France had all expressed great respect for this principle, but their leaseholds and their railroad and non-alienation agreements indicated that these protestations were not to be taken too seriously. It was obvious that an era of special and exclusive privilege was dawning in China. Britain disliked the tendency, for she had more to gain in an open market where all traded on terms of equality. But no power, not even the United States, would align itself with the British. Consequently, Downing Street, having protested, decided to join the robbers.[9] In London, opponents of this policy of imitation spoke in sarcastic terms of "Port Arthur Balfour" and "a triumph of diplomatic incompetency." The Opposition called Wei-hai-wei, "Woe! Woe! Woe!" The fact was that the four great powers of Europe had begun the serious business of tampering seriously with Chinese sovereignty. To be sure, each of the leasehold agreements carefully reserved to China her

[8] Details on railroad concessions in Sun E-tu Zen, *Chinese Railways and British Interests,* 1898–1911 (1954).

[9] On British policy at this time it should be said that the only way to stop Russia in Manchuria was to fight her, and Britain had no intention of doing that. It would have been a dubious undertaking. Geography would have favored Russia.

full sovereignty in the leased areas. But as Langer has said: "This was mere camouflage and the statesmen knew it." The most serious phase of the business was that in 1898 there was no unity of purpose within China herself, no constructive program of reform and resistance, and, in the main, no able leadership.

THE PHILIPPINES

This avalanche of economic and political concession-hunting which had descended upon China in the years 1895 to 1898 was a natural expansive movement, though not necessarily a desirable one, deriving its momentum from the industrial revolution in Europe. Often described by the none too descriptive label, economic imperialism, the movement though basically European had also developed, in addition, by 1898 a somewhat uncertain American base.

It has been said with some truth that in the months that preceded May 1898, no idea was perhaps so remote from the mind of the American people as the conquest and acquisition of the Philippine Islands off the coast of South China. Yet within the year that followed, the United States had taken unto itself a great Asiatic territory 6,000 miles from San Francisco across the Pacific, had projected itself into the main currents of world politics; and had discarded, so it seemed, some of its most deeply rooted traditions. These stirring events came just at the moment when Europe seemed bent on the dismemberment of China.

To Americans there was nothing new in the acquisition of contiguous territory. The nineteenth century was filled with the territorial advance of Americans through Louisiana and Florida, through Texas to the Rio Grande and California, and across the plains of Kansas to Oregon. The movement was completed by mid-century. The thought was that it was now the business of Americans to remain at home to develop what they already possessed. Nevertheless, a new extracontinental, overseas expansion had already been

foreshadowed. In Seward's purchase of Alaska, 1867,[10] there was the suggestion of the earlier ideas of Commodore Perry in Japan and Peter Parker in China that the United States needed coaling and naval stations on far eastern islands: Formosa, the Ryukyus, and the Bonins. As early as 1854 President Pierce and Secretary of State Marcy tried but failed to annex the Hawaiian Islands by treaty. The Midway Islands were easier marks. A thousand miles northwest of Hawaii, they were occupied by an American naval force in August, 1867. In 1878 the American Navy acquired the use of a harbor in the far distant Samoan Islands of the South Pacific, and a decade later the State Department resisted German encroachment there with vigor.[11] This official American interest in Samoa and the harbor of Pago Pago, 5,600 miles from Panama, was significant because it was an

> . . . assertion by the United States, not merely of a willingness, but even of a right to take part in determining the fate of a remote and semi-barbarous people whose possessions lay far outside the traditional sphere of American political interests.[12]

And, if previously Americans had not been seriously interested in annexing Hawaii, the Senate in 1887 secured an equivalent, the exclusive right for the United States to use Pearl Harbor as a naval station, and, by 1893, Americans were debating with a good deal of heat the proposals of the Harrison administration to bring the islands under the American flag. Against the pro-expansionist arguments of Captain Alfred T. Mahan, that

[10] On the Alaska purchase, see V. J. Farrar, *The Annexation of Russian America to the United States* (1937); F. A. Golder, "The Purchase of Alaska," *The American Historical Review* 25 (1920): 411–25; T. A. Bailey, "Why the United States Purchased Alaska," *The Pacific Historical Review* 3 (1934): 39–49; and the popular account in F. R. Dulles, *America in the Pacific* (1932), Chapter 6.

[11] George H. Ryden, *The Foreign Policy of the United States in Relation to Samoa* (1933), Chapters 7–9.

[12] John Bassett Moore, in *The Cambridge Modern History*, VII, 663.

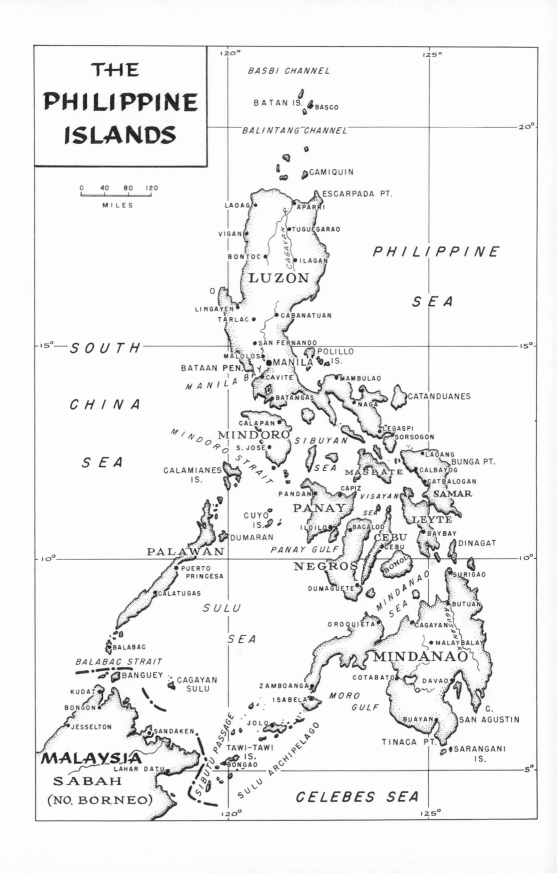

the islands controlled the commerce of the North Pacific and were strategically essential, were those of the anti-expansionists and anti-annexationists: men such as Carl Schurz, E. L. Godkin, editor of *The Nation*, and James Gordon Bennett, Jr., publisher of the Democratic *New York Herald*. This opposition to expansion expressed views running the gamut from the constitutional and ideological objections of Schurz to the polemics of Godkin, who asserted that if Hawaii were admitted to the Union,

> . . . *men would come into our Senate worse than those from Nevada, Wyoming and Idaho and which will be sent from Utah, Arizona, New Mexico and Oklahoma after they are admitted into the Union.*[13]

BLOCKING THE NEW MANIFEST DESTINY

So it was that in the decades immediately preceding the threatened partition of China the American mind had not kept pace with "the march of events in the Pacific." The official arm of the United States had already carried the Stars and Stripes far afield, to Alaska and the Aleutians, to Midway and to Samoa, and finally to Pearl Harbor. Yet the vast majority of Americans had no interest in these places, no understanding of why their government was projecting itself into foreign fields, and certainly no thought of setting up a colony in Asia itself. Disciples of the New Manifest Destiny, of imperialism, there were, but they were few compared with those Americans who followed the more timid philosophy of Grover Cleveland, called by the expansionists "the Buffalo lilliputian!"[14] Even American "big business," usually con-

[13] E. L. Godkin, "Hawaii," *The Nation* 56 (1893): 96.
[14] For further readings on the beginnings of American imperialism in the Pacific, see J. W. Pratt, *Expansionists of 1898* (1936),* Chapter 1, "The New Manifest Destiny"; H. W. Bradley, "The American Frontier in Hawaii," *Proceedings, Pacific Coast Branch, American Historical Association*, 1930, 135–50; Allan Nevins, *Grover Cleveland* (1934), Chapter 30; C. C. Tansill, *The Foreign Policy of Thomas F. Bayard, 1885–1897* (1940), Chapter 12; A. T. Volwiler, "Har-

sidered the spearhead of imperialism, was, with exceptions to be noted later, content to stay at home. In 1893 no less a person than the vice-president of the Great Northern Railroad was saying publicly that

> . . . *he [the Chinaman] is as poor as a rat, and has nothing with which to pay for our high-priced products except silk handkerchiefs and bamboo pipes. . . . The Great Northern is coming here to do business with the Pacific slope, not with Asia.*

THE NEW FAR EASTERN POLICY IN THE MAKING

Nevertheless, a new far eastern policy for the United States was taking shape in the minds of some Americans. It voiced a point of view that added new political ideas to old commercial ones.[15] The patron saint of the new and large policy of expansion, John Louis O'Sullivan, close associate of Polk, Pierce, and Buchanan, and coiner of the phrase "Manifest Destiny," died in 1895; but his philosophy was kept alive by John W. Burgess of Columbia University, under whom Theodore Roosevelt sat as a student, and by Captain Alfred Thayer Mahan, whose lectures at the Naval War College were later published under the title, *The Influence of Sea Power upon History*. The composite doctrine, the larger policy, that emerged from the writings and speeches of these men and others was that the United States had come of age;

rison, Blaine, and American Foreign Policy, 1889–1893," *American Philosophical Society Proceedings*, 79 (1938): 637–48.
[15] A. Whitney Griswold, *The Far Eastern Policy of the United States* (1938),* 8. Thomas J. McCormick, *The China Market: America's Quest for Informal Empire, 1893–1901* (1967) explores the background of the decisions to annex Hawaii, Guam, and the Philippines, and to dispatch the Open Door Notes. He concludes that American action was influenced less by the accidents of war, pressures of public opinion, or force of personalities than by an evolving purpose on the part of the Cleveland and McKinley administrations to discover ways to assist in the development of American foreign trade. Josefa M. Saniel, *Japan and the Philippines, 1868–1898* (1963).

that it could no longer be held within the old continental borders; that the commerce of the world was beckoning to American enterprise; that benighted areas and backward people were calling to the beneficent forces in American civilization; in a word, that we could no longer ignore the responsibilities of the "white man's burden" to civilize and to Christianize less fortunate peoples.

To a notable degree the stage was already set for new adventures in American foreign policy when, on April 19, 1898, the Congress of the United States passed a joint resolution that precipitated the Spanish-American War. Actually, the roots of this war were connected only remotely, if at all, with the white man's burden and the larger policy it entailed. There were few Americans in the spring of 1898 who entertained any notion that the war with Spain would place the United States among the great colonial powers, much less that the principal new colonies would lie on the fringe of Asia. There was in fact no official suggestion that, if war came, it was to lead to colonies at all. On the contrary, the war resolution voiced traditional principles associated with the Monroe Doctrine. It stated that Cuba was and ought to be free "of right"; it demanded the withdrawal of Spain; it instructed the President to secure these ends by use of the armed forces; and it expressly denied any intent on the part of the United States to annex Cuba.

In reality, however, the American policy and purpose which was to emerge during and immediately following the Spanish-American War had a much clearer identity than the vague shibboleths of the "larger policy" would imply. The condition of the American economy after 1870, culminating in the panic of 1893, had suggested to some industrialists and politicians that industrial overproduction could only be cured through over-seas markets. Therefore foreign markets must be kept open to insure equal commercial opportunity for Americans. In the vast Pacific, so it was said, there would be the need for island stepping-stones to major markets such as China which, defeated by Japan in 1895, would surely awaken and throw open her doors to American commerce.

These ideas also found support in the thinking of American naval strategists concerning a possible war with Spain. This thinking included a plan for an attack on the Spanish fleet at Manila, a plan which was known by McKinley as early as September, 1897. Thus a Pacific offensive was already an accepted plan when Theodore Roosevelt became Assistant Secretary of the Navy. Roosevelt wanted a war to annex the Philippines, and the evidence suggests that not only he but others, including perhaps the President himself, were not unaware that the conflict could result in annexation of the Islands. If the opportunity came it would not be unwelcome to many industrialists. Certainly nothing should be done to impede it. Nevertheless, these speculative factors were a secondary consideration in the shaping of war plans. The main objective was quick and effective damage to Spain. When Roosevelt in October 1897, sent George Dewey to command the American Asiatic squadron, and later cabled him, in the event of war, to destroy the Spanish fleet in the Philippines, the basic purpose was to win a war, not to open a market in China.[16]

[16] The last word has not yet been written on American thinking and resulting policy in this period. On the role of naval interests, see W. R. Braisted, *The United States Navy in the Pacific, 1897–1909* (1958). Walter LaFeber, *The New Empire: An Interpretation of American Expansion* (1963)* sets forth the economic underpinnings of American decisions. Thomas McCormick, "Insular Imperialism and the Open Door," *The Pacific Historical Review* 32 (1963): 155–69 applies LaFeber's insights to the annexation of Pacific islands. A lively argument persists between the economic determinists and their critics. The latter admit that the economic transformation of the United States provided stimulus to the new and large policy, but that too much stress has been given to economic arguments. Some of the economic arguments were simply absurd save as corollaries of "duty and destiny." In assessing the force of economic factors, it has been pointed out that the determinists often neglect the differences in means advocated by those who were agreed on the need for increased government aid to business. Some were annexationists, mild or extreme. Others advocated expanding foreign markets through an assertive diplomatic service, or reform of the consular service, or construction of an isthmian canal.

When war did come, Dewey moved his fleet thirty miles up the China coast into the Chinese waters of Mirs Bay, "an isolated locality" where, "independent of international complications," supplies could be received secretly and temporary repairs effected. "We appreciated that so loosely organized a national entity as the Chinese Empire could not enforce the neutrality laws," wrote Dewey.[17]

Dewey's fleet sailed for the Philippines on April 27. On the morning of May 1, while it was yet dark, his ships passed the guns of Corregidor, and sent the Spanish fleet to the bottom as it clung to its base at Cavite. Dewey promptly established a blockade of the bay and city of Manila, while he informed Washington that the city could be taken but that 5,000 men would be needed to hold it. In Washington, the decision to send troops to the support of Dewey involved many questions. No clear political policy as to the future of the Philippines had yet emerged, and even the future of the immediate military policy was in a formative and tentative stage. For what specific purposes were the troops to be sent? Were they to engage in the conquest of the entire archipelago? How many troops would be sent? Illogically, the last question was answered first. The fact was that Dewey's dramatic victory had taken the country by surprise. Neither the government nor the people were prepared for the vital decisions that the victory demanded. Thus McKinley's cabinet, groping for an immediate and future policy, dispatched troops to Manila, where by the end of July some 8,000 had arrived. This was to make possible the eventual capture of Manila, but it did not clarify the political atmosphere in the islands where Filipino nationalists with American encouragement and assistance had taken the field against Spain, and with Dewey's approval harassed the outskirts of Manila while the American commodore awaited the arrival of an American army.

REVOLT IN THE PHILIPPINES

Who were these Filipino patriots, who, like the Americans, were fighting against Spain? Prior to the Spanish conquest of the islands in the sixteenth century there was no strong national or political structure in the Philippines. With the completion of the Spanish conquest, which by the close of the sixteenth century reached all parts of the archipelago save Palawan and the Moro country, the islands passed under a unified control. Slavery was abolished in law if not in fact, and the natives were converted to Catholicism. However, economic progress under the Spanish regime was slow. Agricultural methods remained antiquated until well into the nineteenth century, while excessive restrictions on trade hampered commercial development. Under remnants of feudal practice, Spain at first controlled all the land, conducting its administration through the *encomienda* system. With the failure and subsequent abolition of this system, the control of local affairs passed largely into the hands of the regular clergy (known as the friars). The clergy, as missionaries, were close to the natives; they had mastered the native tongues, and had frequently protected their converts from the injustice of the *encomienderos*. In addition, the union of church and state in the Philippines was even more intimate than the corresponding union in Spain. Thus, while in law the governor general might appear all-powerful, he acted, and usually wished to act, in close collaboration with the hierarchy of the religious orders. The system meant that the Filipino lived through more than two centuries of political stagnation until in the nineteenth century a political awakening began to draw inspiration from liberal movements in Europe and the democratic struggle within Spain itself.

These distinctions are important since they suggest that the emerging American drive to the Western Pacific was based less on rational calculation than it has sometimes been said to be. Note the comments of Marilyn Blatt Young, "American Expansion, 1870–1900: The Far East," *Towards a New Past: Dissenting Essays in American History.* Barton J. Bernstein, ed. (1968),* 176–201, an able criticism of economic interpretations.

[17] *Autobiography of George Dewey* (1916), 175–90.

In part, too, the movement was a revolt against the increasingly oppressive rule of the friars.[18]

Leaders of the Philippine Revolt

The last quarter of the nineteenth century produced a number of Filipino students, writers, and political agitators who became aggressive in their demands for reform. Marcelo H. Del Pilar attacked the friars as the principal enemy of both the church and the state. Jose Rizal wrote political novels revealing the social, political, and economic backwardness of his people. These books, though condemned by the friars, found their way secretly into thousands of homes. Rizal, a man of education, culture, and letters, who had studied abroad, founded in 1892 the Liga Filipina, through which he hoped to raise the economic, social, and educational life of his people. Far more radical in method and purpose were Andres Bonifacio and Emilio Aguinaldo, who were associated with a new secret society, the Katipunan. This organization, definitely plebeian and revolutionary, contemplated destruction of the power of Spain, of the friars, and of the great landlords. Discovery of its plans resulted in a premature revolt in 1896. Rizal, unjustly accused of inspiring the rising, was executed, and thereby was to become the Philippine national hero. During 1897 the revolt was suppressed. But reforms were not forthcoming, and the result was that on the eve of the Spanish-American War sporadic revolts were again occurring even though most of the leaders were in exile.

Aguinaldo, one of the exiles, was at Singapore when Dewey entered Manila Bay. The Commodore, advised of this fact by an American consul, first encouraged and then actively aided Aguinaldo's return to Manila on an American dispatch boat. At Manila, Aguinaldo was assisted further with supplies and rifles from the Cavite arsenal in recruiting a new revolutionary army. In May 1898 Aguinaldo proclaimed his revolutionary government and announced his purpose to liberate the islands from Spain. In June the revolutionary government named Aguinaldo president, and adopted a constitution proclaiming independence. In August this government petitioned foreign powers for recognition of its belligerent status and for recognition of independence in the Philippines. A week later, after the newly arrived American troops had occupied lines that Aguinaldo's insurgents had thrown about the city, Manila capitulated to the American forces. This occurred only a few hours after a protocol of peace had been signed at Washington by the United States and Spain, August 12, 1898 (August 13, 5:30 a.m. Manila time).

THE EMBARRASSMENTS OF VICTORY

From May 1, the date of Dewey's naval victory, until February 6, 1899, when the Senate ratified the Treaty of Paris by a margin of only two votes, the government and the people of the United States were embarrassed by a naval victory which had given them a tropical archipelago and some six to seven million "little brown wards." At first the experience was intoxicating. When the news came of Dewey's triumph,

> . . . the country went wild with excitement. "Dewey Days" were celebrated in the principal cities. Streets were renamed for Dewey. Young women wore "Dewey" sailor hats, sipped "Dewey" cocktails, chewed "Dewey Chewies"—a new brand of gum—and wrote letters on "Dewey blue" stationery. Men smoked cigars made of Sampson Havana filler and Dewey Manila wrappers, while those who were so inclined resorted to the corner saloon and called for Dewey brand whiskey. Meanwhile the President notified Congress that: "At this unsurpassed achievement the great heart of our nation throbs, not with boasting or with greed of conquest, but with deep gratitude that this triumph has come in a just cause . . ."[19]

But the problem of what to do with these Oriental fruits of victory still remained.

[18] Maximo M. Kalaw, *The Development of Philippine Politics, 1872–1920* (1926), 1–19.

[19] H. R. Lynn, *The Genesis of America's Philippine Policy* (University of Kentucky, 1935), in manuscript, 8.

THE EMERGENCE OF A POLICY

207

China,
1890s:
Foreign
Pressures

The expansionists wanted annexation of all the Philippines. Senator Henry Cabot Lodge urged the larger policy on McKinley and his Secretary of State, Judge William R. Day. Then, early in July, the Congress, by joint resolution, annexed the Hawaiian Islands, and by the time Manila fell, public opinion and pressure groups were swinging definitely toward the larger policy. There were petitions to Congress and to the State Department picturing the Philippines as the key to far eastern commerce. Publications of the Protestant churches favored annexation almost unanimously, for church editors saw God's hand and new mission fields in Dewey's victory.

In addition, McKinley was now attaching more and more importance to public opinion. The earlier public clamor for war with Spain was very fresh in his mind. It was easy for him to be persuaded that the people wanted the Philippines and therefore that they should be retained. Some interpretations go so far as to say that McKinley thought only of his own and his party's leadership and was concerned only incidentally about real or imagined interests abroad.[20]

Powerful forces in international politics also exerted pressure on McKinley and his cabinet. Great Britain and Germany were dominated by their bitter colonial rivalry. Each was determined that the Philippines should not fall into the hands of the other if by chance the United States turned them loose. Great Britain, whose attitude when the war began was in doubt, later urged Washington to retain the islands. England did not wish to be placed in a position where she would have to oppose German claims directly. Unquestionably, the Germans were interested. They had hoped to prevent the war. They were alarmed by signs of Anglo-American friendship and the prospects of American commercial rivalry in Asia. During the war German public opinion, favorable to

Spain, had aroused the suspicions of Americans, who were still sensitive over the Samoan affair. Then, too, there was a story, widely believed, that at Manila the German admiral, von Diederich, had interfered with Dewey's blockade, and had withdrawn only when threatened by a British squadron. This was a far cry from what actually happened, but the incident served none the less to arouse American resentment, and so to support the advocates of American annexation.[21] Japan's attitude at the time was not very significant. Her influence, such as it was, was added to England's urging American annexation.

The Protocol of Peace, drawn up by McKinley's cabinet and signed with Spain, August 12, was diplomatically vague concerning the future status of the islands, though it foreshadowed occupation of at least part of them. But the implications of the Protocol were soon reflected in the appointment by McKinley of a peace commission that was dominated by expansionists. While the commissioners sailed toward Paris, John Hay was crossing from the London embassy to become Secretary of State and to be one of the decisive influences on McKinley's final decision (October 26): "The cession must be of the whole archipelago or none."

The Treaty of Paris was not signed until December 10, 1898, for Spain's opposition to relinquishment of the Philippines was persistent and bitter. The Spanish commissioners had not been slow to point out that in their view the United States could not claim the Philippines by right of conquest, since Manila had been captured several hours after the signing of the Protocol of Peace. Thus the Treaty, which set up American sovereignty in the Philippines, Puerto Rico, and Guam and provided for Spain's withdrawal from Cuba, also stipulated that the United States pay Spain $20,000,000.

[20] See Ernest R. May, *Imperial Democracy: the Emergence of America as a Great Power* (1961).

[21] T. A. Bailey, "Dewey and the Germans at Manila Bay," *The American Historical Review* 45 (1939): 59–81; L. B. Shippee, 'Germany and the Spanish-American War," *The American Historical Review* 30 (1925): 754–77.

One more hurdle remained: ratification of the Treaty by the Senate. This was secured February 6, 1899, by the dangerously narrow margin of two votes. It was preceded by some of the most dramatic debates in the Senate, in the press, and on the public platform. The arguments centered primarily on the Philippines. In Congress the opposition to expansion and imperialism was led by Senator George F. Hoar of Massachusetts. His eloquence opposing imperialism failed to curb the popular enthusiasm for empire either within or outside Congress. Even then the result was in doubt until news of the outbreak of the Filipino insurrection against American control (February 4) raised the issue of national honor and strengthened the hands of the annexationists. Certainly one of the most momentous decisions of American history had been made. The United States had acquired a dependency—a dependency that was already in armed revolt against its new master. Truly, this country was entering the arena of world politics the hard way. She had fought a war to free Cuba; what she got was a colony in Eastern Asia. Moreover, this colony was acquired at a rather embarrassing moment. If the United States had any design to protest the inroads of the powers on China, she could now do so with little grace for she herself had become an empire in Asia.

FOR FURTHER READING

CHINA: REFERENCE AND ORIENTATION. Joseph R. Levenson, *Liang Ch'i-ch'ao and the Mind of Modern China* (1953),* an intellectual history of modern China. Liang Ch'i-ch'ao, *Intellectual Trends in the Ch'ing Period*, trans. with introduction and notes by Immanuel C. Y. Hsu (1959) contains the memoirs of one of the leading revolutionaries of the late nineteenth century. Benjamin I. Schwartz, *In Search of Wealth and Power, Yen Fu and the West* (1964).

TRADE, INVESTMENT, TREATIES. C. F. Remer, *The Foreign Trade of China* (1926). C. F. Remer, *Foreign Investments in China* (1933). John van Antwerp MacMurray, *Treaties and Agreements With and Concerning China, 1894–1919* (2 vols., 1921), indispensable for reference. Cheng Yu-kwei, *Foreign Trade and Industrial Development of China: An Historical and Integrated Analysis Through 1948* (1956), a convenient factual summary covering the century of the Western impact, but the interpretations are open to serious qualifications.

THE DIPLOMACY OF THE POWERS. Philip Joseph, *Foreign Diplomacy in China, 1894–1900* (London, 1928). R. Stanley McCordock, *British Far Eastern Policy 1894–1900* (1931). John F. Cady, *The Roots of French Imperialism in Eastern Asia* (1954), a thorough and able study. D. J. Dallin, *The Rise of Russia in Asia* (1949) traces the rise of Russia as an Asiatic power. Andrew Malozemoff, *Russian Far Eastern Policy, 1881–1904 with Special Emphasis on the Causes of the Russo-Japanese War* (1958). G. A. Ballard, *Influence of the Sea on the Political History of Japan* (1921) is a naval rather than an historical analysis. Francis Hilary Conroy, *The Japanese Frontier in Hawaii, 1868–1898* (1953), an account of the establishment of the Japanese community in Hawaii prior to annexation. T. A. Bailey, "Japan's Protest against the Annexation of Hawaii," *The Journal of Modern History* 3 (1931): 46–61. Paul H. Clyde, *International Rivalries in Manchuria* (rev. ed., 1928) is a general survey of international relations affecting Manchuria. Marilyn B. Young, *The Rhetoric of Empire: American China Policy, 1895–1901* (1968). Akira Iriye, "Imperialism in East Asia," *Modern East Asia: Essays in Interpretation*, James B. Crowley, ed. (1970),* 123–50.

China, 1890–1901: Artless Reform and Blind Reaction

chapter 16

China in the last decade of the nineteenth century was a pitiful shadow of a great Confucian civilization. The comfortable and once realistic concept of China as the center of a natural world order, fringed with weaker satellites unable to compare with her in power, wealth, culture, and virtue, had become an empty pretense. For half a century, since 1840, the Manchu-Chinese scholar-officials had fumbled with the task of saving and revitalizing their Confucian vehicle for government and power. To this end they had used the means that were familiar to them: force plus persuasion, conciliation, enticing barbarian to fight barbarian, and finally the long but uneven effort in self-strengthening. All had failed. The onerous defeat at the hands of the despised Japanese, 1894–1895, mocked the very idea of the Middle Kingdom.

Indeed, there was evidence that China, or rather the Ch'ing dynasty, had made its bargain with the West. It had come to accept the foreigner, however unwillingly, with his treaty ports, settlements and concessions, treaty tariffs and extraterritoriality, and his management of the great Imperial Maritime Customs Service under Sir Robert Hart. It was not a happy acceptance, but it was a profitable one for the merchant, whether Chinese or foreign, and there was the possibility that, if the powers were reasonable, acceptance might even strengthen the dynasty. The late nineteenth century was the great day of commercial development between China and the West. It was the era especially of British prosperity in the treaty ports. These commercial good times were shared also by the Chinese merchants of the ports and by political leaders such as Li Hung-chang. It was the continuing support (albeit always for a price) which the powers had given to Peking since the T'ai-p'ing threat and the treaties of 1858 that had enabled the dynasty to live on in smug senility. Thus the bargain was more than a bargain. It was an uneasy and delicate balance of pressures. It was a balance personified by the foreign trader naturally concerned with profits, by the Chinese trader and official torn between profits and cultural humiliation, and by a resourceful concubine in Peking, who, having made herself master of the dynasty, was intent on the single purpose of preserving her court and her power. This temporary equilibrium explains why it was that before 1890 there appeared to be little Chinese response to the West, no answer to the barbarian challenge other than stagnation, no thought of a new China to meet a new world. These complacent trends were the mood of official China when in 1894 the Japanese struck in Korea, ushering in the later scramble of the powers to divide the spoils.[1]

Yet the picture involved more than stagnation. There were men in China who were not content to let time take its course, men who believed that China's salvation lay in ideological and institutional reform. Their influence was becoming positive as the end of the century drew near. There is reason, then, to note who these men were, to examine the nature of the reforms they proposed, and to observe the fate that befell their efforts.

REFORM AND CHRISTIAN MISSIONS

The complex processes through which Western influence stimulated a reform movement in China are known as yet very imperfectly, but it is clear that the Christian missionary, particularly English and American Protestants, played an important part. What the missionary said and did shaped in some major degree the ideas that the Chinese held concerning the West. Moreover, the Protestant missions especially came to have a broad social as well as a religious purpose. They were concerned to improve, through education, the lot of the convert in this world as well as in the world to come. From the earliest days schools were regarded as an essential part of the missionary establishment. Shortly after 1830 two of the first American Protestant missionaries at Canton, David Abeel (1804–1846) and E. C. Bridgman (1801–1861), opened a school and began publication of the famous *The Chinese Repository* (1832–1851). The first American missionary hospital and medical school at Canton was the work of Peter Parker (1804–1888). After the second treaty settlement (1858–1860), which legalized inland missions, there was a marked expansion in both Catholic and Protestant establishments. English and American Protestant missionary

scholars took the lead with the assistance of Chinese associates in publishing Chinese translations and digests of Western books on history, literature, and science. Among the Britishers contributing to this cultural invasion were William Muirhead (1822–1900), Joseph Edkins (1823–1905), Alexander Wylie (1815–1887), James Legge (1815–1897), translator of the Confucian classics, and Timothy Richard (1845–1919), who at the invitation of Li Hung-chang edited a Chinese daily at Tientsin. The Americans included W. A. P. Martin (1827–1916), S. Wells Williams (1812–1884), John Fryer (1839–1923), and Young J. Allen (1836–1907). Fryer and Allen compiled and translated into Chinese the first textbook in science for Chinese students.[2]

However, the cultural influence of the missionary in support of reform was limited in many ways. His direct contacts were confined to the treaty ports and a few inland posts. He reached only a handful of the scholar-official and gentry classes. By the officials and gentry as a whole, the missionary was regarded as a subversive influence, especially when he sought to protect his converts from the course of Chinese justice, a practice especially notable among Catholic missionaries. Furthermore, the religious role of the missionary became in the Chinese mind inseparable from Westernization in general. The consequence was that the growing anti-missionary movement from 1890 onward retarded the entire process of learning from the West, and thereby retarded any genuine reform movement.[3]

[1] These generalizations on China's failure to respond should not be taken in any absolute sense.

[2] See S. Y. Teng and J. K. Fairbank, *China's Response to the West* (1954),* 133–93.

[3] In general the missionary was both a source of ideas on reform and a target of Chinese attack. He was valued by some Chinese reformers for the ideas he might contribute to a new China, but he was resented by the gentry-official class as the agent of foreign and subversive doctrines, religious and political. It is hardly surprising that the Ch'ing dynasty was never able to deal effectively with the problem. Internally it was faced by anti-missionary riots. Externally it was faced by demands from the powers for concessions and for the dismissal of officials who failed to protect the missionary from popular Chinese ire. Edmund S. Wehrle, *Britain,*

The pioneer Chinese reformers were men of agile intellect, though their knowledge of the West was very imperfect. The earliest and most striking among these men was Wang T'ao (1828–1897), an independent scholar and journalist closely associated with the foreigners at Shanghai and Hong Kong. Wang assisted Legge in the translation of *The Chinese Classics*, spent two years in Europe, wrote a book on the Franco-Prussian War, delivered a lecture at Oxford in 1868, visited Japan, and founded his own newspaper in Hong Kong in which he launched his editorial attacks on the Manchu-Chinese administration of the time. While never losing his love of Confucian civilization, he became an ardent admirer of Western law and constitutional government on the British model. Though his comments on Western politics were often acute, his observations on social matters may have been overdrawn, as when he wrote that "most women in the state of Massachusetts have preferred to get concubines for their husbands." [4]

Also an advocate of reform in methods was Hsueh Fu-ch'eng, successively secretary to Tseng Kuo-fan and Li Hung-chang, and later a member of China's diplomatic service

at London and Paris, where he kept a diary. Hsueh remained a staunch opponent of those Western social customs, such as freedom of choice in marriage, which he thought honored woman but degraded man, but, like Wang, he saw in constitutional government the answer to China's ills. In these views Wang and Hsueh went far beyond the technological reforms proposed by their predecessors. Hsueh, like many of the reformers who followed him, was also concerned with a philosophical problem. This was the problem of finding precedent in Chinese history for institutional reform. If such precedent were there, then China could safely learn from the West without surrendering her own foundations. For those who clung to the traditional methods of the past Hsueh remarked that: "We cannot expect to excel others [the Westerners] merely by sitting upright in a dignified attitude."

These men and other reformers such as Ho Kai (or Ho Ch'i, 1859–1917) son of a Hong Kong merchant, disillusioned by the self-strengthening philosophy of most officials, stressed not only the need to develop Chinese commerce, industry, and agriculture, but also to find political solutions to China's ills. Chinese reformism acquired a distinctly political orientation demanding political change and parliamentary institutions as early as the decade that preceded the Sino-Japanese War. [5]

K'ang Yu-wei and other Reformers

China's first heroic efforts toward radical reform are associated with K'ang Yu-wei (1858–1927), a Cantonese of gentry family, and others influenced by him. K'ang was a utopian who had buttressed his Confucian learning with reading of Western books in translation. Perhaps the most significant point in his political philosophy was his interpretation of Confucius as a reformer.

China and the Antimissionary Riots, 1891–1900 (1966). How American pressures were exerted is treated in George E. Paulsen, "The Szechwan Riots of 1895 and American 'Missionary Diplomacy'," *Journal of Asian Studies* 28 (1969): 285–98.

[4] See excerpts from Wang's writings, Teng and Fairbank, *China's Response to the West*, 137–140, and Henry McAleavy, *Wang T'ao: The Life and Writings of a Displaced Person* (London, 1953). Also Paul A. Cohen, "Wang T'ao and Incipient Chinese Nationalism," *Journal of Asian Studies* 26 (1967): 559–74. A central problem in the mind of a nineteenth century Chinese intellectual was that by tradition he tended to view China as a world rather than as a nation. Thus China was not a part of something bigger. Consequently, the Western invitation to China to join the world was incomprehensible, if not impudent. As Chinese reformers moved toward a concept of nationalism, their attitudes toward the West often combined an acute resentment and a grudging respect.

[5] Lloyd E. Eastman, "Political Reformism in China Before the Sino-Japanese War," *Journal of Asian Studies* 27 (1968): 695–710. It was the humiliation suffered by China in the Sino-French War of 1884–1885 that suggested the barrenness of the self-strengthening philosophy (see p. 184) and the need for institutional change.

Therefore he concluded that all intelligent Confucians in a time of troubles should be reformers.[6]

Most notable among K'ang's associates was his student Liang Ch'i-ch'ao (1873–1929), who became a great scholar and a widely read author. Liang in his early career was an ardent reformer seeking a constitutional basis for China's government. In 1896, as editor of a Shanghai newspaper, he attracted the favorable attention of some of the more progressive provincial governors. One of his famous themes was to liken China to a thousand-year-old mansion, decayed and broken. Threatened with collapse of their home, the indifferent inmates merely awaited their doom with weeping or sought to patch up a few holes in the hope that good fortune would catch up with them. Like K'ang Yu-wei, Liang believed that modern reform could be built on Chinese foundations. He attempted to re-evaluate Chinese tradition so that the tradition would justify Western reform. In this pursuit he convinced himself that Confucian teachings had been distorted by faulty texts and dishonest commentators. If the real Confucius were known, it would be obvious that he foretold the coming of science, democracy, and prosperity, the very ideals for which the West stood.[7] To young Chinese students of a reform or revolutionary turn of mind Liang with his command of classical Chinese and his knowledge of the West was an intellectual hero, a sort of universal man joining East and West.

Chang Chih-tung

Reformers at the close of the century were sometimes found among the high and mighty, such as Chang Chih-tung (1837–1909), one of the great Chinese statesmen of the period. Indeed, the diversity of status among the reformers added to the diversity of diagnoses of the disease and the remedies proposed to cure it.

Chang Chih-tung, with all the advan-

tages of a Chinese classical education, was for many years the most powerful and distinguished official in the provinces, where he was governor-general of Kwangtung-Kwangsi (1884–1889) and Hupei-Hunan (1889–1907). In these capacities he was one of the essential advisors of Peking not only on domestic but also on foreign affairs. His fame rested on his capacity as an administrator and on his proposals for reform expressed in frequent memorials to the throne. Of him it has been said that he "was both a liberal official who worked for reforms and a conservative scholar who objected to parliamentary government." [8] In a sense he stood midway between the radicalism of K'ang Yu-wei and the traditionalism of the Court. Chang took the position that China's troubles would be remedied by "Chinese learning for the fundamental principles, Western learning for practical application." Behind this approach was the fact that he did not admire Western political theory and philosophy. He proposed to save China by a threefold assault on her ills. By the first, the Manchu dynasty to which Chang was loyal was to be saved by a revival of Confucianism, with which he found democracy incompatible. The purpose would be to harmonize Confucianism with Western technology and political methods as opposed to political institutions. By his second approach, Chang proposed to rescue China through education, which he promoted unceasingly. Here the limiting factor was that to Chang the goal of education was mastery of the classics and loyalty to the throne. Chang's third approach was to create a new China through industry. His work in this field was notable. He was responsible for the first modern Chinese mint, for the Han Yeh-p'ing steel mills at Wuhan, and the Peking-Hankow railway.

THE HUNDRED DAYS OF REFORM

It was the march of events—China's defeat in the war of 1894–1895 and the subsequent scramble for leaseholds and spheres,

---

[6] Lin Mousheng, *Men and Ideas: An Informal History of Chinese Political Thought* (1942), 215–29, sketches K'ang's career.

[7] Joseph R. Levenson, *Liang Ch'i-ch'ao and the Mind of Modern China* (1953),* 1–2.

[8] Teng and Fairbank, *China's Response to the West*, 164.

1896–1898—rather than the power of the reform movement itself that unexpectedly plunged K'ang Yu-wei and his associates into power and as rapidly into defeat and exile or death. In the spring of 1898 the question of reform as presented in the memorials of K'ang and others touched the imagination of a few progressive officials at the Peking court and, more important, of the Kuang-hsu emperor himself, the nephew of Tz'u-hsi, the Empress Dowager. Since 1889 this weak, ineffectual, and inexperienced but well-intentioned young sovereign had been ruling in his own right. Frightened by the tidings of disaster, and emboldened by the urgings of the reformers, the emperor announced the need for reform by a decree of June 11, 1898. K'ang Yu-wei, Liang Ch'i-ch'ao, and others were appointed to advise the sovereign on proposed reforms and K'ang was allowed to submit memorials directly to the throne. The result was an unparalleled flood of ill-devised reform decrees known as the "Hundred Days of Reform." The problems tackled were as varied as the ills of this sick civilization. China was to have able diplomatic representation abroad, and officials were ordered to recommend men "who are not enveloped in the narrow circle of bigoted conservatism." China was to have a new order in which all the nation would unite in a march to progress. High conservative officials were advised to seek education in Europe. The old education was to be replaced by "practical" subjects; modern schools and colleges were to be established in every province; a transportation and mining bureau would be set up in Peking; the army would be reorganized; useless government posts would be abolished; foreign works on politics and science would be translated. From June to September, some forty decrees attempted to remake an old people into a new. It is small wonder that the effort failed. The reformers lacked experience, and the young emperor was not a magician. Undoubtedly he meant well, but he was emotionally unstable and intellectually diffuse. He possessed no adequate appreciation of the practical difficulties of constructive reform or of the conservative forces,

personified by the Empress Dowager, that would oppose him.[9]

Recognizing that their plans of reform would certainly fail unless this conservative opposition were removed, the reformers conspired to seize the Empress Dowager and Jung-lu, her most trusted adviser and commander of the northern army, and, though the evidence here is conflicting, perhaps to do away with both of them. The plot was discovered; K'ang and some of the reformers fled; and in September the Empress Dowager again seized control of the government. The attempted reform had failed because of the impetuous ineptitude of the reformers, the worthy but misdirected zeal of the emperor, the determined opposition of most of the conservatives, and because the mass of the people had no understanding of, or desire for, reform. Many of the reformers suffered summary execution. But the leaders, K'ang Yu-wei and Liang Ch'i-ch'ao, escaped to British Hong Kong, where in safety they could read the decrees condemning them to death by "slicing." For ten years the Kuang-hsu emperor lived on, a prisoner of the Regent Empress Dowager. That he was permitted even this existence was due, among other things, to the intervention of the powers, the Regent's fear of provoking the southern liberals, and the desire to hide the fact that China was again ruled by a woman.

THE REACTION AGAIN IN POWER

The collapse of the reform movement of the Hundred Days gave renewed evidence

[9] See Meribeth E. Cameron, *The Reform Movement in China* (1931), Chapter 2. K'ang Yu-wei hoped to transform China within the framework of the Confucian tradition. He wanted reform and transformation as opposed to revolution, and he wished the people of China to be active framers of their political future. He was perhaps the last great man of Old China. *K'ang Yu-wei: A Biography and a Symposium,* Jung-pang Lo, ed. and trans. (1967). Recent research on Chinese reform is presented in papers by Richard C. Howard, Yen-p'ing Hao, Hao Chang, Charlton M. Lewis, and John Schrecker in "The Chinese Movement of the 1890's: A Symposium," *Journal of Asian Studies* 29 (1969): 7–54.

of the stubborn power and "the elegant perfumed ignorance" of the court reactionaries. Furthermore, the conflict at Peking for and against reform was merely one aspect of a complex struggle for power between Manchus and Chinese, between Northern and Southern factions at court, and between the personal ambitions of rival officials to insure their own futures. In this context the Empress Dowager symbolized the craving for personal and dynastic power and the aroused inertia of the system-bound eunuchs and officials through whom her influence was maintained.

In the closing months of 1898 it was the fashion among the foreigners in Peking to dismiss Kuang-hsu's reforms as a case of misguided zeal, in the light of which it is easier to understand the determination of the Chinese conservatives to have their way. At the same time the Empress Dowager never ceased to protest her own enthusiasm for reform.

The return of the Empress Dowager to power could not be interpreted as a victory for progressive or patriotic forces in Chinese life, but it was coincident with a stiffening of the government's opposition to further foreign demands. In March, 1899, when Italy demanded the lease of San Men Bay and the setting aside of the greater part of Chekiang province as a sphere of influence, she received a polite but firm refusal. In fact, no further major concessions were secured by the powers during 1899 or the early months of 1900. Nevertheless, as the last days of the year 1899 approached, the far eastern situation was filled with dire forebodings. In addition to the naval leaseholds secured by Germany, Russia, France, and Great Britain, hardly a square foot of Chinese territory remained which was not already claimed or about to be claimed as a sphere of influence. The Russians claimed Manchuria and were extending their influence into Mongolia. From Shantung the Germans were looking westward into the northwest provinces. Great Britain was firmly entrenched in the great Yangtze Valley. France was expanding her concessionary rights in Yunnan, Kwangsi, and the greater part of Kwangtung. Japan, though not as yet a serious contender, had secured in April 1898, China's assurance not to alienate any portion of the province of Fukien opposite Japanese Formosa.

THE THREATENED PARTITION OF CHINA

It has been noted how the Sino-Japanese War, 1894–1895, precipitated a train of events, resulting, in 1896–1898, in a movement threatening the partition of China. This movement, against which the Manchu government seemed helpless, had, by 1899, reduced strategic areas in China to a species of semi-colonial status. For example, Tsingtao, under lease, had become a German city protected by a German squadron; the Chinese derived such consolation as they might from the fact that sovereignty in the abstract was reserved to Peking. Beyond Tsingtao throughout populous Shantung province, the birthplace of Confucius and thus China's Holy Land, German capital had acquired a practical monopoly in railroad and mining development. The stage was thus set in China for an era of special monopolistic privilege for German capital in Shantung, for Russian capital in Manchuria, for British capital in the Yangtze Valley, and for French capital in the areas bordering Indochina.

This state of affairs, whereby large areas of China had fallen into a sort of industrial-investment servitude to the great powers of Europe, would not have come about but for the inability of Peking to protect its territory and to enjoy the respect that power invites. In reality, Peking was not only weak, it was growing weaker. There was no intelligent leadership in China's capital, and popular discontent among the masses suggested that the dynasty had lost the Mandate of Heaven, and that the foreigner, with his leaseholds, his railways, and his Christianity, was not looked upon by the Chinese people as an adequate substitute for Heaven's favor.[10] After 1898 the political and

[10] For background manifestations of political weakness, anti-dynastic, and anti-foreign reactions, see Paul H. Clyde, *United States Policy Toward China* (1940; reissued 1964), Chapter 29.

military impotence of Peking and the lack of a national consciousness served as constant invitations to the great powers in their quest and rivalry for markets that could be controlled politically. Thus, once the first steps had been taken in 1897–1898 to cut the Chinese melon, once the leaseholds and spheres had been acquired, the powers were under the temptation to cut deeper—to make "spheres" into protectorates, and protectorates into annexations. This threat to China's sovereign existence was, it should be remembered, an important by-product not only of China's weakness but also of that intense European rivalry which was to result finally in the World War of 1914. Against the background of this rivalry among the great powers, and of incompetency at Peking, the United States sought to protect its interests by proposing a doctrine designed to create a commercial market in China that was free and open to all comers.

THE OPEN DOOR POLICY

The major interest of the powers in China during the nineteenth century had been in the main commercial. After the first treaty settlement of 1842–1844, these commercial interests were pursued within the limitations imposed by the most-favored-nation clause contained in all the treaties. Commercial privileges or concessions extended by China to one power were thus automatically enjoyed by all. As a result, the principle of equal commercial opportunity was maintained with a fair measure of support from all the powers, and in particular from the United States and Great Britain.[11] When in the winter of 1897–1898 Germany and Russia launched the scramble for naval leaseholds and spheres of influence, the British at first opposed the idea. They were

confident that a free and open market for British commerce and capital was the best guarantee of their continued economic supremacy in China. Realizing, however, that it could not hope for success by playing a lone hand, the British government appealed to the United States in March, 1898, and again in January, 1899, for some form of joint action to maintain an open door.[12] Neither President McKinley nor Secretary of State John Sherman was disposed to act on the British suggestion. Neither possessed any deep understanding of previous American policy in China, and, anyway, American eyes were turned, in the main, toward Cuba, rather than to Kiaochou or Port Arthur. Accordingly, Britain went into the business of leaseholds (Kowloon extension and Wei-hai-wei) and spheres of influence (Yangtze Valley) on a magnificent scale.

In the case of the British overtures, the United States was completely unresponsive to the call of historic American policy. The principle of most-favored-nation treatment was as old as American independence itself and had been applied in European as well as in far eastern treaties. The State Department had been advised repeatedly by Ambassador John Hay in London and Minister Charles Denby in Peking that the leaseholds and the spheres threatened not only equal opportunity in commerce but the territorial and political integrity of China as well.

Only on the basis of a number of factors can this costly mistake of 1898 in failing to defend the principle of equal opportunity be explained. Principal among these were (1) Sherman's incompetence in diplomacy and his fear of being "used" by the British; (2) the preoccupation of government and people with Cuba and the war; and, finally, (3) the fact that the material American commercial stake in China was small—hardly 2 per cent of the total United States foreign trade. Consequently, it was with very hesitant steps that the American government moved to reassert its interests in its historic policy in China. In the winter of 1898–1899 Lord Charles

---

[11] The background of the British attitude is given in Lord Charles Beresford, *The Breakup of China* (1899). On the all-pervading compradore system by which Europeans and Americans conducted their business both economic and sometimes political in China see Y. C. Wang, "Tu Yueh-Sheng (1888–1951): A Tentative Political Biography," *Journal of Asian Studies* 26 (1967): 433–55.

[12] The relevant correspondence is treated in A. L. P. Dennis, *Adventures in American Diplomacy, 1896–1906* (1928), Chapter 8, with documents.

Beresford, returning to England from China, aroused his American friends with a picture of China preserved by an Anglo-American open door policy. The idea fitted well into the new and larger concepts acquired by American businessmen after Dewey's victory of May, 1898, at Manila Bay.[13] The reasonableness of the picture depended on preserving China as a free market. The American government began to react to the pressure of these ideas in the early fall and winter of 1898. The Anglophile John Hay was now Secretary of State. McKinley told the Paris Peace Commission and the Congress that the sale of American products in China could not be prejudiced by exclusive treatment. But the President was still uncertain of his course, for the second British overture for joint action on the open door was rebuffed in January, 1899, despite the fact that more than 1,000 American missionaries in China were at one with American business in wanting a "strong" policy from Washington.

The antecedents from which the reassertion of American policy in China was to emerge must now be related in some detail, since these antecedents and American reactions to them were to exercise an extraordinary influence on twentieth century American policy in the Far East. Principal among these antecedents was the threat to British commercial supremacy in China brought about by the success of the Russian, German, and French drives to create for themselves special positions in China through their respective spheres of influence in Manchuria, Shantung, and Kwangtung-Kwangsi. The British government had reacted to this threat by approaching Washington seeking a joint open door declaration; but at the same time it considered seriously, if reluctantly, the creation of its own sphere in the Yangtze Valley. It was argued that in the new era of railroad and mining enterprise in China there was logic in a system of spheres of concentration as against an open door where the powers would be milling around jostling each other in the scramble for concessions. In other words, so the official British argument ran, it would be useful to keep the open door in matters of trade in consumption goods while protecting future capital investment through the principle of spheres. As a result, the British were not particularly disturbed when Sherman turned them down in March, 1898; but John Hay, American ambassador to London, was disturbed. Hay knew nothing about China, but he thought it poor business to rebuff the British needlessly. The net result was that when Hay became Secretary of State in the summer of 1898 his thoughts were moving toward an open door policy at the very moment when unbeknown to him the British government, while giving the idea lip service, was actually moving away from it by appropriating a Yangtze Valley sphere and by leasing the Kowloon extension across from Hong Kong.

It was at this point that an Englishman, Alfred Hippisley, second ranking official of the Chinese Imperial Maritime Customs Service, returned to England on leave and urged upon his friend W. W. Rockhill, Hay's new adviser on far eastern affairs, that the United States do something to preserve an open door for commerce in China. The spheres, he said, might as well be accepted as realities, and, if they applied only to railroads and mines, might do little harm. What he feared was that the sphere-holding powers would tamper with the Chinese customs administration as the British had already done at Kowloon. These ideas made a strong impression on Rockhill and Hay. At Hay's suggestion, Rockhill prepared recommendations for a policy based on the Hippisley ideas, and these recommendations were approved by the President.[14]

THE HAY OPEN DOOR NOTES

These were the antecedents that produced the Hay Open Door Notes sent to Britain, Germany, and Russia, September 6,

[13] See Julius W. Pratt, *Expansionists of 1898* (1936),* 278.

[14] For the background of the Hay open door policy, see George F. Kennan, *American Diplomacy, 1900–1950* (1951),* 21–37.

1899.[15] These prosaic notes that were to plague American diplomats for half a century began with some background of Hippisley and Rockhill's ideas and with a denial of any American recognition of the spheres, though both Hippisley and Rockhill accepted as axiomatic that the spheres were facts whose existence could only be challenged by force. The real substance of the notes was a three-point technical formula by which each power within its sphere was requested (1) not to interfere with the administration of treaty ports; (2) not to impede the equitable administration of the Chinese Customs; and (3) not to charge discriminatory railroad rates or harbor dues. It would appear that there was no attempt by the government in Washington to appraise the formula in terms of what its practical application in China was likely to be. Actually, the formula seems to have been an expression of what the Chinese Imperial Maritime Customs Service wanted at that particular time. Hippisley had secured the support of the United States without Rockhill or Hay's realizing the degree to which their formula might be contrary to the real purposes of the British government.

By the powers to which they were addressed, the Hay Open Door Notes were received with no enthusiasm, and their replies were plainly evasive. The British response, the most favorable of any, was clearly conditional, accepting the formula in so far as others might accept it. The Russians did not wish to reply at all, and when they did they were completely evasive. As a consequence the replies were all but worthless. Nevertheless, Hay, on March 20, 1900, announced he had received "satisfactory assurances" from all the powers and that he looked upon these responses as "final and definitive." This piece of sheer diplomatic bluff did not deceive the powers, but it did deceive the American people. It created the

impression that the American government by a stroke of diplomatic genius had saved China from the evil purposes of predatory powers.[16]

It is not belittling the Hay policy of 1899 to say that it was inadequate to protect either immediate American commercial interests or the historic American principle of equal opportunity. One need only recall that "in the Far East the powers were dealing with the fate of an empire of upward of three hundred million souls and no less than five major states were disputing the spoils."[17] This was not the sort of thing to be arrested by polite diplomatic notes. The spheres were still there, and they were designed to give preferential treatment in railroad, mining, and investment concessions.[18]

THE BOXER CATASTROPHE

Close on the heels of Hay's timid efforts came the catastrophe of the Boxer rising in North China. The origins of the Boxer movement are not entirely clear, but it is credited generally to a secret society that dated back to the eighteenth century known as the *I-ho-ch'uan*, or Harmonious Brotherhood.[19] Actually, the origins of the

[15] Similar though not identical notes went to Japan (Nov. 13), to Italy (Nov. 17), and to France (Nov. 21). See A. Whitney Griswold, *The Far Eastern Policy of the United States* (1938),* Chapter 2; texts of the Hippisley memorandum, Rockhill memorandum, and drafts of the final notes are in Griswold, 475–500.

[16] Paul H. Clyde, "Historical Reflections on Continuity in United States Far Eastern Policy," *Southeastern Asia in the Coming World*, Philip W. Thayer, ed. (1953), 17–24.

[17] William L. Langer, *The Diplomacy of Imperialism* (1935), II, 677.

[18] It is Langer's conclusion that to this point "the efforts of Hay, then, had no practical bearing on the situation as it was at the turn of the century." *Ibid.*, II, 688. Tyler Dennett, *John Hay* (1933), 295, gives the following comment on the whole negotiation: "It would have taken more than a lawyer to define what new rights had been recognized, or acquired, or even what had actually been said."

[19] Ch'uan signifies defensive calisthenics, hence boxing or boxers. In areas such as Shantung, where the government encouraged the organization of militia to resist the Germans, the Boxers by infiltration acquired a semi-official status as militia. The Boxers were local groups organized to destroy Chinese Christians. Later, under official encouragement, they became the core of a desperate anti-foreign movement. The

uprising, sometimes called the Boxer rebellion, involved far more than the conspiracy of a secret society, since the Manchu court itself was involved in what was soon to transpire. Faced with the imminent breakup of the empire into foreign-controlled spheres and with mounting Chinese antagonism to Manchu rule, the Empress Dowager, having crushed the reforms and the reformers of 1898, threw the weight of her power behind the parties of reaction at court that were bent on the suicidal policy of directing the rising tide of discontent away from the throne and against the foreigners and all their works: their railroads, churches, religion, and converts. This strategy was all too successful.

In June, 1900, the violence, organized and unorganized, began. Boxers by thousands, superstitious and fanatical, and prompted by conservative officialdom, joined in a debauch of slaughter and destruction in Shantung, Chihli, Shansi, and Manchuria. They tore up railroads and telegraphs, burned churches, and murdered Christian missionaries and their converts. This lunacy reached the heart of the Manchu court itself on June 20, when the government declared war on the foreign powers and permitted the Boxers to lay seige to the foreign legations in Peking. A British relief expedition from Tientsin was forced to retire and the siege dragged on until August 14 when an allied army of Americans, British, French, Germans, and Japanese entered Peking. Again, as in 1858, China's inability to adjust to the West, and the blind reaction of court officialdom, had opened the gates of Peking to foreign armies. This time, however, the threat to China's integrity was far greater. In 1858 it was a question of a few commercial concessions. Now in 1900 it was a question whether China as a state should continue to be.

The Boxer outbreak, following closely

---

movement was opposed in varying degrees by Li Hung-chang and Yuan Shih-k'ai in the north and by powerful governors in the Yangtze provinces, such as Chang Chih-tung and Liu K'un-i. Chester C. Tan, *The Boxer Catastrophe* (1955) is a corrective to earlier studies.

on the "final and definitive" assurances Hay had received from the powers, meant that if in 1899 there was little structure on which to hang the open door, there was even less in 1900. The powers were moving toward armed intervention at Peking. The Russians were soon to occupy strategic areas in Manchuria as a result of the Boxers' attack on the Chinese Eastern Railroad, which forced the Russians out of Mukden and Tsitsihar and put Harbin under siege. Kuropatkin, the Russian Minister of War, had exclaimed when he heard of the Boxer outbreak: "This will give us an excuse for seizing Manchuria." By October, 1900, Russia was in complete military control of the Three Eastern Provinces. Certainly there was nothing that was "final or definitive" in what was happening in North China. Moreover, in a presidential election year there was no disposition in Washington to become embroiled with the powers in China, particularly as nobody knew what, if anything, had best be done. During the first half of 1900, Edwin H. Conger, American Minister at Peking, while reporting to his government on the chaos in North China, had cooperated with his diplomatic colleagues in joint protests to the Chinese government. This procedure was in line with the Hay notes of 1899 and had precedent in Burlingame's cooperative policy of the 1860's. Yet between March and June operational procedures were reversed and Conger was told to act "singly and without the cooperation of other powers." Then, on the eve of the attacks on the Peking legations, Rockhill told Hay that the Boxer movement was not likely to "cause any serious complications," and the Department, again partially reversing itself, told Conger that he might act "concurrently" with other powers "if necessity arises."

CHINA'S POLITICAL INTEGRITY

To Hay the time seemed ripe for a clarification of American policy. On July 3, 1900, in a circular to the powers he said, in words designed to be quieting, that the United States had no thought other than

. . . to seek a solution which may bring about permanent safety and peace to China, preserve Chinese territorial and administrative entity, protect all rights guaranteed to friendly Powers by treaty and international law, and safeguard for the world the principle of equal and impartial trade with all parts of the Chinese Empire.

This principle of China's territorial integrity was not new in the language of American policy. It had been expressed by Humphrey Marshall in 1853, and by Anson Burlingame in 1862. It had been absent from, if not repudiated by, the Hay policy of 1899, which tacitly acknowledged the reality of leaseholds and spheres. Now in July, 1900, it was revived in a new and stronger form. Hay invited not only "respect" for China's integrity but also suggested "a collective guarantee" by the powers—a guarantee that was not forthcoming, since, with the exception of Great Britain, none of the powers even replied to the July circular.

Yet the important point is that in late 1900 the threatened partition of China was again arrested temporarily. Why was this? The note-writing of Hay probably had some psychological effect, but it does not appear to have been the determining factor. The determining factor again was the rivalry and the mutual jealousy of the powers, and their retreat from the co-operative policy to bilateral negotiations. England and Japan were slowly drawing together to stop Russia in Manchuria and in the Middle East. Germany's equivocal position in Shantung between Russia and England had resulted on October 16, 1900, in an Anglo-German agreement favoring the open door and the integrity of China, but this was an innocuous affair. John Hay referred to it as "a horrible practical German joke on England." He failed, it would seem, to realize that if this were so, it was an equally horrible joke upon himself and everything he had been attempting to do in China. There was no conversion of the powers to the idea of China's integrity. The business of melon-cutting was stopped temporarily because each of the potential aggressors, fearful of the debacle that would follow, hesitated to make the first move.

Then, ironically, in the midst of this lull, Hay himself joined the concession hunters. In December, 1900, under pressure from the American Navy, he sought a naval coaling station at Samsah Inlet, north of Foochow on the coast of Fukien province. Japan, when consulted, blocked the move, reminding Hay, presumably with some delight, of his own recent efforts to preserve the territorial integrity of China.[20] The incident did not strengthen in subsequent years the moral influence of the United States in the Far East.

THE INTERNATIONAL BOXER SETTLEMENT

With the defeat of the Boxers and the occupation of Peking by an international army the powers set about the long drawn out business of deciding how to punish China and how to provide security for the future. The final settlement embodied in the Peace Protocol of September, 1901, was achieved only after prolonged and involved negotiations. The jealousies of the powers being as they were, it was with the utmost difficulty that agreement was at length reached on the kind and degree of punishment China should suffer.

During the advance of the international relief expedition on Peking there was relative harmony, for the plight of the besieged foreigners in the capital was desperate. The international relief army was one of the most remarkable ever assembled: 8,000 Japanese, 4,500 Russians, 3,000 British, 2,500 Americans, and 800 French. Available German troops were held back to protect Kiaochou

[20] Hay consulted Japan because the latter regarded the province of Fukien, opposite Formosa, as a Japanese sphere of influence. The Chinese Foreign Office in response to a Japanese note had pledged itself, April 26, 1898, never to "cede or lease" any part of the province. MacMurray, *Treaties*, I, 126. Hay's effort to secure Samsah was not made public until 24 years after the event. United States, *Foreign Relations, 1925*, 113–15. The Navy again urged the project on Hay in December, 1901, and in May, 1902. Griswold, *Far Eastern Policy of the United States*, 83–84.

and the coast. The honor of commanding the allied forces had been given, to please the Kaiser, to Field-Marshal Count von Waldersee, who, perhaps fortunately, did not arrive until after Peking was in allied hands. This was a severe blow to German imperialistic pride. The Kaiser was forced to see the glory of leadership go to General Linievitch, the Russian commander. The general tension was increased during the autumn and winter of 1900–1901, when the powers became convinced that Russia was preparing to control not only Manchuria but also the metropolitan province of Chihli. This led to all manner of attempts by the powers for additional concessions. In these unhappy circumstances, suggesting another partition of the empire, the Boxer Protocol was concluded, September 7, 1901.

The terms were severe and humiliating. The wisdom of the settlement has often been called in question. From the standpoint of the powers it could be argued that Peking's responsibility was great. The Manchu government had regarded itself as at war and therefore must now pay the price of its defeat and its treachery. The terms therefore were dictated against a background of punitive expeditions against many localities where foreigners had been attacked, and as allied troops occupied the Imperial City within Peking itself.[21]

In the long view the Boxer uprising was

---

[21] The terms of the Protocol may be summarized as follows: (1) apology to Germany and Japan for the murder of the German minister and the Japanese chancellor of legation, and erection of a memorial to von Ketteler on the spot where he was assassinated; (2) punishment of responsible Chinese officials; (3) erection of monuments in desecrated foreign cemeteries; (4) official examinations to be suspended in all cities where attacks had occurred; (5) China to pay an indemnity of $333,000,000, to create an effective 5 per cent tariff, and to prohibit for at least two years importation of arms, ammunition, and materials for their manufacture; (6) the Taku forts to be destroyed, and a legation quarter to be created in Peking under exclusive control of the powers, which they might make defensible; (7) right of the powers to occupy 13 places as a guarantee of free communication with Peking; (8) China to agree to the amendment of commercial treaties, and to create a ministry of foreign affairs; (9) China to publish preventive

to exert a profound influence upon China's political future. It hastened the end of the Manchu dynasty and the creation of the Republic. In this respect it was a dynamic step in the progress of China's revolution. To be sure, the Boxers were inspired by little more than a "blind and ignorant patriotism," while their patron and defender, Yu Hsien, the Manchu governor of Shantung, was distinguished by nothing save a "policy of blind reaction." The Boxers had no constructive program of reform to offer. They merely attributed China's ills to the "foreign devils" who must be destroyed along with their machines and inventions, "their strange and intolerant religion, their insufferable airs of superiority." [22] Yet, with all its weakness, its lack of constructive program, its blind fanaticism and reaction, the Boxer movement was an unmistakable symptom of China's growing unrest, of her resentment against foreign intrusion and exploitation, and of her will to resist.[23]

---

edicts against further outbreaks; (10) the right of the allies to maintain legation guards at Peking. The American share of the indemnity, $25,000,000, was, as in the case of all the powers, far in excess of justifiable claims. Substantial portions of it were returned to China in 1907 and 1924.

[22] R. F. Johnston, *Twilight in the Forbidden City* (London, 1934), 44.

[23] There have been many points in this study where the reader has been faced with the perplexing historical question: Why, in the late nineteenth and early twentieth centuries, did the Confucian system fail? One answer, frequently encountered, tends to idealize the Confucian tradition and to explain China's recent and contemporary problems as a product of departures from the Confucian tradition, departures brought about either by weak monarchs and scholarbureaucrats within or by the arrival of the Westerners from without. The weakness of this interpretation lies in the fact that the Confucian tradition itself was not lacking in defects. For example, Confucianism of the nineteenth century illustrates almost perfectly an historic Chinese capacity to create and more especially to preserve unworkable systems. The rather inflexible Confucian order based on an agricultural economy was viable while new arable land was available. When such land was no longer available, a system and a tradition which could not adjust to new realities failed. See Harold C. Hinton, "China: An Overview," *Problems of Communism* (May-June, 1969), 45.

CHRISTIAN MISSIONS. Paul A. Varg, *Missionaries, Chinese and Diplomats. The American Protestant Missionary Movement in China, 1890–1952* (1958), useful for factual data. Liu Kwang-ching, "Early Christian Colleges in China," *Journal of Asian Studies,* 20 (Nov., 1960): 71–78. Chen Chi-yun, "Liang Ch'i-ch'ao's Missionary Education: A Case Study of Missionary Influence on the Reformers," *Papers on China,* 16 (1962): 66–125.

CHINESE INSTITUTIONAL CHANGE. Herrlee G. Creel, *Chinese Thought from Confucius to Mao Tse-Tung* (1953),* a well-written non-technical survey. Ralph L. Powell, *The Rise of Chinese Military Power, 1895–1912* (1955) deals with military reorganization and modernization and its political effect. Stanley Spector, *Li Hung-chang and the Huai Army* (1964), a study of Chinese regionalism in the nineteenth century. J. Lossing Buck, *Land Utilization in China* (1937), a principal source on the agrarian economy. Yang Lien-sheng, *Money and Credit in China: A Short History* (1952).*

THE OPEN DOOR AND CHINA'S INTEGRITY. W. W. Willoughby, *Foreign Rights and Interests in China* (2 vols., rev. ed., 1927), reliable on facts rather than interpretation. Paul A. Varg, *Open Door Diplomat: The Life of W. W. Rockhill* (1952). Chang Feng-chen, *The Diplomatic Relations Between China and Germany Since 1898* (1936). Julius W. Pratt, *America's Colonial Experiment* (1950) presents the rise and decline of imperialistic sentiment in the United States.

THE BOXER UPRISING. E. H. Zabriskie, *American-Russian Rivalry in the Far East* (1946). G. N. Steiger, *China and the Occident, the Origin and Development of the Boxer Movement* (1927). Richard H. Wilde, 'The Boxer Affair and Australian Responsibility for Imperial Defense," *The Pacific Historical Review* 26 (1957): 51–65. Victor Purcell, *The Boxer Uprising: A Background Study* (Cambridge, England, 1963), a comprehensive treatment of this upheaval with some new details from contemporary English sources.

China, 1901–1910:
The Empress Dowager
Tries Reform

chapter 17

Until the imminent collapse of the Manchu dynasty during that "midsummer madness" known as the Boxer rebellion, the Empress Dowager had been steadfastly against any significant reform. The failure of the One Hundred Days, in 1898, was due directly to her. Her return to power in the capacity of regent signalized an intensification of reaction. This tendency was given its fullest expression in the policies and actions of the court as the Boxer movement got under way. The Empress Dowager was in full sympathy with the anti-foreign, anti-Christian philosophy of the Boxer patriots. It was not by accident, therefore, that government troops under Tung Fu-hsiang and other sympathizers with reaction were allowed by the Court to join forces with the Boxers.[1] In a word, the Empress Dowager had set her course not only against reform at home but also against the treaty powers that personified the impact of all things Western.

When, in the midst of the Boxer troubles, foreign armies again entered Peking, the Empress Dowager fled for a second time, as in 1860, from the capital. Before her

[1] R. F. Johnston, *Twilight in the Forbidden City* (London, 1934), 46.

return to Peking in January, 1902, Tz'u-hsi professed to be a converted woman. She had hardly become a progressive, for she had no understanding of such things, but she was converted to "reform," at least as she defined that term. From 1901 until three years after her death in 1908, the dynasty, turned in principle to a program that bore striking resemblance to the reforms she had so ruthlessly suppressed in 1898. During 1902, as indicative of things to come, reform edicts removed the ban on intermarriage between Chinese and Manchus, advised the Chinese to abandon the practice of binding the feet of their women, ordered the sending of intelligent Manchus abroad for study, and abolished a number of sinecures. All this seemed to indicate that the Empress Dowager was intent on a housecleaning. There was still, however, the question of the depth and sincerity of her conversion, and whether this masterful but unscrupulous woman had the capacity to rebuild the fortune of the dynasty and the people it ruled. The new reform program was to involve the educational system, the army and navy, the form of government, and a great array of miscellaneous matters including a crusade against the opium traffic.

EDUCATIONAL REFORM

EDUCATIONAL REFORM

The decision to reconstruct China's educational system involved a revolutionary departure from the past. Some rather futile efforts in this direction had already been made in the late nineteenth century. They were important first steps in spite of their failure. The traditional Confucian education leading to the civil service examinations with their eight-legged essays had been sanctified by a thousand years of history and guarded jealously by the ruling scholar-bureaucrats as the fortress of their position and power. A few progressive scholars had dared to say that the classical education alone was no longer adequate for a China harassed by the modern world, but it was not until 1887 that mathematics became a subject for examination. Even then the weight of tradition was so strong that few candidates prepared for it. In 1897 a special examination on political economy was suggested in order that some candidates might be encouraged to learn about current affairs. At the time of the fateful One Hundred Days of Reform, 1898, Liang Ch'i-ch'ao and more than a hundred other progressives asked for abolition of the whole traditional civil service examination system. Nothing came of these preliminaries until 1903, when Chang Chih-tung, governor-general at Nanking, and Yuan Shih-k'ai, governor-general at Tientsin, suggested the gradual abolition of the system. The weight of their prestige encouraged other memorialists, with the result that an imperial decree, September 2, 1905, announced the immediate and permanent end of the examinations.

The Boxer Protocol (1901) had already suspended for five years the civil service examinations in cities where foreigners had been attacked. In 1901, too, an Imperial edict had called for the building of a national school system. Instruction was still to be primarily in the Confucian classics, but it was also to include Chinese and Western history, government, and science. In 1904 this educational plan was revised and extended on the model of the educational system then prevailing in Japan. It was designed to provide for kindergartens, primary schools, middle schools, high schools or provincial colleges, and an Imperial university at Peking. There was a notable lack of provision for the education of women.

There was substantial evidence that many Chinese accepted the new educational reforms with enthusiasm if not always with understanding, but there was also persistent opposition. Fitful waves of reaction followed the first waves of reform. While temples were being turned into schools, and the Empress Dowager was curtailing her theatricals to equip an academy for girls, some of the erstwhile reformers turned conservative, reemphasized Confucian studies, and belittled the Western learning. Still greater opposition came from the local mandarins. Peking might decree reform in education, but it would remain a dead letter until the local officials were prepared to implement it. Even where the local official attitude was favorable, the educational effort frequently dissipated itself in the construction of colleges rather than primary schools.

Of equal difficulty were the problems of financing the new schools and staffing them with trained teachers. Finance was left to the ingenuity of the local community with results that were "precarious and unsatisfactory." In the teacher problem, the missionaries and the native graduates of the mission schools offered the greatest hope. The missionaries, however, were deterred from accepting appointment by a rule forbidding the teaching of religion in government schools. As a result, a large proportion of the new teachers came from Japan. These worked for lower salaries than Westerners, and culturally they fitted more easily into the Chinese environment.

Meanwhile, in 1905, the Empress Dowager, intent on building, through education, a new body of public servants capable of strengthening the dynasty and resisting the pressure of the foreign powers, urged more students to study abroad. At this time there were probably 8,000 Chinese students in Japan. Some undoubtedly profited by the experience, while others were mere adventurers, seeking the prestige that a few months of foreign residence would give. A lesser number of students went to Europe or to the United States. Those who came to America were assisted through Boxer Indemnity funds which the American government returned to China after 1907.[2] On the eve of the Revolution of 1911 there were some 800 Chinese students in the United States and about 400 in Europe.

These were encouraging signs. In the years 1909–1910, China could point to 57,267 schools, 89,362 teachers, and 1,626,529 enrolled students. In the light of only ten years of educational reform the figures seem reasonably impressive until one recalls that China's population was in excess of 400,-000,000, of whom some 65,000,000 were children of school age.

MILITARY REFORM

The need for military reform, for the creation of a national Chinese army, was obvious even to the Manchus. China's military humiliation had reached a new height in the Sino-Japanese war and in the Boxer uprising, while during the Russo-Japanese war the hapless dynasty had no alternative but to open Manchuria to the battling armies of two great foreign powers. There could be little respect for the dynasty at home or for the nation among the powers so long as this military impotence continued.

It will be recalled that China had acquired in the days of the T'ai-p'ing rebellion a number of excellent regional armies that suppressed the rebellion but which in so doing weakened the central government at the very moment they were saving it. The effectiveness of these armies against the T'ai-p'ings naturally suggested a means by which China in time might defend herself against the Western powers. Accordingly Li Hung-chang and others among the new Chinese scholar-militarists had set about to buy

arms and munitions from the West, to seek Western military advisers, and to establish arsenals. All this was without pattern or plan so that, as one observer noted, a small body of troops might carry thirteen kinds of rifles and even more brands of ammunition. The picture was not wholly negative, but as so often in nineteenth-century China, what the right hand acquired the left hand took away. What was learned in the classroom was rarely applied in maneuvers, either because young officers scorned the drill field or because their old-fashioned commanders blocked reform. Since the reform spirit rarely penetrated to Peking, progress, if there was any, was confined at the local level. In the end, the militia armies tended to degenerate once the T'ai-p'ings had been suppressed until with some exceptions they were not much better than the defunct Banners and the Green Standard. Military reform, it would seem, was fashionable only when disaster was imminent.[3]

China's humiliating defeat in the Sino-Japanese war, 1895, and the subsequent scramble of the powers for leaseholds opened a new chapter in the nation's stumbling search for military power. In the first place, there was evidence of some popular demand among the Chinese for reform. In the second, even the Manchu court was no longer wholly blind to the dangers from within or from abroad invited by its military weakness. The central figures in the new military reforms was Yuan Shih-k'ai, who had been Li Hung-chang's agent in Korea in the years before the Sino-Japanese war. Yuan, born in Honan, 1859, in a family of the smaller landed gentry, had failed the literary examinations, and therefore had to purchase his first post and rank in government. He appears to have decided quite early that in the China of his day a career primarily military was the surest path to power. In any event, he became a staff officer in 1880, and between 1882 and 1894 through service in Korea established a reputation as a military man and a diplomat. By 1895 he had formed

---

[2] In 1908 the American Congress by joint resolution authorized President Roosevelt to reduce the United States share of the Boxer Indemnity from $24,440,000 to $13,655,492. The original figure had far exceeded American claims. United States, *Foreign Relations, 1907*, Pt. I, 174–75; *ibid.*, 1908, 64–65, 71–72.

[3] Edward L. Jones, *The Development of Regional Militarism in China, 1850–1927* (Duke University, 1953, in manuscript), 38.

high connections at Peking with such Manchu officials as Prince Ch'ing and Jung-lu, the Manchu president of the Board of War, and was promptly placed in command of an army corps in which many of the young officers were graduates of Li Hung-chang's military school at Tientsin. Yuan set about to make his corps the best-trained, equipped, and disciplined army in China. But it is important to note that because of the political circumstances in which he operated, Yuan was not building a national army but rather was reviving a pattern of principles which had appeared earlier in the days of the T'ai-p'ings, that is, of personal armies operating with Western training and Western arms. From these beginnings there was soon to emerge what was essentially Yuan's own army and his own politico-military cabal of followers.

The One Hundred Days of 1898 made possible Yuan's complete ingratiation with the Manchu dynasty. By this time Yuan had also formed connections with Chinese reformers as well as with the conservatives of the court. His role in the events of 1898 has never been entirely clear, but it is generally assumed that he betrayed the reformers and thus opened the way for the suppression of the reforms and for the return to power of the Empress Dowager. Whatever the truth, Yuan from that time on until 1908 had the confidence of the Manchu court and of the masterful "Old Buddha."

Indeed, Yuan's position at the turn of the century was compounded of the play of multiple forces in delicate balance. He was a Chinese, described by Lord Charles Beresford in 1898 as intelligent, well-informed, patriotic, and deeply concerned for the fate of his country. At the same time Yuan was an individual ambitious to achieve for himself military and political power. His advancement up to 1900 had been due to his ability, energy, and liaison with an ailing dynasty. Yet he had also had close association with Chinese who wanted reform, and, when the Boxer troubles occurred, Yuan displayed a notable independence of judgment. Far from aiding the dynasty in its ill-advised support of the Boxers, Yuan, who had

recently been named governor of Shantung, gave no quarter to the Boxers, maintained order in the province, protected the foreigners, and thus, enjoying the favor of the foreign powers, aided in the return of the fugitive court to Peking after the Boxer settlement. Here then lay the background of the Empress Dowager's new-found ardor after 1901 for military reform, and for the role of Yuan Shih-k'ai in implementing the program.

The Manchu military reform program, 1902–1911, like the other efforts of the dynasty to rebuild its prestige and power, was notable in purpose rather than in performance. Under decrees inspired by the Empress Dowager provincial governors were ordered to modernize their troops. Military schools were to be reformed and the entire program was to be directed by a Commission for Army Reorganization headed by Prince Ch'ing. Meanwhile, Yuan Shih-k'ai, on the death of Li Hung-chang, was named governor-general of the metropolitan province of Chihli and was entrusted with the direction of military and foreign affairs in North China. His own army, now expanded to something between 50,000 and 80,000 men, was commanded by officers who were Yuan's men. Many of these politico-military subordinates were later to hold high office during the early years of the Republic.[4]

It was at this point that the plan of the Manchu court to enforce the general principle of governmental centralization of authority in Peking affected the military reform program. In his rise to power Yuan had made enemies at court, particularly among high Manchu officials. These same officials now found in the idea of centralization a means of wresting from Yuan the command of his army. In 1907, control of some two-thirds of

[4] Feng Kuo-chang was president, 1917–1919; Tuan Ch'i-jui, several times premier and chief executive of the provisional government, 1924–1926; Wang Shih-chen, premier, 1917–1918; Hsu Shih-chang, president 1919–1922; Ts'ao K'un, president 1923–1924. Yuan's military schools graduated other men who figured largely in the subsequent struggle for power: Wu Pei-fu, Sun Chuan-fang, and Feng Yu-hsiang, the "Christian general."

the Peiyang army was assumed by the Ministry of War. A few months later Yuan was further isolated from military power when he was appointed Minister of Foreign Affairs and elevated to the Grand Council. When in 1908 the Empress Dowager died, Yuan was dismissed from office and sent into retirement. With Yuan out of the way, the Ministry of War attempted to organize a national army under its immediate direct control. All manner of elaborate plans were drafted setting forth the control, equipment, and training of this force, including the necessary military industries of munitions and supply. Some progress in fact was made. In 1909 about 700 young Chinese were being trained as officers in Japan. The army itself, however, grew very slowly.

However, these abortive attempts in military reform, like other reform efforts of the Manchus between 1902 and 1911, cannot be appraised in the simple language of success or failure. For example, army reform was not merely a belated effort by the Manchus to preserve the dynasty. It was also a response to a new interest in the defense of China against the foreign powers. The failure of military reform after 1865 and again after 1901 can only be explained when account is taken of (1) the decay of the traditional Manchu military organization, (2) the regional and personal character of the newer militia armies, and (3) the lack of national leadership in the belated Manchu reform program. Nevertheless, the Chinese response to the attempted army reforms signified the beginnings, however feeble, of a new military spirit within China.

CONSTITUTIONAL REFORM

It is perhaps understandable that the Empress Dowager, her frightened dynastic household, and her chief advisers came to grips with the problem of political reform not as a means toward enlightened government but rather as a desperate effort to save the dynasty. As early as January, 1901, "Old Buddha," while still an exile at Sian, had decreed that the best political methods of foreign countries should be studied. The idea

was that there must be some germ of strength in Occidental governments which, if known, would give China strength and re-establish her position of superiority.[5] Accordingly, in 1905 she sent official missions to Europe and the United States to study constitutional government. The reports of these commissions, given to the throne in 1906–1907, revealed the limited steps the dynasty was prepared to take toward constitutional government. Constitutionalism, in so far as it might be adopted, was to be justified on practical rather than theoretical grounds. The commissioners argued that a constitution would make the emperor's powers more effective, and that to give the people some role in political affairs would make them more responsive and productive subjects, thus increasing production and revenue.

The commission was particularly impressed by what it saw in Japan. To the investigators it seemed clear that (1) Japan's strength was due to her adoption of Western institutions, and (2) Japan had provided herself with a constitution without sacrificing the power of the Imperial House. Why then could not the Empress Dowager by similar reforms satisfy her subjects, strengthen the Empire, and preserve her own power? She therefore proceeded on the assumption that real power was to be reserved to the throne, with the people tendering advice when requested to do so through their representatives. Furthermore, she proposed to act slowly in order to placate the conservative opposition. By the close of 1907 three cautious steps had been taken on the road to constitutional government: (1) the principle itself had been accepted; (2) a commission had been created to advise on procedure; and (3) an edict had been issued authorizing a national assembly and also provincial assemblies.

During 1908 these cautious preliminaries assumed more tangible shape. The throne approved specific regulations for provincial assemblies that were to meet within a year. Underlying principles of the future constitution were decided upon and promulgated. A national parliament was to meet after nine years, and a preliminary constitutional pro-

[5] Harold M. Vinacke, *Modern Constitutional Development in China* (1920), 54.

gram to that end was adopted. The new provincial assemblies were to be an integral part of the national machinery, their powers in no case infringing the imperial prerogatives—an indication that the official reformers were under the influence of the Japanese and German models. The assemblies were conceived as sounding boards of provincial opinion. Furthermore, in large part, their discussions were to be limited to matters submitted to them by the viceroy or governor. The right to vote for electors who in turn would choose members of the assembly was strictly limited by property or scholastic qualifications. As time was to show, these assemblies were to make their presence felt in two ways: they reflected a considerable degree of public opinion, and they checked the efforts of the central government to increase its own power.

On the subject of constitutional principles, the court reformers were perfectly clear in their position. "The government of China," said a memorial, "is to be constitutional by imperial decree. . . . The principles of the constitution are the great laws which may not be lightly altered. . . . The constitution is designed to conserve the power of the sovereign and protect the officials and the people." All legislative, executive, and judicial authority was reserved to the Manchu sovereign.

Parliament was given power to propose legislation . . . ; it might adopt measures of government; and it might impeach ministers for illegal acts, but no action it took had any weight or validity save that derived from the Imperial sanction.[6]

As W. W. Rockhill, American Minister at Peking, commented, the purpose of the imperial reformers was "a perpetuation of the existing system under a thin veil of constitutional guarantees."[7]

Application of this program of political reform was to take place gradually over a period of nine years. In 1909 the provincial assemblies met for the first time, conducted themselves with considerable dignity, and led

in the public agitation for early calling of a parliament. The following year the National Assembly held its first meeting (October 3, 1910). Of the 200 members, 100 were chosen by the throne, the remainder by the provincial assemblies from their own members. Contrary to expectation, this Assembly, far from proving a mere rubber stamp, forced the government's decision to convoke a parliament in 1913 instead of 1917. It also forced the throne to consider concessions toward establishment of a responsible ministry. In general it showed a remarkably independent attitude.

The independence shown even by this hand-picked National Assembly of 1910 suggested the appearance of a more general political awakening than the Empress Dowager and her political advisers had been willing to acknowledge. This awakening was already taking the form of an embryonic Chinese nationalism stimulated by the writings of Liang Ch'i-ch'ao, the most effective publicist of the period and an exile in Japan from 1898.

LIANG CH'I-CH'AO

After his escape to Japan in 1898 from the wrath of the Empress Dowager, Liang as a philosopher, writer, and editor moved rapidly forward from the reform philosophy of his teacher K'ang Yu-wei. A reinterpretation of Confucianism was no longer enough for Liang. The Chinese must become a "new people," reborn by a new patriotic and cultural movement. By the force of his reputation as a scholar, and by the vigor of his pen, Liang became the first great teacher of modern Chinese citizenship. He was among the first of the scholar elite to free himself from the Confucian tradition. Probably no Chinese of the time was so influential in popularizing modern knowledge, especially among the student class at home and in Japan. There was little place in Liang's doctrine for the feeble reformism of the Empress Dowager.[8]

---

[6] Vinacke, *Modern Constitutional Development in China*, 77.

[7] Quoted by Vinacke, *op. cit.*, 79.

[8] For an interpretation of Liang, 1898–1911, see Joseph R. Levenson, *Liang Ch'i-ch'ao and*

Of lesser prestige in the eyes of Chinese intellectuals at the turn of the century but of growing influence at home and abroad as a visionary and revolutionist was Sun Wen, or, as he is better known to history, Sun Yat-sen. Sun was born of humble peasant stock in 1866 at Hsiang-shan in the Canton delta of southern China, which had nurtured the T'ai-p'ing rebellion in the neighboring province of Kwangsi. After his early Western schooling at Honolulu, where he acquired a knowledge of English and was converted to Christianity, he studied medicine at British Hong Kong. What Sun had acquired in these years abroad was not primarily a knowledge of medicine but a picture of two contrasting worlds: (1) a Western world of powerful national states, and (2) a moribund China clinging to the Confucian theory of a world community.

As a political agitator, Sun's early political methods followed a conventional Chinese pattern: the formation of a small group of followers, petitions to the authorities, and finally terroristic attacks and flight into exile. By the time of the Sino-Japanese War, 1894–1895, Sun's revolutionary organization had become "modernist, nationalist, and antimonarchial, instead of merely patriotic and antidynastic." [9] His original revolutionary organization, Society for the Regeneration of China (*Hsing Chung Hui*), 1894–1905, drew much of its strength from overseas Chinese. By 1905, when the Empress Dowager was in the midst of her reform program, the Society was reorganized as the League of Common

the *Mind of Modern China* (1953),* 55–169. As an exile in Japan after 1898, Liang became a vigorous exponent of revolutionary ideas, established a school for Chinese students in Tokyo, and eventually became the mentor of a whole generation of young Chinese intellectuals who studied in Japan, particularly between 1903 and 1908. Robert A. Scalapino, "Prelude to Marxism: the Chinese Student Movement in Japan, 1900–1910," *Approaches to Modern Chinese History*, Albert Feuerwerker, ed. (1967), 190–215.

[9] P. M. A. Linebarger, *Government in Republican China* (1938), 34. Note also Key Ray Chong, "Cheng Kuan-ying (1841–1920): A Source of Sun Yat-sen's Nationalist Ideology?" *Journal of Asian Studies* 28 (1969): 247–67.

Alliance (*T'ung Meng Hui*), 1905–1912, and acquired the rudiments of a republican ideology. The object had become the overthrow of the Manchus, the establishment of a republic, and control of the parliamentary regime that would follow. At this stage, Sun's political ideas were still far from mature. His education had been more Western than Chinese, and because of his political exile his audience was composed in the main of overseas Chinese. As a consequence his revolutionary thought often appeared to wander about on an undefined intellectual frontier that lay somewhere between China and the West.

There was much of the cloak and dagger atmosphere in Sun's early revolutionary career. Following some abortive revolutionary efforts in 1885, Sun had moved his base of operations to Japan where, like Liang, he was associated with Japanese Pan-Asiatic advocates in a curious cabal of Chinese revolutionaries and Japanese nationalists, explainable only in relation to the impact of Western imperialism. From 1896 to 1898 Sun was in Europe, where he was released from detention in the Chinese legation in London through the intervention of friends and the British Foreign Office itself. During the Boxer troubles Sun was appealing in vain to Li Hung-chang to break with the Manchus and to support a democratic republic. From 1900 on, Sun's political aims were republicanism and nationalism; the means would be revolution by force. These ends and means were set forth in the Manifesto of the *T'ung Meng Hui* proclaimed at Tokyo in 1905, the year in which the Empress Dowager abolished the Confucian examinations. The Manifesto was one of the great landmarks in Sun Yat-sen's career, for it voiced what was to be the central theory of China's first modern political revolution: (1) the concept of equalization of land rights, and (2) the three stages in the revolutionary process: (a) the period of force and military control, (b) the period of political tutelage during which the people would be instructed in the responsibilities of citizenship, and (c) the final achievement of democratic, constitutional government. Actually, Sun was never a great success as a practitioner of revolution or as a theoretician preparing the ground by the clarity and force of his ideas. Certainly at this early period his aims were ill adapted to traditional China.

At this early formative stage of Sun's ideology, his doctrine of "equalization of land rights," derived from the single tax theory of Henry George, indicated a preoccupation, not with current agrarian problems of China's peasantry, but with the potential problems of a future capitalist society. Indeed, it was not until the 1920's that Sun's party, the *Kuomintang*, acknowledged the immediate and pressing need to assist the peasants. Thus Sun's early thinking leaned toward merely a preventive program against social injustice. He saw social problems largely in Western terms thus losing sight of the immediate realities of China's agrarian maladjustment. Moreover, Sun was a nationalist rather than a social reformer, yet it is significant that in these early years the leadership of the Chinese revolution leaned toward a form of socialism.[10]

ECONOMIC REFORM

Side by side with the Manchu reform program and the revolutionary agitations of Liang and Sun, China witnessed in the first decade of the twentieth century the beginnings of an industrial development. After 1896 nationals of the Treaty Powers enjoyed the right not only to trade, as previously, but also to engage in industry and manufacturing in the treaty ports. The appearance of this new foreign-owned factory industry em-

ploying cheap Chinese labor coincided with the appearance of the foreign naval leaseholds and the spheres of influence in 1898. This industrial activity, so threatening to China's rural handicraft industries, stirred the Manchu-Chinese government to encourage Chinese industry. Invention was invited by the offer of patents and monopolies. By 1906 a Ministry of Agriculture, Industry, and Commerce had been created at Peking; codes of commercial and company law were issued. As a result, there was some growth of Chinese factory industry, including cotton textile mills, electric plants, flour mills, match and tobacco factories, steel mills and silk filatures, and the construction of railroads. Financing of these enterprises was aided, though ineffectively, by the founding of the first modern Chinese banks to compete with the great foreign banking houses of the Treaty Ports. These developments, the beginnings of modern Chinese industrialization, were obviously of great significance, but, in general, the Manchu reform movement was designed not to encourage industry but to save the dynasty. The meager capital accumulation China possessed went into the purchase of land or into usurious loans to the peasantry. Furthermore, China's late nineteenth-century efforts toward industrialization were a part of the "self-strengthening" movement. They were joint official-merchant undertakings, and thus a prelude to the bureaucratic capitalism of republican China.[11]

OPIUM SUPPRESSION

One of the most notable Manchu efforts in reform was directed against the opium traffic which for a century and a half had played havoc with the physical and intellectual well-being of the Chinese people. Under the legalized trade after 1858, importation had continued to increase, reaching

[10] The fame of Sun Yat-sen as the father of China's first modern revolution was due to his skill as improviser, not to the quality of his ideas or his capacity as a political philosopher. At first considered to be no more than an uncouth conspirator, Sun, between 1896 and 1912, had improved greatly his political stature with China's growing and disaffected intellectual elite. It was political style, not ideas, that made him unique. Harold Z. Schiffrin, *Sun Yat-sen and the Origins of the Chinese Revolution* (1968), 1–9. Also Harold Schiffrin, "Sun Yat-sen's Early Land Policy," *Journal of Asian Studies* 16 (1957): 549–64, and Robert A. Scalapino and Harold Schiffrin, "Early Socialist Currents in the Chinese Revolutionary Movement," *Journal of Asian Studies* 18 (1959): 321–42.

[11] Peking's efforts toward industrialization in the first decade of the century may have been aided by the stirrings of nationalism and even by anti-dynastic movements. For background, En-han Lee, "China's Response to Foreign Investment in Her Mining Industry (1902–1911)," *Journal of Asian Studies* 28 (1968): 55–76.

77,966 piculs (a picul equals 133⅓ pounds) in 1888. After this date importations declined substantially but were replaced in part by production within China. The difficulties of the Chinese government in controlling the business were many. Even if it could have suppressed domestic cultivation in the provinces, which is doubtful, the deficit would have been promptly made up by foreign importation which under the treaties China was powerless to control. Furthermore, Peking needed the revenue derived from the import duties and from the taxes on domestic production. In India, from which most of the foreign opium came, the British government saw no reason to discourage production merely to enrich Chinese growers and venal officials. In China there was no disposition to suppress domestic cultivation merely to enrich foreign producers and traders. The heart of the trouble was the Chinese willingness to use opium, and little improvement could be expected until moral sentiment could be linked with effective administrative reforms.

The Chinese program of reform which took shape in the first decade of the twentieth century drew its inspiration from a number of sources. Chinese public sentiment against the drug was stimulated by the report of an American committee seeking to control the traffic in the Philippines. The Indian government, responding to moral sentiment in Britain, showed a disposition to co-operate with China. The first practical step was taken by the Imperial government in 1906, when it adopted a policy of taxing domestic opium out of existence. This was followed almost immediately by a policy designed to stop by gradual prohibition both the cultivation and use of opium. By 1907, encouraging progress had been achieved. Then, as a result of Anglo-Chinese negotiations, an agreement was reached in 1908 whereby Britain would decrease annually the opium exports to China. The arrangement was to run for three years, and to be continued for an additional seven if it was found that China had meanwhile continued effective measures of suppression at home. In 1911 the British government consented to renew the agreement. As a result, too, of findings of an official opium com-

mission, which met at Shanghai in 1909, the International Opium Conference at The Hague, 1911, reached an agreement among the powers having treaties with China whereby they agreed to take more effective measures to stop the smuggling of drugs into China, to close shops and dens in the foreign-controlled areas, and to prevent opium passing through the foreign post offices in China. It was just at this moment, when a victory over opium appeared in prospect, that the Revolution of 1911 occurred, turning, for the time being at least, the thoughts of the nation from social reform to political revolution.

A DECADE OF REFORM IN SUMMARY

China in the years 1901 to 1911 experienced one of the greatest dilemmas in her modern history. Her government sought to resolve a growing crisis through reforms which reached far beyond anything previously undertaken. The Empress Dowager's program was not circumscribed in the manner of "self-strengthening" to the grafting of a few modern institutions on an old Confucian stem. The new reforms looked toward fundamental transformation of the Chinese tradition, and their implementation set in motion or gave impetus to China's twentieth century revolution. Yet, as the Empress Dowager was buried in 1908, it was becoming evident that these reforms had not saved the dynasty. Modernization meant abandonment of the Confucian way. Philosophically the only claim of the alien Manchus to rule in China rested on their historic support of Confucianism.[12]

[12] Ernest P. Young, "Nationalism, Reform, and Republican Revolution: China in the Early Twentieth Century," *Modern East Asia: Essays in Interpretation*, James B. Crowley, ed. (1970),* 151–79.

FOR FURTHER READING

GENERAL. Mary C. Wright, ed., *China in Revolution: The First Phase, 1900–1913* (1968), essays by leading specialists. E.

Backhouse and J. O. P. Bland, *Annals and Memoirs of the Court of Peking* (London, 1914). Hu Shih, *The Chinese Renaissance* (1934; reissued 1963). Robert A. Scalapino and George T. Yu, *The Chinese Anarchist Movement* (1961) depicts the beginnings of the movement among Chinese in France and Japan in the early twentieth century. K'ang Yu-wei, *Ta t'ung shu, The One World Philosophy*, trans. by Lawrence G. Thompson into readable English (London, 1958), a book full of radical ideas written by the conservative scholar in his early years. John Gilbert Reid, *The Manchu Abdication and the Powers, 1908–1912* (1935), a basic and detailed study. Marion J. Levy, *The Family Revolution in Modern China* (1949).* Florence Ayscough, *Chinese Women, Yesterday and Today* (1937).

SUN YAT-SEN.   Sir James Cantlie, *Sun Yat-sen and the Awakening of China* (London, 1912). Hsueh Chun-tu, *Huang Hsing and the Chinese Revolution* (1961), an uneven study of one of Sun Yat-sen's close associates of early revolutionary days. Leng Shao Chuan and Norman D. Palmer, *Sun Yat-sen and Communism* (1960) succinctly defines Sun's connection with Soviet Russia. Marius B. Jansen, *The Japanese and Sun Yat-sen* (1954), a very able study of contacts and conflicts in Sino-Japanese revolutionary thought. S. Y. Teng, "Dr. Sun Yat-sen and Chinese Secret Societies," *Studies on Asia* (1963), 81–99, a challenging research work. Jerome Ch'en, *Yüan Shih-k'ai 1859–1916* (1961).

RELIGION AND REFORM.   Chan Wing-tsit, *Religious Trends in Modern China* (1953). Kenneth Scott Latourette, *A History of Christian Missions in China* (1929).

1902–1910:
Manchuria and Korea

chapter 18

The formal diplomatic settlement of the Boxer affair did not stabilize China's relations with the powers, nor did it implement a real open door policy. The renewed and immediate attack upon equal commercial opportunity in China and upon China's territorial and administrative integrity was centered in Manchuria, which had been occupied by Russia in 1900 as a result of the spread of Boxer outbreaks to areas where the Russians were completing construction of the Chinese Eastern Railway. Before the end of 1900 it was clear that Russia was secretly pressing China for a separate Manchurian agreement that would add greatly to her exclusive rights within her Manchurian sphere. This news was disturbing to Britain, Japan, and the United States, for these three powers had regarded the Boxer negotiations at Peking as providing a common and all-inclusive settlement between China and the powers. A separate settlement by Russia covering Manchuria would destroy this principle of cooperative action. The case was so urgent that Hay again circularized both China and the powers (February, 1901), warning the former

. . . of the impropriety, inexpediency, and even extreme danger to the interests of China of considering any private territorial or financial arrangements, at least without the full knowledge and approval of all the Powers now engaged in [the Boxer] negotiations.[1]

In April, Hay asked Russia for specific assurances that American enterprise in Manchuria would not suffer discrimination. Nevertheless, in November, 1901, the Russian Minister at Peking was standing over the deathbed of Li Hung-chang attempting to extort the dying viceroy's signature on a new Manchurian convention. So matters stood on January 30, 1902, when Great Britain and Japan signed the first Anglo-Japanese Alliance, an agreement which by effecting a complete readjustment in the balance of

[1] A. L. P. Dennis, *Adventures in American Diplomacy, 1896–1906* (1928), 243. For texts of most of the agreements referred to in this chapter, see J. V. A. MacMurray, ed., *Treaties and Agreements with and concerning China, 1894–1919* (2 vols., 1921), I. George A. Lensen, *The Russo-Chinese War* (1967), the most extensive and reliable account of the impact of the Boxer rebellion on Manchuria, holds that Russian policy was partially a response to Chinese opinion which had been organized to oppose foreign control of the Chinese Eastern Railway.

power was to have momentous influence on the future of Europe and the Far East.

The Anglo-Japanese Alliance pledged the signatories in support of "the status quo and general peace in the Extreme East," of the "independence and territorial integrity" of China and Korea, and of the open door there. This was the diplomatic window dressing. The real importance of the alliance was its recognition of the *special interests* of both powers in China, and the *special interests* of Japan "politically as well as commercially and industrially" in Korea. This was a victory for the principle of spheres of influence; it was an equally obvious defeat for the policies of the open door and co-operative action for its maintenance. The alliance went on to pledge each signatory to neutrality if the other was at war, and to come to the other's assistance if attacked by more than one power.[2] Since it was clear that the alliance was aimed at St. Petersburg, Russia and France replied with a declaration (March, 1902) taking cognizance of the alliance and reaffirming their adherence to the status quo and the integrity of China.

FOUNDATIONS OF THE ANGLO-JAPANESE ALLIANCE

How may the appearance of this vital alliance be explained? In its European context the treaty was Britain's first success in the effort to end her isolation. On the other hand, Japan accepted the alliance for considerations that were predominantly far eastern —to advance her interests in Korea, to protect those interests from the Russian threat arising in Manchuria, and, as with the British case, to end her own diplomatic isolation. Even with these interests at stake there was much Japanese opposition to the British alliance, led by Ito, who believed that a settlement should and could be reached with Russia.[3]

The key to official American reactions to the alliance and to American policy in the Far East, 1902–1904, is suggested by the fact that Secretary Hay, inadequately informed by his diplomatic service, was taken by surprise. When Russia, responding to the pressure of the alliance, agreed (April, 1902) to evacuate her troops from Manchuria within eighteen months (that is, by September 8, 1903), Hay appeared to be satisfied. In a letter to President Roosevelt the Secretary of State discussed the purposes of American policy with ungarnished realism.

We are not in any attitude of hostility towards Russia in Manchuria. On the contrary, we recognize her exceptional position in northern China. What we have been working for two years to accomplish, and what we have at last accomplished, if assurances are to count for anything, is that, no matter what happens eventually in northern China and Manchuria, the United States shall not be placed in any worse position than while the country was under the unquestioned domination of China.[4]

There were grounds for some of Hay's optimism, for had Russia carried out her convention with China by withdrawing her troops from Manchuria, there would have been no war. Not a single major power concerned would have disputed the Russian sphere of influence in Manchuria. Furthermore, withdrawal of the Russian troops would have removed the greatest danger to Japanese interests in Korea.

However, Russia did not withdraw. In reality, she reoccupied Manchuria, while at Peking she pressed new secret demands upon China.[5] These demands, which if granted

---

[2] Full text of the alliance in G. P. Gooch and H. W. V. Temperley, *British Documents on the Origins of the War, 1898–1914* (London, 1926–1938), II, 115–20.

[3] For Ito's views and his attempts to reach a settlement with Russia on the eve of the Alli-

ance, see Takeuchi Tatsuji, *War and Diplomacy in the Japanese Empire* (1935), 124–28. The work of the alliance propagandists is ably portrayed by C. N. Spinks, "The Background of the Anglo-Japanese Alliance," *The Pacific Historical Review* 8 (1939): 317–39. Also Ian H. Nish, *The Anglo-Japanese Alliance* (1966).

[4] Roosevelt Papers, printed in Tyler Dennett, *Roosevelt and the Russo-Japanese War* (1925), 135–36.

[5] By these demands China would have agreed, among other things, (1) not to create new treaty ports or admit additional consuls in Manchuria, and (2) to employ no foreigners save

would have ended even the pretense of an open door and China's integrity in Manchuria, have been interpreted variously. Until recently, they were regarded as evidence of a conflict between Russian factions: the one, headed by Witte, favoring gradual economic penetration that would not unduly alarm the powers; the other, led by State Councilor A. M. Bezobrazov, favoring immediate, aggressive economic and political pressure, backed by military force if necessary, to make Russia's position in Manchuria thoroughly secure, and to challenge eventually Japan's position in Korea. More recent research suggests that the Russian policy conceived in 1903 was not based on the whims of adventurers such as Bezobrazov and Admiral Alexieff, later appointed Viceroy of the Far East, but rather was a considered national policy formulated by responsible Russian statesmen.[6]

The failure of Russia to carry out the evacuation, and her presentation of new demands implementing the aggressive policy threatened to make the Manchurian question an exclusive Russo-Chinese concern and to nullify the negotiations for a new Sino-American treaty of commerce already under way. However, this treaty was signed, October 8, 1903, opening Antung and Mukden in Manchuria as treaty ports. This development, however, had no effect either on Russia or on Japan. It did signify that China's foreign policy, however passive, was significant and not entirely lacking in direction.

JAPAN AND RUSSIA

So it was that the way was left open for Japan, backed by the prestige and power of her new alliance with Britain, to challenge Russia, and to do so, ostensibly at least, in defense of the open door. In July, 1903, she opened direct negotiations with Russia for an understanding on both Manchuria and Korea. She proposed an arrangement whereby

(1) Chinese sovereignty and integrity in Manchuria would be respected; (2) the administration of Manchuria would be restored to Chinese hands, Russia retaining only railroad guards; (3) Japan would recognize Russian rights in Manchuria based on recognized treaties; and (4) Russia would recognize Japan's political as well as commercial and industrial interests in Korea as already set forth in the Anglo-Japanese Alliance.

The Russian response was at first dilatory, and when in January, 1904, its official attitude softened, conceding most, if not all, of what Japan had asked, the gesture had no effect since, at the same time, those who were in control at Port Arthur were insisting that Russia would not get out of Manchuria and that there would be no open door there. This meant war.

Japan's policy toward Russia had been fixed with some certainty as early as the spring of 1903. At that time it had been determined "to grant Russia a priority right in Manchuria" while insisting on Japan's unique status in Korea. When negotiations were undertaken with Russia in July, 1903, the Japanese cabinet had already decided to resort to arms, should such negotiations fail. Although this decision was opposed by Ito, it had the vigorous support of General Yamagata. Meanwhile, Japanese public opinion loudly demanded that Russia's advance in Manchuria be stopped. By November, 1903, there was little opposition to this popular, though inspired, public demand, and on February 4, the government reached its decision to sever diplomatic relations on February 6. On February 8, a Japanese squadron delivered a surprise attack on Port Arthur. War was declared on February 10. To neither power did it come as a surprise. Nor does history present a better example of a war fought by both powers for imperialistic ends; but, in assessing the relative responsibility, if this be possible,

. . . it can at least be said for Japan that her policy was based upon a real need. The argument for self-preservation is in her favor.[7]

Russians in Manchuria. United States, *Foreign Relations, 1903*, 53–54.

[6] John Albert White, *The Diplomacy of the Russo-Japanese War* (1964).

[7] W. L. Langer, "The Origins of the Russo-Japanese War" [from the original English manu-

The outbreak of war re-intensified the so-called Chinese question. There was little danger that other European powers would enter the conflict, but since the war was to be fought on Chinese territory, there was very real danger both to the open door and to China's integrity. Accordingly, President Roosevelt reasserted the Hay policy of 1900, asking the powers to respect "the neutrality of China and in all practical ways her administrative entity." Thus, the conception of *de jure* Chinese sovereignty over Manchuria was restored to American diplomacy. In this sense American policy in China was reinforced at least formally, but at the same time it was weakened by evident American willingness "to follow Great Britain's example and abandon . . . [Korea] to its Japanese fate." Russia was quick to ask why the United States opposed her in Manchuria while giving Japan a green light in Korea.[8] At the same time, in far western China the policy of China's integrity was rebuffed by the British. In the course of Anglo-American discussions on Tibet, the British referred to Chinese sovereignty there as a "constitutional fiction" and a "political affectation."

While the Russo-Japanese War was still in progress, the United States made two more efforts to keep alive the principle of China's

script], *Europaische Gesprache* IV, 279–335 (Hamburg, 1926). The more recent study, by Andrew Malozemoff, *Russian Far Eastern Policy 1881–1904* (1958), indicates that in 1903 Russia had no intention of starting aggressive action in Korea. This important work suggests that the motivations, objectives, and degree of Tsarist imperialism were not as constant as has been supposed. Personal records revealing much about the Japanese side of the conflict with Russia are: Sir Ernest Satow, *Korea and Manchuria between Russia and Japan, 1895–1904*, George A. Lensen, ed. (1966); and Albert d'Anethan, *The d'Anethan Dispatches from Japan, 1894–1910*, George A. Lensen, trans. and ed. (1967).

[8] Griswold, A. Whitney, *The Far Eastern Policy of the United States*, (1938) 96–97.* American diplomats in eastern Asia—Griscom at Tokyo, Allen at Seoul, as well as Hay and Rockhill—looked to Japan as the only, if not the most desirable, solution of the Korean problem.

integrity. The first of these was a diplomatic circular, January 13, 1905, similar to that of the previous year. The Russian response gave no satisfaction. The second case was President Roosevelt's demand upon Japan for assurance that she "adhere to the position of maintaining the open door in Manchuria and restoring that province to China." Without this assurance the President was not prepared to act as mediator. It would be foolish, however, to ignore the fact that the open door and the integrity of China meant little to other powers or that they were given more than diplomatic lip-service. Until such time as the United States was prepared to attack the spheres directly, its policies of the open door and China's integrity were destined to savor of the doctrinaire. Moreover, there was nothing to indicate that American public opinion would have sanctioned stronger measures even had the Department of State wished to apply them. Finally, American policy did not always remain true to its own doctrinaire principles. Hay himself became a concession hunter. What is more, he conceded that Chinese integrity in Manchuria was not essential so long as American treaty rights in the area were not infringed.

THE STAKES OF THE RUSSO-JAPANESE WAR

The Russo-Japanese War transformed the political complexion of the far eastern question, and in addition affected issues that were not exclusively far eastern. These issues involved the interests and policies of all the great European powers and the United States. For the moment, however, the complexities of the scene as a whole were overshadowed by the specific purposes of Russia and Japan in Korea and Manchuria. These purposes encompassed the question of Korea's independence and of China's territorial integrity. These questions in turn had already been prejudiced in the case of China by the widespread creation after 1897 of spheres of economic and political interest, and in the case of Korea by Britain's recognition there of Japan's primary interests as expressed in the first Anglo-Japanese Alliance. Control of Manchuria and Korea was the key to control of China. After 1902, Japan held in Korea the advantage given her by the Anglo-Japanese Alliance. After 1900, Russia held in Manchuria the advantage bestowed upon her by the Boxer troubles. She was in a position not only to claim Manchuria as a *de facto* sphere of influence but also to proceed to its political conquest, though she was not prepared to acknowledge Japan's primacy in Korea. Japan in turn was unwilling to share her political interest in Korea with any power. As to Manchuria, though Japan's interests and purposes there were still in the formative stage, it is clear that she wanted a Manchurian foothold. The chance of securing this foothold in the future could be safeguarded only by confining Russia's Manchurian interests within the narrowest interpretation, thus blocking any Russian scheme for a protectorate or for annexation. Consequently, as in 1899 and 1900, Japan appeared to be the spokesman of the open door and the integrity of China.

MILITARY CAMPAIGNS IN MANCHURIA

A major peculiarity of the Russo-Japanese War was that it was fought in Manchuria which was Chinese and hence neutral territory. However, since Russia after 1900 was in partial military occupation of Manchuria, and since Peking lacked the military power to defend the three eastern provinces, there was nothing for China to do but recognize this part of her territory as an area of hostilities and thereby to imply her consent to military operations there by the belligerents.[9]

Only a few of the military events of the war need be mentioned in passing. Japanese troops landed in Korea at Chemulpo, February 8 and 9. Other forces landed at Gensan

[9] Takahashi Sakuye, *International Law Applied to the Russo-Japanese War* (London, 1908), 250; and Amos S. Hershey, *The International Law and Diplomacy of the Russo-Japanese War* (1906), in particular Chapter 9, on China's neutrality.

on Korea's northeastern coast. General Kuroki's army crossed the Yalu River into Manchuria, May 1. A week later a second Japanese army under General Oku landed in South Manchuria (Liaotung) near the Russian leased territory, while another army under General Nodzu landed further east. On May 26 the Japanese cut the Russian lines at Nanshan, thus forcing them to withdraw to Port Arthur, July 31, and a month later the remaining Japanese armies (123,-000) faced the main Russian forces (158,000) under General Kuropatkin south of Mukden. At the Battle of Liaoyang (August 23–September 3), the Russians were forced back, but were not routed. At Sha-ho (October 9–17) the Russians attacked but failed to break the Japanese lines. The campaign was then halted during the bitter Manchurian winter, save at Port Arthur, which fell to the Japanese at terrific cost, January 2, 1905. Japan was thus able to reinforce her northern armies for the Battle of Mukden (February 23–March 10, 1905), in which for the first time she had superiority in numbers (400,000 to 325,000). Again the Russians were forced to retire, this time to Tiehling, north of Mukden. Two months later came Russia's most severe reverse—the destruction of her Baltic fleet in the Sea of Japan.

THE UNITED STATES AND THE PROBLEM OF PEACE

Efforts to find a basis for peace had been undertaken early in the war. Although she had won technical military victories on land and had destroyed Russian sea-power, Japan had failed to destroy the Russian armies. Each victory removed Japanese armies further from their base. At home the nation's economy had been strained to the point of danger. In a military sense, Russia's position showed some improvement as the war dragged on, but her funds were exhausted and French bankers were not disposed to extend further credits. In addition, revolutionary movements within Russia threatened the entire war effort.

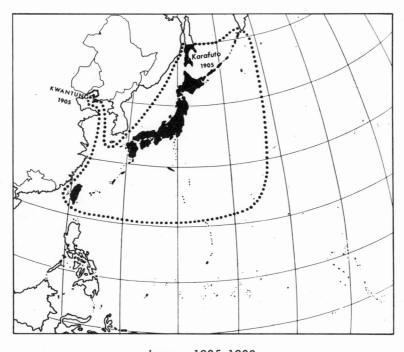

Japan   1905–1909

Reproduced from A War Atlas for Americans *(New York: Simon & Schuster) 1944, with permission from the publisher and from the U.S. Department of State, Division of Map Intelligence and Cartography.*

It was Japan that made the first formal proposal for peace on May 31, 1905, when she requested President Theodore Roosevelt on his own "initiative to invite the two belligerents to come together for the purpose of direct negotiation." Roosevelt's subsequent approach to the tsar was accepted June 6, and two days later the United States sent formal invitations to the belligerents, offering good offices. Both powers accepted. Roosevelt had acted because, as he said:

I believe that our future history will be more determined by our position on the Pacific facing China than our position on the Atlantic facing Europe.[10]

It is unnecessary here to treat in any detail the preliminaries of the peace settlement at Portsmouth, New Hampshire: the appointment of delegates, Witte and Rosen for Russia, Komura and Takahira for Japan;

[10] Dennis, *Adventures in American Diplomacy,* 406.

the death of Secretary Hay, July 1, 1905; the renewal of the Anglo-Japanese Alliance, August 12, 1905, recognizing Japan's "paramount political, military, and economic" interests in Korea; the signing of the secret treaty of Bjorko between the kaiser and the tsar; the alleged success of Witte in capturing American sympathy for Russia's case; the capacity of the Japanese "by their stiffness and taciturnity" to lose in the negotiations the advantage won by their military and naval victories; and the other repeated crises into which the negotiations fell.[11]

[11] Older studies on the war and the peace, Tyler Dennett, *Roosevelt and the Russo-Japanese War* (1925), and Dennis, *Adventures in American Diplomacy* have been superseded in some measure by Raymond A. Esthus, *Theodore Roosevelt and Japan* (1966), and Charles Neu, *An Uncertain Friendship: Theodore Roosevelt and Japan, 1906–1909* (1967). In regard to American public opinion and the Portsmouth Peace Conference, a study of the leading American newspapers shows that there was no "overnight" change in American public opinion. Indeed, the

The Treaty of Portsmouth, September 5, 1905, was destined to become one of the most consequential agreements in the modern history of the Far East. By it Japan acquired from Russia, subject to the consent of China, the Liaotung leased territory, the southern section of the Chinese Eastern Railroad from Kuan-ch'eng-tzu (near Changchun) to Port Arthur, along with certain coal mines which belonged to or were worked by the Russians. Both powers agreed "to evacuate completely and simultaneously Manchuria," except the Liaotung leasehold, within eighteen months after the treaty became effective. Both powers, however, reserved the right "to maintain guards" to protect their respective railway lines in Manchuria. Russia declared that she did not have in Manchuria "any territorial advantages or preferential or exclusive concessions in impairment of Chinese sovereignty or inconsistent with the principle of equal opportunity." Both Japan and Russia engaged "not to obstruct any general measures common to all countries, which China may take for the development of the commerce and industry of Manchuria." The two powers also agreed to "exploit their respective railways in Manchuria exclusively for commercial and industrial purposes and in no wise for strategic purposes with the exception of the railways in the Liaotung leased territory." With regard to Korea, Russia acknowledged that Japan possessed in Korea paramount political, military, and economic interests, and engaged not to obstruct such measures as Japan might deem necessary to take there. The southern half (Karafuto) of the island of Sakhalin was ceded to Japan in lieu of a war indemnity, and Japan was granted fishing rights in certain territorial waters of Siberia on the Pacific. Most important of all, the war had convinced both powers of the futility of working at cross-purposes. Indeed, the Treaty

of Portsmouth opened the door to a period of Russo-Japanese collaboration in Manchuria.

JAPAN'S NEW POSITION IN KOREA

Prior to 1905, Japan considered her primary interests to be in Korea rather than Manchuria. The decade 1894–1904 had been a period of intense but intermittent Russo-Japanese economic rivalry in Korea. The Anglo-Japanese Alliance (1902) recognized that Japan was "interested in a peculiar degree politically as well as commercially and industrially in Korea." With the outbreak of the Russo-Japanese War, Korea proclaimed her neutrality but took no steps to defend it, believing, it would seem, that benevolent protection would come from the United States and the great powers of western Europe. Japan, however, was no longer concerned with Korean neutrality or Korean independence. In the military sphere, Korea was now looked upon as a necessary base of operations against Russia, and in the political sphere the peninsula was soon to be subjected to intimate Japanese control. Japanese forces occupied Seoul (February 8, 1904) the day Togo attacked Port Arthur, and a protocol signed February 23 laid the groundwork for the subsequent Japanese protectorate. Korea was to place "full confidence" in Japan and to "adopt the advice of the latter with regard to improvements in administration." Japan would definitely guarantee the independence and territorial "integrity" of Korea and to this end might interfere in Korean affairs. Korea was pledged not to conclude with third powers any agreement "contrary to the principles" of the protocol. In additional agreements (August 19–22, 1904), Japan was empowered to appoint advisers to the Korean departments of finance and foreign affairs. By the beginning of 1905 Japan had assumed responsibility for policing the Korean capital and had placed a Japanese police inspector in each province. Moreover, international sanction was promptly given to Japan's new position in Korea. William Howard Taft,

---

American public held to well-established pro-Japanese sympathies. See W. B. Thorson, "American Public Opinion and the Portsmouth Peace Conference," *The American Historical Review* 53 (1947–1948); 439–64.

Roosevelt's Secretary of War, in conversations with the Japanese Prime Minister, General Count Katsura, gave his approval, later confirmed by the President, to a Japanese suzerainty in Korea.[12] In August, the renewed Anglo-Japanese Alliance referred to Japan's "paramount" interests at Seoul, and in September, Russia likewise acknowledged Japan's "paramount" position (Article II of the Treaty of Portsmouth). With this international sanction, Japan, through pressure exerted at Seoul, secured from the Korean government an agreement giving Japan control of Korea's foreign relations and the right to appoint a Japanese resident-general at Seoul. On the following day the United States instructed its Minister at Seoul to close the legation. Willard Straight described this diplomatic retreat as "like the stampede of rats from a sinking ship." The establishment of the Japanese protectorate in Korea was thus complete. Having consolidated her position at Seoul, Japan was prepared to implement in South Manchuria the new position which the Treaty of Portsmouth had given her.[13]

STEEL RAILS AND POLITICS
IN MANCHURIA

In general, the Treaty of Portsmouth divided Manchuria into "North Manchuria," where Russia claimed a sphere of influence, and "South Manchuria," where Japan was about to create a sphere.[14] Since Japan had

professed to be fighting for the open door and the integrity of China in Manchuria, the conclusion of peace was greeted with general popular enthusiasm in Europe and America; but American investors and merchants in the Far East disapproved of the treaty because they feared that Japan would now curb their own activity in the Orient, particularly in the promising frontier area of South Manchuria. In its simplest form, the question was whether Manchuria was to be open on terms of equality to the commerce, industry, and capital of all nations, or whether it was to be an exclusive economic preserve of Russia and Japan, buttressed by Russian and Japanese political control in derogation of Chinese sovereignty and administration.

Although ratifications of the Treaty of Portsmouth were exchanged at Washington (November 25, 1905), the former belligerents had agreed to an eighteen-month period in which to complete evacuation of their armies. This meant that for more than a year Manchuria remained partly under military occupation. Although agreements of this type were common at the termination of hostilities, they were often the subject of abuse or of misunderstanding. In the case of South Manchuria, as early as March, 1906 the United States called to Japan's attention charges from American interests in China that Japanese actions could result only in the exclusion of all but Japanese trade by the time the territory was evacuated. Thus within six months of the conclusion of peace the United States was calling upon Japan, as it had previously called upon Russia, to respect the principle of equal opportunity.

THE SINO-JAPANESE TREATY
OF PEKING

The Treaty of Portsmouth had provided that the transfer to Japan of Russian territorial, railway, and other rights in South

[12] H. F. Pringle, *Theodore Roosevelt* (London, 1932),* 384. Japan in turn satisfied Roosevelt by a disavowal of any aggressive purpose in the Philippines. For the nature and meaning of the so-called Taft-Katsura understanding see Raymond A. Esthus, "The Taft-Katsura Agreement—Reality or Myth?" *Journal of Modern History* 31 (1959): 46–51, and Jongsuk Chay, "The Taft-Katsura Memorandum Reconsidered," *Pacific Historical Review* 37 (1968): 321–26.

[13] For a Japanese account of the Korean negotiations, see Takeuchi, *War and Diplomacy*, 160–62.

[14] The line of demarcation between these spheres (North and South Manchuria) was defined in the secret Russo-Japanese treaties of 1907, 1910, and 1912. See E. B. Price, *The Russo-Japanese Treaties of 1907–1916* . . .

(1933). An able pioneering study in a very complex and neglected economic field is Kungtu C. Sun assisted by Ralph W. Huenemann, *The Economic Development of Manchuria in the First Half of the Twentieth Century* (1969).

Manchuria was to be conditional on the consent of China. This consent was secured by Japan's Foreign Minister, Baron Komura, in negotiations with Yuan Shih-k'ai at Peking in a treaty dated December 22, 1905. An additional Sino-Japanese agreement of the same date contained important provisions: (1) China agreed to open sixteen cities in Manchuria to international residence and trade; (2) Japan agreed to withdraw her troops and railway guards (if Russia would withdraw her railway guards) when "China shall have become herself capable of affording full protection to the lives and property of foreigners"; (3) Japan secured the right to maintain the military railway she had built from Antung on the Korean border to Mukden; and (4) China consented to formation of a Sino-Japanese corporation to exploit the Yalu forests.

Moreover, this formal Sino-Japanese treaty and additional agreement were later claimed by the Japanese government to be supplemented by secret "protocols," the most important of which pledged the Chinese government not to construct any mainline railway "in the neighborhood of and parallel to" the Japanese South Manchuria Railway (running from Changchun to Port Arthur and Dalny, now Dairen), or any branch line "which might be prejudicial" to the Japanese line.

To manage the railroad and the other properties acquired from Russia in South Manchuria the Japanese government created the South Manchuria Railway Company—a joint stock company in which the Japanese government owned one-half of the capital stock and controlled appointment of the principal officers. Shareholders were limited to the Chinese and Japanese governments and to subjects of these two countries. The president and vice-president were responsible to the Japanese prime minister. The company was empowered to engage in subsidiary enterprises such as mining, water transportation, electric power, real estate, and warehousing within the railway zone. In addition, the company possessed broad civil administrative powers and authority to collect taxes within the same zone. This company became an amazingly effective agent of Japanese penetration in Manchuria. Protection of the railroad was provided by the government of Japan's leased territory of Kwantung (Liaotung), which was under a governor-general of high military rank who also exercised civil administrative power in the leased territory. Indeed, the development of South Manchurian resources resulting from the capital, the energy, and the efficiency of the South Manchurian Railway Company not only excited the jealousy of other foreign nationals, principally British and American, but also inspired the fear that Japanese railroads using the S.M.R. as the trunk would branch out east and west to the exclusion of all non-Japanese enterprise.

JURISDICTION IN MANCHURIA AFTER 1905

Among the more significant features of Japan's emerging special position in South Manchuria after 1905 were certain jurisdictional powers. Within the Kwantung leased territory she possessed all rights of administration pertaining to sovereignty except the power to alienate the territory. In addition, Japan and Russia exercised special jurisdictional and administrative powers in their respective railway zones. Powers *exercised* by Japan included: ordinary rights of administration pertaining to sovereignty, taxation, police, and transfer of real property; employment of a limited number of railroad guards to protect the railway; and the exercise of ordinary police power and of customary functions of municipal and local administration. Over and above the foregoing powers, Japan enjoyed, as did also other "treaty powers," extraterritoriality and consular jurisdiction long established in China's treaties with foreign powers. In North Manchuria, Russia continued to hold a comparable position save that she no longer possessed a leasehold.

INTENSIFICATION OF INTERNATIONAL RIVALRY

Although in Manchuria after 1905 China's sovereign rights were specifically reserved in the Kwantung territory and the

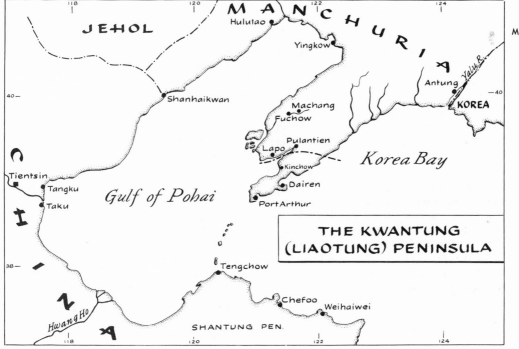

various railway zones, *de facto* administration was exercised by Russia (the Chinese
Eastern Railway) in North Manchuria, and
by Japan (the Government General of Kwantung and the S.M.R.) in South Manchuria.
Far from decreasing foreign (Russian) control in Manchuria, the Russo-Japanese War
had paved the way for Sino-Russian and
Sino-Japanese agreements by which two
powers instead of one claimed spheres of
influence there. In these circumstances there
were few grounds for optimism on the future
of the open door doctrine and the integrity
of China. Foreign business interests in China,
British and American in particular, had anticipated great opportunities for their goods
and capital in South Manchuria once peace
was restored. These opportunities had not
appeared, and the powers were therefore
concerned to discover how far Japan and
Russia were bent on a policy of preference,
if not monopoly, for their own commerce,
industry, and capital. A test case was soon
forthcoming.

BRITAIN AND FRANCE IN MANCHURIA, 1907

The Chinese government in November,
1907, contracted with a British firm to build
a short railroad from Hsinmintun to Faku-
men. In its origins this contract was an out-
growth of agreements made as early as 1898
between the Chinese government and the
(British) Hong Kong and Shanghai Banking
Corporation for the construction of certain
railways in Manchuria. Its revival in 1907
was due to private British and American
interests seeking to challenge Japan's strategic position. The Japanese government
promptly protested that the proposed line
violated the secret "protocols" of 1905, the
new road being in the Japanese view "parallel" and "prejudicial" to the S.M.R. The
success of the Japanese protest was assured
when the British government refused to support the British concessionaires or to call in
question the validity of the "protocol" on
which Japan's protest was based.

Japan's post-war position in Manchuria was reinforced by diplomatic measures far more fundamental than the blocking of a small proposed railway. High on the list of Japanese aims was the problem of coming to workable terms with her recent enemy, Russia. This objective was rendered easier by the fact that statesmen friendly to an entente were in power at Tokyo (Saionji, Hayashi, and Motono) and at St. Petersburg (Iswolsky). This road to a general Russo-Japanese rapprochement was paved by France. France had opposed Japan in 1895 (the Triple Intervention); she was allied with Russia during 1904–1905; and therefore it was now good policy, in view of Japan's victory, for France to clarify her relations with Tokyo, and to aid in creating a Russo-Japanese entente. The Franco-Japanese treaty, which materialized on June 10, 1907, and which was to provide the formula for subsequent Russo-Japanese agreements, is notable ". . . for its complete *sang-froid,* its subtle implications, and its bold assumptions." [15] The two powers, after agreeing "to respect the independence and integrity of China, as well as the principle of equal treatment in that country for the commerce and subjects or citizens of all nations," went on to assert that they possessed "a special interest" in preserving peace and order "especially in the regions of the Chinese Empire adjoining the territories where they possess rights of sovereignty, protection or occupation." These two powers then proceeded to constitute themselves as the guardians of peace in vast areas of China which they later defined as including, in the case of France, the Chinese provinces of Kwangtung, Kwangsi, and Yunnan; and, in the case of Japan, Fukien and "the regions of Manchuria and Mongolia."

Following promptly this remarkable Franco-Japanese treaty came important Russo-Japanese agreements. These included a treaty of commerce and navigation and a fisheries convention,[16] and two political conventions, one public, the other secret. The public convention subscribed, as always, to the "independence and territorial integrity of the Empire of China," and pledged the signatories "to sustain and defend the maintenance of the status quo and respect for this principle by all pacific means within their reach." The secret convention (not revealed until published by the Soviet government, 1918) established precedents of the greatest importance:

1. It drew a line of demarcation between North and South Manchuria (the Russian and the Japanese spheres).
2. North of this line Japan undertook not to seek for herself or her subjects, nor to obstruct Russian efforts there to secure concessions for railroads or telegraphs.
3. Russia undertook neither "to interfere with nor to place any obstacle in the way of the *further development*" of the "relations of political solidarity between Japan and Korea."
4. Japan, "recognizing the special interests of Russia [in Outer Mongolia, undertook] . . . to refrain from any interference which might prejudice those interests." [17]

THE UNITED STATES AND MANCHURIA, 1905–1910

The Franco-Japanese and the Russo-Japanese agreements of 1907 reinforced the doctrine of spheres of influence, and by implication weakened further China's territorial integrity and the principle of equal opportunity. Indeed, what had become of the open door in Manchuria after 1905 has never been described more realistically than by ex-President Roosevelt to his successor, President Taft:

. . . *As regards Manchuria, if the Japanese choose to follow a course of conduct to which we are adverse, we cannot stop it unless we are prepared to go to war. . . . The "Open Door" policy in China was an excellent thing . . . , but as has been proved by the whole history of Manchuria, the "Open Door" policy completely disappears as soon*

[15] Price, *The Russo-Japanese Treaties of 1907–1916 Concerning Manchuria and Mongolia* (1933), 26–31.

[16] MacMurray, *Treaties,* I, 643–48.

[17] Text in Price, *The Russo-Japanese Treaties,* 107–11.

as a powerful nation determines to disregard it, and is willing to run the risk of war rather than forego its intention.[18]

The foregoing explains why the American government under the presidency of Theodore Roosevelt was not prepared to lead any offensive against Japan's claim to special interests in South Manchuria. There were Americans, however, both in and outside government who did attempt to challenge the Japanese position. In 1905, E. H. Harriman, hoping to build a round-the-world transportation system, reached an understanding with Ito and Katsura to finance the reconstruction of the railway (S.M.R.) which Japan hoped to acquire from Russia at the end of the war. After peace came, Japan dropped the scheme. In Tokyo it seemed better policy to secure funds in London, where the Anglo-Japanese Alliance had recently been renewed. Moreover, the scheme probably would have foundered in any event due to rivalry among American bankers.

Far more active than Harriman in furthering American commerce and capital in Manchuria was Willard Straight, Consul-General of the United States at Mukden, 1906–1908. Straight was convinced that the weakness of the United States in the Far East was due to the relatively small American capital investment in China. A Sino-American publicity bureau which he inspired was so active that the Japanese protested and the bureau was liquidated. Straight made little progress with his official superiors as long as Roosevelt remained in the White House. Indeed, the President was less concerned with Japan and American capital in Manchuria than he was with the possibility of hostile Japanese action against the Philippines. Roosevelt's ideas were shaped in part by the crisis of 1906 in American-Japanese relations when the San Francisco School Board segregated Oriental students in the city schools. The "Gentleman's Agreement," 1907–1908, restored in part a sense of diplomatic calm, but war talk was such in

the summer of 1907 that the President sent General Leonard Wood, commanding the troops in the Philippines, special instructions for meeting a Japanese attack, while Taft was again sent to Tokyo (October, 1907), from where he reported that Japan was anxious to avoid war. To meet the crisis in more fundamental ways, Roosevelt decided on two lines of action: (1) he sent the American fleet on a world cruise including Japanese ports (March 1907, to February 1909); and (2) he refused to take the offensive against Japan's position in Manchuria.[19]

While the American fleet pursued its course in foreign waters the President employed the less provocative arts of diplomacy with the Japanese in Washington. A five-year arbitration treaty was concluded with Japan (May, 1908). It was an innocuous affair excluding all questions of "vital interests," but nonetheless a peaceful gesture. This treaty was followed by an exchange of notes between Secretary of State Root and the Japanese Ambassador, Takahira (November 30, 1908), which "was as important for what it left unsaid as for what it definitely stipulated." Since the phraseology of the notes was delightfully general there was ground for the belief that the exchange meant more than appeared on the surface. Certainly it would seem that the Root-Takahira exchange gave some sort of moral sanction to the special position of Japan in Korea and Manchuria. At the same time there is nothing to indicate that Root intended to give Japan a free hand in Manchuria. To the American government the notes meant guarantees on the Philippines, Hawaii, and Alaska, a reiteration of the open door and integrity of China, and a quieting of war talk. To the Japanese the notes gave assurance of peace, a guarantee of Formosa, and acceptance by the United States of the treaties giving Japan a special position in Eastern Asia.[20]

[18] Roosevelt to Taft, December 22, 1910, quoted by Griswold, *Far Eastern Policy*, 132.

[19] T. A. Bailey, *Theodore Roosevelt and the Japanese-American Crises* (1934), Chapters 9, 12.

[20] T. A. Bailey, "The Root-Takahira Agreement of 1908," *The Pacific Historical Review* 9 (March, 1940): 19–35.

The Roosevelt-Root policy toward Japan and Manchuria was soon to give place to a new American strategy. William Howard Taft and Philander C. Knox became President and Secretary of State respectively at a time when American capital was to look increasingly to foreign fields for investment. Government was sympathetic, and, as Taft said later, its policy substituted "dollars for bullets" and combined "idealistic humanitarian sentiments" with "legitimate commercial aims." The commercial machinery of the Department of State was enlarged, and from November, 1908, until June, 1909, its Far Eastern Division was headed by Willard Straight, who worked incessantly to maintain Harriman's interest in Manchurian railway finance and to enlist the interest of New York bankers. Early in 1909 these efforts bore fruit. At the instance of the State Department an American banking group was designated "as the official agent of American railway financing in China," with Straight as its Peking representative. The Department then demanded of China that the American bankers be admitted to the Hukuang railway loan then under negotiation between China and three bankings groups representing British, French, and German interests. The new American policy was thus striking at European financial monopoly in China Proper as well as at the Japanese in Manchuria. This was in line with the objectives of Taft and Knox "to force American capital by diplomatic pressure" into a region of the world where it would not go of its own accord. Also it meant that Secretary Knox was to attempt what was diplomatically impossible, to "smoke Japan out" of her position in Manchuria despite the fact that Japan by 1907 "had given general notice of her determination to dominate as much of Manchuria as she could." [21]

Implementation of the smoking-out experiment was begun by Straight and Harriman, who in 1909 were also attempting to buy the Chinese Eastern Railway from

Russia. What Harriman really wanted was the Japanese S.M.R., but the Japanese had refused to sell. Therefore Harriman would force the sale by buying the Russian road and connecting it with the Gulf of Pechihli by a new line parallel to the S.M.R. from Chinchow (near Shanhaikwan where the Great Wall meets the sea) to Aigun on the Amur. If the threat of construction did not bring the Japanese to terms, then actual construction of the Chinchow-Aigun line would be undertaken. "He [Harriman] would smash competitors in Manchuria exactly as he had smashed them at home." [22] But Harriman died on September 10, 1909, and although Straight secured from the Manchurian government a preliminary agreement to finance (by the American group) and construct (by a British firm) the Chinchow-Aigun line, the bankers in New York without Harriman's leadership became timid. Harriman's railroad politics had failed.

THE KNOX NEUTRALIZATION PROPOSAL

It seemed that if dollar diplomacy had any resources left, this was the time to use them. Accordingly, on November 6, 1909, Secretary Knox made two striking (some would say fantastic) proposals to Great Britain: (1) that the foreign-owned Manchurian railways (C.E.R. and S.M.R. systems) be "neutralized" by providing China with funds to purchase them through a great multipower loan, during the life of which the railroads would be under foreign, international control; and (2) in case "neutralization" proved impracticable, that Great Britain join with the United States in supporting the Chinchow-Aigun project and in inviting powers "friendly to complete commercial neutralization of Manchuria to participate." These propositions were as Gargantuan as they were romantic.

Sir Edward Grey approved "the general principle" of the neutralization proposal but thought it "wiser to postpone" any consideration of its application. As to the

[21] J. G. Reid, *The Manchu Abdication and the Powers* (1935), 75.

[22] Griswold, *Far Eastern Policy*, 152–53; Reid, *Manchu Abdication*, 42.

Chinchow-Aigun proposal, Sir Edward thought nothing should be done until China had agreed to Japanese participation. With this British approval in principle but refusal in fact, Knox approached the Chinese, French, German, Japanese, and Russian governments. Russia and Japan, after consulting with each other, rejected the neutralization scheme in notes that showed a marked similarity. In addition they warned China that they must be consulted before foreign capital was employed in Manchurian railway enterprise. As a result, France and Great Britain gave notice that they would not support the United States in the Chinchow-Aigun line. The plans of Harriman, Straight, and Knox had miscarried. But this was not all. Secretary Knox had hastened, if he did not actually cause, a tightening of the Russian and the Japanese spheres in Manchuria. On July 4, 1910, Russia and Japan signed two conventions, again, as in 1907, one public and the other secret. They announced to the world "the perfecting" of their connecting railway service in Manchuria. They refrained from any mention of China's integrity and the open door, but engaged publicly, in case the status quo should be menaced, to decide "the measures that they may judge necessary to take for the maintenance of the said status quo." Secretly the two powers reaffirmed the line of demarcation drawn between their spheres in 1907, and strengthened their "special position" by recognizing "the right of each, within its own sphere, freely to take all measures necessary for the safeguarding and the defense of those interests." Finally, the secret convention provided for "common action" in defense of their special interests. The significance of dollar diplomacy as practiced by Knox in this instance is that it had not opened—on the contrary, it tended to close—the door to American capital in Manchuria.

Summarized in broad perspective, the years between the end of the Russo-Japanese War and the close of the Taft administration formed a chapter in American far eastern diplomacy distinguished for virility if not for judicious purpose and method.

Japan was creating a new balance of power in Eastern Asia. In China the collapsing Confucian order was giving place to impotency and revolution. Into the tumult of these changes stepped American finance and its government seeking to play a decisive role in Eastern Asia. Leadership was provided by the brilliance of young Willard Straight, hero or evil genius according to interpretation. Although possessed of personal and intellectual charm, Straight was a pathetic failure as diplomat, financial agent, and judge of men and nations. He set the American pattern in anti-Japanese thought which was to be of such consequence in later years. All the efforts of Harriman, Straight, Knox, the bankers, and the so-called Manchurian wing of the Department of State failed to reverse the pattern set by the Root-Takahira exchange. On the contrary, dollar diplomacy in the Far East stimulated the very things it was designed to destroy—Japan and Russia's spheres of influence.[23]

THE ANNEXATION OF KOREA

It will be recalled that by 1905 Korea had become a Japanese protectorate, and was so recognized internationally. Roosevelt had written to Hay (January 29, 1905): "We cannot possibly interfere for the Koreans against Japan. They could not strike a blow in their own defense." Nevertheless, the emperor of Korea persisted in the belief that the United States would come to his country's rescue because of the "good offices" clause in the Korean-American treaty of 1882. The Department of State, however, had taken the view that the earlier Japanese-Korean agreements of 1904 had already created a Japanese protectorate, which Korea had not protested; she had thus deprived herself of any further grounds for appeal under the good offices clause.

Despite the fact that by 1907 the Korean royal palace was guarded by Japanese police,

[23] For an extended study, see Charles Vevier, *The United States and China, 1906–1913* (1955), especially 35–170.

an official Korean delegation, bearing credentials from the emperor and advised by H. B. Hulbert, an American teacher long resident in Korea, arrived at the Hague Peace Conference. The mission was to make known "the violation of our [Korean] rights by the Japanese" and to re-establish "direct diplomatic relations" with the powers. Neither the Conference nor the Dutch government would receive the mission. Japan acted promptly. The Elder Statesmen felt that "the hour had not yet come to push to extreme limits [annexation] the chastisement for the felony committed." Instead "the [Korean] emperor king was forced to abdicate the throne in favor of his son" and a new agreement was concluded "whereby the Japanese resident-general became a virtual regent." Under this agreement all matters of internal administration as well as foreign relations were to be controlled by the resident-general.

With Japanese control tightening its grip on the entire Korean administration, the Korean problem as seen by the Japanese government again became an integral part of the larger Manchurian scene, where Japan and Russia had come to an understanding (in the 1907 and 1910 secret treaties) in order to block the policies of Straight, Harriman, and Knox. As early as the spring of 1909 Foreign Minister Komura had secured the approval of Premier Katsura and Prince Ito to a memorandum "strongly recommending" Korean annexation, a proposal which soon had the approval of the cabinet and the emperor. Meanwhile, Ito, having resigned as resident-general (June, 1909) to become president of the Privy Council, went to Harbin (October, 1909) to meet Russian Minister of Finance Kokovtseff and to prepare the way for a closer understanding with Russia. In July 1909, Viscount Sone, who had replaced Ito in Korea, had already secured an agreement placing the administration of Korean courts and prisons under direct Japanese control. Indeed, every preparation had been made for executing the predetermined policy of annexation. The assassination of Ito by a Korean in Harbin (October 26,

1909) served only to increase the popular and public demand in Japan for immediate annexation. Then on June 24, the day on which the draft Russo-Japanese treaties of July 4, 1910, were shown to the British and French governments, the Korean police were placed under the command of the Japanese resident-general and minister of war. General Terauchi, Minister of War, "under heavy guard," reached Seoul on July 23. "All organs of public opinion had been "suspended or ruthlessly suppressed." In the audience that followed, Terauchi presented the young Korean sovereign with a face-saving means of escape: a request for annexation from the emperor of Korea to the emperor of Japan. The treaty of annexation was signed August 22, 1910, and proclaimed seven days later.

With the annexation of Korea by Japan in 1910, a particular phase of modern Far Eastern history was brought to a close. During the previous thirty years, the traditional Chinese world order had been destroyed, step by step, by Great Britain in Burma, by France in Indochina, and by Japan in Formosa, the Liu-ch'iu islands, and Korea. Moreover, the Powers (France, Great Britain, Germany, Japan, and Russia) had acquired a new influence within China itself through their spheres of influence (see Chapter 15). Even the United States had taken a colony in the Philippines. The old China-centered order had been replaced by the disorder of intense rivalry among the great Western powers and Japan.

China herself had sunk to a status that might almost be called semi-colonialism, while her former tributary states had become, in fact, the colonies of other powers. In general these states lacked both the power and the mot'vation to achieve independence or to maintain it. The case of Korea was notable in this respect. There the Yi dynasty, authoritarian, paternalistic, yet lacking any effective machinery for centralization, had been the prey of its own degenerate court politics for at least three centuries. Thus in the temper of the times, Korea's fate in 1910 was the natural result, however undesirable, of the general march of events.[24]

SUMMATION OF AMERICAN ATTITUDES AND POLICY

The critical posture of popular American reactions to Japan's annexation of Korea was hardly surprising. The honeymoon period in American-Japanese relations had come to an end with Japan's emergence as a so-called great power. Korea now shared with China in American public opinion a "paternalism and a benign sentimentality" which had long marked popular American attitudes toward the Middle Kingdom. Rather mystical feelings of friendship for China had long been nourished by the belief that China was seeking modernization, that she was plagued by dreadful natural calamities, that she was

[24] In a number of phases of modern Far Eastern history, the student will come upon what may be described as the *conspiratorial theory of history*. A case in point is the Japanese seizure of Korea. In this instance the conspiratorial theory postulates that beginning with the early years of Meiji, Japan developed and adhered to a master plan for the conquest of Korea. In reality, this type of interpretation, while having the virtues of simplicity, tends to minimize the play of other very complex forces. Japan's actions in Korea, like the actions of other powers elsewhere, were often treacherous and cruel, but it does not appear that the thesis of "conspiracy" has as yet been proved. The ablest summary of what happened to Korea is C. I. Eugene Kim and Han-kyo Kim, *Korea and the Politics of Imperialism 1876–1910* (1967), 219–23. Note also the fundamental studies by Hilary Conroy, *The Japanese Seizure of Korea: 1868–1910* (1960); and "Lessons from Japanese Imperialism," *Monumenta Nipponica*, 21 (Nos. 3–4): 335–46. Studies which present or which lean toward the conspiratorial theory include, among others, Frederick Foo Chien, *The Opening of Korea: A Study of Chinese Diplomacy 1876–1885* (1967) which makes significant contributions, and the study by Dong Chou, *Japanese Annexation of Korea: A Study of Japanese-Korean Relations to 1910* (1955), published on microfilm, doctoral dissertation ser. No. 16932, 1957. For a summary of conflicting interpretations see the "Review Article," *Journal of Asian Studies* 22 (1963): 469–72.

a victim of European and Japanese aggression, that American, particularly church philanthropy in China, had achieved far more than it actually had, and that these American efforts were in line with the aspirations of the Chinese people. It was quite easy for Americans to assume that the same philanthropic spirit was at the heart of official American policy in China. Paradoxically, this same American public which "believed" so devoutly in China was uninformed about and indifferent to her save in moments of crisis. Actually, American public sentiment and official policy were not one and the same, though they usually appeared to be because the official language used to describe American policy (for example the phrases, "the Open Door," "China's independence and territorial and administrative integrity") implied a concern for China rather than a concern for American interests. Thus, both in the United States and abroad, the impression was created that the United States had become the guardian of China, protecting it from the ravages of European and Japanese aggression. This fanciful myth was to persist in the popular American mind until the communist conquest of China in 1949.[25]

[25] For the full development of the subject see Paul A. Varg, *The Making of a Myth: the United States and China, 1897–1912* (1968), especially 1–13. Thomas J. McCormick, "American Expansion in China," *American Historical Review*, 75 (1970): 1393–96, comments critically on Varg's thesis.

FOR FURTHER READING

GENERAL. Lung Chang, *La Chine à L'Aube Du XX Siècle: Les Relations Diplomatiques De La Chine Avec Les Puissances Depuis La Guerre Sino-Japanaise Jusqu'à La Guerre Russo-Japonaise* (Paris, 1962). Stephen Uhalley, Jr., "The Wai-wu Pu: The Chinese Foreign Office from 1901–1911," *Journal of the China Society*, V (1967), 9–27. George H. Blakeslee, *Japan and Japanese-American*

Relations (1912). Earl Miner, *The Japanese Tradition in British and American Literature* (1958).*

THE RUSSO-JAPANESE CONFLICT. Asakawa Kanichi, *The Russo-Japanese Conflict, Its Causes and Issues* (1904), an important contemporary Japanese view of the causes of the war. Edwin A. Falk, *Togo and the Rise of Japanese Sea Power* (1936), the best account of the life of one of the outstanding naval figures of modern times. Eugene P. Trani, *The Treaty of Portsmouth: An Adventure in American Diplomacy* (1969), a brief, competent study of the president's role.

MANCHURIA. Three legalistic studies: C. Walter Young, *The International Legal Status of the Kwantung Leased Territory* (1931); *Japan's Special Position in Manchuria: Its Assertion, Legal Interpretation and Present Meaning* (1931); and *Japanese Jurisdiction in the South Manchuria Railway Areas* (1931). Owen Lattimore, *Manchuria: Cradle of Conflict* (rev. ed., 1935) presents Manchuria's regional relationship to China. Charles S. Campbell, *Special Business Interests and the Open Door Policy* (1951), an examination of pressures exerted on the American Government by business engaged in China trade. Sun E-Tu Zen, *Chinese Railways and British Interests, 1898–1911* (1954). W. A. Williams, *American-Russian Relations, 1781–1947* (1952). Chang Chiaao, *China's Struggle for Railroad Development* (1943). Ralph E. Minger, "Taft's Missions to Japan: A Study in Personal Diplomacy," *The Pacific Historical Review* 30 (1961): 279–94. Edward H. Zabriskie, *American-Russian Rivalry in the Far East: A Study in Diplomacy and Power Politics, 1895–1914* (1946). Richard T. Chang, "The Failure of the Katsura-Harriman Agreement," *Journal of Asian Studies*, 21 (1961), 65–76.

China, 1911–1916: The Gray Dawn of a Republic

chapter 19

In 1911 the Manchu dynasty had ruled China for 267 years. Like other successful conquerors of the Middle Kingdom, it had recognized the superior cultural attainments of the conquered people, and it had associated Chinese with Manchus in government. Thus the dynasty not only held the Mandate of Heaven but also ruled at times with distinction. By mid-nineteenth century, however, the Manchus faced economic dislocation and bureaucratic ineptitude at home and the impact of the Western world of ideas and power on their seaboard. These conditions called for radical adjustments in China's political, economic, and social structure—adjustments which the Sino-Manchu political hierarchy could neither visualize nor execute. To be sure, in the face of impending disaster, the aging and opportunistic Empress Dowager had sought refuge in reform, but her conversion had failed to halt the decline in Manchu prestige and authority.

A series of events that may be described as the immediate causes of the impending Revolution of 1911 began with the year 1908. There was the death of the unfortunate young Kuang-hsu emperor on November 14, and on the following day the old Empress Dowager died. She had already provided for the succession by unwisely placing an infant on the throne with the Manchu Prince Ch'un as regent. Thus, when death removed the hold of Old Buddha, the helm of state was in the keeping of a child directed by a regent who was to prove devoid of political wisdom. The seriousness of these events should be considered in relation to the complete Chinese picture during the first decade of the century: the abortive reforms of 1898, the disasters of the Boxer revolt, the inroads of the Western powers and Japan, the use of Chinese soil as battlegrounds in the Russo-Japanese War, and the reduction of Manchuria to the status of Russian and Japanese spheres of influence. All of these events called for the appearance of dynamic and far-sighted leadership at Peking. Adding to the political void, however, was the forced retirement of Yuan Shih-k'ai. With Yuan, there also went into retirement many of the abler lesser officials whom he had trained and who were responsive to his leadership. In October, 1909, Chang Chih-tung, the great Yangtze viceroy, died. The result was that, while officially the reform program was continued, it became little more than a succession of edicts and blueprints.

The National Assembly, created by the Manchu reforms and designed to be a willing tool of the dynasty, met for the first time in October, 1910, but, to the chagrin of the court and in spite of all its hand-picked conservatism, it showed a remarkable spirit of independence. It forced the government to promise a parliament in 1913 instead of after the longer nine-year period of preparation provided in the reform program. It threatened to impeach members of the government, and attacked its fiscal and administrative policies with vigor. Early in 1911 it demanded a responsible cabinet, winning the demand, in principle at least, before adjournment.

FLOOD, FAMINE, AND TAXES

Evidence of revolutionary stirrings was not confined to Peking. Recurring crises of famine occasioned by increasing population and by flood and drought were not new to China. In the twenty-five years preceding the Revolution of 1911, population had increased by perhaps as much as 50,000,000. Some of these people found new homes in Manchuria and others in sparsely populated areas of the empire or in immigration abroad to Indochina and the Malay States, but these movements provided no relief for the basic problem of livelihood. The years of 1910 and 1911 marked the culmination of a series of bad seasons. Hundreds of thousands died, and several millions were on the verge of starvation. Those who survived were psychologically prepared for any movement that promised relief.

Throughout China discontent had also been fanned by rising taxes. Every measure in the reform program of 1901 and in subsequent programs had called for more revenue: the new army, new railroads, the new educational system. In addition, there were the charges on the Japanese war indemnity of 1895, and the more onerous charges of the Boxer Indemnity of 1901.

CENTRALIZATION VERSUS
PROVINCIAL AUTONOMY

Closely linked with popular criticism of tax policies was the hard fact that the reform program encroached on the traditional autonomy of the provinces. Insofar as the re-

form program possessed a real purpose other than that of saving the dynasty, it was to give China a national government capable of exercising the sovereignty of the state, and of protecting it from foreign encroachment. This objective required the sacrifice in large measure of the autonomy of the provinces, where vested local interests were loath to part with the prerogatives which time and custom had given them.

The issue came to focus on the question of financing and thus controlling proposed trunk line railroads designed to be the first step in solving China's problem of communications. There had been a strong demand for constructing railroads on a provincial rather than a national basis, and for financing these lines with Chinese rather than foreign funds. It was a natural reaction to foreign concession grabbing and foreign financial control, while at the same time it was an equally natural expression of traditional Chinese political habits. But it was an impractical policy. The huge sums necessary could not be raised in the provinces and even such sums as were collected were dissipated in wild speculation or unadulterated graft. Accordingly, early in 1911 Peking began to pursue with vigor its policy of railroad centralization. Foreign loans were contracted for the Hankow-Canton and Hankow-Szechwan trunk lines. At the same time the government sought to reach a settlement with the provincial interests involved. This proved to be difficult. Official protests were lodged at Peking, and in Szechwan there were public demonstrations on a wide scale.

THE REVOLUTION OF 1911

While the Imperial government was debating measures to settle the railroad troubles in Szechwan, an event of momentous import occurred in the central Yangtze Valley. At Hankow, October 9, a bomb, being manufactured by revolutionaries in the Russian concession, exploded. Investigations led to the arrest and execution of three revolutionaries. These events precipitated a military revolt on the night of October 10 among troops at Wuchang across the river from

Hankow, where leaders of the revolt dragged their commander, Colonel Li Yuan-hung from under his bed and presented him with the choice of immediate death or leadership of rebellion. Being a practical man, though at the time far from a revolutionist, Colonel Li chose the latter. Within a brief period the three Wuhan cities—Hankow, Hanyang, and Wuchang—were in rebel hands.

From this center, the revolt spread rapidly, particularly in the provinces south of the Yangtze. Generally speaking the north remained loyal to the imperial government. The pattern was one of a series of local and largely bloodless rebellions seemingly unco-ordinated and without unified leadership or a predetermined national plan.[1] While the Wuchang group was attempting to co-ordi-nate the movement by inviting provinces which had declared their independence to send delegates to a Wuchang revolutionary council, the revolution spread to Shanghai, where a new rebel government under the leadership of Ch'en Ch'i-mei was organized. Wu T'ing-fang, a Cantonese and former Minister to the United States, was made chief of diplomatic affairs. He attempted to speak for the revolution as a whole. Interrevolu-tionary politics was thus making its appear-ance. The Shanghai group was dominated by Cantonese who were determined that leader-ship in the rebellion should not remain with the Yangtze provinces centered at Wuchang. Fortunately, all the revolutionary groups were at one in their determination that the Man-chus must go. This and Li Yuan-hung's will-ingness to give way to Shanghai's so-called "military government" prevented an open break and permitted the Canton elements to lead.[2]

EFFECTS OF THE REVOLUTION IN PEKING

Peking, fearful of dealing vigorously with the revolt against its railway policies in Szechwan, was even less capable of meeting the anti-dynastic revolts begun at Hankow.

[1] P. M. A. Linebarger, *Government in Re-publican China* (1938), 145.

[2] H. M. Vinacke, *Modern Constitutional De-velopment in China* (1920), 102.

The government was embarrassed also by the reconvening on October 22, less than two weeks after the Wuchang rising, of the Na-tional Assembly. Heartened by the general spirit of rebellion, the Assembly demanded responsible cabinet government; and insisted that a constitution be adopted only with the consent of the Assembly, and that political of-fenders be pardoned. On November 3, the dynasty gave its approval in edicts establish-ing a constitutional monarchy. Meanwhile the regent, Prince Ch'un, had induced Yuan Shih-k'ai to return to Peking by promising him unlimited powers. Yuan promptly re-sumed his command of the military forces, and on November 8 the National Assembly elected him premier.

THE POLICY OF YUAN SHIH-K'AI

Yuan Shih-k'ai's critics have dealt harshly with his record. A soldier and diplomat from the North, he has been characterized as nar-row in outlook, altogether a tradition-bound official, despite his up-to-date ideas—an op-portunist and a realist in politics. Actually, Yuan was far more than these. While he had his limitations, and they were exceedingly large, he had shown progressive tendencies. He was an opportunist and a realist, but he was not altogether tradition-bound. He was a progressive capable of carrying out needed reforms, as the previous decade had shown, and a tried administrator in civil and particu-larly in military affairs. He was not a repub-lican and did not believe in 1911 that repub-licanism was the answer to China's ills, in which view he was by no means alone. Like many other Chinese of sober thought, Yuan seems to have held to the view that it would be fatal for China to attempt a complete break with the spirit or the political ma-chinery of the past, and that the stability of reform would depend in some major degree on Confucian mores and not exclusively on the adoption of Western ideologies.[3] Now that he was invested by the dynasty with supreme powers, and endowed by the Na-tional Assembly with the post of prime minister, Yuan's task was to put a stop to

[3] A. M. Kotenev, *The Chinese Soldier* (1937), 82–83.

rebellion and then to carry on the constitutional reforms of the Assembly. Yuan, however, appears to have entertained purposes more subtle than these. Although he was not as yet seeking the destruction of the dynasty, Yuan was willing to permit the spread of the southern rebellions in order to force the Manchus to accept and play the role of the passive, constitutional monarchy. Yuan's Imperial forces were superior in every respect to the revolutionary armies of Li, yet the northern armies were never permitted to push their advantages to ultimate and decisive victory. So long as these conditions prevailed, Yuan was able to impose his will in Peking.

Opposed to Yuan, to the dynasty, and to the National Assembly stood the rebel armies of Li Yuan-hung, the so-called "military government" (Cantonese) at Shanghai, and the southern provinces that had declared their independence. In October when the Hankow incident occurred, Sun Yat-sen, ideological leader of the southern rebels, was in the United States. Not until two months later (December 24, 1911) did he reach Shanghai.

THE PEACE NEGOTIATIONS

The return of Sun Yat-sen, although inspiring to the revolutionists, did not alter the fact that they were incapable of carrying the revolution to a successful conclusion or of holding its leadership. The balance between the hoary traditions of dynastic rule and the mysteries of republicanism was held not by Sun Yat-sen but by Yuan Shih-k'ai. With a subtle appreciation of his political and military advantage, Yuan attempted to negotiate a settlement with Li Yuan-hung, finally agreeing with Li's consent to deal with the Republican group at Shanghai. Meanwhile, at Li's suggestion, delegates from the "independent" southern provinces assembled at a national convention in Nanking and elected Sun Yat-sen provisional president. It was this more unified republican regime that finally concluded the peace settlement with Yuan's representative, T'ang Shao-yi, an American-educated Cantonese. In these negotiations the

monarchy was brought to an end and a republic, in name at least, was created. Sun Yat-sen stepped down from the presidency, and at his suggestion the Nanking Convention elected Yuan Shih-k'ai first provisional president of the Republic of China. Sun's relinquishment of the presidency could be rationalized by his desire to remain solely the ideological leader of the new China, and by the more decisive factor, the political and military power of Yuan.

The new Republic was to be inaugurated with the arrival of Yuan at Nanking. However, Nanking represented the south and was controlled by the southern republicans, while Yuan's armies were around Peking. This explains why a military mutiny probably engineered by Yuan near Peking made it inconvenient for the new president to leave the old capital. By this means Yuan was able to force the republicans to come to Peking, the home of tradition and conservatism. Furthermore, the abdication edicts, dictated by Yuan himself and promulgated on February 12, 1912, implied clearly that the new president derived his power by transfer from the throne rather than by mandate of the Republic.

The end of dynastic rule and the emergence of Yuan Shih-k'ai as president of the Republic were not due solely to the political and military advantages enjoyed by Yuan within China. Both the Republic and Yuan's leadership therein were in part the creation of the foreign powers. From 1908, and even earlier, the fate of the Manchu dynasty rested on its capacity to prevent further disintegration, to arrest foreign concession hunting, and to forestall the partition of the empire by the foreign powers. However, between 1908 and 1912 the powers failed both singly and collectively to support the Imperial government to these ends. Indeed, the rivalries of the powers in their efforts to control China politically and economically weakened what little prestige was left to the dynasty and thereby invited provincial opposition to Peking's national railway policies. Again, the reforms which Peking planned for the border territories of Tibet, Mongolia, and Manchuria— reforms designed eventually to bring these areas into a national China—were frowned upon by Britain, Russia, and Japan. From the Wuhan rebellion in October, 1911, until the abdication edicts of February, 1912, the powers did nothing to prevent the collapse of the Imperial regime. On the contrary, they assisted Yuan Shih-k'ai in his ambitions to head the new Republic. As a result of conflicting power-interests and of commitments from some of the powers, Yuan was able to count on diplomatic and foreign financial support before the conclusion of his negotiations with the southern republicans and before he had been elevated to the presidency.

EARLY PHASES OF YUAN'S GOVERNMENT

With the establishment of the Republic, China did not enter an era of republicanism but rather one of militarism. The "national" army organized by Li Hung-chang and Yuan Shih-k'ai was a northern army, not a national army; its officers thought of themselves as lieutenants of Yuan, not of the State. In the southern provinces during the revolution, authority had shifted to provincial leaders who could command the personal allegiance of troops in their respective areas. Thus, both during and succeeding the revolution, military authority was also political authority. Since as a result of revolutionary conditions the number of men under arms increased rapidly, there were few checks upon the power of these personal, and in most cases irresponsible, armies.

Not being in a position to destroy or disband these independent provincial armies, Yuan's only recourse was to make allies of them. This he did by appointing their commanders as provincial military governors. Eventually he hoped to replace them by civil administrations responsive to his Peking government. This would be done by coaxing the provincial militarists into various government posts in the capital, thus separating them from their armies, the source of their strength.

Meanwhile, the new government was attempting to get under way at Peking under the terms of a provisional constitution adopted at Nanking in March, 1912. Being the product of southern republicanism, this constitution was shaped with the idea of making the president subject to parliamentary will. In August, Sun Yat-sen announced organization of his new political party, the *Kuomintang*, to which Yuan replied by organizing his own Progressive Party, the *Chinputang*. When a National Assembly under the provisional constitution met early in 1913, the *Kuomintang* held the strongest position but did not have absolute control. Prospects for republican government received a severe blow with the assassination in March, 1913, of Sung Chiao-jen, the parliamentary leader of the *Kuomintang*. After it became known that Yuan's partisans were probably responsible for this deed, a rebellion broke out against Yuan which was supported by part of the *Kuomintang* and a few southern warlords. When Yuan successfully suppressed the outbreak, Sun Yat-sen and some of his followers fled to Japan. In October the remaining members of the Assembly removed Yuan's provisional status by electing him president of the Republic. Less than a month later Yuan ousted from the Assembly those *Kuomintang* members who had not already fled, and banned the *Kuomintang*. Then by presidential decree, January, 1914, he "suspended" the Assembly and replaced it with his own Constitutional Council. This body brought forth on May 1 its own constitution, known as the Constitutional Compact. It created a "presidential government," and "legitimatized" Yuan's dictatorship.[4]

[4] While Sun Yat-sen remained titular head of the revolutionary forces, actual party leadership devolved in considerable measure on Sung Chiao-jen, a Hunanese who had coordinated the uprising in Wuhan, 1911, against the Manchus. It was Sung, not Sun, who advocated parliamentary government, and it was Sung who actually transformed the *T'ung-meng Hui,* a secret society, into an open political organization, the *Kuomintang.* Sung believed that the KMT would become an instrument for strengthening parliamentary government. Sun, on the other hand, advocated strong presidential powers. In 1913, at the height of his powers as a parliamentary leader, Sung was assassinated. See Tamada Noriko, "Sung Chiao-jen and the 1911 Revolution," *Papers on China,* Vol. 21. Published and distributed by the East Asia Research Center, Harvard University (1968), 184–229.

In this manner Yuan was attempting to pave the way for a restoration of monarchy with himself as the monarch. There was much to support the idea that constitutional monarchy as proposed in 1898 by K'ang Yu-wei was more likely to suceed than republicanism. This view was presented to Yuan in a memorandum, August, 1915 by his constitutional adviser, Professor Frank Goodnow. Goodnow pointed out the desirability, viewing China's problem of government in the abstract, "of establishing a constitutional monarchy *if* there was general demand for it rather than of maintaining the trappings of a republicanism without operative democracy." As a result, therefore, of "a circus of plebiscites and constitutional councils," constitutional monarchy was proclaimed in December, 1915. It was short-lived. No considerable body of the Chinese people had any understanding of the relative merits of constitutional monarchy or republicanism, but there were provincial and republican leaders with following enough to oppose Yuan as a monarch of any kind. Revolt promptly flared in Yunnan and spread rapidly through the south. Yuan renounced the throne in March, and died three months later, on June 6, 1916.

DOLLAR DIPLOMACY AND
THE REVOLUTION

The collapse of the Manchu dynasty was due in part to the acquiescence of the powers. In like manner, the hope of a stable regime under Yuan appeared to depend on the financial policies of the same great powers. The new republican government of 1912 was "without funds and with increasing unpaid obligations." China's quest for foreign financial aid, however, could not be divorced from implications of foreign political control. It should be recalled that the Revolution of 1911 was, among other things, a reaction and protest against the foreign scramble for concessions which followed the Sino-Japanese War of 1894–1895, and which continued with increasing intensity in subsequent years. Indeed, the political-financial rivalry of the

powers was so great that they themselves began to favor pooling certain types of loans to China through an international banking agency called the Consortium. This agency was to be composed of groups of bankers designated by their respective governments. Thus, loans made through the Consortium would be subject to a double test: their acceptability to the bankers on economic grounds, and to the powers on political grounds. In its embryonic stage in 1909 the Consortium included only British, French, and German banking groups that were proposing to finance and construct for the Manchu-Chinese government the so-called Hukuang railways in Central and South China.[5] An American group was admitted in 1911 after President Taft had appealed to the Chinese regent.

After the revolution and the establishment of the Republic, the interest of the Consortium, on the surface at least, was directed toward providing the impecunious government at Peking with funds to maintain itself. In principle, the Republic was to be assisted through international financial cooperation. The road to this objective was beset with many obstacles. Russia and Japan, though borrowing countries, demanded admission to the Consortium, and their banking groups were admitted in June, 1912. In the view of the Chinese government and of many foreign bankers not included in the various groups, the Consortium was an attempt to create a monopoly controlling the Chinese loan market.

In the midst of this complicated political-financial wirepulling in Peking, the Wilson administration came into power in Washington. The American banking group asked whether it would continue to enjoy in its China investments the active support of the Department of State. President Wilson replied on March 18, 1913, by withdrawing official support from the American group because he found the control measures of a proposed reorganization loan "to touch very nearly the the administrative independence of China it-

[5] C. F. Remer, *Foreign Investments in China* (1933), 126. Charles Vevier, *The United States and China* (1955), 88–110.

self." Taft had pushed American bankers into China to preserve the open door. Wilson refused to support them there because their activities, along with the activities of the other groups, threatened China's independence. The Reorganization Loan Agreement was concluded without American participation on April 26, 1913.

As for the open door as an instrument of American policy, the best that can be said is that to this point the going had been very rough. Between 1899 and 1910 the so-called policy of the open door and the integrity of China had passed through three phases. The labels used by American politicians remained the same, "the open door" and "the integrity of China," but the policies they represented did not. In the first or Hay phrase, the open door meant the preservation of equal commercial opportunity in an area where there was no equal investment opportunity. For the most part Hay abandoned the integrity of China in the face of Russian power in Manchuria. In the second phase under Elihu Root, it was still assumed that the spheres were facts and that more harm than good would come from any direct attack upon them, but, nevertheless, Root struggled to keep alive the concept of China's integrity. In the third phase, that of dollar diplomacy under Taft and Knox, the open door was supposed to encompass equal investment as well as commercial opportunity thus abolishing the spheres and insuring China's integrity. New policies were simply attached to old words. If Americans did not understand all this, it is hardly surprising that the Japanese were a bit puzzled.[6]

SEPARATIST MOVEMENTS IN BORDER TERRITORIES

The transition from Manchu empire to Chinese republic was the occasion for rebellions and "independence" movements in the former empire dependencies of Mongolia and

[6] Raymond A. Esthus, "The Changing Concept of the Open Door, 1899–1910," *The Mississippi Valley Historical Review* 46 (1959): 452–53.

Tibet. During the decade preceding the Revolution of 1911, the Mongol nobility had grown restive as Chinese settlers encroached on Inner Mongolia and as Peking attempted to extend the government of China Proper to this area. Mongol disaffection was encouraged by Russia, whose agents fostered Mongol nationalism. In December, 1911, an independent Mongol government came into being at Urga. Chinese combatted the movement by attempting to re-establish their authority in Inner Mongolia, only to be countered by Russian recognition of the Urga government in November, 1912. A year later (November, 1913) Russia and the Republic of China agreed that Outer Mongolia was "autonomous" but not "independent." Nearly two years later (June, 1915) Mongolia accepted this status in an agreement involving herself, Russia, and China.

The Revolution of 1911 was also the signal for trouble in Tibet. The Tibetans drove the Chinese garrison from the country and concluded an agreement (January, 1913) with the new Mongolian government. When Yuan Shih-kai sought to re-establish by force China's authority at Lhasa, he encountered British diplomatic opposition. It was not until 1914 that an agreement was worked out among Tibet, China, and Britain whereby western Tibet (Tibet Proper) was to be autonomous, the Chinese maintaining a resident and small guard at Lhasa, while in eastern Tibet the authority of China was to be retained.

ANALYSIS OF THE OLD FIRST REPUBLIC

The years 1911 to 1916 were but a prelude to even more dismal things to come before the final collapse of the old First Republic in 1928. Indeed, it had fallen to Yuan Shih-k'ai to preside over one of the most fantastic failures in modern history. The Chinese Republican Revolution, 1911–1912, was an attempt to set aside the Confucian monarchy and to replace it with a parliamentary constitutional republic. On paper this republic appeared to have everything needed for success: constitutions, parliamentary procedures, codes of law. But the constitutions were not understood, the parliamentary procedures were not followed, and the law codes were never enforced. What the republic did not have was much more important than what it possessed. It did not have a people who understood parliamentary institutions, government by law, or the rudiments of democratic responsible citizenship. When at the beginning of the Revolution of 1911 a council of representatives was convoked by the southern republicans, these representatives were not elected: there was no election machinery in the provinces, and anyway no one knew what an election was. Sun Yat-sen, visionary, genius, Christian, and for the moment provisional president, prayed to his Christian God but also supplicated the spirits of the Ming emperors, the last Chinese rulers of China. Yuan Shih-k'ai rose to the presidency over Sun Yat-sen not by any Mandate of Heaven or mandate of the people but by double-crossing both the dynasty and the republicans through his military power supported later by foreign loans. He dispersed the *Kuomintang*-dominated Assembly and acquired one that would do his bidding. Then, not content with the realism of this presidential dictatorship in a nominal republic, Yuan became a romantic. The scheme to restore the monarchy with himself as monarch failed not because it was a move away from democracy, as so many Americans then and later imagined, but because Peking did not have enough power to suppress southern insurrection. By 1916, when Yuan Shih-k'ai joined the spirits of his ancestors, the old first Republic of China had already been perverted into an immense failure.[7] Moreover,

the effort to find an acceptable relationship between an ailing Confucianism and the new Western world of science and democracy had not been found.

Indeed, the beginnings of the old First Republic remain beset by more historical questions than answers. How did it come about that the ideals of the early revolutionary leadership could produce nothing better than the presidency of Yuan-Shih-k'ai who was neither a revolutionary nor a republican? Was it due to the southern rebels' lack of ideology and organization, to military and financial inferiority, to foreign support of Peking, or simply to the skill of Yuan in turning events to his own advantage (an interpretation which has been overemphasized)? Yuan, it has often been said, maneuvered the court and the revolutionaries into a situation in which they neutralized each other. Then through superior military strength and foreign support, Yuan emerged as president—a first step in his scheme to become emperor. To a degree, all of this was true because Yuan did profit from his talent for intrigue, his position in the North, and his relationship with the Powers. At the same time many other factors entered into his rise to the presidency. He was supported not only by the court but also by many of the southern rebel leaders who, in reality, were not out-maneuvered in giving Yuan the presi-

---

[7] P. M. A. Linebarger, Djang Chu, and Ardath W. Burks, *Far Eastern Governments and Politics* (1954), 120–32.

In the West the distinctive role of the individual in history has made biography a special field in literary and historical writing. In traditional China, on the contrary, where there was no similar cult of the individual, the ultimate purpose of biography was not to portray the individual as a fallible person but to instruct officials in orthodoxy. This explains why a Chinese has been able to write an effective study of Yuan Shih-k'ai as a politician but not as a person. As will be seen later, "in the People's Re-

public of China, biographical writing is largely shaped by a mechanistic view of history which stresses the role of impersonal economic factors in determining the development of social organization and the course of human relations and institutions. Virtue and vice are polarized, the worthy 'model worker' standing in sharp contrast to the socially irresponsible 'bourgeois intellectual,' doomed by his gentry background, his liberalism, and his Harvard Ph.D. Yet the current situation [in Communist China] still contains incongruities. At the same time that both party and academic historians are constrained by the general demands of orthodox Communist doctrine, they also dwell in a specific political environment dominated, in apparent contradiction to that doctrine, by a single individual: Mao Tsetung. Mao himself is not only the exception to all the rules but also, like Confucius, the imposer of new precepts." Howard L. Boorman, "The Biographical Approach to Chinese History," *Journal of Asian Studies* 21 (1962): 454.

dency. The suppression of radical revolutionary forces was effected by other revolutionaries and not primarily by Yuan. Moreover, Yuan's military superiority, if it existed, was not as great as supposed, and he had only limited support from the Powers until after he became president. In a word, Yuan alone did not determine the outcome of the Revolution of 1911.[8]

As a government, the first Republic of China was a failure, but as a symbol of what could happen it was filled with meaning. The fact that the Republic had come into being following two thousand years of Confucian monarchy suggested that a revolutionary process was well underway.

To anticipate and to emphasize the story that will be told later (in Chapter 24), it should be noted that the ascendency of Yuan Shih-k'ai marked the beginning of warlord rule which was to dominate China for nearly forty years, far into the *Kuomintang* era. What the warlords did held significance far beyond their own struggles for power. Their seemingly meaningless warfare, one with another, destroyed the always tenuous internal cohesion of the country, ravaged its economy, and reduced to desperation a large part of its people. In these circumstances, China became very susceptible to a host of new influences, because under warlord leadership power passed to men whose semi-Western military training gave them an awareness of the value of innovation. Their comparative lack of training in neo-Confucian orthodoxy made them more prone to abandon tradition and to adopt new (foreign) ideas in place of those that were Confucian.[9]

[8] See Ernest P. Young, "Yuan Shih-k'ai's Rise to the Presidency," *China in Revolution: The First Phase, 1900–1913*, Mary Clabaugh Wright, ed. (1968), 419–42. The limitations of the revolution are studied in Edward Friedman, "Revolution or Just Another Bloody Cycle? Swatow and the 1911 Revolution," *Journal of Asian Studies* 29 (1970): 289–307.
[9] Donald G. Gillin, "China and the Foreigner, 1911–1950," *South Atlantic Quarterly* 68 (1969): 208–19.

GENERAL. H. F. MacNair, *China in Revolution* (1931); and *Modern Chinese History: Selected Readings* (Shanghai, 1923).* Li Chien-nung, *The Political History of China, 1840–1928*, trans. and ed. by Teng Ssu-yu and Jeremy Ingals (1956),* the work of a Chinese historian who avoided partisan propaganda and undocumented speculation. Pan Wei-tung, *The Chinese Constitution, A Study of Forty Years of Constitution-Making in China* (1945). Franklin W. Houn, *Central Government of China 1912–1928: An Institutional Study* (1957), a rather formal presentation of what was supposed to be rather than what was. Tsao Wen-yen, *The Constitutional Structure of Modern China* (Melbourne, 1948), a study by a legal expert. Joseph R. Levenson, *Confucian China and Its Modern Fate*, I (1958), a thoughtful introduction to Chinese intellectual history. A. N. Holcombe, *The Spirit of the Chinese Revolution* (1930).

SUN YAT-SEN. Lyon Sharman, *Sun Yat-sen, His Life and Its Meaning, A Critical Biography* (1934).* Henry B. Restarick, *Sun Yat-sen: Liberator of China* (1931). Bernard Martin, *Strange Vigour* (London, 1944), a biography of Sun Yat-sen using the Cantlie papers and press notices. P. M. A. Linebarger, *The Political Doctrines of Sun Yat-sen* (1937). Francis Price, trans., *San Min Chu I, The Three Principles of the People* (1928), a translation of Sun Yat-sen's lectures. Leonard Hsu, *Sun Yat-sen, His Political and Social Ideals* (1933). Stephen Chen and Robert Payne, *Sun Yat-sen: A Portrait* (1946), a useful brief introduction to Sun's career and his thought.

OTHER LEADERS. Jerome Ch'en, *Yuan Shih-k'ai, 1859–1916* (1961). Stephen R. Makinnon, "Liang Shih-i and the Communications Clique," *Journal of Asian Studies* 29 (1970), 559–80.

AMERICAN INTERESTS. Roy Watson Curry, *Woodrow Wilson and Far Eastern Policy 1913–1921* (1957). Li T'ien-yi, *Woodrow Wilson's China Policy* (1952). Harold Robert Isaacs, *Scratches on Our Minds: American Images of China and India* (1958).*

Japan, 1889–1918:
Economic Growth and Evolution
of Oligarchical Government

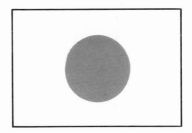

chapter 20

On February 11, 1889 the Meiji emperor bestowed a "gift" upon his people, the nation's first constitution which provided for representative institutions, reflecting concessions to liberal Western ideas, even as it perpetuated and strengthened the myth of the emperor's absolutism. Also in this seemingly paradoxical political picture were officially inspired economic and social factors designed to sustain a modern state: modern education, the skeleton of a national transportation system, basic heavy industries, and expanded and modernized armed forces. Japan, under the direction of a small but able body of former samurai from Choshu and Satsuma, was transforming herself and was entering an era of competition with the West.

Time was to prove that modern Japan's founding fathers worked with consummate skill. The recounting in earlier chapters of Japan's victories over China and Russia, of her acquisition of an empire, and of her claims to special interests in southern Manchuria has suggested how far the nation had already progressed before World War I in her determination to be numbered among the great powers. What remains to be described here are some additional domestic accomplish-

ments in both politics and the economy. For some thirty years, until 1918, the Choshu-Satsuma oligarchs, either in person or through protégés, directed the adaptation of the constitution and the expansion of the economic system. The historical task is to discover the processes through which this continuing transformation took place.

THE BASIS OF OLIGARCHICAL GOVERNMENT

On July 1, 1890, Japan held her first elections under the constitution. It was, in most respects, a model performance. Of the some 450,000 eligible voters (one out of every hundred persons had the right to vote), all but 27,000 resorted in orderly fashion to the polls and cast their ballots. The result was a decided victory for the *Jiyuto* (Liberal Party) and the *Kaishinto* (Reform or Progressive Party), both of which had appeared initially in the 1880s as an opposition to Choshu-Satsuma leadership. As aspirants for parliamentary seats, party candidates in 1890 continued their opposition, attacking the government for failure to abolish the unequal treaties and for grossly inflating national expenditures. Moreover, the force of these attacks was magnified by the election to the House of Representatives of independent opposition candidates, whose numbers swelled the total anti-government membership to more than two hundred of the three hundred contested seats. The government counted in the House only ninety supporters, but it controlled the House of Peers through appointment, thus remaining in a position to block unwelcome legislation.

The appearance of a noisy opposition in a political tradition previously marked by authoritarianism was certainly a notable development. In time this event would become a foundation for democratic institutions, but this was not its immediate significance. Rather, the elections admitted to government members of a small but politically conscious and articulate element that hitherto had been excluded from political leadership. Among this excluded element were men of substantial economic means. As a group drawn from the ranks of ex-samurai, they were also the social equals of the ruling authorities. In effect, by holding elections under the constitution, Japan enlarged substantially the political oligarchy.[1]

Among the older oligarchs were some who believed that the enlarged leadership would strengthen an already thriving state. The opposition, it was said, would be converted to support of the government as power was shared. Furthermore, the parliamentary experiment was to be carefully controlled. The parties' access to power was to be "partial, gradual, and carefully hedged." [2] Actual experience, however, produced results quite different from these expectations. Once in office, the party members were not easily tamed. Within two years, by 1892, a cabinet

[1] Edwin O. Reischauer, *Japan: The Story of a Nation* (1970),* 138–44. From among the original instigators of the Imperial Restoration, Ito Hirobumi, Okuma Shigenobu, Yamagata Aritomo, and Inouye Kaoru were the most important still living. For details on relations between the oligarchs and parties see Hugh Borton, *Japan's Modern Century* (2nd ed., 1970), Chapter 11.

[2] George Akita, *Foundations of Constitutional Government in Japan, 1868–1900* (1967), a recent study of the determination of the oligarchs to share power.

resigned after suffering defeat in the Diet, and this upset was by no means the end of the trouble. Thus the fashioning of a working relationship between the old oligarchs and the parties became one of the first tasks of the new constitutional era.

Other adjustments were required by changes in Japan's older leadership. Prior to 1918 the Choshu-Satsuma oligarchs had lost none of their luster as founding fathers, but their vigor was sapped by advancing age. Those who survived into the new era gradually turned administrative chores over to protégés and, as *Genro* (elder statesmen), gave directions from behind the scenes. Leadership patterns were also changed by the death in 1912 of the Meiji emperor, a vigorous man who sometimes had played a role in decision making. His successor, Taisho Tenno (1912–1926), who had been sickly as a child and who, in later years, was mentally deranged, took little part in decision making. He was relegated largely to a symbolic role. Finally, political processes were also affected by a maturing and growing bureaucracy. In contrast with early Meiji when trained personnel was scarce, Japan after 1890 acquired an expanding and able civil bureaucracy, at the core of which were a few thousand university graduates. Claiming status as "the officials of the emperor," these bureaucrats were conscious of their power and were determined to use it. In this latter respect the civil bureaucracy joined the top officers corp of the military services as important pressure groups within government influencing the national policy.

By 1890, and to an even greater extent by 1918, government operations became far more complex than in the early years of Meiji. This new complexity arose partly because of the constitution itself with its innovation of a bicameral Diet, and also because of a natural institutional growth. As the tasks of government became more numerous, Japanese political administration expanded and specialized. From these developments emerged rival elites (and factions within elites) competing with one another and jockeying for position. Moreover, the very size of government tended to outmode the informal procedures of former time. Controversies moved from the closed committee rooms to the open floor of the Diet. Yet, with all of these changes, it must be remembered that the old oligarchs continued to preside and to control. Japan's government was modernizing, but the spirit remained that of a paternalistic, authoritarian state.

THE OLIGARCHY VERSUS THE PARTIES

The political history of Japan from 1890 until 1918 holds a special interest because it was in these years that the Japanese fashioned the particular structure of political compromise that enabled the constitution to function with notable success. There were three stages in the development of this formula in constitutional compromise. The first, from 1890 to 1895, was marked by antagonism and separation between the ruling oligarchy and the opposition parties. The second, from 1895 to 1900, involved a series of ententes between the parties and the oligarchy. The third, from 1900 to 1918, was distinguished by leadership in which the oligarchy, enlarged by the incorporation of the parties, employed devices of parliamentary government as part of the political process.

The period of complete estrangement between the government oligarchy and the popular parties was of great import because the Japanese learned that compromise was indispensable if there was to be any constitutional government at all. In this particular instance, however, compromise was not easy. The oligarchy, had been entrenching itself in power during all the years that had elapsed since the Restoration of 1867. It was confident of its power. The institution of the cabinet, which continued under the constitution, had been created and had been in operation since 1885, five years in advance of the meeting of the first Diet. The Privy Council, the highest advisory body to the emperor under the constitution, had been created a year before the constitution in order that it might advise the throne on the nature of the document under which it was to be the chief advisory organ. Furthermore, prior to the

meeting of the first Diet, Premier Kuroda Kiyotaka and Ito Hirobumi, president of the Privy Council, had proclaimed the government's policy of "transcendental" cabinets, by which they meant that the government under the constitution derived all its power from the throne and was concerned therefore with all the emperor's subjects rather than with the desires of political parties. This policy was not at variance with the explicit terms of the constitution, but was at variance with the platforms of the *Jiyuto* and the *Kaishinto*, both of which in 1890 made it clear that, given their way, they would use the constitution to subordinate the oligarchy to the rule of party cabinets responsible to the House of Representatives.

So matters stood when in November, 1890, a hostile government, headed by the Choshu militarist, Premier and General Yamagata Aritomo, faced equally hostile parties in the first Diet. The spirit of "arrogance and contempt" with which the Premier addressed the House of Representatives was equalled only by the verbal violence with which the parties used the only constitutional weapon they possessed—a limited power to strike at the government's budget. Yamagata was speaking for the oligarchy and its servants the bureaucracy—the vast body of office holders, great and small—when he called on the House for unity with and unqualified trust in the government and its officialdom. In response, the parties attacked and clipped the budget. In doing this they were not engaging merely in a general assault designed to reduce taxes or to assert their supremacy. The assault was aimed directly at a more specific target. The principal cuts in the budget proposed by the House involved the personal income of officials: salaries, pensions, residence, and travel allowances. Thus the attack, aimed directly at the lesser civil and military bureaucracy, was in the realm of everyday practical politics since it struck at the real and the indispensable foundation supporting the oligarchy. In meeting this attack, the government, as was to be expected, was prepared to use all its resources, fair or foul. As a beginning it employed two devices often resorted to in future years: (1) it stood

firmly on the constitutional provision prohibiting reduction of expenditures already
fixed, and (2) it resorted to intimidation of
members of the parties by hired gangsters, or
soshi. When these methods failed to move the
parliamentarians, the government had recourse to bribery of the weaker party members. A budget more acceptable to the government was then passed.[3]

In the light of Yamagata's unhappy experience, no member of the oligarchy welcomed the prospect of becoming the next
premier. Yet under the policy of the oligarchy
it was inevitable that the post be held by a
member of this group. Thus when Yamagata
resigned, his Minister of Finance, Matsukata
Masayoshi of Satsuma, an able financier but
certainly undistinguished as a political leader,
accepted the premiership, May 6, 1891. When
the second Diet met, it followed precedent by
attacking the government's budget, but in
this case the reductions were leveled at new
expenditures such as the naval program. To
meet this crisis the government dissolved the
Diet and ordered a special election for February, 1892, which turned out to be "the most
brutal election in Japanese history." The
government had decided to show the parties
no quarter and, if possible, to break their
hold on the electorate. Voters were intimidated by hired gangsters, some party candidates were arrested arbitrarily while the
property of others was burned. Before the
election was over at least twenty-five persons
had been killed and nearly 400 wounded.
Yet, the government did not achieve its
purpose. In the new Diet, the parties, with
163 seats, maintained a clear majority.

Thus the battle was soon renewed.
When Matsukata resigned, August, 1892, Ito
accepted the premiership and formed a
cabinet that included most of the *Genro*.

[3] For details of these early party battles
with the oligarchs see Robert A. Scalapino,
*Democracy and the Party Movement in Prewar
Japan* (1953). For a statistical analysis of Japa-
nese national elections, 1892–1937, and their
bearing on Japan's political modernization, see
Robert A. Scalapino, "Elections and Political
Modernization in Prewar Japan," in Robert E.
Ward, ed., *Political Development in Modern
Japan* (1968), 249–91.

This time the House used the ultimate
weapon. It memorialized the throne to impeach the ministry. The emperor's reply, written undoubtedly by the oligarchy, was a
major blow to popular government. The
House was told that its function was "to aid"
the government. Thus a deadlock had occurred when the outbreak of the Sino-Japanese War, 1894, brought peace to internal
Japanese politics. The constitutional question
was forgotten as all factions united in prosecution of the war.

OLIGARCHIC-PARTY ENTENTES, 1895–1900

During the brief period from the close
of the war until the turn of the century, the
oligarchy and parties experimented with political ententes. The first of these was between
the Ito cabinet and the *Jiyuto*. The general
pattern set by this and succeeding ententes
required party support for the government's
program in return for which the party received a post in the cabinet, appointment of
party members to office, and, to phrase the
matter delicately, contributions to the party's
treasury. These shaky alliances did enable a
party to get one foot in the door of administrative authority. On the debit side they contributed little to the advancement of the principle of party government, since neither
oligarchy nor party had surrendered their
extreme and opposing views as to what government should be. Nor did the alliances bring
political stability. From 1895 to 1900 there
were no less than six different cabinets and
four dissolutions of the Diet, leaving chaos
and corruption in their wake. Finally, the
ententes, by providing power and spoils to
only selected members of the parties, increased factionalism among the parties and
destroyed what little chance there was for a
united front among the parliamentarians.[4] It
was at this time, too, that Yamagata, the unrelenting opponent of popular government,

[4] During this period there was a brief interlude of the so-called party cabinet of Okuma
and Itagaki in 1898. The two leaders had recently formed a new constitutional party, the
Kenseito.

gave the military services the advantage in successive administrations when in May, 1900, he secured an Imperial Ordinance requiring that only generals or lieutenant generals on the active list might hold the post of Minister of War and only admirals or vice admirals on the active list the post of Minister of the Navy.[5] The requirement meant that no popular party would be able to form a cabinet unless it complied with the wishes of the military oligarchs.

THE OLIGARCH AS PARTY LEADER, 1900–1918

As the new century opened, Japan's constitutional government, now a decade old, had failed to produce a working pattern for the stress and strain of everyday politics. In this respect the record was one of dismal failure. Yet Japan, through the genius of Ito, was about to find a solution that would give some stability to her constitutional structure. In essence the solution rejected the strong-arm methods of Yamagata and the ententes of recent years. Ito's purpose was to find a means through which a political party might be created as an administration party, thus providing support for the oligarchy. This was not a new idea with Ito. He had been playing with it since the elections of 1892.

In 1900 a faction of the recently formed *Kenseito* party provided Ito with the opportunity to try his idea in practice. Unable to tolerate further the humiliating entente with Yamagata, this faction asked Ito to become its leader. Ito's terms were severe: (1) the party must be dissolved and a new party more representative of all groups in the State put in its place, and (2) party members must accept orders of the leader. The *Kenseito* accepted the terms. On September 16, 1900, a new party was born, the *Rikken Seiyukai* (Association of Friends of Constitutional Government), with Ito as its president. This development meant that the party men (or at

[5] The ordinance was modified in 1913 enabling reserve officers of these ranks to qualify, but reverted to its original form in 1936.

least most of them) had accepted the leadership of one of the most powerful oligarchs without knowing in advance what the policy of its new leader would be. It meant that the *Seiyukai* was willing in some major degree to renounce political principle, if by so doing it might gain access to administrative authority. Yet from the beginning Ito left no doubt as to his purposes. His *Seiyukai* would stand for the "true," that is, the imperial interpretation of the constitution. In summary, the surrender of the *Seiyukai*, the only strong political party, to oligarchic leadership provided a means by which government could be conducted. It did not mean that the struggle for power among political factions was ended.[6] On the contrary, the oligarchy, at the time, was divided into two rival factions under the leadership of Yamagata and Ito. These groups were designated as the "military" and the "civil." From 1901 to 1918 contests between these factions and their successors were a principal feature of Japanese politics.

Ito's first ministry, supported by the *Seiyukai* but racked by internal cabinet discord, survived less than a year. Yamagata, who was the natural successor to Ito in the now well-established process of shuffling premiers among the *Genro*, refused to head the next government. A number of factors influenced this decision: (1) the power of the *Genro* was for the time being secure; (2) Yamagata was of no mind to face the political attacks of Ito and the hostile *Seiyukai* in the Diet; and (3) the time was at hand when younger men were to hold the premiership while the older *Genro* continued their control behind

[6] For conflicting interpretations of the theory of Imperial powers, see H. S. Quigley, *Japanese Government and Politics* (1932), 67–68; R. K. Reischauer, *Japan: Government-Politics* (1939), 167–69; G. E. Uyehara, *The Political Development of Japan 1867–1909* (London, 1910), 19; Nakano Tomio, *The Ordinance Power of the Japanese Emperor* (1923), 5; H. Sato, *Democracy and the Japanese Government* (1920), 1; E. W. Clement, "Constitutional Imperialism in Japan," *Proceedings of the Academy of Political Science* 6 (1916): 325; U. Iwasaki, *Working Forces in Japanese Politics* (1921), Chapter 2. The Japanese doctrine postulating the identity of the emperor and the state is known as *kokutai*.

the scenes. Accordingly, it was a military protégé of Yamagata, General Katsura Taro of Choshu, who became premier in June, 1901. Katsura, faced by parliamentary opposition, was forced like others before him to fall back on the budget of the preceding year. Nevertheless, during 1903 the militarists continued to strengthen their position. Ito was made president of the Privy Council and thus removed from party affiliation. His place as president of the *Seiyukai* went to his civilian protégé, Saionji Kimmochi (a *kuge*), who was eventually to become a full-ranking *Genro*. At this point too, as in 1894, war came to the aid of the militarists. As the tension with Russia increased, the Diet rallied to the financial support of the army. This fervent patriotism continued unchecked until the signing of the Treaty of Portsmouth. Then political peace promptly gave place to violent attacks on government resulting in declarations of martial law. Unwilling to face the hostile Diet, Katsura resigned, and was succeeded by Saionji as premier.

For two and one-half years (January, 1906–July, 1908) Saionji's government, supported by the *Seiyukai*, maintained itself in office. Its fall was due primarily to financial policies that failed to satisfy the military oligarchs. Katsura again succeeded to the premiership, and when in 1909 Ito was assassinated in Harbin, Yamagata, militarist and arch-enemy of all liberal and representative trends, was left as supreme directing head of the *Genro*. As a consequence, Katsura was left free to carry through the annexation of Korea. Far from attacking the policy, the House of Representatives urged Katsura to use the "big stick." [7]

The annexation of Korea, another major victory for the militarists, enabled Katsura to retire with glory, while Saionji again headed the government in August, 1911. It was in this administration that the growing inner conflict within Japan's political machinery was exposed. Yamagata and the Army wanted the creation of two divisions for Korea. Saionji, with the civilians of his cabinet, re-

[7] Takeuchi Tatsuji, *War and Diplomacy in the Japanese Empire* (1935), 166–67.

fused to support this policy. Thereupon, the Minister of War resigned, and when Yamagata and the General Staff refused to name a successor, there was nothing for Saionji and his cabinet to do but resign. The army oligarchs had given a practical demonstration of their power to dominate the civilian wing of government.

With doleful regularity, Katsura again became prime minister (1912), though by this time he was no longer the disciple but rather the rival of the aging Yamagata. This estrangement and his unpopularity with the parliamentarians led Katsura to form his own political party, the *Rikken Doshikai* (Constitutional Fellow-thinker's Society). However, even with lavish use of funds he was unable to secure a majority in the House. He had failed in his challenge to the power of Yamagata and in his efforts to buy parliamentary support.

The *Genro* then turned to Admiral Count Yamamoto Gombei (Satsuma), but when it was discovered that the Navy was implicated in financial scandals touching battleship construction, the Diet refused to pass the budget, and Yamamoto resigned. The next premier was Marquis Okuma Shigenobu (1914), whose command of the Diet during two and a half years was in part due to a new coalition party, the *Kenseikai*.

When Okuma resigned in 1916, the premiership passed with unfailing monotony to one of Yamagata's men, General Terauchi Masatake, a soldier of some reputation but wholly unprepared to meet the political, economic, and social dislocations of a Japan undergoing wartime industrialization. War profiteers had already been the source of popular indignation, and, when the government failed to control the price of rice, the authorities were defied, and rioting spread from city to city. These rice riots, as they were called, were symbolic of new forces stirring within Japan—forces with which the oligarchy lacked the capacity to deal. Accordingly, in September, 1918, Hara Takashi, the first untitled man to hold the office, became premier. Often referred to as Japan's "Great Commoner," Hara was a gifted politician who had achieved leadership of the *Seiyukai* through his ability to command the personal loyalty of his followers.[8] Like many of the military oligarchs who preceded him, Hara was unscrupulous, recognizing loyalty only to party rather than to any abstract program of political ideology. Yet his elevation to the premiership was a significant event. It marked the end of rule by the *Genro* and the clansmen of Satsuma and Choshu. It marked the beginnings of rule by party politicians— men of a new Japan in which the commerce, industry, and finance of a bourgeois society seemed destined to replace the feudal and military traditions perpetuated by the *Genro*.

ECONOMIC AND SOCIAL BASES OF OLIGARCHY

The political battles at the turn of the century to resolve the question of how and by whom Japan should be governed under the constitution were never free from the everyday momentum and temper of a revolutionary age. The last decade of the nineteenth century in addition to shaping constitutionalism in operation, was also giving form to the new industrial system, the foundations of which had been laid in the earlier years of Meiji. The Japanese had been assimilating machine technology, accumulating banking and industrial capital, and increasing the output of textiles and other consumer goods. The Sino-Japanese and the Russo-Japanese Wars stimulated the growth of transport, banking, and strategic industries. By comparison with the giants of the West, Japan's industrial capitalism in 1914 was still weak, but its character, like that of Japan's peculiar constitutionalism, had been formed. Before the turn of the century, Japan had gained relief from the unequal treaties, a matter of first importance in the economy. The Chinese indemnity of 1895 enabled Japan in 1897 to shift to the

[8] Although Hara made much of his lack of title, he actually came from a noble family (a *kaoru*), higher in status than Saionji. This background contributed to the rapid growth of his career in his early years. For the early years see Tetsuo Najita, *Hara Kei in the Politics of Compromise, 1905–1915* (1967).

gold standard. Total production and real income probably increased from 80 to 100 per cent between 1889 and 1914, the first twenty-five years of the constitutional period. Agriculture and fisheries took care of a 25 per cent increase in population, 1894–1914, with some improvement in dietary standards and with only small imports of foodstuffs. Japan's industrial revolution, well under way on the eve of World War I in 1914, included three major lines of development: (1) large-scale industry, (2) agriculture and traditional industries, and (3) the textile trades.

More important to the growth in national productivity in the years up to 1914 was the expansion of Japan's basic economy, including agriculture and small-scale traditional industry. With little increase in farm population, food production increased 35 or more per cent, 1894–1914, due to an increase in cultivated areas, improved credit facilities, scientific intensive methods, and double cropping. There was little change in basic organization. Some 5.4 million farm families cultivated holdings averaging 2.6 acres each. High taxes and interest charges continued to weigh heavily on the farmer. By 1910, 39 per cent of farmers owned no land and 45 per cent of farm lands were tenanted. Tenants paid rents in kind amounting to 45 to 60 per cent of the crop on rice land, and the land tax even after the turn of the century was the principal government revenue to meet the rising armament expenditure. In 1908 the farmer was paying a far larger percentage of his income in taxes than was the merchant or industrialist. In a few cases there was an expanding market for traditional handicrafts such as in Japanese paper, pottery, and fine fabrics. The silk industry and cotton textiles were major examples of adaptation and growth of traditional industries responding to foreign demand. In the growth of the cotton textile industry the technical transformation due to Western influence was much greater than in the case of silk. By 1914 the Japanese cotton textile industry supplied not only the home market but was already invading the foreign field with its products. It was in this period that Japan and India displaced Britain in the cotton yarn market in China. Japan was also beginning to capture the Chinese market in piece goods, especially in coarse goods supplied previously by Americans. In a word, the growth of agriculture and of consumer goods industries enabled Japan at the turn of the century to support a growing population and a large national budget for armaments and colonial expansion.

But expansion constituted only a single feature of Japan's economy. Economic growth was accompanied by strains and instability. For example, it had seemed necessary to increase heavily taxes on low and middle income classes and to resort frequently to foreign borrowing. By 1914 Japan was threatened with a financial crisis, only to be rescued by the outbreak of World War I. The war brought to Japan orders for munitions and other manufactures from the Allies; neutral countries of eastern Asia no longer able to buy from Europe sought their purchases in Japan. As illustrative of what happened, exports of Japanese cotton cloth increased 185 per cent from 1913 to 1918 (412,000,000 to 1,174,000,000 linear yards). The Japanese merchant fleet increased from 1,577,000 gross tons in 1914 to 2,840,000 in 1919. By the end of 1919 Japan's foreign assets exceeded her outstanding debts by 1,300,000,000 yen. Five years earlier Japan had been a debtor by approximately the same figure. These fantastic gains were parallelled by expanded bank credit, price inflation, soaring profits, and wild speculation. Although, as the popular unrest faced by the Terauchi cabinet suggests, Japan's economic difficulties were by no means solved, she had become an industrial power of first rank with a major stake in world markets. Moreover, she was the first and only industrialized nation in East Asia.

Economic expansion gave increased power to the industrial-commercial elements in Japanese society, and paved the way for their growing influence on government policy. Yet it should be emphasized that in exercising this influence Japan's business leaders did not challenge the leadership of the oligarchy. Several factors explain their behavior. In spite of their wealth, they continued to operate under the social stigma attached to business from early Tokugawa days; the business community itself had discovered early in the Meiji era the profit to be realized from deferring to government initiative, subsidy, and protection; and, finally, political initiative was stunted by the weighting of representation in the Diet toward rural landowners. As a result, businessmen largely eschewed political opposition in favor of subtler pressures which promised the least risk and the greatest rewards.

Reinforcing this pattern of subservience were the educational programs that were developed between 1890 and 1918. In the first instance, great progress was made in the national effort to destroy illiteracy. By 1900 some 5,000,000 children were in about 27,000 elementary schools. Above these schools were limited systems of secondary and higher education, the latter available only to the sons of the well-to-do. This system of general and technical education (there were 240 technical schools by 1903) was indispensable to the nation's industrial advance. While technical education rose to increasing standards of excellence, general education, at first strongly influenced by American ideals of freedom, was directed by the oligarchy from 1890 onward toward indoctrination in nationalistic and authoritarian morals. Principles of obedience and subservience to the state, dressed in the garb of Shinto mythology, made education a strong arm of the oligarchy.

Finally, it should be noted that Meiji constitutionalism, subservient as it was to the idea and goal of a centralized, industrial state, was biased in favor of power rather than of the welfare of the common man. This is not to say that the Meiji oligarchy took no steps to curb abuses, yet the first factory labor law drafted by the government in 1898 was not submitted to the Diet because of the opposition of the industrialists. When the Japan Social Democratic Party was formed in 1901 by Katayama Sen and Kotoku Denjiro, it was ordered dissolved by Home Minister Suematsu Kencho, son-in-law of Premier Ito, within three hours of its founding. During the Russo-Japanese War the socialist movement became more radical, international, and intellectual. In 1907, rioting by miners in protest against outrageous working conditions resulted in millions in property damage and in the arrest of more than 200 miners and labor leaders.

This policy of repression directed against socialistic parties and associations was merely an extreme aspect of the oligarchy's attitude toward political freedom in general. Although the constitution made reference to civil liberties, suppression continued after 1890 as it had before. Oftentimes the government, seeking a gradual transition, had a plausible case against the tendency of dissident groups to resort to violence. At first the series of Peace Preservation Laws that were in effect when the constitution was promulgated were opposed bitterly by the parties in the first Diets, and the most obnoxious of the statutes was repealed in 1898 only to be re-enacted two years later in a form vitually precluding the legal organization and maintenance of labor unions. This law persisted until 1926, though it was not always enforced.

FOR FURTHER READING

SOCIAL, ECONOMIC, AND INTELLECTUAL BASES OF POLITICS. For the pattern of Japanese culture, see Ruth Benedict, *The Chrysanthemum and the Sword* (1946).* G. C. Allen, *Modern Japan and Its Problems* (1928) studies the effect of Western influences. W. W. Lockwood, *The Economic Development of Japan* (1954)* provides valuable insights into the political significance of economic processes. On this topic see also Araki Mitsutaro, *Financial System in Japan* (Tokyo, 1933); Yamasaki Kakujiro and Ogawa Gotaro, *The Effect of the War Upon the Commerce and Industry of Japan* (1939); and Ohara Keishi (comp.), *Japanese Trade and Industry in the Meiji-Taisho Era*, trans. and adapted by Okata Tomatsu (Tokyo, 1957).

On the emergence of the labor movement see Katayama Sen, *The Labor Movement in Japan* (1918), and Kohno Mitsu, *Labour Movement in Japan* (Tokyo, 1938). See also Kawabe Kisaburo, *The Press and Politics in Japan, A Study of the Relation Between the Newspaper and the Political Development of Modern Japan* (1921). H. L. Keenleyside and A. F. Thomas, *History of Japanese Education* (Tokyo, 1937) reveals the political philosophy behind the educational system.

HISTORY OF POLITICAL THOUGHT. Ito Hirobumi, *Commentaries on the Constitution of the Empire of Japan*, Miyoji Ito, trans. (Tokyo, 1889). Fujisawa Rikitaro, *Recent Aims and Political Development of Japan* (1923). *The Autobiography of Fukuzawa Yukichi* (Tokyo, 1934). Kawai Tatsuo, *The Goal of Japanese Expansion* (Tokyo, 1938), for the so-called philosophy of musubi. Tokutomi Iidiiro. "The Life of Yoshida Shoin," *Transactions of the Asiatic Society of Japan*, 45, (1917), Part I. Joseph J. Spae, *Ito Jinsai: A Philosopher, Educator, and Sinologist of the Tokugawa Period* (Monumenta Serica Monograph Series 12, Peking, 1948) presents the important position of Yoshida Shoin with a bibliography on Japanese Confucianism.

POLITICAL HISTORY AND GOVERNMENT. R. H. P. Mason, *Japan: First General Election* (1969), the first detailed description in English. See also Yanaga Chitoshi, *Japanese People and Politics* (1956).* Delmar Brown, *Nationalism in Japan: An Introductory Historical Analysis* (1955). C. B. Fahs, *Government in Japan* (1940). Fujii Shinichi, *The Essentials of Japanese Constitutional Law* (Tokyo, 1940). W. W. McLaren, *A Political History of Japan during the Meiji Era, 1867–1912* (London, 1916). Two studies by E. H. Norman. *Japan's Emergence as a Modern State* (1940), and *Soldier and Peasant in Japan: The Origins of Conscription* (1943) deal with the early years of the oligarchy.

Japan and China
in World War I, 1914–1918

chapter 21

Considered in the perspective of its immediate causes and its military and naval campaigns, World War I was primarily a European conflict. No major battles were fought on Asiatic soil or in Asiatic waters. Nevertheless, at one time or another all the major lands and peoples of Asia were aligned with the Allied and Associated Powers. By their participation in the war, the peoples of East Asia were united, formally at least, with the Western democracies in the crusade against German militarism and, after 1917, in the Wilsonian crusade to "make the world safe for democracy." Thus Eastern Asia became a participant in the war despite the fact that it was not intimately concerned with the war's immediate causes.

In contrast with the immediate causes, the more remote causes of the war involved East Asia intimately just as they came eventually to involve the interests of the United States. These remote, underlying causes were concerned with "the psychology of fear, and all other factors which go to make up the somewhat vague conceptions of 'militarism' and 'navalism' as causes of war."[1] They involved the powerful forces of

[1] For a detailed discussion of underlying causes, see Sidney B. Fay, *The Origins of the World War* (2 vols. in one, 1931),* I, 32–49.

nationalism as they developed in the century following the French Revolution, encompassing the political and prejudicial questions of race, religion, democracy, and education.

These underlying causes of conflict had taken root in the political, economic, and cultural soil of East Asia. In 1914 all the great peoples of Asia, the Japanese excepted, were in colonial or semi-colonial status to one or more of the great Western powers or Japan. Therefore, although East Asia could and did remain in relative isolation from the military conflict, it could not be isolated from the consequences of war or from the aspirations which the war or the peace aroused in the minds and hearts of ordinary men and women.

WAR COMES TO EAST ASIA

Japan's entrance into World War I derived its sanction from a double basis: the nation's commitments under the Anglo-Japanese Alliance, and the larger political and military purposes of Japan's emerging Asiatic policy.

On August 7, 1914, three days after her own declaration of war, Great Britain requested Japan to destroy the German fleet in Pacific waters. The decision of the Japanese government, made on August 8, was to

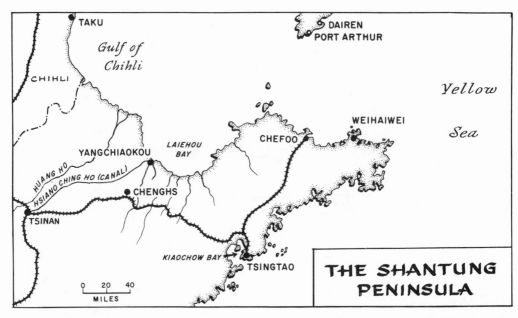

TAKU

Gulf of Chihli

CHIHLI

DAIREN
PORT ARTHUR

Yellow

Sea

WEIHAIWEI

CHEFOO

LAIEHOU BAY

YANGCHIAOKOU

HUANG HO

HSIANO CHING HO (CANAL)

CHENGHS

TSINAN

KIAOCHOW BAY

TSINGTAO

0   20   40
MILES

THE SHANTUNG PENINSULA

demand of Germany not only surrender of its armed ships in Asiatic waters (thus complying with the British request) but also to demand surrender of the Kiaochou leasehold in Shantung. Later in the month, on August 23, as Germany ignored Tokyo's ultimatum, Japan entered the war. This momentous decision to join Great Britain in the war (as explained by Count Kato Takaaki, the Foreign Minister) was not based on legal obligations of the Anglo-Japanese Alliance, for "the general conditions were not such as to impose upon Japan the duty to join the war under treaty obligations," but "as a voluntary expression of friendship toward Great Britain under the Alliance." [2] What Japan meant was that she welcomed an opportunity to destroy German influence in Eastern Asia and to enhance her own international position.

The outbreak of war in Europe had aroused great alarm in Peking. China's interests, so its government reasoned, would best be served by exclusion of her territories and waters from the zone of hostilities. Consequently, Yuan Shih-k'ai enlisted American assistance in seeking from the belligerents declarations of respect for China's neutrality.

[2] Takeuchi Tatsuji, *War and Diplomacy in the Japanese Empire* (1935), 169.

On the assumption, presumably, that the neutrality of China was closely linked with the principle of territorial integrity, dear to American official policy, Secretary of State Bryan sounded the powers. However, when nothing resulted from the American inquiries and the United States declined to take further steps, China had to act alone. Peking first proclaimed her neutrality and later delimited a war zone in the areas adjacent to Kiaochou. The latter step was in line with the precedent set in Manchuria in 1904. But both of these measures were futile. Following promptly on her declaration of war, Japan proceeded to the investment of the Kiaochou leased territory and its port of Tsingtao. With this port under naval blockade, Japanese military forces landed on Chinese soil far to the north, moved to attack Tsingtao from the rear, and to occupy the railway zone reaching from Tsingtao to Tsinan far in the interior of the province.[3] Kiaochou surrendered, November 10, and Japan took over not only the leased territory but also all German interests in Shantung, including the Tsingtao-Tsinan Railway.[4] Japan also took over from the

[3] A small British force was also engaged for "token" purposes.

[4] The nature and scope of German rights which Japan was to claim as a result of her vic-

Chinese, on the plea of military necessity, the policing of the railroads outside the leased territory. Japanese replaced Germans in the Chinese customs house at Tsingtao. Indeed, the ousting of the Germans was thorough and complete. As in 1904, China was unable to keep war from her shores or to control its course within her borders. In the aftermath of the military action, January 7, 1915, she cancelled the war zone on the ground that it was no longer necessary, and this step, as will be seen, was to provide the pretext for further Japanese action.

While Japanese naval and military forces were engaged in the reduction of Tsingtao and in taking over other German interests in Shantung, units of the Japanese navy were operating in the Pacific and Indian Oceans in cooperation with the British against German commerce raiders. Early in these operations, while the Australians were occupying German colonies and islands south of the equator, the Japanese occupied the German islands north

of the equator. These included the Marianas (excepting Guam), the Carolines, and the Marshalls. From this point on, that is from the beginning of 1915, Japan's relationship to the war became essentially noncombatant. On the one hand, Japanese factories equipped the Russian armies on the eastern front; on the other, Japan's policies in China posed a threat not only to Western commerce but also to political principles emerging in the pattern of Allied war aims.

THE TWENTY-ONE DEMANDS

On January 18, 1915, Japanese Minister Hioki at Peking presented to President Yuan Shih-k'ai a group of twenty-one demands designed to "insure" Japan's position in China at a time when Europe was preoccupied with war. These demands, it was asserted, were necessitated by China's cancellation "abruptly and without previous notification" of the war zone in Shantung. Thus, with this Chinese action serving as a pretext, Japan was launched upon new steps in her policy of expansion. In particular she hoped to establish a solid legal basis for her special interests in Manchuria. Although European powers had recognized Japanese claims there, China had not. In consequence, as early as January, 1913, Count Kato Takaaki, before leaving London to become Foreign Minister, informed Viscount Grey that Japan awaited only the "psychological moment" to obtain "permanent occupation of Kwantung Province." [5] A second phase of Japanese policy in 1915 concerned itself with the nation's position and influence south of the Great Wall in China Proper. In the scramble there for railway and mining concessions, Japan as a debtor nation was at a disadvantage against European and American competitors. Moreover, Japanese difficulties were increased by China's tendency to protect herself by seeking American intervention. By the outbreak of World War I many serious and responsible Chinese had construed American support of the open

---

tory were as follows: (1) China had conferred upon Germany a 99-year lease of both sides of Kiaochou Bay, on which Germany erected fortifications and in which Germany had exercised "rights of administration"; (2) within a zone of 50 kilometers of the bay, German troops held the right of freedom of passage, and Chinese administration was subject to German approval; (3) Germany acquired the right to construct certain railroads in Shantung, a provision that resulted in the building of the Tsingtao-Tsinan Railway by a Sino-German concern, the Shantung Railway Company; (4) Germany also acquired the right to mine coal within 30 *li* of the railroads; (5) if Germany desired to return Kiaochou to China before the expiration of the lease, China engaged to lease "to Germany a more suitable place"; (6) Germany had engaged not to sublet the territory to another power, but there was no provision regarding the transfer of the territory by Germany to another power as a result of conquest such as the Japanese action of 1914; (7) if assistance in the form of capital or services or materials were needed for any undertaking in Shantung province, China had agreed to approach German nationals. Under these concessions, Germany had built a modern port at Tsingtao, had extended a railroad far into the interior of the province, and had developed broad commercial undertakings, while at Kiaochou she had created a naval base for the Pacific squadron.

[5] Paul S. Dull, "Count Kato Komei and the Twenty-one Demands," *The Pacific Historical Review* 19 (1950): 151–61.

door to mean that the United States would undertake to guarantee China against any territorial aggression or disregard to its sovereignty.[6] As seen in Tokyo, the weakness of Japan's position could only be corrected by the assertion of specific rights and, if possible, of a general and paramount influence over all of China. To achieve these purposes, Japan presented demands divided into five groups: Group 1 was concerned with the disposition of the former German rights in Shantung; Group 2 related to Japan's position in South Manchuria and eastern Inner Mongolia; Group 3 dealt with a program for Japanese industrial capital in regions of the Yangtze Valley; Group 4 required the nonalienation of Chinese coastal territory; and Group 5 included a variety of subjects, designated as "requests" rather than "demands."

Group 1: Shantung

In these demands, China was required to assent to any subsequent German-Japanese agreement disposing of German rights in Shantung; to agree not to cede or lease any part of Shantung "to any other power"; to agree to Japanese construction of a railroad connecting Chefoo with the Tsingtao-Tsinan line; and finally to consent to the opening of certain cities to "the residence and commerce of foreigners." By these provisions Japan would preclude the return of Germany to Shantung at the close of the war.[7]

Group 2: South Manchuria

In Group 2 Japan demanded that the lease of Port Arthur and Dairen be extended from 25 to 99 years, as also her agreements

[6] United States, *Foreign Relations, 1914* (Supplement), 186–87. How fantastic these Chinese hopes were was revealed by Acting Secretary of State Lansing when he informed the American legation in Peking that although the United States was prepared to promote China's welfare by peaceful methods, "it would be quixotic in the extreme to allow the question of China's territorial integrity to entangle the United States in international difficulties," 190.

[7] The Triple Intervention of 1895 and the Portsmouth Conference of 1905, were usually considered by Japanese statesmen as instances of diplomacy depriving Japan of the rewards of military victory.

covering the South Manchurian Railway and the Antung-Mukden Railway; that Japanese subjects be permitted "to lease or own land" for "commercial and industrial uses or for farming"; that Japanese subjects be accorded "liberty to enter, reside, and travel" in South Manchuria and eastern Inner Mongolia; that Japanese subjects be accorded the right to engage in mining; that China engage to secure Japan's consent before granting to any third power a concession to construct railroads or to extend industrial credits in these areas; that Japan be consulted first if China required foreign advisers in these areas; and finally that control and management of the Kirin-Changchun Railway be placed in Japan's hands for 99 years. These were perhaps the most important of all the Japanese demands. Their purpose was to fulfill a policy that had been pursued since 1904; namely, to establish beyond question Japan's *paramount* interests in these regions.

Group 3: The Han-Yeh-P'ing Company

The third group in the Twenty-one Demands was designed to insure Japan a more adequate source of iron ore by making the Han-Yeh-p'ing Company a Sino-Japanese concern, and by giving the company a mining monopoly in certain regions of the Yangtze Valley. This Chinese company owned some of the richest iron and coal properties in Central China. Japanese concerns had made extensive purchases of these ores since 1899.

Group 4: Nonalienation of Territory

This group consisted of a single article by which China, would engage "not to cede or lease to any other Power any harbour or bay on or any island along the coast of China." This concession would preclude China from making territorial grants to other powers, including the United States.[8]

Group 5: "Wishes" or "Desires"

It was desired that (1) China engage influential Japanese as political, financial, and military advisers; (2) China grant the right to own land to Japanese hospitals, temples,

[8] In this case Japan had in mind John Hay's overtures of 1900 relative to Sam-Sah Inlet.

and schools situated in the interior; (3) China place her police under joint Sino-Japanese administration in designated regions where Sino-Japanese disputes had occurred; (4) China obtain from Japan a supply of arms, or that an arsenal be established under Sino-Japanese administration; (5) Japan be granted a concession to construct certain railways in South China; and (6) the Japanese be granted "the right of preaching in China." Only one article of this group, that dealing with Fukien, became a part of the eventual Sino-Japanese treaty settlement in May, 1915; yet as a result of the sweeping objectives revealed by them, it was with these "wishes" or "desires" that world opinion identified Japanese policy, rather than with the more specific demands relating to Shantung and Manchuria. They justified extravagant speculation as to Japan's real purposes, not excluding the possibility that her motive was creation of a Japanese protectorate over China.

THE COURSE OF NEGOTIATIONS

In two particulars Japanese diplomacy misjudged the problem it faced in China. In the first place, the Okuma cabinet did not anticipate the violent reaction of the Chinese. In the second place, Japan's method of conducting the negotiations with China from January to May, when the resulting treaties were signed, was calculated to increase the apprehension both of China and of the Western powers. The demands were presented directly to President Yuan Shih-k'ai with insistence upon secrecy. This encouraged China to protect herself by permitting the demands to become known through unofficial channels. Garbled accounts appeared in the Chinese and the foreign press. As these unhappy negotiations dragged on, Japan, finding some of China's counter-proposals unsatisfactory, resorted to an ultimatum on May 7. Two weeks later, on May 25, China and Japan signed a number of treaties and notes embodying many, though by no means all, of the objectives set forth in the original Twenty-one Demands.

The more important treaty commitments gained by Japan included: (1) the German leasehold in Shantung was to be returned to China after the close of the war in return for recognition of Shantung as a Japanese sphere; (2) extension of the Kwantung leasehold to 99 years, together with increased railroad and other privileges in South Manchuria; and (3) the right of Japan to be consulted first in case China required foreign capital for railway or harbor construction in Fukien. On paper at least, Japan had won the bases for a commanding position in China.

Before these agreements were reached, however, the United States was to become involved in the negotiations. Since Japan had sought to implement her policy in China at a time when Europe was involved in war, the United States alone was in a position to act in the Far East if she desired to do so. President Wilson had already shown his concern for China. He had been the first to extend formal recognition to the Republic;[9] he had repudiated the Taft-Knox policy in the Consortium which in his view infringed China's administrative independence; and he approved of Secretary Bryan's effort to assist in the maintenance of China's neutrality at the outbreak of war. His policy in the case of the Twenty-one Demands was to "protect China out of sympathy, and American rights out of interest, but to move cautiously lest Japan be antagonized against the United States and be more severe with China." [10] As a result, the policy of the American government was formulated with restraint in a detailed memorandum from Secretary Bryan to the Japanese Ambassador on March 13. The memorandum raised specific objection to several of Japan's demands on the ground that they violated the open door and China's administrative and territorial integrity. To these objections, however, Bryan added an important

[9] Meribeth E. Cameron, "American Recognition Policy Toward the Republic of China, 1912–1913," *The Pacific Historical Review* 2 (1933): 214–30.

[10] Harley Notter, *The Origins of the Foreign Policy of Woodrow Wilson* (1937), 233–34, 241–43, 385–86, 410–11.

observation concerning the areas in which Japan claimed spheres of influence:

> While on principle and under the treaties of 1844, 1858, 1868 and 1903 with China the United States has ground upon which to base objections to the Japanese "demands" relative to Shantung, South Manchuria and Eastern Mongolia, nevertheless, the United States frankly recognizes that territorial contiguity creates special relations between Japan and these districts.[11]

Stated briefly, the United States was offering to strike a bargain with Japan. Insofar as China was concerned, the bargain called for American recognition of Japan's claims to spheres of influence in return for concrete Japanese pledges of support for the open door in the remainder of China. While this offer was undoubtedly more modest than Japan might have wished, it did seem to foretell a significant shift in the policy of the nation which had presented the greatest opposition to the spheres.[12]

But Japan did not respond to the American offer. Thus, later in the negotiations, as a result of Japan's ultimatum to China, the United States appeared less conciliatory. In identical notes to China and Japan on May 11, Secretary Bryan informed these powers that the United States would not recognize

> . . . any agreement or undertaking which has been entered into or which may be en-

[11] Emphasis added.

[12] For the origins of the proffered bargain see Burton F. Beers, "Robert Lansing's Proposed Bargain with Japan," *The Pacific Historical Review* 26 (1957): 391–400. Sir Edward Grey, the British Prime Minister, toyed with the idea of an Anglo-Japanese bargain which was similar in substance to the one hinted by the United States. Grey's idea was to make concessions to Japanese economic interests in areas of China where Britain claimed exclusive investment privileges in return for Japanese pledges foreswearing attacks on British imperial holdings. The idea emerged in the context of British concerns (carefully concealed from Britain's allies) that Japan was behind the rise of Indian nationalism. See Don Dignan, "New Perspectives on British Far Eastern Policy, 1913–19," *University of Queensland Papers: Departments of Government and History*, I, No. 5 (Jan. 31, 1969), 263–302.

tered into between the governments of Japan and China, impairing the treaty rights of the United States and its citizens in China, the political or territorial integrity of the Republic of China, or the international policy relative to China commonly known as the open door policy.[13]

This note was sent after China's acceptance of the ultimatum, but two weeks before the signing of the Sino-Japanese treaties and notes of May 25. The procedure was unusual, and the doctrine that was set forth (that of nonrecognition), though it was later to play a most conspicuous part in American policy, had no immediate effect upon Japan. The United States in 1915, although sympathetic to China and concerned for American interests therein, was not prepared to challenge Japan openly. Moreover, the British government indicated that Japan's demands would not be opposed so long as they did not infringe on British rights in the Yangtze Region. France and Russia were not opposed to the principles of Japanese policy, though they were jealous of her growing influence in China. All these considerations suggested that effective opposition to Japan could come only from China herself.

CHINESE POLITICS, 1915–1917

Although the political and diplomatic turmoil stirred up by Japan's Twenty-one Demands aroused unprecedented resentment among the Chinese people, this popular display of an infant nationalism did not produce an effective national government at Peking. The popular anti-Japanese enthusiasm served for the moment to bring a semblance of greater unity among the politicians, but this was short-lived. President Yuan Shih-k'ai was already planning in the spring of 1915 to set up a monarchy with himself as emperor. Factions representative of the old-style politicians promptly contended with one another for power under the new dispensation. However, Yuan's colorful scheme got nowhere.

[13] United States, *Foreign Relations, 1915*, 146.

Early in 1915 Russia and France were already hoping to bring China into the European war. They considered striking a bargain by which, if China aligned herself with the Entente, the Allies would continue to give their blessing to Yuan and his proposed monarchy. When this scheme failed because of Japanese opposition, the Allies advised Yuan to defer the monarchy plan.[14] The President was indeed forced to hesitate, for the Allies could always threaten to withhold the funds so essential to Peking's bankrupt treasury. Opposition to the proposed monarchy came also from within China and was perhaps as important a factor as foreign pressure. During the early months of 1916, rebellions occurred in many of the southern provinces. These outbreaks were so serious that Peking officially dropped the monarchy plan toward the end of March.

China's political ills, however, were not to be cured by a mere discarding of the monarchy plan. Political disaffection continued to spread through most of the south. At Canton, rebellious provinces organized their own provisional government. Then, in June, death put an end to Yuan Shih-k'ai, and Li Yuan-hung succeeded to the presidency. Again there was a move toward unity, for Li was accepted by most of the rebellious southern provinces. The provisional constitution of 1912 was restored, and on August 1, 1916, the parliament which Yuan had disbanded in 1914 met again in Peking. This session, like the former one, was doomed to fail, for the parliament possessed neither mandate from the people nor military power. Five years of nominal republicanism had not served to transfer the politico-military power either to parliament or to the people. Once held by Yuan, it had now passed to provincial military governors whom he had appointed and controlled.

These military governors were to monopolize the political stage in China for a decade, 1917–1927. Here it is sufficient to note that these local warlords, former henchmen of Yuan Shih-k'ai, made and broke alliances among themselves, and fought for control of Peking with a disregard for fixed principles, loyalty, or sense of responsibility to anyone. And behind the warlords the foreign powers wrestled with each other and with the Chinese for position in and control of China. In the course of this uproar China stumbled into and through World War I.

CHINA ENTERS THE WAR

In the midst of her domestic political chaos, China was called upon in February, 1917, to resolve the question of breaking diplomatic relations with Germany. President Wilson, having announced the severance of American relations with Germany, called upon neutral powers to follow the American example. The American minister at Peking, Paul S. Reinsch, not only conveyed the appeal to the government through Tuan Ch'i-jui, a northern militarist serving as premier, but also proceeded with great zeal to urge its adoption. This pressure from Reinsch touched off a flurry of international activity. Japan, fearing that Reinsch's moves marked the beginning of close Sino-American ties, first sought to block China's break with Germany. Later Japan reversed her course and led the European powers in urging the severance of relations. Thus the way for a diplomatic break between China and Germany had already been paved when on February 24 the torpedoing by a German submarine of the French ship *Athos* in the Mediterranean resulted in the death of 543 Chinese coolies. Thousands of these coolies had been employed by the French and British to work in the Flemish and French military zones in 1916–17. On March 14 China formally terminated relations with Germany. Unknown to China, however, was the price that she had paid for being a party to the maneuvering just described. Before accepting the idea of a break between China and Germany, Japan secretly asked for and obtained (in February and March, 1917) from her European allies pledges of support for her claims

[14] Kwanha Yim, "Yuan Shih-k'ai and the Japanese," *Journal of Asian Studies* 24 (1964): 63–73.

in Shantung as well as in the German islands in the North Pacific (the Marianas, Carolines, and Marshalls).[15]

This was to be only the beginning of Chinese troubles. The question of China's belligerency precipitated a struggle within China itself. Premier Tuan's strategy was to place China in the war in return for Allied loans to maintain his government in power. While there was no real disagreement over the desirability of entering the war, opposition arose in parliament on grounds that Tuan, having acquired financial support, would suppress all rivals to his authority. In consequence, China's leadership split into competing factions. During the summer of 1917, Tuan was forced from office and briefly replaced by another warlord, Chang Hsun, who by a coup restored the Manchu emperor to power for twelve days (July 1–12). This effort resulted in a new coalition of northern warlords who brought Tuan back to office. Tuan's resumption of power thus opened the way for a declaration of war by China on Germany, August 14. Meanwhile President Li Yuan-hung had resigned, and the *Kuomintang* members of Parliament had scurried to Canton where they attempted to launch a government of their own. Clearly, the controversy over the war contributed significantly to the growth of political chaos.

As a belligerent, China was neither able nor willing to contribute much to the war effort except the sending of labor battalions to France, Mesopotamia and Africa. Not until the latter part of 1918, when the collapse of Germany seemed assured, did Tuan's government bestir itself to adopt a vigorous war policy through effective control of enemy aliens and liquidation of enemy property. These tardy steps were a last minute bid for consideration at the forthcoming peace conference. They were also a recognition by the northern warlords that Chinese public opinion was becoming more sympathetic to the

cause of the Allied and Associated Powers. China, however, was not solely responsible for the shortcomings of her war record.

Against the acts of her irresponsible warlord government must be weighed the tortuous diplomacy of the Allied and Associated Powers. Japan, Britain, and France had assisted in pushing China into the war neither for high moral purpose nor in the hope that she would become an effective belligerent, but rather with the specific intent of eliminating German commercial and industrial competition from a post-war China. If American diplomacy was less self-serving, it was also thoroughly ineffective in saving China from the powers or, indeed, from herself. And finally it should be noted that when China issued her declaration of war, she did so without definite assurance of concessions, financial or otherwise, from the West.

PEACE

Although Japan's participation in the war was marginal, Tokyo made extensive preparations for the peace conference. Just as World War I had swept away the old balance of power in Europe, so it had gone far to destroy the balance of power in Eastern Asia. Prior to 1914, Japan had been accorded a nominal status as a so-called great power, a result of victories over China in 1895 and over Russia in 1905. Actually, however, the great powers of Europe had not considered Japan a full ranking member of their select company. It was the World War of 1914 that elevated Japan to a new status. The war had provided Japan with an opportunity to expand her economy and armed forces, as well as to demonstrate her supremacy in China and the Pacific. Japan, therefore, approached the peace conference conscious of her newly found power. She was prepared to seek general recognition of her status as a great power and specific recognition of her hegemony in the Far East.

The opposition to Japan's objectives was to come principally, though not exclusively, from the United States. Since May, 1915, the Wilson administration, concerned with

---

[15] These concessions were the product of diplomacy in which Japan played upon Allied fears that a deal with Germany would take her out of the war. Frank Ikle, "Japanese-German Peace Negotiations during World War I," *American Historical Review* 71 (1965): 62–76.

upholding China's administrative and territorial integrity as well as with the protection of specific American interests, had labored to forestall the establishment of a Japanese political and economic monopoly in China. The United States had urged American investors to underwrite major construction projects and had revived negotiations for the creation of a new Consortium, an organization which would safeguard Peking from financial dependence on Japan. Diplomacy had been employed to obtain pledges limiting Japanese aspirations. But these efforts had been invariably hampered by the war. American investors, for example, had been hard pressed to find funds for China in the face of war demands elsewhere. Again, the necessity of maintaining at least the facade of unity among the Allied and Associated Powers while the war lasted had prevented the United States from exerting much diplomatic pressure at Tokyo. But, in 1917, the United States invited Viscount Ishii Kikujiro to Washington. During the subsequent conversations Secretary of State Robert Lansing urged Japan to relinquish her claims to special privilege in China, but he dared not press too hard, lest Japan withdraw from the war. When Japan refused to yield, Lansing and Ishii signed notes, carefully worded, to conceal the disagreement they embodied. Thus, as the peace conference drew near, the United States, free at last from the responsibility of belligerency, sought new means by which to block Japan in her efforts to gain special privilege in East Asia.

JAPAN AT VERSAILLES

At the Versailles Conference, Japan presented three demands: (1) she asked for cession of the former German islands in the North Pacific Ocean (the Marianas, the Carolines, and the Marshalls); (2) she asked confirmation of her claims to the former German rights in Shantung province; and (3) she asked for a declaration of racial equality among states as a basic principle of the proposed League of Nations. Unassailable as Japan may have believed these objectives to

be, they led nonetheless to widespread and bitter opposition from some of her former allies and associates in arms. The sources of this opposition were many and varied. Japan's claim to the German islands violated the Wilsonian principle of no annexations; her claims to Kiaochou and Shantung ran counter to a young and virile Chinese nationalism; and her demand for a declaration of racial equality raised a storm of protest from some of the British dominions, particularly Australia.

Japan's representatives, Baron Makino Nobuaki and Viscount Chinda Sutemi, approached their task with confidence, for Japan's demands in the case of the German islands and Shantung were supported by powerful legal claims, and, in the case of racial equality, by high moral principles.[16] The German islands and Kiaochou had been captured by Japanese arms and were in Japanese possession. Moreover, Japan's claims were sustained by secret concessions of European Allies and by the treaties and notes signed with China in May, 1915. Whatever moral or legal strength China's resentment against the 1915 treaties may have had, it was weakened seriously in 1918 when China again gave her explicit consent to the transfer of Kiaochou to Japan on the understanding that Japan would in turn restore the leasehold to China but would retain in expanded form Germany's economic rights in the province. Thus Japan's legal case was strong; and despite the desire of the Allies and the United States to block her further expansion, they were not prepared to challenge the legal basis of her claims, lest this challenge rebound upon the whole system of unequal treaties pertaining to China.

CHINA ENTERS THE CONFERENCE

If the demands on which Japan was to insist were brutally clear, they were also a logical result of the policy on which Japan had embarked in 1914–1915 and to which her preparations had been pointed for many

[16] Japan's ranking delegate was Prince Saionji Kimmochi, ex-Premier and *Genro*.

years. In contrast, the role that China might play at the peace table was not so predictable. It is true that by 1918 there was the beginning of a young Chinese nationalism that was extremely vocal, but neither the warlord government at Peking nor the insurgent government, which had been established at Canton, appeared to represent anything with political substance. Indeed, the program that China did present at Paris was a product of opportunism and of particular personalities in her peace delegation. Although the Peking and Canton governments had not achieved unity at home, they presented a facade of unity at Paris, for the Chinese peace delegation was composed of representatives of both governments. In terms of political strategy and showmanship, this Chinese delegation was unsurpassed at Paris, for to the able political strategy of C. T. Wang was added the eloquent English of Wellington Koo. These men fashioned the Chinese program as it was presented. It was the program of a young, progressive, revolutionary, and idealistic China—a program that must have sounded strange in the ears of Peking's warlords. Yet these warlords were the government *de facto* of China; they controlled the administration that was recognized by all the powers; and they were the authority to which the Chinese delegation was responsible. It may be added, too, that no delegation supported with greater eloquence the Wilsonian program. Nevertheless, China's delegation was regarded with suspicion by the European Allies and Japan: first, because in the light of China's internal politics it was questionable whether any delegation could speak for the country; and second, because it was soon evident that Wang and Koo were less concerned with the problem of making peace with Germany than with using the conference to free China from her semi-colonial status. To most of the Allied statesmen this purpose was alarming, for it implied an attack not only on Japan's "special interests" but also upon the larger system of spheres of influence and the "unequal treaties" in general, to which all the victorious great powers were parties. In addition, the mistrust of Japan, England, and France was further aroused be-

cause both before and during the Paris Conference, Wang and Koo systematically set out to cultivate the sympathies and enlist the support of the American delegation, which in turn was not loath to give the Chinese encouragement.

THE DEBATE AT PARIS

Japan's demand for the "unconditional cession" of the German rights in Shantung was made on January 27, 1919. The following day, China's counter-demand that Kiaochou and the German rights be restored directly to China was presented. To President Wilson, the obvious answer to this deadlock between China and Japan was to be found in his own program that promised a new world of international justice under a League of Nations. But Wilson could make no progress against the Japanese on this score while Australia, New Zealand, South Africa, France, Italy, and Belgium remained as insistent on annexing the German colonies in their respective regions as were the Japanese in theirs. The best that Wilson could get eventually was the system of mandates which, with the exception of those in Class A, gave to the mandatory power a control which for practical purposes was hardly to be distinguished from annexation. Under the Class C mandate, Japan acquired the former German islands in the North Pacific and the British dominions got those in the South Pacific.

Having "compromised" by accepting a mandate instead of annexation in the Pacific islands, Japan turned to her third objective. With the approval and aid of President Wilson and Colonel House, her delegation presented as an amendment to the draft covenant of the League of Nations a resolution affirming the principle of racial equality.

This resolution, approved by Wilson, was a logical if not an essential complement to the whole spirit of the Wilsonian program as well as to the League itself; but, in newsroom parlance, it was also a "hot potato." It aroused the unrelenting opposition of Premier William H. Hughes of Australia, who was

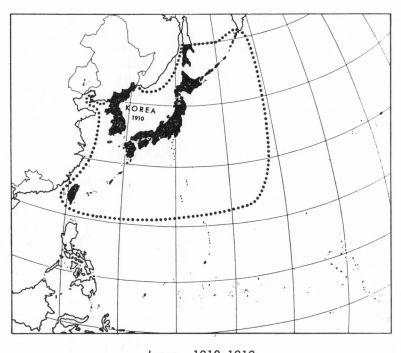

Japan 1910–1919
Reproduced from A War Atlas for Americans *(New York: Simon & Schuster)*
1944, with permission from the publisher and from the U.S. Department of
State, Division of Map Intelligence and Cartography.

supported by the chief British delegates, Arthur Balfour and Robert Cecil. The argument advanced against any provision on racial equality was that it implied the right of the League to interfere in questions concerning immigration and the rights of aliens, which every nation regarded as matters of purely domestic concern. England feared embarrassment in some of the middle eastern colonies. Hughes saw in the resolution a threat to the "white" Australia policy, and he threatened to arouse an outraged public opinion in the British dominions and the United States unless the amendment were dropped. At the same time he stooped to convince the Japanese press that it was the United States and not Australia that was blocking the amendment.

Wilson's dilemma was real. If the racial equality debate was brought into the open, as Hughes threatened to do, what would be the reaction of the American Pacific Coast, especially in California, which had already enacted the discriminatory alien land law of 1913 aimed at the Japanese? But this was not all. American policy at Paris was attempting to hold Japan in check on many fronts. There was Shantung, which Wilson wanted to restore directly to China. There was the prospective Four-Power Consortium, into which he hoped to entice Japan in order to preserve a financial open door in China. There was eastern Siberia (see Chapter 22), which it was hoped could be rescued from Japan's military expansionists despite its occupation at the time by more than 70,000 Japanese troops. And there was the Island of Yap in the Japanese mandate, where it was hoped the United States might be given submarine cable privileges. Would not American policy have a better chance of achieving these objectives if Japanese racial pride were satisfied by even an emasculated concession to the principle of racial equality? Thus, on grounds of high principle and of practical politics Wilson desired adoption of the amendment.

The vote on Japan's amendment [17] was favorable, eleven to six, but Wilson ruled against adoption of the amendment because the vote was not unanimous. For reasons which to him seemed good, Wilson announced defeat of the measure. The newsmen had been right: racial equality was a "hot potato." Wilson could not risk the issue in open debate, and he feared that Hughes would force it into the open if it could be defeated in no other way.

Two of Japan's objectives at Paris had now been disposed of: in the Pacific islands there had been a "compromise" which the Japanese had accepted but did not like; on racial equality Japan had accepted a defeat particularly galling to Japanese pride, since the race issue was a symbol of discrimination, a label of an inferior people. Japan's government was therefore in no mood to accept further reverses as it approached the debate on its next objective: transfer to Japan, in terms of the peace treaty, of the former German rights in Shantung. Here Japan was determined to accept neither compromise nor defeat. The problem was the more difficult because Wang and Koo had by this time gone far beyond their original demand for the direct restoration of Kiaochou and the German rights. Encouraged by the support of public opinion in the West and in China, the Chinese delegates demanded abrogation of all the 1915 treaties and notes. This was a direct thrust not only at Japan's pretensions in Shantung but also at her "special position" in South Manchuria and eastern Inner Mongolia and at her general ambitions in China as a whole. It was a challenge which the Japanese promptly accepted. They stood firm and demanded Shantung, threatening to withdraw from the Conference if it were denied them. Wilson thought that this Japanese stand permitted only one choice—acceptance. In this he differed from some of his close advisers, who felt that the Japanese were bluffing. Wilson, however, was right; his advisers were wrong.[18] With Wilson's

opposition ended, Japan was permitted to insert into the treaty articles giving her free disposal of German rights in return for oral assurances that Chinese sovereignty in Shantung would be restored at some unspecified time. China's response was her refusal to sign the treaty.

CHINA'S BALANCE SHEET OF WAR

Although China refused to sign the Treaty of Versailles between the Allied and Associated Powers and Germany, and although her defeat on the Shantung issue was a reverse of great magnitude, her balance sheet of war was not written wholly in red ink. The war had terminated China's old "unequal" treaties with Germany, Austria, and Hungary, thus opening the way for new treaties with those powers negotiated on a basis of equality.[19] And, more than this, the war contributed in complex ways to the growth of Chinese nationalism. A word about the intellectual foundations of the new China in the aftermath of the Revolution of 1911 will explain this contribution.

In an immediate sense, the Revolution of 1911 was profoundly disappointing to its partisans. While the Manchus had been ousted, the first Republic had not provided the setting for any rapid political transformations in Chinese life. The cold facts were that Chinese society was unchanged; indeed the new political institutions of the Republic itself were attacked by Yuan Shih-k'ai and succeeding warlords. Yet for all its apparent superficiality, the revolution held a deep significance that was manifest even as early as World War I. By sweeping away a dynasty that was foreign but culturally orthodox in subscribing to Confucian traditions, the revolution had encouraged new directions in na-

---

[17] It had become merely an "endorsement of the principle of equality of nations and just treatment of their nationals."

[18] Russell Fifield, "Japanese Policy Toward the Shantung Question at the Paris Peace Conference," *The Journal of Modern History* 23 (1951): 265–72.

[19] China did sign the Treaty of St. Germain with Austria, September 10, 1919; the Treaty of Neuilly with Bulgaria; and the Treaty of Trianon with Hungary. China's war with Germany was ended officially September 15, 1919, by proclamation of the Chinese President.

tionalist thinking even as it removed the stoutest defender of old faiths. Before 1911 opposition to the Manchu had imparted to nationalism a high content of anti-foreignism. With the dynasty gone there was an increased tendency to concentrate on the ills of Chinese society. Similarly young nationalists lost interest in attempts to synthesize Confucian and Western ideas and turned to the examination of foreign ideas which presumably would provide the footings for the new China. In this new context patriotism no longer required the retention of Old China's cultural grandeur. Service to the nation legitimized cultural unorthodoxy.[20]

Leadership in promoting these ideas was provided primarily by an able body of intellectuals fathered at Peking National University. There in September, 1915, the magazine, *New Youth*, founded by Ch'en Tu-hsiu who was both Western educated and a fervent advocate of Western liberalism, began a campaign to direct the rebuilding of China along new lines. Ch'en advocated the destruction of Confucianism and the erection of a society on an entirely fresh base. The first number of the *New Youth* was a call to young Chinese to abandon traditional deference toward elders and to assume the initiative in shaping a new order. Subsequent numbers advocated a modern China built on science and democracy. At about this time Ch'en in collaboration with the American-educated Hu Shih also inaugurated literary reforms aimed at making literature a tool for the remodeling of China. Writers were to compose their works in the vernacular rather than classical Chinese; and they were to express the emotions and thoughts of contemporary China instead of those of the dead past. From these beginnings came the New Culture Movement. Lu Hsun, who joined the movement in 1918 and became one of its leaders, captured one aspect of the thinking of young literati in his popular short stories which depicted the majority in Old China leading dull, meaningless lives amid conditions of poverty, ignorance, and misery. Such attacks on the tra-

ditional order and calls for a new one stimulated endless debates over how Western liberalism, pragmatism, utilitarianism, anarchism, or one of several varieties of socialism might be adapted to Chinese purposes. In short, young intellectuals, rejecting the conservative traditions of the past, embarked upon a search for new standards for Chinese society.

While forces within China provided most of the impetus for the New Culture Movement, the direction of the movement and its impact on the country were affected by events outside the country. During World War I, the emphasis given by the Allied and Associated Powers to democracy and self-determination of people bolstered the orientation of young intellectuals toward the West. By the end of the war, however, it was evident that this orientation was being affected by the Versailles settlement and the spectacle of revolutionary regimes being established throughout Europe. Indeed, young China reacted violently to the provisions of the Treaty of Versailles concerning Shantung. On May 4, 1919, such wild demonstrations were staged against Peking's role at Paris that the entire cabinet was ultimately forced to resign. This marked the first time in the history of the Republic that public opinion had broken the power of a governing clique. But Peking was not the only loser in this episode. Beginning with the May Fourth Movement, the West was included in the attacks of Chinese nationalists. From this point onward young literati increasingly found impossible the achievement of fundamental reforms without the elimination of foreign influence and intervention in Chinese affairs. Moreover, this attack on imperialism was associated with growing skepticism that the West provided useful models for the construction of a new China. For example, Liang Ch'i-ch'ao, formerly a champion of Western liberalism, published in 1920 an article which criticized the development of science and material culture in the West at the expense of human values. According to Liang, Western civilization was bankrupt. As an alternative to Western precedents, some intellectuals were attracted by the Bolshevik experiment. In

[20] Joseph R. Levenson, "The Intellectual Revolution in China," in *Modern China*, Albert Feuerwerker, ed. (1964),* 154–68.

August, 1920, through the so called "Karakhan Manifesto," Moscow announced its intention of relinquishing all special privileges which had been inherited by the Soviet Union from treaties concluded between Czarist Russia and China. Later it will be seen that reservations were attached to this gesture, but these were not immediately apparent. What did seem clear to young Chinese was that the Soviet Union was abandoning imperialism while Japan and the West clung to it. Finally, Chinese thinking was touched by news of successful revolutions not only in Russia but also in Finland and the Dual Monarchy. Whereas the New Culture Movement had been directed initially toward the modernization of China through thought reform, it tended after 1919 toward provision for direct action. One consequence of this was the establishment of numerous groups to promote change on all levels.

Nor were these shifts in the New Culture Movement the only influences on Chinese nationalism deriving from events outside China. The prominence achieved by advocates of the New Culture was itself in some measure related to World War I. Between 1914 and 1919 Western trade with China dropped sharply. As a result, Chinese light industry expanded, swelling the number of factory managers and industrial workers, stimulating migration from the countryside to cities, and causing dislocations in rural economies. One consequence was the weakening of the landlords and gentry, who were prime proponents of the Confucian tradition. At the same time economic and social change presented new opportunities for the cultivation of revolutionary concepts. Thus it appears that World War I created a paradoxical situation for China. Even as the war led to fresh encroachments on Chinese sovereignty, it was indirectly helping to lay the foundations of a new nation.

FOR FURTHER READING

JAPAN AND WORLD WAR I.   Charles R. Hicks, *Japan's Entry into the War, 1914* (1944). For a full study of Japan's ties with Britain see Chang Chung-fu, *The Anglo-Japanese Alliance* (1931). Julian Corbett, *History of the Great War . . . Naval Operations* (3 vols., London, 1920–23), I, and Thomas G. Frothingham, *The Naval History of the World War: Offensive Operations, 1914–1915* (1924) are narratives of the naval situation in the Pacific. Jefferson Jones, *The Fall of Tsingtau* (1915). On politics relating to the war see Shimasa Idditti, *The Life of Marquis Shigenobu Okuma* (Tokyo, 1940), and A. Morgan Young, *Japan Under Taisho Tenno, 1912–1926* (London, 1928), as well as the study by Takeuchi cited in footnotes. A. M. Pooley, *Japan's Foreign Policies* (London, 1920) recounts the growth of ambitions toward China. Ernest B. Price, *The Russo-Japanese Treaties of 1907–1916 Concerning Manchuria and Mongolia* (1933) gives the text of the treaty of 1916 by which Russia and Japan sought further to refine their spheres of influence. Differing interpretations on the origins of this treaty are given in Pauline Tompkins, *American-Russian Relations in the Far East* (1949), and W. A. Williams, *American-Russian Relations, 1781–1947* (1952). Discussion of Japan's secret treaties with her European allies is found in F. S. Cocks, *The Secret Treaties* (2nd ed., London, 1931). Barbara Tuchman, *The Zimmerman Telegram,* (1958)* sifts the evidence on the rumored alliance between Japan and Germany. Ishii Kikujiro, *Diplomatic Commentaries*, trans. and ed. by William R. Langdon (1936), and "The Permanent Bases of Japanese Foreign Policy," *Foreign Affairs* 2 (1933): 220–29, by the same author provide insight into the thinking of a foremost diplomat.

CHINA AND WORLD WAR I.   Thomas E. La-Fargue, *China and the World War* (1937). H. F. MacNair, *China in Revolution* (1931), H. B. Morse and H. F. MacNair, *Far Eastern International Relations* (1931), and H. M. Vinacke, *Modern Constitutional Development in China* (1920) provide useful narratives of Chinese politics. Jerome Ch'en, *Yuan Shih-k'ai, 1859–1916: Brutus Assumes the Purple* (London, 1961), especially useful for the last stages of Yuan's career, though sometimes marred by excessive criticism of the central figure. R. T. Pollard, *China's Foreign Relations, 1917–1931* (1933), superseded by more recent research but useful as a reference. George M. Dutcher, *The Political Awakening of the East* (1925), an early effort to appraise the impact of the war on Asian nationalism. Chow Tse-tsung, *The May Fourth Movement: Intellectual Revolution in Modern China* (1960)* and *Research Guide to the May Fourth Movement* (1963) deal with China's intellectual ferment between 1917 and 1921. Judith Blick, "The Chinese Labor Corps in World War I," *Papers on China*, Vol. 9. Published and distributed by the East Asian Research Center, Harvard University (1955), 111–45, is a well-organized pioneer study on the subject.

AMERICAN FAR EASTERN POLICY. On Wilson's policy see R. W. Curry, *Woodrow Wilson and Far Eastern Policy, 1913–1921* (1957); Li Tien-yi, *Woodrow Wilson's China Policy, 1913–1917* (1952); and Russell H. Fifield, *Woodrow Wilson and the Far East: The Diplomacy of the Shantung Question* (1952; reprinted, 1965). Burton F. Beers, *Vain Endeavor: Robert Lansing's Attempts to End the American-Japanese Rivalry* (1962), more critical of the Wilson policy than any of the foregoing. Note also A. W. Griswold, *The Far Eastern Policy of the United States* (1938).* O. J. Clinard, *Japan's Influence on American Naval Power, 1897–1917* (1947) contains very debatable interpretations. Kamikawa Hikomatsu, ed., *Japan-American Diplomatic Relations in the Meiji-Taisho Era*, trans. by Kimura Michiko (Tokyo, 1958) is based partly on Japanese sources. Paul S. Reinsch, *An American Diplomat in China* (1922), valuable as memoirs and as special pleading rather than history.

VERSAILLES CONFERENCE. This topic is covered in several works already cited. Additional studies are: W. L. Godshall, *The International Aspects of the Shantung Question* (1933). Victor Birdsall, *Versailles Twenty Years After* (1941), an excellent study of the Peace Conference in general with a penetrating chapter on Japanese strategy. A basic work is David Hunter Miller, *The Drafting of the Covenant* (2 vols., 1938). On the disposition of the Pacific islands see Werner Levi "American Attitudes toward the Pacific Islands, 1914–1919," *The Pacific Historical Review* 17 (1948): 55–64; and Paul H. Clyde, *Japan's Pacific Mandate* (1935; reprinted 1967).

The Legacies of War in East Asia, 1919–1924

chapter 22

As World War I receded into the category of things past, new and specific problems, international in character, some created by the war, others magnified by it, appeared to threaten the peace. These new points of friction were by no means limited to particular geographic areas. They were in the Old World and in the New World alike, but they were particularly acute in the sphere of American-Japanese relations. The co-belligerency of the United States and Japan had not served to harmonize their respective policies. The roots of American-Japanese friction had grown lustily since the days of the Russo-Japanese War in 1904–1905. Dollar diplomacy in Manchuria, Oriental immigration in California, and special interests versus the open door in China had already made it quite clear that there was a growing coolness in the traditional nineteenth-century friendship between Japan and the United States. By 1920 there was a widespread popular conviction in the United States and Canada, and to a lesser degree in Great Britain and France, that Japan had shown little interest in the defeat of German militarism and that she had used the war primarily to advance Japanese hegemony in China. In Japan there was a widespread conviction that the Western powers, especially the United States, were seeking to undermine legitimate Japanese aspirations.

The appearance of these recriminatory views was traceable directly and in an immediate sense to the differences that had arisen out of the Twenty-one Demands of 1915, the Lansing-Ishii conversations of 1917, the Japanese programs as presented at Paris, and, finally, out of an episode yet to be discussed—the joint American-Japanese expedition into Siberia in 1918. Underlying the diplomacy of these clashes was the determination of the Japanese military, whose influence on policy had been enhanced by the war, to forestall a resurgence of Western domination in Asia by uniting the Chinese and non-Bolshevik Russians behind Japan. The emerging Japanese military program viewed national security as resting on Japanese leadership of a new Asian "international" order rather than on Japan's co-operation with Europe and the United States. These military views were decidedly at variance with Wilson's vision of a modern China emerging under American tutelage.

The deterioration in American-Japanese relations had not, as yet, produced an extreme crisis. The European war and the Paris Conference, seemingly far removed from Far Eastern affairs, were the principle American concerns prior to 1920. In the early post-war years even questions presenting tangible American interests in the Pacific aroused nothing more than half-hearted public concern. Similarly, the Japanese government and public displayed little inclination to think of war as a means of advancing national interests. Beginning in the autumn of 1918 with the ministry headed by Hara Takashi, Japan's government was led by men, who, while no less determined than their predecessors to defend and to strengthen their country's vital interests, sought their objectives through economic expansion and international co-operation. This new emphasis was derived from a new importance of civilian bureaucrats and politicians in policy making. These men were responsive to manufacturing, mercantile, and banking interests with a stake in international trade and stability. Japanese policy also reflected the conviction that the diplomacy of imperialism had been discredited by Wilsonian internationalism and that a policy embodying old principles could only lead to isolation and trouble.[1] In consequence, Japan, like the United States, had reason to seek a peaceful resolution of international difficulties. But, during the immediate post-war years, 1918–1924, the inclination of both the United States and Japan to move toward an accommodation of their differences was tested by a number of issues of great magnitude and complexity. These issues included the inter-Allied intervention in Siberia, the financing of Chinese national development, naval disarmament with all of its political ramifications, and oriental immigration to the United States.

THE SIBERIAN INTERVENTION

American-Japanese difficulties arising from the inter-Allied intervention in Siberia were full-blown when the war ended. Late in

[1] Akira Iriye, "The Failure of Economic Expansion, 1918–1931" (in manuscript). Papers presented at the Conference on Taisho Japan, Duke University, January, 1968.

1917 the Russian Revolution had created a political vacuum in Siberia and the zone of the Chinese Eastern Railway in north-central Manchuria. During the years 1918–1920 and after, Siberia, North Manchuria, and Outer Mongolia became a confused battleground for armies, political creeds, and irresponsible brigands, in which all the major powers— Great Britain, France, Japan, and the United States—became involved. In tracing these various developments in some detail a word should first be said about events in Siberia itself.

The bonds that had held together Siberia's vast territorial expanse were either weakened or destroyed by the ousting of the Tsarist regime, the collapse of Kerensky's provisional government, and the resulting warfare between revolutionary and anti-revolutionary forces. The collapse of the Imperial government brought first a revival of the late nineteenth-century movement for Siberian autonomy. Opposed to these "regionalists," there was from November, 1917, to the summer of 1918 the rising influence of the local soviets. The defeat of these groups in the summer of 1918 paved the way for the Kolchak White government at Omsk, which claimed all power in Siberia from November, 1918, to January, 1920. Although Kolchak's government was accorded *de facto* recognition by the Supreme Council of the Allied and Associated Powers, it was by no means the only pretender to power. Among the nondescript array of these Siberian pretenders great and small was Cossack Captain Grigorii Semenov, who had been commissioned by Kerensky's provisional government to recruit troops in the Trans-Baikalia. There was also Baron Ungern von Sternberg, who used Mongolia as a base from which he hoped to set up a Pan-Mongolian empire. There were Social Revolutionaries of divergent shades, some of whom operated reluctantly with Kolchak, others with the Bolsheviks. In the Russian railway zone at Harbin there were two principal factions. One was headed by the anti-Bolshevik, Lt. General Dimitrii Horvath, the other by Petr Yakolivich Derber, whose "government" was composed of center-left Social Revolutionaries. In addition to these

THE SINO-RUSSIAN FRONTIER

MILES
0 200 400 600 800

Lake Balkas

U.S.S.R.

Irkutsk
Lake Baikal
• Chita
U.S.S.R.
Amur R.
U.S.S.R.
Khabarovsk •

Urga

MANCHURIA
(Manchukuo, 1932-45)

Tihwa
•

OUTER MONGOLIA
Autonomous, 1912; Soviet Russian
control after 1920 as People's Republic

Harbin •
• Hsinking
to Manchukuo, 1933
Mukden •
Vladivostok

• Kashgar

SINKIANG
Chinese dependency to 1878; then made
19th province of China. Russian influence
dominant by 1941.

Manchu control to 1911; divided into 4 provinces by
Chinese Republic, 1912

INNER MONGOLIA

NINGHSIA

SUIYUAN

CHAHAR

JEHOL

KOREA

JAPAN

CH'INGHAI
(KOKONOR)

KANSU

SHENSI

SHANSI

HOPEH

Peiping •

Yellow R.

SHANTUNG

Yellow
Sea

TIBET
Manchu nominal control
to 1912; Chinese Republic
1912 created provinces
of Ch'inghai and Sikang

INDIA

Lhasa •

SIKANG

SZECHWAN

CHINA

Yangtze R.

HUPEH

HONAN

ANWEI

KIANGSU

Nanking •
Shanghai •

CHEKIANG

HUNAN KIANSI

there were many other groups led by Cossack adventurers more concerned with opportunities for pillage and plunder than with the political stability of Russia. Finally, there were almost innumerable bands of peasant "partisans" who had no understanding of the mad political events in which they were enmeshed and by which they were impoverished.

Another factor complicated conditions in Siberia. Early in World War I a Czechoslovak army was formed in Russia and fought as a division of the Russian army against the Central Powers. During the period of Kerensky's provisional government, this Czech force was increased to some 50,000 men. As the Russian armies disintegrated in the first months of Bolshevik rule, the Czech legions remained intact. They were placed under the Supreme French Command by the Czech National Council in Paris, where the decision was made to transport the force around the world by way of Vladivostok and the Pacific to serve with the French armies on the western front. Permission was granted the Czechs by the Bolsheviks to cross Siberia en route to France. However, in the conditions pre-

vailing, clashes soon occurred between Czech and Bolshevik. During May and June, 1918, anti-Bolshevik governments appeared at Samara and Omsk sheltered by Czech arms.

THE QUESTION OF ALLIED INTERVENTION IN RUSSIA

This checkered pattern of forces and events was a matter of deep concern to Great Britain, France, and Italy, all of whom were hard pressed by the Central Powers. They feared that Germany would use the Bolsheviks to convert Russia into a granary for the Central Powers; would gain control of vast stores of war material at Archangel and Vladivostok; and finally would be free to transfer major reinforcements from the eastern to the western front. They were impressed by reports that the Bolsheviks were planning to spread their revolutionary creed into Central Europe through indoctrination of German and Austro-Hungarian prisoners of war, held in Russian and Siberian camps. In a word, the Allies thought it imperative that Russia be brought back into the war quickly under non-Bolshevik auspices. To this end they urged either that Japan send an expedition eastward to the Ural Mountains or that such an expedition be sent jointly by Japan and the United States. A military expedition, it was reasoned, would provide the dual advantage of reviving the eastern front and providing a rallying point for non-Bolshevik factions.

For seven months, December, 1917, through June, 1918, neither Japan nor the United States yielded to mounting Allied pressure.[2] Although the Japanese army favored intervention on the ground that it would provide a means for combatting Bolshevism and of obtaining a voice in a Russian settlement, the Terauchi Ministry hesitated because the purposes were too large and the results too uncertain for Japan to undertake the risks alone. The American government felt that an expedition was unlikely to revive the eastern front and, in any event, would divert needed energies from the main centers of fighting in Western Europe.

Both Japan and the United States, however, began to shift their respective positions when the Czechs broke with the Bolsheviks in late May, 1918. The Czech hold on the Trans-Siberian Railway and their strategic position in the Volga region provided the first tangible possibility of reopening an eastern front. Moreover, the Wilson administration overcame some of its inhibitions against intervention when the Supreme War Council decided, June 1, to send a force including American troops to Murmansk in northwestern Russia, already held by the British since March, and also to occupy Archangel. Thus, a month later, on July 6, the United States agreed to a Siberian expedition on the grounds that the Czechs needed help. Ostensibly Wilson had accepted the idea that the Allies and Associated Powers could not win on the western front even in 1919 unless the Germans were forced to keep troops in the east.

In reality the President's reasoning was

far more complex than this statement would imply. Wilson feared that a continuation of differences over the Siberian expedition would weaken the united front against the Central Powers. If one was an ally, one must act like an ally. Since the Allies insisted on going into Siberia, the United States would go along with them. Beneath this reasoning were concealed Wilson's apprehensions concerning Japan. While Tokyo had opposed going into Siberia alone, Wilson knew that this stand was closely contested in Japan itself. The Japanese army, riled by the eastward march of Bolshevism, had used every pressure for permission to send troops to Siberia. Indeed, even as the army argued, its agents were contacting Semenov, Horvath, and others in a search for Russian allies. Moreover, in May, 1918, Japan signed agreements with China providing for co-operation in military measures, and granting permission for Japanese troops to move in Chinese territory. The effect of these understandings would be to safeguard the rear of Japanese forces, if they became engaged in Siberia and the Sino-Russian borderlands. Moves such as these cast doubt on any assumption that Japan would long continue to oppose intervention. To Wilson this prospect suggested a final reason for agreeing to the venture. By taking the lead the United States would be able to say later: "Now let us come out," instead of, "now you come out." Convinced that Japanese expansionists would use any intervention for their own purposes, Wilson felt that he could "impose greater restraint on Japan within rather than outside" the intervention. The important thing, he felt, was to maintain the open door in Siberia and North Manchuria against Japanese pretension.[3]

On July 17, 1918, the United States informed the Allied ambassadors of its decision

[2] Both countries wavered during this period. Japan indicated interest in the idea in December, 1917, and again in March, 1918. On this latter occasion the United States considered going into Siberia if Japan acted.

[3] Betty Miller Unterberger, "President Wilson and the Decision to Send American Troops to Siberia," *The Pacific Historical Review* 24 (1955): 63–74, is the clearest statement of the generally accepted interpretation. See Unterberger, "The Russian Revolution and Wilson, Far Eastern Policy," *The Russian Review* (April 1957), 35–46. For a different view of Wilson's motives see Christopher Lasch, "American Intervention in Siberia: A Reinterpretation," *Political Science Quarterly* 77 (1962): 205–23.

to intervene, and of its objectives, to which it asked their adherence.

> *Military action is admissible in Russia . . . only to help the Czecho-Slovaks consolidate their forces and to get into successful cooperation with their Slavic kinsmen and to steady any efforts at self-government or self-defense in which the Russians themselves may be willing to accept assistance. . . . The only legitimate object for which Americans or Allied troops can be employed . . . is to guard military stores which may subsequently be needed by Russian forces and to render such aid as may be acceptable to the Russians in the organization of their own self-defense.*[4]

From August until November, 1918, troops of the Allied Powers—British, Japanese, French, and American—were landed at Vladivostok. It was Wilson's intention to curb the Japanese by an agreement limiting the American and Japanese contingents to some 7,000 troops each. In the end the United States sent 9,000 troops, the Japanese something in excess of 72,000.[5]

THEORY AND PRACTICE IN SIBERIA

Now that Allied contingents were in Siberia, what were they to do? There was as much disagreement on this question as there had been on the original point of intervention. The policy of the American military forces, commanded by Major General William S. Graves, had been determined by Wilson. It required that the troops refrain from "any interference of any kind with the political sovereignty of Russia" and from "any intervention in her internal affairs." Since these American troops were on Russian soil, these were admittedly difficult instructions to follow. Nevertheless, General Graves attempted to carry them out. Where American troops patrolled the railroads, they did so for all Russians, whether White or Red. Graves'

[4] United States, *Foreign Relations, 1918, Russia,* II, 288.

[5] It appears that Japan was careful to reserve the liberty to send additional troops if in her view circumstances demanded it. United States, *Foreign Relations, 1918, Russia,* II, 324–26.

actions in this respect appear to have been proper, but they led to a tense situation, since of all the key personalities in the intervening armies he alone held unswervingly to his instructions and to the announced purposes of the intervention. On the other hand, most of the Allied representatives, including many Americans, completely disregarded the principles of noninterference and neutrality in Russian affairs. The European governments, the Japanese, and some American officials thought the purpose of the intervention was to fight the Reds. The announced purposes of the intervention were no longer to be the real purposes. Thus England, France, and Japan, with the willing support of certain American consular officials and members of the Department of State, became the *de facto* allies of Semenov. Moreover, the Allies, mainly the British and French, had been responsible for bringing Admiral Aleksandr Vasilevich Kolchak to Siberia where they installed him as head of a White government at Omsk. There this well-meaning but mild and ineffectual sailor was surrounded by discredited Russian Whites, and by British and French military missions, which seemed unaware that Russia could not be pressed back into the political and economic mould of the tsars. From November, 1918, until January, 1920, Kolchak, the Czechs, and their British and French allies fought the Bolsheviks, long after Germany had fallen and the need of an eastern front had disappeared. On the part of the European Allies and Japan, the original stated purposes of the intervention had been altered without Wilson's consent, in favor of interference in the internal politics of Russia.

As was inevitable, the Siberian and Chinese Eastern Railways became the focus of these conflicting aims. Whoever controlled these railways controlled Siberia. Late in July, 1918, when Semenov's forces were hard pressed by the Reds, Japan invoked her military agreements with China and dispatched troops to the zone of the Chinese Eastern Railway. These troops soon controlled the line and occupied most of the railway towns. Once established, the Japanese utilized their position to direct supplies to Horvath and other friendly Cossack leaders. From these events it became clear that Japan was expanding her sphere of influence into North Manchuria and was fostering puppet regimes in Siberia.

At first the United States did no more than formally protest these Japanese moves. Presumably the American government feared that uncompromising opposition might so alter the political balance within Japan as to lead to Japanese withdrawal from the war. Later, after the armistice was signed, the American stand was firmer. On November 16, 1918, Secretary of State Robert Lansing stated flatly that Japan's monopoly of the Manchurian railways was opposed by the United States; and he demanded that Japan demonstrate her intention to co-operate by turning over control of the railroads to an inter-Allied commission.[6] In making this demand, the United States was not only taking advantage of the war's end, it was also assuming that America's demonstration of military power in Europe would not be lost on the Japanese. Furthermore, when following the resignation of Count Terauchi on September 29 a new Japanese cabinet was formed by Premier Hara, the United States assumed that the new ministry, less subservient to the army, would seek in some degree to meet American desires. Subsequent events supported the wisdom of these considerations. In December, Tokyo informed the United States of her intention to withdraw more than half of her troops from Siberia and Manchuria. A month later, January, 1919, an inter-Allied railway control board was established with Japan's assent. The Hara government thus made substantial moves to eliminate Siberia as a source of American-Japanese friction.

THE END OF INTER-ALLIED INTERVENTION

Unhappily these steps toward establishing some accord did not bring a fundamental settlement. As the months of 1919 dragged on, evil days settled upon the entire Siberian adventure. The high purposes of military strategy for which it was conceived no longer had any meaning, for Germany had long since collapsed and the war in Europe was over. The real purpose of the European powers and Japan to crush Bolshevism had resulted in dismal failure. By the end of 1919 the remnants of Kolchak's armies were in complete rout before the rising Red tide and the infuriated peasant partisans. The White elements both within and outside Russia had failed to provide a program or a leadership which the Russians would accept. The United States Ambassador Roland S. Morris in Tokyo went far to explain this when he said:

The advent of Allied forces [in Siberia] has led to the hope among former [Russian] officials, civil and military, that they will regain the power and influence they had before the revolution. The attitude of these officials indicates that they will be relentless in their endeavor to suppress all liberal or moderate movements. Possibly nothing but their inevitable failure will bring them to reason.[7]

As for the European Allies and the United States, by 1920 they were tired of the whole business. The scheme for co-operative management of the railways had broken down during the long weeks of the Paris Peace Conference; rivalries among forces in Siberia had intensified. The Western forces therefore were withdrawn, leaving Siberia to the Russians—and to the Japanese.

For two years the Japanese remained. The Japanese government and the army regarded the whole eastern Siberian question as being still very decidedly Japan's business. The growth of the revolutionary ferment in Russia and the discrediting of the Whites appeared as the prelude to a communist society touching the shores of the Pacific which would be a threat to Japan's position in South Manchuria and even to the social fabric and political structure of her society at home. The massacre of Japanese at Nikolaevsk near the mouth of the Amur River, opposite northern Sakhalin in 1920 seemed

---

[6] *Foreign Relations, 1918, Russia,* II, 433–35.

[7] United States, *Foreign Relations, 1918, Russia,* II, 414.

to confirm the wisdom of army expansionists who desired to annex the Maritime Province with Vladivostok. So Japan stayed on, temporarily in control of a great circular area reaching from Vladivostok to Chita, an area traversed by the Chinese Eastern and the Amur Railways. She entertained the hope that a buffer state, friendly to Japan and free of Bolshevik contagion, would yet arise in the Far East. But whatever justification there may have been for this hope, it had already been destroyed by the inter-Allied intervention, for in general the Russians appear to have been just as happy to see the Allies go as the Allied soldiers were to leave. Writing in 1931, General Graves noted that the participating governments seemed to take "very little pride in this venture. Who can blame them?" [8]

THE FOUR-POWER CONSORTIUM

Throughout the two years (1918–1920) of international wrangling in Siberia there had been a continuous sucession of clashes between American and Japanese policy. One such area of conflict was the arena of international finance in China as a whole. It will be recalled that in 1913, President Wilson, disapproving of the control measures employed by the First or Six-Power Consortium as infringement upon the "administrative integrity" of China, informed the American banking group that it would not enjoy official support. In the five years that followed, the basic principles of Wilson's policy toward China—territorial and administrative integrity and the open door —did not change, but his views on the means of achieving and maintaining these principles did change. By November, 1917, the President, though not fully convinced that independent loans to China were impractical as political weapons, had decided to encourage the organization of a new Four-Power Consortium. The following year, on the initiative of the American government, a new American banking group was formed.

[8] William S. Graves, *America's Siberian Adventure* (1931), 356.

The bankers, however, were not of a mind to enter the field of Chinese investments save in concert wih British, French, and Japanese banking groups, and with the assured support of the American government. These conditions the American government accepted, and on its part insisted that in turn the prospective Consortium must respect the well-established principles of American policy in China—principles which were well known to be at variance with Japan's theory of "special interests" and with the theory of the British and the French on spheres of influence.

The reasons for this complete reversal of method by the Wilson administration are significant. The World War had given Japan a free hand in financing China, and it had also destroyed temporarily any possibility of China's receiving British or French credits. But more was involved than the matter of investment. Wilson was forced to recognize that, China's political position being what it was, the political aspects of American policy could no longer be detached with safety from economic considerations. This was made particularly clear during 1918, when as a result of the mysterious maneuverings of Nishihara Kamezo, personal representative in China of Japanese Premier Count Terauchi, the Peking government of Premier Tuan and his Anfu Clique contracted Japanese loans in the amount of about Yen 120 million. These were not investments in the usual meaning of that word. Rather, they were payments to officials then in power in exchange for certain agreements that would promote Japanese policy, particularly in Manchuria.[9] Japan was thus buying an economic and political stake from a Chinese government in Peking that was willing to sell.

Against Sino-Japanese financial politics of this type, doctrinaire slogans of American policy on the open door and the integrity of

[9] For the Japanese origins of the scheme see Frank C. Langdon, "Japan's Failure to Establish Friendly Relations with China, 1917–1918," *The Pacific Historical Review* 26 (1957): 245–58.

China were useless unless implemented by more realistic factors. Therefore Wilson sought to revive and apply international co-operative action through a new Consortium, his hope being that with British and French support Japan could be held in line and her efforts to gain a financial monopoly at Peking frustrated.

Actual negotiations toward the birth of a new Consortium were delayed until the closing days of the Paris Peace Conference; but once started, they appeared at first to progress smoothly. Britain and France agreed to support the American plan for the organization and operation of the Consortium. Japanese bankers also agreed, presumably because they preferred co-operation with rather than competition from their foreign colleagues. Within a short time, however, Japan's position hardened as it became evident the proposed agreement would infringe upon her "special interests." Indeed, it required another year before a compromise agreement for the new Four-Power Consortium could be reached. In this compromise the United States, England, and France pledged their "good faith" to "refuse their countenance to any operation [of the Consortium] inimical to the vital interests of Japan." These powers also agreed to exclusion of the zone of the South Manchuria Railway from the joint activities of the Consortium. It meant that while the powers would now pool all loans, administrative and industrial, in China Proper, south of the Wall, Japan still retained her "special position" in South Manchuria. Contrary, however, to official and popular expectations, China showed no enthusiam for the Consortium and declined to do business with it. Chinese political leaders in general took the view that the Consortium was a "threat of international control of Chinese finance" and a "monopoly or attempted monopoly" designed to deprive China of a free world market where she could borrow on the best terms available. Again it was evident that the problem of "preserving" China and of serving American interests at the same time was not a simple task.

The troubles in Siberia and the arguments over the Consortium only served to underscore another area of friction in American-Japanese relations. As World War I came to a close, Japan and the United States found themselves involved in an appalling naval race. Under the Naval Appropriation Act of 1916 the United States fleet would soon equal and perhaps surpass the British fleet.[10] Japan's building program would enable her to maintain her rank as the third naval power. To what end was this construction now that the war was over? Amicable relations between Great Britain and the United States gave some credance to the suspicion that America and Japan were preparing to fight each other in the Pacific.

The prospect of a naval race was cause for general concern. The United States government was seriously embarrassed since there was reason to doubt that American voters, disillusioned with war as a means of resolving world problems, would continue to support the projected naval construction for a Pacific defense, an area in which the public had shown little interest. Furthermore, the fact that the United States had repudiated the League of Nations and had elected Harding in 1920 did not mean the Wilsonian peace program had been blotted from the American consciousness. Among Harding's advisers and in the Republican Party at large were a number of men such as Charles Evans Hughes, the new Secretary of State, who were committed to the principle of arms reduction and to American leadership to this end.[11] Nor was there much enthusiasm in Japanese government circles for the continuing naval rivalry. The construction of dreadnoughts imposed burdens on an

[10] R. L. Buell, *The Washington Conference* (1922) 139–44; H. C. Bywater, *Sea Power in the Pacific* (1921), 10.

[11] The Republican Platform of 1920, although repudiating the League, had called for "an international association" designed to preserve the peace.

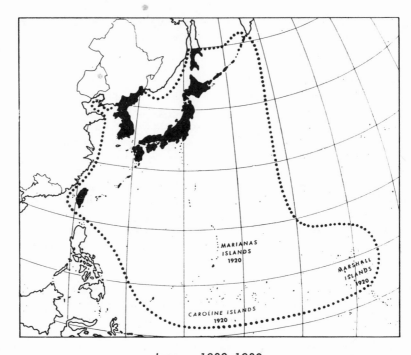

Japan 1920–1930

Reproduced from A War Atlas for Americans *(New York: Simon & Schuster) 1944, with permission from the publisher and from the U.S. Department of State, Division of Map Intelligence and Cartography.*

economy which was sagging as Japan encountered post-war competition. Furthermore, peaceful pursuits such as trade and diplomacy, rather than militarism, were now favored as the means for advancing the national interest. Thus, Japan, like the United States, was prepared to listen at least to proposals for ending the naval race.

The uneasiness in Washington and Tokyo on the naval question was shared by London and the capitals of the Commonwealth nations. London was concerned by reports published in the United States that Great Britain would be involved as the ally of Japan in an American-Japanese war through obligations of the Anglo-Japanese Alliance. These reports, though ill-founded, threatened Anglo-American relations.[12] The Commonwealth countries were troubled by

the prospect of an Anglo-American antagonism upsetting their own amicable relations with the United States. Thus it was that Commonwealth prime ministers, conferring just prior to the Imperial Conference at London, June, 1921, came up with a proposal calling for termination of the Anglo-Japanese Alliance and its replacement by a new and broader agreement covering the Pacific.[13] As a result of this action, Great Britain prodded the United States to call a disarmament conference. Formal invitations to discuss disarmament and problems relating to East Asia and the Pacific were sent from Washington on August 11, 1921 to Great Britain, France, Italy, Japan, and to four lesser powers: Belgium, China, the Netherlands, and Portugal.[14]

[12] A. W. Griswold, *Far Eastern Policy of the United States* (1938),* 168. C. N. Spinks, "The Termination of the Anglo-Japanese Alliance," *The Pacific Historical Review* 6 (1937): 326.

[13] J. Chalmers Vinson, "The Imperial Conference of 1921 and the Anglo-Japanese Alliance," *The Pacific Historical Review* 31 (1962): 257–66.

[14] These latter powers were selected on the

THE WAY TO DISARM IS TO DISARM

It was an illustrious assembly of notables that gathered in Washington's Memorial Continental Hall on November 12, 1921, to hear President Harding's exuberant remarks of welcome. He was followed immediately by Secretary Hughes, chairman of the conference, who, avoiding the platitudes of diplomacy, declared that the nations had come together "not for general resolutions . . . but for action." [15] Thereupon he presented to the startled delegates and the galleries a plan for immediate slashing of naval strength. In brief, the American plan called for:

1. A 10-year naval holiday in capital ship construction.
2. The scrapping of many ships, including some already in commission and others in the process of building.
3. Application of the program of scrapping so as to leave the navies of the United States, Great Britain, and Japan in a ratio of 5–5–3; France and Italy, without scrapping would fit into this ratio as 1.75–1.75.
4. Capital ship replacements limited by treaty to 500,000 tons each for the United States and Great Britain, and to 300,000 tons for Japan.
5. Similar ratios applied to aircraft carriers, cruisers, destroyers, and submarines. [16]

The measured words of Secretary Hughes electrified not only the audience

---

basis of their real or supposed interest in the Pacific. It was not anticipated that they would participate in the arms discussions. Since German and Austrian interests in East Asia had been liquidated by the war, these powers were excluded. The absence of the Soviet Union could be explained only on the basis of a quarantine with which the victorious powers hoped to isolate that government. For another aspect of representation problems see J. Chalmers Vinson, "The Problem of Australian Representation at the Washington Conference for the Limitation of Naval Armament," *The Australian Journal of Politics and History* 4 (1958): 155–64.

[15] *Conference on the Limitation of Armament, Washington, November 12, 1921–February 6, 1922* (1922), 58.

[16] United States, Sen. doc. 126, 67th Cong., 2nd Sess., *Conference on the Limitation of Armament,* 41–63.

---

which sat before him, but also the far larger audience of the world press and public. The impact of the Secretary's plan was suggested by unrestrained applause in the galleries. Yet, in the final analysis, acceptance of the proposed naval ratio would not depend on this emotional response. The armament race had not developed in a vacuum. No great power was prepared to surrender any relative naval advantage it felt it could maintain. Great Britain, however distasteful the idea, was ready for obvious reasons to accept naval parity with the United States, but only if assured of the safety of her interests in the Pacific. Japan, whose armed forces opposed any relative reduction in naval power, would certainly reject any inferior ratio without corresponding compensations. Could the diplomats develop an alternative to the Anglo-Japanese Alliance? Would the conference discover a formula that would reconcile the American traditional policy of upholding China's integrity with Japan's determination to retain her "special interests"? It was upon the answers to be given to questions such as these that the fate of Hughes' disarmament proposal hinged.

THE FOUR-POWER PACT

The conference first approached the troublesome Anglo-Japanese Alliance. Great Britain wanted to expand the Alliance to include the United States, but Hughes would have none of this proposal, for it would have amounted to American recognition of the "special interests" of Japan and Great Britain in East Asia. Rather, Hughes countered with a plan for a Four-Power Treaty (the United States, Britain, France and Japan) which would embody the principles of the Root-Takahira notes of 1908. This idea, which won quick acceptance, became the heart of the Four-Power Treaty, signed December 13, 1921. By this ten-year pact, superseding the Anglo-Japanese Alliance, the signatory powers agreed:

1. To respect one another's rights in the regions of the Pacific in respect to their

"insular possessions and insular dominions."
2. To meet in joint conference "for consideration and adjustment" of any "controversy arising out of any Pacific question and involving their said rights which is not satisfactorily settled by diplomacy."
3. To "communicate with one another fully . . ." if the rights of the contracting parties "are threatened by the aggressive action of any other Power."

The early signature of the Four-Power Treaty materially advanced the fortunes of the conference. The inclusion of France was one of the moves designed to win that country to acceptance of the inferior naval ratio (1.75 as against 5–5–3 for the great powers) assigned to it by the Hughes plan. By ending the Anglo-Japanese Alliance and substituting the broader pledge of "consultation," the treaty went far to remove American and Commonwealth fears of Anglo-Japanese co-operation in some future war. Furthermore, by combining principles of the Root-Takahira notes of 1908 with those of the Bryan treaties of 1914, the United States had been given a renewed pledge against aggression in the Philippines; this was a matter of consequence, since Japan, now in possession of the Marshall, Mariana, and Caroline Islands, lay athwart direct American approaches to Manila.[17]

LIMITING NAVAL ARMAMENT

Japan's assent to the Four-Power Treaty did not mean that Tokyo was prepared to accept without major qualifications the Hughes program of naval limitation. While desirous of ending an unwelcome rivalry, Japan was determined to maintain her own naval supremacy in the western Pacific. To this end she wanted definite assurances that Great Britain and the United States would not develop naval bases at Hong Kong, Manila, Guam, and other Pacific islands. Since this was clearly Japan's price for even

[17] J. Chalmers Vinson, "The Drafting of the Four-Power Treaty of the Washington Conference," *The Journal of Modern History* 25 (1953): 40–47.

considering the principle of the Hughes plan, the Big Three quickly reached agreement on the nonfortification principle which later became Article XIX of the Five-Power Naval Treaty. It was agreed that: "the status quo at the time of the signing of the present Treaty, with regard to fortification and naval bases, shall be maintained" in specified possessions.[18]

The negotiations then shifted to the Hughes naval formula. In consequence of pressure exerted by France, the original plan was whittled down to apply only to capital ships. As finally concluded, the Naval Treaty provided for:

1. A 10-year holiday in capital ship construction.
2. Scrapping specified vessels in commission and under construction (United States, 845,000 tons; Great Britain, 583,000 tons; Japan, 435,000 tons). Under a replacement program to begin after the 10-year construction holiday, battleship tonnage would be limited to: United States, 525,000 tons; Great Britain, 525,000 tons; Japan, 315,000 tons; France, 175,000 tons; and Italy, 175,000 tons. A similar ratio with lower tonnage limitations was specified for aircraft carriers.
3. Limiting the tonnage of individual battleships and aircraft carriers to 35,000 and 27,000 respectively, and the caliber of their guns to 16 and 8 inches respectively.

The treaty was to apply until December 31, 1936, and might be terminated thereafter through two-years' notice by any signatory.

The terms of this epochal treaty are easily stated, but its immediate effect upon the interplay of national policies in the Pacific and the Far East cannot be reduced to simple evaluation. Nonetheless it may be conceded that Japan had won tangible and specific advantages. If her sensitive national pride

[18] Specifically, the territories in which new fortifications were prohibited were: For the United States—the Aleutians, Guam, Pago-Pago, and the Philippines; for Great Britain—Hong Kong and British insular possessions in the Pacific, east of 110 east longitude, excepting islands adjacent to Canada, Australia, and New Zealand; for Japan—the Kurile Islands, Bonin Islands, Amami-Oshima, the Liu-ch'iu (Ryukyu) Islands, Formosa, and the Pescadores.

was wounded by the inferior capital ship ratio, her security was greatly increased by the nonfortification agreement, by her mandate over the former German islands in the North Pacific, and by the resulting liberty she enjoyed to pursue her own specific aims in China.

Britain also profited. Although she did forego the right to add to the fortifications of Hong Kong and islands in the Central Pacific, she retained full liberty to fortify Singapore, Australia, and New Zealand, which were not likely to be threatened so long as Japan observed the nonfortification clause. In a word, Britain gave up little and received much in return. Her advantage was the more striking because East Asia, although of great importance, was of much less significance in British policy than were the Middle East and Europe.

Did the United States win advantages comparable to those gained by Britain and Japan? Conceding that the conference had made Japan the naval master of the western Pacific, the arbiter of China's future, and that the United States had agreed as regards naval fortifications to remain east of Pearl Harbor, it would appear that Secretary Hughes had given much in return for a ten-year naval holiday in capital ship construction. Hughes, however, viewed these concessions in conjunction with the terms of the Nine-Power Treaty, which emerged from the concurrent conference on Far Eastern questions.

THE FAR EASTERN CONFERENCE

This Nine-Power Treaty may best be understood as a culmination of nearly a century of American policy in Eastern Asia. That policy had rested essentially on three principles. The first was the most-favored nation principle, to which in 1899 and 1900 had been added the principles of the commercial open door and the integrity of China. The resulting composite policy was one of self-interest, not sentiment. Practically, it was vulnerable in the highest degree, because American commercial interests in

China were relatively small and because the American people had shown no willingness to defend by force the open door or the integrity of China. Between 1900 and the end of World War I, the powers had violated the open door and China's integrity whenever they regarded it as advantageous to do so and whenever they were not restrained by their mutual jealousies and fears. American policy may have served to retard these encroachments; it did not prevent them.

In negotiating the Nine-Power Treaty, Hughes sought to remedy the weakness by making these principles the heart of a treaty. By so doing, the historic American principles would become international law binding upon each of the signatories. For the first time, Hughes reasoned, Japan and the other powers would be definitely restrained from seeking "special interests" in China.

The conclusion of the Nine-Power-Open-Door Treaty on February 6, 1922, was a signal triumph for Hughes. The signatory powers (the United States, Great Britain, France, Japan, Italy, Belgium, the Netherlands, Portugal, and China) consented to the following provisions:

1. The contracting parties, other than China, agree to respect and support the sovereignty, independence, and the territorial and administrative integrity of China; they further agree to provide the fullest opportunity for China's development and to maintain the principle of equal opportunity for the commerce and industry of all nations in China.
2. No treaty, agreement, arrangement, or understanding infringing the above principles shall be made.
3. The nationals of the contracting parties will not be supported by their governments in any agreement, arrangement, or understanding which infringes the above principles.
4. China's neutrality shall be respected.
5. The parties will consult fully in circumstances requiring the application of the treaty.

Clearly the treaty was, beyond any question, a tangible advance over any previous enunciation of American policy in East Asia.

But, if the United States read the Nine-Power Treaty as limiting Japanese claims in

China, how was the treaty interpreted in Tokyo? Had Japan reversed her policy with respect to her "special interests," abandoning those interests and accepting the American definition of the open door? Publicly Japan did not dispute Hughes' belief that she embraced the American interpretation of the treaty, but privately Japan interpreted the Nine-Power Treaty in a special way. Japanese attention was focused on a clause in Article I in which the signatory powers were pledged to refrain "from countenancing action inimical to the security of the [signatory] States." Since Japan regarded her "special interests" in South Manchuria and Inner Mongolia as vital to her security, she read this clause as modifying the pledge to support the open door. According to this construction, the other parties to the Nine-Power Treaty accepted Japan's claims and were pledged not to interfere with them. Thus to the United States the treaty meant one thing while to Japan it meant quite another. Indeed, Japan's view was that her adherence entailed no basic changes in policy.[19] The American delegation, however, received no intimation of this while the Conference was in session; but several months later during negotiations looking toward the termination of the Lansing-Ishii Notes, Japan once again asserted claims to "special interests." These claims alerted the State Department to the possibility that Japanese policy had shifted less than Hughes had thought.[20] Meanwhile, the apparent agreement which had been achieved enabled the United States and Japan to co-operate in the disposition of several outstanding issues.

Among the questions before the Far Eastern Conference was China's demand for immediate restoration of tariff autonomy and abolition of extraterritoriality. The United States and Japan joined other powers in opposing this demand. The powers were willing to grant only that China be per-

mitted a moderate increase in tariff rates and that commissions be established to study the termination of the extraterritorial system. Nor did China find the powers any more willing to abrogate the Manchurian clauses of the treaties and notes of May, 1915. None of the powers was prepared to concede the Chinese claims that the treaties were invalid because they had been obtained by force. Such an admission might well have opened the way for an attack on practically all the treaties negotiated over nearly a century.

Although the Far Eastern Conference itself did not attempt to deal with the Shantung question, Hughes and Balfour of Great Britain were responsible for bringing the Chinese and Japanese together and for breaking the deadlock between them. At Washington the Chinese were still demanding, as they had at Paris three years earlier, full and direct restoration of former German rights. The Japanese were equally emphatic. They were prepared to restore the leasehold, but only under the terms of the 1915 and 1918 treaties and through direct negotiations with China.[21] The good offices of Hughes and Balfour finally resulted in Sino-Japanese discussions extending through thirty-six meetings with British and American "observers." Even then the negotiations were only sustained through persistent and powerful British and American pressure at Peking and Tokyo. The Sino-Japanese treaty which resulted (February 4, 1922), returned Kiaochou to China. However, Japan would retain control of the Tsinan-Tsingtao Railway for fifteen years, during the life of a loan through which China purchased the road. The settlement was obviously a compromise. Japan retained temporarily a measure of economic and political control, while China had won something more than the mere principle of her claim.

The Conference also provided an opportunity for discussion of two other problems outstanding between the United States and Japan. Hughes won from the Japanese

[19] Sadao Asada, "Japan's 'Special Interests' and the Washington Conference, 1921–1922," *The American Historical Review* 67 (1961): 62–70.

[20] J. Chalmers Vinson, "The Annulment of the Lansing-Ishii Agreement," *The Pacific Historical Review* 27 (1958): 57–69.

[21] The principle was one on which the Japanese had insisted ever since the Shimonoseki negotiations of 1895.

(January 23, 1922) a pledge that their military forces would soon be withdrawn from Siberia and North Sakhalin. In obtaining the pledge Hughes scored another victory in the name of the open door. It appears, however, that pressure from within Japan rather than the diplomacy of Hughes was responsible for Japan's withdrawal. Finally, but not as a part of the Conference, the United States raised again with Japan its claims concerning the island of Yap. These negotiations brought forth an American-Japanese treaty (February 11, 1922), whereby the United States recognized the Japanese mandate over the former German islands in the North Pacific, and Japan in return granted to American citizens residential, cable, and radio rights on Yap.

JAPANESE IMMIGRATION

Only one major issue in American-Japanese relations was not the subject of negotiation at the Washington Conference: Japanese immigration to the United States and American treatment of the Japanese immigrant. The exclusion of the issue from the agenda was due to considerations of tactics rather than lack of concern on either side. The issue had been a serious source of friction during the decade before America's entry into World War I. In the aftermath of war there were signs that it would once again become the source of trouble as Americans, stirred by intense nationalism, agitated for an immigration law which, among other provisions, would exclude Japanese from the United States.

Washington had been embarrassed by the issue since 1906. When, in that year, the San Francisco school board segregated Japanese students on grounds of racial inferiority, President Theodore Roosevelt branded the action a "wicked absurdity" and attempted unsuccessfully to change the board's decision. Roosevelt feared that discriminatory treatment against the people of a vigorous Oriental state would destroy commercial most-favored-nation treatment for American commerce in East Asia and render

illusory the open door in China and the security of the Philippines. To avert possible danger, Roosevelt obtained the amendment of the immigration law of 1902 to stop the entry of Japanese into Hawaii and reached in 1907–1908 an understanding with Tokyo—called the Gentlemen's Agreement—through which Japan herself would refuse passports to laborers seeking residence in the United States.[22] These measures, intended to give assurance to Californians that they would not be overwhelmed by Japanese, did little to calm Western fears, however ill-grounded. In 1913, the California legislature prohibited aliens ineligible for citizenship from owning land and imposed a three year limit on land leases. Since this measure was clearly aimed at the Japanese, it was Woodrow Wilson's turn to be concerned, but, like Roosevelt, he was unable to quiet the anti-Japanese uproar. His efforts were thus confined to trying to soothe Japanese feelings and to head off similar bills in other legislatures.[23]

By the time Congress began consideration of new immigration bills after World War I, Secretary Hughes, aware that the Japanese were acutely sensitive about American treatment of their nationals, was alert lest another affront be given. When, in December, 1923, bills were introduced in the Senate and House denying entry to aliens who were ineligible to citizenship, Hughes himself testified before the House Committee on Immigration. He argued that although

[22] The Gentlemen's Agreement is not contained in a single document. Its text, on the contrary, consists of correspondence exchanged between the United States and Japan during 1907 and 1908. A resumé is printed in United States, *Foreign Relations, 1924*, II, 339–69. It was printed in 1939.

[23] Secret talks held during the closing days of the Wilson Administration resulted in an informal understanding that the United States and Japan would negotiate a treaty covering questions of immigration and discrimination. Neither the Wilson nor the Harding Administrations, however, proved willing to implement the understanding. American interest in settling the issues was linked directly with larger considerations in Far Eastern policy. Kell F. Mitchell, Jr., "Diplomacy and Prejudice: The Morris-Shidehara Negotiations, 1920–1921," *The Pacific Historical Review*, 39 (1970), 85–104.

Japanese immigration should be controlled, the method proposed was inadvisable. In his opinion, it was bad policy to offend Japan unnecessarily when, by assigning Japan an immigrant quota such as those proposed for other nations, not more than 250 Japanese would be admitted annually. Furthermore, the proposed legislation would, the Secretary felt, "largely undo the work of the Washington Conference." Nevertheless, in March, 1924, the House Committee recommended legislation excluding all aliens who were ineligible for citizenship. The bill passed the House on April 12, by the overwhelming majority of 326 to 71.

Simultaneously, the Senate was considering rather favorably Hughes' arguments, when, on April 14, an attack was launched on a memorandum prepared by Japanese Ambassador Hanihara. In this memorandum, which had been sent originally as a note to the State Department, Hanihara reviewed the history of the Gentlemen's Agreement, defined Japan's objections to legislation embodying exclusion, and, in conclusion, "truthfully but most ill-advisedly" referred to "the grave consequences which the enactment of the measure [exclusion law] retaining that particular provision would inevitably bring upon the otherwise happy and mutually advantageous relations between our two countries." Hughes disliked the phrase "grave consequences," for there were few stronger phrases in diplomatic language, but he regarded the Japanese analysis of the Gentlemen's Agreement as sound and so, sent the note to Congress as support for his contentions. Congress however, found the note offensive. It was described as "impertinent," as not to be "tolerated" by even a fourth-class power, and as a "veiled threat." The Hughes compromise was voted down, and on April 16 the Senate followed the House by voting 71 to 4 to exclude aliens who were ineligible for citizenship. Last-minute efforts of President Coolidge to delay application to Japan of the exclusion clause in the hope that a new treaty might be negotiated also failed, and on May 15 the immigration bill emerging from conference was passed by House and Senate, the votes being 308 to 62 and 69 to 9. It was to become effective July 1, 1924. The President, in signing the bill on May 26, announced that had the exclusion clause not been an integral part of the larger bill, he would have vetoed it on the ground that the method adopted by Congress in securing Japanese exclusion was "unnecessary and deplorable at this time."

Immediate reactions to the abrogation of the Gentlemen's Agreement were more pronounced in Japan than in the United States. Japan's official protest was a mild reflection of bitter outbursts in the Japanese press and of deep resentment in the Japanese popular mind. In the United States reactions were varied because the issues involved were more complex. Public opinion throughout the country, though favoring rigid control of Japanese immigration, does not appear to have favored the method used by Congress. Naturally this view was more pronounced in the East than on the Pacific Coast. The Senate, however, was not guided by the general flavor of public opinion, but rather by known public reactions to specific domestic issues. The immigration debate was largely controlled by concurrent domestic reactions that might be expected from "the Southern vote in its relation to the Dyer anti-lynching bill, the issue of Congressional prerogative, the questions of the Senatorial investigations and of party loyalty, the need of thinking of the Pacific Coast's presidential vote, to say nothing of the Pacific Coast's racial future." [24] Undoubtedly many Americans believed, as did *The Cincinnati Enquirer*, that "the crux of this matter is that the United States, like Canada and Australia, must be kept a white man's country." A heroic step, so it was thought, had been taken, not in the implementation of race prejudice but in "producing a civilization peculiar to the American race and suited to a static society." After 1924, influential American groups, business and professional, advocated revision which would give Japan and China a quota. The move was halted by the Manchurian crisis, 1931. Japanese exclusion was not repealed

[24] Rodman Paul, *The Abrogation of the Gentleman's Agreement* (1936), 99.

until 1952, the year in which an American-Japanese peace treaty was signed. In the meantime, during World War II, with the intent of protecting the national security, the United States carried out the relocation to the interior from the Pacific coast of all persons of Japanese extraction. Chinese exclusion was repealed in 1943, and China was assigned an annual immigration quota of 105.

IN SUMMARY

Five years elapsed between the close of the debate on Shantung at Paris and the enactment of the Quota Immigration Act of 1924. For American and Japanese statesmen they were years filled with problems caused or heightened by World War I. How is their work to be viewed? To what extent were they successful in resolving an increasingly troublesome American-Japanese rivalry?

Certainly there was much in the record which pointed to an easing of tensions. The Hara government's effort to co-operate with the United States in the operation of Siberian railways, the compromise on the Consortium, the termination of the naval race, and the signature of the Four- and Nine-Power Treaties contributed to an easing of fears on both sides of the Pacific. Even in the enactment of the exclusion law, the Japanese could take some comfort in the thought that American opinion was divided, and in the hope that the obnoxious measure would eventually be repealed. Moreover, advocates of conciliation were influential in both Washington and Tokyo. Secretary Hughes' determination to achieve limitation of armaments was matched in Japan by the "Friendship Policy" of Baron Shidehara Kijuro, Foreign Minister, 1924–1927. Yet, notwithstanding these hopeful signs, there remained one unresolved issue which had been the root of most American-Japanese problems. Whereas the United States believed that Japan by the Nine-Power Treaty was now pledged to the open door and China's territorial and administrative integrity, Japan was satisfied that the treaty was a guarantee of her own special position. Tensions had been eased but their root cause had not been removed.

FOR FURTHER READING

For details on public reactions to growing American-Japanese tensions see Tokutomi Iichiro, *Japanese-American Relations* (1922); Eleanor Tupper and George McReynolds, *Japan in American Public Opinion* (1937). John Roger Stemen, *The Diplomacy of the Immigration Issue, A Study in Japanese-American Relations, 1894–1941* (Ph.D. dissertation, Indiana University, 1960), draws heavily on Western sources.

SIBERIAN INTERVENTION. George Kennan, *Soviet-American Relations, 1917–1920: The Decision to Intervene* (1958),* based on American, Japanese, and Russian sources. John A. White, *The Siberian Intervention* (1950), especially useful for the study of inter-Allied diplomacy. Betty M. Unterberger, *America's Siberian Expedition, 1918–1920: A Study of National Policy* (1956), the most thorough study of American archival materials. James A. Morley, *Japan's Thrust into Siberia* (1957), indispensable for the development of Japanese policy. The most satisfactory documentary treatment of the period from April to December, 1918 is James Bunyan, ed., *Intervention, Civil War, and Communism in Russia* (1936). Elena Varneck and H. H. Fisher, eds., *The Testimony of Kolchak and Other Siberian Materials* (1935), valuable for the editorial annotation of the sources presented. Clarence A. Manning, *The Siberian Fiasco* (1952).

THE CONSORTIUM. Selected correspondence is in Carnegie Endowment for International Peace, *The Consortium* (1921), and Paul H. Clyde, *United States Policy Toward China* (1940; reissued, 1964). There is a brief exposition in C. F. Remer, *Foreign Investments in China* (1933). F. V. Field, *American Participation in the China Consortium* (1931), a sound specialized study.

WASHINGTON CONFERENCE. On sea power

and politics note E. B. Potter, ed., *The United States and World Sea Power* (1955); and E. A. Falk, *Togo and the Rise of Japanese Sea Power* (1936). J. Chalmers Vinson, *The Parchment Peace: The United States Senate and the Washington Conference* (1955), the most incisive study of American politics in the Washington Conference. Ichihashi Yamato, *The Washington Conference and After* (1928), by a long-time professor of Japanese history and government and secretary to Admiral Baron Kato, Japan's chief delegate to the Conference. Chapter XXI of Takeuchi Tatsuji, *War and Diplomacy in the Japanese Empire* (1935) covers Japanese politics and the Conference. B. E. C. Dugdale, *Arthur James Balfour* (2 vols., 1936), information on the British role. Although outdated in some respects by Vinson's article on the Imperial Conference of 1921 (cited fn. 13, this chapter), J. B. Brebner, "Canada, the Anglo-Japanese Alliance and the Washington Conference," *Political Science Quarterly* 50 (1935): 45–58, is an excellent article. H. F. MacNair and D. F. Lach, *Modern Far Eastern International Relations* (1956), and

George F. Kennan, *American Diplomacy, 1900–1950* (1951)* should also be consulted.

JAPANESE IMMIGRATION. Rogers Daniels, *The Politics of Prejudice: The Anti-Japanese Movement in California and the Struggle for Exclusion* (1962),* the best single study of the problem from its inception through the enactment of the 1924 legislation. The standard study of the Gentlemen's Agreement is T. A. Bailey, *Theodore Roosevelt and the Japanese-American Crises* (1934). A Japanese interpretation is Ichihashi Yamato, *Japanese in the United States* (1932). R. D. McKenzie, *Oriental Exclusion* (1928) presents an able analysis of the working of the 1924 law. E. G. Mears, *Resident Orientals on the American-Pacific Coast* (1928) surveys legal and other relationships of the races. The broad outlines of immigration in the entire Pacific area are given in J. B. Condliffe, ed., *Problems of the Pacific* (1928), 146–161. Basic statistical materials on Japanese migration are given in W. F. Wilcox, ed., *International Migrations* (1929), I, 160–166.

Japan, 1918-1931:
Experiments with Party Government

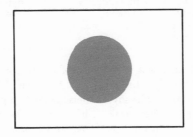

chapter 23

In the years 1918–1931, while the powers searched for a settlement of Far Eastern rivalries, Japan's oligarchs were challenged by a new generation of reformers at home demanding fundamental changes in the policies and procedures of government. High on the reform agenda were demands for an end to imperialism and for the adoption of a co-operative attitude, especially in matters of disarmament. The reformers also wanted a new day in the domestic political process. Stated broadly, Japanese progressives called for government conducted by party cabinets responsible to the majority in the lower house of the Diet, election of the lower house by universal manhood suffrage, and guarantees of civil liberties for the entire population. These proposed advances in democratic and responsible constitutional government were to be joined with internationalism to usher in a new political era. Consequently, in 1918, the downfall of the militarist Terauchi ministry and the selection of Hara Takashi, the untitled president of the *Seiyukai*, as prime minister were hailed by reform-minded Japanese as the dawn of the new era. The stage was seemingly set for the end of rule by oligarchy and for at least the beginnings of more popular interpretations of government under the constitution.

THE BASIS OF THE NEW POLITICS

The new movement for party government recalled the early demands for "restoration" of Imperial rule and for the adoption of Western ideas early in the Meiji era. Like these earlier efforts, the call for party government in 1918, and after, and for a fresh approach to foreign affairs was a product of vital changes in twentieth-century Japanese society. In the background was an intellectual liberalism opposed to state orthodoxy. For example, a theoretical base for curbing absolutism was provided by the theories of Minobe Tatsukichi which held that the emperor was an organ of the state rather than the embodiment of the state. In periodical literature writers such as Yoshino Sakuzo argued for government under party control. Others expounded the theory that German militarism was inferior to Wilsonian idealism.[1] In the background, too, was an expanding elite of business executives, freshly

[1] Frank O. Miller, *Minobe Tatsukichi: Interpreter of Japanese Constitutionalism* (1965); and Bernard S. Silberman, "The Political Theory and Program of Yoshino Sakuzo," *Journal of Modern History* 31 (1959): 310–24.

Year	Prime Minister	Party Affiliation
1918	Hara Takashi	Seiyukai cabinet
1921	Viscount Takahashi Korekiyo	Seiyukai cabinet
1922	Admiral Kato Tomosaburo	nonparty cabinet
1923	Admiral Count Yamamoto Gombei	nonparty cabinet
1924	Viscount Kiyoura Keigo	nonparty Peers cabinet
1924	Viscount Kato Takaaki	Kenseikai cabinet
1925	Viscount Kato Takaaki	Kenseikai cabinet
1926	Baron Wakatsuki Reijiro	Kenseikai cabinet
1927	General Baron Tanaka Giichi	Seiyukai cabinet
1929	Hamaguchi Osachi (Yuko)	Minseito cabinet
1931	Baron Wakatsuki Reijiro	Minseito cabinet
1931	Inukai Tsuyoshi	Seiyukai cabinet

affluent from war profits and boasting a new self-confidence, whose interests called for a larger political role and whose already established connections with the parties provided leverage which they might use on behalf of their stake in world trade.[2] And finally, the rise of party government was hastened by the passing of the *Genro*. By the end of World War I the old oligarchs were all but gone: Yamagata, who died in 1922, and Matasukata, who died in 1924, were old men. Saionji, the only remaining *Genro*, was inclined toward party government.

Thus politics after 1918 rested on foundations quite different from those of 1889, or even 1914. Among the divergent elements in Japan, postwar elite—militarists, bureaucrats, businessmen, and intellectuals—no single group possessed either the prestige or the power of the old oligarchs. Moreover, this new elite, reflecting special interests, lacked the unity of purpose which characterized its predecessors. In these circumstances, the Diet and the party system assumed importance as mechanisms for balancing contending factions within Japan's leadership. The parties also benefited from progressive lowering of property qualifications for voting. By 1918 the bulk of the urban middle class, but not the peasantry or factory laborers, had acquired the franchise. From these latter developments the parties acquired an image as vehicles of

popular government.[3]

Between 1918 and 1932 twelve cabinets guided Japan's destiny. Their average life was little more than one year. Summarized, these cabinets, with the year in which they took office, are shown above. As this record shows, Japan was led by a succession of party or semi-party cabinets, thus making it possible to describe the administration as being in some measure responsible to the Diet. Indeed, the process of governing through party cabinets became so established that it was known as "the normal course of constitutional government." Furthermore, the suffrage was extended, and a conciliatory spirit tended to dominate foreign policy. However, it must also be noted that this era did not bring a complete break with the past or the unqualified achievement of responsible government. The military service ministries remained beyond party control. The principles of oligarchical government remained firmly entrenched in the House of Peers, Privy Council, Imperial Household officials, and among the bureaucrats, and parties themselves were weakened by defects of character and organization.

THE HARA GOVERNMENT, 1918–1921

Hara Takashi symbolized the new forces in Japan. One of the ablest politicians Japan had produced, he entered political life

---

[2] Bryon K. Marshall, *Capitalism and Nationalism in Prewar Japan: The Ideology of the Business Elite, 1868–1941* (1967).

[3] Najita Tetsuo, *Hara Kei in the Politics of Compromise, 1905–1915* (1967); and Peter Duus, *Party Rivalry and Political Change in Taisho Japan* (1968) are the most detailed studies of party development.

in 1900 under the patronage of Ito. Like Saionji, he had shown an early interest in the liberal movement, had worked in the Foreign Office, had become editor of the great daily, the *Osaka Mainichi,* had been a member of the first Saionji cabinet, and had become president of the *Seiyukai* in 1913. As a political leader seeking strength for his party, he traded on the growing spirit of popularism by emphasizing that he was a "commoner," even though he was in fact of noble birth and lacked a title only because he had declined one. His political career was also notable for the contacts he made with the business world. Between 1905 and 1913 he was vice-president of the Furukawa Mining Company. Clearly, Hara differed from the old oligarchs, and it was in part upon these differences that hopes for the new era were built when he took office in 1918.[4]

As premier he was notably successful in reconciling in some degree the contentious factions among Japan's political, business, military, and bureaucratic leaders. This in itself was a rare accomplishment. In matters of policy, however, there was little on which to base his popular title, "The Great Commoner Premier." His cabinet was composed mostly of bureaucrats who had been accepted into the party, and included, as Minister of War, General Tanaka Giichi, the protégé of Yamagata. While his administration made a modest expansion of the franchise and extended the educational system, he promoted an economic policy that favored landowners and businessmen rather than workers, clamped down on socialist activities, and strengthened the government's hand in ideological control. He failed to advance appreciably the theory or practice of responsible government. He made few inroads on the power of the bureaucracy and did nothing to build the prestige of the House of Representatives, which was allowed to consume its energy in debates on trivia and in interparty violence. In fact, he all but ignored his party in policy making. Though doubtless honest himself, Hara

could be blind to corruption among his party colleagues. Yet it is to be remembered that he built the most powerful party Japan had known and that his party was the source of his power as premier. The role played by the *Seiyukai* in the Hara ministry seems all the more significant when it is recalled that the three nonparty cabinets which followed Hara, 1922–1924, were unable to provide even a semblance of leadership. The parties, for all their weakness, could not be ignored, and clearly, the reputation of nonparty forces had declined.

THE KATO GOVERNMENTS, 1924–1926

The prospect for responsible government had never been so high as it was in 1924, when Kato Takaaki formed the country's first coalition party cabinet from the *Kenseikai,* (of which Kato was president), the *Seiyukai,* and *Kakushin Club.*[5] Kato had a long and distinguished political career. From the presidency of the *Doshikai* in 1913 and later of the *Kenseikai,* he had become foreign minister in the second Okuma cabinet 1914, and had challenged, if unsuccessfully, the *Genro* and the militarists on numerous occasions. By 1924, when he became premier, he, having long admired British political institutions, was unquestionably Japan's outstanding exponent of responsible government. Far from being a commoner, he was an aristocrat guided by a philosophy of enlightened conservatism, a quality which enabled him to face the oligarchs without fear.

As a reforming government, Kato's coalition made some notable headway. It responded to economic readjustment with reductions in army and navy budgets; it dropped twenty thousand persons from the overcrowded bureaucracy; and it enacted a manhood suffrage law in 1925. Yet it failed to relieve growing economic distress, and, more important in terms of progress toward responsible government, it failed utterly in its program of Peerage reform. This failure

[4] Lawrence A. Olsen, "Hara Kei: A Political Biography," (Unpublished dissertation, Harvard University, 1954), 176.

[5] Excepting, of course, the period of the Okuma-Itagaki cabinet, 1898.

was of signal importance. With the passing of the *Genro* the importance of the House of Peers as a check upon party government had increased.

When in 1925 Kato formed his second and all-*Kenseikai* ministry, after his coalition had been deserted by the *Seiyukai*, the premier was even less able to advance political or constitutional reform, for he was now more dependent on the bureaucracy and the Peers to maintain his single party government. In these circumstances there was as yet no clear mandate for party government as the custodian of Japan's future. Moreover, the very limited degree of liberalism in the Kato administration was suggested by its passage of a new "Peace Preservation Law," which, though aimed against anarchists and Communists, could be used against the press, the universities, and indeed any movement critical of things as they were.

THE TANAKA GOVERNMENT, 1927–1929

The meaning of Kato's failure to deal with reform of the Peerage was soon evident. On Kato's death, January, 1926, Wakatsuki Reijiro, one of Kato's political protégés, succeeded to the premiership and presidency of the *Kenseikai*. The troubles of government mounted as the army attacked the conciliatory policy toward China of Foreign Minister Baron Shidehara Kijuro; but it was opposition from the Privy Council, which with the House of Peers was the fortress of the Imperial interpretation, that wrecked the Wakatsuki cabinet by the simple expedient of declaring unconstitutional certain emergency measures of the government for dealing with the banking crisis of 1927.

Meanwhile, the *Seiyukai*, thirsting for a return to power and having no leader within its ranks, bestowed its presidency on General Tanaka Giichi. From the beginning Tanaka faced grave problems of political strategy. As a result of the first election under the new manhood suffrage law, the *Seiyukai* held 219 seats, the new *Minseito* (*Kenseikai* plus *Seiyuhonto*) held 217, and the remaining 30

seats were held by independents and representatives of the new labor parties. What followed were legislative scenes of wild uproar. There was the grotesque spectacle of the opposition, presumably the advocates of responsible government, attacking the cabinet for its adherence to the Treaty for the Renunciation of War on the ground that the phrase "in the names of their respective peoples" was an affront to the emperor. With this opposition from the politicians, it was hardly surprising that the Privy Council blocked the treaty until the government gave assurances that this democratic phrase did not apply in the case of Japan.

Even more suggestive of the frail basis of party government was the incident that forced the resignation of the Tanaka cabinet. As prime minister, Tanaka spoke of a "positive foreign policy," of strengthening Japan's position in Manchuria, and of a tougher attitude toward Chinese nationalism. Tanaka's purpose was to reassure his own people, but the hard line provoked anti-Japanese boycotts in China. Further trouble came when conspirators linked with Japan's Kwantung army sought to deal on their own with the dangers of Chinese nationalism by assassinating the Manchurian warlord, Chang Tso-lin.[6] When, however, Tanaka with the support of his entire cabinet, including the service ministers, sought to punish the conspirators and re-establish discipline in the army, he was blocked by the General Staff and the powerful Military Affairs Bureau. The conspirators were not punished and Tanaka's government resigned. Civilian party government had been forced to retreat before the independent power of the army.

THE MINSEITO CABINET, 1929–1931

The surviving *Genro*, Saionji, then recommended a *Minseito* party cabinet with Hamaguchi Yuko, party president, as prime

[6] Paul S. Dull, "The Assassination of Chang Tso-lin," *The Far Eastern Quarterly*, 11 (1952), 453–63, a well-documented essay from Japanese sources.

minister. Coming into office with a strong program calling for clean politics, economy, arms reduction, and a moderate China policy, this cabinet failed more tragically than its predecessors. Its plans to reduce the lesser bureaucracy were challenged successfully, and although the government finally won ratification of the London Naval Treaty, October, 1930, it incurred the wrath of the army and navy and the oligarchs of the Privy Council. In addition, the *Seiyukai*, led by Inukai Tsuyoshi, joined with these bureaucrats in denouncing the government. The real political issue was whether a party cabinet with a majority in the lower House, and with the apparent confidence of the electorate, could challenge successfully the independent and irresponsible power of the militarists and the oligarchs. Hamaguchi maintained that the navy's approval of the London Treaty was beside the point because the constitution provided that the emperor alone on the advice of the cabinet exercised his treaty-making powers. The premier was insisting that in foreign policy the military members of the cabinet did not have a veto.

Hamaguchi's victory was short-lived. In spite of the importance of the constitutional issue involved, the opposition *Seiyukai* did everything in its power to embarrass the government. In addition, economic depression coupled with retrenchment policies were creating alarming unemployment. The oligarchs, most of the bureaucracy, the extreme nationalists and expansionists in the military services, and the secret societies were as one in the belief that the Hamaguchi policies of conciliation toward China and of overriding the advice of the army and navy were subversive, designed to undercut the power of these special groups. Added support for this view came from politicians, the press, and the public, all of whom were sensitive to any implied weakening of Japan's special position in China. Six weeks after his victory on the London Naval Treaty, Hamaguchi was shot at the Tokyo station by a nationalist patriot. While he lingered for nearly a year, he could no longer be an effective leader. Wakatsuki, who followed as premier,

could lead neither the party nor the nation. There was no one to curb the Japanese militarists in Manchuria. On September 18, 1931, these militarists began the seizure of Manchuria. For a brief interlude the *Seiyukai*, under Inukai, returned to office but not to power. The day of party cabinets was ended, and with it the prospect for responsible civilian government.[7]

PARTY GOVERNMENT: A SUMMARY

By 1931, Japan for more than a decade had attempted a transition from oligarchic government to responsible government under a party system. In the early years of the period the parties had revealed a new popular influence as the potential heirs of the *Genro*-sponsored oligarchs. Long before the end of the period, however, there was massive evidence that popular support of the parties was uncertain, that the parties themselves were not dedicated to the principles on which free representative government could survive, that the politicians were unwilling to seek basic constitutional reform, and that though all of the *Genro*, save Saionji, were gone, the principles of oligarchy had not been outlived. Political power had not passed from the bureaucracy and the oligarchs to the representatives of the people.

No simple statement can explain this failure to develop or mature a Japanese democracy. The obstacles in its path were formidable. In the first instance, problems were created by Japan's constitutional structure. The Diet was constitutionally weak. It lacked both legal and financial controls over the cabinet. Such power as was given the elected lower House was shared by the appointed upper House. Moreover, other established centers of authority such as the bureaucracy, the Privy Council, the military services, the *Genro*, and the Imperial Household officials could veto attempts to curtail their power. Second, the political parties, grounded in personal loyalties, and long ac-

[7] Hugh Borton, *Japan's Modern Century* (2nd ed., 1970), 360–62.

customed to subservience to the oligarchy, were ill-equipped to lead an aroused public opinion in obtaining concessions on behalf of popular government. United more by the hope of receiving the crumbs of office than by agreement on principle, the parties battled each other for advantage instead of joining in an attack on arbitrary authority.[8] In addition, the self-seeking appearance projected by the parties seriously limited their popular appeal. It was a fact of more than a little significance that the parties were composed mostly of legislators and their backers. Third, the forces of representative government were frightened into retreat by the labor and radical movements after 1918. The Japanese labor movement, socialist in its origins, grew rapidly during World War I with the organization of the first trade unions. At the same time Marxism had become popular among professors, writers, and university students. The intimate relation between the labor movement and this vocal, proletarian radicalism was as alarming to the political parties as it was to the oligarchs. All agreed that the extension of civil rights might result in radicals overturning the established order. In consequence, both Hara and Kato Takaaki, among the greatest of party leaders, countered each of their measures toward political freedom with new executive powers by which government could control the people. Fourth, compounding all of these difficulties was a social and economic order which provided only a narrow basis for supporting an attack on authoritarian government. The development of a sense of individualism, personal responsibility, and self-confidence, all of which were essential to the proper functioning of responsible government, was

[8] The picture of self-seeking politicians should not be overdrawn. Parties in Japan, it must be remembered, were utterly without historical precedent. Moreover, party members confronted ethical assumptions, such as, for example, sincerity between men, unselfish dedication to serve all of society, and a spiritual consensus based on personal loyalty, which served as obstacles to the operation of parties. See Najita Tetsuo, "Inukai Tsuyoshi: Some Dilemmas in Party Development in Pre-World War II Japan," *American Historical Review* 74 (Dec., 1968): 492–510.

checked in the Japanese populace by the functioning of most social groups. The educational system, as it had since the beginning of the Meiji era, fostered acceptance of oligarchical government. Business mergers tending to enlarge the size and power of the *Zaibatsu* also contributed to the suppression of individualism by promoting inequality of income and perpetuating in industry concepts of status and authority. These were some of the obstacles on the road to representative institutions. When they are seen in the perspective of Japan's international position during the 1920's, the fate of Japanese democracy becomes understandable.

RESPONSIBLE GOVERNMENT AND WORLD POLITICS

The failure of responsible party government was to have a vital bearing on methods used in Japan's foreign policy. In Japan, as in other lands, liberal political reform had not precluded a vigorous policy of expansion. Proponents of party government such as Saionji, after the Russo-Japanese War, and Okuma, in 1915, had not hestitated to implement Japan's special position in China and Manchuria. After World War I, Japanese "liberals" such as Hara, Kato, Shidehara, and Hamaguchi were no more prepared to forego the nation's privileged status in Manchuria than were the militarists, but they were sensitive to the implications of military coercion. So it was that, under their direction, foreign policy in the era of party government became identified with economic rather than military expansion, with informal rather than formal empire. Moreover, this new policy was applied to more than the solution of American-Japanese difficulties. It guided the approach to other fundamental problems: the situation created by the failure of the inter-Allied intervention to topple Bolshevism in Siberia, the extension of naval disarmament, and the challenge to Japanese interests from an ever more vibrant Chinese nationalism. When economic diplomacy failed to produce the promised results, foreign policy and party government alike came under attack.

A striking development in the immediate post-Washington Conference period was the formal improvement in Japan's relations with Soviet Russia. At the end of 1922 the last Japanese forces left the mainland of Siberia. Their withdrawal was due to many pressures. In addition to diplomatic pressure exerted on Japan at the Washington Conference, the Japanese public no longer supported a policy that had cost the taxpayer some 700,000,000 yen, had alienated the Russians and aroused the suspicions of the Western powers, and finally had served to hasten rather than retard the union of eastern Siberia with communist Moscow. The economic as well as the political interests of both Japan and Russia demanded an end to the chaos created by revolution and intervention. As a consequence of protracted negotiations begun in June, 1923, a treaty was signed on January 20, 1925, restoring relations between the two powers.[9]

The rapprochement represented by this treaty was a product of significant and varied forces playing upon Japanese policy. It had become evident even to Japan's chauvinists that military and political intervention had failed utterly to isolate eastern Siberia from the advance of Bolshevism. Furthermore, since there was in Japan an increasing demand for the products of Siberia's mines, forests, and waters, the re-establishment of normal relations in which commerce and industry might develop with some freedom was the natural alternative despite Japan's fear of the infiltration of "dangerous thoughts." Moreover, the success of Russian influence with the Chinese Nationalists at Canton and the conclusion of the Russian treaties with Peking and Mukden in 1924 emphasized Japan's isolation. Indeed, this isolation was now looming much larger in Japanese eyes than it had at the time of the Washington

Conference. There was no longer an Anglo-Japanese alliance as a prop to Japanese policy, and "the insensate method" taken by the American Senate in the Quota Immigration Act of May, 1924, to exclude Japanese from the United States was interpreted by the Japanese press, the government and public opinion as again indicative of an American attitude basically unfriendly to Japan's interests and purposes.

A PERIOD OF SINO-JAPANESE AMITY

The period in which normal diplomatic relations were restored between Japan and Soviet Russia also saw the growth of happier prospects in Sino-Japanese affairs. During the greater part of the decade, 1922–1931, Japan's foreign policy was colored by the personality and the philosophy of Baron Shidehara Kijuro, a career diplomat who had married into the Iwasaki family, which controlled the powerful Mitsubishi trust. Shidehara had become the spokesman of those elements that saw the future of Japan's commercial and industrial expansion in terms of membership in the League of Nations, limitation of naval armament, and the development of a policy of conciliation and adjustment to China's new nationalism without renunciation of Japan's "life line" in South Manchuria. From 1924 to 1927 and from 1929 to 1931, while he was Foreign Minister, Shidehara pursued what came to be known as the "Shidehara policy." Shidehara summarized the principles of the policy before the Japanese Diet in January, 1927:

1. To respect the sovereignty and territorial integrity of China.
2. To promote solidarity and economic rapprochement between the two countries.
3. To entertain sympathetically and helpfully the just aspirations of the Chinese people.
4. To maintain an attitude of patience and toleration in the present situation in China, and to protect Japan's legitimate and essential rights and interests by all reasonable means at the disposal of the government.

[9] George A. Lensen, *Japanese Recognition of the U.S.S.R.: Soviet-Japanese Relations, 1921–1930* (1970), a detailed account of Soviet-Japanese negotiations with the full text of major agreements and extensive quotations from other Japanese and Russian documents.

As applied to the situation in China, these principles produced Japanese co-operation with other powers in modifying rates under treaty tariffs and in expressing readiness to restore tariff autonomy after January, 1929 (concession of autonomy was actually delayed beyond that date). Negotiations on the refunding of the Nishihara and other loans were marked by restraint seldom evident in earlier Sino-Japanese dealings. In Manchuria, Japan's stress on economic rather than military measures was seen in the appointment of additional commercial officers.

On two occasions during Shidehara's first term at the Foreign Office Japan did resort to the use of troops "for the protection of Japanese interests in China." In December, 1925, when Kuo Sung-ling, a lesser militarist in Manchuria, revolted against Chang Tso-lin, Japan dispatched some troops to the Mukden area. Again in April, 1927, Japanese marines were used to resist Chinese mobs attacking the Japanese concession at Hankow. But the Japanese naval forces did not join in the Anglo-American bombardment of Nanking in March, 1927, despite the fact that the Japanese consulate had been attacked by the Chinese and several Japanese nationals had been wounded. The crux of the Shidehara policy was the effort to reconcile China's aspirations with Japan's interest.

TANAKA AND THE POSITIVE POLICY

Shidehara's "weak" policy, which had been pursued in the face of mounting civil war and anti-foreignism in China, aroused bitter opposition among Japanese militarists and bureaucrats and in some business circles. The sentiment was particularly strong in the powerful Privy Council, which forced the resignation of the first Wakatsuki cabinet in April, 1927, thus opening the way for the "positive policy" of Tanaka and the *Seiyukai*. The nature of this so-called "positive policy" toward China merits some further comment.

The *positive policy* distinguished between the attitude Japan would adopt toward China Proper and her attitude toward Manchuria and eastern Mongolia. With re-

spect to China Proper, Tanaka reiterated policies which had been repeatedly announced—noninterference with the Chinese civil war, respect for China's "popular will," sympathy for the demands of the more moderate elements of the *Kuomintang*, and determination to protect Japanese lives and property. In Manchuria and eastern Mongolia, on the other hand, Tanaka emphasized that Japan had "special interests," that it was her duty to maintain peace and order there, "and that her rights and interests in these areas would be protected if threatened by disturbance incident to the Nationalist movement or other civil strife." As guiding principles, these pronouncements were scarcely distinguishable from those of Shidehara. What imparted difference in practice was Tanaka's military background, his party's commitment to a "stronger" policy, and, above all, the application of these principles just as the *Kuomintang* was moving toward military unification of China.[10]

[10] Akira Iriye, *After Imperialism: The Search for a New Order in the Far East, 1921–1931* (1965),* Chapter 4. Associated with the history of the "positive policy" is the so-called "Tanaka Memorial," a document which, purporting to contain the decisions reached at a foreign office conference, first made its appearance in 1929, and after 1931 was reprinted many times and widely circulated as evidence of Japan's predetermined policy vis-a-vis China in general and Manchuria in particular. Japanese policy in Manchuria and China after 1931 bore a striking resemblance to specific points in the "Memorial." The disputed authenticity of the document is discussed by W. W. Willoughby, *Japan's Case Examined* (1940), 146–53. The "Memorial" was a forgery, but the program outlined represented the thinking of some Japanese expansionists. Robert A. Scalapino, *Democracy and the Party Movement in Prewar Japan* (1953), 236.

The "weak" versus the "positive" policies of Shidehara and Tanaka respectively involved more than an argument over principles to be applied in foreign policy toward China. In some considerable measure, Shidehara represented the commercialism of Japan's light industries and their quest for expanding export markets. Tanaka was more closely identified with Japan's heavy industries. A strong armament policy enabled the army and navy to place large contracts with Japan's heavy industries, thus in fact subsidizing them, for which reason the heavy industries tended to be willing to go along with the Tanaka

For Tanaka, as with Shidehara, the problem was to reconcile Chinese aspirations with Japanese interests. Chinese industrialization in Manchuria (particularly the building of Chinese owned railroads) would, it was felt, threaten Japan's South Manchurian Railroad, and therefore her "special position." Moreover, the power of left-wing elements in the *Kuomintang* until 1927 was alarming to the Japanese government and particularly to the leaders of the Japanese Kwantung army in South Manchuria, which consistently urged strong measures. Chinese nationalist tendencies to move away from rather than toward an accommodation with Japan had alarmed Shidehara and had prompted with his blessings a thorough re-evaluation of Chinese relations. Thus it was against a background suggesting that something more must be done that Tanaka approved the use of Japanese troops in Shantung to check the advance of *Kuomintang* forces and thereby prevent the immediate union of Manchuria with the Nationalist cause. The prime minister was less conscious of intervening in China's civil war than of satisfying his own military subordinates and *Seiyukai* colleagues.[11] The effect, nevertheless, was to revive military diplomacy and to enlarge the initiative, exercised by military extremists, especially after the failure to punish Chang Tso-lin's assassins. From this time on, as Tanaka resigned in July, 1929, the course of Japanese foreign policy was under the constant and increasing threat of extreme militarists and of a General Staff that was unable or unwilling to restore discipline in its own service or to permit the civilian wing of government to take steps to that end.

JAPAN AND THE LEAGUE OF NATIONS

As the pendulum of Japanese politics swung uneasily between the "weak" and "strong" policies of Shidehara and Tanaka, Japan had continued to play a respectable and in some cases a distinguished role as a member of the League of Nations. A number of Japan's ablest statesmen, jurists, diplomats, and public men served with the League. Until 1926, Nitobe Inazo, one of the best known of Japan's liberals abroad, served as an Under-Secretary General and as a Director of the International Bureau. He was succeeded by Sugimura Yotaro as Under-Secretary General and Director of the Political Section.

Japan was also active in the field of arbitration and adjudication of international disputes. She was a signatory of the Convention for the Pacific Settlement of International Disputes, a product of the Hague Peace Congress of 1899 and 1907. When, under the League of Nations, the principle of international adjudication acquired new life, Adachi Mineichiro was named a member of the League committee that drafted the statutes for the new Permanent Court of International Justice, commonly known as the World Court. A Japanese, Oda Yorozu, was one of the original eleven judges of the Court. He in turn was succeeded in 1930 by Adachi Mineichiro, who served also as President of the Court. However, on account of the so-called optional clause in the statutes of the Court imposing compulsory acceptance of its jurisdiction in specified cases, Japan did not accept the Court's full jurisdiction.

NAVAL RIVALRY IN THE PACIFIC

The Washington Conference had made a beginning toward holding within bounds the race in naval armament among the great powers. However, after 1924, when the United States passed the Quota Immigration Act excluding aliens who were ineligible for citizenship, there was noticeable tension in American-Japanese relations and a growing interest in the question of armaments. A naval race was still quite possible, for the Washington Conference ratio—5–5–3 for the United States, Great Britain, and Japan—

policy. But in order to justify armaments and preparedness, Tanaka was forced to adopt a "positive" policy, to maintain that a warlike crisis was perpetually just around the corner on the continent of Asia.

[11] Iriye, *After Imperialism*, 146–47.

was applicable only to capital ships. Indeed, the naval race was already under way, for while the United States failed to maintain its naval strength either in auxiliary categories or in the capital ships to which it was entitled under the Washington agreement, the other powers, Japan and Great Britain, continued to build.[12]

Without adequate preparation, President Coolidge on February 10, 1927, invited the powers to a disarmament conference at Geneva. Although France and Italy declined to attend, Great Britain, the United States, and Japan attempted to extend and supplement the principles adopted at Washington. The United States wanted to apply the 5–5–3 ratio to all categories and to reduce total cruiser tonnage. No agreement was reached, however, and the conference ended in failure. This was the more lamentable since there was little doubt that public opinion at this time in all three countries favored further limitation. The conference was defeated both by the naval experts and by lobbyists of special groups.

Anglo-American-Japanese relations continued to deteriorate after the Geneva Conference. There appeared to be no solution to the naval problem so long as Great Britain and the United States remained as far apart as they were at Geneva. By late 1929 this doleful picture had been retouched and brightened. Shidehara was back at the Japanese Foreign Office, and President Herbert Hoover and Prime Minister Ramsay Mac-Donald had talked amicably at the President's fishing camp at Rapidan, Virginia. Evidence of the improved international temper came with a British invitation to the powers, October 7, 1929, to a disarmament conference in London. As at Geneva, this conference was soon mired in the technical details of the experts who again seemed to be "on top" instead of merely "on tap."

[12] For discussions of the growing armament problem, see B. H. Williams, *The United States and Disarmament* (1931); J. W. Wheeler-Bennett, *Disarmament and Security Since Locarno, 1925–1931* (London, 1932), Chapters 1 and 2; Giovanni Engely, *The Politics of Naval Disarmament*, trans. by H. V. Rhodes (London, 1932), Chapters 1, 2, and 3.

Yet, on April 22, 1930, the London Naval Treaty was signed by Britain, the United States, and Japan. France who had demanded a political agreement assuring her of military support, and Italy accepted only part of the treaty. Nevertheless, the results of the conference were positive, if limited. The three major powers had accepted a maximum upper limit in all categories of vessels. Britain acceded to an over-all principle of parity with the United States. Japan accepted a 10–10–6 ratio in heavy cruisers, was granted a 10–10–7 ratio in light cruisers and other auxiliary ships, and parity with the larger powers in submarines. An escalator clause could release any signatory from its obligations if its position was jeopardized by the naval construction of a nonsignatory.

At the London Naval Conference Japan sought "three fundamental claims": (1) a 70 per cent ratio relative to the United States in 10,000-ton, 8-inch-gun heavy cruisers; (2) a 70 per cent ratio in gross tonnage relative to the United States in all auxiliary craft; and (3) parity with Britain and the United States in submarine tonnage at the then high existing strength of some 78,000 tons. This program of the Japanese naval staff, supported by the press, was designed to give the nation greater relative strength in far eastern waters than was provided by the 5–5–3 capital ship ratio of the Washington Treaty. In Japan it was generally regarded as "adequate for defense in any contingency." What Japan achieved by the specific provisions of the 1930 treaty fell short of the 70 per cent ratio in the heavy cruiser class. The United States agreed informally, however, not to complete its heavy cruiser construction schedule until after 1936, thus giving Japan an actual 72 per cent ratio in heavy cruisers vis-à-vis the United States during the life of the treaty (scheduled to terminate with the Washington treaty at the end of 1936). This informal understanding was unacceptable to the naval experts at Tokyo, and the Hamaguchi government met violent opposition from the naval staff and all ultranationalistic groups. Admiral Kato Kanji, chief of the naval general staff, personified the resolute position of the military services and their supporters. The decision to accept the compromise was therefore a major victory for civilian as opposed to military dominance in the government. Furthermore, it strengthened the constitutional theories of Minobe Tatsukichi, the distinguished jurist, who held that the power to determine the military and naval strength of the state did not belong to the supreme command. In this view, it was the prerogative of the cabinet and not of the military services to advise the emperor.

Japan's adherence to the London Treaty marked the high point in the nation's struggle toward responsible government. But as already noted, the victory was fictitious. There was no united public opinion to support a government that was fighting for democratic and responsible control.

FOR FURTHER READING

Tsunoda Ryusaku and others, eds., *Sources of the Japanese Tradition* (1958).° Chapter 26, "The High Tide of Prewar Liberalism" presents pertinent documents and penetrating editorial notes. H. S. Quigley, *Japanese Government and Politics* (1932), a good reference work. R. K. Reischauer, *Japan: Government–Politics* (1939) has an excellent brief chapter on "The Party Politicians in Power, 1918–1932." A useful summary is also to be found in Delmar M. Brown, *Nationalism in Japan: An Introductory Historical Analysis*

(1955). Something of the diversity of Japanese political thinking is suggested by two studies: Douglas H. Mendel, Jr., "Ozaki Yukio: Political Conscience of Modern Japan," *Far Eastern Quarterly* 15 (1956): 343–56; and Walter Scott Perry, "Yoshino Sakuzo, 1873–1933: Exponent of Democratic Ideals in Japan," (1956, University Microfilm Publication 17, 734). A. Morgan Young, *Japan Under Taisho Tenno, 1912–1926* (London, 1928), and *Imperial Japan 1926–1938* (1938), though journalistic, are packed with valuable observations on Japanese politics and the social order. Hugh Byas, *Government by Assassination* (1942) is another valuable journalistic account. Scholarly studies of the social order underpinning politics are John F. Embree's, *Suye Mura; A Japanese Village* (1939),° and *The Japanese Nation, A Social Survey* (1945); and Andrew J. Grad, *Land and Peasant in Japan, An Introductory Survey* (1952). Individual chapters of the following touch on aspects of domestic politics and foreign relations: Yanaga Chitoshi, *Japan Since Perry* (1949); W. G. Beasley, *The Modern History of Japan* (1963).° On Japanese radicalism, see Kawai Tatsuo, *The Goal of Japanese Expansion* (Tokyo, 1938); Hyman Kublin, *Asian Revolutionary, The Life of Sen Katayama* (1964); George M. Beckman and Genji Okubo, *The Japanese Communist Party, 1922–1945* (1969). Peter Duus, "The Era of Party Rule: Japan, 1905–1932," *Modern East Asia: Essays in Interpretation*, James B. Crowley, ed. (1970),° 180–206.

China, 1916-1931:
Warlords, the Kuomintang,
and Nationalism

chapter 24

The China that emerged from the catastrophe of World War I was a paradox of indescribable chaos and of magnificent rebirth. From the death of Yuan Shih-k'ai in 1916 until 1931, China endured civil war, took the first steps toward unity under the revolutionary *Kuomintang*, and began to free herself from the semi-dependent status to which she had succumbed. In some quarters of the Western world it was assumed that in China, as in Japan, responsible government would soon be a fact instead of a hope. These dreams did not become a reality. To understand why this was so, it is necessary to refer to the complex problems which confronted the builders of modern China. Unlike Japan, which in 1918 was an organized and powerful national state, industrialized, and already expanding politically and economically under an able if arbitrary leadership, the new China was as yet formless, unorganized, nonindustrial, and leaderless. Nevertheless, she was about to advance materially the revolution begun in 1911. A unique assortment of movements and personalities was to play its part in this perplexing story. There was the phantom warlord government at Peking, which was the only government recognized *de jure* by

the foreign powers, 1916–1928. There was the insurgent Canton revolutionary government of Sun Yat-sen which, under the *Kuomintang*, was to formalize China's new nationalism at Nanking after 1927. Between these two political movements and within each there were crusades of factionalism, duplicity, civil war, and massacre. And between all of these and the foreign powers there were intrigue and conspiracy in a battle for position, influence, and control in the China that would emerge tomorrow.

AN ERA OF WARLORDISM

In an immediate sense China's warlord era, 1916–1928, was traceable to Yuan Shih-k'ai's ill-favored schemes. Under Yuan's leadership regional armies had been permitted to swell on the theory that China's military power was thereby enhanced. More realistic appraisals revealed that these military increments bolstered local leadership in opposition to the central government, but this development was not immediately apparent. While Yuan lived, he presided over an uneasy coalition, balancing contending forces. Only with his death did Peking lose control and was the stage set for civil war.

Thus, in stimulating militarism Yuan contributed to the chaos that followed his demise. Yet Yuan was himself the victim, not the author, of the deeper revolutionary forces attacking the central authority which until recently had been wielded by the Manchus. The Revolution of 1911 had dealt a death blow to the principle upon which central authority had been based, and for nearly two decades thereafter political authority rested, in the absence of other sanctions, primarily on military power. Not until the *Kuomintang* devised a new program uniting a populace did government issue from something other than a gun.

While warlords were alike as destroyers of political unity, they differed widely in ability, temperament, and ambition. Some entertained no purpose save enjoying whatever fortunes their powers accumulated, but others, though not qualifying for the title of revolutionary, were touched by nationalism and directed their efforts toward regeneration of their country. One such reforming warlord was Yen Hsi-shan, governor of Shansi, 1911–1930. Yen denounced the landowning gentry for their "oppression" of the peasantry, reduced the authority of the gentry in the countryside, and introduced land reforms. He also established a school system with the aim of providing instruction in technology and science, as well as traditional subjects, and promoted modernization of agriculture. Moreover, he gave uncompromising support to the economic modernization of Shansi, irrespective of the cost in terms of traditional values and institutions. Significantly, these steps were not taken as part of any conscious effort to establish a new order in Shansi. Yen, who embraced many of the values of the Confucian gentry and aspired to membership in that class, regarded his actions as necessary to his retention of power. Nevertheless, Yen contributed to change. To many in Shansi his actions suggested that a new society might be built, one which was not Confucian.

Secure in his territorial base, Yen met political changes of the greatest magnitude. Like other warlords, he shifted allies as expediency dictated. Thus, in 1927–1928, unable to check the *Kuomintang's* northern progress, he joined party forces, assisted in the capture of Peking, and accepted a ministry in the *Kuomintang*-Nationalist government. A short time later, following collapse of a coup directed against Chiang Kai-shek, Yen fled to Manchuria, only to return in 1932 to still another alliance with *Kuomintang* leadership. When Japanese troops invaded northern China, Yen's troops joined the Communists in staging a joint defense, but these allies in turn became enemies at the end of World War II. Indeed, it was the Communists who finally ended Yen's political career in Shansi, sending him along with the rest of the *Kuomintang* into refuge on Taiwan.

What Yen's career suggests is that the warlords bequeathed no simple legacy. As independent (the *Kuomintang*-Nationalist government, except in the most nominal sense, never ruled in Yen's Shansi Province) and sometimes brutal leaders, warlords were scorned by Nationalists intent upon ushering China into a new era. It was much later before the more constructive aspects of the reforming warlord regimes were recognized. In an era when Confucianism was destroyed and new values were sought, warlords such as Yen helped introduce some of China's masses to the modern world.[1]

THE GROWTH OF NATIONAL FEELING

Beneath the turmoil of warlordism there were real if submerged strivings toward a new order. The New Culture Movement continued the search for the intellectual underpinnings of a modern China. During the post-war years, three trends were discernible

[1] See Donald G. Gillin, *Warlord: Yen Hsi-shan in Shansi Province, 1911–1949* (1966); James S. Sheridan, *Chinese Warlord: The Career of Feng Yu-hsiang* (1966); and Winston Hsieh, "The Ideas and Ideals of a Warlord: Ch'en Chiang-ming (1878–1933)," *Papers on China*, Vol. 16. Published and distributed by the East Asian Research Center, Harvard University (1962), 198–252.

in Chinese thought. First, disillusionment caused by World War I and the peace settlement prompted some intellectuals, such as Yen Fu, an old-style scholar and translator of Western works, to turn away completely from the West. Yen, once an advocate of evolutionary reform, reaffirmed his faith in traditional government and learning. In so doing he and his colleagues buttressed conservative forces, but they lost all influence in the New Culture Movement. Second, other intellectuals, among whom Ch'en Tu-hsiu was a leader, responded to disappointment over Western behavior by drawing closer to the ideas of Marx and Lenin. Ch'en and Li Ta-chao, the latter of whom was later honored officially by the Chinese Communist Party as its founder, established Marxist study groups.[2] Some indication of the warm feeling that these generated toward communism was to be seen in the unprecedented welcoming ceremonies staged by more than a dozen groups of intellectuals for the Soviet representative, Adolph Joffe, when he arrived in Peking in August, 1922. Third, Hu Shih, who had been one of the early leaders of the New Culture Movement, stood out among those intellectuals continuing to support reform in accord with Western liberal traditions. This position dominated much of the

[2] Ch'en, not Li, was the first leader of the Chinese Communist Party, serving in that capacity from 1921 until his expulsion from the Party in 1927. Communist histories were later to revile him as a "traitorous revisionist." Li's importance in the Party is suggested by his role in negotiating with Sun Yat-sen the coalition between the Communists and the *Kuomintang*. The subsequent reputations of the two men, however, owed less to their actual party roles than to their ideas. Ch'en regarded the total failure of the Chinese traditions as a source of renewal and looked outside China for the basis of the new society. Li, on the other hand, looked to tradition as well as Marxism. Drawing upon his own rural background, Li saw in the peasantry the true spirit of China and the strength for its renaissance. In advancing these latter views, Li anticipated Mao Tse-tung, who in these early party years seved as Li's assistant in the library of Peking University. For a brilliant study emphasizing Li's ideas see Maurice Meisner, *Li Ta-chao and the Origins of Chinese Marxism* (1967).

academic community from the end of World War I until 1949.

In advancing their respective causes there were some things upon which Marxists and liberals alike could agree. Trends in Chinese thought during the 1920s underscored young China's acceptance of certain Western values such as materialism and pragmatism. In 1923, to cite a single example, Ch'en Tu-hsiu and Hu Shih joined the defense against an attempt by Chang Chunmai (Carson Chang) to substitute for materialism a metaphysical system derived from the intuitionism of Henri Bergson and the neo-Confucian School of the Mind. Similarly most young literati could applaud Hu Shih's critical study (*Outline of the History of Chinese Philosophy*) of Confucianism which helped to destroy whatever prestige was retained by the classics and could unite in denouncing the retention by foreign powers of the "unequal treaties." The really crucial differences dividing young intellectuals were concerned with the methods which were to be applied to the problems of Chinese life. Hu Shih was a spokesman for the view that looked toward evolutionary change and stressed individualism. As recently as 1919, a philosophy founded on these concepts had been preached by no less a person than the American philosopher, John Dewey, as he toured China. Marxists, on the other hand, dismissed gradualism with the argument that only radical solutions would serve nationalist aims.

These intellectual strivings toward a New China found popular expression in a literature which built upon reforms of the World War I era. In the post-war years Chinese writers moved beyond earlier attempts to invigorate the vernacular language as a vehicle for spreading Western ideas. Literature followed philosophy in seeking a unique synthesis of new concepts. Literary associations (more than one hundred between 1922 and 1925) sponsored journals reflecting a broad spectrum of opinion. Among young writers were a few concerned with aesthetics alone, but most, figures such as Lu Hsun, Kuo Mo-jo, and Mao Tun, were firmly aligned with the adage, "Art should reform life." On this assumption literature became an ever more self-conscious tool of social reform.[3]

Writers were not the only intermediaries between the intellectuals and masses. Following World War I, this role was assumed increasingly by students. The students' influence was traceable directly to the historic position of scholarship and the scholar in Old China. Many Chinese looked to the students for answers in the chaotic revolutionary years. The students, especially after the demonstrations on May 4, 1919, had shown their power and, in turn, had voiced their opinions with an air of authority. Since some considerable number of them had received a modern education in Japan, Europe, or America, and since in the turmoil of prevailing conditions many graduates could not find jobs which they considered commensurate with their training, they readily became active critics of government. So it was that a growing body of students became revolutionary agents. Among themselves, students did not agree on the details of the revolutionary blueprint, but from their continual, often clamorous, debates a consensus did emerge: China was to be unified, to be relieved of "unequal treaties" which infringed her sovereignty, and to become the seat of a new civilization.

THE NEW KUOMINTANG

It was in these circumstances of warlord politics, of intellectual strivings for a new

order, and of student activism that the *Kuomintang*, China's first Nationalist Party, made its bid for power.[4] During World War I, it had been by no means certain that this party would emerge as an important factor in Chinese politics. After the *Kuomintang* members left the Peking government in 1917 and fled to southern ports, the party went into eclipse. South China, like the North, had its full quota of provincial warlord-governors who made alliances or fought each other for personal advantage under not the slightest control of the "government" in Peking. In this general confusion, Sun Yat-sen and his following made little immediate headway. The *Kuomintang* had no effective organization other than personal bonds of loyalty to Sun. It was filled with factionalism and diverse political creeds and, of course, had no army.

Nevertheless, these dark years created the beginning of a new era in party history. Since, in an age of warlordism, control of Peking offered no sure approach to power, Sun set about creating a military base in the south. A deal was struck with Yunnanese warlords whereby the latter would protect the *Kuomintang* in return for access to public revenues. This proved an unstable arrangement, lasting barely two years, but the alliance gave the *Kuomintang* time to look to its own defense.[5] Important too was the way

[3] Judged by standards of comparable Western literature, the quality of this Chinese writing was pitiful. Russian or Scandinavian works, through which Chinese authors sought inspiration, reached China through poor English or Japanese translations. It would be difficult to find in any of the journals of the 1920s a mature example of literary criticism. See Yi-tsi M. Feuerwerker, "Tradition and Experiment in Modern Chinese Literature," reprinted in *Modern China,* Albert Feuerwerker, ed. (1964),* 169–83. Chinese experiments with scientific ideas during these years reveal little about science but much about young China's search for an identity of its own. See D. W. Y. Kwok, *Scientism in Chinese Thought, 1900–1950* (1965).

[4] *Kuo* means country, *min* means people, and the combination *kuomin* means national (citizen) or as an adjective, nationalist. *Tang* is Chinese for party. Thus *Kuomintang,* the (Chinese) Nationalist Party.

[5] Relations between the Yunnanese army and the *Kuomintang* were not severed by the collapse of the original alliance. The warlord army under several of its old officers was incorporated into the *Kuomintang's* Third National Revolutionary Army. This practice of incorporating old elements without assimilating them completely later served the *Kuomintang* in coming to terms with other warlords. It seemed that the *Kuomintang* was less successful in destroying warlordism than in modifying a system which remained decentralized and militaristic. Donald S. Sutton, "The Kuomintang and Warlordism: The Yunnanese Army in Kwantung, 1923–1925," (in manuscript). Paper presented at the annual convention of the Association for Asian Studies, Philadelphia, March, 1968.

Sun used the interval to link the *Kuomintang* with other revolutionary elements.

Just after World War I, Sun, giving heed to the nationwide student uprising protesting the Shantung settlement at Versailles, brought student leaders into the party, thereby bringing to the movement a younger element ripe for revolution. Then, in 1922, Sun, whose appeals to the Western democracies for aid against the Peking warlords had gone unanswered, met Abram Adolph Joffe, who had been sent by Moscow to cultivate both the Peking regime and the *Kuomintang*. By the following January, Sun and Joffe had reached an agreement. Sun declared that neither communism nor the Soviet system was suitable for China, while Joffe, concurring in this view, assured Sun of Russian sympathy and support in the achievement of China's most pressing needs—national unification and full independence. The Chinese Communist Party, which had been founded in Shanghai during the summer of 1921, pledged support to the *Kuomintang*, and Communists as individuals were permitted to join Sun's forces.

The considerations which prompted this alliance are noteworthy. Both sides saw advantages for themselves. The Comintern, based in Moscow, had picked China as the chief area of activity for the years after 1922. In extending aid to Sun, the objective of the Comintern was to help the Chinese Communist Party establish itself within the *Kuomintang* so as eventually to control it. Sun explained his side of the deal by saying simply that he had to seek help where he could get it. While not subscribing to communism, Sun, especially as the alliance ripened, recognized fully the usefulness of communist methods. The apparent similarity of the communist vision of society and his own principle of People's Livelihood as well as the mutual antipathy to imperialism permitted Sun to believe that the two parties could co-operate. Nor was he concerned that the Chinese Communists might ultimately dominate the *Kuomintang*. The Chinese Communists, Sun believed, were just "youngsters," only some 300 in number in 1922,

(as compared to his own following of 150,-000) whom the Soviet would disavow if necessary in order to maintain its relationship with the *Kuomintang*.

While Sun was overly optimistic about his ability to handle the Communists, he had discovered in his own brand of militarism, in the student movement, and in proffered Russian aid the means for revitalizing his following. Within two years the *Kuomintang* (in theory at least) was a totalitarian party in structure and discipline, though its doctrine had not become communist. Much of this radical reorganization was the work of communist advisers from Moscow headed by Michael Borodin, a revolutionary of international repute. Simultaneously the military leadership for *Kuomintang* armies was trained at the newly founded Whampoa military academy under the command of a young officer just returned from observing the Red Army at Moscow. His name was Chiang Kai-shek. Moreover, Sun, in a series of lectures which he delivered to party officials in 1924, enunciated a basic manifesto that set the frame for future party and government relations. Called the *San Min Chu I,* the Three Principles of the People, this manifesto contained ideas that had been basic with Sun since 1905, but it was not until these ideas were modified and expressed in the context of the post-war years that they became powerful weapons of propaganda.

Sun's first principle was *Min-tsu,* meaning People's Nationhood or Nationalism. In its original form this principle held simply that the Manchus, an alien dynasty, be ousted. Events since 1911, however, had demonstrated that this was not enough to make China a nation. The people remained—in Sun's words—a "sheet of loose sand," lacking solidarity. Thus in its revised form the principle of Nationalism embodied the idea of a unity embracing Chinese, Manchus, Mongols, Tibetans, and various lesser groups. With respect to the principle's internal implications, Sun did not spell out clearly the program for unification, because here he faced problems of extreme delicacy. The question involved not only patriotism to the state but also the problem of what kind of a state. Was it to be a state in which the Chinese, as the overwhelming majority, were to have a corresponding ascendancy over such people as the Mongols? Or was it to be a federated state in which the Mongols and the Tibetans were to have the standing of majorities within their own territories? A number of Mongol-*Kuomintang* followers of Sun believed that the eventual outcome would be a federated state, but for Sun, by 1924, it was extraordinarily difficult to make a decision. Open advocacy of a federated system, in view of China's weakness at the time, might expose the frontier people to annexation or near annexation by foreign powers. If, however, it was difficult for Sun to resolve the internal character of Nationalism, there was no such problem externally. Stung by the way the West had spurned his party, 1919–1924, Sun viewed China's lack of national solidarity as stemming in large measure from the legacy of foreign domination. In consequence, his First Principle was frankly anti-imperialistic. While Sun had once represented the vanguard of Nationalism from the West, he now deprecated the West and sought in Chinese traditionalism a basis for his new Nationalism.

Min-ch'uan, translated as People's Power or Democracy, was Sun's Second Principle. In 1905 Sun proclaimed his support of democracy mainly by attacking advocates of a constitutional monarchy as proponents of "absolutism." By 1924 he was more explicit about what the term meant. His ideas on democracy were derived from four principal sources: (1) Western republicanism, (2) the Swiss doctrine of initiative, referendum, election, recall, (3) Soviet democratic centralism, and (4) Chinese ideas of examination and control. The result was a plan of government which he believed would insure popular control through electoral processes, yet give a strong executive wide powers to deal with the business of government. In operation the plan was to rest on the division of men in Confucian fashion into first, second, and third class citizens. These would be respectively: (1) the leaders, who could

understand the past and thus guide men into the future (a Confucian idea); (2) those who could interpret the leaders to the masses; and (3) the rank and file bereft of understanding but able to say whether they liked what they got. Political power was to be exercised through five branches: three of these—executive, legislative, and judicial— are familiar to students of American government, while the remaining divisions, "examination" and "control", were based on models provided by Chinese history. Training for the exercise of political power would be given to the people by the *Kuomintang* during the period of tutelage that was to follow immediately the military reunification.

The Third Principle was called *Min-sheng* or People's Livelihood, a phrase used to embrace a number of social and economic theories which had attracted Sun's attention. Often Sun and his followers used *Min-sheng* as an equivalent for socialism, drawing upon the popularity of this idea, but Sun rejected Marxism's basic tenets. Drawing upon a work little known in the West, *The Social Interpretation of History* by a Brooklyn dentist, Maurice Williams, Sun refuted the theories of class struggle and economic determinism. More important to Sun were the single tax ideas of Henry George. While Sun never developed a precise economic program, he appears to have envisaged a tax on the unearned increment of land as the means for equalizing land tenure, eliminating inequality in wealth, and providing capital for the expansion of production. To promote China's industrial development, Sun stressed the recovery of tariff autonomy and erection of protective tariffs. Sun's recommendations for agriculture were confined mainly to the need for technological improvement.[6]

[6] Key Ray Chang "Cheng Kuan-ying (1841– 1920): A Source of Sun Yat-sen's Nationalist Ideology?" *Journal of Asian Studies* 28 (Feb., 1969): 247–67; and Stephen Uhalley, Jr. "Sun Yat-sen and Chinese History," *Journal of the Hong Kong Branch of the Royal Asiatic Society* 8 (1968): 109–18, should be read along with the articles cited in Chapter 17.

While his new *Kuomintang* was acquiring a new power, Sun still hoped for the peaceful unification of China through an acceptable agreement with Peking. Late in 1924 the prospect seemed hopeful. The warlord president at Peking, Ts'ao K'un, had been driven from office and his place taken by Tuan Ch'i-jui as provisional chief executive. Accordingly, Sun went to Peking seeking a basis for settlement. There in March, 1925, he died, calling on his followers to carry on the revolution.

The passing of Sun Yat-sen had disrupting effects, all of which were not apparent immediately upon the Nationalist movement and upon the fortunes of the *Kuomintang*. So long as Sun lived, his shortcomings had been obvious not only to many of his immediate followers but also to his enemies. Now that he was gone the failures of the man whom many had regarded as a visionary were forgotten. Sun became the embodiment of all the idealism within the Nationalist movement, and the personification of all the revolutionary fervor of the reconstituted *Kuomintang*. As Confucius had become the sage of ancient China, so would Sun Yet-sen inherit the role in twentieth-century China. Confucianism would give place to Sun Yat-senism. On the other hand, no single leader had emerged to take Sun's place. Rivalry among his immediate associates was therefore a natural consequence—a rivalry that tended to rest its case on divergent interpretations of Sun's political and economic philosophy. Here there was ample ground for ideological warfare and party strife because of the vague, general, uncertain terms in which Sun had so frequently expressed his ideas.[7]

[7] The sources of these intense factional quarrels remain a matter of dispute. Official *Kuomintang* interpretations attribute the trouble to communist plots. Communist versions maintain that Michael Borodin, whom the *Kuomintang* claims was behind the intrigue, did not have much influence in party affairs and that factionalism arose from efforts of "feudal" elements, the bourgeoisie, and imperialist representatives to

For the time being, however, unity as the price of military victory kept factionalism within bounds. The Canton government was declared formally to be the Nationalist government. It was a committee administration with Wang Ching-wei, generally considered to be of the Left as a reformer, as chairman. This Leftist orientation of the *Kuomintang* was unsuccessfully challenged in November, 1925, when a group of Rightist leaders professing to hold a Session of the Central Executive Committee of the Party in the Western Hills at Peking passed resolutions denouncing the Leftists and expelling the Communists. At the Second National Congress of the *Kuomintang*, January, 1926, the sacredness of Sun's teachings, the soundness of the Russian orientation, and the purpose to carry the revolution to the people were all affirmed. The Western Hills group was expelled while more Communists joined the Party. Meanwhile, *Kuomintang* forces had

bolster Chiang Kai-shek. Both of these explanations, however, in keeping with the common tendency of all Chinese to venerate Sun Yat-sen, ignore the roots of factionalism before 1925.

Both the *T'ung Meng-hui* and later the early *Kuomintang* suffered from extreme factionalism throughout their histories, and, indeed, Sun's role in these parties was for a time that of a factional leader. When his leadership was no longer disputed, Sun did not purge the party of dissidents, but rather operated through persuasion and compromise, balancing forces to keep the party intact. While Sun lived, *Kuomintang* elite, who were linked with their chief through personal ties and who conceded his sole authority, held their own rivalries in check. With Sun's death restraints were removed and deeply ingrained rivalries emerged into the open. In these perspectives, intraparty battles assume the appearance less of ideological rivalries than of a search for a leader whose relationship would impart new unity. The difficulties presented by the search are suggested by Wang Ching-wei's observation that the *Tsung-li* (Sun's title as party leader) was not an office but a person. James R. Shirley, "Control of the *Kuomintang* after Sun Yat-sen's Death," *Journal of Asian Studies* 25 (Nov. 1965): 69–82; and George T. Yu's *Party Politics in Republican China: The Kuomintang, 1912–1914* (1966) suggests that western style parties contained no magic solution for Chinese problems.

crushed all military opposition from the Kwangtung and Kwangsi warlords.

With this added security in its southern base, the Nationalist government proposed to move to the military unification of all China. For many reasons the decision was regarded as dubious. Neither the military nor the political position of the Canton regime was strong. The surface unity in the *Kuomintang* did not reflect the factional bitterness beneath. Nevertheless, the military counsel of Chiang Kai-shek, commander of the armies, prevailed. Within three months Nationalist armies were on the Yangtze. The Nationalist government was moved, January, 1927, to the sister cities of Hankow, Hanyang, and Wuchang, where it became known as the Wuhan Regime. Here the growing conflict between Nationalists and Communists came in view. While Wuhan demonstrators (Communists and *Kuomintang* Leftists) attacked foreign concessions at central Yangtze cities and demanded a socialist revolution, Chiang Kai-shek and *Kuomintang* conservatives formed their own National government at Nanking, April 1927, from which it launched widespread attacks on Communists and Leftists in the lower Yangtze.[8] Simultaneously there were further disclosures of Communist and Russian purposes when Chang Tso-lin, the Manchurian warlord, then heading the Peking government, raided the Soviet offices there. Other disclosures came from the Wuhan

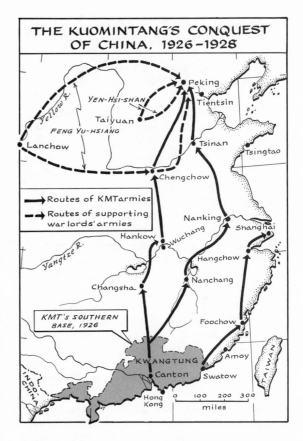

THE KUOMINTANG'S CONQUEST OF CHINA, 1926–1928

Source: I. G. V. Hsü, *The Rise of Modern China* (New York: Oxford University Press, 1970), p. 660.

---

[8] The split with the Communists marked a decided shift in Chiang's political orientation. Chiang was initially an advocate of the left-wing, but his relations with Communists cooled notably after 1925. Both Chiang and the Communists at first were inclined to conceal their differences. When the rivalry broke into the open, an unprincipled struggle for power ensued. Seeking to deny the Communists control of Shanghai, for example, Chiang resorted to deals with the city's extensive underworld, whose forces surprised and defeated Communist forces. For aspects of this struggle see Wu Tien-wei, "Chiang Kai-shek's March Twentieth Coup d'Etat of 1926," and "A Review of the Wuhan Debacle: The *Kuomintang*-Communist Split of 1927," *Journal of Asian Studies* 27 (1968): 585–602; 29 (1969): 125–43.

Regime, which finally expelled its Russian advisers, dissolved itself, reappeared briefly in Canton, and then was reunited with Nanking. On top of these developments the northern march of the Nationalists continued. Some northern warlords, Feng Yu-hsiang, the Christian General, and Yen Hsi-shan, the Model Governor, joined the nationalist cause. Chang Tso-lin, retreated from Peking to Manchuria, where he was slain by the Kwantung (Japanese) army, but his son Chang Hsueh-liang, the Young Marshal, raised the Nationalist flag at Mukden, December, 1928. No southern *Kuomintang* soldier entered Manchuria, but the Republic of China at Peking was dead. The Nationalists had won the war of unification.

CHINA'S REVOLUTION AND
THE FOREIGN POWERS

The perplexing course of China's internal revolution had been watched with anticipation and with fear by the West and by Japan. Would this revolution produce a stable China that would take its place within the international political and legal community of the Western powers? The protestations of Chinese spokesmen at Paris (1919) and Washington (1922) implied that this would be so. Yet there were also dire forebodings of trouble. The revolutionary program of Sun Yat-sen, in particular the principles of nationalism and democracy, was a direct challenge to the unequal treaty system dating back to 1842, to the concessions and foreign settlements, to the naval leaseholds and spheres of influence, and, in fact, to the entire structure of the foreign position and influence through which China had sunk to a semi-colonial status.

Peking's delegates at the Washington Conference on the Limitation of Armaments sought extensive revision of China's treaty structure. The powers, of course, united against these demands, agreeing only to certain steps toward the ultimate relinquishment of their privileges. Subsequently the actions taken at Washington did lead to partial satisfaction of Peking's aims. Before 1922 nearly one hundred foreign post offices operating on Chinese soil were closed.[9] In the same year Japan withdrew her troops from Siberia and the Allied and Associated Powers terminated their control of the Chinese Eastern Railway. Finally, Japan executed her pledge to transfer to China the title to Germany's former "special interests" in Shantung.

These developments, however, were balanced by Peking's unsuccessful efforts in 1923 to reopen with Tokyo the question of the termination of the Sino-Japanese treaties

and notes of May, 1915. Nor was Peking much more successful in concluding other desired agreements. During the Washington Conference, the British had agreed to surrender Wei-hai-wei as a means of facilitating a Sino-Japanese settlement on Shantung. Negotiations were conducted to this end by an Anglo-Chinese Commission, but complete agreement was not reached until April, 1930. Difficulties between the Peking government and France over repayment of the Boxer Indemnity delayed until 1925 the implementation of agreements reached at Washington to raise China's tariff to an effective 5 per cent *ad valorem* level, to return to China the Kwangchow leasehold, and to establish a commission to consider abolition of extraterritoriality. Further disappointment to Chinese nationalists derived from the failure of the Commission on Extraterritoriality to set a date for the termination of foreign jurisdiction in China. The Commission recommended only that the powers co-operate in the progressive modification of their extraterritorial rights. National frustration engendered by this report was not relieved by the recommendations of the tariff conference (convened in Peking, October, 1925) that China should be accorded tariff autonomy on January 1, 1929. Chinese sentiment had been demanding immediate abolition of the conventional tariff along with all other "unequal treaties." As a result, Peking became increasingly aggressive in its efforts to revise China's treaty structure, but with only minor success.[10] When the *Kuomintang* came to power in 1927, the "unequal treaties" were part of its inheritance.

While it was not evident at the time, the foregoing diplomacy was destined to be the least significant aspect of China's foreign relations in the post-war years. As the Nationalist movement at Canton gained momentum after 1920, it was Sun Yat-sen and his heirs supported by an aroused public opinion rather than the warlords at Peking who de-

[9] The exact numbers were: Great Britain, 12; Japan, 66; France, 13; and the United States, 1. The powers were permitted to maintain post offices in leased territories "or as otherwise specifically provided by treaty." Under this provision the Japanese continued to maintain post offices in the zone of the South Manchurian Railway.

[10] A treaty between Austria and China, October 19, 1925, confirmed the war-time ending of Austria's extraterritorial rights. On October 26, 1926, China and Finland negotiated a treaty as equals.

termined what China would or would not do. Until their regime at Nanking was recognized by the powers in 1928, the Nationalists were thorough revolutionaries in diplomacy; thereafter their methods were to be more conservative and conventional. Moreover, China's foreign relations became notable because of the role played by the Soviet Union. Prior to the expulsion of Soviet advisers from Wuhan in 1927, the Soviet Union maintained contact not only with the *Kuomintang* but also with the Republic in Peking and with semi-independent Manchuria.

SOVIET POLICY AND THE CHINESE REVOLUTION

Soviet Russian policy toward China had begun to unfold in 1918 with declarations that appeared to concede China's political rights in the Chinese Eastern Railway zone while reserving Russia's financial and economic interests. Later, in 1920, the Russians went further, declaring null and void all the treaties concluded with China by former Russian governments. Then in 1922 Adolph Joffe arrived in Peking seeking to re-establish diplomatic relations, to get Peking's approval of the new "independent" People's Revolutionary Government which the Russians had set up in Outer Mongolia in 1920, and to regain a position of influence in the Chinese Eastern Railway. Unsuccessful at Peking, Joffe went on to Shanghai to meet Sun Yat-sen. The result of that meeting was the immediate and remarkable growth of Soviet influence in the new *Kuomintang*. Furthermore, the Soviet position was strengthened by Joffe's subsequent visit to Japan and by the adherence to the Soviet Union (1922) of the Far Eastern Republic of Siberia. Accordingly, the Peking Republic was in no position to rebuff further Russian overtures presented by L. M. Karakhan, September, 1923. A treaty concluded by Wellington Koo and Karakhan, May 31, 1924, provided for resumption of formal relations, surrender by Russia of extraterritorial rights and her concessions at Hankow and Tientsin, restoration of Russian lega-

tions and consulates and property of the Orthodox Church, Russian recognition of China's suzerainty in Outer Mongolia, and withdrawal of Russian troops. In addition Russia recognized Chinese sovereignty in the Chinese Eastern Railway zone and agreed that China might redeem the line "with Chinese capital," that the fate of the line would be determined by China and Russia to the exclusion of third parties, and that management of the road would be a joint Russo-Chinese concern.

Since the Chinese Eastern Railway lay in the Manchurian territories of Chang Tso-lin, over which at the time Peking had no control, Karakhan negotiated (September 20, 1924) a separate agreement with the Manchurian dictator. The terms followed in general the previous Peking settlement. Yet they actually did not settle anything. During 1925 and 1926 Sino-Russian relations grew steadily worse. Moreover, by 1926 the Peking government was no longer controlled by the pro-Russian warlord, Feng Yu-hsiang, but by the anti-Bolshevik Chang Tso-lin of Manchuria. Once in Peking, Chang asked the recall of Karakhan and announced that he would rid North China of Bolshevik influence. Russia could afford to accept this reverse, for at Canton her influence was increasing steadily.

Russian diplomacy in North China coincided with the new forms of violence at Shanghai, the center of Western influence where the student movement was both anti-imperialistic and anti-Christian. On May 30, 1925, a Chinese crowd in the Shanghai International Settlement, aroused by student agitators declaiming against the killing of a Chinese in a Japanese cotton mill, was fired upon by Indian and Chinese constables. The order to fire, given by a police inspector of British nationality, resulted in the death of eight demonstrators. Chinese anger at this "inexcusable outrage" took the form of a general strike supported by virtually all sections of the populace. Business in Shanghai was at a standstill and remained so during most of the summer.

Repercussions of the incident were not confined to Shanghai. Anti-foreign outbreaks occurred at widely separated points spreading far into the interior, even to Chungking. The most serious disturbances took place at Canton headquarters of the Soviet-dominated *Kuomintang*. A few foreigners and more than a hundred Chinese were killed when Chinese demonstrators paraded on the Shakee bund opposite the British and French concessions on the island of Shameen. Canton instituted a successful boycott of all British goods, and a general strike of Chinese workmen paralyzed business in British Hong Kong.[11] In the face of these "alarming developments" relations between China and the treaty powers reached a new high point of tension.

THE CANTON SOVIET AND THE POWERS

When, therefore, in 1926 the Nationalists at Canton were preparing for the northern march, they were able to capitalize not only upon the unhappy events just related but also upon a long series of blunders by which the principal powers had shaped their policies toward China. World War I had already done much to destroy the prestige of the white man in the Far East. After the war there was the failure to apply the Wilsonian program of equality and self-determination to Asiatic peoples. Then in 1919 came the failure to restore Kiaochou to China. Lastly, the Washington Conference, while voicing the principle of Chinese sovereignty, perpetuated the unequal treaties under a modest program of prospective revision. The net effect was to drive the *Kuomintang* to make anti-imperialism a clarion call of the Nationalist revolution. Meanwhile the powers knew not what course to pursue, since the end of the unequal treaties was demanded not only by the Communists and the left wing of the *Kuomintang* but also by the center, the conserva-

[11] See the study by Lennox A. Mills, *British Rule in Eastern Asia* (1942). Popular anti-foreign outbreaks, boycotts, etc., were not entirely spontaneous. There was often much organized intimidation of the populace.

tives, and militarists, including Chiang Kai-shek, and the warlord regime at Peking.

The drive of revolutionary forces against Britain's positions, so successfully begun at Canton, was continued with like success at Hankow in December, 1926. A general strike of industrial labor in the Wuhan cities called in November was followed by mass demonstrations in the anti-British crusade. The agitation was so effective that on December 18, 1926, the British government proposed that the Washington treaty powers: (1) legalize what Canton was already doing by agreeing to immediate collection of the Washington surtaxes, (2) recognize and deal with regional governments, (3) implement a grant of tariff autonomy immediately upon China's promulgation of a national tariff, and (4) seek to develop better relations with China even while no national government existed. Britain's gesture of concession, far from satisfying the Nationalists, spurred them to new outbursts of fury. The British policy was described as a design to weaken China by creating regional governments and by encouraging militarists to seize the ports and to profit by collection of the proposed surtaxes.

Before the powers could reply to the British proposal, the anti-British crusade on the upper Yangtze had been carried still further. During the first week of January, 1927, under the threat of mob violence, the British abandoned their concessions in Hankow and Kiukiang. Both concessions were immediately taken over for administrative purposes by the Chinese. Likewise, without waiting for action by the powers, whatever Chinese groups happened to be in control of the treaty ports applied the surtaxes without further ado. This developing situation brought forth hurried assurances from the Japanese and the American governments expressing sympathy with China's "just aspirations" and indicating willingness to aid their attainment in an orderly fashion. In the light of this rising tide of nationalism, Great Britain, already disposed to find a new basis for her relations with China, concluded agreements with the Nationalists during February and March, 1927, handing over the Hankow and Kiukiang concessions.

Almost immediately following these agreements, Britain's policy of conciliation faced new trials at Nanking late in March. No sooner had the old southern capital been captured by the Nationalists than it became the scene of violent and seemingly premeditated attacks by *Kuomintang* troops upon foreign persons and property. Three British, one French, one American, and one Italian national were killed, and a number of Japanese subjects were wounded or subjected to less fatal outrageous treatment. Foreign property was looted. Nor was there an end to these doings of the *Kuomintang* soldiery until British and American gunboats laid a protective barrage about the properties of the Standard Oil Company, where surviving foreigners had taken refuge. The United States, England, France, Italy, and Japan demanded (April 11) an apology, reparations, and guarantees for the future. China's reply was evasive, but despite this the powers did not press for an immediate settlement. To have done so would have strengthened the radical wing of the *Kuomintang*-Soviet leaders at Hankow. Actually, the powers were hoping for the success of a new, conservative, and non-Soviet national regime at Nanking.

NANKING'S NEW TREATY RELATIONS

With the ousting of the old Peking regime, June, 1928, the National Government at Nanking promptly took over the conduct of China's foreign relations. It issued a declaration calling for new treaties negotiated with full regard to the sovereignty and equality of states. Although this declaration was by no means welcome to the powers, they were nevertheless disposed to negotiate. Indeed, there was no alternative unless they proposed to use force to impose the old treaties. Moreover, China's break with Russia and the new conservative orientation of the *Kuomintang* were pleasing to the foreign business groups and, in the main, to their governments.

The United States was the first power to act. By a treaty concluded at Peking on July 25, 1928, this country conceded tariff autonomy to China, subject of course to most-favored-nation treatment. The agreement was one of the most significant in China's foreign relations, for it shattered the old international bloc long opposed to any concessions. The tariff agreement with the United States was followed before the end of 1928 by similar agreements with other powers. Indeed, by January, 1929, Japan was the only power that had not concluded a new tariff agreement. This situation was due to a number of questions outstanding between the two countries. Not until Japanese troops had retired from Shantung and China had agreed to revenue allotments for the security of certain Japanese loans was an agreement reached (May 6, 1930).

The new China tariff treaties with Belgium, Denmark, Italy, Portugal, and Spain contained provisions for abolition of extraterritoriality subject to a similar concession by all the powers. Accordingly, on April 27, 1929, Nanking addressed the United States, Great Britain, and France requesting abolition at the earliest possible date. Similar notes went to Brazil, the Netherlands, and Norway. The replies of Britain, France, and the United States (August 10) were an emphatic denial that China was as yet entitled to full jurisdictional sovereignty. While complimenting China on the progress she had made, they noted that the recommendations of the Commission on Extraterritoriality had not been carried out. In September, 1929, China protested this attitude both directly to the powers and in the Assembly of the League of Nations. In December, Nanking went a step further, announcing the unilateral ending of extraterritoriality as of January 1, 1930, but softening the blow with the assurance that China would negotiate with powers willing to do so.

By the beginning of 1931 there was some reason to believe that China under the Nanking government was finding a new national stability, that the day of the warlord was gone, that the Russian bid for control had failed, that the unequal treaty system would be ended by force plus diplomacy, and finally that Sun Yat-sen's program for a new China was assured.

FOR FURTHER READING

DEVELOPMENT OF NATIONALISM. Nathaniel Peffer. *The Far East: A Modern History* (1958),* perceptive chapters on China in the 1920's. H. F. MacNair, *China in Revolution* (1931), a convenient narrative of events during the warlord period. Two works by A. N. Holcombe, *The Chinese Revolution* (1930), and *The Spirit of the Chinese Revolution* (1931) are of value as introductions. Teng Ssu-yu and Jeremy Ingals, eds. and trans., *The Political History of China, 1840–1928* (1956),* a Chinese account of the national movement. Franklin W. Houn, *Central Government of China, 1912–1928: An Institutional Study* (1957), an excellent account of China's struggle for constitutional government, but the conclusion that the collapse of constitutionalism inclined the country toward communism is debatable. William Ayers, "Shanghai Labor and the May 30th Movement," *Papers on China*, Vol. 5. Published and distributed by the East Asian Research Center, Harvard University. (Cambridge, Mass., 1950), 1–38, informative reference. Edward John Michael Rhoads, "Lingnan's Response to the Rise of Chinese Nationalism: The Shakee Incident," (1925) *Papers on China*, Vol. 15. Published and distributed by the East Asian Research Center, Harvard University, (1961), 115–45, a study correlated with the preceding article. Huang Sung-k'ang, *Lu Hsun and the New Culture Movement* (Amsterdam, 1957), an excellent highly condensed outline of the intellectual revolution as it applied to the modernization of literature, 1917–1930. Amitendranath Tagore, *Literary Debates in Modern China, 1918–1937* (Tokyo, 1967), focuses on the controversies between the right and left. William Theodore de Bary and others, eds., *Sources of Chinese Tradition* (1960),* two chapers—"The Nationalist Revolution" and "The New Culture

Movement"—in which pertinent documents and editorial comment are combined. The student movement is surveyed in Chiang Wen-han, *The Chinese Student Movement* (1948); and T. C. Wang, *The Youth Movement in China* (1927).

RISE OF THE KUOMINTANG. On Sun Yat-sen see: Harold Z. Schiffrin, "The Enigma of Sun Yat-sen," *China in Revolution: The First Phase, 1900–1913*, Mary C. Wright, ed. (1968). P. M. A. Linebarger, *The Political Doctrines of Sun Yat-sen: An Exposition of the San Min Chu I* (1937). Lyon Sharman, *Sun Yat-sen: His Life and Its Meaning* (1934; reprinted, 1965), a full length critical biography; Stephen Chen and Robert Payne, *Sun Yat-sen: A Portrait* (1946), a briefer but suggestive study. Early biographies of Chiang Kai-shek include: Chen Tsung-hsi and others, *General Chiang Kai-shek, the Builder of New China* (Shanghai, 1929); H. K. Tong, *Chiang Kai-shek* (2 vols., Shanghai, 1937); Robert Berkov, *Strong Man of China* (1938). T'ang Leang-li, *Wang Ching-wei* (Peiping, 1931) is by an associate of the subject. P. M. A. Linebarger, *Government in Republican China* (1938), an able and sympathetic account of the National Government's philosophy and structure. On the *Kuomintang's* program see also Sun Yat-sen, *The International Development of China* (Chunking, 1941). For data and interpretations of the period of Soviet orientation see: two studies by David J. Dallin, *The Rise of Russia in Asia* (1949), and *Soviet Russia and the Far East* (1948), which are based on Chinese as well as Russian sources, and exhibit shrewd insights into Soviet thinking. Allen S. Whiting, *Soviet Policies in China, 1917–1924* (1954),* a major work of scholarship. C. Martin Wilbur and Julie Lien-ying How, eds., *Documents on Communism, Nationalism, and Soviet Advisers in China, 1918–1927. Papers Seized in the 1927 Peking Raid* (1956) reveals Communist tactics and intra-party rivalries. T'ang Leang-li, *The Inner History of the Chinese Revolution* (London, 1930) gives a favorable interpretation of the rise of the *Kuomintang* and a justification of both the

Soviet orientation and its later repudiation. Leng Shao Chuan and Norman Palmer, *Sun Yat-sen and Communism* (1960) shows how the Western failure to assess correctly Chinese Nationalism inclined Sun toward the Soviet. Xenia J. Eudin and Robert C. North, eds., *Soviet Russia and the East, 1920–1927* (1957) includes documents pertaining to China. Xenia J. Eudin and Robert C. North, *M. N. Roy's Mission to China, the Communist-Kuomintang Split of 1927* (1963), an important recent study. *Biographical Dictionary of Republican China, Vol. I: Ai-Ch'u*, Howard L. Boorman and Richard C. Howard, eds. (1967), the beginning of an invaluable reference series.

CHINA AND THE POWERS. Robert T. Pollard, *China's Foreign Relations, 1917–1931* (1933), a useful reference. Wesley R. Fishel, *The End of Extraterritoriality in China* (1952), a detailed historical study. See also S. F. Wright, *China's Struggle for Tariff Autonomy, 1843–1938* (Shanghai, 1938). For the special role of the United States see Dorothy Borg, *American Policy and the Chinese Revolution, 1925–1928* (1947). Marius B. Jansen, *The Japanese and Sun Yat-sen* (1954), an important study. In addition to the studies of Sino-Soviet relations listed above note Peter S. H. Tang, *Russian and Soviet Policy in Manchuria and Outer Mongolia* (1959).

The Manchurian Crises,
1929-1937

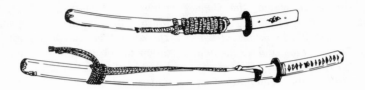

chapter 25

The years during which the *Kuomintang* established its leadership in China were also those in which China sought to strengthen its ties with Manchuria. Although the Manchu dynasty and the later Republic had asserted Chinese sovereignty in Manchuria, Russia and Japan had continued to build spheres of influence there. For these latter two countries, Manchuria had assumed increasing importance. After 1895, Russia, and later Japan, considered Manchuria as the strategic base of East Asian politics. After the Chinese Eastern Railways was built, Manchuria assumed economic importance because of its natural wealth. By 1928, for example, the total value of Manchuria's agricultural products, including such principal crops as soy beans, kaoliang, wheat, millet, and barley, most of which were exported, was some $650,000,000. There had also been extensive exploitation of the rich timber lands and of such minerals as coal, iron, and gold. This development of a frontier region was due in part to the capital and managerial investments of Russia and Japan. Yet while Russia and Japan were busily extending their interests, millions of Chinese peasants from Shantung had taken pos-

session of Manchurian soil and in this sense had made it irrevocably Chinese.[1] Nor did Manchurian politics fall completely under foreign domination. During the years 1905–1928, Manchuria's government was headed by Chang Tso-lin, an erstwhile bandit turned statesman. Although he was long reputed a friend of Japan, he appeared less willing in his later years to permit Japan's "special position" to go unchallenged. It was he who prepared the way for an attack on Russia's Chinese Eastern Railway in 1929 and who initiated a policy of Chinese railway construction "which was to cut off the [Japanese] South Manchuria Railway from some of its feeder districts."[2] His son and successor, Chang Hsueh-liang, also resented the presence of Russia and Japan. In December, 1928, the younger Chang announced his allegiance to the Nanking government, accepted the Nationalist flag, and in turn was made commander-in-chief of the North-Eastern Fron-

[1] By 1931 Manchuria had an estimated population of 30,000,000 persons, of whom some 28,000,000 were Chinese (including a small percentage of native Manchus), 500,000 or more Mongols, 800,000 Koreans, 150,000 Russians, and some 230,000 Japanese.

[2] League of Nations, *Report of the Commission of Inquiry* [The Lytton Commission] (Geneva, 1932), 24–30.

tier (Manchurian) Army and was confirmed as chief of administration of Manchuria and part of Inner Mongolia.

Young Chang's opposition to Russia and Japan was not simply a matter of his conversion to the new nationalism. While his motivation may have had a nationalist tinge, his actions tended to follow the patterns set by other warlords. Chang Tso-lin, his father, had alternately supported, attacked, or declared his territory independent of the Central Government; but this did not mean that he wished to be separated from China or that his goal was to set up a separate nation-state. Rather, it was part of the strategy by which one warlord or another hoped to exterminate his rivals and to emerge as head of a unified national China. Chang Hsueh-liang's maneuvers were prompted by a desire to strengthen his own position by driving out the foreign intruders.[3] The result was that so far as the internal administration of Manchuria was involved, the association with Nanking was nominal rather than real. A Manchurian headquarters of the *Kuomintang* was established, but in reality the old system continued to function without substantial change. The Nanking government merely confirmed what the Manchurian authorities were pleased to do. However, if there was little change in domestic policy, the allegiance of Manchuria to the Nationalist government produced results of great consequence in foreign policy. To the "forward policy" adopted by Chang Tso-lin before his death there was added after 1928 a well organized and systematic *Kuomintang* propaganda which dwelt ceaselessly on the necessity of recovering lost sovereign rights, the abolition of unequal treaties, and the wickedness of imperialism. As in other parts of China, there was a tendency for the official *Kuomintang* line to ascribe to the foreigner and imperialism the blame for all troubles to the exclusion of other contributing factors. This propaganda was extremely effective in Manchuria, where the presence of the foreigner with his special rights was

[3] Akira Iriye, "Chang Hsueh-liang and the Japanese," *Journal of Asian Studies* 20 (1960): 33–43.

more obtrusive than in any other part of China except Shanghai. In consequence, Russians, both Reds and Whites, and Japanese, including Koreans as Japanese subjects, soon felt the effects of persecution manifested in specific acts such as increases in rents or refusals to renew contracts.

THE RUSSO-CHINESE CRISIS OF 1929

Nor were these the only difficulties between China and Russia at the time the *Kuomintang* came to power. Since the expulsion of the Communists from the *Kuomintang* in 1927, Sino-Russian relations had grown progressively worse. In Manchuria, these relations had never been happy even after Chang Tso-lin's agreement with the Soviets in 1924 sanctioning joint Sino-Russian operation of the Chinese Eastern Railway. Chang was bitterly anti-Communist. The Soviet was determined to maintain its right to the railway and it used the railroad zone as a base for Communist propaganda. The conflict came into the open in 1927 when Chang, at the time still master of Peking, raided the Soviet headquarters there, charging Russian violation of the no-propaganda clauses of the 1924 Sino-Soviet agreements. Two years later, in May, 1929, Chang Hsueh-liang entered Soviet consulates along the Chinese Eastern Railway, arrested Communist agents, and seized documentary evidence of Soviet subversion. In July Chang's forces took over the railroad telegraph system and arrested Soviet employees, replacing them with Chinese and White Russians. When China did not respond to an ultimatum addressed to both Nanking and Mukden, the Soviets broke off relations while an informal warfare of raids back and forth broke out on the Siberian-Manchurian border.

These border hostilities were a direct challenge to principles of the recently signed treaty for the Renunciation of War, August, 1928, commonly called the Pact of Paris or the Kellogg-Briand Treaty. Accordingly, the new American Secretary of State, Henry L. Stimson, acting on the theory that the treaty should be "a practical instrument for preserving peace," reminded both Russia and China of their obligations to employ peaceful means of settlement. This appeal, approved by other major signatories, brought assurances from Russia and China that they would resort to force only in self-defense.[4]

Meanwhile, negotiations between the Soviet and local Manchurian officials and between the Russian Ambassador and the Chinese Minister in Berlin were abortive. By November there was open though undeclared warfare on the Manchurian border. A Soviet army invaded Manchuria from the west. The forces of Chang Hsueh-liang retreated in confusion. On December 3, Chang agreed to Russia's demands, and Nanking followed suit on December 22.

The brief undeclared war had shown that (1) in Manchuria, Soviet Russia was as jealous of her interests and as ready to defend them by force as was tsarist Russia before her; (2) the Kellogg-Briand Treaty was an ineffective preventive of war; and (3) the National government at Nanking, involved in suppressing opposition in central and northwest China, was incapable of exerting power in the border provinces of the northeast. These conclusions were not lost on Japan's determined expansionists.

SINO-JAPANESE ISSUES IN MANCHURIA

Manchuria had come to represent, by 1931, a fundamental clash of Sino-Japanese as well as Sino-Russian interests. Chinese nationalism regarded it as the "first line of defense;" Japanese governments, as a "lifeline." Chinese called it the "granary of China," while the migration of Chinese peasants to it was a sort of safety valve easing the pressure in overcrowded areas such as Shantung. Japanese felt that they had won Liaotung in 1895; that they had saved

[4] In the Treaty of Paris the signatories: (1) "condemned recourse to war for the solution of international controversies," (2) renounced war "as an instrument of national policy," and (3) agreed that the settlement of all disputes should be by none but pacific means. All signatories reserved the right of self-defense.

Manchuria from Russia in 1905; that Japanese capital was principally responsible for the development of the country; and that by reason of patriotism, defense, and exceptional treaty rights they had thus acquired there a "special position."

Principal among specific issues were conflicts arising out of the Sino-Japanese Manchurian treaty and notes of May, 1915. Whereas after 1915 Japan insisted upon the fulfillment of the treaty, the Chinese persistently denied its validity. The issues tended to become more acute after 1928 when the *Kuomintang* was established in Manchuria. After 1927, too, there was a movement among the Chinese to divest the South Manchuria Railway of its political and administrative functions, making of it a purely commercial enterprise. This was a natural nationalistic aspiration, but it struck at the very basis of Japan's position, which in Manchuria was definitely political. Furthermore, although the original Russo-Chinese Railway Agreement of 1896 conferred upon the original Chinese Eastern Railway Company the "absolute and exclusive administration of its [railway] lands," the Chinese government denied that this conferred political control in the railroad zone. In addition, the activities of Japanese railway guards, both in and outside the railway zone, and of the Japanese consular police became increasingly irritating as Nationalist sentiment in Manchuria grew. These police were located not only in the railroad areas but also at Japanese consulates in various towns: Harbin, Manchouli, and the Chientao District on the Korean border. A further source of conflict was the presence in Manchuria of 800,000 Koreans, who after 1910 were Japanese subjects. As in the case of Japanese, the Chinese opposed acquisition of land in Manchuria by Koreans. Japan, on the other hand, refused to recognize the naturalization of Koreans as Chinese.

Finally, China and Japan had long quarreled over the construction and financing of railways in Manchuria. Japan, utilizing the tactics which the Russians had employed in operating the Chinese Eastern Railway, obtained from her control of railway transportation in South Manchuria not only profit but also political advantage. The semi-official, efficient, profitable, and wealthy S.M.R. (South Manchuria Railway) made it policy to finance the construction of only such Chinese lines as would be "feeders" to its own road terminating in the great port of Dairen. The increasing power of this transportation system under Japanese ownership and control and, in fact, its very existence were repugnant to Chinese Nationalists. After 1924, the Chinese, in spite of Japanese protests that their action violated the secret protocol of the Sino-Japanese Treaty of Peking, December, 1905, built lines paralleling and competing with the S.M.R. system and connecting with the Chinese controlled ports of Yingkow and Hulutao. These lines were quite successful in diverting traffic from the Japanese roads. But this was not the only aspect of China's offensive. China would neither repay loans of 150,000,-000 yen which had been expended in the construction of four major and a number of lesser Chinese railways, nor appoint Japanese railway advisers who were required by agreements. China contended that the loans were primarily strategic and political, that they had been made by the S.M.R. with the idea of monopolizing railway investments, and that the lines were heavily overcapitalized and could not be put on a paying basis. The legal merits of these disputes were never resolved. Moreover, to this legal tangle there was added a miscellaneous assortment of railway and other disputes involving Sino-Japanese agreements, most of which had political and strategic overtones. One of these, the Wanpaoshan Affair (1931) was of little importance in itself, but it led to anti-Chinese riots and bloodshed in Korea, and from there to an anti-Japanese boycott in China. While this furor was at its height, a certain Captain Nakamura, a Japanese intelligence officer, was killed by Chinese troops in Inner Mongolia.[5]

[5] Daniel B. Ramsdell, "The Nakamura Incident and the Japanese Foreign Office," *Journal of Asian Studies* 25 (Nov., 1965): 51–67, examines the impact of the incident on Japanese policy making.

Thus, the Sino-Japanese-Manchurian question by mid-September, 1931, had produced a collision of "irreconcilable policies." As the tension increased, both sides made some efforts toward peaceful solutions, but these were unproductive. The more rabid Chinese Nationalists had so aroused public opinion as to render negotiations virtually impossible. Among Japanese the disposition to conciliate Chinese nationalism through concession was rapidly fading. This shift away from the Shidehara line was due partly to disappointments with the results of Japan's post-war diplomacy. By 1931, a policy based on international co-operation appeared to have failed on a broad range of issues. Japan's efforts to encourage emigration had been rebuffed in the West; her program of trade expansion had not brought new prosperity; and despite the Washington Conference treaties, Japan had been unable to form with the West a common front in dealing with China. The result of these failures was a deepening sense of frustration. This was a mood, furthermore, which was fed by a social and economic crisis in Japan having its roots in world-wide depression. In such a setting Japanese proponents of territorial expansion had little difficulty in recruiting a large domestic audience.

Moreover, for those who in China and Japan favored and planned a policy of force to settle Manchurian issues, September, 1931, was a time well chosen. In Europe there was economic chaos, which had called forth the Hoover Moratorium. England deserted the gold standard in September, and in both England and the United States there was economic distress with which neither government seemed able to deal. If force were applied in Manchuria, it was unlikely that Europe or America would interfere effectively to stop it.

SEPTEMBER 18, 1931 AND AFTER

On the night of September 18, 1931, the Japanese Kwantung army seized the city of Mukden. The hostilities were precipitated, according to the Japanese, by a Chinese

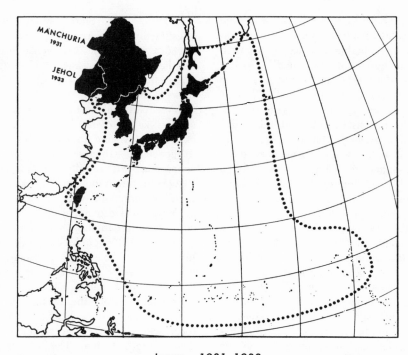

Japan   1931–1933
Reproduced from A War Atlas for Americans *(New York: Simon & Schuster)*
1944, with permission from the publisher and from the U.S. Department of
State, Division of Map Intelligence and Cartography.

attempt to blow up the tracks of the S.M.R. In the light of new materials brought out at the Tokyo War Crimes Trials (diaries, memoirs, and autobiographies), the Manchurian incident of September 18 was engineered by Japanese civilians as well as military extremists who were anxious to find a quick solution to unsolved political problems.[6] Because of advanced preparation for these initial military operations, the Japanese were able to move quickly to seize Changchun and Kirin. During the next three months, the Japanese expanded their operation southward toward the border of China Proper and northward beyond the main line of the Chinese Eastern Railway. On January 2, 1932, the Kwantung army, dispersing the last southern remnants of Chang Hsueh-liang's armies, captured Chinchow, near the Chinese border. As 1932 advanced, Japan

completed her military conquest of Manchuria.[7]

Throughout these months, persistent but ineffective efforts were made to halt the Japanese military and to resolve the issue through peaceful means. Responding to China's appeal under Article XI of the Covenant, the League of Nations tried vainly to interest the powers in imposing sanctions on Japan. On October 24, the League issued an order to the Kwantung army to withdraw to the S.M.R. zone which Japan ignored. Finally, on December 10 a commission was sent to investigate the

[6] Yoshihashi Takehiko, *Conspiracy at Mukden* (1963), offers details not available in other English language sources.

[7] The ultimate intentions of Japan in Manchuria were unclear in September, 1931. It appears, however, that the decision to seize all of Manchuria originated entirely within the Kwantung army and in opposition to the central army authorities and government, both of which sought a settlement on a much more limited scale. Sadako No Ogata, *Defiance in Manchuria: The Making of Japanese Foreign Policy, 1931–1932* (1964), 187.

issue.[8] Meanwhile, the League sought to strengthen its hand by enlisting the support of the United States. The United States, however, concerned lest isolationist sentiment be aroused, maintained that it would act independently and agreed only to consult informally with the League on possible moves. Later, as Japanese operations expanded, Washington took the further step of authorizing Prentiss Gilbert, American Consul in Geneva, to participate in meetings of League Council involving application of the Kellogg-Briand Pact. Apart from its consultations with the League, the United States made representations of its own in Tokyo. The first of these was markedly conciliatory. On September 22, Secretary of State Henry L. Stimson informed the Japanese "that the responsibility for determining the course of events with regard to the liquidating of this [Manchurian] situation rests largely upon Japan," and he hinted that both the Kellogg-Briand Pact and the Nine-Power Open Door Treaty were at stake. At this point Stimson thought it unwise to speak more sternly to the Japanese. The Secretary held that the road to liquidating the Manchurian affair lay in "giving Shidehara and the Foreign Office an opportunity, free from anything approaching a threat or even public criticism, to get control of the situation." It was the difficult problem of letting "the Japanese know that we were watching them and at the same time to do it in a way which will help Shidehara."[9] Later, as it became clear that the Foreign Office would not undo the work of the Kwantung army, Stimson moved toward diplomatic coercion. On January 7, 1932, after informing the British and French of his intention but without waiting for their concurrence, Stimson informed China and Japan that the United States

. . . *cannot admit the legality of any situation* de facto *nor does it intend to recognize any treaty or agreement entered into between those governments, or agents thereof, which may impair the treaty rights of the United States or its citizens in China, including those which relate to the sovereignty, the independence, or the territorial and administrative integrity of the Republic of China, or to the international policy relative to China, commonly known as the open-door policy; and that it does not intend to recognize any situation, treaty, or agreement which may be brought about by means contrary to the covenants and obligations of the Pact of Paris, of August 27, 1928, to which treaty both China and Japan, as well as the United States, are parties.*

The nonrecognition doctrine here asserted was derived from Secretary Bryan's caveat of May, 1915, while the note as a whole was a reassertion of traditional American policy. Stimson assumed that Britain and France would see their far eastern interests as identical with those of the United States and would also make representations in Tokyo, but this assumption was unfounded, for neither country associated itself with this American move.[10]

[8] Detailed treatment is in W. W. Willoughby, *The Sino-Japanese Controversy and the League of Nations* (1935), Chapter 3.

[9] Henry L. Stimson, *The Far Eastern Crisis* (1936), 34–37. For critical comment on the Stimson thesis see George A. Lensen, "Japan and Manchuria: Ambassador Forbes' Appraisal of American Policy toward Japan in the Years, 1931–32," *Monumenta Nipponica: Studies in Japanese Culture* 23 (Nos. 1–2): 66–89.

[10] The ultimate intent of nonrecognition in this instance is not entirely clear. Richard Current has suggested that there were in fact two nonrecognition doctrines. The first was suggested by President Hoover as an alternative to sanctions or militant action. The enunciation of nonrecognition was envisaged by the President as a final measure. Secretary Stimson, on the other hand, saw the doctrine not as an alternative to further action but as a preliminary step to economic and military sanctions, a way of drawing the issue between the United States and Japan. "The Hoover Doctrine and the Stimson Doctrine," *The American Historical Review* 48 (1954): 512–42. Other students of Stimson's diplomacy question whether such a sharp distinction existed between the Secretary and the President. See Robert H. Ferrell, *American Diplomacy in the Great Depression: Hoover-Stimson Foreign Policy, 1929–1933* (1957), 169n; Elting E. Morison, *Turmoil and Tradition: A Study of the Life and Times of Henry L. Stimson* (1960),* 401; and Armin Rappaport, *Henry L. Stimson and Japan, 1931–33* (1963), Chapter 4. For American public reactions to the nonrecognition doctrine see Foster Rhea Dulles, *China and America* (1946).

Toward the end of January, 1932, Sino-Japanese hostilities spread from Manchuria to Shanghai, where a most effective boycott of Japanese goods became the occasion for a naval bombardment of Chinese sections of the city. But, unlike the policy of retreat in Manchuria, at Shanghai a Chinese army (the 19th Route Army) held its position until the arrival early in March of heavy Japanese army reinforcements. Britain, whose interests were now affected seriously, protested Japanese bombings at Shanghai, and concurrently with the United States sent naval and marine reinforcements to the International Settlement. Meanwhile, China invoked Articles X and XV of the Covenant, under which the League was required to assess responsibility and eventually perhaps to apply sanctions. This led to appointment of a League committee at Shanghai consisting of the local consular representatives of the League states to report directly on conditions there. The United States, making use of an open letter from Secretary Stimson to the Chairman of the Senate Foreign Relations Committee, issued on February 24 a general appeal to the powers to associate themselves with the non-recognition doctrine.

For a time there was some improvement. The League Assembly, March, 1932, aligned itself with the nonrecognition doctrine, and in May, China and Japan made peace at Shanghai on terms worked out by the consular committee of the League. But these improvements were at best temporary. The League's disarmament conference in the spring of 1932 revealed the inability of Europe and America to agree on any formula for arms reduction, let alone an effective united front against Japan.[11] As a result, Japan was accorded a virtual free hand in Manchuria. Since the beginning of 1932, the

Japanese had encouraged and promoted the organization of local self-governing bodies throughout Manchuria which had gradually combined into a new "State" that had declared its independence of China and the *Kuomintang*, February 18. On March 9, the former and last emperor of China, known as Henry P'u-yi, became regent of the new state of Manchukuo, and on September 15, Japan in a treaty extended formal recognition to the "offspring of aggression." Less than a month later, October 2, the report of the League's investigating body, the Lytton Commission, made its anti-climactic appearance.

THE REPORT OF THE COMMISSION OF INQUIRY

On the course of immediate events, the report had no influence at all, but as a clarification of the issues at stake, and as a plan for peaceful settlement (for anyone who wanted a peaceful settlement), its importance could hardly be overestimated.[12] The report presented Manchuria as a complex product of historical development involving conditions unparalleled elsewhere, and found that neither a restoration of the *status quo ante* nor the continued maintenance of Manchukuo provided a solution. Japan's reply to the report, November 21, 1932, insisted that Japan alone was the judge whether her military action was justifiable self-defense.

At the League, the report of the Commission was considered by a special Committee of Nineteen, which in February, 1933,

---

[11] Great Britain and the United States did maintain limited naval co-operation in the Pacific aimed at checking Japanese expansion. See Gerald E. Wheeler, "Isolated Japan: Anglo-American Diplomatic Co-operation, 1927–1936," *The Pacific Historical Review* 30 (1961): 165–78.

[12] Members of the Commission included: H. E. Count Aldrovandi (Italian); General de Division, Henri Claudel (French); the Rt. Hon. Earl of Lytton (British), chairman, H. E. Dr. Heinrich Schnee (German); and Major-General Frank Ross McCoy (American), who served with the approval of the Department of State but as an official representative of the League and not of the United States. This was a nice distinction, since the United States was not a member of the League, though in the Manchurian dispute the United States, in the opinion of many, had gone a long way toward entering the League by the back door.

recommended: (1) nonrecognition of Manchukuo, (2) a Manchurian government compatible with Chinese sovereignty, and (3) an invitation to Japan and China to undertake direct negotiations under the good offices of a League commission. Japan's response was the invasion of Jehol province in January, 1933; a dramatic scene at Geneva where the Japanese delegation, headed by Matsuoka Yosuke, walked out of the Assembly, February 24; and finally, March 27, Japan's announcement of her withdrawal from the League, which under terms of the Convenant would become effective in two years' time. Meanwhile, Japanese armies were completing the conquest of Jehol province. Other forces invaded the Peiping area south of the Great Wall, where at Tangku a truce was signed, May 31, 1933, creating a broad "demilitarized neutral" zone from which all Chinese military forces were excluded. This invasion of North China pointed directly toward Japanese control of North China by the creation of an autonomous buffer state.[13]

MANCHURIA: INTERPRETATIONS

By the application of force, Japan had gained control of nearly half a million square miles of territory by means which the international legal opinion of governments did not regard as war, and which the Japanese termed euphemistically an "incident." It was peaceful war, or war that is not war at all. Nevertheless, the effect was to reshape Eastern Asia more radically than any previous "incident" since the British in 1842 had fashioned the Treaty of Nanking. Japan's creation of Manchukuo was an effort to establish a continental power in Asia as a counterbalance to the maritime power which Western nations had exercised over China through nearly a century.[14]

In a broader sense, the Manchurian "in-

---

[13] George E. Taylor, *The Struggle for North China* (1940), 17. On Japan's withdrawal from the League, see League of Nations, *Official Journal* 14 (1933): 657–58.

[14] Owen Lattimore, *The Mongols of Manchuria* (1934), 15.

cident" was a second and more disheartening test of collective security as a principle, and of the means of enforcing it. As Russia used direct action in North Manchuria in 1929, so Japan used force in South Manchuria and North China from 1931 to 1933. Although the League of Nations performed a useful task through the investigations of the Lytton Commission, neither France nor Great Britain, the powers which dominated the League, was prepared to apply sanctions against Japan without the active support of the United States. The question of sanctions was settled for all the powers when they received no encouragement from Washington in 1931. Moreover, while the United States co-operated to a limited degree with the League, this country remained outside the world's only permanent machinery dedicated to the principle of collective security, and the American administration was constantly fearful of public reaction should it appear that it was using Manchuria as a back-door entry into the League. In reality, American policy, as the Manchurian affair developed in 1931, remained true to traditional principles of the open door and the integrity of China as embodied in the Washington Treaties, and it called upon Japan to observe these covenants and the Treaty for the Renunciation of War. It prodded the League toward similar action. Whether more could have been expected from a government representative of the same political faith which a decade earlier had repudiated the Wilsonian program of collective security is a matter on which there has been no general agreement. At all events, neither the League nor the United States nor the two together stopped Japan, and the integrity of China was not preserved by reassertion of the nonrecognition doctrine.

Moreover, the complex causes that led to Japan's seizure of Manchuria will continue to tax the resourcefulness of history. The most widely held and popular interpretation in the years after 1931, especially in the United States, was that Japanese militarism unleashed in Manchuria was simply unprovoked aggression and that these Japanese acts were responsible primarily for the whole later train of events which led to the breakdown of collective security, to the outbreak of war in Europe, and then to Pearl Harbor. The simplicity of this interpretation has been popular in the democracies, but it has been challenged. It was the considered judgment of Joseph C. Grew, American ambassador to Japan from 1932 until Pearl Harbor, that the Lytton *Report,* the primary evidence in Japan's condemnation, was basic but not definitive.[15] Grew emphasized the special importance of the authoritative but unorthodox and unpublicized opinions of John V. A. MacMurray, former United States Minister at Peking and profound student of China, whose unpublished reflections on the Manchurian affair were summarized privately for the Department of State in 1935. In brief it was MacMurray's judgment that (*1*) for nearly ten years Japan tried to preserve the letter and spirit of the Washington Treaties in the face of Chinese intransigence: (*2*) the Treaty Powers sought in the Far East to advance their selfish interests at the expense of collective security; (*3*) when China abrogated unilaterally her treaties with Japan, Japanese forces were bound to act for the protection of life and property; (*4*) the effect of American policy was to condone China's behavior and to encourage her to further recalcitrance; (*5*) the Chinese were willful in their scorn of legal obligations, provocative in their methods, and reckless in resort to violence; and (*6*) the policy of co-operation which might have averted Japanese action was scorned by the Chinese and ignored by the British and the Americans with the result that Japan was finally persuaded she could depend only on force to defend her legal position in China.[16]

CONSOLIDATION OF MANCHUKUO AFTER 1932

Meanwhile, the new state of Manchukuo was the scene of striking developments in the years following 1932. In 1933 its borders were extended by the Japanese conquest of Jehol, a province in eastern Inner Mongolia. On March 1, 1934, Henry P'u-yi, who had served as the Japanese appointed regent, was enthroned as the Emperor Kangte. Under a constitution of the same date, Manchukuo became a monarchy with both executive and legislative authority exercised by the emperor, though the latter powers were subject to the approval of a Legislative Council. Real power, however, remained in the hands of the Japanese Ambassador to Manchukuo who was at the same time commander of Japanese and Manchukuo troops and governor of the Kwantung leased territory.

The subsequent industrial exploitation of Manchukuo represented a fantastic influx of Japanese capital. Prior to the Manchurian incident of 1931, Japanese investments in the South Manchurian sphere of influence amounted to 1,617,000,000 Yen, nearly 50 per cent of which represented outlays of the South Manchuria Railway. In 1938, total Japanese investments in Manchukuo were about 3,441,000,000 Yen and by the end of 1939 the figure had reached 4,500,000,000. Much of this investment took the form of imports of mining, factory, and textile machinery, and of consumer goods.[17]

In line with the American Nonrecognition Doctrine, none of the great powers save Japan at first recognized Manchukuo—and of the small powers, only El Salvador, the Papacy, and the Dominican Republic had extended recognition by 1934. Germany, however, gave qualified recognition in a trade agreement of the same year, renewed for a second three years in 1937; and in November, 1937, Italy formally recognized the puppet state. Full German recognition came on May 12, 1938, and was soon followed by recognition from Poland and Hungary. On February 24, 1939, Manchukuo became a signatory of the Anti-Comintern Pact concluded by Germany and Japan on November 25, 1936. Soviet Russia extended a *de facto* recognition. After two years of negotiations, 1933–1935, Russia sold its

[15] Joseph C. Grew, *The Turbulent Era* (2 vols., 1952), II, 928–29.

[16] Grew, *The Turbulent Era,* II, 929–30.

[17] E. B. Schumpeter, ed., *The Industrialization of Japan and Manchukuo, 1930–1940* (1940), 398.

rights in the Chinese Eastern Railway to Manchukuo, the payment being guaranteed by Japan.

During the decade of the 1930s, the international politics and government of Manchukuo were ordered better than the outside world of nonrecognizing powers was prepared to admit. Under an authoritarian, regimented regime, Manchuria possessed greater stability than at any time in its modern history. Chinese who resisted were hunted down and eliminated. For those who accepted the regime, there could be increased security for life and property.[18]

By 1937 Japan had made considerable progress toward integrating the economic and strategic values of Manchukuo with those of the home land. In general, the idea had been that Manchuria would provide the raw materials in minerals and foodstuffs lacked by Japan's growing industrial society. On the credit side Manchurian population was rapidly increasing, new farm lands were being opened, industry, particularly coal, iron, and steel, was expanding. On the debit side was the instability of the international picture pervaded by the insatiable fever of the Kwantung army to insure the borders of the new state by pushing its boundaries into Mongolia and by forcing the establishment of friendly governments in North China.

FURTHER JAPANESE ADVANCES

Having established herself in Manchuria, Japan also moved into Inner Mongolia. Her interests in that region had been clearly expressed in the Twenty-one Demands of 1915. Inner Mongolia was a potential base from which to control North China, and a barrier against Russian expansion

[18] Although in general this was true, there is also evidence that those who suffered from Japanese rule were not solely those who resisted. See in particular the picture presented by W. I. Ladejinsky, "Manchurian Agriculture under Japanese Control," *Foreign Agriculture* 5 (1941): 309–40. Moreover, there was great economic pressure on the people of Manchuria as Japan's war program developed. These factors all served to keep alive a Manchurian resistance movement.

from Outer Mongolia. Moreover, the Kwantung army believed that it could play upon the existing friction between the Mongol herdsmen and Chinese farmer colonists. After 1912 Chinese farmers had encroached upon Inner Mongolian lands that were marginal between farming and grazing. In the period of republican China after 1912, Inner Mongolia had been incorporated as provinces of China—Jehol, Chahar, Suiyuan, and Ning-hsia. Chinese farmers from heavily populated areas south of the Wall had been encouraged to migrate to these areas.

The first step in Japan's advance was the creation by the Kwantung army of an autonomous Mongol province in western Manchuria incorporating part of Jehol, which had been added to Manchukuo in 1933. Here, by guaranteeing the Mongols possession of their grazing lands, by insuring and respecting their autonomous government, and by fostering the privileges of the Lama priests, the Japanese hoped to appeal to the Mongols in general, including those in Outer Mongolia. The scheme was not entirely successful, since the Mongol princes bargained also with the Chinese Nationalists at Nanking.

Just as the Kwantung army felt it necessary to move westward into Inner Mongolia, so it became even more essential to establish friendly governments in the northeastern sections of China Proper, especially in the provinces of Hopei, Shantung and Shansi. These provinces could be linked, so it was thought, with the Inner Mongolian provinces of Chahar and Suiyuan (yet to be conquered) to give Japan control of all bordering territory to the south and west of Manchukuo. Also, as in the case of Inner Mongolia, Japanese action was declared to be in self-defense. In North China this argument was more plausible, since here the country was controlled after 1932 by Chang Hsueh-liang and his armies, which had retreated from Manchuria. His hopes of regaining his home land and his resistance to the Japanese in Jehol provided the occasion though not the cause for bringing the Kwantung army south of the Wall into the Peiping and Tientsin area where in May, 1933, the Tangku truce was signed. This provided for demili-

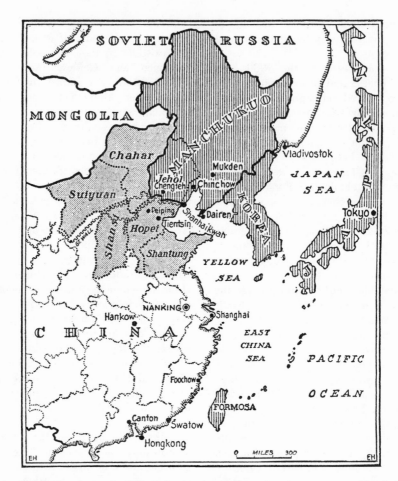

In 1935, Imperialistic groups in Japan favored creation of an autonomous North China, free from the political control of Nanking and under the tutelage of Manchukuo. (Courtesy of the New York Times)

tarization of portions of Hopei province but not for removal of Japanese troops maintained between Peiping and Tientsin under the Boxer Protocol. Chinese police "friendly" to Japan were to maintain order in the demilitarized areas. Confusion was compounded by the fact that the Tangku truce and other agreements subsequently reached were negotiated with local officials whose relationship to the Nanking government was not always clear. Nevertheless, there was temporary improvement since in the two years following the truce postal service and rail traffic, passenger and freight, was resumed between Manchukuo and China, though without the latter extending formal recognition. Underlying friction, however, was unabated, and by 1935 the Kwantung army had exerted enough pressure to force the retirement of more Chinese troops from Hopei and to liquidate the *Kuomintang* in the region. This penetration of North China was all aimed toward the creation of an autonomous North China state to be composed of the five provinces of Chahar, Suiyuan, Shansi, Hopei, and Shantung. This plan was abortive, but it contributed to a general demoralization in North China where the Nanking government sought to preclude exclusive Japanese control by sanctioning local governments that would work with the Japanese.

Simultaneously with the Japanese infiltration into North China came renewed efforts by Japanese diplomacy to reach an understanding with China as a whole. There was always the hope among Japanese statesmen that a workable arangement could be reached for close political and economic planning among Japan, Manchukuo, and China. Japan's success in Manchukuo and the continued factional strife within China lent some encouragement to the Japanese hope. Indeed, on the surface, Japan appeared to make some progress. There were elements within the *Kuomintang*-National Government which were prepared to adopt a policy of appeasement either from personal conviction on the principle of a Pan-Asiatic policy or because they regarded resistance by China as hopeless. Consequently, during 1935, Nanking made some efforts to stop anti-Japanese boycotts, to prevent publication of inflammatory anti-Japanese articles, and to suppress the student movement. Yet Nanking was not entirely subservient. When in 1934 Japan warned the League powers and the United States to follow a policy of "hands off" China, the Nanking government denied the right of Japan to assert a monopoly of political interest in the Far East. It all added up to a situation in North China in which by 1936 there was no Sino-Japanese war but neither was there a Sino-Japanese peace.

FOR FURTHER READING

Peter S. H. Tang, *Russian and Soviet Policy in Manchuria and Outer Mongolia* (1959) has a chapter on the undeclared Sino-Soviet war of 1929. Material on Sino-Soviet difficulties is also to be found in Max Beloff, *Foreign Policy of Soviet Russia, 1929–1941* (2 vols., London, 1953). For interpretations of issues between China and Japan see: H. L. Kingman, *Effects of Chinese Nationalism upon Manchurian Railway Developments, 1925–1931* (1932); K. K. Kawakami, *Manchoukuo: Child of Conflict* (1933), an able Japanese apology; and Seiji G. Hishida, *Japan Among the Great Powers:*

A Survey of Her International Relations (1940). The official Chinese case as presented to the Lytton Commission is *Memoranda Presented to the Lytton Commission* (2 vols., Tokyo, 1932). Oka Takashi, "Saionji and the Manchurian Crisis," *Papers on China*, Vol. 8. Published and distributed by the East Asian Research Center, Harvard University (1953) emphasizes the Japanese political background.

W. A. Williams, "China and Japan: A Challenge and a Choice of the Nineteen Twenties," *The Pacific Historical Review* 26 (1957): 259–79, views Stimson's diplomacy in the light of American policy over the preceding decade. Paul H. Clyde, "The Diplomacy of 'Playing No Favorites': Secretary Stimson and Manchuria, 1931," *The Mississippi Valley Historical Review* 35 (1948) reveals the caution and limited purposes of the Secretary. For an American Ambassador's memoirs see Joseph C. Grew, *Ten Years in Japan* (1944). R. Basset, *Democracy and Foreign Policy: A Case History; The Sino-Japanese Dispute, 1931–33* (1952) studies British public opinion. Harriet L. Moore, *Soviet Far Eastern Diplomacy, 1931–1945* (1945) chronicles what Russia said and did. See also Frank M. Tamagna, *Italy's Interests and Policies in the Far East* (1941). Sara R. Smith, *The Manchurian Crisis, 1931–1932* (1948) is useful chiefly for its discussion of the League of Nations. On legal aspects see Robert Langer, *Seizure of Territory: The Stimson Doctrine and Related Principles in Legal Theory and Diplomatic Practice* (1947).

On Japan in Manchuria after the crisis note: F. C. Jones, *Manchuria Since 1931* (London, 1949); and John R. Stewart, *Manchuria Since 1931* (1936). Norton S. Ginsburg, "Manchurian Railway Development," *The Far Eastern Quarterly*, 8 (1948–49): 398–411, covers the period 1931–45 in the light of Japan's strategic purposes respecting Russia. Ch'ing Hsuan-t'ung, *The Last Manchu*, ed. with an introduction by Paul Kramer; Kuo Ying Tsai, trans. (1967), excerpts from the original manuscript of the last Ch'ing emperor who also served as the titular head of Manchukuo.

Politics in Japan and China,
1931-1941

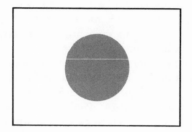

chapter 26

The Manchurian upheaval of 1931 onward was impressive evidence that Japan and China were at war. No matter by what nice terms, legal or political, these events were labeled, the fact was that there had been resort to international hostilities on a large scale, that these hostilities had produced no acceptable solutions for either Japan or China, that the world machinery for collective security had not preserved peace, and that the Far East had become more rather than less explosive. There was also impressive evidence that Japan and China were at war each within and against itself, and it is to the nature of these respective internal conflicts that some attention must now be given. After World War I a newly industrial Japan and a newly national and revolutionary China were achieving a new position in the community of nations and creating new societies at home. Each nation was beset by political, economic, and social instability. In each, men fought with ideas and institutions and guns for political power. In what directions was this turbulence carrying the peoples of Japan and China? What kinds of societies lay just beyond the political horizon? Were they to be authoritarian or responsible, totalitarian or democratic, capitalistic or socialistic, subservient or free?

JAPAN, 1931: THE POLITICAL ATMOSPHERE

When the Kwantung army acted on its own authority in Manchuria in 1931, it had behind it in Japan a people prepared to follow any leadership that offered a positive solution for the nation's ills. Japan was deep in the world depression. Population had been increasing at nearly one million annually, overtaxing the country's food supply. The national economy was not absorbing the more than 400,000 new workers annually who were seeking employment. The farmer, already debt-ridden, faced decreasing income. Capital was concentrated in a few great families. Small business was near bankruptcy and without a voice in economic policy. Hamaguchi's theoretically sound policy of retrenchment and return in 1929 to the gold standard, cut deeply into Japan's exports of goods and doubled her exports of gold, a dire condition for a nation that lived by foreign trade. The whole economic picture with its social implications was fearful. Added to these economic difficulties were frustrations in domestic politics and foreign policy. While party government was not without accomplishments, the political record of the 1920s was marred by vacillation, ineptness, and corruption. Japan's restraint in foreign policy did not forestall anti-Japanese demonstrations in China nor criticism of her ambitions by the West. Thus the stage was set beautifully for those who had long been ready to say that responsible party government was a fraud and that Japan must return to the leadership of her "true" patriots.

By 1931 such critics were rapidly gaining importance. Their themes were not new. In the Meiji era ultranationalists had proclaimed their loyalty to the throne, their mystical belief in Japan's destiny as leader of all Asia, and their conviction that the Japanese possessed superlative inborn qualities which set them apart from others. Proponents of these ideas formed societies aimed at promoting the faith. But these societies were not numerous until the 1920s, when some 600 or more groups were spawned in response to the social and economic changes of the war years. Most societies in the 1920s were short-lived and had little voice in national policy, their views making little impression on those with political authority. The Manchurian incident, however, which resulted partly from plots hatched by members of one of the ultranationalist societies, the *Sakurakai* (The Society of the Cherry), tipped the balance toward the extremists.

As their numbers increased, ultranationalists looked to the military for leadership. Not only were the army and navy held to be less tainted with democratic ideals, but also they were seen as the natural proponents of a "desirable" and continued military expansion. The officer corps, especially junior officers whose education was often narrowly technical, reciprocated by supporting (sometimes even joining) ultranationalist groups. The common ground between civilian extremists and young officers was the conviction that Japan's post-war liberalism and democracy pointed toward national decline. This was a conviction, moreover, which, among the military, was strengthened by sympathy

for the plight of an oppressed peasantry. Since the military drew heavily from a rural and small town populace, the officer corp shared peasant resentment of the businessman's political and economic ascendency. Indeed, after 1931 the military became a champion of agrarian interests against city groups, especially the capitalists.

The pretensions of the civilian and military extremists were encouraged by deeply rooted national traditions. Japanese nationalism in its formative years of the Meiji period was fashioned not primarily by a middle class but rather by military and agrarian leadership which, jealous of the rising power of the commercial urban class, revived the traditional symbols of Shinto, the emperor as ruler and high-priest, and the union of peasant and soldier. These reglorified symbols of an earlier military-agrarian society were never replaced by Western middle-class symbols as Japan moved further into industrialization and modernization. As a result her modern nationalism was less an expression of liberal and democratic principles than of traditional authoritarian concepts. The intellectual soil of Japan in 1931 was deeply infected with the potentials of chauvinism. All that was needed was the intrigue, the conspiracy, and the fanaticism of "true patriots."

THE NEW JAPANISM

The tone and temper of Rightist ultranationalism, the new Japanism was best personified by General Araki Sadao, who had risen from humble birth and from labor in a soya bean sauce factory to become Minister of War, 1931–1934. In appearance and temperament a mild and ascetic priest rather than a saber-rattling samurai, Araki was a soldier, simple in personal habits and single-minded in his devotion to *Kodo*, the Imperial Way. It was Araki who became the spiritual leader and the politico-ethical spokesman of a new Japan. As this Japan faced a world hostile toward her because of her continental expansion, Araki rationalized ultranationalism and foreign conquest in terms of the high ethical principles which clothed the traditional Japanese doctrines of *Kodo* and *Kokutai* (National Polity).[1] The implications of *Kodo* and of *Hakko ichiu* (the world under one roof) were reinterpreted as Japan's universal and benign mission designed to bring peace to the world. In East Asia, this mission would spread the beneficent rule of the emperor to those benighted peoples whose rulers had failed them or who had fallen a prey to Western exploitation and the doctrines of capitalism and liberalism. At home *Kodo* would direct Japanese footsteps into the forsaken paths of her own indigenous culture. From these paths she had been enticed, so it was said, by pernicious Western cults—liberalism, capitalism, democracy, individualism, and even communism—and the result had been a Japan where political life was usurped by corrupt political parties, where capitalists grew wealthy while peasants could not eat the rice they grew—a Japan weakened at home and thus denied the right to rescue Asia from European and American exploitation.[2]

Organizations such as the *Yuzonsha* (Society to Preserve the National Essence) nurtured other national messiahs such as Kita Ikki and Okuwa Shumei, whose writings called for a new authoritarianism under the Emperor's guidance, safeguarding and promoting military power. Other reformers proposed a return to an agrarian-centered economy. In addition to these clearly revolutionary groups, there were conservatives of the oligarchy, the army, the bureaucracy, and business, who, fearing revolution and upholding the Imperial interpretation of the Meiji constitution, were emphatically antidemocratic. The most active personalities of this grouping were organized in the *Kokuhonsha* (National Foundation Society). Among its members were a galaxy of Japanese leaders whose views and interests were

far from identical, such as Admiral Saito Makoto and General Araki Sadao. Clearly the new mood as reflected in the drift of Japan's leadership was suspicious, if not fearful, of democratic trends. By 1933, the *Seiyukai* was parroting the slogans of the young officers, the rabid Nationalists, and was appealing to Japanese education and religion (Shinto) to revive the Japanese spirit and the Imperial Way.

The advocates of ultranationalism were ever alert to ferret out the enemies that bored from within. Those Japanese reputed to be friends of Westernism or democracy and responsible government were especially suspect. They were the purveyors of "dangerous thoughts." The most famous case of this sort of attack on intellectual freedom had as its victim Minobe Tatsukichi, a distinguished professor of constitutional law who had long been known for his constitutional theory of the emperor. His books were widely known and he was a respected member of the Peers. He was not a radical and it would be difficult to know on what grounds he could even be called a liberal. His theory of the emperor was not exactly a democratic doctrine; in its simplest form it was that the emperor was an organ of the State and not the State itself. But this proposition was all that was needed by the superpatriots in their search for subversives. The fact that the doctrine had long been taught and accepted by many respectable men was irrelevant. What did matter was that in 1935 the ultranationalists had made of Minobe a traitor to the Imperial Way. Minobe's logical protest that if the emperor's sovereignty was inherent in his being and person then the Meiji constitution was meaningless, fell on deaf ears. The clamor of the nationalists and also of the *Seiyukai* politicians forced Minobe's resignation from the Peers and from his professorship. Hardly a voice was raised in his defense.[3]

[1] *Kokutai* as used by the Japanese is meant to suggest that unity of the state which results from the unqualified loyalty of the people to the Imperial line "unbroken through ages eternal."

[2] D. C. Holtom, *Modern Japan and Shinto Nationalism* (rev. ed., 1947), 21–23.

[3] Minobe's "organic theory" brought him into direct conflict with the "historical school" of constitutional lawyers who maintained that by his doctrine he had violated the principles and essence of Japanese nationalism known as *national polity*. The advocates of Japanese expan-

Such irresponsible assaults on respectable men did not mean that the chauvinists were all of one mind. Within the top echelons of the army itself were violent factional disputes which were carried in some cases to solution by murder. Furthermore, as the 1930s advanced, there was faltering opposition to the extremes of militarism from conservative officials of the court as well as from other sources. Moreover, while by 1940 the old political parties had dissolved themselves to make way for a single, exclusive, and official political party known as the Imperial Rule Assistance Association, extremists never created in concept or reality a *Fuhrer*. Even General Premier Tojo Hideki, the man who carried Japan into total war in 1941, was never a Hitler. Japan's authoritarianism borrowed from the West but did not imitate the West.

EXTREMISTS SEEK CONTROL

The political history of Japan after 1931 is a history of extreme nationalism nurtured in a strong historical military tradition and directed by a politically minded authoritarian military caste. In 1932, as the success of the Manchurian invasion gave weight to demands for a "stronger foreign policy," the activities of the ultranationalists became violent. On February 9, Inouye Junnosuke, former Finance Minister and manager of the *Minseito*, was murdered, and Dan Takuma, Managing Director of the Mitsui, was murdered on March 5. On May 15, Prime Minister Inukai Tsuyoshi was assassinated by a small band of naval officers and farmers who believed Japan could not be purified until the old politicians and parties were destroyed. Significantly, all of the dead had been outspoken foes of those who sought expansion of Japanese foreign interests through force.

Ten days after Inukai's assassination, the *Seiyukai* cabinet resigned, thus destroying the last vestige of party government. While the fall of the cabinet ended an era begun by Hara in 1918, the event did not mean the immediate adoption of a new theory or structure of government or that the extremists were in unchallenged control. What did happen was an attempted return to tradition, a return to government by elder statesmen who could balance opposing political elites, preserve national unity, and prevent revolution or exclusive army control. When, in 1932, Saionji, the only surviving *Genro*, recommended that the emperor call on Admiral Viscount Saito Makoto to form a national government, he was appealing to Japanese political genius of the late Meiji period. Saito, an admiral, was acceptable to the army though not its choice. He was acceptable in a society where status still prevailed because of his rank and membership in the aristocracy. The bankrupt political parties could accept him because, though not a party man, he had shown them no violent opposition. The court circle, the financiers, and reasonable men of independent judgment saw in Saito the hope of moderation. The Saito cabinet included five party men, three from the *Seiyukai*, two from the *Minseito*, two bureaucrats, three militarists, and three members of the House of Peers. It survived until 1934. Thereafter until 1941 nine governments trampled on the heels of their predecessors. The high mortality in these administrations was symptomatic of the turbulent instability of Japanese political society. Saito's immediate successor, Admiral Okada Keisuke, followed the Saito pattern in cabinet personnel. Thereafter cabinets became less "national" and more representative of the growing power of the militarists and the "fascists." [4]

sionism could not tolerate a philosophy that claimed the emperor was a mere functionary of the state. Frank O. Miller, *Minobe Tatsukichi: Interpreter of Constitutionalism in Japan* (1965). For a study of the opposition to Minobe see George M. Wilson, *Radical Nationalist in Japan: Kita Ikki, 1883–1937* (1969).

[4] On Saito's position, see Ippei Fukuda, *Sketches of Men and Life* (Tokyo, 1933), 27–34. On the fall of cabinet government, Robert A. Scalapino, *Democracy and the Party Movement in Prewar Japan* (1953), 370–71. Premiers who headed "national" cabinets, 1931–1941, included: 1932, Admiral Viscount Saito Makoto; 1934, Admiral Okada Keisuke; 1936, Hirota Koki; 1937, General Hayashi Senjuro; 1937, Prince

Indicative of these trends were efforts to undo the work of the elections of February, 1936, in which the Nationalist parties and the *Seiyukai* lost ground, and in which leftist parties and the more moderate *Minseito* made a surprisingly strong showing. Extremists reacted swiftly to this evidence of continued opposition to their cause. On February 26, four days after the announcement of the election returns, junior officers and a regiment of troops en route to Manchuria attempted by force to overthrow the Okada cabinet. The mutineers murdered Takahashi Korekiyo, the Minister of Finance; Admiral Viscount Saito Makoto, Lord Keeper of the Privy Seal; and General Watanabe Jotaro, Inspector General of Military Education. They attempted to kill Premier Okada but murdered his brother-in-law by mistake. For three days the heart of Tokyo was held by the mutinous troops.

Although for the moment the army's prestige was weakened by these outrages, it soon recovered when apologists painted the assassins as young men pure in heart whose sole motive was to restore the "national spirit." Fundamentally the political picture had not been changed, for although the new government formed by Hirota Koki, March 9, 1936, was composed of moderate militarists and civilian bureaucrats, the influence of the army remained high, each minister having been approved by General Count Terauchi Juichi, the Minister of War. Perhaps more important was the way in which the maneuverings of the moderates versus the extreme militarists added to the confusion of thought and alignment among civilian groups. Factionalism was already present in the bureaucracy, and within the major political parties

Konoye Fumimaro; 1939, Baron Hiranuma Kiichiro; 1940, Admiral Yonai Mitsumasa; 1940, Prince Konoye Fumimaro; 1941, Prince Konoye Fumimaro; 1941, General Tojo Hideki. From 1939 on, cabinet changes hardly affected national policy. Policy was determined not by cabinets but by a small flexible group of military and civilian oligarchs finding some compromise between factions seeking power. It was the *Genro* idea without any genuine *Genro*, since Saionji's power had declined with age and circumstances. He died in 1940.

the *Seiyukai* had long since shown its willingness to support extremes of nationalism. Now there were signs that the great Mitsui house was beginning to look with qualified favor toward extremists at home who could be counted as expansionists abroad. Younger and lesser known capitalists such as Aikawa Yoshisuke, heading army-sponsored industry in Manchukuo, had already accepted army backing as a convenient means of breaking into the industrial monopoly of the established *Zaibatsu* houses. The net result was, as the crosscurrents of domestic conflict increased, that the Hirota cabinet moved steadily toward "bureaucratic totalitarianism." The influence of the Diet continued to decline while military and naval budgets reached an all-time high. Further evidence of the army's involvements in politics came in January, 1937. When the Hirota cabinet resigned, the emperor called upon a moderate, General Ugaki Kazushige, to form a government; but Ugaki was blocked when the army refused to appoint a Minister of War. In February, however, the army did accept the elevation to the premiership of General Hayashi Senjuro, who had been Minister of War. In June, after Hayashi had failed to win the nation's unified support, he was succeeded by Prince Konoye Fumimaro, a member of one of Japan's oldest and most aristocratic families. It was the expectation that Konoye's close family relationship with the Imperial Household would lead the nation to unite politically behind his policies.

The unhealthy state of Japan's domestic politics by June, 1937, continued unabated. Political assassins and terrorists were not a new feature of Japanese life, but their reappearance beginning with the attack on Hamaguchi in 1930 bore a special significance. Always garbed in the role of guardians of the emperor, of the Imperial Way, and of the National Spirit, they served as the shock troops for all those who favored ultranationalism, fascism, or military dictatorship. Each time the terrorists struck, the army and its sympathizers won at least a psychological victory, for the very existence of political terrorism was taken as proof of the depths to which the nation had sunk under the rule of "corrupt" industrial capitalists and political parties. Until 1937 the Japanese electorate showed at times a healthy skepticism toward all moves in the direction of fascism or military dictatorship, but its reluctance to give way to the army at home was forever being weakened by the appeal of military conquest abroad, of the expanding empire in China, and of Japan's benevolent mission to insure the peace and tranquility of the Far East.

CHINESE POLITICS, 1931 AND AFTER

The history of Chinese politics in the 1930s is not easy to describe accurately. Much of the spade work of the historian in this period has yet to be done, but some major aspects of the story are in discernible focus. As a point of departure it may be noted that the Meiji revolution in Japan had produced a modern nation-state which adjusted itself to Westernization through the single-minded leadership of the *Genro*, who knew where they were going and how they proposed to get there. Furthermore, the new Japan achieved an amazing degree of stability by preserving indigenous institutions and symbols surrounding the throne.[5] In contrast, China's modern revolution, coming half a century later, destroyed the moribund Confucian state before there was either a plan or a leadership that could replace it. The vacuum this created was filled for the moment by the political wreckage of Confucianism and by local militarism. Sun Yat-sen's task in nation building was thus immeasurably more difficult than that of the Meiji reformers. The old political China was dead. Sun's revolution faced the triple task of devising a theory and plan for the new China, of suppressing militarism and finally of creating a government that could rule while it built the new political edifice. Sun's theory was reasonably precise by 1923. By

[5] It is true that the *Genro*, particularly Ito and Yamagata, often disagreed violently, but these differences were not permitted to obstruct or to becloud fundamental objectives of policy. They were differences of means rather than of ends.

1927 his followers appeared to have defeated warlordism. By the following year a national government was emerging and the *Kuomintang* was faced with the hard fact that it now had to rule China and at the same time find the means whereby the revolutionary program of Sun Yat-sen—nationalism, democracy, and livelihood—could be made the living and working philosophy of more than 400,000,000 people, most of whom had no understanding of these political doctrines.

From the beginning of the *Kuomintang*-Nationalist era, 1927–1928, the political history of China was therefore a compound of three major ingredients, each amazingly complex in itself. The first was the character of the *Kuomintang* and of the National government which it created and controlled. The second was the nature of the opposition to the *Kuomintang* within China. The third was the obstruction of China's revolution from the outside, principally though not exclusively by Japan.

THE NATIONAL GOVERNMENT AND THE KUOMINTANG

The *Kuomintang*-Nationalist government that ruled over much of China from 1928 until 1949 was the first government to direct China as though it were a Western nation-state. The government structure was established under the First Organic Law of 1928. Under this instrument, power was concentrated at the top and was exercised through five *yuan* (departments or divisions) rather than the three—legislative, executive, and judicial—common to Western government. Of these five, the Executive *Yuan* was in a sense the cabinet. The Legislative *Yuan*, a body of eighty-eight members, was neither a parliament nor a legislature as that term is understood in the West. Basically its function was research on and drafting of legislation. Justice was administered through the Judicial *Yuan*, while the Examination *Yuan* was concerned with applying the merit system to all government officials, excepting the top political positions. Finally, the Control *Yuan*, suggested the Censorate of Old China.

Its function was to denounce (in the modern sense, bring suit against) irresponsible officials. Presiding over this structure until his death in 1943 was President Lin Sen, a scholar and follower of Sun Yat-sen. The First Organic Law provided for extensive presidential powers, but in 1931 the promulgation of the provisional constitution shifted authority to the Executive *Yuan*. Meanwhile the single party rule of the *Kuomintang* from 1928 onward meant that policy decisions belonged to top leaders of the party, men who at times might also hold top offices in the government. In a word, the National government was the creation and the agent of the *Kuomintang*.

This intimate relationship of the National government and *Kuomintang* did not result in the new regime's achieving a singleness of thought and purpose. While the *Kuomintang* had no rivals within the government, the party itself became divided after achieving power. This was partly due to the loss of Sun Yat-sen, whose personality had served as a powerful unifying force. Gone too was the compulsion toward unity which had developed out of the requirements of the Northern Expedition, 1925–1927. But beyond these considerations was the fact that after coming to power *Kuomintang* membership became exceedingly diverse. Among the members the most active were college and middle school graduates, who were employed as party workers, civil servants, teachers, and editors. In time further important categories of membership included small shopkeepers, factory workers, and postal and railway employees. The interests of this membership, which in the 1930s may have totaled more than two million (exclusive of armed forces), were by no means identical. As a result, some members, frightened by Communist activities, pushed the party toward the right to the delight of every opponent of Sun and his revolution. Simultaneously the *Kuomintang* was also pulled toward the left by others inspired by the revolutionary program that had brought the party into being and by the obvious needs for agrarian and labor reforms. Finally, party harmony was taxed by sharp rivalries in its leadership. These rivalries,

however, did not shatter party organization. That structure retained the form given it by Sun Yat-sen. Operating through various levels of authority, the Party extended from the National Congress of the *Kuomintang* and Central Executive Committee at the top to the local party cells. Since the Congress met infrequently and the Central Executive Committee proved cumbersome, authority tended to gravitate to a smaller Standing Committee. Power within the party hierarchy, however, was divided among rival factions. Hu Han-min, a scholar and conservative, Wang Ching-wei, the brilliant and opportunistic demagogue, and Chiang Kai-shek, leader of the armies, were the more outstanding factional leaders. Of these three, the two former later became leaders of the so-called Right and Left factions respectively. Chiang Kai-shek's position was more fluid, his eminence being derived more from his command function than from ideological factors. Lesser factions included the C. C. Clique of Ch'en Li-fu, Minister of Education, and Ch'en Kuo-fu, head of the Central Political Institute, both of whom were master political manipulators; the Regenerationists or Blue Shirts who mimicked a Fascist pattern; the secret police organization; and the milder Political Science Group, which eschewed violence but was hardly revolutionary. During the first years at Nanking, none of these men or factions achieved a position that could control completely the party or the government.[6] Because of the personal basis of Chinese politics, factionalism was to be expected. It was to prove, however, a luxury which the *Kuomintang* could ill afford. Once in power, the party tended to lapse into a mood of assurance, to lose its dynamic character. Factional strife contributed decidedly to this tendency.

[6] The problem of establishing leadership was complicated by the Party's decision that Sun should continue to hold the title *Tsung-li* even after his death. Consequently it was difficult when Sun was gone for anyone to seek exclusive leadership without doing violence to Sun's memory. It was not until 1938 that a new title of leadership, *Tsung-ts'ai*, was created and given to Chiang Kai-shek.

Domestically the *Kuomintang's* program was founded on Sun's Three Principles. Following Sun's example, the Nanking regime placed great emphasis on national unity. Administrative machinery was devised to carry the authority of the central government to the local level. *Hsien* magistrates were placed under orders from Nanking. Separate from the *hsien* government but also responsible to Nanking were local administrative units in charge of military, customs, transportation, and other matters. The *Kuomintang* also maintained party units under central control parallel to governmental administration. Below the *hsien* were further subdivisions leading down to the very households. The theory was that the government through direct administrative contact with the populace was to train the people for self-government during a period of tutelage.

But practice did not measure up to theory. Warlords, who, it must be remembered, had bowed formally to Nationalist authority in order to preserve their own power, often stood between the people and Nanking, especially in regions remote from Nanking. Moreover, bureaucratic power developed more rapidly than democratic processes. The 1930s were marked by a growth of political controls through local police, secret police, press censorship, direction of educational programs, the *poa-chia* (a system borrowed from traditional China in which households were grouped to enable everyone to police everyone else), and other devices. This did not mean, however, that all political opposition was proscribed.

In fact a number of minor parties, consisting usually of a small nucleus of leaders and a few thousand followers and having aims quite different from the *Kuomintang's*, not only operated but also were permitted to form in 1941 a Federation of Democratic Parties, known as the "Democratic League," to oppose one-party rule, party armies, secret police, and corruption. Even so, there were limits beyond which criticism was not tolerated. During the 1930s, opponents of the regime, several of whom were associated with colleges in Peiping, were subjected to mounting pressure. Student critics were jailed, and teachers and editors were intimidated. Accompanying these developments was an attempted revival of Confucianism in the guise of the New Life Movement which sought to instill in the populace a martial spirit and a social consciousness through the resurrection of ancient standards. These were: *li*, defined variously as propriety, "proper behavior according to status," or a regulated attitude; *i* (or *yi*), righteousness or justice (in the Platonic sense); *lien*, integrity; and *ch'ih*, conscience. In order to render these classical concepts more understandable to the masses, some one hundred specific rules were issued as guides in their application. For example, the populace was admonished: do not eat noisily; correct your posture; keep your gown buttoned; do not spit; kill rats and flies. Through such inspiring exhortations Chinese were to be led to practice orderliness and cleanliness. Between 1934 and 1937 the New Life Movement was also responsible for other activities, many of which were of doubtful value in promoting China's regeneration but which certainly did reflect Nanking's tendency to justify itself through authoritarian traditions of Old China.[7] In short, the *Kuomintang*-Nationalist government, operating under a party dictatorship, was largely unsuccessful in advancing toward Sun Yat-sen's goal of People's Democracy. Yet, in noting this failure it is also well to recall that the *Kuomintang*, modeled on authoritarian lines, pulled between the right and left, and divided by personal rivalries, was ill-equipped to pursue Sun's revolutionary program. In addition the pressures exerted by Japan were no boon to political experimentation.

Also disappointing were the government's failures to stimulate economic development. The rise of the *Kuomintang* occurred during a period when light and staple industries, communications systems, and export-import

[7] For a study of a role played by American missionaries in the New Life Movement see James C. Thompson, Jr., *While China Faced West: American Reformers in Nationalist China, 1928–1937* (1969).

firms were continuing the gradual expansion begun during World War I. This trend, however, while it aroused hopes for the future, was developing too slowly to satisfy young China. Thus, as the *Kuomintang* established itself in Nanking, it was assumed popularly that it would quicken and broaden the process of economic modernization. Once in power the *Kuomintang*-Nationalist government did establish some essential foundations for economic growth. There were fiscal reforms such as the centralization of industrial taxation, assertion of national control over tariff policy, and establishment of annual national budgets. Further additions were made to the communications systems and power industries were enlarged. These achievements were publicized as evidence that the new regime was mastering its economic problems. But the reforms, however notable, were not in themselves sufficient to break away from the traditional system and to establish a genuinely modern economy. What was required were far-reaching institutional reforms affecting the very foundations of Chinese life and livelihood. These were not forthcoming. While experiments in rural reconstruction were permitted to function under the auspices of semi-independent provincial governments, they received from Nanking scarcely any encouragement.[8] Land laws aimed at protecting peasants were seldom enforced. Indeed, in some ways Nanking's policies were repressive of economic growth. For example, although heavy expenditures to equip the *Kuomintang's* army did stimulate increased economic activity, they diverted available resources and labor from projects which in the long run could have been more productive of goods and services. The result was that in the years 1932–1936 the gross national product did not keep pace with increases in population, a development which was reflected in deepening popular unrest. The divisions within the *Kuomintang* arising from sharply contrasting views and personal feuds were no more conducive to the creation of new blueprints in economics than in politics. To be

sure, the problem was exceedingly difficult. The *Kuomintang* was called upon to revolutionize China's economy during a period when depression was creating havoc throughout the world and when Japan posed a constant military threat. In addition, the popular demand for economic change was not always matched by a general determination to abandon traditional ways. The nature of this difficulty is suggested by the tendency of educated Chinese to insist upon white-collar jobs that most nearly approximated the prestigious vocations of Old China. Such tendencies, of course, safeguarded individual self-esteem, but they deprived the country of talents badly needed in other areas. Finally, in these years the *Kuomintang*-Nationalist government had to cope with a treaty system which, by giving foreigners and foreign business special privileges, diminished Nanking's authority in the economic realm. When all of these factors are taken into account, it is easier to understand the *Kuomintang's* questionable determination to unite China through military measures rather than to concentrate on political and economic reform.[9]

Indeed, the *Kuomintang's* determination

[8] Lyman P. Van Slyke, "Liang Sou-ming and the Rural Reconstruction Movement," *Journal of Asian Studies* 18 (1959): 457–74.

[9] Cheng Yu-kwei, *Foreign Trade and Industrial Development* (1956), 27–47. See also two articles by Douglas Paauw: "Chinese National Expenditure during the Nanking Period," *The Far Eastern Quarterly* 12 (1952): 3–26; and "The *Kuomintang* and Economic Stagnation," *Journal of Asian Studies* 16 (1957): 213–20. The term "economic stagnation" as applied to China's development is highly relative. In an absolute sense the term was inaccurate for China as a whole. Manchuria under Japanese rule enjoyed an industrial boom. Nor was the term literally accurate even for the regions under *Kuomintang*-Nationalist control. Between 1925–1936 the industrial growth rate was 4.7 per cent; for the years 1931–1937, the figure was 9.3 per cent. Given the militaristic orientation of production underlying these growth figures and *Kuomintang* failures in other fields, these statistics were not a source of pride among young nationalists. Yet these figures should be kept in mind while studying later events in China's revolutionary history. It was a developing country, not one that was standing still economically, which the Communists seized in 1949. John K. Chang, "Industrial Development of Mainland China, 1912–1939," *Journal of Economic History* 27 (1967): 56–81.

becomes even clearer when the party's military program is examined. Here the accomplishments of the Nanking regime were more substantial than in any other area. After 1928 Chiang Kai-shek with the aid of German advisers reorganized the army and strengthened his own position as commander-in-chief. The program of the Army Staff College (*Lu-ta*) was modernized with the result that men trained there, as well as the growing number educated in the finest foreign academies, formed the first competent body of middle-grade officers in China's modern era. Troops were trained in German military methods and equipped with German arms. By 1937 the Central Army numbered about three hundred thousand while more than a half-million men were organized in subsidiary units. A beginning was also made in the organization of a navy and air force. While these units varied greatly in fighting efficiency, training, and equipment, the best of them were excellent, as was demonstrated by the Nineteenth Route Army when it met Japanese forces at Shanghai in January, 1932. Its defense of Shanghai, which was one of modern China's first triumphs over a foreign power, helped to instill confidence in other *Kuomintang* forces. Thus, Nanking faced the future with assurance that the country could be unified by military means.

COMMUNIST OPPOSITION TO THE KUOMINTANG

The power of the *Kuomintang* was affected not only by its own performance as a ruling party but also by the armed challenge of rival revolutionary forces under Communist leadership. Following their ouster from the *Kuomintang* in 1927, the Communists first staged abortive uprisings and then were forced underground. Some Communist Party leaders retreated to the cities where they continued to plot for an urban-based revolution. Another group was established in the mountainous border region of Kiangsi-Hunan provinces a territorial base commanded by Mao Tse-tung as Chairman of the Council of People's Commissars, and by Chu Teh as Commander-in-Chief of the Communist army. From these vantage points the Communist Party increasingly became a contender for leadership of China's revolution.

The appeal of communism to Chinese intellectuals lay partly in its promised solutions to pressing problems; the doctrine's condemnation of the past justified attacks on traditional Confucian values; its justification of force offered a short cut to a modern China; and its demand for an end to colonialism supported the determination of young China to terminate the "unequal" treaty system. Moreover, acceptance of Communist doctrine was encouraged by the New Culture Movement's emphasis on positivism, and materialism. While all of these tenets of a new faith could be embraced by such an eloquent anti-Communist as Hu Shih, for others positivism and Marxism were inseparable as the science of life; pragmatism was identified with Leninism as the means for achieving social revolution; and materialism was a step toward making dialectical materialism a philosophy of life. Finally, some Chinese saw an affinity between the principles of communism and those propounded by Sun Yat-sen. Sun himself had recognized that communism's emphasis on a state-controlled economy, rule by a party elite under strong leadership, and struggle against colonialism could be construed as identical with People's Livelihood, Democracy, and Nationalism.

While these intellectual trends favored the growth of communism, the Chinese Communist Party was unable initially to convert them into a broadly based popular party. At the root of the problem was the party's subservience to Moscow's directives during the first decade after its founding in 1921. First Moscow dictated a united front among all revolutionaries against warlords. The Communists contended that they would represent the workers and poor peasants, while the *Kuomintang* would represent the bourgeoisie. Later, between 1924–1927, the Communist Party members joined the *Kuomintang*, an arrangement by which Moscow hoped to gain control of Sun's organization. After 1927 the Communist Party, then outside the *Kuomintang*, accepted Stalin's view that the revolution must be conducted through conspiracy and armed insurrection. In accord with this new line the party staged the Autumn Harvest Uprising among peasants in Hunan (led by Mao Tse-tung), seized the port of Swatow for a week in September, 1927, and led a four-day uprising in Canton. When these and similar efforts collapsed, the party following still another directive developed in Moscow, attempted to incite the urban proletariat to revolt. These uprisings, which were identified with their leader as the "Li Li-san line," were doomed by labor apathy and vigorous *Kuomintang* suppression. Thus in nearly ten years the Chinese Communist Party could claim no significant victories.

Even so, the party's first decade was not entirely without achievement. The party itself in these years was transformed from a collection of Marxist study groups into a band of professional revolutionaries, disciplined and trained to concentrate on the organization and seizure of power. Unlike the *Kuomintang*, which was given a similar structure but was divided into numerous factions, the Chinese Communist Party was a single ideological unit. Those first years were also marked by appeals for peasant support, the ultimate source of Communist power. In 1925, acting on Lenin's admonition that peasants could help advance revolution, the party with unexpected success began to organize peasant associations in areas which were controlled by revolutionary forces.

Peasants, burdened with extortionate rents and other exactions by landlords and stirred by a tradition of rebellion, responded enthusiastically to Communist leadership in the redistribution of land, the reduction of taxes, and the confiscation of the wealth of local gentry. Within a few months, the peasant associations claimed a membership of 180,000. As the Communists (collaborating with the *Kuomintang*) started the Northern Expedition, so many peasants co-operated with them that the party could not provide adequate leadership to direct the peasant movement. Membership in the peasant associations soon surpassed the three million mark, thus eclipsing the urban labor movement. The party, however, did not immedi-

ately seek to exploit the opportunities of peasant support. Chinese Communist leadership was inclined by background, temperament, and intellectual outlook to regard massive peasant support as a liability rather than an asset. The party's founders, having come mainly from families of landowning gentry or rich peasants, and being bound by the Marxist dogma that the only genuine source of revolutionary initiative was the industrial working class, were unwilling to identify themselves with the peasantry. Party policy subordinated peasant interests to those associated with carrying forward an urban based revolution. Indeed, the "Li Li-san line" was inaugurated partly in an effort to bring the revolutionary effort in the cities abreast of that in the countryside.[10] But if the leadership was unwilling to capitalize on peasant discontent, the possibility of a peasant-based revolution did not escape Mao Tse-tung. As early as 1927, Mao launched a campaign to have the party regard the peasant rather than the industrial worker as the driving force of China's Communist revolution.

While Mao had been active in the Communist cause throughout the 1920s, his rise to prominence in a personal and ideological sense occurred in the party's second decade. Following the collapse of the Autumn Harvest Uprising (September, 1927), Mao, joined by Chu Teh and what was left of Communist forces, retreated to the remote, mountain-girdled plateau region of the Hunan-Kiangsi border. Here a start was made in developing programs that were to give the Chinese Communist movement new life. Careful work converted the Hunan-Kiangsi region into a territorial base.[11] Here in the provincial borderlands Mao determined to construct a bastion within which the Communists could organize the economic basis of power and

[10] Urban Communists, unlike those in the countryside, were unable to offer the masses any immediate benefits as inducements for revolutionary activity.

[11] For a study of the geographic basis of the territorial base in Chinese Communist history see Robert W. McColl, "The Oyuwan Soviet Area, 1927–1932," *Journal of Asian Studies* 27 (1967): 41–60.

defend themselves against attack, and from which Communist rule could be extended to the rest of China. Since Mao and Chu treated the peasants well, the peasantry furnished recruits for the Red Army, supplies, intelligence reports on enemy movements, and concealment for the Communists when they retreated in the face of superior forces. The Red Army in turn was trained to look upon itself as the defender of the peasants and the very embodiment of their aspirations. Wherever the Red Army went, land was redistributed and the powers of landlords, moneylenders, and gentry were broken. These efforts were so successful that by early 1930 the Red Army was conquering large stretches of territory, mostly in Kiangsi but also as far north as Hupeh. During the next two years, three *Kuomintang* invasions were repelled, and scattered territories conquered by the Red Army were consolidated into a unified state under Mao's leadership. But increased power did not automatically convey upon Mao leadership of the Chinese Communist Party. As has been mentioned, the established leaders, aroused by peasant uprisings, strove frantically to stir the city masses. To encourage the urban proletariat, Li Li-san ordered the Red Army to attack the *Kuomintang* armies that were defending the cities. As has also been noted, these latter actions were sanctioned by Moscow, which, while having made some concessions to Mao's views concerning the peasants' place in the revolution, continued to emphasize the primacy of the urban proletariat. Thus it was not until the collapse of the "Li Li-san line" in 1930 that Mao's fortunes improved appreciably within the Party. In 1932 Mao used his new power to force the party's Central Committee to move from Shanghai to the area under his control. Three more years were to elapse before Mao assumed formal control, but in the meantime the Central Committee, having ceased to function as the governing body of the Party, began to act as front men for Mao's *de facto* authority.[12]

[12] Ideological differences were by no means the only trouble between Mao and the Party's Central Committee. Mao was a "non-Bolshevik Revolutionary," who "though an active revolu-

These years of Mao's ascendency were also ones in which the party's fortunes were sharply reversed. In 1934 attacks by the *Kuomintang* on the Hunan-Kiangsi stronghold routed the Communists and forced the beginning of the "Long March." After breaking through encircling *Kuomintang* forces, the Communists marched and fought along a circuitous route of some six thousand miles through China's southwest. Finally, surviving perils that have since become legendary in the Party, Mao and less than twenty thousand followers arrived in northern Shansi late in 1935. Headquarters were transferred a year later to Yenan. Here in the forbidding lands of the northwest the Communists began the dual tasks of creating a new revolutionary base and finding a means of repelling the encroaching Japanese. In devising the means for carrying out these tasks, the leadership acted largely on its own. Relations between Moscow and the Chinese Communist Party were strained, if not completely broken. Moscow, having supported consistently an urban-based revolution in China, had contributed little to Mao's rise. On the contrary, Mao reached the top only after employing threats and violence against Stalin's Chinese supporters. Thus party leaders felt few inhibitions in grounding their programs on

tionary throughout the 1920s, was much too busy to master the fundamental Marxist categories. He was a revolutionary before he became a Communist. A natural leader of men, he found it difficult to subordinate himself to the strict party discipline inherent in a Leninist democratic central regime." He proved to be shrewd and tenacious, bowing to the party leadership whenever that was expedient, but otherwise working steadily to maintain and to increase his own power base. In these latter respects he was not greatly different from such warlords as Yen Hsi-shan or Feng Yu-hsiang. What ultimately distinguished Mao from the warlords was his vision of a transformed China and his ability to marshal mass support. Before he could realize his vision, however, Mao had to fight his way to political power. John E. Rue, *Mao Tse-tung in Opposition, 1927–1935* (1966), 24. See also Hsiao Tso-liang, *Power Relations within the Chinese Communist Movement, Volume I, 1930–1934; Volume II, 1930–1931, The Chinese Documents* (1961–1967).

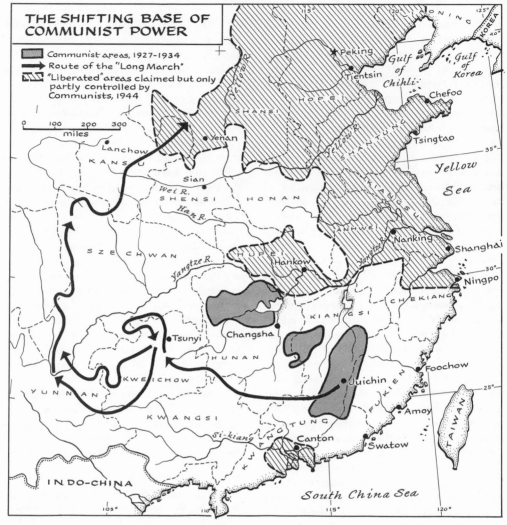

THE SHIFTING BASE OF COMMUNIST POWER

Communist areas, 1927–1934
Route of the "Long March"
"Liberated" areas claimed but only partly controlled by Communists, 1944

Sources: I. C. Y. Hsü, *The Rise of Modern China* (New York: Oxford University Press, 1970), p. 660; and J. K. Fairbank, E. O. Reischauer, and A. M. Craig, *East Asia: The Modern Transformation* (Boston: Houghton Mifflin Co., 1965), p. 853.

peasant support.[13] Their activities appealed to an ever-widening and receptive Chinese audience. Indeed, in the role of radical or progressive reformers the Communists were especially dangerous to a *Kuomintang* no longer dominated by revolutionary zeal.

[13] The thesis that Chinese Communist leadership achieved success by capitalizing on peasant discontent was advanced in Benjamin Schwartz, *Chinese Communism and the Rise of Mao* (1951). A more recent statement of this interpretation is Donald Gillin's "Peasant and Communist in Modern China: Reflections on the Origins of the Communist-led Peasant Movement," *The South Atlantic Quarterly* 60 (1961): 434–46. Conflicting explanations are in Chalmers Johnson, *Peasant Nationalism and Communist Power* (1962), which holds that Communist power capitalized on nationalist feelings stirred by the Japanese invasion; and in Shanti Swarup, *A Study of the Chinese Communist Movement, 1927–1934* (1966) which presents evidence suggesting that the Communists succeeded only when the leadership perceived the necessity of combining national and social revolutions with the operational tactics of warlordism. This perception was uniquely Mao's.

JAPAN AND THE KUOMINTANG

Meanwhile, the position of the *Kuomintang* and the *Kuomintang*-Nationalist government had been challenged from the outside first by Russia in North Manchuria in 1929 and then by Japan in South Manchuria, 1931 and after. In the case of North Manchuria, Nanking could do no more than bow to the terms Russia imposed on Manchurian authorities. In the case of South Manchuria, Nanking could and did appeal to the League of Nations, but Manchuria itself passed into Japanese hands while the Young Marshall, Chang Hsueh-liang, reassembled his army west of Peiping. During 1934–1935, when the Kwantung army attempted to set up an autonomous state around Peiping, the Nationalist government played a delicate game of appeasement, neither obstructing the Japanese completely nor conceding all they asked. To this point the *Kuomintang's* policy was to placate Japan. Confronted with dissension within its own ranks and opposed vigorously by Communists, the party had decided to crush internal foes before turning against foreign invaders.

This policy was soon met with a rising demand throughout China for a united front against Japan. Japanese pressure since 1931 in Manchuria and North China and at Shanghai had gone far to subordinate conflicting groups and class interests of Chinese society and to produce a widespread demand for armed resistance. The popular humiliation before Japanese arms affected all classes, high and low, urban and rural, the *Kuomintang*, the Communists, and others who might be called nonpartisans. A manifestation of this national feeling was a revolt in 1933 in Fukien by *Kuomintang* and other elements demanding resistance to the Japanese and democracy for the Chinese. Later, in 1936, Nanking met revolt by southern generals and their political followers in Kwangtung and Kwangsi who professed to represent regional branches of the Central Executive Committee itself. Again the demand was for resistance to Japan, and again Nanking met the emergency with force, patronage, and assurances that resistance was coming.[14] The culmination of these revolts against the *Kuomintang*-Nationalist government came in December, 1936, when Chiang Kai-shek was seized on a visit to Sian and held prisoner by Chang Hsueh-liang. The kidnapping was clearly a protest against Nanking's orders to fight the Chinese Communists. Chang's commanders and troops were more concerned with fighting the Japanese and regaining their homeland. Indeed, there had been fraternizing rather than fighting between the Manchurian troops and the Communists in the northwest. What Chang wanted was a pledge that the Nanking government would join forces with the Communist Party (an idea which then was supported by the communist leadership) against Japan. Presumably such a pledge was obtained prior to Chiang Kai-shek's release. The *Kuomintang* was clearly being forced to give top priority to the repelling of foreign aggression. It was also evident that Chiang Kai-shek was emerging from the ranks of *Kuomintang* chiefs as the indispensable leader of national resistance.

FOR FURTHER READING

Japan

POLITICS AND GOVERNMENT. A hardheaded scrutiny of Japan's ultranationalistic political organizations and forces during the fate-

[14] The *Kuomintang*-Nationalist government's procrastination eroded its support among educated middle classes and college students. The Communists were slow to exploit this opportunity, but by 1936 they were doing so. Students were in the vanguard of those supporting the Communist call for a united front against Japan. See Jessie Lutz, "December 9, 1935: Student Nationalism and the China Christian Colleges," *Journal of Asian Studies* 26 (1967): 627–48. John Israel, *Student Nationalism in China, 1927–1937* (1966), concludes: "It is quite likely that no government faced with the succession of foreign and domestic crises that plagued the KMT from 1927 to 1949 could have acted to the satisfaction of revolutionary students." Jerome B. Grieder, "Communism, Nationalism, and Democracy: The Chinese Intelligentsia and the Chinese Revolution in the 1920's and 1930's," *Modern East Asia: Essays in Interpretation*, James B. Crowley, ed. (1970),* 207–34.

ful decade of the 1930s is found in Richard Storry, *The Double Patriots: A Study in Japanese Nationalism* (1957). James B. Crowley, "Japanese Army Factionalism in the Early 1930's," *Journal of Asian Studies* 21 (1962): 309–26, modifies the findings of Storry and others on the intraplay of groups within the army. Royal Jules Wald, *The Young Officers Movement in Japan, ca. 1925–1937, Ideologies and Actions* (Unpublished Ph.D. dissertation, University of California, Berkeley, 1949) supplies much information about the various secret organizations among the "young" officers. Pertinent documents and comment on the nature of militarism and the role of the military are contained in Tsunoda Ryusaku and others, eds., *Sources of the Japanese Tradition* (1958),° Chapter 27. John Maki, *Japanese Militarism, Its Cause and Cure* (1945) exemplifies the view of Japanese society as basically autocratic and militaristic. Robert K. Hall, ed., *Kokutai no hongi. Cardinal Principles of the National Entity of Japan,* trans. by John O. Gauntlett, with introduction by the editor (1949) provides a Japanese text published by the Ministry of Education to further nationalism. Charles B. Fahs, *Government in Japan* (1940); Hugh Borton, *Japan Since 1931* (1940); and R. K. Reischauer, *Japan: Government-Politics* (1939), especially Chapter 7, are three studies which supplement each other. See also Evelyn Colbert, *The Left Wing in Japanese Politics* (1952) which traces left wing developments from the 1918 proletarian movement through the 1950 purge. Maruyama Masao, *Thought and Behavior in Modern Japanese Politics,* ed. by Ivan Morris (1963) interprets the rise of ultranationalism.

ECONOMICS. Material on the important and complex economic basis of politics include the following: E. B. Schumpeter ed., *The Industrialization of Japan and Manchukuo* (1940); E. F. Penrose, *Food Supply and Raw Materials in Japan* (1930); Asahi Isoshi, *The Economic Strength of Japan* (Tokyo, 1939); three works by G. C. Allen, *Japan the Hungry Guest* (1938), on Japan's economic needs resulting from industrializa-

tion; *Japanese Industry: Its Recent Development and Present Condition* (1939), on the impact of the Sino-Japanese War on the industrial structure; and *Western Enterprise in Far Eastern Economic Development: China and Japan* (1954), in collaboration with A. G. Donnithorne.

China

ECONOMIC AND SOCIAL CONDITIONS. Cheng Yu-kwei, *Foreign Trade and Industrial Development of China: An Historical and Integrated Analysis through 1948* (1956) painstakingly collects widely scattered data. Shih Kuo-heng, *China Enters the Machine Age* (1944) is useful. On the position of labor see: Augusta Wagner, *Labor Legislation in China* (Peking, 1938); Nym Wales (pseudonym of Mrs. Edgar Snow), *The Chinese Labor Movement* (1945); and Ning Lao-T'ai-t'ai, and Ida Pruitt, *A Daughter of Han* (1945), the autobiography of a Chinese working woman. Victor Purcell, *Problems of Chinese Education* (London, 1936); Chang Jen-chi, *Pre-Communist China's Rural School and Community* (1960); and John DeFrancis, *Nationalism and Language Reform in China* (1950) are suggestive of the role of education in the Nationalist movement. Jerome B. Grieder, *Hu Shih and the Chinese Renaissance: Liberalism in the Chinese Revolution, 1917–1937* (1970).

THE KUOMINTANG. Additional biographies of the *Kuomintang's* military chief are: S. I. Hsiung, *The Life of Chiang Kai-shek* (London, 1948); and Sven Hedin, *Chiang Kai-shek* (1940). P. M. A. Linebarger, *The China of Chiang K'ai-shek* (1941) is an able and sympathetic study. F. F. Liu, *A Military History of Modern China, 1924–1949* (1956) is the first penetrating account of the rise and fall of the Whampoa clique. On this subject see also R. L. MacFarquhar, "The Whampoa Military Academy," *Papers on China,* Vol. 9. Published and distributed by the East Asia Research Center, Harvard University, (1955); and E. F. Carlson, *The Chinese Army: Its Organization and Military Efficiency* (1940). Mary C. Wright, "From Revolution to Restoration: The Transformation of *Kuomintang* Ideology," *The Far Eastern Quarterly* 14 (1955): 515–32, is an important brief study. J. K. Fairbank, *The United States and China* (2nd ed., 1958)° offers chapters placing the problems of the *Kuomintang* and rise of the Communist Party in the broad perspective of Chinese history.

THE COMMUNIST PARTY. "Chinese Communism," in William T. deBary, and Others, eds., *Sources of Chinese Tradition* (1960)° provides an excellent introduction to the relationship of Communist ideology to evolving Chinese thought. On Moscow's link with the Chinese Communists see R. C. North, *Moscow and the Chinese Communists* (2nd ed., 1963)° cited in the footnotes of this chapter. Harold Isaacs, *The Tragedy of the Chinese Revolution* (3rd. ed., 1961); and Conrad Brandt, *Stalin's Failure in China, 1924–1927* (1956) reach opposing views on Stalin's responsibility for Communist failures in China. C. P. Fitzgerald, *The Birth of Communist China* (1966)°; and Franklin W. Houn, *A Short History of Chinese Communism* (1967), offer differing perspectives on the formative years. Chao Ku-chun, *Agrarian Policy of the Chinese Communist Party, 1921–1959* (1960) is most useful for these early years. Hsia Tsi-an, *Enigma of the Five Martyrs: A Study of the Leftist Literary Movement in Modern China* (1962), employs tools of literary criticism to reveal Chinese Communism's intraparty struggles in the 1930s. Edgar Snow, *Red Star Over China* (1944)° gives a sympathetic description of early Communist struggles. C. Martin Wilbur and Julie Lien-ying How, *Documents on Communism, Nationalism, and Soviet Advisors in China 1918–1927* (1956); and Conrad Brandt, B. I. Schwartz, and J. K. Fairbank, eds., *A Documentary History of Chinese Communism* (1952) offers translations of Chinese documents with editorial commentary. O. Edmund Clubb, *Communism in China, As Reported from Hankow in 1932* (1968). Howard L. Boorman, "Mao Tsetung, the Lacquered Image," *The China Quarterly* 16 (1963), 1–55, is a short but carefully documented biography of Mao.

From the Marco Polo Bridge
to Pearl Harbor, 1937-1941

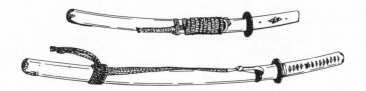

chapter 27

Following Japan's conquest of Manchuria in 1931, politics carried both China and Japan ever closer to a broader conflict. Although China was by no means unified under the new *Kuomintang*-Nationalist government, Chinese nationalism, often unorganized, incoherent, even leaderless, had become vehement against foreign encroachment. There were growing pressures on Nanking to abandon its policy of appeasement in favor of resistance against the Japanese. In Japan, on the other hand, the ascendency of the military portended further changes in foreign policy. From 1933 to 1937 Japan had sought by measures short of open warfare to bind China to her purposes, but the birth of Manchukuo, Japanese penetration of Inner Mongolia, and the effort to create an autonomous state in North China had all failed to create a subservient China. These failures had proved exceedingly irritating to the Japanese army. By 1937, while the military had not established complete control over the Tokyo government, the prominence of military leaders in politics increased the likelihood that solutions to Japan's problems would be sought through armed force. The result was the renewal of Sino-Japanese hostilities on a

grand scale in the bloody though undeclared war of 1937–1941, and the final merging of this conflict with the world conflagration that began with the German invasion of Poland.

MARCO POLO BRIDGE: HOSTILITIES BUT NOT WAR

Japanese expansion into China and, subsequently, into Southeast Asia was rooted in deep-seated feelings of insecurity. In a situation of great social and economic crisis, Tokyo's military leadership won popular support for the theory that Japan, despite a half-century of growth in her international status, was threatened by ever-growing crises. The challenge posed by Chinese nationalism to Japan's leadership in Asia was intensifying. Soviet power, a communist system inimical to Japanese government under an emperor, was firmly established in Siberia. Finally, there was growing suspicion of the United States, a Pacific naval power, which identified its interests with the preservation of China's integrity.[1] According to the mili-

[1] Northern China was not the only target of Japanese military expansionists, 1931–1933. In the aftermath of the Manchurian incident, a faction within the army, the *Koda-ha* (Imperial

tary, Japan could meet these dangers only by establishing her hegemony in Asia. To this end, the Japanese people would submit to the discipline of a planned economy. The ultimate purpose would be to tame Chinese nationalism and to redirect it under Japanese leadership against Western encroachment. Later, from 1940 to 1941, after Europe went to war and the United States threw its support to Great Britain and a Dutch government-in-exile, both of which claimed colonies in Southeast Asia, Japan's military were demanding the elimination of Western "encirclement" from the south. Such was the rationale presented by Japan's military leadership in justification of expansion. It was a view which enabled the military to claim that force was necessary in defense of vital national interests.[2]

On the night of July 7, 1937, in the vicinity of the Marco Polo Bridge about nine miles southwest of Peiping, fighting broke out between a Chinese garrison and a Japanese force. The latter was conducting maneuvers there beyond the localities where foreign troops might be stationed under the Boxer Protocol. The area was important strategically because of the Peiping-Hankow railway. Moreover, without treaty right, the town of Fengt'ai, through which a connecting line passed, had been garrisoned for more than a year by Japanese troops. Although in 1913 the Chinese government had

---

Way), which was organized around such men as General Araki Sadao, demanded a "preventative" war with the Soviet Union. Such was the influence of this faction that tensions in 1933 seemed to foretell a resort to violence. General Araki's dismissal as War Minister, January, 1934, however, was symptomatic of a decline in *Kodaha* fortunes and of a definite shift in Japanese interests toward China. See Ikuhiko Hata, *Reality and Illusion: The Hidden Crisis between Japan and the U.S.S.R., 1932–1934*. Occasional Papers of the East Asian Institute, Columbia University (1967).

[2] Japan's case is explored in two studies by James B. Crowley: *Japan's Quest for Autonomy: National Security and Foreign Policy, 1931–1938* (1966); and "A New Asian Order: Some Notes on Prewar Japanese Nationalism." Paper Presented at the Conference on Taisho Japan, Duke University, January, 1969.

authorized foreign commanders to drill their troops in the region, the magnitude of the Japanese maneuvers following the long period of tension since the Tangku truce of May, 1933 was an invitation to trouble. As on previous occasions, efforts were made in vain to settle the dispute locally. By July 27, Japanese reinforcements reached the Peiping area, and General Kazuki demanded that General Sung evacuate his troops to the south of Peiping and Tientsin. General Sung refused the demand; Peiping and Tientsin were taken by Japanese forces on July 29. The Japanese emperor ordered Prince Konoye to start negotiations with the Nanking government. Nanking, however, having presumably decided that it could tolerate no further erosion of its sovereignty in this region, indicated that it was prepared to use armed force in order to retain North China. Japan's response was to abandon further efforts to control the area through economic and political pressures and to resort to arms herself.

After occupying the area of Peiping and Tientsin, the Japanese troops drove into Inner Mongolia, occupying Kalgan and thus severing China's principal line of overland communication with Soviet Russia. Suiyuan province was overrun and occupied placing the Peiping-Suiyuan railway in Japanese hands. Other Japanese forces moved into Shansi to strike at strongholds of the Chinese Communists both there and in bordering Shensi. But here the Japanese met their first significant reverses at the hands of the 8th Route (Communist) Army, so-called since its nominal incorporation with the Nationalist armies in August, 1937. Employing guerilla tactics against forces overwhelmingly superior both in numbers and weapons, the Communists frustrated Japan's attempt to control northwest China. When the United States entered the war at the end of 1941, Japanese lines in this region were approximately where they had been in 1938.

Meanwhile hostilities had spread to the Yangtze Valley. For this development China was largely responsible. Japanese interests would have been served best by confining the conflict to North China. Nanking, on the other hand, hoped for the involvement

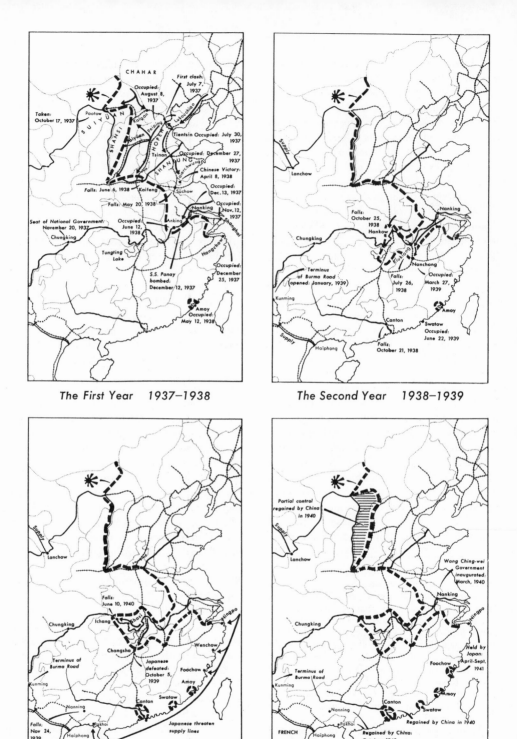

The First Year   1937–1938

The Second Year   1938–1939

The Third Year   1939–1940

The Fourth Year   1940–1941

Reproduced from A War Atlas for Americans *(New York: Simon & Schuster) 1944, with permission from the publisher and from the U.S. Department of State, Division of Map Intelligence and Cartography.*

Hankow and Tientsin-Pukow lines. Five months were required for the Japanese to reach Hankow on the upper Yangtze, which was taken in October, 1938. Ichang still further up the Yangtze was not captured until June, 1940.

This pattern of initial success followed by virtual stalemate was repeated in the south. Canton, the great southern port, fell without resistance in the autumn of 1938, giving credence to reports that the city had been "sold." In November, 1939, the Japanese landed at Pakhoi in Kwangtung. From this base a drive into Kwangsi brought the capitulation of the provincial capital, Nanning. But China's over-all strategy was by then showing improvement. In Hunan province the Japanese were forced to stop their advance on Changsha. Thus, Japan had invaded China on three major fronts, yet Chinese resistance seemed only to stiffen. To meet these difficulties Japan resorted not only to new military measures but also to diplomacy. Bomber raids were launched, especially on the new temporary capital at Chungking and key points on China's supply line from the south, the Burma Road. In February, 1939, the Japanese navy seized the island of Hainan off the South China coast, occupied the Spratley Islands a month later, and continued a blockade of Chinese shipping at principal Chinese ports. Meanwhile the Japanese put forward a series of peace proposals involving Japanese control of strategic Chinese areas, recognition of Manchukuo, and the formation of an economic bloc of China, Japan, and Manchukuo. Although these feelers played upon existing dissensions within the *Kuomintang*, they were all rebuffed by Chiang Kai-shek in December, 1938.

THE PROPAGATION OF PUPPET REGIMES

Having failed to conquer China or to bring her government to acceptance of peace, Japan decided to ignore the *Kuomintang*-Nationalists as a government and to seek the establishment of "a new Chinese regime" which would "do away with the folly of anti-

The Fifth Year   1941–1942

of other powers if Japan disregarded the neutrality of the International Settlement at Shanghai. Unhappily for Nanking, the strategy failed. Again, as in 1932, the Chinese at Shanghai were defeated after heroic resistance, and the Japanese moved up the river to capture Nanking in December, 1937, where local commanders permitted their troops to engage in wholesale acts of brutality against the local Chinese populace. The fall of Nanking, however, did not result in the capture of the *Kuomintang*-Nationalist government. The regime had moved to Hankow before the Japanese arrived and was eventually to retire further westward to Chungking. Nor did the Japanese advance signify the collapse of Chinese resistance in Central China. A humiliating defeat at Taierchwang, near the southern base of the Shantung peninsula, delayed the union of Japan's northern and central armies until May, 1938, when the Japanese won control of the two north-south railways: the Peiping-

Japanism." To this end Japan proposed to set up a puppet government similar to the regime that had functioned in Manchukuo since 1932. The first of these was the Provisional Government of the Republic of China proclaimed at Peking in December, 1937. Its authority and ability to govern the people of North China were successfully challenged from the beginning by a new Chinese administration called the Border Government of Hopei, Shansi, and Chahar, organized by Chinese Communists with initial approval of the *Kuomintang*-Nationalist government. This border government became one of the great forces of guerilla resistance to Japanese penetration in the north.[3]

Since the Provisional Government at Peking never possessed more than a wavering local appeal, it was incumbent on Japan to find a Chinese national personality who could head a new puppet regime at Nanking with some prospect of claiming the allegiance of the Chinese people. Their choice settled upon Wang Ching-wei. Wang had a long and distinguished, if erratic, revolutionary record. An intimate of Sun Yat-sen, he had held many of the highest posts in the *Kuomintang* and the *Kuomintang*-Nationalist government. Although originally a leader of the left wing in the *Kuomintang*, he had come to oppose the Communists, had developed a bitter spirit of rivalry toward Chiang Kai-shek, and had been recognized as the leader of appeasement. Moreover, prior to 1941 Wang had convinced himself that China's future lay in co-operation with Japan. At Nanking, March 30, 1940, the new National (Puppet) Government, under the leadership of Wang, was proclaimed. Declared to be the true guardian of the principles of Sun Yat-sen, this "returned" and "Reorganized Government" retained the *Kuomintang* ideology and the structure of the National Government as it had previously existed at Nanking. Its personnel was composed in considerable part, though not exclusively, of *Kuomintang* members who had deserted with Wang. Wang's government,

soon recognized by Japan, concluded a treaty with Tokyo, November, 1940, providing for joint defense against communism and for co-operation in economic development. Recognition was also accorded to the Wang regime, July, 1941, by Germany, Italy, Spain, Rumania, and other totalitarian governments of Europe.[4]

The area of China thus occupied or controlled by Japan constituted a rich block of territory comprising the Yangtze Valley from Shanghai to Hankow in the south to Peiping and Chahar province in the north. Here Wang's nominal jurisdiction extended over more than a half million square miles of territory with a population of close to 200 million. It included much of the wealthiest and most densely populated areas of China. Japan now turned to economic exploitation that would integrate this area into the co-prosperity framework with Manchukuo and Japan. The groundwork was prepared by intensive campaigns of propaganda to eliminate anti-Japanese sentiment. Against this background the whole economic and commercial structure of central and north-eastern China was reorganized. All forms of communication, and all industry, including mining were to be capitalized and directed by new companies in which Japan held half the stock. Ultimate authority rested with the newly organized China Affairs Board, created

[3] The techniques of resistance as they developed in North China are portrayed by George E. Taylor, *The Struggle for North China* (1940).

[4] For the development of the puppet regime, see Kimitada Miwa, "The Wang Ching-wei Regime and Japanese Efforts to Terminate the China Conflict," *Studies in Japanese Culture*, Joseph Roggendorf, ed. (Tokyo, 1963). The appeal of this government was limited. Japan held that she was creating a new Asian civilization distinct from and opposed to Western civilization. The *Kuomintang*, it was held, advocated a nationalism perverted by "British capitalism, Russian sovietism, and American humanism." Chinese patriots, on the other hand, while critical of Western imperialism, were far from enthusiastic about Asian solidarity under Japanese leadership. F. Hilary Conroy, "Japan's War in China: An Ideological Somersault," *Pacific Historical Review* 21 (1952): 367–79; Akira Iriye, "The Ideology of Japanese Imperialism: Imperial Japan and China," in *Imperial Japan and Asia: A Reassessment,* Grant K. Goodman, comp. Occasional Papers of the East Asian Institute, Columbia University (1967), 32–45.

in Tokyo on December 16, 1938. The general plan contemplated concentrations of high-precision industry in Japan; heavy, chemical, and electrical industry in Manchukuo; and salt production and light industry in North China.

RESISTANCE IN INDEPENDENT CHINA

Both for China and for the world at large the most significant and compelling fact of the four years of undeclared warfare, 1937–1941, was the resistance of independent China. Actually more than half of the territory and population of China Proper remained beyond the control of Japanese arms. In economic wealth, it was much the poorer half. Chinese nationalism thus had no alternative but to base its resistance on the great interior hinterland, where political and economic modernization were all but unknown. To the ancient west country, into the provinces of Szechwan, Kweichow, and Yunnan, trekked an astonishing migration of the wealthy, the educated, the politically influential, students, professors, skilled laborers, and some with no designation other than that of patriot. They travelled by boat, by cart, and on foot, carrying what possessions they could. In the old interior, where ancient and feudal traditions were still predominant they set up the wartime capital at Chungking and reassembled transplanted schools, universities, and factories.

In Northwest China the resistance movement was led by the Communist Party. As the Japanese offensive came to a standstill in Shansi, the 8th Route Army began to push its way back into that province and thence out onto the North China plain. In 1938, this force was joined by the New 4th Army. The Communist objective was to organize war bases in the less accessible border areas between provinces. Beginning with the Shansi-Hopeh-Chahar Border Region set up in 1938 and moving later into the Shansi-Hopeh-Honan-Shantung border area, the Communists by 1941 had organized territory containing a population of about fifty million persons. Within these so-called

"Liberated Areas" Communist troops, having been trained to regard themselves as defenders of the populace, depended upon the civilian population for food and quarters. The utilization of civilian intelligence networks enabled these armies to dispense with much of the usual centralized military organization. In consequence, the Communist armies operated as scattered, mobile forces, appearing and disappearing in the rural areas behind Japanese lines.

Ostensibly the communist resistance effort was linked to *Kuomintang*-Nationalist leadership. Beginning in August, 1935, both the Chinese Communist Party and the Comintern called for a united front against the Japanese, presumably because a nationwide resistance would serve the dual purpose of diverting the Japanese from an attack on the Soviet Union and keeping the *Kuomintang*-Nationalist regime from attacking its Communist opponents. At the end of the following year, more tangible evidence of the Communist desire for a united front was forthcoming as the party leadership helped engineer Chiang Kai-shek's release after the Sian kidnapping. As Japanese pressure increased, the Communists announced, September 22, 1937, their willingness to make peace with the *Kuomintang* on the understanding that the Red Army was to be placed under the Nationalist Government's command as the 8th Route Army, that the Chinese Soviet Republic be disbanded and the territory under its control be organized into a special area government under the Nationalist Government, that the Communists would halt the confiscation of land, and that the Communist Party would subscribe to Sun Yat-sen's "Three Principles." For the *Kuomintang*, Chiang issued a statement endorsing the Communist proposal.

But these steps toward unity did not constitute a genuine political settlement. Relations between the *Kuomintang* and Communists were embittered by ten years of relentless civil war, and each side remained dedicated to the eradication of the other. In these circumstances, the truce, while it produced temporarily closer relations, led eventually to deeper conflicts. The Communists proved unwilling to submit wholly to *Kuomintang* leadership either in military or political matters. The Communist strategy of prolonged resistance through guerilla warfare, which was to be one of China's strongest military weapons, was not supported by the *Kuomintang* leadership. Nor could the *Kuomintang*-Nationalist government fail to be alarmed by the Communist practice of establishing local administrations, loyal to the Communists, in areas liberated by the Red armies. To the *Kuomintang* leadership, it seemed that the Communists were utilizing the war to promote their own political fortunes.[5] After 1938, while the war with Japan went forward, the *Kuomintang* and the Communists diverted some of their best troops to watch each other. From then on there were periodic clashes between *Kuomintang* and Communist armies.

THE SINO-JAPANESE CONFLICT IN WORLD POLITICS

The outcome of the Sino-Japanese conflict, however, was not to be determined solely by events in East Asia. As the two nations sank ever more deeply into the morass of undeclared war, the great Western powers sought to define their interests and positions with respect to the unpredictable contest. The diplomatic maneuvering which resulted from shifting national policies affected profoundly the power balances in East Asia. The world-wide diplomatic struggle that developed along with the undeclared war after 1937, involved the far eastern policies not only of the totalitarian powers but also of Great Britain and the United States between 1932 and 1937.

The historic cleavage which had frequently existed between American and British policy in Asia was not ended with Japan's invasion of Manchuria in 1931. In January, 1932, Great Britain declined to give its formal support when the United States enunci-

ated the so-called Stimson Nonrecognition Doctrine. British policy held that it was not the business of the British government to defend "the administrative integrity of China until that integrity" was "something more than an ideal." [6] The Roosevelt-Hull administration of 1933 recognized that Stimson's provocative note-writing had further irritated the Japanese militarists. It was willing to revise diplomatic tactics, but was not prepared to surrender any principles. Within this framework the United States continued to co-operate with and to bolster the timid efforts of the League for collective security; and on November 16, 1933, it recognized Soviet Russia. Although American recognition was aimed basically towards a revival of foreign trade, its diplomatic significance was not lost upon Japan. The smoothing of relations between two states with which Japan was at odds was a further obstacle to Japan's ambitions. Thus the United States continued to affirm its support of China's territorial and administrative integrity, but the mild measures just noted constituted the limit of the practical steps the American government was prepared to take. In consequence, when British policy in 1935 and 1936 began to shift toward a stiffer resistance toward the Japanese, the United States refused to go along. London, having decided that British interests required an independent Nanking, invited the United States to join an economic mission to China with the aim of rehabilitating the Nationalist government. But the United States, preoccupied with efforts to end the great depression, and leaning heavily toward a political philosophy of pacifism and isolationism, feared the British proposal would lead to involvements Americans had no mind to assume.[7]

These continuing British-American differences over China were a natural product of the failure of the more general peace-

[5] According to Communist claims, the Red Army increased from 80,000 in 1937 to 470,000 by the end of 1943. An army of 1,000,000 was claimed by 1945.

[6] I. S. Friedman, *British Relations with China: 1931–1939* (1940), 18–42.

[7] Nicholas R. Clifford, *Retreat from China: British Policy in the Far East, 1937–1941* (1967), presents the view that joint Anglo-American efforts to check Japanese expansion by means short of war might have worked as late as the year following the Marco Polo Bridge incident.

keeping arrangements that had followed World War I. The years 1932–1937 saw the collapse of limitation on naval armaments. The World Disarmament Conference, meeting in Geneva while Japanese forces consolidated their position in Manchuria and fought with the Chinese at Shanghai, rejected an American proposal either to abolish all offensive weapons or to reduce existing armaments by 33 per cent. In December, 1934, Japan gave the two years' notice of her intent to denounce the Washington Naval Treaty of 1922 and made clear her intent to seek naval parity at the next disarmament conference. Accordingly, when her demand was denied, Japan withdrew from the London Naval Conference of 1935–1936. The treaty agreed upon by Britain, the United States, and France at London, March 25, 1936, without the adherence of Japan and Italy, thus became an empty gesture. Nor was this the only blow to international cooperation. On October 6, 1937, the League of Nations Assembly finally resolved that Japan's invasion of China was a violation of the Nine-Power Treaty and the Pact of Paris, and suggested that the signatories find a solution of the Sino-Japanese dispute. This latter suggestion led to a meeting of nineteen powers in Brussels, from November 3 to November 24, 1937. All original and later signatories of the Nine-Power Treaty were invited and, in addition, Germany and the Soviet Union. Japan declined to attend, since she had already been condemned and since she took the position that the dispute concerned herself and China alone. Germany also stayed away. At Brussels the delegates talked, while some waited for the United States to propose sanctions. In the end the delegates reaffirmed, Italy dissenting, the applicability of the Nine-Power Treaty and went home. Japan was offered no inducement to make peace and there was no thought of collective force if she refused. The Brussels effort was dead before it was born.[8]

[8] While the United States avoided taking any initiative at Brussels, American attitudes were shifting significantly. The Roosevelt administration before 1937 was seriously concerned with Sino-Japanese difficulties, but it tended to

The breakdown of the West's peace-keeping machinery was all the more striking because its deterioration was paralleled by the emergence of a new international force. At Berlin, Japan and Germany on November 25, 1936, signed an Anti-Comintern Pact providing for co-operation in "defense against the disintegrating influence of Communism." This pact, which was followed by a similar one between Japan and Italy, provided Tokyo with safeguards against Soviet Russian interference with her ambitions in China. Indeed, the existence of the Pact encouraged the Japanese the following year to meet Chinese resistance with armed force. Interpreted more broadly, the agreements with Berlin and Rome were the first formal manifestation that Japan's ambitions had been accorded a measure of international acceptance.

THE NEW ORDER IN EAST ASIA

In the autumn of 1938, Japan took stock of its position. It was convinced that the democracies would continue to do nothing and that the Soviet frontier was quiet and

regard the problem as one pertaining primarily to Asia. The outbreak of fighting led the administration to the thesis that the "China Incident" presented broad issues affecting the well-being of all nations. Japan's attack, it was feared, might precipitate a concerted effort by the Axis Powers to overwhelm European democracies. In consequence, the President and Secretary of State assumed personal direction of American Far Eastern diplomacy and began to search for new ways of bolstering the world's peace-keeping machinery. Roosevelt's famed "quarantine" speech, October, 1937, suggesting the isolation of aggressors, represented a possible new direction for American policy, but the idea was not pursued at Brussels because of the sharp reaction of American opinion. Nevertheless, in coming to the view that the Far Eastern crisis was integral to larger threats to world order, the administration had laid the ground for subsequent American resistance to Japanese expansion. The definitive study of the transformation of American policy is Dorothy Borg, *The United States and the Far Eastern Crisis of 1933–1938: From the Manchurian Incident through the Initial Stage of the Undeclared Sino-Japanese War* (1964).

would remain so. But the Japanese conquests in China, which had reached to Canton and Hankow, had not broken Chinese resistance. The *Kuomintang*-Nationalist government had retired to Chungking. The Japanese held the railroads and the big cities, but Nationalist forces and guerillas held the country. Japan had won the battles but she had not won China. The war was a stalemate and seemed likely to remain so indefinitely. Japan therefore sought a new policy to capitalize on her gains in the conquered territories of eastern China. This policy, announced by Premier Konoye, November 3, 1938, was "A New Order in East Asia." Its purpose was to bring stability and co-ordination under Japanese leadership between Japan, Manchukuo, and occupied China.

The hard-core meaning of the New Order was soon evident as Japan attempted to destroy all non-Japanese foreign business in China. The policy and purpose was twofold: to create a near-Japanese economic monopoly and, on grounds of military necessity, to stop foreign aid to the Nationalists. As has already been noted, Japan occupied Hainan Island, February, 1939, and had asserted its claim to the tiny Spratley Islands southeast of Saigon. These were preliminary steps in the Japanese economic offensive. In June, Japan blockaded the British and French concessions at Tientsin, publicly stripping and searching foreigners as they entered or left the concessions. This was an effort to persuade Chinese spectators that Western colonialism was dead and that Japan was the liberator of Asia. Beyond this Japan was trying to force the surrender of the silver bullion held by the British as backing for Chinese currency. The purpose was to destroy this currency in favor of new issues by Japan's puppet governments. Even Germany, Japan's new partner, did not escape injury as the Japanese destroyed the West's economic interests in occupied China. Nevertheless, in spite of Japanese pressure the West did not completely capitulate. Britain refused to give up the bullion, and the United States, responding to the ousting of American business from areas reached by the Japanese army, gave notice that it was terminating its Treaty of Commerce with Japan.

JAPAN STARTS SOUTH

When World War II broke out in late summer of 1939, Japan announced that she would not be involved in the European struggle; she would bend all efforts to settle the China affair. The European war, however, intruded quickly into Asian politics. While officially neutral, the United States, as early as November 4, 1939, began to supply aid to European democracies on a cash-and-carry basis. In May and June, 1940, Holland, Belgium, and France fell before German armies, and the Battle of Britain began. These events gave Japan a freer hand. She was now able to obtain British assent to a suspension of traffic in supplies flowing into Nationalist China from Hong Kong and Burma. In French Indochina, Japanese pressure closed the border into China, secured the use of certain airfields with the right to station troops, and obtained transit rights for troops attacking southwest China. A Japanese economic mission was sent to the Netherland Indies where it bargained, initially without success, for greatly increased quotas of oil. In short, the Japanese army sought in the West's preoccupation with its own war opportunities not only to improve its strategic position but also to augment its slender economic resources by tapping Southeast Asia's rich supplies of oil, bauxite, tin, and rubber.

As early as March, 1939, the Japanese army had been pressing for a full alliance with Germany. Germany had already indicated that she was prepared to overlook the damage done by Japan to her economic interests in China in order to obtain a pact which would give her added weight in Europe. Yet it was not until September, 1940, that the desired treaty, including Italy as a partner, was finally concluded. By that time the pact was aimed clearly at the United States. Germany believed that it would deter the expansion of American aid to Britain. In Japan it was viewed as a warning against American interference with Japanese moves, especially the full-fledged drive into Southeast Asia which the army was then contemplating. The United States, however, was not Japan's only concern. If Japan moved south, what would the Soviet Union do? Japan had been disappointed in her earlier expectation that the Soviet Union would remain quiet. As recently as August, 1939, the prolonged Russo-Japanese rivalry had erupted in a battle along the Manchukuo-Outer Mongolian border in which the Kwantung army suffered some 18,000 casualties.[9] This renewed tension offered the prospect of a Soviet strike in the north when Japan's attentions were directed elsewhere. To eliminate this danger Japan entered protracted negotiations to settle immediate issues related to the northern frontier and, in general, to dispose of the possibility of a general war with the Soviet Union. The key Japanese diplomat in these discussions was Foreign Minister Matsuoka Yosuke, the American-educated firebrand of the civilian ultra-nationalists, of whom Saionji, the last of the *Genro*, had said: "It will improve him if he becomes insane." At Moscow, April 3, 1941, Matsuoka proudly signed the Soviet-Japanese Nonaggression Pact. Japan's northern flank now seemed secure. Only one problem remained—to keep the Americans inactive while Japan took over Southeast Asia and liquidated Chinese resistance.

AMERICA MOVES TOWARD WAR

Meanwhile the United States was moving cautiously away from neutrality. As early as November, 1939, Congress had repealed the arms embargo, enabling Britain and France to purchase and ship war goods in and from the American market. By June, 1940, as all Western Europe save the United Kingdom lay prostrate at Hitler's feet, President Roosevelt promised aid to "the opponents of force" and the speedy rearmament of America itself. Congress followed the President's lead with unprecedented appropriations for the armed services and the first peacetime selective service act. Fifty

[9] Aspects of Soviet-Japanese difficulties are discussed in Alvin D. Coox, "Soviet Ousting of Japanese Consulates, 1937–38," *Orient/West* 9 (1964): 49–58; and Larry W. Moses, "Soviet-Japanese Confrontation in Outer Mongolia: The Battle of Nomonhan-Khalkin-Gol," *Journal of Asian History,* 1, Pt. 1, (1967): 64–85.

overage destroyers still useful for submarine patrol and convoy duty were given to the British in September in return for the right to maintain American military bases in British possessions from Newfoundland to Guiana. Since the destroyer deal was a clear departure from neutrality, it indicated how rapidly the United States was moving toward a shooting war. After the President had been elected for a third term he called for making the United States the "arsenal of democracy." Congress implemented the proposal, March 11, 1941, with passage of the Lend-Lease Act, which meant that the United States would lend goods instead of money to the democracies. Lend lease was a complete denial of neutrality. At the same time British and American military and naval officers were jointly planning the co-ordination of military effort for the time when the United States might enter the conflict. There was close planning for mutual defense between the United States and Canada dating back to August, 1940. By July, 1941, the United States Navy was convoying British lend-lease as far as Iceland. In August, Churchill and Roosevelt issued the Atlantic Charter, proclaiming the goals of the Free World. Thus in early 1941 the United States had moved far along the path to belligerency in the Atlantic. These events encouraged Japanese expansionists to believe that the United States, faced with war in Europe, would not fight in Asia if she were offered some expendable concessions.

The United States policy of aid to Britain in Europe was accompanied by a growing resolve to resist Japanese aims in the Pacific. In July, 1939, Washington gave Tokyo the required six months notice terminating the Japanese-American commercial treaty of 1911 and thus paving the way for economic sanctions. Then in July, 1940, the Roosevelt administration began a policy of progressive economic sanctions against Japan. At first only aviation gasoline and number one grade scrap metal were embargoed, but the following September all scrap metal was placed on the embargo list. Two months later all types of iron and steel were embargoed.

As Japanese-American relations rapidly

deteriorated, unofficial talks were initiated to see if somehow an agreement might take the two governments off a collision course. Two Catholic priests, who had talked with Japanese leaders, Father Drought and Bishop Walsh, arrived in the United States early in 1941 and conferred with Secretary of State Hull and Japanese Ambassador Nomura Kichisaburo. Nomura thereupon drafted a proposal which was presented to Hull and to Tokyo. By its terms Japan would agree to employ only peaceful measures in the Southwest Pacific and would aid Germany under terms of her alliance only if that country were the victim of aggression. The United States in return would restore normal American-Japanese trade, assist Japan in obtaining raw materials in the Southwest Pacific, and press the *Kuomintang*-Nationalist government to make peace. When the Japanese government reviewed these terms, the proposed restrictions on Japan's role under her alliance were omitted, and Tokyo demanded that the United States stop aiding Britain. Furthermore, Japan deleted the pledge prohibiting the use of force in the Southwest Pacific. The United States was to be offered only guarantees on a "neutralized" Philippines.

Secretary of State Hull pursued the American side of the talks by asking Japan's acceptance of four principles which, as he had been saying for years, must be the basis for agreement on specific issues. The first of these was respect for the sovereignty and territorial integrity of nations. The second was the principle of noninterference in the internal affairs of other states. The third was support of the principle of equality, including equality of commercial opportunity. The fourth was nondisturbance of the status quo in the Pacific except as it might be altered by peaceful means. From this confrontation two things were clear: (1) the United States was advancing ethically unimpeachable principles which could become the foundation of a program sharply limiting Japanese expansion, and (2) the Japanese wanted an end to embargoes and to American aid to China, not a debate on principles.

The Hull-Nomura conversations, which began in April just after the conclusion of the Soviet-Japanese Nonaggression Pact, were to continue until the Pearl Harbor attack in December. From beginning to end they were as futile as diplomatic discussions could be. The American refusal to abandon announced principles showed that the Japanese had badly miscalculated the growing seriousness of American intentions in East Asia. At the same time Japan had no intention of getting out of China save on its own terms, or to forego expansion in Southeast Asia. The only virtue of the talks was that they gave both powers more time to prepare for what was coming, and the United States needed that time desperately.

By early summer the march of events was propelling the United States and Japan toward a momentous crisis. Germany's invasion of the Soviet Union, June 22, 1941, without previous advice to Japan, spurred action in Tokyo. On July 2, an Imperial Japanese Conference agreed to advance in Indochina, to observe the Nonaggression Pact with the Soviet Union, and to join in the European war when the defeat of Russia became imminent. General mobilization was ordered. New bases in Indochina were demanded of the Vichy government. By the end of July new Japanese armies were in the French colony. Operational plans were hastened looking to invasion of Malaya, the East Indies, and the Philippines. The navy began practice for an attack on Pearl Harbor, which had been considered as early as January.

On the American side, Roosevelt reacted swiftly to the Japanese occupation of Indochina by issuing, July 26, an executive order freezing all Japanese assets in the United States. The order, which was based on the existence of an "unlimited national emergency," meant the virtual end of trade between the United States and Japan.[10]

[10] Donald S. Friedman, *The Road from Isolation: The Campaign of the American Committee for Non-Participation in Japanese Aggression, 1938–1940* (1968),* is a study of a pressure group seeking the imposition of economic sanctions on Japan. The firm policy advocated by this group and ultimately adopted by the Roosevelt administration was intended to demonstrate its deep concern over the Far Eastern situation and the danger to Japan of violating the princi-

Most important of all, it meant a full embargo on oil. At this point Japanese proponents of a peaceful settlement began what was to be a final effort to avoid war. Premier Konoye Fumimaro proposed in August a meeting with President Roosevelt somewhere in the Pacific. The meeting was never held, for the President informed Nomura that Japan must first stop the military advances and give a clearer statement of her purposes. With the collapse of this proposal the Japanese High Command led by the Minister of War Tojo Hideki and his Kwantung officer clique increased their pressure for a decision on war with America. An Imperial Conference, September 6, concluded that if in a month there was not substantial evidence that the United States would accept Japan's position, war would be forthcoming.[11] The

substantial evidence was not forthcoming. Nomura had nothing to offer that Hull would accept. American principles and Japanese purposes were as far apart as they had been in May. The time had come when Tojo was to have a free hand. The result was that Konoye resigned and on October 18, Tojo became Prime Minister.

The war plans of the Tojo cabinet were approved by another Imperial Conference, November 5. It was agreed that (1) a new proposal would be made to the United States which must be accepted by November 25, and (2) failure would mean war, with simultaneous attacks on Pearl Harbor, Manila, and Singapore. Kurusu Saburo, a special Japanese envoy, reached Washington, November 17, but had no new instructions. To keep the negotiations going while a Japanese fleet moved toward Pearl Harbor, Japan presented new proposals on November 20. They provided an avenue to new troubles rather than an end to old ones. In reply, Hull gave Nomura, on November 26, a comprehensive basic proposal for a general peaceful settlement. It was not an ultimatum, for it left Japan a choice of four alternatives, but it was a denial of everything Japan had set out to do since 1931. She could choose to reverse her policy, to continue the war in China but refrain from further southern advances, to retreat, or to march on. On December 1, an Imperial Conference made the final decision for war with the United States.[12] The American government had long known that zero hour was near. The Japanese codes had been broken. Yet it was not known where the Japanese would strike. Would Congress and the

ples upon which American policy rested. Sanctions presumably would strengthen the hands of those Japanese who opposed war with the United States. In this presumption, the United States probably was wrong. Among the Japanese military, especially middle grade officers, American trade restrictions only "proved" the inevitability of war. Moreover, insofar as American restrictions depleted Japan's ability to wage the "inevitable" war, sanctions gave substance to arguments that Japan was being "encircled" and that she should pursue the southern strategy. Chihiro Hosoya, "Twenty-five Years after Pearl Harbor: A New Look at Japan's Decision for War," *Imperial Japan and Asia: A Reassessment*, Grant K. Goodman, comp. Occasional Papers of the East Asian Institute, Columbia University (1967), 52–63. Joseph C. Grew, the American Ambassador to Japan, was the most important official personage warning that American policy would not deter the Japanese. Citing "psychological factors," Grew reminded Washington that Japan remained a land of "hard warriors," whose values would not permit them to be intimidated by American pressures. Waldo H. Henrichs, *American Ambassador: Joseph C. Grew and the Development of the United States Diplomatic Tradition* (1966).

[11] The timing of the decision was due in part to the fact that until September 4, Tokyo did not believe Hull was serious about incorporating his four principles into an agreement with Japan. When the Japanese government discovered the American intention, its reaction was colored by a belief that the United States had suddenly stiffened its demands. This belief in turn encouraged acceptance of the ideas that the United States was not negotiating seriously and that war was the only recourse. These ideas, it appears, sprang from Tokyo's being misinformed

about the American position. While Hull strove to make clear the American insistence on its principles throughout his talks, Ambassador Nomura, committed personally to a settlement and handicapped by inexperience in diplomacy as well as deficiencies in his comprehension of English, glossed over the Secretary's demands in his reports. Robert J. C. Butow, "The Hull-Nomura Conversations: A Fundamental Misconception," *The American Historical Review* 65 (1960): 822–36.

[12] Nobutaka Ike, *Japan's Decision for War: Records of the 1941 Policy Conference* (1967), a splendid translation of documents revealing the thought of Japanese leadership.

American people support the administration in war on Japan if her next attacks were confined to British and Dutch territories in Southeast Asia? [13] The prevailing assumption in Washington was that Japan would attack British and Dutch but not American territory. Moreover, the American army and navy were demanding more time for preparation. One final effort—if not for peace, at least for delay—was made. On December 6, President Roosevelt sent a direct appeal to the emperor. It reached Grew in Tokyo too late, almost at the moment of the Pearl Harbor attack.

Nomura and Kurusu presented Japan's reply to Hull at 2:20 P.M., December 7. It was a summation of Japan's case against the United States and an announcement that the negotiations were ended. Delays in decoding had prevented its presentation at 1:00 P.M., just in advance of the attack on Pearl Harbor. Thus when the note was presented, Hull knew, but the Japanese envoys did not, that the bombs had fallen. Hull looked at the note (he already knew what was in it), told his callers that it was "crowded with infamous falsehoods," and directed them to leave. Later in the afternoon Japan declared war. The following day Great Britain and the United States declared war on Japan. Germany and Italy declared war on the United States, December 11.

PEARL HARBOR

Japanese planes launched from carriers had crippled the United States Pacific Fleet at Pearl Harbor and had destroyed most American aircraft in the Hawaiian Islands.

[13] While Roosevelt was concerned whether Congress would declare war in response to a Japanese attack on British or Dutch possessions in Asia, he committed his administration to assist Britain in the event of such an attack. The commitment was made informally and was gradually expanded. By December 3, the President promised help even if Britain went to war in response to a Japanese attack on Thailand. Raymond A. Esthus, "President Roosevelt's Commitment to Britain to Intervene in a Pacific War," *The Mississippi Valley Historical Review*, L (1963), 28–38.

The casualties were as staggering as the damage to the fleet: 2,343 dead, 1,272 wounded, 960 missing. That much of the crippled fleet was back in service within a year was belated compensation for the greatest naval disaster in all American history. Providentially, the Japanese did not follow up their victory with an effort to invade the Hawaiian Islands. Having for the time being paralyzed American naval power in the Pacific, Japan was free to pursue her immediate objective, the conquest of southeastern Asia —Hong Kong, Malay, the Philippines, and the Indies.

Responsibility for the Pearl Harbor disaster presents a complex problem in historical interpretation. By July, 1946, there had already been eight official investigations; yet it seemed that the full story had not been revealed. Although the earliest investigations made by the then Secretary of the Navy, Frank Knox, and Associate Supreme Court Justice Owen Roberts, laid the major responsibility on the Pearl Harbor commanders, Admiral Husband S. Kimmel and General Walter C. Short, later investigations, including that of a joint Congressional committee, tended to lay less blame on the commanders and more upon departments and personalities in the government at Washington. Whatever the ultimate verdict of history may be, the Pearl Harbor attack was of tremendous importance not merely as a military catastrophe but also in its political implications. If in the American mind there remained on the morning of December 7 any lingering doubts as to the role of the United States in the struggle against totalitarianism, Pearl Harbor removed them.

Americans sought what satisfaction they could by labelling the catastrophe Japan's "sneak attack." At best, this was consolation only to the thoughtless. At worst it was a convenient diversion from the hard and cold facts that it was the business of the government and of the armed services not to be taken by surprise. There were both immediate and long-range reasons suggesting that the attack should have been anticipated. American carriers in war games in 1932 had carried out a successful Sunday morning attack on Pearl Harbor. Grew had warned the State Department eleven months in advance that if war came Japan might open hostilities with an attack on Pearl Harbor. From September on, intercepted Japanese messages revealed a sharp interest in the location of ships at Pearl Harbor. As the American-Japanese conversations were drawing to a close in November, Grew and Hull had given repeated warnings that the Japanese might depend upon surprise and on simultaneous attack at several points. Such warnings, of course, were not the only ones received. From diplomatic channels and intelligence, the Roosevelt administration obtained a welter of conflicting evidence on what Japan might do. Some of this supported the prevailing assumption that Japan would attack Dutch and British possessions, not American territory. Even so, by early December Washington was sufficiently persuaded of the possibility of war that field commanders were alerted. Yet in spite of this alert both the American government and armed forces were taken by surprise.[14]

[14] History has not yet uncovered the full explanation of Pearl Harbor. Theories and hypotheses have been abundant. Of these the most seductive, especially in times of crisis, has involved what may be called the conspiratorial theory of history. Applied to Pearl Harbor, this theory has been construed to mean that Roosevelt and his top advisers planned, plotted, and permitted the disaster as the only sure means of converting the American people to war against Germany and its Axis partners. Although there was evidence of errors in judgment, bungling, and culpable negligence at Pearl Harbor and at Washington, the hypothesis of conspiracy in 1941 still remains an hypothesis. The conspiratorial theory is developed in varying degrees in George Morganstern, *Pearl Harbor: The Story of the Secret War* (1947); C. A. Beard, *President Roosevelt and the Coming of the War, 1941* (1948); W. H. Chamberlain, *America's Second Crusade* (1950); F. R. Stanborn, *Design for War: A Study in Secret Power Politics, 1937–1941* (1951); C. C. Tansill, *Back Door to War: The Roosevelt Foreign Policy* (1952); H. E. Barnes, ed., *Perpetual War for Perpetual Peace* (1953); R. A. Theobald, *The Final Secret of Pearl Harbor: The Washington Contribution to the Japanese Attack* (1954); H. E. Kimmel, *Admiral Kimmel's Story* (1955). Forrest C. Pogue, *George C. Marshall: Ordeal and Hope, 1939–1942* (1966) contains one of the most

THE SINO-JAPAESE UNDECLARED WAR. Paul H. Clyde, "Japan's March to Empire: Some Bibliographic Evaluations," *Journal of Modern History* 21 (1949): 333–43. Alvin D. Coox, *Year of the Tiger* (1964), excellent essays on such topics as the "rape" of Nanking, *Panay* crisis, and the *Ladybird* affair. F. F. Liu, *A Military History of Modern China, 1924–1949* (1956), one of the fullest accounts of China's mobilization and military effort. Further insight into the Chinese war effort may be had from T. A. Bisson, *Japan in China* (1938); L. K. Rosinger, *China's Wartime Politics, 1937–1944* (1944); H. F. MacNair, ed., *Voices from Unoccupied China* (1944); and E. F. Carlson, *Twin Stars of China* (1940). Yale C. Maxon, *Control of Japanese Foreign Policy: A Study of Civil-Military Rivalry, 1930–1945* (1957) portrays the effect of extremist movements upon national policy.

THE CONFLICT IN WORLD POLITICS. F. C. Jones, *Japan's New Order in East Asia, Its Rise and Its Fall, 1937–1945* (London, 1954) studies Japanese diplomacy from a global viewpoint. Seiji G. Hishida, *Japan Among the Great Powers: A Survey of Her International Relations* (1940), heavy on Japanese official interpretations. A brief and excellent study in German of Japan's dealings with the Soviet Union is Hubertus Lupke, *Japan's Russlandpolitik Von 1939 Bis 1941* (Frankfurt am Main, 1962). Frank W. Ikle, *German-Japanese Relations, 1936–1940: A Study of Totalitarian Diplomacy* (1956); and Ernst L. Presseisen, *Germany and Japan: A Study in Totalitarian Diplomacy, 1933–1941* (The Hague, 1958) are complementary studies emphasizing respectively the Japanese and German sides of diplomacy. Johanna M. Meskill, *Hitler and Japan: The Hollow Alliance* (1966), em-

balanced and coherent accounts of the Pearl Harbor disaster. Roberta Wohlstetter, *Pearl Harbor: Warning and Decision* (1962) is an exhaustive study of what the United States knew of Japanese plans and what happened to the information.

phasizes the failure of the Axis as a military partnership. Paul W. Schroeder, *The Axis Alliance and Japanese-American Relations, 1941* (1958) concludes that the Axis alliance was a lesser factor in Japan's decision to attack the United States than was the rigidity of American policy.

THE UNITED STATES AND JAPAN. W. L. Langer and S. E. Gleason, *The World Crisis and American Foreign Policy: The Challenge to Isolation, 1937–1940,* (Vol. I); and *The Undeclared War, 1940–1941* (Vol. II) (1952, 1953) sets the far eastern crisis in the perspective of world conflict. Herbert Feis, *The Road to Pearl Harbor: the Coming of the War between the United States and Japan* (1950),* an intensive study of American records. Robert J. C. Butow, *Tojo and the Coming of the War* (1961)*; and David J. Lu, *From the Marco Polo Bridge to Pearl Harbor: Japan's Entry into World War II* (1961) are careful studies that lead to different interpretations. On the Japanese attack see Hans L. Trefousse, ed., *What Happened at Pearl Harbor; Documents Pertaining to the Japanese Attack of December 7, 1941, and Its Background* (1958)*; and Paul Burtness and Warren U. Ober, *The Puzzle of Pearl Harbor* (1962).

"Colonial" Southeast Asia
I. The Philippines Under American Rule

chapter 28

Before entering upon the narrative of World War II, some attention must be given to colonial empires in that vast area of the Far East commonly known as Southeast Asia. Southeast Asia is usually defined to include: (on the mainland of Asia) Burma, Siam (Thailand), Malay, Cambodia, Laos, Annam (Vietnam), and Cochin China; and the insular areas of the Philippines and the East Indies, including Indonesia, Borneo, and lesser island groups. This immense geographical region is an area in which China, Japan, and the West have attempted the creation of distinctive international orders. In the late nineteenth century, territories which had been Chinese dependencies became colonial outposts of Britain and France (see Chapter 14). The United States acquired the Philippines. This incorporation of much of Southeast Asia into the Western colonial system was short-lived. On the eve of World War II colonialism, which for a time had ensured in Southeast Asia a measure of stability, was challenged by Japanese expansion, by Chinese nationalism, and by the appearance of independence and nationalistic movements in the lesser states of the region. After the war, the creation of weak inde-pendent states on the Indo-Chinese peninsula was an invitation to further domestic disorder and to a renewal of international rivalry. In presenting the essentials of this story, the present chapter and the one that follows will deal with Western colonial movements and the appearance of various forms of native nationalism. Chapters 36 and 37 will describe the transition from colonialism to "independence" and the resulting struggles for control of Southeast Asia.

THE REPUBLICANS IN THE PHILIPPINES

The beginnings of American rule in the Philippines were a product of many historic factors (see Chapter 15, p. 201): the character of the Spanish colonial system, the birth of native nationalism in the islands, and the unpredictable decision of the United States, in a war designed to free Cuba, to acquire an Asiatic empire. The earliest decisions on American policy and administration in the islands were in a very literal sense determined by the march of events. There was no colonial precedent in the American tradition. Long after the decision to keep the islands had been made, American policy remained a matter of immediate imperatives: to prevent the islands from falling into other hands and to suppress native insurrection against the American conqueror.

Nevertheless, during the years of what may be termed Republican rule in the Philippines to 1913, the United States moved with vigor to form and to implement a positive policy designed to establish political stability, to promote economic growth, to create a system of public education, to transform the pest- and plague-ridden islands into a healthy community, and to prepare the Filipino for self-government at an indefinite future time.

CONSTRUCTION OF A COLONIAL GOVERNMENT

The first task of the United States was to establish its authority. Filipino patriots, having revolted against Spanish authority and having assembled a constitutional convention, were determined not to submit to American rule. Accordingly, on January 21, 1899, only weeks after Spain and the United States had agreed to the transfer of the islands, insurgent leaders announced the establishment of the independent Philippine Republic under the presidency of Emilo Aguinaldo. Moreover, the Republic was to be defended with arms. Thus, American efforts were directed initially to the establishment under General Arthur MacArthur of a military government and to the destruction of the independence movement. The latter outcome was foretold by Aguinaldo's capture in 1901, and the rapid fading of guerilla resistance soon thereafter.

It was against this background of hostilities in the islands and popular opposition to the annexation at home that American policy was shaped. In January, 1899, before ratification of the Treaty of Paris, McKinley appointed a commission of investigation headed by Dr. J. G. Schurman of Cornell University. The preliminary and final reports of this commission, November, 1899, and January, 1900, were a comprehensive and, on the whole, accurate picture of the Philippine problem. While in the islands, the commission had attempted to make clear "the

liberal, friendly, and beneficent attitude of the United States," coupled with the fiat that American "supremacy . . . must and will be enforced." It recommended a territorial form of government since "the Filipinos are wholly unprepared for independence, and if independence were given to them they could not maintain it."

Acting on the report, McKinley appointed a second commission to provide a government in which there should be a gradual swing to civilian in the place of military control. On questions of fundamental and immediate concern, the policy of this second commission, under William Howard Taft, was definite, even arbitrary. In the Philippines the United States was supreme. No promise of independence was to be given.[1] With the exception of trial by jury and the right to bear arms, the Filipino was to enjoy all guarantees of the American Bill of Rights. The Filipino was to be given the greatest possible influence and participation in government for which his education and increasing experience would fit him. Where, however, local customs interfered with "the rule of law and the maintenance of individual freedom," custom was to give way to law.[2]

The second Philippine Commission car-

[1] For many years after Dewey had assisted Aguinaldo's return to Manila, there was much debate on the question: Did the United States promise independence to the Philippines at that time? The answer would seem to be "that the United States by properly accredited agents made no promises of independence, but that the actions of certain Americans led the Revolutionists to draw inferences, exaggerated by their hopes." George A. Malcolm, *The Government of the Philippine Islands* (1916), 121–22. See also Dean C. Worcester, *The Philippines Past and Present* (new ed., 1930), Chapter 2.

[2] It should not be assumed, however, that the political principles enunciated by the Taft Commission were either unfamiliar or unwelcome. By 1901 there already existed in the Philippines an articulate and cohesive native leadership whose political thinking was based on nineteenth-century Western liberalism. Taft, in his need to establish law and order and in a desire to justify imperialism as altruism, presented to this native leadership a program which would win its collaboration. See Bonifacio S. Salamanca, *The Filipino Reaction to American Rule, 1901–1913* (1968).

THE ADVANCE OF COLONIALISM IN SOUTHEAST ASIA

Major colonial areas ca. 1840

Additions by 1900

Sources: J. K. Fairbank, E. O. Reischauer, and A. M. Craig, *East Asia: The Modern Transformation* (Boston, Houghton Mifflin Co., 1965), p. 411; H. J. Benda and J. A. Larkin, *The World of Southeast Asia* (New York, Harper & Row, 1967), p. ix.

ried out its instructions with vigor and, on the whole, with tact. The transition from military to civil government was accomplished on July 4, 1901, when Taft became the first civil Governor. The way was thus paved for the rapid extension of local governing agencies. Prompt steps were taken to suggest that the conduct of colonial affairs was to be in consultation with the populace. To the American membership of the second Philippine Commission were added three Filipinos of wealth who were not advocates of independence: Benito Legarda, Jose R. de Luzuriaga, and T. H. Pardo de Tavera. Legarda and de Tavera were among the organizers of the native *Partido Federalista* (Federal Party), which favored peace, allegiance to the United States, and eventual admission to the Union as a state. The inclusion of Filipinos on the Commission was by no means welcome to all Americans, but Taft, as governor, was less concerned with exploitation of the material resources of the islands than with understanding the character and potentialities of the Filipinos. He was quick to note that they were proud, sensitive, and resentful of any suggestion that their race was inferior. The Commission, therefore, maintained a paternal if not always democratic attitude toward the Filipino, an attitude which Taft liked to express in the phrase "our little brown brothers." This made no appeal either to MacArthur's staff or to the rank and file of the American army of occupation. Soldiers of this young army of imperialism sang with gusto a refrain which ended:

He may be a brother of William H. Taft,
But he ain't no friend of mine!"[3]

THE PERIOD OF THE TAFT POLICY

The administration of the United States in the Philippines from 1901 to 1913 may best be described as the period of the Taft policy. Taft, first as Civil Governor, then as Secretary of War, and finally as President, gave direction and continuity to these years. To be sure, the Taft slogan "The Philippines for the Filipinos," was applied with the utmost caution. By 1907, however, Filipino political aspirations were given some recognition with the election of the first Philippine Assembly, which, as the lower house, was to share the legislative power with the Commission. Since the governor-general did not possess the power of veto, the principal check on legislation rested in the power of Congress to nullify. Taft described the political development of the whole period when he said that it was a process of making a paternal government less paternal.

THE CHANGING PHILIPPINES

During the years that followed Dewey's victory at Manila Bay, the islands and peoples of the Philippines experienced notable development, but in some respects this growth was not an unqualified blessing, since it created new problems with which the American people were not always prepared

[3] Mrs. William Howard Taft, *Recollections of Full Years* (1914), 125.

to deal. First among the notable changes of the twentieth century was the increase of population. In 1903 the islands (115,600 square miles, slightly larger than the state of Arizona) sheltered a population of something more than 7,000,000; by 1918 the figure was 10,314,310; and by 1939 it had reached 16,000,303. Along with increased population came a rising standard of living resulting from expanded agriculture, exploitation of forest resources, and the sale of these products in the duty-free American market. Between 1922 and 1934, sugar, coconut, and tobacco exports increased rapidly. After 1930 a mining industry produced gold, chrome, copper, iron, and manganese. The possibility of developing some light industry also appeared, but with the absence of coking coal there seemed little prospect for heavy industry. Philippine trade statistics provided a measure of economic development. In 1908, Americans sold some $5,000,000 worth of goods to the Philippines; in 1929, $92,592,-000. Philippine exports for the same years were $32,000,000 and $164,446,000.[4]

Most significant, too, was the phenomenal growth in Philippine-American trade. During the first decade of American rule in the Philippines, there was little change in the islands' tariff policy; the treaty of peace with Spain had provided that for ten years Spanish ships and merchandise would be admitted to Philippine ports "on the same terms as ships and merchandise of the United

[4] It is not suggested that Philippine export trade developed exclusively under American rule. The years of Spanish control brought significant economic change. When the Spanish arrived, the native populace resided in isolated, self-sufficient communities (*Barangays*). The resettlement of the populace, which accompanied conquest and Christianization, effected improvements in primitive agricultural technology and introduced limited local commerce. By the 1780s, tobacco and indigo were being cultivated for export to Spain. Fifty years later, Spain, reacting to foreign demands for Philippine products, abandoned efforts to reserve the colonial trade entirely for herself and opened Manila to all shipping. Thus the economic development of the Philippines was less a conscious feature of Spanish colonial policy than it was of American policy.

States." Then, in 1909, Congress established virtually free trade for America with the islands. Full free trade was achieved in 1913 when the quota limitations of the earlier legislation were removed. The result was an American monopoly of the Philippine export market. In 1933, American importers were taking 87 per cent of all Philippine exports. Thus, after some thirty years of American occupation and some twenty years of Philippine-American free trade, the commerce of the Philippine Islands, both export and import, had been channelled almost exclusively to the United States. Trade had indeed followed the flag, and prosperity had been the result, but each year the economic life of the Filipino people became more dependent upon the American market. This condition suggested that the islands were to continue indefinitely as an "unincorporated" territory of the United States.[5]

CHARACTERISTICS OF EARLY AMERICAN POLICY

In the years of Republican rule to 1913, American policy concerned itself primarily with large and basic tasks. The Americans who pioneered in this work left a record of substantial accomplishment. Successive presidents, McKinley, Roosevelt, and Taft, assumed that for some years no purpose was to be served by discussions for independence even as a remote possibility. For the present, it was enough, as Taft had said, that the United States was pursuing a policy of "the Philippines for the Filipinos" and was training them in self-government to open an "era of good feeling." To be sure, this policy was challenged within the United States by the "Anti-Imperialist League," and by the Democratic Party platforms of 1904, 1908, and 1912. Both denounced the idea of permanent

American sovereignty in the islands. Prior to 1912, however, this opposition was impotent. Rather paradoxically, the Republican victory of 1900 meant that the interests of the American electorate in the Philippines were soon to disappear.

Among Filipinos, independence remained a live, though scarcely urgent goal. Some early agitation for independence came from wealthy aristocrats, who with American cooperation had formed the Federal Party. By 1907, following the removal of prohibitions against political activity, a number of groups, including the nationalist revolutionary leaders of Spanish-American War days, had united in a second and stronger party, *Partido Nacionalista* (Nationalist Party), demanding "immediate independence." From 1907 onward, the Nationalists controlled the Philippine Assembly. Their public advocacy of nationhood was combined with a practical co-operation with the regime. The general tone was suggested in an Assembly resolution voting "thanks and appreciation to the American Government for its administration of the islands for the past nine years."[6] Such moderation was due undoubtedly in part to the determination of a Filipino elite to protect its recent gains. Under Spanish rule, the native Filipino aristocracy was expected to assist in the implementation of colonial policy but was unable to influence the content of policy. With the coming of the Americans, Filipinos not only were elevated to high office, but, as the operation of the public education system permitted, they also filled the lower posts of the colonial bureaucracy. Moreover, the socio-economic benefits of American rule soon satisfied Filipino leaders that co-operation with the Americans was the obvious road to national develop-

---

[5] As an "unincorporated" territory, the legal and political position of the Islands and the civil and political rights of the Filipinos under the American flag were determined by Congress, limited only by those provisions of the Constitution which were prohibitive. See J. R. Hayden, *The Philippines* (1942), 763–64.

[6] Onofre D. Corpuz. *The Philippines* (1965),* 65–71. To many Nationalist politicians, the plank of independence was largely a means of getting votes. As one Filipino expressed it, "The peasants remember that they paid heavy taxes under the Spanish regime. They do not pay as much under American rule, and the Nationalist politicians have led them to believe that, when and if independence is achieved, there will be no taxes at all.'" Grayson L. Kirk, *Philippine Independence* (1936), 42.

ment. In consequence, prior to World War I, little occurred in the islands to upset American complacency with its Philippine policy.

THE DEMOCRATS REVIVE INDEPENDENCE

In 1910 the Republicans lost control of the House of Representatives in Washington, and two years later (March, 1912), the Democrats introduced the first Philippine independence bill. This bill, sponsored by Congressman W. A. Jones of Virginia, was reported favorably by the Committee on Insular Affairs but was not acted on by the House. The election of Woodrow Wilson to the presidency was followed shortly by the appointment of Francis B. Harrison as the new governor-general of the Philippines. In his inaugural address at Manila, Harrison expressed the new American policy when he said that every official act would be "taken with a view to the ultimate independence of the Islands and as a preparation for that independence." Independence would be approached as rapidly "as the safety and the permanent interests of the islands will permit." This policy was soon implemented. A native majority replaced the American majority on the Philippine Commission, the upper house of the native legislature; throughout the government Filipinos were appointed to many posts previously held by Americans. President Wilson in August 1916 approved the Jones Act, which provided for widening autonomy in the Philippines and pledged the United States "to recognize their independence as soon as stable government can be established therein." Here for the first time the United States went on record in a qualified promise of eventual independence. After the passage of the Jones Bill, it became the practice of Philippine Nationalists to assert that the "stable government" called for by the act had already been achieved. For the time being, however, nothing could be done while the United States was absorbed in World War I.[7]

[7] See R. W. Curry, "Woodrow Wilson and Philippine Policy," *The Mississippi Valley Historical Review* 41 (1954): 435–52.

Immediately following the war, the Philippine government, encouraged by the Wilsonian principle of self-determination, sent a special mission to Washington. From Europe, Wilson informed the mission that independence was "almost in sight," and, in his annual message to a hostile Congress (December, 1920), he reminded the legislators of "our duty to keep our promise to the people of those Islands." No action, however, was taken, and as the Republicans returned to power, it was again taken for granted that independence had once more become a matter of the distant future.

In 1920, President Harding created a commission headed by General Leonard Wood and former governor W. Cameron Forbes to report on conditions in the islands. The report found that the Harrison administration had proceeded too rapidly in turning the government over to the Filipinos. While General Wood remained in the islands as governor-general with the unpopular task of imposing stricter American executive authority, the Filipino politicos redoubled their independence propaganda in Washington and throughout the United States. It made little headway.

As the Coolidge administration came to a close, the American people were again content to permit Philippine independence to wait for the indefinite future. This was not in itself an unwise resolve. Although the Wood-Forbes and later reports were political documents, they were likewise able analyses of unhappy conditions prevailing in the islands. The real trouble was that the American public in general had long since lost interest in the Philippines. Whether to continue to carry the "White Man's Burden" was, as the average American saw it, something that could be safely left to the government to decide. "Benevolent assimilation" had long since lost its glamour.

INDEPENDENCE AND POLITICAL EXPEDIENCY

American policy on Philippine independence in the decade after World War I was shaped by a peculiar mixture of moral responsibility toward wards and the pressures of interest groups seeking an end to what were styled as the "liabilities" of colonialism. As early as 1921 some farm groups wanted to curtail the importation of Philippine coconut products, but it was not until the period 1928–1929 that the business of putting a stop to the free importation of Philippine agricultural products, was undertaken seriously. Groups other than the farm organizations became interested as it was discovered by so-called patriotic societies and labor that independence was perhaps the speediest and certainly the surest way of putting an end to Philippine immigration. During the decade of the 1920s, Filipinos had migrated to the United States at an average annual rate of slightly less than 5,000. There was wide difference of opinion as to how serious this immigration was either as a labor problem or as a general social problem, but its effect was to revive many of the arguments which had been used effectively against the Chinese and the Japanese.

As the fate of the Philippines was debated in Congress from 1930 on, the question of their independence became less and less a matter of political principle and more and more one of political expediency. In December, 1932, Congress enacted the Hare-Hawes-Cutting Bill. It provided for independence after a transition period of ten years; quota limits were to be applied to Philippine imports; there was to be a gradual application of the American tariff; and finally, the Philippines were to be granted an annual immigrant quota of 50.

The Hoover presidential veto which promptly followed was no surprise, for the firm opposition of the administration to early independence was well known. In one of the ablest state papers of the Hoover regime, the President challenged the statesmanship of virtually every clause of the bill. His over-all denunciation condemned it as a repudiation of the government's moral responsibility to the American people, to the Filipinos, and to the world. As positive alternate proposals the President suggested: (1) a plebiscite to be held in fifteen or twenty years to test

Philippine sentiment, (2) immediate restriction of immigration, (3) gradual reduction of free imports, and (4) gradual enlargement of political autonomy. Eventually commercial relationships would be stabilized on the basis of a fixed mutual preference similar to but broader than that between the United States and Cuba. The Hoover veto was immediately overridden by heavy majorities, and the bill became law, though in reality it satisfied no one. As a result, under the leadership of Manuel Quezon, the offer of independence was rejected by the Philippine legislature on October 17, 1933.

Since there was no likelihood that Congress would change the economic provisions of the law, President Roosevelt suggested the only concession to Philippine sentiment which was likely to win congressional approval. He proposed amendment of the Hare-Hawes-Cutting Act by striking out the provisions for a permanent American military base in the Islands. The question of the American naval establishment was to be left to future negotiations. With this change and some minor revisions of the sugar and coconut oil quotas, the old act, now repassed as the Tydings-McDuffie Law, received presidential approval, March 24, 1934. The law was accepted by the Philippine legislature on May 1, the native leaders being convinced that no better terms would be granted. Then, after having thus provided for Philippine independence following a period of economic transition, Congress surrendered completely to the lobbyists through legislation providing for immediate drastic limitations on Philippine sugar and authorizing a processing tax on all coconut oil imports. The conclusion expressed by the *New York Times* was inescapable: "Congress is indifferent to what may truthfully be called the 'plighted word of the United States Government.'"

THE PHILIPPINES ACCEPT

The Philippines accepted the Tydings-McDuffie Law, May 1, 1934. On July 10, elections for the Constitutional Convention provided for by the Law were held. The Constitution framed by this body was approved by President Roosevelt, and was ratified by the Philippine electorate without opposition. As the Commonwealth of the Philippines was thus inaugurated, Manuel Quezon was elected the first President and Sergio Osmena Vice-President. An amendment to the Tydings-McDuffie Law, the Philippine Economic Adjustment (Tydings-Kocialkowski) Act, was approved by President Roosevelt, August 7, 1939, and accepted by the islands. This was the result of continued efforts to modify the economic clauses of the Independence Law and also of the findings of a Joint Preparatory Committee on Philippine Affairs. A report of this committee showed that even in a period of generally amicable international relations, the abrupt ending of Philippine-American trade preference in 1946 "would endanger the economic and political stability of the independent Philippine state."

After the Japanese invasion of the Philippines, December 8, 1941, the Vice-President and the United States High Commissioner in the Philippines withdrew to the United States, where in Washington a government in exile was set up. On August 2, 1944, Sergio Osmena succeeded to the presidency, following the death of Quezon. The new President was installed at Tacloban, the capital of Leyte, October 10, 1944, during the reconquest of the islands.

THE CONSTITUTION OF THE COMMONWEALTH

Philippine political institutions from the end of the Spanish regime were derived from six basic constitutional documents. The first was the so-called "Malolos Constitution" of the First Philippine Republic of 1899. It was a liberal and democratic document written by Filipino intellectuals voicing their protest against Spanish and American rule.[8] Although somewhat doctrinaire, this constitution revealed broad knowledge of western

[8] The Malolos Constitution is in the *Report of the Philippine Commission*, 1900, I, 189.

political institutions and capacity to modify them to meet Philippine conditions. A second document of constitutional importance was the Instructions to the Second Philippine Commission drawn up by Elihu Root as Secretary of War. These Instructions set forth the principles on which major American policies in and toward the Philippines were to be based. The third and fourth documents were the Organic Act of 1902 and the Organic Act of 1916; both were laws of the United States Congress creating the legal structure within which Philippine government was to be developed. The fifth was the Revised Administrative Code of 1917, an enactment of the Filipino legislature, whereby it created a government taking full advantage of the increased autonomy permitted under the Jones Law. Sixth, and finally, was the Constitution of the Commonwealth of the Philippines of 1935, which, unlike the Constitution of 1899, was drafted by a constitutional convention composed largely of experienced Filipino politicians.[9]

In the Tydings-McDuffie Law, under authority of which the Constitution of the Commonwealth was drafted, the Filipinos were required to provide a constitution, republican in form, containing a bill of rights and providing for complete religious toleration. Since these requirements would have been met regardless of the American mandate, the islands may be said to have been free to form a government expressive of their own political ideals. The result was a constitution resting on the basic political philosophy of Western democracy and providing for a republican state in which sovereignty was declared to reside with the people. The Filipino Bill of Rights was more "extended and explicit" than that contained in American constitutions. Reflecting the period in which it was written, the Constitution of the Commonwealth included concepts designed to create "social justice" for all the people.

[9] Jose M. Aruego, *The Framing of the Philippine Constitution* (2 vols., Manila, 1936), I, 22–23; and Miguel Cauderno, *The Framing of the Constitution of the Philippines* (Manila, 1937) describe the Constitution and the character of the membership of the constitutional convention.

Under this constitution, the Philippine president, elected by the direct vote of the people, was given virtually all the powers possessed by his predecessor, the American governor-general.

The Filipinos wrote into their constitution the principle of the independence and permanence of the merit system as applied to civil service. More important perhaps were the steps subsequently taken by the Commonwealth government to give immediate effect to the civil service provisions of the constitution. These steps resulted in substantial improvement; but, as in the United States, so in the Philippines, the legislature at times refused to classify positions which it was politically expedient to preserve as a part of the spoils systems. Unfortunately, too, for the merit system, Philippine society, being quasi-feudal in its family and class relationships, encouraged the rapid advancement of young men who had the protection of powerful patrons.

Until the establishment of the Commonwealth in 1935, the various legislatures of the islands, from the first elective Assembly of 1907, were marked by two significant characteristics. In the first instance, they were "colonial" legislatures; in the second, they developed as instruments for the securing of independence rather than as the lawmaking body in a state whose constitutional structure was already determined. From 1907 until 1935, with the exception of the Harrison period, the position of the American executive in the Philippine government enabled the governor-general to tender advice on legislative policy and indeed to impose decisions with far greater freedom than could have been exercised by a native executive. Moreover, one party, the Nationalists, enjoyed almost unchallenged control and thus wrote the legislative record of the young nation.

The law of the Philippines and the legal institutions created after 1899 derived their form and substance from a number of sources: from Roman law of Spanish days, from English common law as revealed in American practice, from native Filipino customary law, and from the legal code of the

Koran as it prevailed among the Mohammedans of Mindanao and Sulu. From the beginning of the American occupation, the substance of the Bill of Rights of the American Constitution was extended to the islands. With certain specific exceptions, such as trial by jury, it was included in the Organic Acts of 1902 and 1916; and, with additions, it constituted the new Bill of Rights in the Commonwealth Constitution of 1935.

Under the Commonwealth, the Supreme Court was established by the constitution; inferior courts were provided for by law. All judges were appointed by the president with the consent of a Commission on Appointments of the Congress.

POLITICAL PARTIES IN THE PHILIPPINES

During the period of American rule, Filipinos looked upon their political parties as instruments for political independence. The exception to this generalization was the Federal Party, a party of the conservative upper classes, which in the days of the insurrection was the party favoring immediate peace with the United States. Since peace could only be had by accepting American sovereignty, this party favored statehood in the American Union as the highest status to which the Philippines could aspire.[10] From 1900 to 1905, sometimes called the "period of suppressed nationalism," a great many political groups appeared which favored immediate or early independence; it was in 1907 that these abortive efforts resulted in the union of various groups to form the Nationalist Party. At the same time the Federalists adopted the name *Partido Nacional Progresita* (Nationalist Progressive Party), and thus became the conservative nationalist and independence party. Beginning with the election of the first Philippine Assembly by a semi-popular electorate in 1907, the Nationalists won a majority which it not only held but increased in successive elections. It was this party that succeeded in identifying itself most closely with the cause

[10] Dapen Liang, *The Development of Philippine Parties* (Hong Kong, 1939).

of independence. It was also this party that took the position that it was responsible to the Filipino voters as well as to the American sovereign power that had created the Assembly in which this majority party now functioned.

Until the period 1934 to 1935, when the Tydings-McDuffie Law was accepted by the Filipino people, the history of political parties in the Islands was affected and controlled primarily by (1) the issue of independence and (2) political rivalries within a small elite. During the Commonwealth the factor of personalities did not disappear, but in some degree it was subordinated to the major task of constructing a government capable of meeting new problems inseparable from independence. The need for statesmanship was emphasized by the *Sakdalista* rebellion on May 2, 1935. This was an abortive attempt by underprivileged elements to overthrow the government in Manila. The result was to hasten formation of a limited coalition between the dominant leaders, Quezon and Osmena, and their respective political followings or parties.[11] In the 1941 elections there was no opposition party; to be on the Nationalist list was to be elected.

EDUCATION IN THE PHILIPPINES

Since the beginning of the American occupation of the Philippines, Filipino leaders had favored free public education and the separation of church and state. The broad objectives of the American educational program were to abolish illiteracy, to provide every child with a modern elementary education, to provide a limited secondary and higher education, and to give instruction in the English language for all. In 1925 the accomplishments and failures of the program were revealed by a commission of recognized American educators.[12] In 1939 there were some 1,800,000 students in the Philippine

[11] By this time constant shifts and reunions among political groups had complicated party terminology. Quezon's party was now known as the *Nacionalista-Democrata;* Osmena's as the *Nacionalista-Democrata Pro-Independencia.*

[12] Board of Educational Survey, *A Survey of the Educational System of the Philippine Islands* (Manila, 1925).

public school system, or only 45 per cent of the estimated school population between the ages of 7 and 17. This percentage should be judged in the light of other factors: (1) the inability of the islands to pay for high-school education for all, and (2) consideration for the social, economic, and political problems which would arise if secondary and higher education were extended to greatly increased numbers under existing conditions.

One of the principal tasks of the Commonwealth was to reorganize its vocational schools and courses, to elevate the prestige of vocational training, and to adjust these courses to the practical needs of the country. Despite these efforts, Filipino students still showed a marked preference for the academic course and the prestige which it carried.

THE PHILIPPINE EXPERIMENT IN PERSPECTIVE

To recapitulate, it may be said that the period of American rule in the Philippines, 1898 to 1934, and the first years of the Commonwealth that followed, brought progressive changes to the life of the islands. These changes were often described as substantial foundations for an emerging democratic society. When the Commonwealth came into being in 1934, the new constitution was received as a logical product of American democratic thought, and as a democratic promise for the future. During the Commonwealth, however, this promise was fulfilled to a very limited degree, if at all. Filipino democracy in practice showed little in common with its formal description as given in the constitution. Government possessed the constitutional forms of an American-style democracy, but in actual operation it evolved "into a quasi-dictatorship with democratic embellishments." [13]

From 1934 until the Japanese invasion (December, 1941 to January, 1942), the Commonwealth of the Philippines was put to the hard test of running its own practical politics. President Quezon was the political

[13] Lennox A. Mills, "The Governments of Southeast Asia," *Government and Nationalism in Southeast Asia,* Mills, *et al.,* eds. (1942), 65.

master of the islands. He and a few colleagues controlled the patronage. He was adept at influencing all classes, including the little man who liked his program of "social justice." In the election of 1941, Quezon, without effort, was reelected by 90 per cent of the vote cast. This willingness to accept Quezon and the Nationalist Party was partly a tribute from the nation to those who had won independence, but it also signified how few were those who indulged in independent political thought.[14]

These shortcomings in politics were partly a reflection of failures to integrate all sections of the populace into the national life. Obstacles to the development of strong national and democratic institutions were to be found in the more than forty ethnographic groups and more than eighty languages and dialects which divided the people. Moreover, the barriers separating Christian, Mohammedan, and pagan created serious problems for the young Commonwealth. At the time of the Japanese invasion of 1941, for example, it was as yet too early to evaluate efforts to win the political allegiance of culturally heterogeneous Mindanao, the great southern island. Thus, factors linking the small ruling elite, such as a common ability to communicate in English or Spanish and subscription to similar political principles, were missing among the masses. An educated elite could write into the Constitution of the Commonwealth the Western principle of equality before the law; but there is little

---

[14] Clause A. Buss, "The Philippines," *The New World of Southeast Asia*, Lennox A. Mills, ed. (1940), 38–39. There were, of course, factional quarrels within the Nationalist Party, but the issues were never permitted to become matters of principle or party program. Men such as Quintin Paredes, Jose Yulo, Claro Recto, and Manuel Roxas might feign revolt, but in the end they humbly did the bidding of the single party machine. There were a few minority leaders who refused to join the Nationalists, to bow humbly to its dictates, or to be silenced by its machine: Tomas Confesor, who later won added distinction as a guerilla; Wenceslao Vinsons, a champion of the miners who was elected to the Assembly, though opposed by the Nationalists, and was later killed by the Japanese; and Pedro Abad Santos, who championed the cause of the peasants of Luzon.

---

evidence that this same elite had either the desire or the capacity to implement the principle in the every day life of Philippine society.

THE SOCIOECONOMIC SYSTEM

Although American rule had brought to the Philippines a kind of prosperity, it was not of the sort best calculated to reinforce democratic concepts and practices. Surprisingly, little was done to broaden the base of the islands' internal wealth. The problem was admittedly difficult. The fact was, however, that the United States had not removed the incubus of the old Spanish land grants or dealt effectively with the abuses of landlordism. Thus there was created a paradox in which a humanitarian America built schools, sewer systems, and hospitals while an imperial America tolerated a socioeconomic system suggestive of the Middle Ages.[15] The well-being of landlords and compradors was not shared proportionately by the peasants. Concentrating on money-crop products such as sugar for the American trade, the islands had to import rice that might have been grown at home. Out of these economic maladjustments came the report of the Joint Preparatory Committee on Philippine Affairs and the resulting Economic Adjustment (Tydings-Kocialkowski) Act of 1939 extending the period for favored treatment of Philippine products in the American market beyond the date when the Commonwealth was to give place to the free Republic. By 1941 the Philippine economy was in crisis, and both in the islands and in the United States there was talk of re-examination and of dominion status.

Social conditions in the islands were tied closely to and affected by the antiquated economic structure. In 1941, the American high commissioner described the social and political health in alarming terms. He noted that neither a sizeable independent middle class nor an influential public opinion had developed. The bulk of newly created income had gone to the government, to the landlords, and to urban areas, but had done little to ameliorate living conditions among the

[15] Buss, "The Philippines," 40–41.

peasantry and tenancy. Maldistribution of population, of land, and of wealth in many forms continued. The gap between the mass population and the small governing class had broadened, and social unrest had reached serious proportions.[16]

PARADOXES IN AMERICAN POLICY

It has been said that in the history of the United States and its possessions no chapter can compare in point of "glaring contradictions and inconsistencies" with the chapter on the Philippines. This statement finds its foundation in the fact that while American political policy was directed toward self-government and then toward independence, American economic policy made the islands dependent on a free American market. Interestingly enough, both policies were implemented by the Democratic Party. Moreover, while the Independence Act of 1934 was often described as a pious fulfillment, the motivation behind it was almost wholly the desire of certain American producers to exclude Philippine products. Finally, independence was granted at a time when abler Filipino leaders no longer desired it, and upon terms that were economically disastrous to the islands. The paradox in all this becomes even more pronounced when it is recognized that the American policy of free trade brought a kind of prosperity to the Philippines and limited economic benefits to the United States itself. Furthermore, the persistent Filipino demand for independence was based on psychological rather than economic factors of national politics. In this demand for independence, Filipino politicos outdid themselves. By 1929 they were admitting privately that they would accept a modified dominion status with continued free trade with the United States. These ideas came too late. In the United States the pressures to be rid of the islands were already too strong.[17]

[16] Fifth annual report of the high commissioner for the fiscal year ending June 30, 1941, quoted by Buss, "The Philippines," 42–43.

[17] Julius W. Pratt, *America's Colonial Experiment* (1950), 291–98.

FOR FURTHER READING

SPANISH RULE. Jose Montero y Vidal, *Historia general de Filipinas desde el desubrimiento de dichas islas hasta neustros dias* (3 vols., Madrid, 1887), among the best of the older accounts of the operations of Spanish colonialism. John Foreman, *The Philippine Islands* (1899), is by a foreign visitor and tends to be critical of the Spanish regime. Scholarly and readable accounts of early European activities on the islands are H. De La Costa, *The Jesuits in the Philippines, 1581–1768* (1961), and Rafel Lopez and Alfonso Felix, Jr., *The Christianization of the Philippines* (Manila, 1965). O. D. Corpuz, *The Bureaucracy of the Philippines* (Manila, 1957), and Arthur L. Carson, *Higher Education in the Philippines* (1961) treat Spanish contributions as well as more recent developments. Alfonso Felix, Jr., ed., *The Chinese in the Philippines, 1570–1770* (Manila, 1966), and Edgar Wickberg, *The Chinese in Philippine Life, 1850–1898* (1965) are important contributions to social and economic history under Spanish rule.

EARLY FILIPINO NATIONALISM. Conrad Benitez, *History of the Philippines: Economic, Social, Cultural, Political* (rev. ed., 1954), an original study from pre-Spanish times onward. Gregorio F. Zaide, *Philippines: Political and Cultural History* (rev. ed., 2 vols., Manila, 1957), a detailed and well-documented account by a Filipino historian. Leandro H. Fernandez, *The Philippine Republic* (1926) remains a standard work on the Revolution and First Republic, though it has been superceded by more recent research. Theodoro Agoncillo, *The Revolt of the Masses: The Story of Bonifacio and the Katipuhan* (Quezon City, 1956), and *Malolos: The Crisis of the Republic* (Quezon City, 1960); Cesar Adib Majul, *The Political and Constitutional Ideas of the Philippine Revolution* (Quezon City, 1957); and *Mabini and the Philippine Revolution* (Quezon City, 1960) are four complementary pioneer studies by Filipino historians. While founded on solid research, the volumes are marred by attempts to view the revolutionary movement in terms of class struggle. Pedro de Achutegui, S. J., and Miguel Bernad, S. J., *Religious Revolution in the Philippines: Life and Church of Gregorio Aglipay, 1860–1940* (Manila, 1960) is a valuable chronicle of religious nationalism. The activities of two revolutionary leaders may be glimpsed in Emilio Aguinaldo and V. A. Pacio, *A Second Look at America* (1957), and Jose Rizal, *One Hundred Letters of Jose Rizal* (Manila, 1959), W. H. Gray, "The First Constitution of the Philippines," *The Pacific Historical Review* 26 (1957): 341–51, recounts an early effort to introduce into the islands liberal ideas from Europe.

AMERICAN RULE AND THE COMMONWEALTH. *The Philippines Circa 1900: Book One, Philippine Life in Town and Country*, by James A. LeRoy; *Book Two, Yesterdays in the Philippines*, by Joseph E. Stevens (reprint ed., Manila, 1968). Leon Wolff, *Little Brown Brother: How the United States Purchased and Pacified the Philippine Islands at the Century's Turn* (1961) provides a detailed narrative. On this topic see also Julius Pratt, *Expansionists of 1898: The Acquisition of Hawaii and the Spanish Islands* (1936)° Josefa M. Saniel, *Japan and the Philippines, 1868–1898* (Quezon City, 1963), reveals that Japanese, like Americans, responded positively to the idea of "uplifting" the Filipino. On the development of American colonial policy, 1898–1946, see Garel A. Grunder and William E. Livezey, *The Philippines and the United States* (1951). Frank T. Reuter, *Catholic Influence on American Colonial Policies, 1898–1904* (1967) deals with an important pressure group. Richard L. Deats, *The Story of Methodism in the Philippines* (Manila, 1964) is the first scholarly study of Protestant missionary work in the islands. Pedro E. Abelarde, *American Tariff Policy towards the Philippines, 1898–1946* (1947) is a careful study to 1941, but is weak on the post-war period. Georges Fisher, *Un Cas de Decolonisation: Les Etats-Unis et les Philippines* (Paris, 1960) points up the conflict

between the American political and economic policies. Gerald E. Wheeler, "Republican Philippine Policy, 1921–1933," *The Pacific Historical Review* 28 (1959): 377–90, outlines the considerations leading the United States to slow the progress of the independent movement. See also Shirley Jenkins, *American Economic Policy toward the Philippines* (1954). Theodore Friend, *Between Two Empires: The Ordeal of the Philippines, 1929–1946* (1965) provides discussion of the 1930's which is especially rewarding to the advanced student. Accounts by American colonial officials include: W. Cameron Forbes, *The Philippine Islands* (rev. ed., 1945); and George A. Malcolm, *The First Malayan Republic (The Philippines)* (1951), and *American Colonial Careerist* (1957). Albert Ravenholt, *The Philippines, A Young Republic on the Move* (1962)° is a popular introductory survey. George E. Taylor, *The Philippines and the United States, Problems of Partnership* (1964) analyzes U.S.-Philippine problems and surveys Philippine history from colonial period to the early 1960's.

Among studies of Philippine politics not already cited in footnotes are: Sergio Osmena, *The Problem of Democratic Government in the Philippines: Its Salient Aspects* (1925); Theodore Friend, "The Philippine Sugar Industry and the Politics of Independence," *Journal of Asian Studies*, 22 (1963): 179–192; and David R. Sturtevant, "Sakalism and Philippine Radicalism," *Journal of Asian Studies*, XXI (1962), 199–213. Isabelo P. Caballero and M. deGracia, *Quezon: The Story of a Nation and Its Foremost Statesman* (Manila, 1935) is an uncritical biography. Data on the social basis of politics is given in the following: H. W. Krieger, *Peoples of the Philippines* (1942); Conrad Benitez, *et al., Philippine Social Life and Progress* (1937); and K. K. Kirhara, *Labor in the Philippine Economy* (London, 1945). The reaction to the Japanese invasion is given in Carlos P. Romulo, *I Saw the Fall of the Philippines* (1942).

"Colonial" Southeast Asia
II. The British, French, and Dutch

chapter 29

Four centuries ago adventurous Western navigators seeking a new and more profitable way to put spices on the dinner tables in Europe founded their first trading posts on the shores of Southeast Asia. While from these beginnings there grew in time European empires of great size and wealth, the character of the early Western settlements in Southeast Asia was pre-eminently commercial rather than political. For example, after two centuries of occupation, the Dutch residents in Java still looked upon themselves as merchants staying abroad for purposes of trade. Although on occasion they used their constabulary to subdue unruly native peoples in the neighborhood of the commercial settlements, Dutch traders remained merchants rather than colonizers.[1] In general, too, the Portuguese and British settlements in Southeast Asia were for long merely outposts of their Indian settlements. Europeans seldom went to Southeast Asia with the conscious

[1] The territories were usually referred to as colonies, though in reality they were not colonies because there were no colonists. They resembled colonies because they were not self-governing, but they differed from colonies in being under alien rule and subject to an alien economic system.

or deliberate purpose of building empires, though in the long run that was what they eventually did.

For some three centuries, the importance of the general area of Southeast Asia rested primarily on the spice trade, coffee, and tobacco. The meat and fish which Europeans ate in winter had been preserved without benefit of refrigeration by salting them away in the fall. When later they were brought to the dinner table, the richly aged taste was softened by heavy doses of pepper, mustard, nutmeg, cinnamon, and cloves. Spices, therefore, commanded a price for which men would risk their fortunes and their lives. Control of the spice trade was a major avenue to wealth and power for men and for nations. Since most spices came from the East Indies, as they do even today, Southeast Asia acquired immense political as well as economic importance. In more recent years, the spice trade has declined in relative importance, but this has not decreased the significance of Southeast Asia, which in contemporary times has become a source of rubber, tin, oil, sugar, and many other products. This fact in part explains why alien control of Southeast Asia in one form or another was an issue in World War II. One of Japan's chief objectives was to break the

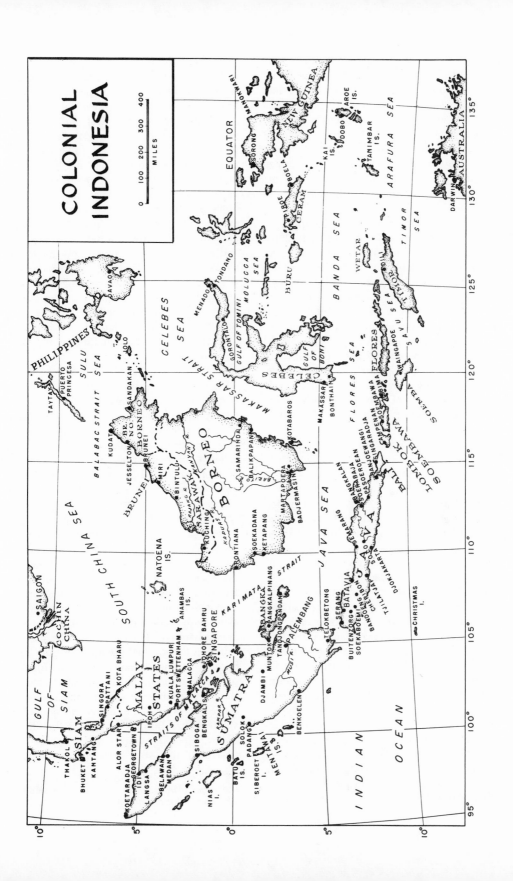

political bonds of Europe and America in Southeast Asia, and, under the guise of bringing freedom to this area, to incorporate it into the Japanese sphere known as Greater East Asia. But even before this struggle came to a crisis in World War II, other conflicting forces of great moment were stirring among the native peoples of Southeast Asia. Principal among these was the appearance of nationalistic movements rebelling against foreign control.

Although the Far Eastern empires of Spain, Portugal, and the Netherlands dated back to the sixteenth and seventeenth centuries, the development of mature patterns of control in Southeast Asia was an achievement of the nineteenth century. These patterns were the work of the Dutch in the East Indies (Netherlands India), of the British in Burma and Malaya, and of the French in Indochina. The British and French systems were closely related to the roles played by these powers in the nineteenth-century opening of China. British policy was also an aspect of Britain's position in India.

NETHERLANDS INDIA

Prior to the arrival of European traders —first the Portuguese and later the Dutch— the development of the East Indies was the work largely of Malay migrants from the Asian continent. The cultural patterns established by these people were complex in that, while there was a basic cultural identity, life on the islands of the far-reaching archipelago encouraged a diversity of language and custom. Moreover, subsequent immigration and trade introduced the influences of Hinduism, Buddhism, and Islam. By the eighth century, commerce and agriculture had developed sufficiently to sustain several competing kingdoms in Java, and by the twelfth century the spice trade with Indian, Arabian, and Persian merchants was flourishing. Government was usually conducted through tiny princely states, but in the fourteenth century the Javanese empire of Majapahit established a measure of unity throughout the islands. It was the decline of this empire and the resumption of local rivalries which facilitated European penetration, leading to conquest and control.

Dutch rule in the East Indies was the product of sustained efforts at economic exploitation. The Dutch East India Company, which carried the flag of the Netherlands into the East, was interested in trade and not in government. Experience suggested, however, that trade was dependent on government. Consequently, by 1750 the Company had gradually shifted to a territorial and political base. Through agreements with native rulers, the Company from its trading posts acquired indirect control over large areas of the islands. But in the process of doing so, its profits declined, and when in time the Company collapsed, the whole undertaking was assumed in 1800 by the Dutch government.[2]

After the Napoleonic Wars, during which the Indies were held briefly by the British, the Dutch, beset in the islands by mounting deficits, devised measures which were intended to increase revenue but which also tightened colonial rule. Under a so-called Culture System, natives placed part of their land and labor at the disposal of government for the cultivation of export crops. The three principal results of this system were: (1) the Dutch treasury prospered; (2) abuses led to exploitation of the peasantry; and (3) general economic development was retarded, seemingly because of the exclusion of private Western enterprise. By mid-nineteenth century, however, demands for reform by Dutch civil servants, along with increased political power at home in the hands of the Dutch middle class, resulted in the gradual abolition of the Culture System, in the entrance into the Indies of private enterprise, and in increased guardianship of the natives by government. This last aspect of policy, the Dutch version of the White Man's Burden, known as the "Ethical Policy," soon became a major characteristic of Dutch rule. By 1910 the proddings of

[2] The best brief account is J. D. Legge, *Indonesia* (1964).* See also Amry Vandenbosch, *The Dutch East Indies* (1942).

"moral duty" and fear of foreign intervention prompted the Dutch, who had preserved in many areas the form of indirect rule used by the East India Company, to extend their authority throughout the islands. This extension of authority coincided with the beginnings of a native nationalism.

Nationalism theoretically challenged Dutch rule in that it fostered organizations which looked toward the creation of a just and prosperous society under native leadership. Moslem members of such organizations as *Sarekat Islam* advocated establishment of an Islamic state, while Communists, whose party was founded in the 1920s, sought a secular policy derived from Western radicalism. Contending with both of these groups were nationalists whose thinking was influenced by nineteenth-century Western liberalism. All nationalists recruited followers through study clubs and privately supported schools. The Dutch, uncertain initially as how to respond to these movements, did not turn to suppression until Communists staged uprisings in 1926 and 1927, after which mass arrests of political leaders resulted in the jailing of such nationalist figures as Achmed Sukarno, Soetan Sjahrir, and Mohammed Hatta. In consequence, the nationalist movement after 1929 appeared to decline. Its later revival in the mid-1930s was on a more co-operative basis with the Dutch as remaining nationalist leaders entered legislative bodies sanctioned by the colonial regime. This tempered attitude of the nationalists was inspired in some degree by the excesses of totalitarianism in Europe and by Japanese expansion in Asia.

Before World War II, the Dutch failed to recognize, in the main, the potential force of the nationalist movement. Although it was assumed that self-government would eventually be granted, there was no thought of conceding independence. Prior to 1941, plans for an Indonesian partnership in a Dutch confederation were debated, but all revolutionary moves were suppressed.[3] Furthermore, education in the Indies under Dutch rule was the reflection of what has been called a philosophy of empire. Whereas in the Philippines American theory held that

383

Southeast
Asia
(British,
French,
Dutch)

an ever-expanding system of schools would provide democratic training for the masses, Dutch education policy was aimed at giving the native greater skill in his traditional calling of agriculture, a Dutch education being reserved for a few potential native leaders and for those entering minor posts in government. The policy, though thoroughly justified in the Dutch view, was not popular because many an Indonesian, like the Burmese and the Filipinos, preferred a literary education leading to the law and government office. The Dutch defended their system by saying that freedom of educational choice would mean economic and social dislocation and the creation of an idle intellectual proletariat. They held, too, that although they did not encourage democratic education, their system was much concerned with improving the native standard of living.

Dutch economic policy was founded on the conception of the East Indies as suppliers of raw products and consumers of foreign manufactures. Under the liberal economic policy adopted in the late nineteenth century, Western enterprise in agriculture and mining prospered. Until 1933, Dutch goods entering the islands paid the same low tariff as goods from other countries. The world depression of the 1930s was, however, a severe blow; the price of raw materials exported by the Indies fell far more rapidly than the price of finished imports. These

[3] On the extent of limited self-government in the Indies, 1925–1941, see Amry Vandenbosch, "Indonesia," *The New World of Southeast Asia*, Lennox A. Mills, ed. (1949), 85–91. See also the exhaustive study by J. S. Furnivall, *Netherlands India: A Study of a Plural Economy* (1944).

conditions forced a departure from the liberal trade policy at a time when Japanese imports of inexpensive manufactured goods were beginning to flood the Indies market. The result was adoption of a quota system resulting in reciprocal trade agreements. As world tensions increased, these agreements became political rather than economic, and were aimed at halting a Japanese economic invasion.

On the eve of World War II, Dutch control was not considered to be in imminent jeopardy, though in the Indies, as in other subject areas, administrators and home government alike were slow to see what they did not want to see. There was no large and stable native middle class and certainly no understanding by the peasant of democracy. The middle-class petty capitalists of the islands were the Chinese, who had not been assimilated into the native population, and whose loyalties were often to China rather than to the Indies. The great natural resources, the wealth of the Indies—rubber, oil, etc.—were owned and operated by the capital and the technical skill of the West. In other words, Indonesia was a plural society comprising three social orders: the native Indonesians, the Chinese, and the Europeans. These social orders lived side by side, but at the same time they lived separately, rarely meeting save in the material and economic sphere. These facts go far to explain why the developing history of Indonesian nationalism before 1941 was marked by lack of purpose on the part of government and lack of confidence on the part of the people.

BURMA

Burma, with an area of 261,000 square miles—about the size of Texas—has two well-defined regions, Upper and Lower Burma. Lower Burma, in the south, comprised the deltas and plains of the Irrawaddy, the Sittang, and the lower Salween, the province of Arakan, and the Tenasserim Peninsula. Here were produced the great crops of rice (prior to World War II Burma was the world's greatest exporter of this grain), tin, and lumber. Upper Burma was a vastly different country, formed of successive narrow valleys and the towering mountain systems of the north and northwest regions. With the exception of tin and oil, most of Burma's extensive mineral wealth was found in Upper Burma. Only coal was lacking to give Burma the common requisites of an industrial civilization.

Burma's long and earlier, as distinct from her short and modern, history reflects her unique location between the two great civilizations of Asia, the Indian and the Chinese. Her early inhabitants migrated primarily from eastern Tibet and western China. To this racial tie with China was added in the eleventh century an even stronger cultural bond with India through the conquest of Burma by Hinayana Buddhism. After the thirteenth century, when the Mongols invaded the country, Burmese history was marked by successive periods of political disintegration interspersed with the appearance of aggressive and strong military rulers whose conquests spread at times far beyond the borders of present-day Burma. Thus Burma, neither Indian nor Chinese, partook of the culture and life of her neighbors. For example, her pre-World War II population, 17,000,000, included a number of language groups, of which the outstanding were the Burmese, about 10,000,000, the Karen, 1,-350,000, the Tai or Shan, 1,000,000 and more than 1,000,000 who used various Indian languages.[4]

Long before the nineteenth century, European traders in the East had a secondary interest in Burmese commerce. As far back as the beginning of the seventeenth century, the English, the French, and the Dutch had exported teakwood from Burma, but the country lay beyond the interests of the spice trade and therefore did not become a major center of European commerce. However, as a prelude to European involvement in Burma's internal affairs, the British and the French, contending for supremacy in India, gave aid respectively to opposing Burmese

[4] John L. Christian, *Modern Burma* (1942), Chapter 1.

factions in the decade of 1750. During the next seventy-five years exaggerated reports reached the outer world of Burma's power and wealth, and eventually frontier incidents provided the occasion for the First Anglo-Burmese War. As a result of three conflicts, the First, the Second, and the Third Anglo-Burmese Wars, 1824–1826, 1852, and 1886, Burma became a British colony; the final steps in annexation (1886) were hastened as a result of French intrigue in Upper Burma.

Under colonial rule there was a marked growth and modernization of Burma's economic and, to a somewhat less degree, of her political life. Burma's economy in pre-British days was semi-feudal, based largely on subsistence agriculture. By the beginning of the twentieth century, however, this agricultural society had been invaded by the aggressive, laissez-faire commercialism of British, Indian, and Chinese traders and businessmen. The development of the teak industry and the transformation of the Irrawaddy delta jungles into rice fields created a new economic picture involving Burmese and Indian labor, Indian merchants and money lenders, British capital, and a British-Burmese civil service. Huge profits made possible large colonial revenues from which came significant public services, such as improved roads and public health services. Meanwhile Burma became a province of the British Indian Empire, a status which it held until 1937. The native populace exercised a measure of self-government, first through the agency of village headmen and later through representative district councils. While neither of these systems enjoyed much success, there was initially little objection to colonialism. During the nineteenth century, most Burmese appeared in general to have welcomed the stability and peace of British control which replaced the factional strife that had existed under native rule.

National feeling became manifest after World War I. Although the achievements of economic modernization under British rule were great, economic and social problems caused popular unrest. In some areas commercial capitalism destroyed traditional occupations; the educational influence of

Buddhist clergy declined; and a migrant working class appeared and contributed to increasing lawlessness. After the Indian moneylender, the landlord, the tax collector, and the Chinese merchant had taken their toll, the peasant had less than enough on which to live until his next crop. Anti-Indian riots in 1930 and 1938 were a result. The British were also a target of resentment, because British courts gave Indians the protection of law. The colonial government was slow to devise solutions to these problems. Since native inertia had to be overcome, and since it was not easy to decide what to do, many basic economic problems (agricultural credit, farm tenancy, immigration) were not grappled with until after 1937.

The settlement of political grievances had been attempted at an earlier date. British policy, which was responsive to the idea of self-government, provided for a new Burmese constitution in 1922. Under this document more than 70 per cent of the Burmese population enjoyed the suffrage, and Burmese held a majority in the newly established legislative council of the central government. The constitution, however, was extremely unpopular, presumably because it set up a dyarchy dividing executive authority into powers reserved to the governor (defense, foreign affairs, finance, higher education, justice, and communications) and those transferred to responsible ministers (agriculture, forests, health, primary education, and local government). Candidates elected to the legislative council were pledged not to accept posts in the transferred ministries. Faced with collapse of the system, the British undertook further reforms. A new constitution of 1935 separated Burma from India and gave her dominion status. Provision was made for the extension of self-government, though ministerial responsibility to an elected legislature was still limited by extensive powers reserved to the governor. The new constitution went into effect in 1937 with the active support of the Burmese electorate.

These steps toward self-government reflected the growing intensity of the Burmese independence movement. By 1930, when

385

Southeast
Asia
(British,
French,
Dutch)

economic distress had added its weight to the general discontent, political groups outside the legislative council had become more noisy than the council itself. A serious rebellion against British authority led by Saya San in 1930 revealed the degree to which popular sentiment was prepared to challenge the established order. Out of the rebellion came the organization of the *Dobama* (We Burmans) Society of young nationalists demanding independence and calling themselves *Thakin* (Lord) in derision of the earlier custom of addressing Britishers by this term. By 1940, the *Dobama* Party had won substantial popular influence, its purposefulness being in marked contrast with the petty and personal rivalry that appeared to control so many Burmese politicians in the legislative council. Thus on the eve of World War II, Burma, if beset by economic and social problems, had achieved a remarkable degree of responsible government and a vital national consciousness.

MALAYA

Prior to World War II, Great Britain held a large and wealthy empire cutting across the tropics of Southeast Asia, composed of Burma, British Malaya, and portions of the great island of Borneo (Sarawak, and British North Borneo). In this empire, the most important area in economic terms was a group of small settlements and protectorates known as British Malaya. Like many another region remote from the Western World, British Malaya was thrust upon public attention by the early military disasters of World War II. Previously this tropical empire was largely taken for granted even by Britishers, and about all the average man knew was that it produced tin and rubber and had a strong naval base.

The Malay Peninsula, with an area of 53,000 square miles, approximately the size of the state of Florida, had a population of about 5,000,000 in 1940 and nearly 8,500,-000 in 1966. It was a region characterized by a central mountain chain with altitudes ranging from 4,000 to 8,000 feet, below

which lie the rolling foothill country and the coastal plains, extremely narrow in some places and as wide as thirty miles in others. It was here on the western shore in the coastal plains and in the undulating terrain of the lower foothills that the rubber-growing lands of Malaya were found. Here, too, in the valleys of the lowlands, were the deposits of tin washed down from the high granite ranges.

In modern times, agriculture in Malaya has consisted of (1) the small plots of the natives (Malays), where, in many cases, rubber is grown together with rice and tropical vegetables, and (2) the large-scale plantations of Europeans and Chinese, where, prior to World War II, about 45 per cent of the world's supply of rubber was produced. In the decade of the 1930s, Malaya held first place in the world's production of tin with 28 per cent of the total output.[5]

The native of the peninsula was the Malay, a descendant of the Proto-Malay with a considerable mixture of Arab, Indian, and Chinese blood. In 1947, the total population of 5,808,000 included: Malays, 2,512,-000, 43 per cent; Chinese, 2,608,000, 44 per cent; Indians, 605,000, 10 per cent; Europeans, principally British, 18,000. Most of the Malays were British subjects or British-protected persons, whereas in the case of the Chinese the majority were foreign residents: 1,000,000 out of a total Chinese population of 1,709,000 in 1931.[6] But although the Chinese formed the overwhelming group in Malaya in the twentieth century, it was Indian rather than Chinese culture that influ-

[5] James C. Jackson, *Planters and Speculators: Chinese and European Agricultural Enterprise in Malaya, 1786–1921* (1968), a pioneering study, shows that Chinese were the first to recognize the possibilities of commercial agriculture under British rule. The Chinese, who were interested primarily in short-term profits and return to their homeland, speculated with tapioca, gambier, and pepper. Their success resulted in Chinese domination of plantation agriculture until the latter part of the nineteenth century when Europeans, experimenting with longer term ventures and larger investments, developed coffee and rubber plantations.

[6] Sir Richard Winstedt, *Britain and Malaya, 1786–1941* (London, 1944), 6.

enced the historic patterns of native Malayan life. Indian commerce, Indian Buddhism, and Hinduism had reached Malaya by sea in the early centuries of the Christian Era.

The Portuguese, the first Europeans to reach China by the all-sea routes, seized Malacca in 1511, some four years before they reached Canton. Under Portuguese control, Malacca soon became the great entrepôt of Lisbon's commerce in the East. Here were handled the nutmegs, mace, pepper, camphor, gold, and silk which for a century made Portugal master of the Eastern trade. A little more than a century later, in 1641, Malacca was captured by the Dutch, who were already strongly entrenched at Batavia. Malacca remained in Dutch hands until the period of the French Revolution when, the Dutch and French Republics having formed an alliance, Malacca was seized and held by the British until 1818 and then returned to Holland, only to be finally ceded to Britain in 1824. By the beginning of the twentieth century, therefore, Malacca had been continuously a European possession for four centuries.

Meanwhile, the British had acquired the island of Penang in 1786, and a strip of land on the opposite mainland known as Province Wellesley in 1800. In 1819 Thomas Stamford Raffles made the first agreements with the Sultan of Johore whereby land was granted for factories on the island of Singapore in return for a small annual allowance. In 1824 Singapore was ceded to Britain in perpetuity. Thus, by that year the English East India Company held in Malaya in the name of Britain the island of Penang and Province Wellesley, Malacca, and the island of Singapore, all of which came to be known collectively as the Straits Settlements.

In 1867 the Straits Settlements were brought under direct British rule when, following the abolition of the East India Company and the failure of a brief attempt to govern the Settlements through the India Office, they were constituted a crown colony. Under this new status the Straits Settlements were administered by a governor who in time was assisted by an executive council com-

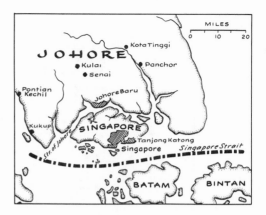

387

Southeast
Asia
(British,
French,
Dutch)

posed of the commandant of the British garrison, leading officials of the administration, and three appointed members supposedly representative of the public. Whereas final legislative authority in the crown colony remained with the British Parliament, this authority was exercised only in emergency. Customarily, local legislation was passed by a local legislative council. In the Settlements this council consisted of the governor, thirteen officials of his administration, and thirteen nonofficials (British subjects), representatives of the public and appointed by the governor. These latter representatives usually included Chinese, British Indians, and Eurasian elements of the population. The governor plus the official members of the council constituted a majority and thus had the controlling voice in all legislation.

With the Straits Settlements serving as a foothold on the coastal region, British authority extended gradually inland. Much earlier in the nineteenth century, officials of the East India Company, acting in the interest of peace among the native states, had arbitrated in boundary disputes, had used force to repel invasions by Siamese forces, had offered protection to certain states in case of attack, and had sometimes determined the succession to native thrones.[7] This policy of directing native affairs was eventually adopted by the British colonial

[7] For a comment on the significance of British pressure prior to 1870 see Nicolas Tarling, "Intervention and Nonintervention in Malaya," *Journal of Asian Studies* 21 (1962): 523–27.

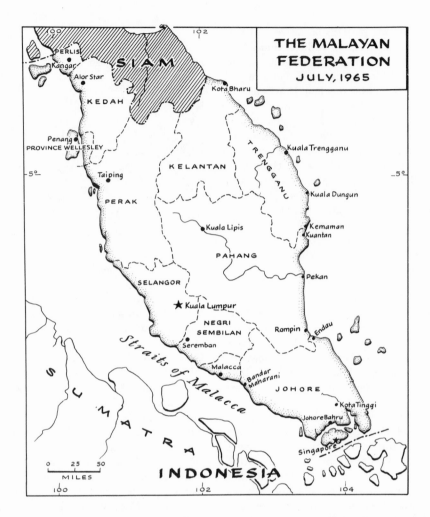

THE MALAYAN
FEDERATION
JULY, 1965

government when it became clear that constant warfare among Malayan states was retarding the development of profitable plantation and mining enterprises. Thus the governor of the Straits Settlements placed British advisers in the native states of Perak (1874), Selangor (1874), and Negri Sembilan (1874–1898), and Pahang (1888). As a result of treaties signed by the British with the native rulers of these four states, it was provided that (1) each native ruler accept a British resident whose advice was mandatory in all matters "other than those touching Malay religion and customs"; and (2) revenues be collected and all appointments made in the name of the respective state sultans. Each of these states had a state

council combining legislative and executive functions, but there was as yet no over-all interstate control, with the result that there were in fact wide variations in law, in taxation, and in administration of land in the various states, despite the presence of a British adviser in each.

To achieve greater uniformity and more effective administration, the four states were federated in 1896 under a common civil service controlled by a resident-general. A federal durbar was also formed with advisory but no legislative powers. In 1909 a federal council was created which, with the purpose of protecting the vested interests of the tin and rubber industries, curtailed further the autonomy of the states. These various moves toward centralization soon led to abuse and eventually to criticism of the entire administration. As a result, in 1935, reforms looking to decentralization were effected.

Five states—Johore, Kedah, Perlis, Kelantan, and Trengganu—remained outside the Federation. However, they received British resident ministers who supervised local affairs, except for native customs and religion. The international status (protectorates) of these states was fixed by treaties similar to those between Britain and the federated states.

British Malaya thus was composed of ten separate governments under three different varieties of administration—a crown colony, protected federated states, and protected unfederated states. The theory of this arrangement was highly complex; the practice was not. The difference between the Straits Settlements, a crown colony of the traditional type, and the protected states was not very great, for in both cases the actual administration adhered closely to the crown colony pattern. Furthermore, the government of the three parts was united in the person of the British governor of the Straits Settlements, who, as High Commissioner, directed the federation government at Kuala Lumpur and the British resident ministers of the unfederated states.

In addition to imposing some measure of political unity over what had been independent sultanates, British rule brought economic, social, and ethnic changes. The colonial government promoted the development of a postal service, a telephone and telegraph system, roads, and a railroad running the length of the peninsula from Singapore to Bangkok. Advances in agricultural science contributed to the development of a plantation economy specializing in production of rubber, sugar, coffee, and coconuts; extractive industries, especially the mining of tin, supplied world markets; a school system was established; medical research fought tropical diseases; and, finally, the introduction of Western law curtailed the arbitrary powers of sultans and protected the individual. Not all of these changes, however, benefitted the native populace. Under British rule Malaya

ceased to be a Malay country. The reduction of the Malay to minority status has already been mentioned. Beyond this, profits from the various modern enterprises went mostly to British, Indian, and Chinese owners.

By World War II, Malay feelings against the Chinese and Indians had become intense as native leaders agitated for a greater share in the development of the country. Unlike the Burmese, however, the Malayans did not generally include the British in their resentment of foreigners. This was due to the British policy in colonial affairs of favoring Malayans culturally and politically. For example, the British supported a Moslem revival by building mosques and permitting religious instruction in schools. As a result, native enmity against Chinese and Indians did not become an assertive nationalism prior to 1941.

SIAM OR THAILAND

Thailand in modern times has been a political curiosity in Southeast Asia—a small independent state wedged between and hedged about by the possessions of Europe and the United States. On the west and northwest, Thailand borders on Burma; on the east and northeast, on Indochina; on the south, it is open to the Gulf of Siam, beyond which is the Malay Peninsula, the South China Seas, the Indies, and the Philippines. This legal, and in some respects actual, independence was not a result of the military prowess of Thailand or the wisdom of its rulers, but rather of agreement between European rivals—England in Burma and Malaya, and France in Indochina—to preserve this small kingdom as a buffer state.

Thailand, with an area of some 200,000 square miles, slightly smaller than Texas, had a natural border of mountains on the west, north, and northwest. In general, the country has three geographical areas. The southwestern delta and plain in the vicinity of Bangkok, the capital, is the region of rice culture; the north is mountainous with steep valleys running north and south; the remainder of the country, chiefly the north-

389

Southeast
Asia
(British,
French,
Dutch)

east, is an area of rolling hills. Thailand, a land of the monsoon, has two rather distinct seasons: the rainy season of the southwest monsoon, May through October; and the dry season of winter, November through February, followed by the early spring heat.

Thailand's population in 1950 was 18,000,000 (in 1967 32,000,000). In 1950, some 3,000,000 of this population were Chinese whose loyalties have usually been to China. There were also other foreign groups including: 700,000 Moslem Malays, 50,000 Vietnamese, and 50,000 Indians. Most of the people are rice farmers; the Chinese are merchants. Life in Thailand has depended almost exclusively on rice culture. Some 95 per cent of the crop land produced rice and, prior to 1940, about one-third of the crop was exported. In the earlier years of the century this export trade went primarily to Europe. After World War I it was diverted to China and India.

Although Thailand had been peopled in the long course by successive immigrant waves of Mongol extraction, the principal stock was the Thai, who spoke a language of the same name. The Thai were among the more recent comers and probably entered the peninsula from Yunnan.

Just as in the seventeenth century it was Thailand's almost incessant military involvement with her neighbors that prompted her to seek aid from Europeans, so it was again in the early nineteenth century when she began to exchange native products for firearms, first secured from the Portuguese. Her first major commercial treaties were made with Great Britain in 1822 and 1826, and with the United States in 1833. This last was the first treaty concluded by the United States with a nation of the Far East. In 1855 and 1856, Britain, France, and the United States concluded further treaties with Thailand containing rights of extraterritoriality and a conventional tariff. On this occasion Townsend Harris was the American envoy.

During most of the nineteenth century, despite these commercial accords, the fate of Thailand as a nation hung in the uneasy balance of Anglo-French rivalry in Southeast Asia. Britain's successive annexations in Burma made her a territorial neighbor of Thailand on the west and north; the advent of France in Cochin China, Cambodia, and Annam brought her to Thailand's border on the north, east, and southeast. Indeed, the French protectorate in Cambodia was achieved by breaking the control of Thailand over that state. Much later in the century (1893), Thailand, in a treaty with France, renounced her claims to territory east of the Mekong (Laos). This territory was ceded technically to Annam, already a French protectorate, and then organized by France as the separate protectorate of Laos. In 1896 growing friction between the European rivals on the borders of Thailand was abated by an Anglo-French treaty which created British and French spheres in western and eastern Thailand respectively. In 1904 France secured at Thailand's expense further cessions of territory to Cambodia and Laos. After these transfers the Anglo-French rivals agreed to annex no further territory in their respective zones of influence. Nevertheless, in 1907 some 7,000 square miles were added to Cambodia, although France restored some territory previously acquired and agreed that Siamese courts should exercise jurisdiction over French Asiatic subjects and protected persons on Siamese soil. Two years later, in 1909, Siam surrendered to British Malaya the states of Trengganu, Kelantan, Kedah, and Perlis. In return Thailand regained jurisdiction over British subjects in her territory.

Twentieth-century Thailand (before 1945) has been confronted with three major political problems: (1) the movement from autocracy to some form of representative government; (2) the effort to create national unification; and (3) the task of maintaining the country's independence, so frequently threatened in the nineteenth and twentieth centuries, at first by the missionary, the mercantile, and the political interests of the Western powers, and then by the expansion of Japan.

A program of modernization in the late nineteenth century effected many changes. Slavery was abolished. Many Siamese studied abroad and returned with new technical skills and new viewpoints toward politics, thus preparing the way for the downfall of absolutism. The gradual creation of a new and more widely selected body of civil servants provided the beginning of a new political group and ultimately a revolutionary party. When in the depression years of the late 1920s the dynasty applied a policy of retrenchment, the "Promoters," as the revolutionary group called itself, including a number of army officers, took over the government in June, 1932, and imposed a constitution upon the king, who himself favored constitutionalism but who had been restrained by members of the royal house. The revolution was entirely peaceful, because both the royal and the revolutionary parties hoped to avoid giving any pretext for foreign intervention. Among the revolutionary leaders were Pridi Phanomyong, a civilian, and Phibun Songgram, a militarist.

The new constitution, which excluded the royal family from political power, placed the new Assembly in the hands of the Promoters. The power of the latter, so long as they remained united, became as absolute as had been the king's. The new government promoted education as an ultimate test for the franchise, sought to implement a national economic policy to provide remunerative work for all, and attempted to stimulate a political consciousness that would eventually express itself through political parties. Meanwhile, however, factionalism had appeared between the civilian and the military wings of the Promoters' party. For five years, 1932–1937, Colonel Phahon Phonphayuhasena, as Prime Minister, held the two groups in unsteady balance. When he was succeeded by Phibun, Thailand entered upon a program of extreme nationalism implemented by the methods of the dictator.

INDOCHINA

Indochina, in the late nineteenth and early twentieth centuries, included five political and administrative divisions: the French possession of Cochin China, and the French protectorates of Tonkin, Annam, Laos, and Cambodia. The total area, 286,000 square miles, was approximately the combined area of Texas and West Virginia. The population in 1941 was some 24,000,000 including nearly 500,000 Chinese, and 42,000 Europeans, almost all of whom were French. The estimated population in 1966 was some 39,-500,000. The concentrations of population were in the Mekong Delta and valleys of the south and the Red River Valley in the north. The central mountainous area had scattered settlements along the seacoast and in the Mekong Valley of the interior. Each of the five states had its own peculiar geographical setting. Life in Tonkin, the northern state, centered in the valley of the Red River and in the cities of Hanoi and Haiphong. Annam was a long, coastal, mountainous area with limited and isolated coastal plains. Laos, to the west in the interior, included the hill country of the upper central Mekong. Cambodia covered the plain of the lower Mekong. Cochin China, with its important city of Saigon, encompassed the delta of this great river. Rice culture, the predominant form of agriculture, was followed by the plantation culture of rubber, tea, and coffee. Mineral wealth was extensive in the north where coal, tin, zinc, tungsten, chromium, iron, and other ores were mined. In Indochina as in Burma there was an extensive export trade in rice.

The political divisions of the area were not coterminous with the complex of racial groups and cultures found in Indochina. The Annamese predominated, making up about 70 per cent of the population. Culturally, Annamese civilization reveals a strong Chinese influence; Annam was for many centuries a tributary state of China. Confucian concepts dominated most phases of Annamite life. Buddhism in modified forms also had a foothold, though it commanded little popular prestige. Taoism was present in some of its lower forms, particularly sorcery. Mixed with these formal religious importations were substantial remnants of many indigenous cults. The resulting religious picture, though somewhat obscure, was distinguished by a comforting absence of fanaticism.[8]

The peoples of Cambodia and Laos, in contrast to the Annamese, were predomi-

[8] Virginia Thompson, *French Indo-China* (1937), 43.

391

Southeast
Asia
(British,
French,
Dutch)

nantly Indian in culture. The Cambodians, the second major racial group, representing some 6 per cent of Indochina's population, included descendants of ancient Khmer stock. At Angkor in Cambodia still remain the magnificent ruins of temples and palaces, built by forced labor, as evidence of the Khmer civilization of eight centuries ago. Feudal relationships, with emphasis on powerful ties of clan, tended to persist strongly among the Cambodians. Brahmanism and Buddhism were the dominating religious philosophies.

The Portuguese, who arrived in the sixteenth century, were the first modern Europeans to reach Indochina. Chinese immigration here as in Malaya, the Philippines, and Indonesia long antedated the arrival of Europeans. The early Chinese immigrants were controlled by the seasons, which prevented merchant vessels from crossing the seas in the months of the typhoons. Hence "factories," or trading posts, were established and grew into Chinese communities. In general they were not militant, and they were unsupported by the home government. Thus in time they disappeared. The Europeans, in contrast, were armed, able to fight off pirates, able to pit local princes against each other, and thereby able to establish permanent posts. Portuguese objectives here, as in China, were trade and the establishment of Jesuit missions.

French missionaries and traders appeared in the seventeenth century, but the real foundations of French political power in Indochina were laid in the years from 1747 to 1858. In the earlier years of this period, 1747 to 1774, France made diplomatic contact with Annam in the hope of opening trade and using the region as a base for attacks on Dutch and British commerce. In 1787 the first treaty between France and Cochin China was signed. This was the work of Pigneau de Behaine, Bishop of Adran, ecclesiastic, diplomat, and soldier of fortune, who aided the king of Cochin China against rebels in the hope of furthering French territorial expansion and the spread of Catholic missions. The early nineteenth century, however, was marked by violent anti-Christian movements and by the refusal of native rulers to receive French diplomatic and naval missions. Later, Napoleon III, failing in 1855 to secure a treaty with Annam that would put an end to the executions of French and Spanish ecclesiastics, in cooperation with Spain dispatched a naval expedition, 1858, at the time of the *Arrow* War in China. Successful campaigns were conducted against Tourane (Da Nang) and Saigon. In 1859 French forces seized Saigon, and in 1862 Annam ceded that city and the three southernmost provinces to France. Annam also guaranteed religious toleration, opened three ports to French and Spanish trade, and paid an indemnity of $4,000,000. The following year Cambodia was made a French protectorate, and soon the remaining provinces of Cochin China were annexed.

From this time until the beginning of the present century, France moved steadily forward to complete the conquest of Indochina, each move seemingly timed nicely by intervals of a decade as though there were some peculiar magic in this regularity. After the French had applied military pressure in 1874, France formally recognized the independence of Annam, and in return Annam opened the Red River in Tonkin to French trade, designated a number of ports open to French commerce, and granted extraterritoriality to Europeans. By the close of another decade, 1884, Annam was forced to become a protectorate of France. Since Annam had been, at least formally, a tributary state of China, this development precipitated Franco-Chinese hostilities, ending in Chinese defeat. In still another decade, 1893, France demanded of Siam (Thailand), in the name of Annam, certain inland territories to the east of the Mekong which were organized as the new French protectorate of Laos. Again in a decade, 1904, further territory held by Siam was ceded to both Cambodia and Laos, and an additional grant to Cambodia at Siam's expense was made in 1907. Thus, by the beginning of the twentieth century, France, by military force, had become the master of an empire in Indochina.

Government in French Indochina was

designed to attain objectives quite different from those sought in neighboring British territories of Southeast Asia. Whereas in the latter, autonomy within the Empire became the goal during the twentieth century, with self-government being introduced by progressive stages, in the former "the intention has been that the dependency should be drawn progressively closer to France as an integral part of a closely knit empire dominated by the mother country." [9] In practice this meant that the governor-general had little local independence, that most natives did not acquire French citizenship but remained subjects, the legislative councils had little authority, and that the very limited representation of the colony (Cochin China) in the French Chamber of Deputies was chosen by and spoke for the French and not the native community.

While Cochin China was administered directly by French officials, the other four provinces of Indochina, technically protectorates, maintained their native administrations, operating under close French supervision and control. Although the native mandarins in the protectorates were not simple figureheads, the power of the French officials was hardly less than it was in the colony of Cochin China, where direct rule prevailed. But even as France perfected the forms of colonial administration, its rule was challenged by the first manifestations of nationalism.

It is hardly possible to generalize on the origins of nationalism in French Indochina. Divergence of race and culture, a product of the many migrations that peopled Indochina, meant that nationalism struggled in an inextricable tangle of minorities or race, language, and religion.

The roots of Annamese nationalism in varying forms may be traced to the distant past when Annam was under the political as well as the cultural .sway of China. In modern times, Annamese nationalism sprang from the influence of the French conquest. Although French administrators never con-

sciously promoted nationalism, "French institutions were so impregnated with the liberal ideas of 1789 that they unconsciously fostered patriotism and a love of political liberty in subject people." [10] Moreover, French rule was the result of a long and bitter conquest in which native resistance was compounded of diverse elements: patriotism, brigandage, and piracy.

Unrest, political and economic in its base, was typical of Indochina in the decade prior to World War I. Stimulation came from Japan's victory in the Russo-Japanese War, but more particularly from a new interest among Annamese intellectuals in the eighteenth-century French political philosophy of Rousseau and Montesquieu. Many native intellectuals, however, were disillusioned in 1908, when, as the result of a conservative reaction among the French in Indochina, Hanoi University was closed. This reactionary trend in French policy was further emphasized a few years later when France used forced Indochinese labor in Europe during World War I. During and after that war, the more rapid economic development of Indochina created additional cause of native resentment.

As in other parts of Southeast Asia, the Chinese in French Indochina were a focal point of native attack. An outstanding case was the anti-Chinese boycott of 1919. The Chinese in Indochina had shown little interest in politics, but they controlled the native rice and fish trade and the sources of native credit. In general the Annamite attitude toward the Chinese was one of admiration of Chinese commercial adeptness. At the same time Annamite nationalists were as much opposed to Chinese economic as to French political control. An additional factor closely linked with the nationalist agitations of the 1920s was the rapid development of the Communist movement.

Prior to World War II, however, the native nationalist movement suffered crip-

393

Southeast
Asia
(British,
French,
Dutch)

---

[9] Lennox A. Mills, "The Governments of Southeast Asia," in *Government and Nationalism in Southeast Asia*, Mills, *et al.*, ed. (1942), 108.

[10] Virginia Thompson, "Nationalism and Nationalistic Movements in Southeast Asia," in *Government and Nationalism in Southeast Asia*, 198; and the same author's larger study, *French Indo-China*, 475–94.

pling disabilities. In the first place, it possessed distinct racial limitations, since it was confined to the Annamese, who continued to regard Cambodians and Laotians as fit only to be subject peoples. Moreover, Annamese nationalists were divided among themselves by jealousies and by the lack of a constructive national program, and they were unsupported by any vital public spirit. Finally, French policy in the pre-war years was rigid and cruel in its suppression of nationalist and Communist groups.

Thus native nationalism posed no immediate threat to French rule. Nevertheless, the philosophy behind French rule in Indochina from the middle nineteenth century until World War II was to have tremendous repercussions on the history of this area in the post-war years. From its beginnings in the nineteenth century, French imperialism in the Far East was motivated primarily by national pride. In general the considerations behind French policy were political rather than economic—the determination not to be outdone by the British. Toward the close of the nineteenth century, the policy matured and expressed itself in a persistent urge to enhance French national prestige and cultural superiority. The reality and substantial character of French motives were attested to by the scholarly achievements of the Ecole Française d'Extrême Orient, which opened at Hanoi in 1898. French imperialists could conceive of no higher goal than the making of brown-skinned Frenchmen out of Annamese in an ever more perfect union with France. Of all Westerners in Southeast Asia, the French were outstanding for their lack of racial prejudice and for their willingness to treat as equals those Asiatics who were equal to the French in education, refinement, or attainment. There was indeed no antagonism to Indochinese nationalists of French education so long as they abstained from political propaganda among the peasantry. What led to persecution was that the Indochinese nationalists, French in almost everything but appearance, learned principally from China that their own political futility would end the moment they became leaders of mass movements. Thus France

in Southeast Asia was trapped by her own logic. She could not admit the possibility of political or cultural equality with herself. Prior to 1941 France had succeeded in indoctrinating native intellectuals with French culture, but by her failure to embody the concepts of this culture in native political institutions, she had failed to win native loyalty.[11]

SOUTHEAST ASIA ON THE EVE OF WORLD WAR II

By the 1930s Southeast Asia had been transformed under Western colonialism. Dynastic states or, as in the case of the Philippines, politically primitive local regimes had been superseded by territorial states with expanded domains and colonial bureaucracies.[12] Livelihood no longer was based exclusively on a subsistence economy but rather was supplemented by the development of exports and imports and on exploitation of the region's rich mineral resources. Moreover, under the impact of the new political and economic orders, population increased and traditional social life eroded. Finally, to the exceedingly rich and diverse Hindu and Confucian cultural influences was added the impact of the West. In a word, Western intrusion into Southeast Asia served as it had in China and Japan to lay the foundations of a new order.

Yet on the eve of World War II colonialism was very much a part of the Southeast Asian picture. Only in the Philippines had the United States made definite commitments to future nationhood. The British were

[11] The definitive study is John F. Cady, *The Roots of French Imperialism in Eastern Asia* (1954),* 294–96.

[12] The penetration of native societies by colonial governments was not always welcomed, even when the aims were benevolent. The Dutch Ethical Policy, for example, which provided for improvements in village life, was met by the jibe that "the villager cannot even scratch his head, unless an expert shows him how to do it and the sub-district officer gives him permission." Quoted in J. S. Furnivall, *Netherlands India* (1939), 389.

directing Burma and Malay toward limited autonomy, while the French in Indochina and the Dutch in the East Indies denied even that much promise. These limited prospects for national independence, however, were not a serious source of friction. While after World War I Western colonialism increasingly met native nationalism, this nationalism was not yet a threatening force. In some areas, such as Laos and Cambodia, nationalism had not even assumed an organized form. Where it was more vibrant, nationalists were divided and often as much at odds with themselves as with the colonial overlords. These were the conditions prevailing when Japan attacked and set in motion forces which destroyed the basis of colonial rule.

FOR FURTHER READING

GENERAL. John F. Cady, *Southeast Asia: Its Historical Development* (1964), a fluent survey written especially for the college level. D. G. E. Hall, *A History of South-East Asia* (2nd rev. ed., 1964) is a standard reference work. Among the shorter and stimulating general treatments are: Brian Harrison, *Southeast Asia: A Short History* (3rd ed., 1966); Nicholas Tarling, *A Concise History of Southeast Asia* (1966); and John Bastin and Harry J. Benda, *A History of Modern Southeast Asia: Colonialism, Nationalism, and Decolonization* (1968).* For useful extracts from the sources see Harry J. Benda and John A. Larkin, eds., *The World of Southeast Asia: Selected Historical Readings* (1967)*; and John Bastin, ed., *The Emergence of Modern Southeast Asia, 1511–1957* (1967).*

For the geographic foundations of society see: Ernest H. G. Dobby, *Southeast Asia* (10th ed., London, 1967); C. A. Fisher, *South-East Asia: A Social Economic, and Political Geography* (1964); and T. G. McGee, *The Southeast Asian City: A Social Geography of the Primate Cities of Southeast Asia* (London, 1967). Bruno Lasker, *The People of Southeast Asia* (1944) is a thoughtful introduction.

395

Southeast
Asia
(British,
French,
Dutch)

Stephen N. Hay and Margaret H. Chase, *Southeast Asian History: A Bibliographic Guide* (1962) lists standard books and articles. D. G. E. Hall, ed., *Historians of South-East Asia* (1962) and Soedjatmoko, et al., eds., *An Introduction to Indonesian Historiography* (1965) are helpful in evaluating literature. *The Journal of Southeast Asian History*, published by the Department of History, University of Singapore, (1960-present) carries recent scholarship of high standard.

PRE-NINETEENTH CENTURY. In addition to the references noted above, the early and pre-Western era in Southeast Asian history is treated in: George Coedes, *The Making of South East Asia*, S. E. Cowing, trans. (1966); Paul Wheatley, *The Golden Khersonese: Studies in the Historical Geography of the Malay Peninsula Before A. D. 1500* (Kuala Lumpur, 1966); and O. W. Wolters, *Early Indonesian Commerce: A Study of the Origins of Srivijaya* (1967). India's cultural impact is studied in George Coedes, *The Indianized States of Southeast Asia*, S. B. Cowing, trans. and Walter F. Vella, ed. (1968); Reginald S. LeMay, *The Culture of South-East Asia; The Heritage of India* (London, 1954); H. G. Quaritch Wales, *The Indianization of China and of Southeast Asia* (London, 1967).

Portuguese intrusions into Southeast Asia have been treated authoritatively in three studies by C. R. Boxer: *Four Centuries of Portuguese Expansion, 1415–1825: A Succinct Survey* (Johannesburg, 1963); *Portuguese Society in the Tropics: The Municipal Councils of Goa, Macao, Bahia, and Luanda, 1510–1800* (1965); and *Race Relations in the Portuguese Colonial Empire, 1415–1825* (Oxford, 1963). See also Ian A. MacGregor, "Notes on the Portuguese in Malaya," *Journal of the Malayan Branch, Royal Asiatic Society*—28, Part 2 (1955): 4–47.

K. N. Chaudhuri, *The English East India Company: The Study of an Early Joint-Stock Company, 1600–1640* (1965); and C. H. Philips, *The East India Company, 1784–1834* (Manchester, 1940) are complementary studies. Serafin D. Quiason, *English*

"Country Trade" with the Philippines, 1644–1765 (Quezon City, 1966) fills out the story of English activity.

C. R. Boxer, The Dutch Seaborne Empire 1600–1800 (1965); Kritof Glamann, Dutch-Asiatic Trade 1620–1740 (Copenhagen and The Hague, 1958); and S. P. Sen, The French in India, 1763–1816 (Calcutta, 1958), focus on the dynamics of Western commercial expansion. Of the same character but broader in the sense that it treats Portuguese, Dutch, and English activities is M. A. P. Meilink-Roelofsz, Asian Trade and European Influence in the Indonesian Archipelago between 1500 and about 1630 (The Hague, 1962). Jacob Cornelis VanLeur, Indonesian Trade and Society: Essays in Asian Social and Economic History (The Hague and Bandung, 1955); and K. M. Panikkar, Asia and Western Dominance: A Survey of the Vasco da Gama Epoch of Asian History, 1489–1945 (2nd ed., London, 1959)* offer Asian-centered perspectives of the period of Western expansion.

BURMA. John F. Cady, A History of Modern Burma (1958) is especially recommended for the years 1800–1885. Frank N. Trager, Burma—From Kingdom to Republic: A Historical and Political Analysis (1966), a detailed and penetrating study. Maung Htin Aung, A History of Burma (1968) presents a Burmese statesman's view. See also the latter author's The Stricken Peacock: Anglo-Burmese Relations, 1752–1948 (The Hague, 1965)* which reveals some of the inadequacies of Western writings without contributing any new research. J. S. Furnivall, Colonial Policy and Practice: A Comparative Study of Burma and Netherlands India (1956) is a work of extraordinary competence. J. Russell Andrus, Burmese Economic Life (1947), and G. E. Harvey, British Rule In Burma, 1824–1942 (London, 1946) are standard references. See also F. S. V. Donnison, Public Administration in Burma: A Study of Development During the British Connexion (London, 1953).

INDOCHINA. Particularly useful for the pre-modern period are: Joseph Buttinger, Viet-nam: A Dragon Embattled (1967)* and Lethanh Khoi, Le Viet-Nam: Histoire et Civilisation (Paris, 1955). Thomas E. Ennis, French Policy and Developments in Indo-China (1936) treats economic and social problems. Details on people, agriculture, industry, and foreign trade are found in F. M. LeBar, and A. Suddard, eds., Laos: Its People, Its Society, Its Culture (1960), David S. Steinberg, et al., Cambodia: Its People, Its Society, Its Culture (1959); Charles Robequain, The Economic Development of French Indo-China (London, 1944), and Olov R. T. Janse, The Peoples of French Indo-China (1944). Selected aspects of French rule are treated in Roger Levy, Guy Lacam, and Andrew Roth, French Interests and Policies in the Far East (1941).

INDONESIA. The standard study is Bernard H. M. Vlekke, Nusantara: A History of Indonesia (1960). See also Eduard Sarvaas DeKlerck, History of the Netherlands East Indies (2 vols., Rotterdam, 1938) Clive Day, The Policy and Administration of the Dutch in Java (reprinted ed., Kuala Lumpur, 1966) provides a brilliant analysis covering the years up to about 1900. See also Harry J. Benda, "The Pattern of Administrative Reforms in the Closing Years of Dutch Rule in Indonesia," Journal of Asian Studies 25 (1966): 589–605. On economic development and problems see: G. C. Allen and Audrey G. Donnithorne, Western Enterprise in Indonesia and Malaya: A Study in Economic Development (1957). A study of the organized activities of the educated native population, 1914–1927, is provided in Robert VanNiel, The Emergence of the Modern Indonesian Elite (1960). A specialized but important study is Clifford Geertz, The Religion of Java (1960).*

MALAYA. For a broad historical introduction see Sir Richard Winstedt, A History of Malay (rev. ed., Singapore, 1962); and K. G. Tregonning, A History of Modern Malaya (1967), and The Malays: A Cultural History (rev. ed., London, 1950). On the British conquest, note C. D. Cowan, Nineteenth-Century Malaya (1961); Lennox A. Mills,

397

Southeast
Asia
(British,
French,
Dutch)

British Malaya, 1824–1867 (Oxford, 1926), and *British Rule in Eastern Asia* (London, 1942); Harry J. Marks, *The First Contest for Singapore, 1819–1824* (The Hague, 1959); C. Northcote Parkinson, *British Intervention in Malaya, 1867–1877* (Kuala Lumpur, 1964). Rupert Emerson, *Malaysia: A Study in Direct and Indirect Rule* (reprinted ed., Kuala Lumpur, 1964)° compares British rule in Malaya with the Dutch in Indonesia. Sir Reginald Coupland, *Raffles, 1781–1826* (Oxford, 1926); and H. P. Clodd, *Malaya's First British Pioneer: The Life of Francis Light* (London, 1948); and two volumes edited by W. R. Roff: *Stories By Sir Hugh Clifford* (Kuala Lumpur, 1966); and *Stories and Sketches By Sir Frank Swettenham* (Kuala Lumpur, 1967) offer personal insights into colonial administration. J. Norman Parmer, *Colonial Labor Policy and Administration: A History of Labor in the Rubber Plantation Industry in Malaya, c. 1910–1941* (1960) focuses on the conditions and control of Indian labor. The Chinese role is treated in Wong Lin Ken, *The Malayan Tin Industry to 1914* (1965) W. R. Roff, *The Origins of Malaya Nationalism* (1967) studies the changes produced by British rule which are productive of national feeling. Fay-Cooper Cole, *The Peoples of Malaysia* (1945) is an anthropological study. E. H. G. Dobby, *Malaya and the Malayans* (London, 1947), a standard text.

THAILAND. Noel F. Busch, *Thailand, An Introduction to Modern Siam* (1959)° and Virginia Thompson, *Thailand: The New Siam* (1941)° provide convenient general surveys. The country's history as seen from the court may be found in Prince Chula Chakrabongse, *Lords of Life: The Paternal Monarchy of Bangkok, 1782–1932, with the Earlier and More Recent History of Thailand* (2nd ed., London, 1967), and Walter F. Vella, *The Impact of the West on Government in Thailand* (1955) and his *Siam Under Rama III* (1957). Abbot L. Moffat, *Mongkut, the King of Siam* (1961);° and A. B. Griswold, *King Mongkut of Siam* (1961) are mainly biographies of the nineteenth-century reformer. See also Donald E. Lord, "The King and the Apostle: Mongkut, Bradley, and the American Missionaries," *The South Atlantic Quarterly* 66 (1967): 326–40. Margaret Landon, *Anna and the King of Siam* (1944)° is a delightful story based on Anna H. Leonowen's book picturing Siam in the 1860s. Thawatt Mokarapong, "The June Revolution of 1932 in Thailand." (Ph.D. dissertation, Indiana University, 1962). James C. Ingram, *Economic Change in Thailand since 1850* (1955) emphasizes changes brought about by world trade. David A. Wilson, *Politics in Thailand* (1963)° is the first book-length study of politics in Thailand. Social problems are treated in Kenneth P. Landon, *The Chinese in Thailand* (London, 1941), and *Siam in Transition: A Brief Survey of Cultural Trends in the Five Years Since the Revolution of 1932* (Shanghai, 1939). G. William Skinner, *Chinese Society in Thailand: An Analytical History* (1957) and his *Leadership and Power in the Chinese Community of Thailand* (1958) are two fine studies in social and anthropological approach.

East Asia
in World War II,
1941-1945

chapter 30

Even as the democracies had been on the defensive ideologically and diplomatically since 1937 and earlier, so for many uncertain months after Pearl Harbor they were to remain on the defensive militarily. The Axis Powers fought with many advantages. They had planned and prepared for war. Their armies were mobilized, and many of their troops had already been tested in battle. Finally, they possessed interior lines of supply contrasting with the far-flung ocean routes on which the anti-Axis group depended. To gain military initiative, the Anglo-American chiefs of staff determined early in 1942 to concentrate first on Hitler while simply holding Japan. Time was to prove the wisdom of this decision, though at the moment it was an anathema to the Chinese and others threatened by Japanese invasion.

MILITARY OFFENSIVES AND THE
DIPLOMACY OF WAR, 1941–1945

Japan's attack immediately following Pearl Harbor spread like a great fan southward and westward to encompass south-

eastern Asia and the island empires that lay off its shores. Co-ordinated attacks were launched not only from the Caroline Islands and Formosa, but also from naval bases and airfields which the Vichy French had permitted Japan to acquire in French Indochina, and from bases acquired in Thailand after December 8. Less than three weeks were required to subdue Hong Kong (on December 25), the island fortress and great commercial city which had been a British possession for a century. Japanese troops, trained for tropical and jungle warfare, moved southward on the Malay Peninsula to capture Singapore on February 15, 1942, and westward into Burma to occupy all of that country by June, 1942. The attack on the Philippines, which came a few hours after the assault on Pearl Harbor, placed these islands, after five months of bitter fighting, under Japanese control. With speed unabated, Japan moved on to the conquest of the rich Netherlands Indies. The Bismarck and Solomon Islands and New Guinea, south and east of the Philippines, were invaded with the ultimate objective of attacking Australia.[1] But here the stubborn, heroic re-

[1] For the techniques of the Japanese occupation, military, political, and economic, see Robert S. Ward, *Asia for the Asiatics* (1945).

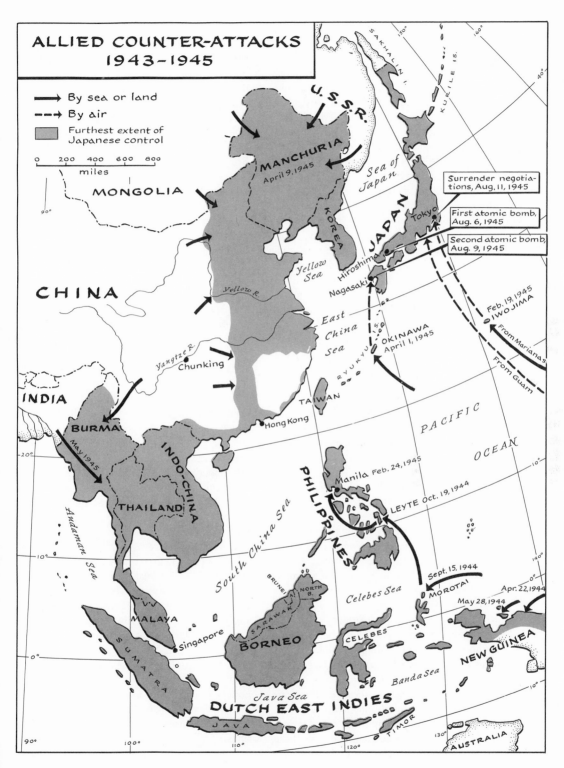

ALLIED COUNTER-ATTACKS
1943–1945

By sea or land
By air
Furthest extent of
Japanese control

0   200   400   600   800
miles

U.S.S.R.

MONGOLIA

MANCHURIA
April 9, 1945

Sea of
Japan

KOREA

CHINA

Yellow
Sea

Yellow R.

JAPAN

Tokyo

Surrender negotia-
tions, Aug. 11, 1945

First atomic bomb,
Aug. 6, 1945

Second atomic bomb,
Aug. 9, 1945

Hiroshima

Nagasaki

East
China
Sea

RYUKYU IS.

OKINAWA
April 1, 1945

Feb. 19, 1945
IWO JIMA

From Marianas

From Guam

Yangtze R.

Chunking

INDIA

BURMA

May 1945

TAIWAN

Hong Kong

PACIFIC

OCEAN

INDO-CHINA

THAILAND

Andaman Sea

PHILIPPINES

Manila Feb. 24, 1945

LEYTE Oct. 19, 1944

Sept. 15, 1944

Apr. 22, 1944

MALAYA

South China Sea

BRUNEI

SARAWAK

NORTH
B.

Singapore

BORNEO

Celebes Sea

MOROTAI

May 28, 1944

CELEBES

NEW GUINEA

Banda Sea

DUTCH EAST INDIES

Java Sea

JAVA

TIMOR

AUSTRALIA

sistance that had been waged since Pearl Harbor by slim forces checked the Japanese. New Guinea remained partly in Allied hands.

On May 7 and 8, in a naval-air battle over the Coral Sea, American planes broke up a Japanese attempt to cut the Australian supply lines across the southwestern Pacific to Honolulu and the American Pacific coast. The first major Japanese reverse was the naval-air battle of Midway, June 4–7, 1942, which inflicted heavy losses (21 ships) on her fleet and prevented the occupation of Midway and possibly the invasion of the Hawaiian Islands. Indeed, this proved to be a pivotal encounter. After Midway, save for their invasion of the Aleutians, the Japanese were no longer a menace in the central or eastern Pacific. Elsewhere, Allied actions in the southwest Pacific (Solomons, Guadalcanal, and New Guinea) and the CBI (China-Burma-India) Theater destroyed Japanese opportunities for driving further toward Australia and India.

The year 1943 thus marked the end of Japan's march to conquest and the beginning of ultimate defeat. In the Pacific and in Asia, as in Europe, however, defeat could not come until the enemies of the Axis had achieved a realistic unity in over-all policy and strategy, had won the battle of production, and had brought this newly created power to bear on far-flung battlefronts on the land, seas, and in the air.

From the beginning of the war in Europe and Asia, it had been the ill-concealed boast of the totalitarian powers that their opponents were incapable of unity in resistance. Nevertheless, in a series of momentous conferences, the principal powers achieved a realistic unity in over-all policy and strategy aimed at winning a speedy military victory and providing the basis of a durable peace. On January 1, 1942, in response to an American proposal, twenty-six governments at war with the Axis pledged their united action in prosecuting the conflict, agreeing to conclude no separate peace. By this means the principles of the Atlantic Charter became a basic manifesto of these United Nations and the preliminary blue-

print for war and eventual peace in Asia as well as in Europe.

At Quebec, August 11–24, 1943, Roosevelt, Churchill, and T. V. Soong approved policies designed to (1) strike at Japan through greater aid to China, (2) achieve closer collaboration with Russia, and (3) speed the invasion of Italy. The Moscow Conference of Foreign Ministers was a logical sequel. There, October 19–30, 1943, Britain, the Soviet Union, and the United States proclaimed the principles of the coming peace. Fascism was to be destroyed and war criminals brought to justice. China also joined in declarations demanding "unconditional surrender" by the Axis and promising a post-war international organization based on the sovereign equality of states to maintain peace and security.

Since Russia was not at war with Japan, the Moscow Conference of Foreign Ministers had not dealt specifically with war plans in Asia. Such plans were the subject of the meeting of Roosevelt, Churchill, and Chiang Kai-shek at Cairo, November 22–26, 1943. The war was to be prosecuted until Japan accepted "unconditional surrender." Japan was to be deprived of all the lands which she had seized since 1894. Korea was "in due course" to be free and independent. Following immediately on Cairo came the first meeting of Stalin with Roosevelt and Churchill at Teheran, December 2–7, which gave final shape to plans for destruction of Hitler's Germany, and produced Russia's first promise to enter the war against Japan.

Meanwhile, at Dumbarton Oaks in Washington, D.C., representatives of the United States, Great Britain, Russia, and China drafted preliminary proposals for an international organization to replace the League of Nations. This organization was later to materialize as the United Nations. Subsequently, at Yalta in the Crimea, February, 1945, Roosevelt, Churchill, and Stalin again met and, among other things, announced a coming international conference at San Francisco to create a charter for the permanent organization of the United Nations.

Even before the achievement of a complete diplomatic and military coalition, the United Nations were winning their first campaigns. In the Pacific, these included, as already noted, the Battle of Midway and the campaigns at Guadalcanal. At the far eastern extremity of the Asiatic and Pacific battlefront in the Aleutian Islands, American forces took the offensive in May, 1943, and by August had reconquered the entire archipelago. Simultaneously, British and American forces broke the German and Italian armies in North Africa (May, 1943). Soviet armies had stopped the German advance at Stalingrad (September-November, 1942), and in 1943 were engaged in the first great Soviet counteroffensive. In September, 1943, came the unconditional surrender of Italy. By the spring of 1944 the Germans had been driven from all of southern Russia.

Axis reverses in Europe permitted the United Nations to mount offensives in three widely separated areas in Asia and the Pacific. In the summer of 1943, American forces advanced through cruel campaigns in New Georgia, Bougainville, and New Guinea toward Rabaul, Japan's principal military and naval base in the Southwest Pacific. To the north, the capture of the Gilbert and Marshall Islands (November, 1943, and February, 1944) was the prelude to a great naval offensive in the summer of 1944. Striking westward toward the China coast, American forces moved to the conquest of the major islands of the Mariana group (Saipan, July 9, and Tinian, July 23) and to the reconquest of Guam (August 3) all of which were captured only after the bitterest fighting and great loss of life. Far to the west in the CBI, offensives —long delayed by impenetrable jungles, devastating heat, disease, scarcity of transportation, and paucity of supplies and troops —were begun in northern Burma and along the Manipur-Imphal front. Especially important in this theater was the work of American and Chinese forces in northern Burma (1944) covering construction of the Ledo Road, the new supply route from India to China.

Other pressures, too, were reducing Japan's power to resist. By the summer of

1944, American submarines had sunk a total of nearly 700 Japanese vessels. These losses contributed to the eventual collapse of Japanese war production at home. To this latter task the United States brought the B-29 bomber which flew from secret airfields deep in China. The first raid by these flying superfortresses against southern Japan was made on June 15, 1944. Later raids struck at the eastern part of North China and Manchuria.

The weight of this military and naval power moved ever closer to the Japan islands in the closing months of 1944 and in 1945. Following successful campaigns in the western Carolines and the Halmahera group off northern New Guinea, the Philippines were invaded (October 19, 1944) in a series of related military and naval operations which resulted in serious Japanese losses at sea and the ultimate destruction of twenty-three Japanese divisions. Meanwhile the capture of Iwo Jima, March 16, 1945, and of Okinawa in the Liu-ch'iu (Ryukyus) on June 21 prepared the way for massive air assaults on Japan's home islands. The first of these in the early months of 1945 were concentrated on industrial centers—Tokyo, Nagoya, Osaka, Kobe, and others—and on the destruction of Japanese airfields, principally in Kyushu. Although American losses in all these attacks were heavy, they could not be compared with the frightful destruction wrought in Japan. By June 1, 1945, more than fifty square miles of Tokyo had been reduced to rubble and ashes. In July, 1945, British carrier planes joined the attack. By the same month, more than 2,000 American planes were sometimes over Japan in a single day. The land-based attacks were supported by naval carrier-plane attacks and by naval bombardment of Japan's coastal cities. The combined Anglo-American Third Fleet in the final two and one-half months of the war destroyed or damaged nearly 3,000 Japanese planes and sank or damaged some 1,600 enemy naval and merchant vessels, thus completing the destruction by August 1, 1945, of Japan's power on the sea and in the air. Moreover, as these great assaults developed, Japan's defenders were struck not only in Japan itself but also on the further edges of her conquered and now crumbling empire—in Bangkok, Formosa, Saigon, Rangoon, Penang, and Kuala Lumpur.

Thus by the summer of 1945, Japan's military position was hopeless. In Europe, Germany had already collapsed (May 7–8, 1945). It was now possible to warn the Japanese people that particular cities would be destroyed. The resulting raids carrying out these threats made it increasingly clear to the Japanese populace that their own defenders were powerless. At least some of Japan's leaders recognized the inevitability of defeat, as indicated by the removal in April 1945 of General Koiso Kuniaki from the Premiership and the installation of Suzuki Kantaro, whose appointment departed from the army's insistence that the Premier be a general in active service. The appointment, however, did not mean that control had passed to peace advocates. As late as June 9, Suzuki, replying to President Truman's warning that Japan would be destroyed unless she surrendered, declared that Japan would fight on. Then, on July 26, during the Potsdam Conference, the United States, Britain, and China delivered a final ultimatum to Japan demanding immediate unconditional surrender.[2] Japan replied (July 30) that she would ignore the demands of the Potsdam Declaration.

While the ultranationalist Japanese fanatics were determined to fight on, other events conspired to end hostilities without an invasion. On August 6 the Japanese city of Hiroshima and its army base were destroyed in the space of minutes by the first atomic bomb used in warfare. Nearly a month earlier (July 13), the Japanese government had asked Russia to intervene with Britain and the United States to bring about peace. Russia's reply, not delivered until August 8, announced immediate severance of her diplomatic relations with Japan and that "from August 9 the Soviet Government will consider itself to be at war with Japan." Within hours of Russia's severance of relations, a second atomic bomb destroyed the

city of Nagasaki and its naval base (August 9). On the same day Russian armies invaded Manchuria, seized the Korean ports of Rashin and Yuki (August 12) and advanced in the southern or Japanese half of Sakhalin Island. On August 10, the Japanese government announced its willingness to accept the Potsdam terms (to which Russia had now subscribed), provided they comprised no "demand which prejudices the prerogatives of His Majesty [the Emperor] as a sovereign ruler." The reply of the United States (August 11) stated that "the authority of the Emperor and the Japanese Government to rule the State shall be subject to the Supreme Commander of the Allied Powers." Japan accepted these terms August 14, and the surrender was effected on board the U.S. battleship *Missouri* in Tokyo Bay, September 2, 1945.

The Japanese decision to surrender was not produced by the atomic bomb or the Soviet Union's declaration of war. These factors, however, intensified an existing crisis, and gave to the Japanese emperor an extraordinary role in a decision that had long been in the making. It was a case in which the personal opinion of the emperor became an Imperial decision and therefore the will of the state. The crisis of July and August gave to the men who had long known that Japan must surrender the chance to stop the fanatics and to allow the historic influence of the throne to end the carnage.[3]

The emperor's announcement of surrender presented the Japanese with one of the great crises of their history. A proud and sensitive people, having met military defeat, was called upon to face a future compounded of social confusion in the homeland and of uncertainty in its relations with the outside world of conquerors. Before passing to the account of the post-war era, however, some further attention must be given wartime developments in Japan and China. In both nations these developments not only affected the conduct of war, but also bequeathed a troublesome legacy to the years of peace.

[2] Text in United States, Department of State, *Occupation of Japan* (1946), 53–55.

[3] Robert J. C. Butow, *Japan's Decision to Surrender* (1954), 228–33.

The political philosophy and the structure of government which had developed in Japan by 1941 and which were to persist throughout the war were in many respects logical developments of earlier steps taken after 1931 toward totalitarian control. Yet neither before nor after 1941 did Japan become a corporate state in the manner of Germany or Italy. She produced no all-powerful Nazi or Fascist party and no single political leader capable of emerging as a dictator. In matters of economics and production, she failed to create the full corporate state in the manner of her European allies. What happened in Japan both before and during the war was influenced by these European pace-setters, but Japanese conditions, problems, and the methods of dealing with them remained essentially Japanese.

When, by her attack on Pearl Harbor, Japan engulfed the Pacific area in World War II, she was operating under a governmental structure that had been altered vastly since the invasion of Manchuria a decade earlier. The movement toward parliamentary government, from which so much had been expected in the decade 1920 to 1930, had been extinguished. The Imperial Diet had declined in political importance, though its entire influence had not been destroyed. The traditional political parties, the *Seiyukai* and the *Minseito*, had abolished themselves under the pressure of extremists in 1940, and the country had returned to nonparty ministries. The armed services had secured increasing control over the civil administration but had been unable to gain a monopoly of political power in the cabinet and especially in the office of the prime minister. The functions of government had been increased greatly, in part by cabinet-inspired legislation in the Diet and by a much greater use of Imperial ordinances, ministerial orders, and departmental regulations. When she attacked Pearl Harbor, Japan seemed to be not far from the goal of the corporate state. Yet, the corporate state that was appearing was peculiarly Japanese in character. The most important results of the governmental changes from 1931 to

1941 were the increase of the number and the power of bureaucratic agencies, the enhancement of the prestige and the political influence of the bureaucracy as a whole, and thus the creation in wartime Japan of what may best be called "a dictatorship of the bureaucracy." [4]

The growth of bureaucratic agencies and of bureaucratic power in Japan after 1931 was not unique. [5] There were similar tendencies in the Western world and particularly in the United States under the New Deal. Nevertheless, throughout the history of modern Japan, bureaucracy had a greater political force, a broader and more complex

[4] Charles Nelson Spinks, "Bureaucratic Japan," *Far Eastern Survey* 10 (1941): 219–25.

[5] The term "bureaucracy" as applied to government in Japan is used in a much broader sense than is common in Western usage. It includes not only the civil servants but also the agents of the military services and, at times, of the political parties and the *Zaibatsu*. Thus, the enlargement of the bureaucracy may be said to have proceeded along two major lines: (1) There was an expansion of ministerial agencies and the creation of extraministerial boards under the jurisdiction of the cabinet. Some of the more important of these created in the immediate prewar years included: the Manchurian Affairs Board, entrusted with the co-ordination of policy between Japan and Manchukuo; the Cabinet Planning Board, a species of politico-economic general staff; the China Affairs Board, responsible for furthering the New Order in occupied China; and the Cabinet Advisory Council, an effort to recognize the modern would-be *Genro* and through them to find a means of reconciling rival bureaucratic factions. (2) Of great importance also was the multiplication of the national policy companies, which were the instruments of Japanese expansion at first in Manchuria and then in occupied China. The idea involved in this kind of an organization was not new. It had been employed early in the Meiji era in such cases as the Hokkaido Development Company and the Yawata Iron Works. As an instrument of national expansion abroad, the system was first fully matured in the South Manchurian Railway Company, founded in 1906, in whose hands Japan's exploitation of the South Manchuria sphere remained a practical monopoly until 1932. The pattern of organization for which the S.M.R. provided the model was that of an official corporation in which the government held a controlling number of shares. In the later national policy companies, the companies were holding concerns controlling subsidiary companies which conducted the business enterprises involved.

mechanism, than in other countries. During the entire constitutional period the ministers of state (the cabinet) were linked more intimately with bureaucratic elements than with the Diet. In addition some factions of the bureaucracy, the army and the navy, enjoyed a position of political independence and power guaranteed by constitutional organization. Again, Japan's bureaucrats enjoyed a unique political strength because of the influence they had wielded in the formulation as well as in the execution of policies. Ministers of state in Japan's bureaucratic cabinets long recognized that the government's fortunes depended less on the adoption of important national policies than on appropriate political recognition of each major bureaucratic group and the maintenance of a balance among these groups. As the bureaucratic agencies of government increased in size and number after 1931 and as the political parties lost influence and finally disappeared, it became the function of the prime minister to act as a mediating officer between these factions of permanent office-holders.

The absence of commanding political leadership in pre-war and wartime Japan was as notable as the power of the bureaucracy. There were efforts, indeed, to perpetuate the *Genro* system. In a limited way it did live on in a loose organization made up of the Lord Keeper of the Privy Seal, former prime ministers, and high representatives of the army and navy. Its influence, however, never equalled or even rivalled that of the Meiji *Genro*. Outstanding among the so-called new *Genro* was Prince Konoye Fumimaro, who headed three cabinets on the eve of the war. Konoye was chosen not because of his ability to lead but because of the aristocratic prestige of his family and his capacity, despite nebulous political thinking, to keep on reasonably good terms with all factions.

As the power of the bureaucracy increased, successive governments after 1932 sought to provide the prime minister with agencies through which he might exercise more effective leadership. A five-minister conference or inner cabinet had become fully established by 1940. In the spring of 1941, Premier Konoye turned to a second expedient, the creation of an unofficial but informally recognized "Big Three of the Cabinet," including the premier, the vice-premier, and the minister of finance. This device, although more flexible than the five-minister conference, also failed. A third device designed to increase the efficiency of Japan's top bureaucratic leadership was the *Taisei Yokusan Kai* or Imperial Rule Assistance Association (IRAA), which made its appearance on the demise of the traditional political parties in 1940. The idea of a single political party had been inspired by the European fascist model. Konoye was prevailed upon to lead the movement. The new association emerged as an agency of "spiritual mobilization" and was soon controlled by the army. Early in the war, the political importance of the IRAA led to the creation of a new and closely related organization, the Imperial Rule Assistance Political Society (IRAPS). This body, at first associated with the efforts of the government to pack the Diet with "approved candidates," enjoyed only a very limited success. As the war progressed, the IRAPS tended to become a species of Diet members' club dominated by conservative, but not extremist, party leaders.

The Economic Pattern

Although political power in prewar Japan had gravitated toward a cumbersome and leaderless bureaucracy, and although there was increasing state intervention in economic life, the nation was still far from possessing a planned economy. As late as 1941, most of the nation's business was financed and operated by private enterprise with only limited government interference. From the autumn of 1940, however, the need for national control of industry became more pressing, but there was no agreement as to the degree of control desirable or as to who should exercise this control. Extremists in the army, the navy, and some factions of the bureaucracy clamored for total control in which the state would simply take over all industry. The business interests, particularly the *Zaibatsu*, were opposed to this program and remained so throughout the war. They were not hostile to greater wartime integration of industry enforced by the state—in fact, they perceived some advantages to themselves in such a system—but they were determined that their ownership and their prerogatives of management should be safeguarded and preserved.

The Search for Effective Government

The Tojo cabinet, which replaced the third Konoye ministry on October 18, 1941, was supposed to be the answer to this riddle of leadership. General Tojo Hideki was a product of the Kwantung Army School, a former commander of the gendarmerie in Manchukuo, Chief of Staff of the Kwantung army, Vice-Minister of War in the first Konoye cabinet, and finally Minister of War in the third Konoye cabinet. He had a reputation as an able administrator, and in his political and economic thinking it was assumed that he shared the attitude of the "state planners" of the Kwantung army in Manchukuo. He was thus acceptable to the militarists and the fascist extremists, but in addition he appears to have been regarded by the *Zaibatsu* as a reliable leader for the greater war ahead. As Japan's wartime premier, Tojo held more offices and acquired greater power than any prime minister in Japan's history. He held concurrently the posts of Premier, War Minister, and Home Minister. After he had relinquished the last of these, he took over the new Ministry of Munitions and became also Chief of Staff. Tojo's accession to power seemed to guarantee the creation in wartime Japan of a full-fledged, military, corporate state, if not a personal dictatorship.

This expectation, however, was not fulfilled. Tojo was confronted with the industrial monopolies of the *Zaibatsu* operating in general as semi-autonomous units linked neither with each other nor with the government through any effectively coercive administrative authority. Even with unprecedented authority at his command, the prime minister proved unable to overcome the problems emerging from this system. Finally, in

January, 1944, after two war years of chaotic administration, the major enterprises were placed under the control of the newly created Ministry of Munitions. This centralized control and relatively efficient management of war production was not a political victory for the militarists and extreme "state planning," but rather an acceptance by the government of control measures proposed by and acceptable to the industrialists, the *Zaibatsu*. Indeed, the Tojo government, whose fumbling in directing home-production contributed to Japan's first military and naval reverses, fell and was replaced in July, 1944.

Although the war thus forced a greater concentration of administrative power than Japan had known previously, the failure of these belated measures to achieve victory, together with the rising specter of defeat, encouraged a return to traditional politics under more conservative guidance of the so-called new *Genro*. When the Tojo cabinet fell, the new ministry that succeeded was still essentially a military cabinet headed by a Kwantung army extremist, General Koiso Kuniaki, but was tempered by the presence of Admiral Yonai Mitsumasa as Deputy Prime Minister and Navy Minister. Koiso's cabinet survived less than a year in the face of mounting military reverses. On April 7, 1945, as has been noted, it was succeeded by a ministry headed by Admiral Baron Suzuki Kantaro. Suzuki was a former Lord Chamberlain who had been attacked by the extremist assassins in 1936. This cabinet represented a careful balancing of conservative bureaucrats, the military services, and the business interests, and a conscious effort by the elder statesmen to defeat all extreme forms of political control. It was the Suzuki cabinet that tendered Japan's surrender in August and then gave place, September 16, 1945, to a new ministry under a prince of the Imperial Household, Higashikuni Naruhiko, a cousin of Emperor Hirohito. The selection of an Imperial prince as premier was an effort to stabilize public opinion as the Japanese people witnessed the occupation of their homeland by a foreign army. Once the first phase of the occupation and demobilization was complete, Higashikuni resigned on October 5. He was succeeded the following day by one of Japan's few surviving "liberals," a man whom the nation had repudiated in 1931, Baron Shidehara Kijuro, who remained in office until April 22, 1946. It was Shidehara who faced the first problems of a defeated and broken Japan—the problems of food, of housing, of inflation in a nation without leadership and without purpose. These crises were beyond the grasp of the aged Shidehara, and in May the premiership passed to Yoshida Shigeru.[6]

Although Japan's unconditional surrender was brought about by the overwhelming powers of American armament, the time and the manner of the surrender were conditioned by the political, economic, and bureaucratic character of the Japanese state. Indeed, Japan's surrender would probably have come earlier if the political structure of the nation had permitted a more rapid and decisive determination of national policies or if the allies had been content with something short of unconditional surrender. As early as mid-1944 those Japanese leaders who possessed the basic information foresaw the economic collapse which was already underway and which assured the coming military disaster. By August, 1945, even without direct air attack, the level of Japan's production would have declined below the peak of 1944 by 40 to 50 per cent solely as a result of the interdiction of overseas imports. As it was, the damage from air attacks approximated that which was suffered by Germany. Approximately 30 per cent of the urban population of Japan lost its homes and much of its possessions. With this appalling physical disaster came declining morale. Japan's civilian casualties numbered about 806,000, of which 333,000 were deaths. A declining belief in the power to win was accompanied by loss of confidence in both the military and the civilian leaders. Although a few of Japan's statesmen foresaw the ultimate defeat as early as February, 1944, it was not until May, 1945, that the

[6] Shidehara died in 1951. See Hugh Borton, *Japan's Modern Century* (2nd ed., 1970), 466–67.

Supreme War Direction Council, a creation of the Koiso cabinet, seriously considered means to end the war.

CHINA DURING THE WAR

For China, the global scale that hostilities assumed by the close of 1941 appeared as a limited blessing. It seemed to foreshadow the ultimate defeat of Japan by Anglo-American arms, the triumph of China's Nationalist revolution, and the elevation of China to the envied position of a great power. These, however, were hopes for the future. Against these hopes, the realities of early 1942 were foreboding. No one was certain when the democracies would win, or indeed, that they would win at all. Moreover, within China, the revolution that began on the Yangtze in 1911 had neither completed its course nor remained united in its objectives. The conditions that created the revolution had not been removed, and Sun Yat-sen's program, which gave the revolution life and purpose, had not been realized. Insofar as resistance to Japan was concerned, the Chinese had preserved a notable unity, but this unity did not mean that China was at peace with herself. There were dissensions and open conflicts within the revolution which the leadership of the *Kuomintang* had not resolved. Moreover, as her own long conflict with Japan became merged with the worldwide struggle against the Axis Powers, China was ill-equipped in the material weapons with which modern nations fight. Her moral strength was symbolized by her ready adherence to the Declaration of the United Nations on January 1, 1942. The darker side of the picture was that China's new allies, the United States and Britain, were unable to give her immediate aid. Independent China remained locked in the great western interior, governed from the fugitive capital at Chungking. China's plight grew progressively worse. Isolation from her allies became almost complete as all of Southeast Asia fell to Japan. For many months after the tide of battle in the Pacific had turned, there could be only limited relief in munitions, guns, or planes for China. Thus, while China was ultimately to share in the rewards of a United Nations victory, conflicts arising from an unfinished revolution and the stress of war sapped the vitality of the *Kuomintang*-Nationalist government and eroded its support among the populace. The *Kuomintang's* chief opponents, the Communists, on the other hand, were able to use the war years to strengthen their position.

Basic in Nationalist China's wartime problems was the deterioration of her economy. The retreat into the undeveloped hinterland, however heroic in terms of human endurance, cut deeply into productive capacity. Government assistance had been given to effect the removal of industries to the interior, but since many coastal enterprises were foreign-owned, only about 600 private factories and 117,300 tons of machinery were actually transferred. While additional plants were built with government capital, the value of total production reached at its peak in 1943 only 12 per cent of prewar levels.[7] Light arms were manufactured, but there was in all China not one factory that could produce a truck, a tank, or an airplane. To meet her most pressing needs, the *Kuomintang*-Nationalist government welcomed such imports as could be obtained from the Soviet Union, the United States, and, after 1941, even Japan.[8] Added to the production crisis were economic dislocations arising from inflation. As the inflationary spiral rose, the hoarding of and speculation in commodities became more profitable than the manufacturing of finished products. Indeed, profiteering among businessmen and government officials was so widespread in the later war years that "National goals were dissipated in making money and protecting special privilege."[9] Inflation also progressively beggarized the new middle class, thus reducing the political influence of the *Kuomintang's* liberal constituency and giving the extreme right wing increased power and authority.

The *Kuomintang*-Nationalist government confronted another problem in rising peasant unrest. After 1937 the horrors of war multiplied the burden suffered by peasants as a result of tenancy and indebtedness. As Japanese forces invaded China, villages were looted and burned and the populace abused. Behind Nationalist lines peasants were indiscriminately conscripted into the army—some provinces were stripped of as many as one-half to two-thirds of the male population of military age—where they were often treated brutally by their officers. Nationalist armies commandeered men, carts, and draft animals without regard to local need or peasant sensibilities. Even worse was the government's use of troops to collect food while peasants starved. To a peasantry thus treated, the Nationalist government assumed the appearance of a devouring tyrant. On occasion peasant mobs attempted to disarm their own troops, and as the war progressed, Nationalist armies became increasingly unreliable as the ranks were filled by sullen, sometimes rebellious peasant conscripts.

Still other problems were connected with the multiple objectives of the Nationalist government's political leadership. The government and the source of its authority, the *Kuomintang*, faced the Herculean task of providing leadership in prosecuting the war and expelling the Japanese. In addition, the *Kuomintang* professed to be the guardian and the vehicle of Sun Yat-sen's continuing revolution. In the context of government under one-party political tutelage, a staggering responsibility rested on the *Kuomintang* hierarchy. This hierarchy professed to maintain its political power on a broad base of popular consent. Yet, to obtain this consent was peculiarly difficult in the atmosphere of wartime China not only because Chinese politics was traditionally a very personal

---

[7] In 1943 Nationalist China produced 147,000,000 kilowatts of electricity, 84,300 tons of pig iron, 10,400 tons of steel, 6,000,000 tons of coal, less than 6,000 tons of basic chemicals, and 14,300,000 gallons of liquid fuel. Cheng Yu-kwei, *Foreign Trade and Industrial Development of China* (1956).

[8] Imports from Japanese sources trickled through long, thinly manned battlelines. Between 1942 and 1945, Nationalist China's imports from the Japanese ranged from 20 to 35 per cent of the total from all sources.

[9] Foster Rhea Dulles, *China and America* (1946), 241.

thing but also because constitutionalism did not yet exist in fact. Those who were beyond the Party and many of the rank and file of the Party, having no effective means of influencing policy, became something less than ardent adherents of *Kuomintang* leadership.[10] This problem of leadership was the more serious because, in addition to the challenge from the Communists, the *Kuomintang* was confronted by a whole group of minor political parties, jealous of *Kuomintang* power, all of which thought they knew what ought to be done. During the early war years beginning in 1937, although the minor parties were allowed no share in the *Kuomintang's* monopoly of political power or in responsibility for the conduct of war, they did seek to co-operate with government even when their status as independent parties was not fully recognized in law. After 1941, however, when the *Kuomintang*-Communist united front failed, the Nationalist government revived a policy of repression which in turn alienated popular support at the very moment it was most needed.[11]

[10] On the structure of the Nationalist government as affected by the Japanese invasion, see Liu Naichen, "The Framework of Government in Unoccupied China," *Voices from Unoccupied China*, H. F. MacNair, ed. (1944), 1–15.

[11] Ch'ien Tuan-sheng, *The Government and Politics of China* (1950), 371–75. A wide array of political ideas and programs were represented by the minor parties. The Young China Party (sometimes called the Chinese Youth Party) had been organized in Paris, 1923. It called itself democratic and filled its platform with vague aspirations, extreme nationalism, and anti-Communism. The National Socialist Party, dominated at the outset by university professors, had been formed in 1931 by Carsun Chang among intellectuals who had been followers of Liang Ch'i-ch'ao. The party was largely an attempt to restore traditional values modified by Western thought. The National Salvation Association was organized by intellectuals at Shanghai, 1936, to promote armed resistance against Japan. Its thinking was Leftist, and for this many of its members were imprisoned, though in reality its objective was unity of the country above all party considerations. During the war the *Kuomintang* continued a policy of suppressing this movement. Two additional minor groups, the National Association for Vocational Education and the Rural Reconstruction Group, favored popularizing vocational education and implementing rural reform respectively.

Also contributing to the *Kuomintang's* difficulties in marshaling broad support was the party's failure to supply dynamic leadership either on the battlefield or in the political realm. The indispensible party leader at the time of the outbreak of war was Chiang Kai-shek, whose emergence from party ranks was due principally, though not exclusively to his status as a soldier. Chiang, the military man, had won a new degree of unity within China by defeating the warlords. The luster derived from this achievement, however, dimmed as Chiang grappled with the exceedingly complex problems of resisting Japan, from 1937 to 1945. For one thing, Chiang's forces, while numerically impressive, were in general unequal to Japanese armies in equipment, training, and morale. Moreover, Chiang's inability to deal effectively with political problems of military control and organization meant that he exercised only limited authority over some of the troops under his command. Thus after 1938, except where a pitched battle and frontal attack on a better equipped enemy appeared mandatory, Chinese troops were ordered to avoid decisive engagements, to yield in the face of Japanese assaults, and to attack only thinly defended points. By such means Chiang hoped to hang on, keeping his armies in the field until help arrived and Japan was overcome by United Nations forces. The strategy was designed to achieve the survival of the National government and, given the handicaps under which Chiang labored, perhaps nothing better could have been devised. Nevertheless, Chiang's essentially defensive effort produced no political-military heroes prepared to pay any price for victory.[12]

These groups were less important as political parties than as symbols of political needs. Finally, the Democratic League, founded in 1941 by progressives of the People's Political Council, had a more valid claim to the label "democratic" than any other political group. In the *Kuomintang*-Communist conflict during and after the war the League was divided between those inclined toward close co-operation with the Communists and those aspiring to be neutral mediators.

[12] P. M. A. Linebarger, "Ideological Dynamics of the Postwar Far East," *Foreign Governments*, F. Morstein Marx, ed. (1949), 555.

However, the conduct of hostilities was only a single aspect of the problem of leadership. In a land where nationalism was still a vibrant, popular aspiration rather than a realized system of administration, Chiang was expected to implement Sun's revolution through appropriate political, economic, and social reforms. These demands for political and social leadership came at a time when nearly half of China's territory was in the hands of the invader, when factionalism within the *Kuomintang* was increasing rather than decreasing, and finally when Chiang's position was constantly under challenge by the Communists and by non-Communists both inside and outside the *Kuomintang*. In 1937 and 1938 Chiang appeared to be rising to the crisis that called him. In response to popular demand he made peace with the Communists and moved in the direction of constitutionalism. He showed some qualities of political as well as military leadership and of ethical stature, but unlike Sun Yat-sen he was not a "political philosopher and utopist" who could stir the loyalty of men by his power of expression, nor was he a saint like Gandhi who could convince a world of his selfless devotions.[13]

Chiang's political creed was revealed not only by what he did, but also by his book, *China's Destiny*, first published at Chungking in Chinese in 1943.[14] It is a textbook on Chinese nationalism in which Chiang appears as a disciple of nineteenth-century nationalism similar to the models pro-vided by Germany, Italy, and Japan. Chiang's program, as presented, was in close parallel to the reform philosophy of Meiji Japan. Emphasis was on "an emotional race and national consciousness with the Yellow Emperor presented as the common ancestor of Chinese, Manchus, Mongols, Tibetans, and Mohammedans, just as Amaterasu, the Sun Goddess, became the ancestress of the Japanese emperor and the Japanese race." Chiang reviewed the decline and the fall of the Manchus, the story of Western imperialism (the unequal treaties), the subversion of the Revolution of 1911 by Yuan Shih-k'ai and the warlords, the reorganization and triumph of the *Kuomintang*, its record of national reconstruction from 1928 to 1937, and, finally, China's achievement of new nationhood signified by termination of the unequal treaties with Great Britain and the United States in 1943. China's revolution, therefore, could be held together no longer by anti-imperialism. It required a new positive nationalism that Chiang proposed to base on Confucian morality, which he believed could still inspire the nation. The weakness of his position lay in the fact that his plea for loyalty to the state was backed by no sound political theory relevant to the wartime China of 1937–1945.[15]

[13] P. M. A. Linebarger, "Government in China," *Foreign Governments*, F. Morstein Marx, ed. (1949), 597.

[14] Editions in English include: (1) Chiang Kai-shek, *China's Destiny* authorized translation by Wang Chung-hui, with an introduction by Lin Yutang, (1947); (2) Chiang Kai-shek, *China's Destiny and Chinese Economic Theory* with notes and commentary by Philip Jaffe (1947). Although there was much controversy as to the relative merits of the two English editions, as a matter of fact "as translations they are about equally faithful to the author's original," despite "the servile acceptance of Lin Yutang" and "the bitterly hostile presentation of Mr. Jaffe." See the evaluation on this point by Earl Swisher in *The Far Eastern Quarterly* 10 (November, 1950): 89–95.

[15] "The weakness and confusion of his [Chiang's] thesis lie in the fact that Confucian morality has been outmoded for several generations of students and political leaders who regard it as old-fashioned, and the additional fact that Confucius' political philosophy is moralistic, non-legal, and anti-state and thus ill-suited to modern nationalism, even of the conventional sort. The fact that Chiang tried to append an argument for a government of law over a government of men only serves to confuse his dominant and basically untenable thesis. . . . No attempt is made to reselect from China's rich tradition those elements that would support a new and modern state; no search is made for the democratic elements in China's history and philosophy." Swisher, *The Far Eastern Quarterly* 10 (November, 1950): 93. The view that Chiang's ideological shortcomings were less serious than his failure to stay in touch with the broad spectrum of political factions is advanced in Pichon P. Y. Loh, "The Politics of Chiang Kai-shek: A Reappraisal," *Journal of Asian Studies* 25 (1966): 431–51.

Whatever may be said of *China's Destiny* as a sincere revelation of Chiang's mind and soul, as a political manifesto it was a lamentable miscarriage. It opposed the intellectual trends of the pre-war years by berating those Chinese who had sought inspiration from the West. It scolded Chinese businessmen of the Treaty Ports for their Western free enterprise while it advocated restriction of private capital and a government-planned economy. It alienated the youth of China by offering it nothing more than an exhortation to obedience and frugality. It sought political and social stability by appeals to tradition which had no meaning in the ferment of modern China and which served only to alienate political allies in the struggle against Communism.

Kuomintang-Communist Strife

Another difficulty besetting the National government's leadership after 1941 was the progressive breakdown of the *Kuomintang*-Communist united front. Proclaimed in September, 1937, the united front rested on an agreement between the *Kuomintang* and Communists to abandon their war against each other and to act jointly in the defense of China. The motivating force behind the agreement was China's growing determination to resist Japanese imperialism; the agreement did not signify any lessening of hostility between the two contending parties. On the contrary, both Chiang and Mao Tse-tung were intent upon resuming their warfare at the earliest feasible moment. The unification movement, therefore, was soon gripped by creeping paralysis. Both the Nationalist government and Communists continued to fight Japan, but the united front after late 1938 became merely a name, and eventually, by 1944, not even that. The total effect was to cripple China's limited powers to resist Japan and to pave the way for renewed civil war.

In contrast to the *Kuomintang*, the Communists during these war years gained strength. As Japanese forces swept into northern Chinese cities, Communist units moved through the countryside behind Japanese lines capturing arms, recruiting troops, and organizing the peasantry. Wherever pos-

sible local governments were established, landholding revised, and tax reforms instituted. These tactics were first employed successfully in the Shansi-Hopeh-Chahar border region. Subsequently vast regions in northern and central China were infiltrated and organized. The united front enabled the Communists to appear as patriots, defending China from her enemy. However genuine this image may have been, it is also clear that the war provided the Communists with opportunities to extend their influence into regions where they had no hold previously.

The Communists capitalized on these opportunities by devising means for consolidating their rule: (1) So-called "border region" governments, consisting of a pyramid of "peoples' councils" each of which was responsible to the one above and which was dominated by the Communist minority in its membership, were set up to administer Communist power; (2) the party membership responsible for the conduct of government was expanded from some 40,000 in 1937 to perhaps as many as 1,200,000 in 1945; and (3) party members, old and new, were given rigorous ideological indoctrination aimed at making them completely obedient to Mao Tse-tung. This latter process, known as the *cheng feng* movement, involved party members in intensive study of authorized texts (such as, for example, Mao's *On the New Democracy*, in which Sun Yatsen's Three Principles of the People were reinterpreted so as to harmonize with Mao's theory of revolution), group discussion, public confession, and self-criticism. By these means dissident elements were eliminated from the party and a fresh sense of revolutionary fervor was injected into the membership. Therefore, when World War II terminated with Japan's surrender there was in China a powerful Communist Party composed of highly trained revolutionists, which claimed an army of more than half a million men and mastery of an area populated by nearly one hundred million people.

The spectre of expanding communism greatly alarmed the Nationalist government and triggered counterefforts. Initially the Nationalists broke up Communist front organizations within their reach and launched guerilla efforts of their own behind Japanese lines, but lacking both an ideology and program of action to match the Communists' in popular appeal, neither of these activities had much success. There followed a military blockade of the Communists' northern stronghold to prevent the infiltration of Nationalist territory. Finally, the expansion of Communist forces outside the regions designated in the truce agreements led to a series of "incidents," which culminated in the pitched battle of the "New Fourth Army incident" of January, 1941, and which led to the beginning of intensified civil war.

Nevertheless, in spite of frequent incidents and continual friction, the stated policy of the Nationalist government remained that of seeking a political settlement with the Communists. At meetings of the People's Political Council, some minor parties attempted mediation with the object of preserving *Kuomintang*-Communist co-operation. On a number of occasions, there were direct negotiations between Nationalist and Communist officials in which suggestions for a "coalition government" were brought forth for the first time. Although no settlement was reached, it did appear that from May to September, 1944, the Nationalist government and the Chinese Communist Party were at least going through the forms of seeking a peaceful settlement. But behind these maneuvers was the government's fear of offending elements within the *Kuomintang* if "radical measures of reform" were passed, and the government's well-justified conviction that the Communists would extend their power at the first opportunity.

Efforts to Bolster China

Although China was isolated from the mainstream of World War II, her war effort was supported by her allies. In the early stages of the Sino-Japanese conflict, the Soviet Union, although officially at peace, provided assistance in the form of $250,000,000 in credits, five air wings with Soviet pilots, and the stationing of Soviet troops at Hami to block Japan's access to Sinkiang. However, this aid, which had been prompted

by fears that the German-Japanese Anti-Comintern Pact of 1936, pointed to an ultimate Japanese assault on the Soviet Union, was not sustained beyond the outbreak of World War II. Beginning in 1941, the United States became the chief source of foreign aid.

At first this American aid was little more than verbal assurance that the war would be fought until Japan was defeated. There followed financial aid, a $500,000,000 loan in 1942.[16] There was also implementation of long-range planning to reopen communications with Chungking. The chief of the American military mission to China, General Joseph Stilwell, became chief-of-staff to Generalissimo Chiang Kai-shek and commander of ground forces in the CBI Theater. After the retreat from Burma, it was Stilwell's task to train Chinese troops for the reconquest, to open air transport from India over the Hump of the Himalayas to Chungking, and to construct the Ledo Road (later known as the Stilwell Road) from Assam through northern Burma to link with the upper Burma Road. One of the heroic stories of the war was written by the Americans who, beginning with scanty equipment, flew lend-lease supplies to Chungking.[17] There was also aid to China from the American Volunteer Group. Under Colonel, later General, Claire L. Chennault, these American "Flying Tigers" had operated prior to Pearl Harbor under contracts with the Chinese government to protect the Burma Road. Later they continued to operate in China as the Fourteenth Air Force of the United States Army Air Forces.

On the political and diplomatic front, the United States also moved to bolster Chinese confidence by discarding the last remnants of the unequal treaty system. Tariff autonomy had already been conceded to China more than a decade earlier. Now, on January 11, 1943, both the United States and Great

[16] Previous loans had been made in the prewar years.

[17] See Charles F. Romanus and Riley Sunderland, *Stilwell's Mission to China* (1953) for an authoritative account of American military aid.

Britain concluded treaties with China providing for immediate relinquishment of their extraterritorial rights and for the settlement of related questions. This act and similar relinquishment of special rights by all the remaining "treaty powers" completed the long process of restoring and recognizing the full sovereignty of China. At the same time, impelled by the pressures of war, Congress ended Chinese exclusion on December 17, 1943. Under the new law, a presidential proclamation fixed an annual quota of Chinese immigrants at 105.

The fuller significance of the ending of extraterritoriality and the exclusion laws was given at the Cairo Conference, November 22–26, 1943, where Roosevelt and Churchill met with Chiang Kai-shek to consider problems of war and peace in the Far East. The implication was that China was now accepted as one of the great powers; that the Nationalist government had the full support of Britain and America; and that the postwar Far East would be built around a fully sovereign, independent, and strong China. Indeed, the year 1943 revealed new heights in America's traditional and sentimental admiration for China. This newly aroused enthusiasm was associated with Madame Chiang Kai-shek, who had come to the United States early in 1943 to win American support for the Nationalist government and to criticize the strategy of merely holding the front against Japan until the defeat of Hitler had been achieved. Her eloquence and charm appeared to personify the heroism of a China that had refused to be beaten. "Chinese unity and Chinese democracy were accepted uncritically under the spell of her magnetic personality." [18] Madame Chiang spoke of the high lights; she avoided the shadows. Neither she nor other spokesmen of the Nationalist government were in a position to say what all knew—that China's prosecution of the war had reached its lowest point since Japan struck at Lukouchiao in July, 1937.

Although there had been warning rumors in 1943, it was not until early in 1944 that an alarming picture of China's deteriorating war effort and morale broke through the Chungking censorship to reach the American public. In the shock of this disclosure, American public opinion swung from emotional admiration to utmost unqualified denunciation. President Roosevelt was afraid that China would not hold together to the end of the war. Vice-President Henry A. Wallace was sent to Chungking to encourage Chiang and to get the Nationalist and Communist armies to stop fighting each other. The American government wanted Chiang to form a combined war council to co-ordinate all Chinese forces against Japan, and under Chiang's authority to place General Joseph W. Stilwell in command. In August, 1944, General Patrick J. Hurley went to Chungking as the President's personal representative to Chiang to sweeten the already bitter relations between Chiang and Stilwell, to keep China in the war, and to unify all Chinese military forces against Japan. Hurley soon came to the view that relations between Chiang and Stilwell over the question of China's war effort and the means of promoting it had deteriorated beyond repair. Accordingly, following Hurley's recommendation, Stilwell was recalled and Major General Albert C. Wedemeyer was designated to replace him as Chiang's chief-of-staff, October, 1944.[19] Coincident with these events, Clarence E. Gauss, ambassador to China, resigned November 1, 1944, and was replaced by General Hurley who continued as

[18] Dulles, *China and America*, 240.

[19] Stilwell's troubles with Chiang were rooted in the American general's proposed military reforms. Stilwell recommended the reduction of China's armies, a thorough retraining of remaining troops, and reorganization of the command structure. To Stilwell these were merely steps toward the creation of an effective fighting force. Chiang, however, perceived that Stilwell's program would certainly undermine the coalition upon which his power rested. Tensions engendered by this basic difference were heightened by deep personal animosity. General Chennault's relationships with the Generalissimo, on the other hand, were uniformly cordial. Chennault proposed to win the war through air assaults, a method which would not require American interference with China's political or military structure. Jonathan Spence, *To Change China* (1969), Chapter 9.

ambassador until November 26, 1945. Hurley's activities included: (1) efforts to mediate between the Nationalists and Communists, and (2) efforts to clarify relations between China and the Soviet Union. By this time however, the American offensive against Japan through the Philippines and the Mandated Islands was reducing the China theater to lesser importance in American military planning. As a result there was less effort to deal with the problem of Nationalist military and political power. General Hurley was instrumental in a resumption of negotiations between the Nationalists and the Communists, but the basic question of power between the two groups remained unresolved. Thus matters stood as, with Japan's sudden surrender, hostilities in the Pacific came to an end.

FOR FURTHER READING

MILITARY AND NAVAL AFFAIRS. Louis Morton, *The War in the Pacific; Strategy and Command: The First Two Years* (1962) offers careful description and analysis of American military policy. Samuel Eliot Morison, *History of United States Naval Operations in World War II* (14 vols., 1947–1960) is the most detailed operational history of American naval warfare. On the United States Army's role, see appropriate volumes in three officially sponsored series: *United States Army in World War II; The Army Air Forces in World War II;* and *Operational Narratives of the Marine Corps in World War II.* Among the more specialized accounts are: Samuel B. Griffith, *The Battle for Guadalcanal* (1963); Stanley L. Falk, *Bataan: The March of Death* (1962); Robert L. Eichelberger, *Our Jungle Road to Tokyo* (1950); Claire Chennault, *Way of a Fighter* (1949); James A. Field, *The Japanese at Leyte Gulf* (1947); W. W. Smith, *Midway: Turning Point of the Pacific* (1966); Masanobu Tsuji, *Singapore, The Japanese Version* (Sidney, Australia, 1960); Hashimoto Mochitsura, *Sunk: The Story of the Japanese Submarine Fleet, 1941–1945.* E. H. M. Colegrove, trans. (1954); George C. Kenney, *The MacArthur I Know* (1951); Frank O.

Hough, *The Island War* (1947); Roy McKelvie, *The War in Burma* (London, 1948); and T'an Pei-ying, *The Building of the Burma Road* (1945). For literature not suggested by the foregoing see Louis Morton, "Britain and Australia in the War Against Japan: Review Article," *Pacific Affairs* 34 (1961): 184–89. The decision to use atomic weapons against Japan has produced historical controversy. Lansing Lamont, *Day of Trinity* (1965) is a readable account of scientific and technological development leading to the bomb. Louis Morton, "The Decision to Use the Atomic Bomb," *Command Decisions*, K. R. Greenfield, ed. (1960) is based on the memoirs of American officials; the complex military, political, and moral issues involved in the decision are treated in Herbert Feis, *The Atomic Bomb and the End of World War II* (rev. ed., 1966); Robert J. C. Butow, *Japan's Decision to Surrender* (1954),° and T. Kase, *Journey to the Missouri* (1950). The timing of the attacks, nature of the orders issued, and other operational details are covered in appropriate volumes of the naval and air force histories cited above. The effect of the bombing is told in John Hersey, *Hiroshima* (1946)°; the recollections of some survivors are in Arata Osada, ed., *Children of the A-Bomb* (1963) and Robert J. Lifton, *Death in Life: Survivors of Hiroshima* (1967). Among volumes sharply critical of the decision to use atomic weapons are: Fletcher Knebel and Charles W. Bailey, *No High Ground* (1961); R. C. Batchelder, *The Irreversible Decision* (1962); and Gar Alperovitz, *Atomic Diplomacy* (1965). The latter argues that the decision was prompted by a desire to pursue a tough line with the Soviet Union, and not to save lives or to hasten peace.

WARTIME DIPLOMACY. Herbert Feis offers the fullest scholarly treatment in a series of four volumes: *The China Tangle: The American Effort in China from Pearl Harbor to the Marshall Mission* (1953) °; *Churchill, Roosevelt, Stalin: The War They Waged and the Peace They Sought* (1957); *Between War and Peace: The Potsdam Conference* (1960); *The Atomic Bomb* (cited above); and *Con-*

test Over Japan (1967).* See also H. F. Angus, *Canada and the Far East, 1940–1953* (Toronto, 1953); Walter Johnson, ed., *Roosevelt and the Russians: The Yalta Conference* (1949); John L. Snell, ed., *The Meaning of Yalta*, with foreword by Paul H. Clyde (1956) *; and Theodore H. White, ed., *The Stilwell Papers* (1948).

POLITICS AND ECONOMICS OF WAR. T. A. Bisson, *Japan's War Economy* (1945) stresses the role of the *Zaibatsu*. Jerome B. Cohen, *Japan's Economy in War and Reconstruction* (1949) is the ablest general study. B. F. Johnston, *Japanese Food Management in World War II* (1953) is a voluminous reference work. Douglas G. Haring, ed., *Japan's Prospect* (1946) is by scholars who trained personnel for military government in Japan. Yale C. Maxon, *Control of Japanese Foreign Policy: Study of Civil-Military Rivalry, 1930–1945* (1957) provides a careful study of a crucial aspect of Japanese politics. J. Morris, *Traveller from Tokyo* (London, 1943), an eye-witness account of Japan at the beginning of the war. William Craig, *The Fall of Japan* (1967)* emphasizes the human dimensions of surrender. Among the apologies written by Japanese leaders are: Shigemitsu Mamoru,

Japan and Her Destiny: My Struggle for Peace (1958); and Togo Shigenori, *The Cause of Japan* (1956).

Graham Peck, *Two Kinds of Time* (1950) * is a reflective account of Chinese life, 1940–1947. A vivid, first-hand report of China's wartime decline is T. H. White and Annalee Jacoby, *Thunder Out of China* (1946).* The story of the ways in which foreign aid was utilized in China is told by a long-time Chinese financial adviser, Arthur N. Young, *China and the Helping Hand, 1937–1945* (1964). Allen S. Whiting and Shen Shih-ts'ai, *Sinkiang: Pawn or Pivot?* (1958) covers the years 1933–1943.

On the Chinese Communists see: Charles McLane, *Soviet Policy and the Chinese Communists, 1931–1946* (1958); Edgar Snow, *Random Notes on Red China, 1936–1945* (1957),* and Fox Butterfield, "A Missionary View of the Chinese Communists (1936–1939)," *Papers on China*, Vol. 15, (1961), 147–99. Published and distributed by the East Asian Research Center, Harvard University. See also John K. Fairbank, Edwin O. Reischauer and Albert M. Craig, *East Asia: The Modern Transformation* (1965), Chapter 8, for a critical evaluation of the Nationalist performance and the Communist challenge.

The Occupation
of Japan, 1945-1952

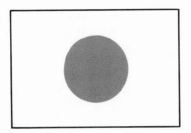

chapter 31

V-J Day, August 14, 1945, ended the hostilities of World War II in the Pacific and the Far East but did not bring peace to Eastern Asia. To be sure, victory in war freed the Orient of the incubus of Japanese militarism, and imperialistic expansion, but the war had not and could not rid Asia of all the ills from which it suffered. In many areas of East Asia, men were still prepared to fight, and they continued to fight to achieve the things they desired. Many of their goals were old and could not be traced exclusively to the recent policies and behavior of Japan. Rather, they were the recurring manifestations of an Asia stirred by a political and social revolution underway before World War II. But if the processes of modernization were not introduced into East Asia by the war, these processes were in many respects accelerated by the conflict, and they continued to operate with even greater force after the hostilities had ceased. Throughout the entire area there was not a single country or a single people unaffected by dynamic forces of change. Thus Japan's surrender was but the first step toward meeting a vast array of perplexing questions which war had not solved, and which in some cases were made more difficult by the war.

Basic in Asia's post-war turmoil were traditional "low" standards of living made even lower by the ravages of war: the destruction of life savings and property, the interruption of trade, the displacement of large segments of population, and the general dislocation resulting from extreme shortages and uncontrolled inflation. Some areas of Eastern Asia were affected more adversely and radically by the war than others. Yet the words of Manuel Roxas, a Filipino leader, that war and the Japanese had brought "physical ruin" to the Philippines could well be applied to larger areas of East Asia. This was not to say that Asia's economic problems had become insuperable. It was, rather, that the destruction wrought by war, added to the relative poverty of Eastern Asia in resources for an industrial society, to its historic problems of population, to the subsistence income of the peasant masses, to the lack of industrial capital, and to traditional historic social habits which had not adjusted themselves to a modern world, made economic rehabilitation and development an exceedingly difficult matter. Clearly, economic independence and new standards of living remained a hope for the distant future.

Politics no less than economics were disrupted by war. Traditional views of Asia's political status became untenable. Japan, the one "great power" of East Asia, was reduced to the status of a third- or fourth-class power. China, for one hundred years a quasi-dependent area, regained her full sovereignty and was dignified with nominal inclusion among the great states. The Philippines became an independent republic. Other native republics, semi-independent in fact, were born in French Indochina and the Netherlands Indies, and independence "in due course" had been promised to Korea. The Mongolian People's Republic acquired nationhood under Soviet patronage. Burma and India entered upon a new and independent political future. These signs of vital political consciousness were partly a result of what loosely may be called nationalism, (a refusal to be governed longer by alien powers), but were also symptoms of a much broader social unrest. The dream of modernization brought Eastern Asia out of her seclusion, affected her intellectual as well as her material life, created the stirrings of a new social consciousness and supplied her with a new intellectual and social leadership, whether in the person of a Chiang Kai-shek, or a Mao Tse-tung in China, a Roxas or a Taruc in the Philippines, a Sukarno in Indonesia, a Ho Chi-minh in Indochina, a Syngman Rhee or a Kim Il-song in Korea. The principle common to all these leaders was the concept of Asia's inherent right to political independence. What they had not resolved was the political, economic, and social structure in which independence was to function.

JAPAN AS A VICTIM OF WAR

The legacies of war in Japan were manifest everywhere. The country that had embarked on arrogant conquest was vastly different from the one that bowed before the victors in 1945—a picture of physical destruction, economic collapse, and social and spiritual emptiness; yet withal a Japan that responded with habitual discipline to the emperor's bidding to surrender. The catalogue of the nation's losses included nearly two million lives and some 40 per cent of the aggregate urban area including 2,000,000 buildings. Nearly 700,000 buildings were destroyed in Tokyo alone where, during the war, population in the terror of bombings attacks shrank from more than 6,500,000 to less than 3,000,000.

Frightful as the physical destruction was, its consequences were by no means so damaging as the breakdown of the economy at war's end. The extraordinary gains of the pre-war decade (1930–1940), during which industrial output doubled, were wiped out by defeat, leaving the nation in 1946 with less than a third of its 1930 production. The only immediately useful vestige of Japan's wealth was the paddy field. The peasant became an important person as desperate city dwellers sought food through the illicit channels of the black market. Prized family possessions were traded for rice; vegetables were grown where houses had stood; inflation consumed the meager savings that millions of little people had gathered through long hard years.

Possibly most damaging of all to a disciplined people was the enforced departure from discipline. Men defied authority, or they perished. It was no longer possible to live within the law. The price was paid in morale and in character. Petty lawlessness and juvenile delinquency flourished, while gangsterism and protection rackets terrorized whole communities.[1]

At the same time, the picture of Japan, as the victors found it, was not hopeless. Millions of Japanese accepted surrender and humiliation with dignity. They met the cruel reality of defeat, surrender, and hunger, and, with little effort to shift the blame to others, accepted it as their own responsibility as well as that of their leaders. Whatever later successes the Occupation enjoyed were attributable in a major degree to this attitude that enabled the Japanese people to co-

[1] A graphic account of Japan in defeat is given by Edwin O. Reischauer, *The United States and Japan* (rev. ed., 1961).* For differing appraisal of the Occupation, see Robert B. Textor, *Failure in Japan: with Keystones for a Positive Policy* (1951), and Kazuo Kawai, *Japan's American Interlude* (1960).

operate with the inevitable. Troops of the Occupation were received without visible animosity: a strange and friendly reception for Americans who had been taught, or had learned in battle, to hate the Japanese.[2]

THE AMERICAN CONCEPT OF OCCUPATION

From the moment of Japan's defeat it was clear that the United States would assume a predominant position in the Occupation. Although America gave assurance that it would consider the wishes of the principal Allied powers, it was emphatic that "in the event of any differences of opinion among them, the policies of the United States will govern." This idea of a completely free hand for the United States in fashioning the new Japan did not meet with international favor. Since the control of Japan would have a direct bearing on larger questions concerning East Asia, it was to be expected that China, Russia, Australia, Great Britain, and France would seek a voice in policies applied in Tokyo. Anticipating such demands, the United States seized the initiative by inviting participation, but the original American proposal for a purely advisory committee representing the chief Allied powers was not received favorably.

The problem was eventually resolved in December, 1945, when the foreign ministers of Great Britain, Russia, and the United States, after consultation with China, agreed upon the creation of a Far Eastern Commission and an Allied Council for Japan. The functions of the Commission, located in Washington, were to formulate policies, to review on the request of any member any directive issued to the Supreme Commander, and to consider other matters referred to it by agreement among the participating powers. Military operations and territorial adjustments were beyond the Commission's powers. After establishment of the Commis-

sion, it still remained the task of the United States to issue directives to the Supreme Commander in accordance with the policy decisions of the Commission. In theory at least, the Commission was a severe limitation on the freedom of the United States to formulate policies, but this did not mean that the United States had lost its predominant position. American directives to General Douglas MacArthur, to whom was assigned the responsibility of Supreme Commander of the Allied Powers (SCAP), continued to be issued in accord with American interpretation of policy decisions, and the Supreme Commander continued to apply the directives according to his own interpretation of them. The Allied Council in Tokyo was designed to be a consultative and advisory body without power to act.

Initial plans to establish in Japan a full-scale military government were altered by Tokyo's sudden surrender and the subsequent peaceful reception accorded American forces.[3] Instead of administering Japan directly through American military officers, authority was to be exercised through the Emperor's government. Under this concept staff sections were created as a part of MacArthur's headquarters to plan the execution of Occupation policy in respect to political, economic, and social problems involved in the remaking of Japan. Corresponding roughly to the ministries in the Japanese Cabinet, these American staff sections were

[2] The operation of military government at the local level is discussed by Ralph J. D. Braibanti, "Administration of Military Government in Japan at the Prefectural Level," *American Political Science Review* 43 (1949): 250–74.

[3] With Japan's surrender the United States faced a situation quite different from the one presented by a defeated Germany. Germany's Nazi Party, for example, could not be equated with any single element in Japan. Nor did Germany have any institution similar to the Japanese Imperial Throne. American planning, therefore, had to take into account such problems as how the emperor was to be treated, the continued existence of the Japanese government as an entity, and the wisdom of direct American rule (as in Germany). For a description of the evolution of American planning by one who participated in it, see Hugh Borton, *American Presurrender Planning for Postwar Japan.* Occasional Papers of the East Asian Institute, Columbia University (1967).* Borton's "Preparation for the Occupation of Japan," *Journal of Asian Studies* 25 (1966): 203–12, contains additional information, especially on the emperor question.

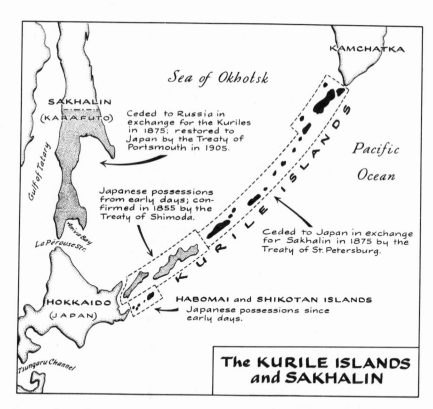

KAMCHATKA

Sea of Okhotsk

SAKHALIN
(KARAFUTO)

Ceded to Russia in
exchange for the Kuriles
in 1875; restored to
Japan by the Treaty of
Portsmouth in 1905.

Gulf of Tatary

Pacific

Ocean

K U R I L E I S L A N D S

Japanese possessions
from early days; con-
firmed in 1855 by the
Treaty of Shimoda.

Aniva Bay

La Pérouse Str.

Ceded to Japan in exchange
for Sakhalin in 1875 by the
Treaty of St. Petersburg.

HOKKAIDO
(JAPAN)

HABOMAI and SHIKOTAN ISLANDS
Japanese possessions since
early days.

Tsungaru Channel

**The KURILE ISLANDS
and SAKHALIN**

to transform policy directives into specific programs and to transmit the programs to the appropriate Japanese agency. In this way the private Japanese citizen acted on instructions from his own government.[4]

The ultimate objectives of the Occupation were to insure that Japan would cease to be a threat to peace and security, and to encourage the development of responsible government supported by the freely expressed will of the Japanese people. These objectives were to be secured by: (1) limiting Japanese sovereignty to her main islands and a few outlying ones, (2) destroying Japan's military establishment and the economic base which supported it, (3) barring from office persons who were associated closely with Japan's militaristic policies and punishing war criminals, (4) encouraging the develop-

[4] In practice this operation was less precise than the description suggests. While Washington regarded the Occupation forces as the instruments of policy and not the determinants of policy, many of the day-to-day decisions were determined by events and by personalities commanding the Occupation forces.

ment of organizations in labor, industry, and agriculture that would facilitate expression of the popular will, (5) promoting policies which would encourage the wide distribution of income and ownership of the means of production and trade, and (6) revamping the educational system to encourage the acceptance of democratic reforms through reorientation of Japanese thought.

The implementation of the Occupation was directed by MacArthur's staff of military officers in key posts and by civilians, some of whom were at relatively high levels. This small group undertook the amazing task of renovating politically, economically, and socially a nation of more than 80,000,000 people. Many members of the Occupation staff were persons with wide or specialized knowledge of Japan; others, although not conversant with Japan, had brilliant records in government, business, or the professions in the United States. To their staggering tasks in Japan they brought not only expert knowledge but also, and perhaps as important, a crusading zeal to create a new and revolutionary, though peaceful and democratic, Japan. As the Occupation continued, however, it became increasingly difficult to procure and hold staff personnel of high competence. In addition, the Occupation by its very nature tended to pervert its own members who enjoyed standards of living no Japanese could afford, whose judgments were always right while the Japanese were always wrong. Nevertheless, it should be added that the "corruption of conquest" would have been far greater had not the majority of Occupation personnel retained their perspective and their honesty of purpose.

Throughout the Occupation, both the staff of SCAP and the Japanese government upon which it operated felt the unique personal influence of MacArthur. To Japanese as well as to Americans, his name was synonymous with military tradition. Entering Japan as conqueror, he came, as it were, with the emperor's approval to assume the role of super-emperor. Autocratic, austere, decisive, always the dramatist, yet benevolent, MacArthur personified qualities which, although respected and admired by the traditional Japanese mind, were not wholly representative of the American democracy which was about to re-educate Japan in peaceful and democratic ways. Certainly, MacArthur was a stabilizing influence on the war-shaken Japanese. They understood his insistence on personal loyalty. His personal leadership and his apparent desire to preserve the emperor reassured them at a time when their own leaders had failed. He became, in brief, a national idol, the spirit of the Occupation and the promise of a new Japan, though not necessarily a democratic one.

THE OCCUPATION AT WORK

The work of remaking Japan, a task of almost inconceivable complexity, was essentially a fourfold undertaking. It involved: (1) the disassembling and demilitarizing of the former Japanese Empire; (2) the building of a new peaceful political structure, presumably democratic; (3) the insuring of

sufficient economic well-being to guarantee survival of the new political edifice; and (4) the fashioning of new social and educational foundations.[5]

Disposal of Japan's territorial empire was forecast by the Cairo Conference, December, 1943; by the Potsdam Proclamation July, 1945, later adhered to by Russia, limiting Japanese territory to Honshu, Hokkaido, Kyushu, Shikoku, and some minor islands; and at the Yalta Conference, February, 1945, where it was agreed that Russia would receive the Kurile Islands and Southern Sakhalin. Since there was no further elaboration on Japan's territorial limits, the ultimate legal disposition awaited a general Japanese treaty. Meanwhile, Japan's overseas territories were taken over by those victors who believed they had a right to them or who were determined to get possession of them anyhow. Korea ceased to be a part of the Japanese empire. Chinese *Kuomintang* forces occupied Formosa, the Pescadores, and part of Manchuria. United States forces remained in the Caroline, Marshall, and Mariana Islands, the Bonin Islands, and the Ryukyu Islands. Russia took *de facto* possession of Southern Sakhalin and the Kuriles.

Demilitarization in the Japanese homeland involved the effort to destroy both the physical machinery of war and the intellectual or spiritual sources of war. It was easy to cope with the former. Those parts of the industrial machine that directly fed the military services were closed, naval bases were destroyed, and the army and navy were disbanded. Atomic research was proscribed. Steel, chemical, and machine tool industries were limited. There remained, however, the second objective, to destroy the authority

[5] Basic documents and commentary on the Occupation to the end of 1947 are in Edwin M. Martin, *The Allied Occupation of Japan* (1948). The period 1948–1950 is covered in Robert A. Fearey, *Occupation of Japan: Second Phase, 1948–1950* (1950). Two major official accounts are of interest: *Summation of Non-Military Activities in Japan,* published by SCAP in 35 vols.; and *Political Reorientation of Japan,* 2 vols. published by SCAP, 1949. Both cover the period to 1948.

and influence of those who had led Japan into attempted world conquest.

The most spectacular phase of this effort in political fumigation was the Tokyo trial of twenty-five Japanese leaders in which the prosecution attempted to show that these men were personally responsible for Japan's misdeeds and were therefore guilty of crimes against humanity. The Tokyo trial was instituted pursuant to the Potsdam Declaration of July 20, 1945, and the Instrument of Surrender of September 2, 1945, and was conducted under the terms of the Charter of the International Military Tribunal for the Far East, approved by the Supreme Commander of the Allied Powers on January 19, 1946, with amendments of April 26. In the indictment, Japan's "major war criminals" were charged with (1) crimes against peace, (2) murder, and (3) conventional war crimes and crimes against humanity. The specific purpose of the trials, as expressed by Joseph B. Keenan, Chief of Counsel, was to confirm the already recognized rule that such individuals of a nation who, either in official positions or otherwise, plan aggressive warfare, especially in contravention of sound treaties, assurances, and agreements of their nations, are common felons and deserve and will receive the punishment of ages meted out in every land to murderers, brigands, pirates, and plunderers.[6]

[6] Documents, including the opening statement of the prosecution, the Charter of the International Military Tribunal, and the indictment, are in *Trial of Japanese War Criminals*. Department of State Publications 2613, Far Eastern Series 12 (1946). See also, *Judgment of the International Military Tribunal for the Far East* (10 vols., 1948).
The case for the natural law school of international law as manifested in the trials in Germany and Japan is J. B. Keenan and Brendan Brown, *Crimes Against International Law* (1950). The juridical basis of the Tokyo War Crimes Trial and of the corresponding earlier trial in Nuremberg was also given by Henry L. Stimson, "The Nuremberg Trial: Landmark in Law," *Foreign Affairs* 25 (1947): 179–89.
For an able attack on the theory of the trials, see Nathan April, "An Inquiry into the Juridical Basis for the Nuremberg War Crimes Trial," *Minnesota Law Review* 20 (1946): 313–31.

The decision of the Military Tribunal handed down in December, 1948, condemned seven defendants to be hanged and consigned the remainder, with the exception of two, to life imprisonment. Along with the trials, there was also the dissolution of some 1300 Japanese chauvinistic societies and organizations and the disbarment of nearly 200,000 persons from public office. These latter were disqualified on grounds of having contributed to militarism and aggression. As was anticipated, these measures contributed to the appearance of new personalities in Japanese politics, men not associated with the military regime. However, if the trial and punishment were designed to convince the Japanese people that the real culprits had been brought to justice, it must be concluded that the effort failed. The Japanese public did not appear to be convinced that the magic of the judicial process had solved the question of war guilt.[7]

THE NEW POLITICAL STRUCTURE

The political policy of the United States for post-war Japan involved some inherent contradictions. The policy was to foster "a peaceful and responsible government" and to see that this government conformed in general "to principles of democratic self-government," while at the same time it assured the Japanese that no form of government would be imposed on them that "was not supported by the freely expressed will of the people." How were these objectives to be brought about with a people who were not democratic, and by means that would not prostitute the essence of democracy itself?

The demilitarization program was the first major, though negative step toward a

[7] Elsewhere in East Asia about 5,000 lesser Japanese figures were placed on trial. For example, in the Philippines, in 1946, a number of Japanese military leaders were tried for alleged war crimes, were sentenced to death, and were executed. Among these were Generals Yamashita Tomoyuki and Homma Masaharu. Other trials were held in Shanghai. See the study by A. Frank Reel, *The Case of General Yamashita* (1949).

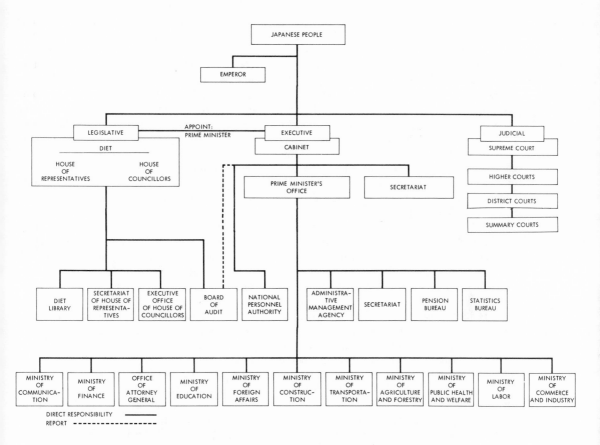

Government of Japan under the Constitution of 1947

democratic political structure. By demilitarization it was hoped to liquidate both the leaders and many of the agencies of totalitarianism. As this ground-clearing proceeded, the Occupation also undertook its positive program to remodel the old political and legal edifice which had been built since the early days of Meiji. The result was the complete revision of the Meiji Constitution, amounting really to the writing of a new constitution, though this was done by procedures well established under the Meiji Constitution: namely, amendments initiated by Imperial Ordinance and later approved by the Diet. The task of revising the old constitution was undertaken at the bidding of SCAP late in 1945, but the results were meager, and a satisfactory draft constitution emerged only after vigorous suggestion and,

indeed, dictation by the Occupation. The new constitution, proclaimed by the emperor with MacArthur's approval, was adopted and became effective, May 3, 1947.[8]

The Constitution of 1947 was, for the Japanese, a revolutionary document. In it, sovereignty reposes with the people, not

[8] The official version of the origins of the new Constitution is given in *Political Reorientation of Japan*, Vol. I, 82–118; the various drafts are in Vol. II, 625–55, 671–77. A useful analysis and a comparison is Harold S. Quigley, "Japan's Constitutions: 1890 and 1947," *American Political Science Review* 41 (1947): 865–74. Observe Quigley's comment, regarding the emperor system, that "there is small likelihood that a Japanese Emperor will seek to govern. The opponent of democracy is not autocracy but bureaucracy." The problem of bureaucracy itself is treated by John M. Maki, "The Role of the Bureaucracy in Japan," *Pacific Affairs* 20 (1947): 391–406.

with the emperor. This popular sovereignty was defined in an extensive bill of rights spelling out such principles as: equality of the sexes; freedom of thought; the right to "minimum standards of wholesome and cultured living"; equality of education; and the right and obligation of the workers to work and organize. The emperor was stripped of the vast constitutional powers he had held under the Meiji Constitution, and became simply the symbol of the State and of the unity of the people. In reality this change in the Emperor's status was theoretical rather than actual, since even under the Meiji Constitution the emperors had not exercised their constitutional powers.

The new constitution also created a new constitutional balance by conferring overwhelming political power upon the Diet, elected by the people, whereas this power had resided formerly with the executive responsible to the emperor. The new Diet remained bicameral but was wholly elective, while the electorate itself no longer labored under disabilities of income, sex, or status in an aristocracy. The lower house, elected for a four-year term, remained known as the House of Representatives; the old House of Peers was replaced by the House of Councillors, elected for six years. The House of Representatives can pass measures over the objections of the House of Councillors by a two-thirds vote, and the budget can be adopted over the objections of the upper house by a simple majority vote in the lower house.

As for the executive branch, the prime minister and his cabinet, the new constitution made it directly responsible to the Diet. The prime minister is selected by the Diet, and a majority of his cabinet must be Diet members. Thus the Diet through its control of the cabinet and the budget was given the constitutional power to direct the formerly all-powerful bureaucracy. The first step taken by the Diet in this direction was enactment of a new civil service code.[9]

[9] On the broad subject of Japanese law, see Thomas L. Blakemore, "Postwar Developments in Japanese Law," *Wisconsin Law Review* (July, 1947): 632–53.

While Diet and Executive suggested the British model, the new Japanese judiciary was patterned after American ideas. Recognition was given to the principle of an independent judiciary, beginning with a Supreme Court, that passes on all questions of constitutionality. The Court also nominates for judgeships in the lower courts, although the actual appointment of the judges is done by the cabinet. Members of the Supreme Court are also appointed by the cabinet, but such appointments are subject to review by the people at the next general election.

Local government, formerly a mere agent of the central power, was strengthened in the new constitution by provision for the popular election of the chief local officials, the abolition of compulsory neighborhood associations, the elimination of the centrally controlled police, and the delegation of larger powers to local legislative bodies.

Finally, in the Constitution of 1947, Japan renounced war and the right of belligerency forever. To some, this clause seemed to have little value beyond an expression of human aspirations for a more decent world. In a sense it recalled the pious hopes embalmed in the Kellogg-Briand Treaty for the Renunciation of War, 1928. It also appeared paradoxical that militaristic Japan should be the first to ban war. Nevertheless, the renunciation appealed to many Japanese as further evidence of Japan's unique character and mission.

EDUCATIONAL REFORMS

Practically all activities of the Occupation were undertaken with the object of bringing about in Japan a reformation by education. The wiser counsels of the Occupation recognized that no paper reforms such as new constitutions, codes, etc. could possibly outlive the Occupation itself unless the Japanese people themselves acquired a sense of democratic values and some experience with democratic ways. Therefore, Japan would be taught the values of democracy. The method seemed well-fitted to the Japanese, a literate nation of tireless readers. Moreover, the moment also seemed opportune because the Japanese, stunned by defeat, appeared to retain little confidence in their own traditional ways. Intellectually, they sought feverishly for new horizons, much as they had done toward the end of the nineteenth century.[10]

In the first years of the Occupation, therefore, the broad educational reform program enjoyed a wide popularity and a measure of success. To the vast majority of the Japanese, democracy (however vague their concept of it might be) appeared as a happy substitute for their own way of life which had led them to war and disaster. At the same time, the business of teaching democracy, always a difficult affair, became even more so by reason of acts of the Occupation itself. Reminiscent of the days of Japan's warlords was the rigid censorship imposed on imported printed matter lest "dangerous thoughts" enter Japan. Criticism of the Occupation and of Allied countries was banned. American Occupation personnel, civilian and military, were themselves subject in word and deed to military controls. They were the agents of a policy, and, of course, it is doubtful whether any policy can be promoted in an occupied country if that policy is not followed at all levels. In occupied Japan the censorship was aimed quite specifically at Communist propaganda. Nevertheless, Occupation personnel, not being free themselves to voice independent judgments, were handicapped from the start in attempting to behave as democrats. In a word, the Occupation found it difficult to pose as a model of democracy in action.

Specific educational reforms effected by the Occupation were aimed at creating a more intelligent and critical public mind and at training the younger public generations for responsible citizenship. The period of compulsory education was extended from six to nine years. Beyond the elementary training required under the old system, there were created a three-year compulsory junior high school, a three-year senior high school, and a four-year college course. An effort was made to equalize the quality of education at all levels, and to provide the fullest opportunity for children of both sexes to pursue programs that would contribute most fully to the development of their individual talents. But these innovations, initially at least, suffered from lack of democratically trained teachers, and from the serious question of how penniless Japan was to pay for this major expansion in schools and curriculum. In the curriculum itself, the traditional emphasis on ethics (a synonym for supernationalism) gave way to concern for social studies. Efforts were also made to rewrite the textbooks, to introduce modern methods of instruction, and to break the stifling centralized control of the old Ministry of Education.

THE NEW SOCIAL AND ECONOMIC PATTERNS

Having set out to remodel Japan's government and its schools, the Occupation, partly by desire, partly by compulsion, found it necessary to go further into the tangled areas of what may be called social reform. A first step was to strike at the traditional form and behavior of the Japanese family. Equality, a strange principle to Oriental ears, was applied to the sexes by the new constitution. Japanese women acquired equal legal rights with men in politics and education. Furthermore, this principle of equality, and the new educational program in general, tended to weaken the control formerly exercised by family heads over the youth and even over other adult members of the family. Tendencies toward individualism which had appeared in Japan long before World War II were encouraged by the Occupation. This shifting from the family to the individual as the basic unit of society was among the most vital effects of the Western impact on East Asia.[11]

[10] The basic treatment on educational reforms is Robert King Hall, *Education for a New Japan* (1949).

[11] Kazuya Matsumiya, "Family Organization in Present Day Japan," *American Journal of Sociology* 53 (1947): 105–10.

Furthermore, the Occupation went far beyond the status of family and of women. It attempted to strike at the high concentration of wealth held by a few families—the *Zaibatsu*—to break up these combines and to encourage a wide distribution of income and the ownership of the means of production. *Zaibatsu* leaders were barred from business and politics; the great central holding companies were dissolved; assets were taken over by the government for later sale; and the great family fortunes were all but wiped out by capital levies, heavy income taxes, and inflation. The attack was then directed against the larger corporations capable of exercising monopoly power in restraint of trade. This latter program, however, was abandoned in 1949 for a variety of reasons relating to Japan's failure to achieve economic recovery and to the appearance of Communist control in China.

On the opposite side of the industrial picture, the Occupation paved the way for Japan's first free development of a labor movement and labor unions, whose membership by 1950 had mushroomed to some seven million. Japanese labor, which lacked tested organization, experience, and leadership, found itself suddenly possessed of a new freedom and power just at the moment when the nation itself was prostrate from defeat and economic collapse. There were efforts by some unions through strikes to take over policy control of an industry. High pressure methods, rather than the slower electoral process diminished the already disastrously low national industrial output. Sabotage under Communist instigation became the policy of some unions. This latter kind of behavior was not tolerated by the Occupation. Instead, in its later stages the Occupation, concerned by labor's growing pains, tended to join forces with Japan's conservatives who had shown little sympathy with a responsible role for labor in either industry or politics.[12]

Finally, among the most striking of all Occupation reforms was the redistribution of agricultural land. Essentially this reform entailed (1) enforced sale to the government of all land held by absentee landlords, (2) resale of these lands to former tenants who had cultivated them, (3) permission for farmer-landlords to retain the land cultivated by their families and in addition some two and one-half acres of tenant-cultivated land. The program of purchase and resale was effected at pre-war values, making it a possible transaction for the tenants but virtual confiscation for the former owners. The extent of this reform was suggested by the fact that by 1952 more than five million acres of land had been purchased from landlords and sold to working farmers. This meant that about 90 per cent of all cultivated land had been acquired by those who worked it, as compared with less than 50 per cent in 1945. Moreover, legislation reduced land rents by about 50 per cent, and provided further protection by means of rent ceilings. Although this land reform implied social consequences of the utmost importance, it was in no sense a magic formula. Japan's basic agricultural problem—how to feed too many people from too little land—was still unsolved.

POLITICS DURING THE OCCUPATION

The effect of the Occupation upon Japanese government and politics was profound from the beginning. SCAP's reforms broke old political patterns and forced many established leaders from office. Communists, who were released from prison or returned from exile, formed their first legal party under Nozaka Sanzo, who was to become one of the ablest post-war political manipulators.[13] The Social Democrats (*Shakaito*), refusing a united front with the Communists, formed their own party drawing strength from intellectuals and labor. More conservative elements were grouped in the Liberal (*Jiyuto*) and the Progressive (*Shimpoto*) parties, the former led by Ashida Hitoshi

[12] Miriam S. Farley, *Aspects of Japan's Labor Problems* (1950), and "Labor Policy in Occupied Japan," *Pacific Affairs* 20 (1947): 131–40.

[13] On Communists in Japan, see Rodger Swearingen and Paul Langer, *Red Flag in Japan . . . 1919–1951* (1952).

and Yoshida Shigeru, the latter by Shide-hara Kijuro. Most of the members of these latter parties had belonged to the old *Seiyukai* or *Minseito*.

While the formation of new political groupings and the reshuffling of old ones imparted a new character to Japanese politics, the parties were not free immediately to seek goals that were entirely of their own devising. In October, 1945, for example, when the Occupation directed implementation of a "Bill of Rights" guaranteeing basic human freedoms, the releasing of political prisoners, and curbing the Ministry of Home Affairs and its powerful centralized police, the surrender cabinet of Prime Minister Higashikuni resigned on the ground that it could not maintain order. The Liberals, whose gains in the election of April, 1946, enabled them to form a ministry headed by Yoshida, were given the responsibility of installing the "MacArthur Constitution," and of carrying the purge of undesirable persons into the area of local politics. While the Yoshida government's popularity suffered from Occupation-imposed policies, the cabinet's eventual collapse was not precipitated by Japan's own political processes. Early in 1947 General MacArthur blocked a general strike called to protest the economic condition of workers. The Communists thus suffered a setback, and the government announced that a new general election was to be held. The latter step, which was in effect a declaration of no confidence in Yoshida, was preliminary to the election of a government headed by Katayama Tetsu, President of the Social Democrats. Not until mid-1949 did MacArthur indicate that close control of Japanese domestic affairs was no longer necessary. By this time Yoshida was back in power with a Liberal party government which he was to lead until 1954. By this time, too, the Cold War was exercising a pronounced influence on Japan's politics. Confronted with the increasing influence of Communism, Japanese political thought and organization became more deeply divided into right and left wings, Communist party strength declined, and conservatism was reborn.

From the beginning of 1948, the Japanese government and the Occupation, deeply concerned by the Communist threat in Asia and by Japan's persistent economic difficulties, gave less attention to reform and more attention to the historic problem of increasing the export of manufactures to pay for imports needed to support a population that had increased by nearly 8,000,000, 1945–1948. American aid had not met the problem and had been in any case a temporary measure. There could be no political stability in a land where prices were completely out of control and bore no recognizable relationship to wages. Thus, the Occupation moved belatedly in 1948 to meet this crisis through an all-inclusive program of stabilization: balance the budget, limit credit, renovate the tax structure, and deal with tax evasion. At the same time the United States encouraged expansion of industrial production and export by favoring the eventual dropping of further reparations payments, extending economic aid, and, when the Korean War broke out, placing orders with Japanese firms. The combined effort resulted by the end of the Occupation in substantial improvement in the country's economic and financial status, though the apparent link between Japan's growing prosperity and American aid (a matter of one and three-quarter billion dollars in goods, 1945–1950) gave rise to the thought that the economy was not yet on a sound foundation.

THE JAPANESE PEACE TREATY

The outbreak of war in Korea emphasized the need, as the United States saw it, of ending the Occupation by concluding a peace treaty with Japan and thereby bringing her into the company of the Free World and against the Communist powers.[14] Earlier

[14] While in general it was true that the decision to terminate the Occupation rested with the Americans, the Japanese influence on the final stages of the Occupation must be noted. By 1949, as the Japanese electorate began to mani-

efforts toward a treaty had broken down in 1948. On American initiative, conversations among the former allies were resumed in September, 1950, which were to result a year later in the San Francisco peace conference and a treaty of peace with Japan. By July, 1951, there was sufficient agreement for the United States and the United Kingdom to issue a joint invitation to the fifty-five powers at war with Japan to a peace conference to be held at San Francisco on September 4, 1951. Suggested revisions of the draft treaty enclosed with the invitations were to be submitted promptly so that the final text might be circulated by August 13. The treaty would thus be completed before the conference assembled.

Accordingly, at San Francisco, September 8, 1951, a peace treaty was signed by Japan and forty-eight nations (Communist powers refused to sign). Japan agreed to seek membership in the United Nations and to respect the civil rights of her own new constitution, to accept the territorial clauses of the Potsdam Declaration, to recognize the independence of Korea, to forgo her claims to Formosa, the Pescadores, the Kuriles and Karafuto (southern Sakhalin), and to agree to a United Nations trusteeship in the Ryukyu and Bonin Islands. The treaty recognized Japan's right of self-defense. Within three months after the treaty was in force,

---

fest a returning self-confidence, Japan's leadership demonstrated some independence of American policy. For example, in an effort to ensure the establishment of democracy, SCAP had shown a preference for working with less conservative elements, but Japanese voters gave a landslide victory to the Liberal-Democratic party (*Jiyu-Minshuto*), which led to the formation of the third Yoshida cabinet. In a word, the shift in Occupation policies after the years 1948–1949 should not be attributed entirely to American reactions to the onset of the Cold War. Conservative forces in Japan, which were beyond American control, were beginning to assert themselves. Thus the student may well ask whether the American Occupation could have been maintained much longer, even if its termination had not proved expedient. Justin Williams, "Completing Japan's Political Reorientation, 1947–1952: Crucial Phase of the Allied Occupation," *The American Historical Review* 73 (1968): 1454–69.

Occupation armies would leave, though limited foreign forces might continue to be stationed there under special agreements. The Occupation came to an end April 28, 1952, the day the treaty became effective. Also on September 8, 1951, Japan and the United States concluded a security agreement permitting American forces to remain in Japan for an unspecified period, which meant that the United States was assuming responsibility for Japan's defense for an indefinite future.

The peace treaty with Japan was a necessary step toward ending the war, but it was not a solution of Japanese problems. Rather, it was merely the formal beginning of Japan's efforts as a sovereign state to chart her course at home and abroad in the postwar world. In so far as the reforms of the Occupation, including the Constitution of 1947, could be taken at face value, Japan was a democracy, but she had had as yet no free experience in making democracy work: Her peoples were not of one mind as to what democracy meant; she did not have a stable and prosperous economy that could afford policies of drift; and in world affairs she was on the explosive Asiatic frontier between Communism and the free world. From 1952 onward, therefore, Japan's political, economic, and social history was to be a reflection of her efforts to find a new life in the ominous turmoil of these pressures.

FOR FURTHER READING

GENERAL ACCOUNTS. For a critical evaluation of the way Western nations have been trying to meet Asian revolution, see W. MacMahon Ball, *Nationalism and Communism in East Asia* (1952). Ball's *Japan: Enemy or Ally* (rev. ed., 1949), and T. A. Bisson's *Prospects for Democracy in Japan* (1949) are critical of American occupation policy. Among other studies of the Occupation not cited in footnotes are Royden J. Dangerfield, *The New Japan* (1953); John D. Montgomery, *Forced to Be Free: The Artificial Revolution in Germany and Japan* (1957); and Edwin Reischauer and others, *Japan* and America Today (1953). Allen S. Clifton, *Time of Fallen Blossoms* (1951) describes the simple dignity of the country people of Japan in the early post-war years. Mishima Sumie, *The Broader Way: A Woman's Life in the New Japan* (1953) portrays life during and after the hostilities. Elizabeth Gray Vining, *Windows for the Crown Prince* (1952) contains delicate and sympathetic sketches of Japan and upper-class Japanese culture by the tutor of the Crown Prince. Frank Gibney, *Five Gentlemen of Japan: The Portrait of a Nation's Character* (1953) tells of the impact of the Occupation on Japanese life through sketches of the Emperor, a farmer, an admiral, a newspaperman, and a steel worker. Robert S. Schwantes, *Japanese and Americans: A Century of Cultural Relations* (1955) deserves careful reading.

GOVERNMENT, POLITICS, AND PARTIES. Paul M. A. Linebarger, Djang Chu, and Ardath Burks, *Far Eastern Governments and Politics: China and Japan* (1954) provides sound analysis. Chitoshi Yanaga, *Japanese People and Politics* (1956)* emphasizes the forces of politics rather than the structure of government. A briefer but enlightening study is Nobutaka Ike, *Japanese Politics: An Introductory Study* (1957). H. S. Quigley and J. E. Turner, *The New Japan: Government and Politics* (1956) is another standard work. An excellent specialized study is Robert E. Ward's "The Origins of the Present Japanese Constitution," *American Political Science Review* 50 (1956): 980–1010. Robert E. Ward and D. A. Rustow, *The Political Modernization of Japan and Turkey* (1964) is the third volume of a series in comparative studies in political development. More emphasis on recent years is Theodore McNelly, *Contemporary Government of Japan* (1963)* which deals with the structure and functions of the government since the last world war. Hans H. Baerwald, *The Purge of Japanese Leaders under the Occupation* (1959) combines a factual account with discussion of the moral and administrative dilemmas implicit in the purge. Evelyn S. Colbert, *The Left Wing in*

Japanese Politics (1952) discusses the role of the Socialist and Communist parties, principally in post-war Japan. William J. Coughlin, *Conquered Press: The MacArthur Era in Japanese Journalism* (1952) focuses on the era after the tight wartime controls were lifted.

ECONOMICS. Edward Ackerman, *Japan's Natural Resources and Their Relation to Japan's Economic Future* (1953) explains Japan's problems in supporting her expanding population on her meager resources. For a statistical analysis of Japan's post-war economic problems, see Jerome B. Cohen, *Economic Problems of Free Japan* (1952). For specialized studies see: T. A. Bisson, *Zaibatsu Dissolution in Japan* (1954); Ronald P. Dore, *Land Reform in Japan* (London, 1959); Laurence I. Hewes, Jr., *Japan—Land and Men: An Account of the Japanese Land Reform Program, 1945–1951* (1955); and Sherwood M. Fine, *Japan's Postwar Industrial Recovery* (Tokyo, 1953).

SOCIAL IDEALS AND RELIGION. Jean Stoetzel, *Without the Chrysanthemum and the Sword: A Study of the Attitudes of Youth in Postwar Japan* (1955) surveys the impact of defeat and occupation on young Japanese. The role of religion in the post-war era is assessed in Richard T. Baker, *Darkness of the Sun: The Story of Christianity in the Japanese Empire* (1947); and Yanaihara Tadao, *Religion and Democracy in Modern Japan* (1948). Herbert Passin, *Society and Education in Japan* (1965),* essays and documents touching traditional and modern Japan to 1947.

THE JAPANESE PEACE TREATY. Bernard C. Cohen, *The Political Process and Foreign Policy: The Making of the Japanese Peace Settlement* (1957) studies the means by which American pressure groups were brought to accept the peace treaty. Also note R. H. Rosecrance, *Australian Diplomacy and Japan, 1945–1951* (1962). Frederick S. Dunn, *et al.*, *Peace-making and the Settlement with Japan* (1963).

From Kuomintang to
Communist China, 1945-1949

chapter 32

The end of hostilities in World War II altered decisively the long-standing conflict between the *Kuomintang* and Chinese Communists. With the removal of Japanese power by surrender, these contending parties abandoned all pretense of a united front and engaged in a violent scramble for Japanese-occupied China, which included Manchuria and the whole area of central and eastern-seaboard China. In this struggle the Communists had advantages they had not possessed in 1937. No longer confined to a relatively small region in the northwest, they controlled the countryside in the north and central regions, thus presenting formidable obstacles to Nationalist occupation efforts. The Communist party, reorganized and strengthened by the *cheng feng* movement, had increased in membership from about 40,000 to more than 1,200,000. While the Red Army remained inferior to the Nationalist force in men and equipment, its size was growing (the Communists claimed a force of 930,000), and it was supported by an effective militia. The *Kuomintang*-Nationalist government, on the other hand, had declined as a vital force. Its status was suggested by loss of fervor in its revolution-

ary program, by widespread corruption, spiraling inflation, and deteriorating morale among the military. In consequence of this new balance of forces, even though the Nationalist government had been accorded by its allies nominal big power status, its survival after 1945 was not assured.

Altered, too, was the international setting of the *Kuomintang*-Communist conflict. With Japan's defeat both the Soviet Union and United States acquired new Asian strongholds from which pressure could be exerted on China. In 1945 the Soviet Union reassumed a position of great strength in northeastern Asia. She entered the war against Japan by invading Manchuria, August 9, 1945, and concluded a Sino-Soviet Treaty of Friendship, August 14, 1945, with the Nationalist government of China. The practical effect was to give Russia immediate control of Manchuria, to restore old historic rights in the Manchurian railways and the Kwantung leased territory, and to guarantee the "independence" of Outer Mongolia under a government controlled by Moscow. In return for these Manchurian and Mongolian concessions Russia was pledged to give moral support and material aid only to the National government as *the* government of China, to respect China's sovereignty in Manchuria, and to refrain from interference in the internal affairs of Sinkiang. These conditions were acceptable to the *Kuomintang*-Nationalist government because they appeared to deny to the Chinese Communists any support from Russia. The fact, too, that Russian military operations in Manchuria and Korea continued long after the Japanese surrender gave to Russia a position of power beyond anything granted in the Yalta Agreement or the Sino-Soviet Treaty. Within a few weeks and with the expenditure of a minimum of effort Russia acquired a stronger position in the limited but key area of northeast Asia than she had ever held before.

Against this focal area of revived Russian power was the even greater though more widely dispersed power of the United States in the Far East. This predominant American position was a creation of the military campaigns of the war and not of an historical development of American policy. Immediately following Japan's surrender, the United States was (1) master of the Philippines and the entire Western Pacific, (2) in a position to set the terms on which the Dutch, French, and the British might reoccupy their empires in Southeast Asia, (3) indispensable to the Nationalist government of China as a source of military transport for purposes of the Japanese surrender, (4) the only external power other than Russia capable of exerting strong pressure on the Nationalist government, (5) the unqualified military and political master of Japan, and (6) in occupation of Korea south of the 38th parallel. This extraordinary position of power did not mean, however, that the United States could dispose of far eastern problems of peace by simple mandate or in complete disregard of forces of opposition which it did not and in all probability could not control. In the Philippines and in Japan the United States was at greater liberty than in other areas to pursue its own purposes, but even in these areas its power was subject to various restraints imposed by local conditions or by the traditions of its own institutions and historic policies. With respect to China, the power of the United States to make decisions designed to influence or to determine the future of that state was limited by (1) the inhibitions of traditional American policy there, (2) the reoccupation of Northeast China by Russia, and (3) the division of Chinese power itself between Nationalists and Communists.

THE NATIONALIST ATTEMPT TO GAIN CONTROL

At the time of the Japanese surrender, Chiang Kai-shek, as Allied Commander-in-Chief in the China Theater and as head of the Nationalist (and recognized) government, was to receive the Japanese surrender in China and in northern Indochina. Three major tasks confronted the Nationalists: (1) to take over the occupied territory from the Japanese armies and restore the administration of the Nationalist government in these areas, (2) to reach a settlement of the Communist problem, and (3) to revive China's war-torn economic and social orders.

For the task of accepting the Japanese surrender, Nationalist forces could hardly have been in a less advantageous position. These forces had been driven by the Japanese invasion into southwestern China. Nevertheless, with substantial American assistance, Nationalist armies were taken to the east and northeast, where they took over the cities and lines of communication the Japanese had held. General rejoicing over the long-awaited victory greeted the Nationalist government's reoccupation of Nanking and the coastal cities. Here the reputation of Chiang Kai-shek, which had suffered in the war years, seemed to be re-established. However, in the northeastern countryside where Communist forces had infiltrated, and where they had not only harried the Japanese but had won the support of the peasantry by implementing their program of agrarian reform, the reception accorded the Nationalists was decidedly cold. Thus, when the Nationalists took over the cities of northeast China, the villages and countryside were unwilling to accept Nationalist authority unless the reformed local governments instituted by the Communists were also accepted.

As a consequence the Nationalist government found itself opposed in the countryside by both the Communists and the peasantry.

Nor were the prospects for economic reconstruction at all bright. While the Nationalist government inherited from the Japanese productive facilities in eastern China, its access to other industrial regions in the north and in Manchuria was impeded by Communist control. To meet pressing needs for immediate relief, the United Nations Relief and Rehabilitation Administration supplied food and repaired power lines and lines of communication in an amount of some $650,000,-000, of which the United States contributed $474,000,000. But this was very limited aid for a country whose economy had been completely devastated. Moreover, the value of this aid was diminished by the Nationalist failure to curb inflation or to make effective use of available revenues and production. The whole general failure was due to the growing power and appeal of the Communists, and to the inability of the Nationalist government and the party that controlled it, the *Kuomintang*, to implement effective measures and thereby to recapture the confidence of the populace.

EFFORTS AT POLITICAL SETTLEMENT

In the closing months of the war, American policy, recognizing that the *Kuomintang* had ceased to be an effective unifying force, and that the Chinese Communists were capitalizing on the resulting demoralization, sought to strengthen the Nationalist government by urging it to effect: (1) economic, administrative, and democratic reforms, and (2) a coalition with other parties, including the Communists, to achieve internal strength and peace.[1] It was this policy

---

[1] For an example of the quality of information on the *Kuomintang*-Communist struggle that was available to American officials, see Lyman P. Van Slyke, ed., *The Chinese Communist Movement. A Report of the United States War Department, July, 1945* (1968). Based on more than 2,500 reports, pamphlets, and books, and completed in June, 1945, this report represented an attempt by the Military Intelligence

which General Patrick Hurley tried to implement between September, 1944, and November, 1945. By this time there was a clear distinction between solutions acceptable to the Communists on one hand and the Nationalists on the other. While the Communists professed a willingness to enter a coalition government and to place their military forces under the control of that government, they demanded guarantees that they would have a position of strength in the new government before giving up control of their armies. The Nationalists, although willing to give political promises to the future, were determined to have military integration first under their own control. In consequence, negotiations were deadlocked when Japan surrendered, and when General Albert C. Wedemeyer, who had succeeded General Joseph Stilwell as American Commanding General in the China Theater, was required to assist in disarming Japanese troops without becoming involved in the *Kuomintang*-Communist conflict. Wedemeyer's task was the more difficult because American policy as applied during the Hurley period was undergoing subtle but significant modifications. As the hope for a coalition between the Nationalist government and the Communists became more remote, Hurley became more sympathetic to the position taken by the *Kuomintang* and exerted less pressure on the Nationalist government to reform itself. Some members of Hurley's staff disagreed with this shift in emphasis. They took the position

---

Division of the War Department to evaluate the strength, nature, and intentions of the Chinese Communist party. Aside from the specific information it contained, the report was very significant because, although clearly anti-Communist and anti-Russian, it did not hesitate to characterize the *Kuomintang*-Nationalist government as an inefficient dictatorship which had alienated every sector of society. The Communists were pictured as politically well-organized, highly disciplined, progressive, and popular. Nevertheless, in a summary based on the report, Brigadier General Peabody emphasized the *Kuomintang*-Nationalist government's legitimacy and international status as though these had some sacred validity which made the concept of revolution unthinkable.

that it was hopeless for the United States to pose as a mediator unless its purposes were regarded as impartial. The reputation of impartiality, they said, could not be maintained if mediation could be approached only on terms set by the *Kuomintang*.[2]

In an effort to revive the mediation policy, President Truman sent General George C. Marshall to China late in 1945 to seek "the unification of China by peaceful, democratic methods." This effort was based on specific premises: (1) that American assistance would not be extended indefinitely to a China that could achieve no unity within itself, and (2) that a united and democratic China was essential to world stability and the proper functioning of the United Nations. Marshall was initially successful in persuading the Nationalists and the Communists to meet, January, 1946, in a body called the Political Consultative Conference (PCC), and to accept three agreements foreshadowing a settlement: (1) a military truce, (2) a political and constitutional agreement, and (3) an agreement on the reorganization and control of military forces.

Under the truce agreement military advances were to be halted while local outbreaks were to be settled by truce teams com-

[2] In his later years Hurley joined partisans of the *Kuomintang* who asserted that the United States had "sold out" China to the Communists. He claimed that his embassy's staff had sabotaged efforts to shape a coalition government. Moreover, he held that State Department career officers had deceived President Roosevelt with respect to the implications for China of the Yalta accords. These later views were at variance with the ones entertained by Hurley while he held office. In 1944–1945, Hurley supported Roosevelt's efforts to bring the Soviet Union into the war against Japan and to win Russian support of the *Kuomintang*-Nationalist government. To these ends, Hurley was prepared to recommend even larger concessions to the Russians than those agreed upon at Yalta. Russell D. Buhite, "Patrick J. Hurley and the Yalta Far Eastern Agreement," *Pacific Historical Review* 38 (1968): 343–53. For a description of Hurley's relationship with his staff, see Robert T. Smith, "Alone in China: Patrick J. Hurley's Attempts to Unify China, 1944–1945," (Unpublished Ph.D dissertation, University of Oklahoma, 1966).

posed of a Nationalist, a Communist, and an American officer. The second or political agreement confirmed the Nationalists or the Communists in control of the territory each held and provided for a State Council in the Nationalist government in which all political groups would have representation. This new body was to determine policy. Moreover, the political agreement provided for a parliamentary system when constitutionalism was achieved. The third or military agreement, to which General Marshall contributed in the discussions, provided an arrangement whereby the Communist army was to become a part of a Chinese national army. All three of these basic and encouraging agreements were interdependent. A failure of one meant a failure of all.

The reasons that were soon to bring this failure were many and complex. They involved disputes over means of control in local and provincial areas and Communist demands for greater representation in the State Council, but the most serious clash concerned the mastery of Manchuria. At the time of Japan's surrender Manchuria was in the hands of the Russian army. The PCC military agreement had set up quotas of Nationalist and Communist troops for Manchuria. The Communists arrived first in greater numbers than had been agreed upon and proceeded to recruit local forces. The Nationalist forces, denied the use of Dairen by the Russians, fought their way into Manchuria. The Russians then turned over the main cities and railroads to the Nationalists as had been agreed, but, at the same time, allowed large quantities of arms surrendered by the Japanese to fall into Communist hands. The Communists were thus fully prepared to challenge the Nationalist bid for control of Manchuria. Then, too, while the Communists were violating the military agreement in Manchuria, the right wing of the *Kuomintang* forced the Nationalist government to disavow the PCC agreements. Each side could accuse the other of bad faith. By the beginning of 1947 all pretense of keeping the agreements had vanished on both sides. To this failure civil war was the answer. American policy had failed to achieve its purpose under Hurley. It failed for a second time under Marshall.[3]

A CASE OF CRUMBLING FOUNDATIONS

Faced by the prospect of a desperate civil war and recognizing at last the need to gain popular support, the Nationalist government sought to save itself by a belated appeal to constitutionalism. A national convention open to all parties, but which was attended only by the *Kuomintang* and some of the minor groups, adopted a constitution generally in line with the principles of the PCC agreements. Providing for a parliamentary system, the constitution became effective, formally at least, in December, 1947, but during the emergency of civil war large special powers were to be retained by Chiang as President.[4]

The efforts toward constitutionalism and parliamentary government in 1947 were doomed from the beginninng. They were made at a time when the Nationalist government was not only beset by civil war but also

[3] John F. Melby, a State Department officer who worked with General Marshall in mediating between the *Kuomintang* and the Communists, recorded in his journal (November 16, 1946): "I suppose coalition had to be attempted, even though it was an impractical notion at best and the very nature of this kind of political struggle has precluded success except on a temporary basis and then only under great stress. I know Marshall now believes he made a mistake in ever thinking coalition was desirable or useful or possible." *The Mandate of Heaven: Record of a Civil War, China, 1945–49* (Toronto, 1968), 172.

[4] The new constitution and the parliamentary system came largely from the efforts of Carsun Chang, head of the Social Democratic party, who had striven to overcome party dictatorship and militarism through adoption of the parliamentary principle. His plan was so modified by the national convention as to subvert largely the representative principle. Thus when the new government under the constitution was formed, many of the minor parties, united in the Democratic League, refused to co-operate and allied themselves with the Communists. See Chang Chia-sen (Carsun Chang), *The Third Force in China* (1952).

when it had already lost the revived prestige it had enjoyed briefly when Japan surrendered in 1945. At that time there was still hope that the government's economic and financial assets, including foreign aid, if used wisely, could provide a sound economic structure, a base for intelligent political reform demanded alike by the business, professional, and intellectual classes. But neither the *Kuomintang* nor the Nationalist government found or effected the means of using these assets wisely. In a period when, if ever, the productive capacity and support of the business community were needed desperately, the government did the very thing best designed to alienate private enterprise. It seized the Japanese industrial plants in occupied China and operated them as state concerns. This amounted to confiscation in some cases, since part of the firms had been privately owned. Even worse was the government's use of foreign aid in support of state owned or controlled undertakings, and its excessive exactions on firms that remained in private hands.

Equally ruinous to *Kuomintang*-Nationalist fortunes was a vicious inflationary spiral. As *Kuomintang*-Communist warfare intensified, Nanking sought to pay its way by printing more and more paper money. In mid-1947, the Chinese national currency rate to the U.S. dollar was 45,000 to 1, and the top had not yet been reached. The foreign financial reserves, which the government held in 1945, had been spent. There was no budget in fact. Expenditures, especially by the military, were wasteful, and in any event no one could tell what proportion of the taxes collected reached the treasury, due to the flagrant dishonesty of tax collectors.

It would appear, however, that the worst effects of inflation were neither economic nor military, but moral. The unending spiral of worthless paper corrupted every man who was forced to use it. For those dependent on salaries and wages the problem was not one of iniquity but of survival. Soldiers, lesser officials, and the intellectuals suffered most. These last, who could have contributed so much to the *Kuomintang*, were at best ignored; at worst they were persecuted or liquidated. These were the men who had recognized that in China ideology was important. They were the carriers of the Chinese revolution that had begun in the nineteenth century. Most of them were not Communists. Perhaps a majority of them were opposed to the civil war and favored compromise with the Communists and the establishment of a truly representative government. When the PCC agreements failed and the full civil war was resumed in 1947, many of these intellectuals were dismissed from their positions or arrested, and some were slain. This type of repression was another example of the forces that had undermined from within the Nationalist government and the *Kuomintang* at the very moment when this Government and Party were to meet in full battle all the power which the Chinese Communists could bring against them.

THE COMMUNIST MILITARY VICTORY

The civil war that followed the failure of the Nationalists and the Communists to effect a political solution was of brief duration, 1947 to 1949, and resulted in the complete defeat of the Nationalist armies. Spreading over thousands of square miles and involving millions of men on both sides, this civil war was really an aggregation of small battles. Communist forces, although numerically inferior at the outset, seized the initiative by subjecting government forces to a continuous series of ambushes, skirmishes, and attacks on isolated garrisons. The Nationalist government's determination to hold as much of China as possible and to defend many critical lines of communication rendered its forces particularly vulnerable to these tactics. In a word, the Nationalists employed a strategy which nullified their superiority in men and arms. Meanwhile the Communists, flushed by an accumulation of minor successes, enlarged their armies, supplied them with equipment turned over by the Russians or captured from the Nationalists, and stepped up their offensive.

Major Nationalist reverses came first in Manchuria. Chiang had sent his best troops into this region over the objections of the United States Military Mission, which argued that the move would overextend Nationalist forces and open supply lines to Communist attack. The disastrous consequences of ignoring American advice were expressed by General Wedemeyer, September, 1947, when he reported to Washington that, in spite of Nationalist efforts to hold Manchuria, (1) Manchuria was on the verge of becoming a Soviet satellite, (2) the Chinese Communists were close to control there and to the setting up of a government, and (3) the result would be agreements between Manchuria, Outer Mongolia, and Russia of the utmost danger to China, the United States, and the United Nations since it could lead ultimately to a Communist-dominated China. Wedemeyer therefore suggested that China ask the United Nations to end Manchurian hostilities and then place Manchuria under a trusteeship composed of China, Russia, the United States, Britain, and France. But the Wedemeyer proposal could not be considered practical politics unless: (1) the Nationalist government was willing to admit that Manchuria was not China, and that it was unable to deal with its own Communists or with Russia, and (2) the United States was willing to pledge military forces in a situation in China which in reality could only be described as civil war. Neither Nationalist China nor the United States was prepared to take these steps, and, in consequence Chiang was advised by Washington to concentrate on strengthening his position in North China. Again, by pursuing the Manchurian conquest, Chiang disregarded the advice, with the result that by 1948 the Communists in the Manchurian countryside were strong enough to cut the railroad lines and thus to make the Nationalist armies in the cities dependent on supplies brought in by air. Further reverses followed when the Nationalist garrisons were forced to evacuate the major Manchurian cities. As a result, large numbers of troops and their American equipment were taken by the Communists. The whole Manchurian fiasco was a disaster from which the Nationalist armies never recovered. The responsibility for this military disaster was attributed by American military observers to incompetent army administration and supply, high officers who lacked ability, unimaginative strategy and tactics, which could not see beyond the holding of major cities, and finally the lack of a sound economic program in support of military action.

In North China, too, the Nationalist forces, denied adequate support, surrendered Peking to the Communists. In December, 1948, the Communists destroyed the main Nationalist armies in central and eastern China. Again Communist strategy won over the superior armament of the Nationalists. At this point Chiang Kai-shek could no longer ignore demands for negotiations. He resigned the presidency. Li Tsung-jen became acting president and opened negotiations with the Communists. In essence, the Communist demands were for unconditional surrender. In April the Communists renewed the attack, penetrating south to Canton and west to Chungking. With the remnants of the Nationalist armies Chiang Kai-shek escaped to Formosa, where, in March, 1950, he resumed the presidency of all that was left of Nationalist China.

THE NATIONALIST DEFEAT IN PERSPECTIVE

The Communist takeover in China fitted neither the traditional Marxist concept of an urban insurrection nor the Maoist vision of a general peasant uprising. Rather the pattern was one of systematic military conquest by armies which moved from rural bases in the North to seize and occupy the remainder of the mainland. It was a victory that resulted from *Kuomintang* failures as much as from Communist power. Indeed, by 1949 the collapse of the Nationalist government was so far advanced that the Communist military often met little opposition. The Communists, in the main, moved into a political vacuum.

While a definitive interpretation of the defeat and the collapse of the *Kuomintang's* army and government must await additional evidence and research, it is possible to set forth many of the major factors involved. To the student who has followed systematically China's journey during the past century into the modern world, it will be apparent that there is no single or simple explanation of the debacle which overtook the *Kuomintang*. Indeed, the search for rational explanations must take account of the full force of the Western impact on China particularly after 1897. It was this impact which aroused the Chinese response, formalized in the program of Sun Yat-sen which, in turn, was to be implemented by his political party, the *Kuomintang*. In the years following Sun's death (1925), the *Kuomintang* and its creation, the National government, appeared to enjoy measurable success (see Chapter 26). However, these successes, more often than not, were nullified by lack of agreement on what Sun's program meant, and by lack of any single leadership that could inspire unity of purpose and patriotic fervor among the Chinese people. China's ancient Confucian values and institutions had already been destroyed or weakened almost beyond recognition. The new values, whatever they were to be, were not made understandable even to contending factions within the *Kuomintang*, far less so to major segments of the populace. This was the great failure of the *Kuomintang*. It was a failure that opened wide the door to Communist or any subversion of Sun's revolutionary program. Admittedly, the task that had faced the *Kuomintang* within China alone was monumental. It was made far more onerous by the Japanese invasion in 1937 and after and the subsequent march of events during World War II. By 1945 the Allied victory had freed the *Kuomintang* from the Japanese conquest, but it was not free from civil war against the Communists, and it was confronted by a new Far Eastern balance of power held by the world giants, the Soviet Union and the United States. To meet these dire crises, the *Kuomintang* was ill-equipped in purpose, in organization, and in spirit.[5]

[5] Pichon P. Y. Loh, ed., *The Kuomintang Debacle of 1949: Conquest or Collapse?* (1965),* summarizes varying interpretations. Seen in their

In the immediate sense, the Communist victory was due to superior military organization and strategy and tactics. But this fact does not explain why the Communists were able to build up an effective military machine and a base of popular support in the areas they controlled, while the *Kuomintang*-Nationalist government, even with American military aid, was unable to do so. The answer to this question may well be found in a failure of the Nationalists to recognize the importance in China of ideology and its application to practical and revolutionary politics.[6]

REPERCUSSIONS IN THE UNITED STATES

The Communist conquest of China was nothing less than a catastrophe in American Far Eastern policy. During the war, from 1941 to 1945, the American people and their government had found comfort in an assumption that, with the defeat of Japan,

---

immediate context, the events of 1949 readily lead to the view that "the victory of the Chinese Communists was a victory of military organization and strategy." See Franz H. Michael and George E. Taylor, *The Far East in the Modern World* (1956), 447. A longer view suggests "that Chinese politics have been primarily a reflex of ideological dynamics, with armies, economics, and governments playing secondary and tertiary roles." See Paul M. A. Linebarger, Djang Chu, and Ardath W. Burks, *Far Eastern Governments and Politics* (1954), 252.

[6] A. Doak Barnett, *China on the Eve of Communist Takeover* (1963),° 5–13. Note also Chalmers Johnson's metaphor picturing the Communists as "fish" swimming and hiding in an "ocean" of overtly neutral civilians. To eliminate the Communists, the Nationalists would have been required to so win civilian loyalists as to convert the "ocean" into a "desert." See "Civilian Loyalties and Guerrilla Conflicts," *World Politics* 4 (1962): 646–61. See also Scott A. and Howard L. Boorman, "Chinese Communist Insurgent Warfare, 1935–1949," *Political Science Quarterly* 81 (1966): 171–95, who conclude that: "Communist victory . . . was not inevitable in China. Nor could the stability required for implementation of social theory and national planning have been implemented by any political coterie without military force. In the end, Chinese Communist insurgent warfare . . . provided 'the ordered application of force in the resolution of a social problem.'"

China's sovereignty would be reborn under the *Kuomintang*, and that this party would direct China's transformation into a strong, democratic, and friendly nation. The assumption, however ill-founded, was a natural corollary to popular American views on historic policies such as the Open Door and China's integrity. Unfortunately popular concepts of the Open Door and China's integrity failed to consider whether these historic principles bore any understandable relationship to what China was in 1949 or, indeed, to what she had been during the previous fifty years. Since these principles of policy had failed time after time in the past there was no reason to suppose they would be effective guardians of American interests in 1949. Yet this was precisely the assumption Americans had been permitted and encouraged to cultivate.

Thus to the overwhelming majority of Americans in 1949, news of the sweeping Chinese Communist victory and the collapse of the *Kuomintang*-Nationalist government was at first simply incomprehensible. For a century the American public had believed that Sino-American relations were based not only on what was considered the justice of American policies but also on a resulting unique Chinese attachment to the United States and its institutions. This public and its government were now faced with policies that lay in ruin and with the prospect that a rising Chinese Communism would recreate the Chinese Empire, aggressive and totalitarian, bent on using Chinese nationalism in the interest of a Communist world revolution. In addition, there was the further frightening prospect of the new Chinese Communist dictatorship expanding its power by communizing its neighbors, thereby converting them into satellites, just as the old traditional Chinese empires controlled their border states by Confucianizing them. There was, furthermore, an even broader sense in which American historical policy lay prostrate. During the twentieth century the United States had sought to preserve a balance of power in Asia by opposing Japan's ambitions in China. World War II had now destroyed Japanese power, but it also destroyed the power of Britain, France, and Holland in the Far East thereby opening the way for a resurgence of the Russian empire on the Pacific. The result was that after the period 1945–1949 Russian and Chinese power replaced Japanese and Western European power in continental Eastern Asia.

In these circumstances, the American government had no alternative other than to attempt belatedly a fundamental reappraisal of American policy, a review which should have been in continuous process since at least the beginning of the century. When this review was undertaken toward the end of the war and after it, it soon became a vast public debate pursued in a manner and in an atmosphere of such irresponsibility and of such unbelievable public recrimination as to suggest that Americans were more afraid of each other than they were of the Chinese or the Russian Communists.

The public crusade to fix responsibility for the tragedy was led by American partisans of the *Kuomintang* both in and outside the Congress. These elements aided and abetted by the so-called China Lobby advanced the theory and the charge that the collapse of the Nationalist government was due not to its own weakness and revolutionary and political vacuity but to the failure of the American government to give it adequate support. This theory, if true, meant that the administration of President Truman, indirectly if not directly, had assisted the Chinese Communists to power. From this position it was charged more specifically that certain conclusions were inescapable. Among these, it was said, either the administration had so miscalculated affairs in China as to bring about the disastrous defeat, or it had knowingly pursued a course that was manifestly easy on communism if not sympathetic with it.[7] To an American public which at no time in its history had given sustained and serious attention to Eastern Asia, these charges seemed plausible enough in 1949 and for some years thereafter. The charges were also

welcomed in greater or lesser degree by a variety of American factions intent on exploiting the tragedy in China for political purposes in the United States.

The flagrant irresponsibility of the great debate to find the American culprits guilty of negligence or foul play in the China tragedy can hardly be understood until it is recalled that the communization of China was the greatest single defeat the foreign policy of the United States has ever suffered. At the same time, the very expression used to describe the tragedy, "we have lost China," suggested clearly that there was a large element of myth in the popular American concept of Sino-American relations. Neither in the nineteenth nor in the twentieth century had the United States ever "possessed" China. One cannot "lose" what one does not possess. But even as late as 1970 there was still a deepseated reluctance to seek for valid answers in the historical record, since the record would doubtless reveal errors of judgment and mistaken actions thereby revealing "the loss of China" not through negligence, treachery, and subversion of "an identifiable group of scapegoats but through Americans themselves, in policies which expressed not only the preferences of the government but the concensus of the people."[8]

The basic reasons for the failure of American policy in China have already been suggested. Here it is only necessary to add that in the years 1940 to 1950 there were fatal weaknesses both in the policy of the *Kuomintang*-Nationalist government and in that of the United States. "Chiang's whole political program was vitiated by a shortsighted determination to hold on tenaciously to his own power and a corresponding refusal to share power and control with political leaders who did not blindly obey and follow him." As a consequence the minor Chinese parties, among whom were many of China's able men, tended to find a community of interest with the Communists rather than with the *Kuomintang*. The repressive measures taken by Chiang toward these minority par-

[7] A statement of this thesis is Anthony Kubeck, *How the Far East Was Lost: American Policy and the Creation of Communist China, 1941–1949* (1963).

[8] Tang Tsou, *America's Failure in China, 1941–1950* (1963),* vii–viii.

ties, indicated a basic weakness in American policy in this period.

Based upon a misunderstanding of the nature of Chinese communism and motivated by a desire to use Communist forces in the war against Japan, American policy failed to distinguish the problem of liberalizing the Nationalist regime to include all non-Communist political elements from the issue of establishing a coalition government with the Communists. As a result, it unwisely demanded the impossible of the Nationalists on the latter issue and did not force them to yield on the former. This failure to separate the two issues enabled Chiang to justify his refusal to liberalize his repressive rule by pointing to the Communist menace and to attribute American criticism of his regime to the inspiration of the Communists. Chiang's policy isolated the Kuomintang *from other non-Communist political groups while American policy failed to build up the power and influence of those non-Communist political elements which were oriented toward the United States but were excluded by Chiang from a fair share of power in the government. Both the Nationalist and American policies worked to the advantage of the Chinese Communist party while each in its own way exacerbated Sino-American relations.*[9]

In principle and in fact, the failure of the American effort in China lay in the disparity between the ends of policy and the means the government and the American people were prepared to use to achieve policy. While the United States held to a vision of the kind of China it desired, there were no systematic, deliberate historical or immediate efforts to employ American power to produce the ends desired. The government of the United States was never of a mind to be a co-belligerent in the *Kuomintang*-Communist civil war and there is no available evidence to indicate that the American people were prepared to abandon this limited policy. Moreover, by 1947–1948 on the eve of the Communist conquest, American diplomatic influence on the Nationalist government was even less effective than it had been while World War II was still in progress. It would thus appear that the factors that brought the collapse of historic American policy toward China were not the product of

[9] Tsou, *America's Failure in China*, 292–93.

subversion at home, but rather the product of a policy whose ends could not be achieved through the means this country was willing to use. Between 1945 and 1949, the United States was unwilling and, at times, unable either to employ measures that were necessary to attain its objectives, or alternatively, to seek objectives which could be supported with limited measures.

COMMUNIST CHINA AND THE POWERS

The Communist military victory and the establishment, October 1, 1949, of a central government at Peking of the People's Republic of China was followed immediately, October 2, by Russian recognition of the new regime. The action was designed to bolster the Peking government, to enable both governments to repudiate the 1945 Soviet-Nationalist treaty, and to permit Russia to join with Peking in attacking the policy of the United States as one of intervention and imperialism. By January of 1950 Mao's government had also been recognized by Russia's satellites, and by India, Burma, Britain, Finland, Sweden, Israel, and Denmark, and soon thereafter recognition was extended by Ceylon, Pakistan, Afghanistan, Indonesia, the Netherlands, and Switzerland. In all cases recognition was extended or withheld as an instrument of national policy. Britain's early recognition was extended in the hope of protecting her territorial and commercial interests, and of counterbalancing the preponderant Russian influence. The Indian position as expressed by Prime Minister Jawaharlal Nehru was that power had passed to the Chinese Communists, that they rather than the *Kuomintang* had popular support, and that the people of Asia must be allowed to decide their political future without foreign interference.

The United States did not recognize the new Communist government. At first the presumption was, though this was not stated explicitly as policy, that the United States would follow its traditional practice of extending recognition when (1) the military outcome was decisive, (2) the stability of the new regime was beyond reasonable doubt, and (3) the new government gave evidence that it could and would be internationally responsible. Actually in the months and even years that followed October, 1949, when the Chinese Communists proclaimed their government, it was never possible for any American administration to approach the subject of extending or withholding recognition on the basis of this foregoing sound and tested formula of American policy. The prominence given by anti-Administration and pro-*Kuomintang* politicians to the general issue of communism so befogged the policy question of recognition that the American government was precluded from dealing with the question in the light of established policy or of national interest. In reality there was small reason at best for the United States to recognize the People's Government. Nevertheless, the fact that the real issues never became the substance of American public debates created in Asia a conviction that the United States would not deal with governments whose institutions and programs were repugnant to American ideas. This obscuring of issues tended also to prolong the hope that nationalism rather than international Communism would predominate in the People's Government and that a Chinese Titoism would be the result. Such a result would have been welcome to American opinion. As it was, American support for the fugitive Nationalist government on Formosa, and the involvement of China in the later Korean conflict stimulated the "Hate America" campaign, drew China closer to Russia, and aided the Communists in their efforts to put the imperialist tag on America. On February 14, 1950, Russia and Communist China concluded a treaty of alliance and mutual assistance. This alliance, directed against a disarmed and an American-occupied Japan, was in reality aimed at the United States. The treaty aligned China in international affairs with the Soviet bloc of states, precluded economic assistance from the United States to Communist China, and drew closer the economic and cultural ties between Mao's government and the Soviet Union. With the backing of this treaty the Chinese Communists were able to continue the charges that America's China policy was one of imperialism. At the same time Mao was willing to tolerate Soviet imperialism in Manchuria, Mongolia, and Sinkiang, even if he did not welcome it.

FOR FURTHER READING

Conrad Brandt, Benjamin Schwartz, and John Fairbank, *A Documentary History of Chinese Communism* (1952) * offers translations of documents relating to the Nationalist-Communist competition that ended in 1949. Chang Chia-ao, *The Inflationary Spiral: The Experience in China, 1939–1950* (1958) is a study of the economic disintegration of the Nationalist government by a former cabinet minister in the government. Ch'ien Tuan-sheng, *The Government and Politics of China* (1950) should be noted for its explanation of Nationalist failures. C. P. Fitzgerald, *Revolution in China* (London, 1952) * focuses skillfully on the indigenous forces underlying the revolution. See also Harold Isaacs, *The Tragedy of the Chinese Revolution* (rev. ed., 1951).* Chiang Chung-cheng (Chiang Kai-shek), *Soviet Russia in China: A Summing-up at Seventy* (1957) * is important as Chiang's explanation of his failure.

For the military climax of the *Kuomintang*-Communist struggle see General L. M. Chassin, *La Conquête de la Chine par Mao Tse-tung, 1945–1949* (Paris, 1952), and Chapter 8 in O. Edmund Clubb, *20th Century China* (London, 1964).* Mr. Clubb, who was the last American Consul General in Peiping, also provides detailed discussions of the crucial Manchurian campaigns in "Chiang Kai-shek's Waterloo: The Battle of the Huai-Hai," *The Pacific Historical Review* 25 (1956): 389–99; and "Manchuria in the Balance, 1945–1946," *The Pacific Historical Review* 26 (1957): 377–89. Robert B. Rigg, *Red China's Fighting Hordes* (1952) describes the leadership, organization and tactics of the Communist armies.

Among significant eyewitness accounts of the Communist conquest are: Derke Bodde,

Peking Diary: A Year of Revolution (1950);* and Jack Belden, *China Shakes the World* (1949). Kuo Ping-chia, *China: New Age and New Outlook* (1956) assesses the events of 1945–1949 against the background of history. Sun K'o, *China Looks Forward* (1944) is a summing-up by the son of Sun Yat-sen of the *Kuomintang's* accomplishments and failures.

Max Beloff, *Soviet Policy in the Far East, 1944–1951* (London, 1953); Aitchen K. Wu, *China and the Soviet Union* (1950); and Henry Wei, *China and Soviet Russia* (1956) offer narratives describing the formation of the Sino-Soviet Alliance of 1950. See also Klaus Mehnert, *Peking and Moscow* (1963);* Harry Schwartz, *Tsars, Mandarins, and Commissars; A History of Chinese-Russian Relations* (1964) and William Mandel, comp., *Soviet Source Materials on USSR Relations with East Asia, 1945–1950* (1950). Herbert Feis, *The China Tangle* (1953) * is an able, dispassionate survey emphasizing the conflicting objectives of American policy. An able and extensive survey of American Far Eastern policy is Harold Vinacke, *Far Eastern Politics in the Postwar Period* (1956). United States Department of State, *United States Relations with China, with Special Reference to the Period 1944–1949* (1949) provides selections from once-secret documents and an official explanation of American policy. Paul H. Clyde, "Historical Reflections on American Relations with the Far East," *The South Atlantic Quarterly* 61 (1962): 437–49, is a critical interpretation.

China under Communism;
1949 and After

chapter 33

The year 1949 was unique in the political traditions of Chinese civilization. When, in that year, the Communist armies drove the *Kuomintang*-Nationalists from continental China, they seemed merely to be repeating what had been done many times in China's long past—destroying a government that had apparently failed and substituting another professing to have the Mandate of Heaven. It suggested the old cyclical theory of Chinese history by which dynasties rose in virtue and fell in decay. This had served as a convenient rationalization of the coming and going of dynasties. After 1911, however, the theory was no longer quite so satisfying. The Republican revolution that year did not propose simply the installation of another dynasty. What it sought was a composite vehicle resting on foundations that were both new and old, on values that were new and Western mingled with others that were old and Chinese. Nor did the Communists in their turn seek the re-establishment of an older order. This latest conquest rested on assumptions of total revolution uninhibited, for the moment at least, by traditions or values of China's great past. Here lay the uniqueness of 1949.

For the tasks of remolding China and uniting a people who in the fullest sense had not lived under a central government since the fall of the Manchu Dynasty, the Communists possessed endowments greater than any other group that had claimed leadership in the twentieth century. Years of bitter struggle had created a leadership, which, initially at least, was remarkably united and determined under Mao Tse-tung. In addition to skills in the politics of opposition and destruction, the Communists came to power with experience derived from actually governing in China's Northwest. Furthermore, from their revolutionary heritage, from the teaching of their ideology, and from study of precedents supplied by the communist state in Soviet Russia, this new leadership had obtained a clear conception of its immediate goals and of the means for achieving them. But would these qualities suffice for the tasks ahead? Would the new regime succeed in casting off the weight of a traditional social order which rested on the inequality of man and of an economy based on subsistence farming so as to achieve the proclaimed goal of a classless society blessed with material abundance? Would revolutionary innovations survive the regime's first years? Indeed, would communism provide answers for China's problems that were any more satisfactory than those of regimes whose failures marked the past half-century? Since the Chinese Communist era is contemporary history, these and similar questions are necessarily lacking in definitive answers. Moreover, knowledge of Communist China is distorted by inadequate or inaccurate data. As in any totalitarian state, the Chinese government controls all media of communication and manipulates the flow of information for its own purposes. These limitations have not been offset by opportunities for first-hand observation. Only limited numbers of outsiders, especially those with training and background for specialized analysis, have been admitted to China since 1949. Of these, few have been American, because the United States, lacking consular and diplomatic officials in China, maintains its own barriers to travel.[1] These and other difficulties suggest the tentative character of scholarship on Communist China.

[1] The limitation imposed on research by the inaccessibility of Communist China has been suggested by Walter Galenson's "The Current State of Chinese Economic Studies," in United States Congress: Joint Economic Committee, *Studies Prepared in the Joint Economic Committee, Congress of the United States: An Economic Profile of Mainland China* (90th Congress, 1st sess.: Joint Committee Print), 2 vols., 1967, I, 3–7, which points out that since 1960, Chinese authorities have published scarcely a single significant figure relating to the country's economy. No public announcements have been made of the magnitude of steel or coal production, of machinery output, or of the size of harvests. Peking has attempted to block the publication of useful data outside the country. Thus, for economists a recent task has been to discover data upon which to base analyses. This job has required quite different skills from those applied in the 1950s to the mass of officially published but often quite unreliable data. Other difficulties have stemmed from the inability of economists to travel to the mainland (statistics ought to be checked against living realities), from the complexities of the Chinese language, and from the unfamiliarity of many economists with Chinese culture.

In 1969, the United States announced that the passports of Americans in certain occupational categories, such as professors or journalists, would be automatically validated for travel in Communist China. Peking, however, made no immediate move to issue visas to such persons.

As the Communists moved toward military victory, 1948–1949, they also prepared for the establishment of a national government. A first step was the convening, September, 1949, of the Chinese People's Consultative Conference which met in Peking and adopted three basic documents: the Common Program of general principles, to serve as an interim constitution; the Organic Law of the Central People's Government, to establish a provisional government; and the Organic Law of the Chinese People's Consultative Conference. In Communist legal theory this Conference and its documentary products imparted to the regime a legitimacy unattainable through military conquest alone. Thus, only after the Conference completed its work did the Communists proclaim on October 1, 1949, the existence of the Chinese People's Republic.

Ostensibly the new government was a broad coalition in which the Communists, functioning as a party of proletarians in alliance with the peasantry, served along with a number of "democratic" parties.[2] These "democratic" parties held seats in the Chinese People's Consultative Conference, and their representatives received appointments to governmental posts. Yet the real substance of the coalition was suggested by the requirement that the "democratic" parties operate under Communist leadership.

[2] The leading "democratic" party was the *Kuomintang* Revolutionary Committee, comprising defectors from the Chinese Nationalist party of Chiang Kai-shek. The Democratic League was made up of intellectuals and bureaucrats of the former regime who had attempted the abortive "third force" movement in 1946–1948. Business interests were grouped in the National Construction Association. Doctors and health specialists dominated the Peasants' and Workers' party, while the Association for Promoting Democracy directed its attention primarily to school teachers. Intellectuals who did not fall into any of the foregoing categories were to be found in the *Chiu San* Society. Allen S. Whiting, "China," in *Modern Political Systems: Asia*, Robert E. Ward and Roy C. Macridis, eds. (1963), 184–86.

These parties generally were not permitted to build grass-roots support or propagandize on their own behalf. They provided window dressing for the claim that the new government represented all people and not a single class. Moreover, insofar as they were compliant tools, these parties assisted in educating and guiding people in the way the Communists wanted them to go; they helped to mobilize enthusiasm and energies for the work of "socialist construction." When they no longer served these purposes, they disappeared.

The Communists also set up mass organizations to assist their rule. Among those organizations deriving membership from definite and permanent interest groups were: the All-China Federation of Democratic Youth, the All-China Federation of Cooperatives, the All-China Federation of Democratic Women, the Peasants' Association, and the National Committee of the (Christian) Churches in China for the Realization of Self-Administration. Other mass organizations, such as the Sino-Soviet Friendship Association, the Red Cross Society of China, or the Chinese People's Committee for World Peace and Against American Aggression, represented some specific purpose. Unlike the "democratic" parties, these organizations—and there was one for nearly every conceivable group or purpose—did not conceal their Communist leadership. The All-China Federation of Trade Unions, for example, had as its honorary chairman, Liu Shao-ch'i, a top party official. The inclusion of practically everybody in one or another of the mass organizations helped to create the impression at home and abroad that the Communists enjoyed overwhelming popular support, and the organizations themselves provided additional mechanisms for publicizing and implementing party programs.

The provisional government established in 1949 was comprised of four main branches. The Central People's Government exercised legislative, executive, and judicial powers. Administrative responsibilities and control of the armies were vested respectively in the Government Administrative Council and the People's Revolutionary Military Council. And finally, complementary to the executive organs but subordinate to them were the Procurator General's Office and the Supreme People's Court. Directly beneath this structure was local government, comprising everything from the provinces on down. In contrast, with the old imperial system which extended only as far as the *hsien* (county), Communist government penetrated the lowest levels to the towns and to the wards and streets in towns.[3] This centralized structure was modified only by the establishment of autonomous local governments in regions inhabited by national minorities. In 1949, however, it was unclear whether the Communists intended to permit these minorities much autonomy.

With the convening of the National People's Congress and the adoption of the constitution, September, 1954, government

[3] The Communists experimented with different administrative systems below the central structure. Upon coming to power they took over nearly intact the existing system having regional, provincial, county, and district divisions. Later the regional divisions were eliminated and changes were made in appointing local officials so as to tighten Peking's control. During the "Great Leap Forward" of 1958, village governments were often consolidated into a single commune congress. Additionally, there were changes in the means of directing this structure. The Chinese initially followed the Soviet example of creating complex bureaucracies for the management of subordinate organs, but in 1956 party members functioning in provincial and local governments were given enlarged authority in making decisions. The latter move did not imply a loosening of central control. Rather it reflected confidence that party members would do the bidding of their leaders. This reliance on the ideological soundness of party members had worked remarkably well in giving direction to scattered bands of revolutionaries before 1949. Moreover, the new system undoubtedly recommended itself to Peking because it contained echoes of traditional Confucian concepts concerning man in government. On this latter point see H. F. Schurmann, "The Roots of Social Policy," *Survey*, No. 38 (1961): 156–69. Richard H. Solomon, "On Activism and Activists: Maoist Conceptions of Motivation and Political Role Linking State to Society," *The China Quarterly* (July-September, 1969), 76–114, studies the influence foreign models and native experience on Mao's theories on the party "activist."

Source: Communist China Map Portfolio (U.S. Central Intelligence Agency, 1967).

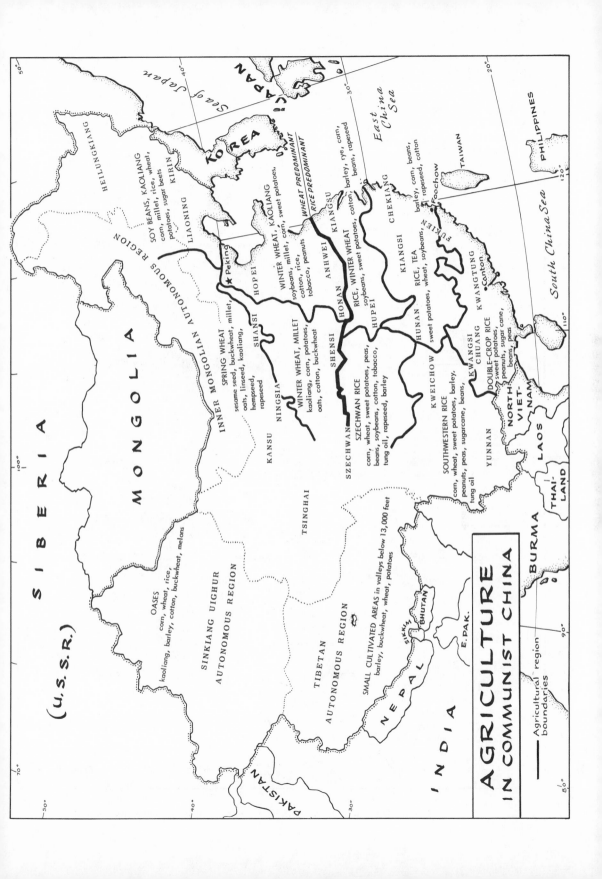

AGRICULTURE
IN COMMUNIST CHINA

——— Agricultural region
       boundaries

(U.S.S.R.)

SIBERIA

MONGOLIA

HEILUNGKIANG

INNER MONGOLIAN AUTONOMOUS REGION

SOY BEANS, KAOLIANG, corn, millet, rice, wheat, potatoes, sugar beets

KIRIN

LIAONING

KOREA

JAPAN

Sea of Japan

Peking ★

HOPEI

WINTER WHEAT, KAOLIANG, soybeans, millet, corn, sweet potatoes, cotton, rice, tobacco, peanuts

WHEAT PREDOMINANT
RICE PREDOMINANT

ANHWEI

KIANGSU

barley, rye, corn, beans, rapeseed

East China Sea

CHEKIANG

barley, corn, beans, rapeseed, cotton

TAIWAN

Foochow

FUKIEN

SPRING WHEAT
sesame seed, buckwheat, millet, oats, linseed, kaoliang, hempseed, rapeseed

SHANSI

WINTER WHEAT, MILLET kaoliang, corn, potatoes, oats, cotton, buckwheat

NINGSIA

SHENSI

HONAN

RICE, WINTER WHEAT, cotton, soybeans, sweet potatoes, peas

HUPEI

KIANGSI
RICE, TEA wheat, soybeans, cotton

KANSU

SZECHWAN RICE
corn, wheat, sweet potatoes, peas, beans, soybeans, cotton, tobacco, tung oil, rapeseed, barley

SZECHWAN

HUNAN
RICE sweet potatoes, wheat, soybeans, cotton

KWEICHOW

KWANGTUNG
Canton

SOUTHWESTERN RICE
corn, wheat, sweet potatoes, barley, peanuts, peas, sugarcane, beans, tung oil

YUNNAN

KWANGSI
CHUANG

DOUBLE-CROP RICE sweet potatoes, peanuts, sugar cane, beans, peas

NORTH VIET-NAM

LAOS

TSINGHAI

SINKIANG UIGHUR AUTONOMOUS REGION

OASES
corn, wheat, rice, kaoliang, barley, cotton, buckwheat, melons

TIBETAN AUTONOMOUS REGION

SMALL CULTIVATED AREAS in valleys below 13,000 feet
barley, buckwheat, wheat, potatoes

NEPAL

SIKKIM

BHUTAN

E. PAK.

INDIA

PAKISTAN

BURMA

THAI-LAND

South China Sea

PHILIPPINES

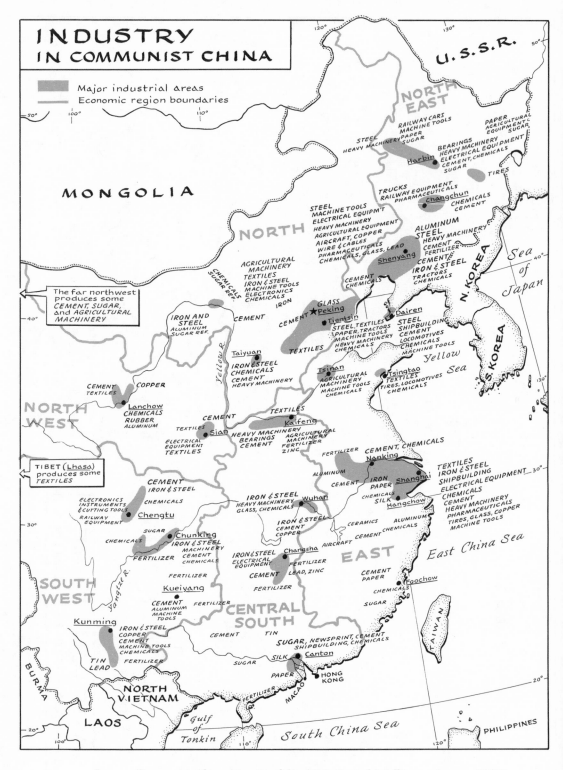

INDUSTRY
IN COMMUNIST CHINA

- Major industrial areas
- Economic region boundaries

U.S.S.R.

MONGOLIA

NORTH EAST

NORTH

STEEL
HEAVY MACHINERY PAPER
SUGAR

RAILWAY CARS
MACHINE TOOLS
PAPER
SUGAR

PAPER
AGRICULTURAL
EQUIPMENT
SUGAR

BEARINGS
HEAVY MACHINERY
ELECTRICAL EQUIPMENT
CEMENT, CHEMICALS
SUGAR

Harbin

TIRES

TRUCKS
RAILWAY EQUIPMENT
PHARMACEUTICALS

Changchun

CHEMICALS
CEMENT

STEEL
MACHINE TOOLS
ELECTRICAL EQUIP'T
HEAVY MACHINERY
AGRICULTURAL EQUIPMENT
AIRCRAFT, COPPER
WIRE & CABLES
PHARMACEUTICALS
CHEMICALS, GLASS, LEAD

ALUMINUM
STEEL
HEAVY MACHINERY
CEMENT
FERTILIZER

AGRICULTURAL
MACHINERY
TEXTILES
IRON & STEEL
MACHINE TOOLS
ELECTRONICS
CHEMICALS

Shenyang

CEMENT
CHEMICALS

IRON & STEEL
TRACTORS
CHEMICALS

N. KOREA

Sea
of
Japan

The far northwest
produces some
CEMENT, SUGAR,
and AGRICULTURAL
MACHINERY

CHEMICALS
SUGAR REF.

IRON

IRON AND
STEEL
ALUMINUM
SUGAR REF.

CEMENT

GLASS
Peking

CEMENT

Tientsin

STEEL, TEXTILES
PAPER, TRACTORS
MACHINE TOOLS
HEAVY MACHINERY
CHEMICALS

Dairen

STEEL
SHIPBUILDING
CEMENT
LOCOMOTIVES
CHEMICALS
MACHINE TOOLS

N. KOREA

S. KOREA

Taiyuan
IRON & STEEL
CHEMICALS
CEMENT
HEAVY MACHINERY

TEXTILES

Tsinan
AGRICULTURAL
MACHINERY
MACHINE TOOLS
CHEMICALS

Tsingtao
TEXTILES
TIRES, LOCOMOTIVES
CHEMICALS

Yellow
Sea

CEMENT
TEXTILES

COPPER

NORTH
WEST

Lanchow
CHEMICALS
RUBBER
ALUMINUM

CEMENT

TEXTILES

Kaifeng

HEAVY MACHINERY
BEARINGS
CEMENT

AGRICULTURAL
MACHINERY
FERTILIZER
ZINC

CEMENT, CHEMICALS

Nanking

TEXTILES
IRON & STEEL
SHIPBUILDING
ELECTRICAL EQUIPMENT
CEMENT
HEAVY MACHINERY
PHARMACEUTICALS
TIRES, GLASS, COPPER
MACHINE TOOLS

TEXTILES
Sian
ELECTRICAL
EQUIPMENT
TEXTILES

TIBET (Lhasa)
produces some
TEXTILES

CEMENT
IRON & STEEL

CHEMICALS

ELECTRONICS
INSTRUMENTS
& CUTTING TOOLS
RAILWAY
EQUIPMENT

Chengtu

SUGAR

CHEMICALS

Chunking
IRON & STEEL
MACHINERY
CEMENT
CHEMICALS

FERTILIZER

IRON & STEEL
HEAVY MACHINERY
GLASS, CHEMICALS

Wuhan

IRON & STEEL
CEMENT
COPPER

ALUMINUM

CEMENT

IRON
PAPER

CHEMICALS
SILK

Shanghai

Hangchow

ALUMINUM

FERTILIZER

CERAMICS

CEMENT

CEMENT
CHEMICALS

IRON & STEEL
ELECTRICAL
EQUIPMENT
CEMENT

Changsha

FERTILIZER
LEAD, ZINC

AIRCRAFT

EAST

CEMENT
PAPER

East China Sea

SOUTH
WEST

FERTILIZER

Kueiyang
CEMENT
ALUMINUM
MACHINE
TOOLS

FERTILIZER

FERTILIZER

CEMENT
PAPER

CHEMICALS

Foochow

CENTRAL
SOUTH

SUGAR

Kunming
IRON & STEEL
COPPER
CEMENT
MACHINE TOOLS
CHEMICALS

CEMENT

TIN

SUGAR, NEWSPRINT, CEMENT
SHIPBUILDING, CHEMICALS

TAIWAN

BURMA

FERTILIZER

TIN
LEAD

NORTH
VIETNAM

SUGAR

SILK

PAPER

Canton

MACAO

HONG
KONG

LAOS

Gulf
of
Tonkin

FERTILIZER

South China Sea

PHILIPPINES

Source: Communist China Map Portfolio (U.S. Central Intelligence Agency, 1967).

was formalized and its structure recast, but there were no fundamental political changes.[4] Aside from imparting to the regime an additional claim to legitimacy, the new constitution chiefly was important as a legal basis for the forthcoming socialist transformation of the national economy, the nationalization of natural resources, and the inauguration of centralized planning. Governmental processes under the constitution also offered elections and opportunities for office holding, both of which provided China's masses with a sense of participation. In this respect, government, like the mass organizations, became an instrument for enlisting popular support.[5]

THE ROLE OF THE COMMUNIST PARTY

For most of the regime's first twenty years, until the advent of the "Great Prole-

[4] Among the changes were: (1) replacement of the Chinese People's Consultative Conference with the National People's Congress; (2) substitution of the State Council, a body which was to function like a cabinet under the direction of a Premier, for the Government Administrative Council; (3) reorganization of military planning and administration under a National Defense Council; and (4) creation of a new institution, the Supreme State Conference, which was to co-ordinate on a high administrative level the work of various agencies. While these alterations appeared extensive, government maintained its original form of a coalition operating under Communist leadership. Arthur H. Steiner, "Constitutionalism in Communist China," *American Political Science Review* 49 (1955): 1–21.

[5] Party theory has embraced two contradictory concepts: on the one hand, the supremacy of the collective interest, popular activism, and popular political consciousness have been stressed; on the other, doctrine has postulated the leading role of the Party. The result in practice has been popular participation more as a matter of form than substance. Thus, Chinese have enjoyed "limited opportunities for participation in the management of minor affairs." Such opportunities, moreover, have been limited to those things which "support socialism as defined by the Party." See James R. Townsend, *Political Participation in Communist China* (1967).* A. Doak Barnett, ed., *Chinese Communist Politics in Action* (1969), a collection of essays dealing with relationships between formal government structure and the populace.

tarian Cultural Revolution," 1966–1968, the Chinese Communist Party was central to the operation of the government, the army, and every other agency by which authority was maintained. The Party's organization was so designed that its reach extended from Peking to the grassroots. Between 1949 and 1961 (the date of the latest official statistics) membership expanded from 4,448,080 to some 17,000,000. Thus the Party was equipped with personnel necessary to control key posts in all organizations. It was through Party members, acting as a cohesive, disciplined body, that public policy was implemented. It also was through control of the Party that Mao Tse-tung and a handful of veteran colleagues, such as Liu Shao-ch'i, Chou En-lai, Chu Teh, Ch'en Yun, Teng Hsiao-p'ing, and Lin Piao, irrespective of official titles, claimed authority to determine national policy, to assign responsibility, and to prescribe—sometimes in minute detail—the ways and means for carrying out decisions.[6]

Leadership during the regime's early years was characterized by a remarkable unity of purpose. Mao's authority was unquestioned, and top officials seemed immune to the devisive influence of factionalism. Throughout the Party, unity and a high level of political consciousness and revolutionary competence were maintained by unremitting indoctrination. Every member constantly engaged in *hseuh-hsi* (study or training) in order to sharpen his perception of Marxist-Leninist principles and the "Thought of Mao Tse-tung." The Party's frequent resort to *cheng-feng*, the rectification campaigns which had proven so effective in building unity, required members not only to intensify their studies but also to expose their innermost thoughts in group meetings directed toward criticism and self-criticism. This latter mechanism proved especially effective in enabling party leadership to

[6] The men cited were members of the Communist party's key organization, the Politburo's Standing Committee, prior to the latter's reshuffling in August, 1966. For a more extensive description of the Party's role in governmental affairs, see Whiting, "China," *Modern Political Systems: Asia,* 154–87.

detect undesirables and to eliminate them from the ranks.

The "Great Proletarian Cultural Revolution," however, marked a fundamental change in politics. Beginning as a rectification campaign designed to heighten revolutionary fervor among intellectuals (hence the name, "Cultural Revolution"), this movement produced by August, 1966 a leadership crisis when the central authority was rent by competing factions vying for power and control over national policy.[7] Most notable was the open break between Mao and his designated heir, Liu Shao-ch'i. But these struggles were not contained at the highest levels. Embattled officials sought allies wherever they could be found among the lower echelons of the Party, governmental bureaucracy, and even the populace itself. By the summer of 1967, the world witnessed the spectacle of millions of young revolutionaries, dubbed "Red Guards," "staging anti-Rightist" demonstrations, "dragging out" and humiliating alleged "powerholders in the Party taking the capitalist road," wresting authority from incumbent officials, and shattering in many provinces party and governmental machinery. Not until 1968 did a coalition composed of the army under Lin Piao and remnants of state and party apparatus restore some semblance of order.

Reliable information on this momentous upheaval was exceedingly rare. In 1970 observers still were trying to assemble a coherent account of events and to interpret their significance. The most plausible theory held that Mao himself had precipitated the crisis when he converted party rectification into a sweeping purge.[8] Once under way

the movement gained unexpected momentum, approaching the status of civil war. Mao seemingly had hit upon these means to revitalize China's revolutionary leadership and to ensure his own command. Prior to the Cultural Revolution the aging dictator confronted a Party elite increasingly disenchanted with such revolutionary excesses as the Great Leap Forward and determined to relegate Mao to a titular capacity. Mao fought back, employing the doctrine of "permanent revolution" to justify the activities of crusading Red Guards.[9] Help was also forthcoming from Lin Piao and the army. The ultimate Maoist victory eliminated from the Party all whose devotion to Mao was suspect, but the Party itself, suffering from the public abuse of its leaders (Mao's friends and foes alike), the rapid turnover of membership, and the interruption of normal

---

[7] The opening rounds of the "Cultural Revolution" are detailed in two articles by Stephen Uhalley, Jr.: "The Wu Han Discussion: Act One in a New Rectification Campaign," *The China Mainland Review*, I, (1966), 24–38; and "The Cultural Revolution and the Attack on the 'Three Family Village,'" *The China Quarterly* (July-September, 1966), 149–61. Franklin W. Houn, *A Short History of Chinese Communism* (1967),* Chapter 7, views the early stages of the "Cultural Revolution" against the background of party rectification.

[8] Earlier rectification campaigns had been controlled by subjecting critics at every level to

the control of senior party officials. In 1966 Mao not only insisted that youths be permitted to detect "rightists," but also that the usual restraints be abandoned.

[9] The doctrine of "permanent revolution" holds that China's social transformation shall extend unceasingly into an infinity of time. In its origins the doctrine takes into account both China's backwardness and the resistance of the old order to change. If China is to advance, her revolutionary leadership must wage a struggle characterized by bitterness and extremism. Moreover, the struggle must extend in time well beyond anything envisaged by other revolutionaries. The peculiar feature of this theory is the open-ended character of the dialectical vision. Western Marxists, while generally viewing revolution as continuing indefinitely, see the dialectic culminating at some point in socialism. Mao holds that the reformation of human character and the transformation of society require a revolutionary drive extending through all time. Such departure from Western theory raises a question whether "Marxism" as applied to China may be more ascriptive than descriptive. See Mark Mancall discussing Stuart R. Schram's *Documents sur la theorie de la "revolution permanente" en Chine: ideologie dialectique et dialectique du reel* (Paris, 1963) in *Journal of Asian Studies* 26 (1966): 109–10; and Maurice Meisner, "Utopian Goals and Ascetic Values in Chinese Communist Ideology," *Journal of Asian Studies* 28 (1968): 101–10. Franz Schurman, *Ideology and Organization in Communist China* (1966)* offers the best discussion of the nature and causes of China's unique patterns.

operations, was displaced from its key role. Lin Piao's designation as Mao's new heir apparent signaled the emergence of the army as a controlling element. Peking boasted that its new leadership was more "Red" than "expert," a characteristic which in Maoist terms was accounted an advantage. The proposition, however, that revolutionary zeal was the main requirement in the solution of China's problems remained untested.[10]

RESHAPING THE MASSES

Attainment of Mao's vision required enthusiastic popular support, not mere acquiescence to his will. Thus, with their power secured after 1949 the Communists applied themselves to the elimination of old loyalties, the arousing of greatly enlarged expectations, and the identification of themselves with those expectations. In pursuing these goals, the Party, especially during its first years in power, sometimes used the harshest tactics. According to Communist theory and practice, enemies of the revolu-

[10] Western observers were sharply divided on the long range implications of the Cultural Revolution. For example, Franz Schurman's "The Attack of the Cultural Revolution on Ideology and Organization," in *China in Crisis: China's Heritage and the Communist Political System*, Ping-ti Ho and Tang Tsou, eds. (1968), 525–64, accepts the Maoist view that the Communist elite had become conservative and was subverting the revolution. Accordingly, temporary reverses stemming from disorder, suspension of schooling, and disruption of production were more than offset by a new leadership possessed of a truly revolutionary drive. On the other hand Chalmers Johnson's "Communist China's Political Turmoil," *SAIS Review* 12, No. 2 (1968): 5–24, argues that China's experience in such episodes as the Great Leap Forward demonstrates that unorganized enthusiasm is a poor substitute for a rational attack on her problems. Mao's purge removed from office the very men who showed promise of making such a rational approach. A similar conclusion is reached by William T. deBary's "The Relevance of Asia," *Liberal Education* (Oct., 1969): 433–40. Note especially the observation that, "For China itself Maoism represents both a rejection of the bourgeois West and a traditional anti-foreignism, essentially defensive and reactionary, shielding the Chinese people from new influences and new options. It cannot, in the long run, succeed."

tion—their identity was determined by the Communists alone—were not entitled to civil rights and were to be treated sternly. Under this rationalization the regime supported in 1951–1953 the extermination of untold numbers of "landlords" and the redistribution of their land. These measures, by destroying a local leadership noted for its conservatism and for its attachments to China's old traditional order, were of the utmost importance in clearing the way for a new era. But, in the balance, propaganda and persuasion proved more important in Communist China than force. China's involvement in the Korean War, for example, while costly in terms of trained military manpower and of resources, provided in the regime's early day an opportunity to rally a patriotic people. Moreover, the Communist leadership's confidence in ideological control (a traditional Confucian method) was bolstered by successes with the *cheng feng* movement of the 1940s and subsequent rectification efforts. It remained, therefore, for the Communists to determine what the new society should be and would be.

Education became a major instrument for introducing the new society. The Communists made every effort to expand and reorganize the school system to accomplish two major aims: (1) the training of a largely illiterate populace in the skills necessary for a modern society, and (2) the inculcating of concepts that would sustain Peking's revolutionary programs.[11] By 1959 there were some 86,000,000 children attending elementary schools, 12,000,000 in middle schools, and 660,000 in college and universities. In addition numerous part-time schools, providing for combined work and

[11] Among reforms were efforts to counteract traditional disdain for manual labor, to stress science and technology (most students in the inherited school system were enrolled in humanities and social studies), to integrate study, research and practical labor, and to emphasize in the circumstances of severe shortage the importance of quantity over quality. Robert A. Barendsen, "Education in China," *Problems of Communism* 13, No. 4 (1964): 19–27. For a fuller study with documents see Stewart Fraser, comp. and ed., *Chinese Communist Education: Records of the First Decade* (1965).*

study, taught basic skills. Measured in quantitative terms (college-level enrollment in 1963 was five times that of 1947, the highest year for the pre-Communist era), these were impressive accomplishments. Yet, generally speaking, the quality of education was not high. Nor was the progress of the first decade sustained into the 1960s. Economic pressures imposed by the Great Leap Forward forced cut-backs in the expansion of the school system. Ever greater damage was done by the Cultural Revolution, during which the school system closed as students were caught up in political agitation.

Beyond the school system the Communists campaigned incessantly and intensively to reshape Chinese thinking. Literature, the press, the stage, films, and radio became evangelists of the new China. The populace was organized by trained staff party workers into groups of a dozen or so for critical discussion and appraisal of their own activities in the light of party directives.[12] The numbers enlisted in campaigns of this kind cutting across the entire society can hardly be estimated. In 1951–1952, the "Three Antis-Movement" was designed to arouse Chinese to expose "corruption, waste, and bureaucracy" in a campaign to eliminate from the Party unworthy Communists and to expose former *Kuomintang* officials the regime had found useful temporarily but who were no longer needed. The "Five Antis-Movement" of the same period, which had for its target "tax evasion, bribery, cheating in government contracts, theft of

economic intelligence, and stealing national property," enlisted public support in driving "enemies" of the state from business. Targets of other campaigns were "feudalism," "American imperialism," and "running dogs of capitalism." During the later 1950s, the period of the Great Leap Forward, increased industrial production became a major propaganda theme. By controlling all the communications media, by piling one campaign on another, by arousing public opinion on behalf of selected objectives, the Communists proposed to keep opponents off-balance and to maintain in their own hands the initiative for transforming China.

The Communist insistence on conformity with the new ideology held special implications for Chinese intellectuals. Traditionally leaders of opinion, the intellectuals presented Peking alternatively with a threat or promise, depending on their attitude toward Communist leadership. The problem was that in 1949 many intellectuals, while disenchanted with the *Kuomintang*, saw little advantage in the new regime. In consequence, this group became a target of intensive persuasion. Among lesser figures conversion was attempted through the pressure of opinion. Meetings were staged at which individuals were subjected to ridicule, urged to confess the erroneousness of their ideas, and encouraged to adopt a new course. These efforts at thought-remolding (or more popularly, brainwashing) were softened somewhat for more prominent personages, but the intent remained the same.[13] Faced with the eradication of free thought, many intellectuals sought escape, but the great majority, for whom escape was undesirable or impractical, remained to serve the Communists. Thus the Peking government achieved a substantial success in an area where the *Kuomintang* had failed. The Communists claimed the services of a considerable

[12] The power of the Chinese Communist Party to effect wide social and intellectual control was due mainly to its trained staff workers, the *kan pu* or cadres. These were young party or sympathetic workers educated for leadership in government and party activities. Their chief qualifications were capacity to develop loyalty, obedience, initiative, and ability in organizing the masses. The Communists had begun the formal training of cadres back in the days at Yenan. This training consisted of both classroom learning and of field work whereby the student acquired a mastery of doctrine and technique and also an intimate knowledge of how the common people lived and thought. This vast army of trained workers was kept "pure" in thought and deed by periodic rectification.

[13] The process of thought-remolding is described by an American scholar who underwent the experience in Harriet Mills, "Thought Reform: Ideological Remolding in China," *Atlantic Monthly* 204 (1959): 71–77. A psychiatric appraisal is given in Robert J. Lifton, *Thought Reform and the Psychology of Totalism: A Study of "Brainwashing" in China* (1960).

portion of the country's modern-trained scholars, although an outburst of criticism from intellectuals during the "Hundred Flowers" campaign of 1957 and the subsequent Cultural Revolution cast doubt on the regime's success in eliminating all independent thought.[14]

THE BALANCE SHEET ON SOCIAL REFORM

By 1970 Communist rule had wrought fundamental social transformations. One of the most significant revolutions, for example, was in family life. Under the Marriage Law of 1950 women gained full equality with men in marriage, divorce, and ownership of property. Communist practice encouraged children to criticize and to inform on parents for persisting in traditional ways. Through the adoption of such measures Peking hoped to eliminate intense loyalties which competed with allegiance to the state. Another ob-

jective was the mobilization of women for productive work outside the home.

Yet in some areas the government's assault on traditional culture was something less than total. While the regime was antireligious and desired the ultimate eradication of what it held to be superstition, campaigns against religious bodies were determined in the light of their probable political effect. Organized cults with no foreign ties, such as Taoism, were severely treated, but outward deference was shown Buddhism and Islam, which claimed many adherents in Southeast Asia and other regions where the Communists also had interests. Toleration and even encouragement were accorded the traditional concepts of political and cultural unity, some traditional etiquette and customs, and much traditional art and literature.[15]

Indeed, only partial success could be claimed by the entire Communist effort to reshape Chinese society. Peasants welcomed enthusiastically the extermination of land-

---

[14] The Hundred Flowers campaign, which drew its name from the ancient saying, "Let a hundred flowers bloom, let a hundred schools of thought contend," represented a momentary relaxation of thought control. Intellectuals, encouraged by party leaders to engage in free discussion, spoke out on every phase of the Communist transformation of China. The criticism, however, apparently became more widespread and intense than was anticipated. The critics went so far as to challenge the relevance of Marxism-Leninism to the Chinese revolution, and anti-Communist demonstrations occurred in several universities. At this point further criticism was forbidden, and those who had spoken were punished. Translations of statements made during the Hundred Flowers campaign are given in R. MacFarquhar, *The Hundred Flowers Campaign and the Chinese Intellectuals* (1960); and Dennis J. Doolin, trans., *Communist China: The Politics of Student Opposition* (1964).* The latter collection suggests a generation gap among Chinese intellectuals. Students were less opposed to communism than their elders. Their criticisms were directed toward disparities between theory and practice, and failures to measure up to the promises of "liberation." For the recollections of an intellectual who served the Communists before becoming disillusioned see Chow Ching-wen, *Ten Years of Storm: The True Story of the Communist Regime* (1960).

[15] While in general tradition was permitted to survive if it served the Communist state, the process of determining what remained and what did not was by no means simple. Ralph C. Crozier's *Traditional Medicine in Modern China: Science, Nationalism, and the Tensions of Cultural Change* (1968), finds that the Communists have sanctioned such traditional medical treatments as acupuncture because, in a country desperately short of medical personnel, they were anxious to provide treatment in which the people had confidence. The past also was used to bolster national feeling. "Popular" and "progressive" factors from tradition were rescued from obscurity and refurbished to demonstrate China's equality with or even superiority to the West. Yet, in resurrecting the past, the Communists invariably were careful to distinguish between those things that were relevant to the present and those that belonged to the past. Thus the memory of Confucius could be honored while his ideas as applied to the modern world were condemned. Joseph Levenson has likened the procedure to a vast "museum" in which artifacts might be admired without their being adopted. The Chinese revolution, Levenson observes, has been "against the world to join the world, against their past to keep it theirs, but past." *Confucian China and Its Modern Fate, Volume III: The Problem of Historical Significance* (1965). See also Ralph C. Crozier, ed., *China's Cultural Legacy and Communism* (1970).*

lords, but they were notably unhappy about the subsequent introduction of co-operatives, collectives, and heavy taxes. Industrial workers discovered little improvement in their conditions under Communism. And national minorities became restive as their so-called autonomous governments lost their autonomy. In consequence, by 1962 the Party, having concluded that the masses were not prepared to embrace the Communist vision of the new China, launched a "Socialist Education Campaign," which was intended to teach the populace to think as Mao's people should think. Under the banner of Socialist Education, the Party attempted to "counter modern revisionism," to train "revolutionary heirs," and to force both intellectuals and party cadre to perform physical labor. This attempt to revitalize the Party and to intensify revolutionary fervor was sustained until mid-1966 when it was superceded by the greater furor of the Cultural Revolution.

ECONOMIC DEVELOPMENT

As Marxists, Peking's leaders identified their society of the future with the world of science and technology and with the triumph of modernization over a backward peasant society. The plentiful peoples' society was to replace the rule of special privilege and poverty. Yet, between this future and a meaner present loomed a perilous struggle not only against internal barriers to progress but also against external enemies who were determined to destroy the revolution. Thus, Peking embarked upon a program of rapid modernization emphasizing initially the building of heavy industry rather than light industry and consumer goods. Agriculture was to be reorganized and updated in support of industrialization. Furthermore, Marxist convictions encouraged the determination to direct the whole process of modernization through centralized planning, decision making, and collectivism.

Lacking both capital and personnel for the material transformation of China, Peking looked to its Communist neighbor, the Soviet Union. Early in 1950, China and the Soviet Union signed a treaty of alliance and a number of collateral economic agreements, providing for a $300,000,000 loan, reciprocal trade, and Soviet technical assistance. Subsequent understandings expanded the amount of Soviet aid. In 1956 alone, for example, provision was made for the exchange of some 2,000 persons. Thousands of Russian technical experts were sent to China, while additional thousands of Chinese went to the Soviet Union for technical education and on-the-job training. Soviet loans to China were estimated to have totaled about two billion dollars for economic development and one billion for military purposes.[16] By the later 1950s, however, Sino-Soviet aid agreements were expiring and were not renewed as tensions strained relations between these allies. In retrospect, while Soviet aid never approached the dimensions desired by China, its effectiveness was enhanced by careful selection of projects and by relatively efficient use of available resources. Without this assistance China's industrial goals would have been far more limited than they eventually were.

The economic system inherited by the Communists bore little resemblance to one they hoped to build. Industrial facilities were comparatively small and localized. A major asset was the heavy industry left by the Japanese in Manchuria. Some light industries, mainly textiles, remained from foreign investment in China's coastal cities, especially in Shanghai and Tientsin. The railway system was concentrated in Manchuria save for the trunk lines in China Proper. Agriculture differed little from that of Old China. Altogether these were limited facilities, and all had suffered the ravages of foreign and civil war. On their takeover the Communists gave particular attention to repair of railways, the construction of new lines, and the administration of barge traffic on the rivers still so important to Chinese transportation. Light industry revived more rapidly than heavy industry. Agriculture responded to a succession of

[16] Hu Chang-tu, *et al.*, *China: Its People; Its Society; Its Culture* (1960), 391.

good crop seasons. Most important, however, in the Communist economic recovery were measures to control inflation. The improvements achieved here were due to rigid restrictions on credit and to government control of prices through the release of major commodities by state trading companies. These measures were bolstered by a firm national budget and a system of national taxation enforced relentlessly. Additional government revenue accrued from fines upon businessmen or confiscation of their property. By 1952 production was nearly at pre-war levels. Moreover, the Communists were in command of the machinery for generating further advances. Trade, industry, and bank loans and deposits were substantially in the hands of government agencies and enterprises. Meanwhile under the Agrarian Reform Act of 1950 landlords were stripped of their property and land was redistributed among millions of peasants. One of the consequences of this step was establishment in the countryside and villages of a ruling peasant class which owed its new status to the Communist regime.

Upon these foundations the new industrialization of China was built. While the Five Year Plan announced in 1953 did not go into specifics, Peking's intent was obviously the establishment of a heavy industrial base in many regions, including the remote and technologically primitive areas of the interior. State control over this expansion was maintained through centralized planning and the socialization of enterprise. Financing was obtained through the imposition of austere living standards which prevented the loss of surplus income through personal consumption. The peasantry was goaded into a forced pace to produce an agricultural surplus that could be converted into foreign exchange, industrial raw materials, and the means for supporting an ever larger population.

In some periods and areas, the accomplishments in industry were both visible and impressive. Steel production, though small, increased from 1952 to 1957 by a total of some 325 per cent, while coal pro-

duction expanded about 200 per cent. A total of 4,084 kilometers of new rail lines were constructed.[17]

During these years, the Communists faced difficulties in agriculture as they attempted to shift from individual enterprise to a collective system. Beginning in 1953, the government announced that small, individualized land holdings were unsuitable for mechanized farming. Individual holdings, which averaged two-and-a-half acres after land redistribution, were pooled so that productivity might be raised through increased use of machines, irrigation, and chemical fertilizers. But the attempt to raise production and to change simultaneously the entire land tenure system by 1957 produced only a widening gap between agricultural output and demand. Complicating this difficulty were declining Soviet aid and the loss of momentum in the expansion of industries.

The "Great Leap Forward"

Faced with these problems, Peking, late in 1957, turned to a crash program of intensive exploitation of Chinese labor. Production goals were revised upward drastically, the populace was remobilized, and the so-called "Great Leap Forward" was launched in 1958. The Communists proclaimed their intention to surpass Britain's industrial production in fifteen years. To this end agricultural productivity was to be raised through large scale irrigation projects, deep plowing, and intensive tillage. The state invested heavily in the expansion of selected heavy industries. Individuals were to work harder than ever at their regular jobs and were to

[17] While these percentage increases were impressive, total production remained extremely small for a country of China's size and population. According to official claims, between 1952 and 1957 the output of key industries rose as follows:

Steel	1.35 to 5.35 million (metric) tons
Pig Iron	1.9 to 5.94 million tons
Coal	63.53 to 130 million tons
Electric Power	7.26 to 19.3 billion KWH
Cement	2.86 to 6.86 million tons
Machine tools	13.7 to 28 thousand sets

assume additional productive tasks. This latter arangement permitted established production facilities to be augmented by thousands of small scale projects utilizing available labor but requiring little investment capital. Workers in their spare time would operate "backyard furnaces" smelting scrap iron, plant tree seedlings, or build water control projects, thereby stimulating the economy through additional labor. For the individual, however, the eight-hour day proclaimed by the Party in 1931 became less than a vision as the workday stretched to fourteen or more hours.

The commune, an administrative unit which in the countryside encompassed on the average 10,000 acres and 5,000 households, became an essential framework for organizing the forced pace of the Great Leap. Although the Communists had little experience with the commune before their attempt to create some 26,000 of them in August, 1958, they were attracted to the device by the possibilites presented for completely mobilizing all available labor. In each commune, workers from 200 to 300 households were formed into a production brigade which was shifted from job to job as need required. This was viewed as an advance over the collectives in that the latter pooled labor only for agricultural purposes. Moreover, by placing large numbers under single direction, the commune was equipped to undertake vast projects (for example, reforestation of an entire watershed). Still other advantages were anticipated from new patterns of communal living: community mess halls would cut household labor and tighten control over food consumption; labor expended on care of the very young and old would be reduced by eastablishment of nurseries and homes for the aged; and de-emphasis of the family as the primary social unit would strengthen work discipline. In short, the commune provided machinery for controlling the individual's economic activity, working conditions, place of residence, and even his family life.

For a time this regimentation of Chinese life resulted in a fury of human activity having few parallels in history. By the end of 1958, Peking was claiming an increase of 100 per cent in agricultural production. The output of iron and steel was said to have doubled. Similar "leaps" were said to have occurred in other key enterprises. Yet as time passed the government's production estimates were reduced, and there were other signs of forced retrenchments. Some features of the commune system, such as community mess halls and rigid direction of work brigades, were modified or abandoned. Many of the much publicized economic experiments, most notably the "backyard furnaces," were accounted failures. It seemed that the Communists had attempted too much too fast. On the credit side, the Great Leap Forward was responsible for increased momentum resulting in temporary increases in industrial production, the establishment of new plants, expansion of transportation facilities, modernization of some aspects of agriculture, and consolidation of the regime's hold on the populace. Nevertheless, many new and staggering problems were created. Beginning in 1959, China experienced a distinct economic setback as plants, whose machinery had been overtaxed to the breaking point, closed for repair and as new construction was cut drastically by general disorganization. Even more serious was a break down in agriculture. In 1960 a drop in grain production to levels achieved eight years earlier created the necessity for importing wheat from Australia, Canada, or wherever it could be obtained.

Retrenchment

To surmount these problems Peking retreated from the more extreme features of the Great Leap Forward. Centralized planning, which had been cast aside in the fury of expansion, was re-emphasized, agricultural production was given priority, and industrial investment was reduced. Official concern for quality and variety replaced an earlier emphasis on rapid growth in output. The Party also acknowledged the necessity of increasing production of consumer goods and of improving market conditions. The greatest transformations, however, occurred in rural communes, where the administrative structure was altered to bring management closer to the producer. Peasants were given private plots to use as they wished.[18]

These retrenchments, 1961–1962, effected a partial recovery. Thereafter the regime moved cautiously in preparing for further development. On the theory that peasant energies, properly channeled, could transform China, the Party looked to the "Socialist Education Campaign" for the psychological preparations of still another economic drive. Meanwhile, pending the establishment of the proper intellectual and emotional climate for that drive, the Party retained many of the adjustments of the retrenchment period—the private plots, rural markets, and local direction of production. Economic progress under these circumstances was such that by 1965 Party officials spoke optimistically of an upsurge that would soon lead to the announcement of a third Five Year Plan. Once again, however, the momentum of economic growth was broken as the Cultural Revolution enveloped the country. The turmoil interfered both with planning and production.[19] Not until 1969 was calm sufficiently restored to enable Peking to resume long range planning.

Despite these reverses, a summation of economic achievements over twenty years of Communist rule revealed notable expansion. In a land where population was expanding by 15,000,000 each year, the growth

[18] For the impact of the Great Leap on traditional patterns in economic behavior and the force of tradition in breaking the Great Leap, see G. William Skinner, "Marketing and Social Structure in Rural China: Part III, Rural Marketing in Communist China," *Journal of Asian Studies* 24 (1965): 371–73; 397–99. Kenneth R. Walker, *Planning in Chinese Agriculture: Socialization and the Private Sector, 1956–1962* (London, 1965) reveals the ways planning has worked.

[19] Dislocations apparently were more serious in industrial than in agricultural production. In its early and most excited stages, the Cultural Revolution shook the cities but left the countryside relatively untouched. Moreover, rural production may actually have benefited by the breakdown of bureaucratic controls. Thus in 1969 the Communists claimed "abundant" grain harvests, a claim which seemed substantiated by modest grain imports from the Western world.

rate meant little in terms of improved living standards, but expansion did supply the basis of new national power as was demonstrated in China's support of the largest conventionally armed force in Asia. Moreover, the detonation of a nuclear device, October, 1964, and a subsequent nuclear testing program, both of which required the products of a broad, modern industrial base and the labor of hundreds of skilled scientists and engineers, illustrated dramatically a growing technical sophistication.

COMMUNIST CHINA IN WORLD AFFAIRS

The significance of this new economic base was evident in Peking's conduct of foreign relations. After 1949 China assumed a variety of faces before the world, ranging from militant advocacy of Communist revolution and war to the softer language of "peaceful co-existence," but whatever the line, the constant purpose was to become the first power in Asia and a world communism leader. China, long at the mercy of the West, proposed to meet the West at least as an equal and to eliminate entirely Western political influence in Asia. By its own avowal, Peking assumed a most vocal role as the chief opponent of what it called "imperialism." The new foreign policy was distinctly ideological, but it was also a policy solidly based in Chinese natonalism.[20]

Chinese Communist foreign policy in its first phase was guided by militant idealism. According to Peking's analysis, nations fell into one of three categories—the Communist bloc, the "imperialist" powers, and the "unliberated" ex-colonial countries of Asia. With respect to the Communist bloc, China would "lean to one side," uniting its forces in revolutionary endeavor with those of the

[20] A basic study is A. Doak Barnett, *Communist China and Asia: Challenge to American Policy* (1960). Tang Tsou and Morton H. Halperin, "Mao Tse-tung's Revolutionary Strategy and Peking's International Behavior," *American Political Science Review* 59 (1965): 80–90, analyzes the projection of Mao's revolutionary experience into the realm of foreign policy.

Soviet Union. Toward the "imperialist" camp, China would wage continuous war. The "unliberated" countries were to be the target of revolutionary efforts to bring them into the Communist world. Basic to this policy was the assumption of a continuing revolution until all countries were "free."

Expressed in more concrete terms, Chinese policy involved aid to "People's Liberation Armies" seeking the overthrow of existing Southeast Asian governments, the buildup of armed forces along the Chinese coast in preparation for an assault against the remnants of the Nationalist forces on Taiwan, and intensive propaganda attacks against Western activities in Japan, the Philippines, and Indochina. Following the outbreak of the Korean War, June, 1950, China first supported North Korea verbally and later intervened on her behalf as fighting tipped in favor of United Nations forces. Meanwhile Sino-Soviet relations had been formalized in a treaty of friendship and alliance.

After 1952, however, Peking adopted the tactics of "peaceful co-existence." While this shift was probably encouraged by the Soviet Union, it was dictated in fact by internal interests. The Peking regime, then preparing to launch its first Five Year Plan, anticipated for the first time sufficient resources for spreading its influence through trade and aid. Furthermore, peaceful co-existence appeared to offer a means for circumventing the countermeasures being developed by the United States against China's militant policy. Thus between 1952 and 1955, China, while not discarding completely her militancy, abandoned at least for the moment efforts to overthrow "bourgeois nationalist" governments in Asia, agreed to a Korean truce, and participated in an international conference in Geneva, which halted fighting in Indochina. In April, 1955, China joined twenty-eight Asian and African states at Bandung, Indonesia, in pledging increased economic and cultural co-operation, respect for human rights and self-determination, and work for peace through universal disarmament. She attempted to implement these principles

through increased trade with nonaligned countries and the extension of economic and technical aid to nations whose peoples were certainly in no greater plight than the Chinese themselves.[21]

But peaceful co-existence was in turn supplanted by still other tactics, some of which, significantly, were not developed jointly with the Soviet Union. International tensions mounted in 1958–1959 as the Chinese Communists opened bombardment of Nationalist-held islands off the mainland coast, employed troops to beat down uprisings in Tibet, and skirmished with Indian forces along the ill-defined Indo-Tibetan border.[22] In Peking's view Taiwan and Tibet, both of which had a history of foreign influence or control, were symbolic of the hated imperialism. Thus it was important to redeem them (India was alleged to be plotting with Tibetan rebels) and to establish China's own definition of her boundaries. The pursuit of these nationalistic goals, however, marked China's unmistakable break with peaceful co-existence and with its sponsor, the Soviet Union. Moscow displayed little enthusiasm for becoming entangled with the United States, Taiwan's protector, over an issue that was so distinctively Chinese. With respect to the border dispute, Soviet policy dictated open sympathy with the Indian cause. From this point onward, China and the Soviet Union became rivals in an emerging bid for leadership of the Communist world.

Sino-Soviet rivalry, as it developed, was expressed publicly as diverging interpretations of Communist doctrine. Thus the Chinese, attacking peaceful co-existence, maintained that Communists ceased to be Communists when they no longer made revolutions. The Russians, on the other hand, affirmed that peaceful co-existence

[21]Among nations receiving aid were: North Korea, North Vietnam, the Mongolian People's Republic, Cambodia, Nepal, Hungary, and Egypt.

[22] Alastair Lamb, *The Chinese-Indian Border: The Origins of the Disputed Boundaries* (1964)* tends to support Chinese claims. Gondkar Narayana Rao, *The India-China Border: A Reappraisal* (Bombay, 1968) is a good statement of the Indian case.

aided revolution because friction within capitalist countries increased when tension outside was reduced. These and other doctrinal points, however, were entangled with important conflicts in the national interests of the two Communist giants. As the leader of a Communist revolution and of the world's most populous nation, Mao aspired at least to equality with his Russian comrades in determining basic Communist bloc policy. The Soviet Union, confident of its own power, and determined to exercise leadership in its own right, was unwilling to give way to Peking. This conflict stemmed from specific issues. By 1958, Chinese Communist leadership had reached the view that China was unequal to taking full advantage of the trade and aid programs of peaceful co-existence. Moreover, it had failed to persuade the Soviet Union either to provide the assistance that would revive the Chinese economy or to alter its doctrinal position. Other differences arose over such questions as to whether the Soviet Union should assist China in attaining nuclear capability; what risks the Russians should take in support of Peking's ambitions to invade Taiwan; the problem of reducing tensions with the United States; and how far the Communist nations should go in encouraging and backing revolutionary armed struggles in underdeveloped regions. In 1969 the Sino-Soviet border became a prime issue as Moscow and Peking accused each other of vast and unjustified territorial designs. Both sides armed the border, and there were brief but sharp clashes along the Manchurian and Sinkiang frontiers. Fighting was followed by an agreement to talk, but the early round of conferences—staged in an atmosphere of intense, public vituperation—held little promise of immediate settlement.[23]

[23] Difficulties presented by border questions were intensified by the absence in the Chinese tradition of the Western concept of a border. Thus, "under the Chinese Republic of 1911, under Sun Yat-sen, and under Mao Tse-tung the view was maintained that it was the duty of China to educate and lead weaker people and to help them achieve independence that could, however, never turn against China." Horst Pommerening, *Der Chinesisch-Sowjetische Grenzkon-*

Toward Southeast Asia and Japan, China mixed reminders of her proximity and power with a display of willingness to settle questions on the basis of mutual accommodation. In the developing nations of Africa, Peking supported revolutionary movements, signed trade and aid pacts, and proclaimed the virtues of Chinese communism. These tactics initially were bolstered by the Communists' success in transforming China's economy and in inaugurating a nuclear test program, which enabled China simultaneously to pose as a model for developing countries and a power to be heeded. In the long run, however, Communist China's appeal abroad dimmed as African leaders discovered that in Peking's eyes they were "enemies of the revolution," as Indonesian militarists attempted to link (the evidence was not conclusive) Peking with an alleged Communist plot to seize their country, and as the vaunted Great Leap Forward delivered less than had been promised.[24] The disorders of the Cultural Revolution also tarnished China's image as a nation to be emulated. Nevertheless, by striking out on her own, by supporting her policies with her military, economic, and ideological resources, China demonstrated her intention of regaining a diplomatic initiative that had been lost more than a century ago. Furthermore, despite reverses, China could claim some success. Her dual challenge to Soviet leadership of the Communist movement and to the West's long standing cultural, political, and economic dominance gave her unprecedented prominence in world affairs.

ASPECTS OF CONTEMPORARY CHINA

By 1970 it was evident that Communist China stood in marked contrast both to Old Confucian China and to the China of

flikt: Das Erbe der Ungleichen Vertrage (Olten, 1968). John Gittings, *Survey of the Sino-Soviet Dispute* (1968) documents the broad range of issues over which the two powers have quarreled.

[24] Guy J. Pauker, "The Rise and Fall of Afro-Asian Solidarity," *Asian Survey* 5 (Sept., 1965): 425–32.

Chiang Kai-shek. The Communists had established a new society based on a rigid totalitarianism reaching from Peking to the remotest village, an economy mobilized for purposes of national power, and a social order motivated by Communist ideology. No longer the decadent state of the later years of the Manchus, China had become a world power.

Yet, if Communist leadership was vital in this Chinese transformation, it must also be remembered that the Chinese revolution was not a Communist creation. Many of the most fundamental innovations of which Peking boasted did not originate with the Communist leadership. As the reader of these pages is well aware, the Communists were by no means the first to seek the development of modern industry or the establishment of modern governmental institutions. Nor did they introduce such concepts as nationalism or patriotism to China. Rather, in fostering the adoption of modern institutions and values, the Chinese Communists, while going further than any of their predecessors, capitalized on changes set in motion by a century of the Western impact on China. Moreover, when viewed in the light of China's long history, even the most modern aspects of the Communist state might be discerned as containing some echoes of the past. While no government of Old China operated with the power or effectiveness of the contemporary regime, Communist China inherited a political tradition dominated by concepts of authoritarianism, centralization of government, and control of the populace. The Communist emphasis on remolding the masses was reminiscent of the Confucian and neo-Confucian stress on ideological orthodoxy, conformity, and thought control. And finally, the individual, now the creature of the state, was traditionally subordinated in China to the family, and to other social groups. Contemporary China, while presenting a new face to the world, remained linked with its history.[25] This is not to say that the Communist state was simply a Confucian state in modern dress or

[25] A. Doak Barnett, *Communist China in Perspective* (1962), 43–50.*

an Eastern copy of another Communist regime such as the Soviet Union. On the contrary, emerging China appeared to be taking shape as a distinctive nation, drawing its inspiration from many sources, old and new, Eastern and Western.[26]

[26] Commenting on the complex interplay of historical and contemporary forces influencing present day China, John K. Fairbank has written:
"The *Kuomintang* was the precursor of the Chinese Communist Party in seeking to train a new type of scholar-bureaucrat in a new ideology, so as to revive the functions once performed by the Confucian literati and the classics. . . . Mao in his turn unified the country as a hero risen from the people, like the founders of the Han and Ming. . . . Mao's armies in the 1940's were not a scourge upon the peasantry but avenged their wrongs. He 'won the hearts of the people' sufficiently to secure food and soldiers from territorial bases. He attracted college students to staff his administration. His ideology claimed the Mandate of History, if not of Heaven. Once in power, his regime surveyed, classified and redistributed both the land and the populace. His example mightily affected the peripheral states. Rising to power with barbarian help, he yet patronized Chinese culture and employed scholars to document the record of previous regimes and point the lesson of its fall. In Peking he built a great Red Square, whither came delegations from Southeast Asia and the Western Regions to watch the great processions.

"The reader can continue for himself to recognize the echoes of the past in China today . . . : (1) a single authority co-terminous with civilization, (2) a balanced economy basically managed by the state, (3) an orthodox doctrine which harmonizes and guides all forms of human activity, including the selection of intellectuals for state service. . . . Yet . . . events have now outstripped the historian's precedents. Institutional changes have broken the cadence, and the differences between past and present are as great as the similarities. . . .

"Values have changed as well as institutions. The K'ang-hsi Emperor never watched the calisthenics of ten thousand selected maidens wearing shorts, nor commended sons for denouncing their fathers. . . . He paid no honors to peasants who exceeded norms nor to the idea of progress or the dialectic, though he would have acknowledged the sequence of *yang* and *yin*.

"Since the patterns of the past cannot be entirely expunged, they remain curiously intertwined with new motifs. Peking today has a Marxist-Leninist-Maoist ideological orthodoxy as vigorous as Confucianism used to be; but it believes in progress toward a future millennium, not cyclical repetition descending from a golden

It has sometimes been assumed that the tribulations arising from the Communist transformation were driving the Chinese masses toward revolt. Under Communism, it was noted, the people not only lacked democratic freedoms, but they were deprived of their land and continued to subsist on meager rations of food, clothing, and housing. The assumption was strengthened by the exodus of refugees to Hong Kong. Yet, while Chinese history was replete with instances of uprisings against unpopular governments, it was also evident that revolution in contemporary China involved more than discontent. The Communists, even as they battled among themselves in the Cultural Revolution, commanded a centralized authority making organized opposition exceedingly difficult. Moreover, in the absense of full and reliable data on Chinese opinion, it was tempting to impute to the Chinese a widespread and deep desire to overthrow a regime which was unpopular in the West, especially in the United States. It was, for example, highly improbable that the Chinese masses, having almost no exposure to the ideas and practice of democracy, were deeply concerned over, let alone aware of, their lack of democratic rights. In the event the Communist leadership were to become complacent, or fail in satisfying at least a minimum of the nation's needs, then rebellion, an honored Chinese political theory, could become a reality.[27]

If the Chinese were controlled by their Communist masters, the Communists, in turn, were the captives of China. The Communist regime has said and promised many things only to see events belie its words. To be sure, some promises materialized, but China has not become the often-promised Utopia. The basic facts of Chinese life cannot be wished away: a Chinese populace still largely without education for a complex industrial society; an industrial base smaller in 1949 than the Russian base of 1917; glaring miscalculations by the Communists themselves on the Great Leap Forward. Finally, the most important limiting factor was the pressure of population on available resources. The first Five Year Plan assumed a population of about 480,000,000, but the census of 1953 revealed a total of some 580,000,000. In subsequent years the Communists faced a population growing at a rate of 2 per cent annually, which meant that there were some 732,000,000 Chinese in 1970 and which, if continued, would place China's population at a billion in 1980. These increases before 1960 created food shortages, aroused popular unrest, and slowed industrialization beyond all expectation. While the grain imports and renewed emphasis on food production mentioned earlier helped remove the sense of impending crisis, these measures failed to solve basic problems since growing production barely kept pace with minimum consumptive needs. As in the past, production might prove adequate to permit further development of China's national power but inadequate to give substance to the promise of a better life for her millions.[28]

---

age. Dynastic absolutism has been replaced by party dictatorship. . . . Merchants continue to be disesteemed, being undoubtedly bourgeois, but soldiers are now glorified. . . . Government used to be thinly spread out and superficial and the peasant passive, a sub-political animal. Today the government penetrates every hut, and peasants are people unless they misbehave." *The United States and China* (rev. ed., 1958), 308–10. Joseph R. Levenson, "The Past and Future of Nationalism in China," *Survey*, No. 67 (1968): 28–40, examines the impact of China's past on the Cultural Revolution.

[27] "Looking to the future, the most likely prospect is for a continuing seesaw contest between the regime and the peasantry—a contest that will probably involve severe tensions between a government driven to increase its controls and pressures on agriculture in order to pursue its industrial goals, and a peasant population that can be expected to continue resisting excessive controls and pressures, even if only by dragging its feet." Barnett, *Communist China in Perspective*, 67.

[28] For differing aspects of China's population problems see Leo A. Orlean, "The 1953 Chinese Census in Perspective," *Journal of Asian Studies* 16 (1957): 565–74; Warren S. Thompson, *Population and Progress in the Far East* (1959); Ho Ping-ti, *Studies on the Population of China, 1368–1953* (1959); and S. Chandrasekhar, ed., *Asia's Population Problems* (1966).

GOVERNMENT. Among translations of Communist documents are John Lewis, ed., *Major Doctrines of Communist China* (1964); Center for International Affairs and the East Asian Research Center, Harvard University, *Communist China, 1955–1959: Policy Documents with Analysis* (1962); Theodore H. E. Chen, *The Chinese Communist Regime: Documents and Commentary* (1967); and K. H. Fan, ed., *The Cultural Revolution* (1968). Peter S. H. Tang, *China Today: Domestic and Foreign Policies* (2nd. rev. ed., 1961) is an exhaustive description of the first decade. See also A. Doak Barnett, *Communist China: The Early Years, 1949–1955* (1964). John W. Lewis, *Leadership in Communist China* (1963) is a brilliant study of politics before the "Cultural Revolution." Ezra Vogel, *Canton Under Communism (Programs and Politics in a Provincial Capital, 1949–1969)* (1969), the first extended study of local government under communism. For insights into the army and its political role, see Samuel B. Griffith, *The Chinese People's Liberation Army* (1967); John Gittings, *The Role of the Chinese Army* (1967); and William Whitson, "The Field Army in Chinese Communist Military Politics," *The China Quarterly*, No. 37 (Jan.–Mar. 1969): 1–30.

ECONOMIC DEVELOPMENT. Rhoades Murphey, "Man and Nature in China," *Modern Asian Studies*, I, No. 4 (1967): 313–33, emphasizes the intellectual underpinnings of the drive to industrialize China. Theodore Shabad, *China's Changing Map: A Political and Economic Geography of the Chinese People's Republic* (1956), a reference work. On the early years of economic transformation, see Li Choh-ming, *Economic Development of Communist China: An Appraisal of the First Five Years of Industrialization* (1959); T. J. Hughes and D. E. T. Luard, *Economic Development of Communist China, 1949–1960* (2nd rev. ed., 1962); and Chen Chi-yi, *La Reforme Agraire en Chine Populaire* (Paris, 1964). Two sophisticated studies of food production having anti-collectiviza-

tion biases are John L. Buck, Owen L. Dawson, and Yuan-li Wu, *Food and Agriculture in Communist China* (1966); and Owen L. Dawson, *Communist China's Agriculture: Its Development and Future Potential* (1970). Alexander Eckstein, *The National Income of Communist China* (1962); and Liu Ta-chung and Yeh Kung-chia, *The Economy of the Chinese Mainland: National Income and Economic Development, 1933–1959* (1965) develop base lines against which development may be measured. See also Alexander Eckstein, "Sino-Soviet Economic Relations: A Reappraisal," in *The Economic Development of China and Japan*, C. D. Cowan ed. (1964).

INTELLECTUAL AND SOCIAL LIFE. Aspects of intellectual developments are presented in C. O. Fitzgerald, *The Chinese View of their Place in the World* (London, 1964); Owen Lattimore, *From China, Looking Outward: An Inaugural Lecture* (Leeds, 1964); Mu Fu-sheng, *The Wilting of the Hundred Flowers: The Chinese Intelligentsia under Mao* (1963); Franklin Houn, *To Change a Nation: Propaganda and Indoctrination in Communist China* (1961); Albert Feuerwerker, ed., *History in Communist China* (1968); Stephen Uhalley, Jr., "The Controversy over Li Hsiu-ch'eng: An Ill-timed Centenary," *Journal of Asian Studies* 25 (1966): 305–17; Merle Goldman, *Literary Dissent in Communist China* (1967); and Francis P. Jones, *The Church in Communist China: A Protestant Appraisal* (1962). See also Cyril Birch, ed., *Chinese Communist Literature* (1963); Wingtsit Chan, *Religious Trends in Modern China* (1953); and Sidney H. Gould, *Science in Communist China* (1961).

Edgar Snow, *The Other Side of the River: Red China Today* (1962) is a sympathetic report by a seasoned journalist. Similarly sympathetic is William Hinton, *Fanshen: A Documentary of Revolution in a Chinese Village* (1966). William T. Liu, *Chinese Society under Communism* (1967) reveals patterns of control. The revolution's impact on family life is treated in Yang Ch'ing-k'un, *A Chinese Village in Early*

Communist Transition (1959). Two important studies pointing to the persistence of traditional legal practices in a revolutionary society are Stanley Lubman, "Mao and Mediation: Politics and Dispute Resolution in Communist China," *California Law Review* 55 (1967): 1284–1359; and Jerome A. Cohen, *The Criminal Process in the People's Republic of China, 1949–1963* (1968).

IDEOLOGY. On Mao and his ideas, see Jerome Chen, *Mao and the Chinese Revolution* (1965); Stuart Schram, *Mao Tse-tung* (1966), and *The Political Thought of Mao Tse Tung* (rev. ed., 1969); Arthur A. Cohen, *The Communism of Mao Tse-tung* (1964); and "What is Maoism: A Symposium," *Problems of Communism* 15 (Sept.-Oct., 1966): 1–30. Chung Hua-min and Arthur C. Miller, *Madame Mao–A Profile of Chiang Ch'ing* (Hong Kong, 1968).

FOREIGN RELATIONS. Robert A. Scalapino, "Tradition and Transition in the Asian Policy of Communist China," in *Symposium on Economic and Social Problems of the Far East, University of Hong Kong, 1961, Proceedings* (Hong Kong, 1963), 262–77, views Communist foreign policy as a product of traditionalism, nationalism, and Communist ideology. An absorbing and comprehensive treatment is Harold C. Hinton, *Communist China in World Politics* (1966). For a study of border problems, see Alastair Lamb, *Asian Frontiers: Studies in a Continuing Problem* (1968); Klaus Menhart, *Peking and Moscow* (1963), a basic study. For aspects of China's nuclear diplomacy, see Alice L. Hsieh, *Communist China's Strategy in the Nuclear Age* (1962); Morton H. Halperin, *China and the Bomb* (1965); and Morton H. Halperin and Dwight H. Perkins, *Communist China and Arms Control* (1965). Military dimensions of foreign policy are treated in Ralph Powell, "Maoist Military Doctrines," *Asian Survey* 8 (1968): 239–62; and Alexander L. George, *The Chinese Army in Action: The Korean War and Its Aftermath* (1967). The impact of the "Cultural Revolution" on foreign relations is studied in Klaus Mehnert, *Peking and the New Left: At Home and Abroad* (1969).

For specialized treatment of Sino-American relations, see Robert Blum, *The United States and China in World Affairs* (1966); William W. Lockwood, ed., *The United States and Communist China* (1965); and Tang Tsou, ed., *China in Crisis: Volume II; China's Policies in Asia and America's Alternatives* (1968).

RECENT DEVELOPMENTS. Allan B. Cole and Peter C. Oleson, comps., *Fifty Years of Chinese Communism: Selected Readings with Commentary*, Publication No. 47, Service Center for Teachers of History: The American Historical Association (1970) serves both as a guide to further reading and an interpretation of Chinese Communist history. Study of the current scene may be pursued in excellent periodicals: *Pacific Affairs; Asian Survey; China Quarterly; Far Eastern Economic Survey;* and *Journal of Asian Studies.* See also annual volumes of collected essays published by the Union Research Institute under the title, *Communist China.*

Toward a New Japan:
1952 and After

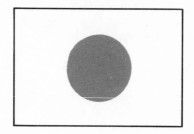

chapter 34

With the ending of the American Occupation in 1952, Japan faced problems as complex as any in her modern history. She was faced with making the transition from a defeated, humiliated, and occupied state under foreign control to a sovereign nation responsible for its own destiny. Immediate tasks included the maintenance of a stable and prosperous economy in islands poor in natural resources, and the organization of an infant democratic political and social order brought to the islands by the Occupation. Moreover, by virtue of its location on the periphery of the Communist world and its treaty obligations to the United States, Japan was involved immediately in tense international questions. Clearly the post-Occupation years were not to be free of the pressures, domestic or foreign, that had been remolding Japanese life for a century. But what was to be the impact of these pressures on the Occupation's reforms? Would democratic institutions survive, or would there be a return to authoritarianism? How durable was an alliance that denied to the Japanese their age-old links with the China mainland? Was Japan capable of supporting an expanding population without resort to another drive for empire? [1]

---

[1] Two brief but basic studies of Japanese development since 1952 are in E. O. Reischauer's *The United States and Japan* (rev. ed., 1961),* 291–337; and *Japan: The Story of a Nation* (1970),* ·242–340.

ECONOMIC RECOVERY

Economic rebuilding was a fundamental task in a land described by Joseph M. Dodge, MacArthur's financial adviser, as having "too many people, too little land, and too few natural resources." While Japanese cities were still scarred by war, the country as a whole suffered less from actual fighting than from the loss of 311,514 square kilometers (46 per cent) of its pre-war territory. No longer did Japan have direct control of the mineral and agricultural resources of Korea and Manchuria, the sugar and rice of Formosa, or the pulp of Sakhalin. Nor could her fishing fleets exploit the waters of Korea and the Kuriles and other shores of the northern Pacific. Complicating the problem of a reduced economic base was the specter of an expanding population. The return of some 6,000,000 Japanese from the colonies, and a continuing high birth rate boosted Japan from a nation of 72,000,000 in 1945 to one of 90,000,000 a decade later. Furthermore, there was the problem of rebuilding foreign markets to provide exchange for the imports Japan must have to survive. Some of Japan's former customers, especially in Southeast Asia, remembering the tragedies of World War II, traded elsewhere. Even worse was the disappearance of Japan's most numerous customers, the Chinese and North Koreans, behind the Bamboo Curtain. Altogether these manifold problems imperiled the economic recovery that had begun in the latter years of the Occupation.

Yet, the economic outlook was not hopeless. Japan retained the skills and energies which had made her a major competitor of the West. In the context of the Cold War her human resources assumed a new importance in the struggle for control of the Western Pacific and Southeast Asia. Japan became a major supplier of industrial goods and services for United States forces in this area. American expenditures, first for direct aid and later for special procurement, reached about $800,000,000 a year in 1952–1953 and continued at better than $500,000,000 annually through 1957. These expenditures provided a powerful stimulus to economic development, enabling Japan to balance her payments and build a surplus in foreign exchange even though imports were generally larger than exports during these years. Furthermore, Japan's industrial experience encouraged exploitation of the latest and most sophisticated industrial techniques. Through the negotiation of technical assistance contracts, Japanese industrialists imported technology and capital from the West, especially the United States, in a wide range of concerns from shipbuilding to electronics. With this help, Japanese enterprise invaded new fields of activity, thus compensating for time lost during the war.

ECONOMIC DEVELOPMENT

Enlightened national fiscal policies provided for economic progress through the encouragement of private investment. Coupled with these measures was a government-assisted search for markets involving not only the sale of Japanese goods to new customers in the West but also intensive efforts to regain old customers in non-Communist Asia. A stimulus was given these efforts when Burma, April, 1955, settled reparation questions and reopened trade, thus clearing the way for similar understandings with other Southeast Asian countries. Another government program emphasized population control as a long-term measure to ease

economic pressures. In giving full support to the Eugenics Protection Law of 1948, whereby both birth control and abortion were encouraged, the average annual increase was lowered to 1 per cent—one of the world's lowest rates. This achievement did not mean an immediate curtailment of larger numbers, but the controls established did promise a leveling off of population at a little over 100,000,000 toward the end of the century.[2]

Beyond these measures, factors over which post-Occupation Japan itself had relatively little control contributed to economic growth. Under the new Constitution prohibiting rearmament, Japan was spared the heavy pre-war costs of maintaining large military forces and conducting overseas operations. Reconstruction of bombed-out industrial facilities provided opportunities for the installation of the latest productive equipment, giving Japanese manufacturers advantages over foreign competitors. Moreover, the Japanese drive to expand exports benefited from a world-wide liberalization of trade policies and a general rise in international trade.[3]

The product of these various programs and events was an unanticipated economic boom regarded as one of the miracles of the post-war era. By 1956 all major Japanese economic indexes, except trade, exceeded pre-war (1934–1936) peaks. Manufacturing and mining outputs were double pre-war levels; the increase in the generation of electric power was even greater; most branches of agriculture, forestry, and fisheries were

[2] Irene Taeuber, *The Population of Japan* (1958), 386–89.

[3] Robert B. Hall, Jr., *Japan: Industrial Power of Asia* (1963),* 54–70. While Japan benefited from liberalized trade and investment policies, Japanese markets, especially capital markets, were protected against foreign competition. By the late 1960s, as the Japanese economy was soundly established, Tokyo came under heavy foreign pressure to liberalize its own policies. The issue was particularly acute in American-Japanese relations and led to negotiations in which Americans were granted some enlarged opportunity. See Leon Hollerman, *Japan's Dependence on the World Economy: The Approach toward Economic Liberalization* (1967).

operating about 30 per cent above the 1934–1936 rate; real national income per capita was up 16 per cent. These figures signified full recovery from the dislocations of war and the beginnings of intensive new development, which by the late 1960s had boosted her Gross National Product to third place among the world's industrial powers and had made her Asia's undisputed industrial leader. For example, Japan produced more than half of the electrical energy generated in all of Asia, excluding Soviet Siberia. Ranked against all nations, Japan was fifth in production of crude steel and fourth in production of cement. She led the world in the manufacture of merchant shipping, and her automobiles, television sets, cameras, and other sophisticated consumer goods were major competitors on world markets.

RISING LIVING STANDARDS

For the Japanese this economic boom was significant in producing a spectacular rise in living standards. The traditional essentials of diet expanded to include milk, butter, cheese, ice cream, and meat. There was an abundance of clothing for all seasons. The demand for housing to replace that destroyed by war and to fill the needs of an expanding populace created a backlog which the building trades reduced slowly. Roads were crowded with far more motorized vehicles—buses, trucks, taxis, private cars, and motor scooters—than before the war. Most Japanese enjoyed more education and more of most other services than ever before. Indeed, along with the populace of highly industrialized Western states, the Japanese by the 1960s were trying to discover what to do with their leisure hours.[4] This was not to suggest, of course, that Japan had become an economic paradise. Slums, malnutrition, and sweatshops were also in the picture, making Japan, compared to the West, still a poor nation. Nevertheless, she was once again the richest Asian country, and her people

[4] See David W. Plath, *The After Hours: Modern Japan and the Search for Enjoyment* (1964).

were sharing in this prosperity to a degree unparalleled in their history.

While popular expectations were geared for new economic achievement, the specter of lean years lurked amid growing plenty. Japan's economy remained a sensitive mechanism requiring complex adjustments. Within the nation, for example, manufacturers faced the necessity of raising productivity in order to compensate for higher labor costs. At the same time, population growth, although checked over the long run, required at least until 1970 the creation of 1,000,000 new jobs every year. Even more difficult than these internal problems were external ones arising from Japan's utter dependence on foreign trade. Without expansion of its trade and industry Japan would be a relatively minor nation, small, overpopulated, and highly vulnerable. Yet, to sustain the industrial miracle upon which her improved standard of living depended, Japan after 1952 had to cope with fresh foreign competition, drives discriminating against Japanese goods, and the establishment of economic blocs, such as the European Economic Community. Moreover, there was an ever present danger of a precipitous decline in the total volume of world trade in which Japan shared. Although none of these problems was peculiar to Japan, they dramatized the unusual degree to which the Japanese were sensitive to global trends and decisions beyond their control. Little in Japan's post-war record suggested how she would respond to sharp pressures on the material basis of her society.[5]

SOCIAL CHANGE

The American Occupation laid the legal foundations of a social revolution designed to uphold democratic political institutions. At the upper levels, the power of the hereditary aristocracy and military elite was broken, and the control of the traditional business leadership was shaken seriously. At lower levels, the Occupation sought to expand individual opportunity, and to build safeguards

[5] For a concise discussion of the crucial importance of trade, see Hall, *Japan*, 93–107.

against a return of authoritarian government by inculcating democratic values. These reforms during the Occupation and after laid the foundations for an evolving society which, while not breaking completely with the past, was new and distinctive both in its organization and outlook.

Among the most important social changes was the appearance of a new middle class. Some middle-class recruits came from the old aristocracy whose wealth and position had been destroyed by the war, inflation, and the Occupation's reforms. Far more numerous, however, were additions from the humbler social orders. In the cities, enlarged opportunities in business and government awaited individuals, irrespective of social origins. In the countryside, upward social mobility was the product of land reform, technological improvement, and unprecedented prosperity. Meanwhile, as the middle class expanded, the lesser social groupings shrank to a point where they constituted a smaller proportion of the populace than before the war.

The tendency toward an economic leveling was also part of a striking transformation in popular attitudes toward authority. While the Japanese remained conscious of class distinctions, the old practices and manners associated with traditional elitist society were eroding. Marked displays of deference shown before the war by inferiors to superiors tended to diminish. As family controls were relaxed, the younger generations spoke with a louder voice in the choice of their schooling, their vocations, and their marriage partners. Women showed an increased self-confidence, assertiveness, and independence not only in feminine fashions but also in politics.[6] Far less formality char-

acterized social contacts and personal relationships. Japanese everyday behavior in personal contacts suggested less of status and more of equality. This new spirit was not as yet a dominant theme but its further development, backed by new legal codes and strengthened by social fluidity, appeared likely.[7]

---

[6] A sampling of voter behavior in 1963 suggests the extent of the transformation wrought by the removal of the sex barrier to political participation. The sample revealed that levels of education and income were more important than sex in determining individual's participation in political processes. In general, Japanese in the lower ranks of education and income, irrespective of sex, participated less than did those in the higher ranks. Alice and Yasumasa Kuroda, "Aspects of Community Political Participation in

Japan: Sex, Education, and Generation in the Process of Political Socialization," *Journal of Asian Studies* 27 (1968): 229–51.

[7] The interplay of traditional and modern behavior in contemporary Japanese life is revealed in patterns among corporate executives. A college graduate typically enters a firm as a staff member immediately after graduation. He works toward appointment as a deputy section manager in seven to ten years and as section manager in an additional four to six years. This latter position represents major achievement for, in addition to having ten to twenty subordinates, the young executive acquires social prestige. Only about two out of ten section managers will continue to rise further along the promotion ladder. Thus, life is extremely competitive. Section managers work hard and socialize with superiors late into the night, sacrificing family life. Yet, once a man joins a firm he rarely leaves it, since frequent job changes are regarded as evidence of undependability. Companies in turn seldom fire an employee unless he performs disgracefully. The ambitious young executive conforms to the seniority system, whereby a junior officer seldom gets more money than his senior regardless of capability. Senior officers not infrequently counsel subordinates in business and personal matters. In consequence, the subordinate develops an obedient, filial relationship with his boss and works hard as a member of a "family" team. The Japanese firm values group spirit more than individual capability or willingness to take responsibility. Such industrial practices reflect the persistence of traditions and attitudes, particularly those of feudal Japan when loyalty and benevolence, duty and respect for authority were social moralities; when lords assured the securities of life in return for the loyalty of vassals. For a case study see John E. Thayer, III, "Tokugawa vs. Madison Avenue: Age-old Traditions Behind East-West Conflicts in a Modern Tokyo Advertising Agency," *Papers on Japan*, Vol. 4. East Asian Research Center, Harvard University (1967): 215–27. Other Aspects of changing social attitudes are treated in two articles by George DeVos and Hioshi Wagatsuma, "Value Attitudes toward Role Behavior in Two Japanese Villages," *American Anthropologist* 63 (1961): 1204–30; and "Attitudes toward Arranged Marriage in Rural Japan," *Human Or-*

Striking too were shifts in Japanese opinion on questions of politics and political theory. Nationalism in its extremer forms was no longer a beloved emotion. Shaken by defeat, and disillusioned by the record of the militarists and the superpatriots, probably most Japanese developed a vigorous skepticism on all overseas adventures. When proposals were advanced to amend the constitution to provide a legal basis for rearmament, there was pronounced opposition. Symptomatic, too, was a notable decline in the habit of flag waving.

A new rejection of political authoritarianism was revealed in the treatment accorded the emperor, formerly the divine personification of the nation before whom all bowed. In his altered status as the "symbol of the State and of the unity of the people," the emperor, whose popularity was attested by crowds greeting his public appearances, continued to be the most powerful focus of political loyalties, but no longer did he receive homage as an awesome symbol of authority. Rather he was popular as the human, democratized figure whose personal life was detailed in the press and whose son, the Crown Prince, took a commoner for his wife.[8]

Still another aspect of post-war political thought was a Japanese world view colored by Marxism. After World War II, Marxism, largely suppressed since its initial appearance in Japan in the 1920s, was seized upon by some Japanese as an alternative to the discredited philosophy of a military nationalism. Japanese Communists and Socialists

_____

ganization 21 (1962): 187–200; and Ezra F. Vogel's "The Democratization of Family Relations in Japanese Urban Society," *Asian Survey* 1 (1961): 18–24. See also Marius B. Jansen, ed., *Changing Japanese Attitudes toward Modernization* (1965).*

[8] Public opinion surveys indicated growing acceptance between 1952 and 1959 of the emperor's status as defined in the new constitution. Takeshi Ishida, "Popular Attitudes toward the Japanese Emperor," *Asian Survey* 2 (1962): 29–39.

achieved a prominence in the press, in university faculties, and in the powerful teachers' union, which imparted to Japanese thought a flavor oddly at variance with Japan's actual political and economic practices. While profits and wages rose to unprecedented heights, Japanese in many walks of life spoke glibly of the collapse of capitalism resulting from the "exploitation" of labor. War and international tensions were frequently ascribed to "capitalist imperialism." Nevertheless, Japanese in general showed more enthusiasm for close relations with the United States and Western Europe than with the Soviet Union.

Finally the Japanese mind in this period was characterized by what Professor E. O. Reischauer has called an "American fixation." [9] Defeat at American hands, the Occupation, and continuation of close ties beyond 1952 created a relationship unparalleled even by historic Sino-Japanese ties. In consequence, to most Japanese the United States appeared to enter and to meddle in every issue. Japanese advocates of nonalignment, of neutrality, or of alignment with the Communist world attacked the Japanese-American Security Treaty and the presence of American bases on Japanese soil. At the other end of the political spectrum, more traditionally-minded Japanese berated the United States as responsible for democratic reforms unsuited to Japan's circumstances and temperament. Others criticized Japan's economic dependence upon the United States. These anxieties, whatever the degree of their significance, made it quite evident that many years after the end of the Occupation the United States was still regarded as playing a key role in Japan's national and international life.

The foregoing suggestions on the nature of the new Japan are subject to many qualifications. For one thing, Japanese political and social thought were far less unified than before the war. The younger generations accepted new attitudes more readily than their parents. Sharp differences among political

[9] *Japan: Past and Present*, (3rd ed. rev., 1964), 256.

parties and their followings accentuated ideological diversity. Egalitarian tendencies made little headway among rural inhabitants and the less educated city dwellers. Nor did old attitudes on authority disappear completely. Village leaders and elders continued to enjoy respect, and large segments of the population continued to regard politics as a matter with which the leaders rather than the average citizen should be concerned. Moreover, as conditions changed, the new attitudes also tended to shift. For example, as Japan's booming economy restored national self-confidence, the appeal of Marxian dogmatism declined measurably. Increased contact with other nations contributed to some fading of the "American fixation." Thus attitudes that were strong during the first post-Occupation decade were by no means constant in subsequent years. Their fate in years ahead would undoubtedly exercise a major influence on Japan's future.[10]

GOVERNMENT AND POLITICS

Although the Japanese political system underwent extensive reform during the Occupation, politics retained a remarkable continuity from pre-war days. If the military elite, uprooted and discredited, no longer was an important pressure group, government continued to be dominated by the bureaucracy and big business. The bureaucracy gained new power because of its near monopoly of expert opinion on the complex problems of modern government. The Diet and cabinet, ill-equipped to deal with these problems, was dependent on bureaucrats in making policy decisions and in formulating legislation. The same voice was also heard from bureaucrats who, upon retirement, filled elective offices. Except for a period of a little over three years, Japanese cabinets after 1945 were headed by former bureaucrats. Ex-bureaucrats were heavily represented in cabinet memberships and in the Diet. Also close, but less well defined were

[10] Reischauer, *Japan: Past and Present*, 246–58.

the ties linking government and the highly integrated management of Japan's larger business firms, a revived *zaibatsu*. Big business became a major source of funds for ruling parties, while party and business leaders maintained the closest co-operation.[11] Against these power combinations, other pressure groups, such as organized labor, were relatively ineffective.

POLITICAL PARTIES

Japan's post-war political parties were likewise rooted in the past. The *Seiyukai* and *Minseito*, the two major pre-war parties, re-emerged after 1945 to dominate party politics as the Liberals (*Jiyuto*) and the Progressives (*Shimpoto*, reorganized in 1947 as the Democratic Party or *Minshuto*). In resuming operations these parties retained much of their old leadership, cultivated their established constituencies in rural Japan, and were financed as before the war largely by business contributions. Left wing groups, Socialists and Communists, similarly could trace their origins to pre-war parties having the support of intellectuals and urban workers. Moreover, like their predecessors, these post-war parties were riddled by factionalism. The Liberal-Democratic party (*Jiyu-Minshuto*), which had been formed by a merger in 1955, was divided during the earlier months of Ikeda Hayato's leadership into no less than eight factions holding seats in the House of Representatives. On the Left, repeated attempts at a "united front" failed to effect a lasting union of Socialists and Communists. Meanwhile Socialist strength was dissipated by party feuds which led successively to the shearing off of splinter groups in 1948; a party split into right and left wing groups, 1950–1955; party reunification; and another

[11] Chitoshi Yanaga, *Big Business in Japanese Politics* (1968). Yamamura Kozo, "*Zaibatsu*, Prewar and *Zaibatsu*, Postwar," *Journal of Asian Studies* 23 (1964): 539–54, rejects "*zaibatsu*" as an appropriate label for post-war industrial combinations.

split in 1960 resulting in establishment of the Japan Socialist Party (*Nihon Shakaito*) and the Democratic Socialist Party (*Nihon Minshu Shakaito*).[12] The chief distinction between the various factions in parties of the Left and Right is not easily summarized. Among Socialists and Communists (the Communists organized under the *Nihon Kysanto*), party factions stemmed for the most part from ideological differences, whereas Liberal-Democratic factions arose almost entirely from more personal rivalries.

Finally, there was continuity in Japanese voting patterns. Politics was dominated by right wing parties, but the Socialists resumed their slow growth in popular support that could be detected before World War II. In national elections the combined vote for all Socialist candidates rose from little better than 20 per cent of the total balloting in 1952 to a little less than 40 per cent ten years later. Even more encouraging to the Socialists was their success in gaining the support of younger voters, an element which was in numerical ascendency. Following the elections of 1963, Socialist leaders predicted control of government within eight years. It remained to be seen, however, whether this trend toward the Socialists would continue, or, indeed, whether the Socialists could attain sufficient unity to hold power if it came within their grasp.[13]

Although American control of Japan's

---

[12] The evolution of post-war parties is traced briefly in Robert E. Ward, *Japan's Political System* (1967).*

[13] See two articles by Robert Scalapino: "Japanese Socialism in Crisis," *Foreign Affairs,* 38 (1960): 1–11; and "The Left Wing in Japan," *Survey,* No. 43 (1962): 102–11. Elections in the late 1960's suggested that the Socialists' optimism was ill-founded. While a burgeoning urban populace harbored resentment against the ruling party, Socialists, divided and doctrinaire, were unable to sustain their appeal to the protest voters. In 1967 Socialist parties lost four seats in the House of Representatives, but a Socialist won the governorship of Tokyo. Disaster struck in the elections of 1969 when Socialists lost fifty seats in the House of Representatives. Some of the more radical Socialists were switching to the Communist Party. Many more drifted toward the conservatives or to the *Komeito,* the political arm of the *Soka Gakkai.*

government was relaxed beginning in 1949 and was withdrawn altogether three years later, Japanese politics still retained the flavor of defeat. Premier Yoshida, whose Liberal party won the nation's first post-Occupation election, October 1, 1952, wrestled with adjustments in the Occupation's reforms, problems of economic recovery, and restoration of normal relations with other nations. In these as in almost every other important issue over the next decade the influence of the United States real or imagined figured prominently.

While the Yoshida Ministry was committed to upholding Japan's new constitution and its bill of rights, the government became identified with the restoration of centralized control. On May Day, 1952, the Communists, who had instigated a number of student strikes, and whose strength at the polls had been growing steadily, organized a mass rally in Tokyo culminating in pitched battles with the police. Yoshida's response was to request parliamentary action on an Anti-subversive Activity Law and a measure increasing the government's control over the police. The first of these was opposed unsuccessfully by organized labor on grounds that a provision giving the cabinet power to ban activities leading to violence would endanger legitimate union operations. The proposed Police Law was more controversial in that it provided for a return of some practices through which the police, operating under the Home Minister, had been a dreaded instrument of an authoritarian state. Protesting vehemently, opponents blocked the bill until 1954, when, following new general elections, additional votes were mustered for its passage.[14] Meanwhile, some voters, reacting apparently to Communist violence at home and abroad, deserted the party. In the election of 1952, the Communists lost all thirty-five of their parliamentary seats, and their portion of the total vote declined to 2.6 per cent.

Controversy also swirled about Yoshida as his government transformed the Police Reserve into a National Security Force and

---

[14] D. C. S. Sissons, "The Dispute over Japan's Police Law," *Pacific Affairs* 32 (1959): 34–45.

approved, March, 1954, a Mutual Defense Assistance Agreement broadening the United States-Japanese Security Treaty into a defensive alliance. Under the agreement's terms the United States renewed its pledge to fight in Japan's defense, while Japan agreed to maintain prohibitions on trade with Communist China and to build its military forces again Communist aggression.

Both the agreement and the transformation of the Police Reserve violated deep Japanese convictions that war was reprehensible and that it might be avoided if Japan remained neutral and unarmed. Moreover, the changed status of the Police Reserve raised questions about the need to revise the constitution to eliminate the article on the renunciation of war. While Yoshida argued that constitutional revision was unnecessary since Japanese forces were purely defensive, he found many political, religious, and social groups arrayed against him. The Communists and left wing Socialists opposed rearmament and closer alliance with the United States, but they were not alone in this position. Many Japanese of other political persuasions feared the economic drain imposed by military reconstruction and resented being used by the United States as a buffer against Communism. Mixed with these fears were others holding that rearmament would lead to renewed military leadership. In contrast with these arguments, a few ultranationalists castigated the measures because they failed to provide for sufficiently rapid militarization.

Yoshida prevailed against the opposition, carrying both controversial measures in the Diet, but the effort weakened his hold on power. Revelation that Japan suffered a trade deficit resulting from a drop in American procurement toppled the Ministry, and in December, 1954, control of the cabinet passed to Hatoyama Ichiro, who once had been president of the Liberal party but was then serving as leader of the Democrats (*Minshuto*).[5] Subsequently Hatoyama's cabinet was backed jointly by the Liberals and Democrats as those parties merged to meet the challenge of a united Socialist party.

Under Hatoyama, Japan tackled unsettled questions arising from the absence of a peace treaty with the Soviet Union. A fisheries agreement, May, 1956, and a joint statement, October 19, 1956, terminating the state of war and re-establishing diplomatic relations served as initial steps toward the opening of limited trade under terms of a commercial treaty concluded at the end of the following year. Meanwhile, Japan joined the United Nations as a result of the Soviet Union's dropping its opposition. These accomplishments failed to produce entirely amicable relations. On the contrary, Japanese opinion was offended by the Russian failure to return several small islands off Hokkaido and by her procrastination in the repatriation of Japanese prisoners.[16] Dissatisfaction with the handling of Soviet affairs turned factions within the ruling party against the prime minister. These difficulties plus Hatoyama's own failing health forced the cabinet's collapse in December, 1956. Liberal-Democratic party leadership, however, continued under governments headed first by Ishibashi Tanzan and then by Kishi Nobusuke.

While Kishi's parliamentary majority was soon confirmed by a Liberal-Democratic victory at the polls, his administration confronted dual hazards arising from factional rivalries within its supporting party base and increased Socialist strength. Furthermore, Kishi came to power as Japanese opinion demanded a new disposition of questions relating to China and the United States as well as the Soviet Union. With respect to China, Socialists and Communists led criticism of the nation's isolation from its neighbor and urged reopening for formal relations. The appeal of these arguments, however, was limited by no means to left wing groups. Among Japanese in general, China was viewed with a peculiar mixture of admiration and con-

---

[15] Hugh Borton, *Japan's Modern Century* (1955), 444–52.

[16] Antipathy toward the Soviet Union was one of the few attitudes common to most Japanese. See James W. Morley, "Japan's Image of the Soviet Union, 1952–1961," *Pacific Affairs* 35 (1962): 51–58.

descension, an attitude encouraging support for the fullest contacts with the source of Japanese civilization. Even right wing businessmen were attracted by the potentialities of the China market. Such sentiments were scarcely satisfied by informal contacts, whereby the Kishi Ministry permitted limited Sino-Japanese trade under private agreement and allowed Japanese delegations to travel to China. Public opinion persisted in looking toward the expansion and formalization of these contacts, even though China's economic limitations promised to curtail trade volume and Peking's motives in promoting the relationship were clearly political.[17] For the Kishi Ministry the problem was one of resolving these pressures while maintaining Japan's treaty commitments to the United States.

Related to but not identical with this problem was one of meeting the increasingly vehement attacks on Japan's close ties with the United States. The Socialist opposition charged that the Japanese-American alliance simultaneously limited Japan's initiative in dealing with nations such as China and threatened Japan with involvement in nuclear war. To a Japanese public already aroused by American nuclear tests in the southwest Pacific and irritated by the presence of American bases in Japan, these were telling arguments. By 1958 criticism was so widespread that the Kishi Ministry and Eisenhower Administration opened negotiations which resulted two years later in the signature of a new Treaty of Mutual Security and Co-operation providing for (1) American consultations with Japan before Japanese bases were employed for war in Asia or nuclear weapons were introduced to Japanese soil, and (2) the imposition of a ten-year limit on American claims to Japanese bases after which either party might

seek a cancellation. These concessions to Japanese sensibilities were intended to ease pressures on the Kishi Ministry, but they failed to meet the basic charge that the alliance was unwise and should be terminated.

The Socialists did not have enough votes to block parliamentary approval of the treaty, but several incidents gained public support for their position and turned opinion against the Kishi Ministry. Early in May, 1960, while a vote was pending, the downing of an American U-2 reconnaissance plane inside of the Soviet Union, the cancellation of a scheduled summit conference between President Eisenhower and Premier Khrushchev, and the intensification of the Cold War dramatized afresh for the Japanese the risks entailed by an alliance with the United States. Amid these events, Premier Kishi, desiring apparently to complete ratification of the new defense treaty before a scheduled visit by President Eisenhower to Japan, called a surprise vote on the treaty while opponents were not on the floor of the House of Representatives. These tactics won the treaty's approval, but the way was opened for a double-barrel attack on the substance of the alliance and the Ministry's "dictatorial" procedures. As the Eisenhower visit approached, demonstrations, which were spearheaded by left wing organizations but supported by a formidable number of persons with more moderate leanings, paralyzed Tokyo, humiliating and intimidating the government. The Eisenhower visit was cancelled at Tokyo's request, and Kishi, badly shaken and confronted with the refusal of key factions within his own party to support his leadership, resigned in favor of the Liberal-Democrat, Ikeda Hayato, another ex-bureaucrat and protégé of Yoshida.[18]

With Ikeda's appointment Japanese

---

[17] Popular enthusiasm for enlarged contacts with China were set back temporarily in May, 1958, when Peking, seizing upon the destruction of a Chinese Communist flag by a rightist youth in Nagasaki, cut off all trade. China's intent was to exert a favorable influence on the left wing vote in Japan's impending parliamentary elections. Not only did the effort fail, as Japanese were outraged by these crude tactics, but trade was slow in rebuilding to its earlier levels.

[18] The coalition opposing the Mutual Security Treaty was unbelievably fragmented and its elements opposed to one another. Yet the opposition was not deadlocked because it was broadly based on a public mood that was concerned not with ideology but with Japan's involvement in nuclear war and with the threat to democracy inherent in the "tyranny of the majority." George R. Packard, *Protest in Tokyo: The Treaty Crisis of 1960* (1966). J. A. A. Stockwin, *The Japanese Socialist Party and Neutralism* (1968).

politics unexpectedly entered a period of smoother sailing. Rioters disappeared, and the aura of crisis no longer colored government operations. General elections in November, 1960, revealed no extensive damage to the Liberal-Democratic party. Its percentage (57.6) of the total popular vote was almost identical with 1958. Among its opponents, the Socialists made slight gains in voting but lost parliamentary seats through a party split, while the Communists managed to poll only 2.9 per cent of all votes cast. These results confirmed the power of a political leadership whose largely rural constituency had remained calm throughout the turmoil. But even more important to the outcome were second thoughts entertained by many who had participated in the demonstrations. Except on the far left, Japanese came to view riots threatening chaos as a dangerous corrective. After 1960 the press, having engaged in public and serious "self-reflection," departed from its customary sharp criticism of government and adopted a more constructive tone.[19] Of importance, too, was the new look in government policies. On assuming office Ikeda announced that he would assume a "low posture," meaning that his Ministry would heed opposition views and avoid highly controversial issues.[20]

Domestically, Ikeda focused attention on "income doubling" within ten years, a popular goal which, in view of Japan's over-all economic growth, appeared attainable. In foreign affairs Ikeda emphasized the enhancement of Japan's international position and attainment of equality in Japan's dealings with the United States. Among the products of these latter efforts were: (1) the settlement on favorable terms of a debt owed the United States for costs of Occupation; (2) the establishment of the United States-Japan Committee on Trade and Economic Affairs, a body composed of cabinet-level officers who were to review periodically problems upsetting commercial relationships; (3) the

exchange of visits by high European and Japanese statesmen; and (4) the membership of Japan in the Organization for Economic Co-operation and Development (OECD), an international body admitting only the most economically advanced states. These steps were accompanied by the appearance of new Japanese attitudes toward their country's position in world affairs. Increasingly, Japan's relations with the United States were described as a "partnership," and, while in Europe in 1962, Ikeda spoke of Japan's serving with the United States and Western Europe as the "three pillars" of the free world. At the beginning of the 1960s, Japan appeared to be entering a new phase of post-war development characterized by a self-assurance that had been missing since the end of World War II.[21]

NEW JAPAN

Indeed, confidence in Japan's future was the keynote of the policies of Sato Eisaku, who became Prime Minister late in 1964 in the place of the ailing Ikeda. While the new ministry pledged close relationship with the United States, it also gave notice of enlarged initiative in shaping its own foreign policies. Nowhere was this new attitude more apparent than in Sato's approach to the problem of Okinawa, an island in which Japan claimed "residual sovereignty" but upon which the United States had constructed a vast military base.[22] In the circumstances of an escalating Vietnam war, the United States was extremely reluctant to modify its control. Yet, as the "reversion" campaign in Japan mounted, it became apparent that the Okinawa question threatened the entire Ameri-

---

[19] The role of the press in the rioting of 1960 is the basis of Edward P. Whittemore, *The Press in Japan Today: A Case Study* (1961).

[20] For interpretations of the political events of 1960, see Reischauer, *Japan: Past and Present*, 276–86.

[21] Reischauer, *Japan: Past and Present*, 286–87.

[22] In 1951 Japan agreed that the United States would retain administrative rights in Okinawa until such time as a plan to place it under a UN trusteeship with the United States as trust power could be approved. President Dwight Eisenhower, however, affirmed in 1957 that Japan possessed "residual sovereignty" over Okinawa. Presidents Kennedy and Johnson subsequently agreed that administrative rights to the island were eventually to revert to Japan.

can-Japanese relationship, especially the chances for renewal of the Treaty of Mutual Security and Co-operation which was due again in June, 1970.[23] In consequence, the United States promised "joint and continuous review" of Okinawa's status, and as a manifest of ultimate intentions, the Johnson Administration permitted the reversion to Japan of the Ogasawara (Bonin) Islands in June, 1968. Negotiations on Okinawa itself, however, were delayed until the Nixon Administration had made public commitments on the withdrawal of American combat forces from Vietnam, thereby presumably reducing the island's prospective value as a base. Accordingly, Sato, November, 1969, received a pledge that administrative control of Okinawa would revert to Japan in 1972. After that date the United States, pending the incorporation of the island into Japan's defense system, would maintain its base under restraints imposed by the Treaty of Mutual Security and Co-operation (see p. 468).[24] Sato capitalized on the victory by calling parliamentary elections which strengthened Liberal-Democratic control.

Japan's new found confidence also was manifest in the assumption of enlarged international responsibilities in financial and technical aid. As she entered the second

[23] Agitation for reversion of the island was conducted initially in Okinawa and among opposition parties in Japan. The issues mounted in Japan as the Liberal-Democratic Party moved against its opponents, taking over the issue for itself. Mikio Higa, "The Reversion Theme in Current Okinawan Politics," *Asian Survey* 7 (1967), 151–64.

[24] The terms of reversion were to be tied to the outcome of the Vietnam war. According to the "Joint Communique" issued on November 21, 1969, "The President and the Prime Minister expressed the strong hope that the war in Viet-Nam would be concluded before the return of the administrative rights over Okinawa to Japan. In this connection, they agreed that, should peace in Viet-Nam not have been realized by the time reversion of Okinawa is scheduled to take place, the two governments would fully consult with each other in the light of the situation at that time so that reversion would be accomplished wihout affecting the United States' efforts to assure the South Vietnamese people the opportunity to determine their own political future without outside interference."

postwar decade, Japan became a provider rather than recipient of foreign assistance. Some Japanese aid was an aspect of private trade and investment. African and Latin American economies, for example, were boosted by the technological advice, capital investment, and export credits provided by Japanese firms. Government programs were more prominent in Southeast Asia. In addition to her membership in the Organization for Economic Co-operation and Development, Japan became a major contributor to the capital funds of the newly established Asian Development Bank and the sponsor of the Ministerial Conference for Economic Development of Southeast Asia. Total governmental funds expended through these agencies—$538,000,000 in 1966—were substantially less than aid budgets of the United States or leading European industrial powers. More important than amounts, however, were indications given by these commitments of Japan's growing determination to make her own way in the world.[25]

Problems Ahead

Japan's reappearance as an Asian power was welcomed by Americans as well as Japanese. The United States received advantages in shifting to Japan some of its repsonsibilities in the maintenance of Asian peace and order. In accepting the partnership the Sato Ministry, however, was anxious to define and limit its own commitments. Japan was willing to expand its homeland defense forces, which by 1969 numbered 285,000 and possessed in conventional weaponry a firepower greater than Imperial forces at their wartime peak, but she was determined that her contribution to regional security were to be economic only. Japan reminded the United States that constitutional restraints prohibited the deployment of forces beyond the Japanese islands. Moreover, she maintained that her economy could not sustain expenditures entailed by larger undertakings.

[25] Edwin O. Reischauer, "Japan Is One of the Biggest Countries in the World," *New York Times Magazine*, Oct. 16, 1966; and Robert A. Scalapino, "In Search of a Role: Japan and the Uncertainties of Power," *Encounter* 27 (1966): 21–27, sketch the basis of Japan's initiatives.

In fact even this limited assumption of responsibilities promised to bring hard decisions on the allocation of national resources. Sato pledged substantially larger amounts to foreign aid even as his Ministry was pressed to spend more at home. Like other highly industrialized nations, Japan was confronted by problems of pollution and blight. Industrialism accelerated urbanization, spawning huge megalopolises while emptying age-old villages. These problems in turn drew attention to inadequate public services at a time when the citizenry was becoming more insistent on its right to enjoy life. As a consequence, government during the 1970s would doubtless be forced to deal with demands for improvements in the physical environment, for the creation of more social capital, and for the solution of problems created by prosperity. Popular concern with these domestic problems presumably would strengthen inward-looking tendencies, thus eroding support for larger international responsibilities.[26]

Japan's Prospects

If the past is any indication, the resolution of these difficulties will certainly be plagued by sharp internal divisions. One consequence of a rapidly changing society was a populace so divergent in outlook that the Japanese foreign minister, searching in 1969 for an apt description, resorted to sociologist Peter Drucker's phrase, "the age

of discontinuity." [27] Further evidence of cleavage was revealed in student demonstrations, which in 1968–1969 sent mobs into streets and partially paralyzed more than one hundred of the nation's some eight hundred colleges and universities. These demonstrations were partly a response to outmoded curricula and educational practices, but they also protested evils beyond the academic world. Students, holding themselves as "pure" popular spokesmen, rallied to the defense of workers or others who were held to be "voiceless" elements in Japanese society.[28] That student protests were directed to tangible needs was apparent in the popular following they attracted. Yet the student movement, largely because the vast majority of Japanese mistrusted the radical excesses of the young, failed to develop a broadly based constituency.

Cleavages also were evident in political divisions, making a genuine national consensus unlikely on almost any issue.[29] If the Socialists and Liberal-Democrats provided the major lines of division, the political spectrum was made more complex by the existence of various splinter groups and by the challenge of the *Komeito* (Clean Government Party), a political offshoot of a "new

[26] The demand for enlarged governmental services seemed likely to be the more insistent because of deeply rooted tradition. While the development of such programs as public welfare assistance was associated mainly with the advent of modern capitalism, these programs were no mere imports from the West. Japanese assistance programs rested upon indigenous and traditional Confucian ethics and motives, theories of the benevolence of the emperor, and the compassion of public officials. Japanese imported techniques and institutions of public assistance but not the theory. See Koji Taira, "Public Assistance in Japan: Development and Trends," *Journal of Asian Studies* 27 (1967): 95–109. Yamamura Kozo, *Economic Policy in Postwar Japan: Growth versus Economic Democracy* (1967) is an analysis emphasizing the importance of new policies that will encourage democratic development.

[27] Kiichi Aichi, "Japan's Legacy and Destiny of Change," *Foreign Affairs* 48 (October, 1969): 21–38.

[28] While student protests focused on a broad array of national and international issues, students were notably silent on discriminatory treatment accorded Koreans living in Japan. See Richard H. Mitchell, *The Korean Minority in Japan* (1967).

[29] Efforts to revise Japan's post-war constitution will illustrate the problem. After seven years of study and discussion, the commission on the constitution made its final report, recommending by a vast majority (31–7) that fundamental changes be made. The majority members, however, were united only by the abstract desirability of change. On particulars—whether revision should be total or partial, what specific points of substance should be altered and in what degree, or whether change should be contemplated immediately or in the indefinite future—their divisions were so numerous, so different, and so cross-cutting as to defy description. Robert E. Ward, "The Commission on the Constitution and Prospects for Constitutional Change in Japan," *Journal of Asian Studies* 24 (1965): 401–29.

religion," the *Soka Gakkai*. In marking out a political ground between the Socialists and Liberal-Democrats, the *Komeito* attracted a steadily growing popular following. By 1970 it had become the third largest party in the Diet (forty-seven seats) and was accounted as the most unpredictable element in Japanese politics.[30] In two decades since the end of the Occupation, these sharp divisions had failed to obstruct normal government operations, but this was due to the clear parliamentary majorities of the conservative parties. Since Japan lacked a broad consensus conducive to the smooth working of a parliamentary system, it was uncertain how she would fare if, as seemed likely, her major political groupings neared equality.

But if difficulties were ahead, Japan's prosperity achieved in spite of great handicaps, the flexibility of her people in adapting to new social and economic circumstances, and her success in governing under the new constitution augured not only the solution of problems but also further development on the basis of the Occupation's reforms. But at the same time post-war Japan was not entirely the master of her own destiny.

FOR FURTHER READING

GENERAL BACKGROUND. Donald Keene, *Living Japan* (1959) offers a delightful introduction to old and new aspects of contemporary Japanese life. More scholarly studies of the new social order are contained in R. P. Dore's two books: *City Life in Japan: A Study of a Tokyo Ward* (1958) *; and

[30] Theologically the *Soka Gakkai* has its origins in Nichiren Buddhism. Its appeal, however, appeared to derive less from a religious than from a social orientation. The membership, which was composed largely of urban lower class or lower middle class, was attracted by an emphasis on simple doctrines of absolute faith that give direction in a confusing age. The *Soka Gakkai* first entered local elections in 1955. The organization's connections with the *Komeito* were severed shortly after the elections in late 1969. For a study analyzing membership and ideology see James W. White, *The Sokagakkai and Mass Society* (1970).

Land Reform in Japan (London, 1959). Excellent descriptive material is found in Richard K. Beardsley, *et al.*, *Village Japan* (1959); and Edward Norbeck, *Changing Japan* (1965). Jean Stoetzel, *Without the Chrysanthemum and the Sword: A Study of the Attitudes of Postwar Japan* (1955) gives perspective to Ruth Benedict's famous study. For specialized aspects of social life, see James C. Abegglen, *The Japanese Factory: Aspects of its Social Organization* (1958): Solomon B. Levine, *Industrial Relations in Postwar Japan* (1958); Arthur M. Whitehill, Jr. and Shin-Ichi Takezama, *The Other Worker* (1968); and Fernando M. Basabe, *Religious Attitudes of Japanese Men, A Sociological Survey* (Tokyo, 1968). Lawrence Olson, *Dimensions of Japan* (1963) brings together perceptive essays by one of the most sensitive and acute observers writing about Japan today.

JAPAN'S ECONOMY. Jerome B. Cohen, *Japan's Postwar Economy* (1958). G. C. Allen, *Japan's Economic Expansion* (1965). William W. Lockwood, ed., *The State and Economic Enterprise in Japan* (1965). Warren S. Hunsberger, *Japan and the United States in World Trade* (1964). Prue Dempster, *Japan Advances: A Geographical Study* (London, 1967). Two articles by John D. Eyre, "Japan's Electric-Power Supply," *Geographic Review*, 55 (1965): 546-62; and "Development Trends in the Japanese Electric Power Industry, 1963–68," *The Professional Geographer*, 22 (1970): 26–30, examine the transformation of a basic industry. Eleanor Hadley, *Antitrust in Japan* (1970), deals with *Zaibatsu* dissolution and its aftermath.

CONTEMPORARY POLITICAL INSTITUTIONS AND PRACTICES. Theodore McNelly, *Contemporary Government of Japan* (1963). Ike Nobutake, *Japanese Politics: An Introductory Survey* (1957). Frank Langdon, *Politics in Japan* (1967). E. Wight Bakke, *Revolutionary Democracy: Challenge and Testing in Japan* (1968). Chitoshi Yanaga, *Japanese People and Politics* (1956).* John M. Maki, *Government and Politics in Japan: The Road* to Democracy (1962)° is an analysis of performance under the new constitution. Nathaniel B. Thayer, *How the Conservatives Rule Japan* (1969) is a detailed analysis of the Liberal-Democratic party's operations. Allan B. Cole provides pioneering studies of political behavior in *Japanese Society and Politics: The Impact of Social Stratification and Mobility on Politics* (1956); and *Political Tendencies of Japanese in Small Enterprises, with Special Reference to the Social Democratic Party* (1959). Aspects of extremist activities are treated in: I. I. Morris, *Nationalism and the Right Wing in Japan; A Study of Post-war Trends* (1960); Robert A. Scalapino, *The Japanese Communist Movements 1920–1966* (1967); and J. A. A. Stockwin, "The Communist Party in Japan," *Problems of Communism*, No. 1, 16 (Jan.-Feb., 1967); Lawrence H. Battistini, *The Postwar Student Struggles in Japan* (1956); and Felix Moos, "Religion and Politics in Japan: The Case of the *Soka Gakkai*," *Asian Survey* 3 (1963): 136–42. Yoshida Shigeru, *The Yoshida Memoirs: The Story of Japan in Crisis* (1962); and Dan Kurzman, *Kishi and Japan: The Search for the Sun* (1960) provide details on two crucial administrations. Arthur T. von Mehren, ed., *Law in Japan: The Legal Order in a Changing Society* (1963).

JAPAN'S RELATIONS WITH THE OUTSIDE WORLD. Robert Scalapino, "The Foreign Policy of Modern Japan," in *Foreign Policy in World Politics*, Roy C. Macridis, ed. (2nd ed., 1962); and "The United States and Japan," in *The United States and the Far East*, Willard Thorp, ed. (2nd ed., 1962).° Douglas Mendel, Jr. *The Japanese People and Foreign Policy* (1961). James W. Morley, *Japan and Korea: American Allies in the Pacific* (1965). Robert S. Schwantes, *Japanese and Americans; A Century of Cultural Relationships* (1955). Donald C. Hellmann, *Japanese Domestic Politics and Foreign Policy: The Peace Agreement with the Soviet Union* (1969).

TRANSLATIONS OF CONTEMPORARY LITERATURE. Tanizaki Junichiro, *Some Prefer Nettles*, Edward Seidensticker, trans. (1957).° Mishima Yukio, *The Sound of Waves*, Meredith Weatherby, trans. (1956).° Donald Keene, trans., *The Old Woman, The Wife, and The Archer: Three Modern Japanese Short Novels* (1961). Jiro Osaragi, *Homecoming*, Brewster Horwitz, trans. (1954).

Note the journals listed at the end of the preceding chapter for articles on current happenings. To this list should be added the *Journal of Social and Political Ideas in Japan* and *Contemporary Japan*.

Korea and Taiwan
since 1945

chapter 35

For Korea and Taiwan the year 1945 marked the end of Japanese colonialism and the beginning of a new and uncertain political future. As hostilities ended, the United Nations implemented the decisions of the Cairo Conference of 1943, whereby Korea "in due course" was to be independent, and Japan was to be deprived of all territory seized since 1894. Korea was divided at the 38th parallel into two zones, the Japanese surrendering in the north to the Russians and in the south to the Americans. Taiwan was occupied by *Kuomintang*-Nationalist armies under authorization of General MacArthur. Thus the ties that had bound Korea and Taiwan to Japan for a half-century were severed, but the end of Japanese colonialism did not mean that either Korea or Taiwan was to become its own master. Located on the border separating the Communist and non-Communist worlds, each was caught in the pressures of the Cold War, which meant that Japanese influences were replaced by those of other great powers now contending for control of East Asia.

KOREA

One of the less obvious but vital results of the outbreak of World War II was a revival of Korean nationalism. Under Japanese rule Korea had suffered a prolonged and systematic attack on her cultural identity and had seen the progressive integration of her economy with Japan's. Operating through a strong central government and an oppressive police system, Japan had held Koreans in subjection, permitting them only limited educational and occupational opportunities.[1] The educational system fostered the Japanization of the Korean populace, while the economy was developed as a source of raw materials and a market for Japanese manu-

[1] Authoritative decisions were made for Korea by the Japanese Imperial government and the Governor-General of Korea. The conduct of Korean foreign relations was controlled entirely by the Japanese Foreign Ministry. Korean participation in decision-making, limited to a small part of the society's elite, was largely consultative and advisory. A council of notables to advise the Japanese Governor-General was established in 1910, and, subsequently, advisory councils were permitted to function in conjunction with lower levels of government. Koreans generally were not permitted to serve in the colonial bureaucracy.

facturers. These measures enabled Japan to suppress an infant national movement. In all the years of colonial rule, the only major outburst of Korean feeling occurred in March, 1919, when the death of the last royal monarch sent a million or more people into the streets.

Firm government, however, did not eliminate widespread resentment of the Japanese or put an end to nationalist movements among Korean exiles. One exile group attempted unsuccessfully in 1919 to plead Korea's case for self-determination before the Paris Peace Conference. A Korean provisional government, unrecognized but nevertheless aided by China, existed first in the International Settlement at Shanghai and later at Nanking and Chungking. In the United States still another group headed by Syngman Rhee sought vainly for American recognition. Thus Korean nationalism survived Japanese repression, but there was no consensus among the nationalists as to Korea's future. At the end of World War II, two years after the Cairo Declaration, neither Korean nationalists in exile nor the Great Powers themselves were agreed on the country's future beyond a commitment to independence. Moreover, the wishes of the Korean people who had lived under Japanese rule were unknown. The only positive step was the understanding reached at Yalta between Roosevelt and Stalin that for a time Korea might be made a trusteeship.[2]

The collapse of Japanese power in Korea was accompanied not only by Russian and American military occupation but also by revolutionary efforts on the part of Korean factions to seize political power. In the north these groups, heavily weighted with Korean Communists returned from exile, were encouraged and given authority by the Rus-

[2] George McCune, "Korea: The First Year of Liberation," *Pacific Affairs* 20 (March, 1947): 3–17, reveals the lack of advance planning with regard to Korea's future. Soon Sung Cho, *Korea in World Politics, 1940–1950: An Evaluation of American Responsibility* (1967) is critical of the American failure to provide effective support during the war years for a unified Korean state.

sians.[3] In the south, revolutionary groups that had formed a People's Republic at Seoul were not accepted by the American occupation forces as a *de facto* government. Indeed, for a time the Americans retained Japanese in administrative posts and then set up an American military government employing Koreans where qualified. The net result was that in the south the government was American in appearance and power, while in the north the government seemed to be Korean, though the actual control was Russian.

Against this background the American and the Soviet commands in Korea were unable to reach any agreement on relations between the two zones. The respective commands failed, in addition, to agree on how to form a provisional government for all Korea or on what Korean parties were to be consulted and allowed to participate toward this end. In consequence the United States took the Korean problems to the United Nations in August, 1947, while Russia proposed that both powers withdraw their military forces. The United States and the United Nations General Assembly rejected this proposal for reasons that were quite clear, namely the Russian success in creating in North Korea a government which it felt could be counted on to do Moscow's bidding and to extend Communist control to the south once American troops had left.

In the southern zone progress toward the appearance of some kind of Korean leadership was much slower than in the north. The United States wanted Korea to build a truly democratic system and government, but it did not wish to turn over authority to a Korean democracy that might be hostile to American policy. Here the dilemma was very real and the ultimate solution not very satisfactory. While the American military government tolerated agitation by all factions, it tended to support the moderate and conservative elements, and as American-Russian relations became more bitter, the Ameri-

[3] See Robert Scalapino and Lee Chong-sik, "The Origins of the Korean Communist Movement," *Journal of Asian Studies* 20 (1960–1961): 9–32; 149–68.

can tendency to bolster the extreme Korean "conservatives" grew. The result was that the American-supervised elections for an interim legislative assembly were regarded as fraudulent even by middle-of-the-road Korean leaders. At the same time the continuing efforts of North Koreans to escape to the south suggested that there were many who preferred to rely on ultimate American purposes rather than on the imposed regime of the Communists.

Aggravating these questions of internal politics operating under the pressure of external power was the country's economic plight. Korea, formerly a kingdom of largely self-sufficient farmers, had experienced an economic transformation under Japanese rule. Industry and mining were established chiefly in the north, while commercialized agriculture was developed in the south. In the post-war era, this modernized system, cut off from Japanese markets, deprived of Japanese capital and technical guidance, and disrupted by division at the 38th parallel, floundered badly. North Korea met the crisis with land reforms, Soviet economic and technical assistance, and the opening of trade with Russia. The American military government in the south saved a far larger population from starvation through the importation of food and fertilizer. Eventually the problem was relieved further by land reform which allotted Japanese-held land to Korean tenants. No fundamental solution to economic problems, however, was attempted while the political situation was deadlocked. This deadlock continued, and a United Nations Temporary Commission, sent late in 1947 to see that freely elected representatives of the Korean people were permitted to determine the form of government for all Korea, was refused admittance to the Russian zone. Elections held in the south in 1948 under the Commission's supervision (with seats reserved for the North) brought into being the first assembly of the Republic of Korea. A constitution having been adopted, July, 1948, the assembly elected Syngman Rhee the first president. Authority of the American military government was transferred to the new regime, which was approved by the United Nations General Assembly as a lawful government, and was soon recognized by most countries other than the Soviet bloc. The Soviet Union's answer to these steps was an election in the north for a Supreme People's Assembly. The Assembly set up a rival constitution and government under Prime Minister Kim Il-song. Once established, this government was recognized by the Communist bloc and received economic aid from the Soviet Union.

Withdrawal of American troops from South Korea was completed in June, 1949, while the Russians had announced that their withdrawal would be complete by the beginning of the year. The resulting balance of power in the peninsula was uneven. In the north what amounted to a single-party Communist regime, backed by Russia, was intent on consolidating its power. In the south the government of Rhee, purportedly a free administration, was attacked from many quarters on the ground that it had gained power by unscrupulous methods, that the cabinet was chosen unwisely, that no North Koreans were included, and that the president and the ministry were concerned primarily with achieving personal power. The United States thus appeared as sponsor of an anti-Communist regime that was accused of having no virtue other than anti-Communism, and was so lacking in popular support as to deny it any claim as a democratic government. The American embarrassment was the more telling at this particular time, because of the fate that had overtaken the *Kuomintang*-National government of China. There followed a cutback in American economic aid to Korea on the theory that American assistance must be used for political and economic rehabilitation and not to advance the political ambitions of individuals or factions. In principle the American position was unassailable; in practice it was an invitation to the North Korean regime to strike South Korea at its most vulnerable spot—its questionable leadership.

War in Korea

North Korean armies, well equipped and reportedly led by Russian officers, struck

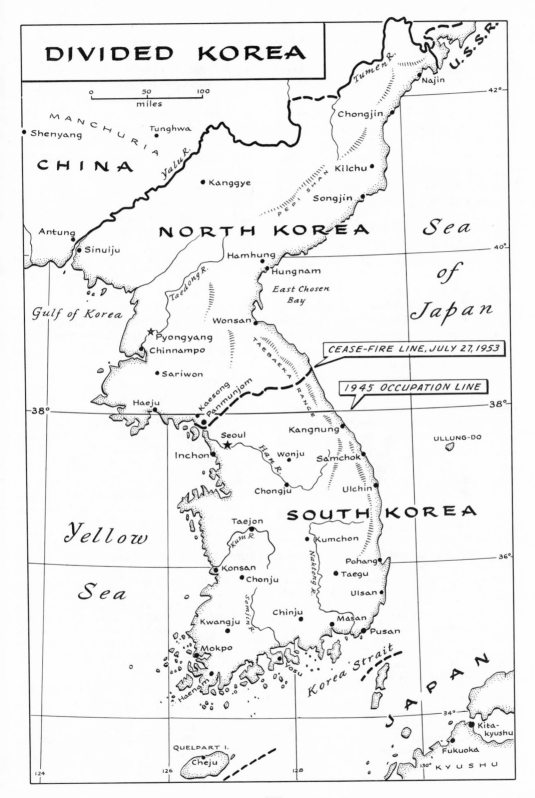

DIVIDED KOREA

0   50   100
miles

MANCHURIA

CHINA

Shenyang

Tunghwa

Yalu R.

Kanggye

Antung

Sinuiju

PEI SHAN

Najin

Tumen R.

U.S.S.R.

Chongjin

42°

Kilchu

Songjin

NORTH KOREA

Sea

of

Japan

Hamhung

Hungnam

40°

Taedong R.

East Chosen
Bay

Gulf of Korea

Wonsan

Pyongyang

Chinnampo

TAEBAEK RANGE

CEASE-FIRE LINE, JULY 27, 1953

Sariwon

Kaesong

1945 OCCUPATION LINE

Haeju

Panmunjom

38°

38°

Seoul

Kangnung

ULLUNG-DO

Inchon

Wonju

Samchok

Han R.

Chongju

Ulchin

SOUTH KOREA

Yellow

Taejon

Kumchon

Kum R.

Sea

Konsan

Chonju

Pohang

Naktong R.

Taegu

36°

Ulsan

Chinju

Somjin R.

Kwangju

Masan

Pusan

Mokpo

Yosu

Korea Strait

JAPAN

Haenam

QUELPART I.

Cheju

34°

Kita-
kyushu

Fukuoka

130° KYUSHU

124

126

128

477

across the 38th parallel in a surprise attack on June 25, 1950. The attack was based presumably on two theories: (1) that the United States, having already excluded Korea from the American security zone, would not intervene with military force, and (2) that a Soviet veto would prevent effective action by the United Nations, or that the United Nations could not act in the absence of one of the great powers, since Russia at the time was absenting herself from the Security Council. However, the Security Council passed a resolution calling on the North Koreans to withdraw, and the United States authorized additional military supplies to the defenders. On June 27 air and sea forces were ordered to cover and support South Korean troops, and when on June 30 it was clear that South Korean forces were facing complete defeat, American ground forces were ordered to Korea. These American actions were in support of the resolution of the Security Council, and in terms of American policy were to halt Communism in its attack upon a free nation.[4] In implementation of policy, the United States, by presidential mandate, proclaimed the neutraliza- of Taiwan. The U.S. Seventh Fleet was placed in the Formosan Straits to prevent hostilities between the Nationalists and Communist Chinese. On July 8 President Truman named General of the Army Douglas MacArthur as commander of United Nations forces in Korea. Russia, on August 1, resumed her seat on the Security Council, taking the

position that the conflict in Korea had been precipitated by a South Korean attack and that the resolutions of the Security Council were illegal. By October, with reversal in the tide of battle, South Korean troops were invading the north. MacArthur had called upon the north to surrender, and had been authorized by the United Nations General Assembly to exercise civil authority on its behalf in the territory north of the 38th parallel.

An entirely new situation was created by the end of October when, as United Nations forces moved across the 38th parallel and as Republic of Korea troops in advance of them neared the Yalu river boundary against Manchuria, Communist Chinese armies, termed "volunteers," joined the North Korean forces.[5] By January, 1951, the Chinese Communists had entered the war in overwhelming force, had driven United Nations forces back to the 38th parallel, and had the power to drive into South Korea. This offensive was contained by April, 1951, when United Nations forces were again north of

[4] "For Americans and others who supported the collective military action, Korea was a test of whether a revolutionary global political movement through the action of its various subcomponents was to impose by violence its political, economic, social, and cultural systems in piecemeal fashion upon a doubtful or reluctant world." Glenn D. Paige, *The Korean Decision (June 24–30, 1950)* (1968), 352. See also the observation of the Korean scholar, Tae-ho Yoo, *The Korean War and the United Nations: A Legal and Diplomatic Historical Study* (Louvain, 1964), 80–81, ". . . in the face of the conflict of the Big Powers, the Korean people had no chance to discuss their problems in their own way, because the problems of the Big Powers were superimposed on the Korean Question."

[5] China's involvement probably reflected both her traditionally deep concerns with "barbarian" dangers on her frontiers and her more contemporary assumption of the inevitability of conflict between Communist and "imperialist" nations. On the American side, the Truman Administration was concerned above all with "solution" of the Korean problem and did not seek a wider war. Thus, the advance of United Nations troops was coupled with repeated American assurances to Peking. The United States, however, apparently did not take into account the possibility that Peking would not be reassured by American professions. Moreover, official Washington enjoyed little success in persuading its field commander, General MacArthur, to observe restraints that might have bolstered China's confidence. On these points, see Allen S. Whiting, *China Crosses the Yalu: The Decision to Enter the Korean War* (1960); and David S. McLellan, "Dean Acheson and the Korean War," *Political Science Quarterly* 83 (1968): 16–39. Matthew B. Ridgway, *The Korean War* (1967), by the general who succeeded MacArthur, condemned his predecessor's incautious approach to the Chinese border. Ridgway contended that MacArthur's disregard of Washington's restraints was founded on a desire to fight a preventative war with Communist China (pp. 143–44). Douglas MacArthur, *Reminiscences* (1964) reveals the general's attitudes.

the parallel. Meanwhile negotiations for a political settlement were inaugurated without success. The United States was prepared to discuss proposals once a cease-fire had been achieved. Russia and Communist China would discuss nothing until there was prior acceptance on their terms of a general Far Eastern settlement. These terms included: (1) evacuation of all foreign troops from Korea, (2) admission of Communist China to the United Nations, (3) termination of American "intervention" supporting the Chinese Nationalists on Formosa, (4) a general Far Eastern conference to seek a comprehensive settlement, and (5) a peace treaty with Japan meeting the wishes of Moscow and Peking. In the face of these demands the United States appealed to the United Nations General Assembly, which on February 1, 1951, found Mao's government guilty of aggression.

If the problem of finding a unified policy for the Korean question was relatively simple for Russia and Communist China, such was not the case with the leadership of the United States and other powers, European and Asiatic, which in general had supported the United States through the United Nations. Many of these governments differed with the United States on principles of policy or on solutions for particular problems. In western Europe there was fear that if the United States became too deeply involved in Asia it would be unable to join in the defense of Europe against Russia. This view was shared by the U.S. Joint Chiefs-of-Staff and expressed by General Omar Bradley when he said participation in a general Far Eastern conflict with Red China would involve the United States "in the wrong war, at the wrong place, at the wrong time and with the wrong enemy." The problem of American policy was also complicated by the so-called neutralism of India and other newly created Asian states. Led by India, these "neutrals" were intent to retain their independence of judgment and not to commit themselves in advance to follow in Far Eastern matters the leadership of the United States, a non-Asiatic state.

The problem of discovering what the United States should and could do to achieve victory in Korea in line with principles enunciated by the United Nations was brought to a head in the spring of 1951 by the position taken by General MacArthur. As steps toward a military victory, MacArthur advocated the broadening of United Nations activities to include: (1) a broad blockade of China, (2) permission for air reconnaissance over Manchuria and the China coast, and (3) authority for the Nationalists on Taiwan to operate against the mainland. These proposals were not considered favorably in Washington. The blockade was not regarded as a weapon that could be immediately effective against the Chinese economy, and the right of reconnaissance was regarded as a first step toward the bombing of Manchurian bases which in turn might well bring Russia into the armed conflict.[6] MacArthur, on the other hand, did not accept as satisfactory the continuing efforts of the United Nations to negotiate a cease-fire, since even if successful the result would be a division at the 38th parallel, which could only be held by forces so strong that they could advance to the Yalu. On this basis, MacArthur asked for more troops and for authority to bomb Manchurian bases. Publication of a letter from MacArthur to Congressman Joseph Martin critical of existing policy brought in Washington the conclusion that the military command was interfering with political decisions. Accordingly, on April 11, President Truman removed MacArthur from command. Renewed efforts for a cease-fire and armistice were undertaken in July, 1951, and continued unsuccessfully for two years while limited hostilities continued along the 38th parallel.

Progress toward an armistice was made only after Dwight Eisenhower succeeded President Truman, and Georgi Malenkov became Soviet Premier. These political shifts cleared the way for a compromise agreement, July 27, 1953, calling for a cease-fire, estab-

[6] John Norman, "MacArthur's Blockade Proposals against Red China," *The Pacific Historical Review* 26 (1957): 161–74.

lishing of a neutral zone on either side of the 38th parallel, and exchanging of prisoners.[7] A subsequent agreement provided for international supervision of these terms as applied, and for a high-level political conference to discuss the peaceful settlement of the Korean question on the basis of reunification. While these understandings terminated hostilities, they failed to usher in a new era in Korean politics. The Korean phase of an international conference meeting in Geneva in 1954 ended in stalemate. Meanwhile, the prospects for Korean reunification were complicated further by the continuing existence of two antagonistic Korean governments, one for the north and another for the south.

Two Koreas

North Korean politics after 1953 were dominated by Kim Il-song. Although Kim had been initially little more than a figurehead operating under Soviet direction, the

[7] American involvement in Korea occurred against the backdrop of a bitter, partisan attack on American Far Eastern policy. Senator Joseph McCarthy, for example, revived amid much fanfare the charge that China "had been lost" to communism because of subversive influences within the American government, especially within the State Department. This campaign was swelled by MacArthur's dismissal at the hands of a Democratic administration. But with the election of Eisenhower, a Republican and World War II hero, Congressional critics of the Truman administration became supporters of an attempt to find a compromise Korean settlement. McCarthy's influence declined, and he ultimately was censured in the Senate on a motion initiated and supported by Republican colleagues. The impact of "McCarthyism" on the American government and on American dealings with Asia, however, did not end with the man. Former Secretary of State Dean Acheson, himself a principal target of McCarthy's attacks, has observed: "McCarthy's name has been given . . . to a phenomenon broader than his own participation in it, the hysteria growing out of fear of Communist subversion. . . . The result was deplorable. The Government's foreign and civil services, universities, and China-studies programs in them took a decade to recover from this sadistic program. . . ." *Present at the Creation* (1969), 369. See also Ronald J. Caridi, *The Korean War and American Politics: The Republican Party as a Case Study* (1968).

close of the Korean War permitted him to eliminate rivals and convert his Communist Workers' party into an instrument for controlling the state.[8] Under his leadership, party enrollment which stood at 360,000 in 1946 swelled by 1961 to 1,311,563, or about 12 per cent of a total population estimated at 10,700,000. The army was guided by party members, and the party directed drastic reforms involving: (1) collectivization of the entire agricultural system; (2) nationalization of existing industry and construction of new plants under a series of long-range plans; and (3) development of a new educational system providing for the socialist reorientation of the populace, revival of Korean nationalism, and instruction in vital technical skills. The Soviet Union supported these programs with aid in the amount of some two billion rubles, the services of 1,500 technicians, and equipment for a variety of industrial enterprises. China and the Communist nations of East Europe together supplied help in roughly an equal amount. In consequence, North Korea's post-war decades were characterized by such expansion and diversification of the industrial system that the country could boast of the production of machine tools, automobiles, tractors, mining equipment, and chemicals. Slender agricultural resources were augmented, though self-sufficiency in producing food and fiber was not attained. Social transformation included declining farm population, growth of an in-

[8] Kim was only one of several Communists to return to Korea with the occupying Soviet forces, and among these his credentials were not the most impressive. Kim Tu-bong, for example, was notable for leadership among Korean revolutionaries in Shanghai and Yenan; and Pak Honyang, a Communist since 1919 and founder of the Korean Communist party, was the most generally acknowledged leader. Kim Il-song, however, as a former exile in Siberia, received Soviet support because he was the Korean Communist whom the Russian military knew best. Once in power Kim posed as the only revolutionary leader of significance before 1945 and as the one who almost single handedly defeated Japanese imperialism. Ching-sik Lee, "Kim Il-song of North Korea," *Asian Survey* 7 (June, 1967): 374–82.

dustrial and clerical labor force, urbanization, and a steady rise in educational levels.[9] These gains were achieved through the well-known methods of the police state. The populace was coerced, deprived of its property, and mobilized into a vast army. While these methods were unpopular, nowhere in North Korea was there an organized opposition to challenge Kim and the Workers' party.[10]

Kim was committed to the reunification of Korea under communism. To this end he supported Soviet proposals at the Geneva Conference of 1954 and, following the withdrawal of Chinese troops in 1958, he indicated a readiness to open trade across the 38th parallel and to discuss establishment of a united Korean government on the basis of free elections, provided United Nations forces were first withdrawn from South Korea. These terms reflected his confidence that the Workers' party would capture any government developed through negotations with South Korea. The founding of a military-controlled regime in Seoul, May 16, 1961, and the south's subsequent attack on elements which had been agitating for negotiations with the north, however, destroyed immediate prospects for the successful conclusion of these plans. In consequence, Kim signed mutual security treaties with the Chinese People's Republic and the Soviet Union and undertook to expand the north's military

[9] Glenn D. Paige, *The Korean People's Democratic Republic* (1966),* Chapter IV. This is not to suggest that North Korea did not have its share of problems in economic development. The goals of the Seven Year Plan of 1961–1967, for example, were not met, and the Plan was extended three years. Soviet aid proved uncertain, since it was linked with North Korea's readiness (not always forthcoming) to submit to Moscow's leadership in world affairs. Economic growth was hampered also by the country's heavy commitment to military spending. By 1969 the pace of economic development had slowed. Yet, even as momentum was lost, it was evident that North Korea had established in a war-ravaged country an embryonic industrial complex that by Asian standards was quite impressive.

[10] B. C. Koh, "North Korea: Profile of a Garrison State," *Problems of Communism* 18 (Jan.-Feb., 1969): 18–27.

forces. This latter effort resulted in a well-trained, Soviet-equipped army of over 350,-000, an air force boasting some 500 jet aircraft, modern air-defense missile complexes, and a militia of more than one million men and women. These forces backed the escalation of violence against the south. North Korean troops clashed with United Nations forces along the 38th parallel; the south's fishing boats were harassed and captured; and North Korean commandos staged raids aimed at the destruction of key facilities and the assassination of South Korean officials (one such squad penetrated to within 800 meters of President Park Chung-hee's residence before being captured).

In a demonstration of Kim's conviction that the United States was his chief opponent, North Korea, January, 1968, seized the American intelligence-gathering vessel, the *Pueblo*, and held its eighty-two crew members prisoners for a year. But with the appearance of Sino-Soviet tensions, North Korea's foreign problems involved more than the opposition of the United States. Sino-Soviet troubles proved especially embarrassing to Kim who embraced theories that linked him ideologically to Mao but who also looked to Moscow for foreign aid. Thus, during the 1960s, North Korea shifted uncertainly between Communist China and the Soviet Union. At the same time, the north's growing military and economic strength contributed to increasingly noisy assertions of its independence of all foreign powers.

North Korea's dependence upon its allies was paralleled in South Korea's relations with the United States. South Korea was the recipient of more than three and one-half million dollars in American economic aid.[11] Moreover, in January 1954, a treaty was concluded whereby the United States was pledged to "act to meet the common danger" in the event of an "armed attack" on South Korean territory. Support of this pledge was

[11] In addition to American financial assistance, South Korea received through a special United Nations rehabilitation agency some $125,000,000 before that agency closed its operations in 1960.

demonstrated in American military aid amounting to some two billion dollars and the stationing of several thousand American troops near the 38th parallel. Yet, while these measures were essential to South Korea's survival, relations between Seoul and Washington were often strained. President Rhee reacted violently to the American decision to agree on a cease-fire short of Korean reunification. He all but ended the armistice negotiations in 1953 by releasing North Korean prisoners in violation of a key understanding, and his constant threats to use South Korean troops in "Marches North," led the United States in the Treaty of 1954 to insist on a prohibition of unilateral South Korean military action. During an official visit to the United States in 1954, Rhee attacked American policy, calling upon Congress and the American people to launch a military crusade against communism on all fronts.

South Korea also was troubled by domestic turmoil. The functioning of democratic political institutions, installed under American guidance, was subverted by authoritarian traditions. The political record became one of constant intrigue and shifting coalitions among rival factions grouped in two loosely organized parties known as the Liberals (headed by Rhee) and the Democrats, two labels that had very little, if any, meaning in Korea.[12] Rhee dominated the government by fair means or foul. For example, when it appeared in 1952 that the National Assembly, acting in its capacity of presidential elector, would not re-elect him, Rhee forced amendment of the constitution to provide for election through a popular vote. He filled administrative posts with ap-

[12] Political factionalism has been a persistent barrier to the development of a consensus on important national questions. In South Korea more than 500 political parties have been identified since 1945. Their sheer number and fluidity indicate the personalized nature of politics and the absence of strong ideological or pragmatic orientations. Even the Communists have not escaped the divisive effects of factionalism. In North Korea, however, since 1945, Kim's systematic elimination of his rivals has been basic to the creation of a seemingly monolithic political system. David I. Steinberg, *Korea: Nexus of East Asia* (1968), 9–17.

pointees whose chief qualification was loyalty to Rhee. The National Assembly, dominated by the Liberal party, was bribed or coerced to do the president's bidding. Notwithstanding his authoritarian tendencies, however, Rhee did not have full dictatorial powers. He was never without a vocal opposition, and in the elections of May, 1956, his hand-picked candidate for the vice-presidency was defeated by the Democratic leader, John M. Chang (Chang Myun). Moreover, Rhee's rule was weakened by confusion and at times by indecision. Lacking capable advisers, he refused to delegate authority, trying unsuccessfully to make all major decisions himself. During the latter years of his administration, bribe-taking and the diversion of foreign aid funds to the private enrichment of favorites became a public scandal.

In spite of this record, Rhee remained in power until April, 1960, a month after his election to a fourth term in balloting marked by police interference and gross corruption. His fall was preceded by mass rioting which the army refused to suppress. The United States at this point also exerted pressure for reforms to meet the public reaction. Rhee in response resigned his office and fled to Hawaii. Following his departure, a new constitution was drawn making the presidency an honorary office and placing authority in the hands of a prime minister responsible to the National Assembly. In July, 1960, a new administration was installed under the control of the Democratic party led by John M. Chang.

While Chang took office pledging widespread reform in government, his task was complicated by the disintegration of his party into feuding factions. The new premier failed to eliminate political malpractice, to arrest growing economic instability, or to prevent Communist infiltration from the north. In the confusion, army leaders entered politics with a bloodless coup, May 16, 1961, that forced Chang from office and dissolved the National Assembly. An interim government functioning through a Supreme Council for National Reconstruction was set up by the military junta. During a period of tutelage that was to end in the summer of 1963, the militarists proposed to punish those guilty of crimes against the state, to institute reforms, and to instruct the populace in the responsibilities of self-government. Former Premier Chang and some of his colleagues were charged with graft, while an extension of the clean-up beyond government circles resulted in the public confession of thirteen business leaders to evasion of several million dollars in income taxes. As a corrective to economic woes, the junta announced both an Emergency Economic Program and a Five Year Economic Reconstruction Plan.

The attack thus launched on basic problems achieved its greatest success in the economic field. Unlike the north where expansion of productive capacity was pressed as early as 1945, South Korea's economic programs before 1960 had emphasized relief and rehabilitation. Once under way, however, the south's development was boosted by the conclusion of a treaty with Japan, June, 1965, restoring relations and providing access to Japanese capital ($300,000,000 in reparations, $200,000,000 in soft loans, and $300,000,000 in commercial credit over a decade). The United States also figured prominently as a source of aid, private investment, and a customer of goods related to the Vietnam war. By the end of the 1960s, South Korea's approach to the goals projected in her economic plans was revealed by a substantial rise in per capita annual income (from $88 to $123), the doubling of foreign exchange reserves in the period 1963–1967, and increases in agricultural production.

This new measure of prosperity created problems of distribution. Economic development produced social dislocations—an urban unemployment rate that sometimes reached 20 per cent, wage levels scarcely above subsistence levels, and a disparity between rich and poor which appeared to increase rather than to diminish. Population pressures added to social tensions. Compounding these difficulties was the failure of the militarist regime to work any magic in Korean politics. Upon seizing power, the militarists had promised an early return to civilian control and in preparation for this move, a new party coalition, the Democratic-Republican party, was formed. Still another revision of the constitution was approved, this one de-

signed to create a government structure not unlike that of the United States. But General Park Chung-hee, who had emerged as strongman, refused to relinquish power and remained as president. His government, like its predecessors, was soon encumbered with factional strife.

Despite these problems, South Korea's mood in 1970 manifested increased self-confidence. As in the north, South Korea took care to demonstrate its independence. President Park travelled abroad, not only in the United States, but also in Southeast Asia and Europe. His government sought to break its almost total dependence on American aid by diversifying its sources of foreign assistance. Moreover, it demonstrated assurance in its own security by sending some 50,000 men to fight in Vietnam. South Korea pictured itself as an influence in Asian affairs.

The emergence of self-confident regimes, north and south, heightened old demands for Korean reunification. Both Korean governments gave priority to unification—but under different auspices and at different times. The south looked toward elections throughout the country under the sponsorship and supervision of the United Nations. These were envisioned for some future time when a less politically fragmented and a more economically powerful south might stand successfully against the north. The north, on the other hand, looked toward reunification without reference to the United Nations or American intervention. The issue of when and how Korea was to be reunited, or, indeed, whether the division was to be ended at all remained, in 1970, beyond the power of Koreans alone to determine. In a world torn by great rivalries, foreign powers were still vitally concerned with Korea's future.

TAIWAN

The history of Taiwan (Formosa) since 1945 is another dramatic chapter in the Cold War.[13] During the immediate post-war years,

[13] "Taiwan" is the mainland Chinese designation for the island. "Formosa" is the name given by Portuguese explorers. The different names assumed contemporary importance in that

and in the absence of a Japanese peace treaty, *Kuomintang*-Nationalist forces administered the island as an army of occupation. This early administration, adept in misgovernment, did not recommend itself to the native population. By January, 1949, however, the Chinese Nationalist government, foreseeing the need for a refuge, appointed one of its ablest officials, Ch'en Ch'eng, as governor. Ch'en eliminated the worst abuses. Later, when Chiang Kai-shek fled to the island with some two million refugees from the the mainland, Taiwan assumed a dual status as a Chinese province and as the seat of the National Republic of China claiming to rule the entire mainland. An additional defense against Communist "liberation" of Taiwan was provided shortly thereafter when the United States, having reexamined its strategic position in East Asia in the light of rising Communist power and the outbreak of the Korean War, set up a naval patrol of the Taiwan Straits and provided fresh military and economic aid to the Nationalists. Thus the march of events dictated that Taiwan was separated from the mainland and dependent on America aid. Taiwan's legal position, however, was not so clear. The decision of the Cairo Conference to restore the island to China seemed clear enough, but after 1949 there was the question of restoration to which China—*Kuomintang* or Communist? Neither Chinese government abandoned in any measure its claim. Moreover, the San Francisco Treaty of 1951, which divested Japan of its rights to Taiwan, did not dispose of the island or contribute to a settlement.[14]

Government on Taiwan after 1949 consisted of a double system wherein a provincial regime governed the island, while Chiang Kai-shek's Republican administration concerned itself in theory with the broader affairs of the lost mainland and its relations with the Powers. Under this division of responsibility, Taiwanese participated in government to the extent of selecting local officials, voting for members of a provincial assembly, and having representation on the Governor's Council. The governor, however, was invariably a mainlander appointed by the Republic. Mainlanders also monopolized positions in the Republic, the governmental structure of which had been transferred almost intact to the island. Remnants of the national assembly, for example, met periodically to discharge such functions as re-electing Chiang Kai-shek, and many administrative officials from mainland days continued to hold titles as provincial governors, customs inspectors, or district magistrates even though the duties of their offices had disappeared.[15] The net result of such a system was to exclude Taiwanese from a major role in government and to create a huge bureaucracy that had too little to do. The rationale voiced by the *Kuomintang*-Nationalist government was the necessity of

islanders seeking an autonomous status for their homeland have used the Portuguese name. Note the usage, for example, in the quarterly publication *The Independent Formosa*, which is published by the "United Formosans in America for Independence." See Douglas Mendel, *The Politics of Formosan Nationalism* (1970), based on extensive interviews both in Formosa and among Formosans living in the United States.

[14] Paul M. A. Linebarger, "The Republic of China on Taiwan: A Descriptive Appraisal," *World Affairs* 126 (1963): 5–16, touches briefly on these legal problems. For still other perspectives see J. P. Jain, "Legal Status of Formosa: A

Study of British, Chinese, and Indian Views," *American Journal of International Law* 57 (Jan., 1963): 25–45; and Douglas Mendel, "Japanese Policy and Views toward Formosa," *Journal of Asian Studies* 28 (May, 1969): 513–34.

[15] Under the Constitution of 1947 the National Assembly was to function as a popularly elected body which would meet every six years to elect a president. The constitution's provisions, however, did not clearly distinguish between the functions of this body and the Legislative Yuan. Thus, in its meetings on the mainland and in Taiwan, the National Assembly sometimes insisted on hearing administrative reports, questioning officials, and passing resolutions. In assuming these additional functions, the National Assembly embarrassed *Kuomintang*-Nationalist officialdom, but such independence never threatened Chiang's re-election. In practice the periodic meetings of the National Assembly reflected more of a commitment to the appearance than to the spirit of constitutional government. Mark A. Plummer, "Chiang K'ai-shek and the National Assembly," *Studies on Asia, 1967*. Sidney Brown, ed. (1967), 119–38.

holding political machinery in readiness for a return to the mainland. Pending that time, the bureaucracy and its army served Chiang on Taiwan as a basis of power.

While local government on the island took on some surface characteristics of a democracy, Taiwan was essentially a police state, though not a fully totalitarian one. The *Kuomintang's* domination of political life was scarcely challenged by the existence of a few opposition parties. *Kuomintang* party cells were organized throughout the island; ambitious local politicians were absorbed into its ranks; and party members holding official posts were safeguarded by laws proscribing discussion of such topics as Chiang's leadership and making candidates criminally liable for their speeches. Other laws providing harsh treatment for Communist sympathizers and limiting civil rights were justified by constant threats of invasion, infiltration, and subversion. Furthermore, as the *Kuomintang* tightened its grip on Taiwan, it became increasingly intolerant of any dissent from Chiang's leadership within its own ranks. In 1955, for example, Sun Li-jen, an able soldier, who objected to the activities of Chiang Ching-kuo (the Generalissimo's son) in the political departments of his army, and who had criticized the Generalissimo, and had expressed doubts about the return to the mainland, was retired in disgrace.[16]

Taiwan's economic progress, however, was substantial. Post-war development was founded on the work of the Japanese colonial regime, which had organized the island under a stable government, had raised the technological proficiency of the populace, and had built farming operations that exported substantial quantities of rice, sugar, and pineapples.[17] In addition, the United States

after 1950 supplied military and economic assistance amounting to more than three billion dollars. These factors combined with favorable governmental programs to produce rapid development. By 1970 Taiwan's productive capacity not only sustained a population of some fourteen million at one of the highest levels (exceeded only by Japan) in all Asia, but it also converted the island into a trade center exporting the more traditional agricultural commodities and a variety of manufactured products.[18] Moreover, the *Kuomintang*-Nationalist government's support of such creative experiments as the industrial processing zone at Kaohsiung (an effort which capitalized on abundant labor by importing raw materials, manufacturing them at the water's edge, and re-exporting them to world markets) demonstrated its commitment to continued growth. In these circumstances of a thriving economy, American economic aid was terminated and Taiwan herself extended technical assistance to developing nations in Africa, the Middle East, and Latin America.[19]

While these accomplishments gave Taiwan a new importance in East Asia, economic problems did not vanish. Population increased at a rate of better than 3 per cent annually, creating the long range task of creating thousands of jobs each year.[20] Furthermore, in addition to the burdens imposed

---

[16] The persecution of Sun Li-jen was not an isolated case. For a brief description of government on Taiwan and its operation see Harold C. Hinton, "China," *Major Governments of Asia*, George McT. Kahin, ed. (2nd ed., 1963), 134–38.

[17] Aspects of Japan's colonial rule are treated in E. Patricia Tsurumi, "Taiwan under Kodama Gentaro and Goto Shimpei," and Ching-chih Chen, "The Police and Hoko Systems in

Taiwan under Japanese Administration," *Papers on Japan*. Vol. 4, published and distributed by the East Asia Research Center, Harvard University (1967), 95–146, and 147–76, respectively. Chang Han-yu and Ramon H. Myers, "Japanese Colonial Development Policy in Taiwan, 1895–1906: A Case of Bureaucratic Entrepreneurship," *Journal of Asian Studies* 22 (1963): 433–49.

[18] Exports from Taiwan in 1952 were valued at $120,000,000. By 1968 their value had reached $842,000, 000 and were continuing to climb. Exports of such agricultural commodities as sugar, tea, rice, and bananas, while reaching all-time records, declined in importance, compared with textiles, plywood, furniture, electrical goods, and canned foodstuffs.

[19] Karl Brandt, "Economic Development: Lessons in Statecraft in Taiwan," *Orbis* 11 (Winter, 1968): 1067–80.

[20] Irene B. Taeuber, "Population Growth in a Chinese Microcosm," *Population Index* 27 (1961): 101–26.

by large bureaucracy, the economy was taxed to support an army of 600,000 men. Yet for understandable political reasons the government delayed until 1968 official support of intensive birth control programs and did not begin reductions in the army's manpower until the following year. The belated decisions in these matters were explained by the official view that rapid population increase and military power were essential to the reconquest of the mainland.[21]

Under Chiang's rule on Taiwan, military and political decisions were directed emphatically toward a return to the mainland. The *Kuomintang*-Nationalist government held that Communist rule had been imposed upon the Chinese people against their will; that the Peking regime was becoming more unpopular as crop failures, coercion, bureaucratic mistakes, and recurrent turmoil compounded human misery; and that throughout China millions were awaiting the moment to revolt. Initially these views were linked to plans for a military invasion. *Kuomintang*-Nationalist policy presumed that troop landings would trigger popular uprisings.[22] In the course of time, however, as the

Chinese People's Republic persisted, *Kuomintang*-Nationalist plans underwent profound changes. During the mainland's Great Proletarian Cultural Revolution, for example, Chiang responded to demands from within his party for an immediate invasion by saying that his plans for the return were 70 per cent political (the nature of the politics was unspecified) and 30 per cent military. In advancing this new formula, Chiang did not alter the contention that his was the only legitimate Chinese government. As such, the *Kuomintang*-Nationalists insisted logically upon retention of China's permanent seat in the Security Council of the United Nations and upon recognition by other nations as the legal government of China.

In 1970, the *Kuomintang*-Nationalist government, entering its third decade in exile, was confronted by unresolved ambiguities. While Taiwan's economic accomplishments were remarkable, the island's continued development—like Japan's—was largely dependent on world conditions well beyond the reach of Chinese leadership. In politics, the regime could boast of having given Taiwan (at least since 1950) a relatively stable, honest, and efficient government, but the old leadership was disappearing. Taiwanese were entering politics on the local and provincial levels, while within the national government men whose reputations had been built upon economic leadership were rising to the top. Chiang at eighty-two years of age remained the titular head of government, but administrative control was devolving upon his son Chiang Ching-kuo.[23] It remained to be seen whether this emerging leadership could command popular loyalty or whether it would continue to regard the return to the mainland as a compelling national goal.[24] Finally, Taiwan's unresolved

---

[21] American military advisers had long advocated reduction in the *Kuomintang*-Nationalist army on grounds that it was too large for the defense of Taiwan and too small to take the mainland. The Chinese decision to undertake the recommended reduction, however, did not reflect an official decision to abandon the return to the mainland. Rather, the *Kuomintang*-Nationalist government adopted in the late 1960s a new formula affirming that the return to the mainland was to be accomplished more by political than by military means. American pledges of new weapons and of facilities enabling the Chinese to manufacture their own helicopters, M-14 rifles, and F-4 fighters also encouraged the shift toward the smaller but more elite force. The *Kuomintang*-Nationalist regime may have been concerned also by the spectre of disloyalty among a force composed almost entirely of Taiwanese enlisted men and commanded by a diminishing supply of mainlanders. Mark A. Plummer, "Taiwan: Toward a Second Generation of Mainlander Rule," *Asian Survey* 10 (January, 1970): 18–24.

[22] This thesis is developed more fully in two articles: Duncan Norton-Taylor, "The Sword at the Belly of China," and Stanley Karnow, "How Communist Economics Failed in China," *Fortune* 67 (1963): 151–53; 154–57.

[23] Chiang Ching-kuo was appointed Minister of Defense in 1965, and in 1969 he became Vice-Prime Minister. His power, however, stemmed less from any particular office than from his parentage and his control of the army and secret police.

[24] The kind of problem created by the crossed purposes of a predominately Taiwanese population and a government dominated by mainlanders was illustrated by the "Great Banana

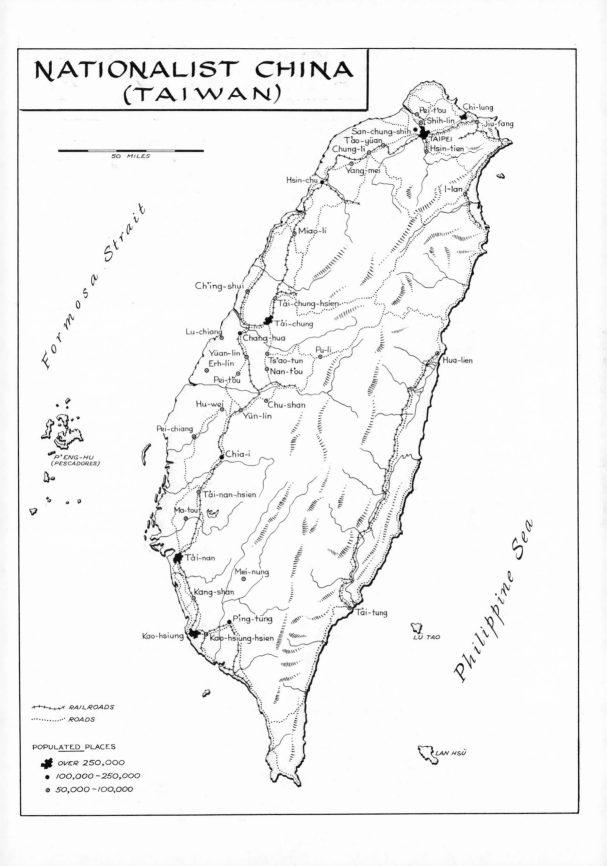

NATIONALIST CHINA
(TAIWAN)

50 MILES

Formosa Strait

Philippine Sea

Pei-t'ou
Chi-lung
Shih-lin
Jiu-fang
San-chung-shih
T'ao-yüan
TAIPEI
Chung-li
Hsin-tien
Yang-mei
Hsin-chu
I-lan

Miao-li

Ch'ing-shui
T'ai-chung-hsien
T'ai-chung
Lu-chiang
Chang-hua
Pu-li
Yüan-lin
Erh-lin
Ts'ao-tun
Nan-t'ou
Pei-t'ou
Hua-lien
Hu-wei
Chu-shan
Yün-lin
Pei-chiang

Chia-i

T'ai-nan-hsien
Ma-tou

T'ai-nan
Mei-nung
Kang-shan
P'ing-tung
T'ai-tung
Kao-hsiung
Kao-hsiung-hsien
LÜ TAO

P'ENG-HU
(PESCADORES)

LAN HSÜ

┼┼┼┼┼ RAILROADS
·········· ROADS

POPULATED PLACES
✦ OVER 250,000
● 100,000 – 250,000
◉ 50,000 – 100,000

legal status was complicated by the continuing failure of the Powers to agree on the identity of the real China. The vote in the United Nations General Assembly, November 11, 1969, on expelling the *Kuomintang*-Nationalist government and seating the Chinese People's Republic (fifty-six against the Communists, forty-eight in their favor, and twenty-one abstentions) provided a measure of the conflicting views. Yet even the persistence of this division was uncertain. In 1969, Canada, Italy, Belgium, Luxembourg, and Portugal—all supporters of *Kuomintang*-Nationalist pretensions to the government of China—were reported to be exploring possibilities in the recognition of Communist China.

These ambiguities in the status of the *Kuomintang*-Nationalist regime were further compounded by qualifications attached to American support. As defined in 1950 (at the outset of the Korean War), American policy included: (1) nonrecognition of the Chinese People's Republic, (2) opposition to a shift in China's representation in the United Nations, (3) economic nonintercourse with mainland China, and (4) material aid to the *Kuomintang*-Nationalist government.[25]

While this policy appeared to support Chiang's determination to return to the mainland, American practice, if not pronouncements, soon revealed definite restrictions on aid to the *Kuomintang*-Nationalist government. American power was employed in the defense of Taiwan and the neighboring Pescadores Islands, but the United States opposed Nationalist ventures which threatened war with Communist China.[26] Thus, despite outward appearances, American policy viewed Chiang less as an alternative and successor to Mao Tse-tung than as head of a government maintaining Taiwan's freedom from Communist control. This view was indicated more explicitly during the late 1960s as searching questions were raised concerning America's Far Eastern policy. The Foreign Relations Committee of the United States Senate in 1966 held nationally televised hearings on American relations with China.[27] Three years later, the Nixon Administration welcomed the resumption of talks in Warsaw between the United States and Communist Chinese ambassadors, and relaxed American prohibitions on travel on the Chinese mainland. As a preliminary to these indications that the American government was willing at least to reconsider its stand on China, Senator J. William Fulbright, Chairman of the Foreign Relations Committee, urged the American people to abandon their "myths" concerning China, to be on guard lest American policies

Case" of 1969. Court actions revealed that Taiwanese banana growers and exporters had succeeded in skimming some $2,500,000 annually off the profits of a $60,000,000 foreign trade. The Taiwanese had connived with key officials, who were lavishly entertained and received expensive gifts. This was the result of a situation in which Taiwanese, enriched by the island's new prosperity, confronted a poorly paid but presumably elite governmental bureaucracy. Plummer, "Taiwan: Toward a Second Generation of Mainlander Rule," *Asian Survey*, 21–22. For other aspects of political tensions see Plummer's "Taiwan: The 'New Look' in Government," *Asian Survey* 9 (1969): 18–22; and Stephen Uhalley, Jr., "Taiwan's Response to the Cultural Revolution," *Asian Survey* 7 (1967): 824–29. In April, 1970, Taiwan's political tensions were demonstrated for Americans as two Formosan Nationalists made an assassination attempt on the life of Chiang Ching-kuo while the latter was visiting New York City.

[25] Harold M. Vinacke, *United States Policy toward China. Occasional Papers—No. 1.* Center for the Study of U.S. Foreign Policy of the Department of Political Science, University of Cincinnati (1961): 28.

[26] American military assistance was extended under a mutual defense treaty (1954). The limitations on American aid under this treaty were illustrated by the reaction of the Eisenhower Administration in 1958 to a Nationalist proposal to bomb the Chinese mainland in defense of Quemoy Island. The United States insisted upon a pledge by Chiang that force would not be "the principal means" of overturning Communist rule. Tang Tsou, "The Quemoy Imbroglio: Chiang Kai-shek and the United States," *Western Political Quarterly*, 12 (1959): 1075–91.

[27] For the full text see *U.S. Policy with Respect to Mainland China* (Hearings before the Committee on Foreign Relations, United States Senate, 89th Congress, Second Session). An edited version of the text with additional material from other hearings is to be found in Akira Iriye, ed., *U.S. Policy toward China: Testimony taken from the Senate Foreign Relations Committee Hearings—1966* (1968).

be "guided by emotionalism" and "thought processes by cliches," and to accept the fact that Red China is likely to be where it is for some time to come.[28]

[28] Concerning China, Senator Fulbright said: "The Far East is another area of the world in which American policy is handicapped by the divergence of old myths and new realities. Particularly with respect to China, an elaborate vocabulary of make believe has become compulsory in both official and public discussion. We are committed, with respect to China and other areas of Asia, to inflexible policies of long standing from which we hesitate to depart because of the attribution to these policies of an aura of mystical sanctity. . . . We have been unwilling to undertake . . . [a critical re-examination of policy] because of the fear of many Government officials, undoubtedly well founded, that even the suggestion of new policies toward China or Vietnam would provoke a vehement public outcry.

"I do not think the United States can, or should, recognize Communist China or acquiesce in its admission to the United Nations under present circumstance. It would be unwise to do so, because there is nothing to be gained by it so long as the Peiping regime maintains its attitude of implacable hostility toward the United States. I do not believe, however, that this state of affairs is necessarily permanent. As we have seen in our relations with Germany and Japan, hostility can give way in an astonishingly short time to close friendship; and, as we have seen in our relations with China, the reverse can occur with equal speed. It is not impossible that in time our relations with China will change again—if not to friendship, then perhaps to 'competitive co-existence.' It would therefore be extremely useful if we could introduce an element of flexibility, or, more precisely, of a capacity to be flexible, into our relations with Communist China.

"We would do well, as former Assistant Secretary Hilsman has recommended, to maintain an 'open door' to the possibility of improved relations with Communist China in the future. For a start, we must jar open our minds to certain realities about China, of which the foremost is that there are really not 'two Chinas,' but only one—mainland China; and that it is ruled by Communists, and is likely to remain so for the indefinite future. Once we accept this fact, it becomes possible to reflect on the conditions under which it might be possible for us to enter into relatively normal relations with mainland China." *Congressional Record*, 88th Cong., 2nd Sess., 110 No. 56 (March 25, 1964): 6028–34. Stefan T. Possony, "The Chinese Communist Cauldron," *Orbis,* 13 (1969): 783–821, a dissenting view.

The reader who will recall the interplay of strength and weakness in America's nineteenth century policies in China may well be forced to the conclusion that the lessons of history are not learned easily if, indeed, they are learned at all.

FOR FURTHER READING

KOREAN WAR. Harold Vinacke, *Far Eastern Politics in the Post-War Period* (1956). Leon Gordenker, *The United Nations and the Peaceful Unification of Korea: The Politics of Field Operations, 1947–1950* (The Hague, 1959). Carl Berger, *The Korea Knot: A Military-Political History* (1957). L. M. Goodrich, *Korea: A Study of United States Policy in the United Nations* (1956). J. W. Spanier, *The Truman-MacArthur Controversy and the Korean War* (1959).* David Rees, *Korea: The Limited War* (1964). William H. Vatcher, Jr., *Panmunjon: The Story of the Korean Military Armistice Negotiations* (1958). Kenneth T. Young, *Negotiating with the Chinese Communists: The United States Experience, 1953–1967* (1968).

KOREA. Shannon McCune, *Korea's Heritage: A Regional and Social Geography* (Tokyo, 1956); and *Korea: Land of Broken Calm* (1966).* George McCune and A. L. Grey, *Korea Today* (1950). Cornelius Osgood, *The Koreans and Their Culture* (1951); and Kim Ik-tal, *Korea: Its Land, People, and Culture of All Ages* (Seoul, 1960). Gregory Henderson, *Korea, The Politics of the Vortex* (1968) relates post-war politics to tradition. Lee Chong-sik, *The Politics of Korean Nationalism* (1963), the standard study. Sih Dae-suk, *The Korean Communist Movement, 1918–1948* (1967). On North Korea, see Philip Rudolph, *North Korea's Political and Economic Structure* (1959); Robert Scalipino, ed., *North Korea Today* (1963); and Joseph S. Chung, *Patterns of Economic Development: Korea* (1966). Lim Youngli, "Foreign Influence on the Economic Change in Korea: A Survey," *Journal of Asian Studies* 28 (1968); 77–99. W. D. Reeve, *The Republic of Korea: A Political and Economic*

Study (1963), useful for the Rhee period. John K. Oh, *Korea: Democracy on Trial* (1968) is critical of achievements to 1967.

TAIWAN. P. M. A. Linebarger, *et al.*, *Far Eastern Governments and Politics* (2nd ed., 1956). On the earlier stages of *Kuomintang*-Nationalist rule, see Norton S. Ginsburg, *Economic Resources and Development of Formosa* (1953); Fred W. Riggs, *Formosa under Chinese Nationalist Rule* (1952); and George H. Kerr, *Formosa Betrayed* (1965). Hsieh Chiao-min, *Taiwan-Ilha Formosa: A Geography in Perspective* (1965). Aspects of agricultural development are treated in Anthony Y. C. Koo, *The Role of Land Reform in Economic Development: A Case Study* (1968); T. S. Shen, *Agricultural Development on Taiwan since World War II* (1964); and Charles Kao, "An Analysis of Agricultural Output Increase on Taiwan, 1953–1964," *Journal of Asian Studies* 26 (1967): 611–26. Norma Diamond, *K'un Shen: A Taiwan Village* (1969),* emphasizes relationships between the economy and social organization. Mark Mancall, ed., *Formosa Today* (1964), a collection of essays generally critical of *Kuomintang*-Nationalist rule. Lung-chu Chen and Harold Laswell, *Formosa, China and the United Nations: Formosa in the World Community* (1967), a justification of Formosan independence.

AMERICAN RELATIONS WITH KOREA AND TAIWAN. Essays by Shannon McCune, Robert Scalapino, and Allen S. Whiting in *The United States and the Far East*, Willard Thorp, ed. (2nd. ed., 1962).* Sheldon Ap-

pleton, *The Eternal Triangle? Communist China, the United States, and the United Nations* (1961) includes American and United Nations documents. Robert P. Newman, *Recognition of Communist China? A Study in Argument* (1961),* a convenient summary of this debate in the United States. Li Thian-hok, "The China Impasse: A Formosan View," *Foreign Affairs* 36 (1958): 437–48. An official statement of American policy is in the United States Department of State, *U.S. Policy on Nonrecognition of Communist China*, Public Services Division, Pub. No. 6705, Far Eastern Series (1958). Conlon Associates, Ltd., *United States Foreign Policy: Asia*, Study No. 5, United States Senate, 86th Cong. 1st Sess. (1959), a critical review made at the request of the Senate Foreign Relations Committee. Robert Blum, *The United States and China in World Affairs* (1966) studies the American commitment to the *Kuomintang*-Nationalist government. Robert Scalapino, "The Question of 'Two Chinas'" in *China in Crisis: China's Heritage and the Communist Political System*, Ho Ping-ti and Tsou Tang, eds. (1968), 109–20, argues for a two-China policy. A. T. Steele, *The American People and China* (1966), an examination of popular attitudes and how they have been formed.

The Transactions of the Korea Branch of the Royal Asiatic Society is an important source for the cultural history of Korea. The *Korean Quarterly* is useful for political events. For current developments in Korea and Taiwan see *Pacific Affairs* and *Asian Survey*.

The New Southeast Asia: 1941 and After

chapter 36

Japan's advance into Southeast Asia brought changes in that vast area that were as striking as those wrought in China and in Japan by World War II. In Southeast Asia in 1941, Western colonial powers enjoyed firm political authority, vital economic stakes, and strategic position symbolized by the great British naval base at Singapore. All of this was swept away by the war. When peace came, the West attempted to re-establish itself in Southeast Asia, but colonialism was opposed by revolutionary nationalism in a great variety of forms. Thus, the years after 1945 witnessed the liquidation of colonial regimes and the creation of new national governments. At the same time, even as Southeast Asia grappled with the complexities of nation building, the newly created states were plunged into rivalries with one another and into the longer struggles among the great powers for control of the area.

THE JAPANESE OCCUPATION

The independence movements which confronted returning colonial authorities in 1945 were in part a product of the Japanese occupation. Between the attack on Pearl Harbor and mid-1942, all of Southeast Asia for the first time was brought under a single authority. Except for Thailand and Indochina where Japanese rule was indirect, the entire region was administered by Tokyo through its army and navy. Japan's immediate purpose was to bind the region to herself in support of the war effort, and to this end her colonial administrations emphasized the production of industrial raw materials and foodstuffs. Generally speaking, these efforts did Japan little good. As the war progressed, shipping shortages and acute economic dislocations denied the Japanese the benefits they sought. Moreover, Japanese policy created new problems as the products of plantation economies were assigned low priorities. The result was widespread hardship which, in turn, fed resistance movements. Thus, well before V-J Day, Southeast Asia's rejection of western colonialism was also directed against continuation of Japanese rule.

Southeast Asian nationalism was heightened by Japan's intense labors to substitute her own cultural influence for that of the old colonial powers. Language instruction, for example, proscribed Western tongues while emphasizing native languages and Japanese. Japanese administrators encouraged the formation of youth organizations, air raid associations, auxiliary police corps, and para-military forces as a popular basis for propa-gandizing the "New Asia" and "Asia for Asiatics." Further distinctions between Ja-panese and Western rule were attempted by enlisting native leaders into government service where they enjoyed some prestige if not much power. These measures, however, like the economic policies, backfired. Japan was unsuccessful in linking Southeast Asians to herself, but she did broaden the popular basis of native nationalism and instilled in native leaders a new sense of self-confidence.[1]

THE PHILIPPINES

Nowhere in Southeast Asia was popular resentment of Japan more intense than in the Philippines. Not only had Japan's propa-ganda emphasizing Asian nationalism and her efforts to establish a "Philippine Repub-lic" under José Laurel held small attraction in the already self-governing commonwealth, but also occupation personnel had belied the image of liberators through extensive looting, exploitation, and destruction. In consequence, resistance movements appeared throughout the islands. The most formidable of these guerrilla operations was the *Hukbalahaps*, or People's Anti-Japanese Army, which operated on the fringes of the Central Luzon plain. Led by Luis Taruc, a labor organizer who had been a Communist since 1939, this force had drawn support from the peasantry through its attacks on landlords as well as on the Japanese. By fighting the Japanese and co-operating with other guerrillas in such operations as secreting American intelli-gence agents, the Huks, as they came to be known, contributed generally to keeping alive Filipino hopes of liberation.

With the American reconquest of the islands, the commonwealth was gradually restored under Sergio Osmeña, who had

[1] John Bastin and Harry J. Benda, *A History of Modern Southeast Asia: Colonialism, National-ism, and Decolonization* (1968),* 123–52.

succeeded to the presidency upon the death of Manuel Quezon. The tenure of this gov-ernment, however, was short-lived, since elections were held in preparation for the establishment of full independence under the Tydings-McDuffie Law. In this first post-war campaign Osmeña, the Nationalist Party candidate, charged that his opponent, the Liberal Party's Manuel Roxas, who had helped to draft the constitution of the Japa-nese puppet republic, had been a collabora-tor. But this allegation was blunted by the rationalization that in view of America's failure to defend the islands successfully, collaboration was the only alternative to Japanese rule.[2] Roxas's patriotism was also vindicated by General MacArthur. Thus, fol-lowing the Roxas victory, collaboration dis-appeared as a political issue, and the new Philippine Republic, proclaimed by the United States on July 4, 1946, turned to its current troubles which were perplexing enough.

The new Philippine Republic was neither free from American influence on the outside nor from disruptive forces at home. While the United States had sought to re-duce Philippine dependence on American trade, American investments retained a spe-cial status. Under the requirement of United States law (the Philippine Trade Act of 1946), the Philippine constitution was amended to permit Americans to enjoy equal rights with Filipinos in industrial exploita-tion. For Filipino nationalists, these special rights for Americans were the more distaste-

[2] Claude A. Buss, "The Philippines," *The New World of Southeast Asia*, Lennox A. Mills, ed. (1949), 44–49. The issues raised by Philip-pine collaboration with the Japanese are ex-ceedingly complex. In 1945, José P. Laurel, then jailed and charged with treason, justified his taking the presidency under the Japanese saying that "forced collaboration is not collaboration." This self-evaluation, however, ignored evidence that Laurel wanted to use the powers of the presidential office, albeit circumscribed by the Japanese, to effect reforms which he believed were essential to the growth of Philippine society. David Steinberg, "José P. Laurel: A 'Collabora-tor' Misunderstood," *Journal of Asian Studies* 24 (1965): 651–65.

ful because American investments tended to increase rather than to diminish.[3] The Philippine Republic was also beset with problems of flagrant corruption. Its own bureaucracy, operating under traditional concepts of obligation to the family rather than to public welfare, found opportunities for personal enrichment exceedingly tempting. Moreover, American aid, which was to assist with rehabilitation and the transition to nationhood, was often misdirected.[4] Payments from this aid exacerbated existing rural problems by strengthening landlords while contributing little to the wellbeing of peasants. The result in Central Luzon was to encourage the Huks to expand their guerrilla campaigns against property and constituted authority. As the only group opposing the landlords, the Huks enjoyed increasing peasant support. By the late 1940s, the "People's Liberation Army," as the Huks called themselves, posed a serious military threat to the Republic.

While these were grave problems, the Philippine government had some resources for dealing with the crisis. The operation of a two-party system, Nationalists and Liberals, contributed to a measure of political stability. The parties smoothed the way for the transfer of power and provided for some expression of genuine popular interests. In addition they succeeded in involving an ever greater portion of the populace in political processes. By the 1960s some 30 per cent of the population voted in presidential elections as compared with only 3 per cent in 1907 and 14 per cent in 1949. Finally, the quality of political leadership on occasion could be outstanding. In the 1950s Raymond Magsay-

say, first as Secretary of Defense and later as President, dealt effectively with the Huks. His tactics included the use of regular troops (rather than the despised local police) against Huk forces, offers of pardons and grants of land and tools so that peasants might establish themselves as farmer-owners. These measures were so successful that the Huks were eventually reduced to a few hundred men hiding in the hills. As President (his term was cut short by a fatal plane crash in March, 1957), Magsaysay demanded integrity of office holders, initiated land reforms, opened credit facilities for the peasantry, and constructed farm-to-market highways. Through these measures and his own magnetic personality, Magsaysay contributed significantly to a growing rapport between the government and the people.

There was the question, however, whether leadership and the party system could sustain the needed level of achievement. A population growth which had produced a nation of 36,000,000 by 1969 and which promised to double that figure within another twenty years denied to the vast majority any substantial benefit from an expanding economy. Indeed, the Philippine political scene was polluted by sprawling, crime-ridden urban slums, by an expanding and largely unmet demand for public services, and by renewed economic pressures on the peasantry. As such conditions intensified, the Huks reappeared as champions of the oppressed. Among more affluent Filipinos, especially educated young "technocrats," there were also indications of political alienation. Increasingly articulate Filipinos condemned both major parties and demanded a search for new political directions. Ferdinand Marcos, following a campaign marred by unprecedented violence, was re-elected in November, 1969, to a second presidential term, but this did not mean that Philippine democracy was secure. What the election seemed to show was that the Philippines for the moment supported a governmenal system bequeathed by their colonial past. However, it was evident also that the Marcos Administration presided over an explosive society.

[3] By 1969, twenty-four of the largest enterprises in the Philippines were American owned. The earlier phases of Philippine reaction to American privilege are suggested in Frank Golay, "Economic Consequences of the Philippine Trade Act," *Pacific Affairs* 28 (1955): 53–70.

[4] The United States continued to assume responsibilities for Philippine defense under a military alliance authorizing American bases. Congress also appropriated, over five years, two billion dollars to compensate Filipinos for war damage and rehabilitation.

The Dutch empire in the East Indies was destroyed in 1941–1942 not by the power of the native nationalism but by a Japanese naval and military invasion. Tokyo, determined to transform the Indies into a Japanese colonial empire, undertook to foment opposition to the Dutch while discouraging independence itself. To accomplish these purposes European residents were publicly humiliated, Moslem leaders were encouraged to assume authority under the Japanese, and, ultimately, a committee to draft a constitution for an independent Indonesia was established. These measures did stimulate native desires to be free, but they failed to engender loyalty toward Japan. The Japanese drained the islands of whatever produce they needed, impoverished the populace, and maintained an oppressive military government until the eve of their defeat.[5]

The first Dutch plans for the post-war Indies were contained, December, 1942, in a vague blueprint for the future proposing a commonwealth. Had this plan been made and acted upon prior to the Japanese attack it might have been the basis of an evolutionary political development. The war, however, created new conditions which the Dutch with signal lack of vision failed completely to anticipate. Dutch policy was to resume control over the islands first and then consider Indonesian demands; Indonesian leadership, however, on August 17, 1945, had already proclaimed the existence of an Indonesian Republic, had organized a militia, and had established a capital in Batavia (renamed Djakarta). The policy of this native leadership, among whom Sukarno and Mohammed Hatta were prominent, was to demand recognition of the independent Republic before negotiating on the future relation of the islands to the Netherlands.

An initial attempt to resolve these differences was embodied in the Linggadjati Agreement of March 25, 1947, which coupled Dutch recognition of the Indonesian Republic with the relegation of that Republic to a subordinate status within a Dutch-controlled political complex. Since this arrangement proved unsatisfactory to all parties, war ensued, and the Dutch, having superior military equipment, drove Republican forces into the hills of central Java. In 1948 the Dutch captured Djakarta and imprisoned Republican leaders. The Dutch then announced that the Republic was destroyed, but in reality they had failed to destroy either the spirit of the Republic or its guerrilla forces.

Indeed, the Dutch had misjudged not only Indonesian resistance but also Western opinion. They soon found it expedient to release Sukarno and others and to agree to a conference at The Hague, October, 1949. Out of this conference came agreement for a United States of Indonesia (the Republic and eighteen states created by the Dutch). This in turn would be a part of the Dutch-Indonesian Union, whose main power was to deal with foreign relations. No settlement was reached concerning Dutch New Guinea (West Irian), claimed by both the Dutch and the Indonesians. It remained under Dutch administration. The Dutch hoped, of course, that the states they had set up would be an effective curb on the Republic. In this they were again wrong. No sooner had The Hague Agreement been effected, December, 1949, than the new Dutch-sponsored states voted under its terms for union with the Republic. By August, 1950, the United States of Indonesia had been replaced by a united and unitary Republic of Indonesia. Four years later, the Dutch-Indonesian Union itself passed into history. Political independence had become a reality.[6]

The form of the new government—a unicameral legislature, a president selected by parliament, a vice-president named by the President but recommended by parliament, and a cabinet responsible to parliament—was derived from Western democratic institutions.

[5] See especially Harry J. Benda, *The Crescent and the Rising Sun: Indonesian Islam under the Japanese Occupation, 1942–1945* (The Hague, 1958); and Benedict R. O. G. Anderson, *Some Aspects of Indonesian Politics under the Japanese Occupation, 1944–1945* (1961).

[6] George McTurnan Kahin, *Nationalism and Revolution in Indonesia* (1952) is an excellent study of the struggle for independence.

The outward appearance of democracy, however, proved easier to approximate than democratic practice. Although members of Parliament resorted to slogans drawn from Western political thought (liberty, democracy, parliament, elections), they had obtained their seats by appointment, not elections, and they were unwilling to hold elections until popular pressures compelled a vote in 1955. Sukarno continued to serve as President, although he had been selected by a group of Nationalist leaders in 1945 rather than by parliament. Compounding these difficulties was chronic instability in cabinet government arising from the failure of any single political party to control a legislative majority. In consequence, the first cabinets were inter-party selections, none of which survived for long. Finally, the government, eminently successful in creating a large bureaucracy, showed far less aptitude for building a strong economy.

The parliamentary elections of 1955, by dividing power among four major parties (Nationalist, Masjumi, Moslem Teachers, and Communists) and several minor ones, only served to deepen the social, economic, and political crisis. Sukarno's remedy for continuing internal division was the expansion of his personal power. In February, 1957, martial law was proclaimed, giving the president and army exceptional powers. Two years later, July, 1959, Sukarno dissolved the Constituent Assembly, which had been drafting a permanent constitution, and ordered restoration of the revolutionary Constitution of 1945. Utilizing the great powers accorded him under that document, Sukarno suspended parliament and created handpicked government organs to collaborate in his rule. Chief support for this experiment in "guided democracy" came from the Nationalists, the Moslem Conservatives, the Communists, and the army. Sukarno presided over these contending groups, preventing any one of them from gaining predominant power, and playing one against the others for his own advantage.[7]

[7] Amry Vandenbosch, " 'Guided Democracy' in Indonesia," *Current History* 41 (1961): 329–34.

In the reshaping of its economic life, Indonesia, like most new states in Southeast Asia, reacted strongly against unfettered private capitalism. Private capitalism was intimately associated in the Indonesian mind with foreign rule. Prior to the war the foreign investor had often been the most outspoken opponent of self-government and independence. Thus the achievement of political independence carried with it the drive to end foreign economic control through economic nationalism operating as state capitalism. This meant the development of a state-planned economy to meet national ends. Complicating the problem of state planning, however, was a rapidly increasing population (a medieval birth rate with a modern death rate), which was a hindrance rather than an aid to economic development. Domestic capital formation in Indonesia under the Republic was negligible, and there was reluctance on the part of the government to give foreign investors the security they desired.[8] Even though Indonesia received much foreign aid, economic development lagged, the transportation system deteriorated, and prices rose as inflation stirred unrest among the salaried classes and urban wage earners.

Adding to these multiplying pressures, the assassination of officers in the Central Indonesian Army Command, October 1, 1965, touched off an extermination campaign in which the army sought, among other things, to eliminate communism as a political influence. More than half of the Communist party's Central Committee was jailed or murdered; surviving members fled into hiding. On the local level the army's campaign degenerated into a blood bath costing thousands of lives.[9] This general blood-letting

[8] B. W. Hodder, "Demographic Influences on Economic Development in Southeast Asia," *Nationalism and Progress in Free Asia*, Philip W. Thayer, ed. (1956), 214–15.
[9] At least a quarter of a million persons are believed to have died. In 1969 some 100,000 others were estimated to remain in jail. Benedict R. O. G. Anderson, "Indonesia's Uncertain Future," *Current History* 57 (1969): 355–60. For descriptive accounts see John Hughes, *Indonesian Upheaval* (1967); and Robert Shaplen, *Time Out of Hand* (1969).

also toppled Sukarno. While the president's role in the turmoil remains obscure, the army, acting on the theory that Sukarno was leagued with Communists, and that the Communists were linked with Chinese expansionism, first restricted his powers and later forced him into retirement.[10] General Suharto, a leader of the coup, was named acting president by a "Provisional People's Consultative Assembly" on March 12, 1967. Subsequently, in 1968, Suharto was confirmed in office and given a five year term.

Claiming that his government would be judged primarily on its performance in economics, Suharto eschewed the flamboyant political posturing of his predecessor and concentrated on more sober planning. An initial task was to check the precipitous economic decline of Sukarno's last years. To this end the regime sought to control inflation, to balance the budget, to bring order into the banking system, to improve the efficiency of the civil service, and to curb corruption. Coordinated with these internal measures were efforts to rehabilitate Indonesia's reputation among foreign creditors. Repayments on the foreign debt of $2,300,000,000 were rescheduled, and private investors whom Sukarno had driven from the islands were offered fresh incentives. As a result of these

[10] By 1965 the *Parti Komunis Indonesia* (PKI) had emerged as a strong political force. Having no more than 5,000 members in 1950, the PKI had grown to more than 2,000,000 by 1963. This achievement owed much to the skill of D. N. Aidit, the party's leader, in blending Communist ideology with Indonesian nationalism and in employing a variety of mass organizations (trade unions, women's movements, youth movements) as a basis for recruiting and retaining members. Relatively little is known either about the development of the PKI or its connections with international communism. Thus, the Indonesian army's allegation that the PKI was linked with the Chinese Communists must be regarded as an hypothesis. For recent studies summarizing and analyzing available evidence, see Donald Hindley, *The Communist Party of Indonesia, 1951–1962* (1964); and two studies by Justus M. Van der Kroef, *The Communist Party of Indonesia: Its History, Program, and Tactics* (Vancouver, 1965); and "The Sino-Indonesian Rupture," *The China Quarterly* (January-March, 1968); 1–30.

measures, a monetary inflation rate which had reached a fantastic 635 per cent in 1966 was cut within two years to 85 per cent, a food crisis was averted, and some foreign capital—mostly American and Japanese—returned. In fact, by early 1969, Suharto was so confident of progress in economic rehabilitation that he announced a five year plan projecting substantial development.

These initial triumphs enabled Suharto to consolidate his power and to arrest political disintegration, but they did not spell an end to the nation's troubles. Long range economic planning had to take into account a population growth rate (census rolls were to swell in 1970 alone by more than 3,000,000) that imposed a most serious strain on available resources. As a result, economic development was dependent not only upon Indonesia's own sound planning but also upon substantial foreign aid. In addition government stability was threatened by Suharto's heavy reliance upon the army, a body which had been united against a Communist threat but which was not at peace either with itself or with the political parties. Moreover, the country's social structure had not recovered from the blood-letting of 1965–1966. It could only be concluded that Indonesia was not far advanced in the tasks of nation building.

BURMA

The Japanese overran Burma in the first six months of 1942. At first they were welcomed and assisted particularly by the extremists of the Thakin party who had been clamoring for independence. In August, 1942, the Japanese military administration recognized Burmese independence under a puppet government headed by Ba Maw, a former premier with a pronounced anti-British record, but Ba Maw's government soon lost its initial popular support.[11] Its

[11] For an interpretation of the relationship between Japanese imperialism and Burmese nationalism see Ba Maw, *Breakthrough in Burma: Memoirs of a Revolution, 1939–1946* (1968). While some critics hold that Ba Maw was an

subservience to the Japanese was clear, while the behavior of the Japanese themselves contradicted their own propaganda that they were the saviors of Asia. The result was that many Burmans who had first assisted the Japanese joined the growing resistance movement organized as the Anti-Fascist People's Freedom League (AFPFL). As finally constituted in 1944, the League was a union of many revolutionary, independence, and Communist groups under the leadership of General Aung San, who only a few years earlier had helped the Japanese conquer Burma. The uniqueness of the AFPFL was that by the time the British returned at the end of the war it was able to confront them with its own effective army.

The immediate British plan for Burma was to restore the pre-war political structure. Burmese parties would then be encouraged to propose and agree on a new constitution, after which there would be negotiations looking to Dominion status. In economic affairs, normal competitive business was to be restored as rapidly as possible. British plans, however, did not meet Burmese realities. The rapid Japanese conquest had destroyed British military and, in a degree, political prestige, while the war experience itself had produced in Burma her own military and political leaders possessed of a limited experience and a boundless determination.

In the circumstances, the British governor, acting on revised plans, created an Executive Council of eleven members, six of whom represented the AFPFL. The British government, December, 1946, affirmed that Commonwealth status or independence, according to Burma's desire, would be granted "by the quickest and most convenient way possible." A subsequent conference at London, in which the Burmese delegation was headed by Aung San, President of the AFPFL, reached a settlement in January,

1947. It provided for an elected constituent Burmese assembly to frame a new independent Burmese government. Provision was also made for a transitional government consisting of a legislative council, a Governor's Executive Council, and a High Commissioner for Burma at London. The British government was to support Burma's application for membership in the United Nations and to invite other governments to establish diplomatic relations with Burma. Although this settlement was opposed by the Communists and other extreme groups, it was accepted by Aung San, the AFPFL, and the country at large. The new constitution was accepted, September, 1947, and Burma's independence dated from an Anglo-Burmese treaty, January, 1948. The transition to this new independent republic, however, was not achieved without violence and bloodshed. In July, 1947, Aung San and six associates in the interim Executive Council were assassinated by U Saw and extremists attempting to take over the government. With the collapse of this abortive coup, leadership passed to U Nu, then Vice-President of the AFPFL, who was to remain, until March, 1962, the outstanding political figure.

Burma's constitutional government was subjected to very severe strains from both the Right and the Left. The former represented elements opposed to the government's socialistic program. The latter was led by Communists who had split into two factions. There was also opposition from the lesser nationalities, especially the Karens, who had approved federation but were reluctant to practice it. The governing AFPFL managed to smother these factional revolts through military action and propaganda, but inefficient political administration, widespread political corruption, and disorders rooted in guerrilla activity and banditry continued to feed public unrest. The result was that U Nu, October, 1958, permitted power to pass to a military caretaker government under General Ne Win.

For two years, 1958 to 1960, his military junta sought to discipline the nation. Army officers, entering every phase of political life, closed newspapers, dealt summarily with in-

opportunistic and unscrupulous collaborator with Japanese fascism, his memoirs present a picture of a deep bond of mutual confidence between his followers and the Japanese, a bond which was based on personal respect and conviction that there was a legitimate commonality of interest between Burma and the Axis cause.

dividuals suspected of corrupt or subversive activity. These measures, however, were avowedly preliminary to the re-establishment of civilian rule. The framework of constitutional government was retained, and, in 1960, elections brought U Nu back into power as prime minister. But it was civilian, not military, government that proved to be temporary. Ne Win seized control on March 2, 1962, this time aiming at permanent retention of power. The General placed elected civilian officials, including Premier U Nu, in "protective custody," abolished parliamentary government, and assumed extraordinary personal powers for dealing with internal disorders.

This formula for resolving Burma's ills embodied in a single-party state applying "the Burmese Way to socialism."[12] Under single-party rule, restrictions on dissent were combined with concessions to the political and economic aspirations of restive elements. After 1966, in another move to create greater national solidarity, Ne Win freed political prisoners, including U Nu, and appointed some of them to study constitutional and administrative reforms. Among Ne Win's economic measures were (1) the nationalization of industry, major trading organizations, and banks; (2) the heavy taxation of the rice trade (and, in consequence, the rice producing peasantry) to provide sorely needed revenues; and (3) the exhortation of the populace to apply itself virtuously to tasks benefiting the nation.

Time showed these measures to have little magic. While the government made much of increased income for peasants and workers, the economy failed to measure up to the demands placed upon it. Severe shortages in government stores nurtured a black market trade. In politics, too, the problem was one of transforming plans into significant action. Government policy succeeded in the

south in winning support among dissident Karens, but in the north, where tribal leadership refused to bow to government leadership, the security threat remained serious. Moreover, difficulties in opening a dialogue between Ne Win and such opponents as U Nu indicated that Burma had yet to discover an acceptable and workable form of government.[13]

MALAYA

Malaya's racial minorities, the Indians and the Chinese, were the first to experience the impact of the Japanese invasion and rule. The Indians benefited from lenient treatment as Japanese military authorities sought a popular base for a contemplated attack on British India. The Chinese, on the other hand, suspect in Japanese eyes because of their long affiliation with Mainland China, were persecuted to such a degree that thousands fled into the countryside where they participated in the creation of a Communist-led guerrilla force. As for the Malay majority, it was brought little change by the Japanese conquest, aside from the impact of economic deterioration. Government continued much as usual because the Japanese, in the manner of the British, chose to rule through native leaders. It was not until late in the war, as Japanese fortunes were reversed and British counterattacks threatened, that Japanese policy sought to cultivate and mobilize the Malays. The small but influential native intelligentsia was encouraged to contact Indonesian Nationalists with the aim of promoting under Japanese leadership, a "Greater Indonesia." Japan's surrender forced an early end to these conversations which, together

---

[12] The attractions of socialism are suggested partly by the fact that in Burma during colonial days private capitalism had operated under British, Indian, or Chinese control. Burmese Nationalist leaders also enjoyed considerable success in linking socialism and Theravada Buddhism. For a study of the latter point see E. Sarkisyanz, *Buddhist Backgrounds of the Burmese Revolution* (The Hague, 1965).

[13] After release from custody in 1969, U Nu publicly questioned the legitimacy of Ne Win's regime and defended the old constitutional system. Ne Win responded with a sharp attack on the record of civilian leadership. The exchange was followed by U Nu's departure from Burma for England where he called for the termination of militarist rule, not its gradual reform. Josef Silverstein, "Political Dialogue in Burma: A New Turn on the Road to Socialism," *Asian Survey* 10 (1970): 133–42.

with Chinese guerrilla operations, were indicators of a nationalism far more vigorous than that with which the British had to deal in 1941.

The British returned to Malaya with plans for a reorganized colonial administration. These called for the simplification and modernization of the cumbersome machinery of indirect government. The separate existence of the several states under British rule was to be ended; various constitutional entities (except for Singapore which was to remain a Crown colony) were to be incorporated into a tightly knit, centralized Malayan Union. Great Britain, however, was eventually pressured into abandoning this scheme. Former colonial administrators campaigned against such an abrupt departure from traditional practice. Moreover, within the colony itself the plan aroused the opposition of British-educated upper class Malays because it promised too much power to Indians and Chinese. Thus, the post-war government system, named the Federation of Malaya, reverted to earlier patterns of colonial rule. The Federation provided for the supremacy of the states and for the safeguarding of Malay rights and privileges, especially with regard to land holding, access to political offices, language, and religion. This new state was put into operation in 1948 with the understanding that Malaya would later have an opportunity to become self-governing.

As the Federation began to govern, Communist-led guerrilla forces launched a violent and prolonged rebellion. The Communist strategy was to terrorize the populace by the murder of officials, plantation owners, businessmen, and supporters of the *Kuomintang*. Within rural bases, the Communists organized (sometimes by force) their Malayan National Liberation Army, whose professed purpose was to set up an independent Malayan People's Democratic Republic with equality for all races. Failing to deal effectively with the crisis through military force, the British turned to more fundamental measures designed to starve out the Communist jungle strongholds by the resettlement of Chinese peasants in government-controlled villages. By 1955, Communist guerrilla strength had not been destroyed, but it had been so reduced as to be no longer a critical threat to the economy.[14]

In spite of strains imposed by the Communist threat, the Federation made progress toward independence. The Malayan Civil Service, a body which before World War II had been noted for excellence, was reconstructed;[15] social welfare and economic development programs were inaugurated; and problems of disunity arising from distinctive racial grouping were met in some degree with the formation of the Alliance Party, a tripartite organization composed of Malay, Indian and Chinese groups which by 1955 had become the major political party. Thus it was amid signs of maturing nationalism that a Constitutional Conference met in London to plan for the transfer of power. These plans were put into operation on August 31, 1957, when the Federation of Malay became a self-governing member of the British Commonwealth of Nations. Within the next two months, Malaya gained admission to the United Nations and signed a defense and mutual assistance treaty with Great Britain. Singapore remained outside the new state

[14] Lucian W. Pye, *Guerrilla Communism in Malaya: Its Social and Political Meaning* (1956) is a detailed study. In the later conflict in Vietnam, some Americans recalling the British experience with Communist insurgency, urged that the United States draw lessons from it. It must be noted, however, that the situations in Malaya and Vietnam differed in several important respects: (1) The insurgents in Malaya were Chinese and, as such, identifiable among the populace. Vietnamese insurgents were not so easily distinguished. (2) Malaya, unlike South Vietnam, was not located next to a Communist state. The Malaya Communists, therefore, experienced great difficulties in obtaining supplies. (3) In Vietnam, the returning French were immediately confronted with armed opposition, while in Malaya the British had almost three years to re-establish control of the administrative framework. (4) The British dealt with the Malayan populace through its own colonial administration. In Vietnam the United States acted in support of a South Vietnamese government. Richard Clutterbuck, *The Long, Long War: Counter-insurgency in Malaya and Vietnam, 1948–1960* (1966).

[15] See Robert O. Tilman, "The Nationalization of the Colonial Services in Malaya," *The South Atlantic Quarterly*, 61 (1962), 183–96.

as a British possession exercising a substantial measure of self-government.

Malaya dealt with its economic problems with a vigor that was unique in postwar Southeast Asia, excepting possibly in North Vietnam. Researchers and technicians were engaged in a far reaching program to sustain rubber exports in an era when synthetics offered increasing competition in world markets. Economic diversification was encouraged through the introduction of new export crops, and priority was given to the expansion of food production. Highway construction linked farms to urban markets, electric power lines were extended into the countryside, and substantial headway was made in building rural schools, health clinics, and agricultural training centers. Most remarkable was Malaya's self-reliance in carrying on these programs. Except for some assistance from a small group of American Peace Corps volunteers and some comparatively small loans from the World Bank and the British Commonwealth, economic development rested to a surprising degree on the nation's own resources. During the 1960s, Malaya's gross national product expanded at a rate of better than 5 per cent each year, an increase which provided the people of West Malaysia (the designation after 1963 for the states located on the Malay peninsula) and Singapore with one of the highest per capita incomes in all of Asia.

Economic development was possible because of a relatively efficient and stable government headed until September, 1970, by Tunku Abdul Rahman as Prime Minister. In the area of politics, however, as contrasted with economics and administration, independent Malaya found no easy answers. The problem was to establish national solidarity in a society where no single race—Malay, Indian, or Chinese—held a clear majority. Under the Tunku government, administration was conducted as an alliance in which a delicate balance was struck among the races. Yet, as the experience of Singapore was to suggest, the maintenance of an equilibrium was no simple matter. Economic factors favored adding Singapore to the Malayan Federation, but the Federation

hesitated because the city's predominantly Chinese population, when added to the Chinese already in Malaya, threatened to submerge the Malays in their own country. It was only with the creation of an enlarged Federation of Malaysia, September, 1963, a state which included two former British colonies in the Indonesian archipelago, Sabah (British North Borneo) and Sarawak, that the incorporation of Singapore seemed feasible. The racial balances of the enlarged Federation prevented the Chinese from having a majority, but even so, a settlement was not assured. By 1965, Singapore's dynamic leader, Lee Kuan Yew, growing restive because he had so little voice in the Malay-dominated government, attempted to unite all Chinese within the Federation under a common front. The effort brought Singapore's prompt expulsion from the Federation, though economic ties were not severed.[16] In May, 1969, the Federation faced further racial troubles when post-election rioting resulted in the death of at least 200 Chinese, the suspension of civil liberties, and the transfer—presumably on a temporary basis—of power to a governing body from which Chinese were excluded. These measures, like Singapore's expulsion from the Federation, restored order, but they did not resolve the basic problem.

INDOCHINA

Nationalism in Indochina, long repressed by French authority, emerged as a

[16] After its expulsion from Malaysia, Singapore retained independent existence as an island republic. Under Lee Kuan Yew, the traditional entrepôt began to transform itself into an industrial center and trade mart. The Vietnam war benefited the city economically and politically, furnishing new jobs which in turn permitted the administration to reinforce its position. Like much the rest of Southeast Asia, however, Singapore was confronted with population growth and a potential unemployment problem. Economic and political stability were viewed by Premier Lee as linked with Singapore's full integration into an expanding world economy. Shaplen, *Time Out of Hand*, 220–29. Alex Josey, *Lee Kuan Yew* (Singapore, 1969), an authorized biography with key documents.

vibrant force during World War II. While its appearance was traceable in an immediate sense to popular resentment of the Japanese invaders, there were also hostile movements against the French. French colonialism, by its political and cultural policy, had failed to win the loyalty of the Annamese, and the economic status of the natives had deteriorated rapidly in the pre-war decade as a result of increasing population without compensating adjustments in the economy. Further damage was done French prestige when the colonial government, following the fall of France in 1940, permitted the Japanese to convert this area into a puppet regime. The willingness of the French to serve Japan enabled Vietnamese nationalism as a revolutionary force to strike at both the Japanese and the French. The organizational basis for these attacks was provided by the Vietnam Independence League (Vietminh), which was composed of a diverse array of patriots under a Communist leadership headed by Ho Chi Minh.[17]

With the collapse of Japanese power the Vietminh sought to establish its own authority. In September, 1945, the Vietminh, having the support of guerrilla fighters, proclaimed the independence of the Democratic Republic of Vietnam. Although this regime was soon in control of Annam, it met resistance from returning French forces. French policy, in principle at least, was willing to accept an autonomous Indochinese federation inside a French federal union, but it remained for France and Vietnam to agree on what the French scheme was to mean. On this point no agreement was ever reached. To the nationalists of the Vietminh, federation meant limited economic co-ordination among the Democratic Republic, Laos, and Cambodia. To the French it meant close co-ordination under a French

High Commissioner who would represent France and the French Union while serving as President of the Indochinese Federation. Another disagreement concerned the establishment of a French puppet regime in Cochin China. Meanwhile, armed clashes were erupting between French and Vietminh forces.

In 1949, France, believing that its only hope was in the establishment of a subservient regime, persuaded Bao Dai, a decendent of the Nguyen dynasty which had ruled in Annam since the eighteenth century, to head a French-sponsored Vietnam government (called the provisional government of Vietnam).

From its beginning, the provisional government rested on foundations of sand. It had no substantial support in either the cities or the countryside. It was operated by a clique of Bao Dai's friends, while the former emperor himself basked in the Mediterranean sunshine of southern France. Its only strength lay in its opposition to the Communist leadership of Ho Chi Minh's republic, but it did not succeed in unifying special groups who were also opposed to communism, such as the native Catholics of Tongkin who followed the political leadership of their own bishops, or the indigenous religious sects of the south, such as the Caodaists and the Hoa Hao.[18]

While the provisional government was failing to gain either popular native support or any real autonomy from French control and was subsisting on what it was against

[17] Ho's party affiliation went back to 1917 when he drew together a group of Vietnamese Communists at Paris where he was a student. He later had Communist schooling at Moscow and was at Canton with Borodin in 1925. While at Canton, he formed a Vietnamese Revolutionary Youth party and secured appointment of Vietnamese cadets for training at the Whampoa Military Academy. Later these men emerged as commanders of the Vietminh army.

[18] Both the Vietminh and the personnel of Bao Dai's regime were drawn from the small Vietnamese upper class which had been educated in French colonial institutions. The Vietminh's leaders had received few social and political rewards from their association with the colonial regime. Impatient for independence and power, this element turned to revolution. The Bao Dai leadership, on the other hand, had a more limited political ambition. While this group believed that France must grant full independence, none subscribed to the idea of a revolution within the country itself. Moreover, the internecine squabbles in which Bao Dai's associates constantly engaged were a further limitation on their political effectiveness. John ᐧT. McAlister, Jr., *Vietnam: The Origins of Revolution* (1969), 6–7.

rather than on what it was for, Ho Chi Minh's republic was casting aside the veil of the United Front, was replacing moderate nationalists with Communists, and accepting publicly the People's Republic of China as its model. Indeed, the Communist victory in China, 1949, was a tremendous boost to the Republic, which was recognized by Peking and Moscow in 1950 and was soon receiving technical military assistance from these sources. As against these gains for Ho in the north, the position of France in the whole of Indochina was weakening. Bao Dai's government together with those of Cambodia and Laos were demanding full independence, which the French now felt it expedient to grant at least formally. At the same time French military prestige suffered a fatal blow when the French garrison at Dien Bien Phu to the west of Hanoi surrendered to Ho's troops.

With both the political and military tide running strongly against them in all Indochina, the French agreed to seek a settlement with the now clearly Communist republic. At a conference at Geneva, beginning in May, 1954, as Dien Bien Phu was falling, an armistice was negotiated. By its terms a military demarcation was drawn just north of Hué near the 17th parallel. The north was assigned to Ho's republic, the south, to Bao Dai's French-supported regime. Each government withdrew its troops from the other's assigned territory. Civilians might move if they so desired. Communist guerrillas were to be withdrawn from Cambodia and Laos, both of which were to gain independence. Finally, there was an agreement providing for the unification of Vietnam through elections, but these were never held.[19]

[19] In the later American debates on Vietnam policy, a question frequently asked was whether the South Vietnamese and the United States had not violated the Geneva accords in failing to conduct the specified elections. The answer would seem to be that (1) the Geneva Conference produced no binding international commitment to elections in 1956, and (2) the provisional government and its followers operating south of the 17th parallel made no promise either to participate in such elections or to respect their results.

Actually, the divergent development of North and South Vietnam made unification a very remote possibility, except through the conquest of one by the other. In the north, Ho Chi Minh and the Communist party, the *Lao Dong* (Worker's party), applied themselves to tasks of consolidation and development. Traditionally oriented village leaders were replaced by trusted personnel; the loyalty of intellectuals and skilled workers was fostered; land reform as a preliminary to efforts to raise agricultural productivity was implemented; state ownership of all levels of business was established; and economic plans emphasizing heavy industry were introduced. These transformations were so fundamental and their implementation was so harsh that the government at first faced widespread uprisings. These, however, were controlled without injury to the Communists' commanding position.[20] Considerable success was achieved also in expanding the regime's economic base. With help from Communist China and the Soviet Union, North Vietnam reopened railway connections with southern China, repaired harbor facilities, and built factories so that by the early 1960s, prior to the onset of Ameri-

This lack of guarantees was in part a reflection of the inability of the conferees to determine the exact purpose of the elections. While the accords set an approximate date, they did not specify the issues that were to be voted upon. That question was to be left to later consultations. In short, the Geneva Conference was more important in defining the terms on which France could withdraw from the fighting than in providing a blueprint for Vietnam's future. McAlister, *Vietnam*, 351–52. George McTurnan Kahin and John W. Lewis, *The United States in Vietnam* (1967),* Chapter 3, presents the view that the Geneva accords did constitute a commitment binding the United States and other powers.

[20] The *Lao Dong* aim in carrying forward these transformations was to win the political commitment of the masses. To achieve this commitment, the *Lao Dong* was primarily concerned not with increasing the welfare of the peasant villagers, but with forging them into a political community. What was sought was a community that commanded loyalty because it rewarded performance by upward mobility, by offering individuals access to the attributes of modernity (literacy, technical skills, etc.), and by political power.

can bombing raids, she could boast of industrial leadership in Southeast Asia. These accomplishments were the more notable because they were carried out in a land that had been stripped of facilities left by the French.[21] North Vietnam's economic development, however, contributed more to national power than to individual well-being. In spite of agricultural expansion, foodstuffs were chronically inadequate; shortages in clothing and virtually all other consumer goods forced severe rationing.

The disciplined development of the north also reflected a notable political stability. Operating initially through a provisional government, the *Lao Dong*, on January 1, 1960, provided for permanent leadership under a constitution that defined the institutions of a single-party dictatorship.[22] The elections which followed sanctioned *Lao Dong* control and confirmed Ho Chi Minh as President. Other key leaders were Pham Van Dong as Premier and Foreign Minister; Vo Nguyen Giap, Army Commander-in-Chief, as Minister of Defense; and Truong Chinh as leader of the National Assembly. Following Ho's death in 1969, these close associates continued the leadership on a co-operative basis.

In South Vietnam there was neither the equivalent of the personal leadership offered by Ho Chi Minh nor a party having the organizational basis or discipline of the *Lao Dong*. While France had treated Bao Dai as legitimate chief of state, his government by 1955 was only one of several factions which in fact exercised authority. Caodaists, Hoa Hao, and Catholics had established para-military forces of their own and had begun to operate from separate territorial bases. Within Saigon, the seat of Bao Dai's

government, a gangster organization known as *Binh Xuyen*, controlled the police. The army Chief of Staff, Nguyen Van Hinh, wanted the premiership for himself. And finally, among and between all these contending forces, dozens of miniscule parties maneuvered for position, each seeking its own advantage. It was from this situation of growing and almost indescribable political chaos that Ngo Dinh Diem, a member of a prominent Roman Catholic family, and his brother, Ngo Dinh Nhu, emerged at the head of such government as South Vietnam was to have in the years 1955 to 1963. Serving first as Bao Dai's premier and then as President of the Republic of Vietnam (established in October, 1955), Diem's political fortunes were supported by aid from the United States during the Eisenhower Administration. But it was an extraordinary capacity for political survival as well as foreign aid that explained Diem's tenure. Attacked on all sides, Diem and his brother played army faction against faction, made and broke alliances with the parties, and used their police and military authority to maintain themselves in power.

Complicating Diem's tasks was the fact that the government over which he presided was at war not only with itself but also with the Communists. While the Communist military in 1954 had followed Ho Chi Minh north of the 17th parallel, party cadres had remained behind in the South Vietnam countryside to organize the populace for the elections scheduled under the Geneva Conference agreements. Although Diem jailed local leaders suspected of Communist sympathies, he was unable to root out the opposition. His own officials were subjected to an escalating series of attacks as they attempted to establish their authority.[23] More-

---

[21] Under the Geneva Agreement of 1954 all public institutions and services were to be handed over to Hanoi, but South Vietnam operating through a "Committee for Defense of the North," carried off or destroyed what it could during division of the country. Hanoi ultimately received 265,000,000 francs in restitution from the French government.

[22] Bernard B. Fall, *The Two Viet-Nams* (1963), 399–416, gives the full text of the constitution.

[23] Responsibility for the initiation of hostilities in the south is a much disputed point. Saigon and Washington have held that the Communists first assumed the offensive. The Communist view holds that warfare resulted from "spontaneous" uprisings which deserved all possible support. Given the confusion in South Vietnam during the latter 1950s and the unreliability of available evidence, no definitive conclusion is presently possible. The official American view is in United

over, by March, 1960, the *Vietcong*, as Diem had dubbed the Communists of the south, through their political agency, the National Liberation Front, had established a political administration of their own. By this means, the *Vietcong* collected taxes, conscripted troops, collected food and supplies, and provided rudimentary public services in territory supposed to be ruled by Diem.

Under Diem, some headway was made in consolidating political leadership in Saigon, but little was done to build a popular basis for rule in the countryside. The quality of local leadership declined as established village chiefs were jailed in Diem's anti-Communist campaigns. A land reform program which was intended to win peasant loyalty through rent reductions and other benefits became, under faulty administration, a source of more political disaffection. Furthermore, the introduction of "strategic hamlets," a system of fortified villages which had served in Malaya to isolate guerrillas and thereby to rob them of their major supply base, failed to check the *Vietcong*. In fact, Diem's major accomplishment was the resettlement from the north of some 745,000 Catholic refugees. It was from among this group and the army that Diem found his major support.

Diem's failure to rally his own people opened the way for the United States to assume an increasingly crucial role in Vietnamese politics. The American government, acting on the assumption that defeat of Ho Chi Minh's forces was essential to the containment of communism, had given substantial military aid to the French. Following the French defeat and the division of Vietnam, American military assistance was directed mainly toward the defense of the south against the north. When it was finally

States Department of State, *A Threat to the Peace: North Viet-Nam's Effort to Conquer South Viet-Nam*, Publication #7308, Far Eastern Series 110 (1961), Part I, 12–13. Kahin and Lewis, *United States in Vietnam*, 384–87, is critical of the official thesis. The Communist view is developed in Wilfred B. Burchett, *The Fugitive War: The United States in Vietnam and Laos* (1963); and *Vietnam: The Inside Story of the Guerrilla War* (1965).

realized that Diem, like his predecessor Bao Dai, was in as great danger from his own people as from the Communist north, American advice and aid were increased and extended to nonmilitary matters in the hope that political and economic reforms might curb the continuous political disintegration. American support, for example, was given to the social and economic reforms associated with the "strategic hamlet" program. The theory of assistance of this kind was undoubtedly sound, but in actual practice the aid was often administered by authorities trusted neither by their own people nor by the government of the United States. During 1962–1963 the political shambles of the Diem government became more and more obvious to the outside world. The *Vietcong* extended the areas of South Vietnam under their control. Diem's own planes bombed the Presidential Palace. Buddhist monks burned themselves to death in the streets of Saigon. To these and similar events Diem replied by narrowing still further his own political base. He arrested unnumbered suspected political opponents and bestowed more power on relatives and a small circle of family friends. Finally, in November 1963, Diem felt it necessary to bring troops into Saigon to protect government offices. At this point, the United States, apparently despairing of Diem's capacity to govern, announced suspension of some American aid. Shortly thereafter a military coup engineered by officers of the South Vietnamese army drove Diem from office and took his life. In the months that followed, South Vietnam appears to have survived only because of the American presence. Even with this presence, nine administrations appeared and fell before a somewhat more permanent leadership was discovered. In June 1965, a new government took office. It included General Nguyen Van Thieu, a Catholic, as Chief of State, and Air Marshall Nguyen Cao Ky, a Buddhist, as Premier.

The beginnings of the Thieu-Ky regime were not encouraging. The government continued to lose territory to the *Vietcong*. Saigon's defense rested with American troops whose numbers multiplied and whose role shifted decisively from advice to combat. By 1970 there were reports of some progress in the tasks of political consolidation. The government's opportunity to retrieve some reputation had come in the aftermath of the *Vietcong's* so-called *Tet* offensive in the spring of 1968. On this occasion, the *Vietcong*, confronted with the loss of military initiative to the Americans, had conducted vast and bloody uprisings throughout South Vietnam. Saigon's security was indeed imperiled, but the *Vietcong* lost much of their own key personnel. Thus, Saigon was enabled to send pacification teams into the countryside and to re-establish its authority in a number of areas. These activities were combined with renewed effort to build an institutional basis for enlisting popular support. Personnel was trained in rural reconstruction and village development with the aim of breathing life into languishing reform programs. President Thieu announced a program of land redistribution, which, if implemented, promised to resolve major peasant grievances, and to rob the *Vietcong* of some of their appeal. Under a constitution adopted in 1967, it was reported that steps would be taken to form a broadly based government. Moreover, Saigon's military power grew as the American decision to "Vietnamize" the war resulted in retraining and resupplying South Vietnamese forces and in transferring to those forces enlarged responsibilities for combat operations. It was thus a government enjoying somewhat improved prospects for survival that joined the United States at Paris in 1968 to begin talks with North Vietnam looking toward an end to the Vietnam war.

LAOS

Laos was the smallest of the countries which gained independence through the Geneva settlement of 1954. The Geneva Conference had attempted to create in this new state an international buffer separating non-Communist South Vietnam, Cambodia, and Thailand from the Communist world of North Vietnam and China. Laos could not

have been more ill-equipped for the role. Natural resources undergirding national power were either missing or undeveloped. The authority of the central government seldom reached beyond a few populated centers. Moreover, the populace itself was divided between the Lao, a people who were linked linguistically and historically with the inhabitants of northeastern Thailand, and the hill people whose homes were scattered through an area adjacent to the Vietnamese border. The gulf between these people had deepened during World War II and the years immediately thereafter as nationalist movements took root. Among the Lao, the *Lao Issara* (Free Laotian Party) first vowed resistance to foreign control and then agreed to modified independence under the French. An opposing group, the *Pathet Lao*, under Vietnamese influence, demanded full independence. Thus, there was some ground for the theory that Laotians seemed more likely to take the part of one or another of their neighbors than to unite against them. In 1954, the Geneva accords acknowledged these divisions in assigning to the *Pathet Lao* provisional control over two northeastern provinces.

France and the United States initially sought to guarantee Laotian neutrality through a coalition in which the *Pathet Lao* under Prince Souhanovong would merge with the followers of neutralist Prince Souvanna Phouma. Such a coalition was indeed formed but was imperiled constantly by ideological differences and factional strife within and among the ruling elite. In time the coalition's stance was altered as right wing elements supporting General Phoumi Nosavan (omitted from earlier negotiations) gained an ascendency. Repeated crises followed, and they were the more serious because the anti-Communists (and American advisers) backed the Right while the Communists (North Vietnamese, Russians, and Chinese) backed the Left. However, in 1962 the United States and the Soviet Union joined in a fourteen nation declaration setting forth a formula for "independence, neutrality, and peace for Laos." Under this formula foreign military missions were to be withdrawn from Laos, an International Control Commission was to be established, and a new coalition constituting the Royal Laotian Government (RLG) was formed from elements of the Right, Center, and Left. International tensions were reduced by this agreement, but Laos was not restored to peace. In 1964 an attempted right wing coup emphasized the precarious tenure of all regimes. By that time too, the *Pathet Lao*, which had boycotted the coalition government, and the RLG once again were at war. Hostilities initially were limited and little territory changed hands. In 1969–1970, however, the *Pathet Lao*, seeking apparently to weaken the RLG and to ensure its control of the jungle paths (supply routes known collectively as the Ho Chi Minh Trail) broadened its offensives. The international aspects of the widened war were evident in reports of the integration of Lao-speaking Thai forces into the armies of the RLG and of American air support for RLG ground operations. North Vietnam was said to have stationed in Laos more than 50,000 troops to guard the Ho Chi Minh Trail and to support the *Pathet Lao*. Laos, it seemed, remained a nation "by diplomatic courtesy" rather than by self-determination.

CAMBODIA

Cambodia, the modern descendant of an ancient Khmer monarchy, was in some respects meagerly endowed for independent status. Her largely agricultural economy supplied only part of the national requirements. The purchase of foreign manufactures was limited by the relatively low earnings of rice and rubber exports. Slim resources also restricted development of schools, communications, and public health services. In politics, while Cambodians were united culturally and through monarchical tradition, they could boast no experience with the technique of modern government. Under French rule the kingship had been retained and native officials served in local posts, but major administrative responsibilities had been reserved to French *residents*. Political

debates in a native consultative assembly had been expressly proscribed.

Despite these handicaps, Cambodia moved without serious incident from colonial dependence to independence. This was due largely to the astute leadership of the young Cambodian monarch, Prince Norodom Sihanouk, whom the French had placed on the throne in 1941. In the immediate post-war era, Sihanouk outmaneuvered rival factions which attempted to align Cambodia with either Thailand or the Vietnamese Communists. Through hard bargaining he also won independence from the French and international recognition (at the Geneva Conference of 1954) of his country's neutrality. Subsequently, having abdicated the throne to become prime minister and then head of state, Sihanouk sought political unity and stability through a highly personalized style of government. The Prince himself presided over the National Congress, the sessions of which were attended by all classes, and was indefatigable as a speechmaker, meeting his people in small audiences throughout the country. Given Sihanouk's own considerable charm and the rural populace's reverence for the royal family, this exercise in personal government served in the absence of a well-developed administrative system as a unifying influence.

By the 1960s, however, opposition was becoming pronounced among the urbanized and more educated Cambodians, many of whom, having completed their schooling, found no positions commensurate with their training. Civilian and military elites were increasingly critical of the Prince's handling of economic and foreign affairs. Since these groups seemed generally to favor close relations with the United States (hoping for economic and military assistance), they deplored Sihanouk's diplomatic break with the American government in 1965 and his professions of friendship for Peking and Hanoi. Meanwhile, North Vietnamese troops and *Vietcong* entered border provinces, from which they launched attacks on South Vietnamese and American forces and gave support to armed Cambodian insurgents known as the *Khmer Rouge*. Under the pressures of these events Sihanouk, in 1969, attempted to open new diplomatic avenues to the United States. By that time, however, Cambodia was in deep economic crisis. In April, 1970, while Sihanouk was in Eroupe, his government was overthrown by a former prime minister, General Lon Nol. This move was countered by Peking's announcement of support for a Cambodian government in exile (with Sihanouk serving as titular head). Furthermore, the nation's troubles were magnified as North and South Vietnamese (the later having American military support) began fighting on Cambodian soil.

THAILAND

On the eve of World War II, Thailand, which had been permitted by Britain and France to maintain a precarious independence, was moving into the orbit of growing Japanese influence. A commercial treaty of 1938 gave Japanese businessmen a favored position and appealed to the Thai as a means of curbing the Chinese. A new Japan-Thailand treaty of friendship concluded in 1940 coincided with Japan's benevolent mediation when Thailand seized the lost Cambodian provinces at the expense of France. Therefore, when Japan, in December, 1941, demanded the right of military transit to attack the British in Malaya, the government of Luang Pibun Songgram after a token resistance consented, allied itself with Japan, and declared war on the United States and Britain (January 25, 1942). From the beginning, however, a civilian faction led by Pridi Phanomyong (Luang Pradit Manudharm), who as a member of Pibun's government had opposed the Japanese demands and the declaration of war, formed a resistance movement that served the Western Allies. At the close of the war the British after accepting the Japanese surrender in Thailand proposed a settlement that would have made Thailand a British protectorate. This plan was opposed by the Thai and by the United States, which had not recognized the Thai declaration of war. As a result, the peace settlement of January, 1946, deprived Thailand of territories she had taken after December 7, 1941, and compensated British subjects for war losses.

The most notable characteristic of Thailand's post-war internal politics was the recurrent outbreaks by which administrations were threatened or overthrown. These so-called revolutions had little if anything to do with nationalism, communism, or even good government. They were in reality a more recent version of the factional struggle for power that had colored the Thai political stage in the 1930's. By 1948 Pibun Songgram, temporarily discredited because of his collaboration with Japan, was back in power with his military faction and the blesssing of the United States and Great Britain. His predecessor Pridi Phanamyong, whose following, at least in theory, favored a more democratic government, had not made democracy work. Thus grounds were furnished for the return of Pibun to power until 1957, when he in turn was overthrown by Sarit Thannarat, field marshal of the army. Sarit charged his predecessor with inefficiency, corruption, and an inept foreign policy, but his own administration bore a striking resemblance to what had gone before. Upon Sarit's death, December, 1963, Thanom Kittakachorn became premier. Despite frequent coups and changes in formal constitutional structure (no less than five constitutions between 1945 and 1968), Thai political history reveals substantial continuity. Thailand's post-war factions were drawn from the small elite which had ruled since the overthrow of absolute monarchy in 1932. Moreover, government retained the essential form of a limited dictatorship operating under an hereditary monarchy.

Economics rather than politics was the focus of change in post-war Thailand. Early in the 1960s, Bangkok adopted programs designed to establish an industrial base. Favorable markets for rice and tin, Thailand's chief exports, provided the foreign exchange to finance these undertakings. Economic strength came also from Thailand's alliance with the United States—more than a half-billion dollars in economic aid by 1969 plus spending by American servicemen stationed in the country or visiting it on leave from Vietnam. Foreign capital investment was attracted by generous tax incentives and the relaxation of duties on industrial raw materials. The new policy and the inducements created a high economic growth rate. By 1968 new industries—plants for the production of tires, pharmaceuticals, light steel goods, electronics, and plastics—accounted for more than 30 per cent of the total national product. While some Thai businessmen were fearful that an American withdrawal from Vietnam would end prosperity, the national economy as a whole was not considered to be dependent upon the United States.

Minority problems, however, continued to be cause for concern. In the northeast, a region inhabited by Lao, and in the south near the Malayan border, the country was faced with repeated armed insurrections. These uprisings were rooted in economic inequities and political neglect. The per capita income in the northeast, for example, was less than half the national average. Moreover, Bangkok had not taken the trouble until recent years to extend basic services—schools, roads, health facilities— into these regions. This neglect was an open invitation to foreign sources of subversion. Terrorist activity in the south stemmed in part from a revival of the communist-directed Malayan People's Liberation Army. In the northeast Bangkok claimed that dissident tribesmen supplied with sophisticated weapons were coming from across the Laotian borders. Government efforts to quell the insurgents emphasized force rather than persuasion.

THE BALANCE SHEET OF THE POST-WAR YEARS

In the early post-war years, Southeast Asia's educated elites, particularly their younger members, entertained high hopes for the creation of a new world. This coming new world, however, was not self-defining. Beyond such slogans as "the end of colonialism and the birth of national independence," there was not much agreement as to what

was to be done or how it was to be done. It was easy for native politicians and their followings to proclaim an era of nation-building. It was more difficult to decide on the materials of construction, on the ultimate shape of the edifice, or on what could be used to pay for it. Moreover, decisions on these matters were called for at a time when each new state was tormented in greater or lesser degree by factionalism, division of purpose, lack of political experience or responsibility, poverty, illiteracy, violence, and the devastations of prolonged civil wars aided and abetted by outside powers.

After 1945 and the collapse of the old colonialism, Southeast Asia stumbled along a rough and often uncharted road compounded of its old traditional cultures on the one hand, and of Western ideologies (state sovereignty, nationalism, constitutionalism, liberty, equality, democracy, socialism, communism, and fascism) on the other. The intellectual problem for such leadership as Southeast Asia had was to determine what of the old should be discarded, what of the new and foreign should be absorbed. Democracy's struggles to get a foothold on this new soil were impeded from the first because democracy was the ideology of the colonial master, because of indigenous authoritarian traditions, because there was no strong and established native middle class or political parties experienced in applying constitutionalism, and because of the wide gulf between the urban and the rural populace neither of which was integrated effectively into a national society.

North Vietnam alone, where communism gained control, suffered none of these problems. The initial objective of Ho Chi Minh and his followers was to seize power, first from the French and then from domestic or other foreign opponents such as the Americans. In pursuit of this objective and in the later consolidation of their regime, the North Vietnamese Communists enjoyed some important advantages. Since they were among the earliest nationalist leaders seeking independence from the French, they assumed the role of "patriots." Among political leaders in Southeast Asia who knew where they were going and how they intended to get there, Ho Chi Minh had a position and reputation that was without rival. He maintained a tough, rigid regime tolerating no domestic opposition. Behind him geographically were the ideological and material resources of Communist China and the Soviet Union. No other Southeast Asian state produced a leadership of comparable force with its own people. Only in the Philippines had infant democracy produced a Ramon Magsaysay but, by 1970, both Magsaysay and Ho Chi Minh were dead. Some Asian leaders were frank to confess that the old nationalist ideologies (democracy, communism, and the like) did not have the answers needed at this stage of Asia's revolution.

FOR FURTHER READING

GENERAL. Rupert Emerson, *From Empire to Nation* (1960) is a classic examination of the development of nationalism. John F. Cady, *Southeast Asia: Its Historical Development* (1964) has an excellent chapter on the Japanese impact. See also Willard Elsbree, *Japan's Role in Southeast Asian Nationalist Movements, 1940–45* (1953). Among recent political analyses are: Hugh Tinker, *Ballot Box and Bayonet: People and Government in Emergent Asian Countries* (1964); Richard Butwell, *Southeast Asia Today—and Tomorrow: A Political Analysis* (1969)*; Robert C. Bone, *Contemporary Southeast Asia* (1962)*; and Michael Brecher, *The New States of Asia: A Political Analysis* (1964). Aspects of forces influencing national development are treated in Gunnar Myrdal, *Asian Drama: An Inquiry into the Poverty of Nations* (3 vols., 1968); S. Chanrasekhar, ed., *Asia's Population Problems* (London, 1968); Cora Dubois, *Social Forces in Southeast Asia* (2nd ed., 1959); Robbins Burling, *Hill Farms and Padi Fields: Life in Mainland Southeast Asia* (1965); Frank M. LaBar, *Ethnic Groups of Mainland Southeast Asia* (1964); Claude A. Buss, *Arc of Crisis* (1961); Frank N. Trager, ed., *Marxism in Southeast Asia: A Study of*

Four Countries (1959). Lois Mitchison, *The Overseas Chinese* (London, 1961); and C. P. Fitzgerald, *The Third China: The Chinese Communities in Southeast Asia* (Vancouver, 1965), are compact and objective analyses of life and politics relating to Southeast Asia. E. H. G. Dobby, *Southeast Asia* (6th ed., London, 1958) surveys economic and social structure. T. H. Silcock, *The Commonwealth Economy in Southeast Asia* (1959) presents uncommon insights into some familiar problems of economic development. C. A. Fisher, *South-East Asia, A Social, Economic and Political Geography* (1964) is a very detailed, useful reference. F. R. Von Der Mehden, *Politics of the Developing Nations* (1964), and Lennox A. Mills, *Southeast Asia: Illusion and Reality in Politics and Economics* (1964). Jan M. Pluvier, *A Handbook and Chart of Southeast Asian History* (Kuala Lumpur, 1967)*, a very slim but useful compilation. S. N. Hay and M. H. Case, *Southeast Asian History: A Bibliographic Guide* (1962).

THE PHILIPPINES. Aspects of Filipino-Japanese relationships are treated in Royama Masamichi and Takeuchi Tatsuji, *The Philippine Polity: A Japanese View* (1967); Grant K. Goodman, *Davao: A Case Study in Japanese-Philippine Relations* (1967); and David J. Steinberg, *Philippine Collaboration in World War II* (1967). Onofre Corpuz, *The Philippines* (1965),* an original and penetrating interpretation emphasizing major themes in Philippine history. Albert Ravenholt, *The Philippines: A Republic on the Move* (1962); and Robert Aura Smith, *Philippine Freedom, 1946–1958* (1958) are good introductions. Specialized aspects of national development are studied in: O. D. Corpuz, *The Bureaucracy in the Philippines* (Manila, 1957); and Frank Golay, *The Philippines: Public Policy and National Economic Development* (1961); Edgar Wickberg, *The Chinese in Philippine Life, 1850–1898* (1965), studies the origins of a contemporary problem. See also Frances L. Starner, *Magsaysay and the Philippine Peasantry* (1961); and Luis Taruc, *Born of the People: An Autobiography* (1953), and

He Who Rides a Tiger: The Story of an Asian Guerrilla Leader (1967). Two excellent introductions to Philippine literature are Leonard Casper, *The Wounded Diamond: Studies in Modern Philippine Literature* (Manila, 1964); and the same author's *New Writings from the Philippines: A Critique and Anthology* (1966). F. Landa Jocano, *Growing Up in a Philippine Barrio* (1969) affords delightful insights into everyday life.

INDONESIA. Jeanne S. Mintz, *Indonesia, A Profile* (1961); J. D. Legge, *Indonesia* (1964)°; and Bruce Grant, *Indonesia* (1967) are sound introductions. Willard A. Hanna, *Bung Karno's Indonesia* (1960) is a collection of perceptive reports. W. F. Wertheim, *Indonesian Society in Transition* (2nd ed., 1959); and P. J. Zoetmulder, "The Cultural Background of Indonesian Politics," *Essay Series* #1, Published by the Institute of International Studies, University of South Carolina (1967) are valuable anthropological studies. Bernard M. H. Vlekke, *Nusantara: A History of Indonesia* (The Hague, 1959) is the standard history of the archipelago available in English. Among more specialized studies are Donald E. Weatherbee, *Ideology in Indonesia: Sukarno's Indonesian Revolution* (1966); John R. W. Smail, *Bandung in the Early Revolution, 1945–1946: A Study in the Social History of the Indonesian Revolution* (1964); Donald Hindley, "Political Power and the October, 1965 Coup in Indonesia," *Journal of Asian Studies* 26 (1967): 237–49. Arnold C. Brackman, *Indonesian Communism: A History* (1963) is especially good for the years since 1947.

BURMA. John F. Cady, *A History of Modern Burma* (1958) is a basic reference. Frank N. Trager, *Burma—From Kingdom to Republic: A Historical and Political Analysis* (1966); and Donald E. Smith, *Religion and Politics in Burma* (1965) are at their best in discussing the post-war years. Short introductions by distinguished writers are provided in J. S. Furnivall, *An Introduction to the Political Economy of Burma* (3rd ed., Rangoon, 1957); D. G. E. Hall, *Burma* (London,

1950). Lucian W. Pye, *Politics, Personality, and Nation-Building: Burma's Search for Identity* (1962) is for sophisticated readers. Maung Maung, *Aung San of Burma*, and *The Trial of in Burma, The Assassination of Aung San* (The Hague, 1962) are both written by an able native legal scholar. William C. Johnstone, *Burma's Foreign Policy: A Study in Neutralism* (1963) is the first complete study of the subject. Kenneth Sein and J. A. Withey, *A Chronicle of the Burmese Theater: The Great Po Sein* (1965), a humanizing supplement to political and religious studies.

MALAYA. Norton Ginsburg and Chester F. Roberts, *Malaya* (1958) surveys the geographic basis of politics. K. G. Tregonning, *A History of Modern Malaya* (1967), a lively narrative that emphasizes the essentials. R. O. Winstedt, *A History of Malaya* (rev. ed., Singapore, 1962), a standard account. Three studies focusing on events of the 1960s are Richard Allen, *Malaysia: Prospect and Retrospect. The Impact and Aftermath of Colonial Rule* (1968); J. M. Gullick, *Malaya* (rev. ed., 1964); and Arnold C. Brackman, *Southeast Asia's Second Front: The Power Struggle in the Malay Archipelago* (1966). T. H. Silcock and E. K. Fisk, eds., *The Political Economy of Independent Malaya: A Case Study In Development* (1964). Robert O. Tilman, *Bureaucratic Transition in Malaya* (1964) views post-colonial governmental structure against its historical foundations. L. A. Sheridan and Harry E. Groves, *The Constitution of Malaysia* (1967), a usable reference. Peter J. Wilson, *A Malay Village and Malaysia: Social Values and Rural Development* (1967), largely descriptive. William R. Roff, *The Origins of Malay Nationalism* (1967).

INDOCHINA. For description of life and customs, see Gerald Hickey, *Village in Vietnam* (1964); Frank M. LeBar and Adrienne Suddard, eds., *Laos: Its People, Its Society, Its Culture* (1960); and David J. Steinberg, *et al., Cambodia; Its People, Its Society, Its Culture* (rev. ed., 1959). Joseph Buttinger, *Vietnam: A Political History* (1968), condensation of a massive and scholarly work.

Ellen Hammer, *Vietnam: Yesterday and To-day* (1966) is a well written and solid introduction. The latter author's *The Struggle for Indochina* (1954); and Allan B. Cole, ed., *Conflict in Indo-China and International Repercussions: A Documentary History, 1945–1955* (1956) are indispensable for the post-war years. For description and analysis of Vietnam (north and south), see Bernard B. Fall, *The Two Vietnams* (2nd rev. ed., 1967). Dennis J. Duncanson, *Government and Revolution in Vietnam* (1968) is useful chiefly for insights into the Diem regime. On North Vietnam, see P. J. Honey, ed., *North Vietnam Today* (1962); Hoang Van Chi *From Colonialism to Communism* (1964); Bernard B. Fall, ed., *Ho Chi Minh on Revo-lution: Selected Writings, 1920–66* (1967); and Jean Lacouture, *Ho Chi Minh: A Political Biography* (1968). Douglas Pike, *Viet Cong: The Organization and Techniques of the National Liberation Front of South Vietnam* (1967), a standard reference. Hugh Toye, *Laos: Buffer State or Battleground* (1968).

THAILAND (SIAM). Wendell Blanchard, *et al. Thailand: Its People, Its Society, Its Culture* (1958) is the most useful single volume. John E. DeYoung, *Village Life in Modern Thailand* (1951) derives from observations in the north. Pierre Fistie, *L'Evolution de la Thailande Contemporaine* (1967) is useful for the period 1932–1958.

The New Southeast Asia
in World Affairs

chapter 37

World War II bequeathed to Southeast Asia a perplexing and a frustrating legacy. War had destroyed the old political order, thus permitting the countries of this vast area to achieve, in theory at least, their political independence from colonial control by the British, the French, the Dutch, the Americans, and finally the Japanese. This new independence was said to have opened the way for the peoples of Southeast Asia to nurture their concepts of freedom, nationalism, and economic and social modernization. War also had bequeathed what may best be described as the gift of political vacuum. Southeast Asia's modern history, in fact most of its history, is a story of dependence on outside control. This control had been exercised at various times by China (the tributary system), by Indian religious and cultural influence, and, in modern times, by the colonial and imperial empires of western Europe, the United States, and, briefly, Japan. In all of these cases the colonial empires were considered to be sources of wealth, prestige, and security. When, therefore, the pre-war colonial empires retreated from Southeast Asia, the resulting political vacuum was an invitation to new contestants:

the United States versus the Soviet Union and Communist China. Southeast Asia was linked to the world-wide Cold War, and extreme ideological differences were added to older rivalries based on economics and security. The student of contemporary history may find it useful to compare recent years in Southeast Asia with the plight of the Balkans following the collapse of the Ottoman Empire.

CO-OPERATION AND RIVALRY IN THE EARLY YEARS OF INDEPENDENCE

Nationalism in the new Southeast Asia was a united force as it opposed any concession to "Western colonialism." It was a divided and weakened force as each state reasserted long-standing claims against its neighbors. The relative strength of these aspects of the new nationalism was revealed in the unsuccessful efforts to forge a united front among the newly established Asian and African states. Conferences convened by India in 1947 to discuss "Asian relations" and in 1949 to demand the departure of the Dutch from Indonesia were early expressions of an "all-Asia" faith and philosophy. In 1953–1954, Asian socialists led representa-

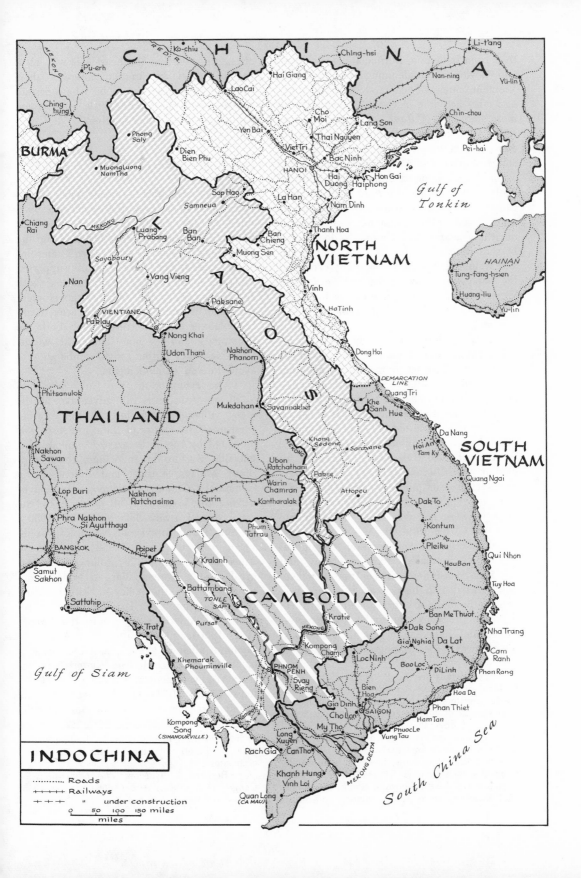

CHINA

Ko-chiu
Pu-erh
MEKONG (RED R.)
Chinghung
Chiang Rai
Chinghsi
Li-t'ang
Nan-ning
Yu-lin
Ch'in-chou
Pei-hai
Yu-lin

BURMA

Hai Giang
LaoCai
Cho Moi
Lang Son
Yen Bai
Thai Nguyen
Viet Tri
Bac Ninh
HANOI
Hai Duong Haiphong
Hon Gai
La Han
Nam Dinh

Phong Saly
Dien Bien Phu
Muongluong NamTha

Gulf of Tonkin

HAINAN
Tung-fang-hsien
Huang-liu
Yu-lin

L A O S

Sop Hao
Samneua
Luang Prabang
Ban Ban
Ban Chieng
Muong Sen
Thanh Hoa

NORTH VIETNAM

Sayaboury
Vang Vieng
Nan

MEKONG

Vinh
Ha Tinh

VIENTIANE
Pak Lay
Nong Khai
Udon Thani
Paksane

Dong Hoi

DEMARCATION LINE
Quang Tri
Khe Sanh
Hue

Phitsanulok

THAILAND

Nakhon Phanom

Mukdahan
Savannakhet

Da Nang
Hoi An
Tam Ky

SOUTH VIETNAM

Nakhon Sawan
Lop Buri
Nakhon Ratchasima
Surin
Ubon Ratchathani
Warin Chamran
Kantharalak
Khong Sedone
Saravane
Pakse
Attopeu

MEKONG

Quang Ngai
Dak To
Kontum
Pleiku
HauBon

Phra Nakhon Si Ayutthaya
BANGKOK
Poipet
Phum Tatrau
Kralanh

Qui Nhon
Tuy Hoa

Samut Sakhon
Sattahip
Trat

Battambang
TONLE SAP
Pursat

CAMBODIA

Kratie
Dak Song
Gia Nghia Da Lat
Bao Loc
Di Linh

Ban Me Thuot

Nha Trang
Cam Ranh

Khemarak Phouminville

Gulf of Siam

MEKONG
Kompong Cham

Loc Ninh
Bien Hoa

Phan Rang
Hoa Da
Phan Thiet

Kompong Song
(SIHANOUKVILLE)
Kampot
PHNOM PENH
Svay Rieng

Gia Dinh
Cho Lon
SAIGON
My Tho

Ham Tan

PhuocLe
Vung Tau

Long Xuyen
Rach Gia CanTho

South China Sea

Khanh Hung
Vinh Loi

Quan Long
(CA MAU)

MEKONG DELTA

INDOCHINA

········· Roads
+++++ Railways
+ + +   " under construction

0   50   100   150 miles
        miles

tives from Indonesia, Burma, India, Pakistan, and Ceylon in condemning the French in Vietnam, nuclear weapons, the arms race, and other activities of the great powers. The most ambitious of these meetings, the Bandung Conference, called by Indonesia in 1955, was a bid for unity among the new states of Asia and Africa. Delegates to this assemblage supported Indonesia's territorial claims in West Irian, the right of North Africans and Palestinian Arabs to self-determination, an end to the production and testing of nuclear weapons, and United Nations membership for such states as Laos, Cambodia, and a united Vietnam. Bandung expressed the hope of destroying the last vestiges of Western authority, but, like earlier meetings, the Conference skirted the problems of the new states.

Indeed, during the early years of independence, the Southeast Asian states seemed unwilling to co-operate on anything other than opposition to colonialism. Thailand pressed Burma and Cambodia for territorial border adjustments; Prince Sihanouk in Cambodia protested alleged Vietnamese expansionism at Cambodia's expense; and the creation of the Malaysian Federation, including North Borneo (Sabah) and Sarawak, brought protests and threats, 1963–1965, from the Philippines and Indonesia. These disputes were not permitted to degenerate into war. After 1964, the Philippines, presumably acting on considerations of political expediency, retreated from its claims; and the Malaysian-Indonesian confrontation likewise drifted into history as Sukarno's successor, the Suharto government, turned to domestic problems. But only one dispute— Thai and Cambodian claims to a Buddhist temple—was settled through adjudication.[1] It

often appeared that Southeast Asia was less a region linked by mutual interests than "merely a place on the globe where certain groups of people, holding little in common, live contiguous to one another." [2]

SOUTHEAST ASIA IN WORLD POLITICS

Despite the new Southeast Asia's aspirations for independence, the region was powerless to act independently of the great powers. The result was that Thailand and the Philippines looked to the United States for military assistance. Great Britain supported Malaysia in the latter's "confrontation" with Indonesia, while the Sukarno government equipped its military with Soviet arms. Cambodia under Sihanouk flirted with both the Communist and the non-Communist worlds. Only Ne Win's Burma sought deliberately to avoid foreign entanglements.

The extension of the Cold War into Southeast Asia took full advantage of the area's vulnerability to internal and external pressures. The nature of these pressures was indicated by the outbreak of Communist-led guerrilla warfare in Indochina, the Philippines, Malaya, Burma, and Indonesia; by Communist China's proclaimed intention of driving the West from all of Asia; by the conclusion of a Sino-Soviet alliance (1950); by Sino-Soviet support of North Korea's invasion of South Korea (1950); and by the American decision (1950), following the outbreak of the Korean War, to extend from Europe to Asia the policy of "containment" of communism. This last decision was reflected in America's entry into the Korean War (1950), in the creation of an American-Japanese alliance (1951), and the dispatch of fresh assistance to the Kuomintang-Nationalist government in Taiwan (Mutual Defense Treaty, 1954). On the theory that the Communist powers were behind guerrilla

---

[1] For details see L. P. Singh, "The Thai-Cambodian Dispute," Asian Survey 11 (1962): 23–26. Territorial disputes, one of the most common sources of trouble in Southeast Asia, were rooted in border lines inherited from colonial days. Modern nationalists advanced claims based on the domains of ancient kingdoms. The actual extent of these kingdoms, however, was usually impossible to determine. The old dynastic states were concerned with the protection of the throne, and, therefore, gave more attention to sources

of income—the commodity trade, trading routes, cities, and entrepôts—than to the mere control of territory.

[2] Bernard K. Gordon, The Dimensions of Conflict in Southeast Asia (1966),* an excellent analysis of regional rivalries.

THE LAOTIAN CRISIS

515

Southeast
Asia
in World
Affairs

activities in Southeast Asia, that region also was incorporated in American policy. Thus the statement (June 27, 1950) announcing American military intervention in Korea further stipulated that the Philippines were to receive expanded military aid, that a military mission was to be dispatched to Indochina where the French were fighting Ho Chi Minh, and that assistance was to be given the Associated States of Vietnam, Cambodia, and Laos. In a related action Thailand was included as a recipient of American aid. In September, 1954, a few months after the Geneva Conference had provided for the establishment of a Communist-led provisional government in North Vietnam and at a time when Chinese Communists seemed to threaten an invasion of Taiwan, the United States met at Manila with Great Britain, France, Australia, New Zealand, the Philippines, Thailand, and Pakistan to form the Southeast Asia Treaty Organization (SEATO). Members of this organization pledged that, in the event of aggression or subversion (presumably Communist), they would "consult immediately" on measures to be taken within the limits of the "constitutional processes." Under a special protocol, the terms of the SEATO treaty were extended to cover Laos, Cambodia, and "the free territory under the jurisdiction of the State of Vietnam." SEATO was a pale reflection of the North Atlantic Treaty Organization. Unlike the latter, SEATO had no armed forces of its own and no explicit pledges of support for its purposes. Moreover, four "neutral" states—India, Burma, Indonesia, Ceylon—pointedly spurned membership in SEATO. In short, SEATO was less a military alliance than a consultative arrangement affirming an American intent to assume enlarged responsibilities in a region evacuated by European colonial power.[3]

The Cold War's extension to Southeast Asia was illustrated further by the clash of the Communist and non-Communist worlds in Laos, a state whose geographic location and political instability invited foreign intervention. In the context of the United States' "containment" policy, Laos had become a neutral buffer on the borders of non-Communist Thailand, Cambodia, and South Vietnam. This status, however, was threatened by the operation of the Communist *Pathet Lao* in eastern border regions and by the stipulation in the Geneva accords that these Communists were to be incorporated into a coalition government. In 1957 the search for such a government produced an arrangement whereby the *Pathet Lao* would renounce their claims to a separate territorial base and would demobilize their guerrilla forces (except for two battalions which were to be integrated into the Royal Laotian army) in return for two of fourteen cabinet posts and the right to operate as a legal party. Soon thereafter the *Pathet Lao* operating through the *Neo Lao Hak Xat* (Lao Patriotic Front) scored heavily in National Assembly elections. These events, promising enlarged power for the *Pathet Lao*, triggered a coup in which the Laotian military, who were the principal beneficiaries of American aid, ousted the coalition leader, Souvanna Phouma, established a right wing government, and renounced neutrality in favor of alignment with the West. Thus, the ground was prepared for civil war, 1959–1961, and a confrontation of the great powers. The new right wing government was supported by a Thai imposed economic blockade against its opponents and by American military aid. The opposing neutralist-*Pathet Lao* coalition ap-

[3] "It was against the threat of aggression that our double-edged policy of containment—of military security and economic and social progress—was directed. Its archetypes were the Truman doctrine and the Marshall Plan. These two ideas have also been fundamental to the evaluation of other programs for regional cooperation in many parts of the world, programs involving economic and cultural cooperation as

well as security." Eugene V. Rostow (Under Secretary of State for Political Affairs), "The United States and the Communist Worlds," Department of State Publication #8388 (1968), 11. Rhodes Murphey, "China and the Dominoes," *Asian Survey* 6 (1966): 510–15, argues that the diversity of Southeast Asia made the area less susceptible to Chinese pressure than American policy would suggest.

pealed for and got foreign assistance in the form of a massive Soviet arms airlift.

In 1961 the Laotian crisis threatened a wider war as the United States appealed to SEATO for help in countering Communist expansion. The British and French, however, believed that the situation required another attempt at resolving Laotian problems on the basis of the Geneva accords. Since the powers desired to avoid a major conflict, and since neither Communists nor non-Communists had achieved in Laos a decisive advantage, both the Soviet Union and the United States agreed to a fourteen nation conference at which (1) the neutrality of Laos was once again defined, (2) guarantees were given against foreign intervention in Laotian politics, and (3) Laotian factions were directed to make a new effort to construct a coalition government. Subsequent events showed that this understanding did not assure a quick resolution of either Laotian problems or international tensions. Negotiations involving three Laotian princes—Boun Oum (Right), Souvanna Phouma (Center), and Souphanouvong (*Pathet Lao*)—periodically appeared to be deadlocked. At one point, May, 1962, American forces (4500 troops, including tactical air units) were rushed to Thailand's northeast border where they were to deal with a *Pathet Lao* offensive that never materialized. Not until mid-1962 did all factions agree on a formula for a coalition. The immediate crisis was resolved, but the conditions from which it sprang were not. It seemed that Laos was likely to continue as a battleground of the Cold War.

THE COLD WAR IN VIETNAM

By the early 1950s, conditions in Vietnam resembled those in Laos. Ho Chi Minh's Communist forces had well established territorial bases while the non-Communist opposition (the French sponsored Bao Dai government) had neither organization nor resolution. Also, as in Laos, the contending forces were supported by foreign powers. The Chinese Communists recognized the Vietminh-created "Democratic Republic of Viet-

nam" in 1950, earlier than the Soviet Union, and began almost immediately to supply it with arms.[4] American policy at this time, 1950–1954, appears to have assumed that France in fighting the Vietminh was chiefly responsible for the "containment" of communism in the Indochina area.

While French forces remained in Vietnam, the American role was largely one of providing military equipment. Following the defeat of France and the division of Vietnam, the United States became the principal support of South Vietnam. Fearful that the Bao Dai regime was about to collapse, the United States entered South Vietnamese politics in support of Ngo Dinh Diem, thus becoming a participant in the Vietnamese civil war that resumed during the late 1950s and in the 1960s. In 1961, as the Eisenhower Administration left office, the United States had less than a thousand officers and men in South Vietnam; at the time of President John F. Kennedy's death in November, 1963 (not long after Diem was ousted from power and killed), American forces numbered more than 15,000. These forces had been assigned as advisers to South Vietnam but were shortly to be involved in combat.

The assumption of these enlarged responsibilities was the American response to South Vietnam's questionable political leadership. It also reflected a determination following the collapse of the anti-Communists in Laos, to make Vietnam the focus of "containment" in Southeast Asia. This new importance of Vietnam in American policy was suggested, August 4, 1964, when President Lyndon B. Johnson announced that in retaliation for reported attacks on two American destroyers patrolling in the Gulf of Tonkin, the United States had raided North

---

[4] For details on Chinese military aid, see Harold C. Hinton, *China's Relations with Burma and Vietnam* (1958), 18; and Richard P. Stebbins, *The United States in World Affairs, 1954* (1956), 217. This Chinese aid was extended during the latter years of the Vietminh's fight with the French. Earlier the Vietminh relied on a wartime stock of light and often obsolete arms secured from Chiang Kai-shek and the Japanese. George McTurnan Kahin and John Lewis, *The United States in Vietnam* (1967), 30.*

Vietnamese military installations, thus for the first time carrying the war outside the south. Shortly thereafter Congress approved the "Gulf of Tonkin Resolution," whereby the administration was authorized to "take all necessary measures to repel any armed attack against the forces of the United States and to prevent further aggression." The United States, the resolution affirmed, was prepared "as the President determines to take all necessary steps, including the use of armed forces, to assist any member or protocol state of the Southeast Asia Collective Defense Treaty requesting assistance in defense of its freedom." [5] Taking note that this resolution had been passed in the midst of a presidential campaign, President Johnson asserted that, "Hostile nations must understand that in such a period the United States will continue to protect its national interests and that in these matters there is no division among us." [6]

Escalation of the American military effort also included, by February, 1965, air strikes against *Vietcong* military installations and troop concentrations in the south and against supply lines, logistical centers, and, eventually, industrial targets, in the north. At the height of these raids, American planes dropped weekly bomb tonnages that exceeded the total used at the peak of the attacks against Germany in World War II. Meanwhile, American ground forces swelled from 16,500 in 1964 to 267,000 in 1966, and to more than 500,000 in 1968. In addition, 44,000 Korean, 4,000 Australian, and small New Zealand, Philippine, and Thai contingents joined the conflict. American policy seemed to presume that these determined efforts would speed the making of peace on

[5] Text of the resolution in *Department of State Bulletin* 5 (August 24, 1964): 268. The resolution passed unanimously in the House of Representatives; the Senate vote was 88-2.

[6] President Johnson's order to strike North Vietnamese military installations improved his political fortunes. The Gallup poll, August 26, 1964, showed that public approval of the President's handling of the Vietnam situation rose from 38 percent to 71 per cent; 16 per cent of the population was unfavorable; and 13 per cent had no opinion.

terms favorable to non-Communist South Vietnam. The immediate result, however, appeared only to intensify the fighting.

Furthermore, in 1965, as large American contingents landed in South Vietnam, the Saigon government was perilously close to defeat. *Vietcong* advances in the countryside isolated and threatened to strangle the government's urban bases; the army appeared to include very few patriots; and in Saigon factional political quarrels raged unabated, suggesting there was no immediate prospect of finding effective non-Communist leadership. Moving into this situation, American forces enjoyed a limited political victory by denying to the Communists a quick military triumph. By 1967 American forces were entering the Mekong Delta area which had long been a *Vietcong* stronghold. Moreover, bombing in the north destroyed much of the industrial and commercial bases that had been so painstakingly constructed since independence. Altogether the American effort provided Saigon with additional time to reorganize and to establish, if possible, its authority. For the Vietnamese, north and south, there was a dreadful price in casualties, both military and civilian, in villages destroyed, in lands laid waste, and in social and moral disintegration.

THE SEARCH FOR PEACE

Since an escalating Vietnam war carried the threat of a wider conflict, there were demands from many sources for an end to the fighting. Thus, the course of hostilities was paralleled by a peace diplomacy involving the United Nations and, at one time or another, virtually all of the world's powers.[7] This movement made no headway until President Johnson, April 1968, offered restrictions in American bombing of North Vietnam in return for negotiations. As a re-

[7] Chester A. Bain, *Vietnam: The Roots of Conflict* (1967),* a convenient summary of offers and counteroffers. Franz Schurman, Peter Dale Scott, and Reginald Zelnick, *The Politics of Escalation in Vietnam* (1966), a critique of the American negotiating positions.

sult, the United States, North Vietnam, South Vietnam, and the National Liberation Front (the *Vietcong's* political arm) came together for discussions at Paris (beginning in late 1968) while hostilities continued south of the 17th parallel.

At Paris, the future of South Vietnam was the fundamental issue. In effect, negotiators were asked to resolve what had not been resolved on the battlefield. The result was the presentation of terms which had no common ground. North Vietnam and the National Liberation Front demanded that Communists be assured a significant role in the formation of a South Vietnamese government. South Vietnam, while accepting in principle a coalition with the *Vietcong*, insisted on a formula that would make the degree and nature of the Communist access to power a matter for future decision. The American negotiating position was somewhat more flexible. Initially, the United States held that members of the National Liberation Front could participate in politics only as individuals, after forsaking war, and under rules to be determined by the Saigon government. By mid-1969, however, the Nixon Administration had invited the National Liberation Front to compete on equal terms with the Saigon regime in elections under rules to be worked out by the Vietnamese themselves. The victors in such an election would be free to change South Vietnam's government without American interference. This proposal, if implemented, would have increased the liklihood of Communists' sharing in political power, but it provided no guarantees. In consequence, the negotiators at Paris found neither in this nor in any other proposal the basis for a ceasefire and the establishment in South Vietnam of a unified government.

At the same time that President Nixon was seeking a settlement through negotiations, his administration began to apply a formula for withdrawing American forces even as Vietnam's struggles continued. On the theory that Saigon was rapidly becoming politically self-reliant and that government forces, freshly trained and supplied, could deal with the *Vietcong* and their North Viet-

namese allies, the United States in 1969 announced a policy to "Vietnamize" the war. Stated simply, "Vietnamization" called for the replacement of American forces with South Vietnamese troops.[8] In practice, however, this transfer of responsibility proved to be remarkably delicate business, because (1) it assumed that the *Vietcong*, having scaled down their military operations after the *Tet* offensive of 1968, would be unable in the near future to launch major operations; (2) it was dependent upon the relatively quick revitalization of a Vietnamese army that since 1965 had played a secondary role; and (3) it was linked to the exercise of stable, effective government under the Thieu-Ky leadership. Failure in any one of these three areas could endanger the entire "Vietnamization" program.

Some of the problems involved in "Vietnamization" and the proposed further withdrawals of American forces were revealed when, beginning in May, 1970, American and South Vietnamese forces invaded Cambodia to destroy command bases and supply depots long maintained in the border jungles of this supposedly neutral state. While critics charged that the invasion broadened the war and held grave implications for Cambodia's future, Washington emphasized its value to the "Vietnamization" program. By destroying supplies, by driving the Communists from sheltered sanctuaries, the invasion would provide additional time, it was said, for strengthening South Vietnamese forces. Furthermore, the action served as a warning that the United States would take whatever steps were required to safeguard American troops as they left Vietnam.

Meanwhile, the United States was formulating a new statement of American Far Eastern policy. In this statement, the United States appeared to be a "Pacific" rather than an "Asian" power; America's future policy was to be keyed to Asian initiatives ("Peace and progress," President Nixon said in Manila, "must be shaped and protected pri-

---

[8] The decision to withdraw 25,000 troops was announced in June, 1969. President Nixon reserved to the future decisions on the timing of further withdrawals.

marily by Asian hands."), but the United States fully intended to honor existing treaties. As applied in Asia, these principles were held to mean that

In some cases, assistance in economic and political development may be enough. In other cases aid in the form of training and equipment may be necessary. But the job of countering insurgency in the field is one which must be conducted by the government concerned, making use of its popular support, its resources, and its men. Large-scale intervention from abroad is, of course, something else again and must be considered against the backdrop of the total obligations and interests of the American people.[9]

The new policy seemed to mean that the United States was attempting the difficult business of closing out the American role in the Vietnam war and of assuring the American people that they would not again be involved in such a venture, while at the same time giving fresh pledges that the United States would not "abandon" Southeast Asia.[10]

INTERNATIONAL PERSPECTIVES ON THE NEW SOUTHEAST ASIA

These prospective limits on American intervention assumed that Southeast Asia

[9] Undersecretary of State Elliot L. Richardson, speaking at a meeting of the International Studies Association. Quoted in *The National Observer*, September 15, 1969.

[10] All that could be said about the motives of the new policy was that few people, inside the Administration or outside of it, could agree on what they were. Washington columnist, Stewart Alsop, for example, argued that, "What the President is really doing is to conduct a great military retreat—the greatest in American history. But for quite natural reasons he doesn't want to admit it—probably even to himself." "Mr. Nixon's Great Retreat," *Newsweek* 75 (May 25, 1970): 120. Former Secretary of Defense, Clark Clifford, on the other hand, viewed the Nixon policy as a repeat of President Johnson's: "One of the deepest concerns I have about our present policy in Vietnam is that President Nixon, while proclaiming his dedication to a political settlement, by his action still seeks to gain the military victory that cannot be won." "Set a Date in Vietnam. Stick to It. Get Out," *Life* 68 (May 22, 1970): 34–38.

during the 1970s would grow in strength and self-confidence. There was some evidence to support this view. Southeast Asia's leadership, once preoccupied with parochial nationalism and anti-Western sloganeering, had begun timidly to support projects encouraging international co-operation. The Asian Development Bank, operated on Asian capital and directed by a Japanese president, was promoting such diverse projects as the Seoul-Inchon expressway, irrigation in Indonesia, Thai industrial expansion, and air-transport in Nepal. Despite the Vietnam war, planning for development of the Mekong River was proceeding on an international basis (Thailand had completed two hydro-electric facilities, and work was underway on two other dams in Laos and Cambodia). Moreover, regional co-operation was exemplified in planning transportation and communication systems to overcome the insularity of the Southeast Asian states. Still other evidence of what Adam Malik, Indonesia's Foreign Minister, described as building a "community of nations" was to be seen in the formation of two regional international organizations: the Asian and Pacific Council (Japan, South Korea, Nationalist China, the Philippines, South Vietnam, Thailand, Malaysia, Australia, and New Zealand) and the Association of Southeast Asian Nations (Indonesia, Malaysia, Singapore, Thailand, and the Philippines), both of which through annual meetings afforded some opportunity for discusion of mutual problems where none had existed previously.

Yet it also was apparent that if regionalism was to be a vital force in Southeast Asia's future, it would not find its strength in historical tradition. Conflicting territorial ambitions remained strong. Thailand and Malaysia, though threatened by guerrilla insurrections in their border areas, did little to meet a common danger. The area's economies had little to sell to each other. Most of them continued to export raw materials and to import manufactured goods. Japanese business capitalized on this situation to succeed where Imperial Japan had failed. In fact, Southeast Asia had not broken the economic pattern of an earlier colonial era. Her new states continued to be linked more closely with industrial powers than with one another.

SOUTHEAST ASIA IN AMERICAN POLICY

From what has been said to this point it should be obvious that the nature and the status of Southeast Asia since World War II had become increasingly complex and uncertain. Even had the area been left to work out its own destiny free from external pressure, there is little in the historical record to suggest that its journey toward modernization would have been in keeping with what the West calls progress. It is well to recall therefore that Southeast Asia since 1941 has been the victim also of a world war, of revolutionary nationalism, of local state struggles for territory, and of great power rivalries waged at the ideological, the political, and the military levels. Since the mid-1950s, the government of the United States and the American people have been deeply involved in this amazing conflict. The verdict of history on whether that involvement was wise will not and cannot be written for many years to come. What can be said now is that despite nearly half a century of American rule in the Philippines, the United States and the American people were ill prepared intellectually for involvement. National educational resources devoted to the schooling of Americans on Southeast Asia had been at best minimal.[11]

[11] "Let us profit by our inadvertent war in Vietnam as an object lesson in historical non-thinking. The history of Vietnam has never been part of history in the USA. Indeed, it has not even been part of American Sinology or East Asian studies. . . . Suppose that our leaders in the Congress and the executive branch had all been aware that North Vietnam is a country older than France with a thousand-year history of southward expansion and militant independence maintained by using guerrilla warfare to expel invaders from China, for example, three times in the thirteenth century, again in the fifteenth century, and again in the late eighteenth century, to say nothing of the French in the 1950's. With this perspective, would we have sent our troops into Vietnam so casually in

For literate and concerned Americans, military involvement in Vietnam was to raise eventually a host of troublesome questions. For example, which Vietnam, North or South, was entitled to rule? Precedents in recognition and legitimacy were provided by American experiences in Europe and in Latin America, but did these precedents apply in Southeast Asia?[12]

Equally troublesome were issues of how the nation's priorities were to be arranged. Were American interests in Southeast Asia more, or less, vital than those in other regions? Could resources expended in Vietnam be used to greater advantage in coping with domestic problems? Was American policy conceived wisely or was it merely the result of an unplanned, creeping involvement? Questions such as these led to one of the most emotional and divisive public debates in American history.

Criticism of the involvement was expressed by marathon "teach-ins" in the colleges, by the public burning of draft cards, and by mass demonstrations, including one at the Pentagon in Washington. As in the case of Korea in 1950, the critics at first were out-voiced by strong public support of official policy; but as casualties increased, as the heavy drain on national resources continued, and as the war seemingly took on an interminable character, public patience was eroded by increasing demands that the

1965? A historical appreciation of the Buddhist capacity for individual self-sacrifice, of the Confucian concern for leadership by personal prestige and moral example, even of the Communist capacity for patriotism, might also have made us hesitate to commit ourselves to bomb Hanoi into submission." John K. Fairbank, "Assignment for the '70's," *American Historical Review* 74 (1969): 873–74.

[12] The theory of legitimacy holds that the operation of one or more of several principles gives a government legitimacy and makes it possible to govern with a minimum of force. If the principles are not appropriate to the situation, there will be need for a maximum force. The problem in applying the theory in Vietnam was to discover what principles should contribute to legitimacy. Could a government sustained by the principles of communism claim legitimacy? How were the claims of a militarist regime to be regarded?

United States extricate itself.[13] Furthermore the Vietnam conflict raised issues of a constitutional nature. The war was said to be illegal because Congress, as required by the constitution, had not declared it formally. The growing criticism was noted by the Senate Foreign Relations Committee which in 1966 conducted hearings that included witnesses critical of the war. In mid-1970, the authority claimed by the President in his role as Commander-in-Chief was said to be challenged by proposed legislation that would place limitations on the use of military funds. There was also pointed questioning of the leadership offered by the American federal bureaucracies. A so-called "Credibility Gap" was said to have resulted from a war which persisted in spite of repeated administration assurances that victory was just around the corner.[14] Finally, criticism of America's part in the war touched on the methods by which the conflict was conducted, the problems of interfering in a civil war, and the alleged neglect of American domestic affairs in favor of foreign entanglements.

[13] By May 1970, nearly 45,000 Americans had been killed in the Vietnam war, some 275,000 had been wounded, and more than one hundred and twenty-five billion dollars had been expended in war costs and aid.

[14] Some American newsmen professed to see deliberate distortion. Samuel G. Blackman, general news editor of the Associated Press, noted of the administration that "its misinformation on the progress of the war in Vietnam has been monumental." "The Gospel According to Blackman," *The Saturday Review* 52 (August 9, 1969): 45. The war between the press and American officialdom is described from the newsman's point of view in David Halberstram, *The Making of a Quagmire* (1965). With respect to charges of lack of frankness, John Mecklin, onetime chief of United States information services in Saigon, commented: ". . . the case against us was more complex than the sin of falsehood. The root of the problem was the fact that much of what the newsmen took to be lies was exactly what the Mission genuinely believed, and was reporting to Washington. Events were to prove that the Mission itself was unaware of how badly the war was going, operating in a world of illusion." *Mission in Torment: An Intimate Account of the U.S. Role in Vietnam* (1965), 100.

The administrative response to persistent public criticism defended presidential powers under the Constitution and also the Gulf of Tonkin Resolution to employ force as circumstances required. Allegations of misconduct in the prosecution of the war were denied with evidence placing responsibility on the *Vietcong*. The United States in this view, was not the aggressor. Saigon had requested the American presence to aid in repelling intervention by North Vietnam, which in turn was supported by the Chinese Communists and the Soviet Union. Thus, if civilian lives were lost, responsibility could not be assigned to circumstances created by the United States. Furthermore, the fortunes of free men were held to be at stake and dependent upon American power. In South Vietnam, it was said, the Communists could simply destroy their opponents. America's allies, some forty in number, would lose faith if the United States did not fulfill its commitments.[15]

The great debate on the Vietnam war was the third occasion (the fall of China to the Communists and the Korean war were the others) since World War II during which American national politics had been stirred profoundly on Asian questions. Why was it that the course of events in East and Southeast Asia always appeared to run counter to American purposes? Did the answer lie in the fact that Americans, having little knowledge of what Asians were or wanted to be, tended to see the area as a large, monolithic, and undifferentiated region?[16]

[15] Thomas A. Bailey, *A Diplomatic History of the American People* (8th ed., 1968), 908–13, a brief narrative of the developing controversy.

[16] An understanding of any part of modern Asia requires more than the assembly of data. Note, for example, "that Western religious values, with their senses of mission and guilt, as well as Western philosophical and scientific concepts of man's capacity to understand and change his natural and social environments and to experience inevitable progress, have greatly influenced Western attitudes toward aid to less developed peoples. The failure of the new states to achieve rapid political development and economic modernization is often attributed . . . to the alleged moral deficiencies and lack of competence of

There can be no doubt that the countries of Southeast Asia would have preferred to find their political salvation independently. Since this was not possible, they have accepted, on occasion, aid from both the Communist and the non-Communist worlds. In this context, Communist Chinese influence in Southeast Asia should not be underestimated. Many Southeast Asians who have no interest in or sympathy with communism, see, nevertheless, in China not only the center of East Asian civilization but also a nation that freed itself from Western semi-colonialism and imperialism, and which now speaks loudly on the world stage. Moreover, the states of Southeast Asia, poor and without strong and democratic political institutions, have not been inclined to dismiss socialist or Communist theory as simply evil and inapplicable.

There are non-Communist Southeast Asians who question American motives in Asia and are therefore not prepared to follow meekly in the footsteps of American leadership. In spite of repeated assurances from the United States, many non-Communist Asians appear to be as suspicious of American imperialism as they are of a Communist imperialism.[17]

Asians and Africans. In turn, the failure of less developed peoples to meet Western expectations has contributed to the reassessments, and reduction of aid programs, both in Western Europe and the United States. Such misgivings about aid . . . do not take sufficient account of the persistence of the characteristics of traditional society which diminish the prospects of rapid development and modernization." Robert L. Pfaltzgraff, Jr., reviewing Theodore Geiger's *The Conflicted Relationship: The West and the Transformation of Asia, Africa, and Latin America* (1967) in the *Journal of Asian Studies* 28 (1969): 833.

[17] "We have just entered a period in which Europeans, including Americans (though many of the latter are slow to realize it) remain in an Asia no longer controlled by the West. . . . If our descendants are to remain there [in Asia] in any numbers they must remain as welcome guests. This task should forcibly remind us of those earlier centuries—the sixteenth, seventeenth, and early eighteenth—during which Europeans became ubiquitous in much of Asia without controlling it. What can we learn from those centuries?" Holden Furber, "Asia and the West as Partners before 'Empire' and After," *Journal of Asian Studies* 28 (1969), 711.

Finally, the evidence of the past twenty years suggests that the goals of the non-Communist World in Southeast Asia are far more difficult to attain than the immediate goal of the Communists—the simple seizure of power. The evidence would also suggest that the outcome will depend on the ability of Asian leadership to inspire and create as much dedication to democratic institutions as Communist Asians have marshaled to the totalitarian cause. Without this dedication, history may some day record that assistance —political, military, and economic—in Southeast Asia fell upon barren soil.[18]

[18] For a full discussion, see Robert Blum's "Commentary" on Walter S. Robertson, "The United States Looks at South and Southeast Asia," *Nationalism and Progress in Free Asia,* Philip W. Thayer, ed. (1956), 1–15.

FOR FURTHER READING

GENERAL. Russell H. Fifield, *The Diplomacy of Southeast Asia, 1945–1958* (1958), the most complete description of post-war international relations. Also recommended, Saul Rose, ed., *Politics in Southern Asia* (1963); and D. E. Kennedy, *The Security of Southern Asia* (1965). J. M. Gullick, *Malaysia and Its Neighbors* (London, 1967), one of the few studies on regional rivalries. Communist activities are studied in Frank N. Trager, ed., *Marxism in Southeast Asia: A Study of Four Countries* (1959); and Robert A. Scalapino, ed., *The Communist Revolution in Asia: Tactics, Goals, and Achievements* (1965). Various aspects of American involvement in the region are treated in Russell H. Fifield, *Southeast Asia in United States Policy* (1963); Fred Greene, *U.S. Policy and the Security of Asia* (1968); Arthur J. Dommen, *Conflict in Laos* (1964); and George Modelski, *SEATO: Six Studies* (Vancouver, 1962). Alastair Buchan, ed., *China and the Peace* (1965), a series of essays. Two fine, specialized studies are Frank Golay, ed., *The United States and the Philippines* (1966); and George E. Taylor, *The Philippines and* the United States (1964). Daniel Wit, *Thailand—Another Vietnam* (1968) argues against American support.

VIETNAM WAR. The literature on the Vietnam war has become so voluminous that it is possible here to list only a few representative examples. Reports on the war itself are in Marguerite Higgins, *Our Vietnam Nightmare* (1967); Robert Shaplen, *The Lost Revolution: The Story of Twenty Years of Neglected Opportunities in Vietnam and of America's Failure to Foster Democracy There* (1966)* and *The Road from War: Vietnam 1965–1970* (1970); and two volumes by Bernard B. Fall, *Hell is a Very Small Place: The Siege of Dien Bien Phu* (1967); and *Viet-Nam Witness: 1953–1966* (1966). Wilfred G. Burchett, *Vietnam: Inside Story of a Guerrilla War* (1965),* an outright pro-Communist account. Marvin E. Gettleman, ed., *Viet Nam: History, Documents, and Opinions on a World Crisis* (1966), a broadly ranging collection of primary materials and interpretative analyses. A similar volume is Wesley R. Fishel, *Vietnam: Anatomy of a Conflict* (1968).* United States Department of State, *Aggression from the North—The Record of North Vietnam's Campaign to Conquer South Vietnam,* Office of Media Services, Publication #7839 (1965), supplies an essential part of official justification for American involvement. United States Senate, Committee on Foreign Relations, *China, Vietnam, and the United States: Highlights of the Hearings of the Senate Foreign Relations Committee* (1966), privately printed excerpts from the much publicized 1966 hearings. Frank N. Trager, *Why Viet Nam?* (1966) supports American involvement. Varying degrees of criticism of American policy may be found in Victor Bator, *Vietnam, A Diplomatic Tragedy* (London, 1967); Malcolm Browne, *The New Face of War* (1965); and Howard Zinn, *Vietnam: The Logic of Withdrawal* (1967). Foreign Policy Association, *Vietnam: Vital Issues in the Great Debate* (1966),* a brief analysis. Important legal aspects are examined in Richard A. Falk, ed., *The Vietnam War and International Law* (1968). George W. Ball, *The Discipline of Power* (1968), perceptive views of Vietnam and other issues by a former Undersecretary of State. Richard M. Pfeffer, ed., *No More Vietnams? The War and the Future of American Foreign Policy* (1968)* excerpts from round-table discussions by leading scholars.

Index

Abeel, David, 75, 210
Abortion in contemporary Japan, 461
Adachi Mineichiro, 307
Adams, John Quincy, 74–75
Afghanistan, recognition of People's Republic of China by, 437
Agrarian Reform Act (China, *1950*), 451
Agriculture
  collectivization of, 450–53, 480
  in Democratic Republic of Vietnam, 503
  in Japan: Meiji, 140–42, 264; post-World War II, 461–62
  in Malaya, 500
  in North Korea, 480–81
  in People's Republic of China, 450–53, 457
  See also Land; Peasantry
Aguinaldo, Emilio, 206, 368
Aigun, Treaty of, 97
Aikawa Yoshisuke, 340
Ainu people (Japan), 40
Alaska, 243
Alcock, Sir Rutherford, 119, 161
Aleutian Islands in World War II, 401
Alexieff, Adm. Yevgeny I., 234
Allied Council for Japan, 417
Allen, Young J., 210
Amherst, Sir William, 63, 68
Amory (China), establishment as trading post of, 73–74
Amur river, Russian exploration of, 96–97
Analects, Confucian, 29
Ancestor worship
  in ancient China, 16
  in ancient Japan, 41
Angell, James B., 165
Annam
  conquest by Mongols of, 15
  French control of, 184, 199–200, 367, 390–91, 500–2
  nationalism in, 393–94, 500–1
  religion in, 391–92
  See also Vietnam
Anti-Comintern Pact *(1936)*, 359, 411
Anti-Fascist People's Freedom League (Burma), 497
Anti-Subversive Activity Law (Japan, *1952*), 466

Arabs
  in Malaya, 386
  Palestinian, self-determination for, 614
  trade with China by, 54
Araki Sadao, General, 337, 338
Architecture in ancient China, 13, 43
Arrow War *(1857–58)*, 90–91, 171
Art, *see* Literature; Painting
Arthur, Chester, 166
Ashida, Hitoshi, 424
Ashikaga shogunate *(1336–1573)*, 48–49
Asia
  geography of, 3–4
  problems in the study of, 2–3
  United States foreign policy in, 520–22
Asian Development Bank, 470, 519
Asian and Pacific Council, 519
Association of Southeast Asian Nations, 519
Astronomy in ancient China, 23
Atlantic Charter, 361, 400
Atomic bomb, use on Japan of, 402
Atomic research, Japanese, proscription by occupation of, 419
Aung San, Gen., 497
Australia
  British fortification of, 293
  SEATO and, 515
  at Versailles, 275–77
  Vietnam and, 517
Autumn Harvest Uprising (China), 346

Ba Maw, 496
Bakufu (Japanese tent government), 47, 49, 100–1, 107, 116
Balfour, Sir Arthur, 200, 277, 294
Bandung conference *(1955)*, 454, 514
Bao Dai (emperor of So. Vietnam), 501–2, 516
Becker, Carl L., 7
Behaine, Pigneau de, 392
Belgium, 276, 321, 360, 488
Bennet, Gordon, Jr., 203
Bentham, Jeremy, 147

Beresford, Sir Charles, 215–16, 225
Bergson, Henri, 312
Berthemy, M., 158
Bezobrezov, A. M., 234
Bill of Rights, Japanese, 425
Binh Xuyen, 503
Birth control: in Formosa, 486; in Japan, 461
Bismark Island in World War II, 398
Bismark, Otto von, 130
Bjorko, Treaty of, 237
"Blue shirts," Chinese, 342
Bogue, Treaty of, 72
Boissanade, Gustave, 147
Bonifacio, Andres, 206
Bonin Islands
  United Nations trusteeship of, 426
  U.S. interests in, 115, 201
  U.S. occupation of, 419, 470
Borneo, 367; British colonial system in, 386
Borodin, Michael, 314
Bougainville (Solomon Islands) in World War II, 401
Boun Oum, Prince, 516
Bourboulon, M. de, 151
Boxer rebellion, 217–20
Bradley, Gen. Omar, 479
Brahmanism in Cambodia, 392
Brandt, von, 195
Brazil, 321
Bridgeman, Elijah C., 75, 210
Brown, M'Leavy, 199
Browne, Horace A., 163
Browne, J. Ross, 165, 169
Bruce, Frederick, 93–94, 151, 158
Bryan, William J., 268, 271–72
Buddhism
  in Annam, 391–92
  In Burma, 385
  in China: ancient, 13, 16, 21; People's Republic of, 449
  in East Indies, 382
  in Japan: ancient, 45, 49, 104; Meiji, 144, 146
  in Malaya, 387
  in Vietnam, 504
  Zen, 49
Bureaucracy
  ancient Chinese: attempt to establish, by Hans, 12; character of, 17–18, 37–38

Japanese: development of, 102–3; Meiji, 133–34; during World War II, 403–4; post-World War II, 465

Burgess, John W., 203

Burlingame, Anson, 151, 158–60, 164–66, 169, 183, 219

Burma
at Bandung conference, 514
British colonial system in, 184, 384–86, 395
economy of, 384–86
independence of, 416, 497
Japanese occupation of, 496
recognition of People's Republic of China by, 437
relations with Japan of, post-World War II, 461
SEATO and, 515
in World War II, 398–402, 411, 496
post-World War II, 496–98, 514–15, 519

Burma Road, 411

Business interests, see Investment; Trade

Cairo conference (1943), 400, 412, 419, 474, 484

Calendar, ancient Chinese, 12–13

Calligraphy: Chinese, 22; Japanese, 45

Cambodia, 367
French colonial system in, 390–92, 394, 506
nationalism in, 502
post-World War II, 506–7, 514–15, 519

Cambaluc (old Peking)
Christian mission at, 59
conquest by Mongols of, 14
Manchu government at, 32
See also Peking

Canada, 488

Canton (China)
anti-foreign demonstrations in, 81–83, 320
crisis at (1834–40), 169–70
fall to Japan of, 355

Canton Soviet, 320–21

Canton trade
Arab, 54
European: early, 55–57, 60; in 18th and 19th centuries, 62–69, 73, 80

Cao Dai (religion), 501, 503

Capitalism, see Investment; Trade

Caroline Islands, 269, 274–75, 292
U.S. occupation of, 419
in World War II, 401

Carpini, John de Plano, 54

Cathcart, Charles, 63

Cecil, Robert, 277

Censorship: in ancient China, 32; in occupied Japan, 423

Cespedes, Gregario de, 183

Ceylon
at Bandung conference, 514

People's Republic of China recognized by, 437
SEATO and, 515

Ch'ang-an (capital of T'ang China), 13

Chang Chih-tung, 196, 199, 212, 223, 249

Chang Chun-mai, 312

Chang Hseuh-liang, 317, 324–25, 328, 333, 349

Chang Hsun, 274

Chang, John M. (Chang Myun), 482

Chang Tso-lin, 302, 306, 317, 319, 324–25

Chapdelaine, Auguste, 89

Chefoo Convention (1876), 163

Ch'en Ch'eng, 484

Ch'en Ch'i-me, 251

Ch'en Kuo-fu, 342

Ch'en Lanpin, 160

Ch'en Li-fu, 342

Ch'en Tu-hsiu, 279, 312

Ch'en Yun, 445

Cheng Kuan-y'ing, 175

Chennault, Claire L., 411

Ch'i-shan, 72

Ch'i-ying, 79, 82, 170

Chiang Ching-kuo, 485–86

Chiang Kai-shek, 311, 314, 320, 342, 416
defeat of, 429–37
government of Formosa by, 484–89
Japanese and, 335, 356
kidnapping of, 349, 357
Kuomintang army reorganized by, 345
nationalism of, 408–9
in World War II, 400, 408–12

Chiang Kai-shek, Madame, 412

Chih Kang, 159

Ch'in-ch'ai (imperial commissioner), 78

Ch'in dynasty (221–207 BC), 12, 29, 31

China
ancient, 10–38: ancient Japan compared to, 39; Ch'in dynasty in (221–207 BC), 12, 29, 31; Ch'ing dynasty in, see Manchu dynasty; Chou dynasty in (1026–256 BC), 12; class structure of, 22–23; government in, local and provincial, 33–35; Han dynasty in (202 BC–220 AD), 12–13, 29; ideas on government in, 17, 26–38; influence on Japan of, 40, 42–44, 46, 49; Manchu dynasty in, see Manchu dynasty; Ming dynasty in (1368–1644), 15; Mongol rule of (1260–1368), 14–15; population of, 15; religion in, 13, 16, 18–22; science in, 23–24; social philosophy of, 16–17; stability of, 2, 10. 15: Sung empire in (960–1279), 13–14; T'ang dynasty in (618–

906), 13; ways of life in, 10–24
Boxer rebellion in, 217–20
dependent states of, 180–83, 232–35
early contacts with West of, 53–58, 168–75
economic interests of West in, 192, 200, 214, 288–89, 318–21
foreign missions in, 158–59
foreign relations of: pre-19th century, 53–58, 63–64, 75–76; 1833–48, 66–69, 75–76, 79–82, 87; 1848–60, 86–99; 1860–90, 158–63, 169–70, 172–74; 1890–99, 185–90, 194–208, 234; 1901–10, 232–47; of People's Republic, 453–55
immigration to U.S. from, 164–65
influence in Indochina of, 181, 401, 406–13
influence of West on, 170–72, 177–78, 210–11, 278–80, 312, 456
Japan and, see Japan
Korea and, 180–83, 185–90
leadership in 19th century, 175–78
legal system of, 65–66, 73, 87–90
militarism in: Kuomintang rule and, 342, 344; in Manchu period, 152, 155–58; reform of, 224–26; after revolution of 1911, 253–54, 257, 273, 310–11
Nine-Power Treaty on (1922), 293–95, 297, 329, 359
People's Republic of: agricultural collectivization in, 450–53, 457; Cambodia and, 506–7; conditions in, after 1949, 440–57; cultural revolution in, 444–46, 449; economy of, 450–53; education in, 447–48, 457; foreign relations of, 453–55; Formosa and, 454, 486, 488; founding of, 437–38, 441; government of, 441–47; Korean conflict and, 447, 478, 480–81; Laos and, 505; North Vietnam and, 502, 509, 516; population growth in, 457; social reform in, 449–50; Southeast Asia and, after World War II, 512–15; Soviet Union and, 437–38, 440, 450, 454–55; United Nations membership denied to, 488; see also Chinese Communist Party
policy of seclusion of, 60–61
reform movements in, 210–13, 222–30
Republic of: birth of, 249–57; Canton government of, 316–17; economy of, 343–44, 406–7, 411, 430, 432; ef-

China (cont.)
fect of World War I on, 278–80; Japanese advances into (1937), 333–35, 353–58, 360, 407; Japanese puppet government in, 355–57; Nanking government of, 317–22; politics in (1931–41), 341–49; resistance to Japanese in, 357–58, 360; Soviet influence in, 305, 312, 314, 319–21, 325–26, 428–29, 431; World War II in, 401, 406–13
revolution of 1911 in, 249–51
tariff policies of, 63–64, 73, 95, 315, 318, 320–21, 344
Twenty-one demands of Japan on, 270–71, 333
war with Japan of (1894–95), 185–90, 195, 224
western ideas about, 53, 61, 169
in World War I, 268–80
See also Canton trade; Kuomintang; Manchuria; Open Door policy; Opium war; T'ai P'ing rebellion
China-Burma-India theater in World War II, 400–1, 411
China's Destiny (Chiang Kai-shek), 409–10
Chinda (Count Sutemi), 275
Chinese (language): adoption by Japanese court of, 42; beginnings of written, 12; difficulty of, 18, 22
Chinese (population): in Burma, 385–86; in East Indies, 385; in Malaya, 386, 389, 498–99; in Thailand, 390
Chinese Communist Party, 312, 314
alliance with Kuomintang, 355–58, 407–11
appeal to peasants by, 346–47, 410–11, 429–30
military victory of, 433–34
opposition to Kuomintang by, 345–48, 428–34
resistance to Japanese by, 349, 353, 357–58, 407–11, 429
role in contemporary China of, 445–47
Soviet Union and, 347
Chinese Eastern Railway, 197–99, 218, 232, 238–39, 244, 283, 286–88, 318–19, 333; Soviet-Chinese-Japanese conflict over, 324, 326–28
Chinese People's Consultative Conference (1949), 441
Ch'ing dynasty, see Manchu dynasty
Chinputang Party (China), 253
Chosen, see Korea
Chou dynasty (1026–256 BC), 12
Chou En-lai, 445
Christianity
in China: exclusion in 18th century, 60; introduction in 16th century, 56; reform movements and, 210; spread in Manchu period, 161; in T'ai-

P'ing Rebellion, 85–86; tolerance provisions in Tientsin treaty, 92, 160–62
in Japan: exclusion in 17th century, 59–60, 100; introduction in 16th century, 58–60; in Meiji period, 148
in Philippines, 377
in Vietnam, 501, 503–4
See also Missionaries
Chu Teh, 345–47, 445
Ch'an-chou (Zayton, China), 54
Chuang-tzu, 28
Ch'un, Prince (Tsai Feng), 174, 176, 249, 251
Chun chi ch'u (grand council), 78
Chungking, Kuomintang headquarters at, 360, 406
Churchill, Sir Winston, 361, 400, 412
Cincinnati Inquirer, The, 296
Civil code, Japanese, 129, 147–48
Civil service: in ancient China, 13, 29, 36; in Meiji Japan, 134
Clarendon, Lord (George Villiers), 160–61
Class structure
in China: ancient, 17–18, 22–23, 34–35; Communist revolution and, 345–48, 429–30, 449–52; effect of World War I on, 280
in Japan: ancient, 44; effect of Meiji restoration on, 125; in Tokugawa period, 103–4, 107–8, 110; after World War I, 299–300; after World War II, 462–63
Cleveland, Grover, 203
Co-hong merchants, 64, 73
Cochin China, 367, 390–91; see also Vietnam
Collectivization, agricultural: in China, 450–53; in Korea, 480
Colonialism in Southeast Asia, 367–94, 512–14; see also Burma; East Indies; Indochina; Malaya; Philippines
Comintern, Chinese policy of, 314
Communes, in People's Republic of China, 452
Communism
in Annam, 393–94
in Burma, 497, 519
in East Indies, 383
in Indonesia, 494–96, 519
in Japan, 423–25, 464–69
in Laos, 505–6, 515–16
in Philippines, 492–93, 519
in Southeast Asia, 508–9, 515, 521–22
in Vietnam, 501–5, 516–18
Communist China, see China—People's Republic of
Confucianism
in ancient China, 12, 20–21: philosophers of, 28–29; political institutions of, 31–38; political thought of, 29–31

in Annam, 391
Chiang Kai-shek's, 409
influence on Sun Yat-sen of, 314–15
in Manchu China, 171, 172
in Meiji Japan, 144
in People's Republic of China, 456
in Republic of China, 343
in Tokugawa Japan, 104–5, 108, 110
Confucius, 12, 18–19, 20–21, 27
Conger, Edward H., 218
Constitutional government
in China, 226–27
in Japan: establishment of, 128–35, 149; reform by occupation of, 420–22
Consumer goods: in contemporary China, 450; in contemporary Japan, 462
Cook, Captain (James Cook), 74
Coolidge, Calvin, 297, 308, 372
Coolie trade, 88, 164; legalization of, 95
Cotton industry in Meiji Japan, 141, 264–65
"Credibility gap," 521
Crimean war, 97
Cuba, 204
"Cultural revolution" in China, 444, 446–47, 450, 457
Culture
in China: ancient, 12–15, 22–23; European interest in, 61
in Japan: ancient, 44–46, 48–49; Tokugawa, 106–7
Cushing, Caleb, 75–76, 82, 170
Customs administration in Chinese treaty ports, 87
Czechoslovakia, 284–86

Daimyo system, Japanese, 101–4, 124–25
Dan Takuma, 339
Davis (Gov. of Hong Kong), 82
Davis, John W., 89
Day, William R., 207
"Democratic League" of China, 343
Democratic Republic of Vietnam (North Vietnam), 501–3
bombing of, 516–17
Cambodia and, 516–17
Laos and, 505–6
Denby, Charles, 188, 215
Dengyo-Daishi, 45
Denmark: People's Republic of China recognized by, 57, 321; trade with China by, 57, 321
Derber, Petr Yakolivich, 283
Dewey, Adm. George, 204–6
Dewey, John, 312
Diederich, Adm. von, 198, 207
Diem, Ngo Dinh, 503, 516
Dien Bien Phu, battle of, 502
Diet (Japanese parliament)
powers of, 132, 134–35, 260–61, 265, 300, 403–4

reform by occupation of, 420–22; post-World War II, 465–66
Disarmament, naval, 289–93, 307–9
Djakarta (Indonesia), 494
Dobama party (Burma), 386
Dodge, Joseph M., 460
"Dollar diplomacy," 244, 254–55, 282
Dominican Republic, 332
Doshikai party (Japan), 263, 301
Drought, Father, 362
Drucker, Peter, 471
Dumbarton Oaks conference (*1944*), 400
Dutch East India Company, 382–83

East Indies, 367, 416
  Dutch colonial system in, 382–4, 395
  economy of, 383–84
  Japanese interest in, 362, 364
  in World War II, 399
Edkins, Joseph, 210
Education
  in China: ancient, 17, 35–36; of Chinese students abroad, 172–73, 223–24, 313; in People's Republic, 447–48; reform of, 223–24; at Tung-wen Kuan, 171–72
  in East Indies, 383
  in Japan: contemporary, 462–63; Meiji policy on, 126, 133, 265, 305; reform by occupation of, 422–23
  in Korea, 474, 481
Eighth Route Army (Chinese Red Army), 353, 357
Eisenhower, Dwight D., 468, 516
El Salvador, 332
Elgin, Lord, 91, 93
Elliott, Capt., 72
Empress of China, The, 57, 74
England
  attack on Choshu by, 119
  attack on Taku by, 93–94
  Boxer rebellion and, 218–19
  colonial system in Southeast Asia of, 184, 384–86, 394–95, 496–97
  control of Burma by, 184, 496–97
  control of Malaya by, 386–89, 499
  control of Sikkim by, 184
  interests in China of, 200, 214, 288–89, 318–21, 437
  intervention in Siberia by, 283–89
  Korea and, 183, 185, 188
  Kowloon leased by, 200–1
  legal disputes with China of, 65–67, 73, 87–88
  Manchuria and, 241–42, 329–32
  missions in China of, 160
  naval disarmament and, 289–93, 307–9
  People's Republic of China recognized by, 437

Philippines and, 207
SEATO and, 515–16
Thailand and, 390, 507
Tibet and, 225
trade with China by: early, domination of, 57, 62–65, 68–69; 19th century, 73–74, 77–79, 81
trade with India by, 68–69
trade with Japan by, 59
treaties between China and, 72, 88–92, 160–61, 163
treaties between Japan and, 115, 118
in World War I, 268–69, 272, 274, 276–77
in World War II, 358–61, 364, 398–402
Yunnan expedition of, 162–63
English East India Company, 62, 64–65, 74, 387
Eugenics Protection Law (Japan, *1948*), 461
European Economic Community, Japan and, 462
Evarts, William M., 166
Extraterritoriality
  in China: abolition of, 318, 321; conflicts over, 87–88
  in Japan, aboliiton of, 129

Family
  in China: ancient, 16–19; People's Republic, 449, 452
  in Japan: Meiji, 145–46; Tokugawa, 106
Far Eastern Commission on Japan, 417
Far Eastern Republic of Siberia, 319
Farmer's Cabinet (publication), 159
Feng Kuei-fen, 171
Feng-Yu-hsiang, 317, 319
Feudal system: Chinese, 12; Japanese, 49–50, 100–3, 123–25
Fillmore, Millard, 113
Finland, 437
"Five Dynasties" of ancient China, 13
Five-year plans in People's Republic of China, 451, 453, 457
"Flying Tigers," 411
Foochow (China), establishment as trading port of, 74–75
Forbes, W. Cameron, 372
Foreign Relations Committee, U.S. Senate, 488, 521
Formosa (Taiwan)
  during World War II, 401
  Japanese possession of, 189
  Korea and, 479
  Kuomintang control of, 419, 426, 474, 479, 483–89
  loss to Japan of, 460, 484
  neutralization of, 478
  People's Republic of China and, 454, 486, 488
  post-World War II, 514: agriculture in, 484; economy of,

485; government of, 484–86; Taiwanese role in, 484; United Nations membership of, 488; U.S. and, 485, 488–89
  U.S. interests in, 115, 182, 201, 243
Four-Power Consortium in China, 288–89, 297
France
  attack on Choshu by, 119
  attack on Taku by, 93–94
  Boxer rebellion and, 218–19
  early trade with China by, 57, 62
  Indochina policies of, 184, 199–200, 362, 390–95, 500–2
  intervention in Siberia by, 283–89
  investment in China by, 288–89
  Japan and, 118, 193–94
  Korea and, 183, 185
  Kwangchow Bay leased by, 199–200, 214
  Manchuria and, 229–31, 241–42
  naval disarmament and, 292
  protection of missionaries in China by, 89, 94, 161
  SEATO and, 515–16
  Thai territory obtained by, 390, 392
  trade with Burma by, 384
  trade with Japan by, 118
  trade treaties with China of, 74, 76, 91–92, 93–95, 321
  Vietnam and, 184, 199–200, 367, 390–91, 500–2, 516
  in World War I, 272–74, 276
  in World War II, 359–60, 398
Franciscan missionaries in Japan, 58–59
Franklin, Benjamin, 74
Frelinghuysen, Frederick T., 185
Fryer, John, 210
Fujiwara clan, 46
Fuken-kai (Japanese prefectural assemblies), 128
Fukien (China): Japanese interests in, 271; nationalist revolt in, 349
Fulbright, J. William, 488–89

Gama, Vasco da, 55
Gauss, Clarence E., 412
Gautama, 21
Geneva conference (*1954*)
  Cambodia and, 506
  Korea and, 481
  Laos and, 502, 515–16
  Vietnam and, 502, 515
"Gentlemen's agreement" between the U.S. and Japan, 243, 295–96
Genro (elder statesmen), 132–33
George, Henry, 315
Germany
  aid to *Kuomintang* by, 345
  Boxer rebellion and, 218–20
  defense pacts with Japan and Italy of, 359–60

Germany *(cont.)*
  interests in China of, 198–99, 214
  Japan and, 19th century, 193–94
  Korea and, 188
  Philippines and, 207
  recognition of Japanese puppet government in China by, 356
  recognition of Manchukuo by, 332
  in World War I, 267–68, 273, 275–78
  in World War II, 361, 398
Ghenghis Khan, 54
Giap, Vo Nguyen, 503
Godkin, E. L., 203
Goodnow, Frank, 254
Gordon, Maj. Charles, 155
Goto Shojiro, 129
Government, ideas on: in ancient China, 26–31; in Meiji Japan, 143–45
Grant, Ulysses S., 130, 182
Graves, Gen. William S., 286, 288
Great Britain, *see* England
"Great Leap Forward" in China, 446, 448, 451–53, 457
Great Wall of China building of, 12
Green Standard Chinese Army of the, 155–56
Grew, Joseph C., 332, 364–65
Grey, Sir Edward, 269, 444
Guadalcanal, campaign of, 400–1
Guam, 292
Guerilla warfare
  in Burma, 514
  in Cambodia, 506
  in Indonesia, 514
  in Laos, 505–6, 515–16
  in Malaya, 499, 514
  in the Philippines, 492–93, 514
  in Thailand, 508, 519
  in Vietnam, 501–5, 516–18
Gulf of Tonkin resolution *(1964)*, 517, 521

Hague Agreement on Indochina *(1949)*, 494
Hague Peace Conference *(1907)*, 246
Hainan Islands, 356, 360
Halmahera Island, 401
Hamaguchi Osachi (Yuko), 300, 302–3, 308, 336
Han dynasty *(202 BC–220 AD)*, 12–13, 29
Han Fei, 28
Hanihara Masanao, 297
Hankow (China), anti-British strike at, 320
Hanoi (Vietnam), 391
Hara Takoshi, 263, 283, 287, 299–301, 304
Harding, Warren G., 289, 291, 372
Harriman, E. H., 243–44
Harris, Townsend, 116-18, 390
Harrison, Francis B., 372
Hart, Sir Robert, 209
Hatta, Mohammed, 383, 494

Hatoyama Ichiro, 467
Hawaii, 207, 243
Hay, John, 207, 215–19, 232, 237, 255
Hayashi (Count Tadasu), 192, 242
Hayashi Senjuro, 340
Hayes, Rutherford B., 165
Hegel, Georg W. F., 147
Heian period (Japan, *794–1185*), 44–45
Heinkyo, Japanese capital at, 45
Hepburn, J. C., 148
Hidetoda (Japanese shogun), 59–60
Hideyoshi Toyotomi, 50, 58–59
Higashikuni Naruhiko, 405–6, 425
Hinduism: in East Indies, 382; in Malaya, 387
Hioki (Japanese prime minister), 269
Hippisley, Alfred, 216–17
Hirohito (Japanese emperor), 405, 464
Hiroshima, atomic bombing of, 402
Hirota Koki, 34
History
  study and teaching of, 1–8
  writing of: in ancient China, 13; in ancient Japan, 43–44
History of Civilization in England (Buckle), 148
History of Civilization in Europe (Guizot), 148
Ho Chi Minh, 416, 501–3, 508–9, 515–16
Ho Chi Minh trail, 506
Ho Kai, 211
Hoa Hoa religion, 501, 503
Hoar, George F., 208
Hokkaido Island, 419, 467
Hong Kong (China)
  anti-foreign demonstrations at, 320
  British possession of, 72, 73
  Chinese refugees in, 457
  Japanese attack on, 364, 398
  naval bases at, 292
Honshu Island, 419
Hoomum Chai, Treaty of, 72
Hoover, Herbert, 308
Horvath, Lt. Gen. Dimitrii, 283, 285–86
House, Col. Edward M., 276
Hoyumi Yatsuka, 147
Hseuh Fu-ch'eng, 211
Hsing Chung Hu (League for the Regeneration of China), 228
Hsu Kwang-chin, 82
Hu Han-min, 342
Hu Shih, 279, 312, 345
Huc, E. R., 37
Hughes, Charles E., 289, 291–97
Hughes, William H., 276–78
Hukbalahaps (Huks), 492–93
Hukuang railways, 254
Hulbert, H. B., 246
Hull, Cordell, 358, 362–64
Hunan (China), peasant uprising in, 346
"Hundred Flowers" campaign, 449
Hung Hsiu-ch'uan, 85–86
Hungary, 332

Hunt's Merchants Magazine, 76
Hurley, Gen. Patrick J., 412, 430, 432
Hyogo (Kobe, Japan), shipbuilding in, 138

I-ho-ch'uan (Harmonius Brotherhood), 217–18
I-hsin, *see* Kung, Prince
Ignatiev, Gen. Nikolai P., 93, 98
Ikeda Hayato, 468–69
Ili Island, 184
Immigration to United States
  from China, 164–65, 282–83
  from Japan, 295–96, 305, 307
  from Philippines, 373
India
  at Bandung conference, 514
  independence of, 416
  influence on Burma of, 384
  influence on China of, 22
  influence on Indochina of, 392, 512
  influence on Malaya of, 386, 389, 498
  influence on Thailand of, 390
  People's Republic of China and, 437, 454
  SEATO and, 515
  trade among China, England and, 68–69
Indochina, 367, 416
  ancient China and, 181
  French colonial system in, 390–94
  French penetration of, 184, 199–200
  Japanese intervention in, 360, 362, 491, 501
  People's Republic of China and, 454–55
  post-World War II, 500–7
  See also Annam; Cambodia; Laos; Vietnam
Indonesia, 367
  Bandung conference called by, 514
  Dutch colonial system in, 383–84, 494
  economy of, 383–84, 495–96
  independence of, 383–84, 495–96
  Japanese rule of, 494
  People's Republic of China recognized by, 437
  SEATO and, 515
  post-World War II, 494–96, 519
Industry
  in Burma, 498
  in China: advocates of, 174–75, 212, 229; government and, in 19th century, 174–75; People's Republic, 450–53; during World War I, 307, 344, 430
  in Democratic Republic of Vietnam, 502–3
  in Japan: contemporary, 461–62, 471; Meiji, 138–39, 264, 304; occupation control of, 419

in North Korea, 480
in Thailand, 507–8
Influence of Sea Power on World History, The (Mahan), 203
Inouye Junnosuke, 339
Inouye Kaoru, 133
Inouye Tsuyoshi, 130
International Control Commission in Laos, 506
International Military Tribunal for the Far East, 420
Inukai Tsuyoshi, 300, 303, 339
Investment
  Japanese: in Africa and Latin America, 470; in Korea, 483
  United States: in China, 275, 288–89; in the Philippines, 492; in Thailand, 508
  of Western powers in China: 19th century, 195, 200, 214; 20th century, 244–45, 275, 288–89, 344
Iron industry
  in China, 174
  in Japan, 138
Ishibashi Tanzan, 467
Ishii Kikujiro, 275, 282
Islam
  in China, 85, 409, 449
  in East Indies, 382–83, 494–95
  in Malaya, 389
  in Philippines, 375, 377
Isolationism,, Japanese, 60, 101–12; collapse of, 112–20
Israel, 437
Iswolsky (Russian foreign minister), 292
Itagaki Taisuke, 128–29
Italy
  interests in China of, 214
  intervention in Siberia by, 284
  pact with Japan of, 359–60
  recognition of Japanese puppet government in China by, 356
  recognition of Manchukuo by, 332
  tariff treaty with China of, 321
  at Versailles, 276
Ito Hirobumi, 129, 133, 139, 142, 149, 186, 193, 233–34, 243, 260, 262; assassination of, 246, 263
Ito Myoji, 130
Iwakura Tomomi, 128
Iwo Jima, battle of, 401
Iyemitsu (Japanese shogun), 60
Iyeyasu, 50, 59

Japan
  ancient, 39–50: ancient China compared to, 39; clan system in, 42; culture of, 44–46, 48–49; feudal society in, 47; Heian period in *(784–1185)*, 44–45; Hojo regency in *(1205–1333)*, 48–49; influence of China on, 40, 42–44, 46, 49, 181; Kamakura military dictatorship in *(1185–1338)*, 46–47; militarism in,

48–49, 103; Mongol invasion of, 40; political institutions in, 46; religion in, 40–42
  Ashikaga Shogunate in *(1336–1573)*, 48, 50
  Boxer rebellion, 218–19
  business elite in, 138–42, 265, 299–300, 340, 405–6, 424, 465
  China and: 19th century, 177–78, 186–90, 192–97, 218–20, 224, 255, 270, 282; 20th century, 303, 305–7, 318, 333–35, 349; during World War II, 353–58, 360, 362, 407; post-World War II, 454–55, 467
  contemporary: foreign investment and loans by, 470, 483, 519; future of, 471–72; living standards in, 462; politics in, 464–72
  early contacts with West of, 57–60
  education in, 126, 133, 265, 304, 462–63
  end of isolationism in, 112–20
  Germany and, 193–94, 359–60
  immigration to United States from, 295–96, 305, 307
  influence of West on, 126–28, 137, 147–49, 177–78, 299, 338
  Korea and, 50, 183–87, 232–38, 245–47, 263; post-World War II, 419, 460
  Manchuria and: 19th century, 189, 193–95, 232–37, 239–47, 269–71, 278; 20th century, 294, 302, 305–7, 324–26, 336, 349; during World War II, 401–2; post-World War II, 460
  Meiji period in *(1867–1918)*: constitution of, 128–35, 149, 258–59, 303; economic and cultural base of, 137–49, 264–66; foreign relations during, 193–95, 233–34, 303–9; government of, 125–35, 257–66
  militarism in, 134, 262–63, 299–300, 302–3, 307–8, 336–41, 352, 403–6
  naval disarmament and, 289–93, 308–9
  occupation by United States of, 415–26, 460–64
  party government period in *(1918–)*: economy of, 301, 305, 336–37, 404–5, 423–25, 461–62, 470, 483, 519; government of, 299–304, 336–41
  peace treaty with, after World War II, 425–26
  reform by occupation of, 422–23
  Russia and, 193–94, 305–7; war between, 235–38, 264–65
  Tokugawa shogunate in *(1603–*

1867): economy of, 105–8; government of, 50, 100–10
  twenty-one demands on China of, 270, 282
  United States and: conflict of interests between, post-World War I, 282–87; ties between, post-World II, 464, 467–70; in World War I, 267–73, 275–80
  in World War II: advances into China by, 333–35, 353–58, 407; allied campaign against, 398–402; attack on Pearl Harbor by, 364–65; effect of war on, 416–17; government of, 403–6; "new order" in Asia of, 359–61, 491–92; occupation of Burma by, 496; occupation of Indonesia by, 494; occupation of Malaya by, 498
  See also Trade, with Japan
Japan Social Democratic Party, 265
Japanese (language), 45–46
Jay, John, 75
Jefferson, Thomas, 74
Jesuits
  as bridge between Europe and Far East, 61, 168
  in China, 56, 58
  in Japan, 58–59
  in Korea, 183
Jiyuto (Liberal) party (Japan)
  in Meiji period, 142–43, 258, 260–62
  post-World War II, 424–25, 465–67, 469–71
  See also: Seiyukai party
Joffe, Abram Adolfe, 312, 314, 319
Johnson, Andrew, 159
Johnson, Lyndon B., 470, 516–17
Jones, W. A., 372
Jung-lu, 213, 225

Kaishinto (Progressive) party (Japan), 142–43, 258, 260
Kakushin club, 301
Kamakura (Japan): culture of, 48–49; Japanese military government at, 48–49
Kamchatka (Russia), settlement of, 96
Kammu (Japanese emperor), 44
Kanagawa, Treaty of, 115
K'ang Yu-wei, 211–12, 227, 254
Kangte, emperor of Manchukuo, *see* P'u-yi, Henry
Karafuto (South Sakhalin Island), 419, 426
Karakhan, L. M., 280, 319
Karens people in Burma, 497–98
Katayama Sen, 265
Katayama Tetsu, 425
Kato Kanji, Adm., 308–9
Kato Takaaki, Viscount, 268–69, 300–2, 304
Kato Tomosaburo, Adm., 300
Katsura (Count Taro), 133, 142, 239, 243, 246, 263

Kearny, Denis, 164–65
Keenan, Joseph B., 420
Kellogg-Briand treaty *(1928)*, 325–26, 329, 422
Keneko Kentaro, 130
Kennedy, John F., 516
Kenseikai party (Japan), 262, 300–2
Kerensky, Aleksandr, 283
Khmer Rouge, 506
Khrushchev, Nikita S., 468
Kiaochou Bay: German possession of, 198; Japanese claims to, 268, 275–78; return to China of, 294, 320
Kim Il-song, 416, 476, 480–81
Kimmel, Adm. Husband S., 364
Kishi Nobusuke, 467
Kita Ikki, 338
Kittakachorn, Thanom, 507
Kiyoura (Viscount Keigo), 300
Knox, Frank, 364
Knox, Philander C., 244–45, 255
Kobe (Japan), in World War II, 401
Kobo-Daishi, 45
Koiso Kuniki, 402, 405–6
Kojiki, 43, 146
Kokinshiu, 45
Kokovtseff, Russian finance minister, 246
Kokuhonsha (National Foundation Society), 338
Kolchack, Aleksandr V., 283, 286–87
Komeito (Clean Government) party (Japan), 471–72
Komura (Marquis Jutaro), 237, 240, 246
Konoye (Prince Fuminaro), 340, 360, 363, 404–5
Koo, V. K. Wellington, 276, 278, 319
Korea
　China, 180–83, 185–87
　England and, 185
　France and, 183, 185
　Germany and, 185
　independence of, 19th century, 189–90
　independence promised to (Cairo agreements), 400, 416, 426, 477
　Japanese intervention in, 50, 183–85, 197–98, 238–39, 245–47, 474
　loss to Japan of, 419, 460
　migration to Japan from, 40
　Mongol conquest of, 14
　North: economy of, 480–81; government of, 475, 481; military in, 481; Soviet intervention in, 429, 474–81
　Russia and, 186, 197–98; Soviet, 474–81
　South: economy of, 481–83; government of, 475–76, 483; Japan and, 483; United States' occupation of, 429; Vietnam and, 517
　Tientsin convention on, 186
　United States and, 183, 185, 188,

235, 238–39, 245–47, 263, 429
　in World War II, 402, 426
Korean conflict, 2, 438, 514–15
　People's Republic of China and, 447, 454, 478
　Soviet Union and, 474–81
　United Nations and, 475–78, 481
　United States and, 474–76, 478–80, 481–83
Kotoku Denjiro, 265
Kowloon (China), concession to British of, 95, 200
Kowtow, 67, 75
Kuala Lumpur (Malaya), 402
　249, 312
Kuang-hsu (emperor of China), 175, 249, 312
Kublai Khan, 14–15, 48, 54
Kung, Prince (I-shin *or* Yi Hsin), 151–52, 157, 159, 172–73, 176–77
Kuo Mo-jo, 312–13
Kuo Sung-ling, 306
Kuo Sung t'ao, 160
Kuomintang, 229, 310–16
　alliance with Chinese Communist party of, 355–58, 407–11
　anti-imperialism of, 320–22
　conflicts within, 342, 406
　failure of, reasons for, 434–35
　founding of, 253
　government of Formosa by, 483–89, 514
　Japanese relations with, 306–7, 334, 349, 353–55, 360, 362, 407
　Manchurian headquarters of, 325–26
　national government of, 341–45
　new program of, 313–16
　occupation of Formosa by, 419, 434, 438
　Soviet influence on, 312, 314–17, 319
　struggle with Chinese Communist party of, 345–49, 428–34
　tariff policies of, 320–21
　in World War II, 406–12: Soviet aid to, 407, 411; United States support of, 407, 411–12
　See also Chiang Kai-shek
Kurile Islands, 419, 426, 460
Kuroda Kiyotaka, 260
Kuropatkin, Aleksai N., 218, 236
Kurusu Saburo, 363–64
Kwangchou Bay, 200, 319
Ky, Nguyen Cao, 504, 518
Kyoto, Japanese capital at, 45, 101
Kyushu Island, 401, 419

Labor movement, *see* Trade unions
Ladrone Islands, 57
Lagrene, Theodore de, 170
Land
　in China: ancient, ownership of, 22–23; purchase by foreigners of, 81; redistribution of, by Chinese Communist party, 346, 410, 429, 447, 451–52;

shortage of, in 19th century, 85; tax on (Sun Yat-sen's program for), 315
　in Japan: ancient, ownership of, 101–2, 107–8, 141; in Meiji period, tax on, 141; redistribution by occupation of, 424
　in Philippines, struggle over, 493
Langer, Frederick D., 201
Language, *see* Chinese; Japanese
Lansing, Robert, 275, 282, 287
Lao Dong (Vietnamese Workers' Party), 502–3
Lao Issara (Free Laos), 505
Laos
　French colonial system in, 390–92, 394
　nationalism in, 502
　post-World War II, 505–6, 515–16, 519
Lao-tzu, 12, 18–19, 28, 30
Laurel, José, 492
Law
　in ancient China, 13, 17–18, 33
　Chinese-foreign disputes over, 65–66, 73, 87–90
　in Japan: influence of West on, 147–48; reform of, 129, 132
League of Nations, 275, 289, 321
　Japan and, 305, 307, 359
　Manchuria and, 329–31
Ledo Road (Stilwell Road), 401, 411
Ledyard, John, 74
Lee Kuan Yew, 500
Legard, Benito, 369
Legge, James, 210
Leibnitz, Gottfried W., 61
Lend-Lease Act *(1941),* 361
Leninism, 312, 345
Li Hung-Chang, 79, 154–56, 159–63, 171–72, 176–77, 184–88, 196, 199, 210, 224, 232
Li Li, 28
Li Li-san, 346–47
Li-Lobanov Treaty *(1896),* 196–97
Li Po, 13
Li Sen, 342
Li Ta-chao, 312
Li Tsung-jen, 434
Li Yuan-hung, 251, 252–53, 273–74
Liang Ch'i-ch'ao, 212, 223, 227, 279
Liaotung Peninsula: Japanese control of, 189, 192–93, 238, 240, 326; Russian interest in, 199
Lin Piao, 445–47
Lin Tse-hsu, 71–72, 78–79, 169
Linggadjati Agreement *(1947),* 494
Literature
　in China: ancient, 13; post-World War I, 312–31
　in Japan: ancient, 45–46, 48; Meiji, 148–49
Liu Ch'iu, *see* Ryukyu Islands
Liu Shao-ch'i, 442, 446
Lodge, Henry Cabot, 207
Lon Nol, Gen., 515
London Naval treaty *(1930),* 303, 308–9, 359

"Long march" of Chinese Red Army, 347
Low, Frederick F., 161–62, 173
Lu Hsun, 279, 312–13
Luxembourg, 488
Luzuriaga, José R. de, 369
Lytton commission, 330–31

MacArthur, Gen. Arthur, 368, 370, 460
MacArthur, Gen. Douglas
  direction of occupation of Japan by, 417–19, 421, 474
  Korea and, 478–79
  Philippines and, 492
Macao, Portuguese settlement at, 55–56, 62, 164
Macartney, George, 63, 68
MacDonald, Ramsay, 308
Magellan, Ferdinand, 57
Magsaysay, Raymond, 493, 509
Mahan, Alfred T., 201, 203
Makino (Baron Nobuaki), 275
Makura-no-soshi, 45
Malacca, European trade at, 387
Malaya, 367
  British colonial system in, 386–89, 395, 499
  economy of, 389, 500
  Japanese invasion of, 362, 364, 498
  post-World War II, 498–500, 514
Malayan People's Liberation Army, 499, 508
Malaysia, Federation of, 500, 514, 519
Malenkov, Georgi, 479
Malik, Adam, 519
Manchu (Ch'ing) dynasty *(1644–1912)*, 15
  decline of, 77, 84–85, 92, 152, 156, 214
  end of, 249–51
  restoration of, 151, 170–71
  See also Boxer rebellion; T'ai P'ing rebellion
Manchukuo (Japanese-controlled Manchuria): consolidation of, 332–33, 356–57; establishment of, 330–31
Manchuria (China)
  crisis of *1929–37* in, 324–25
  inter-allied intervention in, 283
  Korean war and, 479
  Kuomintang policy on, 314–15, 409, 419
  loss to Japan of, 460
  Manchu empire in, 31
  occupation by *Kuomintang* of, 419
  resources of, 324
  Russian interests in, 98, 195–97, 199, 214, 232–38, 240–42, 319
  Soviet military operations in, 427–28, 438
  T'ang empire in, 13
  United States' policy on *(1901–10)*, 232–33, 235, 242–45, 247

in World War II, 401–2
  See also Manchukuo
"Manifest destiny," 87, 203
Manila (Philippines): Japanese interests in, 363; United States' blockade of, 205
Manipur-Imphal front in World War II, 401
Manudharm, Przdit (Pridi Phanomyong), 391, 507
Manyoshu, 44
Mao Tse-tung, 345, 416, 438, 440, 455, 481
  authority of, 445
  cultural revolution and, 446–47
  program for peasant revolution of, 345–47, 410
Mao Tun, 312–13
Marco Polo bridge, 353
Marcos, Ferdinand, 493
Margary, Raymond, 162–63
Mariana Islands, 57; Japanese interests in, 269, 274–75, 292; in World War II, 401, 419
Marshall, Gen. George C., 431–32
Marshall, Humphrey, 89, 158, 219
Marshall Islands: Japanese interests in, 269, 274–75, 292; in World War II, 401, 419
Martin, Joseph, 479
Martin, William A. P., 210
Marxism: in China, 312, 315, 345–46; in Japan, 304, 464–65
Mathematics in ancient China, 13, 23
Matsukata Masayoshi, 133, 261
Matsuoka Yosuke, 331, 361
May Fourth Movement (China), 279
McKinley, William, 2, 204–5, 207, 215–16, 368, 371
McLane, Robert, 89
Medicine in Japan, influence of West on, 148
Meiji government of Japan, 125–28, 299–304, 336–41
  constitution of, 128–35
  economic basis of, 137–43
  political thought of, 143–45
  restoration of, 123–25
  social and cultural base of, 145–59
Mekong delta, 517, 519
Mencius, 30
Merchants: in China, 175, 229; in Japan, 104, 106–9
Midway Islands, 201, 203; battle of, 400–1
Militarism
  in China: *Kuomintang* rule and, 342, 344; in Manchu period, 152, 155–58; reform of, 224–26; revolution of *1911* and, 253–54, 257, 273, 310–11
  in Japan: ancient, 48–49, 103; in Meiji period, 134, 262–63; in *1920s* and *30s*, 299–300, 302–3, 307–8; in World War II, 403–6
  in South Korea, 482–83
  in World War I, 267–80

Mill, J. S., 147
Minamoto Yoritomo, 46–47
Ming dynasty *(1368–1644)*, 15
Mining in 19th century China, 174
Minobe Tatsukitchi, 299, 309, 338
Minseito party (Japan), 300, 302, 339–40, 403, 425
Minshuto (Democratic) party (Japan), 467, 469–71
Missionaries
  in Boxer rebellion, 218
  early contacts with Far East by, 54–57
  exclusion from China of, 60
  executions of, 59–60, 89–90, 162, 218
  in Indochina, 392
  in Japan, 58–60
  in Manchu China, 161–62, 210
  in Philippines, 205–6
  restoration of property to, in China, 95
Mitsubishi family, 140, 305
Mitsui family, 125, 140
Mo Ti, 18, 19, 28, 30
Mollendorf, P. G. von, 186
Mongolia
  independence movement in, 255
  inter-allied intervention in, 283
  Japanese claims in, 278, 294, 306, 333
  Japanese invasion of, 353
  Kuomintang policy on, 314–15, 409
  Manchu rule of, 31
  People's Republic of, 416
  Russian policy in, 96–98, 255, 319, 427, 438
Mongols, ancient, 14–15, 48, 55, 384
Monroe Doctrine, 204
Monte Corvino, John of, 54
Montesquieu, Baron de (Charles de Secondat), 393
Mori Arinori, 184
Morris, Roland S., 287
Morrison, Robert, 161
Moscow conference *(1943)*, 400
Moslems, *see* Arabs; Islam
Mosse, Albert, 148
Muirhead, William, 210
Mukden (Manchuria, China), Japanese seizure of, 327–38
Murasaki no Shikibo, 45–46
Muraviev (Count Nicholas), 96–97
Mutsu (Count Munemitsu), 193
Mutsuhito (Japanese emperor), 123, 130
Mutual Defense Assistance Agreement between Japan and United States *(1954)*, 467
Mutual Security Treaty, U.S. and Japan *(1958)*, 468, 470

Nagasaki (Japan), 116, 138; atomic bombing of, 402
Nagoya, Japan, in World War II, 401
Nanking (China)
  fall to Japan of, 355

Nanking (China) *(cont.)*
  Kuomintang government at, 317–22
  reoccupation of, 429
Nanking, Treaty of, 72, 77, 88
Napier, Lord, 65
Napoleon III, 90, 91
Nara (Japanese capital), 13, 43–44
National Liberation Front of South Vietnam, 504–5, 518
Nationalism
  in Annam, 393–94
  in Burma, 496–97
  in Cambodia, 502
  in China: anti-Japanese, 353, 357–58; Chiang Kai-shek's, 408–9; contribution of World War I to, 267, 278–79; growth of, 311–15, 320–21; in People's Republic, 440, 453, 456; Sun Yat-sen's, 228–29, 313–16
  in East Indies, 383
  in Japan: Meiji education and, 265; Shintoism and, 146–47, 337; in 1930s, 336–41
  in Korea, 475
  in Laos, 502, 505
  in Malaya, 498–99
  in Philippines, 205, 368, 492–93
  in Southeast Asia, 395
Naval disarmament, 289–93, 307–9
Ne Win, Gen., 497–98
Nehru, Jawaharlal, 437
Neo Lao Hak Xat, 515
Nepal, 519
Nertchinsk, Treaty of, 58, 96
Nestorian missions to China, 54
Netherlands
  attack on Choshu by, 119
  early trade with China of, 57, 62
  East Indies colonial system of, 382–84, 395, 512
  People's Republic of China recognized by, 437
  tariff treaty with China of, 321
  trade with Burma by, 384
  trade with Japan by, 59–60, 115, 117
  in World War II, 360
New Culture Movement (China), 279–80, 311–12, 345
New Georgia in World War II, 401
New Guinea: Indonesia and, 494; in World War II, 398–99, 401
New Life Movement (China), 343, 345
New York Times, 373
New Youth, 279
New Zealand, 276
  British fortification of, 293
  SEATO and, 515
  Vietnam and, 517
Nhu, Ngo Dinh, 503
Nien rebellion (China, *1853–68)*, 85
Nihon Minshu Shakaito (Democratic Socialist Party of Japan), 466
Nihon Shakaito (Socialist Party of Japan), 466, 471

Nihon Shoki, 43
Nikolaievsk (Siberia, Russia), founding of, 96
Ningpo (China), established as trade port, 73, 80
Nine-Power Open Door Treaty *(1922)*, 293–95, 297, 329, 359
Nineteenth Route Army (Chinese Red Army), 330, 345
Nishihara Kamezo, 288
Nitobe Inazo, 307
Nixon, Richard M., 470, 488, 518–19
No drama, 49
Nomura Kichisaburo, 362, 364
North Vietnam, *see* Democratic Republic of Vietnam
Northwest rebellion (China, *1862–73)*, 85
Norway, trade with China by, 74, 321
Nozaka Sanzo, 424
Nu, U, 497–98

Oba Nobunaga, 50
Oda Yorozu, 307
Ogasawar Island, *see* Bonin Islands
Okada Keisuke, 339–40
Okinawa Island, in World War II, 469–70
Okuma Shigenobu, 128, 263, 271, 304
Okuwa Shumei, 338
On New Democracy (Mao Tse-tung), 410
Open Door Policy toward China, 217–20, 247, 255, 271, 282, 288, 295, 435
  Nine-Power Treaty on *(1922)*, 293–95
Opium trade, 68–69, 71, 73, 75, 88
  legalization of, 92–93
  prohibited by Harris treaty, 117
  suppression of, 229–30
Opium War, 65, 72
Organization for Economic Cooperation and Development, 469–70
Osaka (Japan): arms industry in, 138; in World War II, 401
Osaka Mainichi, 301
Oshiro Heilbachiro, 108
Osmena, Sergio, 374, 376, 492
O'Sullivan, John L., 203
Oyama Iwao, 133

Pacification program in Vietnam, 504–5
Pago Pago, 201
Pai Sang-ti Hui (Association of God Worshippers), 85
Painting: in ancient China, 22; in ancient Japan, 49
Pakistan
  at Bandung conference, 514
  People's Republic of China recognized by, 437
  SEATO and, 515

Palmerston, Lord (Henry J. Temple), 65
Paris, Pact of, *see* Kellog-Briand Treaty
Paris, Treaty of *(1898)*, 207
Paris Peace Conference, *see* Versailles Conference
Park Chung-hee, 481, 483
Parker, Peter, 201, 210
Parkes, Harry, 90, 120
Partido Federalista (Philippines), 369, 375
Partido Nacionalista (Philippines), 371, 377
Pathet Lao, 505–6, 515–16
Peace Corps, 500
Pearl Harbor, 201, 203; Japanese attack on, 363–65, 403
Peasantry
  in China: ancient, 22; *Kuomintang* and, 407; role in communist revolution of, 345–48, 410, 429–30, 449–52
  in Japan: Meiji, 125, 141; Tokugawa, 104, 106–9
  in Philippines, 493
  in Vietnam, 504
  See also Agriculture; Land
Peasants' Association (China), 442
Peking (China)
  British and French occupation of, 97–98
  communist capture of, 434
  "desertion" of, 151
  Japanese occupation of, 353
  See also Cambaluc
Peking, Treaty of *(1860)*, 94–95
Peking, Treaty of *(1905)*, 239–40
People's Republic of China, *see* China—People's Republic of
Perry, Comm. Matthew C., 113–14, 201
Pescadores Islands
  Dutch trading outpost on, 57
  Japanese possession of, 189
  Kuomintang occupation of, 419, 426, 488
Pham Van Dong, 503
Phanomyong, Pridi (Pradit Manudharm), 391, 507
Philippines
  economy of, 370–71, 377–78
  education in, 376
  effects of World War II on, 415–16
  guerilla warfare in, 492–93, 514
  immigration from, 373
  independence of, 372, 492
  Japanese attack on, 364, 398, 401
  nationalism in, 205, 368, 492–93
  People's Republic of China and, 454
  revolt in, 205–6, 368
  SEATO and, 515
  Spanish conquest of, 157
  U.S. interests in: pre-World War II, 201–2, 243, 292, 295; post-World War II, 362, 370–74, 429, 492
  U.S. rule of, 367–78

post-World War II, 492–93, 509–
15, 519
Phouphayuhasena, Gen. Phahon, 391
Phoumi Nosavan, Gen., 505
Pibun Songgram, Prack, 391, 507
Pierce, Franklin, 115, 201
Pilar, Marcello H. Del, 206
Pin-ch'un, 158
Pinto, Fernám Mendez, 58
Pires, Thomas, 55
Poa-chia system (China), 343
Po Chu-i, 13
Poetry: in ancient China, 13; in
ancient Japan, 44, 45
Poland, 332
Political Consultative Conference
(China), 431–33
Political parties
in Japan: economic base of, 142–
43; emergence of, 129, 142;
government by, 299–304;
during occupation, 424–25;
oligarchy versus, 260–64
in Philippines, 375–76
Political thought, *see* Government—
ideas on
Pollution in contemporary Japan,
471
Polo, Maffeo, 54
Polo, Marco, 54, 168
Polo, Nicolo, 54
Population growth
on Formosa, 485–86
in Indonesia, 495–96
in Japan: contemporary, 460–61;
Tokugawa, 108
in Philippines, 493
in People's Republic of China,
493
Port Arthur: Japanese attack on,
234; Russian lease of, 199
Portsmouth, Treaty of (*1905*), 237–
39
Portugal, 488
China reached by, 55
China trade of, 56, 62, 73
early trade with Japan of, 58–59
exclusion from Japan of, 60
tariff treaty with China of, 321
trade with Indonesia of, 392
trade with Malaya of, 387
trade with Thailand of, 390
Potsdam Conference (*1945*), 402,
419–20, 426
Pottinger, Sir Henry, 72, 170
Printing in ancient China, 13, 23
Privy council, Meiji, 134, 260, 300,
302–3
P'u-yi, Henry, 330, 332
Pueblo incident, 481
Putiatin, Count, 91, 97–98, 115
Putnam's Magazine, 113

Quezon, Manuel, 373–74, 376–77,
492
Quota Immigration Act (United
States, 1924), 296, 305, 307

Racial conflict: in Malaya, 499–500;
in Thailand, 505

Racial equality, Versailles debate on,
275–78
Rahman, Tunku Abdul, 500
Railroads
In China: 19th century, 174, 192,
197, 200, 212, 214, 229;
20th century, 241, 243–45,
251, 254, 355, 450
in Japan, 138
United States, Chinese labor on,
165
See also Chinese Eastern Railway; Southern Manchur:a
Railroad; Trans-Siberian Rail-
road
Ranke, Leopold von, 169
Red Army (Chinese), 433–34, 347,
428
"Red Guards," Chinese, 446
Reed, William B., 89, 91, 93
Reinsch, Paul S., 273
Reischauer, E. O., 464
Religion
in ancient China, 13, 16, 18–22
in Meiji Japan, 144–48
in Philippines, 375, 377
in People's Republic of China, 449
in Vietnam, 501, 503
See also Ancestor worship; Brah-
manism; Buddhism; Chris-
tianity; Confucianism; Hin-
duism; Islam; Missionaries;
Shintoism; Taoism; Zen
Buddhism
Reorganization Loan Agreement
(China, *1913*), 255
Rhee, Syngman, 416, 476, 482
Ricci, Matteo, 56
Richard, Timothy, 210
Richardson, C. L., 118–19
Richterhofen, Ferdinand von, 198
Rikken (Imperialist) party (Japan),
142
Rizal, José, 216
Roberts, Rev. Issachar, 85
Roberts, Owen, 364
Rockhill, W. W., 216, 218, 227
Roessler, Herman, 147–48
Roosevelt, Franklin D., 358, 361–
64, 400, 412, 475
Roosevelt, Theodore, 203, 204, 245,
295: Manchurian policy of,
233, 235, 237–39, 242–43;
Philippine policy of, 371,
374
Root, Elihu, 243, 255, 374
Root-Takahira Agreements (*1908*),
291–92
Rosen, Baron, 196, 237
Rousseau, Jean-Jacques, 393
Roxas, Manuel, 415–16
Royal Laotian government, 506
Rumania, 356
Russia
Boxer rebellion and, 218–19
early contacts with Japan of, 113,
118, 193–94
first contacts with China by, 57–
58
Ili ceded to, 184

interests in Manchuria of, 98,
195–97, 199, 214, 232–38,
240–42
Korea and, 183
Mongolian policy of, 255
Soviet: aid to *Kuomintang* from,
407, 411; Chinese Communist
Party and, 347; crisis with
China of (*1929*), 325–26;
Hokkaido held by, 467; influence on *Kuomintang* of,
312, 314, 316–17, 319; inter-allied intervention in,
283–89; interests in China
of, renunciation of, 280;
Japan and, 305–7, 352, 361,
417; Korean war and, 429,
474–81; Kurile Islands received by, 419, 426; Laos
and, 505, 516; Manchukuo
recognized by, 332; non-ag-
gression pact with Japan of,
362; North Vietnam and,
502, 509, 516; People's Republic of China and, 437–38,
440, 450, 454–55; position
of, post-World War II, 435–
36; in Southeast Asia, 512;
South Sakhalin Island re-
ceived by, 419, 426; United
States' recognition of, 359
territorial expansion of, 95–99
war between Japan and, 235–38,
264–65
in World War I, 272–73
Russo-Japanese war (*1904–1905*),
235–38, 264–65
Ryukyu Islands
China and, 180–82, 419
United Nations trusteeship of, 426
United States' interests in, 115,
182, 201
in World War II, 401

Saigo Takamori, 128
Saigon (Vietnam), 391, 402, 503–5
Saionji Kimmochi, 133, 242, 263,
300, 302, 339, 361
Saito (Viscount Makoto), Adm., 338–
40
Sakhalin Island, 96, 238, 295, 460;
Russian control of, 419, 426;
in World War II, 402
Sakurakai (Society of the Cherry),
337
Samoan Islands, 201, 203
Samuri
effect of Meiji restoration on,
125, 132, 134
militarism of, 128
pre-Meiji, 103–5, 109
role in Meiji restoration of, 122–
23, 137, 145, 259
San Francisco, Chinese immigration
to, 164–65
Sankin Kotai system, 102
Sansom, Sir George, 106, 149
Sato Eisaku, 469–70
Satsuma, house of, 101, 118, 128,
133, 182

Saya San, 386
Schopenhaur, Arthur, 147
Schurman, J. G., 368
Schurz, Carl, 203
Science: in ancient China, 23–24; in Tokugawa Japan, 109–10
SEATO, *see* Southeast Asia Treaty Organization
Sei Shonagon, 45–46
Seiyukai party (Japan), 262–64, 299–303, 307, 338–41, 403, 425
Sekigahara, battle of, 101
Semenov, Capt. Grigori, 283, 285–86
Senate Foreign Relations Committee, 488, 521
Seoul, Russo-Japanese agreement on, 197
Seoul-Inchon expressway, 519
Seward, George F., 162
Seward, William H., 159–60, 165–66, 183, 201
Shakaito (Social Democratic) Party (Japan), 424
Shang Yang, 28
Shanghai (China)
establishment as trading port of, 73–75
international settlement at, 80–81, 319
Japanese bombardment of, 330
T'ai-P'ing rebellion in, 86, 95
Shantung (China)
Japanese demands on, 270–71, 274–75, 277–79
Japanese withdrawal from, 318
Shao Yung, 13
Shaw, Samuel, 74
Shen Pao-chen, 159
Sherman, John, 215
Shidehara (Baron Kijuro), 297, 302, 304–6, 308, 329, 406, 425
Shih Huang Ti, 12, 28
Shikoku Island, 419
Shimbara revolt (Japan), 60
Shimonoseki, Treaty of (1895), 189–90, 192
Shimpoto (Progressive) Party (Japan), 424–25
Shintoism
in ancient Japan, 41, 45
Japanese nationalism and, 146–47, 337
restoration of, 124
Shipbuilding: in 19th century China, 174; in 19th century Japan, 138
Shogunates
Ashikaga (1336–1573), 48–49; decline of, 112, 116, 118–20, 122
Tokugawa (1603–1867), 50, 100–10, 144: rise of, 47–50
Short, Gen. Walter C., 364
Shotoku Taishi, 42
Shufeldt, Robert, 185
Sjahrir, Soeten, 383
Siam, *see* Thailand
Sian, Nestorian monument in, 54; *see also* Ch'ang-an
"Sian incident," 349, 357

Siberia
Far Eastern Republic of, 319
inter-allied intervention in, 283–89
Japanese interests in, 277, 283–88, 295, 318
Russian migration to, 57–58
Siebold, Philip Franz von, 148
Sihanouk, Prince Norodom, 506–7, 514
Sikkim, British control of, 184
Silk: production of, in Meiji Japan, 139, 264; trade in, 55, 69, 74, 120, 192
Singapore (China)
British control of, 293, 499–500
Japanese interests in, 363
in World War II, 398
Sinkiang (China)
Manchu rule of, 31
Soviet presence in, 438
Sino-Japanese war (1894–95), 185–90, 195, 224, 261, 264
Sino-Soviet Treaty of Friendship (1925), 185–90, 195, 224, 261, 264
Smith, Arthur, 66
Social Interpretation of History, The (Williams), 315
Socialism
in Burma, 498
in Japan, 265–66, 304, 464–69
in Southeast Asia, 512–14
Soka Gakkai, 472
Solomon Islands, 398–99; *see also* Bougainville Island
Soong, T. V., 400
Souphanouvong, Prince, 505, 516
South Africa, 276
Southeast Asia
colonialism in, 367–94, 512–14
on eve of World War II, 394–95
Japanese occupation of, 491–92
in World War II, 398–402
post-World War II: politics in, 491–509; in world affairs, 512–22
See also Indochina
Southeast Asia Treaty Organization (SEATO), 515–17
Southern Manchurian Railroad, 239–40, 244, 270, 307
Japanese control of, 327–28, 332
Souvanna Phouma, Prince, 505, 516
Soviet Union, *see* Russia—Soviet
Spain
colonial system of, 367
exclusion from Japan of, 60
exploration of East Asian Islands by, 57
first contacts with Japan of, 57
recognition of Japanese puppet government in China by, 356
tariff treaty with China of, 321
war with United States of, 204–6, 367
Spanish-American war, 204–6, 367
Spencer, Herbert, 147
Spice trade, 380–81, 387
Spratley Islands, 356, 360
Stalin, Joseph, 345–47, 400, 475

Standard of living
in Ch'ing China, 15
in contemporary Japan, 462
in People's Republic of China, 450
in Sung China, 13
Sternberg, Baron Ungern von, 283
Stilwell, Gen. Joseph W., 411–12, 430
Stimson, Henry L., 325–26, 329
Stimson Non-recognition Doctrine, 358
Stirling, Sir James, 115
Straight, Willard, 239, 243–44
"Strategic hamlet" program in Vietnam, 504
Student movement in contemporary Japan, 471
Suematsu Kencho, 265
Sugimura Yotaro, 307
Suharto, Gen., 496, 514
Sui dynasty, 12
Sukarno, 383, 416, 494–96, 514
Sumitomo family, 125, 140
Sun Li-jen, 253
Sun Yat-sen, 228–29, 318, 341–43, 345
new program of, 313–16, 318, 322, 434
passing of, 316–17
principles of, Chinese Communist Party and, 357
revolution of 1911 and, 252–53, 256
Sung Chia-jen, 253
Sung empire (960–1279), 13–15
Supreme Court, Japanese, 422
Supreme People's Court, Chinese, 442
Suzuki Kantaro, 402, 405
Sweden: People's Republic of China recognized by, 437; trade treaty with China of, 74
Swift, John F., 165
Switzerland, 437

Taft, William Howard, 238–39, 244–45, 254–55, 368–71
T'ai-P'ing rebellion (1851–64), 15, 85–86, 95, 98, 224
collapse of, 152–55
effect on foreign interests of, 87
ideology of, 152–53
Taikwa (great reform), 42
Taira Kiyomori, 46
Taisho Tenno, 259
Taiwan, *see* Formosa
Takahashi (Viscount Korekiyo), 300, 340
Takahira (Baron Kogoro), 243
Taku, European attack on, 93–94
Tanaka Giichi, Gen., 300–3
T'ang dynasty (618–906), 13
T'ang Shao-yi, 252
Tanuma Okitsugu, 109
Taoism
in ancient China, 19–20
in Annam, 391
in People's Republic of China, 449
political thought of, 28

Tao-t'ai (intendant of circuit), 77, 81
Tariffs
  in China, 63–64: Chinese view of, 95; demands for autonomy in, 318, 320–21; 5% ad valorem, 73; *Kuomintang* policy on, 315, 344
  in Japan: provisions in Harris Treaty for, 117; post-World War I, 306
  see also Trade
Taruc, Luis, 416, 492
Tavera, T. H. Pardo de, 369
Taxation
  in Burma, 498
  in China: ancient, 34–35; *Kuomintang* policy on, 315, 344; Manchu, 157, 250; reduced by Chinese Communist Party, 345, 410
  in Japan: Meiji, 141, 265; reform by occupation of, 425; Tokugawa, 107–8
Tea trade, 68, 74, 120, 192
"Teach-ins" (on U.S. policy), 520
Technology
  development of, Chinese and Japanese compared, 177–78
  in Japan, 264, 461
  in North Korea, 480
  Western, influence in China of, 171–72
  See also Industry
Teheran Conference (*1943*), 400
Teng Hsiao-p'ing, 445
Terauchi, Juichi, 340
Terauchi (Count Seiki), 246, 263, 287–88, 299
Terranova case, 65
"Tet offensive" in Vietnam, 505
Textile production
  in Meiji Japan, 139, 264
  in 19th century China, 174
  in People's Republic of China, 450
Thailand
  constitutional revolution in, 391
  effects of colonialism on, 389–92
  Japanese intervention in, 491, 507
  United States and, 507–8, 514–15
  Vietnam and, 517
  in World War II, 402
  post-World War II, 507–8, 519
Thakin party (Indonesia), 496
Thannarat, Field Marshal Sarit, 507
Theatre in Japan, 49, 106–7
Thieu, Gen. Nguyen Van, 504–5, 518
"Three Antis-Movement," 448
Thunberg, Carl, 148
Tibet
  independence movement in, 255
  Kuomintang policy on, 314–15, 409
  Manchu rule of, 31
  People's Republic of China and, 454
Tientsin (China)
  foreign concessions at, 80, 319
  massacre at, 162
  Japanese occupation of, 353

Tientsin, Convention of (*1885*), 186
Tientsin, Treaty of (*1858*), 91–92, 97, 99: provisions for religious toleration in, 92, 260–62; supplementary articles to, 159–60
Tinian Island, 401
Tirpitz, Adm. Alfred von, 198
Tojo Hideki, 339, 363, 404–5
Tokugawa Iyeyasu, 50, 100–1
Tokugawa shogunate (*1603–1867*), 50, 100–1, 144
  difficulties of, 109–10, 112, 116, 118–20
  economy of, 105–6
  fall of, 122
  philosophy of, 104–5, 146
  political system of, 101–3
Tokyo (Japan)
  arms industry in, 138
  effect of World War II on, 418
  in World War II, 411
  Yedo renamed as, 124
Tokyo War Crimes Trial, 420
Tong Hak, 187–88
Tonking (Vietnam), 391: French control of, 199–200; *see also* Vietnam
Toshiyori (council of elders), 102
Tozama lords of Japan, 102, 116, 118, 122
Trade
  with Burma, 384
  Canton, *see* Canton trade
  with China: Arab, 54; Dutch, 57, 62, 321; English, 57, 73–74, 88–92, 160–63; French, 57, 62, 74, 76, 91–95, 321; Japanese, 190, 264–65; new ports for, 79–80; Portuguese, 55–56, 62, 73; Roman, 53; Russian, 57–58; Spanish, 57, 321; United States', 57, 69, 74–76; during World War I, 280
  with Indochina, 392
  with Japan, 123–24: Dutch, 59–60, 115, 117; English, 59, 115, 118; French, 118; limitation by shogun of, 60, 101; Portuguese, 58–59
  with Malaya, 387
  opium, 68–69, 71, 73, 75, 88, 92–93, 117, 229–30
  silk, 53, 69, 74, 120, 192
  with Southeast Asia, 381–82, 387, 391
  spice, 380–81, 387
  with Thailand, 390
  tea, 68, 74, 120, 192
  See also Tariffs
Trade unions
  in China: Hankow strike of, 320; People's Republic of, 442
  in Japan: Meiji, 304; post-World War II, 465
Trans-Siberian Railroad, 187, 195–96, 285–86
Trescott, William H., 165

Tribute system in Chinese foreign relations, 67
Truman, Harry S., 402; China policy of, 431–36; Korea and, 478–79
Truong Chinh, 503
Tsai-tien, 174, 176
Ts'ao-kun, 316
Tseng Kuo-fan, 79, 154–56, 159, 171–72, 176–77
Tsingtao (China): German lease of, 214; Japanese occupation of, 268–69
Tso T'sung-t'ang, 171–72, 176
Tsungli Yamen (foreign affairs committee), 77, 152, 159, 170, 173, 189
Tu Fu, 13
Tuan Ch'i-jui, 273–74, 288, 316
T'ung chi, 170–71
Tung Fu-hsiang, 222
T'ung Meng Hui (League of Common Alliance), 228
T'ung-wen Kuan (Interpreter's College), 171–72
Turkestan, T'ang empire in, 13
Twenty-one demands of Japan on China, 269–70, 282
Tyler, John, 75
T'zu-hsi ((Empress Dowager), 174, 176–77, 188, 213–14: death of, 226, 249; reform policies of, 222–30, 250

U2 incident, 468
U Nu, Gen., 497–98
Ugaki Kazushige, Gen., 340
Ukhtomskii, Prince Esper, 196
United Nations, 400, 426, 433
  Chinese membership in, 488
  Korean war and, 475–78, 481
  Laotian, Cambodian, and Vietnamese membership in, 514
  Vietnam war and, 517
United Nations Temporary Commission on Korea, 476
United States
  aid to *Kuomintang* by, 407, 411–12, 429–34, 485
  attack by Japan on, 364–65
  Boxer rebellion and, 218
  Cambodia and, 506–7
  Chinese policy of: 19th century, 75–76, 87–89, 91–92, 158–60, 234; 20th century, 269–78, 282, 288–89, 293–94, 407, 411–12, 429–37, 485, 488–89
  early trade with China of, 57, 69, 74–76
  effect of Chinese Communist victory on, 435–37
  Far Eastern policy of: *1890s*, 202–8, 215–17; post-World War II, 429, 515, 520–22
  immigration from Asia to, 164–65, 282–83, 295–96, 305, 307, 373
  intervention in Siberia by, 283–89

United States (cont.)
   Japanese policy of: 19th century,
      113–18; 20th century, 274–
      78, 282–87, 293–97, 307–9,
      352, 358–65, 415–26, 422–
      23, 460–64, 467–70
   Korean policy of: Korean war,
      474–76, 478–83, 514–15;
      19th century, 183, 184, 188;
      20th century, 235, 238–39,
      245–47, 429
   Laos and, 515–16
   Manchurian policy of, 232–33,
      235, 242–47, 329–32
   mutual defense pacts with Japan
      of, 467–68, 470
   occupation of Japan by, 415–26,
      460–64
   opium trade of, 69
   Philippine policy of: pre-World
      War II, 201–2, 243, 292,
      295; post-World War II, 362,
      367–78
   public opinion in: neglect of
      Asia by, 3, 10; Far Eastern
      policy and, 520–21
   SEATO and, 515–16
   Thailand and, 390, 507–8
   Tientsin Treaty signed by, 93–94
   Vietnam war and, 483, 502–5,
      516–18, 520–21
   war with Spain of, 204–6
   in World War II, 398–402
Urbanization
   in contemporary Japan, 471
   in North Korea, 481

Versailles Peace conference (1918),
   275–79, 282, 475
Viet Cong, 504–5, 517–18; in Cam-
   bodia, 506
Vietminh, 501–2, 516
Vietnam, 367
   Bandung resolution on, 514
   French colonial system in, 184,
      199–200, 367, 390–94, 500–2
   North, see Democratic Republic
      of Vietnam
   South, 519; government of, 501–3,
      516–18
   war in: French, 501–2; Korea and,
      483; Okinawa and, 489–90;
      U.S., 502–5, 516–18, 520–21
Vladivostock (Russia), founding of,
   99

Wakadoshiyori (Council of Junior
   Elders), 102
Wakatsuki (Viscount Reijiro), 300,
   302, 306
Waldersee, Count Alfred von, 220
Wallace, Henry A., 412
Walsh, Bishop, 362
Wang, C. T., 276, 278
Wang Ching-wei, 316, 356
Wang-hsia, Treaty of, 76
Wang T'ao, 211
Wang Wei, 13
Wanpaoshan affair, 327
Ward, Frederick T., 154–55
Ward, John E., 94
Ward, Thomas F., 163, 173
Warlords, see Militarism in China;
   Feudal system, Chinese
Washington Disarmament Conference
   (1921), 289–92, 307–8, 318,
   320, 327, 359
Watanabe Jutaro, 340
Webster, Daniel, 75
Weddell, Capt. John, 57
Wedemeyer, Maj. Gen. Albert C.,
   412, 430, 433
Wei-hai-wei (China), British lease
   of, 200
Wei Ying-wu, 13
Wen-hsiang, 159
Western Hills Group (China), 316
Williams, Maurice, 315
Williams, S. Wells, 75, 165, 210
Wilson, Woodrow, 372
   China policy of, 254–55, 271,
      275–78, 282, 288–89
   Japanese immigration and, 295–
      96
   Siberian intervention and, 285–88
Witte, Count Sergei Y., 195–96, 237
Wo-jen, 172
Wood, George L., 243, 372
Women
   binding of feet of, in ancient
      China, 13
   equality of, in People's Republic
      of China, 449
   Japanese, post-war status of, 463
World Bank, 500
World Court, 307
World Disarmament Conference
   (1933), 359
World War I: effect on Japanese
   economy of, 265; Japan and
   China in, 267–80

World War II
   China during, 401, 406–13
   East Asia in, 398–413
   effect on Japan of, 416–17
   in Europe, 360–61
   Indochina during, 501
   Japan during, 403–6
   Pacific war in, 2, 398–402
   U.S. entry into, 364–65
Wu T'ing-fang, 251
Wylie, Alexander, 210

Xiavier, Francis, 56, 58

Yalta Conference (1945), 400, 429,
   475
Yalu river, 478–79
Yamagata Arimoto, 133, 197, 234,
   260–63, 300
Yamagata-Lobanov Agreement, 197–
   98
Yamamoto (Count Gombei), 263, 300
Yamoto (Japanese state), 41–43
Yangtze valley (China), Japanese
   occupation of, 353
Yap Island, 277
Yasuda family, 140
Yedo (old Tokyo), 59, 101, 105–6
Yen Hsi-shan, 311, 317
Yeh Ming-ch'en, 82
Yen, Duke of, 32
Yen Fu, 312
Yokosuka (Japan), shipbuilding in,
   138
Yonai Mitsumasa, 405
Yoritomo, 46–47
Yoshida Shigeru, 406, 425, 466–67
Yoshino Sakuzo, 299
Young, John Russell, 168
Yu Hsien, 220
Yuan Shih-k'ai, 186, 223–26, 240,
   249, 268–69, 271–74, 278;
   policies in 1911 revolution
   of, 251–57, 310–11, 409
Yung Wing, 160, 172
Yunnan, conquest by Mongols of, 15
Yuzonsha (Society to Preserve the
   National Essence), 338

Zaibatsu (finance capitalists)
   in Meiji Japan, 138–42, 265,
      304, 340, 405–6
   in occupied Japan, 424
   post-World War II, 465
Zen Buddhism in feudal Japan, 49

536

DATE DUE

Demco, Inc. 38-293

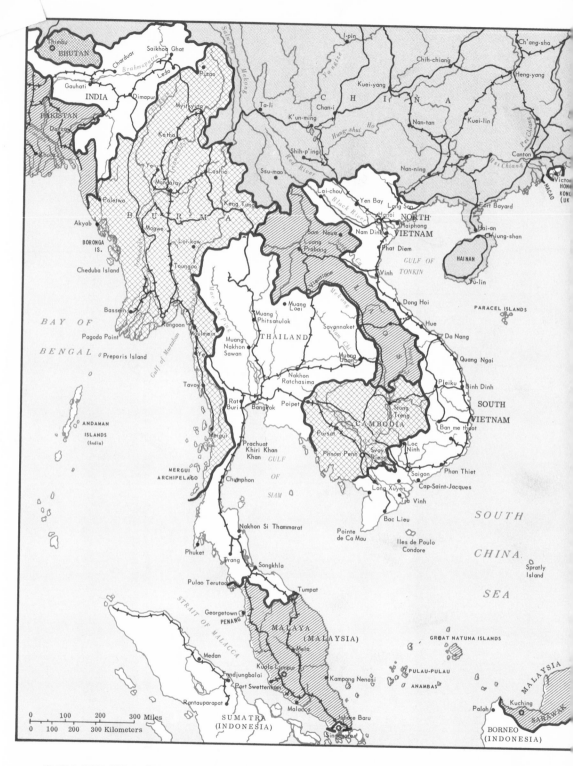

SOUTHEAST

ASIA

┼┼┼┼ Selected railroad ──── Selected road ━━━ International boundar